HOLT McDOUGAL

TEACHER'S EDITION

Discovering FRENCH Today!

FRENCH 3
Rouge

Jean-Paul Valette

Rebecca M. Valette

HOLT McDOUGAL

 HOUGHTON MIFFLIN HARCOURT

From the Authors

DEDICATION

This book is dedicated to our grandchildren in the hope that they will grow to understand and appreciate their French heritage. From left to right: Nico, Téa, Zoé, and Esmé; Jackson and Will; Caroline and Jean-Pierre.

CREDITS T2 (tl, c) ©Rebecca Valette; T2 (tr) ©Janet Valette; T3 (tr) ©Rebecca and Jean-Paul Valette; T2-T3 (bg) ©Sandra Baker/Alamy; T4 (bg) ©Bertrand Gardel/hemis.fr/Getty Images; T4 (c) ©Myrleen Pearson/Alamy; T5 (br) ©Science Photo Library/Alamy; T6 (bg) ©Jeff Hunter/Getty Images; T8 (br) ©Jack Hollingsworth/Photodisc/Getty Images; T11 ©Brand X Pictures/Jupiterimages/Getty Images; T47 (tl) ©Datacraft Co Ltd/Getty Images; T49 (tc) ©Comstock Images/Getty Images; T55 (tr) ©Photodisc/Getty Images; T65 (cl) ©Lebrecht Music and Arts Photo Library/Alamy; T65 (tl) ©Mary Evans Picture Library/Alamy

ISBN 978-0-547-87184-4

1 2 3 4 5 6 7 8 9 10 0914   21 20 19 18 17 16 15 14 13 12

4500357322   ABCDEFG

Dear French Teachers and Friends,

We take this opportunity to welcome you to **Discovering French Today!** You will find that this new edition offers a fresh design with the same clearly presented content and communicative features that you and your students have come to appreciate. In response to your feedback, it also offers a variety of innovative technology resources that reflect the learning styles of today's students.

The organization of **Discovering French Today!** reflects the style and manner in which most French Level Three courses are taught. At this level, the teaching of French is no longer linear, and teachers have great flexibility in choosing the material they want to present and the skills they want to emphasize. **Discovering French Today!** provides a technology-enhanced program that gives the teacher a maximum of flexibility by offering different strands to build upon: vocabulary, language, and daily-life culture as well as French and francophone literature and civilization.

While the units follow a logical progression in terms of increasing complexity, the book need not necessarily be presented in a linear manner. Rather, each teacher is encouraged to establish a Level Three curriculum on the basis of the skills or outcomes to be emphasized in the course of instruction. A teacher who wants to stress oral communication in daily-life situations may wish to concentrate primarily on the *Français pratique* sections. Another teacher, interested primarily in culture, may allocate much more classroom time to the *Interludes culturels*. Still another teacher, preferring to focus on control of structure and building reading skills, will spend more time with the *Langue et communication* sections and the *Lectures*, and will refer as needed to the information contained in the *Interludes culturels* to elucidate specific points of French and francophone cultural background. Again, the key word to success is flexibility.

Although this book is the last volume of the **BLEU, BLANC, ROUGE** trilogy, we hope that it will not mark the end of your students' French studies, but rather that it will further stimulate their interest in French and the culture of the French-speaking world. We hope they will be eager to continue beyond this level, whether in high school or in college.

Bon courage à tous!

Jean-Paul Valette   Rebecca M. Valette

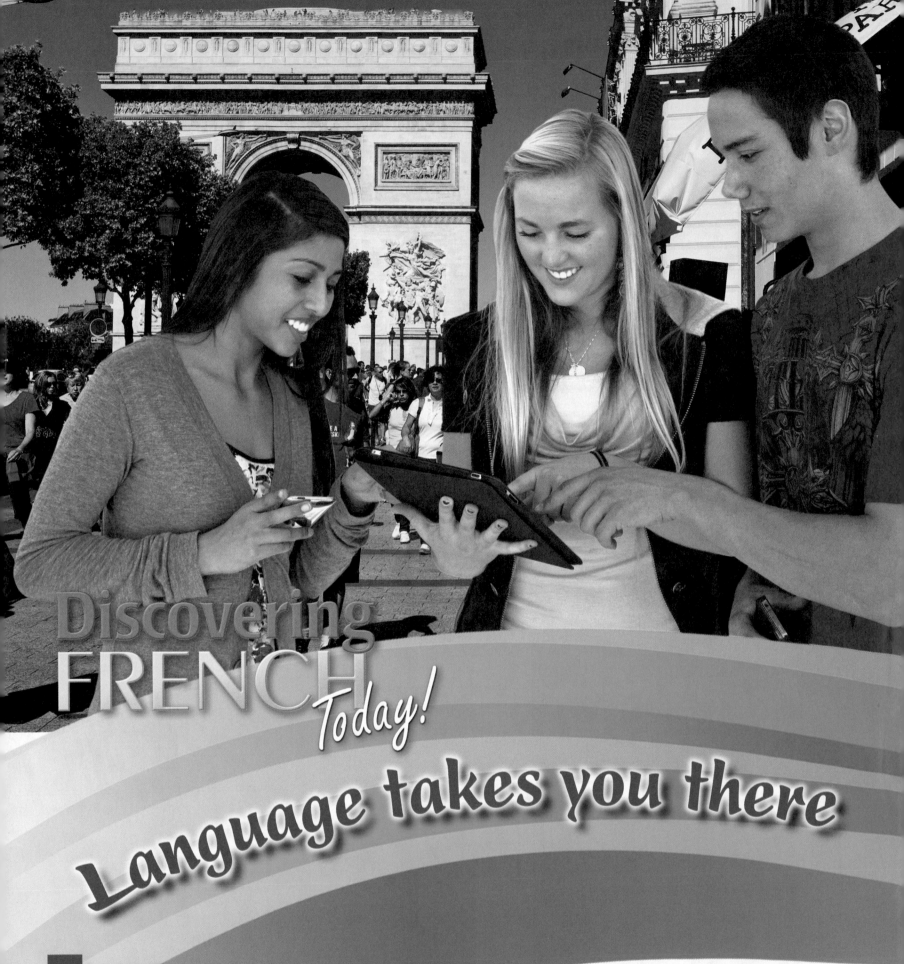

Discovering FRENCH Today!

Language takes you there

Remarkable Culture

Vivid, inspiring, and focused culture goes beyond the textbook with on-site videos, **News**+Networking, and more!

Relevant Instruction

Our proven approach to learning and differentiated practice are amplified with new interactive technology such as **FRENCH InterActive Reader**

Real Interaction

Students show what they know with **performance))space**, a virtual one-to-one environment that allows students to record spoken and written responses.

Contents

Book Organization T7

Program Resources T8

Easy Articulation T12

Grammar Across Levels T14

Scope and Sequence T16

Unit Walkthrough T30

Teacher's Edition Walkthrough T44

Cultural Reference Guide T46

Aligning Language Standards with National Initiatives:
Collaboration is the Key!
  by Barbara Rupert Mondloch T52

Teaching to the Standards in *Discovering French Today!* T55

Differentiation in the French Classroom
  by Leonore Ganschow, Ed.D. and Richard L. Sparks, Ed.D T56

Strategies for Pre-AP® Students by Mary L. Diehl T61

Introduction to French Literature T64

Literature Selections T65

Professional Reference Information T66

Book Organization

Setting your own course goals is easy with
Discovering French Today! **Rouge**

Flexible Modular Units

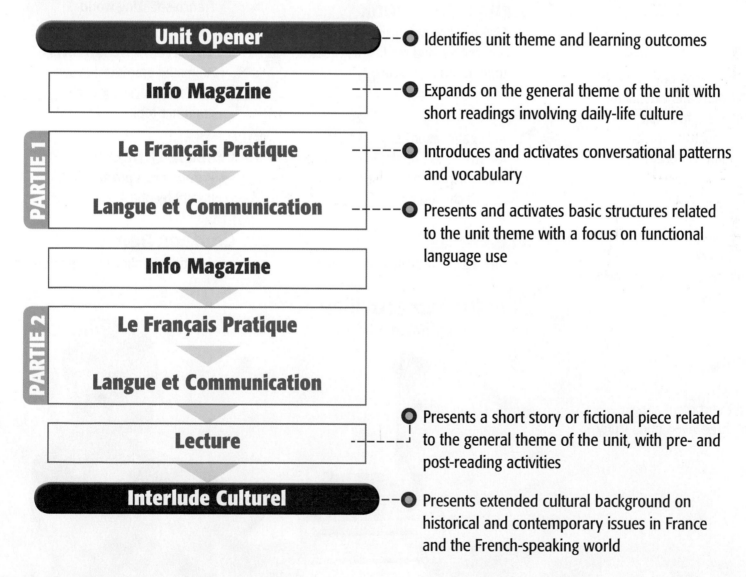

Unit Opener — ● Identifies unit theme and learning outcomes

Info Magazine — ● Expands on the general theme of the unit with short readings involving daily-life culture

PARTIE 1

Le Français Pratique — ● Introduces and activates conversational patterns and vocabulary

Langue et Communication — ● Presents and activates basic structures related to the unit theme with a focus on functional language use

Info Magazine

PARTIE 2

Le Français Pratique

Langue et Communication

Lecture — ● Presents a short story or fictional piece related to the general theme of the unit, with pre- and post-reading activities

Interlude Culturel — ● Presents extended cultural background on historical and contemporary issues in France and the French-speaking world

Digital Resources for the Student at my.hrw.com

Fully Interactive Online Student Edition
- Includes Performance Space and audio and video at point of use

performance space
- Students can submit oral, multiple choice, and short and extended written responses to activities
- Student Dashboard to track completion and feedback

News + Networking
- High-interest articles at appropriate levels of difficulty
- Current cultural and newsworthy videos
- Monitored blogs

FRENCH InterActive Reader
- Authentic texts
- Reading in the content areas
- Practice at three levels of difficulty

@HomeTutor
- Practice at three levels of difficulty, self-scoring, and animations

Online Workbook
- Skill-building practice with grammar, vocabulary, and reading activities at three levels of difficulty

On rappe! (Levels 1–2)
- Video animations of rap songs
- Karaoke track, printable worksheets, interactive practice, and optional French captioning

Flashcards
- Interactive flashcards with audio

À votre tour activities
- Cultural exploration activities

WebQuests
- Cultural activities designed to expand students' knowledge of the countries and communities in the French-speaking world

Grammavision (Levels 1–2)
- Animated grammar presentations with self-checks for each grammar topic

Lesson Quizzes
- Provide extra practice with instant feedback

Composition
- Additional online writing activities

Additional Digital Resources for the Student

Textbooks
- Available for delivery on a variety of devices

Holt McDougal French Apps
- Flashcards with visuals and audio to reinforce learning

Student One Stop DVD-ROM
- Entire Student Edition with audio and video

Print Resources for the Student

Student Edition

Activités pour tous with Review Bookmarks
- Provides vocabulary, grammar, and reading practice at three levels of difficulty

Workbook with Review Bookmarks
- Contains listening, reading, writing and culture activities

Lectures pour tous with audio CD
- Offers reading selections with strategies and tips, as well as test preparation

Digital Resources for the Teacher at my.hrw.com

Online Teacher's Edition

performance))space

- Teacher can give spoken and written feedback to student responses
- Teacher Dashboard to manage student responses

Teacher One Stop (online and on DVD)

- Pre-AP Digital Resources (Level 3)
- All Print Resources
- Audio and Video
- Teacher Edition
- Calendar Planner (on DVD)
- Projectable Transparencies
- Middle School Bridging Packet (Level 1)
- Lesson Plans
- Teaching Proficiency through Reading and Storytelling
- *Français pour hispanophones*
- ExamView Assessment Suite
- Teacher to Teacher Copymasters
- Block Scheduling Copymasters

Interactive Whiteboard Lessons

- Interactive practice and games for the whole class

Pre-AP Digital Resources (Level 3)

- Include readings, audio, printable worksheets, teaching suggestions, and other resources to help prepare students for the new AP French Language and Culture Exam

Video Program (online and on DVD)

- Includes vocabulary video with pop-up words, dramatic vignettes that contextualize new language, and cultural segments

Audio Program

- Provides selections from the Student Edition, Workbook, and Assessment

Online Assessment

- ExamView Assessment Suite
- Holt McDougal Online Assessment
- Generate Success Rubric Generator

Additional Digital Resources for the Teacher

Power Presentations CD-ROM
- Editable PowerPoint slides, projectable transparencies for oral and written practice, and customizable clip art

Sing Along Grammar and Vocabulary Songs Audio CD with Booklet (Levels 1-2)
- Reinforces grammar and vocabulary with lyrics, music sheets, and songs that reflect the diversity of the francophone world

Print Resources for the Teacher

Teacher's Edition

Lectures pour tous Teacher's Edition

Unit Resource Books
- Workbook Teacher's Edition
- *Activités pour tous* Teacher's Edition
- Communipak (Levels 1–2)
- Reading and Culture Activities
- Lesson Plans
- Block Scheduling Lesson Plans
- Family Letters
- Absent Student Copymasters
- Family Involvement
- Video Activities
- Videoscript
- Audioscript
- Assessment
    - Lesson Quizzes
    - Unit Test Forms A & B
    - Listening Comprehension Performance Test
    - Speaking Performance Test
    - Reading Comprehension Performance Test
    - Writing Performance Test
    - Multiple Choice Test Items
    - Test-Scoring Tools

DISCOVERING FRENCH TODAY!

▶ *Discovering French Today!* is a carefully articulated three-level sequence of French instruction. Each level has its own special focus, which builds a spiraling progression across levels.

	CONVERSATION	DESCRIPTION	NARRATION	EXPLANATION
BLEU	Basic communication with learned phrases; simple questions and answers	Simple descriptions of people and things	Simple narration in the present; introduction to past narration	Simple explanations as to why something is done
BLANC	Creative conversation; asking and answering questions	More detailed descriptions, including simple comparisons	Basic narration in the past (*passé composé* and imperfect) and future	Expression of personal wishes and needs
ROUGE	Extended conversation using complex sentences and appropriate pronouns	More complex comparisons of people, things and actions	Extended narration of past, present and future events and corresponding conditions	Expression of emotions, wishes and hypotheses in complex sentences

▶ This chart shows the articulation of basic communication themes and topics across levels. (Only the major entry and reentry points are shown.) These themes and topics are recycled throughout the program in the various exercises, readings and communication activities.

THEMES AND TOPICS	BLEU	BLANC	ROUGE
Greeting and meeting people	Unit 1	Reprise: Rappel 1	–
Time and weather	Unit 2	Reprise: Rappel 1	Unit 3
Family and friends; Family relationships	Unit 1	Unit 1	Reprise A; Unit 9
Food and restaurants	Unit 2 Unit 8	Units 1, 3	Reprise A
Money and shopping	Units 2, 6	Reprise: Rappel 2	Reprise B; Unit 4
School and education	Images: À l'école en France	Reprise: Faisons connaissance	Unit 10
Daily activities	Unit 3	Reprise: Rappel 3	Reprise A
Getting around the city	Unit 3 Unit 5	Unit 2	Unit 8
Describing oneself	Unit 4	Units 1, 7	Unit 1
Home and furnishings	Units 4, 5	Unit 6	Unit 6
Possessions and their description	Unit 4	Reprise: Rappel 2 Unit 2	Reprise A; Unit 2
Sports, fitness, daily routine	Unit 5	Units 5, 8	Unit 1
Medical and dental care	–	Unit 5	Unit 7
Clothing and personal appearance	Unit 6	Unit 7	Reprise A; Unit 4
Leisure activities, music, entertainment	Unit 7	Unit 4	Interlude 4
Vacation and travel	Unit 7	Unit 8	Reprise B; Unit 3
Transportation	Unit 7	Units 8, 9	Unit 5
Jobs and professions	–	Unit 1	Units 2, 10
Helping around the house	–	Unit 2	Unit 2
Nature and the environment	–	Unit 2	Unit 3
Services and repairs	–	–	Unit 4
Hotel accommodations	–	–	Unit 6

FUNCTION	BLEU	BLANC	ROUGE
Greeting people and socializing	Units 1, 2	Reprise: Rappel 1	–
Talking about the present Asking and answering questions Describing people, places and things Describing future plans (Simple description)	Units 3, 4, 5, 6	Reprise: Rappels 2, 3; Unit 1	Reprise A
Narrating past events (Simple narration)	Unit 7	Unit 2	Reprise B
Discussing daily routines (Simple narration)	–	Unit 5	Unit 1
Describing people, places, things (Extended description)	Unit 8	Units 3, 4, 5	Reprise C Units 2, 4
Describing past conditions and narrating past events (Extended narration)	–	Unit 6	Reprise B Units 3, 7
Comparing and discussing people, things and actions (Complex description)	–	Unit 7	Units 6, 9
Discussing future events (Extended narration)	–	Unit 8	Unit 5, 8
Discussing hypothetical conditions and events (Complex discussion)	–	Unit 8	Units 5, 8
Expressing wishes and obligations (Direct statements)	–	Unit 9	Unit 2
Expressing doubts and emotions (Complex discussion)	–	–	Unit 7
Expressing cause and purpose (Complex discussion)	–	–	Unit 10

Discovering French Today!

LEVEL 1 Bleu

Unité 4	Unité 7	Unité 8	
Leçon 10 • Optional presentation of the **passé composé** appears in the Teacher's Edition.	**Leçon 21** • Faire de + sport **Leçon 22** • The **passé composé** of **-er** verbs • Expressions with **avoir** **Leçon 23** • The **passé composé** of **-ir** verbs • The **passé composé** of **-re** verbs • The **passé composé** of irregular verbs • The verb **voir** **Leçon 24** • The **passé composé** with **être**	**Leçon 26** • The verb **prendre** • The verb **vouloir** • The verb **boire** • Partitive article **Leçon 27** • The verbs **pouvoir** and **devoir** • Pronouns **me, te, nous, vous** • Pronouns with commands	**Leçon 28** • The verb **connaître** • The verbs **dire** and **écrire** • Pronouns **le, la, les, lui, leur**

LEVEL 2 Blanc

Unité 1	Unité 2	Unité 3	Unité 4	Unité 5
Leçon 3 • The verb **faire** • The verb **avoir** **Leçon 4** • The verb **aller** • The verb **venir** • The construction **aller** + infinitive	**Leçon 6** • The **passé composé** with **avoir** • The verbs **mettre, permettre,** and **promettre** • The verb **prendre** **Leçon 7** • The **passé composé** with **avoir** *(cont.)* • The **passé composé** with **être** The verb **voir** **Leçon 8** • The **passé composé** with **être** *(cont.)*	**Leçon 10** • The verb **vouloir** • Partitive article • The verbs **pouvoir** and **devoir** **Leçon 11** • The verb **préférer** • The verb **boire** • The verb **acheter** • The verb **payer**	**Leçon 14** • Object pronouns **me, te, nous, vous** • Object pronouns in commands **Leçon 15** • The verb **connaître** • Object pronouns **le, la, les** **Leçon 16** • The verbs **écrire, lire,** and **dire** • Object pronouns **lui, leur**	**Leçon 18** • The pronouns **en** and **y** **Leçon 19** • Definite article with parts of the body • Reflexive verbs: present tense **Leçon 20** • Reflexive verbs: infinitive constructions

LEVEL 3 Rouge

Unité 1	Unité 2 — Recycles *Blanc Unité 9*	Unité 3	Unité 4	Unité 5 — Recycles *Blanc Unité 8*
Partie 1 • Definite article with parts of the body • Reflexive verbs: present tense • Reflexive verbs: infinitive constructions **Partie 2** • Reflexive verbs: **passé composé** • Reflexive verbs: idiomatic usage Recycles some topics from Blanc Unité 5	**Partie 1** • Present subjunctive: regular forms • Usage of the subjunctive after **il faut que** **Partie 2** • Present subjunctive: irregular forms • Usage of the subjunctive after certain impersonal expressions and **vouloir que**	**Partie 1** • Review of the **passé composé** • Review of the imperfect • Contrasting the imperfect and the **passé composé** **Partie 2** • Describing an event using the imperfect and the **passé composé** • Using the imperfect and the **passé composé** in the same sentence • The **passé simple** Recycles some topics from Blanc Unité 6	**Partie 1** • Review of the pronouns **en** and **y** • Indefinite expressions of quantity **Partie 2** • Review of the pronouns **le, la, les, lui, leur** • The order of pronouns • The construction **faire** + infinitive Recycles some topics from Blanc Unité 4	**Partie 1** • Negative expressions • The expression **ne … que** **Partie 2** • The future tense • The future with **si**-clauses • The future with **quand** • The conditional

Grammar Across Levels

Discovering French Today! addresses the challenges of articulation between levels by providing a unique instructional overlap. Much of the grammar and vocabulary taught in Units 7 and 8 of **Bleu** are covered again in **Blanc,** so teachers can choose how far into the grammatical and functional sequence they wish to go. Since the units of **Rouge** are self-contained, they can be taught in any order. Students' study of French can continue seamlessly!

Unité 6	Unité 7	Unité 8	Unité 9
Leçon 23 • The imperfect • Contrasting the imperfect and the passé composé **Leçon 24** • Contrasting the imperfect and the passé composé *(cont.)*	**Leçon 27** • Comparisons with adjectives • Comparisons with adverbs • Superlative constructions **Leçon 28** • Pronouns **lequel** and **celui**	**Leçon 31** • The future tense • The future with **si**-clauses • The future with **quand** **Leçon 32** • The conditional	**Leçon 35** • Present subjunctive: regular forms • Usage of the subjunctive after **il faut que** **Leçon 36** • Present subjunctive: irregular forms • Usage of the subjunctive after **vouloir que**

Unité 6 Recycles *Blanc* Unité 7	Unité 7	Unité 8	Unité 9	Unité 10
Partie 1 • Comparisons with adjectives • Comparisons with adverbs • The superlative **Partie 2** • The pronouns **lequel** and **celui** • Possessive pronouns	**Partie 1** • Concept of the subjunctive • The verbs **croire** and **craindre** • Usage of the subjunctive: emotions, feelings, doubt **Partie 2** • The past subjunctive	**Partie 1** • The construction **si** + imperfect • The **plus-que-parfait** **Partie 2** • Review of the conditional • The conditional in phrases with **si** • Other uses of the conditional **Partie 3** • The past conditional • Summary of tenses with **si**	**Partie 1** • Using reflexive verbs to express reciprocal action • Review of the relative pronouns **qui** and **que** • The construction preposition + relative pronoun • The relative pronoun **dont** **Partie 2** • Summary of relative pronouns • **Ce qui, ce que,** and **ce dont**	**Partie 1** • The construction preposition + infinitive • The past infinitive • The present participle **Partie 2** • The construction conjunction + subjunctive

LEVEL 1 SCOPE AND SEQUENCE

UNITÉ 1 Faisons connaissance • CULTURAL CONTEXT Meeting people

COMMUNICATION: FUNCTIONS AND ACTIVITIES COMPREHENSION AND SELF-EXPRESSION	COMMUNICATION TOPICS THEMATIC VOCABULARY	LINGUISTIC GOALS ACCURACY OF EXPRESSION
Meeting people • Introducing oneself **(Leçon 1A)** • Spelling one's name **(Leçon 1A)** • Asking someone's name **(Leçon 1A)** • Saying where you are from **(Leçon 1B)**	• Adjectives of nationality **(Leçon 1B)**	• **L'alphabet (Leçon 1A)** • **Français / française (Leçon 1B)**
Greeting people • Saying hello **(Leçon 1A)** • Asking how people feel **(Leçon 1C)** • Saying good-bye (Leçon 1C)	• Expressions with **ça va (Leçon 1C)** • Counting 0 to 10 (Leçon 1A) • Counting 10 to 20 (Leçon 1B) • Counting 20 to 60 (Leçon 1C)	
Talking about other people • Pointing people out **(Leçon 2A)** • Finding out someone's name (Leçon 2B) • Saying where a person is from (Leçon 2B)	• People **(Leçon 2A)**	• **Un garçon / une fille (Leçon 2A)** • **Le garçon / la fille (Leçon 2B)**
Introducing one's family • Giving their names **(Leçon 2B)** • Giving their ages (Leçon 2C)	• Family members **(Leçon 2C)** • Counting 60 to 79 (Leçon 2A) • Counting 80 to 100 (Leçon 2B)	• **Mon cousin / ma cousine (Leçon 2C)** • **Ton cousin / ta cousine (Leçon 2C)**

UNITÉ 2 La vie courante • CULTURAL CONTEXT Having a snack in France

Saying you are hungry • Offering a friend something to eat **(Leçon 3A)** • Asking a friend for something to eat (Leçon 3A)	• Foods **(Leçon 3A)**	• **Un sandwich / une pizza (Leçon 3A)**
Saying you are thirsty • Ordering a beverage in a café **(Leçon 3B)** • Asking an adult for something to eat or drink (Leçon 3B)	• Beverages **(Leçon 3B)**	• **S'il te plaît / s'il vous plaît (Leçon 3B)**
Paying at a café in France • Asking what something costs **(Leçon 3C)** • Asking a friend to lend you money (Leçon 3C)		
Talking about time • Asking for the time **(Leçon 4A)** • Indicating the time (Leçon 4A) • Saying when certain events are scheduled (Leçon 4A)	• Expressions of time **(Leçon 4A)**	
Talking about dates • Asking the day of the week **(Leçon 4B)** • Giving the date (Leçon 4B) • Talking about birthdays (Leçon 4B)	• Days of the week **(Leçon 4B)** • Months of the year (Leçon 4B)	
Talking about the weather	• Weather expressions **(Leçon 4C)** • Seasons (Leçon 4C)	

UNITÉ 3 Qu'est-ce qu'on fait? • CULTURAL CONTEXT Daily activities at home, at school, on weekends

COMMUNICATION: FUNCTIONS AND ACTIVITIES COMPREHENSION AND SELF-EXPRESSION	COMMUNICATION TOPICS THEMATIC VOCABULARY	LINGUISTIC GOALS ACCURACY OF EXPRESSION
Describing daily activities • What people do and don't do **(Leçon 5)** • What people like to do and don't like to do **(Leçon 5)** • What you want and don't want to do (Leçon 5)	• Daily activities **(Leçon 5)** • Expressions with faire (Leçon 8)	• Subject pronouns **(Leçon 6)** • The negative **ne… pas** **(Leçon 6)** • Verb + infinitive (Leçon 7) • Regular **-er** verbs **(Leçon 7)** • The verb **faire** **(Leçon 8)**
Talking about where people are	• Places **(Leçon 6)**	• The verb **être** **(Leçon 6)**
Finding out what is going on • Asking yes/no questions **(Leçon 6)** • Asking information questions (Leçon 8)	• Question words **(Leçon 8)**	• Yes/no questions with **est-ce que** **(Leçon 6)** • Information questions with **est-ce que** **(Leçon 8)** • Questions with inversion (Leçon 8)
Inviting friends to do things with you • Extending an invitation **(Leçon 5)** • Accepting an invitation (Leçon 5) • Turning down an invitation (Leçon 5)		• Verb + infinitive **(Leçon 7)**
Expanding one's conversational skills • Answering yes/no questions **(Leçon 6)** • Expressing approval or regret (Leçon 7) • Expressing mild doubt or surprise (Leçon 8)	• Affirmative and negative expressions **(Leçon 6)**	

UNITÉ 4 Le monde personnel et familier • CULTURAL CONTEXT People and their possessions

Describing yourself and others • Physical appearance **(Leçon 9)** • Age (Leçons 9, 10) • Character traits (Leçon 11) • Nationality (Leçon 11)	• People **(Leçon 9)** • Adjectives of physical description (Leçon 9) • Adjectives of personality (Leçon 11) • Adjectives of nationality (Leçon 11) • Adjectives of aspect (Leçon 12)	• Singular and plural nouns **(Leçon 10)** • Definite and indefinite articles (Leçon 10) • The expression **avoir… ans** **(Leçon 10)** • Adjective formation (Leçon 11) • Adjective position (Leçons 11, 12) • Use of **c'est** and **il est** **(Leçon 12)**
Describing your room • What is in it **(Leçon 9)** • Where things are located (Leçon 9	• Room furnishings **(Leçon 9)** • Prepositions of place (Leçon 9)	• The expression **il y a** **(Leçon 9)**
Talking about possessions • Things that one owns and doesn't own **(Leçons 9, 10)** • Whether they work or not (Leçon 9) • Where they were made (Leçon 11) • What they look like (Leçon 12)	• Everyday objects **(Leçon 9)** • Color (Leçon 12) • Aspect (Leçon 12)	• The verb **avoir** **(Leçon 10)** • The negative article **pas de** **(Leçon 10)**
Expanding one's conversational skills • Getting someone's attention **(Leçon 12)** • Making generalizations (Leçon 10) • Expressing opinions (Leçon 12) • Talking about regular events (Leçon 10) • Contradicting a negative statement or question (Leçon 10) • Introducing a conclusion (Leçon 11)	• Attention getters **(Leçon 12)** • Expressions of opinion (Leçon 12)	• Use of the definite article: in general statements to indicate repeated events **(Leçon 10)** • Impersonal **c'est** **(Leçon 12)**
optional: • Talking about past events **(Leçons 10, 11, 12)**		• Conversational introduction: answering questions in the **passé composé** **(Leçons 10, 11, 12)**

UNITÉ 5 En ville • CULTURAL CONTEXT City life—the home, the family and urban activities

COMMUNICATION: FUNCTIONS AND ACTIVITIES COMPREHENSION AND SELF-EXPRESSION	**COMMUNICATION TOPICS** THEMATIC VOCABULARY	**LINGUISTIC GOALS** ACCURACY OF EXPRESSION
Describing your city • Streets and public buildings **(Leçon 13)** • Places you often go to (Leçon 14) • How you get around (Leçon 14)	• City places and buildings **(Leçon 13)** • Transportation (Leçon 14)	• The verb **aller** (Leçon 14) • Contractions with **à** (Leçon 14)
Finding your way around • Asking and giving directions **(Leçon 13)** • Indicating the floor (Leçon 16)	• Giving directions **(Leçon 13)**	• Ordinal numbers **(Leçon 16)**
Describing your home and your family • Your address **(Leçon 13)** • The inside and outside of your home (Leçon 13) • Your family (Leçon 16)	• Neighborhood **(Leçon 13)** • Rooms of the house (Leçon 13) • Family members **(Leçon 16)**	• The expression **chez** (Leçon 14) • Stress pronouns (Leçon 15) • The construction noun + **de** + noun **(Leçon 15)** • Possession with **de** (Leçon 16) • Possessive adjectives (Leçon 16)
Making plans to do things in town • What you are going to do **(Leçon 14)** • Asking others to come along (Leçon 15) • Saying where you have been (Leçon 15)	• Activities: sports, games, etc. **(Leçon 15)**	• **Aller** + infinitive **(Leçon 14)** • The verb **venir** (Leçon 15) • Contractions with **de** (Leçon 15)
Expanding one's conversational skills: • Contradicting someone **(Leçon 15)** • Expressing doubt (Leçon 16) • Expressing surprise (Leçon 15)		
optional: Talking about past events **(Leçons 13, 14, 15, 16)**		• Conversational introduction: answering questions in the **passé composé (Leçons 13, 14, 15, 16)**

UNITÉ 6 Le shopping • CULTURAL CONTEXT Buying clothes

Talking about clothes • What people are wearing **(Leçon 17)** • Whether the clothes fit (Leçon 17) • What they look like (Leçons 17, 19) • What one's preferences are (Leçon 17)	• Clothing and accessories **(Leçon 17)** • Descriptive adjectives (Leçon 17) • Adjectives **beau, nouveau, vieux (Leçon 19)** • Expressions of opinion (Leçon 17)	• The verb **mettre** (Leçon 18) • The verb **préférer** (Leçon 18) • The demonstrative **ce** (Leçon 18) • The interrogative **quel?** (Leçon 18)
Discussing shopping plans • Where to go **(Leçons 17, 20)** • What to buy (Leçon 18)	• Stores that sell clothes **(Leçon 17)** • Verbs like **vendre** (Leçon 20)	• The verb **acheter** (Leçon 18) • Regular **-re** verbs (Leçon 20) • The pronoun **on** (Leçon 20)
Buying clothes • Asking for help **(Leçon 17)** • Finding out prices (Leçons 17, 20) • Deciding what to choose (Leçon 19) • Comparing items (Leçon 19) • Talking about what you need and what you like (Leçon 20) • Giving advice (Leçon 20)	• Numbers 100–1000 **(Leçon 17)** • Money-related expressions **(Leçon 20)** • Verbs like **choisir** (Leçon 19) • Expressions **avoir besoin de** and **avoir envie de** (Leçon 20)	• Regular **-ir** verbs (Leçon 19) • The verb **payer** (Leçon 20) • Comparisons (Leçon 19) • The imperative (Leçon 20)
Expanding one's conversational skills • Emphasizing a remark **(Leçon 18)** • Indicating approval (Leçon 20) • Introducing an opinion (Leçon 19)		
optional: Talking about past events **(Leçons 17, 18, 19, 20)**		• Conversational introduction: answering questions in the **passé composé (Leçons 17, 18, 19, 20)**

UNITÉ 7 Le temps libre • CULTURAL CONTEXT Leisure-time activities

COMMUNICATION: FUNCTIONS AND ACTIVITIES COMPREHENSION AND SELF-EXPRESSION	COMMUNICATION TOPICS THEMATIC VOCABULARY	LINGUISTIC GOALS ACCURACY OF EXPRESSION
Discussing leisure activities • Going out with friends **(Leçon 21)** • Sports (Leçon 21) • Helping around the house (Leçon 21) • How you and others feel (Leçon 22) • Things you never do (Leçon 24)	• Common weekend activities **(Leçon 21)** • Individual summer and winter sports **(Leçon 21)** • Household chores (Leçon 21)	• **Faire de** + sport **(Leçon 21)** • Expressions with **avoir** **(Leçon 22)** • **Ne … jamais** **(Leçon 24)**
Describing vacation travel plans • Travel dates **(Leçons 21, 24)** • How to travel (Leçon 21) • How long to stay (Leçons 21, 23) • What to see (Leçon 23)	• Means of transportation **(Leçon 21)** • Divisions of time (Leçon 21) • Periods of future time (Leçon 23) • Verbs of movement (Leçon 24)	• The verb **voir** **(Leçon 23)**
Narrating what happened • What you did and didn't do **(Leçons 22, 23)** • Where you went and when you returned (Leçon 24) • The sequence in which you did these things (Leçon 22) • Remaining vague about certain details (Leçon 24)	• Adverbs of sequence **(Leçon 22)** • Periods of past time (Leçon 23)	• **Passé composé** of **-er** verbs **(Leçon 22)** • **Passé composé** of **-ir** verbs **(Leçon 23)** • **Passé composé** of **-re** verbs **(Leçon 23)** • **Passé composé** of irregular verbs **(Leçon 23)** • **Passé composé** with **être** **(Leçon 24)** • **Quelqu'un, quelque chose** and their opposites **(Leçon 24)**

UNITÉ 8 Les repas • CULTURAL CONTEXT Food and meals

COMMUNICATION: FUNCTIONS AND ACTIVITIES	COMMUNICATION TOPICS	LINGUISTIC GOALS
Talking about your favorite foods • What you like and don't like **(Leçon 25)** • What you can, should and want to eat (Leçons 25, 26, 27)	• Names of foods and beverages **(Leçon 25)** • Verbs of preference (Leçon 25)	• The verb **vouloir** (Leçon 26) • The verbs **pouvoir** and **devoir** (Leçon 27)
Shopping for food • Making a shopping list **(Leçon 25)** • Interacting with vendors (Leçon 25) • Asking prices (Leçon 25)	• Quantities **(Leçon 25)** • Fruits and vegetables (Leçon 25)	• Partitive article **(Leçon 26)**
Planning a meal • Asking others to help you **(Leçon 27)** • Setting the table (Leçon 25	• Meals **(Leçon 25)** • Verbs asking for service (Leçon 27) • Place setting (Leçon 25)	• Pronouns **me, te, nous, vous** (Leçon 27) • Pronouns with commands (Leçon 27)
Eating out with friends • Ordering food **(Leçon 25)** • Asking the waiter/waitress to bring things for others (Leçon 28) • Talking about people you know (Leçon 27) • Talking about what others have said or written (Leçon 28) •	• Verbs using indirect objects **(Leçon 28)**	• The verb **prendre** (Leçon 26) • The verb **boire** (Leçon 26) • The verb **connaître** (Leçon 28) • The verbs **dire** and écrire (Leçon 28) • Pronouns **le, la, les, lui, leur** (Leçon 28)

LEVEL 2 SCOPE AND SEQUENCE

REPRISE (REVIEW) Entre amis • CULTURAL CONTEXT Getting acquainted

COMMUNICATION: FUNCTIONS AND ACTIVITIES COMPREHENSION AND SELF-EXPRESSION	COMMUNICATION TOPICS THEMATIC VOCABULARY	LINGUISTIC GOALS ACCURACY OF EXPRESSION
Talking about school and classes (Faisons connaissance!)	• School subjects **(Faisons connaissance!)**	
Expressing oneself on familiar topics • Giving the date **(Rappel 1)** • Telling time (Rappel 1) • Describing the weather (Rappel 1)	• Review: numbers 1-100 **(Appendix A)** • Review: days, months (Appendix A) • Review: times of day (Appendix A) • Review: weather (Appendix A)	
Talking about places and things • Describing things you own **(Rappel 2)** • Saying where things are (Rappel 2) • Pointing things out (Rappel 2) • Expressing preferences (Rappel 2)	• Review: common objects and items of clothing **(Appendix A)** • Prepositions of location (Rappel 2) • Review: place names (Appendix A)	• Review: articles and contractions, **ce** and **quel** **(Appendix A)** • Review: possessive adjectives (Appendix A)
Carrying out simple conversations • Asking and answering questions **(Rappel 3)** • Talking about daily activities (Rappel 3) • Talking about places where you go (Rappel 3) • Saying what you like (Rappel 3)	• Review: question words **(Rappel 3)** • Review: common **–er, -ir, -re** verbs **(Appendix A)**	• Review: present tense of regular verbs **(Appendix A)** • Review: interrogative and negative constructions (Appendix A) • Review: subject pronouns and stress pronouns (Rappel 3) • Review: the imperative (Appendix A)

UNITÉ 1 Qui suis-je? • CULTURAL CONTEXT Oneself and others

Presenting oneself and others • Providing personal data **(Leçon 1)** • Identifying one's family (Leçon 1) • Talking about professions (Leçon 1)	• Adjectives of nationality **(Leçon 1)** • Family and friends (Leçon 1) • Professions (Leçon 1)	• The verb **être** **(Leçon 2)** • **C'est** and **il est** **(Leçon 2)**
Interacting with others • Introducing people **(Leçon 1)** • Making phone calls (Leçon 1) • Reading birth and wedding announcements (Leçon 1)		
Talking about oneself and others • Describing looks and personality **(Leçon 2)** • Talking about age (Leçon 3) • Describing feelings and needs (Leçon 3)	• Descriptive adjectives **(Leçon 2)** • Expressions with **avoir** **(Leçon 3)** • Expressions with **faire** **(Leçon 3)**	• Regular and irregular adjectives **(Leçon 2)** • The verb **avoir** **(Leçon 3)** • The verb **faire** **(Leçon 3)** • Inverted questions (Leçon 3)
Describing one's plans • Saying where people are going and what they are going to do **(Leçon 4)** • Saying where people are coming from (Leçon 4) • Saying how long people have been doing things (Leçon 5)	• Expressions with **depuis** **(Leçon 4)**	• The verb **aller** **(Leçon 4)** • The construction **aller** + infinitive **(Leçon 4)** • The verb **venir** **(Leçon 4)** • The present with **depuis** **(Leçon 4)**
READING Getting the gist		

UNITÉ 2 Le week-end, enfin · CULTURAL CONTEXT Weekend activities

COMMUNICATION: FUNCTIONS AND ACTIVITIES COMPREHENSION AND SELF-EXPRESSION	COMMUNICATION TOPICS THEMATIC VOCABULARY	LINGUISTIC GOALS ACCURACY OF EXPRESSION
Talking about weekend plans • Describing weekend plans in the city **(Leçon 5)** • Planning a visit to the country (Leçon 5)	• Going out with friends **(Leçon 5)** • Helping at home (Leçon 5) • The country and the farm (Leçon 5) • Domestic and other animals (Leçon 5) • Expressions of present and future time (Leçon 7)	• The verbs **mettre, permettre,** and **promettre** **(Leçon 6)** • The verb **voir** **(Leçon 7)** • The verbs **sortir, partir,** and **dormir** **(Leçon 8)**
Getting from one place to another • Getting around in Paris **(Leçon 5)** • Visiting the countryside (Leçon 5)	• Getting around by subway **(Leçon 5)**	• The verb **prendre** **(Leçon 6)**
Narrating past weekend activities • Talking about where one went **(Leçons 7, 8)** • Talking about what one did and did not do (Leçons 6, 7, 8)	• Expressions of past time **(Leçon 6)**	• The **passé composé** with **avoir** **(Leçons 6, 7)** • The **passé composé** with **être** **(Leçons 7, 8)** • Impersonal expressions: **quelqu'un, quelque chose, personne, rien** **(Leçon 7)** • **Il y a** + elapsed time **(Leçon 8)**

READING Recognizing word families

UNITÉ 3 Bon appétit! · CULTURAL CONTEXT Meals and food shopping

Planning a meal • Talking about where to eat **(Leçon 9)** • Setting the table (Leçon 9)	• Meals **(Leçon 9)** • Place setting (Leçon 9)	
Going to a café • Ordering in a café **(Leçon 9)**	• Café foods and beverages **(Leçon 9)**	• The verb **boire** **(Leçon 11)**
Talking about favorite foods • Discussing preferences **(Leçon 9)** • Expressing what one wants (Leçon 12)	• Mealtime foods and beverages **(Leçon 9)** • Fruits and vegetables (Leçon 9)	• The verb **préférer** **(Leçon 11)** • The verb **vouloir** **(Leçon 10)**
Shopping for food at a market • Interacting with vendors and asking prices **(Leçon 9)** • Asking for specific quantities (Leçon 9) • Discussing what one can get (Leçon 12) • Talking about what one should buy or do (Leçon 12)	• Common quantities **(Leçon 12)** • Expressions of quantity (Leçon 12)	• Partitive article **(Leçon 10)** • The verbs **acheter** and **payer** **(Leçon 11)** • Expressions of quantity with **de** **(Leçon 12)** • The adjective **tout** **(Leçon 12)** • The verbs **devoir** and **pouvoir** **(Leçon 10)** • The expression **il faut** **(Leçon 12)**

READING Reading by phrase groups

UNITÉ 4 Loisirs et spectacles!   CULTURAL CONTEXT Free time and entertainment

COMMUNICATION: FUNCTIONS AND ACTIVITIES COMPREHENSION AND SELF-EXPRESSION	COMMUNICATION TOPICS THEMATIC VOCABULARY	LINGUISTIC GOALS ACCURACY OF EXPRESSION
Planning one's free time • Going out with friends **(Leçon 13)** • Extending, accepting, and turning down invitations (Leçon 13) • Talking about concerts and movies (Leçon 13)	• Places to go and things to do **(Leçon 13)** • Types of movies (Leçon 13)	
Talking about your friends and your neighborhood • Describing people and places you know **(Leçon 15)**		• The verb **connaître** **(Leçon 15)** • Object pronouns **le, la, les** **(Leçon 15)** • The verb **savoir** **(Leçon 16)**
Discussing relations with others • Asking others for assistance **(Leçon 14)** • Describing services of others (Leçon 16)	• Verbs asking for a service **(Leçon 14)** • Verbs using indirect objects (Leçon 16)	• Object pronouns **me, te, nous, vous** **(Leçon 14)** • Object pronouns **lui, leur** **(Leçon 16)** • Object pronouns in commands (Leçon 14) • Double object pronouns (Leçon 16)
Reading and writing about daily events • Writing a letter to a friend **(Leçon 14)** • Discussing what you like to read (Leçon 16) • Talking about what others have written or said (Leçon 16)	• Expressions used in letters **(Leçon 14)** • Reading materials (Leçon 16)	• The verbs **écrire, lire**, and **dire** **(Leçon 16)**
Narrating what happened • Talking about losing and finding things **(Leçon 15)**	• Verbs used to talk about possessions **(Leçon 15)**	• Object pronouns in the **passé composé** **(Leçon 15)**

READING Inferring meaning

UNITÉ 5 Vive le sport!   CULTURAL CONTEXT Sports and health

Discussing sports • Finding out what sports your friends like **(Leçon 17)** • Talking about where you practice sports and when (Leçon 18) • Giving your opinion (Leçon 18)	• Individual sports **(Leçon 17)** • Adverbs of frequency (Leçon 18) • Expressions of opinion (Leçon 18)	• The verb **courir** **(Leçon 17)** • The expression **faire du** **(Leçon 17)** • The pronouns **en** and **y** **(Leçon 18)**
Discussing fitness and health • Describing exercise routine **(Leçon 17)** • Describing common pains and illnesses (Leçon 17)	• Parts of the body **(Leçon 17)** • Health (Leçon 17)	• The expression **avoir mal à** **(Leçon 17)** • Definite article with parts of the body (Leçon 19)
Talking about one's daily activities • Describing the daily routine **(Leçon 19)** • Caring for one's appearance (Leçon 19) • Giving others advice (Leçon 20) • Asking about tomorrow's plans (Leçon 20)	• Daily occupations **Leçon 19)** • Hygiene and personal care (Leçon 19)	• Reflexive verbs: present tense **(Leçon 19)** • Reflexive verbs: imperative (Leçon 20) • Reflexive verbs: infinitive constructions (Leçon 20)
Narrating past activities • Describing one's daily routine in the past **(Leçon 20)**	• Common activities **(Leçon 20)**	• Reflexive verbs: **passé composé (Leçon 20)**

READING Recognizing prefixes

UNITÉ 6 Chez nous   CULTURAL CONTEXT   House and home

COMMUNICATION: FUNCTIONS AND ACTIVITIES COMPREHENSION AND SELF-EXPRESSION	COMMUNICATION TOPICS THEMATIC VOCABULARY	LINGUISTIC GOALS ACCURACY OF EXPRESSION
Discussing where you live • Describing the location of your house or apartment **(Leçon 21)** • Explaining what your house or apartment looks like (Leçon 21)	• Location of one's home **(Leçon 21)** • Rooms of the house (Leçon 21) • Furniture and appliances (Leçon 21)	• The verb **vivre** **(Leçon 22)**
Renting an apartment or house • Reading classified ads **(Leçon 21)** • Asking about a rental (Leçon 21) • Giving more complete descriptions (Leçon 22)		• Relative pronouns **qui** and **que** **(Leçon 22)**
Talking about the past • Explaining what you used to do in the past and when **(Leçon 23)** • Describing ongoing past actions (Leçon 23) • Giving background information about specific past events (Leçon 24)	• Prepositions of time **(Leçon 23)** • An accident (Leçon 24)	• The imperfect **(Leçon 23)** • Contrasting the imperfect and the **passé composé** **(Leçons 23, 24)**

READING Recognizing partial cognates

UNITÉ 7 Soyez à la mode!   CULTURAL CONTEXT   Clothes and accessories

Talking about clothes • Saying what people are wearing **(Leçon 25)** • Describing clothes and accessories (Leçon 25)	• Clothes and accessories **(Leçon 25)** • Colors (Leçon 25) • Fabric, design, materials (Leçon 25)	
Shopping for clothes • Talking with the sales clerk **(Leçon 25)** • Expressing opinions (Leçon 25)	• Types of clothing stores **(Leçon 25)** • Sizes, looks, and price (Leçon 25) • Numbers 100-1,000,000 (Leçon 26) • Adjectives **beau, nouveau, vieux** **(Leçon 26)**	
Comparing people and things • Ranking items in a series **(Leçon 26)** • Expressing comparisons (Leçon 27) • Saying who or what is the best (Leçon 27) • Referring to specific items (Leçon 28)	• Descriptive adjectives **(Leçon 27)**	• Ordinal numbers **(Leçon 26)** • Comparisons with adjectives (Leçon 27) • Superlative constructions (Leçon 27) • Pronouns **lequel?** and **celui** **(Leçon 28)**
Talking about how things are done • Describing how things are done **(Leçon 26)** • Comparing how things are done (Leçon 27)	• Common adverbs **(Leçon 27)**	• Adverbs ending in **-ment** **(Leçon 26)** • Comparisons with adverbs (Leçon 27)

READING Understanding the context

UNITÉ 8 Bonnes vacances — CULTURAL CONTEXT Travel and summer vacations

COMMUNICATION: FUNCTIONS AND ACTIVITIES COMPREHENSION AND SELF-EXPRESSION	COMMUNICATION TOPICS THEMATIC VOCABULARY	LINGUISTIC GOALS ACCURACY OF EXPRESSION
Discussing summer vacations • Talking about vacation plans **(Leçon 29)** • Planning a camping trip **(Leçon 29)**	• Destinations, lodging, travel documents **(Leçon 29)** • Foreign countries **(Leçon 29)** • Camping equipment **(Leçon 29)**	• Prepositions with names of countries **(Leçon 30)** • The verbs **recevoir** and **apercevoir** **(Leçon 30)**
Making travel arrangements • Buying tickets **(Leçon 29)** • Checking schedules **(Leçon 29)** • Expressing polite requests **(Leçon 32)**	• At the train station, at the airport **(Leçon 29)**	• The use of the conditional to make polite requests **(Leçon 32)**
Talking about what you would do under various circumstances	• Verbs followed by infinitives **(Leçon 30)**	• The constructions verb **+ à** + infinitive, verb **+ de** + infinitive **(Leçon 30)**
Making future plans • Talking about the future **(Leçon 31)** • Setting forth conditions **(Leçon 31)**		• The future tense **(Leçon 31)** • The future with **si**-clauses **(Leçon 31)** • The future with **quand** **(Leçon 31)**
Talking about what one would do under certain circumstances • Discussing what would occur **(Leçon 32)** • Describing conditions **(Leçon 32)**		• The conditional **(Leçon 32)** • The conditional with **si**-clauses **(Leçon 32)**

READING Recognizing false cognates

UNITÉ 9 Bonne route — CULTURAL CONTEXT Getting around by car

Talking about cars • Describing cars **(Leçon 33)** • Having one's car serviced **(Leçon 33)** • Getting one's license **(Leçon 33)** • Rules of right of way **(Leçon 33)**	• Types of vehicles **(Leçon 33)** • Parts of a car **(Leçon 33)** • Car maintenance **(Leçon 33)**	• The verbs **conduire** and **suivre** **(Leçon 33)**
Expressing how one feels about certain events		• Adjective **+ de** + infinitive **(Leçon 34)**
Talking about past and present events • Describing purpose and sequence **(Leçon 34)** • Describing simultaneous actions and cause and effect **(Leçon 34)**	• Prepositions **pour, sans, avant de,** and **en** **(Leçon 34)**	• Preposition + infinitive **(Leçon 34)** • Present participle constructions **(Leçon 34)**
Discussing what has to be done • Expressing necessity and obligation **(Leçon 35)** • Letting others know what you want them to do **(Leçon 36)**	• **Il faut que** **(Leçon 35)** • **Je veux que** **(Leçon 36)**	• Present subjunctive: regular forms **(Leçon 35)** • Present subjunctive: irregular forms **(Leçon 36)**

READING Recognizing figures of speech

REPRISE • OBJECTIVE Light Review of Basic Material (from Levels One and Two)

BASIC REVIEW		CULTURE AND READING
STRUCTURES	**VOCABULARY**	**VACATION OPTIONS** Travel, sports, archaeology, helping others
A. La vie courante Describing the present • Present of regular verbs • **Être, avoir, aller, faire, venir** and expressions used with these verbs • Other common irregular verbs • Use of present with **depuis** • Regular and irregular adjectives • Use of the partitive article	• Daily activities • Food and beverages	The French-speaking world: Its people
B. Hier et avant Describing the past • **Passé composé** with **avoir** and **être** • Imperfect and its basic uses	• Clothes	The French-speaking world: Cultural background
C. Nous et les autres Referring to people, things, and places • Object pronouns • Negative expressions • **Connaître** and **savoir** • Other irregular verbs		**Lecture: *Les trois bagues***

UNITÉ 1 Au jour le jour • MAIN THEMES Looking good; one's daily routine

COMMUNICATION OBJECTIVES		READING AND CULTURAL OBJECTIVES		Interlude Culturel 1
COMMUNICATION: FUNCTIONS AND CONTEXTS LE FRANÇAIS PRATIQUE	**LINGUISTIC GOALS** LANGUE ET COMMUNICATION	**DAILY LIFE** INFO MAGAZINE	**READING** LECTURE	Le monde des arts GENERAL CULTURAL BACKGROUND
Describing people • Their physical appearance **Caring for one's appearance** • Personal care and hygiene • Looking good **Describing the various aspects of one's daily routine** **Expressing how one feels and inquiring about other people**	**Describing people and their ailments** • The use of the definite article **Describing what people do for themselves** • Reflexive verbs **Explaining one's daily activities** • Reflexive verbs: different tenses and uses	**How important is personal appearance for French young people and what do they do to enhance it?** • The importance of **le look** • Clothing and personal style **How have artists expressed their concept of beauty?** **How do people begin their daily routine?**	Ionesco, ***Conte pour enfants de moins de trois ans***	**French modern art** • **Impressionism** and impressionist artists: **Monet, Degas, Renoir, Manet, B. Morisot** • Artists of the **post-impressionist** era: **Van Gogh, Gauguin, Rousseau, Toulouse-Lautrec** • **Surrealism** as an artistic and literary movement: **Magritte** **Poems** • Desnos, *La fourmi* • Prévert, *Pour faire le portrait d'un oiseau*

UNITÉ 2 Soyons utiles! • MAIN THEME Being helpful around the house

COMMUNICATION OBJECTIVES		READING AND CULTURAL OBJECTIVES		Interlude Culturel 2
COMMUNICATION: FUNCTIONS AND CONTEXTS LE FRANÇAIS PRATIQUE	**LINGUISTIC GOALS** LANGUE ET COMMUNICATION	**DAILY LIFE** INFO MAGAZINE	**READING** LECTURE	Les grands moments de l'histoire de France (jusqu'en 1453)
				GENERAL CULTURAL BACKGROUND
Helping around the house • In the house itself • Outside **Asking for help and offering to help** • Accepting or refusing help • Thanking people for their help **Describing an object** • Shape, weight, length, consistency, appearance, etc. • The material it is made of	**Explaining what has to be done** • **Il faut que** + subjunctive **Telling people what you would like them to do** • **Vouloir que** + subjunctive	**Why do French people enjoy do-it-yourself activities?** • What is **bricolage**? • What is **jardinage**? **How should you take care of your plants?** **How do French young people earn money by helping their neighbors?**	*La Couverture* (Une fable médiévale)	**Early French history** • Important events The Roman conquest The Holy Roman Empire The Norman Conquest of England The Hundred Years War • Important people **Vercingétorix** **Charlemagne** **Guillaume le Conquérant** **Aliénor d'Aquitaine** **Jeanne d'Arc** **Literature:** *La Chanson de Roland*

UNITÉ 3 Vive la nature! • MAIN THEMES Vacation and outdoor activities; the environment and its protection

				Interlude Culturel 3
				Les grands moments de l'histoire de France (1453-1715)
				GENERAL CULTURAL BACKGROUND
Talking about outdoor activities • What to do • What not to do **Describing the natural environment and how to protect it** **Talking about the weather and natural phenomena** **Relating a sequence of past events** **Describing habitual past actions**	**Talking about the past** • The **passé composé** • The imperfect • The **passé simple** • Contrastive uses of the **passé composé** and the imperfect **Narrating past events** • Differentiating between specific actions (**passé composé**) and the circumstances under which they occurred (imperfect) • Providing background information (imperfect)	**How do the French feel about nature and their land?** • What is **le tourisme vert**? • What is an **éco-musée**? **How do the French protect their environment?** • What rules to observe on camping trips • What young people do to protect the environment • Who was **Jacques-Yves Cousteau**? **Why do the French people love the sun?**	• Sempé / Goscinny, *King*	**The classical period of French history** • Important periods: **la Renaissance, le Grand Siècle** • Important people: **François Ier, Louis XIV** • French castles, as witnesses of French history **Literature** • La Fontaine, *Le Corbeau et le renard* • Prévert, *Soyons polis* **Film:** Rostand, *Cyrano de Bergerac*

UNITÉ 4 Aspects de la vie quotidienne • MAIN THEME Going shopping and asking for services

COMMUNICATION OBJECTIVES		READING AND CULTURAL OBJECTIVES		Interlude Culturel 4
COMMUNICATION: FUNCTIONS AND CONTEXTS LE FRANÇAIS PRATIQUE	**LINGUISTIC GOALS** LANGUE ET COMMUNICATION	**DAILY LIFE** INFO MAGAZINE	**READING** LECTURE	Vive la musique!
				GENERAL CULTURAL BACKGROUND
Shopping for various items • in a stationery store • in a pharmacy • in a convenience store **Buying stamps and mailing items at the post office** **Having one's hair cut** **Asking for a variety of services** • at the cleaners • at the shoe repair shop • at the photo shop	**Answering questions and referring to people, things, and places using pronouns** • Object pronouns • Two-pronoun sequence **Talking about quantities** • The pronoun **en** • Indefinite expressions of quantity **Describing services that you have done by other people** • The construction **faire +** infinitive	**How are certain aspects of daily life different in France?** • Shopping on the Internet • Shopping in a supermarket • Services at the post office • When to tip and not to tip	*Histoire de cheveux*	**The musical landscape of France and the French-speaking world** • Classical musicians: **Lully, Chopin, Bizet, Debussy** • Historical overview of French songs • Famous French singers of yesterday and today • The multicultural aspect of music from the francophone world: **zouk** (Antilles); **raï** (North Africa); **cajun, zydéco** (Louisiana) **Song: Vigneault, *Mon pays*** **Opera: Bizet, *Carmen***

UNITÉ 5 Bon voyage! • MAIN THEME Travel

				Interlude Culturel 5
				Les grands moments de l'histoire de France (1715-1870)
				GENERAL CULTURAL BACKGROUND
Planning a trip abroad **Going through customs** **Making travel arrangements** • Purchasing tickets **Travel in France** • at the train station • at the airport	**Making negative statements** • Affirmative and negative expressions **Describing future plans** • Future tense • Use of future after **quand** **Hypothesizing about what one would do** • Introduction to the conditional	**What are the advantages of visiting France by train?** • The **TGV** • The **Eurotunnel** **Why do French people like to travel abroad and what do they do on their vacations?** • Impressions of young people visiting the United States	*Le mystérieux homme en bleu*	**The historical foundation of modern France** • Important periods the **French Revolution** the **Napoleonic era** • Important contemporary French institutions • Important people **Louis XVI et Marie-Antoinette Napoléon** **Song: Rouget de Lisle, *La Marseillaise*** **Literature: Victor Hugo, *Les Misérables***

UNITÉ 6 Séjour en France • MAIN THEME Hotels and other places to stay when traveling

COMMUNICATION OBJECTIVES		READING AND CULTURAL OBJECTIVES		Interlude Culturel 6
COMMUNICATION: FUNCTIONS AND CONTEXTS LE FRANÇAIS PRATIQUE	**LINGUISTIC GOALS** LANGUE ET COMMUNICATION	**DAILY LIFE** INFO MAGAZINE	**READING** LECTURE	Les grands moments de l'histoire de France (1870 au présent)
				GENERAL CULTURAL BACKGROUND
Deciding where to stay when traveling **Reserving a room in a hotel** **Asking for services in a hotel**	**Comparing people, things, places and situations** • The comparative • The superlative **Asking for an alternative** • The interrogative pronoun **lequel?** **Pointing out people or things** • The demonstrative pronoun **celui** **Indicating possession** • The possessive pronoun **le mien**	**What inexpensive accommodations are available to students?** • **Auberges de jeunesse** • **Séjour à la ferme** **How does one use the *Guide Michelin* when traveling in France?** • To find a hotel • To choose a restaurant	*Une étrange aventure*	**France in the 20th century** • Important events the two World Wars the economic union of Europe • Important people **Marie Curie** **Charles de Gaulle** **Simone Veil** Literature: **Éluard, Liberté** Film: **L. Malle,** *Au revoir, les Enfants*

UNITÉ 7 La forme et la santé • MAIN THEME Health and medical care

				Interlude Culturel 7 Les Français d'aujourd'hui
				GENERAL CULTURAL BACKGROUND
Going to the doctor's office • Describing your symptoms • Explaining what is wrong • Giving information about your medical history • Understanding the doctor's prescriptions **Going to the dentist** **Going to the emergency ward**	**Expressing how you and others feel about certain facts or events** • Use of the subjunctive after expressions of emotion **Expressing fear, doubt or disbelief** • Use of the subjunctive after expressions of doubt and uncertainty **Expressing feelings or attitudes about past actions and events** • The past subjunctive	**How do the French take care of their health?** • How does the French health system work? • What is the **Sécurité sociale?** • Why do the French consume so much mineral water? • What is **thermalisme?** **How do French doctors participate in humanitarian missions around the world?** • What is **Médecins sans frontières?**	**Maupassant,** *En voyage*	**Modern France as a multi-ethnic and multi-cultural society** • The French as citizens of Europe • The new French mosaic: the impact of immigration on French society • The **Maghrébins** – their culture and their religion • **SOS Racisme** • Two French humanitarians: **L'abbé Pierre** and **Coluche** Song: *Éthiopie*

UNITÉ 8 En ville • MAIN THEME Cities and city life

				Interlude Culturel 8 Les Antilles francophones
				GENERAL CULTURAL BACKGROUND
Making a date and fixing the time and place **Explaining where one lives and how to get there** **Discussing the advantages and disadvantages of city life**	**Narrating past actions in sequence** • The pluperfect **Formulating polite requests** • The conditional **Hypothesizing about what one would do under certain circumstances** • The conditional and its uses • The past conditional • Sequence of tenses in si-clauses	**What does a typical French city look like?** • Its historical development • Its various neighborhoods • Its buildings • The **villes nouvelles** **Why do French people love to stroll in the streets?** • Various street shows • Sculptures to view while walking in Paris	**Theuriet,** *Les Pêches*	**The French-speaking Caribbean islands** • Historical background • Important people **Toussaint Louverture** **Joséphine de Beauharnais** **Aimé Césaire** • Haitian art as an expression of life Literature: **Césaire,** *Pour saluer le Tiers-Monde* Film: **Palcy,** *Rue Cases-nègres*

UNITÉ 9 Les relations personnelles • MAIN THEME Personal relationships, friendships, and family life

COMMUNICATION OBJECTIVES		READING AND CULTURAL OBJECTIVES		Interlude Culturel 9
COMMUNICATION: FUNCTIONS AND CONTEXTS LE FRANÇAIS PRATIQUE	**LINGUISTIC GOALS** LANGUE ET COMMUNICATION	**DAILY LIFE** INFO MAGAZINE	**READING** LECTURE	L'Afrique dans la communauté francophone
				GENERAL CULTURAL BACKGROUND
Describing degrees of friendship **Expressing different feelings towards other people** **Discussing the state of one's relationship with other people** **Congratulating, comforting, and expressing sympathy for other people** **Describing the various phases of a person's life**	**Describing how people interact** • Reciprocal use of reflexive verbs **Describing people and things in complex sentences** • Relative pronouns • Relative clauses	**How important are friends and family to French people?** • The meaning of friendship • Family relationships **How socially concerned are French young people and what type of social outreach do they do?** **What is a typical French wedding like?** • Where French spouses meet one another • Planning the wedding • A French wedding ceremony	M. Maurois, *Le Bracelet*	**The place of Western and Central Africa in the francophone world** • Historical periods and events: prehistory, the **African empires**, colonization, and independence • Basic facts about Western Africa language and culture religions and traditions • **African art** and its influence on European art **African Fable:** *La Gélinotte et la Tortue* **Literature** • **D. Diop,** *Afrique* • **Dadié,** *La légende baoulé*

UNITÉ 10 Vers la vie active • MAIN THEME University studies and careers

				Interlude Culturel 10
				La France et le Nouveau Monde
				GENERAL CULTURAL BACKGROUND
Deciding on a college major • University courses **Planning for a career** • Professions • The work environment • Different types of industries **Looking for a job** • Preparing a résumé • Describing one's qualifications at a job interview	**Describing simultaneous actions** • The present participle **Explaining the purpose of an action** • **Pour** + infinitive • **Pour que** + subjunctive **Explaining the timing, conditions, and constraints of an action** • The use of the infinitive or the subjunctive after certain prepositions and conjunctions	**How important is academic success to French young people?** • The French school system: high schools and universities • **Le bac:** its history and its importance **What does one do after graduation?** • Choosing a profession • **Le service militaire** **How does one interview for a job?** • Preparing for the interview • Writing a résumé in French	Thériault, *Le Portrait*	**The French presence in North America** • Historical background The French in Canada and Louisiana • Important people **Jacques Cartier, Jeanne Mance, Cavelier de La Salle** • Why certain American cities have French names **Song: Richard,** *Réveille* **Literature: La Fayette,** *Lettre à sa femme*

Emphasize Communication

● The *Reprise* unit opens the book with a quick contextualized review of the core material of *Discovering French Today!* Level 2. The *Rappels* review basic structures and expressions in a unique way that allows students to personalize their review.

● **Thematic Units**
Motivating themes set up the situational context of the language.

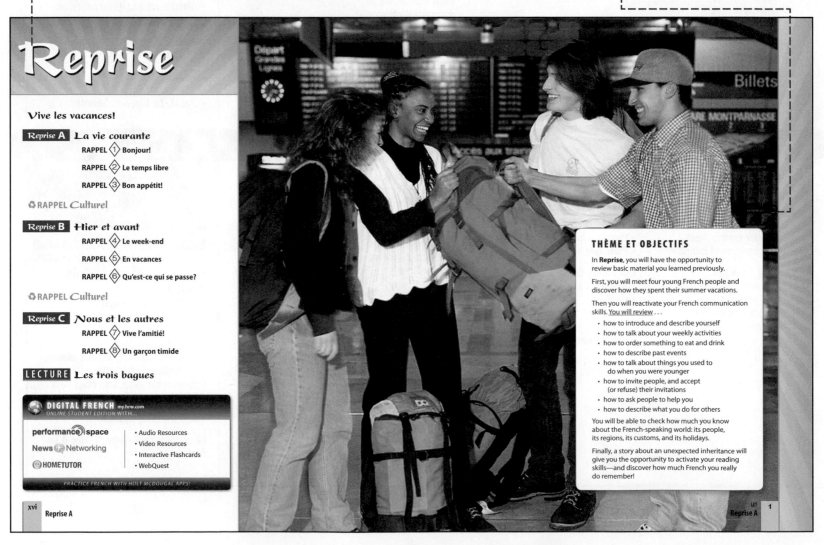

Reprise

Vive les vacances!

Reprise A *La vie courante*
    RAPPEL ① Bonjour!
    RAPPEL ② Le temps libre
    RAPPEL ③ Bon appétit!

✿ RAPPEL *Culturel*

Reprise B *Hier et avant*
    RAPPEL ④ Le week-end
    RAPPEL ⑤ En vacances
    RAPPEL ⑥ Qu'est-ce qui se passe?

✿ RAPPEL *Culturel*

Reprise C *Nous et les autres*
    RAPPEL ⑦ Vive l'amitié!
    RAPPEL ⑧ Un garçon timide

LECTURE *Les trois bagues*

DIGITAL FRENCH my.hrw.com
ONLINE STUDENT EDITION WITH...

performance space   • Audio Resources
News Networking   • Video Resources
                 • Interactive Flashcards
@HOMETUTOR   • WebQuest

PRACTICE FRENCH WITH HOLT MCDOUGAL APPS!

xvi   Reprise A

THÈME ET OBJECTIFS

In **Reprise**, you will have the opportunity to review basic material you learned previously.

First, you will meet four young French people and discover how they spent their summer vacations.

Then you will reactivate your French communication skills. You will review . . .

• how to introduce and describe yourself
• how to talk about your weekly activities
• how to order something to eat and drink
• how to describe past events
• how to talk about things you used to do when you were younger
• how to invite people, and accept (or refuse) their invitations
• how to ask people to help you
• how to describe what you do for others

You will be able to check how much you know about the French-speaking world: its people, its regions, its customs, and its holidays.

Finally, a story about an unexpected inheritance will give you the opportunity to activate your reading skills—and discover how much French you really do remember!

un 1
Reprise A

Unit Structure
Every unit contains:
- Introductory thematic readings
- Practical vocabulary and conversational patterns
- Grammatical structures
- A longer fictional reading
- An extended cultural reading

Unité 5 Bon voyage!

DIGITAL FRENCH
my.hrw.com

INFOMAGAZINE 187
- La passion des voyages
- Leurs destinations préférées
- Impressions d'Amérique

Partie 1 LE FRANÇAIS PRATIQUE **Les voyages** 190

Les voyages
Au contrôle des passeports
À la douane

LANGUE ET COMMUNICATION 192
- A Les expressions négatives
- B L'expression **ne...que**

INFOMAGAZINE 194
- La France en train
- L'Eurotunnel

Partie 2 LE FRANÇAIS PRATIQUE **Partons en voyage** 196

À l'agence de voyages
À l'aéroport
À la gare

LANGUE ET COMMUNICATION 201
- A Le futur
- B L'usage du futur dans les phrases avec **si**
- C L'usage du futur après **quand**
- D Le conditionnel

LECTURE **Le mystérieux homme en bleu** 208

Interlude culturel **Les grands moments de l'histoire de france (1715-1870)** 216

Les dates, les événements, les personnes 216
L'héritage de la Révolution 218
L'histoire de la Marseillaise 222
Les Misérables. 224
Victor Hugo: écrivain et homme politique 224

Unité 5

Bon voyage!

THÈME ET OBJECTIFS

Culture

In this unit, you will discover ...
- what French young people do when they travel abroad and where they go
- why the train is the most popular means of transportation in France
- how the Eurotunnel has linked Great Britain to France and the rest of Europe

Communication

You will learn how ...
- to make travel plans and purchase tickets
- to go through passport control and customs
- to travel by plane and by train

Langue

You will learn how ...
- to discuss future plans
- to talk about future events
- to describe what you would do under certain conditions

DIGITAL FRENCH my.hrw.com
ONLINE STUDENT EDITION with...

performance space
News Networking
@HOMETUTOR

- Audio Resources
- Video Resources
- Interactive Flashcards
- WebQuest

PRACTICE FRENCH WITH HOLT MCDOUGAL APPS!

Goal-Setting Objectives
The culture, communication, and grammar objectives tell students what they will be able to do at the end of the unit.

A variety of **digital resources** supports lesson content.

Strengthen Proficiency

Le Français pratique section introduces students to the lesson vocabulary.

New vocabulary and related conversational patterns are introduced in **thematic context** to help students achieve their communicative goals.

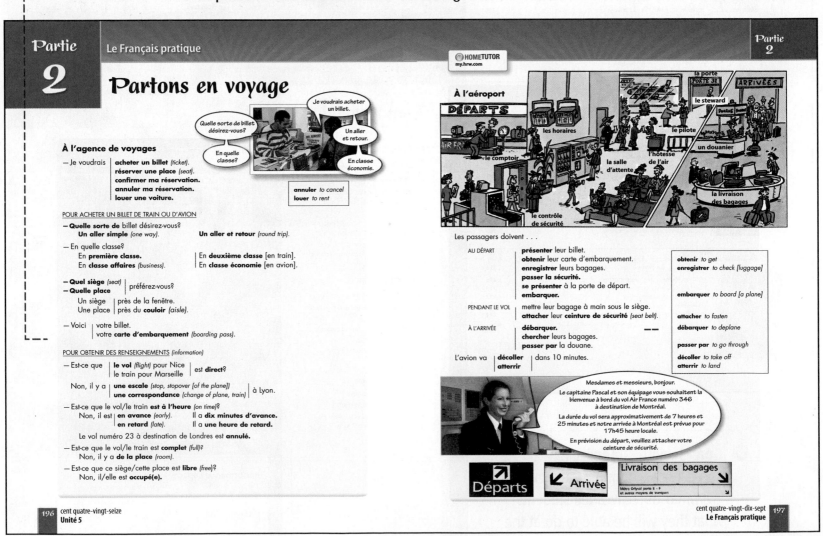

Holt McDougal French Apps

Students can practice vocabulary on the devices they love with Holt McDougal French Apps!

Partie 2 — Le Français pratique

4 **Pas de chance**

Il y a des voyageurs qui n'ont pas de chance. Avec votre partenaire, complétez les échanges suivants.

1. «Est-ce que cette place est libre?»
«Non, – – – .»

2. «Est-ce que le train est à l'heure?»
«Non, – – – .»

3. «Est-ce que le vol à destination de Toronto a été confirmé?»
«Non, – – – .»

4. «Est-ce que le vol est direct?»
«Non, – – – à Genève.»

5. «Est-ce que le train pour Tours est direct?»
«Non, – – – à Saint-Pierre.»

6. «Est-ce qu'il y a de la place sur le prochain vol?»
«Non, – – – .»

5 **Train ou avion?**

Vous voulez visiter l'Europe avec votre partenaire. Vous n'êtes pas d'accord sur le mode de transport que vous allez utiliser pendant le voyage: train ou avion?

Chacun va choisir un mode de transport (train ou avion) et essayer de convaincre *(to convince)* son partenaire. Présentez vos arguments par ordre de préférence. Qui va gagner le débat? Voici quelques idées:

TRAIN
- C'est moins cher.
- On peut mieux voir le paysage.
- On peut faire connaissance de plus de personnes.
- On peut se déplacer *(to get around)* plus facilement.
- **??**

AVION
- C'est plus rapide.
- C'est plus confortable.
- On est moins fatigué.
- On a plus de temps pour visiter le pays.
- **??**

Conversations libres Avec votre partenaire, choisissez l'une des situations suivantes. Composez le dialogue correspondant et jouez-le en classe.

2 | **Trop tard!**

Aujourd'hui vous partez en France. Malheureusement vous arrivez à l'aéroport avec cinq minutes de retard. Votre avion vient juste de partir. Allez au comptoir d'Air France et expliquez la situation à l'employé(e). (Donnez des précisions sur le vol que vous avez raté.) Demandez-lui de vous trouver une place sur le vol suivant.
Rôles: vous / l'employé(e) d'Air France

1 | **Un voyage en avion**

Caroline va aller à la Martinique avec son petit frère Julien, 8 ans. C'est la première fois que Julien prend l'avion. Il pose beaucoup de questions à sa soeur qui lui explique comment va se passer le voyage.
Rôles: Caroline / Julien

3 | **Contrôle de billets**

Vous êtes dans le train Paris-Strasbourg. Vous avez acheté un billet de 2e classe. Vous n'avez pas fait attention et vous êtes allé(e) dans un wagon de 1re classe. Le contrôleur *(conductor)* arrive. Il vous demande de payer un supplément. Vous n'avez pas assez d'argent. Expliquez-lui la situation.
Rôles: vous / le contrôleur

○ **Instant Application**
Situational activities provide opportunities for open-ended communicative pair work.

Build Accuracy

Langue et Communication provides grammar support so students can activate thematic vocabulary.

○ **Clear Grammar Explanations**
Easy outline form helps students assimilate grammar concepts.

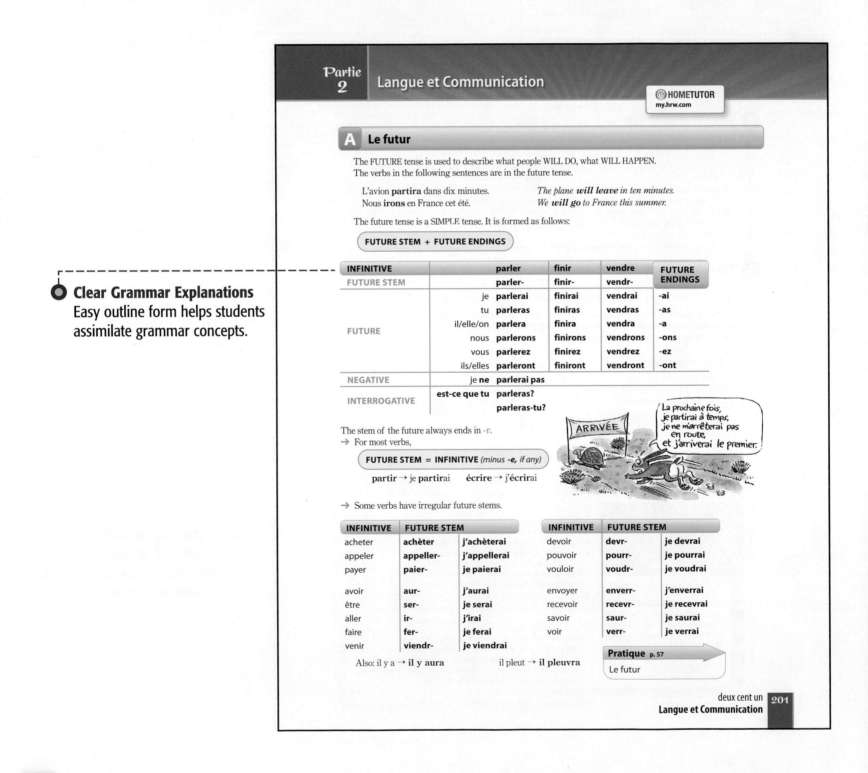

Partie 2 — Langue et Communication

@HOMETUTOR
my.hrw.com

A Le futur

The FUTURE tense is used to describe what people WILL DO, what WILL HAPPEN. The verbs in the following sentences are in the future tense.

L'avion **partira** dans dix minutes. — *The plane **will leave** in ten minutes.*
Nous **irons** en France cet été. — *We **will go** to France this summer.*

The future tense is a SIMPLE tense. It is formed as follows:

FUTURE STEM + FUTURE ENDINGS

INFINITIVE		parler	finir	vendre	FUTURE ENDINGS
FUTURE STEM		parler-	finir-	vendr-	
FUTURE	je	parlerai	finirai	vendrai	-ai
	tu	parleras	finiras	vendras	-as
	il/elle/on	parlera	finira	vendra	-a
	nous	parlerons	finirons	vendrons	-ons
	vous	parlerez	finirez	vendrez	-ez
	ils/elles	parleront	finiront	vendront	-ont
NEGATIVE	je **ne**	parlerai pas			
INTERROGATIVE	est-ce que tu	parleras?			
		parleras-tu?			

The stem of the future always ends in -r.
→ For most verbs,

FUTURE STEM = INFINITIVE (minus -e, if any)

partir → je **part**irai   écrire → j'**écri**rai

→ Some verbs have irregular future stems.

INFINITIVE	FUTURE STEM	
acheter	**achèter**	j'achèterai
appeler	**appeller-**	j'appellerai
payer	**paier-**	je paierai
avoir	**aur-**	j'aurai
être	**ser-**	je serai
aller	**ir-**	j'irai
faire	**fer-**	je ferai
venir	**viendr-**	je viendrai

INFINITIVE	FUTURE STEM	
devoir	**devr-**	je devrai
pouvoir	**pourr-**	je pourrai
vouloir	**voudr-**	je voudrai
envoyer	**enverr-**	j'enverrai
recevoir	**recevr-**	je recevrai
savoir	**saur-**	je saurai
voir	**verr-**	je verrai

Also: il y a → **il y aura**   il pleut → **il pleuvra**

Pratique p. 57
Le futur

deux cent un **201**
Langue et Communication

Interactive Whiteboard Lessons

Get the entire class involved with these vocabulary and grammar lessons.

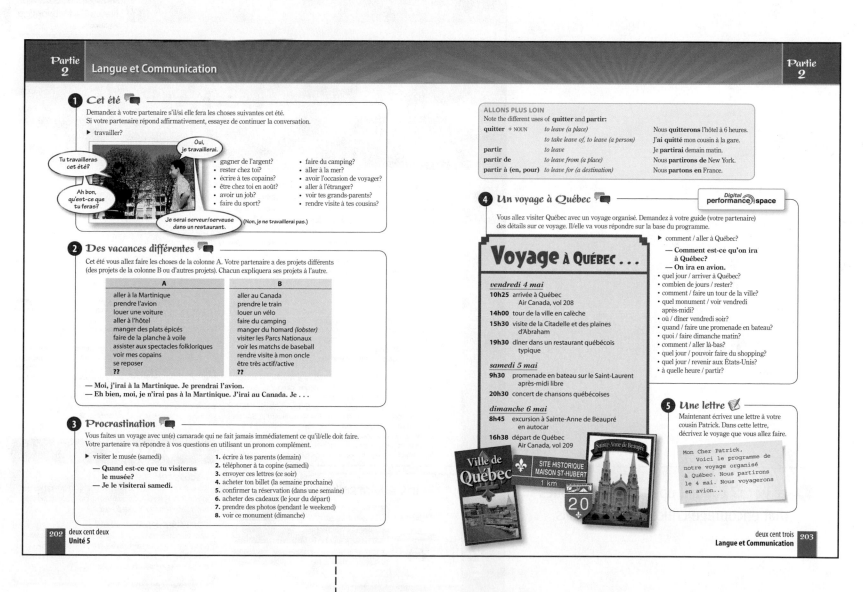

From Recognition to Production
A solid progression of activities from guided practice to open-ended communication

Encourage Reading

INFO Magazines are light culture-based articles that encourage reading practice to reinforce thematic vocabulary and structures.

● *et vous?* contain open-ended activities that encourage critical thinking skills.

INFOMAGAZINE

News ⊕ Networking
my.hrw.com

La France en train

Pour les vacances de Mardi Gras, Marie-Hélène, une étudiante parisienne, est allée chez sa grand-mère qui habite à Marseille. Elle aurait pu° prendre l'avion ou conduire° sa voiture, mais elle a choisi d'y aller en train. Pourquoi? Parce que c'est plus rapide, plus pratique, et plus sûr. Avec le TGV (Train à Grande Vitesse), on peut aller de Paris à Marseille (750 kilomètres) en 3 heures. Il n'y a pas d'embouteillage,° pas de péage° à payer, et on arrive à sa destination frais et dispos.°

■ Le train: c'est plus rapide, plus pratique, et plus sûr!

Le TGV, produit de la technologie française, est ce train super rapide qui circule sur un système spécial de rails et peut rouler° à une vitesse de 300 kilomètres à l'heure. La première ligne (Paris-Lyon) a été inaugurée en 1981, mais aujourd'hui le TGV dessert° presque° toutes les grandes villes françaises. Il y a un TGV Sud-est (orange), un TGV Atlantique (bleu) et un TGV Nord... En fait, 50% du service voyageurs est assuré par le TGV. Les autres trains sont peut-être un peu moins rapides, mais ils sont aussi confortables et aussi pratiques.

Les Français sont très fiers° de leurs trains et ceci pour de bonnes raisons:
● Les trains français sont toujours à l'heure. Ils partent à l'heure indiquée et arrivent à l'heure indiquée. Avec le train, on n'est jamais en retard.
● Les trains sont propres et confortables. Si on a faim, on peut prendre un repas au wagon-restaurant.° Sur les grandes distances, on peut voyager en wagon-lit.°
● Le train est bon marché et très flexible. Il y a des réductions de prix pour les jeunes, pour les familles, pour les personnes âgées, pour les personnes qui voyagent

souvent. Pour toutes ces personnes, les prix des billets varient selon l'époque où on voyage. Ils sont plus élevés° en période rouge (vacances) ou blanche (week-ends), et moins élevés en période bleue (le reste du temps).

Pour les touristes, il y a d'autres services intéressants. Avec «train + vélo» et «train + auto,» on peut voyager en train et louer un vélo ou une voiture quand on arrive à sa destination. Avec «train + hôtel,» on trouve toujours une chambre d'hôtel.

Les jeunes Américains peuvent acheter un Eurailpass. Cette carte leur permet de sillonner° l'Europe pendant plusieurs semaines pour un prix relativement modique°. Pour beaucoup de jeunes qui utilisent ce système, le train est non seulement un moyen° de transport mais c'est aussi un hôtel, un restaurant, une cafétéria et un lieu où ils peuvent rencontrer d'autres jeunes qui, comme eux, viennent découvrir le vieux continent. ■

INFOMAGAZINE

Paris à Marseille

✈	(≈480 km l'heure) 640 km aériens	1h20
SNCF 🚄	(≈250 km l'heure) 750 km	3h00
🚗	(≈100 km l'heure) 773 km	7h35

et vous?

DISCUSSION
Vous allez visiter la France avec votre partenaire. Il/Elle voudrait voyager en avion, mais vous préférez voyager en train. Expliquez-lui les avantages du train. Votre partenaire va poser des questions.

COMPOSITION: UNE LETTRE
Alice, une copine française, va visiter les États-Unis cet été. Elle ne sait pas si elle va voyager en train ou en bus, et elle vous demande votre avis (opinion). Dites-lui quel système vous préférez et expliquez-lui les avantages et les inconvénients de ce système.

aurait pu *could have* **conduire** * *to drive* **embouteillage** *traffic jam* **péage** *toll* **frais et dispos** *fresh and rested* **rouler** = *aller* **dessert** *services* **presque** *almost* **fiers** *proud* **wagon-restaurant** *dining car* **wagon-lit** *sleeping car* **élevés** *higher* **sillonner** = *voyager à travers* **modique** *low* **moyen** *means*

194 cent quatre-vingt-quatorze
Unité 5

News + Networking
my.hrw.com

Find current blogs, videos, and articles on News and Networking.

INFOMAGAZINE

L'EUROTUNNEL

Aujourd'hui, l'Angleterre n'est plus une île. Avec l'Eurotunnel, on peut maintenant franchir° les 50 kilomètres qui séparent Coquelles (France) et Cheriton (Angleterre) sans quitter la terre ferme.° L'idée d'un tunnel sous la Manche est très ancienne. Le premier projet remonte° à Napoléon et date de 1802. Malheureusement, la rivalité franco-britannique, les guerres européennes, les difficultés techniques et l'énorme coût financier ont pendant longtemps empêché° la réalisation de ce projet. Finalement, les travaux ont commencé en 1988 et depuis 1994, l'Eurotunnel est une réalité.

L'ANGLETERRE
Londres
Douvres
Cheriton • • Calais
Coquelles
LA MANCHE
LA FRANCE
Paris

■ Chaque année, dix millions de voyageurs passent sous la mer pour aller de France en Angleterre, ou vice versa, en moins de 20 minutes.

Chaque année, dix millions de voyageurs passent sous la mer pour aller de France en Angleterre, ou vice versa, en moins de 20 minutes. Il y a en réalité deux tunnels, un tunnel nord et un tunnel sud, permettant le trafic dans les deux sens.° Ces deux tunnels sont exclusivement réservés au trafic ferroviaire,° mais les automobilistes peuvent tout de même° utiliser l'Eurotunnel en chargeant° leurs voitures sur des trains spéciaux.

Imaginez, par exemple, que vous habitez à Paris et que vous voulez déjeuner avec votre copain qui habite à Londres. C'est simple. Si vous préférez le train, vous prendrez l'Eurostar à 10 heures et vous arriverez à Londres à midi. Si, au contraire, vous préférez conduire, vous devez partir à sept heures. Vous prendrez l'autoroute° qui va de Paris jusqu'à l'accès de l'Eurotunnel. Là, vous monterez avec votre voiture sur une navette° spéciale qui vous amènera jusqu'au° terminal britannique. De là vous continuerez votre route. S'il n'y a pas trop d'embouteillages° dans Londres, vous serez à votre rendez-vous pour le déjeuner.

L'Eurotunnel est beaucoup plus qu'un grand exploit technique. Autrefois, la Manche représentait une formidable barrière qui protégeait l'Angleterre contre les invasions, mais qui la maintenait aussi dans son «splendide isolement». Aujourd'hui l'Eurotunnel joint l'Angleterre à la France et, par la France, à l'Allemagne, à la Belgique, à la Hollande et à tout le continent européen. C'est le symbole de la Nouvelle Europe, unie et en paix° avec elle-même. ■

QUESTIONS
1. Comment peut-on aller de Paris à Londres par la terre ferme?
2. Quels ont été les obstacles à la construction de l'Eurotunnel?
3. Pourquoi l'Eurotunnel est-il un grand exploit technique?
4. Quel est le symbole politique de l'Eurotunnel?

franchir = traverser **terre ferme** ground **remonte** goes back **empêché** prevented **sens** = directions **ferroviaire** railroad **tout de même** nevertheless **chargeant** loading **l'autoroute** turnpike **navette** shuttle train **jusqu'au** up to **embouteillages** traffic jams **paix** peace

INFOMAGAZINE

cent quatre-vingt-quinze **195**
INFO Magazine

Magazine Format
High-interest articles grab students' attention and hook them into reading.

Develop Reading Skills

The *Lecture* section contains high-interest short stories that are directly related to the unit theme, and recycle lexical and structural elements.

Reading Strategies

Pre- and post-reading strategies help students to be active readers and develop critical reading skills.

French InterActive Reader provides multi-leveled authentic and content-area readings.

● The *Après la lecture* activities expand into speaking and writing projects.

LECTURE

Troisième Partie

Le lendemain à deux heures de l'après-midi, Caroline est allée voir l'inspecteur Legrand au quartier général de la police.
— Bonjour, Inspecteur, j'ai une très bonne nouvelle pour vous.
— Ah bon? Quoi?
— Vous allez pouvoir retrouver la trace de vos voleurs de documents.
— Vraiment? Comment?
Caroline a ouvert son sac d'où elle a tiré° les photos prises hier à l'aéroport.
— Regardez bien ces deux photos. Je les ai fait développer ce matin.
— Mais ce sont des photos de vous!
— Oui, bien sûr, mais regardez de plus près la voiture de sport rouge.
— Je vois bien. C'est une Alfa-Roméo.
— C'est aussi la voiture qu'ont prise le jeune homme et sa véritable° complice à l'aéroport. Prenez votre loupe. Vous pourrez lire très nettement son numéro d'immatriculation.
L'inspecteur Legrand a pris sa loupe.
— Vous avez raison, mademoiselle. Je vais alerter immédiatement tous les postes de gendarmerie pour qu'on retrouve cette voiture et ses occupants.

135

140

145

150

155

Une semaine après, la police a arrêté le chef de bande et sa complice et les documents secrets ont été récupérés.
L'histoire de Caroline a été publiée en première page de tous les journaux. Caroline a donné plusieurs interviews à la radio et à la télévision. Un studio de cinéma lui a proposé un rôle dans un prochain film et une maison d'édition a pris contact avec elle pour publier le récit° de ses aventures.

160

165

a tiré = a sorti   **véritable** = réelle   **le récit** = l'histoire

Avez-vous compris?
1. Qu'est-ce que Caroline a apporté le lendemain?
2. En quoi est-ce que cela a aidé l'inspecteur?
3. Comment s'est terminée l'histoire pour le jeune homme blond? pour Caroline?

Et vous?
Imaginez que vous êtes Caroline. Qu'est-ce que vous allez faire?
• Accepter l'offre du studio de cinéma?
• Écrire le récit de vos aventures?
Pourquoi avez-vous choisi cette option?

LECTURE

APRÈS LA LECTURE

Expression orale

Dramatisation
Avec un groupe de camarades, transformez cette histoire en petite pièce de théâtre et jouez-la.

Situations
Avec votre partenaire, choisissez l'une des situations suivantes. Composez le dialogue correspondant et jouez-le en classe.

1	Un coup de téléphone

Caroline téléphone à un(e) ami(e) québécois(e) pour lui raconter ses aventures. L'ami(e) interrompt souvent et lui pose beaucoup de questions sur ce qui est arrivé.
(Utilisez la forme **tu**.)
Rôles: Caroline, son ami(e)

2	Une interview

Un(e) journaliste pour Radio-Québec a obtenu une interview avec Caroline et lui pose beaucoup de questions. Il/Elle voudrait savoir ce que Caroline fera si elle accepte la proposition du studio de cinéma ou de la maison d'édition. Caroline est très contente de répondre.
(Utilisez la forme vous.)
Rôles: le/la journaliste, Caroline

Expression écrite

L'histoire de «l'homme en bleu» est écrite objectivement, et cependant vous avez pu remarquer que l'auteur décrit les événements du point de vue de Caroline. Utilisez votre imagination pour raconter la même histoire d'un autre point de vue. Voici trois options:

Le rapport de l'inspecteur de police
L'inspecteur Louis Legrand, qui vient de recevoir les photos de Caroline, écrit un rapport à son chef. Dans ce rapport, il décrit ce qui est arrivé et aussi comment il arrêtera les voleurs.

Journal d'un prisonnier
L'homme à la mallette jaune (vous pouvez lui donner un nom) est maintenant en prison. Dans son journal intime, il décrit les événements qui ont mené à son arrestation.

Article de journal
Un(e) journaliste écrit un article où il décrit comment la police a récupéré les documents volés. Il utilise un style très direct.

Experience Culture

The *Interlude culturel* section introduces your students to the richness and variety of French culture while developing reading skills.

Unité 5 — Interlude culturel

L'héritage de la Révolution

La **Révolution** est probablement la période la plus importante de l'histoire de France. Elle met fin° à **l'Ancien Régime*** et à ses abus. Elle établit les bases d'un gouvernement démocratique en affirmant l'égalité de tous les citoyens.° Ce fut pendant la Révolution que furent proclamés la République, l'abolition de l'esclavage° et les droits° de l'homme et du citoyen. La Révolution française fut aussi marquée par un énorme effort de centralisation qui unifia la France en donnant un certain nombre d'institutions communes au pays. La plupart de ces institutions subsistent aujourd'hui. Voici quelques institutions françaises qui remontent° à la Révolution.

La prise de la Bastille

DOCUMENTS — *Déclaration des Droits de l'Homme*

Déclaration des Droits de l'Homme

Article I
«Les hommes naissent et demeurent libres et égaux en droits.»

Article IV
«La liberté consiste à pouvoir faire tout ce qui ne nuit pas à autrui.»

Article IX
«La libre communication des pensées et des opinions est un des droits les plus précieux de l'homme.»

■ **La devise de la France: Liberté, égalité, fraternité**

Cette devise° rappelle les objectifs politiques et sociaux de la Révolution. Elle fut adoptée en juin 1793. Malgré plusieurs interruptions, la fameuse trilogie est restée la devise officielle de la France. Aujourd'hui elle figure° sur les documents officiels et sur les pièces de monnaie.

* L'Ancien Régime: entre le 15e siècle et 1789, la France était une monarchie et la société française était divisée en trois ordres: le clergé, la noblesse (*nobility*) et le Tiers État (*third estate*).

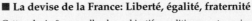

met fin à *puts an end to*   **citoyen** *citizen*   **esclavage** *slavery*   **droits** *rights*   **remontent** *go back*   **devise** *motto*   **figure** *is on*

218 deux cent dix-huit
Unité 5

● **Visual Support**

Relevant documents, paintings, photos, and realia are introduced in context to help students form a deeper understanding of francophone history and culture.

Historical Information

Highlights from the history of France and other French-speaking countries familiarize students with key figures and events.

Les Grands Moments de l'Histoire de France (1715-1870) — Unité 5

La première fête du 14 juillet en 1790

■ La fête nationale du 14 juillet

La **fête nationale** commémore la prise° de la Bastille par les Parisiens le 14 juillet 1789. Par ce geste symbolique, la population mettait en question° le pouvoir° royal. La Bastille fut démolie et ses pierres servirent à la construction de nombreuses maisons parisiennes. Ce n'est qu'en 1880 que la date du 14 juillet a été adoptée comme fête nationale.

La «Fête nationale» aujourd'hui

■ Le drapeau bleu, blanc, rouge

Avant la Révolution, il n'existait pas de drapeau national mais uniquement des drapeaux militaires dont les couleurs et les motifs variaient de régiment à régiment. (Le seul symbole national était alors la personne du roi.) L'origine du drapeau français remonte à la prise de la Bastille le 14 juillet 1789. Les révolutionnaires qui participèrent à cet événement portaient au chapeau une cocarde bleue et rouge, aux couleurs de la ville de Paris. Quelques jours plus tard, le roi Louis XVI ajouta° cette cocarde° bleue et rouge à la cocarde blanche royale (le blanc était alors le symbole de la monarchie française), créant ainsi la cocarde tricolore.

Ces trois couleurs — bleu, blanc, rouge — firent leur apparition sur les drapeaux et les étendards° des armées révolutionnaires. En 1830, le drapeau tricolore à bandes verticales égales devint de façon définitive l'emblème national.

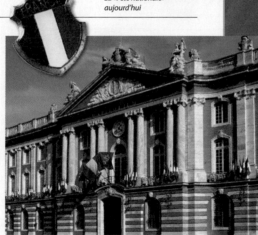

■ Marianne: symbole de la République

Marianne

Cette femme coiffée du bonnet révolutionnaire est le symbole de la République française. (On attribue le nom «Marianne» à une citoyenne de Colmar, Marie-Anne Reubell.) Cette figure allégorique apparut d'abord sur les pièces de monnaie de la Révolution. Elle réapparut brandissant un drapeau dans le fameux tableau de Delacroix, *La Liberté guidant le peuple*. Depuis 1880, les bustes de Marianne ornent° toutes les mairies de France et son portrait est représenté sur les timbres et les pièces de monnaie.

Delacroix «La Liberté guidant le peuple»

prise *taking* **mettait en question** *was questioning* **pouvoir** *power* **ajouta** *added* **cocarde** *cockade* **étendards** *military banners*
ornent = *décorent*

deux cent dix-neuf **219**
Interlude culturel

Introduce Authentic Films

Discovering French Today! takes advantage of students' interest in films to expand their contact with **authentic language and culture.**

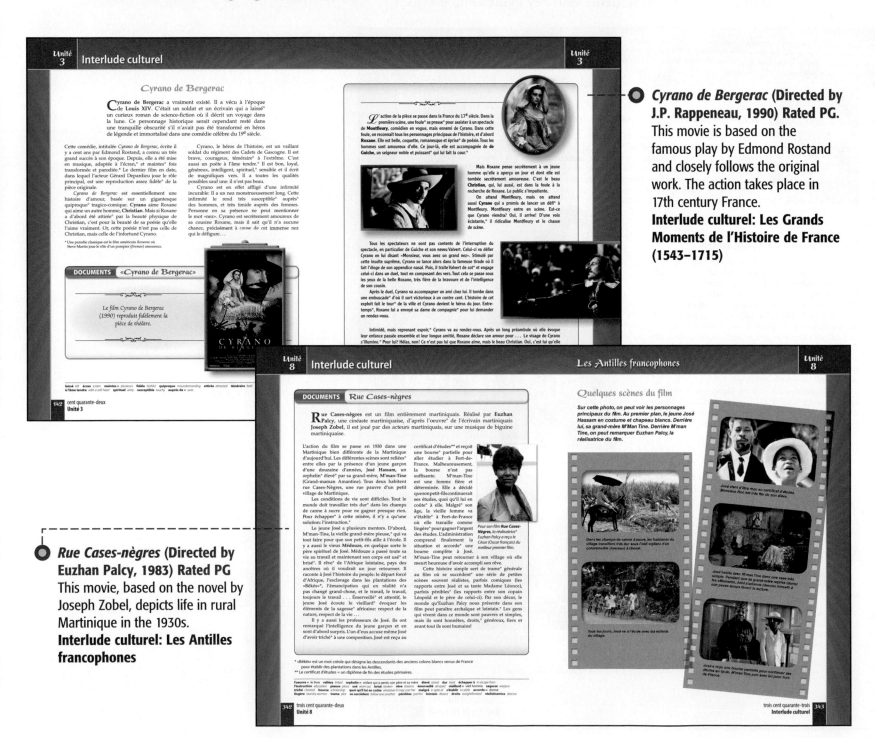

Cyrano de Bergerac **(Directed by J.P. Rappeneau, 1990) Rated PG.** This movie is based on the famous play by Edmond Rostand and closely follows the original work. The action takes place in 17th century France.
Interlude culturel: Les Grands Moments de l'Histoire de France (1543–1715)

Rue Cases-nègres **(Directed by Euzhan Palcy, 1983) Rated PG** This movie, based on the novel by Joseph Zobel, depicts life in rural Martinique in the 1930s.
Interlude culturel: Les Antilles francophones

News ✛ Networking
my.hrw.com

Provides additional cultural videos!

- *Au Revoir, les Enfants* (Directed by Louis Malle, 1987) Rated PG.
This award-winning semi-autobiographical movie is based on a script by Louis Malle. It describes a dramatic incident in a private boys' boarding school during the German occupation of France (1940–1944).
Interlude culturel: Les Grands Moments de l'Histoire de France (1870 au présent)

Deliver Solid Instruction

The comprehensive Teacher's Edition and resource materials provide the support you need to introduce, explain, and expand your lessons.

● The five elements of the **ACTFL Standards for Foreign Language Learning** are correlated to the objectives of each unit.

● **Easy-to-use technology** transforms your classroom to engage students through a variety of devices.

● **21st Century Skills** references make it easy to see how you are meeting the requirements.

Pre-AP® Digital Resources

Provide additional resources and material to help prepare students.

● *Note culturelle* and Teaching **Strategies** found throughout the Teacher's Edition offer more cultural support and teaching ideas.

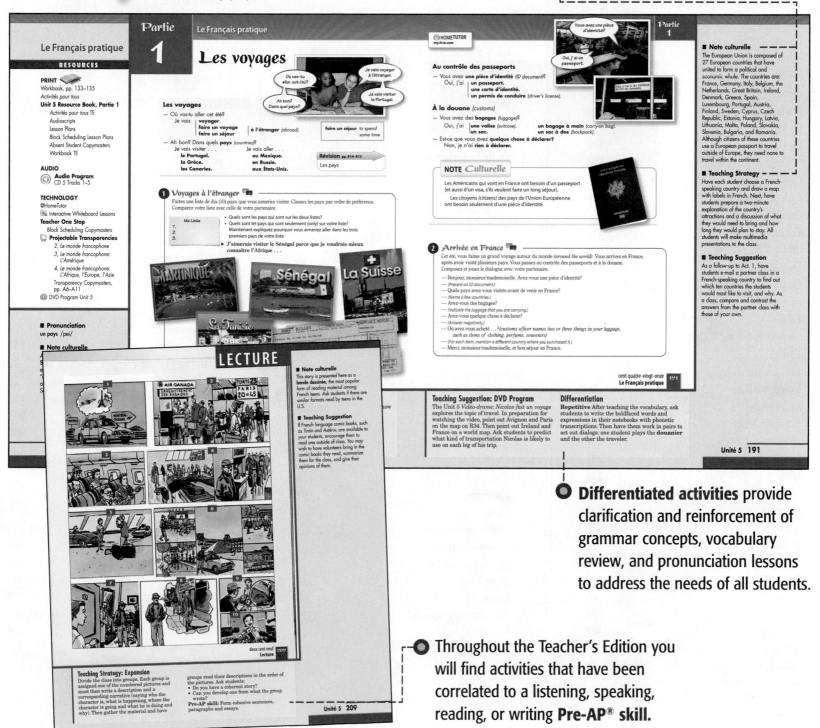

● **Differentiated activities** provide clarification and reinforcement of grammar concepts, vocabulary review, and pronunciation lessons to address the needs of all students.

● Throughout the Teacher's Edition you will find activities that have been correlated to a listening, speaking, reading, or writing **Pre-AP®** skill.

CULTURAL REFERENCE GUIDE

AFRICA

See also: Art, Cities, History, People
Afrique noire	180, 181
Algérie	20
Algérie	21
Algérie	255
Algérie 2	97
Baoulé people	380
Bénin	341
Bénin	372, 373
Bénin	374
Burkina-Faso	375
Cameroun	378
Cameroun	374
Climate	374
Colonisation	252
Colonisation	373
Congo (République démocratique)	374
Côte-d'Ivoire	374
Empire du Ghana	372, 373
Empire du Mali	372, 373
Empire de Songhaï	372, 373
Ethiopia	301
Fable	377
French-speaking countries	20
Griot	377
Independence	252
Independence	255
Independence	337, 338, 340
Independence	373, 378
Maghreb	180, 181
Maghreb	297
Mali	374
Maroc	14
Maroc	297
Masks	20, 379
Mauritanie	376
Niger	375
Sahara	372
Sénégal	20
Sénégal	21
Sénégal	187
Sénégal	181
Sénégal	374, 377, 378

Slavery	373
Tassili	372
Tunisie	297

ANIMALS
Frogs	136

ANTILLES

See also: Art, History, People
Caraïb Indians	335
Guadeloupe	334
Haïti	11
Haïti	334, 338, 339, 340, 341
Haïti	418
Hispaniola	334
Île de la Tortue	334
Martinique	11
Martinique	334
Martinique	335, 336
Martinique	337, 342
Music	180
Saint-Domingue	334, 338
Saint-Domingue	418
Slavery	334, 335, 33

ART

See also: People
African masks	20
African masks	379
African sculpture	379
Bayeux tapestry	104
Bénin bronze	373
Bénin sculpture	35
Chefs-d'oeuvre en péril	3
Cubisme	252
Fauvisme	252
Haitian art	340
Impressionnisme	60–64, 69
Impressionnisme	252
La liberté guidant le peuple	219
Léger, Fernand	256
Mauritanian houses	376
Middle Ages	35
Mona Lisa	35, 141
Musée du Louvre	220

Picasso	176
Post-Impressionism	64–65
Prehistoric art (Tassili)	372
Renaissance Châteaux	140, 147
Sculpture	69
Street artists	320, 321
Surréalisme	66
Surréalisme	252

ASIA
Indochine	252

BELGIUM
Bruxelles	11

CAFÉS
Cafés	151

CANADA

See also: History, People
Acadiens	418, 419
Filles du Roy	411
French colonies	334, 338
Gaspésie	2
Gaspé	410
Laurentides	77
New Brunswick	182
Newfoundland	133
Nouvelle France	20
Quebec	20
Quebec	21
Quebec	203
Quebec	410
Quebec	402
Québec	2
Saint Laurent	133

CHÂTEAUX
Amboise	140, 147
Angers	147
Carcassonne	147
Chambord	140, 147
Château-Gaillard	147
Chenonceaux	140, 147
Chinon	106
Fontainebleau	147
Louvre	220

Vaux-le-Viconte 147
Versailles 140, 141, 147

CINEMA
Au revoir, les Enfants 256–259
César award 342
Cyrano de Bergerac 142–145
Rue Cases-nègres 342, 343

CITIES
Abbeville 93
Abidjan 11
Amboise 233
Bordeaux 303
Bruxelles 11
Clermont-Ferrand 305
Fontevrault 105
Giverny 63
Lafayette, LA 182
Lyon 303
Marseille 303
Menton 283
Montana, Switzerland 11
Montreal 411, 412
Nice 303
Nouvelle-Orléans 412
Nouvelle-Orléans 418
Orléans 98, 107
Paris 115
Paris 303
Rouen 303
Saint-Pierre 335
Sanary-sur-Mer 2
Strasbourg 303
Strasbourg 222
Strasbourg 293
Tombouctou 372
Toulouse 303
Tours 303
Yamoussoukro 375

CITY, COUNTRY AND SUBURBS
City vs. Country 304
French cities 303

French cities 310
Maison des Jeunes 347
Suburbs 311
Villages 246
Villes nouvelles 311

CLOTHING
See also: Style
Accessories 34
Adolescent styles 33-34
Shoes 33

DANCE
Ballet 184

EDUCATION
Africa 374
Areas of study 383, 386
Baccalauréat 383, 384
Écoles du palais 99
Erasmus 293
University 383, 384

ENVIRONMENT
Protection 110, 111, 121

ETHNIC DIVERSITY 4
Ethnic Diversity 296, 297
Ethnic Diversity 300
Ethnic diversity 2, 3

EUROPE
Communauté Économique
Européenne 252
Communauté Européenne 292
Marché Commun 252
Marché Commun 292
Parlement Européen 292
Passports 191

FAMILY
Africa 376
Family life 345
Housework 73, 74, 75
Marriage 358–359
Meeting one's spouse 359

Polygamy 376

FASHION   See Clothing, Style

FOLKLORE
Frogs and weather 136
Griot 21
Griot 377

FOOD
Couscous 298
Frogs' legs 136
Pâté and saucisson 57
Primeurs du Midi 329
Supermarket 149, 151

FRANCE
See also: Cities, Regions and
departments of France
Départements 220
Départements d'Outre-Mer (DOM) 334
Eco-musées 110
Fifth Republic 255
Gaul 98
Immigrants 296, 297
Parks and public gardens 134
Population 20

FRIENDS
Courrier du coeur 353
Friends 345, 346, 348

GEOGRAPHY
African climate 374
Alpes 21
Massif Central 262
Pyrénées 262
Thermal sources 262
Vosges 262

GOVERNMENT
Aix-la-Chapelle (Aachen) 99
Departments 220
Health 261
History 98, 99, 140, 141, 216, 217, 218,
219, 252, 253, 254, 255, 292, 293, 334
Monetary system 221
Marriage, civil 358, 359

CULTURAL REFERENCE GUIDE

HEALTH

Avoiding sunburn	122, 123
Health facts	263
Health services	261
Mal au foie	57
Medical visit	261, 264-266
Mineral water	262
Tuberculosis	283

HISTORY

See also: People

African colonization	373
African independence	373, 377
African prehistory	372
American Revolution	217, 413
Ancien Régime	218
Appel du 18 juin	254
Arab conquest	372
Army	221
Bastille	216
Bastille	219
Bastille	222
Bataille d'Azincourt	98
Bataille d'Orléans	98, 99
Bataille de Hastings	98, 104
Bataille de Valmy	221
Bataille de Yorktown	413, 414
Belle Époque	252
Belle Époque	326
Canada	410, 411
Colonialism	252
Déclaration des Droits de l'Homme	216, 218
Empire de Charlemagne	98
French Revolution	176
French Revolution	216, 217, 218
French Revolution	221
French Revolution	334, 338
French Revolution	336
French Revolution	92
Guerre de Cent Ans	98, 105
Guerre de Cent Ans	140
Guerre de Cent Ans	147
Le Grand Siècle	140–145, 147
Huguenots français	413

Liberation	252, 253
Louis XIV	176
Louisiane	20
Louisiane	418
Middle Ages	303
Middle Ages	98, 99, 102, 103, 104, 105
Middle Ages	176
Middle Ages	92
Napoleonic Empire	336
Normandy Invasion	252
Normandy Invasion	416
Nouvelle France	20
Nouvelle France	412
Omaha Beach	416
Parlement européen	253
Premier Empire	220
Premier Empire (Napoléon Ier)	216, 217
Provincia Romana	98
Renaissance	140
Resistance	67
Resistance	176, 178
Resistance	253, 254
Resistance	256
Resistance	294
Resistance	250
Révolution de 1830	216
Roman invasion	98
Sarrasins	102
Second Empire (Napoléon III)	216, 217
Slavery	373
Third Republic	218, 219, 252, 253, 254, 255
Traité de Paris 1763	412
Traité de Rome	292
World War I	252
World War I	373
World War II	252
World War II	256
World War II	257
World War II	293
World War II	294
World War II	373

HOLIDAYS

Carnaval	21
Fête nationale	219
Quatorze Juillet (la fête nationale)	21

HOTELS

Reservation letter	233
Services	240

INDUSTRY

Michelin	228

INSTITUTIONS

Assemblée nationale	294
Code Napoléon	216
French army	221
French flag	219
Légion d'Honneur	178
Marianne	219
Motto	216
Police nationale, Gendarmerie	313

LANGUAGE

African languages	374
Baoulé	374
Use of vous	95
Wolof	374
Words of Arab origin	298

LEISURE ACTIVITIES

Bricolage	71
Cooking	82
Gardening	725

LITERATURE

See also: People

Académie française	377
Académie française	56
Académie française	326, 366
African	377, 378
Afrique (Diop)	378
Chanson de Roland	103
Chanson de Roland	176
Conte pour enfants de moins de trois ans	57
Cyrano de Bergerac (Rostand)	142
Fabliaux	92
La couverture	92
Le Bracelet	366

Le corbeau et le renard (La Fontaine)	146
Légende baoulé (Dadié)	380
Les Misérables	224, 225
Liberté	256, 257
Lucky Luke	134
Négritude	336
Petit Nicolas	134
Pour Haïti (Depestre)	339
Pour saluer le Tiers-Monde (Césaire)	337
Surréalisme	66-68, 256
Théâtre de l'Absurde	56
Tristan et Yseult	363

MARRIAGE

Marriage in France	358-359

MEDICAL CARE

Baths and springs	262
Dental visit	279
Emergency ward	278
Hospices des vieillards	95
Médecins du monde	277
Médecins sans frontières	276, 277
SAMU	261
Women doctors	261

MILITARY SERVICE

Military service in France	383, 385

MONEY

Earning money	82, 83
French currency	221

MOVIES

See Cinema	

MUSIC

See also: People	
African rhythm	181
Beausoleil	182
Cajun	182
Carmen	185
Carmen (Bizet)	185
"Chat Noir"	176
Éthiopie	301
Fête de la Musique	180

La chanson française	176
Kassav	180
La Marseillaise	222, 223
Malavoi	180
Mano Negra	181
Mon Pays	183
Piano	184
Québec	182
Raï	181
Rap	180
Réveille	419
Soukous Stars	181
Troubadours	176
Yé-yé	177
Zap Mama	181
Zouk	180
Zydéco	182

NAMES

Arab names	299
Baoulé names	374

NATURE

Baobab	378
Baobab	21
Environmental protection	110, 111, 121
Frogs	136
Mont Pelée	334, 335
Plants	72
Sun	122, 123

PARIS

Bateaux-mouche	212
Montmartre	176
Paris	69
Tour Eiffel	91

PEOPLE

Abbé Pierre (Henri Grouès)	294
Aliénor d'Aquitaine	98, 105
Avril, Jane	65
Aznavour, Charles	177
Baker, Joséphine	177, 178
Baudricourt, Sire de	106
Beauharnais, Alexandre de	336
Beausoleil, Capitaine	419
Bénabar	179

Bergen, Candice	258
Bizet, Georges	185
Boulay, Isabelle	182
Bourgeoys, Marguerite	411
Brassens, Georges	177
Brel, Jacques	177
Cadillac, Antoine de la Mothe	417, 418
Cartier, Jacques	133
Cartier, Jacques	410
Cassatt, Mary	60
Césaire, Aimé	336, 337
César (Baldaccini)	69
César, Jules	98, 99
Cézanne, Paul	60, 61
Champlain, Samuel de	410
Charlemagne	98, 99, 102, 103
Charles VII	106, 107
Chénier, Clifton	182
Chopin, Frédéric	184
Claudel, Camille	65
Clovis	98
Colomb, Christophe	334
Coluche (Michel Colucci)	295
Cousteau, Jacques-Yves	120
Cousteau, Jacques-Yves	258
Curie, Marie	253
Curie, Pierre	253
Dadié, Bernard	380
Damas, Léon	336
De Gaulle, Général	254, 255
Debussy, Claude	185
Degas, Edgar	60, 61
Delacroix, Eugène	219
Depardieu, Gérard	142
Depestre, René	339
Désir, Harlem	300
Desnos, Robert	67
Dessalines, Général	340
Dion, Céline	182
Diop, David	378
Du Luth, Daniel	417
Dubuffet, Jean	69
Duffaut, Préfète	341
Eisenhower, General	416
Eisenhower, Général	252

CULTURAL REFERENCE GUIDE

Éluard, Paul	256
Fouquet	147
François Ier	140, 141
François Ier	147
Franklin, Benjamin	413, 414
Fremont, John Charles	417
Garou (Pierre Garand)	182
Gauguin, Paul	35
Gauguin, Paul	64
Goscinny, René	134
Guillaume le Conquérant	98, 104
Henri II	147
Henri IV	140
Henri Plantagenêt	98, 105
Hugo, Victor	224, 225
Hyppolite, Hector	341
Ionesco, Eugène	56
Jay, John	413
Jean sans Terre	105
Jean-Paul II	375
Jeanne d'Arc	98, 99, 106–107
Joséphine, Impératrice	336
Kouchner, Bernard	276
Kunda, Touré	181
La Fayette, Marquis de	20
La Fayette, Marquis de	414, 415
La Fontaine, Jean de	146
La Ramie, Jacques	417
La Salle, Cavelier de	412
Lee, Spike	181
Léonard de Vinci	35
Léonard de Vinci	141
Léonard de Vinci	147
Leroy, Nowell	179
Louis XIII	105, 140
Louis XIII	147
Louis XIV	140, 141, 142
Louis XIV	147
Louis XIV	184
Louis XIV	220
Louis XIV	412
Louis XIV	417
Louis XV	216
Louis XVI	216
Louis XVI	217

Louis XVI	219
Louis XVI	413
Louis XVI	417
Louverture, Toussaint	338
Lully, Jean-Baptiste	184
Maé, Christophe	179
Magritte, René	66–67
Maisonneuve, Paul Chomedey de	411
Malle, Louis	256, 258
Mance, Jeanne	411
Manet, Édouard	60, 61
Marie-Antoinette	217
Marie-Antoinette	13
Marie-Antoinette	417
Marquette, Père	412
Maupassant, Guy de	282
Maurois, André	366
Maurois, Michelle	366
MC Solaar	180
Michelin, André et Édouard	228
Minuit, Peter	413
Modigliani, Amedeo	35
Modigliani, Amedeo	379
Monet, Claude	60, 62–63
Montand, Yves	177
Morisot, Berthe	60, 61
Moulin, Jean	253
Murat, Général	217
Noah, Yannick	179
N'Dour, Youssou	181
Napoléon	195
Napoléon	147
Napoléon	216, 217
Napoléon	222, 224
Napoléon	334
Napoléon	336, 338
Napoléon III	216, 217
Napoléon III	224
Obin, J. M.	340
Palcy, Euzhan	342, 343
Paul, Dieuseul	341
Pershing, General	416
Peters, De Witt	340
Philippe-Auguste, Salnave	340
Piaf, Édith	177

Picasso, Pablo	35, 379
Point du Sable, Jean-Baptiste	21
Prévert, Jacques	68
Renoir, Pierre Auguste	35
Renoir, Pierre Auguste	60, 61
Revere, Paul	413
Richard Coeur de Lion	105
Richard Coeur de Lion	147
Richard, Zachary	182
Richard, Zachary	419
Robespierre	223
Rochambeau, Amiral de	413
Rodin, Auguste	65
Roland	98, 102, 103
Rostand, Edmond	142
Rouget de Lisle, Claude	222, 223
Rousseau, Henri	64
Saint Louis (Louis XV)	417
Saint-Phalle, Niki de	69
Sand, George	184
Sempé, Jean-Jacques	134
Senghor, Léopold	336, 337
Senghor, Léopold	377
Thériault, Yves	402
Theuriet, André	326
Tiffany, Louis	413
Toulouse-Lautrec, Henri de	65
Toussaint Louverture	338
Van Gogh, Vincent	64
Veil, Simone	253, 292
Vercingétorix	98, 99
Vigneault, Gilles	182, 183
Vincennes, Jean-Baptiste	417
Vital, Pauleus	341
Vlaminck, Maurice de	379
Voisine, Roch	182
Washington, George	414
Zaz	179
Zobel, Joseph	342

POST OFFICE

Post Office	149, 150, 152–153

POLYNESIA

Tahiti	20
Tahiti	64

PROFESSIONS

Professions in France ... 385, 387, 394

REGIONS AND DEPARTMENTS OF FRANCE

Alsace ... 21
Auvergne ... 2
Côte d'Azur ... 282, 283
Départements ... 20
Jura ... 2
Lorraine ... 106
Massif Central ... 262
Normandie ... 21
Provence ... 21
Provence ... 98
Savoie ... 20
Savoie ... 21

RELIGION

African masks ... 20
Animism ... 341
Animism ... 375
Catholic ... 375
Catholicism ... 341
Islam ... 11
Islam ... 20
Islam ... 296, 297, 298, 299
Islam ... 375
Jewish ... 296
Vaudou ... 341

RESTAURANTS

Advertisements ... 8

SCIENCE

See also: People
Metric system ... 221
Nobel Prize ... 253

SCHOOL

See Education

SHOPPING

Cleaners ... 166
Food ... 149
Petits commerçants 1 ... 49, 151
Pharmacie ... 153
Photo shop ... 150, 153, 166
Shoe repair ... 166

Shopping ... 149, 150, 152–153
Stationery ... 152, 153

SOCIAL AWARENESS

Beurs 298 ... 298
Chiffonniers d'Emmaüs ... 294
French nobility ... 92
Gavroche ... 225
Helping others ... 3
Helping others ... 276
Helping others ... 346-347
Multi-ethnic France ... 296, 297
Noblesse ... 218
Restos du Coeur ... 295
Restos du Coeur ... 347
Sécurité sociale ... 261
Social classes ... 92
Solidarity ... 301
SOS Racisme ... 300

SPORTS

Camping ... 111, 227
Hiking ... 111, 227
Tour de France ... 21

STYLE AND LOOKS

Beauty ... 35, 40-41
Coiffeur ... 149, 150, 160, 161
Hair styles ... 34
Le "Look" ... 33
Make-up ... 34

SWITZERLAND

Montana ... 11

TECHNOLOGY

Eurotunnel ... 195
TGV ... 20

TRANSPORTATION AND TRAVEL

European passport ... 293
Farm stays ... 227
Michelin Guide ... 228, 229, 233
Plane ... 194
TGV ... 20
TGV ... 194, 195
Tourism ... 230
Train ... 194, 195, 198

Train ... 282
Youth hostels ... 227, 230

UNITED NATIONS

United Nations ... 373

UNITED STATES

See also: History, Music, People
Acadian flag ... 420
Cajun culture ... 182
Cajun origins ... 418, 419
French-Americans ... 410
French impressions ... 189
Huguenots français ... 413
Louisiana ... 334
Louisiana Territory ... 20
Louisiane ... 11
Louisiane ... 412
Statue de la Liberté ... 91
US cities with French names ... 417

VACATIONS

Camping ... 111
Holiday travel ... 187, 188
Les grands départs ... 247
Séjours linguistiques ... 187
Sunbathing ... 122, 123
Tourisme vert ... 109

VIETNAM

Vietnam ... 11

WEATHER

Weather ... 126, 127, 136

WORK

Curriculum vitae ... 393
Finding a job ... 384
Job interview ... 392-393
Job search ... 392, 396–397
Part-time jobs ... 82, 83
Professions ... 385, 387, 394

Aligning Language Standards with National Initiatives: Collaboration is the Key!

by Barbara Rupert Mondloch

Since their release in 1996, the National Standards for World Languages have demonstrated the benefits of using meaningful learning targets and measurable outcomes to drive instruction. As these standards are revised and strengthened to incorporate what educators have learned over the years and to reflect the needs of today's students, The American Council on the Teaching of Foreign Languages (ACTFL) is perfectly positioned to partner with other organizations who are also championing efforts to meet the diverse needs of 21st Century Learners. ACTFL has collaborated to create two important documents that respond to a new era of teaching and learning in the United States: *The 21st Century Skills Map for World Languages* and *Aligning the National Standards for Learning Languages with the Common Core Standards.* Both of these projects demonstrate how learning another language and exploring other cultures are essential components of an education that equips students to thrive in college, careers and life in a global society.

The 21st Century Skills Map for World Languages is the result of a collaborative project between The Partnership for 21st Century Skills (P21) and ACTFL. P21 is a national organization that brings together educators, business leaders and policy makers to advocate for "21st Century Readiness for every student." P21 has joined forces with key national organizations such as ACTFL in order to develop Skills Maps that demonstrate the connections between the core academic subjects and the 21st Century Skills.

P21 has identified Learning and Innovation Skills, referred to as 'the 4Cs':

• Critical thinking and Problem Solving

• Communication

• Collaboration

• Creativity and Innovation

These outcomes, combined with Information, Media and Technology skills, and Life and Career Skills, are integrated with the core academic subjects of Social Studies, English, Math, Science, Geography, World Languages and the Arts, to keep content relevant and engaging in order to prepare our students to succeed in a global society.

The World Languages 21st Century Skills Map, developed by a task force led by Toni Theisen, includes contributions from World Language educators across the country. The map provides a framework that demonstrates how the P21 outcomes and the goals of the Standards for Foreign Language Learning in the 21st Century—Communication, Cultures, Connections, Comparisons and Communities (the 5 Cs), weave together seamlessly to support student success.

The design of the map makes it easy for language educators to connect the P21 learning targets with the World Languages curriculum. Each section of the map starts with a skills statement that describes the 21st Century Learning target in the context of World Languages. For example, under the Creativity and Innovation goal, the statement is, "Students as creators and innovators respond to new and diverse perspectives. They use language in imaginative and original ways to make useful contributions." The specific skills that P21 uses to define each of the 4 Cs are consistent across the core content areas and are generally organized with learner outcomes for grades 4, 8 and 12. However, in the context of the World Languages Map, delineating by proficiency levels, rather than grade levels, makes more sense and aligns with the ACTFL scale. For each of the learner outcomes, there are examples of authentic activities, many contributed by classroom teachers, that demonstrate what the outcome looks like at the novice, intermediate and advanced levels. Icons clearly identify the communication mode (interpersonal, interpretive or presentational) in the sample activities and also note interdisciplinary connections to the P21 themes of Financial, Economic, Business and Entrepreneurial Literacy, Civic Literacy, and Health Literacy all in the context of Global Awareness. The World Languages Map clearly demonstrates how the study of other languages and cultures contribute to the development of 21st Century Skills. It is available for free download at www.p21.org.

> *Students as creators and innovators respond to new and diverse perspectives. They use language in imaginative and original ways to make useful contributions.*

Other organizations are also working to promote and implement clear educational standards across the nation. Over the past couple of decades states have develop their own standards and assessments to measure student achievement. As a result, the standards, curriculum and assessments vary widely in content and rigor, yet the achievement data from 50 different state tests have been used to measure success and compare schools and districts for federal accountability. The National Governor's Association for Best Practices and the Council of Chief States Schools Officers (CCSSO) are working together to develop the Common Core State Standards beginning with English Language Arts and Mathematics. Under the Common Core, students would have a guaranteed and viable curriculum that would be measured consistently from state to state. Similar to the P21 project, the standards are intended to establish clear and consistent goals for learning across the nation that will prepare America's children for success in college, work and the world. At least 45 states have signed on to adopt the Common Core State Standards.

ACTFL, in partnership with the Standards Collaborative Board and both the state supervisors (NCSSFL) and district supervisors (NADSFL), is updating the National Standards for Learning Languages, and creating a crosswalk document to clearly demonstrate the connections between the knowledge and skills identified in the Common Core Standards for English Language Arts and the National Standard for Language Learning. Like the World Languages Map, the crosswalk document is organized to clearly show how World Languages education meaningfully contributes to student success with The Common Core.

Common Core State Standards for English Language Arts and Literacy in History/Social Studies, Science and Technical Subjects contain four strands that are all represented by the Communication goal for learning languages in the 5 Cs. The Common Core strands are:

- Reading
- Writing
- Speaking and Listening
- Language

The other four goals in the National Standards for Learning Languages—Cultures, Connections, Comparisons and Communities also bolster the Common Core.

The crosswalk document is organized so that the reader can see how each of the four strands in the Common Core is addressed through the lenses of the Interpretive, Presentational and Interpersonal Communication Standards for Learning Languages. Examples of standards from all 5 Cs illustrate the tight relationship between the Common Core and Standards for Learning Languages which emphasize using another language in a real world context. For example, a Common Core Standard for Reading: Craft and Structure is: "Assess how point of view or purpose shapes the content and style of a text." Several of the Standards for Learning Languages address the idea of author's purpose and point of view. Some examples from the crosswalk document are:

- Interpretive Communication: Students derive meaning from expressions found in culturally authentic texts.

- Practices and Products of Culture: Students compare and reflect on products, practices, and /or perspectives of the target culture(s).

- Language Comparisons: Students evaluate similarities and differences in language use and idiomatic expressions between target language and student's native language

- Cultural Comparisons: Students evaluate similarities and differences in the perspective of the target culture(s) and his/her own culture(s) as found in multimedia and digital/print resources.

In addition to the alignment of the standards, examples of learning targets at the novice, intermediate and advanced levels represent the trajectory of skills and proficiency the students develop over time. The document called "Alignment of the National Standards for Learning Languages with the Common Core State Standards" is currently in draft form at the time of this writing and is available on the ACTFL website at www.actfl.org.

Under the national pressure of high-stakes testing focused on reading and math, well intentioned decision-makers may look at narrowing the curriculum in an effort to improve scores in tested subjects. *The 21st Century Skills Map for World Languages* and

Aligning of the National Standards for Learning Languages with the Common Core Standards clearly illustrate how learning other languages and studying other cultures contribute to success with the Common Core and are critical skills essential to prepare students for success in a global world. In an ACTFL press release, Dane Linn, Director, Education Division, National Governors Association Center for Best Practices puts it well, "Exposure to a foreign language supports the development of the critical literacy skills outlined in the Common Core Standards as well as critical 21st century skills. These skills will better position students for success in their careers and communities."

Standards for the Learning of French

GOAL 1: Communication Communicate in French	**Standard 1.1 Interpersonal Communication** Students engage in conversations or correspondence in French to provide and obtain information, express feelings and emotions, and exchange opinions. **Standard 1.2 Interpretive Communication** Students understand and interpret spoken and written French on a variety of topics. **Standard 1.3 Presentational Communication** Students present information, concepts, and ideas in French to an audience of listeners or readers.
GOAL 2: Cultures Gain Knowledge and Understanding of the Cultures of the Francophone World	**Standard 2.1 Practices of Culture** Students demonstrate an understanding of the relationship between the practices and perspectives of the cultures of the francophone world. **Standard 2.2 Products of Culture** Students demonstrate an understanding of the relationship between the products and perspectives of the cultures of the francophone world.
GOAL 3: Connections Use French to Connect with Other Disciplines and Expand Knowledge	**Standard 3.1 Making Connections** Students reinforce and further their knowledge of other disciplines through French. **Standard 3.2 Acquiring Information** Students acquire information and recognize the distinctive viewpoints that are available through francophone cultures.
GOAL 4: Comparisons Develop Insight through French into the Nature of Language and Culture	**Standard 4.1 Language Comparisons** Students demonstrate understanding of the nature of language through comparisons of French and their native language. **Standard 4.2 Cultural Comparisons** Students demonstrate understanding of the concept of culture through comparisons of francophone cultures and their own.
GOAL 5: Communities Use French to Participate in Communities at Home and Around the World	**Standard 5.1 School and Community** Students use French both within and beyond the school setting. **Standard 5.2 Lifelong Learning** Students show evidence of becoming life-long learners by using French for personal enjoyment and enrichment.

Teaching to the Standards in Discovering French Today!

GOAL ONE: Communicate in French

From the outset, **Discovering French Today!** students learn to communicate in French. In the *Invitation au français* opening section of Level 1, the focus is on understanding what French young people are saying (in video and audio) and on exchanging information in simple conversations. In units 3–6, the oral skills are supplemented by the written skills, and students learn to read and express themselves in writing.

As students progress through Levels 2 and 3, they learn to engage in longer conversations, read and interpret more challenging texts, and understand French-language films and videos. Teachers who incorporate portfolio assessment into their programs will have the opportunity to keep samples of both written and recorded student presentations. Teachers might also want to use Digital Performance Space for a digital version of the recordings and written work.

GOAL TWO: Gain Knowledge and Understanding of the Cultures of the Francophone World

In **Discovering French Today!** students are introduced to the diversity of the French-speaking world. In Level 1, the emphasis is on contemporary culture — in France, of course, but also in Quebec, the Caribbean, and Africa. Students learn to observe and analyze cultural differences in photographs and on the video program.

GOAL THREE: Use French to Connect with Other Disciplines and Expand Knowledge

It is especially in Level 3 that students have the opportunity to use the French language to learn about history, art, music, social concerns and civic responsibilities. Topics suggested in the student text can be coordinated with colleagues across the school curriculum.

GOAL FOUR: Develop Insight through French into the Nature of Language and Culture

From the outset, **Discovering French Today!** draws the students' attention to the way in which French speakers communicate with one another, and how some of these French patterns differ from American ones (for example, shaking hands or greeting friends with a *bise*). Notes in the *Teacher's Edition* provide suggestions for encouraging cross-cultural observation. English and French usage are also compared and contrasted, as appropriate.

GOAL FIVE: Use French to Participate in Communities at Home and Around the World

In **Discovering French Today!** beginning students are invited to exchange letters with French-speaking pen pals. In addition, students are encouraged to participate in international student exchanges. In Level 3, students are invited to discover French-language videos which in many parts of the country can be found in a local video store. As students experience the satisfaction of participating in authentic cultural situations, they become more confident in their ability to use their skills in the wider global community.

Differentiation in the French Classroom

by Leonore Ganschow, Ed.D. and Richard L. Sparks, Ed.D.

The acquisition of a foreign language in our increasingly multilingual society has emerged as a major goal for today's students. Across the country, states require or are starting to require foreign language study by all students, sometimes beginning as early as middle school. Further, in our public schools the movement towards inclusion—placing students with exceptionalities (special education) in regular classrooms—has received increasing emphasis since the early 1990s. These are real changes from the days when the study of a foreign language was largely reserved for the "college-bound" student. Today's foreign language instructors face increasing teaching challenges as more and more learners of diverse abilities and cultures come together in their classrooms.

In this introduction, an approach is presented for addressing the needs of diverse learners. The term "at-risk language learners" is used to describe students who struggle with languages, native or foreign. The introduction is divided into two themes, both of which are important as underpinnings for helping teachers build successful adaptation strategies in their classroom. The themes are (1) there are well-supported assumptions about at-risk language learners and (2) there are solid principles of instruction for at-risk language learners. Both the assumptions and the principles are based on an extensive body of research and input from numerous foreign language and native language teachers who have had years of experience working specifically with at-risk native language learners.

Assumptions

Why do some students learn a foreign language so easily? They learn the meanings of new vocabulary words quickly and begin to read and spell words in the foreign language easily. They quickly comprehend phrases and questions and sometimes even pronounce words in the foreign language as if they had previously spoken the language. They appear to incorporate most aspects of the new language naturally and without extensive effort. In contrast, foreign language teachers encounter other students who cannot read words in the new language and constantly misspell words even after extensive review. They confuse the meanings of vocabulary words and cannot say or understand simple basic foreign language phrases or basic questions. Despite dogged attempts to learn the language, there is nothing that comes naturally to them.

In past years, most foreign language educators assumed that students who did poorly in language classes displayed low motivation, negative attitudes, or lack of effort. While some poor language learners exhibit these characteristics, foreign language teachers often are baffled because these students want to succeed but simply are unable to do so despite spending extra time studying the course material or even participating in tutoring. Moreover, many of the students who have problems in foreign language classes are otherwise good students who do reasonably well (and even exceptionally) in their other courses.

Over the years, researchers have studied why students with average to above-average intelligence struggle with foreign language learning. The emergence of an extensive body of research on native language learning problems has enabled researchers to draw parallels between native and foreign language learning. Findings indicate that "at-risk" students who have difficulty with foreign language learning exhibit overt or subtle problems with their native language skills. Their problems with native language learning usually occurred when they were much younger (i.e., in the primary or intermediate grades) and affected their skills when they were learning to read, spell, and write their native language. Many of these students then struggled in high school with reading comprehension, and they were poor and/or slow readers. Some of these "at-risk" students may have exhibited speech articulation (pronunciation) deficits that required speech therapy. Others had difficulty learning phonics (i.e., letter-sound relationships) and may have received tutoring to learn how to read and spell their native language. Some "at-risk" students learned to read and spell their native language well but have always had difficulty with comprehending oral and/or written language. Still others have weak vocabulary skills in their native language and do not know the meanings of words that their peers seem to know.

It is not surprising that "at-risk" students who had difficulty learning to read, spell, and write their native language or had previous difficulty with speech articulation or who have weak vocabulary skills have similar difficulties when attempting to learn a foreign language. After all, learning to read, spell, write, speak, and listen to a foreign language is the learning of *language*, albeit a new language. And therein lies the problem. The difficulties that these "at-risk" learners encountered in learning their first language are "re-created" when they face the task of learning a second language.

Generally, "at-risk" students who have difficulty with foreign language learning have language-based problems. These problems can occur in the phonological (sound and sound-symbol), syntactic (grammar), and/or semantic (meaning) components of language. For example, a student who had problems in the phonological component of English in elementary school may have had difficulty learning phonics, i.e., the sounds that letters make. This student will probably have difficulty learning to read and spell words in a foreign language and may also have some problems with the pronunciation of words in the new language. In some cases, for example, a student with serious phonological problems may not even notice that some consonant sounds or most vowel sounds in the foreign language are different from the sounds in their native language. Another student may have had problems with the syntactic component of the native language. He or she may have experienced problems with subject-verb agreement or the understanding of adjectives and adverbs. This student will likely have difficulty with grammatical learning in the foreign language. For example, he or she may struggle conjugating verbs, matching the correct masculine or feminine article with a noun, or placing the adjective in the proper order in a spoken or written sentence in the new language. A third type of student may have adequate phonological skills but have weak native language syntactic (grammar) and semantics (meaning) skills. In the native language, this student has difficulty using appropriate grammar when writing and speaking and also has problems with the efficient comprehension of language when listening to others speak or when reading. In the foreign language, this student may have difficulty comprehending oral questions and written text even though he or she knows the meaning of the vocabulary words. Sometimes, students with semantic difficulties do well in the first semester or year of foreign language learning but begin to struggle when the amount and complexity of listening comprehension, speaking, reading comprehension, and writing increase.

New research findings from several languages show that most "at-risk" language learners have problems primarily in the phonological (sound and sound-symbol) and sometimes syntactic (grammatical) components of language. Generally, students who have problems with foreign language learning do not have the same degree of difficulty learning the semantic (meaning) aspects of the new language as they do learning the new phonological and grammar systems. For example, they tend to learn the meaning of new vocabulary words or basic phrases and questions fairly well. However, their problems with the phonology and grammar of the native language cause them to have problems with reading

> "Foreign language teachers play a crucial role in helping their at-risk language learners attain success in their classrooms."

and spelling words, pronouncing sounds, comprehending questions and sentences, and writing grammatically correct sentences in the foreign language. Most of the time, the problems of these "at-risk" learners become apparent early in the first weeks of the first semester of the foreign language course. Other "at-risk" learners may do average work in the first quarter of the course but begin to exhibit problems soon thereafter.

Researchers have found that "at-risk" students who struggle to learn the phonology and grammar of a new language not only exhibit poor skills in the written aspects (reading and writing) of the foreign language, but also achieve low scores on the oral aspects (i.e., speaking and listening) of learning a new language. That is, they do not learn to speak and interpret the foreign language as well as students who have stronger phonological and syntactic skills. Researchers speculate that students with lower levels of phonology and grammar will be hindered in both the written and oral aspects of foreign language learning.

Each year, foreign language teachers encounter increasing numbers of students in their classrooms classified as learning disabled, at risk, language impaired, or even dyslexic. While each student is unique, most students with language learning problems exhibit similar types of difficulties. Their difficulties are *language-based;* that is, the students have problems with the phonological, syntactic, and/or semantic components of language. Because their problems with the learning of a foreign language originate in weak language skills, the large majority of these "at-risk" learners will benefit from instruction that follows several basic principles.

Principles of Instruction

What can foreign language teachers learn from these findings that apply in their inclusion classrooms? This question can be answered by tying these findings to principles derived from an extensive body of literature on language instruction (listening, speaking, reading, writing) with at-risk language learners in the native language. Further, there is a small body of research indicating that principles of instruction that apply to at-risk learners in the native language are effective with at-risk foreign language learners as well. Drawing upon this research base, foreign language teachers can apply the following eight principles of instruction in working with at-risk language learners by making the learning of a foreign language:

Multisensory
use multiple input/output strategies and involve all of the learning channels—visual, auditory, tactile, and kinesthetic

Repetitive
provide ample opportunities for students to "overlearn" a concept through frequent practice and reviews

Structured
teach language concepts in logical order and help students organize the language into logical categories

Sequential
organize language concepts from simple to complex. Note that the term sequential also applies to the phonological level of language, where at-risk language learners have difficulty learning the sound and sound-symbol system of the foreign language, and to the grammatical level of language, where at-risk language learners have problems recognizing parts of speech (nouns, verbs, adjectives)

Cumulative
build on what at-risk language learners already know

Alphabetic/phonetic
teach students directly and explicitly the sounds of the language and the letters those sounds/sound sequences represent

Metacognitive
teach students how to think about or reflect on the language; thinking about how the language is structured is especially important in grasping grammar concepts (e.g., word order in a sentence)

Synthetic/analytic
help students break language into parts (analytic) and put the parts together again (synthetic). For example, help them recognize parts in a chunk of language (a syllable, a word, a phrase, a sentence) (analytic). Help them put together the sounds of the language to form words and chunk parts of words (prefixes, suffixes, roots) together to form larger words (synthetic).

Instructional adaptations for at-risk language learners, then, should reflect one or more of these guiding principles.

These eight principles provide some direction for teachers, but can these principles really be applied successfully in inclusion settings? In our view, the extent to which instruction can be modified and the types of lesson adaptations that are feasible and desirable depend to a large extent on the *severity* of the at-risk learner's language difficulties and on the *nature* of the learner's language difficulties. In terms of severity, it is helpful to think of a continuum of difficulty/lack of difficulty with language. The following figure visually presents an outline of a severity continuum in relation to the degree of adaptations that might be necessary in inclusion classrooms.

Severity of Language Difficulty				
High Degree				▨
Moderate			▨	
Some		▨		
None	▨			
	Some	**Moderate**	**Intensive**	

Accommodation Needs

In inclusion classrooms, foreign language teachers are likely to experience the most success using accommodations for students with some to moderate difficulties. As the severity of the language difficulty becomes more of an issue, the need for adaptation strategies becomes increasingly critical. For students with a high degree of language difficulty and intensive accommodation needs, teachers should consult with the learning specialist at their school as more intensive modifications may be necessary.

Foreign language teachers play a crucial role in helping their at-risk language learners attain success in their classrooms. In order to do so, however, teachers need an understanding of the nature of these students' learning difficulties and help in developing accommodations that can be successful in helping them learn the foreign language.

General Suggestions for Making Classroom Accommodations

• Provide a simple study guide of the day's activities (structured).

• Present major points simultaneously orally and on overheads; have students repeat important words and phrases and say them again as they write them in their notebooks (multisensory).

• Provide guided pair activities to practice/reinforce a concept (pair strong/weaker language learners) (repetitive).

• Analyze the concept to be learned and talk students through the sequence of steps needed to master the concept (especially important in teaching grammar concepts); have written samples available to work as guides (sequential).

• Require students to keep a notebook and help them organize it (structured).

• Speak slowly and with clear pronunciation, using the same phrases repeatedly (alphabetic/phonetic).

• Provide daily structured written reviews of material covered that day (repetitive, cumulative).

• Use verbal/visual (pictorial) mnemonic devices to assist in memory; let students design their own mnemonic devices and discuss the value of this strategy (metacognitive).

• Show students how parts are added to words to change meaning and how long words can be broken down into parts (i.e., prefixes, suffixes, roots) (synthetic/analytic).

• Use color coding to illustrate grammar and pronunciation (alphabetic/phonetic).

• Provide an opportunity to demonstrate mastery of smaller chunks of information prior to longer, unit exams (sequential, repetitive).

• Provide time for students to reflect on how they best learn and remember language concepts; teach them strategies to help them remember (metacognitive).

Inclusion of Accelerated Language Learners in the French Classroom

Gifted and talented learners have the potential to move through the foreign language curriculum at an accelerated pace; some excel in one language area, such as reading or speaking; others may excel in all language areas. Typically, these students learn new language concepts quickly; they don't need repetition and once they learn something, they remember. They're highly curious, find new information challenging and stimulating, and often ask probing questions. They're also creative and enjoy tackling the unfamiliar. Their approach to problem-solving, including the challenge of a new language, is often unusual because they tend to think "outside the box." On the flip side, if these students are not challenged, they might tune out, stop doing their homework, and become a problem to the teacher.

Principles of Instruction

How, then, might foreign language teachers address the special needs of the accelerated language learner? Educators of the gifted commonly recommend that teachers differentiate their classroom curriculum. Classroom teachers can differentiate the foreign language curriculum by modifying (1) course content, (2) the learning process, (3) the learning environment, and (4) the product or outcome expectations. The following examples demonstrate how teachers can differentiate curriculum in their foreign language classes.

Course Content

Enrichment Through Curriculum Expansion Develop structured opportunities for students to explore the language through an expansion or extension of activities related to a given language concept or topic. Educators of the gifted can be very helpful in setting up these learning experiences.

Enrichment Through In-depth Exploration Develop opportunities for students to deepen their understanding of a language concept or topic through a more in-depth focus. Again, teachers might solicit guidance from an educator of the gifted.

Learning Process

Self-pacing Allow students to move through the textbook and their assignments at an accelerated pace. Allow them to competency-test out of units.

Individualized Learning Once they have mastered a language concept, provide structured opportunities for students to work on their own. Short- and long-term projects can be negotiated through teacher-student contracts.

Self-directed Learning Encourage students to initiate or create their own enrichment activities. The role of teacher becomes negotiating, structuring, and monitoring the learning experience.

Learning Environment

Higher-Level Thinking Encourage students to think about language concepts in increasingly complex ways. In helping students design activities, use the three highest levels of Bloom's taxonomy (analysis, synthesis, evaluation).

Creative Thinking Encourage students to develop unusual or unique approaches to language study. Invite them to problem-solve in figuring out language structures such as grammar concepts and vocabulary connections.

Product/Outcome Expectations

Product Variation Allow students to demonstrate what they are learning in different ways and through a variety of verbal and nonverbal media.

Self-Evaluation Provide opportunities for students to participate in evaluating their own progress and their products.

Initially, implementing these principles will necessitate some extra work by the teacher. However, the experience of providing a motivating and enriched environment will ultimately be fulfilling for the student and allow the foreign language teacher to experience the satisfaction of having challenged the student. Further, the task will become easier as the teacher increases his or her understanding of the specialized needs and capabilities of accelerated language learners and uses this knowledge to build a repertoire of appropriate differentiated curriculum options.

Related References
General
Ganschow, L., & Sparks, R. (2001). Learning difficulties and foreign language learning: A review of research and instruction. *Language Teaching, 34,* 79–98.
Ganschow, L., & Sparks, R. (2000). Reflections on foreign language study for students with language learning problems: Research, issues, and challenges. *Dyslexia, 6,* 87–100.
Sparks, R., & Ganschow, L. (1991). Foreign language learning difficulties: Affective or native language aptitude differences? *Modern Language Journal, 75,* 3–16.
Research
Sparks, R., Artzer, M., Patton, J., Ganschow, L., Miller, K., Hordubay, D., & Walsh, G. (1998). Benefits of multisensory language instruction for at-risk learners: A comparison study of high school Spanish students. *Annals of Dyslexia, 48,* 239–270.
Sparks, R., Ganschow, L., Javorsky, J., Pohlman, J., & Patton, J. (1992). Test comparisons among students identified as high-risk, low-risk, and learning disabled in high school foreign language courses. *Modern Language Journal, 76,* 142–159.

Sparks, R., Ganschow, L., Javorsky, J., Pohlman, J., & Patton, J. (1992). Identifying native language deficits in high and low-risk foreign language learners in high school. *Foreign Language Annals, 25,* 403–418.
Teaching
Ganschow, L., & Schneider, E. (1997). Teaching all students: From research to reality. In A. Vogely (Ed.), *Celebrating languages, opening all minds!* Annual Meeting Series – NO. 14, New York State Association of Foreign Language Teachers, Fall, 1997.
Pritikin, L. (1999). *A policy of inclusion: Alternative foreign language curriculum for high-risk and learning disabled students.* ERIC Clearinghouse on Languages and Linguistics, Center for Applied Linguistics. ED 428 486.
Schneider, E., & Ganschow, L. (2000). Dynamic assessment and instructional strategies for learners who struggle to learn a foreign language. *Dyslexia, 6,* 72–82.
Sparks, R., Ganschow, L., & Schneider, E. (2002). Teaching foreign (second) languages to at-risk learners: Research and practice. In J. H. Sullivan (Ed.), *Literacy and the second language learner* (pp. 55–83). Greenwich, CT: Information Age Publishing.
Sparks, R., & Miller, K. (2000). Teaching a foreign language using multisensory structured language techniques to at-risk learners: A review. *Dyslexia, 6,* 124–132.

Strategies for Pre-AP® Students

by Mary L. Diehl

Integrating Pre-AP® strategies into the *Discovering French Today!* series

The standards-based goals of the **Discovering French Today!** series address the skills necessary for success in Advanced Placement® French Language and Culture. While many instructional approaches exist for developing the skills required in AP, certain strategies prepare students to meet the objectives of the AP course and examination in French language. The **Discovering French Today!** series uses an integrated, thematic approach that combines listening, speaking, reading, writing, and culture. Vertical teaming, beginning with French 1 and continuing through the highest level offered (AP French Language and Culture), is essential in ensuring success. In other words, teachers work together to provide sequential programs that develop language proficiency and challenge all students. **Discovering French Today!** offers important tools for teachers to do just that.

Background Information: The Advanced Placement® French Language and Culture Course and Examination

The AP French Language and Culture Course prepares students for the French Language and Culture Examination, which holistically evaluates proficiency in three modes of communication defined in the *Standards for Foreign Language Learning in the 21st Century* (Interpersonal, Interpretive, and Presentational). In addition to demonstrating linguistic proficiency, students are asked to demonstrate cultural understanding. There are six themes around which the AP French Language and Culture course is structured : Global Challenges, Science and Technology, Contemporary Life, Personal and Public Identities, Families and Communities and Beauty and Aesthetics. During the three-hour exam students will complete a multiple-choice and a free-response section. The skills of listening and reading comprehension are tested in the first part of the exam with multiple-choice items that ask students to respond to questions related to a variety of authentic print and audio materials. These questions may require understanding of cultural or interdisciplinary information. In the second section of the exam students are asked to produce written and spoken responses to demonstrate their Interpersonal and Presentational proficiency. The Multiple Choice and the Free Response sections of the exam are worth 50% each. More detailed information about the exam is available at: http://www.collegeboard.org/

With **Discovering French Today!** you may begin to prepare students in French 1-3 by using strategies and exposing them to the themes that reflect the goals of the AP course and examination.

Grammar and Vocabulary Strategies

Students must develop a command of many grammatical structures and a wide range of vocabulary in order to be proficient in listening, reading, speaking, and writing. Teaching students *about* grammar is not the same as having students *use* the grammar and vocabulary they have learned to carry on conversations, understand what they hear, read and comprehend what they have read, and write coherent sentences, paragraphs, and, later on, compositions. Incorporate the new grammar and vocabulary students learn into the different types of activities students perform. You can provide learner-centered opportunities for Pre-AP students to:

- use a variety of structures and vocabulary, which increase in complexity as the students move from level 1 through level 3.

- recognize errors in forms or usage. On the speaking portion of the Advanced Placement Examination, for example, awareness of error which leads to self-correction shows that the student is cognizant of what is "correct" usage. This student will score at a higher level than one who does not self-correct because he/she is unaware of errors.

- demonstrate knowledge and use of devices that link meaning (transitions).

- use circumlocution. Encourage students to describe in French rather than use English when they don't know a certain word or phrase.

- use a variety of structures and vocabulary at the same time rather than always dealing with one tense, structure, or set of vocabulary items at a time.

Discovering French Today! 1–3 teaches structures and includes many topics ideal for Pre-AP courses. The exercises requiring that the students create with the language rather than merely follow a pattern are crucial. Pre-AP students, especially in level 3, need practice exercises that "mix" a variety of structures and vocabulary. Make students aware of tense usage and the complexities of language structure as their proficiency level increases.

Listening Strategies

The AP listening sections requires students to listen and respond to a variety of authentic audio materials. In the first subsection of the Interpretive Communication section, students are asked to respond to audio recordings that are paired with print materials. In the second subsection, only audio recording is provided. In order to prepare students for these tasks, Pre-AP courses should include a wide variety of listening passages on many different topics. The passages should become longer and more complicated as the student progresses through levels 1, 2, and 3. For example, in **Discovering French Today!** *Bleu* students learn to get the "gist" of passages and then more details as their proficiency increases. By the time students use **Discovering French Today!** *Rouge,* listening passages stress both the main idea and details and involve more complicated material.

You can help Pre-AP students organize information by incorporating sequencing, sorting, and categorizing activities. First, the Pre-AP students learn to summarize what they have heard and later analyze, compare and contrast, and evaluate the information.

Ask questions that range from the concrete and factual to those that ask for implied or inferred information. From the beginning, the Pre-AP student should be given the opportunity to tell "why" and to use higher order thinking skills.

Incorporate these specific strategies to help the Pre-AP student get ready for the listening portion of the AP Examination:

- Conduct your classes in the target language to the greatest extent possible.
- Provide practice in a multiple-choice format as well as the question/answer type free response.
- Have students listen only and not read the text at the same time.
- Teach students to use context cues to determine unknown words or phrases they hear. Encourage students to "guess."
- Teach students to listen for intonation patterns and stress to determine whether they are hearing a question, a statement, and so on. By listening for stress patterns they can also determine if the speaker is talking about the past, present, or future.
- Teach students to listen for background noises or sounds that help determine where a dialogue takes place.
- Provide opportunities for students to practice note-taking skills when listening or viewing.
- Design or choose activities that require the class to listen to a variety of voices including classmates, DVDs, audio, and you, their teacher. Elicit a written or spoken response to what is heard. (Example: Students do oral presentations on travel brochures they have created and classmates list reasons for going to each place. This encourages listening for both general ideas and details.)

- Take advantage of the opportunity to respond to your students' work with a voice message in your Performance Space Teacher Dashboard.

Reading

On the reading section of the AP exam, students read for the main idea, details, and inferred meaning. The passages vary in length and may be cultural or interdisciplinary. Students must have command of grammar and vocabulary in order to understand the reading selections which come from a wide range of sources. Teach your Pre-AP students to:

- identify the main idea and as many details as possible.
- use pre-reading skills such as establishing the purpose, making predictions, looking for cognates, and so on.
- skim and scan.
- read increasingly longer, more complicated passages.
- sequence information.
- use context clues.
- analyze language used (formal, informal, metaphors, similes, etc.)
- make predictions and inferences based on what they have read.
- draw conclusions.
- recreate the text in their own words.
- elaborate when summarizing.
- distinguish fact from opinion.
- determine cause and effect.
- indicate where in the text the answer to a certain question is found. The questions and the answers may express ideas in language using synonyms or circumlocution.

Writing

Students' writing is assessed in Section II of the exam. Students are asked to respond to a written message and to write a persuasive essay in response to three prompts . Students are allotted 40 minutes to complete this section of the exam. Students will do well on this portion of the AP exam if they have been trained from French I in the way they will be evaluated.

In order to prepare your Pre-AP students for these tasks, provide opportunities for them to:

- write in a timed situation.
- use pre-writing skills such as brainstorming, organizing ideas, making outlines.
- organize thoughts and then essays. Know how to write introductions, supporting paragraphs and conclusions.
- write thesis statements.

- support ideas with details.
- use transitions and ways to link paragraphs.
- write relevant and thorough compositions.
- consider the audience (voice) and establish purpose.
- write relevant and thorough responses.
- practice combining sentences
- use a variety of vocabulary and structures to form cohesive sentences, paragraphs and essays.
- show command of the conventions of written language.
- control both simple and complex structures.
- evaluate the writing of others as well as their own writing. (peer-edit and self-edit)
- practice writing in a variety of formats: journals, letters, articles, dialogues, and essays.
- Respond to articles and other students' comments on News and Networking.

Begin with very guided writing activities. In level 1, students write simple information with learned phrases, structures and vocabulary. In level 2, students begin to create with the language, while level 3 students can write about a wider variety of topics using a greater number of structures and transitions. The most important point is to provide many writing opportunities. Use Generate Success to provide graphic organizers so students can organize their thoughts and rubrics to help them more effectively evaluate their own writing

Speaking Strategies

In the Interpersonal Speaking section of the AP exam, students are asked to participate in a simulated conversation by responding to questions. In the Presentational Speaking section, students are asked to respond to a cultural prompt with a 2-minute presentation. To prepare students for this these tasks, have them:

- retell information or stories (move from simple to complex in levels 1–3).
- use pictures as a basis for telling stories or describing.
- respond to questions with thorough answers that are increasingly more complex and correct.
- plan for what will be said by brainstorming answers.
- organize ideas and sequence information.
- vary vocabulary and circumlocute.
- expand, elaborate.
- use intonation and pronounce with care.
- self-correct.
- agree, disagree; approve, disapprove; encourage, discourage.

Teaching Strategy: Challenge

Give students a sentence with includes an indefinite adjective. Ask them to restate the sentence using **en** and an indefinite pronoun. (Give them one or two examples since this concept can be difficult for some students.) **Pre-AP® skill:** Use a variety of structures and vocabulary.

Teaching Strategy: Warm-Up

Put the verbs from p.48 on the board or on a transparency. Have students write a story about what twin sisters, Annique and Hélène, do every day from morning until bedtime. The following day, have students rewrite their story in the past tense. **Pre-AP® skill:** Sequence events.

- give directions, orders, advice.
- relate opinions.
- communicate preferences.
- persuade.
- relate what happened before, what is happening, what will happen next
- participate in pair activities, information gap activities where one student has the information another needs.
- answer within a given time frame.
- take risks and not be afraid to make errors.
- feel comfortable speaking. In linguistic terms, this is "lowering the affective filter."

Using Your Resources

The **Discovering French Today!** series provides a strong foundation for the AP French Language and Culture course and exam. Many of the sections involving speaking (*Tête à tête, À votre tour!*, for example) could easily be targeted for Pre-AP. In addition to the foundation provided with the text, **Discovering French Today!** students and teachers have a wealth of resources to support preparation for the AP Language and Culture exam. Pre-AP Digital Resources available via my.hrw.com provide 4-skill activities related to the AP cultural themes, reading, speaking and listening practice, practice exams and tips, and suggestions for preparing for the exam.

With **Discovering French Today!** you can produce students who understand what they read and hear and who can communicate ideas through speaking and writing and who are ready for the challenges of the AP French Language and Culture course and exam.

Introduction to French Literature

Beginning with Level Three, the teaching of literature becomes a significant objective in the curriculum of many French courses. Because most authentic French literary pieces are linguistically very complex, it is important that the introduction to French literature be done in a *progressive* manner so as to correspond to the linguistic abilities of the students. It should also be done in an *interesting* and *stimulating* way and include a variety of texts that students can relate to easily.

If the initial introduction to literature is successful, students are more likely to develop an interest in the richness of French literature and breadth of francophone culture. Many will be encouraged to continue their study of French, and perhaps make plans to travel or study in a French-speaking part of the world.

The literature-related contents of **Discovering French Today!** Level 3 have been selected to meet the following objectives:

- To *present integral literary pieces that are linguistically accessible* to Level Three students. All the twentieth-century texts are presented as written with only minor occasional abridgments. Because of their lexical complexity, however, the short stories of the nineteenth century have been somewhat adapted.

- To show how *poetry can be used to convey powerful political messages.* Students tend to dismiss poetry as boring and uninteresting. Here they will discover how Paul Éluard's *Liberté* became a call to resistance in World War II, how David Diop and Aimé Césaire used poetry to promote African independence, and how Zachary Richard uses song lyrics to plead for the maintenance of Cajun culture in Louisiana.

- To *introduce longer significant literary works* via summaries and synopses. By encountering some major works of literature through brief summaries, students will broaden their awareness of the breadth of the French cultural heritage and develop a growing interest in French literature.

- To bring students into direct contact with the variety of *the literature of the French-speaking world,* by including authors from France, Africa, the Caribbean and North America. Genres include short stories, fables, legends, letters, poetry, as well as introductions to novels and plays.

The breadth of the literary content of **Discovering French Today!** Level 3 is shown in the following chart on page T65.

Literature Selections in Discovering French Today! Level 3

FRANCE
Moyen Âge   PAGE

- *La Chanson de Roland*
  (introduction)   102
- Fabliau: *La Couverture*   92

17e Siècle

- La Fontaine: *Le Corbeau et
  le renard*   146

18e Siècle

- La Fayette: *Lettre à sa femme*   415

19e Siècle

- Victor Hugo: *Les Misérables*
  (introduction)   224
- Guy de Maupassant:
  En voyage   282
- Edmond Rostand: *Cyrano de
  Bergerac* (introduction au film) 142
- André Theuriet: *Les Pêches*   327

20e Siècle

- Robert Desnos: *La Fourmi*   67
- Paul Éluard: *Liberté*   256
- Eugène Ionesco: *Conte pour enfants
  de moins de trois ans*   56
- Michelle Maurois: *Le Bracelet*   366
- Charles de Gaulle:
  *Appel du 18 juin
  1940* (extrait)   254

                                                 PAGE

- Jacques Prévert: *Soyons polis*   123
- Jacques Prévert: *Pour faire le portrait
  d'un oiseau*   68
- Sempé et Goscinny:
  *King (from Les Récrés
  du petit Nicolas)*   134
- Louis Malle:
  Au revoir, les Enfants
  (introduction au film)   256

AFRIQUE

- Fable: *La Gélinotte et la tortue*   377
- Bernard Dadié: *La Légende baoulé*   380
- David Diop: *Afrique*   378

ANTILLES

- Aimé Césaire: *Pour saluer le Tiers-Monde*   337
- René Depestre: *Pour Haïti*   339
- Joseph Zobel: *Rue Cases-nègres*
  (introduction au film)   342

QUÉBEC

- Yves Thériault: *Le Portrait*   402
- Gilles Vigneault: *Mon Pays*   183

LOUISIANE

- Zachary Richard: *Réveille*   419

Professional Reference Information

Professional Language Organizations

American Association of Teachers of French (AATF)

Mailcode 4510
Southern Illinois University
Carbondale, IL 62901-4510
Phone: (618) 453-5731
www.frenchteachers.org

As an AATF member:
• you will receive subscriptions to the French Review and the AATF
  National Bulletin.
• you will be able to attend local, regional, and national AATF
  meetings where you can share ideas and meet new colleagues.
• you have the opportunity to apply for one of the many summer
  scholarships to France and Quebec offered to AATF members.
• you may sponsor a chapter of the Société Honoraire de Français
  at your school so that your students will then be eligible to
  compete for study abroad travel grants and participate in the SHF
  creative writing contest.
• you can have your students participate in the National French
  Contest and be considered for local, regional, and national awards.
• you can obtain pen pals for your students through the Bureau de
  Correspondance Scolaire.

American Council on the Teaching of Foreign Languages (ACTFL)

700 S. Washington St., Suite 210
Alexandria, VA 22314
Phone: (703) 894-2900
Fax: (703) 894-2905
headquarters@actfl.org
www.actfl.org

Governmental Organizations

Alliance Française

The Alliance Française is a French organization dedicated to the
promotion of French language and culture.
   To obtain the address of the Alliance Française nearest
   you, write:

Federation of Alliances Françaises USA

1800 E. Capitol Drive
Milwaukee, WI 53211
Phone: 800-6-FRANCE (800-637-2623)
Fax: 1-800-491-6980
federation@afusa.org
www.afusa.org

French Cultural Services

The French Cultural Services are very supportive of French teaching
in the United States. For more information, contact the French
Cultural Officer at the French Consulate nearest you or write the
New York office.
   To obtain information about available French cultural
   materials, write:

Cultural Services of the French Embassy

972 Fifth Avenue
New York, NY 10021
Phone: (212) 439-1400
Fax: (212) 439-1455
www.frenchculture.org

Sister Cities International

If your town has a Sister City in a French-speaking country, you
might want to explore the possibility of initiating a youth or
education exchange program. If your town does not yet have a
French-speaking Sister City, you might want to encourage your
community to set up such an affiliation.
   For information on both youth exchanges and the
   establishment of a sister-city association, contact:

Sister Cities International

915 15th Street, NW, 4th Floor
Washington, DC 20005
Phone: (202) 347-8630
www.sister-cities.org
info@sister-cities.org

HOLT McDOUGAL

Discovering FRENCH Today!

FRENCH 3
Rouge

Jean-Paul Valette

Rebecca M. Valette

HOLT McDOUGAL

 HOUGHTON MIFFLIN HARCOURT

Cover photography

Front Cover ©Shaen Adey/Gallo Images/Getty Images
Back Cover Level 1a: ©David Noble/Travel Pictures; Level 1b: ©Patrice Coppee/Workbook Stock/Getty Images; Level 1: ©Travelpix Ltd/Stone/Getty Images; Level 2: ©David Sanger/The Image Bank/Getty Images; Level 3: ©Shaen Adey/Gallo Images/Getty Images

Photography credits appear on page R75.

Printed in the U.S.A.

ISBN 978-0-547-87247-6

1 2 3 4 5 6 7 8 9 10 XXXX   21 20 19 18 17 16 15 14 13 12

4500000000   A B C D E F G

Merci!

We would like to thank the many teachers across the country who have responded to surveys and sent suggestions for this program. In particular, we would like to thank the following people who participated in the development process and provided guidance and encouragement:

Susan Arandjelovic
Dobson High School
Mesa, AZ

Joseph Giorgio Arias
James "Niki" Rowe High School
McAllen, TX

Pat Barr-Harrison
Prince George's County Public Schools
Landover, MD

Beth Bossong
Vestal High School
Vestal, NY

Celeste Carr
Howard County Public Schools
Ellicott City, MD

Betty C. Clough
McCallum High School
Austin, TX

Linda Crecca
Hampton Bays Junior/Senior High School
Hampton Bays, NY

Kay Dagg
Washburn Rural High School
Topeka, KS

Dorothy Davis
Royal High School
Simi Valley, CA

Deborah DeMelfi
Central Columbia High School
Bloomsburg, PA

Janice Dowd
Teaneck High School
Teaneck, NJ

Christiane Fabricant
The Winsor School
Boston, MA

Susan Fritz
Reading Memorial High School
Reading, MA

Susan Hennessey
Reading Memorial High School
Reading, MA

Mary Sue Hoffman
Upper Moreland High School
Willow Grove, PA

Barbara Holohan
Princeton High School
Princeton, NJ

Sheila (Ray) Hutchinson
Kimball High School
Dallas, TX

Belinda Kuck
Clearfield High School
Clearfield, UT

Myrella LeBlanc
Sam Rayburn High School
Pasadena, TX

Lula Lewis
Hyde Park Academy
Chicago, IL

Virginia Mayer
Padua Academy
Wilmington, DE

Patricia McCann
Lincoln-Sudbury High School
Sudbury, MA

William Price
Day Junior High School
Newton, MA

Susan Redd
Mt. Vernon High School
Mt. Vernon, WA

Barbara Reeback
Albuquerque Academy
Albuquerque, NM

T. Jeffrey Richards
Roosevelt High School
Sioux Falls, SD

Virginia Rossy
Simi Valley High School
Simi Valley, CA

Dr. Judith Smith
Baltimore, MD

Kathy Withington
McCluer Senior High School
Florissant, MO

We would also like to thank the following persons for helping us acquire a better insight into their areas of the French-speaking world:

Thierry Gustave *(Martinique)*   **Kouadio Konan** *(Ivory Coast)*
Yasmina Hacien-Bey *(Algeria)*   **Ourida Mostefai** *(Algeria)*

Reprise

Vive les vacances! 2

 **Reprise A** La vie courante 4

RAPPEL ①〉 Bonjour! 4

RAPPEL ②〉 Le temps libre 6

RAPPEL ③〉 Bon appétit! 8

À votre tour! 10

♻ RAPPEL Culturel 11

Reprise B Hier et avant 12

RAPPEL ④〉 Le week-end. 12

RAPPEL ⑤〉 En vacances 14

RAPPEL ⑥〉 Qu'est-ce qui se passe? 16

À votre tour! 19

♻ RAPPEL Culturel 20

Reprise C Nous et les autres 22

RAPPEL ⑦〉 Vive l'amitié!. 22

RAPPEL ⑧〉 Un garçon timide. 24

À votre tour! 26

LECTURE Les trois bagues. 27

Unité **1** *Au jour le jour*

INFOMAGAZINE **33**
- L'importance du «look»
- Les visages de la beauté

Partie 1

LE FRANÇAIS PRATIQUE *La description physique* **36**

LANGUE ET COMMUNICATION **38**
- A L'usage de l'article avec les parties du corps
  «Je ne suis pas très belle.»

LE FRANÇAIS PRATIQUE *La toilette et les soins personnels* **42**

LANGUE ET COMMUNICATION **44**
- A Les verbes réfléchis

INFOMAGAZINE **46**
- À la résidence Bon Repos

Partie 2

LE FRANÇAIS PRATIQUE *La routine quotidienne* **48**

LANGUE ET COMMUNICATION **50**
- A Les passé composé des verbes réfléchis

LE FRANÇAIS PRATIQUE *La condition physique et les sentiments* **52**

Comment demander des nouvelles à un(e) ami(e)
Comment répondre
Comment décrire quelqu'un

LANGUE ET COMMUNICATION **54**
- A L'usage idiomatique des verbes réfléchis

LECTURE *Conte pour enfants de moins de trois ans (Ionesco)*. **56**

Interlude culturel *Le monde des arts* **60**

La révolution impressionniste **60**
Claude Monet: le peintre de la lumière **62**
Après l'impressionnisme **64**
Le surréalisme **66**
Desnos: *La fourmi* **67**
Prévert: *Pour faire le portrait d'un oiseau*. **68**
L'art dans la rue **69**

v

Contents

Unité 2 Soyons utiles!

INFOMAGAZINE **71**
- Les passe-temps actifs
- Soyez bon pour les plantes
- Ça, c'est la justice!

Partie 1

LE FRANÇAIS PRATIQUE *Les travaux domestiques* **74**

LANGUE ET COMMUNICATION **78**
- A La formation du subjonctif (1)
- B Comment exprimer une obligation personnelle:
  L'usage du subjonctif après **il faut que**
- C La formation du subjonctif (2)

INFOMAGAZINE **82**
- Le travail, ça paie!

Partie 2

LE FRANÇAIS PRATIQUE *Pour rendre service*. **84**

Comment demander de l'aide

Comment accepter

Comment refuser … et donner une excuse

Comment remercier … et répondre à quelqu'un
  qui vous remercie

LANGUE ET COMMUNICATION **86**
- A Le subjonctif: formation irrégulière
- B Le subjonctif après certaines expressions impersonnelles
- C L'usage du subjonctif après **vouloir que**

LE FRANÇAIS PRATIQUE *Comment décrire un objet* **90**

LECTURE *La Couverture (une fable médiévale)* **92**

Interlude culturel *Les grands moments de l'histoire
de france (jusqu'en 1453)* **98**

Les dates, les événements, les personnes **98**
Lascaux **100**
Roland, l'homme et la légende **102**
La chanson de Roland. **103**
Quand les rois d'Angleterre étaient français **104**
Jeanne d'Arc à Chinon **106**

Unité 3 Vive la nature!

INFOMAGAZINE **109**

- Oui à la nature!
- Les éco-musées
- Les sept commandements du campeur

Partie 1

LE FRANÇAIS PRATIQUE *Les vacances: Plaisirs et problèmes* **112**

LANGUE ET COMMUNICATION **114**

   A Révision: Le passé composé
   B Révision: L'imparfait
   C L'usage du passé composé et de l'imparfait

INFOMAGAZINE **120**

- Jacques-Yves Cousteau, champion de l'écologie marine
- L'Écologie à la maison
- Le soleil, notre bonne étoile
- J. Prévert, *Soyez polis*

Partie 2

LE FRANÇAIS PRATIQUE *Quoi de neuf?* **124**

Comment décrire un événement, comment raconter
  une histoire
Comment parler de la pluie et du beau temps

LANGUE ET COMMUNICATION **128**

   A La description d'un événement: le passé composé et l'imparfait
   B L'imparfait et le passé composé dans la même phrase
   C Le passé simple

LECTURE *King (Sempé/Goscinny)* **134**

Interlude culturel *Les grands moments de l'histoire
de France (1453-1715)* **140**

Les dates, les événements, les personnes **140**
Film: *Cyrano de Bergerac* **142**
La Fontaine: *Le corbeau et le renard* **146**
L'histoire de France à travers ses châteaux **147**

Contents

Unité 4 Aspects de la vie quotidienne

INFOMAGAZINE **149**

- En France, faites comme les Français!
- Scènes de la vie courante

Partie 1

LE FRANÇAIS PRATIQUE *Comment faire des achats* **152**

À la papeterie
À la poste

LANGUE ET COMMUNICATION **156**

A Révision: Le pronom **y**
B Révision: Le pronom **en**
C Expressions indéfinies de quantité

INFOMAGAZINE **160**

- À chacun son style

Partie 2

LE FRANÇAIS PRATIQUE *Au salon de coiffure* **161**

LANGUE ET COMMUNICATION **162**

A Révision: les pronoms **le, la, les** et **lui, leur**
B L'ordre des pronoms

LANGUE ET PRATIQUE *Services* **166**

Chez le cordonnier
Chez le teinturier
Chez le photographe

LANGUE ET COMMUNICATION **168**

A La construction **faire** + infinitif

LECTURE *Une histoire de cheveux* **170**

Interlude culturel *Vive la musique!* **176**

Histoire de la chanson française. **176**
Les vedettes d'hier **177**
… et les vedettes d'aujourd'hui. **179**
La musique des jeunes. **180**
La musique francophone en Amérique **182**
Vigneault: *Mon pays* **183**
Et la musique classique? **184**

Unité **5** Bon voyage!

INFOMAGAZINE **187**

- La passion des voyages
- Leurs destinations préférées
- Impressions d'Amérique

Partie 1

LE FRANÇAIS PRATIQUE *Les voyages* **190**

Les voyages
Au contrôle des passeports
À la douane

LANGUE ET COMMUNICATION **192**

- A Les expressions négatives
- B L'expression **ne...que**

INFOMAGAZINE **194**

- La France en train
- L'Eurotunnel

Partie 2

LE FRANÇAIS PRATIQUE *Partons en voyage* **196**

À l'agence de voyages
À l'aéroport
À la gare

LANGUE ET COMMUNICATION **201**

- A Le futur
- B L'usage du futur dans les phrases avec **si**
- C L'usage du futur après **quand**
- D Le conditionnel

LECTURE *Le mystérieux homme en bleu* **208**

Interlude culturel *Les grands moments de l'histoire de france (1715-1870)* **216**

Les dates, les événements, les personnes **216**
L'héritage de la Révolution **218**
L'histoire de la Marseillaise **222**
Les Misérables **224**
Victor Hugo: écrivain et homme politique **224**

Unité 6 Séjour en France

INFOMAGAZINE **227**

- Les jeunes touristes en France
- Le *Guide Michelin*
- La société Michelin
- Comment lire le *Guide Michelin*

Partie 1

LE FRANÇAIS PRATIQUE À l'hôtel **230**

Où loger?
À la réception

LANGUE ET COMMUNICATION **234**

- **A** Le comparatif
- **B** Le superlatif

INFOMAGAZINE **238**

- À l'Hôtel de la Plage

Partie 2

LE FRANÇAIS PRATIQUE Services à l'hôtel **240**

Comment demander un service

LANGUE ET COMMUNICATION **242**

- **A** Le pronom interrogatif **lequel**
- **B** Le pronom démonstratif **celui**
- **C** Le pronom possessif **le mien**

LECTURE Une étrange aventure **246**

Interlude culturel Les grands moments de l'histoire
de france *(1870 au présent)* **252**

Les dates, les événements, les personnes **252**
Charles de Gaulle, homme d'action **254**
C. de Gaulle, *Appel du 18 juin 1940* **254**
P. Éluard, *Liberté* **256**
Film: L. Malle, *Au revoir, les Enfants* **258**

Unité 7 La forme et la santé

INFOMAGAZINE **261**
- Les Français et leur santé
- L'eau, c'est la santé
- La France des eaux
- Le savez-vous?

Partie 1

LE FRANÇAIS PRATIQUE *Une visite médicale* **264**

Dans la salle d'attente
Dans le cabinet du médecin

LANGUE ET COMMUNICATION **270**
- A Le concept du subjonctif: temps et modes
- B Les verbes **croire** et **craindre**
- C L'usage du subjonctif: émotions et sentiments
- D Le subjonctif après les expressions de doute

INFOMAGAZINE **276**
- Les médecins et l'action humanitaire
- Médecins Sans Frontières — une organisation humanitaire mondiale

Partie 2

LE FRANÇAIS PRATIQUE *Accidents et soins dentaires* **278**

À l'hôpital
Chez le dentiste

LANGUE ET COMMUNICATION **280**
- A Le passé du subjonctif

LECTURE *En voyage (Maupassant)* **282**

Interlude culturel *Les Français d'aujourd'hui* **292**

Français et Européens **292**
Oui à l'Europe **293**
Nous, c'est les autres! **294**
La France, une mosaïque **296**
Le Maghreb et les Maghrébins **297**
Djamila ou le dilemme de l'intégration **298**
Les cinq principes de la religion musulmane **299**
SOS Racisme **300**
Song: *Éthiopie* **301**

Unité **8** En ville

INFOMAGAZINE **303**

- Les villes françaises
- Ville ou campagne?
- Interview dans la rue

Partie 1   LE FRANÇAIS PRATIQUE *Un rendez-vous en ville* **306**

Comment se donner rendez-vous
Les rencontres et les rendez-vous

LANGUE ET COMMUNICATION **308**

- **A** La construction **si** + imparfait
- **B** Le plus-que-parfait

INFOMAGAZINE **310**

- La géographie des villes françaises
- Les «villes nouvelles»

Partie 2   LE FRANÇAIS PRATIQUE *Comment expliquer où on habite* **312**

LANGUE ET COMMUNICATION **314**

- **A** Révision: Le conditionnel
- **B** Le conditionnel dans les phrases avec **si**
- **C** Le conditionnel: autres usages

INFOMAGAZINE **320**

- Le spectacle est dans la rue
- L'automate

Partie 3   **LANGUE ET COMMUNICATION** **322**

- **A** Le conditionnel passé
- **B** Résumé: l'usage des temps avec **si**

LECTURE *Les pêches (Theuriet)* **326**

Interlude culturel   *Les Antilles francophones* **334**

Un peu d'histoire **334**
La malédiction caraïbe. **335**
Deux Martiniquais célèbres **336**
A. Césaire, *Pour saluer le Tiers-Monde*. **337**
Haïti: Un champion de la liberté: Toussaint Louverture **338**
R. Depestre, *Pour Haïti* **339**
En Haïti, l'art, c'est la vie **340**
Film: *Rue Cases-nègres* **342**

Unité 9 Les relations personnelles

DIGITAL FRENCH
my.hrw.com

INFOMAGAZINE 345

- Les amis et la famille
- Les qualités d'un(e) ami(e)
- Nous et les autres

Partie 1

LE FRANÇAIS PRATIQUE **Les amis, les copains et les relations personnelles** 348

Les personnes qu'on connaît
Les sentiments
Les relations personnelles
Comment féliciter quelqu'un
Comment plaindre et consoler quelqu'un

LANGUE ET COMMUNICATION 352

A Les verbes réfléchis: sens réciproque
B Révision: Les pronoms relatifs **qui** et **que**
C La construction préposition + pronom relatif
D Le pronom relatif **dont**

INFOMAGAZINE 358

- Le mariage en France
- Comment se sont-ils rencontrés?

Partie 2

LE FRANÇAIS PRATIQUE **Les phases de la vie** 360

LANGUE ET COMMUNICATION 362

A Résumé: Les pronoms relatifs
B **Ce qui**, **ce que** et **ce dont**

LECTURE **Le bracelet** *(M. Maurois)* 366

Interlude culturel **L'Afrique dans la communauté francophone** 372

Un peu d'histoire 372
L'Afrique francophone et sa culture 374
Une fable africaine: *La gélinotte et la tortue* 377
D. Diop, *Afrique* 378
L'art africain et son influence sur l'art européen 379
B. Dadié, *La légende baoulé* 380

Unité 10 Vers la vie active

INFOMAGAZINE **383**
- Ce fameux bac!
- Petite histoire du bac
- Il a raté le bac

Partie 1

LE FRANÇAIS PRATIQUE *Études ou travail?* **386**

Les études
Quelques professions

LANGUE ET COMMUNICATION **388**

- **A** La construction préposition + infinitif
- **B** L'infinitif passé
- **C** Le participe présent

INFOMAGAZINE **392**
- Comment se présenter à une entrevue
- Curriculum vitae

Partie 2

LE FRANÇAIS PRATIQUE *La vie professionnelle* **394**

Quelle sorte de travail?
À la recherche d'un emploi

LANGUE ET COMMUNICATION **398**

- **A** La construction conjonction + subjonctif

LECTURE *Le portrait (Thériault)* **402**

Interlude culturel *La France et le Nouveau Monde* **410**

L'histoire franco-américaine en dix questions **410**
Les «Filles du Roy» **411**
La Fayette: *Lettre à Madame de La Fayette* **415**
Villes américaines—noms français **417**
Les héritiers de la Louisiane française **418**
Z. Richard, *Réveille* **419**
Le drapeau acadien **420**

TÊTE À TÊTE PAIR ACTIVITIES **PA1**

Reference Section **R1**

Vous êtes fantastiques!

You are terrific! We would like to welcome you back to DISCOVERING FRENCH TODAY!, but first and foremost we congratulate you on your decision to continue your study of French. As you have discovered, French is a language that broadens your horizons and opens doors to a world of new experiences and opportunities. French offers you the chance to communicate with new people and learn about their culture, the opportunity to explore the wonderful variety of the French-speaking world, and maybe one day the possibility to travel, study or even work in a country where French is spoken... knowing French gives you that extra little "plus" that makes life richer and more enjoyable!

With DISCOVERING FRENCH TODAY! you will learn to communicate on a variety of topics useful when you travel abroad: making a train reservation, staying in a youth hostel, shopping for things you need, asking for services, etc. But you will learn much more than that. First, you will expand your communication and reading skills. You will also learn to express your thoughts more naturally and more effectively. You will increase your awareness of the francophone world and become more familiar with the many contributions that French-speaking people have made in the world of arts, sciences and great ideas.

As you progress in your study of French, we hope that you will be able to put your knowledge into practice. Perhaps you will have the opportunity to visit Quebec on a school trip. Maybe in the summer you will be able to go bicycling in Belgium or study in France or participate in a home stay program in the Ivory Coast. Even if travel is not in your immediate future, you may have the chance to meet French speakers in the region where you live: new American citizens from Haiti, tourists from Quebec or France, foreign students who have studied French. Remember that in the world there are millions of young people who, like you, are learning French! Don't be shy! Use your French! It's a great language!

Jean-Paul Valette   Rebecca M. Valette

Reprise

MAIN THEME

Everyday life (review)

COMMUNICATION
- Accepting and refusing invitations
- Ordering in a café or restaurant
- Asking for help
- Talking about daily life activities
- Describing vacation activities
- Introducing and describing
- Talking about events in the past
- Describing what you do for others

CULTURES
- Learning about French teens' vacation destinations
- Reviewing information about cultural practices in the francophone world
- Learning about French Independence Day
- Learning about the Tour de France
- Reviewing information about cultural products in the francophone world

CONNECTIONS
- Locating areas on a map
- Reading advertisements for information
- Reading realia for information
- Reading a travel itinerary
- Connecting to Geography: Researching information on francophone countries
- Connecting to Language Arts: Writing a group story
- Connecting to Art: Drawing cartoons and writing captions

COMPARISONS
- Comparing talking about the future, present, and past in French and English
- Comparing talking about the duration of an ongoing activity in French and English
- Comparing survey results of Canadian and American teens

COMMUNITIES
- Recreating a French restaurant in a skit performed for the class

Reprise

Vive les vacances!

Reprise A La vie courante

RAPPEL ① Bonjour!

RAPPEL ② Le temps libre

RAPPEL ③ Bon appétit!

♻ RAPPEL *Culturel*

Reprise B Hier et avant

RAPPEL ④ Le week-end

RAPPEL ⑤ En vacances

RAPPEL ⑥ Qu'est-ce qui se passe?

♻ RAPPEL *Culturel*

Reprise C Nous et les autres

RAPPEL ⑦ Vive l'amitié!

RAPPEL ⑧ Un garçon timide

LECTURE Les trois bagues

  DIGITAL FRENCH my.hrw.com
ONLINE STUDENT EDITION WITH...

performance space
- Audio Resources

News + Networking
- Video Resources
- Interactive Flashcards

@ HOMETUTOR
- WebQuest

PRACTICE FRENCH WITH HOLT MCDOUGAL APPS!

🌐 DIGITAL FRENCH

TEACHER TOOLS
- **Teacher One Stop**
- **Interactive Whiteboard Lessons**
- **Generate Success Rubric Generator and Interactive Graphic Organizers**
- **Examview Test Generator**

ALSO AVAILABLE...
- **Online Workbook**
- **French InterActive Reader**
- **@HomeTutor**
- **DVD Program**
- **Power Presentations**
- **Interactive Flashcards**

FRENCH ON THE GO!
- **Performance Space**
- **Holt McDougal French Apps**
- **Discovering French Today eTextbook**

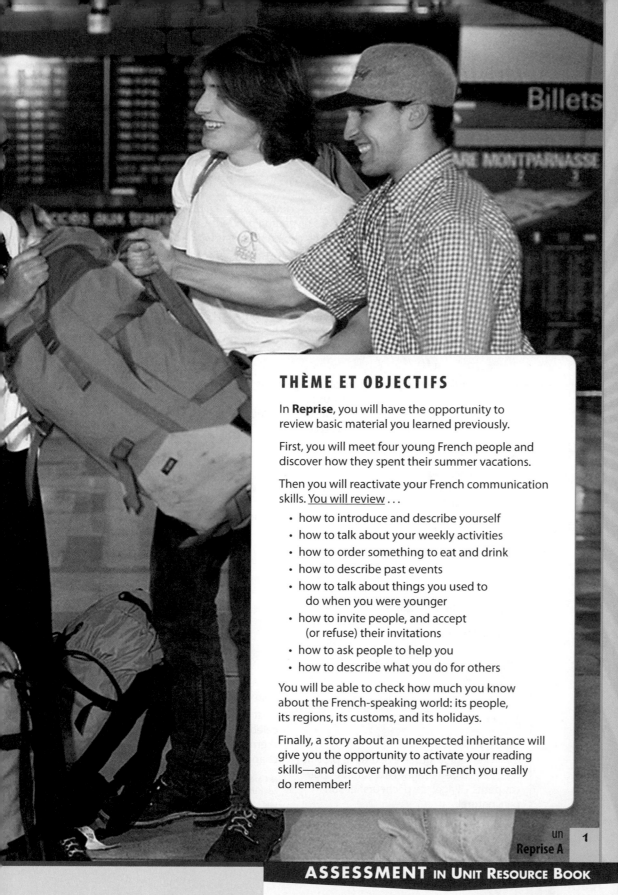

THÈME ET OBJECTIFS

In **Reprise**, you will have the opportunity to review basic material you learned previously.

First, you will meet four young French people and discover how they spent their summer vacations.

Then you will reactivate your French communication skills. <u>You will review</u> . . .

- how to introduce and describe yourself
- how to talk about your weekly activities
- how to order something to eat and drink
- how to describe past events
- how to talk about things you used to do when you were younger
- how to invite people, and accept (or refuse) their invitations
- how to ask people to help you
- how to describe what you do for others

You will be able to check how much you know about the French-speaking world: its people, its regions, its customs, and its holidays.

Finally, a story about an unexpected inheritance will give you the opportunity to activate your reading skills—and discover how much French you really do remember!

un **1**
Reprise A

Print Resources

- **Workbook TE/PE**
- *Activités pour tous* **TE/PE**
- *Lectures pour tous*
- **Unit Resource Book** Audioscripts Video Activities Videoscripts

Achievement Tests

- **Quizzes, Reprise**
- **Unit Test Reprise**
- **Reading and Culture Tests**
- **Assessment Answer Key**

Proficiency Tests

- **Listening Comprehension**
- **Speaking Performance**
- **Writing Performance**
- **Portfolio Assessment**

■ Notes culturelles

- The students are in Paris, at the Gare Montparnasse, the second-largest train station in France after the Gare de Lyon. Other train stations in Paris are: Gare Paris-Nord, Gare de l'Est, and Gare Saint-Lazare.
- **La SNCF (Société Nationale des Chemins de Fer)** is a state-owned company that runs the French railroad system.
- Young people between the ages of 12 and 25 can buy **une carte Inter-rail** *(Eurail pass)* which allows them to travel through France and other countries at lower rates.
- French students are on vacation during July and August. Most French workers have five weeks of paid vacation per year. They generally take four weeks off in July or August, and one week in the winter. The most popular vacation destination is the seashore.

SUPPLEMENTARY VOCABULARY

le sac à dos *backpack*
la casquette (de base-ball) *(baseball) cap*
la chemise à carreaux *checkered shirt*
le gilet *vest*
le jean *jeans*
les chaussures de marche *walking shoes*

21ST CENTURY SKILLS

- **Communication:** SE: pp. 3–5, 7–15, 19, 21, 23, 26–28, 31; TE: pp. 3, 4, 6, 8, 11–12, 16–17, 19, 23, 28
- **Collaboration:** TE: p. 6
- **Creativity and Innovation:** SE: p. 31; TE: pp. 3, 8, 11, 12, 14, 16–19, 23, 30
- **Technology Literacy:** TE: p. 11
- **Flexibility and Adaptability:** TE: p. 8
- **Initiative and Self-Direction:** TE: pp. 6, 11, 19
- **Social and Cross-Cultural Skills:** SE: pp. 11, 20, 21; TE: pp. 4, 14
- **Productivity and Accountability:** TE: pp. 8–10, 12, 19, 23, 29

Reprise 1

Vive les vacances!

■ **Teaching Strategy**
Have students locate the areas
mentioned on the map on p. R34
or in an atlas.

■ **Note culturelle**
UNE CHAPELLE ROMANE
Romanesque chapels are
characterized by their heavy
stone walls, round archways, and
small rounded windows.

Vive les vacances!

C'est la rentrée. Quatre jeunes Français (deux garçons et deux filles)
parlent de ce qu'ils ont fait pendant les vacances.

Jean-Michel Renaudin (15 ans et demi)

Comme d'habitude,° j'ai passé les vacances avec ma famille.
Chaque année, nous allons dans un endroit différent. Cette année,
nous sommes allés à Sanary-sur-Mer où nous avons fait du
camping. J'ai fait un stage° dans un club de planche à voile.
À la fin° du stage, j'ai participé à un championnat et je suis arrivé
troisième. Pas mal pour un débutant!°

comme d'habitude *as usual*   **faire un stage** = suivre des leçons
la fin *end*   **un débutant** *beginner*

Ali Belkacem (18 ans)

Je suis allé au Québec avec un programme d'échange. Nous
étions quatre Français dans notre groupe. Nous avons passé
les deux premières semaines à la ferme Pouliot sur l'Île d'Orléans.
Là, on a cueilli° les framboises et on a fait la récolte° du maïs.°
(On dit «blé° d'Inde» en québécois.)

Après notre séjour° sur l'Île d'Orléans, nous avons visité
la ville de Québec où nous avons loué° un camping-car. Puis,
nous avons fait le tour de la Gaspésie. Partout nous avons été
accueillis° dans les familles québécoises. Les Québécois sont
vraiment des gens formidables!° J'espère bien retourner un jour
dans la «Belle Province»!

cueillir *to pick*   **faire la récolte** *to harvest*   **le maïs** *corn*   **blé** *wheat*
un séjour *stay*   **louer** *to rent*   **être accueilli** = être invité   **formidable** *great, terrific*

FLASH d'information

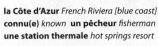

Sanary-sur-Mer
C'est une petite ville de la Côte d'Azur°
située près de Toulon.

Le Jura
Le Jura est une région montagneuse située
à l'est de la France.

La Gaspésie
C'est une région située à l'est de la province
de Québec. Cette région est connue° pour
ses petits villages de pêcheurs° et son
parc naturel.

L'Auvergne
C'est une région du centre de la France,
célèbre pour ses volcans, ses stations
thermales,° ses eaux minérales, ses
chapelles romanes et ses vieux châteaux.

la Côte d'Azur *French Riviera [blue coast]*
connu(e) *known*   **un pêcheur** *fisherman*
une station thermale *hot springs resort*

Teaching Strategy: Warm-Up

Hand out a 5 x 5 grid. Each square of the grid
should have a different verb and sentence
fragment (e.g., **visiter un pays européen**).
Have students stand up, circulate and ask
questions (in **passé composé**) to find out who
did the suggested activities during the summer.
Record the initials of each student in the
appropriate activity box. The winner is the
student who fills in a different student's initials
in every box. **Extra practice:** Ask the winning
student to name who did each activity. Then ask
the student whether or not they did it.
Everyone must answer in complete sentences.

Laurence Legarec (16 ans et demi)

J'ai passé l'été en Auvergne avec les «Chantiers° Histoire et Architecture Médiévales». C'est une organisation qui recrute des volontaires pour restaurer les monuments anciens. Le projet de notre groupe était de restaurer une chapelle romane du XIIe siècle.°

D'abord, on a reconstruit° un mur° qui tombait en ruines. Puis, on a refait le toit°. Le travail était dur, c'est vrai, mais il y avait beaucoup d'avantages. Pour moi, l'avantage principal de cette expérience a été de faire la connaissance° de jeunes d'autres pays européens. Notre groupe était, en effet, très international. Il y avait des Allemands, des Belges, des Hollandais, des Anglais … et un jeune Italien très sympathique avec qui je continue à correspondre!

un chantier *worksite*   **un siècle** = 100 ans   **reconstruire** *to rebuild*   **un mur** *wall*
le toit *roof*   **faire la connaissance** = rencontrer

Valérie Laroze (17 ans)

En juillet je suis restée chez moi. En août, je suis allée dans le Jura où j'ai travaillé comme animatrice° dans une colonie de vacances pour jeunes handicapés mentaux. Nous étions trois animatrices pour accompagner un groupe de vingt jeunes.

Chaque jour, on faisait une randonnée° de 10 à 15 kilomètres dans la montagne. Pendant les haltes, on étudiait la faune° locale. (Je devais° être bien préparée, parce que les jeunes voulaient tout connaître sur les animaux et les oiseaux de la région.) Le soir, j'organisais des activités et des jeux pour le groupe.

Pour moi qui habite dans une grande ville, j'ai bien profité de ces vacances en plein air.° Mais surtout, en aidant ces jeunes handicapés à avoir une vie° normale, j'ai fait un travail utile et intéressant. Et en plus,° j'ai gagné un peu d'argent!

une animatrice *counselor*   **une randonnée** *long hike*   **la faune** = les animaux
je devais *I had to*   **en plein air** = dans la nature   **une vie** *life*   **en plus** *in addition*

À votre avis *(in your opinion)*

Avec un(e) ou plusieurs partenaires, discutez des questions suivantes.

- Qui a fait le voyage le plus long?
- Qui a passé les vacances les plus intéressantes? Pourquoi?
- Qui a fait la chose la plus utile? Pourquoi?
- Vous avez la possibilité de passer les vacances comme ces quatre jeunes Français. Qu'est-ce que vous choisissez de faire? Pourquoi?

À votre tour!

Digital performance space

Maintenant parlez de vos vacances.

1. Êtes-vous resté(e) chez vous ou avez-vous fait un voyage? Si vous avez fait un voyage, où êtes-vous allé(e)? Avec qui? Combien de temps êtes-vous resté(e) là-bas? Qu'est-ce que vous avez vu?

2. Est-ce que vous vous êtes reposé(e) ou est-ce que vous avez travaillé? Si vous avez travaillé, quel travail avez-vous fait? Où? Est-ce que vous avez gagné de l'argent?

3. Qu'est-ce que vous avez fait d'intéressant?

4. Qu'est-ce que vous avez fait d'utile?

■ **Notes culturelles**

- «Chefs d'oeuvre en péril» was a French television program structured as a **concours** *(competition)* to safeguard and protect historical monuments. There are several organizations that recruit young people to work on architectural restoration sites. They include: **R.E.M.P.A.R.T.S.**, **Jeunesse et Reconstruction**, and **Club du vieux manoir**, all located in Paris.

- **Les colonies de vacances** are summer camps organized by cities for children. Being a camp counselor is a typical summer job for a French teen. Teens must be at least 17 and follow a special training course and obtain a certificate. The salary varies from place to place but includes food and lodging.

■ **Compréhension**

1. Avec qui Jean-Michel a-t-il passé ses vacances?
2. Quel sport a-t-il pratiqué?
3. Où est allé Ali avec son programme d'échange?
4. Nommez une activité qu'il a faite pendant ses vacances.
5. Qu'est-ce que c'est que la «Belle Province»?
6. Quel était le but des vacances de Laurence?
7. Est-ce que c'était facile? Pourquoi oui ou non?
8. Dans quelle sorte de colonie de vacances Valérie a-t-elle travaillé?
9. Nommez une activité qu'elle a faite tous les jours.

Teaching Strategy: Pair Practice

Divide the class into pairs and have each pair write a dialog of 10–12 lines between two of the French students on pages 2–3. They should ask and answer questions based on information given, as well as invent possible answers.

(e.g., **Laurence: Pendant combien de temps est-ce que vous avez fait du camping? Jean-Michel: Nous avons fait du camping pendant trois semaines.**)

After 10–15 minutes of preparation time, have students present the dialog to the class.

RESOURCES

PRINT
Workbook, pp. 3–5
Activités pour tous
Reprise Resource Book
   Activités pour tous TE
   Lesson Plans
   Block Scheduling Lesson Plans
   Absent Student Copymasters
   Workbook TE
   Diagnostic Test

■ **Note culturelle**
La Touraine is a region of France, south-west of Paris, around the Loire river.

■ **Teaching Note**
You may have students do their poll first, and then compare their answers with those of the Canadian students.

Reprise A

La vie courante

RAPPEL <1> Bonjour!

① À l'Institut de Touraine

L'Institut de Touraine est une école où beaucoup d'étudiants viennent apprendre le français en été. Vous allez passer un mois à l'Institut de Touraine.

Donnez oralement les renseignements demandés.

> **INSTITUT D'ÉTUDES FRANÇAISES**
> DE TOURAINE
> 1, Rue de la Grandière, 37000 TOURS
>
> **BULLETIN D'INSCRIPTION**
>
> Prénoms et Nom..
> Né(e) le..
> à..
> Nationalité:..
> Profession:...
> Adresse (dans le pays d'origine):......................
> École ou collège d'origine:............................
> Nombre d'années d'étude du français: ....

② Les parents idéaux

Quelles sont les qualités les plus importantes pour la mère idéale ou le père idéal? Un magazine québécois, le *Bulletin Pacijou*, a posé cette question à des jeunes de 13 à 18 ans. Voici les résultats de cette enquête.

LA MÈRE IDÉALE: QUALITÉS ESSENTIELLES			
selon les filles		**selon les garçons**	
compréhensive	29%	gentille	39%
gentille	29%	compréhensive	17%
attentive	15%	joyeuse	17%
confiante°	11%	généreuse	11%
tolérante	9%	patiente	8%
patiente	7%	confiante	8%

LA PÈRE IDÉAL: QUALITÉS ESSENTIELLES			
selon les filles		**selon les garçons**	
gentil	31%	gentil	31%
compréhensif	30%	compréhensif	31%
tolérant	23%	riche et généreux	21%
affectueux	16%	drôle	17%

confiant(e) *trusting*

Maintenant faites une enquête dans votre classe:

- Quelles sont les qualités essentielles pour être la mère idéale?
- Quelles sont les qualités essentielles pour être le père idéal?

> **Révision** p. R7
>
> **Pratique** p. 3
> Les adjectifs réguliers et irréguliers

Teaching Strategies: Pair Practice

Review: Question words. Have students look at the form on p. 4 and figure out what questions need to be asked to get the requested information. Divide the class into pairs and have them ask each other these questions and fill in a copy of the form with their partner's information.

Warm-Up

Give each student (orally or on a slip of paper) an **avoir** expression to act out. Then, have each student give a complete sample sentence (e.g., **Quand j'ai faim, je vais au restaurant**).

3 Notre personnalité

Nous avons tous des qualités, mais nous avons aussi des petits défauts. Choisissez une des personnes suivantes (ou une autre personne de votre choix). Décrivez deux qualités—au moins—et un petit défaut de cette personne.

- moi
- mon copain
- ma copine
- mon cousin
- ma cousine
- mes profs
- mes parents
- mes voisins
- les élèves de cette classe
- ??

En général . . .

☺ QUALITÉS

actif
aimable
amusant
attentif
brillant
compréhensif
consciencieux
courageux
discret
drôle
dynamique
énergique
gentil
généreux
honnête

imaginatif
intéressant
joyeux
optimiste
organisé
patient
poli
ouvert
sensible (sensitive)
sérieux
spirituel (witty)
spontané
sympathique
tolérant
??

mais de temps en temps . . .

☹ DÉFAUTS

bête
distant
égoïste
ennuyeux
impoli
inactif
incompréhensif
indifférent
indiscret
indiscipliné
méchant

paresseux
pénible
pessimiste
prétentieux
renfermé (uncommunicative)
sévère
stupide
timide
triste
vaniteux (vain)
??

Révision p. R3

Pratique p. 4

Avoir et les expressions avec **avoir**

▶ En général, ma cousine Élisabeth est très gentille. Elle est aussi drôle et optimiste. De temps en temps elle est un peu prétentieuse.

4 Que faire?

Choisissez une expression de la colonne A et décrivez votre situation à votre partenaire. Votre partenaire va vous dire ce qu'il faut faire, en utilisant les suggestions de la colonne B.

J'ai chaud!

Eh bien, tu peux ouvrir la fenêtre!

A. Votre situation
- faim
- soif
- chaud
- froid
- sommeil
- besoin d'un livre
- envie de voir un film
- besoin de ??
- envie de ??

B. Conseils
- mettre un pull
- ouvrir la fenêtre
- aller au ciné
- passer à la bibliothèque
- manger un sandwich
- boire un soda
- dormir
- prendre un café
- ??

♻ **RAPPEL**

TO DESCRIBE . . .
- what you ARE GOING TO DO
- what you ARE DOING RIGHT NOW
- what you HAVE JUST DONE

USE . . .
aller + infinitive
être en train de + infinitive
venir de + infinitive

Je vais sortir.
Je suis en train de téléphoner.
Je viens de dîner.

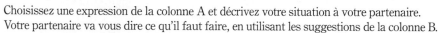

| Il va dîner. | Il est en train de dîner. | Il vient de dîner. |

Révision p. R3

Pratique p. 4

Avoir, être, venir

SUPPLEMENTARY VOCABULARY

coléreux *quick tempered*
fier *proud*
jaloux *jealous*
maladroit *clumsy*
moqueur *mocking*
têtu *stubborn*
franc *frank*
indépendant *independent*
indulgent *lenient*
intelligent *smart*
talentueux *talented*
travailleur *hard-working*

■ **Language Note**

A familiar form for "annoying, bothersome" is **embêtant(e)**.

Expansion

Have students write a list of 10 adjectives, being as creative as possible. Make a list of three to four people or groups of people to be described by the students' adjectives (e.g., **Ma meilleure amie/mon ami idéal/le prof idéal/ les frères et les soeurs**).

Ask students to volunteer their adjectives and copy them onto the board. Finally, have students create negative or affirmative sentences about each of the people/groups of people using the adjectives listed (e.g., **Ma meilleure amie n'est pas méchante**).

RAPPEL ②

RESOURCES

PRINT
Workbook, pp. 5–7

■ Notes culturelles

- **Antoine de Saint-Exupéry** (1900–1944) was an aviator as well as a writer. He described his pioneering flying experiences in several books. When France was occupied by German troops at the beginning of World War II, Saint-Exupéry sought refuge in the United States where he wrote his most famous work, *Le Petit Prince*. In 1943, although he was past the age limit, he volunteered as a pilot with the Free French Forces and died while flying from Africa to France on a secret mission. In 1994, the French government issued a new 50-franc note in his honor.
- For more information on Ionesco, see p. 56.

■ Rappel

You may point out that **depuis** may be followed by a POINT IN TIME or an EXPRESSION OF DURATION. For example, the remark made by the girl in the cartoon can be interpreted in two ways:

I have been waiting for my friend since three o'clock.
I have been waiting for my friend for three hours.

■ Expansion

Have students write letters or e-mails to francophone pen pals asking about the types of information found in Valérie's letter: school, leisure activities, sports, etc.

RAPPEL ② Le temps libre

Bonjour,

Je m'appelle Valérie Dussart. J'ai 17ans et j'habite à Lyon. Je suis élève de première au Lycée Saint-Exupéry où je prépare le bac.

J'ai beaucoup de travail, mais je ne travaille pas tout le temps. Le samedi, par exemple, est un jour que je me réserve entièrement. L'après-midi je vais en ville et je fais du shopping. Quand il y a une bonne exposition, je vais au musée. Le soir, je sors en bande° (J'ai beaucoup de copains et de copines, mais je n'ai pas de «copain» en particulier.) En général, on va voir un film. De temps en temps, on va danser dans une «boîte».

J'ai d'autres loisirs. Je fais du théâtre depuis un an à la Maison des Jeunes. En juin, nous allons présenter «La leçon» une pièce de l'écrivain° Ionesco dans laquelle° je joue le rôle de l'Élève... Je suis° aussi des cours de danse africaine. C'est excellent pour la forme!

Pendant l'année je n'ai pas l'occasion de faire beaucoup de sport, mais en été je me rattrape° Ma passion, c'est la planche à voile. Il y a d'autres sports que j'aimerais faire, comme le parapente. Malheureusement, mes parents ne sont pas d'accord!

Et vous, quels sont vos loisirs préférés?

Valérie

Moi, avec mes amies.

en bande = en groupe   **une boîte** club, nightspot   **un écrivain** = une personne qui écrit
laquelle which   **suivre** to take [a class]   **se rattraper** to catch up with

J'ATTENDS MON COPAIN DEPUIS TROIS HEURES!

♻ RAPPEL

To describe what you <u>have been doing</u> for or since some time, you use:

present + **depuis** + time

Pratique p. 5
Depuis

Teaching Strategy: Challenge

Once students have taken turns reading the letter from Valérie, have them go back to the beginning of the letter and imagine that a friend is asking who the letter is from and what it says. Have students make all the changes necessary to put the letter into the third person in order to tell their curious friend about Valérie and her friends.

RAPPEL

- In French, there are three groups of regular verbs: **-er, -ir, -re**.
- **Vouloir, pouvoir, devoir** and verbs like **sortir** are irregular.
- **Faire**, an irregular verb, is used in many expressions.

Révision p. R2
Pratique p. 6
Verbes réguliers

Révision p. R3
Pratique p. 7
Faire et expressions avec **faire**

Révision p. R2
Pratique p. 6
Quelques verbes irréguliers

 1 et vous?

Répondez au questionnaire suivant. Si vous voulez, comparez vos réponses avec celles de votre partenaire ou de votre groupe.

1. À la maison, quand j'ai du temps libre *(free time)*, je préfère . . .
   - regarder la télé
   - écouter de la musique
   - lire un bon livre
   - **??**

2. Quand je suis en ville, je préfère . . .
   - faire du shopping
   - faire du lèche-vitrine *(window-shopping)*
   - voir une exposition
   - **??**

3. Avec mon argent, je préfère . . .
   - aller au cinéma
   - acheter des vêtements
   - acheter des CD
   - **??**

4. Le samedi soir, je préfère . . .
   - sortir seul(e) *(by myself)*
   - sortir avec mes copains
   - regarder un DVD à la maison
   - **??**

5. Quand je sors avec mes copains, je préfère . . .
   - assister à un concert
   - voir un film
   - aller au restaurant
   - **??**

6. Pour rester en forme, je préfère . . .
   - courir
   - faire du vélo
   - faire des exercices de gymnastique
   - **??**

7. L'après-midi, quand il fait beau, je préfère . . .
   - faire du jogging
   - faire du roller *(roller blades)*
   - jouer au basket
   - **??**

8. Quand je suis à la plage, je préfère . . .
   - nager
   - jouer au volley
   - prendre des bains de soleil
   - **??**

9. Pendant les vacances, je préfère . . .
   - faire un voyage
   - rendre visite à des amis ou à des parents
   - travailler et gagner de l'argent
   - **??**

10. Je voudrais apprendre à . . .
    - jouer de la clarinette
    - faire du parapente
    - piloter un avion
    - **??**

■ Expansion: Activity 1

1. jouer aux jeux d'ordinateur, lire des magazines, téléphoner à mes copains
2. aller dans un café, faire une promenade à pied
3. louer un DVD, aller au restaurant
4. téléphoner à des amis, faire du baby-sitting
5. assister à un match de baseball, aller danser dans une boîte
6. faire de l'aérobic, nager
7. jouer au football, faire du patin à roulettes, faire de la planche à roulettes
8. jouer au frisbee, faire un pique-nique
9. suivre des cours d'été
10. parler japonais, faire du bateau à voile, faire du ski nautique

 **2 Une lettre à Valérie**

Écrivez une lettre à Valérie où vous expliquez . . .

- qui vous êtes
- à quelle école vous allez
- ce que vous faites le samedi
- quels sont vos loisirs
- quels sports vous pratiquez
- ce que vous faites en été

Puis comparez votre lettre avec celle de votre partenaire.

Differentiation

Cumulative Have students write entire conjugations of one regular **-er, -ir,** and **-re** verb in their notebook. Have students underline identical pronunciations.

Have students write entire conjugations of the verbs **vouloir, pouvoir,** and **devoir.** Have students practice them orally in pairs or small groups.

RAPPEL ③

■ **Note linguistique**

fruits de mer = *assorted seafood*
livraison à domicile = *home delivery*

■ **Notes culturelles**

- **Une brasserie** is a type of restaurant that has a relaxed setting. A brasserie usually is open all day and offers the same menu during that time. The word "brasserie" literally means brewery.
- **Couscous** is a staple food from the Maghreb, the region of Northwest Africa which includes Morocco, Algeria, Tunisia, Libya, and Mauritania. Couscous is a pasta made of tiny grains of hard wheat. It is usually served with meat or vegetables spooned on top.

RAPPEL ③ Bon appétit!

1 **Le bon choix**

Regardez les illustrations pour compléter les phrases avec l'option qui convient. Soyez logique.

On va dans ce restaurant si on aime . . .

- la cuisine chinoise
- le poisson et les fruits de mer
- la cuisine mexicaine

La Brasserie de la Gare
vous propose
**Salades • Croque-monsieur
Pizzas • Sandwichs
Grillades
Poissons et fruits de mer**
et aussi un menu enfant
de 11h à minuit

Depuis 1920

> **Révision** p. R11
> **Pratique** p. 8
> Nourriture et boissons

La Dolce Vita

Plus de 20 choix de Pizzas
Pâtes fraîches maison
Salades

ouvert tous les jours
de 11h30 à 22h30
livraison à domicile

3, rue des Amarres
35000 Rennes
02.35.65.03.79

Dans ce restaurant, on peut commander . . .

- des pizzas
- des croque-monsieur
- un steak-frites

MARRAKECH
Spécialités marocaines
Couscous au poulet
Couscous aux légumes
Merguez et Kebab
Thé à la menthe

16, rue des Capucines • 35000 Rennes • 02.36.67.97.44

On va dans ce restaurant si on veut manger . . .

- italien
- des crêpes
- un couscous aux légumes

Dans quel restaurant aimeriez-vous aller manger? Pourquoi?

♻ **RAPPEL**

- To refer to things you like in general, use: **le (l'), la (l'), les.**
  J'aime <u>le</u> poulet, <u>la</u> salade, <u>les</u> frites.

- To refer to a CERTAIN, UNDEFINED QUANTITY or AMOUNT of something, use: **du (de l'), de la (de l'), des.**
  Je voudrais <u>du</u> poulet, <u>de la</u> salade, <u>des</u> frites.

  Note: In negative sentences: **du, de la, des → de**
  Je ne vais pas prendre <u>de</u> fromage.

> **Révision** p. R6
> **Pratique** p. 9
> Les articles définis et partitifs

Teaching Strategy: Groups

Divide students into groups of 2 or 3. Have them pick a restaurant from p. 8, or make up their own, and develop a menu for it. Give students 5 minutes to brainstorm on ideas for the menu, and 10 minutes to begin to develop a dialog between waiter and customer(s). Groups of three should also create a part of the dialog between the two customers about their likes and dislikes before the arrival of the waiter.

In class Day 1: Students brainstorm, take down notes and decide who will do which part of the assignment.

Révision p. R2; pp. R24–R29

Pratique p. 10

Prendre *(to take, to have)*, boire *(to drink)*

2 et vous?

Répondez au questionnaire suivant. Si vous voulez, comparez vos réponses avec celles de votre partenaire ou de votre groupe.

1. Mon repas préféré est . . .
- le petit déjeuner
- le déjeuner
- le dîner

2. Au petit déjeuner, je prends généralement . . .
- des céréales
- des oeufs
- du pain avec du beurre et de la confiture
- ??

3. Avec ça, je bois . . .
- du lait
- du chocolat chaud
- du jus d'orange
- ??

4. Je préfère les sandwichs avec . . .
- du jambon
- du fromage
- du beurre de cacahuète *(peanut)*
- ??

5. Quand je dîne au restaurant, je commande généralement . . .
- de la viande
- du poisson
- des spaghetti
- ??

6. En général, sur mes hamburgers, je mets . . .
- du ketchup
- de la moutarde
- de la mayonnaise
- ??

7. Mon plat favori est . . .
- le steak-frites
- le poulet rôti
- le filet de sole
- ??

8. Il y a certaines choses que je n'aime pas, par exemple, . . .
- les brocolis
- les carottes
- les épinards *(spinach)*
- ??

9. Comme dessert, je préfère manger . . .
- de la glace
- du gâteau au chocolat
- de la tarte aux pommes
- ??

10. Ma cuisine favorite est . . .
- la cuisine italienne
- la cuisine chinoise
- la cuisine mexicaine
- ??

3 Au supermarché

Votre partenaire et vous, vous faites les courses.

Vous passez par les rayons suivants. Chacun va faire une liste des articles qu'il/elle va acheter.

Achetez deux (2) articles par rayon. Puis comparez vos listes:

- Quels produits identiques avez-vous achetés?
- Quels produits différents avez-vous choisis?

← BOISSONS	PRODUITS LAITIERS →
BOUCHERIE CHARCUTERIE FRUITS	BOULANGERIE PÂTISSERIE LÉGUMES

TU VEUX DU LAIT?

OUI, J'EN VEUX!

♻ RAPPEL

- **Y** replaces a NAME OF A PLACE introduced by **à**, **dans**, **chez** . . .
  Je vais <u>au restaurant</u>. → J'**y** vais.
  Je ne vais pas <u>chez Paul</u>. → Je n'**y** vais pas.
- **En** replaces **de**, **du**, **de la**, **des** + NOUN.
  Je mange <u>du pain</u>. → J'**en** mange.
  Je ne bois pas <u>de limonade</u> → Je n'**en** bois pas.

neuf **9**
Reprise A

■ Expansion: Activity 2

3. du café, du thé
4. de la salade de thon, du rosbif, de la dinde *(turkey)*
6. des oignons, des tomates, du fromage, de la laitue, des cornichons *(pickles)*, du sel, du poivre
7. les pâtes *(pasta)*, les légumes
8. le foie *(liver)*, les rognons *(kidneys)*, les petits pois *(peas)*, les choux de Bruxelles *(Brussel sprouts)*
9. des fraises, des framboises
10. la cuisine thaïlandaise, vietnamienne, française

■ Teaching Note

The pronouns **y** and **en** are reviewed here for recognition only. They are actively re-entered in Unit 4.

Homework: Each student takes one part of the assignment and completes it.
Student A: Creates a menu
Student B: Develops dialog between waiter and customer(s).
Student C: Develops dialog between the two customers.

In class Day 2: Give students 10 minutes to pull everything together and practice. Then have them present their skits to the class.

À votre tour!

■ **Teaching Note**
Situation 7
Remind students if necessary *to have breakfast* = **prendre le petit déjeuner.**

Digital **performance** space

À votre tour!

Situations Imagine you are in the following situations. Your partner will take the role of the other person in the dialogue and answer your questions.

4 | You are visiting Quebec City with your friend. It is about one o'clock.

Ask your friend . . .
- if he/she is hungry
- if he/she feels like going to a French restaurant
- what he/she feels like eating.

1 | While on an errand, you see a friend waiting at the bus stop.

Ask your friend . . .
- where he/she is going
- what he/she is going to do there
- how long he/she has been waiting for the bus.

5 | You are making weekend plans with your friend.

Ask your friend . . .
- if he/she is going to go out
- what he/she is going to do
- if he/she feels like going to the movies on Sunda

2 | At a party last weekend, your friend met a French-speaking girl named Juliette. You want to know more about Juliette.

Ask your friend . . .
- how old Juliette is
- if she is French or Canadian
- what she is doing in the United States.

6 | You have invited your friend for dinner next Saturday and want to find out if your friend has any special food preferences.

Ask your friend . . .
- if he/she eats meat
- what desserts he/she likes
- what he/she does not eat.

3 | You are new in town and you would like some information.

Ask your friend . . .
- to which supermarket he/she goes shopping
- where he/she buys her clothes
- what sports one can do in the summer.

7 | You have been invited to spend a week at the home of your French friend. You are asking about meals.

Ask your friend . . .
- at what time they have breakfast
- what they eat
- what they drink.

Differentiation

Multisensory Have students write information questions for when, what, where, for how long, etc., on index cards. Have students write 4 **avoir** and **faire** idioms on index cards as well. Have S1 choose a question card and an idiom card. Have S1 pose a question and have S2 respond. Then ask students to exchange roles.

♻ RAPPEL *Culturel*

Utilisez vos connaissances du monde francophone pour compléter les portraits suivants.

1. Virginie habite à la Martinique. En classe elle parle français, mais avec ses copains elle parle souvent . . .
   a. créole
   b. italien
   c. espagnol
   d. alsacien

2. Nathalie est née à Bruxelles. Elle parle français, mais elle n'est pas française. Elle est de nationalité . . .
   a. belge
   b. suisse
   c. allemande
   d. luxembourgeoise

3. Aya parle français. Elle est d'Abidjan, une grande ville de 2,5 millions d'habitants. Son pays est . . .
   a. l'Algérie
   b. le Nigéria
   c. le Sénégal
   d. la Côte d'Ivoire

4. Albert Bilodeau est un homme de 60 ans. Il habite dans la paroisse d'Iberville où ses ancêtres sont venus il y a plus de deux cents ans. Albert Bilodeau comprend le français et il le parle un peu. Il adore aller aux festivals de musique «cajun» de la région. Albert Bilodeau habite . . .
   a. en Floride
   b. en Louisiane
   c. en Nouvelle-Angleterre
   d. dans la province de Québec

5. Yasmina habite en France avec sa famille. Ses parents qui sont immigrés sont d'origine algérienne. Ils pratiquent la religion de leur pays qui est la religion . . .
   a. catholique
   b. protestante
   c. bouddhiste
   d. musulmane

6. Jean-Philippe habite à Boston, mais il n'est pas américain. Il comprend le français mais il n'est pas français. Il vient d'un pays qui est une ancienne colonie française et qui est devenu indépendant en 1804. Jean-Philippe est . . .
   a. haïtien
   b. martiniquais
   c. portoricain
   d. cubain

7. Gilles habite à Montana dans une région très montagneuse. En hiver, il est moniteur de ski. Là où il habite, on parle français. À l'est, on parle un dialecte allemand. Plus à l'est, on parle italien. Gilles est . . .
   a. canadien
   b. américain
   c. suisse
   d. français

8. Mai Van Lee vient d'un pays d'Asie où beaucoup de gens parlaient *(used to speak)* français. Il est . . .
   a. coréen
   b. vietnamien
   c. thaïlandais
   d. japonais

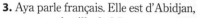
Answers: 1-a; 2-a; 3-d; 4-b; 5-d; 6-a; 7-c; 8-b

onze **11**
Reprise A

Teaching Strategy: Expansion

Assign each student one of the pictures on p. 11 and have them prepare a map (in French) of that person's country including surrounding countries, bodies of water, mountains, major cities. Also have them research two interesting facts (historical, current events, political...) about that country.

For large classes, choose other French speaking regions in addition to those discussed on p. 11 (e.g., **le Luxembourg, la Tunisie, le Québec, le Congo (la République démocratique du Congo), le Cameroun, le Maroc, Madagascar, le Sénégal**). Students can present their maps to the class; the maps make excellent classroom decorations.

Reprise B
RAPPEL ④

RESOURCES

PRINT
Workbook, pp. 11–12

TECHNOLOGY
Teacher One Stop
🖥 **Projectable Transparencies**
  10, *Un week-end à la campagne*
  10(o), *Un week-end à la campagne*
Transparency Copymasters, pp. A22–A23

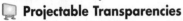

■ **Realia Notes**
- A ticket is **oblitéré** when it is stamped so that it cannot be used again.
- **Les Nouvelles Galeries** is a large supermarket chain that sells clothing and linens as well as food. It is known for its high quality and low prices.
- **Jean-Paul Belmondo** is a famous French movie actor known particularly for his roles in adventure films and comedies. Three of his best-known movies are *À bout de souffle*, *Pierrot le fou*, and *The Siren of Mississippi*.

■ **Looking Ahead**
The **passé composé** with **être** is reviewed in Rappel 5.

Reprise B

Hier et avant

RAPPEL ④ Le week-end

1 **Êtes-vous bon(ne) détective?**

Le week-end dernier, vous avez trouvé un portefeuille dans la rue. Dans ce portefeuille il n'y a pas d'argent, mais il y a les choses suivantes. Regardez bien ces choses. Pouvez-vous décrire ce qu'a fait la personne qui a perdu le portefeuille?

```
** NOUVELLES GALERIES **
COMPACT      18€
LIVRE         9€
TOTAL        27€
CB 5201001190741190
000000002809717 VIV
 *************
    MERCI
```

- Où est-ce que cette personne est allée?
- Qu'est-ce qu'elle a acheté?
- Combien a-t-elle payé chaque objet?

Chez Jacqueline
CAFÉ - RESTAURANT
21, RUE BERTHELOT
01-47-05-69-34

Table n° 4	
1 steak-frites	6 €
1 salade mixte	3 €
1 eau minérale	2 €
Total	11 €

- Où est-ce que cette personne a déjeuné?
- Qu'est-ce qu'elle a mangé?
- Qu'est-ce qu'elle a bu?
- Combien est-ce qu'elle a dépensé pour le déjeuner?

CINÉ-VOX
Festival Belmondo
Les films de la semaine

lundi-vendredi
CARTOUCHE

samedi-dimanche
L'HOMME DE RIO

Séances à 14h30 et 17h

CINÉ-VOX
ENTRÉE
7€
350717

- Où est-elle allée après le déjeuner?
- Qu'est-ce qu'elle a vu?
- À quelle heure est-ce que le film a commencé?

♻ **RAPPEL**

To describe what people DID in the past, use the PASSÉ COMPOSÉ.

- For most verbs,

  passé composé = **avoir** + PAST PARTICIPLE

  Tu as étudié hier. Je n'ai pas étudié.

- For a few verbs like **aller**,

  passé composé = **être** + PAST PARTICIPLE

  Je suis allé(e) au cinéma.

Révision p. R4

Pratique p. 11

Le passé composé des verbes réguliers avec avoir

12 douze
Reprise B

Teaching Strategy: Warm-Up

Have the class write a group story. Each student will contribute at least one sentence. Give them an amusing subject that lends itself to creativity and to action sentences for **passé composé** practice (e.g., tell about what Xavier l'Horrible did and/or didn't do during the weekend that his parents were away). Students can take turns being scribe and copying the story onto the board as it is being developed. Be sure that what is being written is carefully verified for grammatical mistakes by both you and the other students.

2 Oui ou non?

Révision p. R4

Pratique p. 12

Les participes passés
irréguliers

Décrivez deux choses que vous avez faites et une chose que
vous n'avez pas faite le week-end dernier. Utilisez les activités
suggérées ou d'autres activités de votre choix.

- dormir
- ranger ma chambre
- travailler dans le jardin
- acheter des vêtements
- déjeuner dans un restaurant
- visiter un musée
- assister à un concert
- rendre visite à des copains

- lire un livre
- voir un film
- faire des achats
- avoir un rendez-vous
- faire une promenade à la campagne
- faire du camping
- prendre des photos
- ??

3 Un week-end à la campagne

Ces personnes ont passé le week-end à la campagne. Dites ce qu'elles ont fait.

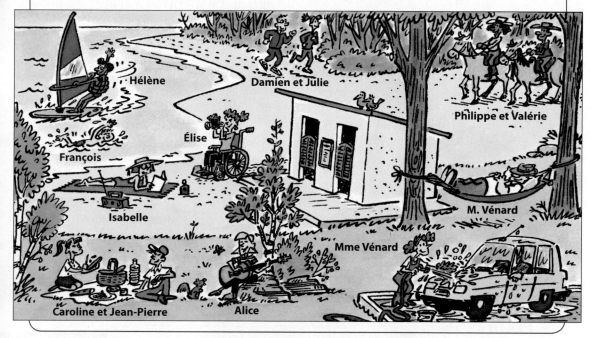

Hélène · Damien et Julie · Philippe et Valérie · Élise · François · M. Vénard · Isabelle · Mme Vénard · Caroline et Jean-Pierre · Alice

♻ RAPPEL

To express HOW LONG AGO
you did something, use:

il y a + time

J'AI ACHETÉ MA VOITURE IL Y A 70 ANS!

Pratique p. 12

Il y a

Teaching Strategy: Extra Practice

Using **Projectable Transparency 10**, have
students in pairs make lists of every activity
they see in 15 minutes.

Variation: Show the transparency for only
20–30 seconds, and have students list as many
activities as they remember. Note: This activity
may also be done as an A/B activity.

Differentiation

Structured Have students make a list of
verbs using **être** in the **passé composé** (see
Rappel 5) in their notebooks. Have students
write infinitives, meanings, and past participles,
including agreement for masculine and
feminine singular and plural forms. Have
them read out loud what they wrote.

aller à la gym *to go to the gym*
aller danser *to go dancing*
cuisiner *to cook*
faire du baby-sitting *to babysit*
louer un DVD *to rent a DVD*
**participer à une compétition
sportive** *to participate in a
competition*
regarder la télévision *to watch TV*
surfer sur l'Internet *to surf the
Internet*
utiliser un ordinateur *to use a
computer*

■ Expansion: Activity 2

Follow up by having students sign
their names next to each activity on
Bingo cards, then call students'
names.

RAPPEL ⟨5⟩

■ **Realia Notes**

• **une Kasbah** une citadelle d'un souverain dans les pays arabes.
• **Fès-el-Boli:** la plus ancienne agglomération de Fès, le centre religieux et économique du Maroc.
• **la Médina:** ville sainte pour les musulmans qui a servi de refuge à Mahomet en 622.
• **Une mosquée** est un temple musulman.
• **Un souk** est un marché, une boutique arabe.

■ **Teaching Strategy: Expansion**

Bring in travel brochures and catalogs. Have students (in pairs) prepare brief oral presentations on their "vacations."

RAPPEL ⟨5⟩ En vacances

1 *Un voyage au Maroc*

L'été dernier, Gabrielle a fait un voyage au Maroc avec un voyage organisé. Voici le programme de ce voyage. Regardez bien ce programme et répondez aux questions.

• Comment est-elle allée au Maroc?
• Quel jour est-elle partie?
• À quelle heure est-elle arrivée à Rabat?
• Qu'est-ce qu'elle a visité dans cette ville?
• Dans quelle ville est-elle allée ensuite?

• Qu'est-ce qu'elle a fait dans cette ville?
• Quelle est la dernière ville qu'elle a visitée?
• Qu'est-ce qu'elle a vu dans cette ville?
• Quel jour est-elle rentrée en France?
• À quelle heure a-t-elle pris son avion?
• À quelle heure est-elle arrivée à Paris?

Agence Maroc-Tours

PRIX SPÉCIAL 480E PAR PERSONNE TOUT COMPRIS

5 jours au Maroc

◈ PROGRAMME DU VOYAGE ◈

VENDREDI, 10 JUIN
matin Départ de Paris, vol Air Maroc 104, 8h35 Arrivée à Rabat, 11h18
après-midi Tour de Rabat en autocar

SAMEDI, 11 JUIN
matin Visite de la Kasbah Musée des Arts marocains
après-midi Libre

DIMANCHE, 12 JUIN
matin Départ pour Fès en autobus, 8h00
après-midi Libre

LUNDI, 13 JUIN
matin Visite guidée de Fès-el-Boli (vieille ville)
après-midi Départ pour Marrakech en avion, 18h35

MARDI, 14 JUIN
matin Marrakech, Visite de la Médina Mosquée de la Koutoubia
après-midi Visite des souks: shopping

MERCREDI, 15 JUIN
matin Libre
après-midi Départ pour Paris, vol Air Maroc 121, 12h35 Arrivée à Paris, 15h21

FLASH d'information

Le Maroc est un pays de 30 millions d'habitants situé au nord-ouest de l'Afrique. La majorité des Marocains sont arabes et pratiquent la religion musulmane.

La capitale du Maroc est Rabat, mais la plus grande ville est Casablanca. Marrakech et Fès sont des villes traditionnelles avec des monuments anciens.

Ancien protectorat français, le Maroc est devenu indépendant en 1956. C'est une monarchie constitutionnelle avec un roi, le Roi Mohammed VI.

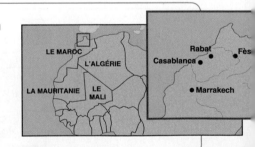

Teaching Strategy: Oral/Aural Practice

Before class, prepare a simple story of about ten negative and affirmative sentences in the **passé composé**. Tell it to the students twice. Ask them to retell the story sentence by sentence in chronological order.

Note: If the story is told in the first person, the students will have the added practice of transforming it into the second person formal since they will now be telling you what you did. You might want to make a transparency of the story (as they will be telling it) so that, as the students come up with the sentences, you can give them the written reinforcement.

♻ **RAPPEL**

When the passé composé of a verb is formed with **être**, the past participle AGREES WITH THE SUBJECT.

Julien <u>est arrivé</u> ce matin.

Pauline et Claire <u>sont arrivées</u> hier soir.

Révision p. R4 →

Pratique p. 13 →

Le passé composé

2 Dialogues

Avec votre partenaire, composez et jouez l'un des dialogues suivants.

Tu <u>as étudié</u> hier soir?

Non, je <u>suis allée</u> au ciné.

Qu'est-ce que tu <u>as vu</u>?

Un film policier.

1.
- rester chez toi ce week-end
- aller à la campagne
- faire
- une promenade à vélo

3.
- rentrer chez toi à midi
- déjeuner au restaurant
- manger
- ??

2.
- sortir avec ton copain samedi
- faire des achats
- acheter
- un blouson

4.
- venir à la boum dimanche
- aller au théâtre
- voir
- ??

3 Pendant les vacances

Pendant les vacances, ces personnes ont fait des choses différentes. Avec un(e) partenaire, choisissez une des illustrations et décrivez-la ensemble. Faites trois ou quatre phrases et utilisez votre imagination.

Où sont allées les personnes? Qu'est-ce qu'elles ont fait?

Paul et Robert

Juliette

Monsieur Ramirez

Alice et Julien

Caroline

Cécile et Sophie

Thomas

Olivier

■ **Vocabulary Notes**

Terms students may find useful for Act. 3:
1. un touriste, prendre des photos de la Tour Eiffel
2. prendre un avion, préparer des valises
3. monter sur un chameau, visiter les pyramides de Gizeh (l'Égypte)
4. faire du vélo, faire un pique-nique (du camping)
5. mettre une échelle, monter dans un arbre, jouer dans une cabane
6. descendre dans une caverne, prendre une lampe de poche
7. monter dans un arbre, perdre son équilibre, sauver un chat, tomber
8. un film d'horreur, avoir peur

quinze **15**
Reprise B

Teaching Strategy: Verb Drill

Draw a 6 x 6 grid on the board. On the vertical axis, write the six subject pronouns. On the horizontal axis, write six different verbs (being careful to use both **avoir** and **être** verbs and verbs with various endings—e.g., **faire, rencontrer, sortir, perdre, prendre, rentrer**).

Choose one of the boxes in the grid and write down the correct conjugation in the **passé composé** on a slip of paper (**tu/faire—tu as fait**). Go around the class and have students try to guess which box/conjugation you have chosen, putting "guesses" in the grid until the conjugation on the slip of paper is finally identified.

RAPPEL ⬦6⬦

PRINT
Workbook, pp. 13–14

TECHNOLOGY
Teacher One Stop
🖥 **Projectable Transparencies**
11, *Plus de peur que de mal*
Transparency Copymasters,
pp. A23–A24

■ **Notes Linguistiques**
• Point out the name of the character to the students. **M. Léveillé** = Mr. "Awakened."
• **Plus de peur que de mal** means "more frightened than harmed."

■ **Teaching Strategy**
Use **Projectable Transparency 11** as an introduction to the story before students read. Make copies of the pictures and have students discuss the sequence.

RAPPEL ⬦6⬦ Qu'est-ce qui se passe?

1 🗨 *Plus de peur que de mal* 🗨

En général, Monsieur Léveillé dort très bien, mais la nuit dernière, il n'a pas bien dormi. Expliquez pourquoi. Avec votre partenaire, décrivez l'histoire en répondant aux questions correspondant à chaque illustration.

Scène A ➡ *Scène B*

1. Quelle heure était-il?
• Il était onze heures.
• Il était minuit.
• Il était une heure du matin.

2. Où était Monsieur Léveillé?
• Il était au salon.
• Il était dans la salle à manger.
• Il était dans sa chambre.

3. Qu'est-ce qu'il faisait?
• Il dormait.
• Il lisait le journal.
• Il écoutait de la musique.

4. Pourquoi est-ce que Monsieur Léveillé s'est réveillé?
• Il avait chaud.
• Il avait mal à la tête.
• Il a entendu un bruit.

Scène C

5. Qu'est-ce qu'il a fait?
• Il est resté au lit.
• Il est descendu.
• Il a téléphoné à la police.

6. Qu'est-ce qu'il avait à la main?
• Il avait un revolver.
• Il avait une batte de baseball.
• Il avait une raquette de tennis.

Teaching Strategy: Expansion

Divide students into pairs and have them draw their own stick figure cartoon with six different scenes. As in the cartoon on pp. 16–17, there should be captions in the **imparfait** and in the **passé composé**.

Have students write captions to their cartoon on six separate pieces of paper. When cartoon and captions are completed, two pairs should exchange their cartoons and captions and try to put the captions to the appropriate pictures. Have both pairs get together afterwards and compare notes.

Note: As with any creative activity, the teacher should circulate constantly in order to verify that vocabulary and structure are correct.

Note culturelle
Raccoons are found in Canada and the United States. They are rare in France.

Scène D

7. Qu'est-ce qu'il a vu?
- Il a vu un homme armé.
- Il a vu une ombre *(shadow)* dans le jardin.
- Il a vu des traces sur le sol.

Scène F

Maintenant racontez la fin de l'histoire.
- Qu'a fait Monsieur Léveillé?
- Et les ratons laveurs?
- Et le chat?

Scène E

8. Qu'est-ce qu'il y avait dans la cuisine?
- Il y avait un fantôme.
- Il y avait un cambrioleur *(burglar)*.
- Il y avait des ratons laveurs *(raccoons)*.

9. Qu'est-ce qu'ils faisaient là?
- Ils dormaient.
- Ils jouaient avec le chat.
- Ils mangeaient la nourriture du chat.

10. Où était le chat?
- Il était sur la table.
- Il était sous la table.
- Il mangeait avec les ratons laveurs.

RAPPEL

> To describe what you USED TO DO, what you WERE DOING, or to describe the CIRCUMSTANCES of an event, use the **imperfect** tense.
>
> **J'allais** au ciné. *I used to go to the movies.*
> *I was going to the movies.*
>
> **Il était six heures**. *It was 6 o'clock.*
>
> → You will learn more about the use of the imperfect in Unit 3.

Révision p. R5

Pratique p. 13

L'imparfait

Teaching Strategy
Have students work on the conclusion in pairs. They may want to illustrate the last scene.

Teaching Note
Activity 2 may be done as an A/B activity.

2 Dialogue

Avec votre partenaire, composez et jouez l'un des dialogues suivants.

▶ — Où étais-tu <u>hier soir</u>?
— J'étais <u>dans ma chambre</u>.
— Qu'est-ce que tu faisais?
— Je <u>lisais un livre</u>.
— Et qu'est-ce que tu as fait après?
— J'<u>ai fini mes devoirs</u>.

1. • cet après-midi
• au café
• attendre un copain
• aller au ciné

2. • à deux heures
• à la bibliothèque
• étudier
• rentrer chez moi

3. • samedi matin
• au centre commercial
• faire du shopping
• **??**

4. • samedi après-midi
• dans le jardin
• aider mon père
• **??**

Teaching Strategy: Pair Practice

Divide students into pairs. One student will be a police officer and one will be an accused criminal. Have them create a dialog in which the police officer questions the accused and he/she gives an alibi: "What were you doing at 10:00 when the victim died?"

Differentiation

Structured Have students review the formation of the **imparfait** (see R5). Have students copy one regular verb in the **imparfait** for each of the 3 verb groups: **-er, -ir, -re**. Have students write endings in red. Have students practice verbs orally and underline all forms pronounced identically in black.

■ **Vocabulary Notes**

Terms students may find useful for
Act. 3:

1. se promener
2. porter des lunettes
3. avoir une raquette à la main
4. avoir un sac; porter une casquette
5. une personne âgée; faire les
   courses
6. aller à la pêche

Terms students may find useful for
Act. 4:

1. un orchestre; jouer du rock;
   danser; boire dans un café
2. une course à vélo; des vaches;
   regarder les coureurs; acheter des
   glaces
3. jouer au volley; faire du ski
   nautique; prendre un bain de
   soleil; faire de la planche à voile
4. la fête de la musique; danser dans
   la rue; faire un film

■ **Notes culturelles**

- July 14 is the national holiday of
  France. Street dances (**les bals
  populaires**) are traditionally
  organized that day as well as
  parades and fireworks.
- **La fête de la musique** is an
  international event, usually
  celebrated on the first night of
  summer.

Révision p. R13

Pratique p. 14

Les vêtements

3 Au café

Vous avez passé l'après-midi à la terrasse d'un café. Vous avez vu
les personnes suivantes passer dans la rue. Décrivez chacune de
ces personnes.

- Il était (quelle heure?)
- J'ai vu (un homme? une dame? . . . ?)
- Il/elle était (jeune? grand(e)? . . . ?)

- Il/elle portait (quels vêtements?)
- Il/elle avait aussi (quoi?)
- Il/elle allait (où?)
- Il/elle allait faire (quoi?)

4 Photo de vacances 📝

Vous avez passé les vacances en France avec votre partenaire. Pendant votre voyage,
vous avez pris les photos suivantes. Choisissez deux photos et décrivez ce qui se passait
(what was going on) quand vous avez pris ces photos. Utilisez l'imparfait.

Teaching Strategy: Expansion

- Use **Projectable Transparency 13**, and
  cover all but one scene at a time. In pairs,
  students list as many details and actions as
  possible. Partners then choose one scene and
  create a story to present to the class.

- Have students bring in four pictures of
  themselves on vacation, at camp, at a party,
  etc. For each picture, students should write a
  4–5 sentence description of the scene using
  imparfait and/or **passé composé**: (e.g., how
  old they were, what season it was, who took
  the picture, etc.).

À votre tour!

Digital performance space

Situations Imagine you are in the following situations. Your partner will take the role of the other person in the dialogue and answer your questions.

1 Your friend just told you that he/she saw a great movie last Saturday.

Ask your friend . . .
• with whom he/she went to the movies
• what movie they saw
• what they did afterwards.

2 For his/her birthday, your friend was invited to a French restaurant.

Ask your friend . . .
• if he/she went to this restaurant for lunch or dinner
• what he/she ate
• what he/she drank.

3 You are phoning your French friend Valérie. Her brother/sister answers the phone and says that Valérie is not at home.

Ask Valérie's brother/sister . . .
• what time Valérie left
• where she went
• when she is coming back home.

4 Your friend came back from spring vacation with a tan and looks great.

Ask your friend . . .
• where he/she went
• what he/she did there
• when he/she came back.

5 Last summer your friend traveled through France with his/her family. You want to know more about their trip.

Ask your friend . . .
• how long they stayed in France
• if they traveled by *(en)* car or by train
• what cities they visited.

6 Last night your friend went to a concert by a French rock group.

Ask your friend . . .
• if the group *(le groupe)* sang in French or in English
• what clothes they were wearing
• how many people there were at the concert.

7 After supper last night you called your friend but nobody answered the phone.

Ask your friend . . .
• where he/she was
• what he/she was doing
• what his/her family was doing.

8 You and your friend are talking about your childhood — when you were eight years old.

Ask your friend . . .
• where he/she used to live
• to which school he/she used to go
• what programs *(quelles émissions)* he/she used to watch on TV.

dix-neuf **19**
Reprise B

À votre tour!

■ Student Portfolios

Use the situations in *À votre tour!* to record audio or video of student conversations for their portfolios. This makes an excellent "benchmark" to be used as a comparison with both the *previous* year's oral work and later work in the current year.

• Have students cut out a comic strip from the newspaper. Tell them to white out all of the captions and create completely new ones in French, using **passé composé** and **imparfait. Note:** Students should not translate the existing captions, but should use only the pictures to create the original captions.

Differentiation

Metacognitive Have students write out the five categories of usage for the **imparfait** (see R5). Have them write 6 clue words (**mots clés**) in English and French that would signify use of the **imparfait:**
always = toujours; often = souvent; usually = d'habitude; etc.

Reprise 19

Rappel Culturel

RESOURCES

TECHNOLOGY
Teacher One Stop
Block Scheduling Copymasters
🖥 **Projectable Transparencies**
1(o), *La France*
2, *Le monde francophone*
3, *Le monde francophone: L'Amérique*
4, *Le monde francophone: L'Afrique, l'Europe, l'Asie*
5(o), *L'Europe*
6, *Paris*
7, *Le métro de Paris*
Transparency Copymasters, pp. A5–A17

■ Teaching Strategy

Have students work in pairs or small groups to find the answers to these questions. Information may be found in the *Images du monde francophone* sections of DISCOVERING FRENCH TODAY!–*BLANC*.

♻ **RAPPEL** *Culturel*

A. FAITS CULTURELS

1. La devise *(motto)* de la France est . . .
 a. Paix et Prospérité
 b. Liberté, Égalité, Fraternité
 c. Je me souviens

2. La France métropolitaine est divisée administrativement en 96 . . .
 a. cantons
 b. départements
 c. provinces

3. Le TGV est . . .
 a. un avion supersonique
 b. une voiture électrique
 c. un train très rapide

4. Si on veut faire du ski en hiver, on peut aller . . .
 a. à Monaco
 b. en Normandie
 c. en Savoie

5. La «Belle Province» est le nom que l'on donne à . . .
 a. la Touraine
 b. la Louisiane
 c. la province de Québec

6. La Polynésie française est un groupe d'îles qui font partie de la France d'outre-mer. La plus grande de ces îles est . . .
 a. Tahiti
 b. la Martinique
 c. Madagascar

7. En 1803, la France a vendu aux États-Unis un vaste territoire pour la somme de 15 millions de dollars. Ce territoire était . . .
 a. la Louisiane
 b. la Caroline du Sud
 c. l'Alaska

8. Ce Français est un héros de la Révolution américaine. Il s'appelle . . .
 a. Cavelier de la Salle
 b. Champlain
 c. La Fayette

9. Le continent où il y a le plus grand nombre de pays qui utilisent le français comme langue officielle est . . .
 a. l'Europe
 b. l'Afrique
 c. l'Amérique du Sud

10. L'Algérie est une ancienne colonie française. Ce pays est situé . . .
 a. en Asie
 b. en Afrique noire
 c. en Afrique du Nord

11. En Afrique, les masques sont considérés comme des objets . . .
 a. religieux
 b. de collection
 c. de la vie courante

12. Au Sénégal, la religion principale est . . .
 a. la religion musulmane
 b. la religion catholique
 c. la religion protestante

13. La population de la France est de . . .
 a. 45 millions d'habitants
 b. 63 millions d'habitants
 c. 100 millions d'habitants

14. La «Nouvelle France» est le nom . . .
 a. d'un grand magasin à Paris
 b. d'un satellite français
 c. de l'ancien empire français en Amérique du Nord

Answers: 1-b; 2-b; 3-c; 4-c; 5-c; 6-a; 7-a; 8-c; 9-b; 10-c; 11-a; 12-a; 13-b; 14-c

Notes culturelles
- **Je me souviens** is the motto of the Canadian province of Quebec.
- **Cavelier de La Salle** (1643–1687) explored the Mississippi region and Louisiana.
- **Samuel de Champlain** (1567–1635) founded the city of Quebec in 1608.
- **La Fayette** (1757–1834) was a French general who took an active part in the American Revolution.

B. SITUATIONS CULTURELLES

1. Les Smith, des touristes anglais, ont visité la France en voiture. À Paris ils ont vu Notre-Dame. En Normandie, ils ont vu le Mont-Saint-Michel. En Provence, ils ont vu le Pont du Gard. *Qu'est-ce qu'ils ont vu en Alsace?*
  a. *Le Futuroscope.*
  b. *Le château de Chambord.*
  c. *La cathédrale de Strasbourg.*

2. Patrick et Jérôme ont passé leurs vacances dans les Alpes. Un jour, ils ont assisté à un grand événement sportif. Pour voir cet événement, ils sont allés sur une route de montagne et là ils ont attendu patiemment avec des milliers d'autres personnes. Enfin, ils ont vu des voitures, des motos, et finalement les coureurs parmi lesquels ils ont reconnu le «maillot jaune».
  À quel événement sportif ont-ils assisté?
  a. *Le Grand Prix de Monaco.*
  b. *Les 24 Heures du Mans.*
  c. *Le Tour de France.*

3. Catherine est une étudiante française. À Noël, elle va généralement faire du ski, mais cette année elle n'a pas fait de ski. Elle a fait un grand voyage, mais elle n'est pas allée à l'étranger. Là où elle est allée, elle a fait de la planche à voile et du ski nautique. Elle est rentrée chez elle très bronzée.
  Où est-elle allée?
  a. *En Savoie.*
  b. *En Normandie.*
  c. *À la Guadeloupe.*

4. Chaque année Claire attend patiemment la période de Carnaval. Finalement le Carnaval est arrivé. Le premier jour, Claire a assisté au couronnement de la reine par «Bonhomme». Les jours suivants, Claire a assisté à la course des canoës sur le Saint-Laurent et elle a admiré les sculptures de glace et de neige.
  Où habite Claire?
  a. *À Québec.*
  b. *À Nice.*
  c. *En Guyane française.*

5. Hier c'était un jour férié *(holiday)*. Le matin, Julien est allé sur les Champs-Élysées où il a assisté au défilé militaire. L'après-midi, il est sorti avec sa copine Véronique. Le soir, les deux amis ont vu les feux d'artifice *(fireworks)*. Ensuite, ils ont dansé dans les rues comme des millions de Français.
  Quelle fête est-ce qu'on célébrait hier?
  a. *La fête du Travail.*
  b. *La fête nationale.*
  c. *La fête de Mardi Gras.*

6. Philippe montre les photos qu'il a prises pendant les vacances. Il explique: «Cet arbre géant est un baobab . . . Le vêtement que porte cette jeune fille s'appelle un boubou . . . Cet homme qui raconte une histoire est un griot.» *Où Philippe est-il allé pendant les vacances?*
  a. *Au Sénégal.*
  b. *En Algérie.*
  c. *À Tahiti.*

7. Il y a environ deux cents ans, Jean-Baptiste Point du Sable, un Français d'ascendance africaine, arrivait dans la région des Grands Lacs. Il a construit la première maison d'un petit village qui allait devenir l'une des plus grandes villes du continent américain. *Quelle est cette ville?*
  a. *Détroit.*
  b. *Chicago.*
  c. *Montréal.*

8. Monsieur Dutour est ingénieur pour une compagnie de prospection pétrolière. Dans sa profession, il voyage beaucoup. La semaine dernière, il est allé dans un pays d'Afrique du Nord qui produit beaucoup de pétrole et de gaz naturel. *Où est allé Monsieur Dutour?*
  a. *Au Congo.*
  b. *En Algérie.*
  c. *En République Centrafricaine.*

Answers: 1-c; 2-c; 3-c; 4-a; 5-b; 6-a; 7-b; 8-b

Notes culturelles

- **Le Futuroscope** is a theme park near **Poitiers**. It presents new and future technologies through attractions like 3-D and IMAX movies.
- **Le Grand Prix de Monaco** and **Les 24 heures du Mans** are famous international car races.

- **Le griot** is a traditional African storyteller. **Griots** are poets and musicians who go from village to village, carrying on the oral traditions and folklore. (Students may remember learning about the **griot** in *Discovering French Today!–Blanc*, p. 426.)

Reprise C

Nous et les autres

RAPPEL ⟨7⟩ Vive l'amitié!

Dans la vie, l'amitié est peut-être la chose la plus importante. Mais attention, il y a toutes sortes d'amis! Par exemple . . .

♻ RAPPEL

When we ask someone to do something for us, we often use
OBJECT PRONOUNS:

   Téléphone-**moi** ce soir.   Prête-**moi** dix dollars.

Note also the constructions:

Tu **me** donnes ton numéro de téléphone?	Tu **nous** invites?
Je **te** donne aussi mon adresse.	Je **vous** invite à ma boum.

- **me, te → m', t'** before a vowel sound.
   Tu **m'**invites?   Oui, je **t'**invite.

Révision p. R8-R9

Pratique p. 15

Les pronoms compléments

Teaching Strategy: Grammar Drill

Read these questions orally and have students replace the d.o. or the i.o. in their answers:

1. **Est-ce que ton ami t'écrit souvent?**
2. **Tu regardes la télé?**
3. **Tu achètes tes livres à la librairie ou à la bibliothèque?**
4. **Est-ce que ton prof de maths aide tes amis et toi avec les devoirs?**
5. **Tes parents te prêtent de l'argent?**
6. **Est-ce que le prof de français vous donne beaucoup de devoirs?**
7. **Est-ce que le président nous connaît personnellement?**

① S'il te plaît

Vous venez d'arriver en France. Demandez à votre copain français (copine française) trois services et expliquez-lui pourquoi.

▶ S'il te plaît, présente-moi à tes copains.

Pourquoi?

Je voudrais rencontrer des jeunes Français.

QUELS SERVICES?
- amener dans une boutique de vêtements
- amener à la banque
- présenter à tes copains
- prêter ton plan *(map)* de la ville
- prêter ton appareil-photo
- donner l'adresse d'un bon restaurant
- montrer où est la poste
- ??

POURQUOI?
- envoyer une lettre
- changer de l'argent
- dîner en ville
- faire une promenade
- prendre des photos
- rencontrer des jeunes Français
- acheter un blouson
- ??

② Échanges 💬

Demandez certains services à votre partenaire. Il/elle va proposer un échange. Acceptez ou refusez.

▶ Dis, Éric, prête-moi ton VTT.

D'accord! Je te prête mon VTT si tu me prêtes tes rollers.

D'accord!

(Non, merci!)

prêter . . .	tes notes
	tes CD
	ton VTT *(mountain bike)*
inviter . . .	chez toi
	à ta fête d'anniversaire
aider . . .	avec le devoir de français
	avec le devoir de maths
présenter . . .	à ton copain
	à ta copine
montrer . . .	tes photos
	tes magazines

TU CONNAIS QUELQU'UN ICI?

NON, JE NE CONNAIS PERSONNE. JE NE SAIS PAS OÙ NOUS SOMMES.

♻ RAPPEL

Although **connaître** and **savoir** both mean *to know,* they are used differently:

Nous **connaissons** Yasmina.
Nous **savons** où elle habite.

Révision p. R8–R9 ➡

Pratique p. 16 ➡

Connaître et savoir

⟳ RAPPEL

quelqu'un *(someone)*	Je vois **quelqu'un.**	**ne . . . personne** *(no one)*	Je **ne** vois **personne.**
quelque chose *(something)*	Je vois **quelque chose.**	**ne . . . rien** *(nothing)*	Je **ne** vois **rien.**

---

8. Tu téléphones souvent à tes amis?
9. Est-ce que tu m'aimes bien?
10. Est-ce que je vous invite régulièrement au restaurant?
Note: Answers to these questions could be put on a transparency ahead of time to give written reinforcement of the correct answers; students could also write out answers on the board.

Differentiation

Repetitive Have students write verbs that take indirect objects on one color of index cards and verbs that take direct objects on differently colored cards (see R8–9). Have students write out questions using the appropriate kind of object (direct or indirect) on each card. S1 asks S2 a question. S2 responds, replacing the object with the appropriate pronoun.

■ **Note culturelle**
Le VTT (= vélo tout terrain) has been popular in France since being imported from the U.S. in 1983.

■ **Expansion: Activity 2**
Students ask their partner why he/she wants to borrow the item. The partner answers.
— Dis, Éric, prête-moi ton VTT.
— D'accord, je te prête mon VTT si tu me prêtes tes rollers.
— Pourquoi?
— Parce que je ne veux pas marcher!

SUPPLEMENTARY VOCABULARY

(Illustration)
l'espace *space*
l'extraterrestre *alien*
le martien *Martian*
l'OVNI (Objet Volant Non Identifié) *UFO*
la planète *planet*
la soucoupe volante *flying saucer*

■ **Expansion: Rappel**
Have students invent a story based on the illustration. What just happened? What is the people's reaction? What do the aliens want? What will happen next?

RAPPEL ⟨8⟩

RESOURCES

PRINT
Workbook, pp. 17–18

■ Notes culturelles
• This type of photo-illustrated story is called **un roman-photo** in France. **Les romans-photos** are mostly published in romance magazines such as **Nous Deux** or **Intimité**.

■ Teaching Strategy
Make copies of the story, cutting apart the captions, pictures, and dialogs. In groups of 4, have students "assemble" the story, then mime the story without words. Have the rest of the class supply the correct caption for each scene.

RAPPEL ⟨8⟩ Un garçon timide

Dans la classe, il y a une nouvelle élève. Elle s'appelle Catherine. Pierre la trouve sympathique, mais il est trop timide pour lui parler.

Je la trouve vraiment très sympa . . .

Qui est ce garçon? Pourquoi est-ce qu'il me regarde tout le temps?

Après la classe, Pierre et Catherine attendent le bus . . .

Je voudrais bien lui parler . . . Oui, mais qu'est-ce que je vais lui dire?

Pourquoi est-ce qu'il ne me parle pas?

Chez lui, Pierre pense toujours à Catherine. Il prend le guide et regarde le programme des films de la semaine.

Il y a un bon film ce soir. Je pense que Catherine aime le cinéma. Est-ce que je l'invite? Courage, je vais lui téléphoner!

Mais Pierre ne téléphone pas à Catherine.

Et si elle me dit qu'elle n'est pas libre . . . Bon . . . Je vais lui téléphoner samedi prochain. C'est promis!

Pierre met sa veste et il va seul au cinéma.

Pendant ce temps, Catherine regarde aussi le journal.

Tiens, il y a un bon film ce soir en ville . . . Je voudrais bien le voir, mais je n'ai pas envie d'aller seule au cinéma . . . Si je téléphonais à ce garçon qui me regarde tout le temps en classe. Après tout, je le trouve bien sympathique.

Catherine cherche le numéro de Pierre sur l'Internet. Puis elle lui téléphone . . .

. . . mais chez Pierre, personne ne répond au téléphone.

DRIN . . . DRIN . . .

Teaching Strategy: Direct Object Pronouns

On a transparency, photocopy or on the board, write a story which repeats the same <u>direct object</u> over and over and read it aloud to the students. Ask them to identify what is wrong with the story. Once they realize the same word is repeated many times, ask them to fix the problem. This is a fairly quick group activity that clearly demonstrates the importance of the direct object pronouns (e.g., **J'ai une nouvelle voiture. J'adore ma voiture. J'ai acheté ma voiture chez Renault. Je vais laver ma voiture tous les jours et je vais garder ma voiture dans le garage...**).

Le lendemain après la classe.

Pierre, il y a un bon film au Rex. Est-ce que tu l'as vu?

Euh oui . . . je l'ai vu. C'est un film vraiment super!

Est-ce que tu veux le revoir avec moi ce soir?

Mais oui, avec plaisir.

Et maintenant, avec votre partenaire, imaginez la suite de l'histoire. Par exemple . . .
• Quand est-ce que Pierre et Catherine sont allés au cinéma?
• Qu'est-ce qu'il lui a dit?
• Qu'est-ce qu'elle lui a dit?
• Est-ce qu'ils ont eu d'autres rendez-vous?

♻ RAPPEL

To refer to people previously mentioned, use:

le / la / les	
Je regarde **Marc**.	Je **le** regarde.
Tu connais **Claire**.	Tu **la** connais.
J'invite **mes** amis.	Je **les** invite.

lui / leur	
Je téléphone **à Marc**.	Je **lui** téléphone.
Tu parles **à Claire**.	Tu **lui** parles.
J'écris **à mes amis**.	Je **leur** écris.

• **le/la/les** may also refer to things.
   Je regarde **la photo**.   Je **la** regarde.
• **le/la → l'** before a vowel sound
   Nous écoutons **le CD**.   Nous **l'**écoutons.

Révision p. R8–R9
Pratique p. 17
   Les compléments d'objet direct et indirect

1 Relations personnelles

Demandez à votre partenaire de décrire ses relations avec l'une des personnes indiquées.

Révision p. R26, R30
Pratique p. 18
   Voir *(to see)*, écrire *(to write)*

▸ — Tu as <u>une cousine</u>?
   — Oui, bien sûr.
   — Tu <u>la vois souvent</u>?
   — Oui, je <u>la vois</u> <u>de temps en temps</u>.
   — Tu <u>lui écris</u>?
   — Non, <u>je ne lui écris</u> <u>jamais</u>.

QUI?	QUOI?	QUAND?
un copain	voir	souvent
des copines	inviter	de temps en temps
une tante	téléphoner (à)	rarement
des cousins	écrire (à)	jamais
une cousine	aider	toujours
des voisins	rendre visite (à)	
	donner des cadeaux (à)	
	donner des conseils *(advice)* (à)	
	demander des conseils (à)	

2 La boum

Vous préparez une boum. Demandez à votre partenaire s'il (si elle) peut vous aider avec les choses suivantes. Votre partenaire va accepter ou refuser.

▸ — Tu peux préparer les sandwichs?
   — Oui, d'accord, je vais les préparer.
   (Je suis désolé(e) mais je ne peux pas les préparer.)

• faire les courses
• acheter les boissons
• laver les verres
• ranger la cuisine
• mettre la table

• décorer le salon
• choisir la musique
• inviter nos amis
• téléphoner aux voisins
• préparer les sandwichs

■ **Teaching Note**
Before doing Activity 1, you may want to review the placement of the object pronoun in front of the infinitive.

■ **Expansion: Activity 2**
In case the request for help is refused, students should be encouraged to invent an excuse, e.g.:
   Je n'ai pas le temps.
   Je dois aider ma mère, etc.

Note: In writing the story, be sure to include sentences in the future, **passé composé**, and negative tenses, etc.

Indirect Object Pronouns
Use the same technique to repeat the same indirect object over and over (e.g., **Ma meilleure amie s'appelle Pauline. Pauline est très sympa. Je téléphone souvent à Pauline. L'autre jour, j'ai téléphoné à Pauline et j'ai demandé à Pauline si elle voulait aller au cirque...**).

À votre tour!

Situations Imagine you are in the following situations. Your partner will take the role of the other person in the dialogue and answer your questions.

1 You are an exchange student in a French lycée. It is your first day at school and you need help.

Ask another student (who, of course, is willing to help you) . . .
- to loan you a notebook
- to give you a pencil
- to show you where the cafeteria is
- to take you *(amener)* to the library.

2 You are spending two weeks at the home of your French cousin who lives in Paris.

Ask your cousin (who will accept or refuse) . . .
- to introduce you to his/her friends
- to loan you something you need
- to show you a place in Paris you would like to visit
- to take you to a show or an event that you are interested in.

3 Your friend has a Belgian neighbor named Béatrice. You would like to know more about their relationship.

Ask your friend . . .
- how long he/she has known Béatrice
- if he/she knows her parents
- if he/she invites her often
- what he/she is going to give Béatrice for her birthday.

4 Your friend has a Canadian penpal, Jean, who coming to visit next weekend. You want to kn what your friend has planned for Jean's visit.

Ask your friend . . .
- to what restaurant he/she is going to invite Jean
- what places *(quels endroits)* he/she is going to show him
- what gift *(un cadeau)* he/she is going to give him

5 You are the manager of a tourist shop in Montreal. You are hiring students for the summer and are interviewing one of the candidates.

Ask the candidate . . .
- if he/she knows how to speak French well
- What other languages he/she knows how to spea
- if he/she knows how to answer the phone in French
- what other things he/she knows how to do.

6 You and your friend are planning a party for next Friday night. You are checking if your friend has done his/her share of the work.

Ask your friend . . .
- if he/she sent the invitations
- if he/she called the neighbors
- if he/she chose the music
- if he/she bought the beverages *(les boissons)*.

7 You are visiting Paris with your friend. It is yo first trip but your friend has visited Paris befo

Ask your friend . . .
- what monuments he/she knows
- if he/she knows how to get to the Eiffel Tower
- if he/she knows if the Louvre is open *(ouvert)* this afternoon

---

À votre tour!

RESOURCES

TECHNOLOGY
Teacher One Stop
📺 **Projectable Transparencies**
LR, *Les trois bagues*
Transparency Copymasters,
pp. A119

■ Teaching Note
- In France, the school cafeteria is called **la cantine**. Une **cafétéria** is a self-service restaurant open to everyone.
- You may want to point out again the false cognate:
 la librairie = bookstore
 la bibliothèque = library

LECTURE

LECTURE

LECTURE

Reading STRATEGY

Reading fiction

Les trois bagues

AVANT DE LIRE

Quand on lit une histoire, il est utile d'anticiper ce qui va se passer d'après les éléments que l'on connaît déjà. Lisez d'abord la **Note culturelle** et **Une annonce**. D'après vous, pourquoi est-ce que les neveux vont aller chez le notaire?

- pour assister à un mariage
- pour vendre la maison familiale
- pour recevoir une somme d'argent
- pour régler *(to settle)* une dispute

Maintenant, continuez votre lecture pour vérifier votre réponse.

NOTE *Culturelle*

Le notaire

Le notaire joue un rôle important dans la vie des familles françaises. Son rôle est d'officialiser un grand nombre d'actes et de contrats de la vie civile (contrat de mariage, testaments,° ventes° de biens immobiliers,° etc.). Un notaire a le titre de **Maître,** Maître Durand, par exemple. Son bureau° s'appelle **une étude.**

testament *will*   **vente** *sale*
biens immobiliers *real estate*
bureau *office*

■ Teaching Note

The purpose of this reading is to review and reactivate some important items and structures in the context of a short and simple self-contained narrative.

In particular, the text exemplifies the contrast between the imperfect and the **passé composé**. It can be used here, or postponed until Unit 3, which focuses on the narration of past events.

■ Note linguistique

Officier is used to mean "to officiate." **Officialiser** means "to make official."

LES TROIS BAGUES

Une annonce

Un jour l'annonce suivante a paru dans *La Nouvelle République* de Tours.

Mots utiles
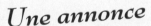

un neveu	*nephew*
un propriétaire	*owner*
un ouvrier	*worker*
gagner sa vie	*to earn one's living*

Héritage

Les neveux de Jules Larivière, né le 18 octobre 1930 à Amboise, sont invités à se présenter le 21 janvier à l'étude de Maître Durand, notaire à Tours.

vingt-sept **27**
Lecture

Notes culturelles

- **Tours** is a city on the Loire southwest of Paris. The inhabitants of Tours are called **les Tourangeaux.**

- **Amboise** is another city on the Loire, famous for its Renaissance castle, and the **Manoir du Clos-Lucé** where the artist **Leonardo da Vinci (Léonard de Vinci)** died in 1519.

■ **Teaching Note**

Since the action of this story takes place in Touraine, you may want to remind students about that region of France: Tours, the Loire valley, and châteaux such as Amboise and Chenonceaux (*Interlude 3*, p. 147).

SUPPLEMENTARY VOCABULARY

le neveu ≠ **la nièce**
l'oncle ≠ **la tante**
célibataire ≠ **marié**
le décès ≠ **la naissance**
l'aîné ≠ **le cadet (la cadette)**

Les trois neveux

Le 21 janvier, trois hommes se sont présentés° à l'étude de Maître Durand. Neveux de Jules Larivière, ils étaient cousins, mais de condition sociale très différente.

Le premier neveu, Roland Larivière, avait 45 ans et était célibataire.° Propriétaire d'un grand hôtel dans le centre de Tours, il était président de la Chambre de Commerce de la ville. C'était un homme riche et influent.

Le second neveu, Henri Larivière, 38 ans, exerçait la profession de pharmacien et gagnait bien sa vie. Marié, mais sans enfants, il habitait avec sa femme dans une jolie maison située en banlieue.°

Le troisième neveu, Jean-Marc Larivière, 28 ans, était un simple ouvrier agricole. Il habitait dans une petite ferme à la campagne° avec sa femme et ses trois enfants.

La secrétaire de Maître Durand a pris le nom, la profession et l'adresse des trois neveux, puis elle les a introduits° dans le bureau du notaire.

5

10

15

se sont présentés = sont venus   **célibataire** = non-marié   **banlieue** *suburbs*
campagne *country*   **les a introduits** *led, introduced them*

■ *Avez-vous compris?*

(Sample answers)

1. Ils vont chez le notaire le 21 janvier, parce qu'ils ont lu l'annonce mise dans le journal par le notaire.
2. Le plus riche est Roland, propriétaire d'un hôtel. Le moins riche est Jean-Marc, ouvrier agricole.
3. *Answers will vary.*
4. *Answers will vary.*

Avez-vous compris?

1. Quand et pourquoi les trois neveux vont-ils chez le notaire?
2. Qui est le plus riche des trois neveux? le moins riche?
3. À votre avis, lequel des trois neveux exerce la profession la plus intéressante? Pourquoi?
4. À vos yeux, lequel est le plus sympathique? Pourquoi?

Anticipons un peu!

D'après vous, qu'est-ce qui va se passer à la fin de l'histoire?

• Les trois neveux vont recevoir la même somme d'argent.
• Le neveu le plus riche va donner sa part *(share)* à ses cousins.
• Le neveu le moins riche va recevoir plus d'argent que ses cousins.
• Autre possibilité? Expliquez votre opinion.

Maintenant, finissez l'histoire et vérifiez si vous aviez raison.

Teaching Strategy: Expansion

Divide the class into groups and assign a group leader and a recorder. First, have students identify each person in the illustration. On what do they base their answer?

Next, have students decide which ring would they choose and why. The recorder should note student answers so that groups can compare and discuss.

Le Testament

Maître Durand a serré la main° des trois neveux et puis il a commencé à parler.

Me Durand	J'ai le regret de vous annoncer le décès° de votre oncle Jules Larivière. Il est mort le 12 décembre dernier au Mexique dans la ville de Cuernavaca où il habitait depuis son départ de France, il y a quinze ans. Il n'avait pas d'enfants. Vous êtes, par conséquent, ses héritiers.

20

Roland L.	Qu'est-ce qu'il nous a laissé?
Me Durand	Il vous a laissé trois bagues.
Roland L.	Trois bagues? C'est tout?!
Me Durand	Non, il vous a laissé aussi une très belle photo de lui.
Roland L.	Est-ce qu'on peut voir les bagues?
Me Durand	Oui, bien sûr.

25

Maître Durand a pris une grande enveloppe dans laquelle il y avait les trois bagues. Il les a mises sur une table et il a continué . . .

30

Me Durand	Voilà les trois bagues. Comme vous pouvez voir, ces bagues sont très différentes. Il y a une bague de diamant, une bague en or et une bague en argent . . .
Roland L.	Mais ces bagues n'ont pas la même valeur.° Le partage° est impossible.

35

Me Durand	Au contraire! Le testament de votre oncle est très explicite. Il stipule que c'est à l'aîné de ses neveux de choisir d'abord.
Roland L.	Alors là, mon oncle a eu une bonne idée!
Me Durand	Monsieur Roland Larivière, vous êtes l'aîné! Quelle bague voulez-vous?

40

Roland L.	Eh bien, c'est facile! Je prends la bague de diamant! Quel merveilleux souvenir de mon oncle!
Me Durand	Voulez-vous aussi la photo de votre oncle?
Roland L.	Euh, non. Je crois que je me souviendrai° mieux de mon oncle avec la bague. Et puis, j'ai assez de vieilles choses chez moi.

45

Maître Durand s'est tourné° ensuite vers Henri Larivière.

Me Durand	Monsieur Henri Larivière, vous êtes le second neveu. C'est votre tour maintenant.
Henri L.	Eh bien, moi, je proteste! Je ne suis peut-être pas l'aîné, mais c'était moi le neveu préféré de mon oncle. Pourquoi est-ce qu'il ne m'a pas donné la bague de diamant? Oui, je proteste!

50

Me Durand	Choisissez, s'il vous plaît! La bague en or ou la bague en argent?

55

Henri L.	Bon, je prends la bague en or, mais . . .
Me Durand	Voulez-vous la photo de votre oncle?
Henri L.	Ah ça, certainement pas! Mon oncle a été trop injuste avec moi!

a serré la main de *shook hands with*   **décès** *death*   **valeur** *value*   **le partage** = la division
je me souviendrai *I will remember*   **s'est tourné** *turned*

Mots utiles

un testament	*will*
un héritier	*heir*
laisser	*to leave*
une bague	*ring*
l'or	*gold*
l'argent	*silver*
l'aîné	= le plus âgé
une clé	*key*
un coffre	*safe*
juste ≠ injuste	*fair ≠ unfair*

vingt-neuf **29**
Lecture

Differentiation

Cumulative Divide the class into groups of 4–5 students. Have each group take a reading passage (teacher distributes photocopied sections). Have each group make a vocabulary list of 5–10 new words and expressions. Have each student in each group be responsible for orally reading 2–3 sentences. Have each group write 4 comprehension questions for their passage. Have each group present to the class as follows: 1) students introduce new vocabulary on the board; 2) students read their sentences orally; and 3) students check class comprehension with questions.

Finalement Maître Durand s'est tourné vers le troisième neveu.

Me Durand	Alors, Monsieur Jean-Marc Larivière, il vous reste° la bague en argent . . . Je suppose que vous non plus, vous ne désirez pas la photo de votre oncle. 60
Jean-Marc L.	Au contraire. Je me souviens bien de lui. C'était un homme très bon et très juste. Je l'aimais beaucoup!
Me Durand	Eh bien, voilà votre bague, et voici la photo de votre oncle.

Anticipons un peu!

D'après vous, qu'est-ce qui va se passer à la fin?

Maître Durand s'est levé,° puis il a serré très fort° la main de Jean-Marc Larivière.

Me Durand	Félicitations, vous êtes maintenant un homme très riche!
Jean-Marc L.	Mais non, je suis seulement un pauvre ouvrier agricole . . .
Me Durand	Oui, mais vous avez la photo. 70
Jean-Marc L.	La photo?
Me Durand	Retournez-la . . . Il y a la clé du coffre de votre oncle. Quand il était au Mexique, votre oncle a fait des investissements très profitables. Il est mort multi-millionnaire et c'est vous qui héritez de sa fortune! 75

il vous reste = vous avez   **s'est levé** got up   **très fort** = avec beaucoup de force

Avez-vous compris?

1. Pourquoi les neveux de Jules Larivière étaient-ils ses héritiers?

2. Quels objets est-ce que Jules Larivière a laissés à ses neveux?

3. En quoi ces bagues étaient-elles différentes?

4. Pourquoi est-ce que les deux premiers neveux n'ont pas pris la photo de leur oncle?

5. Pourquoi est-ce que le troisième neveu a pris la photo?

6. Comment est-ce qu'il a été récompensé *(rewarded)*?

APRÈS LA LECTURE

Expression orale

Discussion

Voici plusieurs morales possibles pour l'histoire que vous avez lue. Avec votre partenaire, déterminez quelle est la meilleure morale et expliquez pourquoi. (Si vous préférez, vous pouvez suggérer une autre morale.)

- Il y a toujours une justice.
- L'avarice (greed) ne paie pas.
- Les riches ont souvent tort.
- L'argent ne fait pas le bonheur.

Dramatisation

Avec vos camarades de classe, jouez la scène du **Testament**. Chaque personne va adopter la personnalité correspondant à son rôle et jouer ce rôle avec beaucoup d'expression.

Situations

Avec votre partenaire, choisissez l'une des situations suivantes. Composez le dialogue correspondant et jouez-le en classe.

1 La bonne nouvelle

Jean-Marc Larivière rentre chez lui et annonce la bonne nouvelle à sa femme qui veut des détails.
Rôles: Jean-Marc Larivière, sa femme

2 Au café

Roland Larivière va au café où il rencontre un(e) ami(e). Il lui raconte l'histoire du testament.
Rôles: Roland Larivière, un(e) ami(e)

3 Un procès

Henri Larivière, très mécontent de ce qui s'est passé, va voir un(e) avocat(e) (lawyer), dans l'intention de faire un procès (suit) à son cousin Jean-Marc. Il explique l'injustice de la situation à l'avocat(e) qui veut des détails.
Rôles: Henri Larivière, l'avocat(e)

Expression écrite

L'héritage

Dans un petit paragraphe, décrivez ce que Jean-Marc Larivière va faire avec l'argent de l'héritage.

Les trois neveux

Sur la base de l'histoire que vous avez lue, faites le portrait des trois neveux (leurs qualités, leurs défauts, ce qu'ils aiment, ce qu'ils n'aiment pas, etc.).

Jules Larivière

Écrivez une courte biographie de Jules Larivière. Utilisez votre imagination. Vous pouvez considérer les questions suivantes:

- Que faisait Jules Larivière avant d'aller au Mexique?
- Pourquoi a-t-il quitté la France?
- Qu'est-ce qu'il a fait à Cuernavaca?

Le testament

Choisissez l'un des personnages suivants: Maître Durand, Roland Larivière, Henri Larivière, Jean-Marc Larivière

Écrivez une lettre dans laquelle vous décrivez l'histoire du point de vue de la personne que vous avez choisie. Comparez votre lettre avec celles que vos camarades ont écrites.

Student Portfolios

Use the *Après la lecture* activities as the basis for portfolio elements. If students prefer, they may also choose to do a recording of the *Lecture*, with students taking turns reading sections of the story aloud.

For writing rubrics, consult the **Generate Success** Rubric Generator on the **Teacher One Stop**. You can also create your own custom rubrics with this tool.

MAIN THEME

Personal appearance
Daily routine

COMMUNICATION
- Expressing how one feels and inquiring about other people
- Caring for one's appearance
- Describing people
- Describing aspects of daily routine

CULTURES
- Evaluating images of beauty in French art
- Learning about French art movements

CONNECTIONS
- Locating cities on a map
- Determining a story's genre based on its title and the author's biography
- Connecting to Language Arts: Learning to list ideas for a writing project
- Connecting to Math: Graphing results of a survey and calculating costs
- Connecting to Science/Health: Learning about personal-care products
- Connecting to Social Studies: Conducting a survey about personal-care products
- Connecting to Art/Music: Creating a travel manual
- Connecting to Technology: Using a computer to design a travel manual

COMPARISONS
- Comparing how French and English speakers refer to parts of the body
- Comparing familiar expressions in
- French and English
- Comparing the use of the definite article, reflexive actions, and stress pronouns in French and English
- Comparing French and American teens' attitudes on style

COMMUNITIES
- Preparing and displaying a travel manual
- Using French to learn about advertising

Au jour le jour

THÈME ET OBJECTIFS

Culture

In this unit, you will discover . . .

- what French people call "le look" and why it is important to them
- how French teenagers care for their personal appearance
- how different artists have expressed the concept of beauty
- what constitutes the daily routine for different French people

Communication

You will learn how . . .

- to describe what a person looks like
- to explain what you do to make yourself look good
- to talk about your daily activities
- to describe how you feel in different circumstances

Langue

You will learn how . . .

- to describe what people do for themselves
- to describe certain aspects of your daily routine
- to express feelings and changes of mood

DIGITAL FRENCH my.hrw.com
ONLINE STUDENT EDITION with...

performance space

News + Networking

@HOMETUTOR

- Audio Resources
- Video Resources
- Interactive Flashcards
- WebQuest

PRACTICE FRENCH WITH HOLT MCDOUGAL APPS!

DIGITAL FRENCH

TEACHER TOOLS
- Teacher One Stop
- Interactive Whiteboard Lessons
- Generate Success Rubric Generator and Interactive Graphic Organizers
- Examview Test Generator

ALSO AVAILABLE...
- Online Workbook
- French InterActive Reader
- @HomeTutor
- DVD Program
- Power Presentations
- Interactive Flashcards

FRENCH ON THE GO!
- Performance Space
- Holt McDougal French Apps
- Discovering French Today eTextbook

L'importance du «LOOK»

Il y a deux semaines, Cédric, 16 ans, avait les cheveux longs. Maintenant, il les a courts.° Cédric change de coiffure° tous les° trois mois. Véronique, 17 ans, dépense son argent en «fringues»° qu'elle achète au moment des soldes.° Pour se composer un «look», Sandrine préfère utiliser sa vaste collection d'accessoires.

Pour les jeunes Français, le «look» est extrêmement important. En fait, l'importance du look marque le passage de l'enfance° à l'adolescence. Avant l'âge de 12 ou 13 ans, ils ne s'intéressent° pas beaucoup à leur apparence. Après, ils y font très attention.

Le look, c'est une façon de personnaliser son apparence physique, de se créer un style. S'il est difficile de modifier son corps,° on peut facilement changer son look. Il suffit° de choisir les vêtements, les accessoires, la coupe° de cheveux correspondant à l'impression qu'on veut donner. Voici, par ordre d'importance, les éléments du look pour les «ados» (les adolescents) français.

"C'est la première impression qui compte"

■ Les vêtements

Avec le choix de ses vêtements, on détermine son style général: sport, classique, romantique, etc. . . Pour les ados, les vêtements les plus importants sont d'abord le jean, uniforme de la jeunesse internationale, et ensuite le blouson, le sweat et le tee-shirt. La marque des vêtements est capitale. On n'achète pas un blouson, mais un Naf Naf ou un Chevignon. On ne porte pas un sweat, mais Go Sport ou un Kookaï. Parce que la marque coûte cher, les ados mélangent° les vêtements de marque avec des vêtements moins chers qu'ils achètent dans les grandes surfaces.°

■ Les chaussures

Les Français sont les plus grands acheteurs de chaussures d'Europe: ils en achètent en moyenne cinq paires par an. Là aussi, la forme, le style et surtout la marque sont très importants.

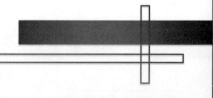

---

courts *short* **coiffure** *hairstyle* **tous les** *every* **fringues** = *vêtements (slang)* **soldes** *sales* **l'enfance** *childhood* **ne s'intéresse** = *ne sont pas intéressés*
corps *body* **suffit** = *il est suffisant* **coupe** *cut* **marques** *designer (boutique) brand names* **mélangent** *mix* **grandes surfaces** *shopping centers*

ASSESSMENT IN UNIT RESOURCE BOOK

Print Resources
- **Workbook TE/PE**
- *Activités pour tous* **TE/PE**
- *Lectures pour tous*
- **Unit Resource Book**
  Video Activities
  Videoscripts
  Audioscripts

Achievement Tests
- **Quizzes, Unit 1**
- **Unit Test 1**
- **Reading and Culture Tests**
- **Assessment Answer Key**

Proficiency Tests
- **Listening Comprehension**
- **Speaking Performance**
- **Writing Performance**
- **Portfolio Assessment**

INFO MAGAZINE

Theme: Personal style

Reading Strategy:
Browsing; reading for cultural information

■ Teaching Strategy
These readings can be done:
- in class or as homework
- at the beginning of the unit or as a wrap-up activity

Note linguistique
Les fringues *(f.)* is a popular slang term for "clothes," almost always used in the plural form. Also frequently used are: **fringuer =** **habiller, se fringuer = s'habiller.**

■ Note culturelle
Chevignon is a clothing label created by the Algerian-born Guy Azoulay. **Naf-Naf** is a clothing label for young people. Naf-Naf is the name of the third little pig in the **Les trois petits cochons** (The Three Little Pigs).

■ Pronunciation
un sweat /swit/
levis /lewis/

21ST CENTURY SKILLS
- **Communication:** SE: pp. 35, 37, 41, 47, 49, 51, 57, 59; TE: pp. 35, 36, 41, 45, 47, 48, 53
- **Collaboration:** TE: p. 49
- **Critical Thinking and Problem Solving:** SE: p. 41; TE: pp. 34, 41, 43, 56
- **Creativity and Innovation:** SE: p. 59; TE: pp. 45, 47, 53
- **Information Literacy:** TE: pp. 37, 39, 41, 46, 56, 62, 66
- **Technology Literacy:** TE: pp. 36, 48, 55, 56, 62, 66
- **Flexibility and Adaptability:** TE: pp. 37, 45, 60, 66
- **Initiative and Self-Direction:** TE: pp. 37, 48, 56, 60, 66
- **Social and Cross-Cultural Skills:** TE: pp. 34, 41, 46, 49, 56, 62
- **Productivity and Accountability:** TE: pp. 41, 44, 48, 50, 56, 59
- **Leadership and Responsibility:** TE: pp. 55, 66

Les styles de mode
fashion styles

le grunge: la chemise à carreaux, le jean déchiré et les godillots *checkered shirt, torn jeans, and [military] boots*

le BCBG (Bon Chic Bon Genre): le tailleur ou le costume, les chaussures de cuir, les accessoires chics (carré Hermès, collier de perles, montre en or) *Upscale style: women's or men's suit, leather shoes, "chic" accessories (Hermès scarf, pearl necklace, gold watch)*

le style rappeur: le pantalon large, la casquette à l'envers, les baskets *large pants, cap "the wrong way," sneakers*

le style techno (pour les amateurs de technologie comme les ordinateurs): le pantalon large, le tee-shirt aux couleurs fluo, les tennis *large pants, brightly colored tee-shirt, tennis shoes*

le style skater (pour les amateurs de skateboard ou de surf): les jeans larges, les tennis et les tee-shirts avec des logos détournés *wide jeans, tennis shoes, and tee-shirts with rewritten logos*

Rétro usually designates the fashions of the 1920s–1970s.

■ Realia note

Jean-Louis David is a popular hairdresser, with salons in all major French and U.S. cities.

INFOMAGAZINE

■ Les accessoires

Colliers, bracelets, boucles d'oreille, bijoux, chapeaux permettent aux filles de se créer un look ou d'en changer rapidement. Pour leur look, les garçons utilisent casquettes,° ceintures, bretelles,° et parfois des boucles d'oreilles. Le sac à dos° est un élément du look plus important pour les filles que pour les garçons. Et n'oublions pas les lunettes. Suivant leur forme et leur couleur, on peut avoir un look sérieux, intelligent, drôle, rétro . . .

■ La coiffure

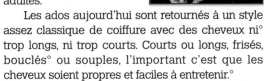

La coiffure fait partie° intégrale du look. C'est aussi une façon° de manifester ses opinions. Les cheveux longs des années 1970 ou le style «punk» des années 1980 marquaient le refus de s'intégrer à la société des adultes.

Les ados aujourd'hui sont retournés à un style assez classique de coiffure avec des cheveux ni° trop longs, ni trop courts. Courts ou longs, frisés, bouclés° ou souples, l'important c'est que les cheveux soient propres et faciles à entretenir.°

■ Le maquillage et les produits de beauté

Aujourd'hui, les jeunes Françaises préfèrent un style naturel. Leur maquillage° et aussi leur parfum restent généralement discrets. Quant° aux jeunes Français, ils utilisent de plus en plus° de produits de beauté: eaux de toilette, crèmes et lotions pour les mains, gels pour les cheveux.

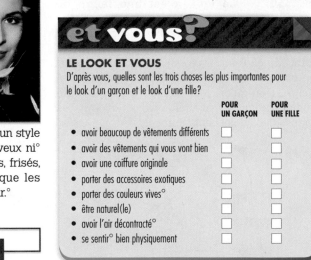

et vous?

LE LOOK ET VOUS
D'après vous, quelles sont les trois choses les plus importantes pour le look d'un garçon et le look d'une fille?

	POUR UN GARÇON	POUR UNE FILLE
• avoir beaucoup de vêtements différents	☐	☐
• avoir des vêtements qui vous vont bien	☐	☐
• avoir une coiffure originale	☐	☐
• porter des accessoires exotiques	☐	☐
• porter des couleurs vives°	☐	☐
• être naturel(le)	☐	☐
• avoir l'air décontracté°	☐	☐
• se sentir° bien physiquement	☐	☐

---

casquettes *caps* **bretelles** *suspenders* **sac à dos** *backpack* **fait partie** *is a component* **façon** = *une manière* **ni** *neither* **bouclés** *wavy* **entretenir** *to take care of* **maquillage** *makeup* **Quant à** *as for* **plus en plus** *more and more* **vives** *bright* **l'air décontracté** *to look relaxed* **se sentir** *to feel*

Teaching Strategy: Warm-Up

Once students have read the cultural information on pages 33–34, ask them to talk about how they would characterize **le look** for themselves, using each category (**les vêtements, les chaussures...**). After this open-ended discussion, compare and contrast French and American adolescent attitudes on style. On theboard, rate each category **as plus important pour les Français...aussi important pour les Français que pour les Américains... plus important pour les Américains.**

Note: Are there other important categories that contribute to **"le look"** that are not mentioned in the article?

Les artistes ont toujours voulu représenter leur idée de la beauté. La beauté a des visages différents à travers les âges et les cultures.

Les visages de la beauté

La beauté, c'est . . .

Pour Léonard de Vinci (1452-1519)

. . . un visage tranquille
. . . des traits° réguliers
. . . un sourire° énigmatique
. . . la discrétion et le mystère

Pour ce sculpteur du Moyen Âge

. . . un visage ovale
. . . des cheveux bouclés
. . . un sourire d'ange
. . . la douceur° et la discrétion

Pour Pierre Auguste Renoir (1841-1919)

. . . un visage rond
. . . des joues° pleines°
. . . un teint° frais
. . . la joie de vivre

Pour Amedeo Modigliani (1884-1920)

. . . un visage ovale
. . . un nez long et fin
. . . des traits symétriques
. . . la délicatesse

Pour Paul Gauguin (1848-1903)

. . . un visage rond
. . . des cheveux abondants
. . . une bouche pleine
. . . la bonté° et la générosité

Pour Pablo Picasso (1881-1973)

. . . un regard profond
. . . des traits marqués
. . . une attitude fière
. . . la personnalité

Pour ce sculpteur anonyme du Bénin

. . . une coiffure° élaborée
. . . un visage altier°
. . . des traits fermes
. . . la noblesse° de caractère

Et ça! C'est le contraire de la beauté!

et vous?

- Parmi les huit visages représentés, lesquels correspondent le mieux à votre idéal de la beauté? Expliquez pourquoi.
- Apportez en classe des photos ou des portraits de personnes que vous considérez être belles. Décrivez ces portraits.

traits *features* **sourire** *mile* **douceur** *kindness* **joues** *cheeks* **pleines** *full* **teint** *complexion*
bonté *goodness* **coiffure** *hairdo* **altier** *proud* **noblesse** *nobility*

INFOMAGAZINE

■ Notes culturelles

- **Léonard de Vinci** was a Renaissance artist known especially for his paintings The Mona Lisa *(la Joconde)* and The Last Supper *(la Cène)*. He was also a designer, sculptor, writer, architect, scientist, musician, and engineer.
- For more information on **Renoir** and **Gauguin**, see pp. 61 and 64 in *Interlude 1*.
- **Bénin** is a country in western Africa. The powerful kingdom of Benin flourished from the 14th through the 17th centuries.
- In the Middle Ages (9th–15th centuries) many great churches and cathedrals were built in Europe. The facades often contained statues of saints and other biblical figures.
- **Amedeo Modigliani** was an Italian painter whose portraits were characterized by elongated forms and warm colors.
- **Pablo Picasso** was a Spanish painter who lived for many years in France. His works can be divided into several periods:
  Blue Period (1901–1904)
  Pink Period (1905–1907)
  Cubism (*Les Demoiselles d'Avignon*, 1907)
  Surrealism and abstraction (1926–1936)
  Expressionism (*Guernica*, 1937), etc.
- The gutters of Notre Dame Cathedral are decorated with statues of fantastic monsters known as gargoyles (**des gargouilles**).

Teaching Strategy: Descriptions

Locate large representations of the illustrations on p. 35. Describe each picture and have students indicate which one is being described (#1–8).

Differentiation

Synthetic/Analytic Have students say and write the vocabulary words defined at the bottom of p. 34. Have students work in pairs to identify the vocabulary words in the passage. Have them write the main points of the passage and share them with the class.

Unité 1   35

PRINT

Workbook, pp. 107–108

Activités pour tous

Unit 1 Resource Book, Partie 1

Activités pour tous TE

Audioscripts

Lesson Plans

Block Scheduling Lesson Plans

Absent Student Copymasters

Workbook TE

AUDIO

Audio Program
CD 1 Tracks 1–3

TECHNOLOGY

@HomeTutor

Interactive Whiteboard Lessons

Teacher One Stop

Block Scheduling Copymasters

Projectable Transparencies

14, *Dix ans après*

14(o), *Dix ans après*

Transparency Copymasters,
pp. A29–A30

■ **Teaching note**

1 kg = 2.2 lb
1 lb = .45 kg
1 m = 3.28 ft
1 ft = .30 m
1 in = 2.54 cm

Par exemple:

5' = 1 mètre 50
5'5" = 1 mètre 63
6' = 1 mètre 80
100 lb = 45 kg
120 lb = 54 kg
160 lb = 72 kg
180 lb = 81 kg

36 Unité 1

La description physique

La figure, le visage

les cheveux
le front
un oeil (les yeux)
le nez
une oreille
la joue
la bouche
le menton
le cou

Un garçon / une fille . . .

	est **brun(e)**	ou	**blond(e)**	
			roux (rousse) *(redhead)*	
LES CHEVEUX	**a les cheveux bruns** ou	**blonds**	**châtain** *(chestnut)*	
		noirs	**châtain clair** *(gold)*	
		roux	**châtain foncé** *(brown)*	
	a les cheveux longs	ou	**courts** *(short)*	
	lisses *(straight)*	ou	**frisés** *(curly, frizzy)*	
			bouclés *(curly, wavy)*	
LES YEUX	**a les yeux noirs**	ou	**bleus** **verts**	
			gris **marron** *(brown)*	
LE VISAGE (LA FIGURE)	**a le visage ovale**	ou	**rond** **rectangulaire**	
			carré *(square)*	
LA TAILLE	**est grand(e)**	ou	**petit(e)**	
			de taille moyenne *(average)*	
L'APPARENCE GÉNÉRALE	est **mince** *(thin)*	ou	**gros(se)** *(heavyset, fat)*	
	maigre *(skinny)*			
	est **athlétique**			
	fort(e) *(strong)*	ou	**faible** *(weak)*	
	costaud(e) *(solid, well-built)*			
LES SIGNES PARTICULIERS	**porte des lunettes**	ou	**des verres de contact**	
			des lentilles *(lenses)* **de contact**	

▶ **À noter** **la taille** *(height)* **Je mesure** 1 mètre 75. *I am 5 feet 10 inches tall.*
le poids *(weight)* **Je pèse** 65 kilos. *I weigh 143 pounds (65 kilos).*

Teaching Strategy: Warm-Up

Before class, cut out pictures from magazines of different types of people. Hold them up in front of the class and have students give complete sentence descriptions of each one. In order to touch on all aspects of descriptions, you can also ask questions such as «**Est-ce qu'elle est blonde?**» «**Non, elle est brune.**»

Alternate: With the class in a circle, have students describe the person to their left in three to five sentences.

Ce monsieur...

 est chauve

 est barbu; a une barbe

 a une moustache

 a une cicatrice *(scar)*

Ce garçon ...
Cette fille ...

a les cheveux en brosse *(crew-cut)*

a une queue de cheval *(ponytail)*

a des taches de rousseur *(freckles)*

a un grain de beauté *(beauty mark)* sur le menton

---

1 Dix ans après

Dix ans séparent ces deux photos. Entre temps, les élèves du lycée Descartes ont beaucoup changé. Choisissez un(e) élève sur la photo de l'école et décrivez-le(la). Votre partenaire va décrire cette personne maintenant.

Au lycée Descartes, il y a 10 ans

Alice   Marc   Sophie   Isabelle   Julien   Jérôme

Maintenant

Alice   Marc   Sophie   Isabelle   Julien   Jérôme

2 Autoportrait — *Digital* performance space

Faites votre autoportrait en donnant le maximum de détails sur votre aspect physique.

Conversations libres Avec votre partenaire, choisissez l'une des situations suivantes. Composez le dialogue correspondant et jouez-le en classe.

1 Rendez-vous

Votre partenaire vous propose d'aller au cinéma avec un(e) jeune Français(e) qu'il/elle a rencontré(e) récemment. Vous voulez avoir des détails sur cette personne.

2 Un(e) enfant perdu(e)

Vous faites du shopping aux Galeries Lafayette avec votre petit(e) cousin(e). Pendant que vous êtes au rayon des jouets *(toys)*, votre cousin(e) disparaît *(disappears)*. Faites une description de votre cousin(e) au détective du magasin (votre partenaire). Il va vous demander des détails.

Teaching Strategy: Game

Have each student write down two people for whom they could create a description. Then demonstrate by beginning the game with someone you have picked out (e.g., Arnold Schwartzenegger). Students have ten questions (**oui/non**) in order to guess the person chosen.

Differentiation

Cumulative Have students mount a photo of a family member or a celebrity on poster board. Have students label as many physical traits in French as they can. Have the class ask questions about the person and have the student respond with the appropriate answers.

■ **Teaching Strategy: Game**
Use the «**Jacques dit**» game to identify physical characteristics.

■ **Expansion**
For extra practice and cultural development, bring to class reproductions of portraits by famous artists and have the students describe the people portrayed. You might select works by the following artists, explaining briefly who they are:

Modigliani (1884–1920)
Picasso (1881–1973)
Renoir (1841–1919)
Matisse (1869–1954)
Van Gogh (1853–1890)
Manet (1832–1883)

As an alternative, have students use the Internet to find portraits by famous artists and ask them to bring printouts of their favorite ones to describe in class.

■ **Note culturelle**
René Descartes (1596-1650) was a French mathematician, physicist, and philosopher. He is the author of the famous statement: «**Je pense, donc je suis.**» (I think, therefore I am.)

■ **Teaching Strategy**
Have students work in pairs to draw and describe each other.
Variation Have students bring in photos of family members or friends to describe.

■ **Note linguistique**
Note that the following types of adjectives are invariable:
• colors derived from nouns: **marron** *(a chestnut)*, **châtain**, **orange**
• colors modified by an adjective: **bleu clair** *(light blue)*, **vert foncé** *(dark green)*

PRINT
Workbook, pp. 19–21, 109
Unit 1 Resource Book, Partie 1
Audioscripts

AUDIO

Audio Program
CD 1 Track 4

TECHNOLOGY
@HomeTutor
Teacher One Stop
📺 **Projectable Transparencies**
15, *Les parties du corps*
15(o), *Les parties du corps*
Transparency Copymasters,
pp. A31–A32

■ **Photo Note**
In two of the pictures, you can see **la Tour Eiffel** and **le Sacré-Coeur** in Paris.

A **L'usage de l'article avec les parties du corps**

Catherine a **les yeux** bleus.	*Catherine has blue eyes. (=* ***Her eyes*** *are blue.)*
Qu'est-ce que tu as dans **la main**?	*What do you have in* ***your hand?***
J'ai une cicatrice sur **le menton**.	*I have a scar on* ***my chin.***

In French the DEFINITE ARTICLE **(le, la, l', les)** is generally used with parts of the body. (In English, we use possessive adjectives.)

1 ❶ **Monsieur et Madame Dupont**

Monsieur et Madame Dupont sont des touristes français. Complétez la description de Monsieur Dupont et ensuite faites la description de Madame Dupont.

Monsieur Dupont a . . . frisés.

Il porte un chapeau sur . . .
Il a une pipe dans . . .
Il a un foulard autour (de) . . .
Il porte son appareil-photo sur . . .
Il a un magazine (à) . . .
Il porte des sandales (à) . . .

Madame Dupont a . . .

la bouche
les cheveux
le cou
l'épaule
la main
les pieds
la tête

♻ **RAPPEL**
à + le → au   de + le → du
à + les → aux   de + les → des

Teaching Strategy: Variations
• Make a transparency of the illustration in Act. 1 and use yes/no, either/or, and open-ended question sequences.
• Ask students to illustrate the sayings in Act. 3, and then circulate the drawings and have students match the drawings with the correct saying.

Differentiation
Cumulative Divide students into 2 teams. Have students write all of the idioms from p. 39, Act. 3 on poster board. Then players show a written idiom to opposite team members. Players read the idiom, guess its meaning and write a sentence using the idiom on the board. Take turns.

② Dommage!

Aujourd'hui ça ne va pas! Choisissez une chose que vous ne pouvez pas faire et expliquez pourquoi.

Je ne peux pas travailler dans le jardin.

Mon/Ma pauvre! Qu'est-ce que tu as?

J'ai mal au dos.

(aux pieds).

Dommage!

Révision p. R3; p. R12
Avoir mal à + les parties du corps

QUELLE ACTIVITÉ?	POURQUOI?
parler	le genou
sortir avec toi	les pieds
dîner avec toi	la main
faire du jogging	le dos
jouer au foot	la gorge *(throat)*
jouer au ping-pong	les jambes
manger des bonbons	le ventre
transporter cette table	les dents
écouter ce CD de rap	la tête
travailler dans le jardin	les oreilles
??	??

③ Enrichissez votre vocabulaire!

Voici certaines expressions que vous pouvez utiliser avec vos amis. Faites correspondre ces expressions avec leurs équivalents anglais.

1. Ne fais pas la tête!
2. Ne mets pas les pieds dans le plat!
3. Tu as un poil *(hair)* dans la main!
4. Tu as les yeux plus gros que le ventre!
5. Tu as le cœur sur la main!
6. Tu coupes les cheveux en quatre.
7. J'ai l'estomac dans les talons *(heels)*.

a. *I am very hungry.*
b. *You are too greedy. (Your eyes are bigger than your stomach.)*
c. *You are really lazy.*
d. *Don't look so upset.*
e. *Don't put your foot in your mouth.*
f. *You are very finicky. (You are splitting hairs.)*
g. *You are a very generous person. (You wear your heart on your sleeve.)*

ALLONS PLUS LOIN: Autres usages de l'article défini

The definite article is used . . .

Pratique p. 19
Usages de l'article défini

- with dates   **le 18 juin**   **le samedi 3 avril**
- with days of the week (or parts of the day) to refer to a repeated or habitual action
  Compare:
    Que fais-tu **le samedi**?   *What do you do **on Saturdays?***
    Que fais-tu **samedi**?   *What are you doing **on (this) Saturday?***
- with geographical names (countries, states, rivers, mountains, etc.), except cities
  le Canada   **les États-Unis**   but   **Israël, Cuba, Tahiti, Haïti**
  la Virginie   **le Mississippi**   **les Alpes**
- with names of languages, colors, and school subjects
  J'étudie **le français** et **les maths.**
  Mes couleurs préférées sont **le bleu** et **le rouge.**
- with certain titles   **le docteur** Mercat   **la reine** Élizabeth
- with nouns indicating a weight, measure, or quantity
  L'essence coûte un euro **le litre.**   *Gas costs one euro **a liter.***

Réponses: Activité 3
1. d
2. e
3. c (= you use your hands so little that hair is growing on your palms)
4. b
5. g
6. f
7. a

SUPPLEMENTARY VOCABULARY

avoir le cœur gros *to be sad*
être tête en l'air *to be forgetful, to have one's head in the clouds*
casser les pieds (de quelqu'un) *to annoy, to be a pain*
avoir bon pied bon œil *to be still in great shape*
donner un coup de main *to lend a hand, to help*
demander la main (d'une jeune fille) *to propose (marriage)*
mettre le nez dehors *to go out*
prêter l'oreille *to listen carefully; "lend an ear"*

■ Teaching note
You may wish to review years:
1998 dix-neuf cent quatre-vingt-dix-huit
2000 deux mille
2012 deux mille douze
2013 deux mille treize

Full dates are expressed as follows:
14/7/1789 le quatorze juillet dix-sept cent quatre-vingt-neuf

Write important dates in the history of France on small strips of paper and ask each student to pick one. Have students use the Internet or the library resources to research the significance of these dates. Have them report back to class orally.

Teaching Suggestion: Extra Practice

Divide the class into groups. Give situations and have students use a complete sentence to describe where they have pain.

1. Après le marathon de Boston, qu'est-ce qu'on a?
2. Après un concert de rock très fort, qu'est-ce qu'on a?
3. Après avoir mangé de la viande verte, qu'est-ce qu'on a?
4. Après avoir crié pendant 5 heures au match de football, qu'est-ce qu'on a?
5. Après un rendez-vous chez le dentiste, qu'est-ce qu'on a?
6. Après avoir lu 200 pages d'un livre sans lunettes, qu'est-ce qu'on a?

Entre nous

■ **Teaching note**
Have students locate where writers are from on the map on p. R34 or in an atlas.

Entre nous «Je ne suis pas très belle»

Juliette a l'impression de ne pas être belle. Elle parle de son problème dans *Le Journal des Copains*. Lisez ce que les lecteurs de ce journal lui ont répondu.

Chers copains,

Quand je me regarde dans la glace, je ne suis pas satisfaite de moi. J'ai le nez trop long, les oreilles trop grandes, le front trop large, les cheveux trop raides°. En un mot, je ne suis pas très belle. J'ai 15 ans, et pour moi, c'est un grave problème.

Juliette

Valérie (Grenoble),
17 ans

Ne t'inquiète pas !° À 15 ans, toutes les filles pensent qu'elles ne sont pas assez belles. C'était mon cas quand j'avais ton âge. Je me suis trouvée° beaucoup plus belle le jour où un garçon m'a invitée. Patiente un peu ! Un jour, ça va être ton tour.

Valérie

raides *straight*   **ne t'inquiète pas** *don't worry*   **Je me suis trouvée** *I found myself*

Teaching Strategy: Writing Practice

- Display pictures from **La belle et la bête,** or of *Quasimodo*, etc., and have students write letters asking for advice.
- Play background music while students sit in a circle and do a "write-around" giving suggestions for responses to Juliette's "problem."

Differentiation

Cumulative Have students work in groups of 5. Each student in a group reads one of the letters on pp. 40–41. They must retell the main points in their own words in French. The rest of the group writes down the main points of the other students' letters.

Cécile *(Pau)*,
16 ans

La beauté, c'est une chose, mais il y a aussi le look. Ça aussi, c'est important. Tu peux changer de coiffure, te maquiller° un peu, porter des accessoires marrants,° choisir des vêtements qui correspondent à ta personnalité... L'essentiel, c'est de se créer un style. Essaie!° Ce n'est pas si difficile!

Cécile

Guillaume
(Bruxelles), **18 ans**

Tu sais, je ne suis pas très beau non plus, mais ce n'est pas si grave que tu penses. En fait, j'ai des tas° de copains et de copines. La clé° du succès, c'est de se sentir° bien dans sa peau.° La vraie beauté n'est pas physique. Elle dépend des qualités que tu as. Mets les tiennes° en valeur. Et n'oublie pas que la beauté ne fait pas nécessairement le bonheur.° Regarde donc Marilyn Monroe!

Guillaume

Philippe *(Nice)*,
17 ans

La beauté est importante, mais ce n'est pas tout. Ce qui compte aussi, c'est le charme et la personnalité. Quand j'invite une fille, ce n'est pas parce qu'elle est super-jolie, mais parce qu'elle est sympa, drôle, et qu'elle aime rire!° Cultive ton sens de l'humour et tu auras toujours des amis!

Philippe

et vous?

EXPRESSION ORALE
D'après vous, quelle lettre offre les meilleurs conseils à Juliette? Expliquez pourquoi.

EXPRESSION ÉCRITE
Écrivez votre propre *(own)* réponse à la lettre de Juliette.

te maquiller *put on makeup*
marrants = drôles *(slang)*
essaie *try*
des tas = quantités
la clé *key*
se sentir *to feel*
dans sa peau *inside (in one's skin)*
les tiennes = tes qualités
le bonheur *happiness*
rire* *to laugh*

Teaching Suggestion: Extra Practice
Pose the following question to students and have them discuss in groups, or write short responses if they prefer:

Philippe dit **«Cultive ton sens de l'humour et tu auras toujours des amis.»**
L'humour est-il une qualité importante ou pas?
Pourquoi?

Differentiation
Metacognitive Have students write two separate lists of traits that define beauty; one for inner beauty and one for physical beauty. Ask them to explain their reasons for the words on each list. Then have students identify a famous person who represents each list and explain why.

■ **Teaching Strategy:
Additional Activities**
- Donnez trois qualités très importantes. Pourquoi sont-elles importantes?
- Donnez un défaut. Pourquoi est-ce un problème?
- Quelle est votre qualité principale?
- Regardez les photos. Qui est le/la plus sympathique? Le plus beau/la plus belle?

■ **Proverbe**
«La beauté ne fait pas le bonheur» is a play on the proverb «L'argent ne fait pas le bonheur.»

■ **Teaching Suggestion**
Have students use the Internet or the library to find other famous quotes or proverbs in French that relate to beauty or happiness. Have them share their findings and discuss the proverbs and quotes as a class.

■ **Irregular Verbs**
(see Appendix C)
rire

Unité 1 41

my.hrw.com

Le Français pratique

La toilette et les soins personnels

■ **Note linguistique**
Compare and contrast:
essuyer *to wipe*
s'essuyer *to dry [one's hands] with a
    towel*
sécher *to dry (out)*
se sécher *to dry [one's hair] with a
    dryer*

■ **Pronunciation**
Eye-liner is pronounced as in English:
/ajlajnœr/

■ **Note culturelle**
Un gant de toilette is a washcloth
that resembles a pocket with a slit for
one's hand.

■ **Teaching Strategy**
Using their flashcards, students set up
pair dialogs: «Qu'est-ce qu'on fait
avec [un séchoir]?» «On se sèche les
cheveux.» (See p. 36)

42 Unité 1

La toilette et les soins personnels

Révision p. R12
Les parties du corps

Olivier utilise . . .   pour . . .

le rasoir	se raser	**se raser** *to shave*
le savon	se laver la figure	
la brosse à dents	se brosser les dents	**se brosser** *to brush*
la serviette	s'essuyer les mains	**s'essuyer** *to (wipe) dry*
les ciseaux	se couper les ongles *(nails)*	**se couper** *to cut*

Charlotte utilise . . .   pour . . .

le shampooing	se laver les cheveux	
le séchoir	se sécher les cheveux	**se sécher** *to dry*
le peigne	se peigner	**se peigner** *to comb one's hair*
le rouge à lèvres	se maquiller	**se maquiller** *to apply makeup*
l'eye-liner	se maquiller les yeux	

Quelques autres articles de toilette et produits de beauté

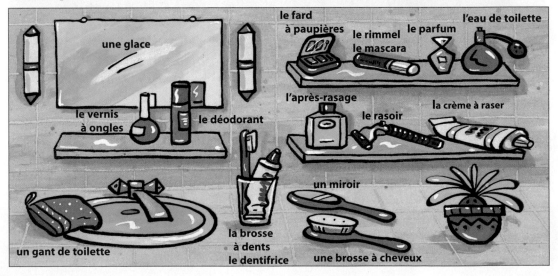

une glace · le fard à paupières · le rimmel · le mascara · le parfum · l'eau de toilette · le vernis à ongles · le déodorant · l'après-rasage · le rasoir · la crème à raser · un miroir · un gant de toilette · la brosse à dents · le dentifrice · une brosse à cheveux

Teaching Suggestion: DVD Program

The *Vidéo-drame: Bonjour, Monsieur Pasquier* in Unit 1 introduces the topic of toiletries and personal care. Students will learn vocabulary that will help them describe their morning routine, as well as typical items found in the bathroom. Show the video once all the way through to familiarize students with the new vocabulary. Next, present the video in short segments, asking students comprehension questions, such as:

Qu'est ce-que Mélanie utilise pour sécher ses cheveux?

1 **La trousse de toilette** *(toiletry kit)*

Ce week-end vous n'allez pas rester chez vous.
Mentionnez cinq articles—ou plus—que
vous allez mettre dans votre trousse de toilette . . .

- si vous allez faire du camping
- si vous allez passer le week-end chez vos cousins.

Maintenant imaginez que vous allez en France cet été.
Faites une liste de dix articles ou produits
que vous allez emporter *(take along)* avec vous.

Comparez vos listes avec celles de votre partenaire.
Combien de choses identiques avez-vous prises?
Combien de choses différentes?

2 **Qu'est-ce qu'ils vont faire?**

Lisez les descriptions suivantes. Puis mentionnez deux ou trois choses que
chaque personne va faire.

▶ **Philippe vient de jouer au foot. Il va dans la douche du stade.**
Il va prendre une douche. Il va se laver les cheveux.
Ensuite, il va se sécher et se mettre du déodorant.

1. Il est sept heures du matin. Monsieur Lebot, président
de la Banque Industrielle, se lève et va dans la salle de bains.
2. Il est onze heures du soir. Jérôme va se coucher. D'abord il va dans la salle de bains.
3. Ce soir, la fameuse chanteuse d'opéra va jouer le rôle de Carmen. Elle est dans sa
loge *(dressing room)* où elle se prépare pour la représentation *(performance)*.
4. Caroline va dîner avec Vincent, son nouveau copain, dans un restaurant très élégant.
Elle se prépare pour l'occasion.

3 **En voyage**

Vous êtes en voyage avec un groupe.
Demandez à votre partenaire l'un des objets
suivants et expliquez pourquoi vous
en avez besoin.

> Tu as
> du shampooing?

Oui,
pourquoi?

Je voudrais me laver
les cheveux.

LE RENDEZ-VOUS LOUPÉ
(Vocabulary/Reflexive verbs)
Ask students to give hypothetical
reasons for the following situations:
1. Oliver didn't get a date with
Charlotte. Why did Charlotte
refuse to go out with him? What
did or didn't he do/use in order
to prepare himself to ask her out?
2. Charlotte didn't get a date with
Oliver. Oliver likes simple/natural
girls. What did/didn't Charlotte
do/use that made Oliver not want
to go out with her?

Teaching Strategy
Use flashcards and a picture of
a trousse de toilette and have
students "fill" it according to
various situations.

■ **Teaching Note**
For Activity 3, present supplementary
expressions as necessary, e.g.: **se
faire les ongles, se mettre du
déodorant, se mettre du parfum, se
regarder,** etc.

SUPPLEMENTARY VOCABULARY

une lame de rasoir *razor*
blade
l'après-shampooing
conditioner
le shampooing colorant
la laque à cheveux *hair spray*
le gel coiffant *styling gel*

la crème *lotion*
le fond de teint *foundation*
la poudre *powder*

le sourcil /surci/ *eyebrow*
le cil /cil/ *eyelash*
la paupière *eyelid*
la lèvre *lip*
la peau *skin*

The DVD contains closed captions in French,
which you can choose to display. You may want
to play a segment once without captions. Then
play the segment a second time while students
do the video activities. The third time through,
display the captions so students can check their
comprehension and correct the video activities
themselves.

Differentiation

Synthetic/Analytic Have pairs of students
write out names of objects and pronominal
verbs on index cards. Have students separate
cards into two piles, one for objects and one for
verbs. Students draw cards from each deck and
try to match objects with appropriate verbs.

■ **Teaching Strategy:
Extra Practice**

(Reflexive verbs: Imperative)
Have students form groups of 2 or 3
and come up with sentences for the
following situations using reflexive
verbs in the imperative:
1. Give 5 suggestions to a friend
   who's going for an interview at a
   trendy fashion magazine.
2. Give 5 suggestions to your friends
   of things the three of you should/
   shouldn't do before going out
   dancing.
As students volunteer their answers,
write them on the board in two
separate columns in order to assist
the visual learners.

**Teaching Strategy:
Extra Practice**

(Reflexive verbs: Future)
Tell students that they have just been
asked out by a famous male/female
star (e.g., Ben Affleck/Gwyneth
Paltrow). Have each student say what
he/she is going to do in order to
prepare for the date. What are
students <u>not</u> going to do? Each
student should give one answer.

A Les verbes réfléchis

REFLEXIVE VERBS are formed with a REFLEXIVE PRONOUN that represents
the same person as the subject.

Je **me** lave.   Monsieur Martin **se** rase.

FORMS

Review the forms of **se laver** in the present and the imperative.

PRESENT				IMPERATIVE	
				AFFIRMATIVE	**NEGATIVE**
AFFIRMATIVE	je	**me**	lave		
	tu	**te**	laves	**lave-toi!**	**ne te lave pas!**
	il/elle/on	**se**	lave		
	nous	**nous**	lavons	**lavons-nous!**	**ne nous lavons pas!**
	vous	**vous**	lavez	**lavez-vous!**	**ne vous lavez pas!**
	ils/elles	**se**	lavent		
NEGATIVE	**je ne me lave pas**				
INTERROGATIVE	**est-ce que tu te laves?** **te laves-tu?**				

INFINITIVE CONSTRUCTIONS

Je vais **me** laver.   Je **ne** vais **pas me** laver les cheveux.
Nous allons **nous** brosser les dents.   Vous **n'**allez **pas vous** raser.

→ In an infinitive construction, the reflexive pronoun comes immediately before the verb
and represents the same person as the subject.

USES

Reflexive verbs are very common in French. They are used:

• to describe actions that the subject is performing on or for himself/herself.
  Catherine **se regarde** dans la glace.   *Catherine **is looking at herself** in the mirror.*
  Je **me fais** un sandwich.   *I **am fixing myself** a sandwich.*

• to describe many aspects of one's DAILY ROUTINE.
  Je **me lève** à sept heures.   *I get up at seven.*

→ Note the use of the DEFINITE ARTICLE after reflexive verbs.
  Tu te brosses **les** dents.   *You are brushing your teeth.*
  Alice se coupe **les** ongles.   *Alice is cutting her nails.*

Teaching Strategy: Warm-Up

Pass out slips of paper with reflexive or
non-reflexive verbs on them to each student in
the class. Ask students to act out their verb so
that the class can guess. As the verbs are
guessed, write two columns on the board—one
with reflexives and one with non-reflexives. At
the end, ask students if they can explain the
difference between the two columns and give
the counterpart to each reflexive or
non-reflexive verb. (e.g., if **laver** is in the
non-reflexive column, have students come up
with the verb **se laver** and give a sentence for
each of them.)

4 Le matin

Choisissez une personne et dites ce qu'elle fait et ce qu'elle va faire après. Soyez logique!

Révision p. R2

Le présent des verbes
comme préférer: se sécher, pp. R20–21
comme payer: s'essuyer, pp. R20–21

Pratique p. 21

Le présent des verbes

QUI?		QUOI?	
moi	Jean-Philippe	• se laver	• se brosser les dents
toi	Madame Lescure	• se raser	• se laver la figure
nous	Monsieur Dupont	• se maquiller	• se laver les mains
vous	Éric et Thomas	• se peigner	• se laver les cheveux
Alice	Sylvie et Catherine	• s'essuyer	• se couper les ongles
		• se regarder dans	• se brosser les cheveux
		la glace	• se sécher les cheveu

▸ **Tu te sèches les cheveux. Après, tu vas te peigner.**

5 Publicité 📝

Composez des slogans publicitaires pour les produits suivants.

Radio-Symphonie	se raser
le savon SAMBON	se laver
le dentifrice SOURIRE	se laver les cheveux
l'eau de toilette VÉSUVE	se maquiller
le shampooing CAPILLO	se couper les ongles
le séchoir SAHARA	se couper les cheveux
le rasoir BLIP	se brosser les dents
les ciseaux CLIP	se parfumer
la brosse à dents BRIL	se sécher les cheveux
le fard CLÉOPÂTRE	se réveiller en musique

▸ **Mesdemoiselles, maquillez-vous avec le fard Cléopâtre!**

6 Baby-sitting 💬

Vous faites du baby-sitting pour l'enfant de vos voisins français. Dites-lui de faire les choses suivantes. L'enfant (votre partenaire) va vous répondre qu'il/elle ne peut pas. Puis, il/elle va vous donner une excuse.

ACTIONS	EXCUSES POSSIBLES
• se peigner	Je ne trouve pas . . .
• se laver les mains	Je ne sais pas où est . . .
• se laver les cheveux	Je ne peux pas trouver . . .
• s'essuyer les mains	J'ai perdu . . .
• se brosser les dents	
• se sécher les cheveux	

▸ — <u>Brosse-toi les dents!</u>
    — Je ne peux pas me brosser les dents!
    — Et pourquoi donc?
    — <u>J'ai perdu</u> ma brosse à dents.
       (<u>Je ne trouve pas</u> le dentifrice.)

ALLONS PLUS LOIN

To express what you or other people can do by themselves, use the construction:

STRESS PRONOUN + **même(s)**

    J'ai réparé mon vélo **moi-même**. *I fixed my bike* **by myself**.

→ **Même** is also used to reinforce a stress pronoun referring to the subject.
    Jérôme parle toujours **de lui-même**. *Jérôme always talks* **about himself**.

Pratique p. 22

Moi-même, toi-même, etc.

■ Variation

Have one student give the first sentence, and then call on another student to provide the second sentence.

■ Allons plus loin

If you decide to assign further practice, you may want to present the complete chart:
    moi-même, toi-même, lui-même, etc.

■ Teaching Strategy: Game

Using three dice, one black, one red, one green, have students construct sentences (they may be absurd!): black=subject; red=first action; green=second action.

■ Teaching Strategy: Expansion

Divide the class into groups. Students create an ad and a short **publicité** to present to the class.

■ Variation: Activity 6

Give the following instructions: Demandez à votre partenaire s'il/elle fait les choses suivantes. Il/Elle répond négativement et donne une raison. Exemple:
—Est-ce que tu te brosses les dents?—
    Non, je ne me brosse pas les dents.
—Pourquoi?
—Parce que j'ai perdu ma brosse à dents!

Verb Drill

Using specific hand motions which should remain constant throughout the year, drill the class to practice reflexive conjugations. Example: SE LAVER

Point one finger to yourself: say **je me lave**	Point two fingers (two hands) to yourself: say **nous nous lavons**
To the class: say **tu te laves**	to the class: say **vous vous lavez**
To the right: say **il se lave**	to the right: say **ils se lavent**
To the left: say **elle se lave**	to the left: say **elles se lavent**

For the negative, use the same motions but shake your head. Also: switch the order of the conjugations, speed up the pace, or put students in pairs. This is a fast and efficient drill.

INFO MAGAZINE

Theme: Daily activities

RESOURCES

TECHNOLOGY

Teacher One Stop

Projectable Transparencies

17, *La Résidence Bon Repos*

Transparency Copymasters,
pp. A36–A38

■ Teaching Strategy

These readings should be an interesting "break" in the teaching sequence and provide both enjoyment and practice for students.

■ Notes linguistiques

• Generally, **une résidence** is a group of homes (houses or apartments). **Une résidence secondaire** is a country home.

• **Un(e) banlieusard(e)** is a person who lives in the Paris **banlieue**.

■ Teaching Suggestion

Have students research **résidences secondaires** for sale in various regions of France on the Internet. Have them choose a home they like and bring the ad to present it in class, explaining why they like this particular region and/or home.

À LA RÉSIDENCE
BON REPOS

Aujourd'hui, les gens des villes habitent généralement dans des immeubles.° Ces immeubles ont beaucoup d'avantages . . . et quelques petits inconvénients.

Un jour comme un autre à la résidence° «Bon Repos» dans la banlieue° parisienne. Il est six heures du matin. Tout est calme. . . Tout d'un coup°. . .

SIXIÈME ÉTAGE

Drin. . . Drin . . . Un réveil° sonne° chez Monsieur Léveillé. Drin. . .Drin. . . Monsieur Léveillé se réveille en sursaut°. . . Puis il se lève, met sa robe de chambre° et va dans la salle de bains. Il se regarde dans la glace, se brosse les dents. Ensuite, il branche° son rasoir électrique et commence à se raser. Zzz. . . Zzz. . .

CINQUIÈME ÉTAGE

Le bruit° du rasoir électrique de Monsieur Léveillé réveille Madame Dumoulin. Elle ouvre un oeil, puis l'autre, et attend deux ou trois minutes. Finalement, elle se lève et va dans la cuisine pour se préparer une tasse de café. Elle branche son nouveau moulin° électrique. Grr. . . Grr. . .

QUATRIÈME ÉTAGE

Le moulin à café de Madame Dumoulin réveille Mademoiselle Lasouplesse. Elle se lève, enfile° un short et un tee-shirt, met un DVD de gymnastique et commence ses exercices. Une, deux. . . une, deux. . . une, deux . . .

TROISIÈME ÉTAGE

Quand il entend Mademoiselle Lasouplesse faire sa gymnastique, Monsieur Trémolo se réveille. Il va dans la salle de bains et prend une douche. Quand il se lave, Monsieur Trémolo adore chanter ses airs d'opéra favoris: «Toréador, toréador. . .»*

* «Toréador» is a well-known aria from Bizet's **Carmen.**

DEUXIÈME ÉTAGE

La belle voix de Monsieur Trémolo réveille Madame Bellamy. Elle se lève, prend un bain, et se lave les cheveux. Puis, elle s'habille, se peigne et se maquille. . .

À huit heures et demie, tous les locataires° de la résidence «Bon Repos» sont partis pour leurs occupations de la journée. . . Tous sauf° un. C'est Monsieur Morphée, le locataire du premier étage. Il travaille comme portier° de nuit dans un grand hôtel. À l'heure où les autres locataires se rendent° à leur travail, lui, il rentre chez lui. Là, il se déshabille et prend un bon bain. «Quelle chance d'habiter dans une résidence si calme» pense-t-il. Puis, il va dans sa chambre, met son pyjama, se couche et s'endort° d'un profond sommeil.

Une journée comme les autres vient de commencer.

---

immeubles *apartment buildings* **résidence** = *l'immeuble* **banlieue** *suburbs* **Tout d'un coup** *all of a sudden*
réveil *alarm clock* **sonne** *rings* **en sursaut** *with a start* **robe de chambre** *bathrobe* **branche** *plugs in*
bruit *noise* **moulin** *coffee grinder* **enfile** = *met* **locataires** *tenants* **sauf** = *excepté* **portier** *doorman*
se rendent = *vont* **s'endort** *falls asleep*

Notes culturelles

• In Greek mythology, **Morpheus (Morphée)** is the god of sleep. You may want to explain this term and others to students.

• Remind students that in France, the first floor corresponds to the second floor in an American building. The ground floor is called **le rez-de-chaussée**.

• **Georges Bizet** (1838–1875) wrote **Carmen** in 1875. For more information on Bizet, go to p. 185.

Teaching Strategy
Make copies of the illustrations and cut them up. Read the descriptions and have students put the "floors" in the correct order.

Follow-Up
In groups of 4 or 5, have students describe their own routine and create an "apartment" story.

et vous?

À VOTRE TOUR
- Dites à quelle heure vous vous levez d'habitude et ce que vous faites après.
- Dites comment vous trouvez l'histoire que vous avez lue: réaliste? amusante? triste? exagérée? Expliquez pourquoi.

EXPRESSION ÉCRITE
Décrivez les habitudes des personnes de votre famille. Dites à quelle heure chaque personne se lève et ce qu'elle fait ensuite. (Votre description peut être réaliste ou imaginaire.)

Teaching Strategy: Expansion Questions

1. Qui se réveille en premier?	M. Léveillé
2. Qu'est-ce qui réveille Mlle Lasouplesse?	Le moulin à café de Mme Dumoulin
3. Qu'est-ce que Mme Dumoulin se prépare?	Elle se prépare une tasse de café.
4. Qu'est ce que M Léveillé fait avant de se brosser les dents?	Il se regarde dans la glace.
5. Est-ce que M Morphée se réveille à 8h30?	Non, il se couche.
6. Est-ce que M Trémolo prend un bain?	Non, il prend une douche.
7. Que fait Mlle Lasouplesse quand elle se réveille?	Elle fait sa gymnastique.
8. Qu'est-ce qui réveille Mme Bellamy?	La belle voix de M Trémolo.

48 Unité 1

La routine quotidienne

Je me réveille à 7 heures et quart. Je me lève, et puis je me lave.

Il y a beaucoup de choses qu'on fait tous les jours. Ces choses font partie de la routine quotidienne *(daily)*. Ici Stéphanie explique sa routine quotidienne:

Le matin . . .
    Je me réveille à 7 heures et quart.
    Je me lève.
    Je me lave.
    Je prends **un bain** *(bath)* ou **une douche** *(shower)*.
    Je m'habille.

se réveiller *to wake up*
se lever *to get up*
se laver *to wash*
s'habiller *to get dressed*

Après le petit déjeuner . . .
    Je me prépare.
    Puis, **je me rends** à l'école.
    Je me dépêche pour être à l'heure.
    (Si je suis en retard, **je m'excuse.**)

se préparer *to get ready*
se rendre à *to go to*
se dépêcher *to hurry*
s'excuser *to apologize*

En classe . . .
    J'étudie.
    À midi, **je m'amuse** avec mes copains.

s'amuser *to have fun*

L'après-midi, après les cours . . .
    Je me promène en ville.
    Je m'arrête parfois chez le marchand de glaces,
        et je m'achète une glace.
    Je rentre et **je me repose** un peu.

se promener *to take a walk*
s'arrêter *to stop*
s'acheter *to buy (oneself)*
se reposer *to rest*

À sept heures et demie . . .
    Je me mets à table
        et je dîne avec ma famille.
    Puis je fais mes devoirs.

se mettre à table *to sit down to eat*

Le soir, **vers** *(at about)* onze heures . . .
    Je me déshabille.
    Je me couche.

    Et finalement **je m'endors.**

se déshabiller *to get undressed*
se coucher *to go to bed*
s'endormir *to go to sleep*

Teaching Suggestion: DVD Program

The *Vidéo-drame: Bonjour, Monsieur Pasquier* in Unit 1 focuses on the daily routine of the Pasquier family. Note that the verbs in these expressions are reflexive. You may want to list some of the verbs that students should listen for, such as **s'habiller, se laver,** and **se dépêcher** before playing the video.

Differentiation

Synthetic/Analytic Have students write pronominal verbs in their notebook. Have them put an asterisk next to spelling change or irregular verbs. Have students practice the full conjugation of these verbs orally. Have students write each verb's past participle.

Révision pp. R20–21

Pratique p. 23

Verbes comme *acheter, se lever, se promener*

1 et vous?

Décrivez certains aspects de votre vie. Comparez vos réponses avec celles de votre partenaire.

1. En semaine, je me réveille . . .
   • avant sept heures
   • à sept heures
   • ??

2. Je me rends à l'école . . .
   • à pied
   • en bus
   • à vélo
   • ??

3. Le soir, je me couche . . .
   • avant dix heures
   • après onze heures
   • ??

4. Généralement, je m'endors . . .
   • vite *(fast)*
   • assez vite
   • difficilement
   • ??

5. Le dimanche, je ne me lève jamais . . .
   • avant huit heures
   • avant neuf heures
   • ??

6. Quand j'ai du temps libre, je préfère . . .
   • me reposer
   • me promener en ville
   • me rendre chez mes amis
   • ??

7. Quand je me promène en ville, j'aime mieux m'arrêter . . .
   • dans les magasins
   • dans un fast-food
   • ??

8. Avec mon argent, je préfère m'acheter . . .
   • des jeux vidéo
   • des vêtements
   • des magazines
   • ??

9. Je me dépêche le plus pour aller . . .
   • à l'école
   • à un rendez-vous
   • à un concert
   • ??

10. En général, je m'excuse quand . . .
   • j'ai tort
   • je suis en retard
   • ??

Conversations libres

Avec votre partenaire, choisissez l'une des situations suivantes. Composez le dialogue correspondant et jouez-le en classe.

Digital performance space

1 Camarade de chambre

Vous êtes étudiant(e) à l'université de Montréal. Vous cherchez un(e) camarade de chambre pour le trimestre prochain. Expliquez votre routine quotidienne à un(e) autre étudiant(e) (votre partenaire). Ensuite, posez-lui des questions sur sa routine.

2 Activités du dimanche

Vous avez invité un(e) camarade français(e) (votre partenaire) à passer le week-end chez vous. Expliquez-lui ce que vous faites le dimanche. Demandez-lui s'il/si elle fait les mêmes choses.

quarante-neuf **49**
Le Français pratique

SUPPLEMENTARY VOCABULARY

s'allonger *to lie down*
s'entraîner *to train, practice (a sport)*
s'étirer *to stretch*
se changer *to change (clothes)*
se démaquiller *to take off one's makeup*
se doucher *to take a shower*
se relaxer *to relax*

■ **Verb Forms** You may have students review the forms of **mettre** (p. R2) and **s'endormir** (like **sortir,** p. R2).

■ **Variation: A/B Pair Activity**

Votre partenaire répond à la question, puis vous demande si vous faites la même chose. Exemple:
—(Je me réveille avant sept heures.) **Et toi? Est-ce que tu te réveilles avant sept heures en semaine?**
—Oui, je me réveille avant sept heures./Non, je ne me réveille pas avant sept heures, je me réveille à huit heures.

■ **Teaching Note**

You may want to review the formation of information questions:
À quelle heure est-ce que tu te lèves?

■ **Teaching Suggestion**

Have a francophone exchange student visit your class. Students can ask the exchange student about his/her leisure activities, school, home, community, and other topics of interest.

Teaching Strategy: Warm-Up

Put the verbs from p. 48 on the board or on a transparency. Have students write a story about what twin sisters, Annique and Hélène, do every day from morning until bedtime. The following day, have students rewrite their story in the past tense.
Pre-AP skill: Sequence events.

Differentiation

Sequential Have one student interview another student. Have them change the verbs on p. 49, Act. 1 to the informal second person. Exchange roles. Ask them to take notes on what each other says. Then ask them to review their notes out loud with their partner.

PRINT

Workbook, pp. 23–24, 113

Unit 1 Resource Book, Partie 2

Audioscripts

AUDIO

Audio Program
CD 1 Track 12

TECHNOLOGY

@HomeTutor

■ **Teaching Note**

The agreement of the past participle depends on whether the reflexive pronoun functions as a direct or indirect object pronoun.

• DIRECT object = AGREEMENT
Catherine **s'est lavée.**
  She washed herself.
Nous **nous sommes amusés.**
  We amused ourselves.

• INDIRECT object = NO AGREEMENT
Catherine **s'est lavé** les mains.
  She washed the hands (belonging to herself).
Nous **nous sommes acheté** des vêtements.
  We bought clothes for ourselves.

Since the agreement of the past participle requires sophisticated grammatical analysis, you may want to present the above explanation only to advanced students.

Variation: Game

Activity 1 may be done as "Signature Bingo/Lotto." Call the names of students, who give personalized responses to the questions.

A Le passé composé des verbes réfléchis

The PASSÉ COMPOSÉ of reflexive verbs is formed with **être**.

AFFIRMATIVE	je **me suis** lavé		je **me suis** lavée	
	tu **t'es** lavé		tu **t'es** lavée	
	il/on **s'est** lavé		elle **s'est** lavée	
	nous **nous sommes** lavés		nous **nous sommes** lavées	
	vous **vous êtes** lavé(s)		vous **vous êtes** lavée(s)	
	ils **se sont** lavés		elles **se sont** lavées	
NEGATIVE	je ne me suis pas lavé		je ne me suis pas lavée	
INTERROGATIVE	est-ce que tu t'es lavé?		est-ce que tu t'es lavée?	
	t'es-tu lavé?		lavée?	

Usually, <u>but not always</u>, the past participle agrees with the subject.

Éric s'est promené.   **Anne et Claire se sont promen**ées avec lui.

→ There is <u>no agreement</u> when the reflexive verb is directly followed by a NOUN. Compare:

Stéphanie **s'est lav**ée.   Elle **s'est lav**é <u>les mains.</u>

Note also:
Catherine et Sophie **se sont achet**é <u>des vêtements.</u>

1 Samedi dernier

Demandez à votre partenaire s'il/si elle a fait les choses suivantes samedi dernier. Votre partenaire peut donner des précisions correspondant aux questions.

▶ se lever tard (à quelle heure?)

1. se promener (où?)
2. s'acheter des vêtements (quels vêtements?)
3. s'acheter autre chose (quoi?)
4. s'amuser (comment?)
5. se reposer (quand?)
6. se coucher tard (à quelle heure?)

> Est-ce que tu t'es levée tard samedi dernier?

> Non, je ne me suis pas levée tard.
> Je me suis levée à 8 heures.

Teaching Strategy: Warm-Up

Put the story about Annique and Hélène (see page 48) on a transparency before class. Tell students that this is not what they do every day but simply what they did yesterday. Have the students put the story into the **passé composé** sentence by sentence.

Differentiation

Repetitive Have students review the **passé composé** with pronominal verbs and then review the rules of agreement. Have students write examples with and without agreement in their notebook under the headings Agreement/No Agreement.

2 Qu'est-ce qu'ils ont fait?

Informez-vous sur les personnes suivantes et dites
ce qu'elles ont fait. Pour cela, utilisez les verbes suggérés.

▶ Monsieur Marty a pris son rasoir.   **Il s'est rasé.**

1. Caroline a pris le dentifrice.
2. Tu as pris tes vêtements.
3. Nous avons entendu le réveil *(alarm clock).*
4. À minuit, tu es allé dans ta chambre.
5. Vous avez pris une semaine de vacances.
6. Nous sommes allées à la campagne.
7. Marc et Philippe ont vu un film très drôle.
8. Dans le bus, j'ai marché *(stepped)* sur les pieds
   de quelqu'un.
9. Le chauffeur de bus a vu le feu-rouge *(red light).*
10. Tu as pris les ciseaux.
11. Vous avez voulu être à l'heure au rendez-vous.

s'amuser
s'arrêter
se brosser les dents
se coucher
se couper les ongles
se dépêcher
s'excuser
s'habiller
se promener
se raser
se reposer
se réveiller

3 La journée d'un mannequin

Christine est mannequin *(model)* pour un magazine de mode. Lisez comment elle
décrit sa journée:

Je me réveille à huit heures. Je ne me lève pas immédiatement.
J'attends dix minutes. Ensuite je me lève et je vais dans la salle de bains.
Là, je prends une douche et je me lave les cheveux. Ensuite je me maquille
et je m'habille. Vers neuf heures, je descends dans la cuisine et
je me prépare un petit déjeuner très léger *(light)*. Après, je regarde
le journal. Je téléphone à mon magazine pour faire mes rendez-vous.
Je réponds à mon courrier *(mail)*.

Vers dix heures et demie, je sors et je fais les courses. Je rentre
chez moi, mais je ne déjeune pas. À une heure, je prends un taxi. Je vais
directement au magazine pour les séances *(sessions)* de photo.
Je travaille tout l'après-midi.

À sept heures, je rentre chez moi et je dîne. Ensuite je regarde un film
à la télé. À onze heures je me couche et je m'endors.

Chaque jour, Christine suit la même routine. Décrivez ce qu'elle a fait hier.

▶ **Hier, Christine s'est réveillée à huit heures . . .**

4 Ma routine personnelle

Décrivez votre routine personnelle. Pour cela, composez un petit paragraphe où vous
racontez ce que vous avez fait hier. (Si nécessaire, utilisez votre imagination!) Ensuite,
comparez votre journée avec celle de votre partenaire.

▶ **Hier, c'était samedi [dimanche]. Je me suis réveillé(e) à . . .**

cinquante et un   **51**
Langue et Communication

■ Conjugation Drill
Give students the verb to be
drilled: SE MAQUILLER. See
p. 45 for Verb drill.

■ Note linguistique
Un mannequin (model) is
always used in the masculine
form. **Un mannequin** also
means "mannequin."

■ Teaching Strategy: Variation
Activity 3 may be presented as a
dictée or cloze activity.

■ Teaching Strategy: Variation
Do Activity 4 as an A/B activity.

Teaching Strategy: Game
Verbal Hot Potato
Students stand in a circle holding pictures of
actions. The teacher says «**Hier, je me suis ...**»
and the student holding that picture says
«**Non, je ne me suis pas ..., je me suis ...**»
Play passes to another student.

Differentiation
Metacognitive Divide students into groups.
Have students in each group take turns reading
lines from Act. 3, p. 51. (project story from a
transparency and ask students to point to the
line that is being read) as other students act
out the story. As students do this task, ask
them to explain what is happening in their own
words.

SUPPLEMENTARY VOCABULARY

Also: **en bonne/mauvaise**
santé
Ça sent bon/mauvais.
avoir l'air ...
soucieux(se) *worried*
détendu ≠ agité
tranquille ≠ irrité

■ **Note linguistique**
avoir l'air + ADJECTIVE
The adjective can:
• remain masculine (to agree with **air**)
Pauline a l'air **fatigué**.
• agree with the subject
Pauline a l'air **fatiguée**.

La condition physique et les sentiments

COMMENT DEMANDER DES NOUVELLES À UN(E) AMI(E)

Ça va?
Comment te sens-tu? | *How do you feel?*
Qu'est-ce que tu as? | *What's the matter?*
Qu'est-ce qu'il y a? | *What's wrong?*

| **se sentir** *to feel* |

COMMENT RÉPONDRE

Ça va. :)

Je me sens | **bien.**
en forme (*in shape*)

décontracté(e) (*relaxed*)

Je suis | **heureux (heureuse).**
content(e)
de bonne humeur
(*in a good mood*)

Ça ne va pas. :(

Je me sens | **mal.**
malade
fatigué(e) (*tired*)
tendu(e) (*tense, uptight*)

Je suis | **malheureux (malheureuse).**
triste (*sad*)
de mauvaise humeur (*in a bad mood*)
énervé(e) (*upset*)
furieux (furieuse)
en colère (*angry*)

COMMENT DÉCRIRE QUELQU'UN

Ton ami(e) | **semble** **calme.**
a l'air

Il/Elle | **semble**
a l'air | **perplexe.**
préoccupé(e) (*worried*)
inquiet (inquiète) (*worried*)
déçu(e) (*disappointed*)

| **sembler** *to seem*
avoir l'air *to look, appear* |

 À noter

Sentir is conjugated like **dormir**.
sentir | *to smell* | Est-ce que **tu sens** cette bonne odeur?
se sentir (+ adjective | *to feel* | Est-ce que **tu te sens** fatigué?
or expression) | | **Je me sens** en forme.
ressentir (+ noun) | *to feel (a pain or an emotion)* | **Je ressens** beaucoup d'admiration pour cette personne.

Teaching Strategy: Dialog Development

Have students in pairs develop and present two 10-line dialogs:
• One dialog asking about each other and how things are going
• One dialog asking about a mutual friend who seems mad, sad, upset, angry...

Differentiation

Cumulative Have students ask the person to the right of them how things are going. The student asking the question holds a thumb up or thumb down signal and the student answering must respond accordingly.

1 Ça va?

Choisissez trois des situations suivantes. Décrivez votre condition ou vos sentiments dans chacun des cas.

- Vous êtes en vacances.
- Vous avez un examen.
- Vous avez un rendez-vous.
- Vous faites du sport.
- Vous mangez trop.
- Vous étudiez trop.
- Vous avez une bonne note à un examen.
- Vous étudiez beaucoup mais vous avez une mauvaise note.

- Vous vous disputez avec votre copain (copine).
- Votre copain (copine) n'est pas à l'heure à un rendez-vous.
- Votre frère (soeur) oublie votre anniversaire.
- Le professeur est malade.
- Votre cousin(e) vous téléphone à une heure du matin.
- Vos professeurs sont contents de vous.
- Vos amis vous critiquent.

▶ Quand j'ai un examen, je me sens malade (je me sens tendu(e), décontracté(e) . . .)

2 Qu'est-ce qu'ils ont?

Décrivez les personnes suivantes. Avec votre partenaire, trouvez deux raisons pour cette situation.

▶ — Monsieur Moreau a l'air en colère.

— C'est parce qu'il a eu un accident de voiture.

— Non, je ne suis pas d'accord. C'est parce que son fils est rentré à deux heures du matin.

M. Moreau   Thomas   Pauline   Juliette

Jean-Philippe   Mme Tessier   Charlotte   Christophe

3 Créa-dialogue

C'est lundi matin. D'habitude votre partenaire est toujours de bonne humeur. Mais aujourd'hui il/elle est de mauvaise humeur. Vous voulez savoir pourquoi.

— Ça va?

— Non, ça ne va pas.

— Qu'est-ce que tu as?

— Je suis triste.

— Et pourquoi donc?

— Mon copain a oublié la date de mon anniversaire.

- *Use another expression.*
- *Express another feeling: anger, disappointment, worry . . .*
- *Give an original and appropriate reason.*

Teaching Strategy: Comprehension

Use enlarged versions of the art in Activity 2 for input:

«Regardez M. Moreau.
Qu'est-ce qu'il a?
Il a l'air en colère.
Je me demande pourquoi.»

Differentiation

Synthetic/Analytic, Gifted & Talented Have students write a humorous poem, skit, or short story illustrating the difference between **sentir** and **se sentir**.

PRINT
Workbook, pp. 25–26, 114
Unit 1 Resource Book, Partie 2
Audioscripts

AUDIO
 Audio Program
CD 1, Track 16

TECHNOLOGY
@HomeTutor
🖵 Interactive Whiteboard Lessons
Teacher One Stop
Teacher to Teacher
Copymasters, *Jumeaux/Jumelles,*
pp. 11–14

■ Notes linguistiques

• Sometimes a reflexive construction in French corresponds to a passive construction in English. Compare:
Cela **ne se fait pas.**
*That is **not done.***
La fête nationale **se célèbre** le 14 juillet.
*The national holiday **is celebrated** on July 14.*

• Some reflexive verbs are considered idiomatic because their English equivalents do not express a reflexive action. However, in many of these verbs a reflexive meaning is implied (i.e., the subject is acting on itself):
Elle **se rend** au bureau.
*She **brings herself** to the office.*
Il **s'impatiente.**
*He **makes himself** impatient.*
Tu **t'excuses.**
*You **excuse yourself.***

■ Verbs

s'asseoir
s'inquiéter   (see **préférer**)
se taire

@**HOMETUTOR**
my.hrw.com

A L'usage idiomatique des verbes réfléchis

NE T'INQUIÈTE PAS!

Reflexive verbs are used:

• to describe certain MOVEMENTS

| se rendre à | *to go to* | Mme Meunier **se rend à** son bureau. |

• to describe FEELINGS or changes in feelings

| s'impatienter | *to get impatient* | Pourquoi est-ce que tu **t'impatientes?** |

• to describe certain other actions and situations

| s'excuser | *to apologize* | Tu as tort! **Excuse-toi!** |
| se trouver | *to be (located)* | Où **se trouve** la pharmacie? |

VOCABULAIRE Quelques verbes réfléchis

MOVEMENT

s'asseoir	*to sit down*	s'approcher (de)	*to come closer*
se lever	*to stand up*	s'arrêter	*to stop*
		s'en aller	*to go away*

FEELINGS

s'amuser	*to have fun*	s'inquiéter	*to worry*
s'embêter	*to get bored*	se mettre en colère	*to get angry*
s'impatienter	*to get impatient*	se sentir (triste . . .)	*to feel (sad)*
s'énerver	*to get upset*		

OTHER MEANINGS

s'appeler	*to be called, named*	se rappeler	*to remember; to recall*
se trouver	*to be (located)*	se souvenir (de)	*to remember*
s'intéresser à	*to be interested in*	se rappeler	*to remember; to recall*
s'occuper de	*to be busy with; to take care of*	se taire	*to be quiet; to shut up*

→ The verb **se souvenir** is conjugated like **venir.**

PRESENT: **je me souviens**   **nous nous souvenons**   **elles se souviennent**
PASSÉ COMPOSÉ: **je me suis souvenu(e)**

→ The following irregular verbs are commonly used in the imperative:

s'en aller	se taire	s'asseoir
Va-t'en!	Tais-toi!	Assieds-toi!
Allez-vous-en!	Taisez-vous!	Asseyez-vous!

✚ Transports Québec

AU QUÉBEC, LA PRUDENCE FAIT TOUTE LA DIFFÉRENCE!

⚜ Je me souviens

ALLONS PLUS LOIN

Reflexive verbs are also used to express a reciprocal action, that is, an action in which two or more people interact with one another.

Philippe et Claire **se téléphonent.**	*Philippe and Claire **phone each other.***
Marc et moi, **nous nous** voyons souvent	*Marc and I often **see each other.***
Où est-ce que vous allez **vous retrouver?**	*Where are you going **to meet (each other)?***

Révision p. R20–21

Pratique p. 25

Le présent des verbes *s'appeler, se rappeler* (comme *appeler*)

Teaching Strategy: Accordian Vocabulary Drill

Have students fold a piece of paper in three columns. In the first column, have them write 10–15 of the verbs which they anticipate having difficulty memorizing, and exchange the list with someone else in the class.

The students, who now have someone else's list, will write the English equivalent of the given vocabulary in the second column and fold down the first column so that only the English and a blank column is showing. (Be sure that the students verify that their answers are correct.)

Finally, hand this list back to the originating student. This student must now write

1 Une question de personnalité

Analysez la personnalité des personnes suivantes et dites si oui ou non elles font les choses entre parenthèses.

▶ Tu es toujours calme. (s'inquiéter?)
Tu ne t'inquiètes pas.

1. Tu as une excellente mémoire. (se souvenir de tout?)
2. Vous n'aimez pas attendre. (s'impatienter?)
3. Alice est optimiste. (se sentir triste?)
4. Philippe est très irritable. (se mettre souvent en colère?)
5. Nous sommes curieux. (s'intéresser à tout?)
6. J'aime étudier. (s'embêter en classe?)
7. Tu es très patient. (s'énerver?)
8. Nous avons toujours raison. (se tromper?)

2 Que dire?

Qu'est-ce que vous allez dire à votre ami français dans les circonstances suivantes? Utilisez l'impératif affirmatif ou négatif des verbes de la liste. Soyez logique dans votre choix!

▶ Votre ami est furieux.   **Ne te mets pas en colère!**
▶ Il a tort.   **Excuse-toi!**

- Il parle trop.
- Il attend sa copine depuis une heure.
- Il est insupportable *(unbearable)* avec vous.
- Il a un problème avec ses parents.
- Il va à une boum.
- Il a un examen de maths.
- Il est fatigué.
- Il a une entrevue professionnelle dans une semaine.

s'amuser
s'asseoir sur cette chaise
s'en aller
s'excuser
s'impatienter
s'inquiéter
se mettre en colère
se souvenir de la date
se taire
se tromper dans les calculs

3 Et vous?

Complétez les phrases suivantes avec une expression personnelle. Ensuite, comparez vos réponses avec celles de votre partenaire.

1. Je m'intéresse à . . .
2. Je me souviens toujours de . . .
3. Je m'amuse quand . . .
4. Je m'embête quand . . .
5. Je m'inquiète quand . . .
6. Je me sens triste quand . . .
7. Je me sens heureux (heureuse) quand . . .
8. Je me mets en colère quand . . .
9. Je me sens fatigué(e) quand . . .
10. Je ne me tais pas quand . . .

4 Zut alors!

Aujourd'hui les personnes suivantes ont eu des problèmes. Expliquez leurs problèmes. Attention: les phrases peuvent être affirmatives ou négatives!

▶ Philippe / s'amuser à la boum
Philippe ne s'est pas amusé à la boum.

1. vous / s'énerver pendant l'examen
2. moi / se souvenir de mon rendez-vous
3. les élèves / se tromper dans l'exercice
4. Alice / se mettre en colère
5. nous / s'impatienter
6. toi / s'embêter pendant la classe
7. Pierre et Robert / se sentir malades au restaurant
8. Isabelle / se sentir en forme

---

the French for the words given in the third column. Students thus practice the words with which they anticipated having difficulty.

Note: This drill can continue by folding the paper and turning it over. It can also be done at home as a useful vocabulary review tool.

Game: Silent Partner

The "Spokesperson" sits in a chair with the "Silent Partner" standing behind. The class asks questions. If the "Spokesperson" gives incorrect information, the "S.P." taps on the left shoulder; if correct, taps the right shoulder. Pairs of students take turns.

Unité 1

Interdisciplinary/ Community Connections

Create a manual of items for personal care and well-being that can be used while traveling in France.

Language Arts
Make a list of daily personal care and health-related activities you perform every day.

Math
Based on the survey, graph how many people thought each product was a necessity or a luxury. Then calculate the cost of items considered necessary and display your information in a chart.

Science/Health
Consult a health professional for information about first-aid products and motion-sickness remedies.

Social Studies
Create a survey asking which products people think are necessary and which are luxuries. Interview classmates and family members.

Art/Music
Design your travel manual.

Technology
Implement your design using the computer.

Community
Print out your class travel manual and display in the French classroom or school library for others to use.

SUPPLEMENTARY VOCABULARY

s'éloigner *to go away*
se déplacer *to move (over)*
se calmer *to get calm*
se réjouir *to be happy*
s'ennuyer *to be/get bored*
se rendre compte *to realize*
s'apercevoir *to notice*

Reading **STRATEGY**

Reading fiction

RESOURCES

PRINT
Activités pour tous

TECHNOLOGY
Teacher One Stop
📺 **Projectable Transparencies**

L1, *Conte pour enfants de moins de trois ans*

Transparency Copymasters, pp. A120–A121

French InterActive Reader

■ **Note culturelle**
Le Théâtre de l'Absurde also includes novels and essays, sometimes called **la littérature de dérision.** Some of its authors are Beckett, Obaldia, and Marguerite Duras.

■ **Additional Information**
Ionesco wrote the following plays: **La Leçon, La Cantatrice chauve, Les Chaises, Rhinocéros.** Encourage students to read excerpts from other works by Ionesco outside of class.

■ **Teaching Suggestion**
Have students research other **Académiciens** and ask them to prepare short illustrated biographies of them. You may wish to display the biographies in your classroom or share them with other French classes at your school via a class website.

LECTURE

Eugène Ionesco

Conte pour enfants de moins de trois ans

Eugène Ionesco (1912-1994) est né en Roumanie. Il fait des études de français à l'université de Bucarest, et devient lui-même professeur de français. En 1938, il quitte son pays menacé par le nazisme et vient s'installer en France. Il commence alors une brillante carrière littéraire qui lui vaudra d'être nommé à l'Académie française.

Ionesco est l'auteur de 33 pièces de théâtre. Dans ses pièces, il dénonce la banalité ou l'angoisse de l'existence avec une arme très puissante: l'humour. Combattant l'absurde par l'absurde, Ionesco a créé un théâtre entièrement nouveau que ses critiques ont justement appelé «Le Théâtre de l'Absurde».

AVANT DE LIRE

Dans ce conte, Ionesco met en scène un père et sa petite fille, âgée de deux ans et demi, dans une situation ordinaire de l'existence. Un matin, papa et sa fille se trouvent seuls à la maison. Pour une raison inexpliquée, la maman est partie chez sa mère. (Il y a peut-être eu une dispute dans le couple.) La petite fille, inquiète° de l'absence de sa mère, veut rester tout près de son père, mais celui-ci, qui veut se laver, n'a pas besoin d'elle. Pour être seul, il joue sur la psychologie des enfants: ce qui est absurde ou illogique pour un adulte peut sembler tout à fait° naturel et logique pour un enfant.

Pour mieux comprendre une histoire, il est utile de savoir quel genre° d'histoire c'est. À votre avis, d'après le titre, les illustrations et la note biographique sur Ionesco, quel genre d'histoire allez-vous lire?

- une histoire réaliste?
- une histoire humoristique?
- un drame psychologique?
- un conte fantastique?
- un récit d'aventures?

inquiète *worried*   **tout à fait** = complètement   **genre** = sorte

NOTE *Culturelle*

L'Académie française
Créée en 1635, l'Académie française a pour but° de préserver la langue française. Cette prestigieuse institution a 40 membres, appelés les «Immortels». Ce sont généralement des écrivains français très connus. Eugène Ionesco est l'un des rares Académiciens d'origine étrangère.
but = objectif

Mots utiles

avoir mal à l'estomac	*to have an upset stomach*
avoir mal à la tête	*to have a headache*
empêcher de	*to stop, keep from (doing)*
frapper	*to knock*
pleurer	*to cry*
profiter de	*to take advantage of*

Notes culturelles

Les membres de l'Académie française sont élus à vie. On les appelle «Immortels» car quand un Académicien meurt, ses collègues élisent un successeur. Parmi les Académiciens d'origine étrangère: Julien Green (américain), Léopold Senghor (sénégalais), Marguerite Yourcenar (belge).

Differentiation

Metacognitive Have students identify the country of origin of Ionesco (top p. 56) on a map. Have students read his biographical information and explain in French what the Académie Française is and why it was unusual for Ionesco to have been named an "Académicien." Ask them to explain the purpose of this exercise.

Conte pour enfants de moins de trois ans

Ce matin, comme d'habitude,° Josette frappe à la porte de la chambre à coucher de ses parents. Papa n'a pas très bien dormi. Maman est partie à la campagne* pour quelques jours. Alors papa a profité de cette absence pour manger beaucoup de saucisson, pour boire de la bière, pour manger du pâté de cochon,** et beaucoup d'autres choses que maman l'empêche de manger parce que c'est pas bon pour la santé.° Alors, voilà, papa a mal au foie,** il a mal à l'estomac, il a mal à la tête, et ne voudrait pas se réveiller. Mais Josette frappe toujours° à la porte. Alors papa lui dit d'entrer. Elle entre, elle va chez son papa. Il n'y a pas maman. Josette demande:

— Où elle est maman?

Papa répond: «Ta maman est allée se reposer à la campagne chez sa maman à elle.»

Josette répond: «Chez Mémée?»°

Papa répond: «Oui, chez Mémée.»

— Écris à maman, dit Josette. Téléphone à maman, dit Josette.

Papa dit: «Faut pas téléphoner.»

Josette dit: «Raconte une histoire avec maman et toi, et moi.»

— Non, dit papa, je vais aller au travail. Je me lève, je vais m'habiller. Et papa se lève. Il met sa robe de chambre° rouge, par-dessus° son pyjama, il met dans les pieds ses *poutouffles*.° Il va dans la salle de bains. Il ferme la porte de la salle de bains. Josette est à la porte de la salle de bains. Elle frappe avec ses petits poings,° elle pleure.

Josette dit: «Ouvre-moi la porte.»

Papa répond: «Je ne peux pas. Je suis tout nu,° je me lave, après je me rase.»

Josette dit: «Tu laves ta figure, tu laves tes épaules,° tu laves tes bras, tu laves ton dos, tu laves ton *dérère*,° tu laves tes pieds.

— Je rase ma barbe, dit papa.

— Tu rases ta barbe avec du savon, dit Josette. Je veux entrer. Je veux voir.

---

* **La campagne.** In French, the term **la campagne** (the country) is used to refer to any area outside **la ville** (the city).

** **Mal au foie.** The French believe that eating too many fatty foods, such as **saucisson** (sausage) and **pâté de cochon** (a type of meatloaf made of ground pork and served cold), and drinking too much wine or beer leads to **mal au foie** (abdominal pain indicating liver trouble).

comme d'habitude *as usual*   **santé** *health*   **toujours** = sans arrêter   **Mémée** = grand-mère   **robe de chambre** *bathrobe*
par-dessus = sur   **poutouffles** = pantoufles *slippers*   **poings** *fists*   **nu** *naked, nude*   **épaules** *shoulders*   **dérère** = derrière *behind, rear end*

Avez-vous compris?

1. Comment le Papa de Josette se sent-il ce matin-là? Pourquoi?

2. Qu'est-ce que Josette demande d'abord à son père?

3. Selon vous, pourquoi est-ce que Josette veut rester près de son père?

Anticipons un peu!

Imaginez que vous êtes dans une situation semblable à celle du Papa. Vous êtes dans la salle de bains où vous vous habillez pour aller à un rendez-vous. Vous vous dépêchez parce que vous avez peur d'être en retard . . . Votre petit(e) frère (soeur) veut entrer dans la salle de bains. Il/elle pleure, mais vous savez que ce n'est pas trop grave. Qu'est-ce que vous allez faire?

• fermer la porte à clé?

• dire à votre petit(e) frère (soeur) de se taire?

• ouvrir la porte et lui donner une sucette *(lollypop)*?

• sortir de la salle de bains pour lui raconter une histoire?

• trouver une autre solution plus originale? laquelle?

Maintenant, lisez la deuxième partie pour voir ce que le papa de Josette a fait.

■ Teaching Strategy

The language used by Ionesco to represent Josette is purposely childish and ungrammatical. You may want to present the corresponding correct forms.

For example:

C'est pas bon pour la santé.
Ce n'est pas bon pour la santé.

Faut pas téléphoner.
Il ne faut pas téléphoner.

Il met dans les pieds ses poutouffles.
Il met ses pantoufles.

Tu laves ta figure.
Tu te laves la figure.

Tu rases ta barbe.
Tu te rases la barbe.

Où tu es?
Où es-tu?

Où elle est maman?
Où est maman?

■ Note linguistique

Mémée is the affectionate term used by children for their grandmother. **Mamy** is another one. The grandfather is called **Pépé** or **Papy**.

■ Avez-vous compris?

(Sample answers)

1. Il ne se sent pas bien, parce qu'il a trop mangé et trop bu.

2. Elle demande où est sa mère.

3. Elle veut rester près de son père parce que sa mère est partie, et les enfants n'aiment pas rester seuls.

Differentiation

Alphabetic/Phonetic Have students note the difference between **étrange** and **étrangèr(e)** ("strange" and "foreign"). Have them ask the person to their right: **Êtes-vous d'origine étrangère?** Students answer: **Oui, je suis américain(e).** Then start in the other direction and have students ask: **Êtes-vous étrange?** Students answer: **Non, je ne suis pas étrange.**

Repetitive Have students read along as you read the Ionesco short story aloud. Have individual students repeat a line after you and answer a short comprehension question: e.g., **Maman, où est-elle allée?** Pourquoi? (Variation: Have a student formulate a question after he or she repeats a line.)

Unité 1   57

■ Irregular Verbs

(see Appendix C)
courir
revenir (see **venir**)

■ Note linguistique

Un buffet is used to put away dishes and silverware. **Une armoire** is used for linens or clothing.

un canapé

un buffet

les casseroles

le four

le paillasson

Mots utiles

aller voir	*to go look*
courir*	*to run*
crier	*to yell, shout*
embrasser	*to kiss*
être tranquille	*to be alone, undisturbed*
revenir*	*to come back*
sauter	*to jump*
à travers	*across, through*
de nouveau	*again*
ne . . . plus	*no longer, not anymore*

II

Papa dit: «Tu ne peux pas me voir, parce que je ne suis plus dans la salle de bains.»

30 Josette dit (derrière la porte): «Alors, où tu es?»

Papa répond: «Je ne sais pas, va voir. Je suis peut-être dans la salle à manger, va me chercher.»

Josette court dans la salle à manger, et papa commence sa toilette. Josette

35 court avec ses petites jambes, elle va dans la salle à manger.

Papa est tranquille, mais pas longtemps. Josette arrive de nouveau devant la porte de la salle de bains, elle crie à travers la porte:

Josette: «Je t'ai cherché. Tu n'es pas dans la salle à manger.»

Papa dit: «Tu n'as pas bien cherché. Regarde sous la table.»

40 Josette retourne dans la salle à manger. Elle revient.

Elle dit: «Tu n'es pas sous la table.»

Papa dit: «Alors va voir dans le salon. Regarde bien si je suis sur le fauteuil, sur le canapé, derrière les livres, à la fenêtre.»

Josette s'en va. Papa est tranquille, mais pas pour longtemps.

45 Josette revient.

Elle dit: «Non, tu n'es pas dans le fauteuil, tu n'es pas à la fenêtre, tu n'es pas sur le canapé, tu n'es pas derrière les livres, tu n'es pas dans la télévision, tu n'es pas dans le salon.»

Papa dit: «Alors, va voir si je suis dans la cuisine.»

50 Josette dit: «Je vais te chercher dans la cuisine.»

Josette court à la cuisine. Papa est tranquille, mais pas pour longtemps. Josette revient.

Elle dit: «Tu n'es pas dans la cuisine.»

Papa dit: «Regarde bien, sous la table de la cuisine, regarde bien si je

55 suis dans le buffet, regarde bien si je suis dans les casseroles, regarde bien si je suis dans le four avec le poulet.»

Josette va et vient. Papa n'est pas dans le four, papa n'est pas dans les casseroles, papa n'est pas dans le buffet, papa n'est pas sous le paillasson, papa n'est pas dans la poche de son pantalon. Dans la poche du pantalon,

60 il y a seulement le mouchoir.

Josette revient devant la porte de la salle de bains.

Josette dit: «J'ai cherché partout. Je ne t'ai pas trouvé. Où tu es?»

la poche, le mouchoir   **une armoire**   **un tapis**   **une poubelle**

Papa dit: «Je suis là.» Et papa, qui a eu le temps de faire sa toilette,
qui s'est rasé, qui s'est habillé, ouvre la porte.
Il dit: «Je suis là.» Il prend Josette dans ses bras, et voilà aussi
la porte de la maison qui s'ouvre, au fond du couloir,° et c'est maman
qui arrive. Josette saute° des bras de son papa, elle se jette° dans les bras
de sa maman, elle l'embrasse, elle dit:
— Maman, j'ai cherché papa sous la table, dans l'armoire, sous
le tapis, derrière la glace, dans la cuisine, dans la poubelle,
il n'était pas là.
Papa dit à maman: «Je suis content que tu sois revenue. Il faisait
beau à la campagne? Comment va ta mère?»
Josette dit: «Et Mémée, elle va bien? On va chez elle?»

au fond du couloir *at the end of the hall* **saute** *jump* **se jette** *throws herself*

> ### Avez-vous compris?
> 1. Quel stratagème est-ce que le père utilise pour être tranquille?
> 2. Est-ce que ce stratagème réussit? Pourquoi, selon vous?
> 3. Comment se termine l'histoire?

APRÈS LA LECTURE

Expression orale

Situation

Avec votre partenaire, composez un
dialogue correspondant à la situation
suivante. Utilisez votre imagination.

Au bureau

Le papa de Josette parle de son week-end avec un(e) collègue de
bureau qui veut des détails. Il décrit . . .

- pourquoi sa femme n'était pas là (il ne dit pas la vérité), et où elle était
- ce qu'il a bu et mangé
- ce qu'il a fait avec sa petite fille
- ce qu'il a fait d'autre

Rôles: le papa, le/la collègue

Théâtre

Avec votre partenaire, composez une
scène semblable au conte que vous
avez lu sur le thème suivant: Stéphanie
(18 ans) fait du baby-sitting pour
Dominique (3 ans). Elle veut téléphoner
à son copain, mais Dominique ne la laisse
pas tranquille. Pour se libérer, Stéphanie
utilise un stratagème semblable à celui de
l'histoire. (Variation: c'est Stéphane qui
fait du baby-sitting, et il veut téléphoner
à sa copine.)

Expression écrite

Un peu d'humour

Décrivez brièvement les éléments de l'histoire que vous avez trouvés drôles.

Une lettre

Imaginez que vous êtes la mère de Josette. Vous écrivez à votre cousine pour lui expliquer
les événements du week-end. Vous pouvez mentionner. . .
- la raison de votre dispute avec votre mari (Inventez!)
- où vous êtes allée et ce que vous avez fait (Inventez!)
- quand vous êtes rentrée chez vous et pourquoi vous étiez heureuse de rentrer

cinquante-neuf **59**
Lecture

■ **Avez-vous compris?**

(Sample answers)
1. Il dit à Josette de le chercher dans toutes les pièces de la maison.
2. Le stratagème réussit, parce que les enfants très jeunes ne savent pas que les parents ne disent pas toujours la vérité.
3. L'histoire se termine bien: le père est habillé et la mère revient à la maison.

■ **Teaching Strategy: Expansion**

Assign the following activity to students:
Finissez l'histoire. Josette dit: «Et Mémée, elle va bien? On va chez elle?» Que répond Maman? Vont-ils aller chez Mémée? Quand? Que va dire Josette à Mémée?

■ **Expression écrite**

For writing rubrics, consult the **Generate Success** Rubric Generator on the **Teacher One Stop.** You can also create your own custom rubrics with this tool.

Student Portfolios

Use the *Après la lecture* activities as the basis
for preparing either a written or recorded
portfolio piece to begin the year's collection of
student work. Allow students to choose their
preferred presentation mode in this case, but
be sure to monitor the portfolio contents on a
continuing basis to assure that a variety of
materials is collected.

Interlude culturel

RESOURCES

TECHNOLOGY
Interactive Whiteboard Lessons
Teacher One Stop
Pre-AP Digital Resources
▶ DVD Program, Unit 1, Vignette culturelle

■ General Synopsis of Interlude 1
French Modern Art
- *Impressionism:* Monet, Degas, Renoir, Manet, B. Morisot
- *Post-Impressionism:* Van Gogh, Gauguin, Matisse, Rousseau, Toulouse-Lautrec
- *Surrealism* as an artistic and literary movement: Magritte

Poems
- Desnos, *La fourmi*
- Prévert, *Pour faire le portrait d'un oiseau*

■ Note linguistique
Les nymphéas = water lilies (Monet's painting, top of page)

■ Teaching Strategy
The material presented in the *Interlude* should remain enjoyable for students and not overwhelming. Ask students to scan the entire *Interlude*, looking at the illustrations, noting familiar and unfamiliar items, and making a list of names they recognize. Ask them to suggest the theme of the *Interlude*.

This *Interlude* is an excellent starting point for an interdisciplinary project. Work with your school's Art and History teachers to develop an appropriate project.

Monet «Les Nymphéas»

La Révolution impressionniste

L'art moderne est né en France dans les années 1870. C'est à cette époque, en effet, qu'un groupe d'artistes, nommés «les **Impressionnistes**», a présenté au monde une nouvelle façon° de concevoir la peinture. Avant eux, la peinture° était très traditionnelle. Les artistes essayaient d'imiter la réalité en reproduisant de façon très exacte et avec beaucoup de détails les sujets qu'ils peignaient. Ils apprenaient leur métier° dans des «académies», c'est-à-dire dans des écoles où ils copiaient minutieusement des modèles sous la direction de maîtres sans grande imagination. Pour ces artistes, l'essentiel dans la peinture était la forme.

Au lieu de° s'intéresser à la forme, les Impressionnistes se sont intéressés à la couleur, et surtout aux effets de la lumière° sur les objets qu'ils représentaient. Au lieu de peindre des scènes de bataille ou des héros de l'Antiquité, ils ont peint des scènes de la vie courante,° des portraits d'amis, et surtout la nature. Au lieu de travailler dans des ateliers,° ils ont travaillé en plein air.° Cette façon simple et naturelle de peindre a révolutionné le monde des arts.

À l'origine, cependant, les Impressionnistes n'ont eu aucun° succès. C'est par dérision° qu'un journaliste leur a donné le nom d'«impressionnistes». Ces peintres ne pouvaient même pas exposer leurs toiles° dans les salons officiels patronnés par le gouvernement. Ils ont donc organisé leurs propres° expositions chez des amis. Il y a eu huit expositions impressionnistes entre 1874 et 1886, mais ces expositions ont été

des échecs.° La peinture impressionniste choquait trop le sens esthétique de l'époque!

Peu à peu, les critiques d'art ont finalement compris l'importance de la «révolution» impressionniste. Les collectionneurs ont commencé à acheter les tableaux° de ces peintres. Aujourd'hui, ces tableaux valent° des fortunes. On peut les admirer dans les plus grands musées du monde: à Paris, à New York, à Londres, à Chicago, à Boston, à Saint Pétersbourg.

Les peintres impressionnistes sont considérés parmi° les plus grands artistes de tous les temps: **Monet, Manet, Cézanne, Renoir, Degas...** Parmi ces artistes, il y avait des femmes: **Berthe Morisot** et une Américaine, **Mary Cassatt.** Mary Cassatt, fille d'un riche banquier de Philadelphie, était venue étudier l'art à Paris. En faisant connaître° l'impressionnisme aux États-Unis, elle en a assuré le triomphe dans le monde.

façon *manner* **peinture** *painting* **métier** *trade* **au lieu de** *instead of* **lumière** *light* **vie courante** *daily life* **ateliers** *studios* **en plein air** *outdoors* **aucun** *no* **dérision** *mockery* **toiles** *paintings (canvases)* **propres** *own* **échecs** *failures* **tableaux** *paintings* **valent** *are worth* **parmi** *among* **en faisant connaître** *by making known*

Teaching Suggestion: DVD Program
Use the Unit 1 *Vignette culturelle* video segment on *l'impressionnisme* to help students understand the Impressionist movement and to identify some of the French artists associated with it. The video will include such artists as Monet, Degas, Renoir and Morisot.

Before showing the video to students, brainstorm a list of French Impressionists and write their names on the board.

Quelques peintres impressionnistes

Degas «*Répétition d'un ballet*»

■ Edgar Degas (1834-1917)

Degas était le fils d'un banquier. Sa mère était issue d'une riche famille de La Nouvelle-Orléans. Degas a étudié le droit°, mais il a abandonné ses études pour se consacrer à la peinture. C'était aussi un sculpteur. Ses sujets préférés étaient les danseuses de l'Opéra, les scènes de café et les chevaux.

Manet «*Le fifre*»

■ Édouard Manet (1832-1883)

Manet voulait être officier de marine, mais après un voyage au Brésil, il a décidé de se consacrer à la peinture. Ses premiers tableaux, de couleurs violentes, ont provoqué l'hostilité du public et des critiques, mais l'admiration de jeunes peintres alors inconnus: Monet, Renoir, Cézanne. C'est ainsi qu'il est devenu le chef d'un nouveau mouvement qui allait être l'impressionnisme. Manet a peint toutes sortes de sujets: portraits de ses amis, scènes de la vie courante et familière, paysages° divers.

Renoir «*La Danse à Bougival*»

■ Pierre-Auguste Renoir (1841-1919)

Renoir a commencé par peindre des devantures° de café, puis il est allé à l'École des Beaux-Arts. Ce peintre aimait les couleurs chaudes. Ses sujets principaux sont les enfants, les jeunes filles, les femmes, les fleurs, les scènes de café et les bals populaires.

■ Berthe Morisot (1841-1895)

Berthe Morisot était la belle-sœur d'Édouard Manet. Elle s'est intéressée très jeune à la peinture. Comme beaucoup d'artistes de l'époque, elle a commencé à copier les tableaux du musée du Louvre. C'est là qu'elle a fait la connaissance de Manet. Elle a alors rejoint le groupe des peintres impressionnistes. Elle a peint avec eux et elle a participé à leurs expositions. Berthe Morisot aimait utiliser les couleurs claires.° Ses sujets principaux sont les fleurs, les paysages, les scènes de la vie champêtre° et les portraits de jeunes filles.

Morisot «*Sous l'oranger*»

droit *law* **devantures** *store fronts* **paysages** *landscapes* **claires** *light* **champêtre** = *rurale*

soixante et un **61**
Interlude culturel

■ Notes culturelles

• When Degas visited the US in 1872, he stayed in New Orleans.

• **Le fifre** is a small flute or the player of this flute. This painting represents an army boy (**un enfant de troupe**) of the Imperial Army (**la garde impériale**) under Napoléon III (1808-1873). **Le Fifre** was rejected by the jury of the 1866 Salon. This rejection prompted an article by Émile Zola, in which he praised the beauty and simplicity of Manet's work. Zola concluded his article with this prophetic line: «**La place de Manet est marquée au Louvre.**»

• Renoir's son, Jean Renoir (1894-1979), became an acclaimed filmmaker. Among his works are the classics **La Grande illusion** and **La Règle du jeu**.

• Manet made several portraits of Berthe Morisot. She is also represented in his painting called **Le Balcon.**

• **Les Beaux-Arts** is a famous art school in Paris where Delacroix, Matisse, and Braque studied.

Expansion

Internet Connection – Interlude 1
Visit **http://my.hrw.com** for more information and useful links about French Impressionism.

Cultures
Standard 2.1 Students demonstrate an understanding of the relationship between the practices and perspectives of the cultures of the francophone world.

■ **Contexte historique:**
19th century in France

1815– : Fall of the Emperor Napoléon 1er.

1830– : Louis Philippe becomes king after a revolution.

1830–1848: Beginning of the Industrial Revolution in France. Romanticism prevails in all arts.

1838– : Beginning of photography, with the **daguerréotypes** invented by Jacques Daguerre.

1852–1870: Napoléon III, nephew of Napoléon 1er, reigns as the emperor of France. Haussman landscapes Paris, widening its streets, and creating large avenues as well as the Parc du Bois de Boulogne. The railroad system is put into place.

1870–1871: Third Republic. After a war with Germany (1870), France loses the eastern regions of Alsace and Lorraine.

1871: A socialist revolution, called **La Commune de Paris,** is violently repressed.

1880– : Elementary school becomes mandatory and free in France.

1889– : The new Eiffel Tower is the talk of the Paris Exhibition.

1894–1899: The Dreyfus Affair divides public opinion and becomes a great scandal.

1895– : The **Brothers Lumière,** Louis Jean and Auguste, show the first movie in Paris.

Claude Monet: le peintre de la lumière

C'est un tableau de **Monet** intitulé «**Impression, soleil levant**»° qui a donné son nom à l'impressionnisme. Monet (1840-1926) était fasciné par les effets de la lumière. Il pensait qu'on pouvait reconstituer les reflets de la lumière sur les objets en décomposant celle-ci° en ses couleurs fondamentales. Il a donc inventé une technique qui consistait à peindre par petites taches° de couleur: du jaune, du rouge, du bleu, du vert, de l'orange et aussi du blanc et du noir.

Monet «*Impression, soleil levant*»

Claude Monet *(1840-1926)*

Monet aimait peindre et repeindre les mêmes scènes sous des lumières différentes: à midi, très tôt le matin, le soir, au printemps, en plein été, sous la neige. Il a ainsi exécuté des séries entières d'un seul° sujet peint à différents moments de la journée ou de l'année. Monet a peint surtout des paysages, mais il a peint aussi des scènes urbaines très célèbres: **la cathédrale de Rouen, la Gare Saint Lazare** à Paris, **la Tamise°** à Londres.

Pendant de longues années, Monet est resté très pauvre, mais avec le succès de l'impressionnisme, il a finalement connu la célébrité, la gloire et la fortune. Après des années de misère, il est devenu un véritable héros national.

Monet «*Gare Saint Lazare*»

soleil levant *rising sun*   **celle-ci =** *la lumière*   **taches** *spots*   **un seul** *only one*   **la Tamise** *Thames (River)*

Teaching Strategy: Groups

Divide the class into groups, or allow the class to choose project teams. Have each team choose a different artist and research the artist's style and works, producing a timeline of the artist's life and a presentation of his/her work. Some students may be able to provide demonstrations of particular styles for the class.

Monet a vécu° longtemps dans une maison de campagne située à **Giverny**, à 60 kilomètres de Paris. Devant cette maison, il avait créé un superbe jardin avec une très grande variété de fleurs qui changeait de couleur avec les saisons. C'est ce jardin aux couleurs chaudes et variées que Monet a peint dans de nombreux tableaux. À Giverny, Monet aimait recevoir ses amis et aussi beaucoup de jeunes peintres qui venaient écouter ses conseils.° Parmi ces peintres, il y avait une colonie d'artistes américains qui s'étaient installés dans un hôtel près de la maison de l'artiste. Vers° la fin° de sa vie, malheureusement, ce grand artiste de la lumière était devenu aveugle,° et ne pouvait plus peindre.

    Après la mort de Monet, la maison de Giverny et son jardin ont été abandonnés. Heureusement, grâce à° la générosité d'une riche Américaine, cette maison a été récemment restaurée et le jardin recréé dans sa splendeur originale. Aujourd'hui des centaines de milliers de visiteurs venus du monde entier viennent chaque année à Giverny saluer la mémoire du grand artiste français et admirer son merveilleux jardin.

Maison de Monet à Giverny

Renoir, *«Monet peignant dans son jardin»*

Monet, *«Le pont japonais»*

Le jardin de Monet à Giverny

---

vécu *lived* **conseils** *advice* **vers** *towards* **fin** *end* **aveugle** *blind* **grâce** à *thanks to*

Notes culturelles

Giverny is a small town (547 inhabitants) in Normandy. Rouen, the city where Joan of Arc was executed in 1431, is also in Normandy.

In 1892, Monet painted the cathedral of Rouen forty times, each painting done at a different time of day and thus in a different light.

Après l'Impressionnisme

Une conséquence importante de l'impressionnisme a été de libérer l'art des normes esthétiques traditionnelles. Ce mouvement a donc ouvert° des voies° nouvelles à d'autres artistes qui ont pu exercer librement° leur imagination et leur créativité. Après l'impressionnisme, d'autres mouvements artistiques sont nés en France. Vers 1900, Paris était devenu la capitale universelle des arts, attirant° des artistes de tous les pays du monde.

■ **Anecdote**

On December 24, 1888, Van Gogh assaulted Gauguin and tried to kill him. To beg his forgiveness, Van Gogh cut off part of his ear and sent it to Gauguin.

Van Gogh «*La nuit étoilée*»

■ **Vincent Van Gogh** (1853-1890):
Le génie de la folie

Van Gogh était hollandais, mais c'est en France qu'il a peint ses tableaux les plus célèbres. Comme les Impressionnistes, il avait un sens profond de la lumière et des couleurs brillantes, mais il est allé plus loin qu'eux. Van Gogh voulait non seulement peindre ce qu'il voyait, mais cherchait aussi à exprimer les sensations° étranges qu'il éprouvait.° Pour cela, il exagérait l'intensité des couleurs et il donnait un mouvement aux choses inanimées. Ses représentations de la lune° et des étoiles° tournant dans le ciel° sont particulièrement hallucinantes.

■ **Note culturelle**

L'archipel des Marquises is a group of ten volcanic islands, and belongs to French Polynesia.

■ **Paul Gauguin** (1848-1903):
Le peintre de l'exotisme

Gauguin travaillait dans une banque où il gagnait bien sa vie. Un jour, à l'âge de 35 ans, il a décidé de tout abandonner, travail, famille, enfants, vie confortable, pour se consacrer totalement à la peinture. Il a rejoint les peintres impressionnistes, mais c'est dans l'exotisme qu'il a cherché son inspiration. Il est allé à Panama, à la Martinique, à Tahiti et, finalement, dans une petite île des Marquises.*
Là, loin de la civilisation et en compagnie de gens simples, mais nobles et généreux, il a peint ses plus belles toiles.

* Les Marquises: a group of islands in the South Pacific

Gauguin «*Femmes de Tahiti*»

ouvert *opened* **voies** *ways* **librement** *freely* **attirant** *attracting* **sensations** *feelings* **éprouvait** *experienced, felt*
lune *moon* **étoiles** *stars* **ciel** *sky*

■ Toulouse-Lautrec (1864-1901): Le peintre de la vie parisienne

Henri de Toulouse-Lautrec est né dans une famille aristocratique très illustre et très ancienne. À l'âge de 14 ans, il a eu un accident de cheval qui l'a rendu infirme° pour le reste de sa vie. Encouragé par sa mère, il a décidé de devenir artiste et il est allé étudier à l'École des Beaux Arts à Paris. Toulouse-Lautrec aimait fréquenter° les cafés, les cabarets et les music-halls, comme le Moulin Rouge pour lequel° il a dessiné des affiches célèbres.

Dans ses tableaux, il a surtout représenté les scènes de spectacle auxquels il assistait: théâtre, music-hall, cirque, vélodrome°. . . Il a immortalisé les artistes de ces spectacles, comme Jane Avril, dans de nombreux portraits.

Toulouse-Lautrec «Jane Avril au Jardin de Paris»

■ Henri Rousseau (1844-1910): Le douanier inspiré

Pendant la semaine, **Henri Rousseau** était un bureaucrate dont° le travail consistait à contrôler le trafic des marchandises à l'entrée de Paris (d'où son surnom de «douanier»).° Le dimanche, cet employé modèle quittait la ville avec sa boîte de peintures pour aller peindre en plein air. Comme il n'avait jamais étudié dans une école d'art, Rousseau utilisait une technique très rudimentaire où la perspective n'existait pas. Si son style était simple, «naïf», son imagination était débordante.° Ses tableaux les plus célèbres représentent des paysages irréels peuplés° d'animaux exotiques.

Rousseau «La bohémienne endormie»

■ Camille Claudel (1864-1943): L'élève, égale au maître

Comme beaucoup de jeunes filles de son époque, **Camille Claudel** voulait être artiste. Comme elle s'intéressait à la sculpture, elle a décidé d'aller à Paris pour étudier sous la direction d'Auguste Rodin, le plus grand sculpteur d'alors. D'élève, Camille Claudel est devenue l'assistante et l'inspiratrice du maître. Son influence est présente dans un grand nombre de sculptures de Rodin.

Camille Claudel était elle-même un grand sculpteur, mais ses oeuvres,° produites dans l'ombre° d'un homme que l'on considérait comme l'un des grands génies de son temps, sont longtemps restées ignorées. Un film sur sa vie tragique a fait redécouvrir le talent de cette artiste méconnue.°

Claudel «La Petite Châtelaine»

---

infirme crippled   **fréquenter** = visiter   **lequel** which   **vélodrome** bicycle racetrack   **dont** whose   **douanier** customs officer
débordante overflowing   **peuplés** populated   **oeuvres** works   **ombre** shadow   **méconnue** unrecognized

Notes culturelles

• Dans le film *Camille Claudel* (1988), réalisé par Bruno Nuytten, **Isabelle Adjani** joue le rôle principal de Camille Claudel.

• **Auguste Rodin** (1840–1917) est surtout connu pour sa sculpture *Le Penseur*.

Le surréalisme

Peinture . . .

Regardez bien ce tableau. Il représente un homme avec un chapeau sur la tête et une pomme verte. La juxtaposition de cette personne réelle avec un objet réel constitue une situation qui n'est pas réelle. C'est une situation surréelle ou «**surréaliste**».

L'artiste qui a peint ce tableau est l'un des plus grands peintres surréalistes. Il était belge et s'appelait **René Magritte**. Magritte ressemblait beaucoup à l'homme du tableau. Il portait souvent une cravate, un manteau et un chapeau, même° quand il peignait. Il n'avait pas de studio. Il peignait ses tableaux dans sa cuisine ou dans son salon. Quand il ne travaillait pas, il aimait faire les courses ou promener son chien Loulou, comme les gens du quartier où il habitait. Cet homme à l'apparence très ordinaire faisait des tableaux absolument extraordinaires.

Les peintres surréalistes comme Magritte voulaient choquer le public en créant° des scènes bizarres à partir° d'éléments étrangement réels. Quand on regarde un tableau surréaliste, on reste perplexe et on veut savoir ce que veut représenter l'artiste. Quelle est la signification° des scènes qui apparemment n'ont pas de sens? La réponse est donnée par Magritte lui-même. Quand les gens lui demandaient d'expliquer ses tableaux, il répondait: «C'est simple! L'explication, c'est qu'il n'y a pas d'explication!»

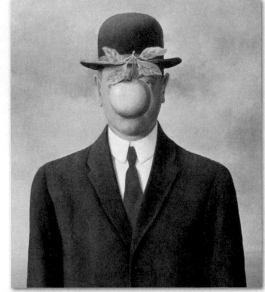

Magritte, *«La Grande Guerre»*

Magritte, *«Carte Blanche»*

René Magritte (1898–1967)

même *even*   **en créant** *by creating*   **à partir de** *from*   **signification** *meaning*

... et littérature

Le surréalisme est un mouvement à la fois° artistique et littéraire. Ce mouvement est né en Belgique et en France vers 1920, quelques années après la première guerre mondiale.* Les artistes et les écrivains surréalistes se sont révoltés contre tous les aspects de la société d'alors, responsable, selon eux, de cette terrible guerre.

Pour les surréalistes, le monde tel qu'on le connaît° est une création artificielle. La véritable réalité vient du subconscient qu'on peut atteindre° par le rêve.° Le surréalisme rejette la raison et la logique. La seule° source d'inspiration est l'imagination, mais celle-ci° doit être libre de tout contrôle et de toute convention. Comme les enfants, et comme dans les rêves, les surréalistes ont construit un monde imaginaire où tout est possible.

* La première guerre mondiale *(World War I)*: 1914-1918.

à la fois *at the same time*   **tel qu'on le connaît** *as we know it*   **atteindre** *to reach*   **rêve** *dream*   **seule** *only*   **celle-ci** = *l'imagination*

DOCUMENTS — La fourmi

LA FOURMI

Une fourmi de dix-huit mètres
Avec un chapeau sur la tête,
Ça n'existe pas, ça n'existe pas.

Une fourmi traînant un char
Plein de pingouins et de canards,
Ça n'existe pas, ça n'existe pas.

Une fourmi parlant français,
Parlant latin et javanais,
Ça n'existe pas, ça n'existe pas.

Eh! Pourquoi pas?

Robert Desnos (1900-1945)

Robert Desnos est l'un des fondateurs du surréalisme. Pendant la deuxième guerre mondiale, il a participé à la Résistance contre les Allemands. Fait prisonnier, il est mort dans un camp en Tchécoslovaquie.

Dans ce petit poème très simple, Desnos pose la question fondamentale du surréalisme: **Où est la réalité? Dans ce que nous voyons ou dans ce que nous imaginons?**

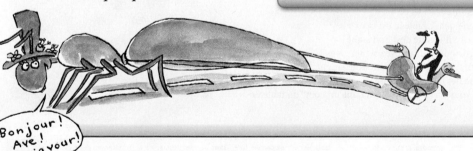

Bonjour!
Ave!
Bavonjavour!

■ **Pour en savoir plus**

For more information on World War II and the Resistance, see *Interlude 6*, pp. 252–259.

■ **Teaching Note**

18 mètres = 59 feet

■ **Note linguistique**

Javanais is the Indonesian dialect of the island of Java. However, for those of Desnos's generation, **javanais** was a coded French slang, similar to Pig Latin, in which the syllables **av** or **va** are inserted after each consonant sound. For example, in **javanais**, **bonjour** becomes **bavonjavour**.

Pour en savoir plus

Oeuvres: **Paroles** (1946),
Spectacle (1951), **La Pluie et le
Beau Temps** (1955), **Fatras** (1966)
Films: **Drôle de drame,
Les Visiteurs du soir,
Les Enfants du paradis**
(de Carné); **Remorques, Lumière
d'été** (de Grémillon)

Note linguistique

la bête = animal

Teaching Strategy

Have students try to guess the
meanings of the words marked with
(°) by looking at the illustrations; if
they are not sure, they can refer to
the glosses to verify their guesses.

DOCUMENTS Pour faire le portrait d'un oiseau

Pour faire le portrait d'un oiseau

Peindre d'abord une cage
avec une porte ouverte
peindre ensuite
quelque chose de joli
quelque chose de simple
quelque chose de beau
quelque chose d'utile
pour l'oiseau

placer ensuite la toile° contre un arbre
dans un jardin
dans un bois°
ou dans une forêt
se cacher° derrière l'arbre
sans rien dire
sans bouger°. . .

Parfois l'oiseau arrive vite
mais il peut aussi bien mettre de
longues années
avant de se décider

Ne pas se décourager
attendre
attendre s'il le faut pendant des
années
la vitesse° ou la lenteur° de l'arrivée
de l'oiseau n'ayant aucun rapport°
avec la réussite du tableau

Faire ensuite le portrait de l'arbre
en choisissant la plus belle de ses branches
pour l'oiseau
peindre aussi le vert feuillage° et la fraîcheur° du vent
la poussière° du soleil
et le bruit des bêtes de l'herbe dans la chaleur° de l'été
et puis attendre que l'oiseau se décide de chanter
Si l'oiseau ne chante pas
c'est mauvais signe
signe que le tableau est mauvais
mais s'il chante c'est bon signe
signe que vous pouvez signer
alors vous arrachez° tout doucement
une des plumes de l'oiseau
et vous écrivez votre nom dans un coin° du tableau

Jacques Prévert (1900-1977)

Jacques Prévert
(1900-1977) est
un autre poète
surréaliste. Il a
aussi écrit des
chansons et des
scénarios° de
films. Dans ce
poème, il
explique de façon humoristique
comment peindre° un oiseau.

Quand l'oiseau arrive
s'il arrive
observer le plus profond silence
attendre que l'oiseau entre dans
la cage et quand il est entré
fermer doucement° la porte avec
le pinceau°
puis
effacer° un à un tous les barreaux
en ayant soin de ne toucher aucune
des plumes de l'oiseau

---

scénarios *scripts* **peindre** *to paint* **toile** *canvas* **bois** *woods* **se cacher** *hide* **sans bouger** *without moving* **vitesse** *speed*
lenteur *slowness* **aucun rapport** *no relationship* **doucement** *gently* **pinceau** *brush* **effacer** *erase* **feuillage** *leaves*
fraîcheur *coolness* **poussière** *dust (visible in the rays of sunlight)* **chaleur** *warmth* **arracher** *pull out* **coin** *corner*

Teaching Strategy: Game

Questions

• Prepare "Jeopardy"-type answers for the
material in the *Interlude*. Group students in
three teams, who compete by supplying
questions.

• Have students memorize lines or sections
from the poem. Each student presents his/her
segment and students identify the lines in
the written poem on the board or on a
transparency.

L'art dans la rue

Quand on veut voir les oeuvres° des grands artistes, on va dans les musées. À Paris, on va au Louvre pour admirer les chefs-d'oeuvres° classiques, au Musée d'Orsay pour regarder les peintures des Impressionnistes et des grands artistes du 19e siècle, et au Centre Pompidou si on veut voir des tableaux modernes. Si on s'intéresse à l'art moderne, on peut aussi se promener dans la rue.

Cette sculpture mobile flottante se trouve° près du **Centre Pompidou**. C'est la création de **Niki de Saint-Phalle**, une artiste qui a aussi créé des bijoux très originaux.

Cette sculpture, intitulée «Hommage à Picasso», représente un centaure, créature imaginaire, mi-homme,° mi-cheval. C'est l'oeuvre du sculpteur **César Baldaccini**. Dans ses sculptures, César utilise toutes sortes de matériaux. Il est connu en particulier pour ses sculptures faites avec des voitures compressées.

Cette sculpture est l'oeuvre du peintre et sculpteur **Jean Dubuffet**. Elle est typique de son style, caractérisé par l'utilisation de lignes parallèles ou concentriques bleues et rouges sur un fond° blanc.

Cette sculpture, oeuvre du sculpteur **Arman,** se trouve près de la **Gare Saint Lazare**. Intitulée «Heure de tous», elle rappelle° peut-être aux voyageurs l'importance d'arriver à l'heure.

---

oeuvres *works* **chefs-d'oeuvres** *masterpieces* **se trouve** *is located* **mi-homme** *half man* **fond** *background* **rappelle** *reminds*

Notes culturelles

Niki de Saint-Phalle (1930–1991), peintre et sculpteur français, membre du groupe des Nouveaux Réalistes des années 60.

Jean Dubuffet (1901–1985), peintre, sculpteur et écrivain français, s'est d'abord inspiré des graffiti et des dessins d'enfants. En 1962 il a commencé à faire des sculptures en matière plastique peinte, comme celle de l'Hôtel de la Monnaie.

César Baldaccini (1921–1999), sculpteur français, apparenté aux Nouveaux Réalistes. Il a surtout travaillé les métaux et les matières plastiques.

Unité 2

MAIN THEME

Being helpful around the house

COMMUNICATION

- Asking for help and offering to help
- Telling people what to do
- Helping around the house
- Describing objects
- Explaining what has to be done
- Expressing opinions

CULTURES

- Learning about pastime activities
- Learning about jobs for French teenagers
- Learning about French fables
- Learning about Astérix
- Learning about *La Chanson de Roland*

CONNECTIONS

- Locating *Les Pyrénées* on a map
- Connecting to Geography: Learning about the *Laurentides* region in Quebec
- Connecting to History: Learning about major events and important people in French history
- Connecting to Language Arts: Learning to brainstorm ideas
- Connecting to Math: Learning to do business math
- Connecting to Science/Health: Learning about occupational safety precautions
- Connecting to Social Studies: Learning about career demographics
- Connecting to Art/Music: Learning to design a brochure
- Connecting to Technology: Researching how inventions make some jobs easier

COMPARISONS

- Comparing French and English use of the subjunctive
- Comparing French and American pastimes
- Learning about the influence of Roman culture on France

COMMUNITIES

- Implementing a service-related business
- Exploring service-related jobs

■ Teaching Strategy: Expansion

Ask students what they think the teens in the picture are doing and why. Why are they wearing name tags?

70 Unité 2

Soyons utiles!

THÈME ET OBJECTIFS

Culture

In this unit, you will discover . . .

- what the French call "bricolage"
- what types of creative activities they engage in at home
- how French young people earn spending money by performing services for their neighbors

Communication

You will learn how . . .

- to talk about various chores and activities around the home
- to ask others to help you, and to give excuses if you cannot be of service to them
- to describe objects: their shape, dimensions, weight, and construction

Langue

You will learn how . . .

- to describe what you have to do
- to ask others to do certain things for you
- to express opinions about situations and events

DIGITAL FRENCH my.hrw.com
ONLINE STUDENT EDITION with...

performance space

News + Networking

@HOMETUTOR

- Audio Resources
- Video Resources
- Interactive Flashcards
- WebQuest

PRACTICE FRENCH WITH HOLT MCDOUGAL APPS!

DIGITAL FRENCH

TEACHER TOOLS

- Teacher One Stop
- Interactive Whiteboard Lessons
- Generate Success Rubric Generator and Interactive Graphic Organizers
- Examview Test Generator

ALSO AVAILABLE...

- Online Workbook
- French InterActive Reader
- @HomeTutor
- DVD Program
- Power Presentations
- Interactive Flashcards

FRENCH ON THE GO!

- Performance Space
- Holt McDougal French Apps
- Discovering French Today eTextbook

Les passe-temps actifs

Le samedi, Catherine, 15 ans, sort rarement avec ses copains. Avec sa soeur Mélanie, 16 ans, elle préfère passer son temps à perfectionner Gustave, un robot de leur invention qui peut se déplacer° sur simple commande vocale. Et quand il y a quelque chose à réparer à la maison, un meuble, un appareil électrique ou même° la voiture de Papa, c'est Catherine ou Mélanie qui s'en charge.° «Nous nous amusons et nous apprenons en même temps» déclare Catherine pour expliquer son goût° pour les travaux manuels.

Le cas de Catherine et de Mélanie n'est pas unique. En France il y a des milliers de jeunes qui préfèrent les passe-temps actifs aux passe-temps passifs comme la télévision et la lecture. Voici deux passe-temps qui sont à la fois créatifs et récréatifs:° le bricolage° et le jardinage.°

■ Le bricolage est une des occupations favorites des Français de tout âge.

Le bricolage

Bricoler, c'est faire toutes sortes de petits travaux manuels. Quand on est un peu créatif et pas trop maladroit,° il y a beaucoup de choses qu'on peut faire chez soi.° On peut peindre° sa chambre, construire des étagères,° installer un système hi-fi ou un système d'alarme, réparer la télé ou la machine à laver, ... Mais attention, quand on démonte° quelque chose, il faut aussi savoir le remonter.° Et surtout, il ne faut pas le casser!°

Le bricolage est une des occupations favorites des Français de tout âge. Et cette occupation n'est pas l'exclusivité des hommes. Aujourd'hui, 75% des Françaises bricolent (et 85% des Français). Pour subvenir° aux besoins des bricoleurs, tous les grands magasins et beaucoup de supermarchés ont un rayon «bricolage» où on trouve l'équipement et les outils° nécessaires. Pour les spécialistes, il y a aussi des magazines comme *Bricolage-Service*. Et pour les passionnés,° il y a à Paris chaque année un Salon° du Bricolage qui attire° des milliers de visiteurs.

---

se déplacer *move around* **même** *even* **s'en charge** *= s'en occupe* **goût** *taste* **récréatifs** *recreational* **le bricolage** *fixing and building things*
le jardinage *gardening* **maladroit** *clumsy* **chez soi** *= à la maison* **peindre** ✻ *to paint* **construire** ✻ *to build* **étagères** *shelves*
démonte *takes apart* **remonter** *to put back together* **casser** *break* **subvenir** ✻ *to meet* **les outils** *tools* **les passionnés** *real devotees*
un Salon *show* **attire** *attracts*

INFOMAGAZINE

INFO MAGAZINE

Theme: Favorite French pastimes

Reading Strategy:
Reading for pleasure; browsing

■ Photo Note
The teens pictured are packing **des boîtes de conserve** *(cans)* and **des tubes de dentifrice** *(toothpaste).*

■ Teaching Strategy
These readings can be done:
- in class or as homework
- at the beginning of the unit or as a wrap-up activity

■ Notes linguistiques
- Le grille-pain (toaster) is invariable: **les grille-pain.**
- Also **une bricole** = a trinket, an insignificant matter

■ Notes culturelles
- BHV **(Bazar de l'Hôtel de Ville)** and **Mr Bricolage** are two store chains catering to the needs of **les bricoleurs.**

■ Irregular Verbs
(see Appendix C)
peindre
construire *(see **conduire**)*
subvenir* *(see **venir**)*
* Note that **subvenir** has **avoir** as an auxiliary.

21ST CENTURY SKILLS

- **Communication:** SE: pp. 72, 73, 79, 83, 85, 87, 91, 94, 96, 97; TE: pp. 83, 85, 86, 91, 97
- **Collaboration:** TE: pp. 77, 83, 106
- **Creativity and Innovation:** SE: p. 97; TE: pp. 79, 80, 83, 81, 91
- **Information Literacy:** TE: pp. 83, 91, 99, 100
- **Technology Literacy:** TE: pp. 77, 83, 91, 97, 98, 99
- **Flexibility and Adaptability:** TE: pp. 80, 83, 91
- **Initiative and Self-Direction:** TE: pp. 77, 80, 83, 91, 92, 97
- **Social and Cross-Cultural Skills:** TE: pp. 96, 98, 100
- **Productivity and Accountability:** TE: pp. 75, 80, 83, 92
- **Leadership and Responsibility:** TE: pp. 91, 106

ASSESSMENT IN UNIT RESOURCE BOOK

Print Resources
- **Workbook TE/PE**
- *Activités pour tous* **TE/PE**
- *Lectures pour tous*
- **Unit Resource Book**
  Audioscripts
  Video Activities
  Videoscripts

Achievement Tests
- **Quizzes, Unit 2**
- **Unit Test 2**
- **Reading and Culture Tests**
- **Assessment Answer Key**

Proficiency Tests
- **Listening Comprehension**
- **Speaking Performance**
- **Writing Performance**
- **Portfolio Assessment**

Le jardinage

Quand on voyage en France au printemps ou en été, on peut admirer les fleurs de toutes les couleurs qui ornent° les parcs publics, les jardins privés et les balcons des maisons. Les Français adorent les fleurs et 60% d'entre° eux pratiquent le jardinage.

Ce n'est pas surprenant° dans un pays où la majorité des gens habitent une maison individuelle et disposent° d'un jardin où ils peuvent planter des fleurs et faire pousser° des légumes. Le jardinage n'est pas seulement une activité manuelle. C'est un loisir écologique qui nous rapproche de la nature et qui est aussi esthétique ... et nutritif. Quoi de plus beau qu'un bouquet de fleurs et quoi de meilleur qu'un plat de tomates qui viennent de son jardin!

et vous?

DÉFINITIONS

Définissez les mots et les expressions suivants. Quand c'est possible, illustrez avec un exemple.

- un robot
- les travaux manuels
- un passe-temps
- le bricolage
- le jardinage
- un loisir écologique

EXPRESSION PERSONNELLE

- Faites-vous des petits travaux manuels chez vous? Qu'est-ce que vous aimez faire et qu'est-ce que vous n'aimez pas faire?
- À votre avis, quel est le passe-temps le plus intéressant: le jardinage ou le bricolage? Expliquez pourquoi.
- Connaissez-vous une personne qui aime bricoler comme Catherine et Mélanie? Décrivez ce que cette personne a fait.

Soyez bon pour les plantes

Les Français aiment beaucoup les plantes. Dans chaque maison française, il y a, en moyenne,° sept plantes.

Les plantes ont beaucoup d'avantages:
— Elles décorent votre chambre.
— Elles purifient l'air que vous respirez.°
— Elles demandent° une attention minime.
— Elles sont propres.°

Les plantes sont des êtres° vivants.° Comme nous, elles ont besoin qu'on s'occupe un peu d'elles. Alors, si vous avez une plante, soyez bon pour elle.

Voici quelques conseils élémentaires:

✿ Arrosez°-la régulièrement. Mais attention: certaines plantes ont très soif. D'autres ont besoin seulement d'un petit peu d'eau.

✿ Si elle aime le soleil,° mettez-la près de la fenêtre. Si elle préfère l'obscurité, ne l'exposez pas à la lumière.°

✿ De temps en temps, mettez-lui de la musique. Les plantes adorent la musique douce.° Elles aiment la musique classique, mais elles détestent le rock et le rap.

✿ Parlez-lui souvent. Chaque jour, dites-lui bonjour et bonsoir.

✿ Ne la maltraitez pas.

✿ Ne l'insultez pas.

✿ Soyez toujours poli et attentif avec elle.

✿ Dites-lui souvent «Je t'aime.»

et vous?

- Est-ce qu'il y a des plantes chez vous? Quelles plantes? Dans quelles pièces sont-elles?
- Avez-vous des plantes ou des fleurs dans votre chambre? Qu'est-ce que vous faites pour elles?
- Pensez-vous que les plantes sont des êtres sensibles *(that have feelings)*? Expliquez votre position.

---

ornent = *embellissent*   **d'entre** *among*   **surprenant** *surprising*   **disposent** = *ont*   **pousser** *to grow*   **en moyenne** *on the average*   **respirez** *breathe*
demandent = *nécessitent*   **propres** *clean*   **êtres** *beings*   **vivants** *living*   **arrosez** *water*   **le soleil** *sun*   **la lumière** *light*   **douce** *soft*

SUPPLEMENTARY VOCABULARY

les plantes vertes *potted plants*
l'engrais *(m.) fertilizer*
la feuille *leaf*
le pot *pot*
la terre *soil*
la tige *stem*
le géranium *geranium*
le lierre *ivy*
la fougère *fern*

General Teaching Strategy: Info Magazines

Although the *Info Magazine* is presented as a light, pleasurable introduction and expansion of the unit theme, some teachers like to check comprehension with a few short questions using the *Info Magazine* quizzes. These quizzes may also be used as a basis for class discussion.

The *Et vous?* activities may be used to encourage class discussion, or as the basis for out-of-class writing assignments.

Ça, c'est la JUSTICE!

Aujourd'hui, Madame Chauvat a beaucoup de travail. Elle demande à ses enfants Victor et Stéphanie de l'aider, mais ce n'est pas facile de les convaincre.° Elle s'adresse° d'abord à Victor qui regarde la télé au salon.

— Dis, Victor, qu'est-ce que tu fais?
— Tu vois, je regarde la télé.
— C'est bien, mais moi, j'ai besoin de toi.
— Pourquoi donc?
— Pour passer l'aspirateur.°
— Alors ça, c'est pas juste!°
— Comment ça?
— C'est pas juste parce que c'est moi qui ai passé l'aspirateur samedi dernier. Alors, cette fois-ci, c'est pas mon tour.° C'est le tour de Stéphanie. Elle ne fait jamais rien!
— Ah oui, c'est vrai, j'ai oublié! Je vais demander à ta soeur.

Victor pousse un soupir de soulagement° pendant que sa mère monte chercher Stéphanie. Celle-ci° est dans sa chambre en train de jouer à un jeu électronique.

— Dis donc, Stéphanie. Je voudrais que tu passes l'aspirateur au salon…
— Ah non, maman. Ça, c'est pas juste… C'est moi qui fais tout dans cette maison!
— Qu'est-ce que tu as fait récemment?
— Eh bien, par exemple, j'ai fait la vaisselle hier.
— Ah oui, c'est vrai… Bon, je te laisse° le choix: la vaisselle ou l'aspirateur.

Stéphanie réfléchit° un instant.

— Mais dis, il y a beaucoup de casseroles° à laver?
— Oui, y en a plein l'évier.°
— Alors, dans ce cas, je suis d'accord pour passer l'aspirateur.

Madame Chauvat redescend au salon.

— Dis, Victor, est-ce que tu peux éteindre° la télé et faire la vaisselle?
— La vaisselle? Mais pourquoi, maman?
— Parce que c'est ton tour.
Et ça, c'est la justice!

et vous?

EXPRESSION ORALE
Comment sont distribuées les tâches domestiques (chores) chez vous? (Décrivez les tâches de chaque personne.) À votre avis, est-ce que cette distribution est juste ou non? Expliquez.

EXPRESSION ÉCRITE
Imaginez que vous êtes Victor ou Stéphanie. Dans une lettre à un copain (une copine) vous décrivez ce qui est arrivé aujourd'hui.

convaincre ✣ *to convince*   **s'adresse** = *parle*   **l'aspirateur** *vacuum cleaner*   **juste** *fair*   **tour** *turn*   **un soupir de soulagement** *breathes a sigh of relief*
celle-ci = *Stéphanie*   **laisse** *leave*   **réfléchit** = *pense*   **casseroles** *pots*   **y en a plein l'évier** *the sink is full (of pots)*   **éteindre** ✣ *to turn off*

■ **Teaching Strategy**
Divide the class into pairs.
• Have students identify all vocabulary that represents a chore.
• Have students identify the expressions that are excuses.
• Have students prepare short dialogs and present them to the class.

N
F
O
MAGAZINE

■ **Irregular Verbs**
(see Appendix C)
convaincre
éteindre   (*see* **peindre**)

Teaching Strategy: Challenge
Have students notice the differences between *casual* French usage, and *standard* French usage:
Pre-AP skill: Analyze language used.

CASUAL FRENCH	STANDARD FRENCH
Pourquoi donc?	**Pourquoi?**
C'est pas juste.	**Ce n'est pas juste.**
Comment ça?	**Pourquoi?**
Y en a plein l'évier.	**Il y en a plein l'évier.**
	L'évier en est plein.

Les travaux domestiques

> Oh là là, j'ai beaucoup de travail aujourd'hui.

Est-ce que . . .

la chambre est **propre** *(clean)* ou sale *(dirty)*?
le salon est **rangé** *(picked up)* ou **en désordre**?
Oh là là, j'ai beaucoup de **travail** aujourd'hui.

le travail *work*	
les travaux domestiques *household chores*	

Dans la chambre et la salle de bains, je dois . . .

faire le ménage *(to clean up)*	**ranger les vêtements**
faire le lit	**nettoyer le lavabo** *(sink)*

ranger *to put away*	
nettoyer *to clean*	

Dans le salon, je dois . . .

ranger les magazines	**nettoyer les vitres** *(windows)*
passer l'aspirateur *(to vacuum)*	**vider la corbeille** *(wastepaper basket)*

vider *to empty*

Dans la salle à manger, je dois . . .

mettre la table	**débarrasser la table**
mettre le couvert *(silverware)*	

débarrasser *to clear*

Dans la cuisine, je dois . . .

couper le pain	**essuyer la table**
laver les légumes	**balayer le sol** *(floor)*
éplucher les carottes	**vider les ordures** *(garbage)*
faire la vaisselle	**sortir la poubelle** *(trash can)*
ranger la vaisselle	
essuyer les verres	

couper *to cut*	
laver *to wash*	
éplucher *to peel*	
essuyer *to wipe, dry*	
balayer *to sweep*	
sortir *to take out*	

Dans **la lingerie** *(laundry room)*, je dois . . .

laver le linge *(laundry)*	**repasser les chemises**

repasser *to iron*

PRINT

Workbook, pp. 115–116
Activités pour tous
Unit 2 Resource Book, Partie 1
   Activités pour tous TE
   Audioscripts
   Lesson Plans
   Block Scheduling Lesson Plans
   Absent Student Copymasters
   Workbook TE

AUDIO
Audio Program
CD 2 Tracks 1–3

TECHNOLOGY
@HomeTutor
Interactive Whiteboard Lessons
Teacher One Stop
   Block Scheduling Copymasters
   Teacher to Teacher Copymasters,
   Les travaux domestiques,
   pp. 15–17
DVD Program, Unit 2

■ Notes linguistiques
- Le couvert = le couteau, la fourchette, la cuillère (à soupe et à café)
- Compare:
  une fenêtre *window*
  une vitre *window pane*
- Note the forms of the **passé composé:**
  sortir *to go out*
     Alice **est sortie** hier.
  sortir *to take out*
     Alice **a sorti** la poubelle.

■ Teaching Suggestion
Play the video with the sound muted. Tell the class to write conversations based on what they see. Afterward, play the video with the sound on to see how close their conversations come to the one on the video.

74 Unité 2

Teaching Suggestion: DVD Program

In the *Vidéo-drame: Nicolas a du travail* in Unit 2, students will learn about household chores. As they watch Mélanie and Nicolas prepare the house for a party, have students write down the chores/tasks they hear. After viewing the video, discuss with the students *their* daily chores around the house.

> Je dois aussi m'occuper des animaux.

Dehors *(outside)*, dans le jardin, je dois . . .

laver la voiture	**couper l'herbe** *(grass)*
arroser | **les plantes**	**tondre la pelouse** *(lawn)*
| **les fleurs** *(flowers)*	**tailler les arbustes** *(shrubs)*

arroser *to water*	**tondre** *to mow, to cut very short*
tailler *to prune*	

Je dois aussi **m'occuper des animaux.** Je dois . . .

promener le chien	
donner à manger | **au chat**	
| **au lapin**	
vider | **l'aquarium**	
remplir |	
nettoyer la cage | **de l'oiseau**	
| **de la perruche** *(parakeet)*	

s'occuper de *to take care of*

donner à manger à *to feed*

remplir *to fill*

1 et vous?

Révision p. R21
Verbes en –ger *(ranger)*

Indiquez comment vous participez aux travaux domestiques.
Comparez vos réponses avec celles de votre partenaire.

1. En général, ma chambre est . . .
   • propre
   • rangée
   • en désordre
   • ??

2. Je fais mon lit . . .
   • le matin
   • le soir
   • jamais
   • ??

3. Je range ma chambre . . .
   • tous les jours
   • toutes les semaines
   • une fois par mois
   • ??

4. Quand j'aide à faire le ménage, je préfère . . .
   • passer l'aspirateur
   • vider les corbeilles
   • nettoyer les vitres
   • ??

5. Quand j'aide mon père (ma mère) dans la cuisine, je préfère . . .
   • éplucher les légumes
   • essuyer les assiettes
   • nettoyer l'évier *(kitchen sink)*
   • ??

6. Quand j'aide avec les repas, je préfère . . .
   • mettre le couvert
   • débarrasser la table
   • faire la vaisselle
   • ??

7. Quand je travaille dans le jardin, je préfère . . .
   • tondre la pelouse
   • arroser les plantes
   • tailler les arbustes
   • ??

8. Le travail que je déteste le plus est de . . .
   • balayer le garage
   • sortir les poubelles
   • vider les ordures
   • ??

Teaching Strategy: Vocabulary Support

Use pictures or transparencies to present the vocabulary. Do frequent comprehension checks by personalizing questions to students about their own chores.

You may also have each student make a list of the people in their family across the top of a piece of paper, then list the chores each person does. After five minutes, ask questions and have students answer (in complete sentences) based on their lists.

■ **Variation**

PAIRED FORMAT
Vous cherchez l'une des personnes de l'illustration. Demandez à votre partenaire où est cette personne et ce qu'elle fait.
— Où est le grand-père?
— Il est dans le jardin.
— Qu'est-ce qu'il fait?
— Il taille les arbustes.
CONVERSATION FORMAT
— Qu'est-ce que tu vas faire cet été?
— Je vais travailler ...
— Ah bon? Qu'est-ce que tu vas faire?
— Je vais ...
— Et toi, qu'est-ce que tu vas faire cet été?
— Je vais travailler ... (etc.)

■ **Note linguistique**

Remind students that **un boulot** is also a familiar form of "work."

2 La famille Duboulot

Aujourd'hui, tout le monde est très occupé chez les Duboulot. Choisissez deux personnes et dites où sont ces personnes et ce qu'elles font.

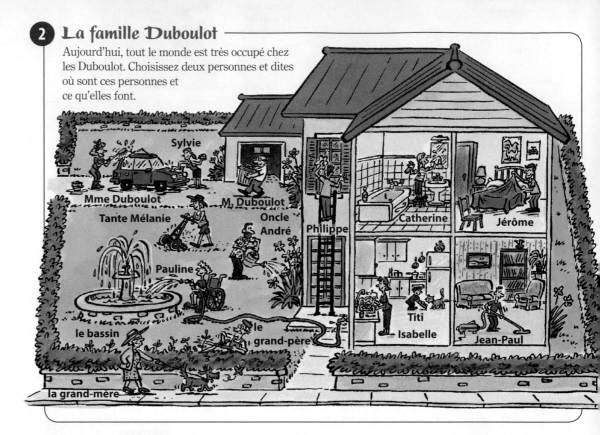

3 Jobs d'été

Votre partenaire et vous, vous allez travailler cet été. Choisissez un job de la colonne A. Votre partenaire va choisir un job de la colonne B. Expliquez ce que vous allez faire. Donnez deux ou trois exemples.

▶ — Moi, je vais travailler dans la cuisine d'un restaurant. Je vais éplucher les légumes et faire la vaisselle. Je vais aussi . . .
— Et moi, je vais travailler dans un zoo. Je vais . . .

Digital performance space

A. Vous	B. Votre partenaire
• travailler dans la cuisine d'un restaurant	• travailler dans la salle *(dining room)* d'un restaurant
• travailler pour les jardins publics de la ville	• travailler dans un zoo
• travailler pour une entreprise de nettoyage *(cleaning)* de bureaux	• travailler comme jardinier *(gardener)* dans un hôtel
• travailler chez un marchand d'animaux domestiques *(pets)*	• être concierge dans un immeuble *(building superintendent)*
• être garçon d'étage *(femme de chambre)* dans un hôtel	• travailler dans une blanchisserie *(laundry)*
	• travailler pour les voisins

76 soixante-seize
Unité 2

Teaching Strategy: Warm-Up

Use the transparencies of the illustration in Act. 2, **Projectables Transparencies 19, 19(o),** to re-enter the vocabulary on pp. 74–75.

Then have each student write a chore on a slip of paper. Collect the slips in a container and have each student choose one. Students then mime their chores one by one, with the rest of the class guessing until it is identified.

Quelques objets utiles

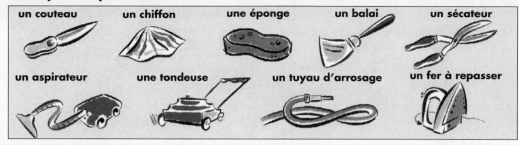

un couteau   un chiffon   une éponge   un balai   un sécateur

un aspirateur   une tondeuse   un tuyau d'arrosage   un fer à repasser

4 Le bon objet

Choisissez un objet de la liste et dites pourquoi vous avez besoin de cet objet.

♻ RAPPEL

de + le → du
J'ai besoin du couteau.

J'ai besoin de . . .

- l'aspirateur
- le balai
- le fer
- la tondeuse
- le sécateur
- le tuyau d'arrosage
- un chiffon
- un couteau
- une éponge

pour . . .

- essuyer la table
- nettoyer la chambre
- laver la voiture
- éplucher les carottes
- repasser cette chemise
- tondre la pelouse
- nettoyer le lavabo
- tailler le rosier (rose bush)
- balayer le garage

5 Le chalet des Laurentides 💬

Vous passez l'été dans la région des Laurentides. Il y a beaucoup de travail dans le chalet que vous avez loué avec vos cousins. Malheureusement, vos cousins ne sont pas très coopératifs. Quand vous leur demandez de faire quelque chose, ils trouvent une excuse. Jouez les dialogues avec votre partenaire.

Dis, Annie, est-ce que tu peux essuyer la table?

Je voudrais bien, mais j'ai un problème.

Quoi?

Je ne trouve pas l'éponge.

TRAVAUX	EXCUSES
• tondre la pelouse	• Le chiffon est sale.
• arroser les fleurs	• L'aspirateur est cassé (broken).
• tailler les arbustes	• Le fer ne fonctionne pas.
• essuyer la table	• La tondeuse ne marche pas.
• essuyer les assiettes	• Je ne trouve pas l'éponge.
• éplucher les pommes de terre	• J'ai perdu le sécateur.
• balayer la terrasse	• Je n'ai pas de couteau.
• repasser les serviettes (napkins)	• Je ne sais pas où est le balai.
• nettoyer le salon	• Il y a un trou (hole) dans le tuyau.
• ??	• ??

NOTE *Culturelle*

Située dans la province de Québec, la région des **Laurentides** est populaire à la fois pour ses stations de ski en hiver et pour ses stations d'été

PRINT
Workbook, pp. 27–28

TECHNOLOGY
@HomeTutor

■ Looking Ahead

Unit 2 presents the formation of the present subjunctive and focuses on its two main uses: to express NECESSITY and to express EMOTION.

The difference between the SUBJUNCTIVE and the INDICATIVE will be developed in Unit 7.

■ Note linguistique

You may point out to students that with **-er** verbs, the present tense and the subjunctive forms are the same for **je, tu, il,** and **ils.**

Je travaille.
Il faut que je travaille. etc.

A La formation du subjonctif (1)

The sentences below express a NECESSITY or OBLIGATION. In sentences of this type, the French use a verb form called the SUBJUNCTIVE.

Il faut que **je finisse** mon travail.　*It is necessary that **I finish** my work.*
(I have to finish my work.)

Il faut que **vous aidiez** vos parents.　*It is necessary that **you help** your parents.*
(You have to help your parents.)

The SUBJUNCTIVE is a verb form that occurs frequently in French. It is used after certain verbs and expressions in the construction:

VERB OR EXPRESSION	+	**que**	+	SUBJECT	+	SUBJUNCTIVE VERB . . .
Il faut		**que**		Marc		**tonde** la pelouse

→ The subjunctive is almost always introduced by **que**.

FORMS

For all regular verbs and many irregular verbs, the subjunctive is formed as follows:

SUBJUNCTIVE STEM	+	SUBJUNCTIVE ENDINGS
ils-form of present minus **-ent**		-e, -es, -e, -ions, -iez, -ent

Note the subjunctive forms of the regular verbs **parler, finir, vendre,** and the irregular verb **dire**.

INFINITIVE		parler	finir	vendre	dire	SUBJUNCTIVE ENDINGS
PRESENT STEM	ils	**parlent**	**finissent**	**vendent**	**disent**	
		parl-	finiss-	vend-	dis-	
SUBJUNCTIVE	que je	**parle**	**finisse**	**vende**	**dise**	-e
	que tu	**parles**	**finisses**	**vendes**	**dises**	-es
	qu'il/elle/on	**parle**	**finisse**	**vende**	**dise**	-e
	que nous	**parlions**	**finissions**	**vendions**	**disions**	-ions
	que vous	**parliez**	**finissiez**	**vendiez**	**disiez**	-iez
	qu'ils/elles	**parlent**	**finissent**	**vendent**	**disent**	-ent

DIS, JULIEN, IL FAUT QUE TU ARROSES LA PELOUSE.

OUI, ... MAIS IL NE FAUT PAS QUE TU ARROSES MON CHAT!

Teaching Strategies: Drill and Homework

To drill subjunctive formation, use the **Multi-colored dice** (p. 45), **"Hot potato"** (p. 51), **"Signature Bingo/Lotto"** (p. 50), or line-up drills (p. 45). As a homework assignment, have students cut out a comic strip from the newspaper, cover the captions, and write *new* ones in French, using at least two verbs in the subjunctive.

Differentiation

Multisensory Divide the class into 2 teams. Have a student from each team stand at the board. Read aloud a sentence, leaving out the verb (e.g., **Je veux que vous — français.**). The student who writes the correct verb first wins a point.

① Le subjonctif, s'il vous plaît!

Révision pp. R26–27

Pratique p. 28

Dire, lire, écrire

Pour chaque verbe du tableau, donner la forme **ils** du présent. Ensuite, complétez les phrases avec le <u>subjonctif</u> de ces verbes.

INFINITIF	PRÉSENT	SUBJONCTIF
▶ laver	ils <u>lavent</u>	Il faut que (nous) <u>lavions</u> la voiture.
1. aider	ils . . .	Il faut que (tu, nous, vous) . . . les voisins.
2. réussir	ils . . .	Il faut que (je, vous, les élèves) . . . à l'examen.
3. répondre	ils . . .	Il faut que (je, Pauline, nous) . . . à cette lettre.
4. attendre	ils . . .	Il faut que (nous, tu, les voyageurs) . . . le train.
5. lire	ils . . .	Il faut que (je, Charlotte, vous) . . . cet article.
6. écrire	ils . . .	Il faut que (tu, nous, mes copains) . . . à Philippe.
7. partir	ils . . .	Il faut que (je, Olivier, nous) . . . à six heures.
8. mettre	ils . . .	Il faut que (je, tu, vous) . . . la table.
9. se laver	ils . . .	Il faut que (tu, vous, ce garçon) . . . les cheveux.
10. se dépêcher	ils . . .	Il faut que (Pierre, nous, vos amis) . . .

② Avant de partir ce week-end

Expliquez ce que chacun doit faire avant de partir ce week-end.

▶ Claire   **Il faut que Claire range sa chambre. Et puis, il faut qu'elle . . .**

Claire	**moi**	**toi**
• ranger sa chambre	• finir mes devoirs	• laver la cage du lapin
• laver son linge	• écrire une lettre	• remplir l'aquarium
• passer l'aspirateur	• téléphoner à mon copain	• donner à manger au chat

Éric et Vincent	**vous**	**nous**
• tailler les arbustes	• finir la vaisselle	• regarder la carte *(map)*
• tondre la pelouse	• vider les ordures	• choisir notre itinéraire
• arroser les fleurs	• sortir la poubelle	• préparer la voiture

③ Après la fête

Votre partenaire et vous, vous avez organisé une fête chez vous. Maintenant vous devez ranger. Vous vous distribuez les tâches. Choisissez une tâche de la colonne A pour votre partenaire. Il/elle va choisir une tâche de la colonne B pour vous.

A	B
• ranger le salon	• ranger la cuisine
• laver les assiettes	• passer l'aspirateur
• laver les verres	• laver les casseroles *(pots)*
• débarrasser la table	• mettre les chaises à leur place
• vider les ordures	• sortir la poubelle
• **??**	• **??**

Teaching Strategy: Expansion

Divide students into groups of two and have them draw their own stick figure cartoon with six different scenes. At least three of the captions should be in the subjunctive. Have students write the captions to their cartoons on six separate pieces of paper. When cartoon and captions are completed, two pairs should exchange their cartoons and captions and try to match the captions with the pictures.

Note: As with any creative activity, the teacher should circulate constantly to verify that structures and vocabulary are correct.

■ Photo Note

The car pictured is a **Citroën 2 CV (Deux-Chevaux)**. Manufactured for the first time in 1939, it was designed to be a mass-market car. Its affordable price and durability made it a popular model for decades. Young people liked it for the same reasons (plus it is a convertible!). The 2 CV is no longer being made in France, but the old model still has its loyal fans.

■ Teaching Note

Before doing items 9 and 10 in Activity 1, you may want to present the complete conjugation pattern of a reflexive verb:

   Il faut que je me lave.
   Il faut que tu te laves.
   etc.

RESOURCES

PRINT
Workbook, pp. 28–30, 116
Unit 2 Resource Book, Partie 1
Audioscripts

AUDIO

Audio Program
CD 2, Tracks 4–5

TECHNOLOGY

@HomeTutor

■ Note linguistique

You may wish to contrast:
Il faut **travailler.**
  *You [people in general]
  have to work.*
Il faut **que tu étudies.**
  *You [a specific person]
  have to work.*

■ Variation

PAIR WORK
Student A describes the message
conveyed by one of the signs.
  Student B identifies which sign is
being described (or draws a copy of
the appropriate sign).

■ Note linguistique

The one-way sign is called
un sens interdit. It indicates **une rue
à sens unique** *(one-way street).*

B Comment exprimer une obligation personnelle: l'usage du subjonctif après *il faut que*

Note the use of the subjunctive in the following sentences:

Il faut que je **parte.**   *I have to (I must) **leave.***
Il faut que vous **travailliez.**   *You have to (you must) **work.***

To express what people HAVE TO or MUST DO, use the construction:

> **il faut que** + SUBJUNCTIVE

→ Personal obligations can also be expressed with **devoir** + INFINITIVE.
  Je dois **partir.**   *I have to **leave.***
→ Note that il faut + INFINITIVE is used to express a GENERAL obligation.
  Il faut **étudier.**   *One has to (one should) **study.***   *You [people in general] have to **study.***
→ The negative **il ne faut pas que** + SUBJUNCTIVE expresses a PROHIBITION or INTERDICTION.
  Il ne faut pas que tu **dormes** en classe.   *You should not **sleep** in class.*

> **ALLONS PLUS LOIN**
> The following expressions are used to express the LACK OF OBLIGATION:
>
> **Il n'est pas nécessaire que** tu partes.
> **Tu n'es pas obligé(e) de** partir.
> **Tu n'as pas besoin de** partir.
> **Tu n'as pas à** partir.
>
> *You don't have to leave.*

4 Obligations?

Voici certains travaux domestiques.
Faites une liste des cinq principaux
travaux que vous devez faire.
Classez-les par ordre d'importance.
Puis comparez votre liste avec celle
de votre partenaire.

- ranger le salon
- laver la vaisselle
- débarrasser la table
- laver le linge
- sortir la poubelle
- arroser les plantes
- tondre la pelouse
- passer l'aspirateur
- mettre le couvert
- ranger ma chambre
- vider les ordures
- donner à manger au chien/chat
- **??**

MA LISTE
IL FAUT QUE JE...
1
2
3
4
5

5 C'est interdit

Vous êtes en France avec des copains. Vous voyez les panneaux *(signs)* suivants.
Expliquez ce que vous ne devez pas faire.

INTERDICTION DE . . .

| **fumer** | **marcher sur la pelouse** | **entrer ici** | **tourner à gauche** | **déposer des ordures** | **écrire sur les murs** |

▶ — Il ne faut pas que nous . . .

Teaching Strategy: Groups

Divide the class into groups. Each group
brainstorms to come up with a variety of new
signs, one for each group member. Next, have
students make their own "traffic signs" for
success in French class.
  (Ex: «**Il ne faut pas que nous parlions
anglais.**»)

Differentiation

Synthetic/Analytic Have students write
English sentences in the construction: I want
you, him, her, them + infinitive (regular **-er, -ir,
-re** verbs only or **dire**) on cards. S1 chooses a
card and reads the English sentence. S2
translates the sentence with the subjunctive
construction: **il faut que** + subjunctive (Ex. I
want him to finish. = Il faut qu'il finisse.).

C La formation du subjonctif (2)

Révision pp. R24–31

Boire, prendre, apprendre, voir

Some verbs like **venir** have different stems in the **ils-** and **nous**-forms of the present. Verbs of this type have TWO STEMS in the subjunctive. (Note that the following verbs all have <u>regular subjunctive endings</u>.)

INFINITIVE	venir		
PRESENT	ils	**viennent**	
	nous	**venons**	
SUBJUNCTIVE	que je	**vienn**e	
	que tu	**vienn**es	
	qu'il/elle/on	**vienn**e	
	qu'ils/elles	**vienn**ent	
	que nous	**ven**ions	
	que vous	**ven**iez	

Il faut que . . .

acheter	j'**achète**	nous **achetions**
espérer	j'**espère**	nous **espérions**
appeler	j'**appelle**	nous **appelions**
payer	je **paie**	nous **payions**
boire	je **boive**	nous **buvions**
voir	je **voie**	nous **voyions**
prendre	je **prenne**	nous **prenions**

6 Chez le médecin

Vous êtes médecin. Donnez des conseils à un patient, Monsieur Grosjean, qui n'est pas en forme. Commencez vos phrases par **il faut que vous . . .** ou **il ne faut pas que vous . . .**

▶ boire trop de café
Il ne faut pas que vous buviez trop de café.

- boire beaucoup d'eau minérale?
- se lever tôt?
- se lever tard?
- dormir bien?
- acheter un vélo?
- apprendre à nager?
- prendre des vitamines?
- s'inquiéter trop?
- payer ma note (bill)?
- revenir dans un mois?

7 La meilleure solution

Avec votre partenaire, choisissez une des situations et décidez ensemble des choses que les personnes doivent faire **(il faut que . . .)** ou ne pas faire **(il ne faut pas que . . .).**

1. Philippe veut rentrer chez lui, mais il n'a pas la clé.
   - attendre sa mère?
   - casser (break) une fenêtre?
   - retourner à l'école?
   - **??**

2. Valérie a dîné au restaurant. Elle a oublié son portefeuille.
   - partir sans payer?
   - téléphoner à son copain?
   - travailler dans la cuisine?
   - **??**

3. Les touristes sont à l'hôtel. Ils voient de la fumée (smoke).
   - sortir par la porte?
   - sauter (jump) par la fenêtre?
   - attendre l'arrivée des pompiers?
   - **??**

4. Marc est secrètement amoureux de Stéphanie mais il est très timide.
   - lui écrire un poème?
   - lui envoyer une lettre d'amour anonyme?
   - prendre des leçons de danse et inviter Stéphanie dans une discothèque?
   - **??**

5. Hélène et Catherine ont eu un accident avec la voiture de leur mère.
   - dire la vérité à leur mère?
   - voir un garagiste?
   - payer la réparation?
   - **??**

6. Thomas et Julien ont trouvé un portefeuille dans la rue.
   - apporter le portefeuille à la police?
   - mettre une annonce dans un journal?
   - garder (keep) le portefeuille?
   - **??**

Teaching Strategy: Writing Practice

Divide the class into groups of six. Give each group a "situation sheet." As music plays, students take turns writing sentences to solve the situation. When the music stops, each group reads its situation and suggested solution.

Differentiation

Structured Have students practice pronouncing irregular subjunctive forms of the verbs **venir** and **acheter** (with two stems).

Have students write the subjunctive stems of all infinitives in Act. 7 with the appropriate subject pronoun.

■ Vocabulary Expansion

Also:
croire
  que **je croie**
  que **nous croyions**
recevoir
  que **je reçoive**
  que **nous recevions**

■ Note linguistique

Verbs ending in **-ger** and **-cer** have only one subjunctive stem:
ranger (nous rangeons)
  que **je range**
  que **nous rangions**
commencer (nous commençons)
  que **je commence**
  que **nous commencions**

■ Teaching Strategy: Challenge

As homework or as a written assignment, students can create new situations and suggest additional possible solutions.

Le travail, ça paie!

Aux États-Unis, beaucoup de jeunes travaillent régulièrement dans les supermarchés, les restaurants ou les stations-service. En France, les jeunes n'ont pas de travail régulier pendant l'année scolaire. (Ils ont trop de devoirs à faire à la maison!) Mais certains ont des jobs qui leur permettent de gagner un peu d'argent. Voici le cas de cinq jeunes Français qui ont découvert° que le travail, ça paie!

Camille, 15 ans, adore les animaux. Un jour, elle espère être vétérinaire. En attendant,° elle a transformé son amour° des animaux en job.

《*Dans mon quartier, il y a beaucoup d'animaux, mais leurs propriétaires° n'ont pas toujours le temps de s'occuper d'eux. Alors, c'est moi qui le fais. Quand les gens partent le week-end, par exemple, je vais chez eux pour donner à manger à leurs chats et je promène leurs chiens. Je préfère les gros° chiens, comme les dobermans et les bergers allemands.° D'abord, ça a plus d'allure° et puis les pourboires° sont meilleurs.*

Je pourrais° gagner plus d'argent si je pouvais garder° les animaux chez moi. Malheureusement, mon père n'est pas d'accord. Il veut bien° que je gagne de l'argent, mais il refuse absolument que je transforme la maison en chenil.° Dommage!》

Pour Jean-François, 15 ans, la cuisine n'a pas de secret, mais c'est dans la pâtisserie qu'il excelle.

《*J'ai toujours aimé faire des gâteaux. Quand j'étais petit, je passais mon temps dans la cuisine à regarder ma mère. C'est elle qui m'a appris à faire les mousses, les brioches,* les tartes aux fruits, les gâteaux à la crème ou au chocolat, et surtout les crêpes créoles,** une spécialité de la Martinique. Je cuisine° pour m'amuser, mais aussi pour gagner un peu d'argent. Quand les gens du quartier préparent une fête, c'est souvent à moi qu'ils font appel° pour les pâtisseries. (Ils savent que mes gâteaux sont meilleurs et moins chers que ceux du boulanger du coin!°) La semaine prochaine, par exemple, je dois faire les pâtisseries pour une réception de 50 personnes. J'espère que ma mère va me donner un coup de main!°*》

Pendant l'année scolaire, Aïcha, 16 ans, n'a pas de job, mais en juillet et août, elle est très occupée. Aïcha explique:

《*Quand les gens sont en vacances, moi je travaille. Chaque été, je m'occupe, en effet, d'une vingtaine de jardins. Je tonds les pelouses, je taille les arbustes, j'arrose les plantes et les fleurs. Vingt jardins, ça représente beaucoup de travail. Quand j'ai trop à faire, je recrute des assistants. En général, ce sont mes copains de lycée. Ils m'appellent "Aïcha l'arrosoir,°" mais quand ils ont besoin de gagner un peu d'argent, ils sont bien contents de me trouver!*》

*Une brioche is a light, sweet pastry prepared as a bun or a round bread. **Une crêpe créole is made with coconut milk and is flavored with cinnamon and nutmeg.
découvrir ✹ *to discover* **En attendant** *In the meantime* **amour** *love* **propriétaires** *owners* **gros** = *grands* **les bergers allemands** *shepherd dogs* **plus d'allure** *look more impressive* **les pourboires** *tips* **pourrais** *could* **garder** *keep* **Il veut bien** = *il est d'accord pour* **chenil** *kennel* **cuisine** = *fais la cuisine* **font appel** = *appellent* **du coin** = *quartier* **un coup de main** = *m'aider* **l'arrosoir** *watering can*

RESOURCES

TECHNOLOGY
Teacher One Stop
 **Projectable Transparencies**
  20, *Le travail, ça paie!*
  20(o), *Le travail, ça paie!*
  Transparency Copymasters,
  p. A44

■ Teaching Strategy

These readings can be done:
• in class or as homework
• at the beginning of the unit or as a wrap-up activity

As *optional* material, you may wish to use them as practice in reading for pleasure, or as the basis for class discussion.

  To verify comprehension, you may ask students to write two sentences (using the subjunctive) which best summarize, advertise, and/or explain each of the jobs.
Camille:
  Il faut que je promène les animaux des autres.
  (Il ne faut pas que je garde les animaux chez moi.)

■ Irregular Verbs

(see Appendix C)
découvrir   *(see* **ouvrir***)*

Notes culturelles

By law, a French teen must be at least sixteen to be able to apply for a full-time job. One can, however, ask for a special authorization by the **Inspection du Travail,** or Labor Department. As of April 2011, the minimum legal compensation for anyone 18 and older was 9€/hour (about \$12.80/hour). The minimum wage is increased as needed to keep up with inflation. A teen between the ages of 17 and 18 must receive at least 90% of the minimum wage, and a teen under 17 at least 80%.

Avec le premier argent qu'il a gagné, Fabien, 16 ans, a acheté l'équipement dont il a besoin pour son job: une échelle° en aluminium avec laquelle il lave les vitres. Il explique comment il a commencé:

« *Un jour de printemps, il y a deux ans, ma mère m'a demandé de laver les vitres de l'extérieur. C'était un samedi. Il faisait très beau, et j'avais l'intention de faire un tour à vélo avec mes copains. Évidemment, j'étais furieux, mais je n'avais pas le choix. Je suis allé dans le garage. J'ai pris l'échelle, une vieille échelle en bois° très lourde,° et j'ai commencé mon travail. Une voisine m'a vu et m'a demandé: "Dis, Fabien, est-ce que tu veux laver mes vitres aussi? Pour ta peine,° je te donnerai 20 euros." Quand j'ai fini chez moi, je me suis précipité° chez la voisine. Pendant que je lavais ses vitres, j'ai reçu° trois offres d'autres voisins. Depuis ce jour, je suis occupé presque tous les samedis et je vais bientôt avoir assez d'argent pour m'acheter une moto.* **»**

Danièle, 17 ans, et son frère Vincent, 16 ans, ont leur carte professionnelle, leur uniforme et leur compagnie: Ado-Services.*
Danièle explique:

« *Aujourd'hui, les adultes travaillent énormément. Quand ils rentrent chez eux le soir, ils sont trop fatigués pour passer l'aspirateur et faire le ménage. Et le week-end, ils ont des choses plus intéressantes à faire. Mais nous, les ados, nous avons du temps libre et nous avons aussi besoin d'argent. Pourquoi ne pas aider les adultes dans leurs tâches domestiques?*

Un jour, j'ai mis une annonce° dans un supermarché pour offrir mes services. J'ai attendu trois semaines avant de recevoir mon premier coup de téléphone.° Ma première cliente m'a recommandée à une amie qui m'a recommandée à une voisine… Bref,° je me suis vite constitué une petite clientèle.

Bientôt, j'ai eu trop de travail pour moi seule. Alors, j'ai demandé à mon frère Vincent s'il voulait m'aider. D'abord, il a hésité. «Je ne suis pas une femme de chambre»° m'a-t-il dit. Mais, comme il avait besoin d'argent, il a fini par accepter. Maintenant nous travaillons en équipe. Je range le salon, je passe l'aspirateur dans les chambres. Vincent, lui, s'occupe de la cuisine. Il fait la vaisselle, range les assiettes, lave le sol° et sort les poubelles.

Aujourd'hui, notre compagnie Ado-Services marche très bien. Nous refusons même des clients. À un moment, je pensais engager des employés, mais il fallait° assurer leur formation,° prendre des assurances,° acheter du matériel,° etc… J'ai renoncé° à ce projet pour le moment. Mais, si je rate° mon bac l'année prochaine, je sais ce que je vais faire! **»**

et vous?

DÉFINITIONS
Définissez, en français, les mots ou expressions suivants.

- un(e) vétérinaire
- un buffet
- une échelle
- une pâtisserie
- un pourboire
- un hors-d'œuvre
- une femme de chambre
- un boulanger
- un chenil
- une réception
- une équipe

EXPRESSION ORALE
1. Des jeunes Français décrits dans le texte, qui, selon vous, a le job le plus intéressant? Expliquez pourquoi.
2. Votre partenaire et vous, vous allez choisir d'être l'un des adolescents décrits dans le texte. Chacun va décrire le job qu'il/elle a et expliquer les avantages et les inconvénients de ce job.
3. Préférez-vous avoir un job où vous travaillez à votre compte (comme les adolescents décrits dans le texte) ou un job où vous travaillez pour quelqu'un d'autre (par exemple, pour un fast-food, une boutique, une station-service, etc.)? Expliquez votre choix. Considérez les éléments suivants:
   - l'intérêt du travail • la flexibilité des heures de travail
   - le salaire • l'indépendance

EXPRESSION ÉCRITE
Vous avez un job (réel ou imaginaire). Écrivez une lettre à votre ami(e) français(e) où vous décrivez:
- comment vous avez trouvé ce job
- ce que vous faites
- les avantages et les inconvénients de ce job

---

*Ado-Services: le terme **ado** est souvent utilisé pour désigner **un adolescent** (comparez **teen** qui désigne un **teenager**).
une échelle: ladder **en bois** wood **lourde** heavy **peine** = travail **précipité** = dépêché d'aller **recevoir** ❋ to get, receive **une annonce** notice, ad
coup de téléphone phone call **Bref** In brief **une femme de chambre** = chamber maid **le sol** floor **il fallait** = il était
nécessaire **formation** training **assurances** insurance **du matériel** equipment **renoncé** gave up **rate** flunk

■ **Teaching Strategy: Expansion Expansion**

EXPRESSION ORALE
- Imaginez que vous êtes l'un des adolescents décrits dans le texte. Expliquez à un(e) ami(e) (votre partenaire) les avantages et les inconvénients de votre job.
- Imaginez que vous êtes un(e) adulte vivant en France. Vous avez besoin d'un service offert par l'un de ces adolescents (joué par votre partenaire). Expliquez le service dont vous avez besoin. Votre partenaire va demander les détails, proposer un prix et accepter ou refuser le travail.

■ **Teaching Suggestion**

Have students search the online employment classified ads of a francophone newspaper and select an ad for a job they might be interested in. Have them create the "perfect" applicant's curriculum vitae. (You may wish to provide models.) Then, in pairs, have students role-play a mock interview between the applicant and the person in charge of hiring. Have volunteers record the interviews so that you can replay them later for peer critique. As an alternative, share the videos via a website with francophone partner students for their feedback.

■ **Irregular Verbs**

(see Appendix C)
recevoir *(see* **voir***)*

French teens work mostly during the summer months, when they are on vacation and have free time. Jobs are not readily available and competition is intense. Typical jobs for young people include delivering pizzas (**livrer des pizzas**), baby-sitting, au-pair work, summer camp counselor (**moniteur/monitrice de colonie de vacances**), harvesting (mostly grapes), or working in a fast-food restaurant (**dans la restauration rapide**).

Pour rendre service

> Est-ce que tu peux m'aider?

> Oui, bien sûr.

■ Photo Note

a wheelchair = un fauteuil roulant

SUPPLEMENTARY VOCABULARY

**Je te demande pardon,
mais ...** *I'm sorry, but*
C'est dommage, mais ... *It's
too bad, but*
Je suis déjà pris(e). *(busy)*
**Je ne peux pas me le
permettre.** *I can't afford it.*
**C'est impossible. Je suis
débordé(e)!** *I'm swamped!*

COMMENT DEMANDER DE L'AIDE

Est-ce que tu peux | **m'aider?**
| **m'aider à** nettoyer le salon?
| **me donner un coup de main**
    (give me a hand)?
| **me rendre service**
(do me a favor)?

COMMENT ACCEPTER

Oui, | **bien sûr.**
| **d'accord.**
| **je veux bien.** *(I'd love to)*

Volontiers! *(With pleasure)*
Avec plaisir!

COMMENT REFUSER . . . ET DONNER UNE EXCUSE

Non, vraiment je ne peux pas.

Écoute, | j'aimerais bien, mais . . . | je suis **occupé(e)** *(busy)*.
| je voudrais bien, mais . . . | je ne suis pas **libre** *(free)*.
| je suis **désolé(e)**, mais . . . | je n'ai pas **le temps** *(time)*.
| **je m'excuse**, mais . . . | j'ai **d'autres choses à faire.**
| **je regrette**, mais. . . | je dois sortir/étudier.

COMMENT REMERCIER . . . ET RÉPONDRE À QUELQU'UN QUI VOUS REMERCIE

C'est | **gentil!**
| **sympa!**

Merci | **beaucoup.**   **De rien.** *(You're welcome.)*
| **mille fois.**   **Il n'y a pas de quoi.**

Je te remercie.   **Je t'en prie.**

Teaching Suggestion: DVD Program

In this section, *Vidéo-drame: Nicolas a du travail* in Unit 2, students will concentrate on expressions used in requesting help, accepting or rejecting an invitation, and showing gratitude. Take note of the varied responses one can use to get the same idea across.

Differentiation

Cumulative Have students say and copy expressions from each section on differently colored index cards and place them in 4 piles: **demander; accepter; refuser; remercier.** S1 chooses question card and reads it aloud. S2 chooses response card (**accepter** or **refuser**) and reads it aloud. Exchange roles.

1 Créa-dialogue

C'est samedi aujourd'hui et vous passez l'après-midi chez votre cousin(e) français(e). Il/elle vous demande de l'aider. Avec votre partenaire, composez un dialogue et jouez-le en classe. Votre partenaire va jouer le rôle de votre cousin(e).

— Dis, est-ce que tu peux m'aider?
— Oui, bien sûr. Où es-tu?
— Je suis au salon.
— Qu'est-ce que je peux faire pour toi?
— Est-ce que tu peux nettoyer les vitres?
— Je voudrais bien, mais je n'ai pas de chiffon.

• Use another expression.
• Use another expression.
• Name another part of the house or yard.
• Mention a chore that needs to be done there.
• Accept or refuse. If you refuse, give an explanation. If you accept, your partner will thank you.

Conversations libres

Avec votre partenaire, choisissez l'une des situations suivantes. Composez ensemble un dialogue correspondant à cette situation et jouez ce dialogue en classe.

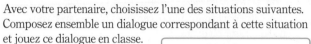

Digital **performance space**

1 À l'université

Jean-Jacques et Christophe sont camarades de chambre à l'université. Jean-Jacques aime l'ordre. Christophe, au contraire, est un garçon très désordonné. Chacun critique les habitudes de l'autre.
Rôles: Jean-Jacques, Christophe

2 Après la soirée

Thomas et Isabelle ont organisé une soirée chez eux. La soirée est finie et Thomas et Isabelle doivent ranger l'appartement qui est vraiment en désordre. Ils discutent de la répartition *(distribution)* des tâches, mais ils ne sont pas d'accord!
Rôles: Thomas, Isabelle

3 Argent de poche

Jean-Philippe veut gagner de l'argent de poche cet été. Il va voir ses voisins pour leur offrir ses services. Madame Brunet répond et veut savoir ce que Jean-Philippe sait faire.
Rôles: Mme Brunet, Jean-Philippe

4 La visite des grands-parents

Les grands-parents de Catherine et de Jean-François vont venir passer le week-end à la maison. Madame Thibault demande à ses enfants de l'aider pour préparer la maison et le jardin. Catherine a d'autres projets et Jean-François est un garçon paresseux.
Rôles: Mme Thibault, Catherine, Jean-François

5 «Le bistrot»

Monsieur Labouffe est propriétaire du restaurant «Le bistrot». Chaque été, il recrute des étudiants pour travailler dans la cuisine et la salle du restaurant. Il explique le travail à deux jeunes employés, Mélanie et Philippe. Ceux-ci demandent des précisions.
Rôles: M. Labouffe, Mélanie, Philippe

6 Drôles de vacances

Robert passe ses vacances chez sa tante Amélie qui a une ferme à la campagne. En réalité, ce ne sont pas de véritables vacances parce que Tante Amélie a toujours des projets pour Robert. Aujourd'hui, Tante Amélie a préparé une longue liste de choses à faire. Robert a décidé de refuse de travailler. Pour chaque chose, il a une excuse.
Rôles: Tante Amélie, Robert

■ Teaching Strategy: Vocabulary Practice

Vocabulary Practice
Before class, write out each of the expressions from p. 84 on pieces of paper and distribute them evenly throughout the class. Ask one student to stand up and show the class his/her expression. Then ask each student who has a synonymous expression to stand also. Have a pre-selected secretary copy the expressions onto the board, thus recreating the vocabulary list from p. 84. Alternately, you may also write the categories on the board and have students list their expression under the appropriate heading.

■ Teaching Strategy: Expansion

(a) Travail au pair
Patrick, un jeune étudiant américain, va travailler comme jeune homme au pair *(helper)* dans une famille française. Il demande à Madame Dumont, sa patronne, de lui expliquer son emploi du temps *(work schedule)*.
   Rôles: Patrick, Madame Dumont

(b) Joyeux anniversaire!
Demain, c'est l'anniversaire de Madame Blanchet. Comme surprise, ses enfants Claire et Julien décident de nettoyer l'appartement et de préparer le repas. Ils se distribuent les tâches.
   Rôles: Claire, Julien

(c) La villa à la mer
Charlotte, Juliette et leurs cousins Laurent et David ont loué une villa à la mer pendant les vacances. Ils discutent de la répartition *(distribution)* des travaux domestiques.
   Rôles: Charlotte, Juliette, Laurent, David

Teaching Strategy: Pairs

Divide the class into pairs; have each pair develop a 20-line dialog between a parent and child. The parent asks to have chores done. The student makes up an excuse, using vocabulary from pp. 74–75 and p. 84. The dialog should include at least two sentences in the subjunctive. This activity might also be done with puppets, either by the teacher or by pairs of students.

RESOURCES

PRINT
Workbook, p. 31

TECHNOLOGY
@HomeTutor
Interactive Whiteboard Lessons

■ **Teaching Strategy**

The subjunctive forms of **savoir**, **vouloir**, **pouvoir**, and **devoir** are not active. You may, however, wish to introduce them here.

que **je veuille**
que **nous voulions**
que **je doive**
que **je puisse**
que **je sache**

■ **Note linguistique**

tant pis ≠ **tant mieux**
too bad ≠ so much the better

■ **Variation: Activity 3**

PAIR WORK

Avec votre partenaire, discutez des choses que vous devez faire pour une des périodes suivantes. Ensuite, écrivez ce que chacun doit faire. Commencez vos phrases par **il faut que ...**

A Le subjonctif: formation irrégulière

The subjunctive forms of **être**, **avoir**, **aller**, and **faire** are irregular.

	être	avoir	aller	faire
que je (j')	**sois**	**aie**	**aille**	**fasse**
que tu	**sois**	**aies**	**ailles**	**fasses**
qu'il/elle/on	**soit**	**ait**	**aille**	**fasse**
que nous	**soyons**	**ayons**	**allions**	**fassions**
que vous	**soyez**	**ayez**	**alliez**	**fassiez**
qu'ils/elles	**soient**	**aient**	**aillent**	**fassent**

1 **Tant pis!** *(Too bad!)*

Invitez votre partenaire à faire certaines choses avec vous.
Il/elle va refuser en donnant une excuse.

INVITATIONS
• sortir
• jouer au volley
• déjeuner
• aller au ciné
• venir chez moi
• faire une promenade
• ??

EXCUSES
• faire mes devoirs
• faire des achats
• aller au supermarché
• aller chez un copain
• être chez moi à midi
• être à un rendez-vous
• ??

2 **Que faire?**

Lisez ce que les personnes suivantes vont faire et dites ce qu'elles doivent faire.

▶ Tu vas ranger la cuisine. (faire la vaisselle)
Il faut que tu fasses la vaisselle.

1. Je vais voir un film. (aller au ciné / être à l'heure)
2. Tu vas organiser un pique-nique. (aller au supermarché / faire les courses)
3. Nous sommes invités à dîner. (avoir un cadeau / être polis)
4. Vous allez prendre l'avion. (faire vos valises / aller à l'aéroport)
5. Mélanie va faire du parapente. (faire attention / avoir du courage)
6. Anne et Thomas vont participer à un marathon. (être en bonne forme / faire du jogging régulièrement)

3 **Choses à faire**

Choisissez une période de temps et nommez deux ou trois choses que vous devez faire en utilisant

il faut que je . . .

• ce soir
• avant le week-end
• ce week-end
• la semaine prochaine
• avant les vacances
• cet été

Teaching Strategy: Warm-Up

Brainstorm a short series of situations in which the subjunctive would be used. Then help students to recognize the subjunctive forms of verbs in sentences.

Differentiation

Alphabetic/Phonetic Have students copy irregular subjunctive forms of **être, avoir, aller,** and **faire** in their notebook. Have students write phonetic transcriptions next to each form (**sois=[swah]; aie=[ay]**). Students should write silent letters in red and underline identical pronunciations for each verb in black.

B L'usage du subjonctif après certaines expressions impersonnelles

Note use of the subjunctive in the following sentences.

Il est important **que nous soyons** à l'heure.	*It is important **that we be** on time.*
Il est bon **que vous fassiez** du sport.	*It is good **that you do** sports.*
Il est dommage **que tu partes.**	*It is too bad **that you are leaving.***

In French, the subjunctive is used after certain impersonal expressions of OPINION when they are referring to specific people.

→ When the expression of opinion is used in a GENERAL sense, it is followed by **de** + INFINITIVE. Compare:

Il est utile **de parler** français.	*It is useful (in general) to **speak** French.*
Il est utile **que Marc parle** français.	*It is useful **that Marc speaks** French.*

VOCABULAIRE — Quelques expressions d'opinion

il est bon que	**il est utile que**	**il est dommage que**
il est important que	**il est naturel que**	**il vaut mieux** (it is better) **que**
il est essentiel que	**il est normal que**	
il est indispensable que	**il est juste** (fair) **que**	

4 D'accord ou non?

Exprimez votre opinion sur l'un des sujets suivants. Votre partenaire va être d'accord ou pas d'accord avec vous. (Ajoutez d'autres sujets à la liste si vous voulez.)

▶ — **Il est important (utile, indispensable) que j'aille à l'université.**
— **Je suis d'accord avec toi. Il est important que nous allions à l'université.**
(**Je ne suis pas d'accord avec toi. Il n'est pas important que nous allions à l'université.**)

- aller à l'université
- être en bonne santé *(health)*
- aider mes parents
- être ponctuel en classe
- avoir beaucoup d'amis
- être riche
- réussir aux examens
- faire des progrès en français
- aller en France
- trouver un job cet été
- avoir mon diplôme
- **??**

5 Pour rester en forme

Votre partenaire veut commencer un programme pour rester en forme. Il/elle hésite entre plusieurs options. Donnez-lui votre opinion en commençant votre suggestion par **il vaut mieux que . . .**

▶ jouer au volley ou au basket?

Je voudrais rester en forme.
Je ne sais pas si je dois jouer au volley ou au basket.

Il vaut mieux que tu joues au volley.

1. manger des fruits ou de la viande?
2. boire du thé ou de l'eau minérale?
3. faire du jogging ou de la musculation?
4. aller à la piscine ou au club de sport?
5. acheter un vélo ou des haltères *(weights)?*
6. faire du golf ou du tennis?

■ **Note linguistique**
When **il vaut mieux** is used in the general sense, it is followed directly by the infinitive:
Il vaut mieux être à 'heure.

■ **Teaching Strategy: Challenge**
Encourage students to continue their conversations from Act. 4:
— **Pourquoi?**
— **Parce que je veux être ingénieur …**
— **Pourquoi pas?**
— **Parce que je veux trouver un job après le lycée.**

Teaching Strategy: Group Practice

D'accord ou non?
Divide the class into two or three groups. Using the expressions in Act. 4, students write as many correct responses as possible. At the end of the pre-determined time period, the group that has used the largest number of expressions wins.

This activity may be done using expanded vocabulary as a "challenge" activity.

RESOURCES

PRINT
Workbook, pp. 32–33, 118
Unit 2 Resource Book, Partie 2
Audioscripts

AUDIO
Audio Program
CD 2, Tracks 9–10

TECHNOLOGY
@HomeTutor
Teacher One Stop
Teacher to Teacher Copymasters,
Et maintenant ..., pp. 23–25

■ **Teaching Strategy: Challenge**

PAS D'ACCORD!
Julien voudrait faire certaines choses mais sa mère n'est pas d'accord. Jouez les deux rôles avec votre partenaire.

- **sortir ce soir**
  JULIEN: **Je voudrais sortir ce soir.**
  SA MÈRE: **Eh bien, moi, je ne veux pas que tu sortes ce soir!**

1. prendre la voiture
2. acheter une moto
3. faire du karaté
4. apprendre à faire du deltaplane *(hang-gliding)*
5. avoir un boa dans ma chambre
6. être cascadeur *(stuntman)*

C · L'usage du subjonctif après *vouloir que*

Note the use of the subjunctive in the sentences below.

Je **voudrais que tu viennes** chez moi.   *I **would like you to come** to my house.*
Éric **veut que je sorte** avec lui.   *Éric **wants me to go out** with him.*
Mon frère **ne veut pas que je prenne** sa voiture.   *My brother **does not want me to take** his car.*

In French, the SUBJUNCTIVE is used **after vouloir que** to express a WISH.

→ Note that the wish must concern someone or something OTHER THAN THE SUBJECT. When the wish concerns the SUBJECT, the INFINITIVE is used. Contrast:

The wish concerns the subject: INFINITIVE	The wish concerns someone else: SUBJUNCTIVE
Je veux **sortir.**	**Je** veux que **tu sortes** avec moi.
Mon père veut **prendre** sa voiture.	**Mon père** ne veut pas que **je prenne** sa voiture.

→ The subjunctive is also used after **je veux bien (que).**

— Est-ce que je peux sortir?   *Can I go out?*
— Oui, **je veux bien que tu sortes.**   *Sure, **it's OK with me** **if you go out.***

QUELQUES EXPRESSIONS DE DÉSIR ET DE VOLONTÉ
(par ordre d'intensité)

je préfère que . . .	j'aimerais que . . .
je souhaite que . . . *(I wish)*	je veux que . . .
je désire que . . . *(I wish)*	j'insiste pour que . . .
je voudrais que . . .	j'exige que . . . *(I demand)*

6 Chez vous

Votre camarade français(e) (votre partenaire) est chez vous. Il/elle vous demande la permission de faire certaines choses. Acceptez ou refusez.

▶ regarder tes photos

Est-ce que je peux regarder tes photos?

Oui, je veux bien que tu regardes mes photos.

(Pas question! Je ne veux pas que tu regardes mes photos!)

1. mettre un CD?
2. faire un sandwich?
3. lire ton journal *(diary)*?
4. téléphoner à un copain en France?
5. emprunter ton vélo?
6. aller dans la chambre de tes parents?
7. aider avec la vaisselle?
8. promener ton chien?
9. donner à manger à ton chat?

Teaching Strategy: Warm-Up

Write out all the different expressions of *wish* or *desire* from p. 88, both with and without **que**, on separate pieces of paper. Distribute to the class, and ask each student to make a sentence with his/her expression.

Put two columns on the board, one for the expressions with **que** and one for the expressions without **que**. Have the students write their sentences on the board in the appropriate column. When completed, ask students to identify the difference between the two columns.

7 Oui ou non?

Décrivez les souhaits *(wishes)* des personnes suivantes. Utilisez **vouloir que** affirmativement ou négativement. Et soyez logique!

▶ le professeur / les élèves (étudier? dormir en classe?)

Le professeur veut que les élèves étudient.
Il ne veut pas qu'ils dorment en classe.

1. nous / le professeur (être très strict? donner de bonnes notes?)
2. le médecin / ses patients (faire du sport? fumer?)
3. Caroline / son copain (être loyal? sortir avec une autre fille?)
4. tu / ton frère (lire ton journal *[diary]*? casser *[to break]* ta tablette?)
5. je / mes amis (dire des mensonges *[lies]*? être patients avec moi?)
6. mes parents / je (avoir de bonnes notes? être impoli?)

8 D'accord, mais . . .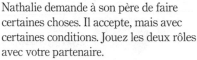

Nathalie demande à son père de faire certaines choses. Il accepte, mais avec certaines conditions. Jouez les deux rôles avec votre partenaire.

1. prendre la voiture
   mettre ta ceinture
   (seatbelt)
2. aller au ciné
   finir tes devoirs
3. inviter des copains
   ranger le salon

4. organiser une boum
   faire la vaisselle
5. faire du parapente
   être très prudente
6. acheter une moto
   porter un casque
   (helmet)

Dis, Papa, je voudrais <u>sortir</u>.

Écoute, je veux bien que tu sortes, mais à une condition!

Quelle condition?

Il faut que <u>tu rentres avant onze heures</u>.

D'accord, Papa.

9 C'est vous le patron (la patronne)! *(You're the boss!)*

Choisissez l'une des situations suivantes. Donnez à un(e) jeune employé(e) deux ou trois tâches à faire. Vous pouvez utiliser les expressions du Français pratique à la page 74/75.

Vous êtes . . .
- le chef d'un restaurant
- le directeur (la directrice) d'un zoo
- le chef jardinier du parc municipal
- le directeur (la directrice) d'une campagne de nettoyage *(clean-up campaign)*
- le patron (la patronne) d'une teinturerie *(dry-cleaner's)*

▶ **Je voudrais que tu . . .   J'aimerais aussi que tu . . .**

10 Expression personnelle

Choisissez une personne et exprimez certains souhaits pour cette personne.

je { souhaite / désire / voudrais } que
- mes parents . . .
- le professeur. . .
- mon copain . . .
- ma cousine . . .
- les voisins . . .

11 Exigences

Expliquez les exigences *(demands)* d'une des personnes suivantes à votre égard.

mon père
ma mère
mes profs
mon meilleur ami
ma meilleure amie
{ exiger / insister pour / ne pas vouloir } que je . . .

■ **Teaching Notes**
- Before doing Activity 7, you may want to quickly review the present of **vouloir**.
- Students may also use **désirer, souhaiter.**

■ **Expansion: Activity 8**
Encourage students to invent their own "conditions."

See if students can then transform the sentences so they could be placed in the opposite column. Remind students that the meaning of their sentence will change (e.g., **Je voudrais que tu viennes chez moi ce soir.** would become **Je voudrais venir chez toi ce soir.**)

Differentiation

Structured Have students copy the infinitives from Act. 7 with the subjunctive stem on a piece of paper (have students place an asterisk next to verbs with 2 stems). Then have students write out a complete answer.

Le Français pratique
Comment décrire un objet

■ Teaching Note
This section is optional, for vocabulary expansion and enrichment.

■ Notes linguistiques
- **Gros** *(big, fat)* is used when referring to the volume, width, or general size of something.
- **Grand** *(tall, big)* refers more to the height of a person or thing: **Le Saint-Bernard est un gros chien. La Tour Eiffel est une grande tour.**
- **poli** comes from **polir** *(to polish)*
  poli also means *polite* (= in a polished manner)

Comment décrire un objet

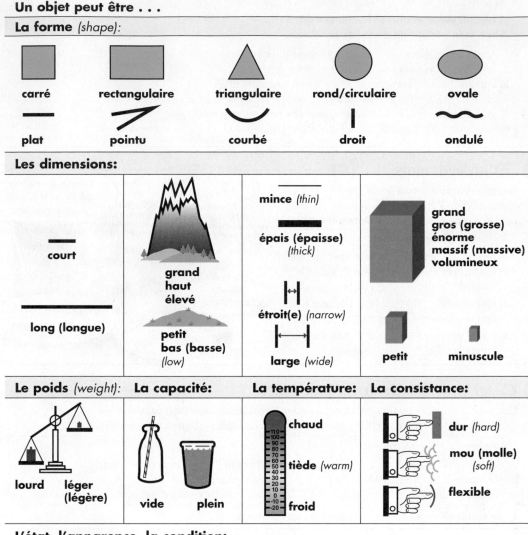

Un objet peut être . . .

La forme *(shape)*:

carré — rectangulaire — triangulaire — rond/circulaire — ovale

plat — pointu — courbé — droit — ondulé

Les dimensions:

court
long (longue)

grand
haut
élevé
petit
bas (basse)
(low)

mince *(thin)*
épais (épaisse) *(thick)*
étroit(e) *(narrow)*
large *(wide)*

grand
gros (grosse)
énorme
massif (massive)
volumineux
petit
minuscule

Le poids *(weight)*:
lourd   léger (légère)

La capacité:
vide   plein

La température:
chaud
tiède *(warm)*
froid

La consistance:
dur *(hard)*
mou (molle) *(soft)*
flexible

L'état, l'apparence, la condition:

solide	≠ fragile
sec (sèche) *(dry)*	≠ mouillé *(wet)*, humide
lisse *(smooth)*, poli *(polished)*	≠ rugueux (rugueuse) *(rough, uneven)*
brillant *(shiny)*	≠ terne *(dull)*
neuf (neuve) *(new)*	≠ vieux (vieille), ancien (ancienne) *(old)* d'occasion *(secondhand, used)* usagé *(worn)*

Pratique p. 33
Comment décrire un objet

Teaching Strategy: Warm-Up
The vocabulary in this section is for enrichment. It can be presented (and practiced) with classroom objects or things which you can bring to class:

une montre
une bague
un bâton de craie
une balle de ping-pong

un ballon de foot
une fenêtre
une porte
un sac

You may also mention an adjective and ask students to name objects that exhibit that feature:

chaud → le thé, le café
froid → la glace, le thé glacé

La matière:

—En quoi est cet objet?
Il est **en plastique.**

le papier	**le bois** *(wood)*	**le métal (les métaux)**
le carton *(cardboard)*	**la pierre** *(stone)*	**l'acier** *(steel)*
l'étoffe *(fabric)*	**la brique** *(brick)*	**le fer** *(iron)*
le caoutchouc *(rubber)*	**le verre** *(glass)*	**le cuivre** *(copper)*
le plastique		**le plomb** *(lead)*
la matière synthétique		**l'aluminium**

En quoi est cet objet?

Il est en plastique.

1 Qui suis-je?

Faites correspondre chaque monument avec sa description.

1. la Tour Eiffel   **2. La Statue de la Liberté**   **3. le bâtiment des Nations Unies**   **4. L'Arche de Saint Louis**

(a) Je suis en métal. Je suis mince, plate et assez étroite. À l'intérieur, je suis vide. Je ne suis ni pointue, ni droite, ni ondulée. Ma caractéristique principale est que je suis courbe.

(b) Je suis élevé et droit. Je suis rectangulaire et plat. Le matin et l'après-midi, je suis plein, mais la nuit, je suis généralement vide. Je ne suis pas entièrement en métal. Je ne suis pas en pierre non plus.

(c) Mon socle *(pedestal)* est en pierre, mais je suis en métal. Je suis verte parce que je suis en cuivre. Je suis grande, mais je ne suis pas très épaisse. Ma figure n'est pas carrée. Ma couronne *(crown)* est circulaire.

(d) Je suis très haute—j'ai 300 mètres de hauteur—mais je ne suis pas grosse. Je suis plutôt mince. Je suis lourde parce que je pèse 7300 tonnes, mais je suis relativement légère. Je ne suis pas en verre. Je suis en fer.

2 Qu'est-ce que c'est?

Choisissez un de ces objets. Puis décrivez cet objet sans mentionner son nom.
Votre partenaire va deviner ce que c'est.

un clou   **un fer à repasser**   **une bouteille**   **une scie**   **une ballon**   **un parachute**   **un réfrigérateur**

Differentiation

Multisensory, Gifted & Talented Have students research and give a presentation on one of the materials listed on p. 91. Students should report on the properties, production, and uses of the material they choose to research.

Unité 2

Interdisciplinary/ Community Connections

Create a class brochure, in French, of services students can perform around the house or at school.

Language Arts
Brainstorm two lists: things that students can do, and things that need doing.

Math
Calculate the costs of supplies of the different jobs, and decide how much pay each task merits.

Science/Health
Find out about safety precautions and the ingredients in various cleaning products.

Social Studies
Investigate who has traditionally done these jobs. Why has this changed?

Art/Music
Design a brochure advertising student services.

Technology
Research how the invention of new technologies has made these jobs easier.

Community
Students may volunteer their services, or charge a modest fee, to people unable to do chores themselves.

SUPPLEMENTARY VOCABULARY

acéré *sharp*
émoussé *blunt*
compact *compact*
dense *dense*
le papier émeri *emery paper*
le marbre *marble*
le nickel
le cuir *(leather)*

■ **Pronunciation**
caoutchouc /kautʃu/

■ **Réponses: Activité 1**
1-d, 2-c, 3-b, 4-a

Unité 2 91

RESOURCES

PRINT
Activités pour tous

TECHNOLOGY
Teacher One Stop
💻 **Projectable Transparencies**

L2, *La Couverture*

Transparency Copymasters,
p. A122

French InterActive Reader

■ Teaching Strategy

- For a broader historical context, you may first have students read *Interlude 2*, pp. 98–107.
- Use the overhead visuals and activities to encourage students to prepare to be attentive and retentive readers.
- Ask students:
  – What is a fable?
  – What can be expected to happen in a fable?
  – Who are the characters in a fable?
  – Is there a moral?

■ Teaching Suggestion

Encourage students to read some of Jean de la Fontaine's fables outside of class.

LECTURE

Additional readings @ **my.hrw.com**
FRENCH
InterActive▐Reader

fable du Moyen Âge

La Couverture

AVANT DE LIRE

Le texte que vous allez lire est basé sur une fable très ancienne, puisqu'elle a été écrite au 13e siècle par un certain Bernier. Au Moyen Âge°, les fables ou **fabliaux** étaient très populaires en France, surtout dans la région du Nord. La fable est une histoire, généralement assez courte, qui a pour objet d'illustrer une vérité morale importante pour les gens de l'époque. Les personnages de fables peuvent être réels ou imaginaires. Dans *La Couverture*, les personnages sont intéressants parce qu'ils sont réels et qu'ils représentent assez bien la vie et la société au Moyen Âge.

le Moyen Âge *Middle Ages*

Anticipons un peu!

Dans la première partie de la fable, un père, qui est commerçant, apprend que son fils veut se marier avec une fille d'une classe sociale plus élevée. Malheureusement, ce fils, qui vient de terminer ses études, n'a ni argent ni maison. Que doit faire le père?

- Conseiller à son fils de trouver une femme qui soit de la même classe sociale que lui.
- Donner sa maison au jeune couple et acheter pour lui une maison plus petite, tout en continuant son commerce.
- Vendre son commerce et en donner les profits ainsi que sa maison au jeune couple.

Maintenant, lisez la première partie de la fable pour voir quelle décision le père a prise.

NOTE *Culturelle*

La noblesse

Avant la Révolution de 1789, la société française était divisée en trois groupes qui n'avaient pas les mêmes droits: **la noblesse** (militaire), **le clergé** (religieux) et **le peuple**. En général, les gens nobles ne se mariaient pas avec les gens du peuple.

Dans ce texte, la différence de classe sociale entre le marchand et le noble est reflétée dans le langage que chacun utilise pour parler à l'autre:

- **Brave homme** *(my good man)* est une expression condescendante.
- **Messire** (dérivé de **monsire** et **monseigneur**) était le terme utilisé au Moyen Âge pour parler à une personne noble. (C'est la forme ancienne de **monsieur**, qui aujourd'hui n'exprime pas la supériorité sociale.)

Notes culturelles

- The most famous French fabulist is **Jean de La Fontaine** (1621–1695). In his fables, animals personify personalities of his time such as the king and his courtesans. Among his 230 fables are **Le Corbeau et le Renard** (The Crow and the Fox), and **La Cigale et la fourmi** (The Cricket and the Ant).

- The university of **La Sorbonne** was founded in 1257 in Paris. At the time, it offered three degrees: **la déterminance, le baccalauréat, and la licence.**

LA COUVERTURE

I

À Abbeville* vivait autrefois° un homme heureux. C'était un marchand qui avait un commerce de tissus.° Il avait peu de biens, mais, grâce à son travail, il gagnait honnêtement sa vie. Cet homme était marié à une femme qu'il adorait. Ils avaient un fils unique. Ce garçon était beau, fort, intelligent et respectueux de ses parents. Chaque jour, le marchand et sa femme rendaient grâce à Dieu° de leur bonheur. Ce bonheur, malheureusement, n'a pas duré éternellement. Un jour, la femme du marchand est tombée malade d'une fièvre subite°. Une semaine plus tard, elle était morte . . . Inconsolable, notre marchand continua° à travailler dur et à s'occuper de l'éducation de son fils. Quand celui-ci eut° dix-huit ans, il l'envoya° à Paris faire des études de droit.

Après deux ans d'études, le jeune homme revient à Abbeville pour travailler comme clerc de notaire. Un dimanche, pendant la messe,° il remarque une très belle jeune fille qui est assise au premier rang° de l'église. Il s'enquiert° de l'identité de celle-ci. On lui dit qu'elle est orpheline et qu'elle vient d'une famille très noble mais sans fortune.

Les dimanches suivants, le jeune homme revoit la jeune fille qui lui sourit°. Il tombe éperdument amoureux° d'elle. Finalement il se décide à lui parler et il se rend compte que la jeune fille l'aime aussi. Alors, un jour il lui demande: «Voulez-vous m'épouser?» La jeune fille lui répond: «Je voudrais bien vous épouser, mais vous n'êtes pas noble. Il faut donc que votre père aille voir mon frère aîné et obtienne le consentement de celui-ci.»

Le jeune homme va trouver son père pour lui expliquer la situation. Le marchand, qui veut faire le bonheur de son fils, va chez le frère de la jeune fille. Celui-ci écoute sa requête, hésite et finalement dit:

— Brave homme, je veux bien que ma soeur épouse votre fils, mais à deux conditions.

— Quelles sont ces conditions, messire?

— D'abord, je veux que vous donniez votre maison à votre fils pour que ma soeur soit chez elle et non chez vous.

*Abbeville. Abbeville est une petite ville de Picardie, une province située dans le Nord de la France. Au Moyen Âge, cette ville avait une industrie textile très importante.

autrefois = dans le passé   tissus *fabrics*
rendaient grâce à Dieu *gave thanks to God*   subite *sudden*
continua = a continué   eut = a eu   envoya = a envoyé
la messe *(Catholic) Mass*   rang *row*
s'enquiert de = pose des questions concernant
sourit *smiles*   éperdument amoureux *hopelessly in love*

Mots utiles

les biens	*wealth*
le bonheur	*happiness*
une couverture	*blanket*
un marchand	*merchant*
appartenir à	*to belong to*
avoir lieu	*to take place*
durer	*to last*
épouser	*to marry*
remarquer	*to notice*
se rendre compte	*to realize*
celui-ci, celle-ci	*the latter*
grâce à	*thanks to*

■ Notes linguistiques

- This introduction to the fable is written in the past. The second paragraph contains three examples of the **passé simple**:
  il continua
  celui-ci eut 18 ans
  il l'envoya
  The **passé simple** is formally introduced in Unit 3, p. 133.
- The remainder of the fable is written in the historical present.

■ Irregular Verbs

- **s'enquérir** *(to ask for information)* is conjugated like **acquérir** *(to acquire):*
  je m'enquiers
  il s'enquiert
  nous nous enquérons
  ils s'enquièrent
- **appartenir** (see **tenir**)
  (see Appendix C)

- In the 13th century, universities were privately owned and autonomous. Most were located in Paris, in the **Quartier Latin,** so named because all scholars spoke Latin.
- The main objective of the **French Revolution** was to establish equality among all people, and, therefore, to abolish the privileges enjoyed by the nobility and the clergy. This is reflected in the second term of the French motto: **Liberté, Égalité, Fraternité.**
(For more information on the French Revolution, you may want to refer students to *Interlude 5,* pp. 216–225.)

Unité 2 93

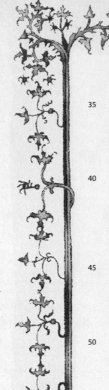

— C'est facile! Tout ce qui m'appartient appartiendra à mon fils. Je lui
donnerai ma maison la veille° même de son mariage. Et la seconde condition,
messire?

— Je veux que vous me donniez 10.000 écus d'or.**

    — Mais, c'est impossible, messire. Je n'ai pas cette somme sous la main.°

    — Que faites-vous dans la vie, brave homme?

    — Je suis marchand de tissu.

    — Eh bien, il faut que vous vendiez votre commerce et que vous
m'apportiez le produit de cette vente°.

    — Je ferai tout ce que vous voulez pour assurer le bonheur de mon fils.

Comme convenu°, le marchand vend son commerce et donne sa maison
à son fils. Le mariage a lieu. Les jeunes époux viennent habiter chez l'ancien
marchand qui leur laisse sa chambre, la plus belle pièce de la maison.

Au début, tout se passe bien. Le jeune couple est heureux. L'ancien
marchand, qui n'exerce plus sa profession, aide son fils et sa belle-fille dans
tous les petits travaux de la vie domestique. Il bricole, répare les ustensiles de
cuisine, coupe du bois pour le chauffage° de la maison, nourrit° les animaux,
s'occupe du jardin. Quand le premier enfant du couple naît, il cède° sa
chambre au bébé et va habiter dans une chambre plus petite. C'est lui qui
s'occupe de son petit-fils. Il joue avec l'enfant, il le promène, il lui apprend à
marcher et à parler.

10 000 écus d'or. L'écu était une pièce de monnaie utilisée en France jusqu'à la Révolution en 1789.
Dix mille écus d'or représentaient une somme considérable.

la veille = le jour avant   **sous la main** at hand, available   **vente** sale   **comme convenu** as agreed   **vente** sale
chauffage heating   **nourrit** = donne à manger à   **cède** = donne

Avez-vous compris?

1. Pourquoi est-ce que le marchand était un homme heureux?
2. Quels sont les sentiments du jeune homme et de la jeune fille? Quel est l'obstacle à leur mariage?
3. Pour le marchand, laquelle des deux conditions émises (expressed) par le noble est la plus difficile à réaliser? Pourquoi?
4. Que fait le marchand après le mariage de son fils? Décrivez sa vie.

Anticipons un peu!

Dans la deuxième partie de la fable, le grand-père, qui est maintenant âgé et très infirme, habite encore chez son fils. Malheureusement, la femme trouve de plus en plus difficile de s'occuper du grand-père malade. Que doit faire le fils?

- Engager une infirmière pour s'occuper du vieillard.
- Garder (keep) le grand-père à la maison et demander à toute la famille de faire le sacrifice nécessaire pour s'en occuper.
- Envoyer le grand-père dans un hospice pour gens âgés.
- Autre solution?

■ Avez-vous compris?

(Sample answers)

1. Il était heureux parce qu'il avait une femme qu'il adorait, un bon fils, et il gagnait bien sa vie.
2. Ils s'aiment, mais la jeune fille est noble, et le jeune homme ne l'est pas.
3. Les 10 000 écus d'or sont la condition la plus difficile, parce qu'il ne les a pas.
4. Il donne sa maison à son fils et sa belle-fille. Il habite avec eux et il les aide beaucoup: il coupe le bois, nourrit les animaux, il répare les outils de cuisine.

Notes Culturelles

- You may point out to the students the many different household chores that were necessary in the past. These included chopping wood (which was used not only for heating, but also for cooking), taking care of the animals raised for food (chickens, ducks, geese, rabbits), and tending the vegetable garden and the orchard.

II

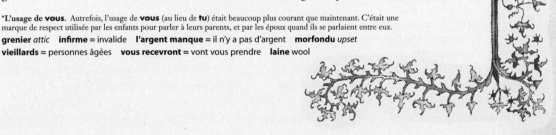

55 *L*es années ont passé et la situation a bien changé à la maison. Il y a maintenant cinq enfants. Le grand-père habite une chambre minuscule au grenier.° Il est vieux et infirme° et il ne peut plus travailler comme avant. Son fils n'a pas réussi dans ses affaires et l'argent
60 manque° à la maison. La femme de celui-ci a perdu sa beauté. Elle est devenue dure et méchante, et elle ne peut plus supporter la présence de son beau-père à la maison. Un jour, elle parle à son mari:

— Votre* père est devenu une charge inutile. Il faut qu'il quitte la maison.
65 — Mais, mon amie . . .

—Oubliez-vous qui vous avez épousé? Il faut que vous choisissiez: votre père ou moi!

Le fils est morfondu.° Il va trouver son père et essaie de trouver une excuse.
70 — Père, il faut que vous* quittiez votre chambre.

— Mais, mon fils, pourquoi veux-tu que je la quitte?

— Père, nous avons besoin d'argent. Il faut que nous louions cette chambre.
75 — Écoute, mon fils, je veux bien aller loger dans l'étable avec les chevaux…

— Père, c'est impossible!

— Et pourquoi donc me chasses-tu?

Embarrassé, le fils doit avouer la vérité: «Père, ma femme exige que
80 vous partiez.»

Le vieillard, consterné, regarde son fils. «Et où veux-tu que je loge?»

—Vous irez à l'hospice des vieillards.° Ils vous recevront.°

— Mais, il fait froid là-bas.
85 Le fils appelle son fils aîné, un garçon de quatorze ans, celui-là même que son grand-père avait élevé quand il était petit.

— Fils, va dans ma chambre. Dans l'armoire, tu trouveras une grande couverture de laine.° Prends-la et donne-la à ton grand-père.

*L'usage de **vous**. Autrefois, l'usage de **vous** (au lieu de **tu**) était beaucoup plus courant que maintenant. C'était une marque de respect utilisée par les enfants pour parler à leurs parents, et par les époux quand ils se parlaient entre eux.
grenier *attic*   **infirme** = invalide   **l'argent manque** = il n'y a pas d'argent   **morfondu** *upset*
vieillards = personnes âgées   **vous recevront** = vont vous prendre   **laine** *wool*

Mots utiles

les affaires	*business*
une charge	*burden*
un couteau	*knife*
la moitié	*half*
dur	*hard-hearted*
méchant	*mean, nasty*
allumer un feu	*to light a fire*
avouer	*to admit, avow*
élever	*to raise (children)*
exiger	*to insist*
expliquer	*to explain*
garder	*to keep*
loger	*to live, lodge*
supporter	*to bear, stand*

■ **Teaching Strategy: Expansion**

Le fils a besoin d'argent. Il veut louer la chambre de son père. Que pourrait-il faire d'autre pour gagner de l'argent?

• Country houses generally had stables (**des étables**), since horses were needed for transportation as well as for farm work.

• In the Middle Ages, many towns had shelters (**des hospices**) for indigent old people, but the living conditions they offered were very rudimentary.

■ **Teaching Strategy**

Ask students to identify uses of the **passé composé** and the subjunctive in the story.

■ **Avez-vous compris?**

(Sample answers)

1. Le père est vieux et infirme. L'argent manque.
2. Il dit qu'il a besoin d'argent. Il veut louer la chambre.
3. Il doit prendre une couverture de laine. Il coupe la couverture en deux.
4. Il explique que son père aura besoin de l'autre moitié un jour.
5. L'histoire finit bien. Le père va rester à la maison.

■ **Teaching Strategy: Expansion**

Ask students:

• D'après vous, comment est le petit-fils? Quelles sont ses qualités?
• Pensez-vous que le petit-fils va envoyer son père à l'hospice plus tard? Pourquoi?

90   Le garçon monte dans la chambre de ses parents, ouvre l'armoire et prend la couverture. Puis, il prend son couteau et coupe la couverture en deux. Il descend dans la cour° et donne la moitié de la couverture à son grand-père.

Son père, surpris, lui demande:

— Fils, pourquoi as-tu coupé la couverture en deux? Et pourquoi
95 n'en donnes-tu que la moitié à ton grand-père?

— Parce qu'un jour, vous aurez besoin de l'autre moitié.

L'homme regarde son fils sans comprendre.

—Il faut que tu t'expliques! Quand donc aurai-je besoin de cette couverture?

100   —Quand vous serez devenu vieux et quand, à mon tour, je vous enverrai à l'hospice des vieillards.

L'homme finalement comprend son ingratitude. Il s'excuse et va embrasser son père qui fond en larmes.° Puis, il va trouver sa femme pour lui dire qu'il a décidé de garder son père à la maison. Celle-ci, qui a vu toute
105 la scène de sa fenêtre, a aussi compris. Elle monte dans la chambre de son beau-père pour allumer un bon feu de cheminée,° puis elle va préparer un grand repas. Une nouvelle vie familiale commence . . .

cour *courtyard*   **fond en larmes** *breaks into tears*   **cheminée** *fireplace*

Avez-vous compris?

1. Qu'est-ce qui a changé à la maison du marchand? Décrivez un ou deux de ces changements.

2. Quelle excuse est-ce que le fils donne à son père quand il lui demande de quitter sa chambre?

3. Qu'est-ce que le petit-fils doit faire dans la chambre de son père? Qu'est-ce qu'il fait en plus?

4. Qu'est-ce que le garçon explique à son père?

5. Comment finit l'histoire?

Notes culturelles

Until 30 or 40 years ago, most French children carried a pocket knife (**un couteau de poche** or **un canif**), especially in the rural areas. They used these knives for all sorts of purposes: slicing bread, eating at the table, sharpening pencils, making whistles, whittling wood, etc.

Would this have been true in rural areas in the United States also? Ask students to compare/contrast.

APRÈS LA LECTURE

Expression orale

Dramatisation

Avec votre partenaire, choisissez une scène de la fable que vous avez trouvée intéressante et jouez-la en classe.

Situations

Avec votre partenaire, choisissez l'une des situations suivantes. Composez le dialogue correspondant et jouez-le en classe.

1	Rencontre

Après sa visite au noble, le marchand rencontre un(e) ami(e) qui est marchand(e) aussi. Il explique sa décision de vendre son commerce. L'autre marchand(e) essaie de le dissuader.
Rôles: le marchand de tissus, un ami(e)

2	Explication

Après la scène de la couverture, le petit-fils explique à un(e) jeune frère (soeur) ce qui s'est passé. Celui-ci (celle-ci) veut des détails.
Rôles: le petit-fils, un frère (une soeur)

Discussion: La morale de l'histoire

Comme nous l'avons vu, l'objet d'une fable est généralement d'illustrer un certain principe moral.

A. Voici plusieurs morales possibles pour la fable que vous avez lue.
- Les gens riches ne sont jamais heureux.
- Il ne faut pas se marier avec une personne d'une autre classe sociale.
- Les jeunes sont charitables; les adultes sont égoïstes.
- Tout est bien qui finit bien.
- On ne peut pas compter sur ses enfants. Pour cela, toute personne raisonnable doit garder ses biens jusqu'à sa mort.
- Il ne faut pas faire aux autres personnes ce qu'on ne voudrait pas qu'elles nous fassent à nous.

Choisissez la morale qui, selon vous, correspond le mieux au récit de *La Couverture*. (Ou, si vous voulez, trouvez une autre morale.) Expliquez votre choix à votre partenaire.

B. D'après vous, quelle était la morale de cette histoire au Moyen Âge? (Pour connaître cette réponse, allez au bas de la page.)

Expression écrite

D'un autre point de vue

Imaginez que vous êtes le petit-fils ou la petite-fille du marchand de tissu. Dans une lettre à un(e) ami(e), vous racontez de votre point de vue la scène de la couverture.

En famille

Décrivez la vie de la famille <u>après</u> l'incident. Pour cela, composez un texte où vous décrivez ce que chacun fait à la maison pour aider les autres.

Fable moderne

Transformez *La Couverture* en fable moderne. Pour cela, composez une nouvelle fable que vous situerez à l'époque actuelle en gardant la morale générale de l'histoire.

D'un oeil critique

Expliquez pourquoi *La Couverture* est une fable très ancienne. Pour cela, faites une liste de tous les détails qui indiquent que l'action de cette fable se passe autrefois plutôt que maintenant.

LA MORALE DE L'HISTOIRE
L'auteur du Moyen Âge qui a écrit cette fable voulait conseiller aux parents de garder leurs biens et leurs ressources pour leurs vieux jours.

■ **Note linguistique**

The original text, transcribed in modern French, reads:
«Mirez-vous dans ce miroir, vous qui avez des enfants à marier. Ne suivez pas l'exemple du vieillard. Si vous êtes en avant, ne vous mettez pas en arrière. Méfiez-vous: les enfants sont sans pitié. Ils en ont assez de leurs pères quand ceux-ci ne sont plus bons à rien. Se mettre à la merci d'autrui, c'est s'exposer à grande affliction.»

■ **Expansion**

Students may wish to compare *La Couverture* to Shakespeare's *King Lear*.

■ **Expression écrite**

For writing rubrics, consult the **Generate Success** Rubric Generator on the **Teacher One Stop.** You can also create your own custom rubrics with this tool.

Student Portfolios

The activities in the *Après la lecture* section may be used as the basis for student portfolio projects, either written or recorded. A group project involving a debate using the *Discussion* topic could be staged within the class or between two French classes. Suggest that a student volunteer videotape the results.

Interlude culturel

■ **Note linguistique**

In 1990, the **Conseil Supérieur de la Langue Française** announced that the word **événement** could also be written **évènement** (with a grave accent on the second "e"). You may allow your students to use either spelling.

■ **Notes historiques**

• **La Gaule** was renamed **Francia Occidentalis** (Franks from the West) after a treaty signed in Verdun, in 843.

• The name "France" comes from the Franks, one of the Germanic tribes that invaded Gaul in the fifth century.

■ **Notes culturelles**

• **Nîmes** and **Arles** are two cities in the south of France where one can admire great Roman ruins, such as arenas.

• The battle of Azincourt is the main scene in Shakespeare's play *Henry V*.

Les dates

20 000	av. J.-C. *Lascaux*
200	av. J.-C.
151	*Provincia Romana*
52	*Vercingétorix*
0	*à Gergovie*
450	apr. J.-C.
508	Clovis, roi des Francs
778	Roland à Roncevaux
800	*Sacre de Charlemagne*
1066	Guillaume le Conquérant: Bataille de Hastings
1152	Aliénor d'Aquitaine épouse Henri Plantagenêt
1337	
1429	*Jeanne d'Arc délivre la ville d'Orléans*
1453	

Période gallo-romaine

Empire de Charlemagne

Guerre de Cent Ans

Les événements

La période romaine (200 av. J.-C. - 450 apr. J.-C.)

Les premières légions romaines arrivent dans le sud de **la Gaule** (l'ancien nom de la France) au deuxième siècle avant Jésus-Christ. En 151 av. J.-C., Rome annexe cette région qui devient «Provincia Romana» ou Provence. En 58 av. J.-C., **Jules César** arrive en Gaule pour conquérir le reste du pays. Ses troupes sont victorieuses, malgré la résistance héroïque du chef gaulois, **Vercingétorix**.

Les Romains construisent de nombreux monuments, visibles encore aujourd'hui: arènes, amphithéâtres, arcs de triomphe, temples . . . Ils apportent aussi leur langue, le latin, qui est la base du français moderne.

À partir de 400, une série d'invasions met fin à la civilisation gallo-romaine. Les Francs, tribu d'origine germanique, conquièrent la Gaule. En 508, **Clovis,** leur roi, choisit Paris comme capitale. La Gaule va devenir la France.

L'Empire de Charlemagne (800-814)

En 800, **Charlemagne,** ou Charles le Grand, roi des Francs, est sacré empereur de l'Occident. Son empire est immense: il comprend la France, l'Allemagne, la Belgique, la Hollande, l'Italie du Nord et le nord de l'Espagne. Avec Charlemagne, l'unification de l'Europe est pour la première fois réalisée.

La Guerre de Cent Ans (1337-1453)

Cette guerre représente plus de 100 ans de conflits franco-anglais. Elle commence en 1337 quand **Édouard III,** roi d'Angleterre, veut devenir roi de France. Les armées anglaises débarquent en France et remportent de brillantes victoires à **Crécy** (1346), à **Poitiers** (1356) et à **Azincourt** (1415). Les Anglais occupent une grande partie du territoire français et dévastent le pays.

Finalement la chance tourne. En 1429, **Jeanne d'Arc,** une jeune fille de 19 ans, rallie l'armée française, qui va peu à peu libérer la France.

Teaching Strategy

This *Interlude* may be used in a wide variety of ways, but the presentation should remain enjoyable and not overwhelming. You may wish to begin by showing students segments of a film on Joan of Arc, sharing information on the discovery of the Lascaux caves, or comparing historical events in other parts of the world.

The *Interlude* quizzes may be used to assess comprehension rather than as a grading tool. Research projects may also be assigned, or creative writings where students imagine what it would have been like to live in this period.

Les personnes

Vercingétorix: un général de 20 ans

Vercingétorix (72-46 av. J.-C.) est le premier héros national français. En gaulois, son nom signifie «chef suprême des combattants». En 52 av. J.-C., il a vingt ans. Jeune et courageux, il décide de se révolter contre l'occupant romain. Il rallie les tribus gauloises, devient leur chef et attaque les légions romaines. **César** contre-attaque. Malgré la supériorité des Romains, Vercingétorix est victorieux à **Gergovie**. Mais le combat est inégal et finalement, quelques mois plus tard, Vercingétorix est capturé. Enchaîné, il est emmené à Rome où il figure au triomphe de César, puis il est exécuté.

Pour les Français, Vercingétorix symbolise le courage, le patriotisme, l'esprit d'indépendance et la résistance contre l'ennemi.

Vercingétorix (72 - 46 av. J-C) le premier héros national français

Charlemagne: Empereur de l'Occident

Charlemagne (747-814) est un grand conquérant et un grand administrateur. Pour gouverner son très vaste empire, il établit sa capitale à **Aix-la-Chapelle** au centre de cet empire et crée une administration centralisée.

Charlemagne (742 - 814), Empereur de l'Occident

Charlemagne fonde aussi un grand nombre d'écoles, les «écoles du palais». C'est un homme cultivé qui parle latin et grec et s'intéresse aux sciences. Il encourage la littérature, la philosophie, les sciences, la médecine, les arts, l'architecture. Dans sa capitale, il fonde une Académie où viennent les plus grands savants° du monde.

Jeanne d'Arc: héroïne et martyre

On trouve la statue de **Jeanne d'Arc** (1412-1431) dans toutes les églises de France. C'est non seulement une sainte de l'église catholique, mais aussi la grande héroïne française. Jeanne a seulement 17 ans quand le roi de France lui donne le commandement de son armée. Elle rallie les troupes démoralisées par de nombreuses défaites. Puis, elle délivre **Orléans**, assiégée par les Anglais, et va de victoire en victoire. Elle est finalement capturée par des soldats

Jeanne d'Arc (1412-1431), grande héroïne française

bourguignons° qui la vendent à leurs alliés anglais. Elle est jugée, accusée de sorcellerie° et condamnée à être brûlée.° La mort héroïque de Jeanne d'Arc, à l'âge de 19 ans, ne profite pas aux Anglais qui sont définitivement chassés de France quelques années plus tard.

---

savants *scientists* **bourguignons** = de Bourgogne *(Burgundy)* **sorcellerie** *witchcraft* **brûlée** *burned at the stake*

FRANCE
Lascaux

Une galerie d'art préhistorique: Lascaux

■ La découverte de Lascaux

Souvent, les grandes découvertes sont le résultat du hasard. C'est, par exemple, le cas d'une très grande découverte préhistorique: la grotte de Lascaux.

Nous sommes au mois de septembre en 1940. À Montignac, un petit village dans le sud-ouest de la France, c'est encore la période des vacances. Un après-midi, Marcel Ravidat, un garçon du village, décide de faire une promenade sur la colline° de Lascaux avec son chien, Robot. Quand il veut rentrer chez lui, il s'aperçoit que son chien n'est pas avec lui. Il l'appelle «Robot! Robot! Robot!» Mais Robot ne répond pas. Finalement, il retrouve Robot près d'un trou°. Quand il examine le trou, Marcel remarque qu'il y a une très grande cavité derrière. Il pense que c'est l'entrée d'un tunnel, peut-être d'un souterrain secret vers l'ancien château de Montignac.

Marcel Ravidat décide d'explorer le mystérieux passage souterrain avec son ami Jacques Marsal et deux autres garçons du village. Quatre jours plus tard, les quatre jeunes partent pour la colline équipés d'un long couteau, d'une pelle° et d'une lampe à huile que Marcel a fabriquée pour l'occasion. Avec le couteau et la pelle, ils élargissent le trou, puis ils pénètrent dans la cavité. Ils ne sont pas dans un tunnel, mais dans une très longue grotte. Les garçons avancent lentement. Avec sa lampe à huile, Marcel éclaire° les murs. Tout d'un coup, il remarque quelque chose d'étrange sur un mur, une sorte de dessin°. Les garçons s'approchent et voient que c'est la représentation très réaliste d'un bison. Il y a d'autres bisons, des bisons rouges, des bisons jaunes, des bisons noirs. La peinture semble presque fraîche. Qui a peint ces animaux?

Les jours suivants, les garçons retournent à la grotte et continuent leur exploration. Ils découvrent d'autres peintures: des chevaux, des cerfs°, et toujours des bisons. Il y a au total plus de mille animaux. Les garçons veulent garder le secret de leur découverte, mais quand ils rentrent chez eux tard et couverts de poussière°, leurs parents demandent des explications. Ils sont obligés de dire où ils sont allés et ce qu'ils ont fait. Finalement ils révèlent leurs découvertes.

Alerté, l'instituteur° du village comprend immédiatement l'importance de ces découvertes. Il prend contact avec l'abbé Henri Breuil, le grand spécialiste de la préhistoire. Quand celui-ci pénètre dans la grotte et voit les peintures, il est stupéfait par leur abondance et leur quantité. Il explique aux garçons que ces peintures datent de 20 000 ans et représentent le plus bel et le plus grand ensemble d'art pictural préhistorique. Il compare leur découverte à un autre grand chef-d'oeuvre° artistique, la Chapelle Sixtine de Rome.

Deux mois plus tard, la grotte de Lascaux est classée Monument historique par le Gouvernement français. Elle est aujourd'hui classée au Patrimoine mondiale de l'UNESCO.

---

colline *hill* **trou** *hole* **souterrain** *underground passage* **pelle** *shovel* **éclaire** *lights up* **dessin** *drawing* **cerfs** *deer* **poussière** *dust*
instituteur *teacher* **chef-d'oeuvre** *masterpiece*

■ L'art préhistorique

Il y a 20 000 ans, des tribus préhistoriques habitaient dans le sud-ouest de la France. Ce peuple a laissé de nombreuses traces d'art pictural dans les grottes de la région, principalement des peintures réalistes de taureaux°, de chevaux et de cerfs. Les experts ne sont pas d'accord sur la signification de ces peintures, mais on pense généralement qu'elles avaient une fonction rituelle et religieuse plutôt° que décorative.

■ Teaching Note

• To further acquaint students with prehistoric cave paintings, encourage students to see the documentary "Cave of Forgotten Dreams" directed by Werner Herzog. This film was made with the special permission of the French government and was sponsored by the French Ministry of Culture and Communication. The 3-D film takes viewers into the Chauvet cave in Southern France.

■ Après la découverte

La découverte de Lascaux a lieu pendant la Seconde Guerre Mondiale. En 1940, la France est occupée partiellement par l'armée allemande. En 1943, les Allemands décrètent que tous les jeunes Français doivent aller travailler en Allemagne. Marcel Ravidat refuse de partir. Au lieu d'obéir, il s'engage° dans la Résistance et combat les Allemands.

Après la guerre, Marcel retourne à Montignac où il retrouve son ami Jacques Marsal. Les deux jeunes gens deviennent les guides officiels de la grotte de Lascaux qu'ils ont découverte. Chaque année, des milliers de touristes viennent admirer les peintures

préhistoriques. Un jour, Marcel remarque une minuscule tache° verte sur une peinture. Les jours suivants la tache progresse et recouvre bientôt toute la peinture. D'autres taches apparaissent.

Des microbologistes viennent de Paris et découvrent l'origine du problème. Le gaz carbonique dégagé par les milliers de visiteurs favorise le développement d'algues microscopiques qui attaquent les peintures. Cette «maladie verte» menace de détruire les magnifiques fresques préhistoriques. Si on veut préserver cet extraordinaire patrimoine culturel et artistique, il y a une seule solution. Il faut interdire l'accès de la grotte au public.

Aujourd'hui la grotte de Lascaux est fermée mais les amateurs de préhistoire peuvent retrouver l'atmosphère et les peintures de la cavité originale. Dans les années 1980, on a construit **Lascaux II** qui est une réplique exacte de la grotte et de ses trésors artistiques.

---

taureaux *bulls* **plutôt** *rather* **s'engage** *joins* **tache** *spot*

Notes culturelles

• Approximately 350 caves have been discovered in Spain and France that contain prehistoric cave paintings. Of that number, about half of these caves are located in France. One of these, the Chauvet cave, is a fairly recent discovery. Discovered in 1994 in Southern France, the Chauvet cave paintings are believed to be the oldest known cave art.

• A few of the numerous sites with prehistoric art in France include the Font-de-Gaume cave, the Niaux cave, the Cosquer cave, and the cave of Tuc d'Audoubert.

Roland, l'homme et la légende

Roland est à la fois un personnage historique et le héros d'une des plus grandes légendes françaises.

Roland son... son oliphan...

■ L'histoire

Nous sommes en l'an 778. **Charlemagne** est en Espagne où il fait la guerre° à des princes arabes. Une insurrection éclate° dans son royaume.° Charlemagne retourne précipitamment en France avec ses meilleures troupes, mais il ne peut pas emmener ses bagages, qui sont trop lourds.° Il confie° leur transport à **Roland**, l'un de ses officiers.

Dans les Pyrénées, le convoi de bagages est attaqué par une bande de pillards° qui capturent le butin° et tuent° Roland.

■ La légende

La légende embellit les faits historiques et le rôle de Roland. Dans la légende, Roland est le neveu préféré de Charlemagne. C'est aussi le plus noble et le plus brave de ses chevaliers.° Il accompagne l'empereur dans toutes ses expéditions militaires. Il est avec lui en Espagne où les Francs combattent les Sarrasins,* ennemis de la chrétienté.°

Comme dans l'histoire, Charlemagne doit rentrer à la hâte en France. C'est à Roland qu'il confie son arrière-garde.° Roland est trahi° par l'infâme **Ganelon**, son beau-père. À **Roncevaux**, son armée de 20 000 hommes tombe dans une embuscade° tendue par 400 000 Sarrasins. Quand **Olivier**, le loyal compagnon de Roland, voit l'arrivée des ennemis, il demande à Roland de sonner° son oliphant (un cor° en ivoire d'éléphant) pour appeler Charlemagne. Homme d'honneur, Roland refuse: il préfère se battre.°

Les Francs et les Sarrasins en combat.

L'infâme Ganelon

Charlemagne et son neveu préféré, Roland

* **Sarrasins:** nom donné aux conquérants arabes venus en Europe au 8e siècle.

---

guerre *war* **éclate** *breaks out* **royaume** *kingdom* **lourds** *heavy* **confie** *entrusts* **pillards** *looters* **butin** *booty* **tuent** *kill* **chevaliers** *knights* **chrétienté** *Christendom* **arrière-garde** *rear guard* **trahi** *betrayed* **embuscade** *ambush* **sonner** *to blow* **cor** *horn* **se battre** *to fight*

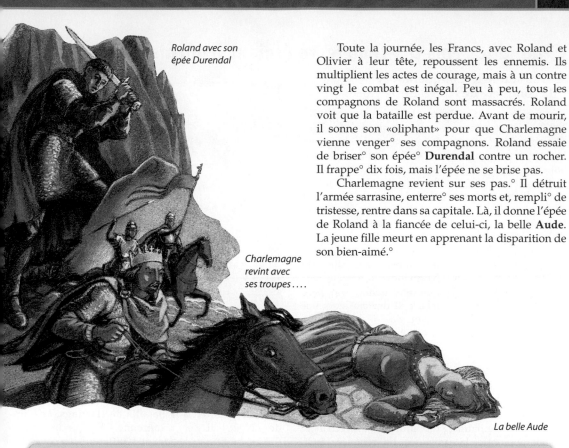

Roland avec son épée Durendal

Charlemagne revint avec ses troupes….

La belle Aude

Toute la journée, les Francs, avec Roland et Olivier à leur tête, repoussent les ennemis. Ils multiplient les actes de courage, mais à un contre vingt le combat est inégal. Peu à peu, tous les compagnons de Roland sont massacrés. Roland voit que la bataille est perdue. Avant de mourir, il sonne son «oliphant» pour que Charlemagne vienne venger° ses compagnons. Roland essaie de briser° son épée° **Durendal** contre un rocher. Il frappe° dix fois, mais l'épée ne se brise pas.

Charlemagne revient sur ses pas.° Il détruit l'armée sarrasine, enterre° ses morts et, rempli° de tristesse, rentre dans sa capitale. Là, il donne l'épée de Roland à la fiancée de celui-ci, la belle **Aude**. La jeune fille meurt en apprenant la disparition de son bien-aimé.°

La Chanson de Roland

Au 12e siècle, c'est-à-dire plus de 300 ans après les faits historiques, un moine° anonyme écrit *La Chanson de Roland*. C'est un long poème épique de 4 000 vers qui relate en détail la légende. *La Chanson de Roland* est la première grande oeuvre littéraire écrite en langue française. Elle a un succès immédiat dans tout le monde occidental.° Pour certains historiens, les raisons de ce succès sont politiques. Au 12e siècle, en effet, les chevaliers chrétiens partent en croisade pour délivrer Jérusalem prise par les Turcs. Ils sont inspirés par *La Chanson de Roland* qui représente un épisode de la guerre sainte des Chrétiens contre les Musulmans.

Un troubadour médiéval

---

venger *to avenge* **briser** *to break* **épée** *sword* **frappe** *strikes* **pas** *steps* **enterre** *buries* **rempli** *filled* **bien-aimé** *beloved* **moine** *monk*
occidental *western*

Quand les rois d'Angleterre étaient français

■ Guillaume le Conquérant et la conquête de l'Angleterre (1066)

Les ancêtres de **Guillaume le Conquérant** (1028-1087) sont scandinaves. Ce sont ces terribles «**Normands**» (homme du Nord) qui, venus de Norvège° et du Danemark sur leurs **drakkars**, ont attaqué et dévasté l'ouest de la France au 9e siècle. Ils ont pris et brûlé° Orléans, Tours et Paris. Pour avoir la paix,° le roi de France a donné à leur chef le duché de Normandie . . . et la main de sa fille. Les Normands sont devenus de bons et loyaux vassaux° du roi de France.

«Drakkar» scandinave

Guillaume est le fils de Robert Ier, duc de Normandie. Il a seulement huit ans quand son père meurt. Il devient alors lui-même duc de Normandie. Jeune homme, il fait un voyage en Angleterre pour rendre visite à son cousin, le roi **Édouard**. Celui-ci lui promet la couronne d'Angleterre à sa mort. Mais il y a un autre prétendant: **Harold le Saxon**. Un jour, Harold vient en Normandie où il est immédiatement fait prisonnier. Guillaume lui propose un échange: la liberté contre la promesse de renoncer à la couronne° d'Angleterre. Harold accepte l'échange, retourne en Angleterre, et là il oublie sa promesse.

Quand Édouard meurt en 1066, Harold se fait nommer° roi. Guillaume apprend cette trahison.° Furieux, il décide de punir Harold et de conquérir l'Angleterre par la force. Pour cela, il organise une formidable expédition. Le 23 septembre, ses bateaux chargés° de soldats arrivent en Angleterre. Le 14 octobre, il défait l'armée d'Harold à **la bataille de Hastings**. Le jour de Noël, il est couronné à Londres roi d'Angleterre sous le nom de **Guillaume Ier**.

Une conséquence de la conquête est que le français va devenir pendant plusieurs siècles la langue de la cour d'Angleterre.

L'histoire de la conquête de l'Angleterre par Guillaume est représentée graphiquement dans une très belle tapisserie° de 70 mètres de long, la tapisserie de Bayeux. C'est, en quelque sorte, la première «bande dessinée» de l'histoire.

Scène de la tapisserie de Bayeux, la première «bande dessinée»

Norvège *Norway* **brûlé** *burned* **paix** *peace* **vassaux** = sujets **couronne** *crown* **se fait nommer** *has himself named*
trahison *betrayal* **chargés** *loaded* **tapisserie** tapestry

---

Notes culturelles

The tapestry of Bayeux was said to have been stitched by Queen Mathilde, the wife of William the Conqueror. In fact, it was ordered by the Bishop of Bayeux from Saxon embroiderers. The tapestry features 626 characters in 72 different scenes.

This scene of the Battle of Hastings shows the English foot soldiers of King Harold (on the right) forming a wall with their shields to defend themselves against the attack of the mounted knights of William the Conqueror.

■ Aliénor d'Aquitaine: Reine de France et Reine d'Angleterre

Elle a été reine° de France, puis reine d'Angleterre. C'est aussi la mère de deux rois d'Angleterre.

Fille et héritière° du duc d'Aquitaine, **Aliénor** (1122-1204) est une princesse d'une grande beauté. À l'âge de quinze ans, elle épouse° le roi de France, **Louis VII**, avec qui elle part en croisade contre les Turcs. Après leur retour de Terre Sainte,° Aliénor et Louis ont deux filles, mais le roi, qui veut des fils, fait annuler le mariage.

Quelques semaines plus tard, Aliénor se remarie avec **Henri Plantagenêt**, duc de Normandie, qui devient roi d'Angleterre en 1154. À leur tour, leurs fils, **Richard Coeur de Lion** et **Jean sans Terre** vont aussi être rois d'Angleterre. À cette époque, les rois d'Angleterre possèdent de vastes territoires en France: la Normandie, l'Anjou, l'Aquitaine. Cette situation est une des causes principales de la **Guerre de Cent Ans**.

Aliénor d'Aquitaine est très belle, très intelligente et très cultivée. En France et en Angleterre, elle crée une cour brillante où elle protège les poètes et les artistes. Princesse libérale, elle donne beaucoup de libertés aux habitants des villes qu'elle possède. À la fin° de sa vie, elle se retire en France, dans son abbaye de Fontevrault, où sont enterrés° deux rois d'Angleterre, son mari et son fils, Richard.

À la cour d'Aliénor d'Aquitaine

---

reine *queen*   **héritière** *heiress*   **épouse** *marries*   **Terre Sainte** *Holy Land*   **à la fin** *towards the end*   **enterrés** *buried*

■ Notes historiques

ALIÉNOR D'AQUITAINE ET SA FAMILLE:
- **Louis VII** (1120–1180)
- **Henri II Plantagenêt** (né au Mans 1133, mort à Chinon 1189)
- **Richard Ier Coeur de Lion** (né à Oxford 1157, mort à Châlus 1199)
- **Jean sans Terre** (né à Oxford 1167, mort en Nottinghamshire 1216). En 1215, il a été contraint à accepter la **Grande Charte** (*Magna Carta*). C'est contre le roi Jean que luttait **Robin des Bois** (*Robin Hood*).

■ Teaching Strategy: Expansion

Ask students:
- Quel âge avait Aliénor d'Aquitaine quand elle a épousé Henri Plantagenêt?
- Quelle âge avait-elle à la naissance de son fils Richard? de son fils Jean?
- À quel âge est-elle morte?

Jeanne d'Arc à Chinon

Un jour, Jeanne a entendu des voix.

Le château de Chinon

Jeanne d'Arc est née en 1412 à Domrémy, un petit village de Lorraine. À cette époque, la France était occupée par les Anglais. Un jour, Jeanne a entendu des voix. Elle a reconnu Sainte Catherine, Sainte Marguerite et Saint Michel. Ces voix lui ont dit: «Jeanne, c'est toi qui vas délivrer le pays!»

«Moi? Mais je suis une paysanne° qui sait à peine° lire et écrire,» a répondu Jeanne.

Mais les voix ont insisté: «Jeanne, va chez le roi et dis-lui que c'est Dieu° qui t'envoie.».

Jeanne et le sire de Baudricourt.

Jeanne a accepté la mission, mais maintenant elle est inquiète°. «Aller chez le roi? Oui, mais comment? Le roi habite si loin et les routes sont pleines° de brigands.»°

Jeanne va trouver un seigneur° local, le sire de Baudricourt.

— Messire, donnez-moi une escorte. Je veux aller chez le roi de France.

— Et qui t'envoie?

— Le Roi du Ciel.°

Baudricourt se moque de° Jeanne et la renvoie chez elle. Jeanne revient. Elle insiste et finalement elle obtient une escorte. C'est avec cette escorte de six hommes qu'elle arrive devant le château de Chinon où réside Charles, roi de France, avec sa cour. Immédiatement elle demande d'être présentée au roi.

Jeanne et son escorte arrivent au château de Chinon.

paysanne *peasant girl* **à peine** *hardly* **Dieu** *God* **inquiète** *worried* **pleines** *full* **brigands** = *bandits* **seigneur** *lord* **Messire** = *Monsieur* **Roi du Ciel** *King of Heaven* **se moque de** *makes fun of*

■ Teaching Suggestion
Divide the class into small groups and assign a francophone country other than France to each group. The groups should research the history of their assigned countries and prepare multimedia or Powerpoint® presentations highlighting the major events. Invite another French class to come join your class on the day of the presentations or video the presentations and share them with francophone partner students for their feedback.

Notes culturelles

• Chinon is a city in Touraine, on the Vienne river. Its fortress, built between the 10th and 15th centuries, still stands, comprised of three castles, including the one where Joan of Arc met the king.

• **La fleur de lys** has been the symbol of the French monarchy since the 8th century. This flower represents holiness and purity.

• Charles VII was crowned in Reims on July 17, 1429.

• Reims became the traditional crowning site for the French kings after King Clovis was baptized there in 496.

Jeanne a reconnu le vrai roi malgré ses humbles apparences.

Le roi Charles est un roi sans royaume.° Il a perdu sa capitale. Paris est occupé par les Anglais, qui ont choisi un autre roi de France, un roi anglais, bien sûr. Charles est un jeune homme timide et sans énergie. Il ne croit plus en la victoire et certainement pas aux miracles. «Qui est cette Jeanne et qu'est-ce qu'elle veut de moi?»

Un courtisan, Bernard de Chissay, suggère au roi de jouer un bon tour° à Jeanne. «Déguisons-nous! Je vais mettre vos vêtements et vous, vous allez vous déguiser en simple courtisan. Nous allons voir si cette petite paysanne va reconnaître le vrai roi.» Bernard de Chissay met les vêtements du roi alors que° Charles met un simple vêtement noir. Jeanne entre dans la grande salle° du château. Il y a plusieurs centaines de dames et de chevaliers. Bernard de Chissay, magnifiquement habillé, reçoit les hommages des courtisans. Charles, le vrai roi, est au fond° de la salle, mais c'est vers lui que Jeanne s'avance.

— Gentil roi de France, le Roi du Ciel m'envoie vers vous.

— Mais ce n'est pas moi, le roi. Le roi est là-bas.

— C'est vous le roi, et pas un autre . . .

Oui, Jeanne a reconnu le vrai roi malgré° ses humbles apparences. Charles est très impressionné. Il décide d'écouter Jeanne. Jeanne et Charles ont une longue conversation secrète. Charles est maintenant convaincu.° Jeanne est l'envoyée° de Dieu.

Jeanne devant la ville d'Orléans.

Le roi lui donne une armée. Jeanne d'Arc, qui a seulement 17 ans, prend le commandement des troupes royales. Elle part délivrer Orléans, assiégée par les Anglais. Arrivée devant la ville, elle exhorte ses compagnons d'armes: «Entrez hardiment° parmi° les Anglais!» Surpris par le courage de cette jeune fille, les soldats attaquent. Le lendemain, Orléans est délivrée!

Charles est couronné roi de France.

La libération de la France vient de commencer. Jeanne d'Arc gagne d'autres batailles. Son grand triomphe a lieu quelques mois après l'entrevue de Chinon quand Charles est solennellement couronné roi de France dans la cathédrale de Reims.

■ **Note historique**

Jeanne d'Arc assiste au sacre de Charles VII à Reims le 17 juillet 1429, mais peu après, son armée échoue devant Paris. En mai 1430, elle est faite prisonnière. Les Anglais la font juger comme sorcière devant un tribunal ecclésiastique à Rouen. Déclarée hérétique, elle fut brûlée le 30 mai 1431.

---

sans royaume *without a kingdom* **tour** *trick* **alors que** *whereas* **salle** *hall* **au fond** *in the back* **malgré** *in spite of*
convaincu *convinced* **l'envoyée** = la messagère **hardiment** *boldly* **parmi** *among*

Teaching Strategy: Game

Prepare **"Jeopardy"**-style answers for the material in the *Interlude*.

Group students in three teams. The teams compete by supplying questions to the answers previously prepared.

Unité 2 107

Unité 3

MAIN THEME

Vacation, outdoor activities
The environment

COMMUNICATION

- Talking about weather, natural phenomena
- Relating a series of past events
- Talking about outdoor activities
- Describing the natural environment and how to protect it
- Describing habitual past actions

CULTURES

- Learning about eco-tourism
- Learning about French attitudes and practices regarding the environment
- Learning about *les éco-musées*
- Learning about *Cyrano de Bergerac*
- Learning about French *châteaux*

CONNECTIONS

- Researching information for a report on a trip to a big city
- Researching information on Jacques-Yves Cousteau
- Reading news articles for information
- Locating *La Gascogne* on a map
- Connecting to Language Arts: Writing a story; writing to organizations and clubs
- Connecting to Math: Compiling statistics and calculating travel time
- Connecting to Science: Learning about weather patterns in different seasons
- Connecting to Social Studies: Writing the history of a person, building, or organization
- Connecting to Art/Music: Collecting images and choosing music selections

COMPARISONS

- Comparing verb meanings in French and English
- Comparing talking about the past in French and English
- Comparing idioms in French and English
- Comparing how people in France and the United States protect the environment
- Comparing French and English fables
- Learning about French influence on English words and English influence on French words

COMMUNITIES

- Writing a report on ways to protect the environment
- Creating a class newspaper
- Using French to describe vacation photos

108 Unité 3

Unité 3

Vive la nature!

THÈME ET OBJECTIFS

Culture

In this unit, you will discover . . .

- why the French people feel close to their roots
- how the French incorporate «tourisme écologique» into their vacation plans
- how the French people feel about their environment
- why Jacques Cousteau is so well known and what important work he did
- what the «culte du soleil» represents for French people

Communication

You will learn how . . .

- to talk about vacation activities
- to tell people who are on vacation that they should take certain precautions and avoid dangers
- to describe weather conditions and natural phenomenon

Langue

You will learn how . . .

- to narrate a sequence of past events
- to describe the setting of these past events
- to read literary accounts of past events

 DIGITAL FRENCH my.hrw.com
ONLINE STUDENT EDITION with...

performance))space

News + Networking

@HOMETUTOR

- Audio Resources
- Video Resources
- Interactive Flashcards
- WebQuest

PRACTICE FRENCH WITH HOLT MCDOUGAL APPS!

 **DIGITAL FRENCH**

TEACHER TOOLS

- **Teacher One Stop**
- **Interactive Whiteboard Lessons**
- **Generate Success Rubric Generator and Interactive Graphic Organizers**
- **Examview Test Generator**

ALSO AVAILABLE...

- **Online Workbook**
- **French InterActive Reader**
- **@HomeTutor**
- **DVD Program**
- **Power Presentations**
- **Interactive Flashcards**

FRENCH ON THE GO!

- **Performance Space**
- **Holt McDougal French Apps**
- **Discovering French Today eTextbook**

OUI à la nature!

Les racines°

Cécile Pécoul, 25 ans, est infirmière. Elle habite et travaille à Paris, mais c'est à la campagne qu'elle se sent vraiment bien. Elle explique: «J'ai besoin d'air pur.° Alors, le week-end, je pars souvent en Normandie* avec mes copains. Parfois je vais faire de l'escalade° dans la forêt de Fontainebleau.** Et en été, je passe les vacances dans la ferme de mes grands-parents en Auvergne.*** C'est là d'où vient ma famille. C'est donc là où je suis vraiment chez moi, parce que c'est là où sont mes racines.»

Aujourd'hui, la majorité des Français habitent dans des grandes villes mais, comme Cécile, ils restent très attachés à leur province d'origine. Ils y retournent à l'occasion des vacances, pour retrouver leurs racines, mais surtout pour établir un contact avec la nature. Cet amour de la terre° et de la nature explique le succès du tourisme «vert» ou du tourisme «écologique».

■ Deux adeptes de la randonnée pédestre

Le tourisme vert

Il y a différentes façons de pratiquer le tourisme écologique. La forme la plus simple est évidemment la marche à pied.° Si on aime celle-ci,° on peut faire de la «randonnée pédestre°» le long° des milliers de kilomètres de sentiers° ruraux. On part le matin, sac au dos.° On marche pendant 35 à 40 kilomètres. On s'arrête le soir dans un gîte° rural où on passe la nuit. En dix jours, on peut ainsi visiter toute une région «de l'intérieur», sans rencontrer beaucoup de gens. Un avantage de la randonnée pédestre est qu'on peut la pratiquer à tout âge. C'est une activité très populaire en France. La Fédération Française de la Randonnée Pédestre compte plus de 200 000 membres.

Quand on passe les vacances à la montagne, celle-ci offre une grande variété d'activités qui nous mettent en contact direct avec notre milieu naturel. En plus° de la randonnée pédestre, on peut faire du VTT, du ski sur l'herbe,° de l'escalade, de l'alpinisme° et, si on aime les sensations fortes, du delta-plane et du parapente.°

■ L'escalade en montagne

---

*Normandie une région à l'ouest de Paris **Fontainebleau une forêt au sud de Paris où il y a des rochers ***Auvergne une province au centre de la France
racines roots pur fresh l'escalade rock climbing la terre land la marche à pied walking celle-ci the latter la randonnée pédestre hiking
le long along sentiers trails sac au dos with a back pack un gîte simple lodging En plus In addition l'herbe grass l'alpinisme mountain climbing
parapente parasailing

ASSESSMENT in Unit Resource Book

Print Resources
- **Workbook TE/PE**
- *Activités pour tous* **TE/PE**
- *Lectures pour tous*
- **Unit Resource Book**
  Audioscripts
  Video Activities
  Videoscripts

Achievement Tests
- **Quizzes, Unit 3**
- **Unit Test 3**
- **Reading and Culture Tests**
- **Assessment Answer Key**

Proficiency Tests
- **Listening Comprehension**
- **Speaking Performance**
- **Writing Performance**
- **Portfolio Assessment**

INFO MAGAZINE

Theme: Outdoor activities; the environment

Reading Strategy: Reading for pleasure; browsing; scanning for information

■ **Teaching Strategy**
Have students scan for cognates and look at the photos for content clues.

■ **Notes linguistiques**
- **35 à 40 km** = 21.7 to 24.8 miles
- **VTT** = Vélo Tout Terrain
- **la Terre** = Earth, soil, land
- **pratiquer** is a false cognate.
  pratiquer un sport = to play a sport; s'entraîner, s'exercer = to practice

■ **Notes culturelles**
- **L'Auvergne** is located in the **Massif Central**. It is known for its spas and springs, such as **Vichy** and **Volvic**.

21ST CENTURY SKILLS
- **Communication:** SE: pp. 110, 113, 115, 119, 123, 125, 127, 129, 139; TE: pp. 114, 120, 123, 125, 126, 127, 130, 145, 147
- **Collaboration:** SE: p. 110; TE: pp. 110, 115, 121, 140
- **Creativity and Innovation:** TE: pp. 111, 117, 119, 123, 125, 127, 129, 133, 138, 144, 147
- **Information Literacy:** TE: pp. 111, 115, 119, 120, 127, 133, 140, 147
- **Technology Literacy:** TE: pp. 111, 115, 119, 120, 123, 125, 133, 140, 142, 147
- **Flexibility and Adaptability:** TE: pp. 125, 127, 133, 142
- **Initiative and Self-Direction:** TE: pp. 111, 121, 133, 147
- **Social and Cross-Cultural Skills:** TE: pp. 121, 123, 140
- **Leadership and Responsibility:** TE: pp. 111, 121, 123

INFO MAGAZINE

Teaching Strategy

Divide the class into groups and assign each group to prepare a definition of the key words in the *Et vous?* activity:

Définitions

- Nos **racines,** c'est là d'où vient notre famille.
- On fait du **tourisme écologique** quand on passe ses vacances en contact avec la nature, par exemple en faisant de la randonnée pédestre.
- La **randonnée pédestre,** c'est quand on marche sur des sentiers spéciaux à la campagne.
- On peut explorer toute une région en marchant sur ces sentiers spéciaux, qui s'appellent des **sentiers ruraux.**
- Un **gîte rural** est une sorte d'auberge très simple, sans luxe, qu'on trouve à la campagne et où on peut passer la nuit quand on fait une randonnée pédestre.
- Un **parc national** est une réserve naturelle pour protéger les plantes et les animaux. On ne peut pas y camper, et il ne faut pas toucher les plantes et les animaux.
- On appelle la **faune** les animaux qui vivent dans un endroit naturel.
- Dans un **éco-musée,** on peut voir comment on vivait à la campagne autrefois.

Expansion: Expression écrite

In the letters or e-mails, have the students ask their French friends about ecotourism opportunites where they live.

La protection de la nature

Quand on aime la nature, il faut la protéger. À cet effet, le gouvernement français a créé des réserves naturelles et de grands parcs nationaux. Ces parcs sont situés principalement dans les zones de montagne (Alpes, Pyrénées, Massif Central). Là, tout est fait pour préserver la faune° et la flore° typiques de la région, et en particulier les espèces en danger. Il est interdit de camper, de faire du feu,° de toucher à la végétation et de déranger° les animaux.

Évidemment, la protection de la nature n'est pas seulement l'affaire° du gouvernement. C'est l'affaire de tout le monde. Pour 80% des Français, l'environnement est «un problème immédiat et urgent.» Cette préoccupation explique sans doute le succès des partis° écologiques. Aux élections, les «écolos» ou les «verts» obtiennent généralement 10% ou 12% des voix. Ce n'est pas beaucoup, mais c'est assez pour avoir une action politique efficace. Cette action se porte° sur beaucoup de domaines: protection de l'environnement, lutte° contre la pollution, limitation et contrôle de l'énergie nucléaire, aide et subventions° pour le développement de l'énergie solaire. Si on veut préserver la qualité de la vie de demain, c'est aujourd'hui qu'il faut agir!°

Les éco-musées

Une autre forme de tourisme écologique consiste à visiter les «éco-musées». Le but de ces musées est de préserver la vie rurale d'autrefois quand la majorité des Français habitaient à la campagne. Ces musées sont souvent des reconstructions de fermes et de villages anciens où l'on peut voir les outils,° les instruments, les ustensiles qu'on utilisait à l'époque.

et vous?

DÉFINITIONS

Définissez en français les mots et expressions suivantes:

- les racines
- le tourisme écologique
- la randonnée pédestre
- un sentier rural
- un gîte rural
- un parc national
- la faune
- un éco-musée

EXPRESSION ORALE

- À votre avis, est-ce que les Américains ont «l'amour de la terre»? Expliquez.
- Avez-vous jamais fait du camping ou de la randonnée pédestre? Décrivez cette expérience.
- Avec votre partenaire, discutez des différentes façons de protéger l'environnement. Préparez un rapport.

EXPRESSION ÉCRITE

Dans une lettre à un(e) ami(e) français(e), vous expliquez comment on peut faire du «tourisme écologique» dans la région ou l'état où vous habitez.

la faune *wildlife* **la flore** *plant life* **feu** *fire* **déranger** *bother* **l'affaire** *business* **des partis** = partis politiques **se porte** = concerne
lutte *fight* **subventions** *subsidies* **agir** *to act* **outils** *tools*

Notes culturelles

- **Le Jour de la Terre** (Earth Day) has been celebrated in France since 1990.
- **"Les Verts"** (officially known as **Europe Écologie Les Verts** or **EELV**) is a French political party with a platform based on the protection of the environment and on social justice.

Ask students if they are familiar with any local, national, or international organizations for the protection of the environment.

Les sept commandements
du campeur

Chaque année, des millions de Français font du camping. Si vous venez un jour en France, vous aurez peut-être l'occasion d'en faire aussi. Voici quelques consignes° à observer.

1. Respectez les règlements.°

En France le camping est en principe libre° sur le territoire public . . . sauf° là où il est interdit. Le camping est interdit sur les plages de mer, dans les réserves naturelles, près des points d'eau utilisés pour la consommation, près des monuments historiques. Et si vous campez sur un terrain privé, n'oubliez pas de demander l'autorisation au propriétaire.°

2. Faites attention au feu.

L'incendie est la plus grande menace qui existe pour la forêt. Chaque année, des milliers d'hectares de forêts sont détruits° par des incendies° causés par des campeurs imprudents.°

3. Préservez l'environnement.

La nature est fragile et a besoin de notre protection. Alors, préservez la végétation au lieu de° la détruire. Ne cassez° pas les branches des arbres. N'arrachez° pas les plantes. Ne cueillez° pas les fleurs, qui ne sont pas pour vous seulement, mais pour tout le monde.

4. Ne dérangez pas les animaux.

Les animaux sont chez eux et vous, vous êtes sur leur territoire. Ce sont vos hôtes. Agissez° avec eux en invité° respectueux, et non pas en barbare.

5. Ne contaminez pas l'eau.

L'eau est une ressource précieuse non seulement pour les humains, mais aussi pour tous les habitants de la nature. Pensez aux animaux qui viennent boire tous les jours dans les rivières et les lacs.

6. Ne laissez pas de déchets.°

Emportez° vos déchets avec vous. Déposez-les dans les réceptacles spéciaux que vous trouverez sur les routes. Surtout, ne laissez pas d'objets en plastique. Le plastique n'est pas biodégradable et il peut provoquer la mort° des animaux qui le mangent.

7. Ne faites pas de bruit.

Si vous avez décidé de faire du camping, c'est pour profiter du calme de la nature et non pas pour écouter de la musique. Alors, laissez votre radio chez vous et n'oubliez pas que le bruit est une forme de pollution.

et vous?

D'après vous, quels sont les trois commandements les plus importants? Expliquez pourquoi.

INFOMAGAZINE

---

consignes *rules* **règlements** *rules* **libre** = *autorisé* **sauf** = *excepté* **propriétaire** *owner* **détruire** ✲ *to destroy* **incendies** *fires*
imprudents = *qui ne font pas attention* **au lieu de** *instead of* **casser** *to break* **arracher** *pull up* **cueillir** *to pick* **agir** *to act* **invité** *guest*
déchets *trash* **emporter** *to take along* **la mort** *death*

■ **Realia Note**
La Camargue is a region in the south of France, not far from Marseille, famous for its swamps and ponds and herds of horses and bulls. The town of **Saintes-Maries-de-la-Mer** is host to a large gypsy pilgrimage in May. Part of the region is a natural park.

■ **Irregular Verb**
(see Appendix C)
détruire (*see* **conduire**)

Teaching Strategy: Interdisciplinary/Community Connections

Combine activities related to environmental protection with your school's science department. Students can create posters in French, either on computer, with magazine and newspaper illustrations, or using their own artwork.

Display the posters, accompanied by a "matching" cognate activity for students who are *not* taking French, and award prizes for the highest score.

@HOMETUTOR
my.hrw.com

Les vacances: Plaisirs et problèmes

RESOURCES

PRINT

Workbook, pp. 121–122
Activités pour tous
Unit 3 Resource Book, Partie 1
  Activités pour tous TE
  Audioscripts
  Lesson Plans
  Block Scheduling Lesson Plans
  Absent Student Copymasters
  Workbook TE

AUDIO

Audio Program
CD 3, Tracks 1–4

TECHNOLOGY

@HomeTutor
Interactive Whiteboard Lessons

Teacher One Stop
  Block Scheduling Copymasters
  Teacher to Teacher Copymasters,
  La nature, pp. 30–32; *Trouver*
  celui qui ..., pp. 33–34

 Projectable Transparencies
  23, *Les vacances: Plaisirs et*
    problèmes
  24, *En vacances*
  Transparency Copymasters,
  pp. A49–A52
DVD Program, Unit 3

■ Notes linguistiques

- The term **plongée sous-marine** is used both for scuba diving and snorkeling, although technically, **faire de la plongée sous-marine autonome** = scuba diving.
- **un homme-grenouille** = scuba diver *(frogman)*
- **le tuba** = snorkel
  le masque = mask
  les palmes *(f.)* = flippers

Quand on est en vacances, on peut faire beaucoup de choses. Mais il faut aussi **éviter** certains dangers et faire attention!

éviter *to avoid*

Au bord de la mer, on peut . . .

nager
se baigner

bronzer
prendre un bain de soleil
  (sunbath)
faire une promenade en
  bateau *(boat)*

faire de la planche à voile
faire de la plongée
  sous-marine *(scuba diving)*

Mais attention! Il ne faut pas . . .

se noyer

attraper un coup
  de soleil *(sunburn)*

avoir le mal de mer
tomber dans l'eau
perdre l'équilibre

se baigner *to go swimming*
se noyer *to drown*
bronzer *to get tan*
attraper *to catch, get*
avoir le mal de mer *to be seasick*
perdre l'équilibre *to lose one's balance*

À la campagne, on peut . . .

se promener
faire un tour *(walk)*
  | **dans les champs** *(fields)*
  | **dans la forêt**
  | **dans les bois** *(woods)*

faire un pique-nique
  sur l'herbe

faire du camping
observer les animaux

Mais attention! Il ne faut pas . . .

se perdre

être piqué par des
  moustiques *(mosquitos)*

mettre le feu
marcher sur un serpent

se perdre *to get lost*

piquer *to sting*
mettre le feu *to set a fire*
marcher sur *to step on*

À la montagne, on peut . . .

faire de l'escalade
  (rock climbing)
faire de l'alpinisme
  (mountain climbing)
aller à la pêche *(fishing)*

Mais attention! Il ne faut pas . . .

glisser
tomber
se blesser
se casser la jambe

glisser *to slip*
se faire mal *to get hurt*
se blesser *to injure oneself*
se casser *to break (a leg)*

Et dans tous les cas, il faut . . .

respecter | **la nature**
protéger | **l'environnement**

Il ne faut pas . . .

polluer
laisser | **des déchets** *(refuse)*
jeter | **des vieux papiers**
détruire la végétation
casser les branches des
  arbres
faire peur aux animaux

polluer *to pollute*
protéger *to protect*
laisser *to leave*
jeter *to throw*
détruire* *to destroy*
casser *to break*
faire peur à *to scare*

Révision et Expansion pp. R20–23

Les formes des verbes:
jeter, détruire

Teaching Suggestion: DVD Program

The *Vidéo-drame: Un accident* in Unit 3 presents the topic of outdoor activities. After playing the video once without interruption, review some of the new vocabulary heard in the video. Play the video a second time. Next, ask students comprehension questions like:

Où est-ce que Malik et Nicolas vont samedi?
Pourquoi est-ce que les deux garçons sont trempés (soaked)?

1 et vous?

Complétez les phrases en exprimant votre opinion personnelle.
Comparez vos réponses avec celles de votre partenaire.

1. Je préfère passer les vacances . . .
   - à la mer
   - à la montagne
   - à la campagne
   - ??

2. Quand je suis à la plage,
   je préfère . . .
   - me baigner
   - prendre des bains de soleil
   - faire de la planche à voile
   - ??

3. Pour me protéger contre les coups de soleil . . .
   - je porte un chapeau
   - je garde *(keep on)* mon tee-shirt
   - je mets de la crème solaire
   - ??

4. Quand je vais à la campagne, je préfère . . .
   - me promener dans les champs
   - faire un tour dans les bois
   - faire de l'escalade
   - ??

5. Quand on se perd à la campagne,
   l'objet le plus utile est . . .
   - une boussole *(compass)*
   - une carte de la région
   - une lampe de poche
   - ??

6. Ce que je déteste le plus est de (d'). . .
   - attraper un coup de soleil
   - être piqué(e) par les moustiques
   - me baigner dans l'eau froide
   - ??

7. Quand on fait un tour dans une forêt, la chose
   la plus stupide est de . . .
   - laisser des vieux papiers
   - casser les branches des arbres
   - faire peur aux animaux
   - ??

8. Quand on fait du camping, la chose la plus
   stupide est de . . .
   - détruire la végétation
   - jeter des déchets
   - mettre le feu à la forêt
   - ??

Conversations libres

Avec votre partenaire, choisissez l'une des situations suivantes.
Composez le dialogue correspondant et jouez-le en classe.

Digital performance space

1 Deux week-ends différents

Samedi dernier Catherine est allée à la campagne
où elle a passé une journée très agréable. Son
cousin Guillaume est allé à la plage où il a passé
une très mauvaise journée. Catherine et Guillaume
se téléphonent pour décrire leur week-end respectif.

Rôles: Catherine, Guillaume

2 Escalade

Carole, une jeune fille très sportive, adore faire
de l'escalade. Elle veut enseigner *(to teach)* ce
sport à son copain Bertrand. Bertrand, qui
n'est pas très courageux, refuse absolument,
expliquant les dangers de ce sport.
Rôles: Carole, Bertrand

3 Camping dans la forêt

Florence est monitrice dans une colonie de vacances. Elle organise
un week-end de camping dans la forêt. Maintenant elle explique
aux jeunes ce qu'ils doivent faire et ce qu'ils ne doivent pas faire.
Ils veulent savoir pourquoi. Florence répond.
Rôles: Florence, une campeuse

cent treize **113**
Le Français pratique

Notes linguistiques
- **l'alpinisme** comes from the adjective **alpin**, meaning "from the Alps." Another related word is: **un(e) alpiniste** (mountain climber).
- **escalader** = to climb (rocks, mountains). **Les alpinistes escaladent l'Everest.**

SUPPLEMENTARY VOCABULARY

<u>Il ne faut pas marcher dans ...</u>
   les orties *nettles*
   l'herbe à puce *poison ivy (Canadian expression)*
<u>On peut être piqué par...</u>
   un insecte
   une abeille *bee*
   une guêpe *wasp*
   une fourmi *ant*
<u>Quelques animaux qu'on peut voir à la campagne:</u>
   un cerf /sɛr/ *stag*
   un chevreuil *deer*
   un corbeau *crow*
   un coyote /kɔjɔt/ *coyote*
   un écureuil *squirrel*
   un élan *elk*
   un lapin *rabbit*
   un loup *wolf*
   un ours /urs/ *bear*
   un raton laveur *raccoon*
   un renard *fox*
   une grenouille *frog*
   une loutre *otter*
   une marmotte *groundhog, woodchuck*
   une tortue *turtle*
<u>À la montagne, il ne faut pas ...</u>
   déraper *to slip, slide down*

Teaching Strategy: Expansion

Pas d'accord
Ce week-end, Charlotte veut aller à la plage. Jean-Louis n'est pas du tout d'accord. Il veut aller à la campagne. Chacun présente les avantages de son projet et les désavantages du projet de l'autre.
   Rôles: Charlotte, Jean-Louis

Teaching Strategy: Game

Charades: Present the vocabulary using **Projectable Transparencies 23** and **24**; then have each student act out one of the verbs from p. 112. Begin the game by acting out one of the verbs and having the students guess which verb you are depicting. Once the students guess, have them give a complete sentence that accurately and precisely uses the verb. (e.g., you act out **nager**. A student says **"nager... Je nage dans la piscine."**)

The student who guesses correctly now chooses a verb to act out in front of the class (Have the students preselect a few verbs so that the game will not drag.)

Langue et Communication

■ **Révision**
Optional, for reference and quick review.

■ **Notes linguistiques**
• Also: **jamais** *(ever)*
Est-ce que tu as **jamais** visité Paris?
• Other adverbs usually come after the past participle, but may come before, depending on emphasis or the rhythm of the sentence.
Il a couru **rapidement**.
Il a **rapidement** compris la question.

■ **Allons plus loin**
The same distinction exists with **rentrer** *(to go home, to take in)* and **retourner** *(to return, to turn over)*.
Pierrre <u>est rentré</u> chez lui. Il <u>a</u> <u>rentré</u> son vélo au garage.
Corinne <u>est retournée</u> au salon. Elle <u>a retourné</u> le tapis.

A Révision: Le passé composé

Révision p. R4
Les participes passés irréguliers; verbes conjugués avec **être**
(participes passés) p. R4, pp. R22–31
(verbes / être) p. R4

The PASSÉ COMPOSÉ is used to describe what people DID, what HAPPENED. Review the forms of the passé composé:

voyager	aller	s'amuser
j'**ai voyagé**	je **suis allé(e)**	je me **suis amusé(e)**
tu **as voyagé**	tu **es allé(e)**	tu t'**es amusé(e)**
il/elle/on **a voyagé**	il/elle/on **est allé(e)**	il/elle/on s'**est amusé(e)**
nous **avons voyagé**	nous **sommes allé(e)s**	nous nous **sommes amusé(e)s**
vous **avez voyagé**	vous **êtes allé(e)(s)**	vous vous **êtes amusé(e)(s)**
ils/elles **ont voyagé**	ils/elles **sont allé(e)s**	ils/elles se **sont amusé(e)s**
je n'**ai** pas **voyagé**	je ne **suis** pas **allé(e)**	je ne me **suis** pas **amusé(e)**
est-ce que tu **as voyagé?**	est-ce que tu **es allé(e)?**	est-ce que tu t'**es amusé(e)?**
as-tu voyagé?	**es**-tu allé(e)?	t'**es**-tu amusé(e)?

→ Review the following expressions:

déjà	*ever*	Est-ce que tu as **déjà** visité Paris?
ne ... **jamais**	*never*	Non, je n'**ai jamais** visité Paris.
déjà	*yet, already*	Est-ce que vous avez **déjà** vu ce film?
ne ... **pas encore**	*not yet*	Non, je n'**ai pas encore** vu ce film.

→ Note the position of the following ADVERBS in the passé composé.

AFTER the past participle:	**tôt** *(early)*, **tard** *(late)*
Je me suis levé **tôt**.	Éric s'est couché **tard**.
BEFORE the past participle:	**bien, mal, souvent, beaucoup, trop, assez**
Sophie a **beaucoup** aimé ce film.	Nous nous sommes **bien** amusés.

ALLONS PLUS LOIN
Depending on their meaning, the following verbs may be conjugated with **être** or **avoir**:

	(avoir)		(être)
monter	*to take or carry something up*	*or*	*to go up*
descendre	*to take or carry something down*	*or*	*to go down*
sortir	*to take something out*	*or*	*to go out*
passer	*to spend [time]*	*or*	*to pass by*

Pauline **a sorti** la poubelle. *Pauline **took** the trashcan **out**.*
Après, elle **est sortie**. *After that she **went out**.*

1 Oui ou non?

Il y a beaucoup de choses qu'on peut faire en vacances. Demandez à votre partenaire s'il (si elle) a fait une des choses suivantes. En cas de réponse affirmative, demandez des précisions: où? quand? à quelle occasion? avec qui?

▶ faire du ski nautique?

• visiter la Floride?	• monter dans un hélicoptère?	• avoir le mal de mer?
• aller en Suisse?	• faire une promenade à cheval?	• se perdre dans une forêt?
• faire de l'alpinisme?	• se promener à dos de chameau *(camel)*?	• se casser la jambe?
• voir un ours *(bear)*?	• faire de la plongée sous-marine?	

Est-ce que tu as déjà fait du ski nautique?

Oui, j'ai déjà fait du ski nautique.

Ah bon? Où ça?

(Non, je n'ai jamais fait de ski nautique.)

Dans le Michigan.

Teaching Strategy: Dialog Development
Divide students into pairs and have them write a twenty-line dialog in which the students compare notes concerning their ideal winter vacation. They should be sure to use as much vocabulary from p. 112 as possible, using the **passé composé.**

Differentiation
Structured Write verbs on the board and have students tell whether they are conjugated with **être** or **avoir**. Have them generate the stem for each infinitive, and then write the full conjugations in their notebook.

2 Créa-dialogue: Pas de chance!

Avec votre partenaire, composez un dialogue où vous décrivez un problème.

— Où es-tu allé(e) ce week-end?
— Je suis allé(e) à la montagne avec ma cousine.
— Ah bon? Qu'est-ce que vous avez fait?
— Nous avons fait de l'alpinisme.
— Vous vous êtes amusé(e)s?
— Oui, mais il y a eu un problème.
— Ah bon? Quoi?
— Ma cousine a glissé et elle s'est cassé le bras.
— C'est vraiment pas de chance!

Choose another time.
Choose another place: beach, city . . . Choose another person.
Choose an appropriate activity.
Describe another problem corresponding to the situation.

3 Une lettre de Paris

Amélie, une jeune Canadienne, vient d'arriver à Paris avec son frère Pascal. Elle écrit une lettre à son amie Gabrielle. Complétez la lettre d'Amélie avec le passé composé des verbes entre parenthèses.

Ma chère Gabrielle,

Eh bien, voilà! Je suis à Paris depuis deux jours avec mon frère Pascal. Nous _____ (arriver) avant-hier mais nous _____ (déjà faire) beaucoup de choses.

Hier matin, nous _____ (se lever tôt) et nous _____ (se promener) dans le quartier Latin. Nous _____ (prendre) le petit déjeuner dans un café où nous _____ (rencontrer) un groupe de jeunes Français. Pascal, qui ne perd pas de temps, _____ (donner) rendez-vous à une jeune fille très sympathique.

Après, nous _____ (s'arrêter) dans une boutique où j' _____ (acheter) des cartes postales. À midi, nous _____ (déjeuner) dans un restaurant algérien. J'_____ (manger) un couscous et j' _____ (boire) du thé à la menthe. C'était délicieux!

L'après-midi, nous_____ (faire) une promenade en bateau sur la Seine et ensuite nous _____ (monter) à la Tour Eiffel. Du sommet on a une vue splendide sur Paris. Évidemment, j'_____ (prendre) beaucoup de photos. Quand nous _____ (descendre), Pascal _____ (vouloir) téléphoner à sa nouvelle amie. Il _____ (chercher) son portefeuille, mais il _____ (ne pas le trouver). Alors, il _____ (remonter) au sommet et heureusement il _____ (trouver) son portefeuille!

Le soir, Pascal _____ (sortir) avec la jeune fille. Moi, je_____ (ne pas sortir) avec eux. Je _____ (rester) à l'hôtel et j'_____ (écrire) des lettres. À onze heures, je _____ (se coucher) et j'_____ (dormir). Ce matin, je _____ (se réveiller) à huit heures. Pascal, qui _____ (rentrer) très tard hier soir, dort encore!

Je t'embrasse,   *Amélie*

4 Et vous?

Écrivez une lettre où vous décrivez une journée que vous avez passée dans une grande ville au cours *(during)* d'un voyage (réel ou imaginaire).

■ Réponses: Activité 3

...nous *sommes arrivés*
...nous *avons déjà fait*
...nous nous *sommes levés tôt*
...nous nous *sommes promenés*
...Nous *avons pris*
...nous *avons rencontré*
...de temps a *donné*
...nous *sommes arrêtés*
...*ai acheté* des cartes
...nous *avons déjeuné*
...J'*ai mangé*
...j'*ai bu*
...nous *avons fait*
...nous *sommes montés*
...*j'ai pris*
...nous *sommes descendus*
...*Pascal a voulu téléphoner*
...*Il a cherché*
...*il ne l'a pas trouvé*
...*il est remonté*
...*il a trouvé*
...*Pascal est sorti*
...*je ne suis pas sortie*
...*Je suis restée*
...*j'ai écrit*
...*je me suis couchée et j'ai dormi.*
...*je me suis réveillée*
...*est rentré*

■ Expansion: Activity 4

Have students send the letters to a francophone pen pal, and have them ask the pen pal to describe a similar day.

■ Notes culturelles

• **Le couscous** is a North African specialty made of semolina grain served with vegetables and meat (lamb or chicken) in a spicy sauce.
• You can tour the Seine River in Paris on a **bateau-mouche,** a sight-seeing boat.

Student Portfolios

Using Act. 4 as a basis for the project, have students prepare their letters and add illustrations, maps, and realia related to their travel. Some research should be involved. If they wish, students may use the Internet to search for information, in addition to using resources such as the **Guide Michelin**.

For writing rubrics, consult the **Generate Success** Rubric Generator on the **Teacher One Stop**. You can also create your own custom rubrics with this tool.

@HOMETUTOR
my.hrw.com

RESOURCES

PRINT
Workbook, pp. 37

TECHNOLOGY
@HomeTutor

■ **Révision**

1. You may have students review other imperfect stems in the verb appendix.
2. You may point out the imperfect forms of verbs ending in **-ger, -cer**:
   manger: nous mangeons
   je mangeais,
   tu mangeais,
   il mangeait,
   ils mangeaient
   BUT: **nous mangions,**
   vous mangiez
   commencer:
   nous commençons
   je commençais
   tu commençais
   il commençait
   ils commençaient
   BUT: **nous commencions**
   vous commenciez
3. In Act. 6, make sure your students repeat the subject before each verb.
   ▶ **Après, je me lavais et je prenais mon petit déjeuner.**

■ **Vocabulary Expansion**

Also:
pleuvoir → il pleuvait
falloir → il fallait

B Révision: L'imparfait

The IMPERFECT is used to describe:

• what people USED TO DO, what USED TO BE
  Quand j'**étais** petit,   *When I **was** little,*
  je **jouais** au Monopoly.   *I **used to play** Monopoly.*

• what people WERE DOING, what WAS GOING ON, what WAS HAPPENING
  Hier soir, je **n'étais pas** chez moi.   *Last night I **was not** home.*
  Je **dînais** avec un copain.   *I **was having** dinner with a friend.*

Review the formation of the imperfect.

dîner	faire	se promener
nous **dînons**	nous **faisons**	nous **nous promenons**
je **dînais**	je **faisais**	je **me promenais**
tu **dînais**	tu **faisais**	tu **te promenais**
il/elle/on **dînait**	il/elle/on **faisait**	il/elle/on **se promenait**
nous **dînions**	nous **faisions**	nous **nous promenions**
vous **dîniez**	vous **faisiez**	vous **vous promeniez**
ils/elles **dînaient**	ils/elles **faisaient**	ils/elles **se promenaient**

→ The imperfect stem is formed as follows:

  nous-form of the present minus **-ons**

→ **Être** is the only verb with an irregular imperfect stem: êt- → **j'étais   nous étions**

IMPERFECT STEMS

visiter	je **visitais**
finir	je **finissais**
vendre	je **vendais**
avoir	j'**avais**
faire	je **faisais**
aller	j'**allais**
être	j'**étais**
venir	je **venais**
sortir	je **sortais**
mettre	je **mettais**
vivre	je **vivais**
savoir	je **savais**
recevoir	je **recevais**
prendre	je **prenais**
boire	je **buvais**
lire	je **lisais**
dire	je **disais**
écrire	j'**écrivais**
voir	je **voyais**
connaître	je **connaissais**

5 En 1900

Imaginez la vie en 1900. Dites ce qu'on faisait et ce qu'on ne faisait pas.

▶ on / utiliser des ordinateurs?   **On n'utilisait pas d'ordinateurs.**

1. tout le monde / avoir des voitures?
2. les gens / voyager en train?
3. on / travailler beaucoup?
4. les gens / respecter l'environnement?
5. on / consommer beaucoup d'essence *(gas)*?
6. beaucoup de gens / habiter à la campagne?
7. les jeunes / faire de la planche à voile?
8. on / être plus heureux qu'aujourd'hui?

6 En colonie de vacances

Marc est allé en colonie de vacances cet été. Il décrit ce qu'il faisait.

▶ En général, nous (se lever à 6 heures et demie)   **En général, nous nous levions à 6 heures et demie.**

1. Après, je (me laver et prendre mon petit déjeuner)
2. Le matin, on (aller à la plage et se baigner)
3. De temps en temps, mes copains (faire une promenade en bateau)
4. D'habitude, on (déjeuner à midi et après faire la sieste)
5. Après la sieste, nous (nous promener dans les bois et observer les animaux)
6. Parfois, on (faire une promenade dans la montagne et faire de l'escalade)
7. Le week-end, nous (prendre nos tentes et faire du camping)
8. D'habitude, tout le monde (se coucher à 10 heures et dormir très bien)

Si vous avez été en colonie de vacances, racontez votre propre expérience en décrivant votre routine quotidienne.

Teaching Strategy: Warm-Up

Have each student give two sentences that describe themselves and/or their families and what they do in the *present tense*. Then, ask them to tell you how this person was or what they used to do 10 years ago.
(e.g. **Aujourd'hui ma mère est blonde et elle a 40 ans.**

Il y a 10 ans, ma mère était brune et elle avait 30 ans.)
This drill should be done quickly so that the idea of the imperfect as the tense of description in the past is confirmed.

7 Souvenirs d'enfance 💬 ✏️

Posez des questions à votre partenaire sur son enfance.
Il/elle va vous poser les mêmes questions.

▶ où / habiter?

1. à quelle école / aller?
2. comment / aller à l'école?
3. à quelle heure / se lever?
4. à quelle heure / se coucher?
5. à quels jeux *(games)* / jouer?
6. quels sports / faire?
7. quelles émissions / regarder?
8. qui / être ton acteur favori?
9. qui / être ta chanteuse favorite?
10. quels objets / collectionner?
11. où / passer les vacances?
12. quel animal domestique / avoir?

Si vous voulez, écrivez un petit paragraphe où vous décrivez les similarités et les différences entre votre enfance et celle de votre partenaire.

Où est-ce que tu habitais?

J'habitais à Charleston. Et toi?

Moi, j'habitais à Savannah.

8 Pourquoi personne n'a répondu . . . ?

Hier après-midi vers deux heures, Pierre a voulu téléphoner à ses copains. Personne n'a répondu. Expliquez pourquoi en disant où chacun était et ce qu'il faisait. Soyez logique!

Qui?	Où?	Quoi?
toi	à la plage	déjeuner
nous	à la piscine	lire un livre
vous	à la campagne	tondre la pelouse
Béatrice	au restaurant	faire des achats
Jean-Paul	dans le jardin	faire un pique-nique
Philippe et Claire	en ville	faire de la plongée sous-marine
Marc et Alice	à la bibliothèque	prendre un bain de soleil
Jérôme et Stéphanie	dans les bois	se baigner
		se promener

▶ **Moi, j'étais à la plage. Je me baignais.**

9 Tout change! 💬

Tout change avec le temps. Avec votre partenaire comparez les photos et décrivez les différences entre aujourd'hui et autrefois.

Maintenant...

Maintenant, Monsieur Lescroc est riche. Il est assez gros et . . .

Maintenant, Valérie . . .

Maintenant Madame Leblanc . . .

Autrefois...

Autrefois, il était jeune. Il était grand et mince . . .

Autrefois, elle . . .

Autrefois, . . .

Teaching Strategy: Expansion

Ask students to respond to the following, either orally or in written form:

Et vous? Dites ce que vous faites et comment vous êtes maintenant. Puis, dites ce que vous faisiez et comment vous étiez autrefois.

Teaching Strategy: Writing Practice

Have the class write a group story. Each student will contribute at least one sentence. Give them an amusing subject that lends itself to creativity and to action sentences for **passé composé** practice.
(e.g. Describe Keira Knightley as a little girl and tell about a vacation that she took at the beach when she was 15 years old. Remind the students that this should be fictitious. It is not necessary for them to have facts.)
Students can take turns being scribe and copying the story onto the board as it is being developed.

RESOURCES

PRINT
Workbook PE, pp. 38, 123
Unit 3 Resource Book, Partie 1
Audioscripts

AUDIO
Audio Program
CD 3, Tracks 5–7

TECHNOLOGY
@HomeTutor
Teacher One Stop
Teacher to Teacher Copymasters,
Et maintenant ..., pp. 35–36

■ Note linguistique

Note that English does not always make the same distinctions that French does.

Pierre **avait peur**.
  Pierre *was scared*.
Pierre **a eu peur** quand il a vu le fantôme.
  Pierre *was (got) scared* when he saw the ghost.

C L'usage du passé composé et de l'imparfait

In talking about the past, the French use the IMPERFECT and the PASSÉ COMPOSÉ. The choice of tenses reflects the type of action or events that are being described.

IMPERFECT	PASSÉ COMPOSÉ
• HABITUAL OR REPEATED ACTIONS *(what people **used to do**)* Le samedi soir nous **allions** au ciné D'habitude on **faisait** de la planche à voile.	• SPECIFIC ACTIONS *(what people **did**)* Samedi dernier, je **suis allé** à un concert. Un jour, on **a fait** de la plongée sous-marine.
• PROGRESSIVE ACTIONS *(what **was going on**)* Je **me promenais** sur la plage. Nous **faisions** du camping.	J'**ai rencontré** un copain. Nous **avons vu** un ours *(bear)*.

→ Depending on how the speaker interprets the action, the passé composé or the imperfect may be used.

Hier à 9 heures, nous **dînions**.	*Yesterday at nine we **were eating dinner**.*
Hier nous **avons dîné** à 9 heures.	*Yesterday we **ate dinner** at nine.*
Tous les jours j'**allais** à la plage.	*Every day I **used to go** to the beach.*
Tous les jours je **suis allée** à la plage.	*Every day I **went** to the beach.*

10 Une explosion

Tout le monde parle de l'explosion qui a eu lieu hier soir dans le quartier Saint Victor. Dites ce que chaque personne faisait au moment de l'explosion et ce qu'elle a fait immédiatement après.

▶ Monsieur Duval (travailler dans le jardin / rentrer chez lui)
  Monsieur Duval travaillait dans le jardin. Il est rentré chez lui.

1. nous (dîner / regarder par la fenêtre)
2. vous (faire la vaisselle / téléphoner à la police)
3. moi (me promener / aller sur la scène de l'incident)
4. toi (rentrer chez toi / prendre des photos)
5. mes parents (regarder la télé / sortir sur le balcon)
6. mon grand-père (dormir / se réveiller)

11 Allô! 💬

Téléphonez à votre partenaire pour lui demander ce qu'il/elle faisait à certains moments. Il/elle va répondre avec les réponses suggérées ou des réponses de son choix.

▶ — Où étais-tu <u>hier soir</u>?
  — J'étais <u>chez moi</u>.
  — Qu'est-ce que tu faisais?
  — J'<u>étudiais</u>.
  — Et après, qu'est-ce que tu as fait?
  — J'<u>ai regardé un film à la télé</u>.

1.	3.
• ce matin	• après le pique-nique
• dans le jardin	• dans la forêt
• tondre la pelouse	• observer les animaux
• se promener	• prendre des photos

2.	4.
• cet après-midi	• avant le dîner
• à la plage	• chez un copain
• bronzer	• regarder ses photos
• se baigner	• rentrer chez moi

Teaching Strategy: Extra Practice

Find or prepare a story that uses verbs in both the **passé composé** and in the **imparfait**. Tell this story to the class orally *twice*. As you tell the story the second time, write one key word per sentence on the board as a means for students to remember the sentence. Once you have repeated the story twice and written the words on the board, ask the students to tell you the story as you told it.

For written practice, have students write the sentence on the board next to the appropriate key word.
Pre-AP skill: Listen for main idea and details.

12 L'été dernier

Décrivez ce que les personnes ont fait ou faisaient l'été dernier. Utilisez
le passé composé ou l'imparfait.

1. tous les jours / nous / aller à la plage
2. un jour où il faisait très chaud / Julien / attraper un coup de soleil
3. le samedi / mes copains / faire une promenade en bateau
4. pendant la promenade / Pierre / tomber dans l'eau

5. le 14 juillet / Catherine et Pauline / assister aux feux d'artifice *(fireworks)*
6. le week-end / vous / faire du camping
7. pendant la nuit / toi / être piqué par un moustique
8. nous / rentrer chez nous / à la fin de juillet

13 Souvenir de vacances

Monsieur Mercier raconte un souvenir de vacances. Complétez son histoire en mettant
les verbes au passé. Utilisez l'imparfait ou le passé composé.

Quand j' _____ (être) étudiant, je _____ (passer) mes vacances à
Annecy. En général, je _____ (ne pas me lever) avant dix heures du matin.
L'après-midi, je/j' _____ (aller) à la piscine où je _____ (prendre) des bains
de soleil. Parfois, je/j' _____ (faire) de la planche à voile sur le lac. Le soir,
je _____ (sortir) avec mes copains et je _____ (rentrer) tard chez moi.

Un jour, un copain m' _____ (inviter) à faire de l'escalade avec lui.
Le lendemain, je _____ (me lever) tôt et je _____ (partir) avec mon copain.
Malheureusement, pendant l'escalade, je/j' _____ (glisser) et je _____
(me casser) la jambe. À l'hôpital où je/j' _____ (aller), je/j' _____ (rencontrer)
une jeune infirmière très sympathique. Un jour, je lui _____ (demander) si elle
voulait se marier avec moi. Elle _____ (accepter) et aujourd'hui, c'est ma femme!

■ **Note culturelle**

The city of Annecy is located on the
Swiss border in the French Alps. The
lac d'Annecy is a popular tourist
attraction.

14 Photos de vacances ✍️

Pendant vos vacances en France, vous avez pris des photos de vos amis français.
Pour chaque photo, dites:
- où vous étiez
- ce que chaque personne faisait au moment de l'incident
- ce que ces personnes ont fait après

Utilisez votre imagination.

Pierre et Caroline

Juliette et Jérôme

Christine et Jean-Pierre

Student Portfolios

Ask students to bring in a vacation photo, or use
illustrations from travel brochures, magazines, or
newspapers. Have them write a short paragraph
describing the activites shown and giving details
as in Act. 14. If students prefer, they may record a
vacation description rather than writing it.

Differentiation

Sequential Give a list of verbs that can be
used to describe habitual or progressive actions,
and have students place them in the
imparfait. Give a list of verbs that could be
used to describe specific actions, and have
students put them in the **passé composé.** Ask
them to then order the sentences to create a
logical sequence.

INFO MAGAZINE

Theme: Ecology

■ Teaching Strategy

- Begin by asking students to look at the photographs, then ask them what they know about Jacques Cousteau. Then have them skim the article and summarize.
- Next, have students compose short descriptive paragraphs or oral presentations on Cousteau's work.
- You may wish to mention that Jacques Cousteau passed away on June 25, 1997. He was born June 11, 1910.

■ Teaching Suggestion

Have students research the flora and fauna of Madagascar and prepare multimedia or Powerpoint® presentations to be shared in class or uploaded on a class website.

■ Additional Information

For more information on l'**Académie française**, see p. 56.

■ Irregular Verbs

entreprendre (see **prendre**)
élire (see **lire**)

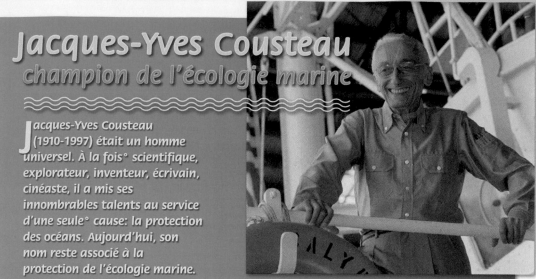

Jacques-Yves Cousteau
champion de l'écologie marine

Jacques-Yves Cousteau (1910-1997) était un homme universel. À la fois° scientifique, explorateur, inventeur, écrivain, cinéaste, il a mis ses innombrables talents au service d'une seule° cause: la protection des océans. Aujourd'hui, son nom reste associé à la protection de l'écologie marine.

◼ Jacques-Yves Cousteau

Cousteau a d'abord été officier dans la Marine française. C'est à cette époque qu'il a inventé le scaphandre autonome (ou SCUBA* en anglais), permettant l'exploration des espaces sous-marins. Au cours de° ses expéditions sur ses fameux bateaux, la Calypso, l'Alcyone, la Calypso II, Cousteau a exploré les fonds° marins un peu partout dans le monde, en France, en Grèce, en Égypte, au Brésil, à Madagascar, dans l'Atlantique, le Pacifique et l'Océan Indien. De ces expéditions, il a rapporté° de nombreux films documentaires. Ces films, comme *Le monde du silence* et *Le monde sans soleil,* et plus tard ses séries télévisées *Découvertes du monde,* ont fait connaître° au grand public l'univers merveilleux de la mer.

> «Il faut sauver les océans! Il faut sauver notre planète, la Terre!»

Mais Cousteau ne s'est pas contenté° d'être l'un des grands explorateurs de ce siècle. Il a aussi entrepris° une croisade mondiale pour la protection de l'environnement. Son message est simple: À long terme,° l'avenir° de l'humanité dépend de la préservation de notre environnement naturel et, en particulier, du monde marin. Aujourd'hui, celui-ci° est menacé non seulement par la pollution, mais aussi par une exploitation économique incontrôlée. Il faut donc le protéger. Il faut sauver les océans! Il faut sauver notre planète, la Terre! Cousteau s'est engagé° totalement dans cette croisade. Pour cela, il a créé une fondation internationale, la Fondation Cousteau, et aussi la «Cousteau Society» qui a 200.000 membres aux États-Unis. Dans son travail, il était secondé par son fils, Jean-Michel Cousteau, qui habite en Californie.

◼ Jacques-Yves Cousteau et son fils, Jean-Michel

◼ Le commandant Cousteau à bord de la Calypso.

Jacques-Yves Cousteau faisait aussi partie° de l'élite littéraire. Pour son oeuvre°, il a été élu° membre de l'Académie française, le plus prestigieux groupe d'écrivains français.

à la fois *at the same time*   **d'une seule** *only one*   **au cours de** = durant   **les fonds** *depths*   **rapporté** *brought back*   **faire connaître** *made known*
contenté = limité   **entreprendre** ✱ *to undertake*   **À long terme** *In the long run*   **l'avenir** *future*   **celui-ci** = le monde marin
engagé *committed himself*   **faisait partie** = était membre   **oeuvre** *work*   **élire** ✱ *to elect*
*Un acronyme pour Self-Contained Underwater Breathing Apparatus.

120 cent vingt
Unité 3

Notes culturelles

Madagascar is a French-speaking island to the west of the coast of Mozambique, Africa. Deforestation is the greatest problem on the island, depriving Madagascar's unique fauna of its natural habitat. Madagascar is the only place in the world where lemurs live.

L'Écologie à la maison

Préserver l'environnement, ce n'est pas difficile. Il suffit d'y penser.° L'écologie commence à la maison. Des jeunes Français expliquent comment ils pratiquent l'écologie chez eux.

Stéphanie:

≪Je recycle le verre. Ce n'est pas compliqué! Il suffit de séparer les bouteilles et de les déposer dans les réceptacles spéciaux qu'on trouve partout dans les villes, et même à la campagne. **≫**

Danièle:

≪J'ai demandé à ma mère de n'acheter que° des produits favorables à l'environnement. J'ai un argument convaincant:° Je refuse de faire la vaisselle ou de laver le linge° avec des produits qui contiennent des phosphates, nocifs° à l'environnement. **≫**

Xavier:

≪J'essaie de conserver l'eau au maximum. Par exemple, au lieu de° prendre des bains, je prends des douches qui utilisent moins d'eau. Quand je me lave les mains, je ferme l'évier.° Quand je me brosse les dents, je ferme le robinet.° J'économise un peu d'eau chaque fois et, à la longue,° ça compte! **≫**

Vincent:

≪Quand j'achète quelque chose, je fais attention aux produits qu'il contient.° En général, je donne la préférence aux produits recyclables ou recyclés. Et j'utilise toujours des emballages° en papier, jamais en plastique. **≫**

Zoé:

≪Je n'utilise plus d'aérosols, parce que les CFC (chlorofluorocarbures) qu'ils contiennent détruisent l'ozone de l'atmosphère. Et les savons, les shampooings, les dentifrices et les produits de beauté que j'utilise sont toujours à base de produits naturels. **≫**

et vous?

Faites une liste des choses que vous faites pour pratiquer l'écologie chez vous.

Il suffit d'y penser. *You just have to think about it.*   **contenir ✳** *to contain*   **emballages** *packaging*   **au lieu de** *instead of*   **l'évier** *sink*   **robinet** *faucet*   **à la longue** *in the long run*   **que** *only*   **convaincant** *convincing*   **linge** *laundry*   **nocifs** *harmful*

■ **Culture Note**

In almost every French city you will find large green hexagonal bins for recycling glass and plastic containers.

■ **Notes linguistiques**

• The term **la lessive** *(laundry detergent)* is more commonly used than **la poudre à laver**. **La lessive** also designates the clothes to be washed.

• **l'essuie-tout** *(m.)* = paper towels, from **essuyer** *(to wipe)* and **tout** *(everything)*.

■ **Teaching Suggestion**

Have students send the survey they created to several francophone partner classes as well. Analyze the responses, as a class, and compare and contrast with the responses received at your school.

■ **Irregular Verbs**

(see Appendix C)
contenir   (see **tenir**)

Teaching Strategy: Expansion

After reading the different ways in which the five French students contribute to the preservation of the environment, have students prepare a list of different things that can be done to be "environment-friendly." Students will prepare a class survey and then compare results with another French class.

This activity is useful for a reading comprehension check, as a vocabulary builder and as a cultural reinforcement activity.

Unité 3   121

Interdisciplinary/ Community Connections Project

This article provides an interesting subject for a short research project in conjunction with science or health classes.

Le soleil, notre bonne étoile

Chaque jour, le soleil nous donne sa lumière,° sa chaleur° et son énergie. Il est source de toute vie.° Sans lui, il n'y aurait pas° de plantes, pas de fleurs, pas d'arbres, pas d'animaux et, évidemment, pas de vie humaine. C'est lui qui cause la pluie, le vent, les différences de climat et les changements de saison. Grâce à° lui, les rivières coulent° et les plantes poussent.° Le soleil est vraiment notre bonne étoile!°

À cause de ses innombrables bienfaits,° les civilisations anciennes ont créé un culte du soleil. Pour les Égyptiens, Amon-Râ, le soleil, était le dieu° suprême. En Amérique, les Incas et les Aztèques adoraient aussi le soleil.

Aujourd'hui, le culte du soleil existe toujours, mais il a pris une forme nouvelle. Chaque année, par exemple, des millions de Français vont sur les plages de l'Atlantique et de la Méditerranée pour se baigner, mais surtout et avant tout pour bronzer au soleil. On peut aussi bronzer à la piscine, à la montagne, dans son jardin, ou même sur son balcon.

Il y a différentes raisons pour lesquelles° les Français s'exposent au soleil. Selon une enquête,° 50% des personnes interrogées° trouvent que c'est agréable, 22% pensent que c'est bon pour la santé,° 18% déclarent qu'être bronzé, c'est à la mode. Le bronzage fait en effet partie du «look».

Si le soleil est indispensable au succès des vacances, il peut aussi créer des problèmes pour les personnes imprudentes.° La lumière solaire contient, en effet, des rayons ultra-violets (UV). Quand ces rayons sont trop intenses, ils sont dangereux pour la peau° et pour les yeux. Si on ne fait pas attention, on peut attraper un coup de soleil ou, chose plus grave, être victime d'une insolation.° À long terme, le soleil contribue au vieillissement° de la peau. Le soleil est aussi un facteur de risque important du cancer cutané.°

lumière *light* **chaleur** *heat* **vie** *life* **il n'y aurait pas** *there wouldn't be* **Grâce à** *Thanks to* **coulent** *flow* **poussent** *grow* **étoile** *star*
bienfaits *benefits, blessings* **le dieu** *god, deity* **lesquelles** *which* **enquête** *survey* **interrogées** *asked* **santé** *health*
imprudentes *who are not careful* **peau** *skin* **insolation** *sunstroke* **vieillissement** *aging* **cutané** *of the skin*

Notes culturelles

• **Amon-Râ**, or **Rê**, was the Egyptian sun-god. He was often represented as a man with the head of a falcon.
• The Aztecs dominated Mexico until Cortés led the Spanish conquest in 1521. The Aztec sun-god was called Huitzilopochtli.

• The Incas ruled Peru until Pizarro's arrival in the 16th century. The Inca religion was based on the worship of the sun, which they called Huiracocha. The emperor, or Inca, was also the religious leader and was considered to be **le fils du Soleil.**

Avant de s'exposer au soleil, il est donc important de prendre quelques précautions élémentaires. Voici certains conseils:

✳ Évitez° de vous mettre au soleil entre 11 heures du matin et 2 heures de l'après-midi. C'est à ce moment que les rayons ultra-violets sont les plus intenses.

✳ Protégez-vous la tête avec un chapeau à large bord° et les yeux avec de bonnes lunettes de soleil qui les recouvrent entièrement.

✳ Utilisez une bonne crème solaire. Les crèmes solaires filtrent les rayons ultra-violets. Choisissez une crème solaire adaptée à votre peau.

✳ N'utilisez pas de produits qui contiennent des substances photosensibilisantes, comme l'eau de cologne ou certains parfums. Ces substances sont à l'origine de réactions cutanées anormales.

✳ Soyez vigilants en hiver aussi bien qu'en été. La neige reflète les rayons ultra-violets plus que le sable.° Si la lumière est intense, portez des lunettes de soleil.

et vous?

DÉBAT: LE SOLEIL: AMI OU ENNEMI?
Prenez une position sur ce sujet et débattez-le avec votre partenaire (qui prendra la position contraire). Présentez vos arguments par ordre d'importance.

EXPRESSION ÉCRITE
Êtes-vous un(e) «adorateur(trice) du soleil»? Composez un paragraphe où vous allez expliquer ...
• pourquoi vous aimez le soleil
• où et quand vous bronzez
• quelles précautions vous prenez

Évitez Avoid **bord** brim **sable** sand

Jacques Prévert (1900-1977) est un écrivain et aussi l'auteur de chansons populaires et de plusieurs scénarios de films. Dans ses poèmes, il décrit avec humour et fantaisie les thèmes simples de l'existence: la nature, l'amour, l'amitié, l'enfance, la réalité de tous les jours.
    Dans cet extrait, Prévert explique:
■ pourquoi il faut être poli avec la terre et le soleil
■ les relations personnelles qui existent entre la terre, le soleil et la lune

SOYEZ POLIS

Le soleil est amoureux de la terre
La terre est amoureuse du soleil
Ça les regarde
C'est leur affaire
Et quand il y a des éclipses
Il n'est pas prudent ni discret de les regarder
Au travers de sales petits morceaux de verre fumé
Ils se disputent
C'est des histoires personnelles
Mieux vaut ne pas s'en mêler
Parce que
Si on s'en mêle on risque d'être changé
En pomme de terre gelée
Ou en fer à friser

Le soleil aime la terre
La terre aime le soleil
C'est comme ça
Le reste ne nous regarde pas
La terre aime le soleil
Et elle tourne
Pour se faire admirer
Et le soleil la trouve belle
Et il brille sur elle
Et quand il est fatigué
Il va se coucher

Et la lune se lève
La lune c'est l'ancienne amoureuse du soleil
Mais elle a été jalouse
Et elle a été punie
Elle est devenue toute froide
Et elle sort seulement la nuit
Il faut aussi être très poli avec la lune
Ou sans ça elle peut vous rendre un peu fou
Et elle peut aussi
Si elle veut

Vous changer en bonhomme de neige
En réverbère
Ou en bougie

Prévert, Histoires (Paris: Gallimard, 1963, pp. 66-69)

cent vingt-trois **123**
INFO Magazine

Additional Information
Jacques Prévert wrote the classic French movies: *Les Visiteurs du soir* and *Les Enfants du paradis*.

Notes linguistiques
le verre fumé = tinted glass
le fer à friser = curling iron
Ça ne nous regarde pas = It's none of our business.
le réverbère = street light

Irregular Verbs
Point out that **contenir** is conjugated like **tenir**. Remind students of the irregular imperative forms of **être**: **sois, soyons, soyez.**

Teaching Strategy: Additional Activities
• Votre partenaire et vous, vous passez les vacances de printemps à la Martinique. C'est votre premier jour là-bas. Votre partenaire a décidé d'aller à la plage. Faites-lui au moins cinq recommandations importantes.
• Faites une enquête dans votre classe. Déterminez:
  – combien de temps par jour vos camarades bronzent en été
  – pourquoi ils aiment bronzer
  – les précautions qu'ils doivent prendre en ce qui concerne leur santé
  Comparez les résultats avec ceux de l'enquête faite en France.

Student Portfolios
Ask students to write a poem or a song about some aspect of nature or the environment. They may illustrate or record these materials for inclusion in their personal portfolios.

For writing rubrics, consult the **Generate Success** Rubric Generator on the **Teacher One Stop**. You can also create your own custom rubrics with this tool.

RESOURCES

Quoi de neuf?

Devine!

Quoi de neuf?

PRINT

Activités pour tous

Unit 3 Resource Book, Partie 2

Activités pour tous TE

Lesson Plans

Block Scheduling Lesson Plans

Absent Student Copymasters

Workbook TE

TECHNOLOGY

@HomeTutor

Interactive Whiteboard Lessons

Teacher One Stop

Block Scheduling Copymasters

DVD Program, Unit 3

COMMENT DÉCRIRE UN ÉVÉNEMENT, COMMENT RACONTER UNE HISTOIRE

— **Quoi de neuf?** *(What's new?)*
  Devine!

> **deviner** *to guess*

— Je ne sais pas!
  Qu'est-ce qui est arrivé? **Qu'est-ce qui a eu lieu?**
  Qu'est-ce qui s'est passé? **Qu'est-ce qu'il y a eu?**

> **arriver** *to happen*
> **se passer** *to happen*
> **avoir lieu** *to take place*
> **qu'est-ce qu'il y a** *what's happening*

J'ai **assisté à**
J'ai **été témoin de** } quelque chose de bizarre.
J'ai **vu**

> **assister à** *to be present at, to see*
> **être témoin de** *to witness*

■ **Note linguistique**

In 1987, the **Académie française** announced that the word **événement** could also be written **évènement** (with a grave accent on the second "e"). You may allow your students to use either spelling.

— Ah bon? Quand?
  C'est arrivé   } **hier**   **lundi dernier**   **il y a** deux heures
  Ça s'est passé } **hier soir**   **la semaine dernière**   **il y a** dix jours
  Ça a eu lieu   } **avant-hier** **le mois dernier**

— Où étais-tu?
  J'étais   } **dehors** *(outside)*   dans un magasin
  Je me trouvais   } en ville   chez un copain

> **se trouver** *to be*

— Alors, raconte! Qu'est-ce que tu as fait?
  Eh bien, **d'abord** *(first)*, j'ai téléphoné à . . .
    puis *(then)* . . .   **enfin** *(at last)* . . .
    ensuite *(next)* . . .   **finalement** *(finally)* . . .
    après *(after, afterwards)* . . .

> **raconter** *to tell (what happened)*

Quelques événements

un accident	**un événement** *(event)*
un incendie *(fire)*	**un fait** *(fact)*
un cambriolage *(burglary)*	**un fait divers** *(minor news item)*

SUPPLEMENTARY VOCABULARY

Quelques événements
une altercation *dispute*
une bonne action *good deed*
une catastrophe *catastrophe*
une collision *collision, crash*
un défilé *parade*
un vol *robbery*
un vol à l'étalage *shoplifting*
un vol à la tire *purse snatching*

Teaching Suggestion: DVD Program

In the Unit 3 *Vidéo-drame: Un accident*, students will learn expressions that will help them tell a story or describe an event. This section focuses on Malik and Nicolas explaining the accident that took place on their fishing excursion. You may want to point out to students the use of the **passé composé** versus the imperfect when posing and answering the question **Qu'est-ce qui s'est passé?**

Comment exprimer la surprise

Vraiment?	*Really?*	**C'est incroyable!**	*That's unbelievable!*
Pas possible!	*That's not possible!*	**Ce n'est pas croyable!**	*That's not for real!*
Mon Dieu!	*My goodness!*	**Tu plaisantes!**	*You're kidding!*

1 Journalisme

Vous êtes journaliste pour le magazine RADAR. Dites quand et où les événements de la colonne A ont eu lieu en choisissant un élément des colonnes B et C. Soyez logique.

A: QUOI?	B: QUAND?	C: OÙ?
un cambriolage	ce matin	à l'église St. Charles
un accident	à deux heures cet après-midi	sur l'autoroute A4
un incendie	hier soir	dans une galerie d'art
un violent orage *(storm)*	vendredi dernier	dans la région de Toulouse
une avalanche	le week-end dernier	dans la forêt d'Amboise
un ouragan *(hurricane)*	la semaine dernière	dans les Alpes
le mariage de l'acteur	l'hiver dernier	à la Martinique
Georges Belhomme	en avril dernier	au zoo de Vincennes

▶ **Un accident a eu lieu ce matin (à deux heures cet après-midi) sur l'autoroute A4 (dans la forêt d'Amboise).**

2 Créa-dialogue

Avec votre partenaire, choisissez un événement au bas de la page (ou imaginez un événement original). Composez le dialogue où vous racontez cet événement.

— Quoi de neuf?
— Devine!
— Je ne sais pas! Qu'est-ce qui est arrivé?
— J'ai rencontré le président!
— Tu plaisantes! Quand?
— Ce matin.
— Où étais-tu?
— Je me trouvais à l'aéroport.
— Qu'est-ce que tu as fait alors?
— J'ai pris une photo et j'ai demandé un autographe.
— C'est incroyable!

• *Use another expression.*
• *Imagine a different event.*
• *Use another expression of surprise.*
• *Mention another time.*
• *Mention another place.*
• *Mention two things you did.*
• *Use another expression of surprise.*

Événements
• J'ai rencontré Oprah Winfrey.
• J'ai vu un OVNI *(UFO)*.
• J'ai été témoin d'un cambriolage.
• J'ai assisté à un accident spectaculaire.
• J'ai assisté au mariage de . . .(?)
• J'ai découvert un trésor.

Teaching Strategies: Warm-Up

• Divide the class into groups of three and have each group write an original dialog using EVERY vocabulary word/expression from pp. 124–125. When there are synonymous expressions, they should still incorporate each of them logically into the dialog. Encourage students to be creative.

• Divide the class into groups of two or three to create a class newspaper. The newspaper should have a variety of columns: weather, news article of accidents, news articles, comics. Give each group one of these sections.

• If you have the opportunity to go to a computer center with the class as a whole, this can make the activity more meaningful and will allow the students to produce a final product that can be displayed and distributed.

Note culturelle

All French super highways are designated by the letter **A** (for **Autoroute**) followed by a number. The A4 (**l'A4**) links Paris to Metz in the east.

Differentiation

Alphabetic/Phonetic On photocopies of pages 124–125, have students mark liaisons for all vocabulary. Have them write out phonetic transcriptions for the following: **a eu lieu; avant-hier; un incendie; Mon Dieu**. Go over pronunciation of all vocabulary.

PRINT
Workbook, pp. 124–126
Unit 3 Resource Book, Partie 2
Audioscripts

AUDIO
 Audio Program
CD 3, Tracks 8–12

TECHNOLOGY
@HomeTutor
Interactive Whiteboard Lessons
Teacher One Stop
Projectable Transparencies
  25, *Le temps*
  1, *La France*
  1(o), *La France*
  Transparency Copymasters,
  pp. A53–A54; A5–A6

SUPPLEMENTARY VOCABULARY

une étoile filante *shooting star*
il fait gris *it's a cloudy day*
une éclaircie *bright interval of sun*
la tornade *tornado*
l'ouragan *(m.)* *hurricane*
une averse *shower*

■ Note linguistique
La météo is the abbreviation of **la météorologie** (meteorology, weather forecasting).

■ Teaching Strategy: Vocabulary Building
• Why is an umbrella called **un parapluie**?
It protects *"against-the-rain."*
• Similarly: **un parachute** (**une chute** *fall*)
Also *lightning rod:*
un paratonnerre
• What is **un gratte-ciel**?
(**gratter** *to scratch*)

126 Unité 3

@HOMETUTOR
my.hrw.com

Comment parler de la pluie et du beau temps

Pour le week-end, **la météo** *(weather forecast)* **a prédit:**

du beau temps	**du mauvais temps**	
du soleil *(sun)*	**de la pluie** *(rain)*	**de la neige** *(snow)*
un ciel *(sky)* **bleu**	**du vent** *(wind)*	**une tempête de neige**
des nuages *(clouds)*	**un orage** *(thunderstorm)*	**du verglas** *(sheet ice)*
de la brume *(mist)*	**une tempête** *(storm)*	
du brouillard *(fog)*	**un ouragan** *(hurricane)*	

prédire *to predict*

Quand il fait beau . . .

Le soleil **brille**.
Le ciel est bleu.

Quand il fait mauvais . . .

Le ciel est **couvert** *(overcast)*.
La pluie tombe.

Quand il y a un orage . . .

Le vent **souffle**.
On voit **des éclairs** *(lightning)*.
On entend **le tonnerre** *(thunder)*.

Quand il fait nuit …

Il fait noir.
On voit **la lune** *(moon).*
et **les étoiles** *(stars).*

Quand il fait froid . . .

La neige **tombe**.
Il y a de **la glace** *(ice).*
Le lac est **gelé** *(frozen).*

briller *to shine*
souffler *to blow*
il fait noir *it is dark*

AUJOURD'HUI		HIER	DEMAIN
il pleut	il pleuvait	il a plu le matin	il va pleuvoir
il neige	il neigeait	il a neigé à midi	il va neiger
il y a eu un orage	il y a un orage	il y a eu un orage dans la nuit	il va y avoir un orage

---

Teaching Strategy: Warm-Up
Use the **Projectable Transparencies** to introduce the weather. Then have students develop short weather dialogs in which they phone a friend living in another part of the country that has weather conditions that are very different from their own.

3 Une question de temps

Complétez les phrases en décrivant
le temps (ou le moment de la journée).

1. Je mets mes lunettes de soleil quand . . .
2. Je mets mon imperméable quand . . .
3. On peut faire du ski quand . . .
4. On peut voir des éclairs quand . . .
5. On ne voit pas le soleil quand . . .
6. On voit des étoiles quand . . .
7. La visibilité sur la route est mauvaise
   quand . . .
8. On peut faire du patinage *(go skating)*
   sur un lac quand . . .

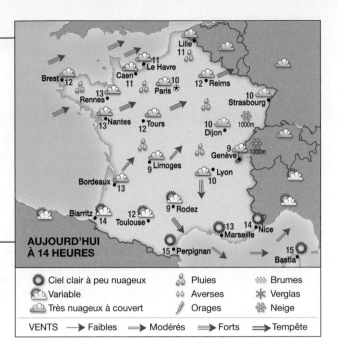

AUJOURD'HUI
À 14 HEURES

☀ Ciel clair à peu nuageux	☔ Pluies	≋ Brumes
☁ Variable	⬮⬮ Averses	✳ Verglas
☁ Très nuageux à couvert	✎ Orages	❄ Neige

VENTS → Faibles ⇒ Modérés ⇛ Forts ⇛ Tempête

Conversations libres

Avec votre partenaire, choisissez l'un des sujets suivants. Composez
le dialogue correspondant à la situation et jouez-le en classe.

Digital performance space

1 Les vacances de printemps

Béatrice passe les vacances de printemps
à la Martinique où il fait très, très beau.
Xavier les passe au Québec où il fait très,
très froid. Les deux cousins se téléphonent
et parlent du temps.
Rôles: Béatrice, Xavier

2 Un ouragan

Nous sommes en septembre. Carole,
une étudiante française, visite la
Floride. Aujourd'hui, il y a un terrible
ouragan. Elle téléphone à son père
qui veut avoir des détails.
Rôles: Carole, son père

3 Week-end

Votre partenaire et vous, vous avez
décidé de passer la journée de samedi
ensemble. La météo a prédit un temps
incertain. Discutez de ce que vous allez
faire suivant le temps.
Rôles: vous, votre partenaire

■ Réponses: Activité 3

Encourage students to find several
completions for each sentence.
Sample answers might include:

1. Je mets mes lunettes de soleil
   quand il fait beau (quand le soleil
   brille).
2. Je mets mon imperméable quand
   il pleut (quand le ciel est couvert).
3. On peut faire du ski quand il a
   neigé (quand il neige).
4. On peut voir des éclairs quand il
   y a un orage.
5. On ne voit pas le soleil quand le
   ciel est couvert (quand il fait nuit).
6. On voit des étoiles quand il fait
   nuit (quand il fait noir).
7. La visibilité sur la route est
   mauvaise quand la neige tombe
   (quand il fait noir, quand il y a du
   brouillard).
8. On peut faire du patinage sur un
   lac quand le lac est gelé.

■ Teaching Suggestion

Have students find weather forecast
maps for various francophone
countries on the Internet. Have them
bring printouts to class and give the
forecast, as if they were
meteorologists for a television
channel in those countries.

Expansion: Les proverbes

Give several examples of French proverbs:

- **Après la pluie, le beau temps.** (Joy comes after sadness.)
- **Autant en emporte le vent.** (Gone with the wind.)
- **Le soleil luit pour tout le monde.** (The sun shines on everyone.)

Ask students to come up with their own new proverbs—these may be serious or silly!

Langue et Communication

RESOURCES

PRINT
Workbook, pp. 39

TECHNOLOGY
@HomeTutor

Teacher One Stop
🖥 **Projectable Transparencies**
   26, *Un mauvais témoin*
   Transparency Copymasters,
   pp. A55–A56

A La description d'un événement: le passé composé et l'imparfait

The following sentences tell about an accident.
   The sentences on the left give the <u>main facts</u>.
   The sentences on the right describe the <u>scene</u> and the <u>background</u>.

MAIN EVENTS	BACKGROUND AND DESCRIPTION
J'**ai vu** un accident.	C'**était** samedi soir. Il **était** 8 heures. Il **pleuvait**. La visibilité **était** mauvaise. J'**allais** à un rendez-vous. Je **voulais** être à l'heure.
Une voiture **est rentrée** dans un arbre.	C'**était** une voiture de sport. Le conducteur **était** un jeune homme blond.
J'**ai téléphoné** à la police qui **est arrivée** immédiatement.	Le jeune homme ne **portait** pas de ceinture de sécurité. Il **était** légèrement blessé.
The PASSÉ COMPOSÉ tells WHAT HAPPENED and narrates the ACTION	The IMPERFECT sets the SCENE and gives the BACKGROUND
It is used to describe: • SPECIFIC EVENTS • the ACTIONS which constitute the STORY LINE	It is used to describe: • EXTERNAL CONDITIONS date weather time scenery • DESCRIPTIONS OF THE CHARACTERS age physical traits health attitudes appearance clothing feelings intentions • BACKGROUND ACTIVITIES what people were doing what was going on

1 Une question de temps

Expliquez logiquement les actions suivantes en décrivant le temps qu'il faisait.

CE QUI EST ARRIVÉ	QUEL TEMPS?
• J'ai glissé.	Il pleut.
• Stéphanie a bien bronzé.	Il fait noir.
• Nous avons fait du ski.	Il est gelé.
• Vous avez pris vos imperméables.	Il y a du verglas.
• Patrick a pris sa lampe de poche *(flashlight)*.	Il y a de la neige.
• On n'a pas vu le sommet de la montagne.	Il y a des nuages.
• Nous avons fait du patin à glace sur le lac.	Il y a de la brume.
• J'ai entendu l'avion mais je ne l'ai pas vu.	Il y a beaucoup de soleil.

▶ J'ai glissé parce qu'il y avait du verglas.

Teaching Strategy: Warm-Up

Passé Composé/Imparfait
Ask students:
• What they were doing at 8:00 last night
• What they were doing when their mother/father got home yesterday
• What they did this past weekend
• What they ate for dinner yesterday

• What they used to do with their friends after a day at grammar school
• Where they were yesterday afternoon at 3:00
• When they began high school
• What they looked like when they were ten years old
• Where they went on vacation last year

■ **Variation: Activity 2**
Have students work in pairs. One looks at the picture while the other reads the text. The student looking at the picture corrects the mistakes as his/her partner reads.

2 Un mauvais témoin

Monsieur Loiseau a été témoin d'un cambriolage samedi dernier. Malheureusement il n'a pas bonne mémoire. Lisez son témoignage *(account)* et rectifiez-le.

Monsieur Loiseau:

«Il était une heure et demie de l'après-midi. Il faisait beau. Il n'y avait pas de voitures dans la rue. Le bandit est sorti par la porte. C'était un homme petit et assez gros. Il avait une barbe noire. Il portait un masque de ski. Il portait un pull. Sa complice l'attendait derrière la banque. C'était une jeune fille brune. Elle avait les cheveux courts et frisés. Elle portait un collier autour du cou. Elle n'avait pas de lunettes. Le bandit et sa complice sont partis en voiture.»

▸ **Mais non! C'est faux! Il n'était pas une heure et demie. Il était trois heures! . . .**

3 Pourquoi?

Demandez à votre partenaire pourquoi il/elle a fait les choses suivantes. Il/elle va répondre avec l'explication suggérée (ou une autre explication de son choix).

▸ aller au café   — **Pourquoi est-ce que tu es allé(e) au café?**
  (j'ai soif)   — **Parce que j'avais soif.**
                         (Parce que je voulais rencontrer mes copains, . . .)

1. aller au restaurant
   (j'ai faim)

2. aller à la plage
   (il fait beau)

3. mettre de la crème solaire
   (il y a du soleil)

4. aller à la disco
   (j'ai envie de danser)

5. rentrer chez toi
   (il est minuit)

6. se dépêcher
   (je veux être à l'heure)

7. téléphoner à ta cousine
   (c'est son anniversaire)

8. prendre de la dramamine
   (j'ai le mal de mer)

■ **Variation: Activity 3**
Demandez à votre partenaire pourquoi il/elle n'a pas fait les choses suivantes. Il/Elle vous répond en utilisant l'explication suggérée ou une explication de son choix.
Exemple:
– Pourquoi n'es-tu pas allé(e) au café?
– Parce que je n'avais pas soif. (Parce que je ne voulais pas rencontrer mes copains, ...)

Write some of the answers on the board in two separate columns—**passé composé** and **imparfait.** Ask students to explain why the sentences belong in each category.

Differentiation

Cumulative, Gifted & Talented Review quickly the formation of the **imparfait.** Then do Act. 1 aloud with the class, writing the answers on the board. Have students then create their own **imparfait** activity, using Act. 1 as a model.

RESOURCES

PRINT
Workbook, pp. 40–41

TECHNOLOGY

@HomeTutor

 Interactive Whiteboard Lessons

Teacher One Stop

Teacher to Teacher Copymasters,
Et maintenant ..., pp. 39–42;
Jumeaux/Jumelles , pp. 43–46

 **Projectable Transparencies**

27, *L'orage*

Transparency Copymasters,
pp. A57–A58

■ **Vocabulary Expansion**
les pompiers *firefighters*

4 Une promenade romantique?

Pierre habite à Annecy. L'été dernier, il s'est acheté un bateau. Voilà ce qui lui est arrivé un jour.

C'est samedi. Il est sept heures du soir. Il fait beau. Pierre est chez lui. Il a envie de sortir. Il téléphone à Armelle, sa nouvelle copine. Il lui propose de faire une promenade en bateau sur le lac d'Annecy. Armelle accepte. Pierre prend sa moto et il va chercher Armelle. Il arrive chez elle. Armelle l'attend. Elle porte une belle robe rouge à fleurs et ses nouvelles chaussures.

Pierre et Armelle arrivent au lac. Ils montent dans le bateau de Pierre. Pierre prend sa guitare. Il chante des chansons romantiques. Le ciel est clair. La lune et les étoiles brillent dans le ciel. Armelle écoute Pierre. Elle est très contente.

Tout d'un coup° Pierre fait un mouvement brusque. Il tombe dans l'eau. Armelle perd l'équilibre et tombe dans l'eau aussi. L'eau est très, très froide. Pierre et Armelle nagent jusqu'à la plage. Armelle est trempée° . . . et furieuse. Sa robe et ses nouvelles chaussures sont fichues°. Elle demande à Pierre de la raccompagner chez elle. Pauvre Pierre, il n'a pas de chance!

tout d'un coup *(all of a sudden)*   **trempée** *(soaked)*   **fichues** *(ruined)*

▶ Maintenant, mettez l'histoire au passé.
C'était un samedi pendant les vacances. . . .

5 Faits divers

Vous avez été témoin des faits divers suivants. Votre partenaire va choisir un de ces faits et vous poser des questions comme:

- C'était quand?
- Où étais-tu?
- Qu'est-ce que tu faisais?
- Qu'est-ce qui s'est passé?
- Qu'est-ce que tu as vu?
- Qu'est-ce que tu as fait?

Répondez à ses questions en utilisant votre imagination.

INCENDIE

Un incendie a eu lieu dans la nuit du 5 février aux établissements Dumoulin. Cet incendie, provoqué,° semble-t-il, par un court-circuit, a détruit l'atelier° de constructions mécaniques et a fait un million d'euros de dégâts.°

provoqué *caused*
atelier *workshop*
dégâts *damages*

ACCIDENT

Un accident de la circulation a eu lieu hier après-midi vers trois heures à l'intersection de la rue Victor Hugo et l'avenue de la République. Une voiture de tourisme, conduite par Monsieur Picard, professeur au lycée Descartes, est entrée en collision avec un camion de l'armée. L'accident, provoqué par la neige, n'a pas fait de victime.

CAMBRIOLAGE

Un cambriolage a eu lieu le week-end dernier dans un magasin d'antiquités de la rue de la Paix. D'après les déclarations de Madame Durand, la propriétaire, les cambrioleurs ont emporté° quelques statues sans valeur mais ont laissé une collection de monnaies° anciennes estimée à deux cent mille euros.

emporter *to carry off, steal*
monnaies *coins*

MARIAGE PRINCIER

Le mariage de la princesse Sophie a été célébré le 15 juin dans la chapelle du château de Rambucourt. La princesse, vêtue de satin blanc, a été accompagnée à l'autel° par son père, l'archiduc Ferdinand.

autel *altar*

---

6 À votre tour

Racontez un événement de votre vie. Décrivez la scène et les événements principaux. Vous pouvez décrire, par exemple . . .

- un accident
- un anniversaire
- un mariage
- une fête familiale
- un événement sportif auquel vous avez participé
- un concert ou un spectacle

Teaching Strategy: Expansion

Have the students draw or cut out from magazines or newspapers a picture that they could then describe using ten sentences in both the **passé composé** and the **imparfait**. Their sentences should include a description of the background scene and background information as well as an explanation of the specific action that is taking place in the picture. The next day in class they should show their pictures to the class and present their description without reading the prepared sentences.

B   L'imparfait et le passé composé dans la même phrase

In describing a past event, we may use both the PASSÉ COMPOSÉ and the IMPERFECT in the same sentence.

SPECIFIC ACTION *(what people did)*	ON-GOING OR PROGRESSIVE ACTION *(what was happening)*
J'**ai vu** un accident . . .	pendant que j'**attendais** le bus.
Le cambrioleur **est entré** . . .	pendant que les voisins **dormaient**.
Quand tu **as téléphoné**, . . .	je **regardais** la télé.
Quand l'orage **a commencé**, . . .	nous **nous promenions**.

The relationship between events and the corresponding choice of the passé composé or the imperfect can be illustrated as follows:

SPECIFIC ACTION   J'**ai vu** un accident   Quand tu **as téléphoné**   J'**ai observé** un oiseau

PROGRESSIVE ACTION   pendant que j'**attendais** le bus.   je **regardais** la télé.   qui **chantait** dans un arbre.

→ Depending on what action is being described, either the PASSÉ COMPOSÉ or the IMPERFECT may be used after **quand**.

| J'ai téléphoné **quand tu regardais** la télé. | *I called **when you were watching** television.* |
| Je téléphonais **quand tu es parti.** | *I was talking on the phone **when you left.*** |

Les expressions de temps

PREPOSITION (+ noun)		
pendant	*during*	Qu'est-ce que tu as fait **pendant** les vacances?

CONJUNCTION		
pendant que	*while*	Qu'est-ce que tu as fait **pendant que** je jouais au golf?
lorsque	*when*	J'ai rencontré Paul **lorsqu**'il travaillait à Paris.
au moment où	*just as*	Je suis arrivé à la gare **au moment où** le train partait.

7 Où étais-tu?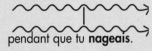

Demandez à votre partenaire où il/elle était quand certaines choses sont arrivées. Il/elle va répondre en utilisant l'expression suggérée ou une expression de son choix.

Où étais-tu quand j'ai téléphoné?

Qu'est-ce que tu faisais?

J'étais dans ma chambre.

Je dormais.

1.
- je suis passé(e)
- au jardin
- tondre la pelouse

2.
- tu as vu l'incendie
- dans la rue
- me promener

3.
- tu t'es cassé la jambe
- à la montagne
- faire de l'alpinisme

4.
- tu as vu l'ours *(bear)*
- à la campagne
- faire du camping

5.
- le cambrioleur est entré
- dans la salle de bains
- se laver les cheveux

6.
- l'homme s'est noyé
- à la plage
- prendre un bain de soleil

■ **Note linguistique**

It is also possible for two specific actions or two progressive actions to occur in the same sentence.

Je **suis parti**

quand tu **es rentré**.

Je **prenais** un bain de soleil

pendant que tu **nageais**.

RESOURCES

PRINT
Workbook, pp. 41–44, 126
Unit 3 Resource Book, Partie 2
  Audioscripts

AUDIO
 Audio Program
  CD 3, Tracks 13–14

TECHNOLOGY
@HomeTutor

■ **Teaching Note**
120 kilomètres à l'heure =
74.5 mph

8 **Rencontres de vacances**

Décrivez les rencontres suivantes.

▶ à la plage / Thomas / parler à une fille / prendre un bain de soleil
  À la plage, Thomas a parlé à une fille qui prenait un bain de soleil.

1. à la montagne / nous / voir des gens / faire de l'escalade
2. pendant l'excursion / Philippe / rencontrer un camarade / se promener dans les bois
3. à la mer / tu / prendre des photos d'un ami / faire de la planche à voile
4. au café / nous / écouter un étudiant / jouer de la guitare
5. au musée / vous / parler à des touristes / visiter la ville
6. dans la rue / Sophie / rencontrer des copains / aller au cinéma

9 **Zut alors!**

Certaines choses arrivent toujours au mauvais moment. Décrivez ce que les personnes faisaient quand certaines choses sont arrivées.

▶ Je visite la Guadeloupe / quand / il y a un ouragan
  Je visitais la Guadeloupe quand il y a eu un ouragan.

1. Philippe regarde les filles / quand / il tombe dans l'eau
2. Mon cousin va à 120 à l'heure / lorsque / la police l'arrête
3. Nous faisons une promenade à pied / quand / l'orage commence
4. Thomas écrit à sa copine / au moment où / le professeur lui pose une question
5. Marc gagne le match de tennis / lorsque / il glisse et se casse le bras
6. Jérôme embrasse *(kisses)* Alice / au moment où / le père d'Alice entre

10 **D'autres mésaventures**

Décrivez les mésaventures *(mishaps)* suivantes au passé.

1. Nous montons à la Tour Eiffel. Pendant que nous sommes dans l'ascenseur, il y a une panne d'électricité.
2. Caroline et Sandrine font du camping. Pendant qu'elles dorment, un raton laveur *(raccoon)* mange leurs provisions.
3. Monsieur Malchance monte sur le toit pour réparer l'antenne de télévision. Pendant qu'il la répare, un vent fort souffle et l'échelle *(ladder)* tombe. Monsieur Malchance reste toute la nuit sur le toit.
4. Roméo va sous le balcon de Juliette et lui chante une chanson d'amour. Pendant qu'il chante, le père de Juliette lui jette un seau *(bucket)* d'eau sur la tête.

C Le passé simple

Expansion pp. R32-33

Passé simple

Like the PASSÉ COMPOSÉ, the PASSÉ SIMPLE is used to describe what people DID, what HAPPENED.

Although you do not need to learn how to write the passé simple, you should be able to recognize its forms since the tense is often used in written narration and literary texts.

Note the passé simple of regular verbs:

INFINITIVE		parler	finir	répondre
PASSÉ SIMPLE	je	parl**ai**	fin**is**	répond**is**
	tu	parl**as**	fin**is**	répond**is**
	il/elle/on	parl**a**	fin**it**	répond**it**
	nous	parl**âmes**	fin**îmes**	répond**îmes**
	vous	parl**âtes**	fin**îtes**	répond**îtes**
	ils/elles	parl**èrent**	fin**irent**	répond**irent**

→ For most irregular verbs, the stem of the passé simple is similar to the past participle:

aller **(allé)** → il **alla**   ils **allèrent**   prendre **(pris)** → il **prit**   ils **prirent**
avoir **(eu)** → il **eut**   ils **eurent**   recevoir **(reçu)** → il **reçut**   ils **reçurent**

Note the following common irregular forms:

être → il **fut**   ils **furent**   venir → il **vint**   ils **vinrent**
faire → il **fit**   ils **firent**   voir → il **vit**   ils **virent**

11 Un peu d'histoire

Lisez l'histoire d'une exploration importante. Puis, racontez cette histoire à votre partenaire en remplaçant le passé simple par le passé composé.

Jacques Cartier (1491–1557) est l'un des grands explorateurs français. Il naquit à Saint-Malo en 1491. Dans sa jeunesse, il alla au Portugal, au Brésil et probablement dans la région de Terre-Neuve.° En 1534, le roi de France lui donna la mission d'explorer les côtes° de l'Amérique du Nord. Cartier et ses hommes partirent de Saint-Malo le 20 avril et arrivèrent dans la région de Gaspé au Canada le 25 juillet. Cartier descendit à terre, planta une croix dans le sol et prit possession de la région au nom du roi de France. L'expédition revint en France où elle fut reçue en triomphe. Jacques Cartier fit un second voyage en 1535 avec la mission cette fois de chercher de l'or et des pierres précieuses. Il ne trouva pas d'or mais il découvrit un immense fleuve qu'il nomma Saint-Laurent. Cartier remonta le fleuve jusqu'au site d'un village indien, Hochelaga, aujourd'hui Montréal. Les premiers colons français s'installèrent au Canada 70 ans plus tard. C'est ainsi que le Canada devint un territoire français.

Terre-Neuve *(Newfoundland)*   **les côtes** *(coast)*

Teaching Strategy: Extra Practice

For additional recognition practice, have students identify the infinitives of the following **passé simple** forms:

il crut (croire)   **il dit** (dire)
il but (boire)   **il lut** (lire)
il partit (partir)   **il mit** (mettre)

Have students guess:
il écrivit (écrire)
il découvrit (découvrir)
il construisit (construire)
il mourut (mourir)

Unité 3

Interdisciplinary/ Community Connections

Create a travel brochure or video, in French, for French-speaking visitors to your area.

Language Arts:
Have students write to various organizations and clubs in your town for sites and activities.

Math:
Compile statistics for busiest times of year. Or calculate travel time between sites and use this information to plan daily itineraries.

Science:
Find out about weather patterns during different seasons to include in the brochure.

Social Studies:
Write a brief history of an important person, building, or organization in town.

Art/Music:
Collect photos, maps, and illustrations to use in the brochure. Or gather props and background music selections typical of your area to be used in a video.

Technology:
Use a computer to implement the design of the brochure, or use a video camera to record a video. Or investigate how technology has affected your town.

Community:
Donate the brochure or videotape to a local travel agency or tourism bureau.

■ Note culturelle

Jacques Cartier died in Saint-Malo, France, after having made another trip to Canada.

LECTURE  Sempé et Goscinny

King

AVANT DE LIRE

L'histoire suivante est extraite d'un album humoristique intitulé
Les Récrés du petit Nicolas. Le petit Nicolas est un peu l'équivalent
français de «Denis la Menace». C'est un garçon de 6 ou 7 ans. Il est
généreux, affectueux, vif d'esprit,° parfois turbulent, mais sans
méchanceté.° Il adore ses parents, aime les animaux, et il a toute une
bande de copains. Comme à tous les enfants de son âge, il lui arrive
parfois de° «faire des bêtises»,° ou bien, très innocemment, de créer
des situations plus ou moins embarrassantes pour ses parents, ses
voisins ou ses professeurs.

Notez que dans ce récit, c'est le Petit Nicolas qui parle. Les impressions
présentées et le style utilisé sont, par conséquent, ceux d'un jeune
enfant français.

Les divers albums relatant
les aventures du *Petit Nicolas*
sont le produit de la
collaboration d'un illustrateur et
d'un écrivain. **Jean-Jacques
Sempé** (né en 1932),
l'illustrateur, a collaboré à de
nombreux magazines. Il est aussi
le père d'un fils qui s'appelle …
Nicolas. **René Goscinny**
(1926-1977), l'écrivain, a créé
d'autres personnages très
célèbres en France comme
Astérix et le cow-boy *Lucky Luke*.

NOTE *Culturelle*

Le jardin public

Les villes françaises ont généralement un **jardin** ou
parc public où les petits enfants viennent jouer, les
personnes âgées se reposer, et les gens de tout âge
se promener. Ces jardins publics sont généralement
très bien entretenus° et très bien équipés. On y trouve
généralement des massifs de fleurs,° des pelouses de
gazon,° une pièce d'eau° avec une fontaine, des jeux
pour les petits enfants, et des bancs.° Pour maintenir
le bon usage de ces jardins, un grand nombre
d'activités sont interdites.° Il est interdit, par exemple,
de faire de la bicyclette dans les allées, de marcher sur
les pelouses, de jouer au frisbee ou au volley, de faire
des pique-niques et d'aller à la pêche dans les pièces
d'eau.

Les jardins publics sont généralement placés
sous la surveillance d'un gardien. Le gardien est
souvent un homme âgé (un ancien militaire, par
exemple). Il porte un uniforme et une casquette
et, pour maintenir l'ordre, il utilise un sifflet.

Anticipons un peu

Pour mieux comprendre une histoire, il est
parfois utile de participer indirectement à cette
histoire en prenant la place d'un observateur et
en essayant d'anticiper ce qui va arriver.
Imaginez, par exemple, que vous êtes le frère
aîné ou la soeur aînée du petit Nicolas. Vous
avez appris que celui-ci est parti faire une
promenade avec ses copains dans un endroit
où il y a un étang.° Connaissant bien votre petit
frère, vous vous doutez bien° qu'il va rapporter
quelque créature vivante de cette promenade.
Avant de lire l'histoire, essayez de deviner°…
- quel animal le petit Nicolas va rapporter
  de l'étang
- qu'est-ce qu'il a l'intention de faire avec
  cet animal
- comment vos parents vont réagir°

---

vif d'esprit *alert*   **méchanceté** = *malice*   **il lui arrive parfois de** *it sometimes happens that he*   **bêtises** = *choses pas très intelligentes*
entretenus *maintained*   **massifs de fleurs** *flower beds*   **gazon** *grass*   **pièce d'eau** *pool*   **banc** *bench*   **interdites** *forbidden*   **étang** *pond*
vous vous doutez bien = *vous êtes assez sûr*   **deviner** *guess*   **réagir** *to react*

134 cent trente-quatre
Unité 3

Teaching Strategy

This story uses a variety of verb forms: the
present, the *passé composé*, the *imperfect*, the
pluperfect, the *subjunctive*, and also the *future*
and *conditional*. With respect to the future and
conditional forms in the text, you may …
- simply treat them as vocabulary items;

- BRIEFLY review the basic forms of the future,
which were presented in Unit 8 of DISCOVERING
FRENCH TODAY!–*BLANC*;
- BRIEFLY present the future and conditional
as anticipatory structures (cf. Unit 5, pp. 201,
204, 207).

■ **Note linguistique**
Le square is a small public park, generally fenced.

Mes copains et moi, nous avons décidé d'aller à la pêche!

Il y a un square° où nous allons jouer souvent, et dans le square il y a un chouette étang. Et dans l'étang il y a des têtards, et c'est ça que nous avons décidé de pêcher. Les têtards, ce sont de petites bêtes qui grandissent
5 et qui deviennent des grenouilles.

À la maison, j'ai pris un bocal à confitures° vide et je suis allé dans le square, en faisant bien attention que le gardien ne me voie pas. Le gardien du square a une grosse moustache, une canne, et un sifflet à roulette comme celui du papa de Raoul, qui est agent de police.° Le gardien nous
10 gronde° souvent, parce qu'il y a des tas de choses qui sont défendues dans le square: il ne faut pas marcher sur l'herbe, monter aux arbres, arracher les fleurs, faire du vélo, jouer au football, jeter des papiers par terre, et se battre.° Mais on s'amuse bien quand même!

Édouard, Raoul, et Clotaire étaient déjà au bord de l'étang avec leur
15 bocaux. Alceste est arrivé le dernier—il nous a expliqué qu'il n'avait pas trouvé de bocal vide et qu'il avait dû en vider un. Il avait encore plein de° confiture sur la figure, Alceste.

Comme le gardien n'était pas là, on s'est tout de suite mis à pêcher.

C'est très difficile de pêcher des têtards! Il faut se mettre à plat ventre°
20 sur le bord° de l'étang, plonger le bocal dans l'eau, et essayer d'attraper les têtards qui bougent et qui n'ont pas du tout envie d'entrer dans les bocaux. Le premier qui a eu un têtard, c'était Clotaire, et il était tout fier, parce qu'il n'est pas habitué° à être le premier en quoi que ce soit.°

Et puis, à la fin, nous avons tous eu notre têtard. C'est-à-dire
25 qu'Alceste n'a pas réussi à en pêcher un, mais Raoul, qui est un pêcheur formidable, en avait deux dans son bocal, et il a donné le plus petit à Alceste.

— Et qu'est-ce qu'on va faire avec nos têtards? a demandé Clotaire.

Mots utiles

un têtard	
une grenouille	
un étang	
un bocal	
un sifflet à roulette	

aller à la pêche	*to go fishing*
emmener	*to bring*
grandir	*to grow (in size)*
se mettre à *	*= commencer à*
pêcher	*to fish*
plonger	*to plunge*
vider	*to empty*
défendu	*forbidden*
fier (fière)	*proud*
vide	*empty*
quand même	*anyhow*

■ **Irregular Verbs**
(see Appendix C)
mettre

Langage familier

une bête = un animal
chouette = super
rigolo = amusant
des tas de = beaucoup de

square = jardin public   **confitures** *jam*   **un agent de police** *policeman*   **gronde** *scolds*   **se battre** *to fight*   **plein de** = beaucoup de
se mettre à plat ventre *lie down on your stomach*   **bord** *edge*   **habitué à** *accustomed, used to*   **quoi que ce soit** *whatever it is*

If you prefer, you may hold this reading until after Unit 5 where the future and conditional are formally introduced.

30 — Ben, a répondu Raoul, on va les emmener chez nous, on va attendre qu'ils grandissent et qu'ils deviennent des grenouilles, et on va faire des courses. Ce sera rigolo.

— Et puis, a dit Édouard, les grenouilles, c'est pratique, ça monte sur une petite échelle et ça vous dit le temps qu'il fera!

— Et puis, a dit Alceste, les cuisses de grenouilles, avec de l'ail, c'est

35 très, très bon!

Et Alceste a regardé son têtard, en se passant la langue° sur les lèvres.

langue *tongue*

NOTE *Culturelle*

Les grenouilles sont des animaux très communs en France. On les trouve un peu partout: dans les étangs, dans les lacs, dans les rivières. Les grenouilles font partie du folklore français.

• **Les grenouilles et la météo**
D'après le folklore, on peut prédire le temps en observant les grenouilles. Si les grenouilles restent dans l'eau, il va faire beau. Si les grenouilles sortent de leur étang pour chercher un terrain sec,° il va pleuvoir. Autrefois, on mettait une grenouille dans un grand bocal avec de l'eau et une petite échelle. Si la grenouille montait à l'échelle, c'était un signe d'orage.

• **La course de grenouilles**
Traditionnellement, à la campagne, les enfants attrapaient des grenouilles et organisaient des courses pour voir laquelle irait le plus vite.

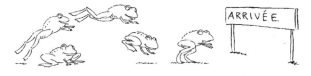

• **Les cuisses de grenouilles**
Contrairement à ce que pensent beaucoup d'Américains, les cuisses de grenouilles ne sont pas un plat typiquement français. En fait, pratiquement aucun° restaurant français ne sert ce plat.

sec *dry* **aucun** *no*

■ *Avez-vous compris?*

(Sample answers)

1. Un têtard, c'est un petit animal qui devient une grenouille plus tard.
2. Le gardien du square surveille les gens qui viennent dans le square. S'ils font des choses défendues, il utilise son sifflet.
3. Ils ont attrapé les têtards dans des bocaux de confiture vides.
4. Pour obtenir un bocal vide, Alceste a mangé toute la confiture!
5. Il n'a pas attrapé de têtard, mais Raoul lui en a donné un.
6. Ils veulent les emmener chez eux et attendre qu'ils deviennent des grenouilles.

Avez-vous compris?

1. Qu'est-ce que c'est qu'un têtard?
2. En quoi consiste le travail du gardien du square?
3. Comment Nicolas et ses copains ont-ils attrapé les têtards?
4. Qu'est-ce qu'Alceste a fait pour obtenir un bocal vide?
5. Comment Alceste a-t-il eu un têtard?
6. Qu'est-ce que les enfants veulent faire avec leurs têtards?

Anticipons un peu

Quelle va être la réaction de la mère du petit Nicolas quand elle va voir le têtard?
• Elle va être heureuse que son fils s'intéresse à la nature.
• Elle va acheter un aquarium pour le têtard.
• Elle va demander à son fils de se débarrasser de *(to get rid of)* cet animal immédiatement.
• Elle va se débarrasser elle-même de l'animal.
• Autre possibilité?

Notes culturelles

French children are very familiar with frog stories, such as those in the fables of La Fontaine: **La grenouille qui voulait se faire plus grosse que le boeuf** and **Les grenouilles qui voulaient un roi.**

Ask students if they know any frog stories in English. (Students will know Kermit, from Sesame Street, of course!)

2.

Et puis nous sommes partis en courant parce que nous avons vu
le gardien du square qui arrivait. Dans la rue, en marchant, je voyais mon
têtard dans le bocal, et il était très chouette. Il bougeait° beaucoup, et j'étais
40 sûr qu'il deviendrait une grenouille formidable, qui allait gagner toutes les
courses. J'ai décidé de l'appeler King; c'est le nom d'un cheval blanc que j'ai
vu jeudi dernier dans un film de cow-boys. C'était un cheval qui courait très
vite et qui venait quand son cow-boy le sifflait. Moi, je lui apprendrai à faire
des tours, à mon têtard, et quand il sera grenouille, il viendra quand je
45 le sifflerai.

Quand je suis entré dans la maison. Maman m'a regardé et elle s'est
mise à pousser des cris: «Mais regarde-moi dans quel état tu t'es mis!
Tu as de la boue° partout, tu es trempé comme une soupe! Qu'est-ce
que tu as encore fabriqué?»

50 C'est vrai que je n'étais pas très propre, surtout que j'avais oublié
de rouler° les manches° de ma chemise quand j'avais mis mes bras dans
l'étang.

— Et ce bocal? a demandé Maman, qu'est-ce qu'il y a dans ce bocal?

— C'est King, j'ai dit à Maman en lui montrant mon têtard. Il va
55 devenir grenouille, il viendra quand je le sifflerai, il nous dira le temps
qu'il fait, et il va gagner des courses!

Maman a fait une tête avec le nez tout chiffonné.°

— Quelle horreur! a crié Maman. Combien de fois faut-il que je te
dise de ne pas apporter des saletés° dans la maison?

60 — Ce n'est pas des saletés, j'ai dit, c'est propre comme tout, c'est tout
le temps° dans l'eau, et je vais lui apprendre à faire des tours!

— Eh bien, voilà ton père, a dit Maman; nous allons voir ce qu'il en
dit!

Et quand Papa a vu le bocal, il a dit: «Tiens! C'est un têtard.» Et il est
65 allé s'asseoir dans le fauteuil pour lire son journal. Maman était toute
fâchée.

— C'est tout ce que tu trouves à dire? elle a demandé à Papa. Je ne
veux pas que cet enfant ramène toutes sortes de sales bêtes à la maison!

— Bah! a dit Papa, un têtard, ce n'est pas bien gênant…

bougeait *was moving around* **boue** *mud* **rouler** *to roll up* **manches** *sleeves* **chiffonné**
wrinkled **une saleté** *something gross, dirty* **tout le temps** = toujours

Mots utiles

faire des tours	*to do tricks*
pousser des cris	*to scream*
prévenir *	*to warn*
ramener	*to bring back*
siffler	*to whistle*
fâché	*upset*
gênant	*bothersome*
parfait	*perfect*
propre ≠ sale	*clean ≠ dirty, nasty*
trempé	*soaking wet*
partout	*everywhere*
puisque	*since*

Langage familier

fabriquer = faire

Avez-vous compris?

1. Pourquoi les enfants ont-ils quitté l'étang en courant?
2. Quel nom le petit Nicolas a-t-il donné à son têtard et pourquoi?
3. Dans quel état le petit Nicolas est-il rentré chez lui?
4. Quelle a été la réaction de sa mère quand elle a vu le bocal?
5. Quelle a été la réaction de son père?

Anticipons un peu

D'après vous, que va faire le père du petit Nicolas pour résoudre le conflit?

■ **Irregular Verb**

(see Appendix C)
prévenir *(see* **venir***)*

■ *Avez-vous compris?*

(Sample answers)

1. Ils ont quitté l'étang en courant parce que le gardien arrivait, et c'est interdit de pêcher dans l'étang.
2. Il l'a appelé King, le nom d'un cheval qui courait très vite dans un film de cowboy, un nom de champion!
3. Il est rentré très sale et trempé.
4. Sa mère n'a pas été contente. Elle a dit que c'était une saleté.
5. Il a dit: «Tiens! C'est un têtard.» et il a commencé à lire son journal.

Teaching Strategy

Point out some familiar French expressions
from the text. Have students infer their
meaning:

- **Il était très chouette**. (It was really great.
  chouette = owl)
- **pousser des cris** (to scream)

- **être trempé comme une soupe** (to be soaking wet)
- **C'est propre comme tout**. (It's very clean.)

3.

70   Eh bien, parfait, a dit Maman, parfait! Puisque je ne compte pas, je ne dis plus rien. Mais je vous préviens, c'est le têtard ou moi!

Et Maman est partie dans la cuisine.

Papa a poussé un gros soupir° et il a plié son journal.

— Je crois que nous n'avons pas le choix, Nicolas, il m'a dit. Il va falloir se débarrasser de cette bestiole.°

Moi, je me suis mis à pleurer. J'ai dit que je ne voulais pas qu'on fasse du mal à King, et que nous étions déjà copains tous les deux. Papa m'a pris dans ses bras.

75   — Ecoute, mon petit bonhomme,° il m'a dit. Tu sais que ce petit têtard a une maman grenouille. Et la maman grenouille doit avoir beaucoup de peine d'avoir perdu son enfant. Maman ne serait pas contente si on t'emmenait dans un bocal. Pour les grenouilles, c'est la même chose. Alors, tu sais ce qu'on va faire? Nous allons partir tous les deux et nous allons remettre le têtard où tu l'as pris, et puis tous les dimanches tu

80   pourras aller le voir. Et en revenant à la maison, je t'achèterai une tablette° de chocolat.

Moi, j'ai réfléchi un moment, et j'ai dit: «Bon, d'accord.»

Alors, Papa est allé dans la cuisine et il a dit à Maman, en riant, que nous avions décidé de la garder, et de nous débarrasser du têtard.

85   Maman a ri aussi. Elle m'a embrassé et elle a dit que pour ce soir elle ferait un gâteau. J'étais très consolé.

Quand nous sommes arrivés dans le jardin, j'ai conduit Papa, qui tenait le bocal, vers le bord de l'étang. J'ai dit: «C'est là.» Alors, j'ai dit au revoir à King, et Papa a versé dans l'étang tout ce qu'il y avait dans le bocal.

90   Et puis nous nous sommes retournés pour partir et nous avons vu le gardien du square qui sortait de derrière un arbre avec des yeux ronds.

— Je ne sais pas si vous êtes tous fous, ou si c'est moi qui le deviens, a dit le gardien, mais vous êtes le septième bonhomme, y compris° un agent de police, qui vient aujourd'hui jeter le contenu d'un bocal d'eau à cet

95   endroit précis° de l'étang.

a poussé un gros soupir *let out a large sigh* **une bestiole** = une petite bête
bonhomme = homme **tablette** *bar* **y compris** *including* **cet endroit précis** *this very spot*

■ *Avez-vous compris?*

(Sample answers)

1. Il lui explique qu'il ne peut pas garder le têtard à la maison.
2. Il se met à pleurer.
3. Il dit que la maman grenouille est triste parce que le têtard est parti.
4. Elle rit, et elle dit qu'elle va faire un gâteau.
5. Il a vu sept hommes qui ont jeté le contenu de bocaux dans l'étang. Il pense qu'ils sont fous parce qu'il ne sait pas qu'il y a des têtards dans les bocaux.

■ Irregular Verbs

(see Appendix C)
conduire
rire
tenir

Mots utiles

avoir de la peine	= *être triste*
conduire *	*to lead*
se débarrasser	*to get rid of*
faire du mal à	*to hurt*
plier	*to fold (up)*
réfléchir	*to think things over*
rire *	*to laugh*
tenir *	*to hold*
verser	*to pour*
fou (folle)	*crazy*
vers	*toward*

Avez-vous compris?

1. Qu'est-ce que le père du petit Nicolas explique à son fils?
2. Quelle est la première réaction du petit Nicolas?
3. Quels arguments le père utilise-t-il pour convaincre son fils de remettre le têtard dans l'étang?
4. Que fait la mère lorsqu'elle apprend la bonne nouvelle?
5. Qu'est-ce que le gardien du square a vu? Pourquoi pense-t-il que ces gens sont fous?

Teaching Strategy: Expansion

Divide the class into groups. Have students brainstorm an expansion on the story by imagining an additional scene. After each group has come up with a scenario, have them present it to the class.

Scenario: Le lendemain, Petit Nicolas rencontre son ami Alceste. Ils racontent et comparent ce qui s'est passé quand ils sont rentrés chez eux et ont montré le têtard à leurs parents.

Rôles: Petit Nicolas, Alceste

APRÈS LA LECTURE

Expression orale

Expérience personnelle

Quand vous étiez petit(e), avez-vous trouvé un jour un animal que vous avez voulu apporter à la maison? Décrivez ce qui est arrivé. Par exemple . . .

- Quel animal était-ce?
- Où l'avez-vous trouvé?
- Quelle a été la réaction de votre père/mère?
- Qu'est-ce que vous avez fait de l'animal? Est-ce que vous l'avez gardé? Sinon, qu'est-ce que vous avez fait de lui?

Situations

Avec votre partenaire, choisissez l'une des situations suivantes. Composez le dialogue correspondant et jouez-le en classe.

---

1   Au marché

Au marché, la mère du petit Nicolas rencontre la mère d'Alceste. Elles parlent de ce que leurs enfants ont fait hier et quelles ont été leurs réactions.

Rôles: la mère de Nicolas, la mère d'Alceste

---

2   Au café

Le père du petit Nicolas et le père de Raoul se rencontrent au café et parlent de ce qui s'est passé. Ils décrivent…

- ce que leurs enfants ont fait
- comment leurs épouses ont réagi *(reacted)*
- comment le problème a été résolu *(solved)*

Rôles: le père de Nicolas, le père de Raoul

Expression écrite

Le sens de l'humour

Les Récrés du petit Nicolas sont un livre humoristique. Décrivez deux ou trois scènes ou situations qui vous paraissent humoristiques dans le récit que vous avez lu et expliquez pourquoi vous les trouvez drôles.

Une lettre

La mère du petit Nicolas écrit une lettre à sa soeur. Elle lui explique ce qui s'est passé hier.

Le rapport du gardien

Le gardien écrit un rapport sur ce qu'il a vu hier dans le square. Il décrit . . .

- où il était
- ce qu'il faisait
- ce qu'il a vu
- pourquoi c'était bizarre

—> **Hier, j'ai été témoin de quelque chose de bizarre. . . .**

■ **Expansion**

__Expérience personnelle__
Suggestions:
un oiseau blessé *(injured)*
une salamandre
un petit écureuil
une tortue
un lapin
une souris
une grenouille
un serpent
un petit chat

■ **Le sens de l'humour**

Exemples de situations comiques:
- comment Alceste a trouvé/obtenu un bocal vide
- ce que les enfants projettent de faire avec leurs têtards
- comment le petit Nicolas essaie de convaincre sa mère
- comment le père essaie de convaincre son fils
- pourquoi le gardien du square est surpris

■ **Realia Note**

Sur la couverture du livre **Les récrés du petit Nicolas**, on voit les enfants jouer au football et jouer à saute-moutons *(to play leapfrog)*.

■ **Expression écrite**

For writing rubrics, consult the **Generate Success** Rubric Generator on the **Teacher One Stop**. You can also create your own custom rubrics with this tool.

Student Portfolios

Ask students to respond to the following questions in a short story format:
- Y a-t-il un animal chez vous?
- Quel animal est-ce?
- Comment l'avez-vous eu?
- Comment s'appelle-t-il?
- Vos parents ont-ils accepté cet animal tout de suite? Pourquoi ou pourquoi pas?

The completed story should be included in the student's portfolio.

Interlude culturel

RESOURCES

TECHNOLOGY
Teacher One Stop
Pre-AP Digital Resources
 Projectable Transparencies
H2, *Histoire de France*
(1453–1715)
1, *La France*
1(o), *La France*
Transparency Copymasters,
pp. A5–A6, A139–A140

■ **Looking Ahead**
The **châteaux** of France are featured
on p. 147 of this *Interlude*.

■ **Teaching Suggestion**
Divide the class into small groups
and have them research important
events that occurred during the same
time period in other francophone
countries. Have the groups prepare
Powerpoint® presentations about
these events. If possible, film the
presentations and post them for
feedback from your francophone
partner classes.

Les dates

1453 *in de la*
Guerre
de Cent Ans

1515

La Renaissance

Règne de
François Ier

1547

1589

Règne
d'Henri IV

1610

Règne de
Louis XIII

1643

Le Grand Siècle

Règne de
Louis XIV

1715 *Mort de Louis XIV*

Les événements

La Renaissance (1500-1570)

Après la Guerre de Cent Ans et la reconquête
de son territoire, la France est finalement en
paix. La période qui commence s'appelle
la «**Renaissance**», c'est-à-dire le renouvellement.
C'est une période de grande activité artistique et
culturelle. C'est à cette époque que les rois de
France ont habité en Touraine où ils ont construit de
magnifiques châteaux: **Chenonceaux, Amboise,
Chambord.**

La cour de François Ier

*Le château de Chambord est immense,
avec plus de 400 pièces et 365 cheminées.*

Le Grand Siècle (1643-1715)

Le **Grand Siècle**, c'est le siècle de **Louis XIV**, ou «**Roi-Soleil**». C'est aussi la
période la plus brillante de l'histoire de France. Louis XIV est devenu roi à
l'âge de cinq ans et il a régné sur la France
pendant 72 ans. Pendant son règne, il a
encouragé les arts et les sciences. Il a créé des
académies de peinture, de sculpture, de
sciences, d'architecture. Avec Louis XIV, le
prestige de la culture française s'est répandu°
dans toute l'Europe. Mais Louis XIV était aussi
un roi autoritaire et ambitieux. De son château
de **Versailles** il exerçait un pouvoir absolu sur
le reste du pays. C'est lui qui a dit: «L'État, c'est
moi!» Louis XIV a engagé la France dans de
nombreuses guerres qui ont fini par ruiner le pays.

Louis XIV à la guerre

s'est répandu *spread*

Teaching Strategy: Interdisciplinary/Community Connections

Since history is sometimes difficult for students,
you may wish to do an interdisciplinary
presentation in conjunction with the history
department. Use **Projectable Transparency
H1** and an overlay that shows historical events
in other parts of the world. You may also begin
by showing sections of the movie version of
Cyrano (see pp. 142–143) to spark student
interest. (Students may know the Steve Martin
film *Roxanne* as a version of *Cyrano.*)

Les personnes

François Ier et Mona Lisa

Le roi **François Ier** (1494-1547) était très grand, très beau et très athlétique. Il aimait tous les sports de son époque, et en particulier le jeu de paume, l'ancêtre du tennis actuel. Sa grande passion était la chasse° qu'il pratiquait dans les forêts de ses châteaux de **Chambord** et d'**Amboise**.

C'était aussi un esprit fin° et cultivé qui aimait la musique, les arts et les lettres. Il a fait venir° dans son château d'Amboise le grand artiste italien **Léonard de Vinci** à qui il a acheté la «**Joconde**» ou «**Mona Lisa**», aujourd'hui le portrait le plus célèbre du monde.

Jean Clouet «François Ier

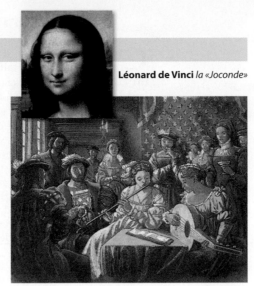

Léonard de Vinci *la «Joconde»*

La vie de cour sous François Ier

Louis XIV et sa cour

La cour de Louis XIV à Versailles

Louis XIV (1638-1715) a longtemps vécu au château de **Versailles**. Il a construit ce château non seulement pour son plaisir, mais pour attirer les nobles du pays. C'était une façon de les contrôler et de les empêcher° de se révolter contre lui. Trois mille personnes vivaient au château de Versailles.

À la cour de Louis XIV, tout était organisé autour de la personne du roi. Les événements de sa vie quotidienne° étaient des cérémonies officielles, réglées par° une étiquette très stricte. C'était un privilège d'assister au lever, au dîner, au souper, au coucher du roi. Seuls les grands seigneurs° étaient invités.

Louis XIV

Patron des arts et des lettres, Louis XIV s'intéressait personnellement à la musique, au théâtre et surtout au ballet. Parfois, il participait lui-même aux représentations. Un jour, il a paru sur scène déguisé en soleil, d'où son nom de «**Roi-Soleil**». Ce nom est avant tout° symbolique. Louis XIV brillait sur sa cour, sur la France et sur le monde. Il se considérait vraiment comme le centre de l'univers.

---

la chasse *hunting* **fin** *refined* **fait venir** *brought* **empêcher** *to prevent* **quotidienne** *daily*
réglées par *structured according to* **seigneurs =** *nobles* **avant tout** *above all*

■ Notes historiques

• C'est au nom de François 1er que Jacques Cartier prit possession du Canada en 1534.

• En 1682, Cavelier de La Salle prit possession d'un vaste territoire en Amérique du Nord qu'il appela Louisiane en l'honneur de son roi, Louis XIV.

• Louis XIV a survécu à son fils et à son petit-fils. À sa mort, ce fut son *arrière-petit-fils* qui a pris sa succession sous le nom de Louis XV.

■ Notes culturelles

• Léonard de Vinci a peint le tableau *La Joconde* vers 1499-1512. François 1er l'a acheté en 1517 pour un prix de 4000 florins d'or, soit 15 kilos *(33 lbs)* d'or. Léonard de Vinci est mort en France, en 1519, près de la ville d'Amboise. *La Joconde* est aujourd'hui l'attraction principale du musée du Louvre à Paris.

• Le château de Versailles était un modeste pavillon de chasse du roi Louis XIII. Le palais devint un musée de l'histoire de France en 1887. En 1783, la France reconnaît l'indépendance des treize colonies américaines et signe le traité de Paris au château de Versailles.

Expansion

Internet Connection – Interlude 3
Visit **http://my.hrw.com** for more information and useful links about French history from 1453–1715.

Communication

Standard 1.2 Students understand and interpret spoken and written French on a variety of topics.

Teaching Note

Students should be encouraged to see Rappeneau's movie version of *Cyrano de Bergerac*, which is available on DVD. If the film is used in class, you will want to focus on those scenes where the dialog is clear and understandable, and view rapidly (or skip) those passages which are well above the students' linguistic level.

■ Notes culturelles

• Edmond Rostand (1868-1918) was a member of the **Académie française**. He wrote **Cyrano de Bergerac** in 1897.

• **Savinien de Cyrano de Bergerac** (1619-1655) wrote several plays as well as imaginary travel logs such as **Histoire comique des États et Empires de la lune**, and **Histoire comique des États et Empires du soleil**.

• Jose Ferrer won the Oscar for Best Actor for his interpretation of the title role in the 1950 movie *Cyrano de Bergerac*.

■ Teaching Strategy: Expansion

Have students look at the movie poster and give their opinion. What do they think the movie is about? Does the poster make them feel like going to see this movie? Why or why not?

Cyrano de Bergerac

Cyrano de Bergerac a vraiment existé. Il a vécu à l'époque de **Louis XIV**. C'était un soldat et un écrivain qui a laissé° un curieux roman de science-fiction où il décrit un voyage dans la lune. Ce personnage historique serait cependant resté dans une tranquille obscurité s'il n'avait pas été transformé en héros de légende et immortalisé dans une comédie célèbre du 19ᵉ siècle.

Cette comédie, intitulée *Cyrano de Bergerac*, écrite il y a cent ans par Edmond Rostand, a connu un très grand succès à son époque. Depuis, elle a été mise en musique, adaptée à l'écran,° et maintes° fois transformée et parodiée.* Le dernier film en date, dans lequel l'acteur Gérard Depardieu joue le rôle principal, est une reproduction assez fidèle° de la pièce originale.

Cyrano de Bergerac est essentiellement une histoire d'amour, basée sur un gigantesque quiproquo° tragico-comique. **Cyrano** aime Roxane qui aime un autre homme, **Christian**. Mais si Roxane a d'abord été attirée° par la beauté physique de Christian, c'est pour la beauté de sa poésie qu'elle l'aime vraiment. Or, cette poésie n'est pas celle de Christian, mais celle de l'infortuné Cyrano.

Cyrano, le héros de l'histoire, est un vaillant soldat du régiment des Cadets de Gascogne. Il est brave, courageux, téméraire° à l'extrême. C'est aussi un poète à l'âme tendre.° Il est bon, loyal, généreux, intelligent, spirituel,° sensible et il écrit de magnifiques vers. Il a toutes les qualités possibles sauf une: il n'est pas beau.

Cyrano est en effet affligé d'une infirmité incurable: Il a un nez monstrueusement long. Cette infirmité le rend très susceptible° auprès° des hommes, et très timide auprès des femmes. Personne en sa présence ne peut mentionner le mot «nez». Cyrano est secrètement amoureux de sa cousine Roxane, mais il sait qu'il n'a aucune chance, précisément à cause de cet immense nez qui le défigure. . .

* Une parodie classique est le film américain *Roxanne* où Steve Martin joue le rôle d'un pompier (*fireman*) amoureux.

DOCUMENTS | **«Cyrano de Bergerac»**

Le film Cyrano de Bergerac (1990) reproduit fidèlement la pièce de théâtre.

GÉRARD DEPARDIEU

CYRANO
DE BERGERAC

A film by JEAN-PAUL RAPPENEAU
JACQUES WEBER · ANNE BROCHET · VINCENT PEREZ · ROLAND BERTIN

---

laissé *left* **écran** *screen* **maintes** = plusieurs **fidèle** *faithful* **quiproquo** *misunderstanding* **attirée** *attracted* **téméraire** *bold*
à l'âme tendre *with a soft heart* **spirituel** *witty* **susceptible** *touchy* **auprès de** = avec

*L'*action de la pièce se passe dans la France du 17e siècle. Dans la première scène, une foule° se presse° pour assister à un spectacle de **Montfleury**, comédien en vogue, mais ennemi de Cyrano. Dans cette foule, on reconnaît tous les personnages principaux de l'histoire, et d'abord **Roxane**. Elle est belle, coquette, romanesque et éprise° de poésie. Tous les hommes sont amoureux d'elle. Ce jour-là, elle est accompagnée de **de Guiche**, un seigneur noble et puissant° qui lui fait la cour.°

Mais Roxane pense secrètement à un jeune homme qu'elle a aperçu un jour et dont elle est tombée secrètement amoureuse. C'est le beau **Christian**, qui, lui aussi, est dans la foule à la recherche de Roxane. Le public s'impatiente.

On attend Montfleury, mais on attend aussi **Cyrano** qui a promis de lancer un défi° à Montfleury. Montfleury entre en scène. Est-ce que Cyrano viendra? Oui, il arrive! D'une voix éclatante,° il ridiculise Montfleury et le chasse de scène.

Tous les spectateurs ne sont pas contents de l'interruption du spectacle, en particulier de Guiche et son neveu Valvert. Celui-ci va défier Cyrano en lui disant «Monsieur, vous avez un grand nez». Stimulé par cette insulte suprême, Cyrano se lance alors dans la fameuse tirade où il fait l'éloge de son appendice nasal. Puis, il traite Valvert de sot° et engage celui-ci dans un duel, tout en composant des vers. Tout cela se passe sous les yeux de la belle Roxane, très fière de la bravoure et de l'intelligence de son cousin.

Après le duel, Cyrano va accompagner un ami chez lui. Il tombe dans une embuscade° d'où il sort victorieux à un contre cent. L'histoire de cet exploit fait le tour° de la ville et Cyrano devient le héros du jour. Entre-temps°, Roxane lui a envoyé sa dame de compagnie° pour lui demander un rendez-vous.

Intimidé, mais reprenant espoir,° Cyrano va au rendez-vous. Après un long préambule où elle évoque leur enfance passée ensemble et leur longue amitié, Roxane déclare son amour pour . . . Le visage de Cyrano s'illumine.° Pour lui? Hélas, non! Ce n'est pas lui que Roxane aime, mais le beau Christian. Oui, c'est lui qu'elle aime et si elle est venue voir Cyrano, c'est pour lui demander de prendre Christian sous sa protection. Celui-ci va, en effet, entrer au régiment des Cadets de Gascogne, le régiment de Cyrano.

---

foule *crowd* **se presse** *hurries* **éprise** *enamoured* **puissant** *powerful* **lui fait la cour** *is courting her* **lancer un défi** *to challenge*
éclatante *very loud* **sot** = *stupide* **embuscade** *ambush* **fait le tour** *goes around* **entre-temps** = *pendant ce temps*
dame de compagnie *lady-in-waiting* **espoir** *hope* **s'illumine** *brightens*

■ **Notes linguistiques**
- In the 17th century, **un cadet** was a young nobleman who served in the army to begin his military career.
- **La Gascogne** is an area between the French regions of Aquitaine and Midi-Pyrénées. Have students locate it using the map on p. R34.

DOCUMENTS «Cyrano de Bergerac»

Cyrano promet de protéger Christian, mais c'est déçu° et triste qu'il va rejoindre ses compagnons d'armes. Tout le monde le salue en héros. Cyrano, trop peiné,° ne fait pas attention. Soudain, Christian, la nouvelle recrue du régiment, entre dans la salle d'armes.° Ne connaissant pas Cyrano, il se moque de lui, répétant sans cesse le mot «nez». L'assistance° est pétrifiée! Que va-t-il se passer? Est-ce que Cyrano va tuer° Christian? Non! Fidèle° à la promesse faite à Roxane, Cyrano traite son rival en ami et en frère.

Dès lors,° Cyrano va assister Christian dans toutes ses démarches amoureuses° auprès de Roxane. Christian avoue° qu'il est sot, qu'il n'a pas d'éloquence, qu'il ne sait pas parler aux femmes. Que cela ne tienne!° C'est Cyrano qui sera sa voix, son porte-parole.° C'est lui qui écrira à Roxane les lettres d'amour que Christian ne sait pas écrire. L'inspiration lui est facile puisque,° lui aussi, il aime éperdument° Roxane.

Les lettres de Cyrano, signées Christian, enflamment de plus en plus le coeur de Roxane qui consent à accorder° un rendez-vous au beau Christian. Celui-ci va seul au rendez-vous, mais sans l'éloquence de Cyrano, il ne dit que des banalités. Roxane, qui s'attendait° à des torrents de déclamations lyriques, est déçue et renvoie° le jeune homme.

Christian obtient un nouveau rendez-vous, mais cette fois, avec l'assistance de Cyrano, qui lui souffle° chaque mot de sa déclaration d'amour, il réussit à conquérir Roxane dans la célèbre scène du balcon. Au cours de° cette scène, Christian monte au balcon de Roxane, entre chez elle où les deux amants sont mariés par un prêtre envoyé par de Guiche, toujours° amoureux de Roxane.

■ **Note culturelle**

Arras is a city in northern France that fell under Spanish rule in 1492. It was reconquered by Louis XIII in 1640.

■ **Note linguistique**

L'expression **à l'insu de** vient du participe passé de **savoir (su)** et du préfixe **in- (sans)**. Autre usage: **à mon/votre insu** (*without my/your knowledge*).

---

déçu *disappointed* **peiné** *in pain* **salle d'armes** *fencing hall* **l'assistance** = les personnes dans la salle **tuer** *to kill* **fidèle** *faithful* **dès lors** *from then on* **démarches amoureuses** *steps in his courtship* **avoue** = admet **que cela ne tienne** *that won't matter* **porte-parole** *spokesperson* **puisque** *since* **éperdument** *madly* **accorder** *to grant* **s'attendait à** *was expecting* **renvoie** *sends away* **souffle** *prompts* **au cours de** = pendant **toujours** *still*

De Guiche arrive lui-même chez Roxane où il apprend le mariage. Furieux et jaloux, il annonce qu'il vient d'être nommé commandant de l'armée française chargée de déloger les Espagnols de la ville d'Arras. Il décide d'y envoyer sur le champ° le régiment des Cadets de Gascogne, séparant ainsi Christian de sa nouvelle femme.

L'action change de lieu.° Nous sommes maintenant à Arras où le régiment de Christian et de Cyrano est cantonné.° La guerre a mal tourné pour les Français. Assiégés par les Espagnols, les fougueux° soldats de Gascogne meurent de faim.° Cyrano veut tenir la promesse qu'il a faite à Roxane. Chaque jour, elle reçoit une lettre de Christian. En réalité, c'est toujours Cyrano qui lui écrit, évidemment à l'insu de° son ami, des billets° d'un lyrisme magnifique.

Dans le camp français, la situation est maintenant désespérée. Sur les ordres de de Guiche, le régiment de Gascogne doit être sacrifié. Cyrano écrit à Roxane une dernière lettre d'adieu, toujours signée du nom de Christian. Entre-temps, émue° par l'intensité des lettres poétiques de son mari, Roxane décide de tout risquer pour le rejoindre à Arras. Elle traverse° les lignes espagnoles et arrive dans le camp quelques heures avant la bataille finale. En présence de Cyrano, elle avoue à Christian que ce n'est plus pour sa beauté qu'elle l'aime, mais pour sa poésie, et qu'elle l'aimerait même s'il était laid.° Déconcerté par cet aveu,° Christian part à l'assaut. Au cours de l'engagement,° il est blessé.° Il meurt, réconforté par l'amour de Roxane et l'amitié de Cyrano. La bataille finale a lieu. Pendant cette bataille, Cyrano et de Guiche combattent héroïquement. Christian est mort, mais sa femme et ses amis sont sauvés.

Quinze ans ont passé. Roxane a pris le deuil de° Christian et s'est retirée dans un couvent. Là, elle reçoit régulièrement la visite de ses deux amis, de Guiche, devenu duc et maréchal de France, et Cyrano, pauvre, mais toujours aussi fier.° Un jour, celui-ci arrive en retard au rendez-vous. Il a été blessé dans une embuscade tendue par ses ennemis et il va mourir.

Ce jour-là, Roxane comprend enfin que c'est bien lui l'auteur des merveilleuses lettres d'amour qu'elle recevait de Christian. Cyrano meurt dans ses bras, finalement aimé par celle qu'il avait aimée toute sa vie.

---

sur le champ = immédiatement   **lieu** *location*   **cantonné** *quartered*   **fougueux** = braves   **meurent de faim** *dying of starvation*
à l'insu de *without the knowledge of*   **billets** = lettres   **émue** *moved*   **traverse** *crosses*   **laid** *ugly*   **aveu** *admission*
au cours de l'engagement = pendant la bataille   **blessé** *wounded*   **a pris le deuil de** *is in mourning for*   **fier** *proud*

Ask students if they like the ending of the movie. What could the other possible endings be? Which one would they prefer and why?

Give students the following assignment:

Faites la critique de ce film. Jugez si, d'après vous, c'est un bon film ou non et expliquez pourquoi. Allez-vous recommander ce film? Combien d'étoiles lui donnez-vous?
(cinq étoiles = super; aucune étoile = nul)

■ Notes linguistiques

- **Maître** est aujourd'hui le titre honorifique des avocats et des notaires; au 17ᵉ siècle, ce titre était donné au gens de condition moyenne.
- **Monsieur du Corbeau** est un titre cérémonieux de noblesse.
- **Le phénix** est un oiseau fabuleux de la mythologie qui, d'après la légende, renaît de ses propres cendres.

■ Teaching Strategy: Expansion

Expliquez: «Tout flatteur vit aux dépens de celui qui l'écoute.» Êtes-vous d'accord? Pourquoi ou pourquoi pas?

DOCUMENTS | **Le corbeau et le renard**

Le corbeau et le renard

À l'école, tous les jeunes Français apprennent par coeur les fables de La Fontaine. Leur auteur est l'un des écrivains les plus célèbres du siècle de Louis XIV. À travers° ses portraits d'animaux, **Jean de La Fontaine** (1621-1695) voulait critiquer les défauts de ses contemporains. La morale de ses fables est en réalité éternelle.

La fameuse fable *Le corbeau et le renard*° s'adresse aux gens qui ont besoin d'être admirés.

Le corbeau et le renard

Maître Corbeau, sur un arbre perché,
*   Tenait° en son bec un fromage.*
Maître Renard, par l'odeur alléché,°
*   Lui tint à peu près ce langage:°*
*   «Hé! bonjour, Monsieur du Corbeau,*
Que vous êtes joli! que vous me semblez beau!
*   Sans mentir,° si votre ramage°*
*   Se rapporte° à votre plumage*
Vous êtes le phénix° des hôtes de ces bois.
À ces mots, le Corbeau ne se sent pas de joie;°
*   Et pour montrer sa belle voix,*
Il ouvre un large bec, laisse tomber° sa proie.°
Le Renard s'en saisit,° et dit: «Mon bon Monsieur,
*   Apprenez que tout flatteur*
*   Vit° aux dépens° de celui qui l'écoute:*
Cette leçon vaut° bien un fromage, sans doute.»
*   Le Corbeau, honteux° et confus,°*
Jura,° mais un peu tard, qu'on ne l'y prendrait plus.°

(*Fables choisies, Livre I*, 1688)

à travers = avec **le corbeau et le renard** *the crow and the fox* **tenait =** avait **alléché =** attiré **lui tint à peu près ce langage =** lui parla ainsi
sans mentir = en vérité **ramage =** chant **se rapporte =** est égal **le phénix =** l'oiseau le plus fabuleux **ne se sent pas de joie =** est transporté de joie
laisse tomber *drops* **proie =** le fromage qu'il a trouvé **s'en saisit =** la prend **vit** *lives* **aux dépens** *at the expense* **vaut** *is worth*
honteux *ashamed* **confus** *upset* **jura** *swore* **on ne l'y prendrait plus** *he wouldn't be taken in again*

Note culturelle

- Quelques châteaux de la Loire célèbres construits sous François 1ᵉʳ: Amboise (en photo), Blois, Azay-le-Rideau, Chambord, Chenonceaux (en photo).
- Nicolas Fouquet (1615–1680), Vicomte de Vaux, devint le surintendant des finances en 1653. Grand amateur d'art, il protégea de nombreux artistes dont Molière, La Fontaine et Poussin. À la suite d'une fête grandiose dans son château de Vaux, Louis XIV devint jaloux de sa fortune. Il accusa Fouquet de fraude et de rébellion puis le condamna à l'exil, avant de changer cette condamnation en une peine de prison. Fouquet fut enfermé sous des conditions rigoureuses au fort de Pignerol où il mourut.

L'histoire de France à travers ses châteaux

Carcassonne

Comme beaucoup de villes médiévales, Carcassonne était entourée de hauts remparts qui la protégeaient contre d'éventuels envahisseurs.° Elle résista aux Anglais pendant la Guerre de Cent Ans.

Chenonceaux

Le château de Chenonceaux est de pur style Renaissance. Sur ses murs on peut y lire encore des graffiti (en anglais) laissés par les gardes écossais° du roi Henri II.

Angers

Angers était la capitale des Plantagenêts, ducs d'Anjou et futurs rois d'Angleterre. Avec ses grosses tours rondes, le château est un bel exemple d'architecture féodale.

Fontainebleau

Maintes fois transformé, Fontainebleau a servi de résidence à plus de 20 rois de France, parmi lesquels François Ier et Louis XIII, père de Louis XIV. C'est ici que Napoléon a fait ses adieux avant de partir en exil.

Château-Gaillard

Construit en 1198 par Richard Coeur de Lion, Château-Gaillard dominait la Seine et barrait la route entre Paris et Rouen. Dix ans plus tard, le château tomba dans les mains des Français et il n'en reste aujourd'hui que d'imposantes ruines.

Vaux-le-Vicomte

Le château de Vaux-le-Vicomte a été construit par Nicolas Fouquet, surintendant des finances du royaume de France. Un jour, Fouquet eut la mauvaise idée d'y inviter le jeune roi Louis XIV. Celui-ci, jaloux de la richesse de son ministre, le fit emprisonner.

Amboise

Le château d'Amboise est situé sur un rocher qui domine la Loire. Sa grosse tour ronde permettait aux cavaliers° et aux carrosses° d'accéder directement au château. C'est au château d'Amboise que le roi François Ier recevait Léonard de Vinci.

Versailles

Toute la majesté de Louis XIV et la puissance de la France sont exprimées dans la splendeur du château de Versailles et de ses magnifiques jardins. C'est ici que vivait le roi, entouré de milliers de courtisans.

envahisseurs *invaders*　**cavaliers** *horsemen*　**carrosses** *horse-drawn carriages*　**écossais** *Scottish*

■ Anecdote

En 1814, Napoléon est vaincu et Louis XVIII accède au trône. Napoléon est à Fontainebleau où il essaie de s'empoisonner. Le poison étant trop vieux, il n'agit pas et Napoléon doit faire ses adieux à sa garde avant de partir en exil pour l'île d'Elbe.

■ Note culturelle

In the 17th century, food and drinks were usually served cold in Versailles because the kitchens were too far away from the dining rooms.

■ Teaching Note

Ask students:
Regardez les photos des châteaux. Lequel préférez-vous et pourquoi?

■ Teaching Suggestion

Divide the class into eight groups and assign one of the castles featured on this page to each group. Students should further research their castles on the Internet or at the library and then prepare illustrated brochures about them. Display the brochures in class or upload them to a class website or blog to be shared with other French classes at your school.

Teaching Suggestion: DVD Program

To learn about these and other French **chateaux** not listed in the textbook, please refer to the *Vignette culturelle: Les châteaux de la Loire* of the Unit 3 video.

MAIN THEME

Shopping
Asking for services

COMMUNICATION

- Buying stamps/mailing at the post office
- Asking for services at shops, cleaners, etc.
- Shopping in a stationery store, pharmacy, and convenience store
- Having items fixed or cleaned
- Having one's hair cut

CULTURES

- Learning about shopping in France
- Learning about French songwriting

CONNECTIONS

- Locating *Lac Léman* on a map
- Connecting to Language Arts: Listing ideas for a services directory
- Connecting to Math: Creating a chart of service costs
- Connecting to Science/Health: Finding out about health-related services
- Connecting to Social Studies: Researching training requirements for service-related jobs
- Connecting to Art/Music: Designing a services directory
- Connecting to Technology: Finding out about technological services

COMPARISONS

- Comparing object pronouns in French and English
- Comparing how French and English express having something done
- Comparing spoken and written language
- Comparing shopping in France and U.S.
- Comparing French and American music
- Learning about English words imported into Canadian and French phrases

COMMUNITIES

- Creating a services directory
- Learning how to shop for basic necessities

■ Photo Notes

- The green cross is an emblem found on every French pharmacy.
- The word **la maroquinerie** (leather goods, leather goods store) comes from **maroquin**, a type of sheep or goat leather that was made in **Maroc** (Morocco).

148 Unité 4

Unité 4

Aspects de la vie quotidienne

THÈME ET OBJECTIFS

Culture

In this unit, you will discover . . .

- where to buy various items and obtain various services
- how shopping habits differ in France and the United States

Communication

You will learn how . . .

- to buy stamps and mail letters
- to purchase small items you might need
- to have items fixed or cleaned
- to get a haircut
- to ask for various services

Langue

You will learn how . . .

- to answer questions using one or more pronouns
- to talk about numbers of people and things without specifying exact quantities
- to describe actions that people have others do for them

DIGITAL FRENCH my.hrw.com
ONLINE STUDENT EDITION with...

performance)space

News + Networking

@HOMETUTOR

- Audio Resources
- Video Resources
- Interactive Flashcards
- WebQuest

PRACTICE FRENCH WITH HOLT MCDOUGAL APPS!

 **DIGITAL FRENCH**

TEACHER TOOLS

- Teacher One Stop
- Interactive Whiteboard Lessons
- Generate Success Rubric Generator and Interactive Graphic Organizers
- Examview Test Generator

ALSO AVAILABLE...

- Online Workbook
- French InterActive Reader
- @HomeTutor
- DVD Program
- Power Presentations
- Interactive Flashcards

FRENCH ON THE GO!

- Performance Space
- Holt McDougal French Apps
- Discovering French Today eTextbook

EN FRANCE, FAITES COMME

les Français!

Il y a beaucoup d'endroits où nous devons aller régulièrement pour répondre aux besoins de la vie quotidienne.° Nous allons au centre commercial pour faire nos achats, au supermarché pour faire les courses, à la poste pour acheter des timbres,° à la banque pour déposer ou retirer° de l'argent. Et de temps en temps, nous allons chez le coiffeur pour nous faire couper les cheveux.° Si les Français font les mêmes choses que les Américains, ils les font parfois un peu différemment.

Un jour vous irez peut-être en France. Voilà quelques conseils pour vivre° «à la française».°

■ Si vous allez au supermarché, n'oubliez pas de prendre de la monnaie.° Pour obtenir° un chariot,° vous devrez, en effet, déposer une pièce d'un euro. Quand vous passerez à la caisse,° n'attendez pas° à ce que la caissière empaquette° vos achats. Vous devrez faire cela vous même. Et si vous voulez récupérer l'euro que vous avez déposé pour votre chariot, n'oubliez pas de rapporter votre chariot à l'endroit où vous l'avez pris.

■ Si vous préférez un service plus personnalisé, allez chez les petits commerçants du quartier où vous habitez. Là, les prix sont plus élevés,° mais la qualité est souvent meilleure. Et vous pouvez faire la connaissance des gens de votre quartier. Évidemment n'oubliez pas de dire bonjour et au revoir à la marchande et aux clients qui se trouvent dans la boutique. Sinon, vous serez considéré comme une personne mal élevée.°

---

quotidienne *daily* **timbres** *stamps* **retirer** *to withdraw* **faire couper les cheveux** *to get a haircut* **vivre** *to live* **«à la française»** = *comme les Français*
monnaie *change* **obtenir** *to get* **chariot** *cart* **caisse** *check-out* **n'attendez pas** *don't expect* **empaquette** *bag* **élevés** *high* **mal élevée** = *impolie*

INFOMAGAZINE

INFO MAGAZINE

Theme: Shopping in France

Reading Strategy:
Skimming, browsing

SUPPLEMENTARY VOCABULARY

À la banque
l'argent liquide *cash*
le distributeur automatique de billets *ATM*
la carte bancaire *bank card*
le chéquier *checkbook*
le compte-chèques *checking account*
le retrait *withdrawal*

■ **Notes linguistiques**
• **Les soldes** is almost exclusively used in the plural form.
• **Le pressing** (*dry cleaner's*) is from the English verb "to press."
• **La teinturerie** offers the dyeing of clothes. (**la teinture** = *dyeing, dye*).

■ **Irregular Verbs**
(*see Appendix C*)
obtenir (see **tenir**)
empaqueter is conjugated like **jeter**

21ST CENTURY SKILLS

• **Communication:** SE: pp. 150, 155, 159, 165, 167, 171-175; TE: pp. 151, 154, 160, 169, 174
• **Critical Thinking and Problem Solving:** SE: pp. 172, 173; TE: pp. 151, 167, 169, 170, 181
• **Creativity and Innovation:** SE: p. 175; TE: pp. 151, 154, 155, 167, 170, 175, 183
• **Information Literacy:** TE: pp. 155, 167, 169
• **Technology Literacy:** TE: pp. 167, 169, 175, 176, 181
• **Flexibility and Adaptability:** SE: p. 175; TE: pp. 151, 169, 183
• **Initiative and Self-Direction:** TE: pp. 169, 174, 183
• **Social and Cross-Cultural Skills:** TE: pp. 151, 167, 181, 182
• **Productivity and Accountability:** TE: pp. 156, 157, 158, 164, 168
• **Leadership and Responsibility:** TE: pp. 169, 183

INFOMAGAZINE

ASSESSMENT IN UNIT RESOURCE BOOK

Print Resources
• **Workbook TE/PE**
• *Activités pour tous* **TE/PE**
• *Lectures pour tous*
• **Unit Resource Book** Audioscripts Video Activities Videoscripts

Achievement Tests
• **Quizzes, Unit 4**
• **Unit Test 4**
• **Reading and Culture Tests**
• **Assessment Answer Key**

Proficiency Tests
• **Listening Comprehension**
• **Speaking Performance**
• **Writing Performance**
• **Portfolio Assessment**

■ **Teaching Strategy**
Ask students to create their own
cartoons illustrating cultural «**faux
pas.**»

■ Si vous allez chez le coiffeur, n'oubliez pas de donner un pourboire° à la personne qui vous a coupé les cheveux, même si vous n'êtes pas très satisfait du résultat. Mais au café et au restaurant, vous n'êtes pas obligé de laisser de pourboire. Il est compris° dans l'addition.

■ Si vous avez besoin d'une photo d'identité, ne perdez pas votre temps à chercher un photographe. Allez dans un grand magasin. Là vous trouverez un «Photomaton» où vous aurez votre photo en cinq minutes. Dans ce même magasin, vous trouverez aussi d'autres services très pratiques: une photocopieuse, un service de réparation de chaussures, un service de reproduction de clés.°

**Maintenant vous savez comment
vivre en France. C'est simple.
Faites comme les Français!**

et vous?

DÉFINITIONS
Donnez une définition des mots et expressions
suivantes.

- un centre commercial
- une poste
- une banque
- un supermarché
- un chariot
- la caisse
- un coiffeur
- un pourboire
- l'addition

SITUATIONS
1. Vous habitez en France. Vous faites les courses avec un(e) ami(e) américain(e) qui vous rend visite. Expliquez à votre ami(e) — votre partenaire — les différences entre un supermarché en France et aux États-Unis.

2. Un(e) ami(e) français(e) vous rend visite. Expliquez à votre ami(e) — votre partenaire — dans quelles circonstances on donne un pourboire aux États-Unis.

3. Imaginez que vous allez passer deux ou trois mois en France. Est-ce que vous pourrez vous adapter facilement à la vie quotidienne décrite dans le texte?
   - Quels aspects vous semblent pratiques et intéressants?
   - Avec quels aspects auriez-vous des difficultés?

pourboire *tip* **compris** = inclus **clés** *keys*

Notes culturelles
- Although a tip is always included on the bill in France, it is customary to leave additional extra change on the table of the café or restaurant upon leaving.
- **Le photomaton** is the name of the machine (booth) that takes pictures automatically.

The same word is also used for photographs taken by such a machine.
- **La carte à puce** (microchip) was invented by a Frenchman, Roland Moréno, in 1974. It has been in use since 1985. These types of cards have many uses, such as banking, for identification, or as key cards for buildings.

Scènes de la vie courante

■ **Teaching Strategy**
Using American examples, have students create a series of **scènes de la vie courante** for French speaking visitors.

Au supermarché

une touche

Au rayon des fruits et légumes, tout est «self-service». Le client doit peser° les différentes choses qu'il achète. Pour cela, on met chaque produit sur une balance° automatique et on appuie° sur une touche correspondant à ce produit. La balance imprime° un ticket qu'on colle° sur le produit.

la balance — *le ticket*

Si on veut utiliser un chariot, il faut payer une caution.° Pour cela, on introduit une pièce dans un petit réceptacle qui se trouve sur le chariot. Celui-ci se débloque° automatiquement. Quand on a fini ses courses, on rapporte le chariot à l'endroit où on l'a trouvé et on récupère son argent.

Chez les petits commerçants

Chez les petits commerçants, le service est plus personnel. En parlant avec les gens, on y apprend les nouvelles du quartier où on habite.

Au café

Partout° en France, il y a des cafés. On va au café non seulement pour prendre une boisson ou un sandwich, mais aussi pour bavarder.°

À la banque

Pour retirer° de l'argent, on utilise le distributeur automatique de billets° ou DAB. D'abord, on introduit la carte bancaire°. Ensuite, on choisit le montant° d'argent que l'on veut prendre, par exemple 40 euros. On tape° le code secret de la carte bancaire. Au signal, on retire° la carte et finalement on retire les billets.

retirer *to withdraw*   **distributeur automatic de billets** *ATM*   **carte bancaire** *bank card*   **montant** *amount*   **tape** *type*   **retire** *take out*

Teaching Strategy: Dialog Development

Divide the class into groups of two or three, giving each one a paragraph about daily life in France. Each group prepares a skit presenting the information from their paragraph. The skit should be short, but should clearly and accurately demonstrate the important cultural information. Then ask the class to explain the differences between the French and American customs in each situation.

Comment faire des achats

RESOURCES

PRINT
Workbook, pp. 127–128
Activités pour tous
Unit 4 Resource Book, Partie 1
- *Activités pour tous TE*
- Audioscripts
- Lesson Plans
- Block Scheduling Lesson Plans
- Absent Student Copymasters
- Workbook TE

AUDIO
Audio Program
CD 4, Tracks 1–4

TECHNOLOGY
@HomeTutor
Interactive Whiteboard Lessons
Teacher One Stop
- Block Scheduling Copymasters
- Teacher to Teacher Copymasters, *Comment faire des achats*, pp. 47–49; *Trouver celui qui …*, pp. 50–51 *Jumeaux/Jumelles*, pp. 54–57
- **Projectable Transparencies**
  - 28, *À la papeterie*
  - 29, *À la poste*
  - 30, *À la pharmacie*
  - 31, *À la supérette*
- Transparency Copymasters, pp. A59–A65
- DVD Program, Unit 4

■ Teaching Note
Contrast:
avoir besoin de + NOUN
  J'ai besoin de papier à lettres.
il me faut + PARTITIVE + NOUN
  Il me faut du papier à lettres.

À la papeterie

— Vous désirez?
  | Je voudrais
  | Pouvez-vous me donner | du papier à lettres.
  | S'il vous plaît, donnez-moi

— Vous désirez? | quelque chose d'autre *(something else)*?
  | autre chose?

  Oui, | donnez-moi aussi | un stylo à bille.
  | j'ai besoin d'
  | il me faut *(I need)*

— **Et avec ça?**
  C'est tout, merci!
  Ça fait combien?
  Combien est-ce que je vous dois?
— **Ça fait 6 euros cinquante.**
  Voici 10 euros.
— Et voici **votre monnaie** *(change)*.
  Merci.

devoir *to owe*

Speech bubbles:
- Vous désirez?
- Pouvez-vous me donner du papier à lettres?
- C'est tout?
- Oui, c'est tout, merci!

À la poste

— **C'est votre tour** *(it's your turn)*, Mademoiselle.
  Je voudrais **des timbres** *(stamps)* à 67 centimes.
— **Combien en voulez-vous?**
  Donnez-m'en dix, s'il vous plaît.
— **Voilà. C'est tout?**
  Non, je voudrais aussi . . .

  | envoyer | cette lettre.
  | | cette carte postale.
  | | ce colis *(package)*.
  | | ce paquet *(package)*.
  faire **des photocopies.**
  prendre **mon courrier** *(mail)* à la poste restante *(general delivery)*.

Speech bubbles:
- C'est votre tour, Mademoiselle.
- Je voudrais des timbres à 67 centimes.
- Combien en voulez-vous?
- Donnez-m'en dix, s'il vous plaît.

Teaching Suggestion: DVD Program

In the Unit 4 *Vidéo-drame: Mélanie fait les courses,* students will have a chance to go shopping with Mélanie for some typical items for the home. This section is rich in useful expressions for shopping and dealing with money. As you watch the video, have students write down the new expressions they hear.

During this time, you may also ask them comprehension questions like:
  Qu'est-ce que Mélanie achète chez le photographe?; Où est-ce que Mélanie va pour acheter des articles comme le shampooing et le dentifrice?

Quelle boutique? Quel rayon (department)?	Quels articles (items)?	Quelles quantités?
À la papeterie Au rayon «Papeterie»	un carnet (notebook) un crayon un stylo à bille (ballpoint pen) du papier, du papier à lettres des enveloppes de la colle (glue) du scotch (scotch tape) un trombone (paper clip) un élastique (rubber band)	un bloc de papier un paquet d'enveloppes un tube de colle un rouleau de scotch une boîte | de trombones | d'élastiques
Chez le photographe Au rayon «Photo»	une carte de mémoire (memory card) une pile (battery)	
À la pharmacie Chez le pharmacien Chez la pharmacienne Au rayon «Produits d'Hygiène»	du dentifrice de l'aspirine, des vitamines du shampooing de l'eau de toilette un coton-tige (cotton swab) un mouchoir en papier (tissue) de l'ouate (cotton) un pansement adhésif (Band-aid)	un tube | de dentifrice | d'aspirine une bouteille | de shampooing | d'eau de toilette | de parfum une boîte | de coton-tiges | de mouchoirs un paquet | d'ouate | de pansements
À la supérette Au rayon «Produits d'entretien» «Produits de maison»	du savon de la lessive (detergent) du papier hygiénique (toilet paper) du Sopalin (paper towels) de la ficelle (string) une allumette (match) une épingle (pin) une épingle de sûreté (safety pin)	un paquet de lessive un rouleau | de papier hygiénique | de Sopalin une pelote (ball) de ficelle une boîte | d'allumettes | d'épingles

■ **Note linguistique**

Paquet is the general term for *package*. **Colis** usually refers to a package which is sent by mail.

■ **Notes culturelles**

• In France, the post office also functions as a bank. Many French people have a **compte-chèques postal** (also called **le CCP**). All related banking transactions are done at the post office.

■ **Anecdote**

In 1962, Jacques Marette, Minister of the PTT, decreed that all letters sent to Santa Claus should be answered by a postcard. Since then, children from any country who write a letter to Santa in the care of the French post office receive a card. Each year, **la Poste** sends about 500,000 cards to children.

■ **Note linguistique**

Sopalin est le nom d'une marque (brand) de papier absorbant. Maintenant on utilise ce nom d'une manière générique.

SUPPLEMENTARY VOCABULARY

À la papeterie
le (stylo-) feutre *felt-tip pen*
la cartouche (d'encre) *ink cartridge*
À la poste
faire la queue *to wait in line*
affranchir (une lettre) *to stamp (a letter)*
le chronopost *express-mail delivery*
À la pharmacie
le démêlant *conditioner*
le démaquillant *makeup remover*
un flacon (small bottle, flask)
　d'eau de cologne / de parfum
du fil *thread*
une aiguille *needle*
un bouton *button*

Notes culturelles

• **Le chronopost** (note: no **e** at the end) is an express-mail delivery system set up by the French post office in 1986.

• In 1991, the Ministry of **Postes et Télécommunications** (also known by its former logo **PTT** or **Poste, Télégraphe et Téléphone**) was split into two independent Government-controlled entities: **La Poste** (for mail service, as well as money orders and postal savings accounts) and **France-Télécom** (for phone services). In 1997, France-Télécom was partially privatized, with its capital open to individual investors.

■ **Variation: Activity 3**

Dites dans quel magasin ces jeunes Français doivent aller et ce qu'ils doivent y acheter pour pouvoir faire les choses suivantes.

- Lucas veut écrire à ses amis pour les inviter à son anniversaire. [à la papeterie: un bloc de papier à lettres, un paquet d'enveloppes, un stylo à bille]
- Samantha veut laver son vélo. [à la supérette: un paquet de lessive, un rouleau de Sopalin]
- Amélie veut prendre des photos au mariage de sa soeur dimanche prochain. [chez le photographe: une carte de mémoire, des piles]
- Stéphane veut fabriquer une marionnette en papier. [à la papeterie: un tube de colle, un rouleau de scotch, du papier]
- Ahmed vient de tomber en faisant du roller. Son genou est égratigné *(scratched)*. [à la pharmacie: un paquet de pansement, un paquet d'ouate]

---

1 **Votre liste** 💬

Vous allez passer les vacances de printemps à la Martinique avec votre partenaire. Chacun va faire une liste de dix articles qu'il va emporter *(take along)* avec lui. Utilisez le tableau qui figure à la page 153.

Puis comparez vos listes:

- Qu'est-ce que vous avez pris de semblable *(similar)*?
- Qu'est-ce que vous avez pris de différent?

2 **Aux Galeries Lafayette**

Vous êtes allé(e) aux Galeries Lafayette, un grand magasin à Paris. Là, vous avez acheté l'un des articles suivants. Dites . . .

- à quel rayon vous êtes passé(e)
- ce que vous avez acheté (nommez l'article)
- deux autres choses que vous avez achetées à ce rayon.

▶ **Je suis passé(e) au rayon «Papeterie». J'ai acheté une boîte de trombones. J'ai aussi acheté . . .**

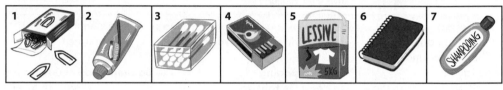

3 **Achats**

Un groupe d'étudiants américains visite la France. Ces étudiants passent dans un grand magasin. Déterminez les besoins de chacun. Dites à quel rayon il passe et ce qu'il achète.

▶ Betty veut prendre des photos du groupe.
Elle passe au rayon «Photo» où elle achète une carte de mémoire.

1. John veut écrire à ses parents.
2. Jim veut laver ses chemises.
3. Elizabeth a perdu sa trousse de toilette *(toiletry kit)*.
4. Anne a mal à la tête.
5. Jacqueline a des ampoules *(blisters)* aux pieds.
6. Cindy éternue *(sneezes)* constamment.
7. Alice veut se laver les cheveux.
8. Robert veut faire un paquet qu'il va envoyer à ses parents.

Teaching Strategy: Warm-Up

Divide the class into groups of three. Each group will prepare two short dialogs based on the following situations (or original scenarios if preferred).

- You need supplies for a first aid kit for a camping trip.

- A friend is leaving for college and needs supplies.
- You have a new penpal in Senegal and you are going to the post office to send a letter.
- You are making a collage of photos with captions for a friend's birthday.

4 À la poste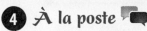

C'est votre première semaine à Paris. Vous allez à la poste pour certaines choses. Composez le dialogue suivant avec votre partenaire qui va jouer le rôle de l'employé(e) de poste.

Employé(e):	*Say hello.*
Client(e):	Say hello and ask for stamps at 50 centimes.
Employé(e):	*Ask how many stamps the client wants.*
Client(e):	Mention a number.
Employé(e):	*Ask if that is all.*
Client(e):	Say that you have something to mail (mention the item: a letter? a postcard? a package?).
Employé(e):	*Determine the price of the items requested and ask the client for the money.*
Client(e):	Pay the postal clerk the sum requested.

4 Créa-dialogue

C'est samedi aujourd'hui et vous avez beaucoup d'achats à faire. Choisissez une boutique où vous allez faire quelques achats. Avec votre partenaire, composez un dialogue pour cette boutique et jouez-le en classe. Votre partenaire va jouer le rôle du vendeur (de la vendeuse).

▶ — Vous désirez, <u>mademoiselle</u>?
— Je voudrais <u>un tube de dentifrice</u>.
— Et avec ça?
— J'ai besoin aussi <u>d'une bouteille de shampooing</u>.
— Voici <u>le dentifrice et le shampooing</u>.
— Merci. C'est combien, s'il vous plaît?
— <u>11 euros cinquante centimes</u>.
— Voici <u>vingt euros</u>.
— Et voici votre monnaie: <u>8 euros et cinquante centimes</u>.

- *Use appropriate greeting.*
- *Mention another product.*
- *Use another expression.*
- *Use another expression and name another product.*
- *Give client the items requested.*
- *Use another expression.*
- *Give a price under 100 euros.*
- *Give a bill to cover the amount.*
- *Return the correct change.*

Conversations libres

Avec votre partenaire, choisissez l'une des situations suivantes. Composez le dialogue correspondant et jouez-le en classe.

Digital performance space

1 Shopping

Vous êtes un(e) étudiant(e) français(e). Vous venez d'arriver à cette école avec un programme d'échange. Faites une liste de trois ou quatre choses dont vous avez besoin et demandez à votre partenaire où vous pouvez les acheter.

2 Une erreur

Vous êtes allé(e) dans un grand magasin où vous avez acheté plusieurs articles. Quand vous rentrez chez vous, vous vous rendez compte *(realize)* que vous avez pris le sac d'une autre personne. Téléphonez au magasin pour expliquer la situation. L'employé(e) va vous demander ce que vous avez acheté et ce qu'il y a dans le sac que vous avez ramené chez vous.

3 Camping

Ce week-end vous allez faire du camping ave votre partenaire. Pour la préparation de cette expédition, votre partenaire veut acheter toutes sortes d'articles. Vous dites que ce n'est pas nécessaire et vous donnez des raisons *(reasons)*.

- You have a summer job in an office and have been asked to pick up some essential desk supplies.
- Your sister or brother has just moved into a new apartment and needs to shop for kitchen and bathroom supplies.

■ **Teaching Suggestion**
Have students go to the website for **La Poste** in France or Switzerland or **Postes Canada** to find out about current services, products, and postal rates.

■ **Note linguistique**
le postier/la postière = l'employé(e) de la poste

■ **Additional Information**
Some popular French brands:
Toothpaste: **Fluocaril**
Shampoo: **L'Oréal, Klorane,**
Beauty products: **Nivea, Lancôme, Vichy**

■ **Note culturelle**
French **parfums** and **eaux de toilette** are known all over the world. The perfume industry developed in the 18th century around the city of **Grasse** in Provence, with the cultivation of large fields of flowers used in the manufacture of essence extracts.

Students may be familiar with the following names of French companies which make perfumes and colognes.
Cacharel (Anaïs)
Chanel (Chanel No. 5)
Dior (Miss Dior, Eau Sauvage)
Givenchy (Ysatis, Le De)
Lancôme (Ô, Ô oui, Poème, Trésor)
Guy Laroche (Fidji)
Rochas (Homme)

Langue et Communication

■ Notes linguistiques

- The pronoun **y** is commonly used with verbs indicating movement or location:
  aller (à, chez)
  entrer (à, dans)
  monter (à, sur)
  partir (à)
  se rendre (à, chez)
  rentrer (à)
  retourner (à)
  se trouver (à, dans, sous)
- To refer to people, the construction **à** + STRESS PRONOUN is used.
  Je pense **à mon copain.**
  Je pense **à lui.**
  Je pense **à mon travail.**
  J'**y** pense.
- To refer to people, the construction **de** + STRESS PRONOUN is used.
  Je parle **de mon prof d'anglais.**
  Je parle **de lui.**
- Other verbs with **à**:
  répondre à (une lettre)
  s'intéresser à
- Other verbs with **de**:
  sortir de
  se souvenir de
  s'approcher de
  s'occuper de

■ Proverbe

Qui s'y frotte, s'y pique. Gather thistles, expect prickles.

156 Unité 4

A Révision: Le pronom *y*

The object pronoun **y** replaces a noun or noun phrases introduced by a preposition of place (**à, en, dans, chez, sur, sous,** etc.). It is the equivalent of *there*.

Tu vas **au** supermarché?	Oui, j'**y** vais.
Tu es passé **chez le pharmacien**?	Non, je n'**y** suis pas passé.

→ **Y** is also used to replace **à** + NOUN referring to a THING.

Tu vas participer **au championnat**?	Oui, je vais **y** participer.

> Verbs used with **à**
> **jouer à**
> **participer à**
> **croire à**
> **penser à**
> **assister à**
> **faire attention à**

B Révision: Le pronom *en*

The object pronoun **en** replaces **du, de la, de l', des, de** + NOUN. It is the equivalent of *some, any*.

Tu prends **des vitamines**?	Non, je n'**en** prends pas.
Tu as acheté **du dentifrice**?	Oui, j'**en** ai acheté.

→ **En** is also used to replace:

- the preposition **de** + NOUN

Tu viens **de la pharmacie**?	Oui, j'**en** viens.
Tu as besoin **de ton stylo à bille**?	Non, je n'**en** ai pas besoin.

- a noun introduced by **un** or **une**

Tu as **une guitare**?	Oui, j'**en** ai **une.**

- a noun introduced by a NUMBER

Marc a acheté **deux cartes postales**.	Moi, j'**en** ai acheté **trois.**

- **de** + NOUN after an expression of quantity

Tu as **beaucoup d'argent**?	Non, je n'**en** ai pas **beaucoup.**
Vous voulez **deux kilos d'oranges**?	Oui, j'**en** veux **deux kilos.**
Combien de tubes de dentifrice as-tu pris?	J'**en** ai pris **un tube.**

→ Note the use of **en** with **il y a** and **donnez-moi.**

Il y a une papeterie dans mon quartier.	Il y **en** a une.
Donnez-moi deux blocs de papier.	Donnez-m'**en** deux.

> Verbs used with **de**
> **venir de**
> **parler de**
> **avoir besoin de**
> **avoir envie de**
> **avoir peur de**

♻ RAPPEL

The pronouns **y** and **en** come BEFORE the verb, <u>except</u> in affirmative commands. Compare:

Tu vas à la papeterie?	Tu **y** vas?	Vas-**y.**
Tu achètes des enveloppes?	Tu **en** achètes?	Achètes-**en.**

Teaching Strategy: Expansion

In affirmative commands, have the students note the liaison /z/ sound and the addition of an "s" in the affirmative imperative before **y** and **en.**
Va à la boulangerie. **Vas-y.**
Achète des croissants. **Achètes-en.**

Differentiation

Synthetic/Analytic Write a sentence using **de + noun** on the board and have students identify each part. Underline the part to be replaced by **en**, and have students generate a sentence using it. Then, under the labeled sentence, write elements of sentences and have students generate sentences, writing them down in their notebooks after practicing orally.

1 La vie de star 🗨

Vous interviewez un(e) star de cinéma français(e) sur sa vie. Votre partenaire va vous répondre affirmativement en donnant des précisions et en utilisant **y** ou **en**.

Vous allez souvent au concert?

Oui, j'y vais souvent avec mes amis.

▶ aller souvent au concert? (avec mes amis)

1. aller au cinéma? (de temps en temps)
2. jouer au tennis? (pendant les vacances)
3. faire du jogging? (tous les matins)
4. faire attention à votre santé? (tout le temps)
5. boire de l'eau minérale? (à tous les repas)
6. manger des fruits? (beaucoup)
7. donner des interviews? (de temps en temps)
8. participer au festival de Cannes? (tous les ans)
9. avoir une voiture de sport? (une)
10. avoir des admirateurs? (beaucoup)
11. avoir besoin d'encouragement? (souvent)

■ **Teaching Note: Activity 1**
You may encourage your more creative students to expand the dialog by giving original answers.

■ **Note culturelle**
Le festival de Cannes is an international film festival started in 1946. It takes place every May and is attended by movie makers and actors from all over the world. The best movie wins **la Palme d'or**.

2 Les courses 🗨

Vous passez les vacances dans un petit village de Normandie. Votre partenaire a fait les courses ce matin. Demandez-lui ce qu'il/elle a acheté.

▶ — **Tu es allé(e) <u>à la papeterie</u>?**
— **Oui, j'y suis allé(e).**
— **Tu as acheté <u>des enveloppes</u>?**
— **Oui, j'en ai acheté <u>un paquet</u>.**

1. • à la poste
   • des timbres
   • vingt

2. • chez le photographe
   • des cartes de mémoire
   • deux

3. • à la pharmacie
   • du shampooing
   • une bouteille

4. • au marché
   • des tomates
   • deux kilos

5. • chez le crémier
   • des oeufs
   • une douzaine

6. • à la boulangerie
   • des croissants
   • six

3 Camping 🗨

Maintenant vous allez faire du camping. Votre partenaire vous demande ce qu'il/elle doit prendre. Répondez-lui en lui donnant des quantités. Soyez logique!

Je prends des allumettes?

Oui, prends-en une boîte.

(deux boîtes)

QUOI?	QUELLE QUANTITÉ?
du dentifrice	un paquet
de la lessive	un tube
du shampooing	une boîte
des coton-tiges	une bouteille
de la ficelle	une pelote
de l'ouate	un rouleau
des pansements	
du Sopalin	
des allumettes	
du papier hygiénique	

Teaching Strategy: Game
Make a line down the middle of the classroom using tape or string. Tell the students that one side of the line is the **en** side and the other side is the **y** side. Have all the students stand on the line. Present sentences that necessitate **y** or **en** and ask the students to go to the side of the line that represents the correct pronoun. (*Right side of the line is **en**. Left side of the line is **y**.*)

You say: **Je vais en Italie.** The students go to the <u>left</u> side of the line.
You say: **Nous avons acheté des fleurs.** The students go to the <u>right</u> side of the line.
Once all students are on the correct side, ask one student to give the sentence with the correct pronoun.

RESOURCES

PRINT
Workbook, pp. 48, 129
Activités pour tous
Unit 4 Resource Book, Partie 1
  Audioscripts

AUDIO
  Audio Program
  CD 4, Tracks 5–6

TECHNOLOGY
@HomeTutor
Teacher One Stop
  Teacher to Teacher Copymasters,
  Trouver celui qui ..., pp. 50–51;
  Et maintenant ..., pp. 52–53

@HOMETUTOR
my.hrw.com

C Expressions indéfinies de quantité

Indefinite expressions of quantity refer to an undetermined number of people or things.

ADJECTIVE (+ NOUN)		PRONOUN	
quelques . . .	*some, a few*	quelques-uns quelques-unes }	*some, a few*
un(e) autre . . . d'autres . . .	*another* *other, some other*	un(e) autre d'autres	*another one* *others, some others,* *other ones*
plusieurs . . .	*several*	plusieurs	*several*
certain(e)s . . .	*some, several*	certain(e)s	*some, certain ones*
la plupart de . . .	*most of*	la plupart	*most (of them)*

The above expressions of quantity can be used either as subjects or as objects.

ADJECTIVE	PRONOUN
SUBJECT	
Quelques amies sont venues.	**Quelques-unes** sont venues.
Plusieurs lettres sont arrivées ce matin.	**Plusieurs** sont arrivées ce matin.
OBJECT	
J'ai invité **quelques** amis.	J'en ai invité **quelques-uns.**
Nous avons visité **plusieurs** monuments.	Nous en avons visité **plusieurs.**

→ Note that **en** is used with the indefinite <u>pronouns</u> of quantity when these expressions are the direct object of the verb.

4 🗨 S'il te plaît!

Vous êtes chez votre partenaire. Il/elle vous offre à nouveau certaines choses. Acceptez-les (ou refusez, en expliquant pourquoi).

▶ une limonade
— **Tu veux une limonade?**
— **Oui, donne-m'en une autre, s'il te plaît.**
  (Non, merci, je n'ai pas soif.)

1. un hamburger
2. un jus d'orange
3. une part de pizza
4. un sandwich
5. une tasse de café
6. un thé glacé

Teaching Strategy: Challenge

Give students a sentence which includes an indefinite adjective. Ask them to restate the sentence using **en** and an indefinite pronoun. (Give them one or two examples since this concept can be difficult for some students.) **Pre-AP skill:** Use a variety of structures and vocabulary.

Differentiation

Structured Have students write down the indefinite expressions of quantity on cards. On a second set of cards, have them write down nouns. Working in pairs, have them combine the cards to create sentences, paying careful attention to agreement.

5 Un après-midi à Montréal

Vous êtes à Montréal avec votre partenaire. Cet après-midi, vous êtes resté(e) à votre hôtel, mais votre partenaire est sorti(e). Demandez-lui ce qu'il/elle a fait.

▶ acheter des souvenirs (quelques-uns)

1. prendre des photos (quelques-unes)
2. écrire des lettres (quelques-unes)
3. envoyer des cartes postales (plusieurs)
4. acheter un guide de la ville (un autre)
5. acheter des CD (plusieurs)
6. rencontrer des jeunes Canadiens (quelques-uns)

> Oui, j'en ai acheté quelques-uns.

> Tu as acheté des souvenirs?

Notes culturelles

- **Montréal** started as a small colony called **Ville-Marie de Montréal**. It was founded in 1642 by **Paul de Chomedey, sieur de Maisonneuve**.
- The **Vieux-Port** is a popular tourist attraction, offering many sights and activities. For example, you can shop at a flea-market, visit the replica of a 1693 tall ship, cruise the harbor, or rent a bicycle. Carriage rides are also a popular way to discover **la vieille ville**.

News + Networking
my.hrw.com

INFO MAGAZINE

Theme: Personal style

■ **Note linguistique**

Un(e) visagiste is a hairstylist who enhances the natural characteristics of a face by choosing an appropriate hairstyle.

■ **Teaching Note**

For a review of related vocabulary, see Unité 1, p. 36.

À chacun son style

COIFFURE

FEMME

ÉTUDIANTE

HOMME

Dans notre apparence personnelle, nous sommes tous un peu différents. Chacun peut choisir son style de vêtements, son style de chaussures et son style de coiffure.

Quel style de coiffure demanderiez-vous à votre coiffeur si vous étiez en France? Aimeriez-vous avoir . . .

les cheveux en brosse

les cheveux au carré

une raie sur le côté

un style punk

une frange sur le devant

des tresses très serrées

des mèches

une permanente

Teaching Strategy: Expansion

You may wish to use this short optional article to personalize the practical situational vocabulary presented on p. 161.

Ask students to look at the pictures and choose the hairstyle that is closest to their own.

Have students imagine they are in a hair salon in France and ask them to prepare short dialogs.

Au salon de coiffure

Pouvez-vous me couper les cheveux?

Oui, bien sûr.

COIFFEUR VISAGISTE

Marini Paris Coiffure

Marini Paris Coiffure
64 avenue Jean Moulin
75014 Paris
01-99-20-20-22

Promotion Spéciale Vacances

Coiffure femme € 30,00
Coiffure homme € 22,00
Coiffure enfant € 12,00

ACCUEIL | LES PRODUITS | LES COLLECTIONS | RELOOKING | CONTACT

— **C'est votre tour,** monsieur (mademoiselle).

Pouvez-vous me couper les cheveux?

Est-ce que vous pouvez me faire

une coupe de cheveux *(haircut)*?
une coupe-brushing (*haircut and blow-dry)***?
un shampooing?
une permanente?
une mise en pli *(set)*?

— Comment est-ce que je vous coupe les cheveux?

Dégagez-les	**sur les côtés** *(on the sides).*	**dégager** *to cut back,*
Coupez-les-moi courts	**sur le devant** *(in front).*	*shorten (hair)*
Laissez-les-moi longs	**sur le dessus** *(on top).*	**laisser** *to leave*
Ne me les coupez pas trop courts	**derrière** *(in back).*	

1 *Chez le coiffeur (At the hairdresser)*

Digital **performance space**

Vous êtes dans un salon de coiffure. Votre partenaire va jouer le rôle du coiffeur (de la coiffeuse). Inventez votre dialogue.

Coiffeur(se): *Tell the client that it is his/her turn.*
Client(e): Ask for a haircut.
Coiffeur(se): *Ask if the client wants something else (for example, a shampoo).*
Client(e): Accept or refuse politely.
Coiffeur(se): *Ask how the client wants his/her hair cut.*
Client(e): Tell the hairdresser how to cut your hair.

cent soixante et un **161**
Le Français pratique

Le Français pratique

RESOURCES

PRINT
Workbook, p. 130
Activités pour tous
Unit 4 Resource Book, Partie 2
Activités pour tous TE
Audioscripts
Lesson Plans
Block Scheduling Lesson Plans
Absent Student Copymasters
Workbook TE

AUDIO
Audio Program
CD 4, Tracks 7–9

TECHNOLOGY
@HomeTutor
Interactive Whiteboard Lessons
Teacher One Stop
Block Scheduling Copymasters
Projectable Transparencies
33, *Au salon de coiffure*
Transparency Copymasters,
pp. A68–A69

SUPPLEMENTARY VOCABULARY

mettre un après-shampooing to condition, to use a conditioner
faire une décoloration to bleach (one's hair)
faire des mèches to streak (one's hair)
colorer les cheveux to color one's hair

Also:
Faites-moi | **une raie** part
| **une frange** bangs
| **des boucles** curls
| **des nattes, des tresses** braids
Tressez-moi les cheveux braid my hair

Langue et Communication

■ Teaching Notes

You may review the forms of the object pronouns very quickly. The focus in this section is on the contrast between these pronouns and **y** and **en**. The next section practices word order in sentences with two object pronouns.

LE, LA, LES

- You may remind students that direct objects answer the questions *whom? what?*
- Remind students that **le** and **la** become **l'** before a vowel sound:

  Cécile: Je **la** connais. Je **l'**invite au concert.

  Vincent: Je ne **le** connais pas. Je ne **l'**invite pas à la boum.

- In French, the past participle agrees with a preceding direct object.

  Quelle veste as-tu acheté**e**?

  Où est la veste **que** tu as acheté**e**?

LUI, LEUR

- You may remind students that indirect objects answer the question *to whom?*
- The following verbs are frequently used with indirect objects:

dire à	promettre à
écrire à	rendre visite à
parler à	répondre à
permettre à	téléphoner à
obéir à	désobéir à
donner à	demander à
montrer à	envoyer à

- Remind students that there is no agreement of the past participle with **lui, leur**.

162 Unité 4

A   Révision: les pronoms *le, la, les* et *lui, leur*

LE, LA, LES

Le, la, les are direct-object pronouns.
They replace PEOPLE or THINGS.

Tu vois **cette fille** là-bas?	Oui, je **la** vois.
Tu vois **ces maisons**?	Oui, je **les** vois.

→ Compare the use of **en** and **le, la, les**.

Tu achètes **le journal**?	Oui, je **l'**achète.
Tu achètes **du pain**?	Oui, j'**en** achète.

> **Pratique** p. 49
> L'accord du participe passé

→ In the passé composé, the past participle agrees with **le, la, les,** but not with **en**.

Tu as pris **la carte postale**?	Oui, je **l'**ai **prise**.
Tu as pris **mes photos**?	Oui, je **les** ai **prises**.
BUT: Tu as pris **des photos**?	Non, je n'**en** ai pas **pris**.

LUI, LEUR

Lui and **leur** are indirect-object pronouns.
They replace **à** + NOUN designating PEOPLE.

Tu as écrit **à tes cousins**?	Non, je ne **leur** ai pas écrit.

→ Compare the use of **y** and **lui, leur**.

Tu as répondu **à Pauline**?	Oui, je **lui** ai répondu.
Tu as répondu **à cette lettre**?	Oui, j'**y** ai répondu.

→ Note that **lui, leur** are not used with **penser**.

Tu penses **à tes amis**?	Oui, je pense **à eux**.

♺ RAPPEL

> Object pronouns always come BEFORE the verb, <u>except</u> in affirmative commands.
> Compare:
>
> | | | |
> |---|---|---|
> | Je prends ces magazines? | Ne **les** prends pas. | Oui, prends-**les**. |
> | Je téléphone à Christine? | Ne **lui** téléphone pas. | Oui, téléphone-**lui**. |

Teaching Strategy: Game

Les pronoms

Prepare a variety of sentences that include direct and indirect objects and phrases that begin with **de** and **à**. Cut apart the sentences, place each group of pieces in an envelope and give one or two envelopes to each pair of students. Prepare several copies of all the pronouns and put these in front of the classroom. Students must put together their sentences using the appropriate pronouns. The first pair to finish successfully wins. All students must then show their completed sentences and the words that were replaced to the class.

1 Au revoir!

Vous avez visité Genève avec vos amis. C'est bientôt *(soon)* le départ. Dites que vos amis ont fait les choses suivantes en répondant affirmativement aux questions. Utilisez le pronom qui convient (**l', les, lui, leur, en, y**).

▶ Catherine a acheté du parfum?   **Oui, elle en a acheté.**

1. Julien a fait ses valises?
2. Pauline a téléphoné à sa mère?
3. Pierre est allé à l'agence de voyages?
4. Marc et Éric ont acheté leurs billets?
5. Claire a trouvé son passeport?
6. Thomas a pris des photos?
7. Isabelle a acheté des souvenirs?
8. Antoine a dit au revoir à ses amis?
9. Alice a acheté un foulard?
10. Véronique a écrit plusieurs cartes postales?

2 Le week-end dernier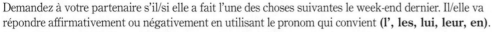

Demandez à votre partenaire s'il/si elle a fait l'une des choses suivantes le week-end dernier. Il/elle va répondre affirmativement ou négativement en utilisant le pronom qui convient (**l', les, lui, leur, en**).

▶ — Est-ce que tu as écouté de la musique classique le week-end dernier?
— Oui, j'en ai écouté. (Non, je n'en ai pas écouté.)

- lire le journal du dimanche?
- regarder les bandes dessinées?
- acheter des vêtements?
- voir un film?
- voir tes voisins?
- téléphoner à ton copain/ta copine?
- ranger ta chambre?
- écouter de la musique classique?
- écouter du rap?
- faire du jogging?
- écrire à ta cousine?
- rendre visite à tes grands-parents?
- aider tes parents?
- ??

3 Pourquoi pas?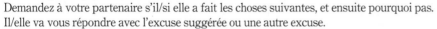

Demandez à votre partenaire s'il/si elle a fait les choses suivantes, et ensuite pourquoi pas. Il/elle va vous répondre avec l'excuse suggérée ou une autre excuse.

▶ inviter Pauline
   (elle est trop snob)

— **Tu as invité Pauline?**
— **Non, je ne l'ai pas invitée.**
— **Mais pourquoi est-ce que tu ne l'as pas invitée?**
— **Elle est trop snob.**

1. téléphoner à tes copains
   (ils ne sont pas chez eux)
2. laver ta voiture
   (elle n'était pas sale)
3. acheter de la limonade
   (je n'avais pas soif)
4. faire les courses
   (j'ai dîné au restaurant)
5. aller chez le coiffeur
   (je n'ai pas les cheveux longs)
6. écrire à Catherine
   (j'ai perdu son adresse)
7. prendre des photos
   (je n'avais pas mon appareil)
8. finir tes devoirs
   (j'avais mal à la tête)
9. tondre la pelouse
   (la tondeuse est cassée)
10. aller à la pharmacie
    (elle est fermée aujourd'hui)

4 L'assistant(e)

Vous êtes l'assistant(e) du président (de la présidente) d'une compagnie française. Demandez-lui si vous devez faire les choses suivantes. Votre partenaire va répondre affirmativement ou négativement.

▶ téléphoner à Madame Simon (oui)

1. répondre à ces clients (oui)
2. copier ces documents (oui)
3. répondre à cette lettre (non)
4. écrire à Madame Susuki (oui)
5. inviter Monsieur Schmidt (non)
6. passer à la poste (oui)
7. acheter des timbres (oui)
8. envoyer ce chèque (non)
9. aller à la papeterie (oui)
10. commander du papier à lettres (oui)
11. acheter des enveloppes (non)
12. acheter votre billet d'avion (oui)
13. réserver une chambre d'hôtel (oui)
14. confirmer la réservation (non)

> *Je téléphone à Madame Simon?*

> *Oui, téléphonez-lui!*

cent soixante-trois 163
Langue et Communication

■ **Teaching Note**
These activities practice and contrast the use of the various pronouns reviewed: **y, en, le, la, les, lui, leur.**

■ **Expansion: Activity 2**
Encourage students to continue their conversation, e.g.:
Quelles bandes dessinées est-ce que tu as lues?
J'ai lu …
Est-ce que tu les as trouvées drôles? etc.

Teaching Strategy: Personalization
In Activity 3, encourage students to invent original excuses.

■ **Expansion: Activity 4**
Also:
faire attention à
Nous faisons attention **à eux.**
s'intéresser à
Paul s'intéresse **à eux.**

Notes culturelles

- The south shore of the **Lac Léman** is French. The north shore is Swiss. The part of the lake nearest the city of **Genève** is also called **le lac de Genève**.
- **Berne** is the capital of Switzerland.
- Ask students to use the map in their text to locate Switzerland, or use **OHT 1** and **1(o)** to point out **Lac Léman**.

■ **Note linguistique**

The past participle always agrees with a preceding direct object, even in sentences where there are two object pronouns.

J'ai prêté **mes piles** à Paul.
Je **les** lui ai **prêtées**.

■ **Teaching Strategy: Grammar Drill**

Have students write their names on a slip of paper and put them into a hat. Have them write the name of an item on another slip of paper and put these into another hat. Ask each student to pick one piece of paper from each hat. They must then make a complete sentence using the item as a d.o., the student name as an i.o., and using the verb **donner** (**Je donne les fleurs à Catherine**). Then, have each student hand the papers they chose to the student whose name appears while they replace the d.o. and i.o. with pronouns. (e.g., **Je les lui donne...** Hands the papers to Catherine.)

B L'ordre des pronoms

Sometimes a sentence may contain <u>two</u> object pronouns. Note the sequence of these pronouns in the following sentences:

DIRECT- AND INDIRECT-OBJECT PRONOUNS

le la les	before	lui leur	Je prête **mon vélo à Alice.**	Je **le lui** prête.
			Tu envoies **cette carte à tes cousins.**	Tu **la leur** envoies.
			Nous montrons **nos photos à Éric.**	Nous **les lui** montrons.

→ This order is also used in affirmative commands.

Montre **la photo à Catherine.** Montre-**la-lui.**

me te nous vous	before	le la les	Vous **me** donnez **le journal.**	Vous **me le** donnez.
			Le coiffeur **te** coupe **les cheveux.**	Il **te les** coupe.
			Paul **nous** vend **sa tablette.**	Paul **nous la** vend.
			Sylvie **vous** prête **ses CD.**	Elle **vous les** prête.

→ Note the order in affirmative commands:

| le la les | before | moi nous | Donne-**moi ton adresse.** | Donne-**la-moi.** |
| | | | Montre-**nous ces photos.** | Montre-**les-nous.** |

OBJECT PRONOUNS AND **Y, EN**

le/la/les lui/leur me/te/nous/vous	before	y en	J'amène **mes amis au concert.**	Je **les y** amène.
			Je donne **des conseils à Marc.**	Je **lui en** donne.
			Alice **me** prête **de l'argent.**	Elle **m'en** prête.
			L'employé **nous** vend **des timbres.**	Il **nous en** vend.

→ This order is also used in affirmative commands.

Donne **des timbres à Catherine.** Donne-**lui-en.**
Donne-**moi du papier à lettres.** Donne-**m'en.**

ALLONS PLUS LOIN

When two pronouns are used with a reflexive verb, the reflexive pronoun always comes first.

Je m'achète des vêtements.   Je **m'en** achète.
Alice s'est coupé les cheveux.   Elle **se les** est coupés.

Comment est ce que je vous les coupe?

Differentiation

Metacognitive Teach the order of pronouns. Copy the charts on the board and have students explain to you the positions. Have them copy the chart in their notebooks. Then, write elements of a Sentence and have them generate sentences with the correct order of pronouns.

5 Conversation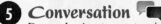

Demandez à votre partenaire s'il/si elle fait les choses suivantes. Il/elle va répondre affirmativement ou négativement.

▶ prêter ton portable à ton copain?
   — **Est-ce que tu prête ton portable à ton copain?**
   — **Oui, je le lui prête. (Non, je ne le lui prête pas.)**

1. prêter de l'argent à tes copains?
2. montrer ton journal *(diary)* à ta copine?
3. montrer tes notes *(grades)* à tes parents?
4. emprunter la tondeuse à tes voisins?

5. demander des conseils à ton prof?
6. donner de l'argent aux pauvres?
7. dire la vérité à tes amis?
8. couper les cheveux à ton petit frère?

6 Échanges

Votre partenaire va vous demander de lui prêter une des choses suivantes. Négociez un échange avec lui/elle. Votre partenaire va accepter ou refuser.

▶ — **Dis, prête-moi ton portable**
   — **D'accord, je vais te le prêter si tu me prêtes ta bicyclette.**
   — **Bon, je vais te la prêter.**
          (Non, je ne veux pas te la prêter.)

7 Oui ou non?

Répondez aux questions suivantes, affirmativement ou négativement. Utilisez les pronoms **lui/leur** et **en.** Soyez logique!

▶ Est-ce qu'on donne de l'aspirine à un malade?
   Oui, on lui en donne.

1. Est-ce qu'on donne des allumettes aux enfants?
2. Est-ce qu'on parle de ses problèmes à ses amis?
3. Est-ce qu'on offre du chocolat à une personne qui est au régime *(on a diet)?*
4. Est-ce qu'on demande des conseils à ses parents?
5. Est-ce qu'on raconte des histoires de fantômes à une personne impressionnable?
6. Est-ce qu'on envoie des cartes de voeux *(season's greetings)* à ses amis?
7. Est-ce qu'on donne un bon pourboire à un serveur désagréable?
8. Est-ce qu'on sert de la viande à un végétarien?
9. Est-ce qu'on écrit des poèmes à une personne qu'on aime?

8 À Paris

Vous travaillez à Paris dans l'un des endroits suivants. Offrez certains services à votre partenaire, qui va accepter. (S'il/si elle refuse, votre partenaire va vous donner une explication.)

▶ — **Je vous apporte le menu?**
   — **Oui, apportez-le-moi, s'il vous plaît.**
          (Non, pas maintenant! Je vais attendre un peu.)

AU RESTAURANT	CHEZ LE COIFFEUR
▶ • apporter le menu	• faire un shampooing
• décrire le plat du jour	• couper les cheveux très courts
• donner du pain	• mettre du gel
• servir du café	

À L'HÔTEL
• montrer votre chambre
• monter vos bagages
• préparer votre note *(bill)*
• commander un taxi

Le Français pratique
Services

RESOURCES

PRINT
Workbook, pp. 131–132
Unit 4 Resource Book, Partie 2
Audioscripts

AUDIO
Audio Program
CD 4, Tracks 12–14

TECHNOLOGY
@HomeTutor
Interactive Whiteboard Lessons
Teacher One Stop
Projectable Transparencies
 34, *Services et réparations*
 35, *Chez le photographe*
 Transparency Copymasters,
 pp. A70–A73

coudre (recoudre) ce bouton *to sew
 this button (back on)*
réparer la fermeture éclair
 to fix the zipper

■ Notes linguistiques
- **La cordonnerie** est la boutique du
 cordonnier.
- **La teinturerie** est la boutique du
 teinturier. On porte des vêtements
 chez le teinturier/à la teinturerie.

Services

Est-ce que vous pouvez réparer ces chaussures?
Oui, bien sûr.
Quand est-ce que ce sera prêt?
D'ici une semaine.

Chez le cordonnier
(At the shoe repair shop)

— Est-ce que vous pouvez | **réparer** ces chaussures?
 | **changer les talons** *(heels)*?

| **réparer** *to fix* |

— Quand est-ce que **ce sera prêt** *(when will it be ready)*?
 Tout à l'heure! *(In a little while!)*
 Dans deux jours.
 D'ici une semaine. *(A week from now.)*

Est-ce que vous pouvez enlever cette tache?
Oui, mademoiselle.

Chez le teinturier *(At the cleaners)*

— Est-ce que vous pouvez | **nettoyer** cette veste?
 | **laver** ces chemises?
 | **repasser** ce pantalon?
 | **enlever cette tache**
 | *(spot, stain)*?

| **repasser** *to iron*
enlever *to remove* |

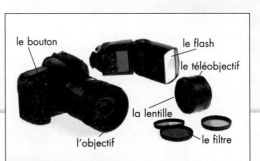
Est-ce que vous pouvez développer ces photos?
Oui, monsieur.

Chez le photographe

— Est-ce que vous pouvez **développer ces photos**?
 Est-ce que vous pouvez aussi **réparer mon appareil-photo**?
 Oui, quel est le problème?
 Qu'est-ce qu'il y a?
 Qu'est-ce qui ne marche pas?
 Le flash | **est cassé.**
 | **ne fonctionne pas.**
 | **ne marche pas.**

| **marcher** *to work,
 to function* |

La pile est **usée** *(worn out)*.

le bouton
le flash
le téléobjectif
la lentille
l'objectif
le filtre

Teaching Strategy: Warm-Up
Use actual items to spark student interest: a pair of shoes, a suit to be cleaned, a camera, a bike, a T.V., a pair of pants to be cleaned or ironed...
 Ask students to come to the front of the class and explain what is wrong with the item and what needs to be done, using the vocabulary from pp. 166–167 in their demonstration.

■ **Variation: Activity 1**
- mon ordinateur
- mes rollers *(rollerblades)*
  les roues? les freins?
  la chaussure?
- mon caméscope *(camcorder)*
  le zoom? l'objectif? la prise de
  son? *(sound recorder)*

1 Réparations 💬

Vous avez un objet à réparer et vous allez chez un spécialiste. Avec votre partenaire, choisissez un des objets suivants et composez le dialogue correspondant.

▶ — S'il vous plaît, est-ce que vous pouvez réparer <u>mon ordinateur</u>?
   — Oui, bien sûr. Quel est le problème?
   — <u>Le modem</u> ne marche pas.
   — Bon, je vais voir ça.

les freins
la roue

la télécommande
l'écran
la prise

le micro
l'ampli   le haut-parleur

le flash
l'objectif
la carte de mémoire

- **mon appareil-photo**
  le flash? l'objectif?
- **ma chaîne stéréo**
  le micro? l'ampli?
  le haut-parleur?
- **ma télé**
  l'écran?
  la prise?
- **mon vélo**
  les freins? la roue?

2 Créa-dialogue 💬

Lisez le dialogue «Chez l'électricien». Puis, avec votre partenaire, choisissez une autre boutique et préparez un nouveau dialogue. Par exemple, vous allez chez le teinturier, chez le photographe, ou chez le cordonnier.

«CHEZ L'ÉLECTRICIEN»	
— Bonjour, <u>madame</u>. Est-ce que vous pouvez <u>changer cette prise (plug)</u>?	• *Use the appropriate form of address.* • *Ask for a service available at the shop.*
— Bien sûr, <u>monsieur</u>. Ce sera tout?	• *Use the appropriate form of address.*
— Non, est-ce que vous pouvez aussi <u>réparer cette lampe</u>?	• *Ask for another service.*
— D'accord, je vais faire ça.	
— Quand est-ce que ce sera prêt?	
— <u>D'ici dix jours</u>.	• *Give the number of days from now.*
— Ce n'est pas possible avant?	
— Si, peut-être. Revenez <u>lundi prochain</u>.	• *Give another day closer in time.*

Student Portfolios

Ask students to make up their own proverbs, using the following as an example:

Les cordonniers sont les plus mal chaussés.
Shoemakers are always the worst shod.

Have students illustrate their proverbs. For students who prefer working on computer, borders, clip art, and scanned photos or illustrations can be included. The final product can be displayed in the classroom or put directly in the portfolios.

Workbook, pp. 51–54, 132

AUDIO
🔊 **Audio Program**
CD 4 Tracks 15
Audioscript, URB 4

TECHNOLOGY
@HomeTutor
Teacher One Stop
Teacher to Teacher Copymasters, *Jumeaux/Jumelles,* pp. 54–57

SUPPLEMENTARY VOCABULARY

faire savoir *to let (someone) know*
Faites-le moi savoir dès que possible.
faire faire *to have done, made*
Je me suis fait faire une robe.
faire construire *to have built (a house)*
Ils ont fait construire (la maison) l'année dernière.

■ Teaching Strategy: Challenge
Ask students to look at the following sentence and notice that there is no agreement of the past participle:

[ma montre] **Je l'ai fait réparer.**

There is no agreement of the past participle in the **faire** + INFINITIVE construction. This is because the pronoun **le/la/les** is not the direct object of **faire**, but rather the direct object of the infinitive.

The reflexive pronoun is generally omitted before an infinitive introduced by **faire:**

Je l'ai fait asseoir.
Elle s'était levée, mais le docteur l'a fait coucher.

168 Unité 4

A La construction faire + infinitif

Note the use of the construction **faire** + INFINITIVE.

Je **fais développer** les photos.	*I am having* the pictures **developed.**
Tu **as fait réparer** ton vélo.	*You **had** your bicycle **fixed.***
Nous allons **faire laver** notre voiture.	*We are going **to have** our car **washed.***

The construction **faire** + INFINITIVE is used to describe actions that people have done by someone else.

→ In this construction, it is the verb **faire** that is used:
  • in the negative

Je fais réparer ma télé.	Je **ne fais pas** réparer mon portable.

  • with pronouns

Ma montre était cassée.	Je l'**ai fait réparer.**
Ta voiture est sale.	**Fais-la** laver.

> **Pratique** p. 51
> Faire + infinitif

The construction **faire** + INFINITIVE is also used to describe actions that we make or have other people do.

Le professeur **fait étudier** les élèves.	*The teacher **makes** the students **study.***

ALLONS PLUS LOIN

• The construction **faire** + INFINITIVE is used in certain expressions:

faire cuire *to cook*	**faire frire** *to fry*	**faire bouillir** *to boil*

Also: **faire marcher** *to operate (equipment)*   **faire voir** *to show*

• Note the use of **se faire** + INFINITIVE to describe actions that people are having done for themselves.

Je vais **me faire couper les cheveux.**	*I am going **to have my hair cut.***

Differentiation

Cumulative, Gifted & Talented Review the conjugation of the verb **avoir**, writing it on the board and having students copy it into their notebooks. Then, write a list of infnitives on the board, and ask students to generate sentences with **faire + infinitive.** Then, collect students' sentences and redistribute them.

Have students write a story using the **faire + infinitive** sentences they received.

1 Services 🗨

Demandez à votre partenaire pourquoi il va à certains endroits. Il/elle va répondre logiquement.

▶ — Tu vas à la teinturerie?
— Oui, je vais faire nettoyer mon blazer.

OÙ?	POURQUOI?
• à la station-service	• réparer mon vélo
• chez le mécanicien	• réparer mon séchoir
• à la teinturerie	• changer cette serrure *(lock)*
• chez le photographe	• nettoyer mon blazer
• à la laverie *(laundry)*	• laver mon linge
• à la boutique d'appareils électriques	• laver ma voiture
• chez le serrurier *(locksmith)*	• vacciner mon chien
• chez le vétérinaire	• développer mes photos

2 Que faire? 🗨

Votre partenaire vous explique certains problèmes. Dites-lui ce qu'il/elle doit faire.

▶ — Ma montre est cassée.
— Fais-la réparer.

PROBLÈMES	QUE FAIRE?
• Ma montre est cassée.	changer . . .
• Ma veste a une tache *(spot)*.	couper . . .
• Mes cheveux sont trop longs.	nettoyer . . .
• Mon MP3 ne marche pas.	réparer . . .
• La pile de mon appareil-photo est usée *(worn out)*.	vacciner . . .
• Mon chien n'a pas eu ses piqûres *(shots)*.	

«Ma montre est cassée.»

«Mes cheveux sont trop longs.»

«Ma veste a une tache.»

«Mon chien n'a pas eu ses piqûres.»

Unité 4

Interdisciplinary/ Community Connections

Create a directory, in French, of services available in your town. Include picture as well as words for those who do not speak French.

Language Arts
In small groups, list and describe all the services available in your town.

Math
Find out the cost for each service and list in a chart.

Science/Health
Be sure to find out about health clubs, gyms, and emergency and non-emergency health care providers in the area.

Social Studies
Choose one of the services you have identified and report on the training and education needed for the job.

Art/Music
Design the directory, including pictures or icons representing different services.

Technology
Find out about computer and other tech services in the area.

Community
Donate your directory to the local library, a travel agency, or the chamber of commerce.

Expansion: Activity 2

Have each pair of students come up with an original problem scenario and then exchange with another pair of students. Then ask pairs to develop a dialog giving an original solution.

This activity can be an amusing one to video and use as a problem-solving authentic assessment piece. Play the problem scenario first, then stop the video and ask students to offer solutions. Finally, play the video to show the original solution; compare and contrast.

■ Realia Notes
- **UV** means that the place offers a tanning booth.
- **Le hammam** is a place to have a steam bath. **Hammam** is a turkish/arabic word meaning "hot bath."
- **Le cireur** = shoeshiner (**cirer:** to wax, to polish; **la cire** wax, shoe polish)
- **Le voiturier** = car service

LECTURE

Comédie en 4 scènes

Additional readings @ my.hrw.com
FRENCH
InterActive 📘 **Reader**

Une histoire de cheveux

AVANT DE LIRE

Le titre et le sous-titre de ce texte indiquent qu'il s'agit° d'une histoire plutôt humoristique avec pour sujet un événement assez ordinaire de la vie quotidienne: une coupe de cheveux.

Pour vous mettre dans l'esprit de cette histoire, répondez aux questions suivantes.

- Est-ce que vous attachez beaucoup d'importance à votre coiffure? Pourquoi ou pourquoi pas?
- Quel style de coiffure préférez-vous?
- Est-ce que vos parents sont toujours d'accord avec ce style? (Si non, pourquoi pas?)
- Quel coiffeur vous coupe les cheveux habituellement? Combien de fois par an (ou par mois) y allez-vous?
- Si votre coiffeur était indisponible° un jour, est-ce que vous permettriez à quelqu'un d'autre (un copain ou une copine, votre soeur ou votre frère, votre mère ou votre père…) de vous couper les cheveux? Pourquoi ou pourquoi pas?

il s'agit de *it is about* **indisponible** *unavailable*

Alain
MAITRE BARBIER COIFFEUR
"SALON MUSEE"
DU MARDI AU SAMEDI DE 9H15 A 19H
8 rue St Saint-Claude 01 42 77 55 80
75003 Paris

MARC DELACRE
Coiffure et Soins Esthétiques
Pour Hommes
Soins Cheveux Corps Visage
Manucure Pédicure Médicale
UV, Sauna, Hammam
Restaurant, Cireur, Voiturier
17 av George V
75008 Paris.................................. 01 40 99 77 70

Une histoire de cheveux
Comédie en 4 scènes

Teaching Strategy

Use the *Avant de lire* questions to focus student interest on the theme of the story and generate a pre-reading discussion.

As a follow-up, students may write their own **Histoire de cheveux**. Personalizing the reading can help students to pay closer attention to the storyline and develop their reading skills.

Scène 1

Patrick, 15 ans, a un problème commun à tous les jeunes de son âge.
Il n'a jamais assez d'argent. Alors, de temps en temps, il en demande à son père.
Malheureusement, aujourd'hui, celui-ci n'est pas d'humeur généreuse.

— Dis, Papa, tu peux me donner un peu d'argent?

— Mais, je t'ai donné vingt euros la semaine dernière.

— S'il te plaît, papa, c'est la dernière fois que je t'en demande.

— N'insiste pas, Patrick, la dernière fois, c'était la dernière
    fois…

Le père de Patrick examine son fils de plus près.

— Dis donc, Patrick, tourne-toi un peu.

Patrick se retourne.

— Tu as les cheveux drôlement longs.

— Mais Papa, c'est la mode.

— Eh bien, moi, je n'aime pas tellement la mode des cheveux longs…
    Il faut absolument que tu ailles chez le coiffeur.

— Tu oublies que je n'ai pas d'argent.

— Ah oui, c'est vrai. Combien est-ce que ça coûte, une coupe de cheveux?

— Dans les° quinze euros.

— Bon. Eh bien, voilà. Je te donne vingt euros, mais je ne veux plus voir
    cette horrible tignasse!

— Merci, papa, à ce soir!

dans les = approximativement

une tignasse

Mots utiles	
l'humeur	*mood*
se tourner	*to turn around*
de près	*closely, from close up*
de temps en temps	*from time to time*

Langage familier

drôlement = vraiment
tellement = beaucoup

Avez-vous compris?

1. Qu'est-ce que Patrick demande à son père?
2. Pourquoi est-ce que le père refuse?
3. Qu'est-ce qu'il remarque quand il examine Patrick de près?
4. Qu'est-ce qu'il demande à son fils de faire?
5. Combien d'argent lui donne-t-il?

Anticipons un peu!

Selon vous, est-ce que Patrick va aller chez le coiffeur ou non? Expliquez pourquoi.

■ *Avez-vous compris?*

(Sample answers)

1. Il lui demande de l'argent.
2. Il refuse parce qu'il lui a donné vingt euros la semaine dernière.
3. Il remarque que Patrick a les cheveux longs.
4. Il lui demande d'aller chez le coiffeur.
5. Il lui donne vingt euros.

■ **Teaching Strategy**

Ask students to discuss the following questions:

• Quelle coupe de cheveux est à la mode en ce moment? Décrivez-la.
• Aimez-vous cette coupe?
• La prochaine fois que vous allez chez le coiffeur, quel type de coupe allez-vous choisir?

Scène 2

25   Patrick prend le billet de vingt euros que son père a sorti de son portefeuille, puis il met son blouson et quitte la maison. En route, il rencontre Béatrice, une nouvelle élève du lycée où il va. C'est une grande fille brune avec de merveilleux yeux bleus. Patrick la trouve très

30   sympa et très mignonne, mais jusqu'ici, il n'a pas eu vraiment l'occasion de lui parler.

    — Salut, Béatrice! Ça va?

    — Oui, ça va.

35   — Dis donc, où est-ce que tu vas comme ça?

    — Je vais au ciné.

    — Qu'est-ce que tu vas voir?

    — Le dernier film de Depardieu. Il paraît° que c'est génial… Si tu veux, on peut y aller ensemble.

40   Patrick voudrait bien accepter la proposition de Béatrice. Malheureusement, il y a cette maudite° coupe de cheveux.

    — Euh, c'est que je dois aller chez le coiffeur.

    — Mais, pourquoi? Je t'aime bien comme ça avec tes cheveux longs…

    Patrick rougit.

45   — Malheureusement, j'ai un père qui préférerait me voir avec les cheveux courts.

    — Ah bon, je comprends… Écoute, j'ai une idée!

    — Quoi donc?

    — On peut aller au ciné, et puis après, on peut aller chez moi. Mon

50   père est coiffeur. Il va te faire une coupe super… Et, en plus, tu économiseras ton argent.

    — Ben, oui, c'est une idée! Tu es bien sûre que ton père sera chez toi tout à l'heure?

    — Absolument! C'est son jour de congé aujourd'hui.

55   — Alors, dans ce cas, j'accepte!

il paraît que = on dit que   maudite *darned*

Mots utiles

un jour de congé	*day off*
rougir	*to blush*
jusqu'ici	*until now*
tout à l'heure	*in a while*

Avez-vous compris?

1. Qui est Béatrice et qu'est-ce que Patrick pense d'elle?
2. Pourquoi Patrick n'accepte-t-il pas immédiatement la proposition de Béatrice?
3. Selon vous, pourquoi Patrick rougit-il?
4. Quelle solution Béatrice propose-t-elle à Patrick?

Anticipons un peu!

Selon vous, qu'est-ce qui va se passer après le film?

■ Notes linguistiques

- **Un congé** is a short period of time taken off from work, such as a national holiday, or a weekend. **Les vacances** implies a longer period of time off.
- **se rendre compte** = to realize (**Rappel: réaliser** = to achieve)

■ *Avez-vous compris?*

(Sample answers)

1. Béatrice est une nouvelle élève du lycée. Patrick la trouve très sympa et mignonne.
2. Il n'accepte pas immédiatement la proposition de Béatrice parce qu'il doit aller chez le coiffeur.
3. Il rougit parce que Béatrice lui dit des choses gentilles et il est un peu amoureux d'elle.
4. Elle propose que son père, qui est coiffeur, coupe les cheveux de Patrick après le cinéma.

172 Unité 4

Teaching Strategy: Expansion

Expansion linguistique

Remind students of the difference between forms in written and spoken French. Ask students if similar differences exist in spoken and written English; ask for examples.

Then point out the abbreviations used in spoken French which appear in this story:

sympa (sympathique)
le ciné (le cinéma)
Et aussi: **T'en fais pas** (**ne t'en fais pas** **s'en faire** = to worry *fam.*),
c'est pas si mal (**ce n'est pas si mal**).

Scène 3

Patrick et Béatrice sont allés au cinéma. Après le film, Patrick a invité Béatrice dans un petit restaurant italien où ils ont mangé une pizza. Ensuite, ils sont allés chez Béatrice. Là, ils ont une mauvaise surprise: il n'y a personne à la maison. Patrick s'inquiète.

— Où est ton père?

— Je ne sais pas! Il a dû faire un tour en ville avec ma mère. Ne t'inquiète pas. Je suis sûre qu'ils rentreront bientôt.

Une heure passe, et toujours personne. Finalement, le téléphone sonne. C'est la mère de Béatrice qui lui dit de ne pas l'attendre. Elle et son mari sont invités à dîner chez des amis. Ils ne vont pas rentrer avant onze heures. Béatrice se rend compte du problème.

— Dis, Patrick, mes parents ne vont pas rentrer ce soir.

— Et ma coupe de cheveux?

— T'en fais pas! C'est moi qui vais te les couper.

— Comment? Tu sais couper les cheveux, toi?

— Ben oui, tu sais, j'ai souvent regardé mon père.

Patrick n'est pas très rassuré, mais il n'a pas le choix. Il est bien obligé d'accepter l'offre de Béatrice.

Béatrice va chercher les ciseaux de son père. Elle demande à Patrick de s'asseoir sur un tabouret. Puis, elle commence à lui couper les cheveux. Clic, une mèche par ci! Clac, une mèche par là. Clic! Clac! Clic! Clic! Il est bien évident que Béatrice n'a jamais coupé de cheveux de sa vie et le résultat est un véritable désastre. Elle a beau° passer° de l'eau et du gel fixatif sur les cheveux de Patrick, elle n'arrive pas à masquer les échelles qu'elle a faites de tous les côtés.

Patrick se regarde dans la glace. Il comprend alors l'ampleur° de la catastrophe.

— Mon Dieu, qu'est-ce que je vais faire?

Béatrice essaie de le rassurer.

— Écoute, c'est pas si mal que ça! Mets-toi un peu dans l'obscurité°… Non, ce n'est pas trop mal. Un conseil: quand tu seras chez toi, ne te mets pas trop près de la lumière, et personne ne verra rien.

Mais Patrick n'écoute pas. Il prend son blouson et sort de chez Béatrice, très inquiet…

Mots utiles

un côté	side
un désastre	= une catastrophe
la lumière	light
arriver à	to manage to
sonner	to ring

Langage familier

t'en fais pas = ne t'inquiète pas

un tabouret

une mèche

des échelles

elle a beau = c'est en vain qu'elle essaie de
passer = mettre
ampleur *extent*
l'obscurité = un endroit où il fait noir

Avez-vous compris?

1. Pourquoi est-ce que Patrick s'inquiète?
2. Qu'est-ce que la mère de Béatrice annonce à sa fille quand elle lui téléphone?
3. Qu'est-ce que Béatrice fait pour résoudre le problème de Patrick?
4. Comment réussit-elle dans ce projet? Expliquez.
5. Qu'est-ce qu'elle conseille à Patrick de faire pour ne pas être trop visible?

Anticipons un peu!

Selon vous, quelle va être la réaction du père de Patrick quand il va voir son fils? Est-ce qu'il va être heureux? furieux? perplexe? Expliquez pourquoi.

■ *Avez-vous compris?*

(Sample answers)

1. Il s'inquiète parce que les parents de Béatrice ne sont pas chez eux.
2. Elle lui dit qu'elle et son père rentreront tard.
3. Béatrice coupe elle-même les cheveux de Patrick.
4. C'est une catastrophe! Elle coupe trop, et mal, elle fait des échelles de tous les côtés.
5. Elle lui dit de ne pas se mettre près de la lumière.

■ **Verb**

s'inquiéter is conjugated like **espérer**:
je m'inquiète
nous nous inquiétons
ils s'inquiètent

■ **Teaching Strategy: Expansion**

Ask students:
Pourquoi Patrick est-il obligé d'accepter de se faire couper les cheveux par Béatrice?

Scène 4

Vingt minutes après, Patrick arrive chez lui. 100
Il a l'air vraiment pitoyable. Sa mère ne peut
pas s'empêcher de rire.

— Mon pauvre Patrick! Tu as l'air d'un
chat qui est tombé dans l'eau…
Qui est-ce qui t'a coupé les cheveux? 105
Allez, dis-moi la vérité.

Patrick hésite un peu. Puis, il raconte à sa
mère ce qui s'est passé.
Celle-ci essaie de le consoler.

—Tu as de la chance! Ton père n'est pas encore rentré! En 110
attendant qu'il rentre, je vais essayer d'arranger cela!

Elle va dans la salle de bains chercher la tondeuse qu'elle utilisait
quand Patrick était petit. Puis elle commence l'opération… En cinq
minutes, elle a complètement tondu le crâne de Patrick.

— C'est un peu court, mais au moins ça peut passer… 115

Puis elle va ranger la tondeuse pendant que Patrick va se regarder
dans la glace.

— J'ai la boule à zéro! Qu'est-ce que mes copains vont penser
de moi?

— Ils vont trouver ça très bien. Je suis sûre que tu vas lancer 120
une nouvelle mode… Tiens, voilà ton père.

Le père de Patrick vient en effet de rentrer. Il regarde Patrick avec
surprise.

— Bravo, mon garçon! Tu as beaucoup de courage… Je te
félicite! Tiens, pour te récompenser, je vais t'emmener au 125
cinéma ce soir. Est-ce que tu veux aller voir le dernier film de
Depardieu? Il paraît que c'est très bon!

— Merci, Papa, …mais j'ai des devoirs à faire!

— Comme tu veux! Et excuse-moi d'avoir été un peu brusque
avec toi cet après-midi. 130

la tondeuse

le crâne

avoir la boule à zéro

Teaching Note

For an overview of a Gérard
Depardieu movie, see **Cyrano de
Bergerac**, pp. 142–145.

Verb

Convaincre is conjugated like
vaincre:
je convaincs
il convainc
nous convainquons
ils convainquent

Avez-vous compris?

(Sample answers)
1. Elle rit.
2. Elle utilise la tondeuse.
3. Il a le crâne complètement tondu,
«la boule à zéro».
4. Il est surpris et fier de son fils. Il
admire son courage.
5. Il lui propose d'aller voir le
dernier film de Depardieu
avec lui.
6. Patrick répond qu'il ne peut pas
parce qu'il a des devoirs. Mais la
vraie raison, c'est qu'il vient de
voir ce film avec Béatrice.

Irregular Verb

(see Appendix C)
rire

Mots utiles

arranger	*to fix*
s'empêcher de	*to stop, prevent oneself from*
lancer	*to launch*
récompenser	*to reward*
rire *	*to laugh*
tondre	*to clip very short*
pitoyable	*pitiful*

Avez-vous compris?

1. Quelle est la réaction de la mère de Patrick quand elle voit
son fils?
2. Qu'est-ce qu'elle fait pour aider Patrick?
3. Quel est le résultat de cette action?
4. Quelle est la réaction du père de Patrick?
5. Qu'est-ce qu'il propose à son fils?
6. Qu'est-ce que Patrick répond à l'invitation de son père?
Quelle est la véritable raison de son refus?

APRÈS LA LECTURE

Expression orale

Dramatisation

En petits groupes, préparez une lecture dramatique de cette histoire. Chaque groupe présentera une scène.

- D'abord, choisissez un narrateur et distribuez les autres rôles.
- Pendant les parties «narratives», les acteurs feront les gestes et montreront les émotions indiquées.
- Pendant les dialogues, chaque acteur lira son texte avec beaucoup d'expression.

Situations

Avec votre partenaire, choisissez l'une des situations suivantes. Composez le dialogue correspondant et jouez-le en classe.

1   Au téléphone

Le soir, après le dîner, Béatrice téléphone à Patrick pour lui demander ce qui est arrivé quand il est rentré chez lui. Patrick le lui explique.

Les rôles: Béatrice, Patrick

2   En classe

Le lendemain, un(e) camarade de classe de Patrick est très étonné(e) de voir son ami avec «la boule à zéro». Il/ Elle lui demande ce qui s'est passé. Patrick lui répond. (Patrick peut lui dire la vérité ou bien il peut inventer une histoire complètement différente.)

Les rôles: le/la camarade de classe, Patrick

3   La nouvelle mode

Maintenant, Patrick est très fier de sa nouvelle coiffure. Il explique à un autre copain les avantages d'avoir «la boule à zéro» et il essaie de le convaincre de faire la même chose. Le copain n'est pas tellement convaincu.

Les rôles: Patrick, le copain

Expression écrite

Imaginons un peu

Quelle va être la réaction des copains de Patrick quand celui-ci ira au lycée demain matin? Qu'est-ce que Patrick va leur dire? À vous d'écrire la Scène 5.

Page de journal

Imaginez que vous êtes Patrick ou Béatrice. Écrivez une page ou deux dans votre journal intime *(diary)* où vous ferez un résumé des événements de la journée.

■ **Teaching Notes**

- You may wish to use the short **Lecture** quiz as a comprehension check or as an assessment option. Use the **Transparency Copymasters** to expand/retell the story.

■ **Teaching Strategy: Expansion**

Pose this problem scenario to students:

Votre meilleur(e) ami(e) arrive à l'école avec la boule à zéro. Quelle est votre réaction? Que lui dites-vous? Imaginez votre dialogue.

Rôles: Vous, votre ami(e)

■ **Expression écrite**

For writing rubrics, consult the **Generate Success** Rubric Generator on the **Teacher One Stop**. You can also create your own custom rubrics with this tool.

Student Portfolios

Use the *Situations* to prepare dialogs on audio or video for portfolios or presentation.

Use the *Page de journal* above as the basis for student writing samples. If your students enjoy performing, you may also use the *Expression orale* suggestion as the basis for recording or presenting a dramatic reading of the story.

■ **Pour en savoir plus**
Much of the historical material mentioned in this text is developed in other *Interludes culturels:*
• la Chanson de Roland, pp. 102–103
• le Moyen Âge, p. 98
• Louis XIV, p. 140–141
• la Révolution française, p. 216
• la Résistance et la guerre de 1940, pp. 252–256

Use the **Projectable Transparencies** to help students situate the various musical periods within a larger historical context.

■ **Note culturelle**
Beaumarchais codified the saying "tout finit par des chansons" in his play *Le mariage de Figaro* (1778).

■ **Teaching Note**
Introduce students to such hits as *Les Passants* by Georges Brassens, *Les Grands Boulevards* by Yves Montand, and *Quelque chose de Tennessee* by Johnny Hallyday.

Histoire de la chanson française

Un proverbe français dit que «tout finit par des chansons». On pourrait° dire aussi que tout a commencé par une chanson. L'histoire de la chanson française est en effet un peu l'histoire de France. La première grande oeuvre° littéraire française date du douzième siècle.° C'était une chanson: *La Chanson de Roland*.

Troubadour du Moyen Âge

Au Moyen Âge,° les **«troubadours»** allaient de cour° en cour en chantant des poèmes qu'ils composaient. Au dix-huitième siècle, les soldats allaient à la guerre en chantant des chansons comme «Malbrough s'en va-t-en guerre»° ou «Auprès° de ma blonde». En 1789, les Français ont fait la Révolution en chantant «Ça ira!»° Pendant la guerre de 1940, le «Chant des partisans» était le cri de ralliement° de la Résistance contre les troupes allemandes.

Mais la chanson n'est pas seulement un phénomène historique. C'est aussi un art populaire et un spectacle. Les premiers chanteurs populaires chantaient dans la rue. Ils recevaient un peu d'argent si leurs chansons étaient bonnes… et parfois un seau° d'eau sur la tête si leurs chansons étaient mauvaises.

Plus tard, la chanson a fait son entrée dans les **«cabarets»**. Le cabaret le plus célèbre était un cabaret de Montmartre qui s'appelait le «Chat noir». C'était un cabaret artistique où se réunissaient° les peintres, les musiciens, les poètes, les étudiants pour écouter les «chansonniers» de l'époque. Ces chansonniers chantaient surtout des chansons politiques, des chansons satiriques et parfois des chansons comiques.

Picasso *«Femme à la Mandoline»*

Le *«Chat Noir»*, cabaret artistique à Montmartre.

pourrait *could* **oeuvre** *work* **siècle** *century* **au Moyen Âge** *in the Middle Ages* **cour** *court* **s'en va-t-en guerre** *goes off to war* **auprès de** *next to*
ça ira *things will go well* **cri de ralliement** *rallying cry* **seau** *bucket* **se réunissaient** *used to get together*

Teaching Strategy: Cultural Connection

You may wish to begin the presentation of this *Interlude culturel* by bringing in recordings of French songs to class. The songs listed under *Leurs grands succès* are appropriate, but you may want to introduce other songs that you particularly like. The recordings may be from any of the periods or artists mentioned. Students should scan the information in the *Interlude* while listening to the music.

Leurs grands succès

Édith Piaf:
La vie en rose
Mon légionnaire, Milord
Non, je ne regrette rien

Yves Montand:
Les feuilles mortes
Les grands boulevards
À Paris
Mon manège à moi

Georges Brassens:
Chanson pour l'Auvergnat
Une jolie fleur
Auprès de mon arbre
Les croquants

Jacques Brel:
Ne me quitte pas
Amsterdam
Le plat pays

Charles Aznavour:
La Mamma
Il faut savoir
Tu te laisses aller

Le grand public, lui, allait au «café-concert» ou au «music-hall». Dans les années 1930, la grande vedette° était **Joséphine Baker**, une danseuse noire américaine que tout le monde applaudissait quand elle chantait «J'ai deux amours: mon pays et Paris». Peu après, les Français ont découvert **Édith Piaf**, célèbre pour ses robes noires et sa voix terriblement poignante. Dans les années 1960, avec le développement de l'amplificateur et le succès de la guitare électrique, une nouvelle forme de chanson est apparue en France. C'était la chanson «yé-yé». Ce qui comptait,° ce n'était plus° le texte de la chanson, mais son rythme et surtout les contorsions du chanteur ou de la chanteuse sur scène° . . . La vedette de l'époque était **Johnny Hallyday** qui en quelques mois est devenue l'idole des jeunes Français. La chanson personnelle n'a cependant pas disparu. Elle est restée vivante° et variée avec **Georges Brassens**, l'anarchiste sympa, **Yves Montand**, le gentleman romantique, **Jacques Brel**, le poète venu du pays des brumes,° et **Charles Aznavour**, le petit bonhomme° à la voix grêle.°

Yves Montand   *Georges Brassens*   *Jacques Brel*   *Charles Aznavour*

Les vedettes d'hier . . .

Édith Piaf (1915-1963)

Édith Piaf a disparu il y a plus de quarante ans, mais sa voix est restée immortelle. Pour les millions de gens qui ont écouté cette voix vibrante d'émotion, elle est toujours la plus grande des chanteuses françaises. Édith Piaf a eu une enfance° misérable. Elle est née dans la rue et c'est dans la rue qu'elle a commencé à chanter pour gagner quelques pièces d'argent.° Un jour, alors° qu'elle chantait au coin° du boulevard MacMahon à Paris, le directeur d'un cabaret célèbre l'a entendue. Ému° par sa voix poignante, il l'a immédiatement engagée.° La phénoménale carrière de Piaf venait de commencer.

Le succès de ses chansons est facile à expliquer. Édith Piaf a chanté passionnément sa vie passionnée. Cette vie a été faite de moments heureux et surtout de moments tragiques. C'est donc avec une extraordinaire sincérité qu'Édith Piaf pouvait chanter le bonheur et le malheur, la fatalité et l'espoir,° l'amour merveilleux et l'amour désespéré. Quand Édith Piaf était sur scène, le public ne pouvait pas faire la différence entre sa vie et ses chansons.

---

vedette *star* **ce qui comptait** *what counted* **plus** *no longer* **sur scène** *on the stage* **vivante** *alive* **brumes** *fog, mist*
bonhomme = *homme* **grêle** *frail* **enfance** *childhood* **pièces d'argent** *coins* **alors que** *while* **au coin** *on the corner*
ému *moved* **embauchée** *hired* **espoir** *hope*

■ Notes linguistiques

- **Le café-théâtre** is a café where people can watch new plays or performance artists.
- **Le music-hall** generally presents variety and vaudeville acts, reviews, and singers.

■ Notes culturelles

- Up to 1914, French people could go to le **café-concert** (or **le caf'conc'**) to watch vaudeville acts.
- **Jacques Brel** was born in Brussels in 1929. The quality and poignancy of his lyrics made him one of the best French songwriters. He spent his last years living on the Marquesas Islands (**les îles Marquises**) before dying in France in 1978.
- **Georges Brassens** (1921–1981) sang his poems accompanying himself on an acoustic guitar. He was able to play with and manipulate the French language into witty lyrics, expressing gentle mockery and nonconformism.
- **Yves Montand** was born in Italy in 1921. He made his career in France as a singer and actor, playing leads in such movies as **Le Salaire de la peur** (Wages of Fear). He died in 1991.
- **Charles Aznavour** is a singer and actor. He was born in Armenia in 1924.

Expansion

Internet Connection – Interlude 4
Visit **http://my.hrw.com** for more information and useful links about French music.

Connections
Standard 3.1 Students reinforce and further their knowledge of other disciplines through French.

■ **Anecdote**

Jean-Claude Baker, one of Joséphine Baker's adopted sons, runs a French restaurant in New York City called **Chez Joséphine**.

Joséphine Baker (1906–1975)

Joséphine Baker sur scène

Joséphine Baker était une artiste de music-hall. Pour des millions de Français, elle a aussi été une grande héroïne nationale. Pourtant Joséphine Baker n'était pas d'origine française, mais américaine. Elle est née dans une famille pauvre de la ville de Saint Louis dans le Missouri. À seize ans, elle est partie à New York pour faire une carrière dans le théâtre. Mais là, victime de la discrimination et du chômage,° elle n'a pas trouvé de travail.

Heureusement, un jour, la chance° lui a souri.° Un imprésario français l'a embauchée° pour faire une tournée° en France avec un groupe d'artistes noirs américains. Joséphine a fait ses débuts au Théâtre des Champs-Élysées en octobre 1925. Chacune° de ses entrées en scène était un triomphe. Pendant cette tournée, Joséphine Baker est tombée amoureuse° de Paris et Paris est tombé amoureux de «l'oiseau des îles». Joséphine Baker était la grande star du spectacle. Tous les soirs, elle donnait aux Français des leçons de danse. Bientôt, toute la France s'est mise° à danser le charleston. En quelques semaines, Joséphine Baker est devenue la reine° de Paris. Elle avait tout juste vingt ans.

Joséphine Baker a fait de nombreuses tournées à travers° l'Europe, mais c'est en France qu'elle se sentait chez elle.° En 1937, elle a décidé d'adopter la nationalité française. Pendant la guerre, fidèle° à son nouveau pays, elle a travaillé dans la Résistance. Pour ses services, elle a reçu les deux plus hautes décorations françaises: la Légion d'honneur et la Médaille de la Résistance. Pour la cérémonie, Joséphine Baker portait son uniforme de lieutenant de l'Armée de l'Air Française.

Après la guerre, Joséphine Baker a voyagé aux États-Unis. En butte° à nouveau à la discrimination, elle a décidé de se fixer° définitivement en France et de consacrer sa vie et sa fortune aux oeuvres° de charité. Elle a acheté un château pour accueillir° une douzaine d'orphelins de différentes races qu'elle avait adoptés et sauvés de la faim° et de la misère. C'était sa «tribu arc-en-ciel».° Ses ressources financières n'étant plus° suffisantes, elle est remontée sur scène à l'âge de 69 ans pour subvenir aux besoins° de sa famille d'adoption. À nouveau elle a connu le succès et c'est en plein triomphe qu'elle est morte en 1975.

Le jour de son enterrement,° la France entière a pris le deuil.° À Paris, une foule° immense a suivi le cortège funèbre.° Vingt et un coups de canon° ont été tirés° en son honneur: le plus grand adieu° français réservé à une femme américaine!

Joséphine Baker et sa «tribu arc-en-ciel»

---

chômage *unemployment* **chance** *luck* **souri** *smiled* **embauchée** *hired* **tournée** *tour* **chacune** *each one* **tombée amoureuse de** *fell in love with*
s'est mise à *began to* **reine** *queen* **à travers** *across* **se sentait chez elle** *felt at home* **fidèle =** *loyale* **en butte à** *faced with* **se fixer** *to settle*
oeuvres *works* **accueillir** *to provide shelter* **faim** *hunger* **arc-en-ciel** *rainbow* **n'étant plus** *no longer being* **subvenir aux besoins** *meet the needs*
enterrement *funeral* **pris le deuil** *went into mourning* **foule** *crowd* **cortège funèbre** *funeral procession* **vingt et un coups de canon** *21-gun salute*
tirés *fired* **adieu** *farewell*

... et vedettes d'aujourd'hui

Yannick Noah

Yannick Noah a deux passions: le tennis et la musique. À l'âge de trois ans, il va au Cameroun, pays d'origine de son père. Là, il est découvert par Arthur Ashe, le grand champion américain de tennis. Rentré en France, il devient quatre fois champion national et gagne le French Open à Roland-Garros.

Puis il se tourne vers la musique. Avec des albums comme *Charango* (2006) et *Frontières* (2010), c'est l'un des chanteurs français les plus populaires. Son style évoque le soul, le reggae et la chanson traditionnelle française. Ses chansons, inspirées par sa double origine, africaine et européenne, ont des thèmes humanitaires. Généreux, Yannick Noah est actif dans les organisation caritatives° comme «Les Enfants de la Terre» créée par sa mère.

Nowell Leroy

Nowell Leroy est née en Bretagne. À seize ans, elle découvre les États-Unis avec un programme d'échange du Rotary Club. À l'université, elle étudie le droit international, mais elle préfère la musique. De sa voix chaude et mélodieuse, elle chante ses propres° compositions et aussi les chansons du folklore breton sur des rythmes de musique celtique. Elle chante en français, en anglais, en breton et aussi en gaélique irlandais.

---
caricatives *charitable*   **propres** *own*

Bénabar

Bénabar s'appelle en réalité Bruno Nicolini. Il commence sa carrière dans le cinéma avec des petits films. Puis il commence à écrire des chansons qui évoquent avec humour les événements de la vie quotidienne. Parmi° ses grands succès, on peut citer *Dis-lui oui!*, *Le Dîner*, *L'Effet papillon°* et *Quatre murs° et un toit°*.

Zaz

Zaz est la grande révélation musicale de l'année 2010. De son vrai nom, elle s'appelle Isabelle Geffroy. Très jeune, elle étudie le piano, le violon et la guitare au Conservatoire de la ville de Tours. Puis, elle va à Paris où elle compose des chansons qu'elle chante dans le rues avec des amis musiciens. Son premier disque, *Je veux*, connaît un succès extraordinaire avec une vente° de plus d'un million d'exemplaires. Dans cette chanson, Zaz exprime son désir de vivre une vie simple pleine de joie et d'amour.

Christophe Maé

Très jeune, Christophe Maé doit abandonner le sport à cause d'une maladie chronique. Il apprend alors à jouer de la guitare et de l'harmonica. Inspiré par la musique de Stevie Wonder et de Bob Marley, il commence à chanter. Aujourd'hui il compose ses propres chansons. Ses singles, comme *Demoiselle* et *Dingue,° Dingue, Dingue*, connaissent un succès phénoménal. En 2011, il est décoré par le gouvernement français et devient "Chevalier des arts et des lettres".

Parmi *Among*   **papillon** *butterfly*   **murs** *walls*   **toit** *roof*   **vente** *sale*
Dingue *crazy*

SUPPLEMENTARY VOCABULARY

le CD *CD, compact disc*
la compilation (la compil) *compilation*
le compositeur *composer*
le disque d'or/de platine *gold/platinum record*
le single *single (record)*
le tube *(fam.) hit*
la vedette *star*

■ Note linguistique

Le hit-parade (*pl.* **les hit-parades**) lists the top singers, songs, actors, or movies of the moment. The French government recommends the use of **le palmarès** instead of **le hit-parade**.

RESOURCES

TECHNOLOGY

Teacher One Stop

▶ DVD Program, Unit 4 *Vignette culturelle*

SUPPLEMENTARY VOCABULARY

le clip *video clip*
le hip-hop *hip-hop music*
rapper *to sing/play rap music*
le rapper *rap artist*
la tournée *tour*

■ Notes culturelles

- **MC Solaar** is the stage name of **Claude M'Barali**. He pronounces MC as in English: "emcee."
- **Ménélik** is a French rap artist, originally from Cameroon. His album **O.Q.P.** is available in the U.S. as is MC Solaar's album **Le tour de la question**.
- Since January 1, 1996, at least 40% of the songs played on French radio stations must be in French. This new law has boosted French rap sales and widened its audience by giving it more air time.
- Other French-speaking African artists whose albums are sold in the US: **Ismael Lo** was dubbed the Bob Dylan of Senegal. Album: **Iso** (Mango records). **Salif Keita**, from Mali, has worked on the music of Disney's Lion King *(Le Roi Lion)*. Album: Folon (**"le passé,"** Mango Islands records).

La musique des jeunes

«De la musique avant toute chose» a dit un poète français.* Aujourd'hui, la musique fait partie de la vie de tout le monde, et en particulier des jeunes. À la maison, on peut écouter des CD et télécharger de la musique sur son ordinateur. Quand on se promène dans la rue ou quand on fait du jogging, on peut écouter son lecteur MP3.

Pour exprimer leur amour de la musique, les Français organisent chaque année une grande fête nationale appelée «la Fête de la Musique». Cette fête a lieu le vingt et un juin. Dans toutes les villes de France, il y a des concerts publics gratuits.° Ce jour-là, tous les Français sont dans la rue. Ils dansent, chantent, ou bien, ils écoutent la musique des orchestres° qui jouent un peu partout° dans les villes. Le slogan du jour est: «Pour la Fête de la Musique, faites de la musique.»

Quelle musique écoute-t-on en France quand on est jeune? En tête° du hit-parade, viennent les stars de la chanson française: **Yannick Noah, Nowell Leroy, Christophe Maé, Bénabar, Zaz...** Mais à côté° de cette musique relativement traditionnelle existe une autre musique très populaire chez les jeunes. Cette musique reflète la réalité multiculturelle de la France d'aujourd'hui. La France est, en effet, une mosaïque de gens d'origines très différentes. À côté des Français de souche,° il y a aussi les immigrés venus d'autres pays européens, du Maghreb,** d'Afrique Noire, d'Asie. . . Chaque groupe a apporté sa culture et, en particulier, sa musique.

La musique française s'est enrichie de ces apports° et aussi des influences d'autres musiques populaires dans le monde: musiques américaine, anglaise, espagnole. . . . Elle est ainsi devenue une musique originale et variée.

■ L'influence américaine: le rap

Le rap est né aux États-Unis dans les années 1980 et depuis il a fait le tour du monde. En France, il est représenté par **MC Solaar**. Ce «Monsieur Rap» est un Français d'origine tchadienne.*** Dans ses chansons, il exprime des messages sociaux positifs où il met en garde° les jeunes contre la violence et la délinquance.

MC Solaar, «Monsieur Rap»

  * Paul Verlaine (1844-1896)
 ** Le Maghreb: l'Algérie, le Maroc, la Tunisie. Ces pays, en majorité arabes et musulmans, sont d'anciennes colonies ou protectorats français.
*** le Tchad: un pays d'Afrique

■ L'influence antillaise: le zouk

Le groupe Kassav

Le zouk vient des **Antilles françaises (Martinique et Guadeloupe)**. Pour les Antillais, «zouk» signifie «fête». Le zouk est donc une musique de fête où s'expriment la joie, l'humour et la fierté° d'être ce qu'on est.

La musique de zouk est typiquement antillaise. Expression de la culture martiniquaise et guadeloupéenne, elle représente la fusion d'éléments caraïbes, africains, français et espagnols. Dans un orchestre de zouk, le chanteur chante en créole. L'instrument principal est le tambour° ou la batterie° qui donne un rythme fort. Les autres instruments sont le synthétiseur, la basse, la guitare et parfois le piano.

Né il y a dix ans, le zouk est très populaire chez les jeunes Français. Il est représenté par des groupes comme *Kassav* (Martinique et Guadeloupe) et *Malavoi* (Martinique). Ces groupes ont fait connaître° le zouk en dehors° de la France et, en particulier, sur la côte est des États-Unis. Aujourd'hui, le zouk a un succès international.

gratuits *free*	**orchestres** *bands*	**partout** *everywhere*	**en tête** *on top*	**à côté** *besides*
de souche *native born*	**les apports** *contributions*	**met en garde** *warns*	**la fierté** *pride*
le tambour *drum*	**la batterie** *drums*	**fait connaître** *made known*	**en dehors** *outside*

Teaching Suggestion: DVD Program

To familiarize students with French music and artists, play the Unit 4 *Vignette culturelle* video segment about *La fête de la musique*.

■ L'influence arabe: le raï

Le raï vient d'**Afrique du Nord** et plus particulièrement d'**Algérie**. Il exprime la mélancolie mais aussi la joie et l'espoir° des jeunes **Maghrébins**. C'est un peu leur «soul music». Le chanteur de raï chante en arabe et parfois en français ou même en anglais. Il est accompagné d'instruments traditionnels et aussi de guitare et de synthétiseur. Les grands représentants du Raï, **Khaled, Faudel** et **Cheb Mami,** sont Algériens ou d'origine algérienne.

Khaled

■ L'influence africaine: le rythme

Depuis une vingtaine d'années, **la musique africaine** a beaucoup de succès en France. Très variée, elle est représentée par un grand nombre de musiciens et de groupes qui viennent des différents pays de l'Afrique francophone.

1. **Touré Kunda** vient du **Sénégal** et chante en wolof,* sa langue maternelle,° et en français. Sa musique est traditionnelle et raffinée.
2. **Youssou N'Dour** vient aussi du **Sénégal**. Ses disques ont été produits aux États-Unis par le cinéaste américain, Spike Lee.
3. Le groupe **Soukous Stars** vient du **Zaïre** et joue de la musique africaine très rythmée avec beaucoup de tambour.
4. Les chanteuses du groupe **Zap Mama** sont d'origine européenne (belge) et africaine (zaïroise). Elles reprennent les chants traditionnels des peuples d'Afrique centrale. Dans d'autres chansons, elles mélangent° le français, l'espagnol, l'arabe et les langues africaines.

■ MANU CHAO

Né en France de parents espagnols, Manu Chao a passé son enfance° dans la banlieue° parisienne. Influencé par le rock anglais, il a fondé° Mano Negra, un groupe de rock alternatif très populaire. Il a quitté ce groupe pour voyager en Espagne, en Amérique latine et en Afrique de l'Ouest. Là, il a enregistré les musiques locales sur un studio portable. Riche de ses expériences, il a décidé de chanter en solo.

Manu Chao écrit et chante en plusieurs langues (français, espagnol, anglais...). Ses chansons parlent de l'état du monde, des immigrants, de solidarité entre les peuples et de la lutte pour la vie°. Quelle que soit° la langue dans laquelle° il est exprimé°, ce message est universellement compris.

Manu Chao

* la principale langue du Sénégal

espoir *hope* **la langue maternelle** *native language* **mélangent** *mix* **enfance** *childhood* **banlieue** *suburbs* **a fondé** *founded* **la lutte pour la vie** *struggle for survival* **quelle que soit** *whatever* **laquelle** *which* **exprimé** *expressed*

■ Notes culturelles

- **Raï** is an Arab word that means "opinion." Raï takes its roots in the music of the Bedouins, the nomadic people of the desert. In the Maghreb, raï was a poetic improvisation sung by its author who used this medium to share his vision of the world. Today, raï reflects the diverse influences of new rhythms, such as pop, reggae, and soul music.
- En mai 1997, le président Laurent Kabila a changé le nom du Zaïre en République démocratique du Congo (le Congo démocratique).

■ Teaching suggestion

Have the students give group presentations on the styles of music mentioned on pages 180–181. They could find samples of recordings at online music stores, or at a public or college library. Ask them what similarities and differences they see between this music and music from their own culture. They can use French search engines to look for information on specific artists.

Teaching Strategy: Community Connections

Ask students if they are familiar with any of the musicians or groups mentioned. If so, they may be able to bring in recordings to share with the class. While playing music, ask students to compare the music from the francophone world to music they listen to at home. Do they see similarities? What differences can they point out? Have each student discuss his/her personal reaction.

Notes culturelles

- **Céline Dion**, born into a French-speaking Quebec family, now sings in English as well as French. She became internationally known for singing the title songs of popular movies such as *Beauty and the Beast* (**La Belle et la Bête**) and *Titanic*.
- **Gilles Vigneault** was born in Natashquan, Quebec, in 1928.
- **Laissez les bons temps rouler**, the literal translation of "Let the good times roll," is the unofficial motto of New Orleans.

Notes linguistiques

- Notez qu'en Louisiane, on prononce **les haricots** avec liaison: /lezarico/.
- Certains attribuent une origine plus ancienne au mot **zydéco** qui pourrait être un terme africain.
- Le terme **la-la** est encore utilisé par les francophones d'origine africaine. Il désigne une musique de danse, voisine du zydéco, ou la danse elle-même.
- En pays cajun, particulièrement dans les zones rurales, il y avait de nombreuses familles d'origine africaine dont la langue maternelle était le français. Certains de leurs descendants parlent encore français.

La musique francophone en Amérique

La chanson québécoise

Au Québec, chanter c'est affirmer son identité et sa culture, c'est exprimer sa fierté° d'être différent, c'est manifester° sa joie de vivre. Les interprètes de la chanson québécoise sont nombreux: **Gilles Vigneault**, le «poète de la chanson» qui chante son pays, **Isabelle Boulay**, **Garou** (de son vrai nom, **Pierre Garand**) et **Céline Dion**, qui est devenue une grande vedette° aux États-Unis.

Il faut également° mentionner les chanteurs acadiens du Nouveau Brunswick comme **Roch Voisine**, devenu une «idole» en France.

Céline Dion

La musique cajun

En pays cajun, on travaille dur,° mais on aime aussi la nourriture, la fête, la musique et la danse. Il n'est donc pas surprenant° que le grand événement de l'année soit le festival de musique cajun qui a lieu au mois de septembre à Lafayette.

On vient de toute la région pour écouter la musique et danser aux sons° des orchestres de musique cajun et de zydéco.

La musique cajun est une musique de fête, très rythmée, où les musiciens utilisent des instruments traditionnels comme le violon, l'accordéon et la guitare, et où le chanteur mélange° l'anglais, le vieux français et le français moderne. Cette musique descend directement de la musique acadienne d'autrefois, mais au cours° des siècles et au contact de groupes ethniques différents, elle s'est enrichie d'éléments anglais, espagnols, indiens et africains. Aujourd'hui, grâce° à ses interprètes comme **Zachary Richard** et le groupe **Beausoleil**, la musique cajun connaît un regain° de popularité non seulement en Louisiane, mais dans tout le monde francophone.

Un orchestre joue du zydéco au festival

Le zydéco

Le **zydéco** tire son nom du mot français «les haricots» et plus précisément du titre d'une chanson célèbre «Les haricots sont pas salés» composée par le légendaire **Clifton Chénier** (1925-1987). Le zydéco est né en Louisiane dans la région de Lafayette. C'est la forme moderne du **la-la**, musique de danse traditionnelle des Louisianais francophones d'origine africaine.

Le zydéco est une variété de musique cajun, encore plus rythmée avec des accents de rock et de blues. Le chanteur chante en français ou en anglais et s'accompagne toujours d'un accordéon qui est l'instrument caractéristique du zydéco.

Clifton Chénier

la fierté *pride* **manifester** *montrer* **vedette** *star* **également** *aussi* **dur** *hard* **surprenant** *surprising* **les sons** *beat* **mélange** *mixes* **au cours** *across* **grâce à** *thanks to* **regain** *renewal*

Teaching Strategy: Challenge

Ask students to compare the Canadian and French phrases. Are there particular usages (such as the importation of English words) that seem more frequent in one than the other?

Quelques expressions canadiennes:	Expressions françaises correspondantes:
faire du magasinage	faire du shopping/des achats
la fin de semaine	le week-end
séraphin *(adj.)*	avare
la gang	la bande d'amis/de copains
le fun	l'amusement
le char	la voiture

Une chanson: Mon pays ✳ ✳ ✳ ✳ ✳ ✳ ✳

Mon pays ce n'est pas un pays c'est l'hiver
Mon jardin ce n'est pas un jardin c'est la plaine
Mon chemin ce n'est pas un chemin c'est la neige°
Mon pays ce n'est pas un pays c'est l'hiver

Dans la blanche cérémonie
Où la neige au vent° se marie
Dans ce pays de poudrerie°
Mon père a fait bâtir° maison
Et je m'en vais être fidèle°
À sa manière à son modèle
La chambre d'amis sera telle°
Qu'on viendra des autres saisons
Pour se bâtir à côté° d'elle

Mon pays ce n'est pas un pays c'est l'hiver
Mon refrain ce n'est pas un refrain c'est rafale°
Ma maison ce n'est pas une maison c'est froidure°
Mon pays ce n'est pas un pays c'est l'hiver

De mon grand pays solitaire
Je crie° avant que de me taire
À tous les hommes de la terre
Ma maison c'est votre maison
Entre mes quatre murs de glace°
Je mets mon temps et mon espace
À préparer le feu° la place
Pour les humains de l'horizon
Et les humains sont de ma race

Mon pays ce n'est pas un pays c'est l'envers°
D'un pays qui n'était ni pays ni patrie°
Ma chanson ce n'est pas ma chanson c'est ma vie
C'est pour toi que je veux posséder mes hivers

Gilles Vigneault

Dans les chansons qu'il compose, Gilles Vigneault exprime l'amour, l'amitié, la joie, l'attachement à son pays. Voici l'une des ses chansons les plus connues: *Mon pays*.

la neige *snow* **le vent** *wind* **la poudrerie** *powdery snow* **bâtir = construire** **fidèle** *faithful* **telle** *such* **à côté de** *next to* **rafale** *gust of wind*
la froidure *cold weather* **crie** *scream* **la glace** *ice* **le feu** *fire* **l'envers** *reverse* **la patrie** *motherland*

Teaching Strategy: Expansion

There are many excellent recordings of *Mon pays* which may be played for students. If any of the students play an instrument or sing, perhaps they might perform the song, giving their own interpretation. Illustrations of the song may also be created and displayed in the classroom, or used for Parents' Night activities.

Et la musique classique?

Quand on pense à la musique classique, on pense généralement aux grands compositeurs allemands (Mozart, Beethoven . . .) ou italiens (Vivaldi, Verdi . . .). À tort,° on a tendance à oublier la musique classique française. Pourtant, au cours° des siècles, la France a produit de grands musiciens dont° les oeuvres° sont toujours au répertoire des plus grands orchestres du monde.

Aujourd'hui, la musique classique connaît un regain° de popularité chez les Français de tout âge et de toute condition sociale. Pour un quart d'entre° eux, c'est la musique qu'ils écoutent le plus souvent. Et, contrairement à ce qu'on peut penser, les jeunes ne lui sont pas hostiles. En fait, la musique classique vient au cinquième rang de leurs préférences musicales, après le rock et les chansons bien sûr, mais avant le jazz et la musique populaire.

Lully et le ballet

Le ballet est né en Italie, mais c'est en France qu'il s'est développé à l'époque de **Louis XIV** (1638-1715). Ce roi était un grand patron des arts et il aimait particulièrement la musique et la danse. Pour mettre en musique les comédies-ballets dans lesquelles° il jouait parfois lui-même, il a fait appel° à **Jean-Baptiste Lully** (1632-1687), un musicien d'origine italienne. Celui-ci a composé un grand nombre de ballets et d'opéras. C'est sous son influence que le ballet s'est codifié et a acquis sa technique classique. Le ballet était alors un spectacle à la fois grandiose et formel où les danseurs entraient en scène masqués et habillés des magnifiques costumes de l'époque.

Un ballet de Lully présenté à la cour de Louis XIV

Chopin: le poète du piano

T. Kwiatkouski *«La polonaise de Chopin»*

Frédéric Chopin (1810-1849) est né en Pologne° d'un père français et d'une mère polonaise. Enfant prodige, il compose et donne son premier concert à l'âge de neuf ans. À vingt ans, il quitte son pays, emportant dans une urne un peu de la terre° natale qu'il ne reverra° jamais.

Chopin s'établit° à Paris où il rencontre les artistes et les écrivains les plus célèbres de son époque. Parmi ceux-ci, il y a une jeune femme, **George Sand**, pour qui il va éprouver° une grande passion. Inspiré par l'amour et plus tard par la tristesse de la séparation, il compose pour le piano des oeuvres d'une grande intensité émotionnelle: études, ballades, nocturnes, fantaisies, préludes, impromptus, sonates et aussi polonaises et mazurkas en l'honneur de son pays natal. De santé° délicate et miné° par la tuberculose, il meurt à Paris à l'âge de 39 ans.

À tort *wrongly* **au cours** *across* **dont** *whose* **les oeuvres** *works* **un regain** *renewal* **d'entre** *of* **lesquelles** *which* **a fait appel** *asked*
Pologne *Poland* **la terre** *soil* **ne reverra jamais** *will never see* **s'établit** *settles* **éprouver** *feel* **la santé** *health* **miné** *weakened*

Note culturelles

- **George Sand** was the pseudonym of Aurore Dupin (1804–1876). She wrote many books, including **La Mare au diable, La Petite Fadette, François le Champi.**
- **Chopin** was a leader of a new musical movement called **la musique romantique.** In this genre, music becomes descriptive and tries to express the feelings of its composer. At 19, Chopin was the best pianist in Poland. He left on November 1, 1830 to study abroad, but never returned to his homeland. He composed 14 **polonaises**, and 20 **nocturnes**.

■ **Note historique**

The introduction of the "tutu" dates to 1830 and the Romantic ballets of that period. In the late 19th century, what we know as classical ballet was perfected in Russia, maintaining French terminology and basic French steps.

«Carmen» présenté à New York (Metropolitan Opera)

Bizet et l'opéra romantique

Tous les amateurs d'opéra connaissent l'air° célèbre «Toréador, en garde, Toréador! Toréador!» Cet air est tiré° de l'opéra *Carmen*, oeuvre du compositeur **Georges Bizet**.

Bizet (1838-1875) était un prodige musical. Il est entré au Conservatoire de Paris à l'âge de neuf ans et il en est sorti à dix-huit ans avec le premier Grand Prix de Rome, distinction réservée aux meilleurs jeunes musiciens de l'époque. De ses nombreuses compositions, la plus connue reste *Carmen*, opéra romantique plein° de passion, d'émotions intenses et d'action dramatique. Jugé immoral, cet opéra n'a pas eu de succès à l'époque de sa création. Très affecté par cet échec,° Bizet est mort trois mois après la première représentation° de son chef-d'oeuvre.°

Aujourd'hui, *Carmen* est le plus populaire des opéras français. Modernisé, il a été adapté pour le cinéma dans plusieurs versions.

Carmen

Une affiche: «Carmen» vers 1900

L'action se passe à Séville dans l'Espagne romantique du dix-neuvième siècle. L'héroïne est Carmen, une gitane° belle, fière, passionnée, mais d'humeur changeante ... Carmen travaille dans une manufacture de tabac. Un jour, elle blesse° une de ses collègues d'un coup de couteau à la joue. Le brigadier Don José vient l'arrêter. Pendant qu'elle est sous sa garde, Don José tombe éperdument amoureux de la belle gitane et il la laisse s'échapper. Il déserte lui-même et s'enfuit avec Carmen dans les montagnes où ils rejoignent une bande de contrebandiers.° Don José devient alors contrebandier.

Un jour, Micaela, une jeune fille du village où il habitait vient annoncer à Don José que sa mère est sur le point° de mourir. Celui-ci retourne dans son village pour voir sa mère. Pendant ce temps, Carmen va à Séville avec ses amies pour assister à une corrida. Là, elle n'a d'yeux que pour le héros de la corrida, le toréador Escamillo, qui est son nouvel amour. Don José revient pour chercher Carmen. Il la trouve à la corrida et il la tue° dans une crise° de jalousie. Puis, il se livre° à la police.

Debussy et la musique impressionniste

On considère **Claude Debussy** (1862-1918) comme l'un des fondateurs de la musique moderne. Élève au Conservatoire de Paris, il étudie les oeuvres des grands compositeurs, mais il refuse absolument d'imiter leur style ou leur technique. Il se révolte en particulier contre la musique romantique dominée par l'intensité dramatique et l'émotion.

Claude Debussy (1862-1918)

Comme l'ont fait les peintres impressionnistes pour la peinture, Debussy veut libérer la musique de tout principe, de toute convention, de toute tradition. En rejetant, par exemple, la règle des accords° progressifs et en utilisant les dissonances et les silences, il donne à la musique des sonorités nouvelles qui ont pu sembler étranges aux gens de son époque. La musique de Debussy, exemplifiée par son célèbre poème symphonique «La Mer», est une musique fluide, délicate, toute en nuances, où l'impression produite remplace l'émotion.

---

l'air *aria* **tiré de** = vient **plein** *full* **un échec** *failure* **la représentation** *performance* **le chef-d'oeuvre** *masterpiece* **gitane** *gypsy* **blesse** *wounds*
contrebandiers *smugglers* **sur le point** *is going* **tue** *kills* **une crise** *fit* **il se livre** *gives himself up* **accords** *chords*

• **Debussy** was a composer of **musique impressionniste**, a music written in small **touches** as if to capture colors. (For more on the Impressionist movement, see pp. 60–63.)
• **Lully** was a composer of **musique baroque**, an ornate style of music developed in Italy.

• Some other famous French composers are:
Hector Berlioz (1803–1869): *Symphonie Fantastique*
Charles Gounod (1813–1893): *Faust*
Paul Dukas (1865–1935): *L'Apprenti Sorcier*
Maurice Ravel (1875–1937): *Boléro*

Unité 5

MAIN THEME

Travel

COMMUNICATION
- Going through customs
- Making travel arrangements
- Traveling in France
- Planning a trip abroad

CULTURES
- Learning the importance of travel for young French people
- Learning about transportation in France
- Learning about *L'Eurotunnel*
- Learning about *les bandes dessinées*

CONNECTIONS
- Determining the meaning of French signs
- Locating countries on a world map
- Connecting to Geography: Researching a French-speaking country
- Connecting to Art: Drawing a map of an airport or train station
- Connecting to Language Arts: Writing about and planning a class trip
- Connecting to Math: Calculating costs
- Connecting to Science: Researching the history of modes of transportation
- Connecting to Social Studies: Researching a museum or historic site
- Connecting to Technology: Using a computer to make travel plans

COMPARISONS
- Comparing limiting expressions in French and English
- Comparing ways to express the future and the conditional in French and English
- Learning how the United States compares to France according to French exchange students
- Comparing the French and American national anthems
- Learning about American influence on the French Revolution

COMMUNITIES
- Preparing a travel log or research notes
- Exploring a travel destination
- Learning to read a travel itinerary

Unité 5

Bon voyage!

THÈME ET OBJECTIFS

Culture

In this unit, you will discover . . .

- what French young people do when they travel abroad and where they go
- why the train is the most popular means of transportation in France
- how the Eurotunnel has linked Great Britain to France and the rest of Europe

Communication

You will learn how . . .

- to make travel plans and purchase tickets
- to go through passport control and customs
- to travel by plane and by train

Langue

You will learn how . . .

- to discuss future plans
- to talk about future events
- to describe what you would do under certain conditions

DIGITAL FRENCH   my.hrw.com
ONLINE STUDENT EDITION with...

performance)space
- Audio Resources

News + Networking
- Video Resources

@HOMETUTOR
- Interactive Flashcards
- WebQuest

PRACTICE FRENCH WITH HOLT MCDOUGAL APPS!

 DIGITAL FRENCH

TEACHER TOOLS
- Teacher One Stop
- Interactive Whiteboard Lessons
- Generate Success Rubric Generator and Interactive Graphic Organizers
- Examview Test Generator

ALSO AVAILABLE...
- Online Workbook
- French InterActive Reader
- @HomeTutor
- DVD Program
- Power Presentations
- Interactive Flashcards

FRENCH ON THE GO!
- Performance Space
- Holt McDougal French Apps
- Discovering French Today eTextbook

La Passion des Voyages

Pour les jeunes Français, le terme «vacances» est synonyme de «voyage.» Ceux qui restent en France vont bronzer sur les plages de l'Atlantique et de la Méditerranée ou faire de la marche à pied dans les Alpes et les Pyrénées. Mais aujourd'hui, ceux qui vont à l'étranger sont de plus en plus nombreux. Aller dans un pays où la langue, les gens, et les coutumes sont différents, ça, c'est l'aventure!

Suivant° leurs objectifs, on peut classer ces jeunes voyageurs en différentes catégories.

■ Pour ces jeunes voyageurs, «vacances» est synonyme de «voyage»!

Les «linguistes»

Les «séjours linguistiques» représentent la majorité des voyages à l'étranger. La formule classique consiste à passer deux ou trois semaines dans une famille en Angleterre (l'anglais étant° la langue la plus étudiée dans les lycées français).

Aujourd'hui, avec le développement des tranports aériens et la diminution° du prix des voyages, les jeunes Français vont de plus en plus loin pour perfectionner° leur anglais. Patrick, par exemple, a passé le mois d'août dans une famille de Denver. Le haut point de son voyage a été la dernière semaine où la famille est allée faire du rafting dans le Colorado. Charlotte, elle, est allée en Australie dans une famille de ranchers. Là, elle a participé à toutes les activités, y compris la tonte des moutons.°

Les «actifs»

Ce sont ceux qui ont un projet particulier. Certains font un «stage» payé ou non payé dans une entreprise. Catherine a ainsi passé un mois en Allemagne à mélanger des colorants° dans une compagnie de produits chimiques. Là, elle a appris les dangers de la pollution et les moyens° de contrôler celle-ci.

Pour d'autres, leur projet a un objectif humanitaire. Jean-Baptiste, un lycéen de 17 ans, est allé au Sénégal avec une bande de copains de son lycée. Il explique: «Notre but° n'était pas de faire du tourisme, mais d'accomplir quelque chose d'utile. Nous avons participé à la construction d'un système d'irrigation dans un petit village. Pendant notre séjour, nous avons travaillé très dur, mais aussi nous avons découvert un mode° de vie tout à fait° différent et nous avons fait connaissance de gens absolument extraordinaires. Pendant ces trois semaines, nous avons appris plus que pendant un an au lycée!»

---

suivant *according to* **étant** *being* **diminution** *decrease* **perfectionner** *improve* **tonte des moutons** *sheep shearing* **mélanger des colorants** *to mix dyes* **moyens** *means* **but** = objectif **mode** *way* **tout à fait** *quite*

ASSESSMENT IN UNIT RESOURCE BOOK

Print Resources
- Workbook TE/PE
- *Activités pour tous* TE/PE
- *Lectures pour tous*
- Unit Resource Book Audioscripts Video Activities Videoscripts

Achievement Tests
- Quizzes, Unit 5
- Unit Test 5
- Reading and Culture Tests
- Assessment Answer Key

Proficiency Tests
- Listening Comprehension
- Speaking Performance
- Writing Performance
- Portfolio Assessment

INFO MAGAZINE

Theme: Travel

Reading Strategy: Browsing, reading for pleasure, scanning

■ **Proverbe**
Les voyages forment la jeunesse.

■ **Teaching Strategy**
These optional readings can be done:
- in class or as homework
- at the beginning of the unit or as a wrap-up activity

■ **Note linguistique**
la marche à pied = hiking
le stage = training course, work placement

■ **Notes culturelles**
- Les langues les plus étudiées par les étudiants français sont: l'anglais, l'espagnol, l'allemand, l'italien, le russe, le portugais, l'hébreu moderne et le chinois.
- Les étudiants français sont obligés d'étudier au moins une langue étrangère.

21st CENTURY SKILLS
- **Collaboration:** TE: pp. 188, 191, 203, 206
- **Critical Thinking and Problem Solving:** SE: pp. 194, 208, 215; TE: pp. 188, 191, 194, 216, 222, 223
- **Technology Literacy:** TE: pp. 189, 191, 206, 207, 215, 216 (Civic Literacy), 223, 225
- **Flexibility and Adaptability:** TE: pp. 191, 197, 203, 204, 207, 215
- **Social and Cross-Cultural Skills:** SE: pp. 190 (Global Awareness), 216–223 (Civic Literacy); TE: pp. 188, 189, 190, 194 (Financial Literacy), 195, 203, 207, 209, 216, 223
- **Productivity and Accountability:** TE: pp. 192, 204, 209
- **Leadership and Responsibility:** TE: p. 207

Unité 5 187

■ Teaching Note

In Activity 1, p. 190, students list countries that they would like to visit. You may want to compare those lists to the one on this page.

■ Note linguistique

Le trekking (or **le trek**) is a difficult hike high up in the mountains.

■ Irregular Verbs

(see Appendix C)
parcourir *(see* **courir***)*

Leurs destinations préférées

☐ = 1 semaine
○ = 2-3 mois

Dans quel pays ou région du monde aimeriez-vous passer vos vacances? Évidemment votre choix dépendra du temps que vous aurez à votre disposition. Voici les destinations préférées des Français.

VACANCES D'UNE SEMAINE

1. l'Espagne, le Portugal
2. l'Angleterre
3. l'Italie
4. la Grèce
5. la Martinique, la Guadeloupe
6. les pays scandinaves*
7. l'Allemagne
8. les États-Unis
9. la France
10. l'Algérie, le Maroc, la Tunisie

VACANCES D'UN OU DEUX MOIS

1. la Martinique, la Guadeloupe
2. les États-Unis
3. le Canada
4. les pays d'Amérique latine**
5. la Grèce
6. le Mexique
7. l'Espagne, le Portugal
8. les pays scandinaves*
9. les pays d'Afrique noire***
10. l'Italie

* le Danemark, la Suède, la Norvège
** le Pérou, l'Argentine, le Brésil, l'Equateur, le Costa Rica, etc.
*** le Sénégal, la Côte d'Ivoire, le Cameroun, etc.

Les «explorateurs»

Ceux-là renouvellent la tradition des explorateurs français d'autrefois. Ils partent à l'aventure, sac au dos,° sans but précis pour des destinations mystérieuses. Julien, un étudiant en médecine, a parcouru° les hauts plateaux du Pérou en bus et en autostop. Marthe et Véronique, deux étudiantes d'une école de commerce, ont fait du trekking dans l'Himalaya. Elles sont parties du Népal et sont allées à pied par des sentiers° de haute montagne jusqu'au Tibet.

Pendant des semaines, les parents de ces voyageurs intrépides n'entendent pas parler° d'eux et s'inquiètent.° Mais finalement, ils reviennent, bronzés, heureux et avec plein° d'anecdotes sur les dangers qu'ils ont évités° et les rencontres qu'ils ont faites pendant leur fabuleux voyage. ■

DISCUSSION

Avec votre partenaire, imaginez que vous allez visiter la France (ou un autre pays francophone) cet été. Est-ce que vous voyagerez plutôt comme «linguiste,» comme «actif,» ou comme «explorateur»? Expliquez vos projets.

COMPOSITION

Décrivez des vacances «actives» que vous avez passées.

sac au dos *with a backpack* **parcourir** ☞ *to travel through* **sentiers** *trails* **n'entendent pas parler** *do not hear* **s'inquiètent** *worry*
plein = beaucoup **évités** *avoided*

Teaching Strategy: Cultural Comparisons

Put two categories on the board:
VACANCES DE DEUX SEMAINES
VACANCES DE DEUX MOIS
Ask students to indicate their preferred destinations in each category, then compare with the ones chosen by French students.

Are the kinds of activities and destinations similar or quite different? Ask students to suggest reasons for differences (Ex: geographically closer etc.). Have students do a survey of other French classes and compile the results.

Impressions d'Amérique

Les États-Unis ont toujours fasciné les jeunes Français. Chaque été, ils sont toujours plus nombreux à réaliser leur rêve:° faire un voyage aux «States.» Nous sommes à Roissy, l'aéroport international de Paris. Un groupe de jeunes Français de 15 à 18 ans vient de débarquer° d'un vol° Air France qui arrive de New York. Ils ont passé six semaines dans des familles américaines avec un programme d'échange. Voici quelques-unes de leurs impressions.

Jean-Pascal «Les États-Unis sont un pays vraiment gigantesque. Là-bas, tout est grand: les gens, les maisons, les voitures, les distances. C'est aussi un pays magnifique. J'ai eu la chance d'aller dans une famille qui habite au Nouveau Mexique. Les villages indiens, les canyons, le désert, c'est fabuleusement beau!»

Émilie «Moi, ce qui m'a frappée,° c'est la variété ethnique des Américains. Ce qui est formidable,° c'est que toutes les races de la terre° y sont représentées. À Boston, par exemple, la ville où je suis restée, j'ai pu parler français avec des Haïtiens, et espagnol avec des Portoricains. Ça, c'est super.»

Christophe «Les Américains sont des gens vraiment sympas et hospitaliers. Ils sont beaucoup plus ouverts et plus décontractés° que nous. Aux États-Unis, par exemple, il est tout à fait facile de lier conversation° avec des gens qu'on ne connaît pas. En France, c'est quasi-impossible. Les Américains sont honnêtes. Ils disent toujours ce qu'ils pensent… Pendant mon séjour, il y a une seule chose que je n'ai pas aimée: la bouffe.»°

Sibylle «Je ne suis pas d'accord avec Christophe. La bouffe américaine n'est pas si mauvaise que ça, et puis, elle est très bon marché. Et il ne faut pas manger tout le temps des hamburgers ou des hot-dogs. Il y a des tas° de restaurants italiens, chinois, mexicains, thaïlandais, où on peut manger des choses absolument délicieuses. On n'est pas obligé de prendre ses repas que dans les fast-foods!»

Arnaud «Les Américains sont des gens dynamiques et superactifs. Malheureusement, ils sont obsédés° par l'argent. Et ils sont stressés parce qu'ils travaillent trop. Dans la famille où j'étais, la mère retournait à son bureau le samedi pour finir ce qu'elle n'avait pas terminé pendant la semaine. Et le fils travaillait dans un supermarché. La détente,° ça n'existe pas. Et puis, la vie de famille est limitée. Le soir, par exemple, les parents et les enfants faisaient réchauffer° des portions de pizza qu'ils mangeaient séparément. Il n'y avait jamais de repas commun.»

Sonia «Les États-Unis sont un pays très intéressant. Ce serait° un pays presque° parfait s'il n'y avait pas autant° de violence. Dans les journaux et à la télévision, on ne parle que° de crime. Et le soir, dans la ville où j'étais, il n'est pas recommandé de sortir seule. J'ai aimé mon voyage, mais je suis bien contente de rentrer en France.» ∎

et vous?

SUJET DE DISCUSSION
Avec votre partenaire, choisissez deux des jeunes Français qui ont visité les États-Unis et analysez leurs impressions. Dites si vous êtes entièrement, partiellement ou pas du tout d'accord avec eux. Expliquez.

COMPOSITION: UNE LETTRE
Un copain français va venir passer un mois dans votre région. Vous voulez lui donner une bonne impression de cette région. Écrivez-lui une lettre où vous allez parler des sujets suivants:

- le pays
- les gens
- la nourriture
- les activités

---

rêve *dream* **débarquer** *to land* **vol** *flight* **frappée** *struck* **formidable** = *super* **terre** *earth* **décontractés** *relaxed* **lier conversation** = *parler* **bouffe** *food (slang)* **des tas** = *beaucoup* **obsédés:** *obsessed* **détente** *relaxation* **faisaient réchauffer** *would reheat* **serait** *would be* **presque** *almost* **(s'il n'y avait pas) autant** *not that much* **ne...que** *only*

INFOMAGAZINE

Notes linguistiques

- Le nom des états américains en français:
  le Nouveau-Mexique,
  la Caroline du Nord/du Sud,
  la Floride, la Louisiane,
  la Géorgie, la Californie,
  la Pennsylvanie, la Virginie.
  (All other state names remain the same in French as in English.)
- The expression **la bouffe** comes from the verb **bouffer** (*to puff up*) by analogy, since the cheeks of someone who eats are puffed up with food. Consequently **bouffer** also means to *eat*.

Sujets de discussion

- Décrivez une région des États-Unis que vous avez visitée. Comment avez-vous trouvé le pays? les gens? la nourriture? Quelles autres impressions avez-vous de cette région?
- Un jour, vous visiterez peut-être la France. Avec votre partenaire, discutez des impressions que vous avez déjà sur ce pays. Vous pouvez donner vos impressions sur:
  - le pays
  - les gens
  - la nourriture
- Quand on visite un pays étranger, on découvre des similarités et des différences avec son propre (*own*) pays. Choisissez un pays que vous aimeriez visiter. Quelles similarités et quelles différences pensez-vous rencontrer? Expliquez votre opinion. Vous pouvez considérer les éléments suivants:
  - le pays
  - la nourriture
  - les voitures
  - les villes
  - les gens
  - le confort

Teaching Strategy: Pair Practice

Divide the class into pairs and assign each pair one of the French students from p. 189. In each group, one student is to be an interviewer and the other is to be a French student. Have the students prepare an interview which will appear on their school's radio station. They are to ask and answer questions that could be answered by reading and/or logically expanding on the quotation given. The "interviews" may be recorded and retained in student portfolios.

RESOURCES

PRINT

Workbook, pp. 133–135

Activités pour tous

Unit 5 Resource Book, Partie 1

Activités pour tous TE

Audioscripts

Lesson Plans

Block Scheduling Lesson Plans

Absent Student Copymasters

Workbook TE

AUDIO

Audio Program
CD 5 Tracks 1–5

TECHNOLOGY

@HomeTutor

Interactive Whiteboard Lessons

Teacher One Stop

Block Scheduling Copymasters

Projectable Transparencies

2, *Le monde francophone*

3, *Le monde francophone: L'Amérique*

4, *Le monde francophone: L'Afrique, l'Europe, l'Asie*

Transparency Copymasters, pp. A6–A11

DVD Program Unit 5

■ **Pronunciation**

un pays /pei/

■ **Note culturelle**

According to tradition, the name **Sénégal** comes from the Wolof expression: **Sunu Gaal**, which means "our **pirogue** *(canoe)."* (**Wolof** is one of the main tribal languages of Senegal.)

Les voyages

> Où vas-tu aller cet été?
>
> Je vais voyager à l'étranger.
>
> Ah bon? Dans quel pays?
>
> Je vais visiter le Portugal.

Les voyages

— Où vas-tu aller cet été?

Je vais | **voyager**
| **faire un voyage** | **à l'étranger** *(abroad).*
| **faire un séjour**

| **faire un séjour** *to spend some time*

— Ah bon? Dans quels **pays** *(countries)*?

Je vais visiter . . .   Je vais aller . . .

le Portugal.   **au Mexique.**

la Grèce.   **en Russie.**

les Canaries.   **aux États-Unis.**

> **Révision** pp. R14–R15
>
> Les pays

---

1 Voyages à l'étranger

Faites une liste de dix (10) pays que vous aimeriez visiter. Classez les pays par ordre de préférence. Comparez votre liste avec celle de votre partenaire.

> *Ma Liste*
> 1.
> 2.
> 3.

- Quels sont les pays qui sont sur les deux listes?
- Quels sont let pays qui sont seulement *(only)* sur votre liste? Maintenant expliquez pourquoi vous aimeriez aller dans les trois premiers pays de votre liste.

▶ **J'aimerais visiter le Sénégal parce que je voudrais mieux connaître l'Afrique . . .**

Teaching Strategy: Warm-Up

Ask the class to suggest 15 countries to visit. List them on the board, then ask students to provide the correct country name in French (including article!), and to locate the countries on a world map. Ask if any students have traveled to one or more of the locations, or know of someone who has. What were their impressions? Do they have photographs or realia to share with the class?

Au contrôle des passeports

— Vous avez **une pièce d'identité** (ID document)?

Oui, j'ai | **un passeport.**
| **une carte d'identité.**
| **un permis de conduire** (driver's license).

À la douane (customs)

— Vous avez des **bagages** (luggage)?

Oui, j'ai | **une valise** (suitcase). **un bagage à main** (carry-on bag).
| **un sac.** **un sac à dos** (backpack).

— Est-ce que vous avez **quelque chose à déclarer?**

Non, je n'ai **rien à déclarer.**

NOTE *Culturelle*

Les Américains qui vont en France ont besoin d'un passeport
(et aussi d'un visa, s'ils veulent faire un long séjour).

Les citoyens (citizens) des pays de l'Union Européenne
ont besoin seulement d'une pièce d'identité.

2 ## Arrivée en France

Cet été, vous faites un grand voyage autour du monde (around the world). Vous arrivez en France,
après avoir visité plusieurs pays. Vous passez au contrôle des passeports et à la douane.
Composez et jouez le dialogue avec votre partenaire.

— Bonjour, monsieur/mademoiselle. Avez-vous une pièce d'identité?
— (Present an ID document.)
— Quels pays avez-vous visités avant de venir en France?
— (Name a few countries.)
— Avez-vous des bagages?
— (Indicate the luggage that you are carrying.)
— Avez-vous quelque chose à déclarer?
— (Answer negatively.)
— Où avez-vous acheté . . . ?(customs officer names two or three things in your luggage,
     such as items of clothing, perfume, souvenirs)
— (For each item, mention a different country where you purchased it.)
— Merci, monsieur/mademoiselle, et bon séjour en France.

■ Note culturelle

The European Union is composed of
27 European countries that have
united to form a political and
economic whole. The countries are:
France, Germany, Italy, Belgium, the
Netherlands, Great Britain, Ireland,
Denmark, Greece, Spain,
Luxembourg, Portugal, Austria,
Finland, Sweden, Cyprus, Czech
Republic, Estonia, Hungary, Latvia,
Lithuania, Malta, Poland, Slovakia,
Slovenia, Bulgaria, and Romania.
Although citizens of these countries
use a European passport to travel
outside of Europe, they need none to
travel within the continent.

■ Teaching Strategy

Have each student choose a French-
speaking country and draw a map
with labels in French. Next, have
students prepare a two-minute
explanation of the country's
attractions and a discussion of what
they would need to bring and how
long they would plan to stay. All
students will make multimedia
presentations to the class.

■ Teaching Suggestion

As a follow-up to Act. 1, have
students e-mail a partner class in a
French-speaking country to find out
which ten countries the students
would most like to visit, and why. As
a class, compare and contrast the
answers from the partner class with
those of your own.

Teaching Suggestion: DVD Program

The Unit 5 *Vidéo-drame: Nicolas fait un voyage*
explores the topic of travel. In preparation for
watching the video, point out Avignon and Paris
on the map on R34. Then point out Ireland and
France on a world map. Ask students to predict
what kind of transportation Nicolas is likely to
use on each leg of his trip.

Differentiation

Repetitive After teaching the vocabulary, ask
students to write the boldfaced words and
expressions in their notebooks with phonetic
transcriptions. Then have them work in pairs to
act out dialogs: one student plays the **douanier**
and the other the traveler.

Langue et Communication

RESOURCES

PRINT
Workbook, pp. 55–56, 135
Unit 5 Resource Book, Partie 1
Audioscripts

AUDIO
Audio Program
CD 5 Tracks 6–7

TECHNOLOGY
@HomeTutor

■ Notes linguistiques

- **Personne** and **rien** may also be used after a preposition.
  Je n'ai parlé **à personne.**
- The expressions **aucun** and **ni ... ni** may introduce the subject.
  Aucun invité n'est venu.
  Ni Pierre **ni** Marc **n**'est venu.
- They may also be used with prepositions. Note the word order:
  Je n'ai parlé à **aucun** invité.
  Je n'ai parlé **ni** à Pierre **ni** à Marc.

■ Teaching Note

Have students note in the **passé composé:**
Je n'ai **rien** fait d'intéressant.

■ Teaching Strategy: Challenge

You may also want to present the construction **ne faire que:**
Je ne fais que travailler.
The only thing I do is work.
Tu ne fais que te plaindre.
The only thing you do is complain.

A Les expressions négatives

Note the following negative expressions and their use in the present and the passé composé.

AFFIRMATIVE	NEGATIVE	
quelqu'un *(someone, somebody)*	**ne ... personne** *(no one, nobody)*	Je **ne** connais **personne** ici. Je **n**'ai rencontré **personne.**
quelque chose *(something)*	**ne ... rien** *(nothing)*	Je **n**'ai **rien** à déclarer. Je **n**'ai **rien** acheté.
quelque part *(somewhere)*	**ne ... nulle part** *(nowhere)*	Je **ne** me promène **nulle part.** Je **ne** suis allé **nulle part.**
quelque(s) *(some)*	**ne ... aucun(e)** *(no, not any)*	Je **n**'ai **aucune** idée. Je **n**'ai acheté **aucun** cadeau.
et / ou *(and/or)*	**ne ... ni ... ni** *(neither ... nor)*	Je **ne** vais **ni** au ciné **ni** au théâtre. Je **n**'ai visité **ni** Paris **ni** Québec.

→ In the passé composé, negative expressions come AFTER the past participle, except **rien** which comes before.
  Nous **n**'avons vu **personne.**   BUT: Nous **n**'avons **rien** vu.

→ **Personne** and **rien** can be used as subjects.
  Personne n'a téléphoné.   **Rien n**'est impossible.

ALLONS PLUS LOIN
Note the following constructions:

quelqu'un, quelque chose, personne, rien } + **de** + masculine adjective   J'ai rencontré **quelqu'un d'intéressant.**

quelqu'un, quelque chose, personne, rien } + **à** + infinitive   Nous **n**'avons **rien à déclarer.**

B L'expression *ne ... que*

The expression **ne ... que** is not a negative expression. It is a limiting expression that means *only.* Its equivalent is **seulement.** Note its use in the following sentences.

Je parle français.
Je **ne** parle **que** français.   *I speak **only** French.*
Je **ne** parle français **qu**'en France.   *I speak French **only** in France.*
Je **ne** parle français en France **qu**'avec mes amis.   *I speak French in France **only** with my friends.*

→ Note the word order with **ne ... que:**
  • **ne** comes before the verb
  • **que** comes before the word or phrase to which the restriction applies.

→ Since **ne ... que** is not a negative expression, the indefinite and partitive articles do not change after the verb.
  Je mange **des légumes.**   Je **ne** mange **que des légumes.**

Teaching Strategy: Warm-Up

Divide the class into pairs and have them draw a cartoon representing a good person and a bad person at the top of a piece of paper. Then, using the negative expressions listed on p. 192, have them write sentences in the affirmative and the negative that describe what each of these people does or doesn't do.

Differentiation

Structured Have students write the affirmative expressions from the chart on p. 192 on cards. Have them work in pairs; one student asks a question using the affirmative expression, and the other answers in the negative.

1 C'est évident!

Informez-vous sur les personnes suivantes et dites ce qu'elles ne font pas. Utilisez les verbes entre parenthèses et une expression négative: **ne . . . personne, ne . . . rien, ne . . . nulle part**.

▶ Jean-Pierre est timide. (parler à)
Il ne parle à personne.

1. Carole se repose. (faire)
2. Pauline est très malade. (manger)
3. Marc n'est pas sociable. (inviter)
4. Thomas reste chez lui. (aller)

5. Antoine n'a pas soif. (boire)
6. Philippe ne voyage pas cet été. (partir)
7. Bernard est un nouvel élève. (connaître)
8. Catherine n'a pas d'argent. (acheter)

2 Une mauvaise surprise

Quand Brigitte est rentrée du concert, elle a trouvé la porte et les fenêtres de son appartement grandes ouvertes *(wide open)* et les lumières allumées *(turned on)*. Elle appelle un inspecteur de police qui lui pose les questions suivantes. Brigitte répond négativement. Jouez le rôle de Brigitte.

▶ L'inspecteur: Avez-vous entendu quelque chose?
Brigitte: **Non, je n'ai rien entendu.**

1. Avez-vous vu quelqu'un quand vous êtes rentrée?
2. Avez-vous observé quelque chose d'anormal?
3. Avez-vous remarqué quelqu'un de suspect?
4. Est-ce que vous avez donné votre adresse à quelqu'un récemment?
5. Est-ce que vous avez fait quelque chose de spécial hier soir?
6. Est-ce que vous avez invité quelqu'un chez vous la semaine dernière?
7. Est-ce que quelqu'un vous a téléphoné dans l'après-midi?
8. Est-ce que quelque chose d'important a disparu *(disappeared)*?
9. Est-ce que quelqu'un est venu réparer l'électricité récemment?
10. Est-ce qu'il y avait quelque chose de grande valeur *(value)* dans votre appartement?

3 À la douane

Vous arrivez à l'aéroport de Dorval à Montréal. Le douanier (joué par votre partenaire) vous pose certaines questions. Répondez-lui en choisissant une expression entre parenthèses.

▶ Vous avez des bagages?

Digital performance)space

Je n'ai qu'un bagage à main.
(Je n'ai que deux valises.)

QUESTIONS	RÉPONSES
Vous avez des bagages?	(deux valises / un sac à dos / un bagage à main)
Vous avez une pièce d'identité?	(mon passeport / mon permis de conduire / une carte d'étudiant)
Vous avez des cadeaux?	(du parfum / des chocolats / des t-shirts)
Vous avez de l'argent?	(des dollars / des travellers chèques / une carte de crédit)
À part l'anglais, vous parlez d'autres langues?	(espagnol / allemand / français)
Vous allez rester longtemps?	(3 jours / 2 semaines / un mois)
Vous allez visiter plusieurs villes?	(Québec / Montréal / Toronto

■ **Réponses: Activité 1**
1. Elle ne fait rien.
2. Elle ne mange rien.
3. Il n'invite personne.
4. Il ne va nulle part
   (Il ne va chez personne).
5. Il ne boit rien.
6. Il ne part nulle part.
7. Il ne connaît personne.
8. Elle n'achète rien.

■ **Note culturelle**
The most common form of identification used in France is **la carte nationale d'identité**. It is the only ID card a French person needs to travel through all the countries of the EU.

Student Portfolios

Using the same French-speaking country that students chose for the assignment suggested on p.191, have them write you a postcard/letter. On the postcard they should tell you what they did and didn't do/see/like/eat, etc. There should be at least six sentences (more if necessary)

using all of the affirmative and negative expressions from p. 192. These postcards may be displayed in the classroom or saved in the student portfolios.

La France en train

INFO MAGAZINE

Theme: Train Travel

■ Teaching Strategy

Ask students to look at the illustrations, scan for cognates, and guess the theme of the article before reading.

■ Note culturelle

Each year, French students get two weeks off around the time of Mardi Gras (February/March). These vacations are also called **les vacances d'hiver.** Many French people use this time to go skiing.

■ Interdisciplinary Connection: Mathematics

Ask students to convert from kilometers to miles:

650 km = 403 miles;
640 km = 397 miles;
600 km = 372 miles
480 km/h = 298 mph;
300 km/h = 186 mph;
200 km/h = 124 mph;
100 km/h = 62 mph;
50 km/h = 31 mph

Pour les vacances de Mardi Gras, Marie-Hélène, une étudiante parisienne, est allée chez sa grand-mère qui habite à Marseille. Elle aurait pu° prendre l'avion ou conduire° sa voiture, mais elle a choisi d'y aller en train. Pourquoi? Parce que c'est plus rapide, plus pratique, et plus sûr. Avec le TGV (Train à Grande Vitesse), on peut aller de Paris à Marseille (750 kilomètres) en 3 heures. Il n'y a pas d'embouteillage,° pas de péage° à payer, et on arrive à sa destination frais et dispos.°

■ Le train: c'est plus rapide, plus pratique, et plus sûr!

Le TGV, produit de la technologie française, est ce train super rapide qui circule sur un système spécial de rails et peut rouler° à une vitesse de 300 kilomètres à l'heure. La première ligne (Paris-Lyon) a été inaugurée en 1981, mais aujourd'hui le TGV dessert° presque° toutes les grandes villes françaises. Il y a un TGV Sud-est (orange), un TGV Atlantique (bleu) et un TGV Nord... En fait, 50% du service voyageurs est assuré par le TGV. Les autres trains sont peut-être un peu moins rapides, mais ils sont aussi confortables et aussi pratiques.

Les Français sont très fiers° de leurs trains et ceci pour de bonnes raisons:

● Les trains français sont toujours à l'heure. Ils partent à l'heure indiquée et arrivent à l'heure indiquée. Avec le train, on n'est jamais en retard.

● Les trains sont propres et confortables. Si on a faim, on peut prendre un repas au wagon-restaurant.° Sur les grandes distances, on peut voyager en wagon-lit.°

● Le train est bon marché et très flexible. Il y a des réductions de prix pour les jeunes, pour les familles, pour les personnes âgées, pour les personnes qui voyagent souvent. Pour toutes ces personnes, les prix des billets varient selon l'époque où on voyage. Ils sont plus élevés° en période rouge (vacances) ou blanche (week-ends), et moins élevés en période bleue (le reste du temps).

Pour les touristes, il y a d'autres services intéressants. Avec «train + vélo» et «train + auto,» on peut voyager en train et louer un vélo ou une voiture quand on arrive à sa destination. Avec «train + hôtel,» on trouve toujours une chambre d'hôtel.

Les jeunes Américains peuvent acheter un Eurailpass. Cette carte leur permet de sillonner° l'Europe pendant plusieurs semaines pour un prix relativement modique°. Pour beaucoup de jeunes qui utilisent ce système, le train est non seulement un moyen° de transport mais c'est aussi un hôtel, un restaurant, une cafétéria et un lieu où ils peuvent rencontrer d'autres jeunes qui, comme eux, viennent découvrir le vieux continent. ■

Paris à Marseille

✈	(≈480 km l'heure) 640 km aériens	1h20
SNCF	(≈250 km l'heure) 750 km	3h00
🚗	(≈100 km l'heure) 773 km	7h35

et vous?

DISCUSSION

Vous allez visiter la France avec votre partenaire. Il/Elle voudrait voyager en avion, mais vous préférez voyager en train. Expliquez-lui les avantages du train. Votre partenaire va poser des questions.

COMPOSITION: UNE LETTRE

Alice, une copine française, va visiter les États-Unis cet été. Elle ne sait pas si elle va voyager en train ou en bus, et elle vous demande votre avis (opinion). Dites-lui quel système vous préférez et expliquez-lui les avantages et les inconvénients de ce système.

---

aurait pu *could have* **conduire** * *to drive* **embouteillage** *traffic jam* **péage** *toll* **frais et dispos** *fresh and rested* **rouler** = *aller* **dessert** *services*
presque *almost* **fiers** *proud* **wagon-restaurant** *dining car* **wagon-lit** *sleeping car* **élevés** *higher* **sillonner** = *voyager à travers* **modique** *low*
moyen *means*

INFOMAGAZINE

L'EUROTUNNEL

Aujourd'hui, l'Angleterre n'est plus une île. Avec l'Eurotunnel, on peut maintenant franchir° les 50 kilomètres qui séparent Coquelles (France) et Cheriton (Angleterre) sans quitter la terre ferme.° L'idée d'un tunnel sous la Manche est très ancienne. Le premier projet remonte° à Napoléon et date de 1802. Malheureusement, la rivalité franco-britannique, les guerres européennes, les difficultés techniques et l'énorme coût financier ont pendant longtemps empêché° la réalisation de ce projet. Finalement, les travaux ont commencé en 1988 et depuis 1994, l'Eurotunnel est une réalité.

L'ANGLETERRE

Londres⭐

Douvres •
Cheriton • • Calais
Coquelles •

LA MANCHE

LA FRANCE

Paris⭐

■ Chaque année, dix millions de voyageurs passent sous la mer pour aller de France en Angleterre, ou vice versa, en moins de 20 minutes.

Chaque année, dix millions de voyageurs passent sous la mer pour aller de France en Angleterre, ou vice versa, en moins de 20 minutes. Il y a en réalité deux tunnels, un tunnel nord et un tunnel sud, permettant le trafic dans les deux sens.° Ces deux tunnels sont exclusivement réservés au trafic ferroviaire,° mais les automobilistes peuvent tout de même° utiliser l'Eurotunnel en chargeant° leurs voitures sur des trains spéciaux.

Imaginez, par exemple, que vous habitez à Paris et que vous voulez déjeuner avec votre copain qui habite à Londres. C'est simple. Si vous préférez le train, vous prendrez l'Eurostar à 10 heures et vous arriverez à Londres à midi. Si, au contraire, vous préférez conduire, vous devez partir à sept heures. Vous prendrez l'autoroute° qui va de Paris jusqu'à l'accès de l'Eurotunnel. Là, vous monterez avec votre voiture sur une navette° spéciale qui vous amènera jusqu'au° terminal britannique. De là vous continuerez votre route. S'il n'y a pas trop d'embouteillages° dans Londres, vous serez à votre rendez-vous pour le déjeuner.

L'Eurotunnel est beaucoup plus qu'un grand exploit technique. Autrefois, la Manche représentait une formidable barrière qui protégeait l'Angleterre contre les invasions, mais qui la maintenait aussi dans son «splendide isolement». Aujourd'hui l'Eurotunnel joint l'Angleterre à la France et, par la France, à l'Allemagne, à la Belgique, à la Hollande et à tout le continent européen. C'est le symbole de la Nouvelle Europe, unie et en paix° avec elle-même. ■

QUESTIONS
1. Comment peut-on aller de Paris à Londres par la terre ferme?
2. Quels ont été les obstacles à la construction de l'Eurotunnel?
3. Pourquoi l'Eurotunnel est-il un grand exploit technique?
4. Quel est le symbole politique de l'Eurotunnel?

franchir = traverser   **terre ferme** *ground*   **remonte** *goes back*   **empêché** *prevented*   **sens** = directions   **ferroviaire** *railroad*   **tout de même** *nevertheless*
chargeant *loading*   **l'autoroute** *turnpike*   **navette** *shuttle train*   **jusqu'au** *up to*   **embouteillages** *traffic jams*   **paix** *peace*

■ **Teaching Strategy: Challenge**

Initiate a discussion on the different modes of transportation used in the United States, and how and why these differ from those most commonly used in France. (e.g.: Do we use the train or the plane more in the United States? What about France? Why the difference? Do we have anything like the TGV or the EuroTunnel here in the U.S.?)

■ **Note culturelle**

Le TGV qui relie Paris et Londres s'appelle l'Eurostar.

INFOMAGAZINE

Notes culturelles

- It is as fast to take the TGV from Paris to London via the Eurotunnel as to fly the same distance and then take a taxi or a train to London. Both trips take about three hours.
- Eurostar (or **TGV Transmanche**) is the name of the high-speed train that travels between Paris and London.

- A total of 139 plans have been made since 1802 to build an underwater connection between France and Great Britain. The first project (1802) called for a stone-paved road in a underground passageway under the Channel. The second project (1803) called for a tunnel made of metal tubes.

■ Teaching Note

You might want to remind students that all schedules in France are posted in the 24-hour time system

---

Partons en voyage

À l'agence de voyages

— Je voudrais | **acheter un billet** *(ticket).*
réserver une place *(seat).*
confirmer ma réservation.
annuler ma réservation.
louer une voiture.

> **annuler** *to cancel*
> **louer** *to rent*

POUR ACHETER UN BILLET DE TRAIN OU D'AVION

—**Quelle sorte de** billet désirez-vous?
Un aller simple *(one way).* | **Un aller et retour** *(round trip).*

— En quelle classe?
En **première classe.** | En **deuxième classe** [en train].
En **classe affaires** *(business).* | En **classe économie** [en avion].

—**Quel siège** *(seat)*
—**Quelle place** | préférez-vous?

Un siège | près de la fenêtre.
Une place | près du **couloir** *(aisle).*

— Voici | votre billet.
| votre **carte d'embarquement** *(boarding pass).*

POUR OBTENIR DES RENSEIGNEMENTS *(information)*

— Est-ce que | **le vol** *(flight)* pour Nice | est **direct?**
| le train pour Marseille |

Non, il y a | **une escale** *(stop, stopover [of the plane])* | à Lyon.
| **une correspondance** *(change of plane, train)* |

— Est-ce que le vol/le train **est à l'heure** *(on time)?*
Non, il est | **en avance** *(early).* Il a **dix minutes d'avance.**
| **en retard** *(late).* Il a **une heure de retard.**

Le vol numéro 23 à destination de Londres est **annulé.**

— Est-ce que le vol/le train est **complet** *(full)?*
Non, il y a **de la place** *(room).*

— Est-ce que ce siège/cette place est **libre** *(free)?*
Non, il/elle est **occupé(e).**

Speech bubbles:
Je voudrais acheter un billet.
Quelle sorte de billet désirez-vous?
En quelle classe?
Un aller et retour.
En classe économie.

Teaching Suggestion: DVD Program

In the Unit 5 *Vidéo-drame: Nicolas fait un voyage,* students will learn about traveling in France. They will become familiar with making reservations and preparing for a trip, as well as useful phrases such as **réserver une place** and **confirmer ma réservation**. As you play the video, listen carefully to Nicolas and Malik as they make a plane reservation. As students watch the video, ask: **Qu'est-ce qu'il faut faire avant de monter dans le train? Où est-ce que Nicolas va pour prendre le train?**

HOMETUTOR
my.hrw.com

À l'aéroport

les horaires — le comptoir — la salle d'attente — le contrôle de sécurité — l'hôtesse de l'air — le pilote — le steward — la porte — PORTE 32 — ARRIVÉES — DOUANE — un douanier — la livraison des bagages

Les passagers doivent . . .

AU DÉPART	**présenter** leur billet. **obtenir** leur carte d'embarquement. **enregistrer** leurs bagages. **passer la sécurité.** **se présenter** à la porte de départ. **embarquer.**	**obtenir** *to get* **enregistrer** *to check [luggage]* **embarquer** *to board [a plane]*
PENDANT LE VOL	mettre leur bagage à main sous le siège. **attacher** leur **ceinture de sécurité** *(seat belt).*	**attacher** *to fasten*
À L'ARRIVÉE	**débarquer.** **chercher** leurs bagages. **passer par** la douane.	**débarquer** *to deplane* **passer par** *to go through*

L'avion va | **décoller** | dans 10 minutes.
         | **atterrir** |

décoller *to take off*
atterrir *to land*

Mesdames et messieurs, bonjour.

Le capitaine Pascal et son équipage vous souhaitent la bienvenue à bord du vol Air France numéro 346 à destination de Montréal.

La durée du vol sera approximativement de 7 heures et 25 minutes et notre arrivée à Montréal est prévue pour 17h45 heure locale.

En prévision du départ, veuillez attacher votre ceinture de sécurité.

Départs

Arrivée

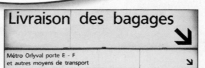
Livraison des bagages
Métro Orlyval porte E - F
et autres moyens de transport

Teaching Strategy: Group Practice
Divide students into groups of 4 or 5. One person from each group will be the travel agent working behind the counter at the airport/train station. The other 3 or 4 people will be travelers in need of information. The travel agent should ask at least one question of each person and answer all of their questions. Each person should ask at least two questions of the travel agent. In the dialogs, the students should attempt to be as original as possible and use as much vocabulary from the text as possible.

Irregular Verb
(See Appendix C.)
obtenir is conjugated like **tenir**.

Language Note
l'équipage *(m.)* = crew

Photo Note
Orlyval is the subway line that connects Orly airport to Paris.

Teaching Strategy: Expansion
Have students draw a map or illustration of an airport and train station, adding the following labels:

À L'AÉROPORT la piste de décollage/d'atterrissage
           (take off/landing) runway
           la tour de contrôle *control tower*
           la boutique hors-taxe *duty-free shop*
EN VOITURE la voiture de location *rental car*
           le kilométrage illimité *unlimited mileage*

EN AVION le stand-by *stand-by*
           la classe affaires *business class*
           la soute à bagages *cargo bay*
EN TRAIN la couchette *berth*
           le compartiment *compartment*
           le wagon *(train) car*

RESOURCES

TECHNOLOGY
@HomeTutor

■ Interactive Whiteboard Lessons

Teacher One Stop

Teacher to Teacher Copymasters, *Bon voyage*, pp. 58–60; *Trouver celui qui...*, pp. 61–62

💻 **Projectable Transparencies**

37, *À la gare*

38, *Jeunes voyagers*

Transparency Copymasters, pp. A76–A80

▶ DVD Program, Unit 5

■ **Notes culturelles**

• In every French station, you will find **un composteur** on your way to the platforms. It is an orange-colored machine (see illustration and photo) in which the traveler inserts his train ticket to have it automatically stamped with the time and date.

• **Lille** is the main city in the north of France. It is located just below the Belgian frontier.

■ **Note linguistique**

Un **haut-parleur** *(loudspeaker)* est utilisé pour annoncer les départs et les arrivées *(voir photo)*.

Les passagers doivent . . .

acheter un billet.
composter le billet.
monter dans leur train.
descendre de leur train à l'arrivée.

Mais attention, il ne faut pas **rater** le train.

Si on rate le train, il faut | **prendre** | **le prochain train.**
| **attendre** | **le train suivant.**

| **composter** *to punch [a ticket]*
monter(dans) *to get on [a train]*
descendre (de) *to get off [a train]*

rater *to miss* |

NOTE *Culturelle*

Avant de monter dans le train, les voyageurs doivent composter leurs billets. Le composteur indique l'heure et la date à laquelle le billet a été composté. Pendant le voyage, le contrôleur *(conductor)* passe dans les wagons pour contrôler les billets. Si on n'a pas composté son billet, on reçoit une amende *(fine)*.

Attention, attention!
Quai numéro 12.
Le train à destination de Lille va partir.
Attention au départ.

Teaching Strategy: Game

Charades

Write each of the vocabulary words from pp. 196–198 on an index card. Distribute two to every member of the class (more if the class is small). Students must attempt to act out a word so that the class can guess it. (If they have **la salle d'attente** they could sit down, look around, look bored, look at the clock and whistle.) Whoever guesses correctly is the next one to act out his/her word. The game continues until everyone has acted out all of his/her words.

1 Un voyage en avion

Vous êtes à Genève avec votre partenaire. Demain, vous avez l'intention d'aller à Nice en avion. Décrivez toutes les étapes *(steps, stages)* de ce voyage en avion en mettant les activités suivantes dans l'ordre chronologique.

- attacher nos ceintures de sécurité
- aller à l'aéroport
- débarquer
- embarquer
- dormir un peu
- passer par la douane
- aller à la porte 18
- chercher nos places dans l'avion

- passer le contrôle de sécurité
- aller au comptoir d'Air France
- montrer notre carte d'embarquement à l'hôtesse
- enregistrer nos bagages
- réserver deux places pour Nice
- sortir de l'aéroport
- téléphoner à l'agence de voyages
- chercher nos valises à la livraison des bagages

▶ **D'abord, nous allons téléphoner à l'agence de voyages. Nous allons . . .**

2 Un voyage en train

Maintenant vous allez de Nice à Cannes en train. Avec votre partenaire, décrivez ce que vous allez faire pendant ce voyage, dans l'ordre chronologique.

3 Club Vacances

Le site Club Vacances offre des voyages très bon marché. Choisissez un voyage et une date de départ. Avec votre partenaire, complétez le dialogue correspondant et jouez-le en classe. (Votre partenaire va jouer le rôle du représentant de Club Vacances à qui vous allez téléphoner.)

L'AGENT: Où désirez-vous aller, monsieur/ mademoiselle?

VOUS: – – –

L'AGENT: Quel jour désirez-vous partir?

VOUS: – – –

L'AGENT: Désirez-vous un aller simple?

VOUS: – – –

L'AGENT: En quelle classe?

VOUS: – – –

L'AGENT: Quelle place préférez-vous?

VOUS: – – –

L'AGENT: Désirez-vous louer une voiture? (Quelle voiture?)

VOUS: – – –

CLUB VACANCES

Profitez des prix exceptionnels offerts par Club Vacances et découvrez de nouveaux pays dans un confort grand luxe !

DESTINATIONS	DÉPARTS	
Dakar	3 juin	4 juillet
Marrakech	10 avril	5 septembre
Québec	8 juillet	2 août
Hong Kong	1er août	3 septembre
Buenos Aires	6 mai	4 juin
Djerba	12 juin	10 août
Fort-de-France	1er juillet	10 septembre

cent quatre-vingt-dix-neuf 199
Le Français pratique

■ **Note linguistique**

In Canada, **un guichet automatique** is an ATM machine. It is called **le distributeur de billets** or the **guichet automatique de banque (GAB)** in France. **Le guichetier/la guichetière** is the person who works behind the counter in a train station, a bank, or a post office.

■ **Note culturelle**

Dakar is the capital of Senegal. **Marrakesh** is famous for its large and labyrinthine souk (traditional market) in Morocco. **Fort-de-France** is the main city of Martinique

Teaching Strategy: Groups

Divide the class into groups. Ask students: Regardez les symboles (pictogrammes) à la page 198. Pouvez-vous deviner *(guess)* ce qu'ils représentent sans lire l'explication? Quels autres symboles de ce type connaissez-vous? Décrivez-les en français. *(fork and knife: restaurant; bed: hotel; tent: campground; gas pump: gas station.)*

Have students create their own new icons.

4 **Pas de chance**

Il y a des voyageurs qui n'ont pas de chance. Avec votre partenaire,
complétez les échanges suivants.

1. «Est-ce que cette place est libre?»
   «Non, – – – .»
2. «Est-ce que le train est à l'heure?»
   «Non, – – – .»
3. «Est-ce que le vol à destination de
   Toronto a été confirmé?»
   «Non, – – – .»
4. «Est-ce que le vol est direct?»
   «Non, – – – à Genève.»
5. «Est-ce que le train pour Tours est direct?»
   «Non, – – – à Saint-Pierre.»
6. «Est-ce qu'il y a de la place sur le prochain vol?»
   «Non, – – – .»

5 **Train ou avion?**

Vous voulez visiter l'Europe avec votre partenaire. Vous n'êtes pas d'accord
sur le mode de transport que vous allez utiliser pendant le voyage: train ou avion?

Chacun va choisir un mode de transport (train ou avion) et essayer de convaincre
(to convince) son partenaire. Présentez vos arguments par ordre de préférence.
Qui va gagner le débat? Voici quelques idées:

TRAIN
- C'est moins cher.
- On peut mieux voir le paysage.
- On peut faire connaissance
  de plus de personnes.
- On peut se déplacer *(to get
  around)* plus facilement.
- **??**

AVION
- C'est plus rapide.
- C'est plus confortable.
- On est moins fatigué.
- On a plus de temps pour visiter
  le pays.
- **??**

Conversations libres Avec votre partenaire, choisissez l'une des situations suivantes.
Composez le dialogue correspondant et jouez-le en classe.

1	Un voyage en avion

Caroline va aller à la Martinique
avec son petit frère Julien, 8 ans.
C'est la première fois que Julien
prend l'avion. Il pose beaucoup
de questions à sa sœur qui lui
explique comment va se passer
le voyage.
Rôles: Caroline / Julien

2	Trop tard!

Aujourd'hui vous partez en France. Malheureusement vous
arrivez à l'aéroport avec cinq minutes de retard. Votre
avion vient juste de partir. Allez au comptoir d'Air France
et expliquez la situation à l'employé(e). (Donnez des
précisions sur le vol que vous avez raté.) Demandez-lui
de vous trouver une place sur le vol suivant.
Rôles: vous / l'employé(e) d'Air France

3	Contrôle de billets

Vous êtes dans le train Paris-Strasbourg. Vous avez acheté un
billet de 2e classe. Vous n'avez pas fait attention et vous êtes
allé(e) dans un wagon de 1re classe. Le contrôleur *(conductor)*
arrive. Il vous demande de payer un supplément. Vous n'avez
pas assez d'argent. Expliquez-lui la situation.
Rôles: vous / le contrôleur

@HOMETUTOR
my.hrw.com

A Le futur

The FUTURE tense is used to describe what people WILL DO, what WILL HAPPEN.
The verbs in the following sentences are in the future tense.

L'avion **partira** dans dix minutes.   *The plane **will leave** in ten minutes.*
Nous **irons** en France cet été.   *We **will go** to France this summer.*

The future tense is a SIMPLE tense. It is formed as follows:

> **FUTURE STEM + FUTURE ENDINGS**

INFINITIVE		parler	finir	vendre	FUTURE ENDINGS
FUTURE STEM		parler-	finir-	vendr-	
FUTURE	je	**parlerai**	finirai	vendrai	-ai
	tu	**parleras**	finiras	vendras	-as
	il/elle/on	**parlera**	finira	vendra	-a
	nous	**parlerons**	finirons	vendrons	-ons
	vous	**parlerez**	finirez	vendrez	-ez
	ils/elles	**parleront**	finiront	vendront	-ont
NEGATIVE	je ne	**parlerai pas**			
INTERROGATIVE	est-ce que tu	**parleras?**			
		parleras-tu?			

The stem of the future always ends in -r.
→ For most verbs,

> **FUTURE STEM = INFINITIVE** *(minus -e, if any)*

partir → je **partir**ai   **écrire** → j'**écrir**ai

La prochaine fois,
je partirai à temps,
je ne m'arrêterai pas
en route,
et j'arriverai le premier.

ARRIVÉE

→ Some verbs have irregular future stems.

INFINITIVE	FUTURE STEM	
acheter	**achèter-**	**j'achèterai**
appeler	**appeller-**	**j'appellerai**
payer	**paier-**	**je paierai**
avoir	**aur-**	**j'aurai**
être	**ser-**	**je serai**
aller	**ir-**	**j'irai**
faire	**fer-**	**je ferai**
venir	**viendr-**	**je viendrai**

INFINITIVE	FUTURE STEM	
devoir	**devr-**	**je devrai**
pouvoir	**pourr-**	**je pourrai**
vouloir	**voudr-**	**je voudrai**
envoyer	**enverr-**	**j'enverrai**
recevoir	**recevr-**	**je recevrai**
savoir	**saur-**	**je saurai**
voir	**verr-**	**je verrai**

Also: il y a → **il y aura**   il pleut → **il pleuvra**

Pratique p. 57
Le futur

Differentiation

Structured Teach the future tense. Have students copy one regular verb in the future for each of the 3 verb groups: **-er, -ir, -re.** Have students write endings in red. Have students practice verbs orally and underline all forms pronounced identically in black.

Langue et Communication

■ Teaching Strategy: Game

Le futur
Draw a 6x6 grid on the board with subject pronouns on the vertical axis and six different verbs on the horizontal axis. Write down on a slip of paper the future conjugation from one of the boxes of the grid and ask each student to guess which conjugation you have chosen: «Est-ce que c'est....» Write that conjugation into the appropriate box on the grid but say «Non, ce n'est pas...» The game continues until a student guesses the conjugation that you had written down. That student then takes your place.

■ Note culturelle

Le Lièvre et la tortue is a famous fable by French author Jean de La Fontaine (see pp. 136 and 146 for more information). It is the story of how a hare lost a race to a turtle. The hare was so sure of his speed that he took a rest along the way. When he finally realized that the turtle would win the race, it was too late for him to catch up. The moral of the fable is: **Rien ne sert de courir, il faut partir à point** *(on time).*

RESOURCES

TECHNOLOGY

@HomeTutor

Teacher One Stop

🖵 **Projectable Transparencies**

*3, Le monde francophone:
L'Amérique*

Transparency Copymasters,
pp. A8–A9

■ **Notes linguistiques**

épicé = spicy, hot
une épice = spice
épicer = to spice

■ **Teaching Note**

Activity 3 reviews object
pronouns.

---

① Cet été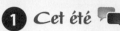

Demandez à votre partenaire s'il/si elle fera les choses suivantes cet été.
Si votre partenaire répond affirmativement, essayez de continuer la conversation.

▸ travailler?

Tu travailleras cet été?

Oui, je travaillerai.

Ah bon, qu'est-ce que tu feras?

Je serai serveur/serveuse dans un restaurant.

(Non, je ne travaillerai pas.)

- gagner de l'argent?
- rester chez toi?
- écrire à tes copains?
- être chez toi en août?
- avoir un job?
- faire du sport?

- faire du camping?
- aller à la mer?
- avoir l'occasion de voyager?
- aller à l'étranger?
- voir tes grands-parents?
- rendre visite à tes cousins?

② Des vacances différentes

Cet été vous allez faire les choses de la colonne A. Votre partenaire a des projets différents
(des projets de la colonne B ou d'autres projets). Chacun expliquera ses projets à l'autre.

A	B
aller à la Martinique	aller au Canada
prendre l'avion	prendre le train
louer une voiture	louer un vélo
aller à l'hôtel	faire du camping
manger des plats épicés	manger du homard *(lobster)*
faire de la planche à voile	visiter les Parcs Nationaux
assister aux spectacles folkloriques	voir les matchs de baseball
voir mes copains	rendre visite à mon oncle
se reposer	être très actif/active
??	??

— Moi, j'irai à la Martinique. Je prendrai l'avion.
— Eh bien, moi, je n'irai pas à la Martinique. J'irai au Canada. Je . . .

③ Procrastination

Vous faites un voyage avec un(e) camarade qui ne fait jamais immédiatement ce qu'il/elle doit faire.
Votre partenaire va répondre à vos questions en utilisant un pronom complément.

▸ visiter le musée (samedi)

   — **Quand est-ce que tu visiteras
   le musée?**
   — **Je le visiterai samedi.**

1. écrire à tes parents (demain)
2. téléphoner à ta copine (samedi)
3. envoyer ces lettres (ce soir)
4. acheter ton billet (la semaine prochaine)
5. confirmer ta réservation (dans une semaine)
6. acheter des cadeaux (le jour du départ)
7. prendre des photos (pendant le weekend)
8. voir ce monument (dimanche)

Notes culturelles

- In a typical restaurant in Quebec, you will be
served **la poutine**, a dish consisting of french
fries topped with melted white cheese and
brown gravy. (Even McDonald's in Montreal
serves this typical side dish.)

- Two Canadian baseball teams are the
Toronto Blue Jays and the Montreal Expos.

ALLONS PLUS LOIN

Note the different uses of **quitter** and **partir**:

quitter + NOUN	*to leave (a place)*	Nous **quitterons** l'hôtel à 6 heures.
	to take leave of, to leave (a person)	J'**ai quitté** mon cousin à la gare.
partir	*to leave*	Je **partirai** demain matin.
partir de	*to leave from (a place)*	Nous **partirons de** New York.
partir à (en, pour)	*to leave for (a destination)*	Nous **partons en** France.

4 **Un voyage à Québec**

Digital **performance space**

Vous allez visiter Québec avec un voyage organisé. Demandez à votre guide (votre partenaire) des détails sur ce voyage. Il/elle va vous répondre sur la base du programme.

▶ comment / aller à Québec?

— **Comment est-ce qu'on ira à Québec?**
— **On ira en avion.**

- quel jour / arriver à Québec?
- combien de jours / rester?
- comment / faire un tour de la ville?
- quel monument / voir vendredi après-midi?
- où / dîner vendredi soir?
- quand / faire une promenade en bateau?
- quoi / faire dimanche matin?
- comment / aller là-bas?
- quel jour / pouvoir faire du shopping?
- quel jour / revenir aux États-Unis?
- à quelle heure / partir?

Voyage à Québec ...

vendredi 4 mai

10h25 arrivée à Québec
Air Canada, vol 208

14h00 tour de la ville en calèche

15h30 visite de la Citadelle et des plaines d'Abraham

19h30 dîner dans un restaurant québécois typique

samedi 5 mai

9h30 promenade en bateau sur le Saint-Laurent
après-midi libre

20h30 concert de chansons québécoises

dimanche 6 mai

8h45 excursion à Sainte-Anne de Beaupré en autocar

16h38 départ de Québec
Air Canada, vol 209

5 **Une lettre**

Maintenant écrivez une lettre à votre cousin Patrick. Dans cette lettre, décrivez le voyage que vous allez faire.

Mon Cher Patrick,
Voici le programme de notre voyage organisé à Québec. Nous partirons le 4 mai. Nous voyagerons en avion...

Notes linguistiques
le **voyage organisé** = package tour
1 km = 0.6214 mile
la **calèche** = carriage

■ Expansion: Activity 4

- Have students use the Internet to do research on taking a trip to Quebec. They can check flight information on the French-language version of the airline's website, study the websites of the sites mentioned in the brochure, and search for current cultural activities and other places to visit on the city's official tourism website. (You may want to locate and bookmark useful websites in advance.) They could also e-mail hotels and places of business to ask for information or brochures. Have each student prepare a personal itinerary for the trip.

■ Student Portfolios

Have students prepare the letters they have written in Act. 5 for inclusion in their portfolios.

■ Rubrics: Activity 5

For writing rubrics, consult the **Generate Success** Rubric Generator on the **Teacher One Stop**. You can also create your own custom rubrics with this tool.

Notes culturelles

- The British built **la Citadelle** in 1759 after the battle between the French and the British. Its purpose was to protect Quebec City from further attack. Visitors can see the changing of the guard (**la relève de la garde**) by the Royal 22nd Regiment.
- The Quebec National Battlefields Park (**le Parc des Champs de bataille**) is located on **les plaines d'Abraham**, commemorating the battle of 1759. It is now a favorite spot for strollers, joggers, picnickers, and tourists.
- **Sainte-Anne de Beaupré:** Pilgrims have come to this church since the 17th century to pay their respects to Saint Anne, the mother of the Virgin Mary.

■ **Teaching Strategy: Expansions linguistiques**

• You may point out that, depending on emphasis, the **si**-clause may come in first <u>or</u> second position.
Je passerai chez toi si j'ai le temps.
• The **quand**-clause may come before or after the main clause.

■ **Teaching Strategy: Expansions**

Si, used as a conjunction, is different from both **si** used as an adverb of degree, and **si** used to replace **oui** in answering a negative question. Examples:

• CONJUNCTION
Si je n'ai plus mal aux dents, j'irai au restaurant avec vous.

• ADVERB
J'ai si mal aux dents que je ne peux rien manger.

• REPLACES **OUI**
Tu n'as plus mal aux dents? Si! (phrase word)

B   L'usage du futur dans les phrases avec *si*

Note the use of the future in the following sentences.

Si le bus **n'arrive pas,** nous **prendrons** le train.
*If the bus **does not come,** we **will take** the train.*

Si je **passe** par l'agence de voyages, j'**achèterai** les billets.
*If I **go** by the travel agency, I **will** buy the tickets.*

The above sentences express what WILL HAPPEN *if* a certain condition is met. They consist of two parts:

• the **si** *(if)* clause, which expresses the condition
• the result clause, which tells what WILL HAPPEN

In French, as in English, the pattern of tenses is:

si-clause: PRESENT	result clause: FUTURE
Si j'**ai** de l'argent,	je **voyagerai.**

C   L'usage du futur après *quand*

Compare the use of tenses in French and English in the following sentences.

J'attacherai ma ceinture **quand** l'avion **partira.**
*I **will fasten** my seat belt **when** the plane **leaves.***

Quand nous **arriverons** à Paris, nous **passerons** par la douane.
***When** we **arrive** in Paris, we **will go** through customs.*

When referring to future events, the French use the future tense in <u>both</u> the **quand** *(when)* clause and the main clause. The pattern is:

quand-clause: FUTURE	result clause: FUTURE
Quand j'**aurai** de l'argent,	je **voyagerai.**

→ The future is also used after **quand** when the main clause is in the IMPERATIVE and a future event is implied.

Écris-moi quand tu **seras** à Nice.
***Write me** when you **are** in Nice.*

VOCABULAIRE   Quelques conjonctions de temps

lorsque	when	**Lorsque** j'aurai mon passeport, je partirai.
dès que	as soon as	J'écrirai à Sylvie **dès que** j'aurai son adresse.
aussitôt que	as soon as	Nous vous téléphonerons **aussitôt que** nous serons à Nice.

→ The future is used after these conjunctions, as it is after **quand.**

Differentiation

Synthetic/Analytic, Gifted & Talented
Write an example of a **si**-clause and result clause sentence on the board and have students label the parts of the sentence. Then have pairs of students formulate and test a scientific hypothesis worded as a **si**-clause. (Consult a science teacher at your school for classroom-appropriate experiments.) Have students present the results of their experiment to the class.

6 Attention!

Quand on voyage, il faut faire certaines choses sinon on aura un problème.
Exprimez cela pour les personnes suivantes.

PERSONNES	CHOSES À FAIRE	PROBLÈMES
vous	arriver à l'heure	rater la correspondance
nous	se dépêcher	rater le train
Béatrice	réserver à l'avance	ne pas trouver de place
les touristes	confirmer la réservation	payer un supplément
M. Duval	composter le billet	avoir une amende *(fine)*
	avoir un passeport	ne pas pouvoir voyager
	présenter la carte	monter dans l'avion
	d'embarquement	devoir les mettre sous le siège
	enregistrer les bagages	

▶ **Si M. Duval ne se dépêche pas, il ratera la correspondance.**

7 Une question de circonstances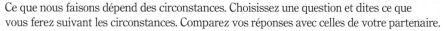

Ce que nous faisons dépend des circonstances. Choisissez une question et dites ce que
vous ferez suivant les circonstances. Comparez vos réponses avec celles de votre partenaire.

1. Qu'est-ce que tu feras ce week-end . . .
- s'il pleut?
- s'il fait beau?
- si tu restes chez toi?

3. Qu'est-ce que tu feras après l'école secondaire . . .
- si tu vas à l'université?
- si tu veux gagner ta vie?
- si tu ne trouves pas de travail?

2. Qu'est-ce que tu feras cet été . . .
- si tu travailles?
- si tu as assez d'argent?
- si tu vas à la mer?

4. Qu'est-ce que tu feras plus tard . . .
- si tu es marié(e)?
- si tu gagnes beaucoup d'argent?
- si tu n'aimes pas ton travail?

8 Projets de voyage

Choisissez une personne et dites ce qu'elle fera quand elle sera dans un certain endroit.

nous	aller	(l') Égypte	assister à (une corrida, ??)
vous	être	(la) France	voir (les pyramides, ??)
Pauline	visiter	(le) Canada	aller à (un match de hockey, ??)
mes cousins		(les) États-Unis	visiter (le Grand Canyon, ??)
		(l') Espagne	parler (français, ??)
		(le) Mexique	acheter (du parfum, ??)
		(la) Chine	manger (du poulet frit, ??)

▶ **Quand Pauline sera en Espagne, elle parlera espagnol. Elle mangera . . .**

■ Teaching Strategy

Have students prepare a tourist brochure — with illustrations — inviting French visitors to your city or region. Use the future tense to explain what the tourists will be able to do.
Venez visiter Boston! Vous vous promenerez dans la vieille ville. Vous visiterez Fanueil Hall et King's Chapel. Vous verrez … *etc.*

Scan the finished product and e-mail it to a partner class in a French-speaking country to get some feedback on the brochure and see if students in the partner class would be interested in visiting your region.

■ Student Portfolios

Have students keep their letters from Act. 11 for their portfolios. Remind them that a French letter starts with:
Cher/Chère + prénom or
Mon cher…/ Ma chère + prénom. It can be ended with one of the following expressions: **Amitiés, Affectueusement, Bien à toi, Sincèrement,** or, if you are very familiar with the person, **Bisous, or Grosses bises** *(kisses).*

206 Unité 5

---

9 S'il te plaît! 🗨

Votre partenaire vous dit ce qu'il/elle va faire. Demandez-lui de faire les choses suggérées (ou d'autres choses de votre choix).

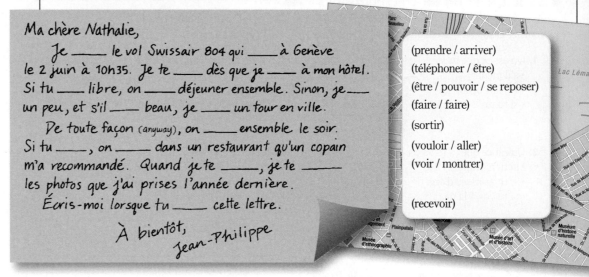

> Je vais aller à la poste.
>
> Eh bien, quand tu iras à la poste, envoie cette lettre, s'il te plaît.
>
> D'accord, j'enverrai cette lettre.

1. partir
   (fermer la porte)
2. faire les courses
   (acheter du fromage)
3. passer à la bibliothèque
   (rendre ce livre)
4. aller à la gare
   (prendre les billets)
5. aller à l'agence de voyages
   (réserver les places)
6. voir Patrick
   (l'inviter à la boum)

10 Une visite à Genève

Jean-Philippe, un étudiant belge, va aller à Genève. Il écrit à sa copine Nathalie qui habite dans cette ville. Complétez sa lettre avec le présent ou le futur des verbes indiqués.

Ma chère Nathalie,

Je _____ le vol Swissair 804 qui _____ à Genève le 2 juin à 10h35. Je te _____ dès que je _____ à mon hôtel. Si tu _____ libre, on _____ déjeuner ensemble. Sinon, je _____ un peu, et s'il _____ beau, je _____ un tour en ville.

De toute façon (anyway), on _____ ensemble le soir. Si tu _____, on _____ dans un restaurant qu'un copain m'a recommandé. Quand je te _____, je te _____ les photos que j'ai prises l'année dernière.

Écris-moi lorsque tu _____ cette lettre.

À bientôt,
Jean-Philippe

(prendre / arriver)
(téléphoner / être)
(être / pouvoir / se reposer)
(faire / faire)
(sortir)
(vouloir / aller)
(voir / montrer)

(recevoir)

11 Bienvenue chez nous! ✏️

Votre amie française Frédérique va passer le week-end dans votre ville. Préparez un programme d'activités que vous ferez ensemble et écrivez une lettre à Frédérique où vous expliquez ce programme. Utilisez des verbes comme **aller, voir, visiter, faire, dîner, déjeuner, prendre, se promener, s'arrêter.**

Digital performance space

Ma chère Frédérique,
Je suis très content(e) que tu passes le week-end dans ma ville. J'irai te chercher à l'aéroport [à la gare / à la station de bus] vendredi soir. Voici ce que nous ferons lorsque tu seras ici. Samedi matin, nous …

Warm-Up/Pre-Teaching

Draw a picture on the board/transparency of a person who needs a lot of help. He/she could have a horrible hair style, pants too short, or a test on which he/she received a 40/100. Have students suggest additional problems and illustrate each one on a separate piece of paper.

Collect all the papers. After presenting the conditional (p. 207), have the students individually or in pairs write **si** clause sentences beginning with something like
«**Il/elle serait plus belle si…**» or
«**Il/elle aurait plus d'amis si…**»

D Le conditionnel

In the sentences below, the verbs in heavy print are in the CONDITIONAL.

Si c'était les vacances, ...	*If it were summer vacation, ...*
• je **voyagerais**	• *I would travel*
• nous **irions** au Sénégal	• *we would go to Senegal*
• vous **n'étudieriez pas**	• *you would not study*

The CONDITIONAL is used to describe what people WOULD DO, what WOULD HAPPEN if a certain condition were to be met.

The CONDITIONAL is a simple tense which is formed as follows:

```
FUTURE STEM + IMPERFECT ENDINGS
```

INFINITIVE		parler	finir	vendre	aller	IMPERFECT ENDINGS
FUTURE	je	**parler**ai	**finir**ai	**vendr**ai	**ir**ai	
CONDITIONAL	je	**parler**ais	**finir**ais	**vendr**ais	**ir**ais	-ais
	tu	**parler**ais	**finir**ais	**vendr**ais	**ir**ais	-ais
	il/elle/on	**parler**ait	**finir**ait	**vendr**ait	**ir**ait	-ait
	nous	**parler**ions	**finir**ions	**vendr**ions	**ir**ions	-ions
	vous	**parler**iez	**finir**iez	**vendr**iez	**ir**iez	-iez
	ils/elles	**parler**aient	**finir**aient	**vendr**aient	**ir**aient	-aient
NEGATIVE	je **ne**	**parler**ais pas				
INTERROGATIVE	est-ce que tu	**parler**ais?				
		parlerais-tu?				

→ Verbs that have an irregular future stem keep the same stem in the conditional.

avoir **aur-** j'**aur**ais   être **ser-** je **ser**ais

12 Vivement les vacances! *(Waiting for summer vacation)*

Les personnes suivantes rêvent des vacances. Dites ce qu'elles feraient et ce qu'elles ne feraient pas. Soyez logique!

▶ Mme Leduc (travailler? se reposer?)
  Mme Leduc ne travaillerait pas. Elle se reposerait.

1. nous (préparer l'examen? voyager?)
2. les élèves (aller à la plage? étudier?)
3. vous (rester chez vous? faire du camping?)
4. Marc (être tout le temps à la plage? regarder la télé?)
5. toi (te lever tôt? dormir jusqu'à dix heures?)
6. moi (faire mes devoirs? sortir avec mes copains?)

Pratique p. 60
Le conditionnel

Teaching Strategy: Expansion

Ask students:
Que feriez-vous si vous étiez riche? Répondez aux questions affirmativement ou négativement en formant des phrases complètes. **Si j'étais riche,...**

1. acheter des vêtements au marché aux puces? (j'achèterais.../ je n'achèterais pas de...)
2. avoir un ordinateur portable? (j'aurais/je n'aurais pas d'...)
3. être généreux(euse) avec vos amis? (je serais/ je ne serais pas...)
4. utiliser une petite voiture? (j'utiliserais/je n'utiliserais pas de...)
5. prendre beaucoup de vacances? (je prendrais/ je ne prendrais pas...)
6. sortir tous les soirs? (je sortirais/je ne sortirais pas...)

Unité 5

Interdisciplinary/ Community Connections

Plan several possible class trips, each focusing on a different mode of transportation (bus, train, plane). Display the finished plans in the school library for future classes, or develop into a formal presentation to school governing bodies to gain approval for a trip.

Language Arts
In small groups, write why you want to travel, what you hope to learn, and how you might raise funds.

Math
For each destination, calculate the cost of travel, food, lodging, and entertainment.

Science
Choose several modes of transportation, and investigate the history of each. Then, in small groups, figure out where you could travel from your town using that mode of transportation, and choose destinations.

Social Studies
Choose a museum or historic site at your destination and explain why you want to visit it.

Technology
Use the Internet to do research or make travel reservations. Create your plans for the trip collaboratively via a class wiki page.

Community
If you take a trip, keep a log to share with future classes.

■ Teaching Notes

- The conditional is presented here primarily for recognition. The use of the conditional is presented in more detail in Unit 8.
- To review the imperfect tense, see Unité 3, page 116.

Unité 5   207

 **Reading STRATEGY**

Reading fiction, extended reading

RESOURCES

PRINT
Activités pour tous

TECHNOLOGY
Teacher One Stop
🖥 **Projectable Transparencies**

L5, *Le mystérieux homme en bleu*

Transparency Copymasters,
pp. A127–A128

French InterActive Reader

■ **Note linguistique**
Familles de mots:
l'inspecteur, inspecter,
l'inspection *(f.)*
l'espion, espionner,
l'espionnage *(m.)*
le voleur, voler, le vol

■ **Irregular Verbs**
(see Appendix C)
disparaître *(see* **connaître***)*

Additional readings @ **my.hrw.com**
FRENCH
InterActive ▌Reader

LECTURE

Le mystérieux homme en bleu

AVANT DE LIRE

Quand on lit une histoire illustrée, il est important de regarder les illustrations pour comprendre le sens général. Si on peut deviner° plus ou moins ce qui va arriver, il est beaucoup plus facile de comprendre les détails.

Le mystérieux homme en bleu est une histoire policière illustrée. Avec votre partenaire, regardez bien les illustrations pour avoir une idée générale de ce qui se passe. Avant de commencer la lecture de l'histoire à la page suivante, essayez de répondre aux questions suivantes.

1. **Qui est le mystérieux homme en bleu?**
   • un détective privé
   • un inspecteur de police
   • un espion international

2. **Qui est Caroline?**
   • une jeune touriste
   • la complice de l'homme en bleu
   • la cousine de l'homme à la mallette jaune

3. **Pourquoi est-ce que la chambre de Caroline est en désordre?**
   • Des voleurs sont entrés pour voler ses chèques de voyage.
   • La police est venue chercher des documents volés.
   • L'homme à la mallette est venu chercher son passeport.

Maintenant lisez l'histoire et voyez si vous aviez raison.

deviner *to guess*

Mots utiles

LES PERSONNAGES		LES ACTIONS	
un détective privé	*private eye*	**récupérer**	*to get back, recuperate*
un inspecteur de police	*police detectivet*	**arrêter**	*to arrest*
un(e) espion(ne)	*spy*	**cacher**	*to hide*
un voleur (une voleuse)	*thief*	**voler**	*to steal*
un(e) complice	*accomplice*	**sauver**	*to save*
une bande	*gang*	**disparaître ***	*to disappear, to go away*

QUELQUES OBJETS	
une loupe	*magnifying glass*
une mallette	*briefcase*
une plaque d'immatriculation	*license plate*

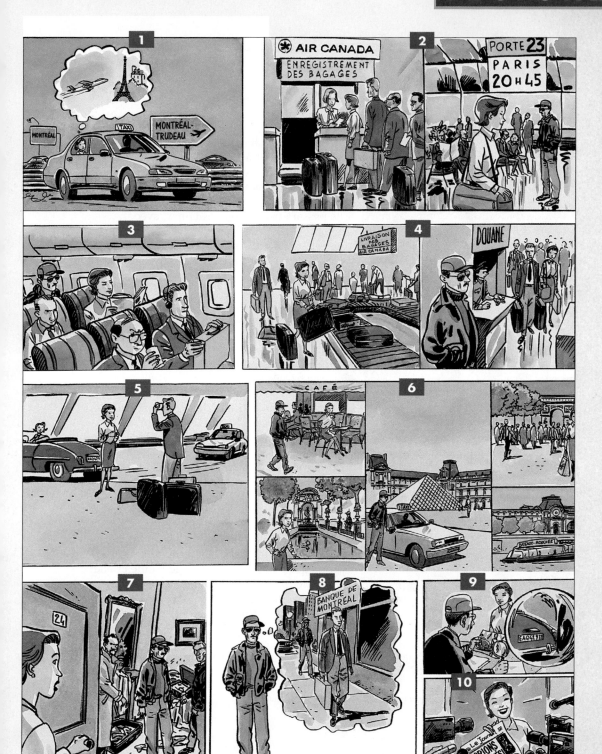

■ **Note culturelle**
This story is presented here as a **bande dessinée,** the most popular form of reading material among French teens. Ask students if there are similar formats read by teens in the U.S.

■ **Teaching Suggestion**
If French language comic books, such as *Tintin* and *Astérix*, are available to your students, encourage them to read one outside of class. You may wish to have volunteers bring in the comic books they read, summarize them for the class, and give their opinions of them.

Teaching Strategy: Expansion

Divide the class into groups. Each group is assigned one of the numbered pictures and must then write a description and a corresponding narrative (saying who the character is, what is happening, where the character is going and what he is doing and why). Then gather the material and have groups read their descriptions in the order of the pictures. Ask students:
• Do you have a coherent story?
• Can you develop one from what the group wrote?
Pre-AP skill: Form cohesive sentences, paragraphs and essays.

Unité 5   209

Le mystérieux homme en bleu

Première partie

Caroline a fait ses valises. Puis elle a pris son passeport et son billet d'avion et elle a appelé un taxi pour aller à Montréal-Trudeau, l'aéroport international de Montréal. Dans le taxi, Caroline pense au voyage qu'elle va faire. [5] C'est la première fois qu'elle va en France. Elle passera trois semaines là-bas, avec l'argent qu'elle a économisé pendant l'année. Elle espère faire un excellent voyage. Ce sera peut-être un voyage plein d'aventures [10] extraordinaires. Qui sait?

Caroline est arrivée à l'aéroport une heure avant le départ de l'avion Montréal-Paris. Elle est allée au comptoir d'Air Canada où elle a présenté son billet [15] et son passeport et elle a enregistré ses bagages.

Puis, elle est allée dans la salle d'embarquement. Là, elle a immédiatement remarqué un mystérieux homme vêtu de [20] bleu:° pantalon bleu, pull bleu, blouson bleu, casquette bleue et lunettes de soleil. «Quel homme étrange!» a pensé Caroline.

Bientôt° on a annoncé le départ pour Paris. Caroline et les autres passagers sont montés dans l'avion. L'homme en bleu aussi. [25]

Caroline est allée à sa place. Le mystérieux homme en bleu est venu s'asseoir derrière elle. Pendant le voyage, Caroline a regardé quelques magazines, puis elle a dîné et elle a vu le film. Après le film, elle a dormi un peu. [30] Quand elle s'est réveillée, Caroline a regardé derrière elle. L'homme en bleu n'était plus là… il avait changé de place.

Finalement, après six heures de vol, l'avion est arrivé à Roissy, l'aéroport de Paris. [35]

vêtu de bleu = qui portait des vêtements bleus **bientôt** = dans peu de temps

Notes culturelles

- The international airport of Montreal is named **Montréal-Trudeau** in honor of **Pierre Trudeau**, a former Prime Minister of Canada. Ask students to locate Montreal on a map. Have any students in the class visited Montreal?

- There are two main airports in Paris: **Roissy-Charles de Gaulle** (north of the city) and **Orly** (south of the city).

Caroline a pris son sac à main et elle est sortie de l'avion. Puis elle est allée chercher ses deux valises. Malheureusement, celles-ci sont très lourdes et Caroline n'est pas très forte. Voyant° l'embarras° de Caroline, un grand jeune homme blond avec une mallette de cuir jaune s'est approché d'elle.

— Est-ce que je peux vous aider avec vos valises? **40**

— Ah oui, s'il vous plaît.

— Tenez, prenez ma mallette et moi, je vais porter vos valises.

Caroline a pris la mallette du jeune **45** homme et le jeune homme a pris les valises de Caroline. Ils sont passés ensemble par la douane, sans problème.

De l'autre côté de° la douane, il y avait l'homme en bleu. Il a regardé longuement Caroline, puis il a disparu. «Ce type° est vraiment bizarre,» a pensé Caroline. **50**

Caroline et son compagnon sont sortis de l'aéroport. Une femme très élégante, dans une petite voiture de sport rouge, attendait le jeune homme. Elle avait l'air un peu irritée de voir Caroline. Le jeune homme a posé les valises de Caroline par terre° et il a appelé un taxi pour elle. **55** Caroline a remercié le jeune homme et elle lui a demandé un petit service.

— J'ai promis à mes amies de leur envoyer des photos de moi à Paris. Voici mon appareil. Est-ce que vous pouvez prendre une ou deux photos?

— Mais, bien sûr! Avec plaisir! **60**

Caroline s'est mise° à côté de la voiture de sport et le jeune homme a pris plusieurs photos.

— Merci beaucoup.

— Bon séjour en France!

Le jeune homme est monté dans la voiture de sport qui est partie très vite. **65** Caroline est montée dans le taxi et elle est allée directement à son hôtel.

voyant = quand il a vu **l'embarras** = la difficulté **de l'autre côté de** = après **ce type** = cette personne
a posé = a mis **par terre** = sur le trottoir (*sidewalk*) **s'est mise** = est allé se placer

---

Avez-vous compris?

1. À quelle occasion est-ce que Caroline a rencontré l'homme en bleu pour la première fois? Décrivez-le.

2. Qu'est-ce que Caroline a fait dans l'avion Montréal-Paris?

3. À l'arrivée à l'aéroport, que fait le jeune homme blond pour aider Caroline? Qu'est-ce qu'elle fait en échange?

4. Quel service est-ce que Caroline demande au jeune homme à la sortie de l'aéroport?

À votre avis

Pourquoi la femme élégante était-elle irritée de voir Caroline?

• Elle était jalouse de Caroline.

• Elle était très pressée (*in a hurry*) de partir.

• Elle avait une autre raison. Laquelle?

■ **Irregular Verb**

(See Appendix C.)
promettre is conjugated like **mettre**

■ **Avez-vous compris?**

(*Sample answers*)

1. Elle l'a vu pour la première fois dans la salle d'embarquement de l'aéroport de Montréal. Il était habillé tout en bleu: pantalon, pull, blouson, casquette, tout était bleu. Il portait des lunettes de soleil.

2. Elle a regardé des magazines, elle a dîné et elle a vu le film.

3. Il porte les valises de Caroline, qui sont très lourdes. En échange, elle porte la mallette du jeune homme.

4. Elle lui demande de prendre des photos d'elle parce qu'elle veut les envoyer à ses amies.

■ **Teaching Strategy: Expansion**

Ask students:

Pourquoi Caroline pense-t-elle que l'homme en bleu est mystérieux? Et vous? Auriez-vous remarqué cet homme? Pourquoi?

LECTURE

■ **Illustrations**

Clockwise from bottom left:
- Caroline au jardin du Luxembourg
- Caroline à la terrasse d'un café
- la pyramide dans la cour Napoléon au musée du Louvre
- l'Arc de Triomphe au bout des Champs-Élysées
- le bateau-mouche sur la Seine.

Deuxième Partie

À l'hôtel, Caroline a défait ses valises. Elle a changé de vêtements et elle est sortie. Elle est allée d'abord dans un café où elle a commandé un café et des croissants. Quelques minutes après, l'homme en bleu est, lui aussi, entré dans le café. 70

«Encore lui!° Mais qu'est-ce qu'il fait ici?» a pensé Caroline. 75

Elle a fini son café et ses croissants, et elle est sortie du café en vitesse.°

Caroline est allée au jardin du Luxembourg où elle a fait une promenade. Derrière, il y avait l'homme en bleu. Elle a pris un taxi et elle est allée au musée du Louvre. L'homme en bleu est sorti d'un autre taxi et il est entré au Louvre. 80

«Zut, zut et zut! Pourquoi est-ce que ce type me suit partout?» Caroline est sortie

du musée et elle a pris un bus pour aller aux Champs-Elysées. Elle a regardé derrière elle. Cette fois-ci, l'homme en bleu ne la suivait pas. «Je l'ai finalement perdu… Je suis sauvée!» a-t-elle pensé. 85

À sept heures, Caroline a décidé de dîner sur un bateau-mouche.* Quelle façon magnifique de passer une première soirée à Paris! Finalement, à onze heures, elle est rentrée à son hôtel. Pas de trace de l'homme en bleu! 90

Quand Caroline a ouvert la porte de sa chambre, elle a tout de suite° vu que celle-ci° était dans le désordre le plus complet. Et debout,° au milieu de la chambre, était l'homme en bleu accompagné de deux hommes en imperméable beige.

«Qu'est-ce que vous faites dans ma chambre? a crié Caroline. Si vous ne sortez pas immédiatement, j'appellerai la police.» 95

«Mais, mademoiselle, a répondu l'homme en bleu, nous sommes de la police.»
Et il a montré sa carte de police à Caroline.

— Qu'est-ce que vous voulez?
— Nous voulons savoir où est la mallette. 100
— Quelle mallette?
— La mallette de cuir jaune que votre complice vous a donnée.
— Je ne comprends pas. De quel complice parlez-vous?
— Allons, mademoiselle, ne faites pas l'innocente.°
— Mais je suis innocente! 105
— Alors, qui est ce jeune homme blond qui est sorti de l'aéroport avec vous ce matin?
— Mais, je ne sais pas! Je ne le connais pas!

---

* Les bateaux-mouches sont des bateaux touristiques qui traversent Paris. Le soir, on peut y dîner.
encore lui = toujours la même personne   **en vitesse** = rapidement   **tout de suite** = immédiatement
celle-ci *the latter* [= sa chambre]   **debout** *standing*   **ne faites pas l'innocente** *don't act innocent*

Notes culturelles

- Spacelab, or le **Labo Spatial**, is a European space laboratory which is regularly launched into space and retrieved. Its crew of four performs diverse scientific tests and experiments. Spacelab can remain in orbit for up to 30 days.

- The French space agency is called le **CNES (Centre national d'études spatiales)**. There are three French space centers: Toulouse, Évry, and Kourou in French Guiana. The satellite launch rocket, the **Ariane**, always takes off from Kourou.

L'homme en bleu a compris que Caroline disait la vérité. Alors, il a expliqué: 110

«Je suis l'inspecteur de police Louis Legrand. Il y a un mois, des documents secrets très importants ont été volés au Ministère des Transports. Ces documents 115 concernent la construction de la station spatiale franco-canadienne. La semaine dernière, un de nos agents a signalé la présence à Montréal du chef de la bande responsable de ce vol. Cette personne, c'est 120 le jeune homme blond avec qui vous étiez ce matin. Samedi dernier, je suis allé à Montréal pour prendre contact avec notre agent. Grâce aux renseignements,° j'ai pu retrouver la trace du jeune homme en question. Je l'ai suivi quand il a pris l'avion Montréal-Paris.

«À Roissy, il vous a donné la mallette dans laquelle sont les documents. J'ai pensé 125 que vous étiez sa complice. En réalité, il a profité de vous pour passer la mallette par la douane sans problème. Je vous ai suivie parce que je pensais que vous aviez toujours° la mallette. J'ai fait erreur et je m'excuse. Évidemment, le problème pour nous, c'est que nous avons perdu la trace de ce dangereux bandit et de la mallette.»

«Je crois que je peux vous aider,» a répondu Caroline. 130

— Mais comment?

— Attendez demain, et donnez-moi votre adresse.

L'inspecteur Legrand a donné sa carte à Caroline et il a quitté l'hôtel, accompagné de ses deux assistants.

grâce aux renseignements = avec l'information qu'il m'a donnée   **toujours** *still*

Avez-vous compris?

1. Où est-ce que Caroline a revu l'homme après être sortie de l'hôtel? Où est-ce qu'elle l'a perdu?
2. Quelle surprise Caroline a-t-elle eue quand elle est rentrée chez elle?
3. Comment est-ce que l'homme en bleu et ses assistants ont justifié leur présence dans la chambre de Caroline?
4. D'après l'homme en bleu, qui est le jeune homme blond? Pourquoi a-t-il pensé que Caroline était sa complice?

Anticipons un peu!

Comment est-ce que Caroline va aider les policiers à retrouver le jeune homme blond?
- Elle a sa photo.
- Elle a son adresse.
- Elle a un autre renseignement. Lequel?

■ Avez-vous compris?

(Sample answers)
1. Elle l'a revu dans un café, puis au jardin du Luxembourg et au musée du Louvre. Elle l'a perdu quand elle a pris un bus pour aller aux Champs-Élysées.
2. Quand elle est rentrée à l'hôtel, elle a trouvé l'homme en bleu et deux autres hommes dans sa chambre, qui était dans un grand désordre.
3. Ils ont dit qu'ils étaient de la police.
4. Le jeune homme blond est le chef d'une bande qui a volé des documents très importants. L'homme en bleu a pensé que Caroline était sa complice parce qu'elle portait la mallette.

- In many Parisian cafés, you will find a basket filled with croissants on the table. You may help yourself, but they are not free! The waiter will know how many croissants you have eaten by counting those that are left.

214 Unité 5

Notes linguistiques

- Le numéro d'immatriculation est inscrit sur la plaque d'imma-triculation, aussi appelée la plaque minéralogique.
- Un inspecteur de police est un policier en civil *(in civilian clothes)* qui est chargé de mener les enquêtes. Le commissaire de police est chargé des travaux de police administrative. L'agent de police porte un uniforme.

Avez-vous compris?

(Sample answers)
1. Elle a apporté les photos prises par le jeune homme blond.
2. Sur les photos on voyait la voiture rouge des bandits et on pouvait lire son numéro d'immatriculation.
3. Le jeune homme a été arrêté, et Caroline est devenue célèbre. On lui a proposé un rôle dans un film, et elle va écrire le récit de ses aventures.

Troisième Partie

Le lendemain à deux heures de l'après-midi, Caroline est allée voir l'inspecteur Legrand au quartier général de la police. 135

— Bonjour, Inspecteur, j'ai une très bonne nouvelle pour vous. 140

— Ah bon? Quoi?

— Vous allez pouvoir retrouver la trace de vos voleurs de documents.

— Vraiment? Comment?

Caroline a ouvert son sac d'où 145
elle a tiré° les photos prises hier à l'aéroport.

— Regardez bien ces deux photos. Je les ai fait développer ce matin.

— Mais ce sont des photos de vous!

— Oui, bien sûr, mais regardez de plus près la voiture de sport rouge.

— Je vois bien. C'est une Alfa-Roméo. 150

— C'est aussi la voiture qu'ont prise le jeune homme et sa véritable° complice à l'aéroport. Prenez votre loupe. Vous pourrez lire très nettement son numéro d'immatriculation.

L'inspecteur Legrand a pris sa loupe.

— Vous avez raison, mademoiselle. Je vais alerter immédiatement tous les postes 155
de gendarmerie pour qu'on retrouve cette voiture et ses occupants.

Une semaine après, la police a arrêté le chef de bande et sa complice et les documents secrets ont été récupérés.

L'histoire de Caroline a été 160
publiée en première page de tous les journaux. Caroline a donné plusieurs interviews à la radio et à la télévision. Un studio de cinéma lui a proposé un rôle dans un prochain 165
film et une maison d'édition a pris contact avec elle pour publier le récit° de ses aventures.

a tiré = a sorti **véritable** = réelle **le récit** = l'histoire

Avez-vous compris?

1. Qu'est-ce que Caroline a apporté le lendemain?
2. En quoi est-ce que cela a aidé l'inspecteur?
3. Comment s'est terminée l'histoire pour le jeune homme blond? pour Caroline?

Et vous?

Imaginez que vous êtes Caroline. Qu'est-ce que vous allez faire?
- Accepter l'offre du studio de cinéma?
- Écrire le récit de vos aventures?

Pourquoi avez-vous choisi cette option?

APRÈS LA LECTURE

Expression orale

Dramatisation

Avec un groupe de camarades, transformez cette histoire en petite pièce de théâtre et jouez-la.

Situations

Avec votre partenaire, choisissez l'une des situations suivantes. Composez le dialogue correspondant et jouez-le en classe.

1	**Un coup de téléphone**
Caroline téléphone à un(e) ami(e) québécois(e) pour lui raconter ses aventures. L'ami(e) interrompt souvent et lui pose beaucoup de questions sur ce qui est arrivé. (Utilisez la forme **tu**.) *Rôles: Caroline, son ami(e)*	

2	**Une interview**
Un(e) journaliste pour Radio-Québec a obtenu une interview avec Caroline et lui pose beaucoup de questions. Il/Elle voudrait savoir ce que Caroline fera si elle accepte la proposition du studio de cinéma ou de la maison d'édition. Caroline est très contente de répondre. (Utilisez la forme **vous**.) *Rôles: le/la journaliste, Caroline*	

Expression écrite

L'histoire de «l'homme en bleu» est écrite objectivement, et cependant vous avez pu remarquer que l'auteur décrit les événements du point de vue de Caroline. Utilisez votre imagination pour raconter la même histoire d'un autre point de vue. Voici trois options:

Le rapport de l'inspecteur de police

L'inspecteur Louis Legrand, qui vient de recevoir les photos de Caroline, écrit un rapport à son chef. Dans ce rapport, il décrit ce qui est arrivé et aussi comment il arrêtera les voleurs.

Journal d'un prisonnier

L'homme à la mallette jaune (vous pouvez lui donner un nom) est maintenant en prison. Dans son journal intime, il décrit les événements qui ont mené à son arrestation.

Article de journal

Un(e) journaliste écrit un article où il décrit comment la police a récupéré les documents volés. Il utilise un style très direct.

■ Student Portfolio

These closing activities may be used for portfolio assessment.

■ Notes linguistiques

éditer/publier *to publish*
l'édition *publishing*
l'éditeur *publisher*
Note: **le réviseur/ le correcteur** *editor/ proofreader*
le rédacteur *editor (of a magazine)*

■ Expression écrite

For writing rubrics, consult the **Generate Success** Rubric Generator on the **Teacher One Stop**. You can also create your own custom rubrics with this tool.

Teaching Strategies: Expansions

- Now that your students know the story, have them go back to the comic strip on p. 209. In pairs or groups, have them make up captions and/or speech bubbles in French for each numbered frame.

- If your school has the appropriate audio-visual equipment, you could use this story as the basis for a short video. Students can participate as script writers, actors, directors, set designers, costume people, etc.

Interlude culturel

RESOURCES

TECHNOLOGY
Teacher One Stop

Pre-AP Digital Resources

 Projectable Transparencies

1(o), La France

6, Paris

H3, Histoire de France
(1715–1870)

Transparency Copymasters,
pp. A5–A6, A13–A14, A141–
A142

■ Note linguistique
le moulin à vent = windmill

■ Note historique
Après sa défaite à Leipzig
(Allemagne) en 1814, **Napoléon** est
exilé à l'île d'Elbe. Il revient en
France en mars 1815 et remonte sur
le trône, mais son nouveau règne ne
dure que cent jours. Son armée est
vaincue à **Waterloo** (Belgique) le 18
juin 1815, et Napoléon est exilé à
Sainte-Hélène où il passera la fin de
sa vie.

■ Irregular Verb
conquérir is conjugated like **acquérir**:

je conquiers
il conquiert
nous conquérons
ils conquièrent

Les dates

- 1715

Règne de
Louis XV

- 1774

Règne de
Louis XVI

- 1789: Prise
de la Bastille

**Révolution
française**

- 1804

**Premier Empire:
Napoléon Ier**

- 1814

- 1830 Révolution

- 1852

Second Empire
Napoléon III

- 1870

Les événements

La Révolution française (1789–1799)

La Révolution française est peut-être la période la plus
importante de l'histoire de France. Cette révolution a été inspirée
par la Révolution américaine. Le 14 juillet 1789,
les Français ont pris **la Bastille**, une prison qui
était le symbole de l'autorité royale. Le 26 août
de la même année, ils ont voté la **Déclaration
des Droits de l'Homme et du Citoyen** qui
proclamait un principe nouveau: l'égalité et la
liberté pour tous les hommes.

Trois ans plus tard, les Français ont
aboli la monarchie et ont institué la
République. C'est la Révolution qui a
donné à la France sa devise:° «**Liberté,
Égalité, Fraternité**».

La Révolution a aussi divisé la
France en «départements» et a
institué le système métrique.

L'épopée napoléonienne (1799–1815)

Napoléon Bonaparte (1769–1821) était le plus brillant général de la
Révolution française. En 1799, à l'âge de 30 ans, il a pris
le pouvoir° absolu. Cinq ans plus tard, en 1804, il s'est proclamé
empereur des Français sous le nom de **Napoléon Ier**.

À cette époque, la France avait beaucoup
d'ennemis: tous les pays d'Europe étaient
coalisés° contre elle. Allant de victoire en
victoire, «l'Aigle» (c'était le nom que les
soldats avaient donné à Napoléon) a battu ses
adversaires les uns après les autres. Au
passage, Napoléon annexait les pays qu'il
venait de conquérir. En dix ans, il a conquis
presque toute l'Europe. Mais finalement la
chance a tourné et l'armée de Napoléon a
été défaite en Russie. Prisonnier des Anglais,
Napoléon est mort en exil sur une petite île
loin de la France.

Génie militaire, Napoléon a été aussi un grand administrateur.
Il a développé l'industrie. Il a encouragé les sciences. Il a ouvert
de nombreuses écoles d'ingénieurs. Il a établi une solide
administration. Il a institué le **Code Napoléon** qui reste la base du
système de justice en France.

devise motto **pouvoir** power **coalisés** = alliés **chance** luck

---

Teaching Strategies

Interdisciplinary/Community Connections
Prepare a combined project with the history,
social studies and English teachers to help
students understand the importance of the
French revolution. Ask students to prepare a
comparative time line showing world events,
U.S. events, and overlay the French timeline.

Expansion
Play recordings of *La Marseillaise* and *Les
Misérables* while students scan the *Interlude*.

Les personnes

Marie-Antoinette, Reine de France

Marie-Antoinette (1755–1793) est peut-être la figure la plus tragique de l'histoire de France. C'était une princesse autrichienne,° mais elle avait autant de sang° français que son mari, **Louis XVI**. Elle a épousé° celui-ci à l'âge de 15 ans et est devenue reine° à 19 ans.

Idéaliste et généreuse, elle a pris parti pour la cause des insurgés américains. C'est en partie grâce à° son influence que Louis XVI a envoyé sa marine et ses meilleures troupes aider les Américains pendant la Guerre d'Indépendance.

Romantique, très belle et pleine° de vie, elle aimait les fêtes. Pendant la Révolution, la famille royale a tenté, sans succès, de s'échapper de France. Arrêtée, Marie-Antoinette a été accusée d'avoir aidé les ennemis de la patrie. Elle a été emprisonnée, jugée, condamnée à mort et guillotinée.

Marie-Antoinette (1755–1793)

Napoléon couronné empereur

L'Empereur Napoléon et sa famille

Napoléon (1769–1821) est né en Corse,° une petite île au sud de la France. À l'âge de dix ans, il est allé en France faire ses études dans une école militaire. Ses camarades se moquaient° de lui parce qu'il parlait français avec l'accent corse. Napoléon, lui, pensait à sa famille à laquelle il était très attaché.

Vingt-cinq ans plus tard, quand il a été couronné empereur, toute sa famille était présente. Napoléon avait trois frères: **Joseph**, **Louis**, **Jérôme**. Quand il a conquis l'Europe, il a donné à chacun un royaume.° C'est ainsi que Joseph est devenu roi d'Espagne, Louis, roi de Hollande, et Jérôme, roi de Westphalie.

Napoléon avait une famille encore plus grande qui était son armée, la «**Grande Armée**». Il a couvert d'honneurs ses généraux victorieux, et il leur a donné des titres rappelant° leurs victoires ou leurs campagnes. Son meilleur général, **Murat**, était aussi son meilleur ami et le mari de sa soeur, Caroline. Napoléon l'a nommé maréchal, grand amiral, prince d'Empire, grand duc de Berg et finalement roi de Naples.

Napoléon avait un fils, qu'il a nommé Roi de Rome à sa naissance, mais qui n'a pas régné. Son neveu, **Charles Louis Napoléon**, est devenu empereur des Français en 1852, sous le nom de **Napoléon III**.

---

autrichienne *Austrian* **sang** *blood* **a épousé** *married* **reine** *queen* **grâce à** *thanks to* **pleine** *full*
Corse *Corsica* **se moquaient de** *were laughing at* **royaume** *kingdom* **rappelant** *recalling*

Notes historiques

- **Louis XVI:** fils de Louis XV et d'une princesse polonaise, Louis XVI avait seulement un grand-père français.
- **Marie-Antoinette:** fille de l'impératrice autrichienne Marie-Thérèse et de François, duc de Lorraine, Marie-Antoinette avait une grand-mère et un grand-père français.
- La ville de **Marietta** (Ohio) est nommée en l'honneur de Marie-Antoinette.
- **La guillotine** est une machine servant à exécuter les condamnés à mort. Elle a été inventée pendant la Révolution par un certain docteur Guillotin, qui a été lui-même guillotiné.
- Les autres membres de la famille de Napoléon:
  - **Lucien** Bonaparte, prince de Canino
  - **Elisa** Bonaparte, grande duchesse de Toscane
  - **Pauline** Bonaparte, duchesse de Guastalla
  - **Caroline** Bonaparte, reine de Naples

NOTE: Napoléon III était le fils de Louis Bonaparte.

Photo Note

In his painting called *Le Sacre* (coronation), French artist Louis David recorded the coronation of Napoleon in the Cathedral of Notre-Dame in Paris. Napoleon is shown crowning his wife, Joséphine, after he crowned himself Emperor of the French.

Expansion

Internet Connection – Interlude 5
Visit **http://my.hrw.com** for more information and useful links about the French Revolution and other moments in French history from 1715–1870.

Communication

Standard 1.2 Students understand and interpret spoken and written French on a variety of topics.

■ **Additional Information**
Charles Dickens' novel *A Tale of Two Cities* is set during the French Revolution.

L'héritage de la Révolution

La **Révolution** est probablement la période la plus importante de l'histoire de France. Elle met fin° à l'**Ancien Régime*** et à ses abus. Elle établit les bases d'un gouvernement démocratique en affirmant l'égalité de tous les citoyens.° Ce fut pendant la Révolution que furent proclamés la République, l'abolition de l'esclavage° et les droits° de l'homme et du citoyen. La Révolution française fut aussi marquée par un énorme effort de centralisation qui unifia la France en donnant un certain nombre d'institutions communes au pays. La plupart de ces institutions subsistent aujourd'hui. Voici quelques institutions françaises qui remontent° à la Révolution.

La prise de la Bastille

DOCUMENTS | *Déclaration des Droits de l'Homme*

Déclaration des Droits de l'Homme

Article I
« Les hommes naissent et demeurent libres et égaux en droits. »

Article IV
« La liberté consiste à pouvoir faire tout ce qui ne nuit pas à autrui. »

Article IX
« La libre communication des pensées et des opinions est un des droits les plus précieux de l'homme. »

■ **La devise de la France: Liberté, égalité, fraternité**

Cette devise° rappelle les objectifs politiques et sociaux de la Révolution. Elle fut adoptée en juin 1793. Malgré plusieurs interruptions, la fameuse trilogie est restée la devise officielle de la France. Aujourd'hui elle figure° sur les documents officiels et sur les pièces de monnaie.

* L'Ancien Régime: entre le 15e siècle et 1789, la France était une monarchie et la société française était divisée en trois ordres: le clergé, la noblesse *(nobility)* et le Tiers État *(third estate).*

met fin à *puts an end to* **citoyen** *citizen* **esclavage** *slavery* **droits** *rights* **remontent** *go back* **devise** *motto* **figure** *is on*

Note culturelle

The fortress of the Bastille was built between 1370 and 1382. Originally designed as a citadel to house soldiers and protect the city, it became a jail under Louis XIII (1601–1643). Soon it came to symbolize royal power in its most abusive form. Most prisoners in the Bastille were of noble origins. There were also dissenting writers such as Voltaire. When the Parisians stormed the Bastille, they found only seven prisoners within its walls: four counterfeiters, two insane persons, and one young noble who was in too much debt.

■ La fête nationale du 14 juillet

La **fête nationale** commémore la prise° de la Bastille par les Parisiens le 14 juillet 1789. Par ce geste symbolique, la population mettait en question° le pouvoir° royal. La Bastille fut démolie et ses pierres servirent à la construction de nombreuses maisons parisiennes. Ce n'est qu'en 1880 que la date du 14 juillet a été adoptée comme fête nationale.

La première fête du 14 juillet en 1790

La «Fête nationale» aujourd'hui

■ Le drapeau bleu, blanc, rouge

Avant la Révolution, il n'existait pas de drapeau national mais uniquement des drapeaux militaires dont les couleurs et les motifs variaient de régiment à régiment. (Le seul symbole national était alors la personne du roi.) L'origine du drapeau français remonte à la prise de la Bastille le 14 juillet 1789. Les révolutionnaires qui participèrent à cet événement portaient au chapeau une cocarde bleue et rouge, aux couleurs de la ville de Paris. Quelques jours plus tard, le roi Louis XVI ajouta° cette cocarde° bleue et rouge à la cocarde blanche royale (le blanc était alors le symbole de la monarchie française), créant ainsi la cocarde tricolore.

Ces trois couleurs — bleu, blanc, rouge — firent leur apparition sur les drapeaux et les étendards° des armées révolutionnaires. En 1830, le drapeau tricolore à bandes verticales égales devint de façon définitive l'emblème national.

■ Marianne: symbole de la République

Cette femme coiffée du bonnet révolutionnaire est le symbole de la République française. (On attribue le nom «Marianne» à une citoyenne de Colmar, Marie-Anne Reubell.) Cette figure allégorique apparut d'abord sur les pièces de monnaie de la Révolution. Elle réapparut brandissant un drapeau dans le fameux tableau de Delacroix, *La Liberté guidant le peuple*. Depuis 1880, les bustes de Marianne ornent° toutes les mairies de France et son portrait est représenté sur les timbres et les pièces de monnaie.

Marianne

Delacroix *«La Liberté guidant le peuple»*

■ Note culturelle

Delacroix's painting *La Liberté guidant le peuple* commemorates the July Revolution (**La Révolution de Juillet**) that took place in 1830.

---

prise *taking* **mettait en question** *was questioning* **pouvoir** *power* **ajouta** *added* **cocarde** *cockade* **étendards** *military banners*
ornent = *décorent*

Note culturelle

The statues of Marianne are changed regularly, and Marianne takes on a new appearance, generally that of a famous Frenchwoman of the time. Brigitte Bardot, Catherine Deneuve (see blue stamp pictured), and fashion model Inès de la Fressange have been models for Marianne.

■ Additional Information

- Since 1989, the pyramid in front of the Louvre has been the entrance to new underground galleries. It also provides light for the galleries. The pyramid and new galleries were designed by the Chinese-American architect I.M. Pei.

  The Louvre is famous for its extensive collections of Egyptian artifacts, Greek and Roman antiques, as well as the Mona Lisa by Da Vinci.

- Martinique, Guyane, Guadeloupe and Réunion are also French **départements**. They are called **les départements d'outre-mer**, or **DOM**. France also governs the following territories: Wallis et Futuna, Nouvelle-Calédonie, Polynésie française, terres australes et antarctiques. They are called **les territoires d'outre-mer (TOM)**. Overseas departments and territories are generally referred to as **les DOM-TOM**.

■ Le musée du Louvre

Situé dans l'ancien palais royal du **Louvre**, le musée du Louvre est une création de la Révolution. Construit au 12e siècle, le Louvre était à l'origine une forteresse. Embelli et maintes° fois transformé, il a été pendant longtemps la résidence des rois de France. Quand Louis XIV a installé sa cour à Versailles, le Louvre est laissé plus ou moins à l'abandon. En 1793, le gouvernement de la Révolution a décidé d'en faire un grand musée national où le peuple pouvait admirer les collections confisquées aux rois de France.

Sous l'Empire, le Louvre est devenu le Musée Napoléon. Napoléon y apportait les trésors d'art qu'il avait saisis° au cours de ses campagnes à travers° l'Europe. Plus tard, le Louvre s'est enrichi

Le Louvre et la pyramide du Louvre

d'antiquités romaines, grecques, égyptiennes et orientales. Aujourd'hui, c'est l'un des plus grands musées du monde.

■ Les départements français

Les **départements** ont remplacé les «généralités» de l'Ancien Régime. Leur création est le résultat d'une réforme proposée peu avant la Révolution et mise en place en 1790. Le découpage° de la France en départements permettait une administration plus facile du pays. (Il était possible à un homme à cheval de parcourir° un département en une journée.) À l'origine, il y avait 83 départements. Aujourd'hui, il y a 96 départements métropolitains.

---

maintes = beaucoup de **saisis** = pris par force **à travers** *across* **le découpage** = la division **parcourir** *to travel across*

■ Le franc et la monnaie française

Avant la Révolution, la monnaie consistait en une multitude de pièces d'or, d'argent et de bronze (écus, louis, sous, deniers, liards**) dont la valeur et le poids° pouvaient varier. La Révolution française uniformisa le système monétaire en adoptant une unité décimale, le **franc**, divisible en décimes et centimes. Le franc est resté la monnaie nationale jusqu'° en 2001.

* **Écus, louis, sous, deniers, liards:** ce sont les noms de ces diverses pièces de monnaie.

■ Le système métrique

Avant la Révolution, on utilisait des unités de distance, de poids et de volume qui variaient de région en région. Ainsi, suivant les provinces, le pied pouvait représenter 10 ou 12 pouces°. Suivant les villes, la livre° pouvait représenter 12, 14 ou 15 onces . . . Le gouvernement révolutionnaire décida de créer un système simple et uniforme. C'est ainsi que fut créé en 1793 le système métrique décimal.

■ L'armée nationale

Avant la Révolution, l'armée était un privilège de la noblesse. Pour être officier, il fallait être noble ou acheter sa charge.° Les soldats étaient des engagés° et des mercenaires étrangers. Les armées de la Révolution incorporèrent les Français de toute condition sociale. À la bataille de Valmy (20 septembre 1792), l'armée française crie pour la première fois: «Vive la Nation!»

La bataille de Valmy, 1792

jusqu' *until*   **poids** *weight*   **pouces** *inches*   **la livre** *pound*   **charge** *rank*   **engagés** = *volontaires*

■ Note culturelle

In 2002, the franc was replaced by the euro, which was officially adopted as the currency of France in 1999.

■ Note linguistique

Literally, the word **pouce** means *thumb*. In the old measurement system, **un pied** was the length of a man's foot, and **un pouce** was the length of the last joint of the thumb.

■ Photo Notes

- The *aires* on the French autoroutes are rest stops that offer a variety of facilities. Some have only picnic or rest areas while others have shops or gas stations.
- Putot-en-Auge, Dives-sur-Mer and Dozulé are all located in the Basse-Normandie region of France.

■ Teaching Note

Rappel:
   1 mile = 1.609 kilomètres;
   1 pied = 30 centimètres
      (0.3 mètre);
   1 livre = 453 grammes
      (0.453 kilogramme)

■ Note historique

The French army regained confidence after its victory against the Prussians at **Valmy**. This battle stopped their advance and prevented the occupation of France by the Prussians.

■ **Note linguistique**

au petit matin = très tôt le matin
le délire = frenzy, great joy/
excitement

■ **Teaching Strategy:
Expansion**

Ask students:
- À votre avis, est-ce une bonne idée de changer les paroles d'un hymne national?
- Doit-on garder l'hymne national sans y toucher? Pourquoi?
- Connaissez-vous l'hymne de votre pays?
- Souhaiteriez-vous le changer? Pourquoi?

LA FRANCE

L'histoire de la «Marseillaise»

La «Marseillaise» est **l'hymne national** de la France. Elle a été composée pendant la Révolution, mais, malgré° son nom, elle n'est pas d'origine marseillaise. Où donc est née cette célèbre chanson et dans quelles circonstances? Voici son histoire.

Avril 1792. Nous sommes en pleine effervescence révolutionnaire. La France vient de déclarer la guerre à l'Autriche.° Pour protéger la frontière,° une armée, l'armée du Rhin, a été cantonnée° à Strasbourg. Il y a des soldats partout° dans les rues. Le 24 avril, le maire° de Strasbourg offre un grand banquet aux officiers de la garnison. On mange, on boit, on chante, et on crie des slogans: «Vive la patrie!», «À bas° la tyrannie!», «À bas les ennemis de la France!» La ferveur patriotique et révolutionnaire est à son comble.°

Parmi° les officiers, il y a un jeune capitaine. Il s'appelle **Rouget de Lisle.** Militaire, il aime aussi la poésie et il joue du violon. Le maire de Strasbourg s'adresse à lui: «Dites donc, Rouget, vous êtes bien poète et musicien. Alors, pourquoi est-ce que vous ne composez pas quelque chose pour ces braves soldats qui vont défendre la patrie?»°

Rouget de Lisle ne dit rien, mais, rentré chez lui, il prend son violon et joue quelques notes. Puis il prend une plume° et écrit ces mots sur une feuille de papier: «**Allons, enfants de la patrie. . . Le jour de gloire est arrivé**. . . » Toute la nuit, il travaille et retravaille les paroles et la musique d'un puissant° chant de guerre. Au petit matin, il a fini.

À dix heures, il se présente chez le maire. «Monsieur le maire, j'ai votre chanson.» Il se met° au piano et commence: «Allons, enfants de la patrie. . .» Chez le maire, c'est l'enthousiasme général. Rouget joue et rejoue l'air qu'il a intitulé «Chant de guerre pour l'armée du Rhin».

Le lendemain, le texte de cette chanson est imprimé° et distribué. Quelques jours plus tard, la musique de la Garde Nationale joue cet hymne révolutionnaire sur la place d'Armes° de Strasbourg. Dans la foule,° c'est le délire. Tout le monde reprend en choeur «Marchons, marchons. . .»

Bientôt° le «Chant de guerre pour l'armée du Rhin» est dans la bouche de tous les soldats. Il passe de garnison en garnison. Partout il enflamme les esprits. En juin 1792, la chanson arrive à Marseille. Là, un régiment de volontaires l'adopte comme son chant de marche. Ces soldats marseillais montent à Paris en chantant la redoutable chanson. Le chant de l'armée du Rhin devient le «Chant des Marseillais», puis, plus simplement la «Marseillaise».

Le 14 juillet 1795, jour anniversaire de la Prise de la Bastille, la Marseillaise devient officiellement l'hymne national, mais pour quelques années seulement. En 1799, la Révolution est terminée. Un peu plus tard, Napoléon devient empereur. Général issu de la Révolution, il se méfie° maintenant de la révolution en général et des chants révolutionnaires en particulier. Il interdit° de jouer la Marseillaise.

La Marseillaise n'est plus l'hymne national français, mais elle devient un hymne révolutionnaire universel. C'est aux accents° de la Marseillaise que se font les révolutions du 19e siècle, en Allemagne, en Italie, dans le monde entier. . . Finalement, la République est rétablie en France et la Marseillaise redevient l'hymne national, mais seulement en 1879.

Depuis 1792, de nouvelles strophes° ont été ajoutées° au texte de la Marseillaise. Aujourd'hui, ce texte est l'objet de controverse. La Marseillaise est, en effet, un hymne terriblement guerrier° qui incite à la lutte° sans merci contre les ennemis de la patrie. À l'heure actuelle, la France n'a plus d'ennemis et elle veut la paix dans le monde. Pourquoi ne pas transformer la Marseillaise en un hymne pour la paix en changeant le texte? Beaucoup de Français seraient d'accord, mais beaucoup d'autres préfèrent garder ce texte traditionnel.

---

malgré *in spite of* **Autriche** *Austria* **frontière** *border* **cantonnée** *stationed* **partout** *everywhere* **maire** *mayor* **à bas** *down with* **à son comble** *at its height* **parmi** *among* **patrie** *homeland* **plume** *(quill) pen* **puissant** *powerful* **se met** = s'assied **imprimé** *printed* **place d'Armes** *parade ground* **foule** *crowd* **bientôt** *soon thereafter* **se méfie** *is distrustful* **interdit** *prohibits* **accents** *tune* **strophes** *verses* **ajoutées** *added* **guerrier** *warlike* **lutte** *fight*

Teaching Suggestion: DVD Program

Play the Unit 5 *Vignette culturelle* about *La Marseillaise* for more information.

DOCUMENTS «La Marseillaise»

La Marseillaise

Allons, Enfants de la Patrie,
Le jour de gloire est arrivé!
Contre nous de la tyrannie,
L'étendard sanglant° est levé,
L'étendard sanglant est levé.
Entendez-vous dans les campagnes
Mugir° ces féroces soldats?
Ils viennent jusque dans nos bras
Égorger° nos fils, nos compagnes.
refrain:
Aux armes, Citoyens!
Formez vos bataillons!
Marchons, marchons!
Qu'un sang impur abreuve nos sillons°!

Claude Joseph Rouget de Lisle (1760–1836)

Dans sa vie, le compositeur de la Marseillaise n'a pas eu de chance. Rouget de Lisle était d'origine noble. Quelque temps après avoir composé le célèbre hymne révolutionnaire, il est accusé d'être royaliste et, paradoxalement, d'être un ennemi de la Révolution. Condamné à mort, il échappe in extremis à la guillotine. (C'est la mort du dictateur Robespierre qui le sauve!)

Rouget de Lisle reprend l'uniforme et il est blessé° au combat. Il quitte l'armée et retourne à sa véritable vocation: la poésie et la musique. Il compose des chansons et écrit des pièces de théâtre, mais celles-ci n'ont pas beaucoup de succès. Vers° la fin de la vie, il n'a plus d'argent, mais beaucoup de dettes. Il meurt dans la misère.

---

blessé *wounded* **vers** *towards* **étendard sanglant** *blood-stained battle flag* **mugir** *roar* **égorger** *to slit the throats of*
qu'un sang impur abreuve nos sillons *may the impure blood [of our enemies] soak the furrows [of our fields].*

■ **Teaching Strategy**
Play a recording of the *Marseillaise* for students. Next, play a recording of the *Star-Spangled Banner* and *O Canada*. Ask students to compare and contrast these national anthems, describing similarities, and differences in tone, subject matter, etc.

■ **Note linguistique**
In extremis is a commonly used adverbial phrase. These latin words literally mean "at the extremity." The expression itself means *at the last minute.*

Note culturelle

In 1974, French president Giscard d'Estaing ordered the Marseillaise to be reorchestrated, following the rhythm of an older version. It was reinstated as a military march in 1981.

Before the Revolution, different religious hymns were used as anthems. They were picked according to the circumstances (parades, war...).

DOCUMENTS «Les Misérables»

Chef-d'oeuvre° de la littérature française, *Les Misérables* a été adapté plus de 30 fois au cinéma. Plus récemment, une comédie musicale, tirée° du roman, a connu un succès retentissant° en France, en Angleterre et aux États-Unis.

L'action des *Misérables* se passe en France et se déroule° sur une période d'une vingtaine d'années au début du 19e siècle. Le personnage principal s'appelle **Jean Valjean**. Dans sa jeunesse, il a été arrêté pour avoir volé° un pain, un jour d'hiver. Arrêté pour ce menu° larcin,° il a été condamné au bagne* où il passe dix-neuf ans. Après plusieurs tentatives d'évasion,° il est finalement relâché,° mais il sera poursuivi toute sa vie par un policier implacable nommé **Javert**.

Sans argent, Jean Valjean va demander l'aumône° à la porte d'un évêque.° Celui-ci est un homme bon qui non seulement reçoit Jean Valjean, mais le traite comme un égal, l'invite à sa table et lui offre l'hospitalité. La nuit, Jean Valjean quitte la maison de l'évêque en emportant° des plats d'argent. Il est arrêté par la police et reconduit chez l'évêque. Au lieu de l'accuser, ce personnage charitable explique aux policiers qu'il a donné les plats d'argent à Jean Valjean et qu'il n'y a par conséquent aucune raison de l'arrêter.

* **Le bagne:** Lieu où on envoyait les hommes condamnés à des travaux forcés. On appelait ces prisonniers des «bagnards» ou des «forçats».

Victor Hugo, écrivain et homme politique

Victor Hugo (1802–1885), l'auteur des Misérables, est l'un des géants de la littérature française. C'est peut-être le plus grand écrivain du 19e siècle. Chef de l'école romantique, il a écrit un grand nombre de poésies, de romans et de pièces de théâtre qui ont fait scandale à l'époque pour leur audacité et leur caractère révolutionnaire.

Victor Hugo a aussi joué un rôle politique important. C'était le fils d'un général de Napoléon. S'il admirait beaucoup cet empereur, il détestait profondément son neveu, Louis-Napoléon, qui avait lui-même pris le pouvoir° par un coup d'état et était devenu empereur sous le nom de Napoléon III. Condamné pour ses idées républicaines, Victor Hugo a été obligé de s'enfuir° en Angleterre où il a passé plusieurs années d'exil.

Victor Hugo est rentré en France après l'abdication de Napoléon, acclamé comme un héros. Devenu sénateur, il a pris le parti des opprimés°, des déshérités, des gens sans protection et sans ressources et il s'est battu° pour la liberté, l'égalité et la justice. C'est cet esprit de compassion pour les petits gens qu'il manifeste dans sa grande oeuvre° *Les Misérables*.

Victor Hugo (1802–1885)

chef-d'oeuvre *masterpiece* **tirée de** = basée sur **retentissant** = très grand **se déroule** *takes place* **volé** *stolen* **menu** = petit **larcin** *theft*
tentatives d'évasion *escape attempts* **relâché** *released* **l'aumône** = la charité **évêque** *bishop* **emportant** = prenant avec lui **pouvoir** *power*
s'enfuir *to flee* **opprimés** *oppressed* **s'est battu** *fought* **oeuvre** *work*

Disney made an animated movie, loosely based on Victor Hugo's novel *Notre-Dame de Paris* called *The Hunchback of Notre-Dame*. Victor Hugo wrote *Les Misérables* in 1862. French artists Alain Boublil and Jean-Michel Schonberg wrote the book and music of the musical **Les Misérables**.

■ **Note culturelle**

Victor Hugo est aussi connu pour son roman du Moyen Âge, *Notre Dame de Paris*, avec Quasimodo, le sonneur de Notre-Dame, et la belle Esmeralda qui se promène à travers Paris avec sa chèvre.

224 Unité 5

Note culturelle

When Victor Hugo died, his body lay in state under the Arc de Triomphe in Paris. He was then given a magnificent national funeral before being brought to the Panthéon, where he was laid to rest beside France's greatest figures, such as Voltaire, Rousseau, Bonaparte, and La Fayette.

You may wish to show a picture of the **Panthéon**, or ask students to locate it on a map of Paris.

Cet acte généreux va transformer Jean Valjean. Il prend le nom de **Monsieur Madeleine** et sous ce nom devient un personnage riche et respecté de tous. Élu° maire° de sa ville, il mène° une vie simple et exemplaire. À son tour, il est charitable et généreux avec tout le monde.

Un jour, il apprend qu'un homme vient d'être arrêté pour un vol° que lui, Jean Valjean, a commis autrefois. Pris° de remords, il va se dénoncer à la police. Condamné cette fois à la prison à vie, il arrive° à s'évader,° toujours poursuivi par Javert.

Gavroche, gamin de Paris

Immortalisé par Victor Hugo dans Les Misérables, Gavroche est l'éternel «gamin° de Paris». Il a une douzaine d'années. On ne sait où il vit, ni de quoi il vit. Sa vraie famille, c'est le petit peuple du quartier où il passe ses jours et ses nuits. C'est un rebelle, mais il n'est pas révolté. Il siffle,° il chante. . . Il est libre, insouciant,° joyeux. . . Il n'a peur de rien. Quand la révolution éclate, il monte sur les barricades. Frappé° par une balle,° il meurt héroïquement, en chantant une chanson.

Les années ont passé. Jean Valjean habite maintenant à Paris. Il a recueilli° **Cosette**, une petite orpheline dont il a connu la mère autrefois. Cosette est fiancée à **Marius**, un étudiant aux idées révolutionnaires. Un jour la révolution éclate.° Marius prend la tête d'une barricade. Javert est fait prisonnier par les insurgés, mais Jean Valjean intervient en sa faveur et lui sauve la vie.

Marius est blessé lors d'une contre-attaque des forces gouvernementales. Averti° par **Gavroche**, un gamin° de Paris, Jean Valjean arrive. Il prend Marius dans ses bras et le transporte pendant des kilomètres à travers les égouts° de Paris. Javert l'attend. Il reconnaît l'ancien bagnard évadé. Les deux hommes se font face. Javert n'ose° pas arrêter l'homme qui lui a sauvé la vie. Il se suicide. . . Peu après, Marius et Cosette se marient, et Jean Valjean meurt, heureux d'avoir contribué à leur bonheur.

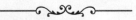

élu *elected* **maire** *mayor* **mène** *leads* **vol** *theft* **pris par** *seized by* **arrive à** *manages to* **s'évader** *to escape* **recueilli** = *adopté*
éclate *breaks out* **averti** *notified* **gamin** *kid* **égouts** *sewers* **ose** *dares* **siffle** *whistles* **insouciant** *carefree*
frappé *hit* **balle** *bullet*

- **Teaching Strategy**
Play portions of a recording of *Les Misérables* for students.

- **Note culturelle**
Parts of the sewers of Paris are open to the public. Visitors can even take an underground boat ride!

- **Irregular Verbs**
(See Appendix C).
Commettre *(to commit)* is conjugated like **mettre**
(See Appendix C).
Intervenir *(to intervene)* is conjugated like **venir**

- **Note historique**
This is the revolution of 1830, during which the Parisians deposed King Charles X.
(See historical time line on p. 216.)

Notes culturelles

- Eugène Delacroix (1798–1863) painted *La Liberté guidant le peuple* shortly after the events of July 1830.

- In his depiction of Gavroche, Victor Hugo was probably inspired by the young boy in the Delacroix painting. For a full picture of Delacroix's painting, see p. 219.

MAIN THEME

Places to stay when traveling

COMMUNICATION
- Asking for hotel services
- Deciding where to stay
- Reserving a hotel room

CULTURES
- Learning about the *Guide Michelin*
- Learning about hotels in Amboise

CONNECTIONS
- Using the *Guide Michelin* to make a hotel reservation
- Connecting to Art: Creating a travel brochure
- Connecting to Language Arts: Brainstorming ideas for a restaurant guide
- Connecting to Math: Creating a chart showing typical meal prices
- Connecting to Science: Judging how health-conscious menu items are
- Connecting to Social Studies: Researching the history of a restaurant
- Connecting to Art: Critiquing a restaurant's ambiance
- Connecting to Technology: Finding out about technology used in restaurants
- Connecting to History: Researching and writing a report about World War II

COMPARISONS
- Comparing comparative and superlative constructions in French and English
- Comparing demonstrative and possessive pronouns in French and English
- Comparing ghost stories in French and American culture

COMMUNITIES
- Using French when making a phone call
- Learning about World War II
- Prioritizing hotel preferences
- Responding to Chamber of Commerce tourism inquiries
- Enjoying readings and music from the French Resistance period

Séjour en France

THÈME ET OBJECTIFS

Culture

In this unit, you will discover . . .

- the different places where you can stay while visiting France
- how to use a French guidebook to find a hotel

Communication

You will learn how . . .

- to reserve a hotel room
- to ask for services in a hotel

Langue

You will learn how . . .

- to compare people or things
- to express who or what is the best
- to indicate what belongs to you and what belongs to other people
- to point out specific people or things and ask questions about them

DIGITAL FRENCH my.hrw.com
ONLINE STUDENT EDITION with...

performance space

News + Networking

@HOMETUTOR

- Audio Resources
- Video Resources
- Interactive Flashcards
- WebQuest

PRACTICE FRENCH WITH HOLT MCDOUGAL APPS!

DIGITAL FRENCH

TEACHER TOOLS
- Teacher One Stop
- Interactive Whiteboard Lessons
- Generate Success Rubric Generator and Interactive Graphic Organizers
- Examview Test Generator

ALSO AVAILABLE...
- Online Workbook
- French InterActive Reader
- @HomeTutor
- DVD Program
- Power Presentations
- Interactive Flashcards

FRENCH ON THE GO!
- Performance Space
- Holt McDougal French Apps
- Discovering French Today eTextbook

Les Jeunes touristes en France

Chaque année, soixante-quinze millions de touristes étrangers visitent la France. Ces touristes viennent principalement d'Allemagne, d'Angleterre, de Belgique, de Hollande et d'Italie, mais il y a aussi beaucoup de touristes américains, canadiens, japonais … Pour accueillir° ces millions de touristes, la France dispose° d'un grand nombre d'hôtels de toutes catégories. Il y a des hôtels très simples et des hôtels très luxueux. Le sommet du luxe consiste à passer quelques jours dans un château historique datant du seizième ou du dix-septième siècle. Là, vous serez vraiment traité comme un prince — ou une princesse! Évidemment, tout le monde n'a pas les moyens° financiers de se payer «la vie de château.» Heureusement, pour les jeunes qui préfèrent l'aventure au confort et au luxe, il y a d'autres solutions moins chères et aussi intéressantes. En voici quelques-unes.

Le séjour à la ferme

Si on aime le grand air et si on n'a pas besoin de grand confort, on peut faire un séjour dans une ferme. Pendant les vacances, beaucoup de fermiers louent des «chambres d'hôte»° pour des prix très raisonnables. Le petit déjeuner est généralement compris° dans le prix de la chambre. Si on veut, on peut prendre les autres repas à la ferme aussi. L'ambiance est familiale et les produits de la ferme (souvent des spécialités régionales) sont absolument délicieux!

En été, il y a beaucoup de travail à faire dans les champs. Les fermiers ont souvent besoin de main d'oeuvre.° Ils recrutent parfois des étudiants pour participer à ces travaux. Dans ce cas le logement et la nourriture sont gratuits° et, en plus,° on reçoit° un peu d'argent.

Le camping

Il y a différentes façons de faire du camping. On peut aller dans un terrain de camping aménagé.° En France il existe des milliers° de terrains de camping équipés d'eau courante, de WC et de douches. Si on préfère la nature ou la solitude, on peut aussi faire du «camping sauvage.» Dans ce cas, on plante sa tente là où on veut: dans une prairie, dans une forêt, près d'une rivière.… Mais attention! Si on est sur une propriété privée, il faut demander et obtenir° l'autorisation du propriétaire.°

Les auberges de jeunesse

Ce sont des hôtels très bon marché réservés aux jeunes touristes qui sont de passage dans une ville. Certaines auberges ont des chambres individuelles, mais généralement on dort dans un dortoir pour 6 à 10 personnes. L'atmosphère des auberges est sympathique et communale: on rencontre d'autres jeunes venus de tous les pays du monde, on fait la cuisine et on mange ensemble. On parle de ses voyages, on raconte des histoires et on rit° beaucoup. Si le confort est élémentaire,° la bonne humeur est toujours présente.

Pour aller dans les auberges de jeunesse, il faut posséder une carte de la FUAJ (Fédération Unie des Auberges de Jeunesse).

DISCUSSION

Avec votre partenaire, discutez le sujet suivant:
• Vous allez faire un voyage en France cet été, mais vous n'avez pas beaucoup d'argent. Quelle solution allez-vous choisir pour votre logement? (faire du camping? aller dans les auberges de jeunesse? prendre une chambre dans une ferme? trouver une autre solution?) Expliquez les avantages et les inconvénients de la solution que vous avez choisie.

---

accueillir ✳ *to welcome*   **dispose** = *a*   **moyens** = *les ressources*   **rire** ✳ *to laugh*   **élémentaire** = *rudimentaire*   **aménagé** = *équipé*
milliers *thousands*   **obtenir** ✳ *to get, obtain*   **propriétaire** *owner*   **chambres d'hôte** *guest rooms*   **compris** = *inclus*   **main d'oeuvre** = *travailleurs*
gratuits *free*   **en plus** *in addition*   **reçoit** = *gagner*

ASSESSMENT IN UNIT RESOURCE BOOK

Print Resources
• Workbook TE/PE
• *Activités pour tous* TE/PE
• *Lectures pour tous*
• Unit Resource Book
  Audioscripts
  Video Activities
  Videoscripts

Achievement Tests
• Quizzes, Unit 6
• Unit Test 6
• Reading and Culture Tests
• Assessment Answer Key

Proficiency Tests
• Listening Comprehension
• Speaking Performance
• Writing Performance
• Portfolio Assessment

INFO MAGAZINE

Theme: Student travel in France

Reading Strategy: Scanning, browsing, reading for information

■ Warm-Up
After students look at illustrations and compile lists of cognates, ask them to guess the meaning:
• **le tourisme vert** = séjours à la ferme ou dans un petit village, pour redécouvrir la nature et la campagne française
• **le tourisme du souvenir** = visite des champs de bataille et des sites historiques
• **le tourisme industriel** = visite d'usines ou de manufactures locales

■ Irregular Verbs
(see Appendix C)
accueillir   (*see* **cueillir**)
rire   (*see* **dire**)
obtenir   (*see* **tenir**)
recevoir

21ST CENTURY SKILLS
• **Communication:** SE: pp. 227, 229, 232, 233, 235, 237, 239, 241, 247, 248, 250, 251; TE: pp. 231, 232, 233, 237, 240, 241, 245, 250, 258
• **Critical Thinking and Problem Solving:** SE: pp. 229, 246, 249, 251; TE: pp. 238, 250, 251, 257
• **Creativity and Innovation:** SE: pp. 232, 251; TE: pp. 231, 233, 238, 240, 241, 245, 250, 257
• **Information Literacy:** SE: pp. 229, 251; TE: pp. 233, 238, 241, 245
• **Media Literacy:** p. 241
• **Technology Literacy:** TE: pp. 233, 238, 241, 245
• **Flexibility and Adaptability:** SE: pp. 229, 232, 233, 245; TE: pp. 233, 237, 238, 241, 254, 256
• **Initiative and Self-Direction:** TE: pp. 238, 241, 245, 254, 256
• **Productivity and Accountability:** TE: pp. 231, 234, 244, 256

RESOURCES

TECHNOLOGY
Teacher One Stop
💻 **Projectable Transparencies**
39, *Le guide Michelin*
Transparency Copymasters,
pp. A81–A83

■ **Notes culturelles**

There are two types of *Michelin* guides:
- the **Guide Rouge** which lists and rates the hotels and restaurants
- the **Guides Verts** which describe the main tourist attractions of a particular area.
- Michelin's logo, the tire man, is called **le bonhomme Michelin**, or **le bibendum Michelin**.

■ **Irregular Verbs**

(see Appendix C)
suivre
atteindre   *(see* **peindre***)*

■ **Language Note**

100 km/h = 62 mph

■ **Note linguistique**

Le best-seller (pl. **les best-sellers**) is more commonly used in France than its French equivalents **le succès de librairie** or **le livre à gros tirage**.

Le Guide MICHELIN

France 2011
🍴
HÔTELS & RESTAURANTS

Quand on voyage, il est utile d'avoir des renseignements° pratiques sur les villes qu'on va visiter. Par exemple: Quelles sont les choses les plus intéressantes à voir? Quel est l'hôtel le plus confortable, ou le moins cher? Où sont les meilleurs restaurants? Pour obtenir ces renseignements, on peut téléphoner au bureau de Tourisme de la ville ou on peut suivre° les recommandations d'un ami, mais le plus simple est d'acheter un guide. Le plus célèbre guide français est *Le Guide Michelin*.

Pour chaque ville, *Le Guide Michelin Rouge* présente une sélection d'hôtels et de restaurants (et, si la ville est assez grande, un plan de la ville). Pour chaque hôtel et chaque restaurant de cette liste, tous les renseignements nécessaires sont donnés: adresse, qualité, prix, etc.... Les touristes peuvent facilement choisir les hôtels et les restaurants qui correspondent à leurs goûts... et à leurs ressources financières.

Le Guide Michelin est publié chaque année. Pour s'assurer de la qualité d'un restaurant ou du confort d'un hôtel, les inspecteurs Michelin visitent régulièrement, mais à l'improviste,° ces établissements. Suivant° les résultats de l'enquête, un restaurant ou un hôtel peut monter ou descendre de catégorie. Pour les grands restaurants, la classification dans *Le Guide Michelin* est extrêmement importante. Une étoile signifie le succès, deux étoiles l'honneur, trois étoiles la gloire. Dans toute la France, il y a seulement 22 restaurants «trois étoiles.»

une étoile   deux étoiles   trois étoiles

La société Michelin

Michelin est l'une des plus grandes entreprises françaises. Son activité principale n'est pas la publication de guides touristiques, mais la fabrication des pneus.° Aujourd'hui Michelin est le deuxième producteur de pneus du monde avec 18% de la production mondiale.

Le succès de cette firme remonte° à l'invention en 1891 du pneumatique démontable° avec chambre à air° par deux frères, André et Édouard Michelin. Cette invention a d'abord été appliquée à la bicyclette, puis à la voiture à cheval et finalement à l'automobile. Premier succès: en 1895, une voiture équipée de

pneus Michelin a terminé la course Paris-Bordeaux-Paris, faisant ainsi la preuve° qu'on pouvait rouler° sur de l'air. En 1899, grâce° au pneu, une autre automobile, la «Jamais Contente» a atteint° pour la première fois la vitesse° alors inimaginable de 100 kilomètres à l'heure.

Pour encourager la vente des pneus, il fallait encourager le tourisme. Pour cela, les frères Michelin ont eu l'idée géniale de publier des cartes et des guides touristiques (les Cartes et les Guides Michelin). Le Guide Michelin a été créé en 1900. Jusqu'en 1920, il était distribué gratuitement° à tous les automobilistes. Aujourd'hui, c'est le «best seller» français: 1.500.000 exemplaires° du fameux guide rouge sont vendus chaque année dans le monde!

renseignements = informations   **suivre** ✲ *to follow*   **l'improviste** *unannounced*   **suivant** *according to*   **pneus** *tires*   **remonte** *goes back*
démontable *which can be removed*   **chambre à air** *innertube*   **preuve** = *prouvant*   **rouler** *drive*   **grâce à** *thanks to*   **atteindre** ✲ *to reach*
vitesse *speed*   **gratuitement** *free of charge*   **exemplaires** *copies*

Expansion culturelle

- The **Clos-Lucé**, seen on the map of Amboise, is the manor where François 1er spent part of his youth, and where the great artist **Leonardo da Vinci** died in 1519.
- The castle at Amboise was built between 1492 and 1498. Its architecture foreshadows

that of the Renaissance, giving for the first time some emphasis on comfort. Its two large towers have spiral staircases with ramps instead of steps so people could climb up on horseback. See p. 147 for a photo and description.

Comment lire le Guide Michelin

Les catégories

🏰 *Grand luxe et tradition*

🏨 *Grand confort*

🏛 *Très confortable*

🏢 *De bon confort*

🏠 *Assez confortable*

♨ *Simple mais convenable*

L'installation

🌳 *Repas au jardin ou en terrasse*

⚕🎾 *Salle de remise en forme - Tennis*

🏊 🏊 *Piscine en plein air / couverte*

🚊 *Jardin*

⬍ 🗔 *Ascenseur - Air conditionné*

🚭 *Chambres pour non-fumeurs*

📞 *Prise Modem dans la chambre*

P P 🚗 *Parking - Parking clos - Garage*

♿ *Chambres accessibles aux handicapés physiques*

TV *Télévision dans la chambre*

☕ *Petit déjeuner*

GB *Carte Bancaire*

Imaginez que vous allez visiter le château d'Amboise, près de Tours. Vous avez réservé une chambre à l'hôtel Belle Vue. Voici la description de cet hôtel:

Un hôtel à Amboise

Amboise est une petite ville très touristique, à cause de son impressionnant château royal. Voici la description d'un hôtel à Amboise, l'Hôtel Belle Vue, dans le *Guide Michelin*.

┌──1──┐┌──2──┐   ┌──3──┐   ┌4┐┌5┐
🏢 **Belle Vue** sans rest, 12 quai Ch. Guinot 📞 02 47 57 02 26, Fax 02 47 30 51 23 – ⬍ TV. GB.
┌────6────┐ ┌7┐ ┌──8──┐
15 mars-15 nov. – ☕ 6 – **32 ch** 46/57.
   ◆ Hôtel simple en bordure de Loire. Les chambres, assez grandes, sont de bon confort.
Sur l'arrière, elles sont plus calmes et offrent une jolie vue sur le château.

1   la catégorie
L'hôtel Belle Vue est un hôtel confortable.
(C'est un hôtel de bon confort.)

2   le restaurant
Cet hôtel n'a pas de restaurant.
(Il est sans restaurant.)

3   l'adresse
Cet hôtel est situé 12, quai Charles Guinot.
Le numéro de téléphone est le 02 47 57 02 26.
Le numéro de fax est le 02 47 30 51 23.

4   l'installation
Il y a un ascenseur. Les chambres ont la télévision.

5   mode de paiement
On accepte les cartes bancaires.

6   période d'ouverture
L'hôtel est ouvert du 15 mars au 15 novembre.

7   le petit déjeuner
Le petit déjeuner coûte 6 euros.

8   le nombre et le prix des chambres
Il y a 32 chambres. Le prix des chambres est
de 46 à 57 euros par jour.

et vous?

1. Selon vous, quels sont les trois éléments les plus importants de l'installation d'un hôtel? Pourquoi?

2. Imaginez que vous allez visiter Amboise (ou une autre ville française.) Avec un(e) camarade, consultez le «Michelin Guide Rouge» sur l'Internet et choisissez un hôtel. Expliquez votre choix.

■ **Additional Information**
Michelin publishes road maps of cities, regions, and countries throughout the world. Its green guides are also published in English.

■ **Teaching Strategy**
You may wish to bring in a copy of a **Guide Michelin** if available so that students can see the many different kinds of information listed.

SUPPLEMENTARY VOCABULARY

payer en liquide *to pay cash*
la suite *suite*
la chambre climatisée *air-conditioned room*
la télévision avec câble *cable T.V.*
le bain à remous *whirlpool bath*
le jacuzzi *jacuzzi*
le forfait *package deal*
un grand lit *double bed*
un lit double
des lits jumeaux *twin beds*
donner sur *to look out on, to have a view over*
  une chambre qui donne sur la mer

Partie 1

À l'hôtel

Où loger?

On peut	aller		dans	un hôtel de luxe.	**loger** *to stay*
	loger			un hôtel bon marché mais confortable.	**séjourner** *to stay*
	séjourner			une auberge *(inn)* à la campagne.	
	passer la nuit			une auberge de jeunesse *(youth hostel)*.	

À la réception *(reception desk)*

— Bonjour, mademoiselle/monsieur. Vous désirez?
  Je voudrais
  Je voudrais **réserver** | une chambre.

— **Quel genre** *(type)* de chambre désirez-vous?
  J'aimerais une chambre . . .

	pour une personne	**pour deux personnes**
	à un lit	**à deux lits**
avec	**douche**	**la climatisation** *(air conditioning)*
	salle de bains	**l'air conditionné**
	téléphone	**un balcon**
	télévision	**une belle vue** *(view)*

Teaching Suggestion: DVD Program

The Unit 6 *Vidéo-drame: À l'hôtel* focuses on hotel lodging. Students will accompany the Pasquier family on their trip as they check in to their hotel. Before playing the video, brainstorm a list of possible amenities one would find at a hotel. Next, have students give the French equivalent of each amenity listed.

— **Combien de temps Jusqu'à** (until) **quand** | **comptez**-vous rester?

| compter *to plan, to count on* |

Je compte rester . . .

deux nuits	jusqu'à mardi
une semaine	jusqu'au 12 juillet
	du 2 au 15 juin

— Comment allez-vous payer?
Je vais payer . . .

| **en espèces** (cash) | **avec des chèques de voyage** |
| **par chèque** | **avec une carte de crédit** |

— Vous avez la chambre 315.
Voici votre **clé** (key).

RENSEIGNEMENTS SUPPLÉMENTAIRES

— Est-ce que l'hôtel a . . .

| **une piscine** |
| **une salle d'exercices** |
| **le service dans les chambres** (room service) |
| **un ascenseur** |
| **un accès pour personnes handicapées** |

PETIT DÉJEUNER

— Est-ce que je pourrais avoir une chambre . . .

plus grande	**plus claire**
plus spacieuse	**mieux située**
plus confortable	**moins chère**
plus calme	**moins bruyante**

| **spacieux** *roomy* |
| **clair** *sunny* |
| **bien situé** *well located* |
| **bruyant** *noisy* |

— Combien coûte . . .

| la chambre | **la pension complète** (full room and board) |
| le petit déjeuner | **la demi-pension** (room, breakfast and dinner) |

Hôtel du **Centre**
Confort Calme Luxe

Chambres claires et spacieuses
(wifi – télévision par satellite)

Restaurant – Salle de remise en forme – Piscine – Spa – Ascenseur

Place de la République
Paris
Réservation 01-46-77-52-51

deux cent trente et un **231**
Le Français pratique

▶ **SUPPLEMENTARY VOCABULARY**

À NOTER:
l'hôtel particulier *large private house in a city, owned by one family*
l'hôtel de ville *town hall*
l'hôtel-Dieu *city hospital (generally founded in a past century)*

■ **Teaching Strategy**
Have the students fold a piece of notebook size paper into three columns. In Column 1, have them write 15 vocabulary words they find most difficult (with their books open). Then, have them exchange these papers with the person next to them who must write the English translation and draw a picture representing the French word in Column 2. Once the second column is completed and verified by the students, the paper should go back to its original owner with the first column folded under so it can't be seen. The original student must then, in Column 3, write the French word that he/she had already written in Column 1.

■ **Notes linguistiques**
• In Canada, you might hear the expressions **le petit déjeuner continental**, **le garage** *(parking lot)*
• W.C. = **le water closet** (or **les water-closets**).

Teaching Strategy: Warm-Up

Divide the class into groups and ask each group to develop a short hotel scenario. Have groups exchange their scenarios. Using the new vocabulary presented on these pages, have students create a dialog appropriate to their scenario. Encourage students to be creative. You may wish to put additional vocabulary on the board or on a transparency for reference. Each group will present to the whole class.

■ **Teaching Notes: Activity 1**
The pictograms show the following:
un climatiseur
un lavabo
une bicyclette (un vélo) d'intérieur
deux flèches
un téléphone
une personne handicapée/un
    fauteuil roulant
un poste de télévision *(T.V. set)*
un plongeur/une piscine
une terrasse/une chaise-longue
une femme de chambre

The corresponding amenities
are *(left to right):*
l'air conditionné
une salle de bains
une salle d'exercices
l'ascenseur
le téléphone dans la chambre
l'accès pour les personnes
    handicapées
la télévision
la piscine
une belle vue
le service dans les chambres

1 La chose la plus importante

Quand on voyage, il est toujours agréable de séjourner dans des hôtels confortables. Voici certains éléments de confort symbolisés par des illustrations.

Liste
1.
2.
3.
4.
5.
6.

Quels sont les six éléments que vous considérez être les plus importants pour vous?

- Établissez votre liste en écrivant le nom de ces éléments par ordre d'importance.
- Comparez votre liste avec celle de votre partenaire.
- Quels sont les éléments que vous avez en commun avec votre partenaire?

2 Créa-dialogue: À l'hôtel Saint-François

Les touristes suivants veulent réserver une chambre à l'hôtel Saint-François. Choisissez l'un(e) de ces touristes. Avec votre partenaire, composez et jouez le dialogue entre ce/cette touriste (T) et le/la réceptionniste (R) de l'hôtel.

R: Allô, ici Hôtel Saint-François, bonjour!
T: *Say hello and say that you would like to reserve a room.*
R: *Ask what type of room the client would like.*
T: *Describe the room you would like to have, giving as many details as you wish.*
R: *Ask how long the client wants to stay.*
T: *Answer by giving the length of your stay.*
R: Je peux vous réserver une chambre *(give a price between 50 and 200 dollars).*
T: *Say whether you are going to take the room or not. If not, say thank you and good-bye.*
R: *If the client accepts, ask how he/she is going to pay.*
T: *Indicate your mode of payment.*
R: Parfait! Je vous réserve votre chambre.

TOURISTES
- un(e) étudiant(e) qui n'a pas beaucoup d'argent
- un professeur de français en vacances
- un(e) représentant(e) de commerce *(travelling salesperson)* en voyage d'affaires *(business trip)*
- un(e) journaliste
- un(e) millionnaire avec sa femme/son mari
- un couple de jeunes mariés *(newlyweds)*
- un couple de retraités *(retired couple)*

Teaching Strategy
Divide the class into groups. Make a set of cards (using the icons from Activity 1) for each group of students. One student from each group distributes one or more cards to each member of the group, then takes the role of the desk clerk at a hotel. The other students arrive, greet the clerk, and request the services on their card. The clerk may respond positively or negatively.

③ Une lettre de réservation

Vous voulez passer plusieurs jours cet été dans la ville d'Amboise avec votre cousin(e). Écrivez une lettre de réservation à l'Hôtel Belle Vue en consultant le Guide Michelin à la page 229. Suivez le modèle proposé.

---

938 Grant Place
Boulder, CO 80302 USA
le 10 avril 2012

Novotel
Route de Chenonceaux
37400 Amboise, France

Monsieur, Madame,

Je voudrais réserver une chambre non-fumeur pour une personne. Je préférerais une chambre avec une vue sur le château. J'arriverai à Amboise le 21 juillet et je partirai le 23.

Dans l'attente de votre confirmation, je vous prie d'agréer, Monsieur, Madame, l'expression de mes sentiments distingués.

Patricia McDougall

Patricia McDougall

Note linguistique

Rappel:
la déception *disappointment*
la fraude/la tromperie *deception*
tromper *to deceive*
décevoir *to disappoint*

Notes culturelles

• You may point out that the French **code postal** (here, 37400) precedes rather than follows the name of the city. The first two digits of the code indicate the **département.**

    37 = Indre-et-Loire
    37000 = Tours (chef-lieu
              du département)
    37400 = Amboise

• In French, business letters end with a long closing sentence.

Conversations libres

Avec votre partenaire, choisissez l'une des situations suivantes. Composez le dialogue correspondant et jouez-le en classe.

1   Un touriste difficile

Vous êtes réceptionniste dans un hôtel à Québec. Un(e) touriste très difficile veut une chambre. Vous lui montrez plusieurs chambres, mais le/la touriste difficile veut toujours quelque chose de différent. Il/elle n'est jamais satisfait(e).
Rôles: le/la réceptionniste, le/la touriste

2   Une auberge de campagne

Vous voyagez en France avec toute votre famille — 5 personnes au total. Un soir vous arrivez dans une petite auberge de campagne. Vous n'avez pas réservé. L'hôtelier *(innkeeper)* vous informe qu'il y a seulement deux possibilités: une très petite chambre sans confort et un grand appartement très confortable mais très cher. Négociez avec lui.
Rôles: le/la touriste, l'hôtelier

3   Une erreur

Vous avez réservé une chambre bon marché dans un grand hôtel à la Martinique. Quand vous arrivez, on vous donne un magnifique appartement avec plage privée. Vous vous installez. Dix minutes après, la réceptionniste vous téléphone pour vous dire qu'il y a erreur et que vous devez changer de chambre. Négociez avec la réceptionniste pour garder votre appartement.
Rôles: la réceptionniste, le/la touriste

4   Déception

Vous allez passer deux semaines en Normandie avec votre famille. Avant votre départ, votre agence de voyages vous a réservé des chambres dans «une auberge de campagne très pittoresque». En réalité, c'est un vieil hôtel sans confort situé près d'une gare où passent des trains toute la nuit. À votre retour, vous passez chez votre agent de voyages pour vous plaindre *(to complain)*.
Rôles: le/la touriste, l'agent de voyages

5   La note

Vous venez de passer une semaine dans une petite auberge en Touraine. Au moment de payer, vous présentez votre carte de crédit américaine. La propriétaire vous dit que l'hôtel accepte seulement l'argent français. Expliquez la situation et négociez une solution.
Rôles: le/la touriste, la propriétaire

Rubrics

For writing rubrics, consult the **Generate Success** Rubric Generator on the **Teacher One Stop.** You can also create your own custom rubrics with this tool.

Student Portfolios

Using the francophone country previously chosen by students, have them create a travel brochure. The brochure should describe the different types of lodging possibilities, and give a sample of a Michelin Guide entry for an interesting hotel; also highlight local features. The brochure should have pictures, captions, and explanations.

Langue et Communication

■ Notes linguistiques

- **Moindre** is the comparative of **petit.** It is used when **petit** conveys the meaning of inferiority, or something smaller in size or quantity. Examples: **C'est la moindre des choses.** *It's the least I can do.* **Le moindre bruit la réveille.** *The least noise wakes her.*
- In a list of several comparisons, **plus/moins/aussi** must be repeated with each adjective. Example: **Il est plus généreux, plus intelligent, plus gentil et plus patient que son frère aîné.**
- The other forms are regular:
  moins bon(ne) que
  aussi bon(ne) que
  moins bien que
  aussi bien que

■ Proverbes

- On ne trouve jamais meilleur messager que soi-même.
- Le mieux est l'ennemi du bien.

■ Illustration Note

un break *station wagon*
une enseigne *(store) sign*

---

234 Unité 6

A Le comparatif

Comparative constructions are used to compare people or things.

Cet hôtel est **aussi moderne que** l'autre.　*This hotel is **as modern as** the other one.*
J'ai **moins d'argent que** vous.　*I have **less money than** you.*

ADJECTIVES AND ADVERBS

+	plus	}	ADJECTIVE		**plus** moderne **(que)**	*more* modern *(than)*
–	moins	}	(OR ADVERB)	(+ que)	**moins** moderne **(que)**	*less* modern *(than)*
=	aussi	}			**aussi** moderne **(que)**	*as* modern *(as)*

→ STRESS PRONOUNS are used after **que.**
   Je suis aussi intelligent **que toi.**

→ The comparative of the ADJECTIVE **bon/bonne** is **meilleur/meilleure.**
   The comparative of the ADVERB **bien** is **mieux.**
   Compare:
   Je suis **meilleur** en tennis **que** toi.　*I am **better** at tennis **than** you.*
   Je joue **mieux.**　*I play **better.***

NOUNS

+	plus de	}			**plus** d'argent **(que)**	*more* money *(than)*
–	moins de	}	NOUN	(+ que)	**moins** d'argent **(que)**	*less* money *(than)*
=	autant de	}			**autant** d'argent **(que)**	*as much* money *(as)*

1 Ah, le bon vieux temps!

Monsieur Ladoux a passé toute sa vie dans le même village. Il se souvient du bon temps de sa jeunesse où tout était meilleur qu'aujourd'hui. Jouez le rôle de Monsieur Ladoux. Soyez logique!

▶ air / pur?

Autrefois, l'air était plus pur.

1. les rivières / polluées?
2. les produits / artificiels?
3. la nourriture / bonne?
4. les jeunes / sérieux?
5. les gens / préoccupés par l'argent?
6. les relations entre les gens / bonnes?
7. la société / matérialiste?
8. les problèmes de l'existence / compliqués?
9. la vie / simple?

234

Teaching Strategy: Warm-Up

Have the students bring in five pairs of pictures that can be compared to each other. For each picture have them write three comparative sentences using **plus ...que, moins ...que** and **aussi ...que**, as well as **meilleur ...que** and/or **mieux ...que** comparing, for example, two famous people.

Differentiation

Metacognitive Ask students to generate some adjectives. Teach comparisons with adjectives. Then, ask 1 or 2 students to create a chart on the board, showing the placement of the elements of a comparative sentence. Have them write this chart in their notebooks.

2 *Où loger?*

Vos amis et vous, vous voyagez en Touraine. Où allez-vous loger? Dans une auberge de campagne *(country inn)* ou dans un grand hôtel à Tours? Avec votre partenaire (ou votre groupe), faites une liste des avantages que vous désirez et classez-les par ordre d'importance. Faites votre choix sur la base de cette liste.

Auberge de campagne	Grand hôtel en ville
• C'est moins cher.	• C'est plus luxueux.
• C'est plus calme.	• C'est plus confortable.
• On s'y repose mieux.	• Les chambres sont mieux équipées.
• La nourriture est meilleure.	• La piscine est plus grande.
• On mange plus de produits naturels.	• Le service est mieux organisé.
• L'air est plus pur.	• On est servi plus rapidement.
• Les chambres sont moins bruyantes.	• On visite plus facilement la ville.
• Le service est plus personnalisé.	• Il y a plus de choses à faire.
• On dort mieux.	• Il y a plus de choses intéressantes à faire.
• ??	• ??

3 *Décisions, décisions*

Avec votre partenaire, discutez les choix suivants. Chacun va expliquer son choix et essayer de convaincre l'autre personne. Utilisez les suggestions suivantes ou votre imagination.

> Tu vas visiter le Canada ou le Mexique?
>
> Je vais visiter le Mexique.
>
> Ah bon? Pourquoi?
>
> C'est un pays plus accueillant!
>
> D'accord, mais le Canada est un pays aussi accueillant et plus pittoresque....

▶ Visiter le Canada ou le Mexique? C'est un pays (intéressant? pittoresque? accueillant *[welcoming]*?...)

1. Visiter San Francisco ou New York? C'est une ville (jolie? grande? intéressante? polluée?...)
2. Prendre l'avion ou le train? C'est un transport (cher? rapide? dangereux? polluant?...)
3. Étudier le japonais ou l'espagnol? C'est une langue (facile? difficile? utile?...)
4. Dîner dans un restaurant italien ou chinois? La nourriture est (bonne? légère? riche en calories? chère? naturelle?...)
5. Manger du poulet frit ou de la sole? C'est un plat (bon? naturel? léger? riche en calories?...)
6. Apprendre à faire du parapente ou de la voile? C'est un sport (facile? dangereux? spectaculaire?...)

4 *C'est évident!*

Comparez les choses ou les personnes suivantes en utilisant l'adjectif entre parenthèses. Faites une autre comparaison en utilisant la phrase qui suit. Soyez logique!

▶ Jacques (+ pauvre) Annie / Il a de l'argent.
  Jacques est plus pauvre qu'Annie. Il a moins d'argent.

1. Nathalie (+ sportive) Philippe / Elle fait du sport.
2. Roger (+ économe) Antoine / Il dépense de l'argent.
3. Albert (= brillant) Thérèse / Il a des idées originales.
4. Sandrine (− heureuse) Sophie / Elle a des problèmes.
5. les voitures américaines (= économiques) les voitures japonaises / Elles consomment de l'essence *(gas).*
6. l'hôtel Méridien (+ grand) l'hôtel Ibis / Il a des chambres.

■ **Teaching Strategy: Activity 4**

Be sure students do not use articles after **plus/moins/autant de.**
1. Elle fait plus de sport.
2. Il dépense moins d'argent.
3. Il a autant d'idées originales.
4. Elle a plus de problèmes.
5. Elles consomment autant d'essence.
6. Il a plus de chambres.

RESOURCES

PRINT
Workbook, pp. 64–65, 141
Unit 6 Resource Book, Partie 1
Audioscripts

AUDIO
Audio Program
CD 6, Tracks 6–7

TECHNOLOGY
@HomeTutor

■ **Note linguistique**

If the adjective normally precedes the noun, the superlative construction may either precede or follow it, depending on the emphasis: **le plus petit hôtel** or **l'hôtel le plus petit.**

With other adjectives, however, the superlative always follows the noun: **la ville la plus intéressante.**

B Le superlatif

Superlative constructions are used to compare people or things with the rest of a group.

Voici l'hôtel **le plus moderne de** la ville.   *Here is **the most modern** hotel **in** the city.*
Et voilà **le plus petit** hôtel.   *And here is **the smallest** hotel.*

ADJECTIVES

le/la/les $\left\{ \begin{array}{l} \text{plus} \\ \text{moins} \end{array} \right\}$ + ADJECTIVE (+ de)	le/la/les plus moderne(s) **(de)** *the most modern **(in)***
	le/la/les moins moderne(s) **(de)** *the least modern **(in)***

→ After a superlative construction, **de** is used to introduce the reference group.
→ The superlative of **bon / bonne** is **le meilleur / la meilleure** *(the best).*
     Voici **le meilleur** restaurant du quartier.

→ In a superlative construction, the position of the adjective (<u>before</u> or <u>after</u> the noun) is usually the same as in the regular construction. Note that when the adjective comes after the noun, the article (**le, la, les**) is used twice.

     le plus grand musée   le musée **le plus** intéressant

→ A superlative construction may be introduced by a possessive adjective.
     Compare: **ma plus belle** veste   **mon** livre **le plus intéressant**

ADVERBS

$\left. \begin{array}{l} \text{le plus} \\ \text{le moins} \end{array} \right\}$ + ADVERB	Qui voyage **le plus** souvent?
	Qui voyage **le moins** vite?

→ The superlative of **bien** is **le mieux.**
     C'est moi qui joue **le mieux** au volley.

NOUNS

$\left. \begin{array}{l} \text{le plus de} \\ \text{le moins de} \end{array} \right\}$ + NOUN	C'est moi qui ai **le plus d'idées**
	mais **le moins d'argent.**

VOICI LA CHAMBRE LA MOINS CHÈRE DE L'HÔTEL.

C'EST AUSSI LA PLUS BRUYANTE!

5 **Compliments**

Faites un compliment à votre partenaire.
Il/elle va vous faire un compliment aussi.

• amusant	• intelligent
• sympa	• patient
• gentil	• étonnant *(amazing)*
• drôle	• mignon
• intéressant	• dynamique
• sportif	• ??

Alice, tu es la fille la plus intelligente de mes amies.

Et toi, David, tu es le garçon le plus drôle de mes amis.

Expansion linguistique

When a superlative construction is followed by a relative clause, the verb is usually in the subjunctive if the speaker has used the superlative to express an opinion. Compare:
     Paris est **la plus belle ville que je connaisse**. *(This is my opinion, based on cities I am familiar with.)*

Paris est **la plus grande ville que j'ai visitée** cet été. *(This is a fact.)*
The superlative may also be used when only two people or things are involved.
     Il y a deux hôtels dans le quartier.
     There are two hotels in the neighborhood.
     Lequel est **le plus moderne?**
     *Which one is the **most modern**?*

6 Au Bureau de Tourisme

Vous travaillez au Bureau de Tourisme. Des touristes (vos partenaires) cherchent des hôtels avec l'une des caractéristiques suivantes. Renseignez-les.

▶ — Je cherche un hôtel.
— Quelle sorte d'hôtel cherchez-vous?
— Un hôtel <u>calme.</u>
— L'hôtel le plus calme de la ville est l'hôtel Bellevue.

- calme
- grand
- cher
- confortable
- bon marché
- petit

Bureau de Tourisme				
HÔTEL	NOMBRE DE CHAMBRES	CONFORT	CALME	PRIX DES CHAMBRES
Hôtel Ibis	45	✳✳	🐌	60€
Hôtel Napoléon	150	✳✳✳	🐌 🐌	120€
Hôtel d'Isly	18	✳	🐌	85€
Hotel Bellevue	30	✳✳✳✳	🐌 🐌 🐌	125€

7 Le meilleur choix

Vous voyagez avec votre partenaire. Expliquez-lui pourquoi vous faites certains choix.

▶ aller dans cet hôtel   (moderne / la ville)
— Allons dans cet hôtel!
— Pourquoi cet hôtel?
— C'est l'hôtel le plus moderne de la ville.
— Alors, d'accord!

1. visiter ce musée (intéressant / la région)
2. prendre ce train (rapide / la journée)
3. acheter ces souvenirs (bon marché / le magasin)
4. dîner dans ce restaurant (bon / le quartier)
5. choisir ce plat (typique / le menu)

8 Les Oscars

Dites qui à votre avis est le/la meilleur(e) dans les catégories suivantes.

- un bon acteur
- une bonne actrice
- un athlète sympathique
- une comédienne amusante
- un bon film de l'année
- une comédie drôle
- une émission (TV program) intéressante
- un sport intéressant
- une classe facile
- une bonne équipe de basket

▶ Quel est le sport le plus intéressant?
À mon avis, c'est le football.
(C'est le sport le plus spectaculaire.)

9 Au Syndicat d'Initiative
(At the Chamber of Commerce)

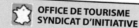

Vous travaillez pour le Syndicat d'Initiative de votre ville. Votre bureau vient de recevoir la lettre suivante d'un(e) touriste français(e). Répondez à sa lettre.

Monsieur, Madame,
Nous pensons visiter votre ville le mois prochain. Pourriez-vous nous indiquer:

un hôtel moderne
un bon restaurant
des boutiques intéressantes
des endroits pittoresques.

En vous remerciant de votre attention, je vous prie de croire, Monsieur, Madame, à l'expression de mes sentiments distingués.

Jacques Delavigne
Jacques Delavigne

⬡ **OFFICE DE TOURISME SYNDICAT D'INITIATIVE**

Monsieur,
Nous vous remercions de l'intérêt que vous portez à notre ville. Permettez-moi de répondre à vos questions. L'hôtel le plus moderne est . . .

En espérant que les renseignements vous seront utiles, nous vous prions de croire, Monsieur, à l'expression de nos sentiments distingués.

Note culturelle

Since its inception, the value of the euro has varied between $1. and $1.60. Check for its current valuation.

■ Expansion: Activity 7

Additional items for Activity 7:
6. acheter ces cartes postales (joli/ le magasin)
7. aller voir ce film (bon/la semaine)
8. aller dans ces magasins (grand/ le quartier)

■ Teaching Strategy

Activity 8 may also be conducted as a class poll. Have students make two or three nominations in each category and then vote on the choices. Tally the results on the board or overhead projector. If you have more than one Level Three class, students may be interested in comparing the results between classes.

Teaching Strategy

Divide the class into groups of five. Have each group create five sentences (three comparative and two superlative) about their group. Each student should be mentioned at least once. Have Group 1 write the five adjectives they used on the board. The other groups will write down the comparisons.

Differentiation

Multisensory Have students write elements of superlative sentences on cards. Working in pairs, have them combine cards to create superlative sentences, adding an ending of their choice. Have them call out their sentences while you write them on the board.

Unité 6   237

À l'Hôtel de la Plage

Après une année de dur° travail, finalement arrive l'époque heureuse des vacances. Quand on décide de partir, on peut faire du camping ou louer une villa, mais l'idéal est d'aller à l'hôtel. Là, il n'y a pas de travaux domestiques à faire, pas de repas à préparer, pas de problèmes à résoudre.° Comme tout est fait pour vous, vous pouvez profiter° complètement et totalement d'un repos bien mérité.

Parfois, l'hôtel réserve quelques surprises aux touristes inexpérimentés.° Prenons, par exemple, le cas de Monsieur et Madame Lagarde. Les Lagarde ont réservé une chambre pour deux semaines à l'Hôtel de la Plage, réputé, d'après la brochure, pour le bon air marin qu'on y respire.° Mais quand ils arrivent à leur destination, ils ont la mauvaise surprise de découvrir que l'Hôtel de la Plage est situé près d'une voie de chemin de fer.° Quant à° la plage …

Florida et gab...
10 Rue Joliot...
29138 Lescon...
(Finistère)
Tél. 02.98.87...

* À l'hôtel, le meilleur accueil est réservé aux heureux voyageurs.
* À l'hôtel, vous profiterez du calme et de la tranquillité absolus.
* Les hôtels de qualité offrent à leurs clients tout le confort de la vie moderne.
* Le grand air de la campagne vous permettra de dormir comme si vous étiez un enfant.
* La nuit personne ne viendra troubler votre sommeil.°
* Les hôtels offrent un service complet à des prix très raisonnables.

* À l'hôtel, le meilleur accueil est réservé aux heureux voyageurs.

* À l'hôtel, vous profiterez du calme et de la tranquillité absolue.

— Où est la plage?
— La plage, la plage … eh bien, elle est à trois kilomètres d'ici. Quand il fait beau, on la voit très bien du sixième étage. … Ah, je vois que votre chambre est au deuxième… Si vous vouliez voir la mer, il fallait réserver plus tôt.

— Oh, excusez-moi! Je reviendrai faire la chambre plus tard.

✳ Les hôtels de qualité offrent à leurs clients tout le confort de la vie moderne.

✳ Le grand air de la campagne vous permettra de dormir comme si vous étiez un enfant.

— Oh là là, chéri!° Quelle chaleur!° Peux-tu vérifier si le climatiseur° fonctionne?
— Oui, il fonctionne, mais c'est de l'air chaud qui sort!

— Je n'arrive pas° à dormir. Qu'est-ce que c'est que ce bruit? Est-ce qu'il y a des souris° ici?
— Mais non, ce sont les voisins d'à côté° qui mangent des chips.

✳ La nuit personne ne viendra troubler votre sommeil.°

✳ Les hôtels offrent un service complet à des prix très raisonnables.

— Bonjour, Monsieur Martin. Vous m'avez demandé de vous réveiller à cinq heures et demie. Bonne journée!
— Alllô! Quoi! Qu'est-ce que vous dites? Martin? Vous faites erreur! Je suis Monsieur Lagarde!

— Comment? vingt euros pour le petit déjeuner? Je croyais que tout était compris dans le prix! Et cette taxe locale de 5%! Qu'est-ce que c'est?

et vous?

EXPRESSION ORALE

Vous êtes Monsieur ou Madame Lagarde. Pour chaque épisode, vous téléphonez au directeur de l'hôtel (joué par votre partenaire) pour expliquer le problème. Le directeur essaie de trouver une solution.

EXPRESSION ÉCRITE

• Vous êtes Monsieur ou Madame Lagarde et vous écrivez à un(e) ami(e). Dans votre lettre, vous parlez des problèmes que vous avez eus pendant votre séjour.

• Décrivez un problème (réel ou imaginaire) que vous avez eu pendant un voyage et comment vous avez résolu ce problème.

dur hard **résoudre** ✳ to solve **inexperimentés** = sans expérience **respire** breathes **profiter** to enjoy **chemin de fer** railroad track **Quant à** As for **accueil** welcome **chéri** darling **chaleur** heat **climatiseur** air conditioner **Je n'arrive pas** = je ne peux pas **souris** mice **d'à côté** next door **sommeil** sleep

■ **Note culturelle**
The tax in France is called the **T.V.A. (Taxe à Valeur Ajoutée)**. Its rate is generally 19.6%.

■ **Irregular Verb**
(see Appendix C)
résoudre

INFOMAGAZINE

2 Services à l'hôtel

> Bien sûr, monsieur, tout de suite.

> Pouvez-vous m'apporter une couverture?

@HOMETUTOR
my.hrw.com

COMMENT DEMANDER UN SERVICE

Au garçon *(bellboy)*

Pouvez-vous | **monter** / **descendre** | mes bagages?

monter *to bring up, carry up*	
descendre *to bring down, carry down*	

À la femme de chambre *(chambermaid)*

Pouvez-vous m'apporter
- **une couverture** *(blanket)*?
- **un drap** *(sheet)*?
- **un oreiller** *(pillow)*?
- **une serviette** *(towel)*?
- **un portemanteau** *(hanger)*?
- **un cintre** *(hanger)*?

Pouvez-vous | **mettre** / **augmenter** / **baisser** | **le chauffage** *(heat)*? / **la climatisation**? / **l'air conditionné**?

mettre *to turn on*
augmenter *to turn up, raise*
baisser *to turn down, lower*

Au (à la) réceptionniste

Pouvez-vous | me **servir** le petit déjeuner dans la chambre? / m'**appeler** un taxi?

servir *to serve*
appeler *to call*

Au standard *(operator)*
Pouvez-vous me **réveiller** à six heures et demie?

réveiller *to wake*

Au (à la) gérant(e) *(manager)*
Pouvez-vous préparer ma **note** *(bill)*?

Teaching Suggestion: DVD Program

In the Unit 6 *Vidéo-drame: À l'hôtel,* students will concentrate on hotel services and how to ask for what they need. You may want to ask students some comprehension questions based on the vocabulary in this section.

Differentiation

Cumulative, Gifted & Talented Have students work in small groups to write a mystery or a ghost story that takes place in a hotel. Students should use the vocabulary from pp. 230–231 and pp. 240–241.

1 Que dire?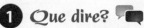

Vous voyagez en France et vous êtes à l'hôtel. Qu'est-ce que vous allez demander dans les circonstances suivantes? (Votre partenaire va jouer le rôle du personnel de l'hôtel.)

▶ Vous arrivez à l'hôtel avec deux grosses valises.
— **Est-ce que vous pouvez monter mes bagages, s'il vous plaît?**
— Oui, mademoiselle (monsieur). Tout de suite.
— Merci bien.

- Vous voulez payer.
- Vous avez un train à 6h30 demain matin.
- Il fait très, très chaud dans votre chambre.
- Vous avez froid.
- Vous voulez rester au lit tard, mais vous voulez prendre votre petit déjeuner.
- Vous avez payé votre note et vous voulez aller à l'aéroport.
- Il va faire froid cette nuit.
- Vous devez quitter l'hôtel mais les bagages dans votre chambre sont très lourds.
- Vous avez beaucoup de vêtements que vous voulez pendre *(to hang up)*.

Veuillez faire la chambre s.v.p.

S.V.P NE PAS DÉRANGER

Hôtel du Centre
Confort Calme Luxe

Hôtel du **Centre**

Place de la République
Paris
Réservation 01-46-77-52-51

ACCUEIL | CHAMBRES | SERVICES | SITUATION | TARIFS | RÉSERVATION

Bienvenue à l'Hôtel du Centre.

Situé en plein cœur de la ville de lumière, il est idéal pour allier travail et plaisirs. Doté d'une connexion Wifi gratuite à travers tout l'hôtel et d'un centre d'affaires avec stations de travail, imprimante et fax, il est idéal pour les voyages d'affaires. Sa situation en plein centre de la capitale en fait une destination rêvée pour ceux d'entre vous qui veulent profiter des musées, magasins et autres divertissements parisiens.

Ses chambres sont claires et spacieuses, avec connexion Wifi, télévision par satellite, salle de bains privée, plateau café et thé. En outre, toutes les chambres ont récemment été refaites et offrent tout le confort moderne souhaité.

Avec son restaurant, sa salle de remise en forme, sa piscine et son spa, vous pourrez vous détendre en toute quiétude.

Teaching Strategy
Bring in as much tourist information on francophone countries as possible from local travel agents, magazines, web sites, and newspapers. Ask students to create an advertisement for a hotel to appeal to different types of travellers (families, students, groups, etc.) The ads may be in any form: music, print, informational statistics, etc. Then ask students to look at the material you brought to class and attempt to categorize the real ads in a similar way.

Teaching Strategy
Ask students:
- Regardez le site web du Hôtel du Centre à la page 241. Choisiriez-vous cet hôtel si vous alliez en vacances en France? Pourquoi?
- Quels services particuliers offre-t-il?

Realia Note
S.V.P. = s'il vous plaît

Culture Note
Most kings of France were crowned in **Reims**, a city which is also known for its local wine: **le champagne**.

Teaching Suggestion
Play the video with the sound muted. Tell the class to write conversations based on what they see. Afterward, play the video with the sound on to see how close their conversations come to the one on the video.

Teaching Strategy: Warm-Up
Have the students think of original questions/ comments that they would ask/say to each of the hotel workers listed on p. 240. **(Au standard: Quel est le numéro pour service dans les chambres?)** Encourage them to use the vocabulary from pp. 230–231. Once they have thought up one question/comment per hotel employee, have them volunteer to read each one so that the class can guess to whom this question/comment would be directed.

Langue et Communication

■ Notes linguistiques

- **Lequel** and its forms can also be used as relative pronouns.
- You may remind students that when a preposition (**à, de, avec,** etc.) is used in a question, it must come at the beginning of the question:
  À qui parles-tu?
  De quoi as-tu besoin?
- You may also wish to remind students that the demonstrative pronouns are a combination of **ce** + the third person stress pronouns:

ce + lui	→	celui
ce + elle	→	celle
ce + eux	→	ceux
ce + elles	→	celles

A Le pronom interrogatif *lequel?*

The interrogative pronoun **lequel?** *(which one?)* replaces **quel?** + NOUN.

Quel hôtel préfères-tu?   **Lequel** préfères-tu?

Lequel? has the following forms:

	MASCULINE	FEMININE
SINGULAR	lequel?	laquelle?
PLURAL	lesquels?	lesquelles?

→ The pronoun **lequel** consists of two parts, both of which agree with the noun it replaces:

$$\text{lequel} = \text{le} + \text{quel}$$

→ Note how **à** and **de** contract with **lequel** to give the following forms:

à + lequel	→	**auquel**	de + lequel	→	**duquel**
à + lesquels	→	**auxquels**	de + lesquels	→	**desquels**
à + lesquelles	→	**auxquelles**	de + lesquelles	→	**desquelles**

Il y a deux concerts.   **Auquel** veux-tu aller?   (= à quel concert?)

J'ai plusieurs cartes de la région.   **Desquelles** as-tu besoin?   (= de quelles cartes?)

B Le pronom démonstratif *celui*

The demonstrative pronoun **celui** *(this one, the one)* replaces **ce** or **le** + NOUN.

Celui has the following forms:

	MASCULINE	FEMININE
SINGULAR	celui	celle
PLURAL	ceux	celles

Celui is never used alone. It occurs in the following combinations:

- **celui-ci, celui-là** *(this one, that one)*
  — Ta valise, c'est **celle-ci**?   *Your suitcase, is it **this one**?*
  — Non, c'est **celle-là**.   *No, it's **that one**.*

- **celui de** *(that of, the one belonging to)*
  Ce n'est pas mon passeport.
  C'est **celui de** Valérie.   *It's **Valérie's**. (= that of Valérie)*

  J'ai raté le train de 10 heures.
  Je prendrai **celui de** 11 heures.   *I will take **the 11 o'clock**.*
          (= the one of 11 o'clock)

Teaching Strategy

Before class, draw, cut out or bring in two like objects (two hats: one red, one blue). Place the objects at different spots around the room: some next to each other, some under or on top of the desk, etc. Then ask: **Aimez-vous le chapeau?** To answer your question they will have to ask you: **Lequel?** You can then answer: **Celui qui est bleu.** Continue, asking them **Lequel est plus grand?** Students must answer with **Celui qui.../celui de...** You can also bring in a pen and a pencil and ask the students **Est-ce que vous vous servez des stylos? des crayons?...**

■ **Note linguistique**
Note also the expression **celui où:**
   J'aime bien ce restaurant mais
   je préfère **celui où** nous avons
   dîné hier.

• **celui qui, celui que** *(the one who(m), the one that)*
   J'aime les hôtels confortables,
      mais je préfère **ceux qui** ont   *I prefer **those (the ones) that***
         une belle vue.   *have a nice view.*

❶ Préférences

Vous faites du shopping avec votre partenaire.
Vous discutez des choses que vous voyez.

   1. ces chaussures / plus élégantes
   2. ce vélo / plus solide
   3. ces livres / plus intéressants
   4. cette voiture / plus rapide
   5. cet ordinateur / plus moderne
   6. ces tee-shirts / plus à la mode

❷ Comparaisons

Lisez les descriptions suivantes et comparez
ces choses à celles qui sont indiquées entre
parenthèses.

▶ Ma maison est grande.
   (mon meilleur ami?)

   **Ma maison est plus (moins / aussi)
   grande que celle de mon meilleur
   ami.**

   1. Notre voiture est grande.
         (les voisins?)
   2. Ma chambre est spacieuse.
         (mes parents?)
   3. Mes progrès en français sont rapides.
         (les autres étudiants?)
   4. La cuisine de ma mère est bonne.
         (la cafétéria?)
   5. L'air de la campagne est pollué.
         (la ville?)
   6. Le climat de la Nouvelle-Angleterre
         est agréable.
         (la Floride?)
   7. Les monuments de Paris sont beaux.
         (New York?)

❸ Au choix

Vous voyagez à Paris avec votre partenaire. Vous
avez le choix entre deux possibilités. Demandez
à votre partenaire de choisir.

▶ deux hôtels (l'un a une grande piscine /
   l'autre, des chambres confortables)
      — Il y a deux hôtels. Auquel veux-tu aller?
      **— Je préfère aller à celui qui a
         des chambres confortables.
         (Je préfère aller à celui qui a
         une grande piscine.)**

   1. deux restaurants
         (l'un sert des spécialités françaises /
            l'autre, des spécialités vietnamiennes)
   2. deux musées
         (l'un a une exposition de photos /
            l'autre, une exposition d'art moderne)
   3. deux piscines
         (l'une est au centre-ville /
            l'autre, dans la banlieue)
   4. deux cinémas
         (l'un joue une comédie /
            l'autre, un western)
   5. deux boutiques
         (l'une vend des jeans /
            l'autre, des chaussures)

■ **Teaching Strategy:
   Expansion**

The conversations in Activity 3 could
be expanded to a negotiation
situation in which the two students
come to an agreement.

Duquel vous servez-vous le plus souvent?
This will give them further practice using/
hearing the contractions with **lequel.** As
students use the important expression, write it
on the board for visual reinforcement.

RESOURCES

PRINT
Workbook, pp. 67–68, 144
Unit 6 Resource Book, Partie 2
Audioscripts

AUDIO
Audio Program
CD 6 Tracks 12–14

TECHNOLOGY
@HomeTutor

■ Pronunciation Note

Be sure that students pronounce **nôtre** and **vôtre** with the closed /o/: **nôtre** /notʀ/ and **vôtre** /votʀ/.

■ Expansion linguistique

Possessive pronouns are used less frequently in French than in English.

• The possessive pronoun is not used after **être** when the subject is a noun or a personal pronoun. Instead French uses the construction **être à** + STRESS PRONOUN.
  Ce livre **est à moi.** That book is **mine.**

However, possessive pronouns are used after **c'est/ce sont.**
  C'est le mien.
  It's **mine.**

• Note the following constructions:
  une de mes amies
  a friend of mine
  des amis à nous
  friends of ours
  un de ses cousins
  a cousin of his/hers
  des cousines à lui
  cousins of his

C Le pronom possessif *le mien*

POSSESSIVE PRONOUNS replace nouns introduced by a possessive adjective. Note the forms of the French possessive adjectives in the following sentences.

Ce n'est pas ta guitare.	C'est **la mienne.**	It's **mine.**
Marc écoute ses CD.	Anne écoute **les siens.**	Anne is listening to **hers.**
Votre chambre est grande.	**La nôtre** est confortable.	**Ours** is comfortable.

	SINGULAR		PLURAL	
	MASCULINE	**FEMININE**	**MASCULINE**	**FEMININE**
mine	**le mien**	**la mienne**	**les miens**	**les miennes**
yours	**le tien**	**la tienne**	**les tiens**	**les tiennes**
his, hers, its	**le sien**	**la sienne**	**les siens**	**les siennes**
ours	**le nôtre**	**la nôtre**	**les nôtres**	
yours	**le vôtre**	**la vôtre**	**les vôtres**	
theirs	**le leur**	**la leur**	**les leurs**	

→ Possessive pronouns consist of two parts, both of which agree with the noun they replace:

le + POSSESSIVE WORD

→ Note how **à** and **de** contract with the possessive pronoun:

à + le mien	→	**au mien**	de + le mien	→	**du mien**
à + les miens	→	**aux miens**	de + les miens	→	**des miens**
à + les miennes	→	**aux miennes**	de + les miennes	→	**des miennes**

Pratique p. 67 →
Pronoms possessifs

---

4 Possessions

Insistez sur la propriété des choses suivantes.

▶ Ce sont mes clés.
  Ce sont les miennes!

▶ C'est la voiture de mes parents.
  C'est la leur!

1. C'est ma serviette.
2. Ce sont tes lunettes de soleil.
3. C'est sa valise.
4. Ce sont ses CD.
5. Ce sont vos bagages.
6. C'est notre sac.
7. C'est l'ordinateur de Paul.
8. C'est le vélo d'Alice.
9. C'est le portable de Jérôme.
10. C'est la maison de tes cousins.
11. Ce sont les valises de Pierre et d'Isabelle.
12. C'est la tondeuse de nos voisins.

Differentiation

Alphabetic/Phonetic. Have students write out phonetic transcriptions for each form of **le mien.** Have them underline the nasal **n** each time it occurs, in a colored pencil. Have them repeat each 3 times, stressing the nasal and non-nasal **n**'s.

5 Camping

Vous faites du camping avec votre partenaire. Vous avez oublié certaines choses.
Demandez à votre partenaire si vous pouvez prendre les siennes.

▶ mon couteau
— Dis, Daniel, j'ai oublié mon couteau.
Est-ce que je peux prendre le tien?
— Le mien? Oui, d'accord!
(Le mien? Ça non, pas question!)

1. ma lampe de poche
2. mon sac de couchage
3. mes jumelles *(f. binoculars)*
4. ma serviette
5. mon savon
6. mon dentifrice
7. ma guitare
8. mes vitamines *(f)*

6 À qui est-ce?

Vous faites un voyage au Canada avec votre école. Vous avez trouvé certains objets mais
vous ne savez pas à qui ils sont. Votre partenaire va vous aider à identifier le propriétaire.

▶ — C'est ta serviette?
— Non!
— Tu es sûr(e)?
— Absolument! La mienne est
plus grande.
— Alors, c'est celle de François.
— Oui, c'est probablement la sienne.

1. • ton sac
   • moins grand
   • Philippe

2. • ton appareil-photo
   • plus petit
   • Isabelle

3. • tes lunettes de soleil
   • noires
   • Claire

4. • ta veste
   • verte
   • David

5. • ta caméra
   • moins chère
   • Éric et Thomas

6. • tes valises
   • jaunes
   • Alice et Pauline

7 À l'aéroport

Vous êtes à l'aéroport avec votre partenaire.
Il/elle vous dit ce qu'il/elle va faire. Dites-lui
que vous allez faire les mêmes choses.

1. Je vais téléphoner à mes cousins.
2. Je vais dire au revoir à ma mère.
3. Je vais prendre une photo de ma soeur.
4. Je vais m'occuper de mon billet.
5. Je vais m'occuper de mes valises.
6. Je vais écrire une carte postale à mon professeur.

▶ *Je vais téléphoner à mon copain.*

Eh bien, moi, je vais aussi téléphoner au mien.

• With more advanced students, you may contrast the
following constructions:

This is *her* suitcase.	C'est **sa** valise.
It is *hers.*	C'est **la sienne**. (or: **Elle** est **à elle.**)
It is not *Catherine's.*	Ce n'est pas **celle de Catherine**.
	(or: Elle n'est pas **à Catherine.**)

Interdisciplinary/Community Connections

Create a restaurant guide for your
area. In small groups, visit
restaurants and note all your
opinions for the class guide. Publish
the ratings and comments in a class
newsletter.

Language Arts
Brainstorm a list of local restaurants
by using online resources, contacting
the chamber of commerce, and
asking family members for names of
restaurants. Then, as a class, develop
a checklist of categories on which to
rate the establishments.

Math
Note and list in a chart the prices of
a typical meal at each restaurant
visited.

Science/Health
When visiting the restaurant, note if it
is possible to create a balanced
meal, and if the restaurant offers
health-conscious items.

Social Studies
Include a history of the restaurant, or
information about ethnic foods served
there.

Art/Music
Comment on the decor and
background music of the eatery, and
describe how each affects the
ambiance of the place.

Technology
Observe and ask about how
technology is used in the restaurant:
in entering orders with the kitchen? in
recording reservations? in placing
orders with suppliers?

Community
Publish your comments and ratings in
a newsletter to share with other
French classes.

Reading
STRATEGY

Reading fiction

RESOURCES

PRINT
Activités pour tous

TECHNOLOGY
Teacher One Stop
Projectable Transparencies
L6, Une étrange aventure
Transparency Copymasters,
pp. A129–A130
French InterActive Reader

LECTURE

Une étrange aventure

AVANT DE LIRE

Le titre d'une histoire donne parfois aux lecteurs une idée générale du contenu et du ton de l'histoire. Elle leur permet ainsi d'anticiper ce qui va arriver. C'est le cas, par exemple, du titre «Une étrange aventure».

- Vous savez que vous allez lire une **aventure**, c'est-à-dire un récit où l'<u>action</u> joue un rôle important.
- Vous savez aussi qu'au cours du récit quelque chose d'**étrange** va arriver.

En général, les histoires de ce genre commencent de façon très normale, très ordinaire. Puis, un petit problème survient et le mystère commence.

Au début (Partie I)
Déterminez le cadre général de l'histoire.
- Qui sont les protagonistes?
- Qu'est-ce qu'ils vont faire? Où vont-ils?
- Quel problème rencontrent-ils?

Au milieu (Partie II)
À mesure que l'histoire se développe, essayez de déterminer . . .
- les éléments qui vous semblent réels, vrais, ordinaires
- les éléments qui vous semblent étranges, mystérieux, irréels, bizarres

À la fin (Partie III)
Essayez . . .
- d'anticiper ce qui va se passer ensuite
- de trouver une solution au mystère de l'histoire

NOTE *Culturelle*

Les villages en France

Autrefois, la France était un pays rural. La majorité des Français habitaient dans des petits villages de moins de 2 000 habitants. Construits généralement autour d'une église, ces villages étaient reliés° entre eux par des petites routes le long desquelles° se trouvaient des fermes isolées. Les cafés, les boutiques, les petits commerces de toutes sortes, les nombreux ateliers d'artisan° donnaient beaucoup de vie et d'animation aux villages d'autrefois.

Avec l'exode rural et le développement des grandes villes, ces villages ont perdu de leur importance et surtout de leur animation. Aujourd'hui, la vie y est calme et monotone. La nuit, leurs rues sont complètement désertes.

reliés *linked* **le long desquelles** *along which* **ateliers d'artisan** *workshops*

Teaching Strategy

The students will better appreciate the strange ending of this story if they are somewhat familiar with the Nazi occupation of France and the French Resistance in World War II. You may first want to read *Interlude 6*, especially the texts *Les Guerres Mondiales* (p. 252) and *Jean Moulin* (p. 253).

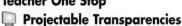

Une étrange aventure

I

John et Bob, deux étudiants américains, sont arrivés à Paris à la fin de juin. Là, ils ont acheté un scooter d'occasion avec l'intention de visiter la France pendant l'été. Ils sont partis de Paris le premier juillet dans la matinée°. Ils espèrent être à Clermont-Ferrand dans la soirée. Ils ont un copain là-bas qui les a invités.

Hélas, John et Bob ne savent pas que le premier juillet, c'est le jour des grands départs.* Il y a beaucoup de circulation sur les autoroutes et même sur les routes nationales. Alors, John et Bob décident de prendre des petites routes. Là, il y a moins de circulation, mais le scooter n'avance pas vite.

Il est neuf heures du soir maintenant. La nuit commence à tomber et les deux garçons sont encore loin de leur destination. C'est John qui conduit le scooter. Il demande à Bob: «Tu sais où nous sommes?»

Bob regarde la carte.

— Non, pas exactement. Dis, est-ce que tu as encore de l'essence?

— Euh non! Pas beaucoup.

— Alors, il faut s'arrêter au prochain village. J'espère qu'il y a une station-service.   25

— . . . Ou un hôtel!

Au prochain village, il y a bien une station-service, mais elle est fermée . . . et il n'y a pas d'hôtel. John demande:

— On continue?   30

— Oui, on continue . . . on n'a pas le choix.

Il fait maintenant nuit noire.° Pas une voiture sur la route. John aperçoit une toute petite lumière au loin.

— Regarde la lumière là-bas!   35

— C'est probablement une ferme. Nous avons de la chance!

Les deux garçons arrivent à la ferme. Ils frappent à la porte. Toc, toc, toc . . . Une voix d'homme répond: 40

— Qui êtes-vous? Et qu'est-ce que vous voulez?

— Nous sommes Américains. Nous sommes perdus.

— Américains? Attendez! Je vous ouvre.   45

*Le jour des grands départs: Le jour où des millions de Français partent en vacances.
la matinée = le matin   il fait . . . nuit noire *it is pitch black*

Avez-vous compris?

1. Qui sont John et Bob?
2. Comment vont-ils voyager en France?
3. Pourquoi est-ce qu'ils décident de prendre des petites routes?
4. Qu'est-ce qu'ils doivent trouver avant la nuit?
5. Qu'est-ce qu'ils font quand ils ne trouvent pas d'hôtel?

Mots utiles

une autoroute	*superhighway*
la circulation	*traffic*
l'essence	*gas*
une ferme	*farm*
une lumière	*light*
apercevoir *	*to notice*
conduire *	*to drive*
au loin	*in the distance*
d'occasion	*second-hand, used*

deux cent quarante-sept   **247**
Lecture

■ Notes linguistiques

- **Un artisan** is a craftsman who generally owns his shop, such as a locksmith (**le serrurier**) or a cobbler (**le cordonnier**).
- **L'exode rural** is the expression used to describe the massive migration of people from the countryside to the big cities, mostly to find work, thus emptying villages and swelling urban areas.

■ *Avez-vous compris?*

(Sample answers)
1. John et Bob sont des étudiants américains en vacances en France.
2. Ils vont voyager en scooter.
3. Ils décident de prendre les petites routes parce qu'il y a trop de circulation sur les autoroutes et les routes nationales.
4. Avant la nuit, ils doivent trouver de l'essence ou un hôtel.
5. Ils continuent leur route et ils arrivent à une ferme.

■ Irregular Verbs

(see Appendix C)
apercevoir (*see* **recevoir**)
conduire

Notes culturelles

- Scooters and mopeds are popular means of transportation among French teens since they are unable to hold a driver's license before the age of 18.
- **Clermont-Ferrand** is a city in **Auvergne**, a central region of France. It is located 388 km (241 miles) south of Paris.
- The speed limit on a French highway varies between 110 and 130 km/h (68-80 mph). On a **route nationale** the speed is limited to 90 km/h (55 mph), and to 50 km/h (30 mph) when crossing a village.

la cheminée

un feu

une chandelle

des meubles rustiques

II

La porte de la ferme s'ouvre.

— Entrez vite . . . La nuit, cette route est très dangereuse, surtout pour vous!

50 John et Bob entrent dans la ferme. À l'intérieur, il y a un homme et une femme, le fermier et la fermière. Ils sont habillés en noir, comme les paysans d'autrefois. C'est la femme qui parle:

55 — Vous avez certainement faim. Hélas, nous n'avons pas grand-chose.° Je vais vous préparer des pommes de terre avec du lard.° Mon mari va vous chercher une bouteille de cidre à la cave.

John et Bob examinent la salle où ils sont. Les meubles sont rustiques et très anciens. Dans la 60 cheminée, il y a un feu et sur la table il y a des chandelles.

L'homme revient avec la bouteille de cidre. La femme apporte le plat de pommes de terre. John et Bob mangent avec grand appétit.

65 — Merci, c'est délicieux!

L'homme parle: «Pourquoi merci? Nous sommes tellement heureux de vous recevoir! Mais vous êtes probablement très fatigués . . . Je vais vous montrer votre chambre.»

70 L'homme prend une chandelle et accompagne les deux garçons jusqu'à leur chambre.

— Excusez-nous, mais nous n'avons plus d'électricité. Je vous laisse la chandelle . . . 75 Bonne nuit!

Puis l'homme descend les escaliers.

Bob dit à John:

— C'est rustique ici!

— Oui, c'est vraiment la campagne. Nous 80 avons de la chance d'avoir trouvé cette ferme.

— Ces gens sont pauvres, mais ils sont vraiment généreux!

Quand Bob et John se réveillent le lendemain, il fait grand jour.°

85 — Quel jour sommes-nous?

— Nous sommes le deux juillet!

— Au fait, tu as entendu les voitures qui se sont arrêtées devant la ferme pendant la nuit?

— Oh là là, oui! Quel bruit!

— Qu'est-ce que disaient les passagers? 90

— Je ne sais pas. Ils ne parlaient pas français. Je n'ai pas compris. Mais vraiment ils avaient l'air furieux!

— Je me demande bien qui c'était.

— Dis, il faut partir maintenant. 95

— C'est vrai! Il est dix heures déjà!

Bob et John descendent dans la salle où ils étaient hier. Mais il n'y a personne.

— Où sont nos hôtes? 100

— Je ne sais pas. Appelons-les.

— Monsieur? Madame?

Silence. Ils crient plus fort: «Monsieur! Madame!» Personne ne répond.

— Ils sont peut-être partis travailler dans les 105 champs.

Bob et John sortent de la ferme, mais il n'y a personne dans les champs.

— Qu'est-ce qu'on fait?

— Il faut partir. On va laisser un mot sur la 110 table et quand on reviendra à la fin de juillet, on s'arrêtera pour remercier ces gens de leur hospitalité.

— Bonne idée!

grand-chose = beaucoup

du lard salt pork

il fait grand jour the sun is up and shining

Mots utiles

un bruit	noise
les champs	fields
un paysan	peasant, farmer
apporter	to bring
remercier	= dire merci
le lendemain	= le jour suivant
fort	loudly

Note linguistique

le lard bacon
le bacon Canadian bacon
le saindoux/la graisse de porc lard

■ *Avez-vous compris?*

(Sample answers)

1. Les habitants de la ferme sont un homme et une femme. Ils sont habillés en noir.

2. L'atmosphère est ancienne: les meubles sont rustiques, et il y a un feu dans la cheminée. Il n'y a pas d'électricité, on utilise des chandelles.

3. Ils sont très gentils envers les jeunes Américains.

4. Le repas consiste en des pommes de terre et du cidre.

5. Après le dîner, John et Bob vont dormir dans une chambre.

6. Ils entendent des voitures, et aussi des gens furieux qui ne parlent pas français.

7. Le lendemain ils ne trouvent personne dans la ferme ou dans les champs.

Avez-vous compris?

1. Qui sont les habitants de la ferme? Décrivez-les.
2. Quelle est l'atmosphère générale de la ferme? Décrivez-la.
3. Quelle est l'attitude du fermier et de la fermière envers *(toward)* les jeunes Américains?
4. En quoi consiste le repas?
5. Que font John et Bob après le dîner?
6. Qu'est-ce qu'ils entendent pendant la nuit?
7. Quelle surprise les attend le lendemain?

Expansion linguistique

• **Le cidre** is a drink made with fermented apple juice. It is produced mainly in Normandy **(la Normandie)**, where there are many apple orchards.

III

Bob et John sont partis vers onze heures. Ils ont trouvé une station d'essence au prochain village et ils ont continué leur route . . .

20 Pendant quatre semaines ils ont parcouru la France en scooter. C'est maintenant la fin des vacances et le retour vers Paris. Bob et John pensent à leur aventure du premier juillet . . . Ils ont acheté des cadeaux pour leurs hôtes: une

25 bouteille de cognac pour le fermier et un joli vase de cristal pour sa femme.

John regarde la carte. Dans dix minutes, ils seront à la ferme. Ils pourront finalement remercier leurs hôtes de leur hospitalité . . .

30 — Je reconnais bien la route maintenant.
— Moi, aussi.
— Regarde les grands arbres là-bas. La ferme est juste en face.

Le scooter s'est arrêté devant les grands arbres, mais il n'y a pas de ferme. 135
— Tu es sûr que c'est ici?
— Absolument certain!

À la place de la ferme, il y a une haie d'arbustes et devant cette haie, une stèle avec une inscription. 140
— Dis, Bob, va voir ce qui est écrit.
Bob descend du scooter et va regarder l'inscription. Il revient vite, très, très pâle.
— Mon Dieu, c'est impossible!
— Qu'est-ce qu'il y a? 145
— Va voir toi-même!

■ Note culturelle
Le cognac is a brandy made from wine. It comes from the region around Cognac, in southwestern France.

une haie d'arbustes

une stèle

Mots utiles

un mot	= une note
un cadeau	gift, present
parcourir *	to travel across
en face	opposite

Anticipons un peu!

Avant de tourner la page, essayez de deviner ce que Bob a vu sur la stèle.

■ Irregular Verb
(see Appendix C)
parcourir (*see* **courir**)

John descend à son tour du scooter. Il lit l'inscription suivante:

ICI REPOSENT
EUGÉNIE ET MARCEL DUVILLARD
HÉROS DE LA RÉSISTANCE
FUSILLÉS° PAR LES NAZIS
LE DEUX JUILLET 1944
POUR AVOIR HÉBERGÉ°
DES PARACHUTISTES
AMÉRICAINS

À L'EMPLACEMENT°
DE CETTE STÈLE
S'ÉLEVAIT LEUR FERME
QUI FUT INCENDIÉE°
LE LENDEMAIN.
PASSANTS,° PRIEZ° POUR EUX!

Avez-vous compris?

1. Que font Bob et John avant de quitter la ferme?
2. À la fin des vacances, pourquoi est-ce qu'ils veulent retourner à la ferme?
3. Quelle surprise les attend?
4. Qu'est-ce qui s'est passé à la ferme au début de juillet 1944?

fusillés *shot and killed*   **pour avoir hébergé** *for having sheltered*
emplacement = endroit   **s'élevait** *stood*   **incendiée** *burned to the ground*   **passants** = vous qui passez par ici   **priez** *to pray*

LECTURE SUPPLÉMENTAIRE

L'histoire que vous avez lue évoque une époque très tourmentée de l'histoire de France: **l'Occupation** par les Allemands (1940-1944), puis la **Libération** par les Alliés (principalement des soldats américains et anglais), et par la **Résistance française**. Voir Interlude 6, pp. 252-255.

Pour découvrir un autre récit concernant cette période, lisez le texte *Au Revoir, les Enfants* (pp. 256-259).

■ ***Avez-vous compris?***

(Sample answers)

1. Ils laissent un mot sur la table.
2. Ils veulent retourner à la ferme pour remercier le fermier et la fermière de leur hospitalité. Ils ont acheté des cadeaux pour eux.
3. Il n'y a plus de ferme. Il y a une stèle avec une inscription.
4. Le fermier et la fermière ont été fusillés par les nazis parce qu'ils ont aidé des parachutistes américains, et la ferme a été incendiée.

Teaching Strategies

Ask students:
- À votre avis, quelle est la réaction de John et Bob quand ils lisent l'inscription de la stèle?
- Est-ce qu'ils ont peur? sont curieux?
- Est-ce qu'ils pensent qu'ils rêvent *(dream)*?

Divide the class into groups. Ask students to imagine their own reactions as if they were characters in the story. Each group may present a short scenario to the class.
Pre-AP skill: Expand, elaborate.

APRÈS LA LECTURE

Expression orale

Discussion

Selon vous, est-ce que l'histoire que vous avez lue est possible ou impossible? Discutez votre opinion avec un(e) partenaire qui n'a pas la même opinion que vous.

Débat

Dans beaucoup de cultures, on peut trouver des «histoires de fantômes» *(ghost stories)* semblables à l'histoire racontée dans **Une étrange aventure.**
Vous-même, croyez-vous aux fantômes ou non? Exprimez votre opinion sur ce sujet et débattez la question avec un(e) partenaire qui n'a pas la même opinion que vous. Si possible, donnez des exemples en support de votre opinion.

Situations

Avec votre partenaire, choisissez l'une des situations suivantes. Composez le dialogue correspondant et jouez-le en classe.

1	Devant la stèle.

Bob et John sont devant la stèle. Ils viennent de lire l'inscription et maintenant ils essaient d'interpréter ce qui est arrivé lors de leur passage la nuit du premier juillet, en fonction des événements qui ont eu lieu les 1er et 2 juillet 1944. Par exemple:
- pourquoi le fermier a dit que la route était dangereuse
- selon les fermiers, qui étaient Bob et John et pourquoi ils étaient heureux de les recevoir
- qui étaient les gens qui étaient venus dans la nuit et qu'est-ce qu'ils cherchaient
- pourquoi le fermier et sa femme n'étaient pas là le lendemain matin

Rôles: Bob, John

2	Aux États-Unis.

En rentrant aux États-Unis, John a une conversation avec son grand-père qui lui aussi a été parachuté en France lors de l'invasion en 1944. Au cours de cette conversation, l'ancien soldat raconte ses aventures de guerre, par exemple, comment il a été recueilli *(picked up)* par les Résistants français.

Rôles: John, son grand-père

Expression écrite

Un peu d'histoire

Écrivez un petit rapport sur l'histoire de France entre 1940 et 1944. Dans ce rapport, expliquez en particulier le rôle ...
- des Allemands
- des Américains
- de la Résistance française

(Source: Encyclopédies, Manuels d'histoire)

Une étrange aventure

Écrivez votre propre «étrange aventure». Commencez par une situation très réaliste. Ensuite, ajoutez un élément mystérieux ou bizarre. Utilisez votre imagination.

■ Teaching Strategies

- DISCUSSION
  As a preliminary step, you may conduct a poll:
  - **Qui croit que cette histoire est possible?**
  - **Qui croit qu'elle n'est pas possible?**
  Group students according to their responses.

- EXPANSION
  Autre dialogue: John raconte son aventure à un(e) ami(e) qui ne le croit pas. John essaie de le/la persuader qu'il a rencontré deux fantômes. L'ami(e) exprime ses doutes et pose des questions à John qui y répond en détail.
  Rôles: John, son ami(e)

- ASSESSMENT
  You may wish to use the *Lecture* quiz as a basis for discussion or as a quick comprehension check.

■ Expression écrite

For writing rubrics, consult the **Generate Success** Rubric Generator on the **Teacher One Stop.** You can also create your own custom rubrics with this tool.

Student Portfolios

Using either the *Situations* or the *Expression écrite* activities, have students prepare these materials to be included in their portfolios. If students frequently choose the oral activity, suggest that they change to a written activity and expand their portfolios in a new direction.

TECHNOLOGY

Teacher One Stop

Pre-AP Digital Resources

 **Projectable Transparencies**

H4, *Histoire de France* (1870–présent)

Transparency Copymasters, pp. A143–A144

■ **Pre-reading Questions**

Pouvez-vous répondre aux questions suivantes?

• Quel pays d'Asie a été colonisé par la France?

• Où est situé Utah Beach?

• Qu'est-ce que le «Marché Commun»?

■ **Notes historiques**

• Les événements du 6 juin 1944 (D-Day ou **Jour-J**) ont été immortalisés dans le film *Le jour le plus long*.

• La Cochinchine, l'Annam, le Tonkin, le Cambodge et le Laos formaient l'Indochine française.

■ **Pour en savoir plus**

• Les étapes de l'unification européene sont résumées dans *Interlude 7*, p. 292.

• Pour des renseignements sur les mouvements artistiques mentionnés, voir *Interlude 1*, p. 60.

Les dates   ## Les événements

1870 *La France devient une république*

La Belle Époque

La Belle Époque (1870-1914)

C'est une époque de prospérité économique et d'intense création artistique, littéraire et scientifique. D'importants mouvements artistiques (**impressionnisme, fauvisme, cubisme, surréalisme**) naissent en France. Paris devient la capitale mondiale des lettres et des arts.

À l'extérieur, la France s'engage dans des expéditions coloniales et se construit un empire en Afrique occidentale et en Asie (Indochine).

Paris à la Belle Époque, représenté par le peintre Jean Béraud

1914 Première Guerre Mondiale

1918

Les guerres mondiales (1914-1918 et 1939-1945)

Ces deux terribles guerres opposent la France et l'Allemagne impériale (Première Guerre Mondiale) puis l'Allemagne nazie (Deuxième Guerre Mondiale). Dans ces deux guerres, l'intervention américaine est décisive.

En 1940, la France est occupée par les Allemands. Le 6 juin 1944, les troupes alliées commandées par le Général Eisenhower, débarquent sur les plages de Normandie: Utah Beach, Omaha Beach . . . La Libération de la France commence.

1939 Deuxième Guerre Mondiale

Soldats américains défilant sur les Champs-Élysées

1945

La France moderne (1945 - présent)

Ruinée par la guerre, la France reconstruit son économie. La construction de la France moderne passe par deux étapes° importantes.

1957 *Marché Commun*

1960 *Fin de l'ère coloniale*

• La décolonisation (1945-1962). Les anciennes colonies françaises d'Afrique du Nord, d'Afrique occidentale, et d'Asie deviennent des républiques indépendantes.

1979 *Premier Parlement Européen*

• L'intégration à l'Europe (1957 - présent). En 1957, la France devient membre de la **Communauté Économique Européenne** ou «**Marché Commun**». La création de cette grande zone de libre-échange permet l'expansion commerciale et industrielle de la France. Intégrée à l'Europe, la France est aujourd'hui un pays moderne avec l'un des niveaux de vie° les plus élevés du monde.

1993 *Formation de l'Union Européenne*

2002 *Mise en circulation de l'euro*

Le Louvre et sa pyramide, symboles du passé et de l'avenir

étapes *steps, stages*   **niveau de vie** *standard of living*

Notes culturelles

• Parmi les artistes étrangers qui viennent en France et qui ont constitué **l'École de Paris**, on peut mentionner: **Picasso** (Espagne), **Modigliani** (Italie), **Diego Rivera** (Mexique), **Foujita** (Japon), **Soutine** (Lithuanie), **Chagall** (Russie).

• Quelques anciennes colonies et protectorats français:
Afrique du Nord: **Maroc, Algérie, Tunisie**
Afrique occidentale: **Sénégal, Côte d'Ivoire**, etc.
Asie: **Vietnam, Cambodge, Laos**

Les personnes

Marie Curie (1867-1934)

Marie Curie, née Sklodowska, est l'un des grands génies scientifiques des temps modernes. D'origine polonaise, elle vient à Paris en 1891 pour continuer ses études scientifiques. En 1895, elle épouse son professeur, **Pierre Curie**. Ensemble, ils découvrent le radium et le polonium, auquel elle donne le nom de son pays d'origine. En accord avec l'esprit scientifique, les Curie refusent de prendre une patente sur leur découverte et d'en tirer° tout° bénéfice commercial.

En 1898, Pierre et Marie Curie reçoivent le Prix Nobel de Physique pour leurs travaux sur la radioactivité. Après la mort accidentelle de son mari en 1905, Marie Curie continue ses travaux, isole le radium et reçoit le Prix Nobel de Chimie en 1911.

Marie Curie dans son laboratoire

Jean Moulin, héros de la Résistance

Jean Moulin (1899-1943)

Jean Moulin est le héros de **la Résistance** française pendant la Deuxième Guerre Mondiale. En 1941, il se rallie au gouvernement de la France Libre, dirigé à Londres par le **Général de Gaulle**. Parachuté en France, il organise la Résistance contre les Allemands. Il est arrêté et torturé par la Gestapo.* Après sa mort, la Résistance continue. Les résistants, organisés en «maquis»° harcèlent les troupes d'occupation et préparent la **Libération**.

Simone Veil (1927-   )

Simone Veil est une championne de l'Europe unie et des droits de la femme. Pendant la Deuxième Guerre Mondiale, elle est déportée dans un camp de concentration nazi. Après la guerre, elle fait de brillantes études de droit et de sciences politiques. À l'âge de 20 ans, elle devient attachée auprès du Ministre de la Justice. De 1974 à 1979, elle est nommée Ministre de la Santé. En 1979, elle est élue Député au Parlement européen et elle en est la première présidente. En 2008, elle devient membre de l'Académie française.

Simone Veil et le drapeau européen

---

* La Gestapo (Geheime Staats Polizei = police secrète d'état) était l'instrument le plus dangereux du régime policier nazi.

tirer *to derive*   **tout** *any*   **maquis** *guerrilla groups*

■ Notes culturelles

- **Jean Béraud** (1849–1935) was a successful French painter, born in Saint Petersburg. He painted many scenes of daily life, representing people in their homes, on the street, or at the theater.
- **Dwight David Eisenhower** was the 34th president of the United States (1953–1961).
- **Marie Curie** was the first woman to hold a chair at the Sorbonne University in Paris.
- **Irène Joliot-Curie**, daughter of Pierre and Marie Curie, became a scientist herself, and won the Nobel prize for Chemistry in 1935, along with her husband (**Frédéric Joliot-Curie**) for discovering artificial radioactivity.

Expansion

Internet Connection – Interlude 6
Visit **http://my.hrw.com** for more information and useful links about the people mentioned (de Gaulle, Curie, Malle, etc.) in this Interlude.

Comparisons
Standard 4.2 Students demonstrate understanding of the nature of culture through comparisons of francophone cultures with their own.

Unité 6   253

■ Notes culturelles

Les endroits suivants sont nommés en l'honneur de Charles de Gaulle:
- l'aéroport Charles de Gaulle (ou Roissy, l'aéroport international de Paris)
- la place Charles de Gaulle (ou Place de l'Étoile, en haut des Champs-Élysées)

■ Additional Information

General De Gaulle was born in Lille in 1890, and died in Colombey-les-Deux-Églises in 1970.

Charles de Gaulle, homme d'action

Charles de Gaulle est peut-être l'homme qui a eu la plus grande influence sur l'histoire de la France du vingtième siècle. Jeune officier, il est fait prisonnier par les Allemands pendant la première guerre mondiale. Plus tard, il préconise° une stratégie militaire basée sur l'utilisation massive des tanks, mais on ne l'écoute pas.

Charles de Gaulle, Président de la République

En 1940, la France capitule et est occupée par l'armée allemande. De Gaulle refuse d'accepter la défaite et part pour l'Angleterre. Le 18 juin 1940, il lance° à la radio de Londres son célèbre appel où il demande à tous les Français de continuer le combat contre l'Allemagne nazie. Pour cet acte de rébellion contre l'autorité officielle, il est condamné à mort par le gouvernement français d'alors. Il organise la Résistance et crée un gouvernement de la «**France Libre**».

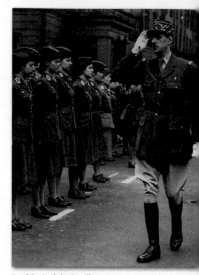

Le Général de Gaulle passe en revue les volontaires féminines de la France Libre.

DOCUMENTS | Appel du 18 juin 1940

Appel du 18 juin 1940

Moi, Général de Gaulle, actuellement à Londres, j'invite les officiers et les soldats français qui se trouvent en territoire britannique ou qui viendraient à s'y trouver, avec leurs armes ou sans leurs armes, j'invite les ingénieurs et les ouvriers spécialistes des industries d'armement qui se trouvent en territoire britannique ou qui viendraient à s'y trouver, à se mettre en rapport avec moi. Quoi qu'il arrive,° la flamme de la résistance française ne doit pas s'éteindre° et ne s'éteindra pas.

Général de Gaulle

préconise *advocates*   **lance** *sends out*   **quoi qu'il arrive** *whatever happens*   **s'éteindre** *to go out, to be extinguished*

Teaching Strategy

Ask students to research in their own families and communities, interviewing people who experienced the events leading up to and including World War II. Relatives may be willing to talk to the class about their experiences.

Local veterans groups may also be contacted. It is important for students to make these events in the recent past as personal and as real as possible.

En août 1944, le Général de Gaulle rentre dans Paris libéré par les troupes alliées. En 1945, il est élu président provisoire de la République française, mais il démissionne° parce qu'il n'a pas les pouvoirs° de gouverner.

Peu après, la France connaît deux longues et tragiques guerres coloniales, d'abord la guerre d'Indochine, puis la guerre d'Algérie. L'Algérie est alors un territoire français avec une population en majorité musulmane.° Les Algériens musulmans veulent leur indépendance et décident de prendre les armes contre la France. Le gouvernement français ne sait pas comment arrêter cette guerre impopulaire. La France est au bord° de la guerre civile.

Les Français font appel à de Gaulle qui devient Président de la République en 1959. De Gaulle comprend que l'ère coloniale est finie. Il négocie l'indépendance avec l'Algérie, puis avec les colonies françaises d'Afrique Noire qui deviennent des républiques amies de la France.

De Gaulle veut restaurer la grandeur de la France. Il comprend que l'avenir° de la France dépend de son intégration dans une Europe forte et indépendante. Il mène° alors une politique marquée par la réconciliation avec l'Allemagne et une certaine distance vis-à-vis des États-Unis. De Gaulle veut aussi réformer les institutions françaises. Beaucoup de Français n'acceptent pas ses réformes et protestent en organisant de violentes manifestations en mai 1968. Peu après, de Gaulle se retire de la vie publique.

Le Général de Gaulle sur les Champs-Élysées à la Libération de Paris en 1944

Le Général de Gaulle avec un chef d'état africain

Les manifestations à Paris, mai 1968

démissionne *resigns* **pouvoirs** *powers* **musulmane** *Moslem*
au bord de *on the edge of* **l'avenir** *= le futur* **il mène** *= il fait*

Note culturelle

The revolution of May 1968 (**la Révolution de Mai 68**), started with demonstrations in high schools and universities in January 1968. In May, students in the Latin Quarter set up barricades and organized demonstrations that became violent. Student leader Daniel Cohn-Bendit was then deported to Germany, his native country. Workers joined the students, and many strikes paralyzed the country. One of the most significant consequences was the reform of the educational system. Universities, which were still operating as they did under Napoleon 1st, became less elitist, more accessible and more affordable.

Liberté, liberté

Pour l'humanité, la liberté est le bien° le plus précieux. C'est le principe fondamental de la démocratie. Dans la *Déclaration d'indépendance* américaine et dans la *Déclaration des droits de l'homme* de la Révolution française, la liberté est un droit inaliénable et imprescriptible.°

Pourtant,° tous les êtres humains ne sont pas libres. Les Français, par exemple, ont perdu leur liberté quand leur pays a été occupé par les troupes allemandes entre 1940 et 1944. Ils rêvaient° alors de cette liberté qu'il fallait reconquérir et beaucoup sont morts pour elle en combattant dans la Résistance.

Paul Éluard

Paul Éluard, auteur du poème *Liberté*, était un poète surréaliste et un membre très actif de la Résistance. Il a publié ce poème pendant l'occupation dans un livre intitulé *Poésie et vérité 1942*. Interdit° par la censure allemande, ce livre était distribué clandestinement et parachuté en milliers d'exemplaires° par l'aviation alliée.

Illustrations du poème par l'artiste Fernand Léger

un bien = *une possession*   **imprescriptible** *which cannot be legally taken away*
pourtant *however*   **rêvaient** *dreamed*   **interdit** *forbidden*   **exemplaires** *copies*

Au Revoir, les Enfants

Au Revoir, les Enfants est un film réalisé par le cinéaste français contemporain **Louis Malle**. C'est un film autobiographique dans lequel Louis Malle évoque un épisode dramatique de sa jeunesse.

Louis Malle, réalisateur du film, avec deux des acteurs principaux

256 deux cent cinquante-six
Unité 6

Teaching Suggestion: DVD Program

Use the Unit 6 *Vignette culturelle* about *La libération* to help students understand more about the liberation of France at the end of WWII.

DOCUMENTS Liberté

Liberté

Paul Éluard

Sur mes cahiers d'écolier
Sur mon pupitre° et les arbres
Sur le sable° sur la neige
J'écris ton nom

Sur toutes les pages lues
Sur toutes les pages blanches
Pierre sang° papier ou cendre°
J'écris ton nom

Sur les images dorées°
Sur les armes des guerriers°
Sur la couronne° des rois
J'écris ton nom

Sur la jungle et le désert
Sur les nids° sur les genêts*
Sur l'écho de mon enfance
J'écris ton nom

Sur mes refuges détruits
Sur mes phares écroulés°
Sur les murs de mon ennui
J'écris ton nom

Sur l'absence sans désirs
Sur la solitude nue°
Sur les marches° de la mort
J'écris ton nom

Sur la santé revenue
Sur le risque disparu
Sur l'espoir° sans souvenirs
J'écris ton nom

Et par le pouvoir° d'un mot°
Je recommence ma vie
Je suis né pour te connaître
Pour te nommer *Liberté.*

**Genêt or broom is a European shrub with bright yellow flowers that grows wild in the woods and uncultivated fields

pupitre *school desk* **sable** *sand* **sang** *blood* **cendre** *ashes* **dorées** *gilded* **guerriers** *warriors* **couronne** *crown* **nids** *nests*
phares écroulés *lighthouses that have collapsed* **nue** *naked* **marches** *steps, stairs* **espoir** *hope* **pouvoir** *power* **mot** *word*

Le film se passe au cours de° l'hiver 1944. À cette époque la France est occupée par les Allemands qui ont imposé la loi° hitlérienne partout. Les Juifs,° en particulier, sont traqués,° et quand ils sont pris, ils sont envoyés dans les camps d'extermination. Les Français qui les aident ou les abritent° sont, eux aussi, passibles de mort.

Parmi les Français, il y a ceux qui résistent aux Allemands, et ceux qui collaborent avec eux, mais la majorité attend passivement l'arrivée des Alliés et la fin de la guerre.

La vie est difficile. Comme la nourriture manque,° le marché noir s'installe partout. De plus en plus fréquemment, la population civile est soumise aux bombardements de l'aviation alliée . . .

au cours de = *pendant* **loi** *law* **Juifs** *Jews* **traqués** *hunted down* **abritent** *shelter* **manque** *is lacking*

Teaching Strategies

- If students are interested, you might draw their attention to how the poem begins with familiar images of childhood, and then moves to more violent images (**sang, cendre**) and scenes of destruction (**mes refuges détruits**), before ending on a note of hope.
- Special project: Have students select one phrase from the poem and illustrate it in a poster.

- Ask students the following questions:
  - Et vous? Qu'est-ce que la liberté pour vous?
  - Donnez-votre définition de la liberté et des exemples.
- Point out that **soumettre** (*p.p.* **soumis**) is conjugated like **mettre**. (See Appendix C.)

Sur les merveilles des nuits
Sur le pain blanc des journées
Sur les saisons fiancées
J'écris ton nom

Sur tous mes chiffons d'azur
Sur l'étang soleil moisi
Sur le lac lune vivante
J'écris ton nom

Sur les champs sur l'horizon
Sur les ailes des oiseaux
Et sur le moulin des ombres
J'écris ton nom

Sur chaque bouffée d'aurore
Sur la mer sur les bateaux
Sur la montagne démente
J'écris ton nom

Sur la mousse des nuages
Sur les sueurs de l'orage
Sur la pluie épaisse et fade
J'écris ton nom

Sur les formes scintillantes
Sur les cloches des couleurs
Sur la vérité physique
J'écris ton nom

Sur les sentiers éveillés
Sur les routes déployées
Sur les places qui débordent
J'écris ton nom

Sur la lampe qui s'allume
Sur la lampe qui s'éteint
Sur mes maisons réunies
J'écris ton nom

Sur le fruit coupé en deux
Du miroir et de ma chambre
Sur mon lit coquille vide
J'écris ton nom

Sur mon chien gourmand et tendre
Sur ses oreilles dressées
Sur sa patte maladroite
J'écris ton nom

Sur le tremplin de ma porte
Sur les objets familiers
Sur le flot du feu béni
J'écris ton nom

Sur toute chair accordée
Sur le front de mes amis
Sur chaque main qui se tend
J'écris ton nom

Sur la vitre des surprises
Sur les lèvres attentives
Bien au-dessus du silence
J'écris ton nom

DOCUMENTS   *Au Revoir, les Enfants*

L'action du film a lieu dans une école catholique de garçons dont le directeur, **le père Jean**, est un prêtre° d'une grande intégrité morale. Le héros du film est un jeune garçon d'une douzaine d'années, **Julien Quentin** (c'est, bien sûr, Louis Malle lui-même), qui est pensionnaire° avec son frère aîné François dans cette école.

[1] Le film commence à la rentrée des classes après les vacances de Noël. Dans la première scène, Julien est à la gare. Il dit au revoir à sa mère, puis il prend son train. Quand il arrive au collège, il retrouve tous ses copains. Dans la classe, il y a un nouvel élève qui s'appelle [2] **Jean Bonnet.** C'est un garçon timide et réservé qui ne parle jamais de sa famille. C'est aussi un brillant élève, en maths, en français, en musique. Julien, qui était jusqu'alors° le meilleur élève de la classe, sent en lui un rival. Il questionne Jean sur son passé, mais celui-ci lui répond d'une façon évasive.

Louis Malle (1932-1995)

Louis Malle est l'un des grands réalisateurs° du cinéma français moderne. Il a d'abord fait des films documentaires, comme son premier film *Le monde du silence*, réalisé en coopération avec Jacques-Yves Cousteau, l'explorateur du monde marin.°

Dans ses films plus récents, Louis Malle a traité de thèmes personnels comme celui évoqué dans *Au revoir, les Enfants*.

Louis Malle était marié avec l'actrice américaine Candice Bergen et habitait à New York.

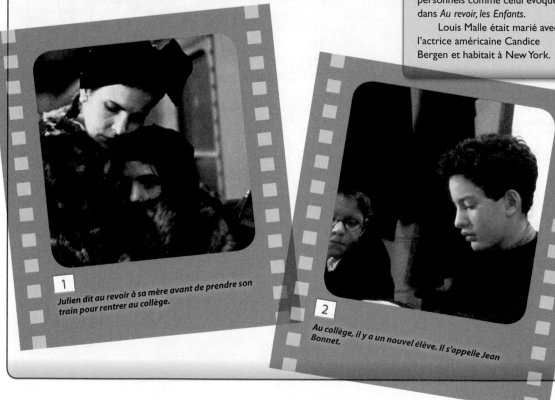

1 Julien dit au revoir à sa mère avant de prendre son train pour rentrer au collège.

2 Au collège, il y a un nouvel élève. Il s'appelle Jean Bonnet.

réalisateur *director*   **marin** = *de la mer*   **prêtre** *priest*   **pensionnaire** *boarding student*   **jusqu'alors** *until then*

IMPORTANT TEACHING NOTE

Although the film *Au Revoir, les Enfants* is rated PG, it contains some language which may be INAPPROPRIATE and OBJECTIONABLE for a class viewing.

Before deciding to show the film in class, you should definitely <u>preview</u> it carefully, paying attention to the dialogs between the boys at the school. If you decide to show the movie, you should be prepared to deal with the objectionable language, or use only selected scenes for class viewing.

3

Les deux garçons deviennent amis.

Un jour, Julien découvre la vérité: Jean Bonnet s'appelle en réalité Jean Keppelstein et il est juif. Les prêtres l'ont recueilli° avec deux autres enfants juifs pour le soustraire° à la police allemande. Au collège, il est en sécurité tant que° sa véritable identité reste cachée.° Depuis cette découverte, les relations entre les deux garçons changent et ils deviennent amis.

Un samedi, au cours d'une sortie, ils se perdent dans la forêt. Julien arrête une voiture de patrouille allemande. Jean veut s'échapper, mais il est rattrapé.° Les soldats allemands ramènent les deux garçons à l'école. Cette fois-ci, il y a plus de peur° que de mal!° Un autre jour, la famille de Julien invite Jean à déjeuner dans un grand restaurant. Jean assiste à une scène pénible° où un client juif, décoré de la Légion d'Honneur,* est insulté par un Milicien, auxiliaire français de la police allemande.

Les jours passent . . . Un employé de l'école est renvoyé° pour avoir fait du marché noir avec les élèves. Pour se venger, il dénonce la présence d'enfants juifs à l'école. La police allemande arrive et encercle l'école. Un soldat entre dans la salle de classe pour arrêter Jean. D'autres soldats fouillent° l'école. Les deux autres élèves juifs sont découverts et arrêtés ainsi que° le père Jean qui était membre de la Résistance. Au moment de quitter l'école, escorté par des soldats allemands, le père Jean dit un dernier au revoir à ses élèves: «Au revoir, les enfants! À bientôt!»

> *Personne ne reviendra. Jean et ses deux camarades juifs mourront à Auschwitz. Le père Jean mourra au camp de Mauthausen.*

4

Un soldat allemand arrive pour arrêter Jean.

5

Le père Jean dit un dernier au revoir aux élèves de l'école.

* La Légion d'Honneur: haute distinction donnée aux gens qui ont servi la France.

recueilli *taken in*   **soustraire à** *to protect from*   **tant que** *as long as*   **cachée** *hidden*   **rattrapé** *caught*
peur *fright*   **mal** *harm*   **pénible** *painful*   **renvoyé** *fired*   **fouillent** *to search*   **ainsi que** *as well as*

MAIN THEME

Health and Medical Care

COMMUNICATION
- Going to the doctor's office
- Going to the emergency room
- Going to the dentist

CULTURES
- Learning about the organization *S.O.S. Racisme*
- Learning the importance of mineral water to the French

CONNECTIONS
- Using a monolingual French dictionary to determine word meanings
- Connecting to Language Arts: Brainstorming a list of common injuries and ailments
- Connecting to Math: Tallying injuries and ailments in a community
- Connecting to Science: Interviewing a health professional for information
- Connecting to Social Studies: Researching the requirements to be an interpreter
- Connecting to Art/Music: Creating health-related drawings or icons
- Connecting to Technology: Finding out about technology used in hospitals

COMPARISONS
- Comparing similar words in French and English
- Comparing the past subjunctive in French and English
- Comparing the medical systems in France and in the United States
- Comparing immigration issues in France and in the United States

COMMUNITIES
- Discovering the origins of supermarket products
- Writing an emergency services guide
- Creating logos and mottos to promote peace
- Using French to test one's knowledge of health facts

La forme et la santé

THÈME ET OBJECTIFS

Culture

In this unit, you will discover . . .

- how the French take care of their health
- why the French drink mineral water
- how the French help provide health care to less fortunate people around the world

Communication

You will learn how . . .

- to see a doctor or dentist and explain what is wrong
- to follow the doctor's instructions

Langue

You will learn how . . .

- to express your doubts and fears
- to affirm your beliefs
- to let people know how you feel about both present and past events

 **DIGITAL FRENCH**

TEACHER TOOLS
- Teacher One Stop
- Interactive Whiteboard Lessons
- Generate Success Rubric Generator and Interactive Graphic Organizers
- Examview Test Generator

ALSO AVAILABLE...
- Online Workbook
- French InterActive Reader
- @HomeTutor
- DVD Program
- Power Presentations
- Interactive Flashcards

FRENCH ON THE GO!
- Performance Space
- Holt McDougal French Apps
- Discovering French Today eTextbook

Les Français et leur santé

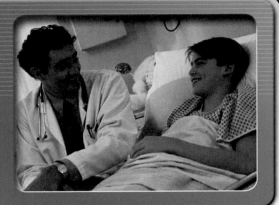

En France comme ailleurs,° la santé et la forme sont la préoccupation de tout le monde. Pour rester en forme, les jeunes Français pratiquent toutes sortes de sports: la natation en été, le ski en hiver, le foot, le basket, le vélo, le jogging, la marche à pied en toute saison. Il arrive° cependant que les personnes en excellente santé tombent malades. Il faut alors aller voir un médecin.

Pour les maladies ordinaires, on va voir un médecin généraliste. Pour les maladies spécifiques, on doit consulter un spécialiste: oculiste pour les yeux, cardiologue pour le coeur, dermatologue pour les maladies de peau,° stomatologue pour la bouche, gastro-entérologue pour l'estomac … Si on a besoin d'une radio,° on va chez un radiologue.

En cas d'urgence° ou d'accident sérieux, on peut téléphoner au SAMU (Service d'Aide Médicale Urgente). Il suffit de composer le numéro 15. Le SAMU est un service public rattaché à un hôpital. Suivant la gravité du problème, le SAMU envoie un médecin d'urgence, une ambulance de réanimation ou une ambulance ordinaire.

Les femmes-médecins

Aujourd'hui, il y a beaucoup de femmes-médecins en France. C'est seulement en 1870 que la première femme a reçu son diplôme de médecin de la Faculté de Médecine de Paris. Cette jeune femme n'était d'ailleurs pas française, mais anglaise!

Le système médical français a le grand avantage d'être presque gratuit.° La majorité des Français sont inscrits° à la Sécurité Sociale. Avec la Sécurité Sociale, le gouvernement français prend en charge les dépenses médicales et la santé de ses citoyens.° Les gens qui vont chez le médecin ou chez le dentiste remplissent° une feuille de Sécurité Sociale qui leur permet° d'être remboursés à 75%. Et quand ils vont chez le pharmacien, les médicaments° sont aussi remboursés.

Les Français aiment se soigner.° En général, les médicaments qu'ils prennent, comme l'aspirine ou les vitamines, sont fabriqués par les grandes compagnies pharmaceutiques. Ils prennent aussi toute une variété de médicaments à base de produits naturels (fruits, fleurs, plantes, herbes sauvages,° feuilles° ou écorce° d'arbre, etc.). Ce sont des infusions pour la digestion, l'insomnie ou la migraine, des pilules° pour le foie,° des pastilles° et des sirops pour la toux,° des crèmes et des pommades° pour la peau, etc.... En pratiquant cette médecine «écologique,» ils redécouvrent° les secrets des remèdes traditionnels.

et vous?

DÉBATS
Choisissez un des sujets de débat et prenez une position pour ou contre. Débattez votre position avec votre partenaire. Si possible, utilisez des exemples pour établir votre position.
1. Les Américains consomment trop de médicaments.
2. Le sport est la meilleure prévention contre la maladie.
3. Quand on est malade, il est préférable d'utiliser des médicaments naturels.

---

ailleurs *elsewhere* **il arrive** *it happens* **peau** *skin* **radio** *x-ray* **cas d'urgence** *emergency* **gratuit** *free of charge*
inscrire ✳ *to register* **citoyens** *citizens* **remplissent** *fill out* **feuille** *form* **permettre** ✳ *to allow* **médicaments** *medicine, drugs*
se soigner *to take care of one's health* **sauvages** *wild* **feuilles** *leaves* **écorce** *bark* **pilules** *pills* **le foie** *liver* **des pastilles** *tablets*
la toux *cough* **des pommades** *ointments* **redécouvrir** ✳ *to rediscover*

ASSESSMENT IN UNIT RESOURCE BOOK

Print Resources
- **Workbook TE/PE**
- *Activités pour tous* **TE/PE**
- *Lectures pour tous*
- **Unit Resource Book** Audioscripts Video Activities Videoscripts

Achievement Tests
- **Quizzes, Unit 7**
- **Unit Test 7**
- **Reading and Culture Tests**
- **Assessment Answer Key**

Proficiency Tests
- **Listening Comprehension**
- **Speaking Performance**
- **Writing Performance**
- **Portfolio Assessment**

■ Teaching Strategy
These readings can be done:
- in class or as homework
- at the start of a unit or as wrap-up

■ Note culturelle
The **pharmacies de garde** are open nights and Sundays for people who need emergency medical attention.

■ Débats
- Les compagnies pharmaceutiques s'intéressent plus à leurs profits qu'à la santé de la population.
- En quoi le système médical français est-il différent du système américain?

■ Irregular Verbs
(see Appendix C)
inscrire	*(see **écrire**)*
permettre	*(see **mettre**)*
redécouvrir	*(see **ouvrir**)*

21ST CENTURY SKILLS
- **Communication:** SE: pp. 261, 263, 267, 268, 269, 275, 277, 279, 283, 285, 287, 291; TE: pp. 261, 266, 268, 269, 271, 272, 275, 277, 278, 281, 296
- **Critical Thinking and Problem Solving:** SE: pp. 261, 282, 285, 287, 291; TE: pp. 261, 284, 286, 288, 290, 296
- **Creativity and Innovation:** SE: p. 291; TE: pp. 266, 268, 278, 279, 290, 296, 300, 301
- **Information Literacy:** TE: pp. 281, 293, 296
- **Technology Literacy:** TE: pp. 266, 267, 268
- **Flexibility and Adaptability:** SE: pp. 262, 277; TE: pp. 268, 281, 293
- **Initiative and Self-Direction:** TE: pp. 276, 281, 293, 301
- **Social and Cross-Cultural Skills:** TE: p. 296
- **Productivity and Accountability:** TE: pp. 262, 264, 266, 270, 277, 280,
- **Leadership and Responsibility:** TE: pp. 276, 281, 301

Unité 7 261

RESOURCES

TECHNOLOGY
Teacher One Stop
□ **Projectable Transparencies**

1, *La France*
1(o), *La France*

Transparency Copymasters,
pp. A5–A6

■ **Additional Information**

Perrier water comes from a spring in Vergèze (Gard). It owes its name to the original owner of the spring: Docteur Louis Perrier. The bottled water is naturally carbonated. Other popular French spring waters sold in American supermarkets are Vichy and Evian.

■ **Notes linguistiques**
Définitions

- **Un minéral:** un élément de la terre
- **Un rhumatisme:** quand on a un rhumatisme, on a mal aux genoux ou aux mains, par exemple
- **Une source thermale:** dans une source thermale, il y a des minéraux bons pour la santé
- **Une cure thermale:** on fait une cure thermale quand on utilise les sources thermales pour se soigner ou se mettre en forme
- **La thalassothérapie:** un traitement par l'eau de mer et l'air marin
- **Un sauna:** un bain de vapeur très chaud
- **Un bain de boue:** pour un bain de boue, on ne se baigne pas dans de l'eau, mais dans de la boue
- **Le stress:** c'est quand on est fatigué parce qu'on a trop travaillé, par exemple, ou parce qu'on a beaucoup de problèmes

L'eau, c'est la santé

Au café ou au restaurant, Stéphanie commande généralement de l'eau minérale. Sandrine en boit un grand verre le matin quand elle se lève, et le soir quand elle se couche. Quant à° Christophe, il ne va jamais au lycée sans emporter° une bouteille d'eau minérale dans son sac. L'eau minérale est la boisson favorite des Français. Ils en boivent en moyenne° 140 litres par personne (hommes, femmes, et enfants) et par an. Ce sont les champions du monde de la consommation d'eau minérale.

■ Au café, les jeunes commandent de l'eau minérale.

L'eau a de nombreux avantages. C'est le plus naturel des produits. Elle contient° zéro calorie. Elle facilite l'élimination des toxines et la régénération des cellules de notre corps. (N'oublions pas que le corps° humain est composé de deux tiers° d'eau!)

En outre,° les eaux minérales ont certaines propriétés thérapeutiques qui dépendent des minéraux qu'elles contiennent (magnésium, calcium, potassium, sodium, etc.) Certaines eaux sont bonnes pour la digestion, d'autres pour le foie° ou les reins.° Certaines sont recommandées pour les rhumatismes, d'autres pour les maladies de peau.° En France, il existe des centaines d'eaux minérales différentes. Ces eaux viennent de sources° thermales situées principalement dans les zones montagneuses: Massif Central (Vichy), Alpes (Évian), Vosges (Vittel, Contrexéville), Pyrénées (Amélie-les-Bains).

La façon la plus normale d'utiliser une eau minérale est d'en boire tous les jours. Une autre façon consiste à faire une «cure» dans la région qui produit° une eau particulière. Là, non seulement on boit de grandes quantités d'eau minérale, mais on utilise celle-ci pour prendre des bains et pour se faire faire des massages. Cette tradition remonte° aux Romains qui connaissaient bien les vertus de l'eau et qui ont découvert° un grand nombre de sources thermales en Gaule il y a 2000 ans. Aujourd'hui des centaines de milliers de Français vont chaque été faire une cure dans les stations thermales spécialisées.

D'autres personnes préfèrent aller à la mer et pratiquer la «thalassothérapie.» Cette méthode consiste à profiter des avantages combinés de l'eau de mer, de l'air et du climat marins. On peut prendre des bains de mer très chauds, des saunas ou des bains de boue.° La thalassothérapie est recommandée pour les personnes qui souffrent° de fatigue ou de stress, pour celles qui veulent se remettre° en forme, et aussi pour les athlètes professionnels.

INFOMAGAZINE

La France des eaux

Il existe plus de 100 stations thermales en France. Chacune a sa spécialité.

- Si vous avez des problèmes de digestion, allez à Vichy, Vittel, Évian ou Contrexéville.
- Si vous avez de l'asthme, allez à Amélie-les-Bains.
- Si vous avez une peau délicate, allez à la Bourboule.
- Si vous avez des rhumatismes, allez à Aix-les-Bains, comme autrefois la reine Victoria, ou à Plombières, comme l'empereur Napoléon III.

PROJET
Allez dans un supermarché et faites une liste des eaux minérales qu'on y vend. Indiquez l'origine géographique de ces eaux minérales.

quant à *as for* **emporter** *to take along* **en moyenne** *on the average* **contenir** ✱ *to contain* **le corps** *body* **deux tiers** *two-thirds* **en outre** = *en plus* **le foie** *liver* **les reins** *kidneys* **la peau** *skin* **les sources** *springs* **produire** ✱ *to produce* **remonte** *dates back* **découvrir** ✱ *to discover* **boue** *mud* **souffrir** ✱ *to suffer* **se remettre** ✱ *to get back (into shape)*

Teaching Strategy: Warm-Up

As homework, have the students read pp. 261–262, and ask them to prepare five to ten questions per page. Have each student ask one of his/her questions and choose a student to answer. Repeat this until all the questions have been asked and answered.

Le savez-vous?

Que savez-vous de votre santé et de la santé en général? Faites le test suivant. Combien de phrases pouvez-vous compléter? [Pour connaître les réponses, allez au bas de la page.]

1. Le matin, notre température normale est de ...
   a. 35 degrés
   b. 37 degrés
   c. 40,2 degrés

2. En moyenne, un adolescent de 16 ans a besoin de ... par jour.
   a. 1.500 calories
   b. 2.800 calories
   c. 3.400 calories

3. Notre niveau d'adrénaline augmente quand ...
   a. on a faim
   b. on a la grippe
   c. on se met en colère

4. La grippe est une maladie causée par ...
   a. un virus
   b. le froid
   c. la mauvaise hygiène

5. Un dermatologue est un médecin qu'on peut consulter quand on a ...
   a. de l'acné
   b. des rhumatismes
   c. mal à la tête

6. Le calcium est l'élément principal du squelette et des dents. Une excellente source de calcium est ...
   a. le lait
   b. la viande
   c. le poisson

7. Il ne faut pas fumer parce que le tabac est un poison qui peut provoquer beaucoup de maladies sérieuses, en particulier ...
   a. l'anémie
   b. la tuberculose
   c. le cancer du poumon

8. La pénicilline est un antibiotique. Son rôle est de ...
   a. faciliter la digestion
   b. éliminer les produits toxiques
   c. détruire les bactéries qui provoquent les infections

9. Quand on est à la plage, il est prudent de se protéger contre le soleil. À long terme, l'exposition trop longue au soleil peut provoquer ...
   a. l'insomnie
   b. la polio
   c. le cancer de la peau

10. Les personnes qui ont un problème avec leur cholestérol doivent éviter *(avoid)* de manger ...
    a. des fruits
    b. des légumes
    c. des oeufs

11. La mononucléose est une maladie qui affecte ...
    a. le sang
    b. les muscles
    c. l'estomac

12. Le jogging, le cyclisme, et la gymnastique sont des activités aérobiques. Le résultat principal d'une activité aérobique est ...
    a. de développer nos muscles
    b. d'augmenter notre rythme cardiaque
    c. d'éliminer les toxines

13. En cas de transfusion sanguine, il est important de connaître son groupe sanguin. Le groupe sanguin le plus rare est ...
    a. le groupe A
    b. le groupe B
    c. le groupe O

14. Quand on est diabétique, il est déconseillé de manger ...
    a. du pain
    b. du sucre
    c du fromage

RÉPONSES: 1b, 2b, 3c, 4a, 5a, 6a, 7c, 8c, 9c, 10c, 11a, 12b, 13b, 14b

■ **Proverbe**
Santé passe richesse. *(Health before wealth.)*

■ **Note linguistique**
Traditionnellement, au nouvel an en France, on dit «Bonne année, bonne santé» aux membres de sa famille et à ses amis.

■ **Language Note**
35°C = 95°F; 37°C = 98.6°F; 40,2°C = 104.3°F

■ **Note culturelle**
Spa is a city in Belgium, renowned for its **station thermale**. The waters from the seven main springs of Spa are said to help people with rheumatism.

Une visite médicale

PRINT
Workbook, pp. 145–146
Activités pour tous
Unit 7 Resource Book, Partie 1
Activités pour tous TE
Audioscripts
Lesson Plans
Block Scheduling Lesson Plans
Absent Student Copymasters
Workbook TE

AUDIO
 Audio Program
CD 7, Tracks 1–4

TECHNOLOGY
@HomeTutor
Interactive Whiteboard Lessons
Teacher One Stop
Block Scheduling Copymasters
Projectable Transparencies
43, *Chez le médecin*
Transparency Copymasters,
pp. A91–A93
DVD Program, Unit 7

Dans la salle d'attente *(waiting room)*

— Avez-vous **un rendez-vous** *(appointment)*?
Oui, j'ai un rendez-vous avec
le docteur Lavie à deux heures.

Avez-vous
un rendez-vous ?

Oui, j'ai un rendez-vous
avec le docteur Lavie
à deux heures.

le médecin	**le/la chirurgien(ne)** *surgeon*
le/la dentiste	**l'infirmier(ère)** *nurse*
le spécialiste	**l'oculiste**

FMP (FÉDÉRATION
MUTUALISTE PARISIENNE

CENTRES OPTIQUE MÉDICALE

24 r St Victor 75005 P_____ 01 40 46 11 37
10-12 av Georges Clémenceau
93139 Noisy le Sec_____ 01 48 44 00 32

Dans le cabinet *(office)* **du médecin**

— Comment allez-vous?
Comment vous sentez-vous?

Ça va, | **je me sens bien.**
| je me **porte** bien.
| je suis **en bonne santé** *(health).*
| je suis **bien portant(e)** *(in good health).*

Ça ne va pas. | **Je ne me sens pas bien.**
Je suis | **malade** *(sick).*
Je me sens |

se sentir *to feel*
se porter bien *to be in
good health*

fatigué	**faible** *weak*
nerveux	**déprimé** *depressed*

— Avez-vous **de la fièvre?**
Oui, j'ai de la fièvre.
J'ai **39 degrés de température.**

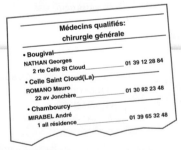

Médecins qualifiés:
chirurgie générale

• Bougival
NATHAN Georges
2 rte Celle St Cloud_____ 01 39 12 28 84

• Celle Saint Cloud(La)
ROMANO Mauro
22 av Jonchère_____ 01 30 82 23 48

• Chambourcy
MIRABEL André
1 all résidence_____ 01 39 65 32 48

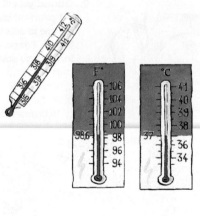

le médecin généraliste
le neurologue
le pédiatre
le cardiologue
le psychiatre

J'ai bonne mine. *I look good/
healthy.*
J'ai mauvaise mine. *I look bad/sick.*

■ **Teaching Suggestion**
Play the video with the sound muted.
Tell the class to write conversations
based on what they see. Afterward,
play the video with the sound on to
see how close their conversations
come to the one on the video.

Teaching Suggestion: DVD Program

In the Unit 7 *Vidéo-drame: Nicolas est malade*,
students will go with Nicolas to the doctor.
They will hear Nicolas identify his symptoms,
and see the doctor prescribe the appropriate
treatment. After watching the video, have
students pair up and re-enact a doctor's visit
based on the video. Encourage them to make
up different symptoms and treatments.

@HOMETUTOR
my.hrw.com

Qu'est-ce qui ne va pas?

Je tousse.

— Est-ce que **ça vous fait mal?**
   Aïe *(Ouch)!* Oui, ça fait mal.
   Non, ça ne fait pas mal.

faire mal *to hurt*

— Où **avez-vous mal?**

J'ai mal à la tête.
   à la gorge *(throat).*
   au ventre *(stomach).*

J'ai mal au coeur *(I feel nauseous).*

Révision p. R12

Les parties du corps

— **Qu'est-ce qui ne va pas?** *(What's wrong?)*

Je tousse.

tousser *to cough* **éternuer** *to sneeze*
vomir *to throw up* **saigner** *(to bleed)* **du nez**

J'ai **un rhume** *(a cold).* Je suis **enrhumé(e).**
J'ai **une douleur** *(pain)* dans le dos.

des nausées
de l'eczéma
des vertiges *dizzy spells*
des boutons *a rash*

— Quelles **maladies** *(diseases)* **d'enfance** avez-vous eues?
   J'ai eu **la rougeole** *(measles).*

les oreillons *mumps*
la varicelle *chicken pox*
la rubéole *German measles*
la coqueluche *whooping cough*

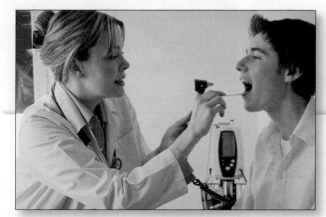

deux cent soixante-cinq **265**
Le Français pratique

Teaching Strategy

Divide the class into pairs and have each pair of students role play the dialogs from the vocabulary. Encourage students to use gestures to clarify meaning and to make the dialogs more fun. Ask each pair to choose their most successful and amusing dialog to present to the class. Use **Projectable Transparency 43** and the **Transparency Copymasters** to extend and expand the dialogs.

SUPPLEMENTARY VOCABULARY

Ouille! /uj/ *ouch!*
transpirer *to sweat*
C'est douloureux. *It's sore.*
Ça gratte. *It's itchy.*
Ça démange. *It's itchy.*
un bleu *bruise*
une égratignure *scratch*
une brûlure *burn*
une ampoule *blister*

Language Note

Write this pun on the board and ask students if they understand the play on words: «**Comment vous santé vous?**» (**Comment vous sentez-vous?**)

Additional Information

Penicillin was discovered in 1928 by Alexander Fleming, a British physician. Fleming received the Nobel Prize in Medicine in 1945.

Notes culturelles

- The first inoculation was made in 1796 by British physician Edward Jenner (1749–1823).
- French scientist **Louis Pasteur** (1822–1895) discovered the vaccine against rabies (1885). He also discovered two other vaccines, the process now called **la pasteurisation**, and founded the **Institut Pasteur** in 1888 in Paris. There are many branches of the Institute around the world serving as major research and vaccine production centers.
- Often, a French person will subscribe to **une mutuelle**, private insurance which will supplement the reimbursement of medical care made by the **Sécurité Sociale**.

Unité 7 265

— Est-ce que vous pouvez **ouvrir la bouche?**

avaler *to swallow*
respirer *to breathe, breathe in*
tousser

— Je vais vous

examiner.
prendre la température.
prendre la tension *(blood pressure).*
faire une analyse de sang *(blood test).*
faire une piqûre *(shot, injection).*
faire une radio *(x-ray).*

— Vous avez **une pneumonie.**

un rhume	**une angine** *strep throat*
de l'asthme	**une bronchite**
la grippe *flu*	**la mononucléose**

— Je vais vous **soigner** *(to treat).*
Voici **une ordonnance** *(prescription).*
Prenez **ce médicament** *(medicine)* . . .

le matin et le soir.
deux fois *(times)* **par jour.**
toutes les 4 heures.

de l'aspirine	**ces comprimés** *pills*
cet antibiotique	**ces cachets** *tablets*
ces vitamines	**ces gouttes** *drops*

— Vous devez

vous reposer.
vous soigner.
rester au lit.
prendre rendez-vous
revenir

dans une semaine.

se reposer *to rest*
se soigner *to take care of oneself*

Voici une ordonnance. Vous devez prendre rendez-vous dans une semaine.

Merci, docteur.

Teaching Strategy

Divide the students into pairs and give each of them an imaginary health problem: earache, nausea, fever, cough, cold, etc. Have each group invent a product that will treat their problem, give this product a catchy name, and create a T.V. commercial advertising it, using as much vocabulary from pp. 264–266 as possible.

Differentiation

Alphabetic/Phonetic Model the sounds of the more difficult vocabulary (**rhume, mononucléose, piqûre, pneumonie**). Have them pronounce the vocabulary 3 times, then write the word in their notebooks and include their own phonetic transcription.

1 Qu'est-ce qu'ils ont?

Choisissez l'option **a**, **b** ou **c** qui correspond logiquement à chaque situation.

1. Thomas va chez l'oculiste.
a. Il va bien.
b. Il a les oreillons.
c. Il a mal aux yeux.

2. Roger a 39 degrés de température.
a. Il est bien portant.
b. Il a de la fièvre.
c. Il a froid.

3. J'ai des difficultés à avaler.
a. J'ai une angine.
b. J'ai la rubéole.
c. J'ai une crampe d'estomac.

4. Ma petite soeur tousse tout le temps.
a. Elle a la varicelle.
b. Elle a une bronchite.
c. Elle est déprimée.

5. Thierry a envie de vomir.
a. Il éternue.
b. Il a de la tension.
c. Il a mal au coeur.

6. Vous avez des boutons.
a. Vous avez la grippe.
b. Vous avez la rougeole.
c. Vous ne respirez pas bien.

7. Je me mets des gouttes dans le nez.
a. J'ai un rhume.
b. Je prends des cachets.
c. J'ai besoin de vitamines.

8. L'infirmière m'a fait une radio.
a. Je prends des comprimés.
b. J'ai beaucoup de tension.
c. Je me suis cassé le bras.

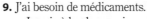

9. J'ai besoin de médicaments.
a. Je vais à la pharmacie.
b. Je vois le chirurgien.
c. Je suis en bonne santé.

10. Je voudrais voir le médecin.
a. Je me soigne.
b. Je me sens bien.
c. Je dois prendre rendez-vous.

2 Créa-dialogue 💬

Aujourd'hui vous ne vous sentez pas bien du tout. Regardez la liste et choisissez une maladie ou un malaise. Décrivez vos symptômes à votre partenaire.

Ça va?

Qu'est-ce que tu as?

Tu es sûr(e)?

Non, je ne me sens pas bien.

Je crois que j'ai le rhume des foins.

Oui, j'éternue tout le temps et j'ai mal aux yeux.

la grippe	**la mononucléose**	**un rhume**	**une bronchite**
une angine	**une indigestion**	**de l'asthme**	**une pneumonie**
le rhume des foins (hay fever)		**une allergie**	**??**

Notes linguistiques
Définitions
• **Un médecin généraliste:** quelqu'un qui soigne les maladies ordinaires
• **Un médecin spécialiste:** quelqu'un qui soigne des maladies spécifiques
• **Un médecin d'urgence:** quelqu'un qui s'occupe des cas d'urgence, des accidents
• **Le SAMU:** c'est le Service d'Aide Médicale Urgente
• **La Sécurité Sociale:** c'est une assurance qui rembourse les dépenses médicales
• **Une compagnie pharmaceutique:** une compagnie qui fabrique des médicaments
• **La médecine «écologique»:** c'est basée sur des produits naturels (plantes, fruits, etc.) et des remèdes traditionnels

Note culturelle
Quand quelqu'un éternue en France, il est poli de dire «À vos (tes) souhaits!» ou bien: «Santé!»

Anecdote
The stethoscope was invented by the French physician **René Laennec** (1781–1826).

Student Portfolios

Using Activity 2 as a base, have students record their dialogs for inclusion in their portfolios. If possible, have students extend or adapt the basic format to include more symptoms, a suggestion to visit the doctor or hospital, etc.

3 À la clinique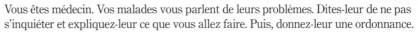

Un(e) malade va dans une clinique où il/elle a rendez-vous.
Avant de voir le médecin, l'infirmier(ère) lui pose des questions.
Complétez le dialogue et jouez-le en classe avec votre partenaire.

Infirmier(ère):	Vous avez un rendez-vous?
Malade:	*Answer affirmatively and give the time.*
Infirmier(ère):	Comment vous sentez-vous?
Malade:	*Say how you feel.*
Infirmier(ère):	Avez-vous de la fièvre?
Malade:	*Give your temperature.*
Infirmier(ère):	Où avez-vous mal?
Malade:	*Explain.*
Infirmier(ère):	Avez-vous d'autres symptômes?
Malade:	*Give at least two symptoms.*
Infirmier(ère):	Quelles maladies d'enfance avez-vous eues?
Malade:	*Mention two.*
Infirmier(ère):	Est-ce que vous avez été malade cet hiver?
Malade:	*Answer affirmatively and explain.*
Infirmier(ère):	Est-ce que vous prenez des médicaments?
Malade:	*Answer affirmatively and explain.*
Infirmier(ère):	Merci. Le médecin va vous examiner.

Clinique de **La Muette**

4 C'est vous le médecin!

Vous êtes médecin. Vos malades vous parlent de leurs problèmes. Dites-leur de ne pas
s'inquiéter et expliquez-leur ce que vous allez faire. Puis, donnez-leur une ordonnance.

- Je tousse tout le temps.
- J'ai de la fièvre.
- J'ai des boutons.
- J'ai des vertiges.
- J'ai des difficultés à respirer.
- J'ai des douleurs dans le dos.
- J'ai été mordu *(bitten)* par
  un chien.
- J'ai des palpitations
  (rapid pulse).

▶ Je me sens très faible.

Ne vous inquiétez pas.

Je vais vous prendre la tension.

Si c'est nécessaire, je vais vous faire
une analyse de sang. Voici une ordonnance.

Prenez ces cachets deux fois par jour.

Teaching Strategy

Divide the class into groups; try to include
varied students in each group. Have students
assign tasks within their groups. Each group
will develop a guide to local emergency services
(in French, of course!). The format of the guides
can differ according to the group's ideas.
Variations may include an online guide, a
printed guide, a recorded guide, or a series of
posters.

Conversations libres 💬 Avec votre partenaire, choisissez l'une des situations suivantes. Composez le dialogue correspondant et jouez-le en classe.

Digital
performance space

1 — Zut alors!

Vous voyagez en France. Un jour vous vous réveillez avec un malaise généralisé et des boutons sur la figure. Vous téléphonez au médecin qui vous demande des détails.
Rôles: le/la touriste, le médecin

2 — Un(e) malade imaginaire

Ce matin, il y a un examen de maths très important que vous n'avez pas préparé. Vous allez voir l'infirmier(ère) de l'école. Vous lui expliquez que vous êtes très malade. (Inventez des symptômes pour cette maladie imaginaire.) L'infirmier(ère) a des doutes sur votre maladie.
Rôles: l'élève, l'infirmier(ère)

3 — Histoire médicale

Vous êtes infirmier(ère) dans une école française. Vous interviewez un(e) candidat(e) pour l'équipe de foot. Posez-lui des questions sur son état général, par exemple . . .

• s'il (si elle) a des problèmes de santé
• s'il (si elle) a mal quelque part
• quelles maladies d'enfance il(elle) a eues
• s'il (si elle) a été malade cet hiver
• s'il (si elle) prend des médicaments, etc.

Rôles: l'infirmier(ère), l'athlète

4 — Une cure miracle

Un charlatan prétend avoir inventé une cure miracle pour toutes sortes de maladies. Un journaliste très incrédule lui pose des questions.
Rôles: le charlatan, le journaliste

PHARMACIE DU GARDET

Mehdi Akrout, Docteur en pharmacie, est heureux de vous accueillir avec son équipe. En collaboration avec votre médecin, votre pharmacien est là pour vous fournir les médicaments et vous conseiller sur leur utilisation. Si vous avez une question au sujet de : votre santé au quotidien, vaccins, préparation d'un voyage, ou effets secondaires d'un médicament, n'hésitez jamais à lui demander conseil.

Horaire :

	Du lundi au vendredi	Samedi
	9h00 à 12h30	9h00 à 12h30
	14h00 à 20h00	14h00 à 19h00

162 rue Aimé Ramond 11000 Carcassonne Tél : 04 68 24 39 71 Fax : 04 68 29 04 64

Sidebar

■ **Additional Topic**

À L'INFIRMERIE
Vous êtes infirmier(-ère) dans une colonie de vacances. Un matin, un(e) enfant vient vous voir avec des symptômes étranges. Faites-lui un examen complet.

■ **Note culturelle**

Le caducée is the universal symbol of the medical profession. This ancient symbol represents a snake wrapping itself around a staff, topped by "the mirror of Prudence." In mythology, both Hermes and Mercury carried a **caducée.** Today, every French doctor has this symbol on the windshield of his car, as a sign of his profession.

■ **Notes linguistiques**

• **La clinique** is generally a privately owned hospital. **L'hôpital** is public.
• **Le diététiste** (*dietician*—Canada) is called **le diététicien** in France.
• **L'éducateur physique** *physical therapist*

Teaching Strategy

Have students conduct a health survey in class. Each group of students should write five questions for the survey. Compile all questions, discarding duplicates and asking for replacement questions. After the survey form is complete, all students should fill it out (no names used). Ask student volunteers to compile the results and use them as a basis for class discussion.

Langue et Communication

RESOURCES

PRINT
Workbook, pp. 69–70

TECHNOLOGY
@HomeTutor

■ **Proverbe**

Il faut qu'une porte soit ouverte ou fermée. *(There can be no middle ground.)*

A Le concept du subjonctif: temps et modes

When we use verbs, we use them in a certain TENSE and a certain MOOD.

- The TENSE of a verb indicates when the action takes place.
  The PRESENT, the PASSÉ COMPOSÉ, the IMPERFECT and the FUTURE are tenses.
- The MOOD reflects the attitude of the speaker or the subject toward the action.

  The INDICATIVE and the SUBJUNCTIVE are moods.

  The INDICATIVE MOOD is *objective*.
  It is used to describe *facts*. It states what is considered to be *certain*.
  It is the mood of *what is*.

  The SUBJUNCTIVE MOOD is *subjective*.
  It is used to express *feelings, judgments,* and *emotions* relating to an action.
  It states what is considered to be *desirable, possible, doubtful,* or *uncertain*.
  It is the mood of *what may or might be*.

→ Although the subjunctive is rarely used in English, it is a mood frequently used in French. Compare the moods in the following sentences:

(fact)	Je sais que tu **es** généreux.	*I know that you **are** generous.*
(wish)	Je souhaite que tu **sois** plus patient avec moi.	*I wish that you **were** more patient with me.*

Both the indicative and the subjunctive may occur in a dependent clause introduced by **que**. The choice between the indicative and the subjunctive depends on what the subject or speaker expresses in the main clause.

MAIN CLAUSE (the subject expresses …)	DEPENDENT CLAUSE
• a **fact**, a **belief**	→ INDICATIVE
• a **wish**, a **necessity**, an **obligation** • an **emotion** or **feeling** • a **doubt** or **possibility**	→ SUBJUNCTIVE

Révision pp. R19, R21; R23-31

Le subjonctif:
  formation régulière
  formation irrégulière

Differentiation

Metacognitive, Gifted & Talented Have students generate some clauses in English that express feelings, judgments, emotions, wishes, necessity, obligation, doubt or possibility. Then ask them to generate some in French, followed by clauses that express certainty. Write all the clauses on the board in columns under the headings Subjunctive and Indicative. Have students create cartoons similar to the one on p. 270 using the clauses.

1 *Chez le médecin*

Vous êtes médecin. Choisissez un patient et dites ce qu'il doit faire et ne pas faire.

PATIENTS		ACTIVITÉS	
	tu	faire du sport	manger trop
il faut que	vous	aller à la piscine	manger des produits
il ne faut pas que	M. Marcoux	être déprimé(e)	naturels
	Mme Lenoir	être nerveux(se)	boire de l'eau minérale
	ces enfants	être optimiste	prendre ces médicaments
	ces malades	avoir trop de	se coucher tard
		tension	se reposer
		avoir peur de la	se soigner
		piqûre	

B Les verbes *croire* et *craindre*

	croire *(to believe)*		craindre *(to fear, to be afraid of)*	
PRÉSENT	je **crois** nous **croyons**		je **crains** nous **craignons**	
	tu **crois** vous **croyez**		tu **crains** vous **craignez**	
	il/elle/on **croit** ils/elles **croient**		il/elle/on **craint** ils/elles **craignent**	
PASSÉ COMPOSÉ	j'**ai cru**		j'**ai craint**	

Verbes conjugués comme **craindre:**

plaindre *(to be sorry for)*   **peindre** *(to paint)*
se plaindre de *(to complain about)*   **éteindre** *(to turn off, to extinguish)*

2 *Vive la différence!*

Chacun fait des choses différentes. Exprimez cela en faisant les substitutions suggérées.

1. Jérôme se plaint de sa copine.
(les élèves - le professeur / le professeur - l'administration / toi - tout)

2. Isabelle croit à son horoscope.
(moi - l'avenir [*future*] / vous - l'amitié / Roméo et Juliette - l'amour éternel)

3. Marc peint un tableau *(picture)*.
(vous - la cuisine / moi - mon bureau / ces artistes - des portraits)

4. J'ai peint ma chambre en bleu.
(mes cousins - en jaune / vous - en gris / nous - en rouge)

■ Teaching Notes
This is a review of **croire**. **Craindre** is a new verb.
Atteindre *(to reach)* is conjugated like **craindre**.
   Les alpinistes **atteignent** le sommet de la montagne.
Also conjugated like **craindre**:
contraindre *to force*
   (someone to do something)

Teaching Strategy
Give pairs of students the following scenarios:
   Vous allez partir camper dans la forêt. Avant de partir, vous demandez à vos compagnons de voyage ce qu'ils craignent. Avec un partenaire, formez les questions et les réponses d'après les suggestions données.

Exemple: tu/les araignées?
      (non)

Est-ce que tu crains les araignées?
Non, je ne crains pas les araignées.

1. vous/les animaux sauvages (non)
2. Paul/les incendies de forêt (oui)
3. Ashley et Laura/les moustiques (oui)
4. toi/l'isolement (non)
5. vous/les disputes (non)
6. nous/les serpents (oui)

Unité 7 271

■ **Note linguistique**

Some subjunctive forms have become word-phrases in French, e.g. **Soit!** *(So be it!)* or **Vive le roi!** *(Long live the King!).* **Note: vive** comes from the verb **vivre**. Agreement can be made or not, e.g. **Vive les vacances!** or: **Vivent les vacances!** *(Three cheers/hooray for the holidays!)*

SUPPLEMENTARY VOCABULARY

le bonheur *(happiness)*
  être enchanté
  se réjouir

la honte *(shame)*
  avoir honte
  être gêné *(bothered)*
  être embarrassé

la tristesse
  être navré *(very sorry)*

l'émotion
  être ému *(moved)*

■ **Teaching Strategy**

Tell students:
Pour chaque illustration de la page 272, exprimez ce qui arrive au personnage en utilisant une des expressions correspondantes et votre imagination! Exemples: Il est content d'avoir une lettre. Il est surpris d'entendre la nouvelle.

C L'usage du subjonctif: émotions et sentiments

Note the use of the subjunctive in the following sentences.

Je suis content **que tu sois** en bonne santé.	*I am happy **that you are** in good health.*
Nous sommes tristes **que vous partiez.**	*We are sad **that you are** leaving.*
Le médecin craint **que j'aie** les oreillons.	*The doctor fears **that I have** mumps.*

THE SUBJUNCTIVE is used after a verb or expression of EMOTION (happiness, sadness, fear, surprise, anger, regret, . . .), when the emotion concerns someone or something *other than the subject*.

→ When the emotion concerns the subject itself, an infinitive construction is used. Compare:

INFINITIVE	SUBJUNCTIVE
Je suis content d'**aller** en France.	Je suis content **que tu ailles** en France.
Alice a peur d'**être** malade.	Le médecin a peur **qu'Alice soit** malade.

VOCABULAIRE Verbes et expressions d'émotion

la joie
  être content
  être heureux(se)
  être ravi *(delighted)*

l'étonnement *(amazement)*
  être surpris
  être étonné *(astonished)*

l'orgueil *(pride)*
  être fier (fière)

la tristesse et le regret
  être triste
  être malheureux(se)
  être désolé *(very sad)*
  regretter
  déplorer

la crainte *(fear)*
  avoir peur
  craindre

la colère *(anger)*
  être furieux(se)

3 Consultations

Vous êtes médecin. Votre partenaire
va décrire un symptôme.
Vous allez exprimer votre diagnostic.

▶ — **Je tousse tout le temps.**
— **J'ai peur que vous ayez une bronchite.**

SYMPTÔMES	DIAGNOSTIC
• éternuer	• une allergie
• avoir mal au ventre	• une indigestion
• avoir très mal à la gorge	• une angine
	• une bronchite
• tousser tout le temps	• la grippe
• avoir des boutons	• la mononucléose
• se sentir très faible	• le rhume des foins *(hay fever)*
• avoir de la fièvre	• **??**

4 Mes sentiments

Décrivez vos sentiments dans les circonstances suivantes.
Choisissez une des options entre parenthèses ou une option de votre choix.

▶ (heureux ou triste?) Mes copains vont en France cet été.
   Je suis heureux/heureuse que mes copains aillent en France cet été.

1. content ou jaloux? (Mes cousins ont une voiture de sport.)
2. désolé ou surpris? (Mon frère ne dit pas la vérité.)
3. triste ou content? (Le professeur est malade aujourd'hui.)
4. furieux ou étonné? (Ma copine/mon copain ne vient pas au rendez-vous.)
5. content ou désolé? (L'examen de français est annulé.)
6. surpris ou fier? (L'équipe de baseball de l'école gagne le championnat.)

5 Leurs réactions

Décrivez les réactions des personnes suivantes aux situations entre parenthèses.
Utilisez une expression d'émotion du Vocabulaire.

▶ Alice (Son copain sort avec une autre fille.)
   Alice est triste (furieuse) que son copain sorte avec une autre fille.

1. Thomas (Sa copine française écrit toutes les semaines.)
2. Le médecin (Monsieur Larose fait des exercices.)
3. Stéphanie (Marc vient à sa boum.)
4. Monsieur Dupont (Sa fille a le premier prix du conservatoire.)
5. Le professeur (Le mauvais élève réussit à l'examen.)
6. Nathalie (Jean-Pierre est en retard au rendez-vous.)
7. Catherine (Sa cousine oublie la date de son anniversaire.)
8. Les supporteurs *(fans)* (Leur équipe perd le match.)
9. Les écologistes (On fait des économies d'énergie.)

■ **Notes linguistiques**

• **Le conservatoire** est une école spécialisée où on apprend la musique, la danse et le théâtre.
• **Le supporteur**, ou **le supporter**, encourage (supporte) son équipe sportive favorite. **Le fan** est un admirateur enthousiaste de quelqu'un ou quelque chose.

Teaching Strategy

This mnemonic device is a good point of departure for quick reference on the subjunctive.

W	wishes	**J'aimerais que...Je voudrais que...**
E	emotions	**Je suis triste que...J'ai peur que...**
I	impersonal expressions	**Il faut que...Il est important que...**
R	relative clauses	**Nous cherchons un secrétaire qui sache taper.**
D	doubts	**Je doute que...Je ne pense pas que...**
O	orders	**J'exige que...J'ordonne que...**
S	superlatives	**C'est le meilleur restaurant que je connaisse.**

@**HOMETUTOR**
my.hrw.com

D   Le subjonctif après les expressions de doute

Compare the use of the INDICATIVE and the SUBJUNCTIVE in the sentences below.

CERTAINTY OR BELIEF (INDICATIVE)	DOUBT, DISBELIEF OR UNCERTAINTY (SUBJUNCTIVE)
Je crois que tu **es** fatigué.	Je doute que tu **sois** malade.
Le médecin pense que j'**ai** la grippe.	Il ne pense pas que j'**aie** la mononucléose.
Il est sûr qu'Alice **est** trop pâle.	Il n'est pas sûr qu'elle **soit** déprimée.
Tu crois que tu **es** très intelligent!	Crois-tu que tu **sois** sympathique?

The INDICATIVE is used after verbs and expressions of CERTAINTY or BELIEF.
   The SUBJUNCTIVE is used after verbs and expressions of DOUBT and UNCERTAINTY.

→   Verbs like **croire, penser, être sûr, être certain,**
    and expressions like **il est sûr, il est certain,**
    are used to convey belief, knowledge, or conviction of certain facts.

   • When used in the AFFIRMATIVE, they are followed by the INDICATIVE.
   • When used in the INTERROGATIVE or the NEGATIVE, however, these verbs
    and expressions may convey an element of doubt or uncertainty.
    In this case they are followed by the SUBJUNCTIVE.

ALLONS PLUS LOIN

Depending on the level of certainty or doubt that the speaker wants to convey,
certain expressions may be followed by the indicative OR the subjunctive.
Compare:

   Il semble que tu **as** raison.   *It seems that you are right.* (This is pretty sure.)
   Il semble que tu **aies** raison.   *It would seem that you are right.* (It is much less sure.)

Teaching Strategy

Tell the students about various problems that you or someone you know is having at home, at school, with their children, etc. Ask the students to make suggestions to solve the problems. Each sentence/suggestion should use an expression that requires the subjunctive. You may also give situations concerning cruel or kind things that someone did to you and ask them to use the subjunctive expressions to explain their feelings about this person.
Pre-AP skill: Give directions, orders, advice.

■ **Teaching Note**
Autres expressions de certitude:
  Je suis convaincu(e)
  Je suis persuadé(e).

VOCABULAIRE Verbes et expressions de certitude et de doute

EXPRESSIONS DE CERTITUDE (+ INDICATIF)	EXPRESSIONS DE DOUTE (+ SUBJONCTIF)
je sais que . . .	**je doute que . . .**
je dis que . . .	
je crois que . . .	**je ne crois pas que . . .**
	crois-tu que . . . ?
je pense que . . .	**je ne pense pas que . . .**
	penses-tu que . . . ?
je suis sûr(e) que . . .	**je ne suis pas sûr(e) que . . .**
	es-tu sûr(e) que . . . ?
il est sûr / vrai / certain que . . .	**il n'est pas sûr / vrai / certain que . . .**
	est-il sûr / vrai / certain que . . . ?
il est clair que . . .	**il est douteux que . . .**
il est probable que . . .	**il est possible que . . .**
il est évident que . . .	**il est impossible que . . .**

6 ## L'optimiste et le pessimiste

L'optimiste voit l'existence sous un aspect positif. Le pessimiste voit l'existence sous un aspect négatif. Avec votre partenaire, jouez le rôle de l'optimiste et du pessimiste.

▶ la vie / être belle

1. les gens / être généreux
2. les jeunes / avoir un idéal
3. les parents / faire le maximum pour aider leurs enfants
4. la situation économique / être excellente
5. on / faire des progrès dans tous les domaines

Je crois que la vie est belle.

Je doute que la vie soit belle.

6. les journalistes / dire la vérité
7. le président / être honnête avec le public
8. le monde / être moins dangereux qu'avant
9. on / découvrir prochainement *(soon)* une cure contre le cancer

■ **Note linguistique**
Un optimiste voit la vie en rose. Un pessimiste voit tout en noir.

7 ## Êtes-vous d'accord?

Voici quelques propositions. Choisissez une proposition et exprimez votre opinion sur ce sujet. Pour cela, utilisez l'une des expressions du vocabulaire. Si possible, illustrez votre opinion en formulant une réflexion personnelle.

▶ la majorité des gens / être superstitieux?
**Je ne pense pas que la majorité des gens soient superstitieux.
Moi, par exemple, je n'hésite pas à voyager le vendredi 13.**

1. l'argent / faire le bonheur?
2. les gens / être fondamentalement honnêtes?
3. les gens idéalistes / être naïfs?
4. la liberté / être un mythe?
5. les femmes / avoir les mêmes responsabilités que les hommes?

6. les extra-terrestres / exister?
7. il / être facile de changer son destin?
8. il / être possible d'éliminer la violence dans la société?
9. tout le monde / avoir les mêmes choses?

deux cent soixante-quinze **275**
Langue et Communication

Teaching Strategy

Using Activity 7 as a base, divide the class into pairs and have each partner express a different opinion. Add the following as expansion scenarios:
• nous/être plus heureux qu'il y a cent ans?
• le président/être concerné par les problèmes des jeunes?

• nous/faire assez d'efforts pour assurer la paix dans le monde?
• le professeur de français/avoir des problèmes avec sa classe?
• toi/vouloir habiter à l'étranger?

INFO MAGAZINE

Theme: Humanitarian aid

Reading Strategy: Reading for information

RESOURCES

TECHNOLOGY
DVD Program, Unit 7, *Vignette culturelle*

■ Notes culturelles

- **Le Biafra** is a region located in the southeast of Nigeria, in Africa.
- Kurdistan is an area under Iranian, Turkish, and Iraqi rule. Its inhabitants, the Kurds, have been vying for independence since 1945.
- **Bernard Kouchner** helped create **Médecins sans Frontières** in 1970.
- **Médecins sans Frontières** was awarded the international Nobel Peace Prize in Oslo, Norway on October 15, 1999. This award honors the organization's relief workers who provide medical and humanitarian assistance in more than 80 countries worldwide.
- Some useful addresses for additional information:
  Médecins sans Frontières
  8 rue Saint-Sabin
  Paris 75011
  Médecins du monde
  62 rue Marcadet
  Paris 75018

■ Irregular Verbs

(see Appendix C)
obtenir (*see* **tenir**)
souffrir (*see* **ouvrir**)
vivre

Les médecins et l'action humanitaire

Nathalie, 27 ans, vient d'obtenir° son diplôme de médecin. Dans quelques semaines elle va partir pour l'Afghanistan. Hélène, une infirmière de 35 ans, rentre de Thaïlande où elle a passé dix mois dans les camps de réfugiés. Emmanuel, 25 ans, n'a pas de spécialité médicale, mais il a passé deux ans au Bangladesh avec «Médecins sans frontières.»° Nathalie, Hélène, Emmanuel: trois exemples parmi° des milliers de Français qui ont décidé de faire quelque chose pour les oubliés° de la terre.°

■ «Médecins sans frontières,» Pakistan

Nathalie explique: «Comme médecins, notre premier rôle est d'aider les gens qui sont dans la détresse. Aujourd'hui, la détresse humaine existe

■ Les organisations comme «Médecins du monde,» «Les Médecins aux pieds nus,» et «Médecins sans frontières» envoient des volontaires dans les régions où il y a une urgence médicale.

partout° dans le monde, et spécialement dans les pays du tiers-monde° où des centaines de milliers de gens souffrent° de la misère, de la faim et de la maladie. Dans ces pays, les catastrophes naturelles, les épidémies, la guerre° civile font des millions de victimes chaque année. Nous autres° citoyens° des pays dits *civilisés*, nous ne pouvons pas rester insensibles° au sort° de ces êtres° humains qui sont nos frères et nos soeurs. Nous devons agir°. Malheureusement, les besoins sont immenses et nos ressources très limitées. Nous sommes là non seulement pour soigner les gens, mais pour leur redonner° l'envie° de vivre.»°

Plusieurs organisations ont été créées en France pour répondre aux besoins de santé des pays du tiers-monde. Ces organisations envoient des volontaires dans des régions où il y a une urgence médicale, et plus spécialement dans des pays d'Afrique et d'Asie: en Éthiopie, en Somalie et au Libéria, au Pakistan, au Cambodge, par exemple.

obtenir ✲ *to get, obtain* **frontières** *borders* **parmi** *among* **les oubliés** *forgotten people* **la terre** *earth* **partout** *everywhere* **tiers-monde** *third world* **souffrir** ✲ *to suffer* **la guerre** *war* **autres** *others* **citoyens** *citizens* **insensibles** *insensitive* **au sort** *fate* **êtres** *beings* **agir** *to act* **pour leur redonner** *to give back* **l'envie** *desire* **vivre** ✲ *to live*

Teaching Strategy

Ask students to scan the article and illustrations and guess the main theme. Then ask each student to list five ways they would *personally* choose to help those less fortunate than themselves. Assign two secretaries to list all suggestions on the board or on a transparency. Ask students if they would like to choose one activity to participate in/ donate to as a class (be sure to clear with school administrators).

Pour être volontaire, il n'est pas nécessaire d'être médecin ou infirmier. Il suffit° d'être une personne de bonne volonté° et de croire à la solidarité des peuples de la terre. Les organisations les plus connues sont «Médecins sans frontières» qui intervient° dans plus de 60 pays, «Médecins du monde» qui a 7000 volontaires dans 40 pays, et «Les Médecins aux pieds nus.»° L'originalité de cette dernière organisation est d'utiliser des médicaments d'origine végétale ou animale et les techniques traditionnelles des pays d'intervention, comme par exemple, l'acupuncture dans les pays d'Asie.

MÉDECINS
SANS FRONTIÈRES

DÉFINITIONS

Définissez les mots ou expressions suivants. (Quand c'est possible, donnez des exemples.)

- un(e) volontaire
- la bonne volonté
- une épidémie
- la solidarité
- un réfugié
- l'action humanitaire
- les pays du tiers-monde
- une catastrophe naturelle
- la guerre civile

EXPRESSION ÉCRITE

1. Imaginez que vous voulez être volontaire pour l'une des organisations mentionnées dans le texte. Écrivez une courte lettre où vous expliquez ...
   - pourquoi l'action humanitaire vous intéresse
   - dans quel pays vous voudriez aller et pourquoi
   - ce que vous voulez faire pour aider les gens de ce pays
2. Imaginez que vous collectez des fonds pour "Médecins Sans Frontières." Dans une lettre à un ami, vous décrivez cette organisation.

"Médecins Sans Frontières" — une organisation humanitaire mondiale

Malgré° le progrès scientifique, le monde moderne n'échappe° pas aux catastrophes humaines et naturelles de toutes sortes: guerres,° révolutions, tremblements de terre,° inondations,° famines, épidémies... Ces catastrophes n'ont pas de frontières, mais elle affectent généralement les pays les plus pauvres et créent des urgences médicales pour les populations les plus vulnérables: enfants, femmes et personnes âgées. Pour répondre à ces urgences, il faut agir° rapidement et indépendamment de toute considération politique.

Dans ce but,° un groupe de médecins français a créé en 1971 une organisation qui a pour mission d'envoyer des volontaires partout° où les populations sont en danger. Cette organisation, appelée "Médecins Sans Frontières," est maintenant une organisation internationale. Chaque année, 27 000 volontaires—médecins, chirurgiens, infirmières—partent en mission à travers° le monde. Leur but est non seulement d'apporter une aide médicale à ceux qui en ont besoin, mais aussi de faire respecter la dignité humaine. Présents sur tous les continents, les "Médecins Sans Frontières" sont intervenus en Somalie, en Éthiopie, au Congo, en Afghanistan, en Palestine... Pour son travail humanitaire, cette organisation a reçu le prix° Nobel de la Paix° en 1999.

---

il suffit = il est suffisant **volonté** will **intervenir ✷** to intervene **pieds nus** bare feet **malgré** in spite of **échappe (à)** escapes (from) **guerres** wars
tremblements de terre earthquakes **inondations** floods **agir** to act **dans ce but** to this end **partout** everywhere **à travers** across **prix** prize **paix** peace

---

■ Teaching Note

The **Définitions** activity encourages students to paraphrase. With open-ended activities of this kind, you may wish to encourage students to consult a monolingual dictionary (e.g., *Le Petit Robert* series). These dictionaries motivate students to "think in French" and serve as a useful vehicle to improve their overall proficiency/fluency.

■ Expansion

Imaginez que vous êtes membre du comité qui décerne le Prix Nobel de la Paix. Votre candidat pour ce prix est le docteur Kouchner. Expliquez aux autres membres du comité (les élèves de la classe) pourquoi vous l'avez choisi.

■ Irregular Verb

(see Appendix C)
intervenir (*see* venir)

■ Notes Culturelles

- The doctors of **Médecins sans Frontières** and **Médecins du Monde** are sometimes referred to as "the French doctors" since the French created this type of humanitarian aid.
- It takes about eight years of study in France to become a doctor. Doctors who go on missions with **Médecins sans Frontières** are all volunteers. They may volunteer for three months, six months, or two years, depending on their commitment. After three months, they receive a small stipend.

Teaching Suggestion: DVD Program

To see *Médecins sans frontières* in action, play the Unit 7 *Vignette culturelle*.

RESOURCES

PRINT
Workbook PE, pp. 148–150
Activités pour tous
Unit 7 Resource Book, Partie 2
  Activités pour tous TE
  Audioscripts
  Lesson Plans
  Block Scheduling Lesson Plans
  Absent Student Copymasters
  Workbook TE

AUDIO
 Audio Program
  CD 7 Tracks 9–13

TECHNOLOGY
@HomeTutor
  Interactive Whiteboard Lessons
Teacher One Stop
  Block Scheduling Copymasters
  Teacher to Teacher Copymasters,
  Les accidents, pp. 84–85
  Projectable Transparencies
    45, *Qu'est-ce qui est arrivé?*
    46, *Problèmes de santé*
    Transparency Copymasters,
    pp. A96–A99

SUPPLEMENTARY VOCABULARY

se tordre le poignet *to sprain
  one's wrist*
avoir une entorse *to have a sprain*
boîter *to limp*
le service des urgences *emergency
  room*
le brancard *stretcher*
le brancardier *stretcher-bearer*

■ Notes linguistiques

• **plâtrer**—Le médecin m'a plâtré
  le poignet.
• **marcher avec des béquilles**
• **suturer (une plaie)** *to stitch (a cut)*

278 Unité 7

---

2 Accidents et soins dentaires

À l'hôpital
Cette personne est **blessée** (injured, hurt).
Elle vient de **se blesser** (to get hurt).
Elle s'est cassé le bras.

se blesser à la tête	**se casser** (to break) **la jambe**
se couper (to cut) **à la main**	**se fracturer l'épaule**
se brûler to get burned	**se fouler** (to twist) **la cheville** ankle

L'infirmier(ère) va lui **faire une radio** (x-ray).

faire un plâtre	cast	**faire un pansement**	bandage
donner des béquilles	crutches	**mettre des sutures**	stitches

Aïeee!

Cette personne est blessée.

On va lui faire une radio.

1 *Créa-dialogue: Qu'est-ce qui est arrivé?*

Vous rencontrez les personnes suivantes. Avec votre partenaire, choisissez l'une des illustrations. Composez le dialogue correspondant et jouez-le en classe. Utilisez votre imagination pour expliquer l'accident!

—Eh Antoine, ça va?
—Hm, comme ci comme ça.
—Pourquoi est-ce que tu <u>as un plâtre?</u>
—Je <u>me suis cassé le bras.</u>
—Comment est-ce que c'est arrivé?
—Eh bien, voilà. Je <u>faisais de l'alpinisme
samedi dernier et je suis tombé.</u>

1. Juliette

2. Thomas

3. Jean-Pierre

4. Véronique

5. Grégoire

6. Vanessa

Teaching Strategy: Warm-Up

Have the class write a group story. Each student will contribute at least two sentences. Tell them that the story is to take place in the emergency room of the local hospital. You might want to give them the first sentences: «**L'autre jour, Raoul est allé à l'hôpital.** **Il est tombé dans l'escalier.**» Have them include dialog in the story, as much vocabulary as possible and a minimum of four verbs in the subjunctive. Students can take turns being scribe and copying the story onto the board as it is being developed.

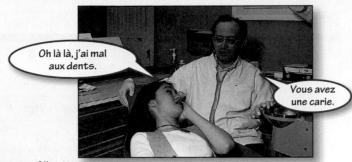

Oh là là, j'ai mal aux dents.

Vous avez une carie.

Chez le dentiste

— Oh là là, j'ai **mal aux dents**.

Vous avez **une carie** *(cavity)*.

Je vais vous | faire **un plombage** *(filling)*.
faire **une piqûre de novocaïne**.
enlever *(to remove)* | **cette dent.**
cette dent de sagesse *(wisdom tooth)*.

---

2 Chez le dentiste

Avec votre partenaire, composez le dialogue suivant entre le/la dentiste et le/la patient(e).

Dentiste: *Ask the patient what's wrong.*
Patient: *Say that you have a toothache.*
Dentiste: *Ask patient to open his/her mouth.*
Say that the patient has a cavity and explain what you are going to do.
Patient: *Ask if it is going to hurt.*
Dentiste: *Say no, and tell your patient that you will give him/her a shot of novocain.*
Patient: *Say that you are not feeling well . . . and then faint.*

Conversations libres

Avec votre partenaire, choisissez l'une des situations suivantes. Composez le dialogue correspondant et jouez-le en classe.

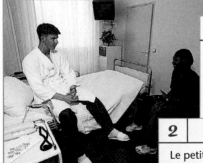

Digital performance) space

1 Accident de moto

Xavier a eu un accident de moto. Le lendemain, son amie Florence lui rend visite à l'hôpital et lui pose des questions. Xavier explique ce qui est arrivé et ce que le médecin a fait.
Rôles: Xavier, Florence

2 Visite chez le dentiste

Le petit Pierre (6 ans) a mal aux dents. Sa mère pense qu'il a probablement une carie et veut l'amener chez le dentiste. Pierre a peur, et sa mère essaie de le rassurer en expliquant ce que le dentiste va faire. Pierre n'est pas du tout rassuré.
Rôles: la mère, Pierre

deux cent soixante-dix-neuf **279**
Le Français pratique

■ **Teaching Strategy**
You may want to review
the agreement of the past participle:

- Verb conjugated with **avoir** →
Agreement with preceding direct object (if any):
Karine **a fait** du ski.
La pierre? Elle ne l'**a pas vue.**
- Verb conjugated with **être** →
Agreement with subject:
Elle **est tombée.**
- Reflexive verb →
Agreement with reflexive pronoun
(= subject) when it is a direct object:
Elle **s'est blessée.**
Elle **s'est cassé** la jambe.

Teaching Strategy: Drill
Tell the students which you will be drilling first: past or present. Then show them the hand signals you'll be using to represent the subject pronouns je .../ tu .../ il .../ elle .../ nous .../ vous .../ ils .../ elles ...
Give them a verb, then begin doing the hand signals so that they give you the verb in the present/past subjunctive for the subject indicated. Start out slowly, with few verb changes, doing the pronouns in order. As they (and you) get better at it, speed up, switch verbs frequently, and mix up the order.

280 Unité 7

A Le passé du subjonctif

FORMS

The past subjunctive is a compound tense formed according to the pattern:

> present subjunctive of **avoir** or **être** + past participle

parler	aller	s'amuser
que j'**aie parlé**	que je **sois allé(e)**	que je me **sois amusé(e)**
que tu **aies parlé**	que tu **sois allé(e)**	que tu te **sois amusé(e)**
qu'il **ait parlé**	qu'il **soit allé**	qu'il se **soit amusé**
qu'elle **ait parlé**	qu'elle **soit allée**	qu'elle se **soit amusée**
que nous **ayons parlé**	que nous **soyons allé(e)s**	que nous nous **soyons amusé(e)s**
que vous **ayez parlé**	que vous **soyez allé(e)(s)**	que vous vous **soyez amusé(e)(s)**
qu'ils **aient parlé**	qu'ils **soient allés**	qu'ils se **soient amusés**
qu'elles **aient parlé**	qu'elles **soient allées**	qu'elles se **soient amusées**

→ The agreement of the past participle in compound tenses also applies to the past subjunctive.

Je suis content que tu **aies téléphoné** à ces filles.

Je suis heureux que tu les **aies invitées** à la boum.

USES

Compare the use of the present and the past subjunctive.

Je doute que Paul **téléphone** ce soir.   *I doubt that Paul **will call** tonight.*
Je doute qu'il **ait téléphoné** hier.   *I doubt that he **called** yesterday.*

Je regrette que vous **ne veniez pas** cet après-midi.   *I am sorry that you **are not coming** this afternoon.*
Je regrette que vous **ne soyez pas venu** samedi.   *I am sorry that you **did not come** on Saturday.*

The past subjunctive is used instead of the present subjunctive to refer to past events or situations.

1 Drôles d'excuses!

Votre partenaire n'est pas venu(e) à une répétition *(rehearsal)* de la chorale samedi dernier. Il/elle va choisir une (mauvaise!) excuse. Vous êtes le directeur/la directrice et vous avez des doutes.

▶ — Je ne suis pas venu(e) à la répétition parce que j'ai raté le bus.
— Ah oui? Écoute, Christophe, je doute que tu aies raté le bus.

EXCUSES
- J'ai eu la grippe.
- Je me suis foulé la cheville.
- Je suis tombé(e) dans les escaliers.
- Je suis allé(e) chez le dentiste.
- J'ai raté *(missed)* le bus.
- Le bus a eu un accident.
- Mon réveil *(alarm clock)* n'a pas sonné.
- Ma cousine s'est mariée.
- Mon arrière-grand-mère est morte.

Differentiation

Synthetic/Analytic Write out a sentence in the **passé subjonctif** on the board and classify each part of speech. Then ask students to generate some new sentence elements for each part of speech. Then, combine to form sentences. Students write the new sentences in their notebooks.

2 Réactions!

Votre partenaire va décrire un événement (imaginaire) qui lui est arrivé.
Exprimez votre réaction. Pour cela, choisissez une expression de la page 272.

ÉVÉNEMENTS

- mon oncle / avoir un accident
- ma cousine / se marier
- mon copain / voir un OVNI (UFO)
- ma grande soeur / gagner une bourse (scholarship) pour l'université
- ma grand-mère / se casser le bras
- ma copine / oublier la date de mon anniversaire
- mes parents / rencontrer le président des États-Unis
- ma tante / m'acheter une voiture de sport

Ma tante m'a acheté une voiture de sport!

Ah oui? Écoute, je doute qu'elle t'ait acheté une voiture de sport.

RÉACTIONS

joie?
tristesse?
surprise?
doute?

(Eh bien, bravo! Je suis ravi(e) qu'elle t'ait acheté une voiture de sport.)

3 Ce qu'ils pensent

Décrivez ce que pensent les personnes suivantes.

▶ l'infirmière / craindre / tu / te fouler la cheville.
   L'infirmière craint que tu te sois foulé la cheville.

1. le médecin / ne pas croire / je / me casser la jambe.
2. je / être content / tu / venir à la boum
3. Pauline / être heureuse / Jérôme / lui écrire une lettre
4. vous / être surpris / l'équipe / gagner le match
5. le guide / avoir peur / les alpinistes (mountain climbers) / se perdre dans la montagne
6. le professeur / douter / vous / faire vos devoirs
7. Madame Dumont / être fière / sa fille / réussir à l'examen d'ingénieur

4 Les mystères de l'univers

Beaucoup de mystères n'ont pas été élucidés (cleared up). Avec votre partenaire, choisissez un des sujets suivants et discutez-le. Exprimez votre opinion en utilisant une expression de doute ou de certitude, et le passé du subjonctif ou le passé composé de l'indicatif.

▶ les Vikings / découvrir l'Amérique?
   Je doute (je ne crois pas / il est douteux) que les Vikings aient découvert l'Amérique. ou: Je suis sûr(e) (il est probable) que les Vikings ont découvert l'Amérique.

1. les Égyptiens / utiliser l'électricité?
2. Dracula / exister?
3. un écrivain inconnu (unknown) / écrire les pièces de Shakespeare?
4. des navigateurs romains / explorer l'Amérique du Sud?
5. des extra-terrestres / venir sur la Terre?
6. des ingénieurs russes / inventer la bombe atomique?

Unité 7

Interdisciplinary/ Community Connections

Invite a speaker from a local hospital to discuss the need for volunteers to speak and interpret foreign languages at the hospital.

Language Arts
Brainstorm a list of common minor injuries and ailments.

Math
Research how many of each type of illness or injury occur each year in your community.

Science/Health
Interview a health professional and find out first-aid treatments for these problems.

Social Studies
Research the education/training needed to be a foreign-language interpreter at a hospital.

Art/Music
Create simple drawings or icons to represent common information a health-care worker would need to ask about.

Technology
Research how technology is used at a local hospital: Is this facility linked via computer to other hospitals? Are there new hi-tech diagnostic tools being used?

Community
Invite a speaker to address a community gathering and present a plan for volunteers for the program.

■ **Language Note**

OVNI is an acronym for **O**bjet **V**olant **N**on-Identifié.

Teaching Strategy

You may wish to add the following information when using Activity 4 in class:

- Dracula is the main character of a novel created by British author Bram Stoker (1847–1912).
- Some people believe that Francis Bacon (1561–1626), a philosopher and essayist, wrote the plays attributed to Shakespeare.
- The first atomic bomb was designed in the U.S. by a team of American and exiled European scientists led by J. Robert Oppenheimer in 1945. It was called the Manhattan Project.
- President J.F. Kennedy was assassinated on November 22, 1963 in Dallas by Lee Harvey Oswald.

Unité 7 281

RESOURCES

PRINT
Activités pour tous

TECHNOLOGY
Teacher One Stop
💻 **Projectable Transparencies**
    L7, En voyage
    Transparency Copymasters,
    pp. A131–A132
French InterActive Reader

LECTURE

Additional readings @ my.hrw.com
FRENCH
InterActive Reader

Guy de Maupassant

En voyage

AVANT DE LIRE

L'histoire que vous allez lire est racontée par un médecin au cours d'un voyage en train. Les autres passagers du compartiment où il se trouve ont déjà fait le récit d'aventures plus ou moins rocambolesques° dont ils sont évidemment les héros. Ces histoires ont un point commun: elles se passent toutes dans un train.

C'est maintenant le tour du médecin. L'histoire qu'il choisit de raconter est une histoire d'amour, l'amour simple et purement spirituel unissant un homme et une femme qui se sont rencontrés dans un train.

rocambolesques = avec beaucoup d'incidents extraordinaires

NOTE *Culturelle*

Guy de Maupassant (1850-1893) a écrit des romans et des pièces de théâtre, mais il est surtout célèbre pour les centaines de contes et nouvelles qu'il a publiés. Maupassant utilise un style clair, objectif et impersonnel. Il décrit avec précision les faits, laissant au lecteur le souci° de découvrir les sentiments qui animent les personnages de ses contes.
souci *care*

Le contexte historique

Pour comprendre une histoire, il faut la situer dans son contexte historique. L'action de l'histoire racontée par le médecin se passe à la fin du 19e siècle dans un train qui va de Russie jusqu'à la Côte d'Azur en France. Les voyages de ce genre étaient très longs. Ils étaient relativement sûrs,° mais de temps en temps les trains étaient attaqués par des bandits ou par des révolutionnaires, alors particulièrement actifs dans les pays de l'Europe de l'Est et surtout en Russie.

Parmi° les passagers du train, il y a une jeune femme mariée à un aristocrate russe. Très malade, elle va en France pour se soigner. Comme les gens riches de l'époque, elle est accompagnée de ses serviteurs et elle a réservé un wagon pour elle seule.

sûrs *safe* **parmi** *among*

Anticipons un peu!

Imaginez que vous êtes la jeune femme russe. Au cours du voyage, un homme fait irruption dans le compartiment où vous êtes seule. Il est très pâle, paraît confus et vous remarquez qu'il est blessé. Cet homme vous demande de l'aider.
Qu'est-ce que vous allez faire?
- tirer la sonnette d'alarme
- appeler vos serviteurs
- aider l'homme

À supposer que vous avez décidé d'aider cet homme, qu'est-ce que vous allez demander à cet homme de faire?
- se livrer à la police
- aller à l'hôpital
- ne jamais plus vous parler

Teaching Strategy

This story is longer and linguistically more sophisticated than the prior selections. To read it fluently, students need to be able to understand the **passé simple**. You may want to review this tense in Appendix C (pp. R32–R33).

Use **Projectable Transparency L7** and the **Transparency Copymasters** to help students retain important elements of the story. Use the *Anticipons un peu* activities to set the stage for the reading.

EN VOYAGE

1

Le médecin commença ainsi son histoire:

«Moi, je n'ai pas d'aventure extraordinaire à vous raconter.
Je vais seulement vous parler d'une jeune femme que j'ai connue,
une de mes clientes, à qui il arriva la chose la plus singulière°
5 du monde, et aussi la plus mystérieuse et la plus attendrissante.°

C'était une Russe, la comtesse Marie Baranow, une très grande
dame, d'une exquise beauté. Vous savez comme les Russes peuvent
être belles, avec leur nez fin, leur bouche délicate, leurs yeux d'une
indéfinissable couleur, d'un bleu gris, et leur charme à la fois tendre
10 et sévère, que les Français trouvent tellement séduisant.

La comtesse Marie souffrait depuis plusieurs années de tuberculose.
Pour la soigner, son médecin, qui la savait très malade, voulait l'envoyer
dans le sud de la France, mais elle refusait obstinément de quitter Saint
Pétersbourg. Finalement, l'automne dernier, le docteur, réalisant la gravité
15 de l'état° de sa patiente, parla à son mari qui ordonna à sa femme de partir
pour Menton.

Résignée, elle prit le train. Elle était seule dans son wagon, ses gens de
service° occupant un autre compartiment. Elle restait contre la portière, un
peu triste, regardant passer les campagnes et les villages de la Russie. Elle
20 se sentait bien isolée dans la vie, sans enfants, sans parents et avec un mari
qui ne l'aimait plus et qui avait décidé de l'exiler à des milliers de
kilomètres de son pays.

À chaque station, son serviteur Ivan venait voir si elle avait besoin de
quelque chose. C'était un vieux domestique, totalement dévoué, à qui elle
25 pouvait demander n'importe quoi.

singulière = étrange   **attendrissante** touching   **l'état** = la condition   **gens de services** = domestiques

Mots utiles

la comtesse	*countess*
la portière	= la porte d'un train
souffrir *	*to suffer*
dévoué	*devoted*
exquis	*exquisite*
séduisant	*attractive*
à la fois	*at the same time*
n'importe quoi	*anything*

NOTES *Culturelles*

La tuberculose La tuberculose est une maladie très grave qui
attaque les poumons.° Au 19e siècle, c'était une maladie très
commune et, comme il n'y avait pas de vaccin et pas
d'antibiotiques, elle était généralement mortelle. Pour se soigner,
les gens riches allaient dans les régions où l'air était pur et le
climat sain°: dans les Alpes, par exemple, ou sur la Côte d'Azur.

Saint Pétersbourg Saint Pétersbourg, ou Pétersbourg, était la
capitale de la Russie impériale. C'était là que les tsars et les
aristocrates russes avaient leurs palais.°

Menton et la Côte d'Azur Menton est une petite ville très
pittoresque située sur la Côte d'Azur ou Riviera française.
Aujourd'hui, cette région attire° des millions de touristes chaque
année. Au siècle dernier, les seuls visiteurs étaient des familles
anglaises et des aristocrates russes qui venaient là à cause du
climat. Dans le cimetière de Menton, on peut voir encore
aujourd'hui de nombreuses tombes aux inscriptions russes.

poumons lungs   **sain** healthy   **palais** palaces   **attire** attracts

Avez-vous compris?

1. Qu'est-ce que le médecin pense des femmes russes?
2. Quelle était la maladie de la comtesse?
3. Qu'est-ce que son docteur en Russie voulait qu'elle fasse?
4. Avec qui a-t-elle fait le voyage?
5. Quels étaient les sentiments de la comtesse quand elle était dans le train?
6. Est-ce qu'elle avait une vie familiale intéressante? Expliquez.

Anticipons un peu!

Quelque chose de dramatique va arriver dans la scène suivante. Selon vous, qu'est-ce qui va se passer?

■ Note linguistique
The adjective **rocambolesque** comes from **Rocambole**. Rocambole was the hero of a popular series of more than thirty novels written by Ponson du Terrail (1829-1871).

■ Additional Information
Other works by Maupassant include:
Boule-de-Suif
Le Horla
Bel-Ami
Contes du jour et de la nuit

■ Irregular Verb
(see Appendix C)
souffrir   (*see* **ouvrir**)

SUPPLEMENTARY VOCABULARY

la locomotive à vapeur
steam engine

■ *Avez-vous compris?*
(Sample answers)
1. Il pense qu'elles sont très belles.
2. La comtesse avait la tuberculose.
3. Il voulait l'envoyer se soigner dans le sud de la France.
4. Elle a fait le voyage avec des serviteurs.
5. Elle était triste, elle se sentait seule.
6. Elle n'avait pas une vie familiale intéressante: elle n'avait plus de parents, elle n'avait pas d'enfants, et elle pensait que son mari ne l'aimait plus.

Notes culturelles

- Saint Petersburg was renamed Petrograd in 1914 before becoming Leningrad in 1924. Saint Petersburg is 2143 km (1331 miles) away from Paris, France.
- France and Russia became allies in 1881. Russia needed French funds, and France was hoping that, with the help of Russia, it would win back Alsace and Lorraine from Germany.
- Chopin, Musset, Molière, and Kafka died of tuberculosis.

2

La nuit commençait à tomber. Le train allait maintenant très vite. Très énervée,° la comtesse ne pouvait pas dormir. Elle eut alors l'idée de compter l'argent que son mari lui avait donné avant son départ. Elle ouvrit son sac, en vida le contenu sur ses genoux et commença à compter les pièces d'or.

Tout d'un coup, la comtesse Marie sentit un vent froid sur son visage. Elle leva la tête et elle vit un homme qui venait d'entrer dans son wagon. Il était grand, bien habillé, et il était blessé à la main. Il referma la porte, s'assit en face de la comtesse et la regarda de ses grands yeux noirs. Puis, il prit un mouchoir dans sa poche et en enveloppa son poignet pour arrêter le sang qui coulait. 3

La jeune femme eut très peur. Cet homme certainement l'avait vue compter son or. Il était venu pour la voler, ou, pire encore, pour la tuer. Il la regardait fixement, essoufflé,° le visage convulsé, prêt, sans doute, à l'attaquer.

Il dit brusquement: 40

— Madame, n'ayez pas peur.

Elle ne répondit rien, incapable d'ouvrir la bouche. Son coeur battait et ses oreilles bourdonnaient.°

L'homme continua:

— Je ne suis pas un malfaiteur°, madame. 45

Elle ne disait toujours rien, mais ses genoux tremblaient tellement que tout l'or tomba sur le sol° du wagon.

Surpris, l'homme regarda ce flot° de métal, puis il se baissa pour ramasser les pièces.

Prise de panique, la comtesse se leva. Elle courut vers la portière 50 pour sauter du train. L'homme comprit ce qu'elle voulait faire. Il l'attrapa, la saisit dans ses bras, et l'obligea à s'asseoir.

— Écoutez-moi, madame, dit-il. Je ne suis pas un malfaiteur. La preuve° c'est que je vais ramasser cet argent et vous le rendre. Je suis moi-même en grand danger. Si vous ne m'aidez pas à passer 55 la frontière, je suis un homme mort. Dans une heure, nous serons à la dernière station russe. Dans une heure dix, nous serons dans un autre pays. Si vous ne me secourez° pas, je suis condamné. Je ne peux pas vous expliquer pourquoi, mais croyez-moi. Je n'ai pas tué. Je n'ai pas volé, et je n'ai rien fait de mal. Je vous jure que je suis 60 un homme d'honneur, mais je ne peux pas vous en dire plus.

énervée = nerveuse **essoufflé** out of breath **bourdonnaient** were buzzing **malfaiteur** = criminel
sol floor **flot** stream, cascade **preuve** proof **secourez** = aidez

■ Note linguistique
Pire is the comparative and superlative of **mauvais**.

■ Irregular Verb
(see Appendix C)
battre

Mots utiles

un coin	corner
une frontière	border
le genou; les genoux	knee; lap
un mouchoir	handkerchief
une pièce d'or	gold coin
le poignet	wrist
se baisser	to stoop, bend down
battre *	to beat
compter	to count
couler	to flow
envelopper	to wrap
jurer	to swear
ralentir	to slow down
ramasser	to pick up
remplir	to fill
rouler	to roll (along); to travel
sauter	to jump
siffler	to whistle
tuer	to kill
vider	to empty
voler	to steal
muet (muette)	silent
pire	worse

Teaching Strategy: Expansion
Ask students the following questions:
• À votre avis, pourquoi l'homme a-t-il besoin d'aide?
• Que pensez-vous qu'il ait fait?
• Que se passera-t-il à la frontière si elle ne l'aide pas?

Expand by asking students to write a short paragraph giving their opinions and the reasons behind their views.

L'homme se mit à genoux. Comme il l'avait dit, il ramassa toutes les pièces d'or, et en remplit le sac qu'il donna à la comtesse. Puis il alla s'asseoir à l'autre coin du wagon.

La comtesse Marie ne bougeait° pas. Immobile et muette, elle retrouva peu à peu son calme. L'homme ne faisait pas un geste pas un mouvement. Il restait droit,° les yeux fixés devant lui. De temps en temps, elle le regardait rapidement. C'était un homme de trente ans environ.° Il était très beau, avec l'apparence d'un gentilhomme. 65

Le train continuait à rouler très vite dans la nuit. Puis, il siffla plusieurs fois, ralentit et finalement s'arrêta. 70

bougeait = changeait de position   **droit** *sitting upright*   **environ** = approximativement

---

Avez-vous compris?

1. Qu'est-ce que la comtesse faisait quand l'homme est entré dans le wagon?
2. Quelle était l'apparence physique de cet homme? Décrivez-le.
3. Quelle a été la réaction de la comtesse quand elle a vu cet homme? Pourquoi?
4. Qu'est-ce que l'homme a fait quand l'argent a roulé sur le sol?
5. Qu'est-ce que la comtesse a voulu faire ensuite?
6. Quel service est-ce que l'homme a demandé à la comtesse?

Anticipons un peu!

À votre avis, est-ce que la comtesse va protéger l'inconnu?
- Si oui, comment?
- Si non, qu'est-ce qu'elle va faire?

■ **Note culturelle**
La monnaie russe s'appelle le rouble. Il y a cent kopecks dans un rouble.

■ *Avez-vous compris?*
(Sample answers)
1. Elle comptait des pièces d'or.
2. Il était grand, beau, bien habillé. Il avait les yeux noirs. Il était blessé.
3. Elle a eu très peur, parce qu'elle pensait qu'il allait voler son argent ou la tuer.
4. Il l'a ramassé.
5. Elle a voulu sauter du train.
6. Il lui a demandé de l'aider à passer la frontière.

3

Ivan, le vieux serviteur, parut à la portière du wagon pour prendre les ordres de la comtesse. Celle-ci regarda son étrange compagnon, puis elle dit à son serviteur d'une voix brusque:

— Ivan, je n'ai plus besoin de toi. Tu vas retourner à Saint Pétersbourg.

Le serviteur, très surpris, ouvrit des yeux énormes. Tremblant d'émotion, il put à peine dire:

— Mais, madame . . . Je pensais que . . .

D'un ton très assuré, la comtesse répondit:

— J'ai changé d'avis. Tu ne viendras pas avec moi à Menton. Je veux que tu restes en Russie… Tiens, prends cet argent pour payer ton billet de retour. Et donne-moi ton manteau, ta casquette et ton passeport.

Ivan enleva sa casquette et son manteau qu'il lui donna, sans comprendre, à la comtesse. Il lui tendit son passeport et, puis, les larmes aux yeux, descendit du train.

Le train repartit vers la frontière. Alors, la comtesse dit à son voisin:

— Mettez ce manteau et cette casquette. Vous êtes maintenant Ivan, mon serviteur. Je mets une seule condition à ce que je fais pour vous: vous ne me parlerez jamais. Je ne veux pas que vous me disiez un seul mot, même pour me remercier.

L'inconnu s'inclina,° sans prononcer un mot. Bientôt le train s'arrêta de nouveau. Des policiers en uniforme entrèrent dans le wagon. Ils regardaient partout comme s'ils cherchaient quelqu'un. La comtesse leur dit d'un ton impérieux:

— Je suis la comtesse Baranow de Saint Pétersbourg, et voici mon domestique Ivan.

s'inclina *bowed*

Mots utiles

une casquette	*cap*
un inconnu	*stranger*
une larme	*tear*
changer d'avis	*to change one's mind*
enlever	*to take off*
paraître*	*to appear*
rompre	*to break*
tendre	*to hand, give*
à cause de	*because of*
à peine	*hardly, scarcely*
debout	*standing*

■ **Irregular Verb**

(see Appendix C)
paraître *(see* **connaître***)*

Teaching Strategy

Divide the class into groups. Have each group discuss the following questions and prepare answers to present to the class:

• À votre avis, pourquoi Ivan pleure-t-il?

• Est-ce parce qu'il est triste de quitter la comtesse ou est-ce parce qu'il est heureux de rentrer en Russie?

• Y a-t-il une autre explication possible? Laquelle?

Puis elle tendit les passeports à un officier qui les lui rendit en saluant. Les hommes sortirent du wagon et continuèrent leur ronde d'inspection. Après une heure d'arrêt, le train se remit en route. 100

Pendant toute la nuit, l'homme et la femme restèrent en tête-à-tête,° muets tous les deux. Le matin, le train s'arrêta dans une gare allemande. L'inconnu descendit du wagon. Debout, sur le quai, il dit à la comtesse:

— Pardonnez-moi, madame, de rompre ma promesse, mais à cause 105
de moi, vous avez perdu votre domestique. Il est juste que je
le remplace. Avez-vous besoin de quelque chose?

Elle répondit froidement:

— Allez chercher ma femme de chambre.

Il y alla, puis il monta dans un autre wagon. 110

Quand elle descendait à quelque buffet° de gare, elle le voyait de loin qui la regardait . . . Le train arriva finalement à Menton.

en tête-à-tête *face to face*   **buffet** *food wagon*

Avez-vous compris?

1. Qu'est-ce que la comtesse demande à Ivan, son vieux serviteur?
2. Comment est-ce que l'inconnu échappe *(escapes)* au contrôle des policiers?
3. Quelle promesse est-ce que la comtesse exige de l'inconnu?
4. Que fait l'inconnu quand le train s'arrête à la gare allemande?

Avez-vous compris?

• D'après vous, est-ce que l'inconnu va tenir *(keep)* sa promesse?
• Comment va se terminer cette histoire?

■ **Note linguistique**
rompre sa promesse ≠ tenir sa promesse

■ *Avez-vous compris?*
(Sample answers)
1. Elle lui demande de retourner à Saint Pétersbourg.
2. Il échappe au contrôle des policiers parce qu'il a mis la casquette et le manteau d'Ivan.
3. Elle exige qu'il ne lui parle jamais.
4. Il descend du train et monte dans un autre wagon.

4

Le docteur toussa, puis il continua son histoire:

Un jour que je recevais mes clients dans mon cabinet, j'eus la visite d'un grand garçon que je n'avais jamais vu. Il me dit:

— Docteur, je viens vous demander des nouvelles de la comtesse Marie Baranow. Elle ne me connaît pas. Je suis un ami de son mari. C'est lui qui m'envoie.

Je répondis:

— La comtesse est très, très malade. Je doute qu'elle rentre un jour en Russie.

À ces mots, cet homme se mit à pleurer comme un enfant. Il se leva et sortit brusquement de mon cabinet.

Ce soir-là, comme d'habitude, je rendis visite à la comtesse dans son hôtel. Je lui dis qu'un étranger était venu m'interroger° sur sa santé. Elle parut émue et me raconta toute l'histoire que je viens de vous dire. Puis elle ajouta:

— Cet homme que je ne connais pas me suit maintenant comme mon ombre. Je le rencontre chaque fois que je sors. Il me regarde d'une étrange façon, mais il ne m'a jamais parlé.

Elle réfléchit, puis ajouta:

— Je parie qu'il est sous mes fenêtres.

interroger = poser des questions

Mots utiles

un baiser	*kiss*
un être	*human being*
un fou	*crazy person*
une ombre	*shadow*
un sourire	*smile*
ajouter	*to add*
deviner	*to guess*
gâter	*to spoil*
parier	*to bet*
pleurer	*to cry*
se retourner	*to turn back*
réfléchir	*to think, reflect on*
suivre *	*to follow*
bouleversé	*overwhelmed*
douloureux	*painful*
ému	*moved, touched*
jusqu'au bout	*to the end*

Elle quitta sa chaise longue, alla à la fenêtre et me montra, en effet, l'homme qui était venu dans mon cabinet. Il était assis sur un banc et regardait dans la direction de l'hôtel. Quand il nous vit, il se leva et partit sans se retourner.

J'assistai ainsi à une chose surprenante et douloureuse, à l'amour muet de ces deux êtres qui ne se connaissaient pas.

Il l'aimait passionnément, avec la reconnaissance° et la dévotion d'un animal sauvé de la mort. Chaque jour, il venait me demander «Comment va-t-elle?», comprenant que j'avais deviné leur amour. Et il pleurait affreusement quand il apprenait qu'elle était chaque jour plus faible et plus pâle.

Elle me disait: «Je ne lui ai parlé qu'une seule fois, mais il me semble que je le connais depuis toujours.»

Et quand ils se croisaient° dans la rue, elle lui rendait son salut avec un sourire grave et charmant. Je sentais qu'elle était heureuse, elle qui savait qu'elle était perdue. Oui, je la sentais heureuse d'être aimée ainsi, avec ce respect et cette constance, avec cette poésie exagérée, avec cette dévotion totale et absolue. Et pourtant, elle refusait désespérément de le rencontrer, de connaître son nom, de lui parler . . .

Elle disait: «Non, non, cela me gâterait cette étrange amitié. Il faut que nous restions étrangers l'un à l'autre.»

Lui aussi continua à garder ses distances. Il voulait respecter jusqu'au bout l'absurde promesse de ne jamais lui parler, promesse qu'il avait faite dans le wagon.

Souvent, pendant ses longues heures de faiblesse, elle se levait de sa chaise longue et allait à sa fenêtre pour voir s'il était là. Et quand elle l'avait vu, toujours immobile sur son banc, elle revenait se coucher avec un sourire aux lèvres.

Elle est morte un matin vers dix heures. Comme je sortais de l'hôtel, il vint vers moi, le visage bouleversé. Il savait déjà la nouvelle.

— Je voudrais la voir une seconde seulement, en votre présence, dit-il.

Je lui pris le bras et rentrai dans la maison. Quand il fut devant le lit de la morte, il lui prit la main et l'embrassa d'un interminable baiser. Puis il se sauva° comme un fou. Je ne l'ai jamais revu.

la reconnaissance = la gratitude   **se croisaient** = se rencontraient   **se sauva** = partit

Teaching Strategy

Make copies of the illustrations from the **Transparency Copymasters**, one set for each group of four or five students. Have each group put the pictures in order, adding a short description for each section of the story. Groups should then peer-check each other's work.

■ Note linguistique

The adverb **mi-** is used with nouns as a prefix, meaning *half*. **Examples: à mi-chemin** *(halfway)*, **en mi-juillet** *(in mid-July)*, **la mi-temps** *(halftime of a game)*, **travailler à mi-temps** *(to work part time)*.

Le docteur toussa de nouveau, et il dit:

— Voilà certainement la plus singulière aventure de train que je connaisse. Il est vrai que les hommes sont un peu fous.

Une femme dit à mi-voix.°

— Ces deux êtres-là étaient moins fous que vous ne croyez . . . Ils étaient . . . ils étaient . . .

Et elle se mit à pleurer, sans terminer sa phrase. On changea de conversation pour la calmer. Personne n'a su ce qu'elle voulait dire.

à mi-voix *in a low voice*

■ *Avez-vous compris?*

(Sample answers)

1. Il dit qu'il est un ami du mari de la comtesse, et que c'est le mari qui l'envoie demander des nouvelles.
2. Elle explique que l'homme la suit toujours. Il est sur un banc sous la fenêtre de la comtesse.
3. Elle éprouve de l'amitié pour lui. Elle aime son amour platonique. Elle pense que parler changerait les choses.
4. Il a peut-être compris qu'elle était morte parce qu'elle n'est pas venue à la fenêtre ce matin-là. Il demande au médecin s'il peut la voir.
5. *Answers will vary.*

Avez-vous compris?

1. Sous quel prétexte l'inconnu va-t-il voir le médecin? Quelle est sa réaction quand il apprend la vérité?
2. Qu'est-ce que la comtesse explique au médecin ce soir-là? Où était l'inconnu à ce moment-là?
3. Quel sentiment est-ce que la comtesse éprouve *(feel)* pour l'inconnu? Comment explique-t-elle son refus de lui parler?
4. À votre avis, comment est-ce que l'inconnu a appris la mort de la comtesse? Qu'est-ce qu'il demande au médecin?
5. À votre avis, est-ce que l'inconnu était un fou ou un héros? Expliquez pourquoi?

Teaching Strategy: Expansion

Ask students to complete the following activities:

- *Expression écrite:* L'inconnu décrit la scène du train dans son journal. Écrivez cette page.
- Complétez la phrase de la jeune femme à la fin de l'histoire avec votre opinion personnelle.

- Avez-vous aimé cette histoire? Expliquez pourquoi.

These questions may be answered as a group activity if students prefer to debate their answers and opinions.

APRÈS LA LECTURE

Expression orale

Dramatisation

Avec un(e) partenaire, jouez la scène du train (partie 3 de l'histoire).

Sujets de discussion

A. L'inconnu du train

Avec votre partenaire, créez une identité et une personnalité à l'inconnu du train. Imaginez, par exemple:

- qui il est
- d'où il vient
- comment, pourquoi, et dans quelles circonstances il a été blessé?
- comment et pourquoi il est entré dans le wagon où était la comtesse?
- pourquoi il a demandé sa protection?

Rappelez-vous: L'inconnu a dit qu'il était un homme d'honneur, qu'il n'avait pas tué, qu'il n'avait pas volé, et qu'il n'avait rien fait de mal.

B. L'amour platonique

Un amour platonique est un amour purement spirituel, comme l'amour qui unit l'inconnu et la comtesse russe.

- Pensez-vous que cet amour soit réel?
- Pensez-vous qu'un tel amour puisse exister aujourd'hui?

Prenez une position pour ou contre et illustrez-la avec des exemples.

Situations

Avec votre partenaire, choisissez l'une des situations suivantes. Composez le dialogue correspondant et jouez-le en classe.

1   Une visite

La comtesse sait qu'elle va mourir. Quelques jours avant sa mort, elle accorde *(grants)* une visite à l'inconnu du train en lui demandant d'expliquer ses actions.
Rôles: la comtesse, l'inconnu

2   Explications

La comtesse vient de mourir. Rentré chez lui, le docteur raconte à sa femme les faits de la journée. La femme du docteur demande des explications.
Rôles: le docteur, sa femme

3   Il y a trente ans . . .

Trente ans ont passé. Au lieu de retourner en Russie, l'inconnu est resté en France. Un jour, il raconte l'histoire à un(e) ami(e) qui demande des détails.
Rôles: l'inconnu, son ami(e)

Expression écrite

Notice nécrologique *(Obituary)*

Vous êtes journaliste. Écrivez une brève notice nécrologique sur la comtesse Marie Baranow. (Inventez-lui une biographie.)

Journal intime

Dans son journal intime, la comtesse décrit la scène du train. Écrivez cette page de journal.

Lettre d'adieu

Sachant que la comtesse va mourir, l'inconnu lui écrit une lettre où il avoue ses sentiments. (Évidemment il ne la lui enverra pas, parce qu'il respecte la promesse qu'il a faite.) Écrivez cette lettre d'adieu.

Student Portfolios

Using either the *Situations* or the *Expression écrite* activities, have students prepare these materials for inclusion in their portfolios. If students prefer to work on an alternate activity suggested by the story (an original story or poem, a song or piece of music, a short scene on video, a series of illustrations with captions), they may do so.

Interlude culturel

RESOURCES

TECHNOLOGY
Teacher One Stop
  Pre-AP Digital Resources
  🖥 **Projectable Transparencies**
    1, *La France*
    1(o), *La France*
    5, *L'Europe*
    5(o), *L'Europe*
    Transparency Copymasters,
    pp. A5–A6, A12–A13

■ **Anecdote**

To prepare for the switch
from francs to euros in 2002, the
French created a converting machine.
This credit-card size calculator is able
to convert any amount instantly from
francs into euros and vice-versa.

Français et Européens

Pour les Français d'aujourd'hui, l'Europe est une réalité bien concrète. Ils portent des chemises italiennes et des imperméables anglais. Ils mangent des oranges espagnoles et du fromage hollandais. Au café, ils commandent de la bière belge ou irlandaise. Ils conduisent des voitures allemandes et suédoises. Ils voyagent avec un passeport européen et passent leurs vacances en Grèce, au Portugal ou en Finlande. Là, ils paient leurs dépenses avec une monnaie unique: l'euro. Avec le programme **Erasmus**, les jeunes Français peuvent faire des études universitaires dans une vingtaine de pays différents. Quand ils ont leur diplôme, ils peuvent travailler dans le pays de leur choix sans la nécessité d'un permis de travail.

La construction de l'Europe a commencé après la Deuxième Guerre Mondiale°, avec la création du **Marché Commun** qui réunissait la France, l'Allemagne, l'Italie, la Belgique, les Pays-Bas et le Luxembourg. Le but° principal de cette union était de faciliter les échanges commerciaux et d'unifier les institutions de façon à promouvoir° l'expansion économique dans tous les pays membres.

Depuis, l'**Union Européenne** s'est agrandie. Elle comprend maintenant 27 pays représentant plus de 500 millions d'habitants. Ces pays restent indépendants, mais sont unis par les mêmes° intérêts et la même vision du monde. L'objectif de l'Union Européenne est d'assurer le progrès économique et social. Sa mission consiste aussi à formuler une politique européenne commune sur les grandes questions d'aujourd'hui: respect des droits° humains et de la diversité culturelle, promotion de la liberté et de la démocratie, maintien de la paix et de la sécurité, protection de l'environnement.

L'Union Européenne

PAYS	POPULATION
Allemagne	82 000 000
France	65 000 000
Royaume Uni	61 000 000
Italie	51 000 000
Espagne	47 000 000
Pologne	39 000 000
Roumanie	22 000 000
Pays-Bas	17 000 000
Grèce	11 000 000
Portugal	11 000 000
Belgique	10 000 000
République Tchèque	10 000 000
Hongrie	10 000 000
Suède	9 000 000
Autriche	8 000 000
Bulgarie	8 000 000
Danemark	6 000 000
Slovaquie	6 000 000
Finlande	5 000 000
Irlande	4 000 000
Lituanie	4 000 000
Lettonie	2 000 000
Slovénie	2 000 000
Estonie	1 000 000
Chypre	1 000 000
Luxembourg	500 000
Malte	400 000

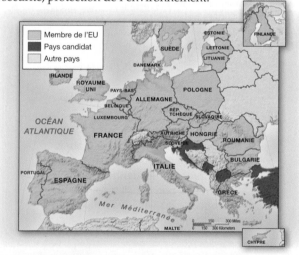

Deuxième Guerre Mondiale *World War II* **but** *objective* **de façon à promouvoir** *in order to promote* **mêmes** *same* **droits** *rights*

Notes culturelles

- The European **flag** bears 12 stars, regardless of how many member states there may be in the Union. This flag was originally designed for the Council of Europe in 1949.
- Other European countries may eventually join the **European Union.** To qualify, a country must meet certain economic conditions and the people must vote affirmatively in a referendum on the question.
- The four countries which did not adopt the **euro** in 1999 were Denmark, Greece, Great Britain and Sweden.

■ Oui à l'Europe!

Les Français sont généralement très favorables à l'Europe. Nous avons demandé à quatre Français d'âges différents d'expliquer pourquoi.

Un lycéen (14 ans)

Pendant les vacances de printemps, je suis allé passer dix jours en Hollande avec les élèves de ma classe. Je ne me suis pas senti dépaysé° du tout. Évidemment, les Hollandais parlent une autre langue, et leur nourriture est différente, mais en général nous avons beaucoup de points communs avec eux. Et je suis sûr que c'est la même chose avec les Allemands, les Anglais et les Italiens. Nous sommes tous européens!

Une étudiante (21 ans)

Je suis étudiante à l'IEP (Institut d'Études politiques) de Strasbourg. Dans ma classe, il y a 25 pour cent d'étudiants étrangers, surtout allemands, anglais et belges. Moi-même, je vais passer l'année prochaine à l'université de Fribourg en Allemagne. Tout ça, grâce au programme *Erasmus*, qui facilite les échanges entre les universités européennes. Avec *Erasmus*, l'Europe est une réalité bien concrète pour nous, étudiants.

Une jeune cadre° (28 ans)

Je suis diplômée d'une école de commerce française, mais maintenant je travaille en Allemagne pour une compagnie anglaise. J'ai un job intéressant et je gagne très bien ma vie. Si un jour je décide de changer d'entreprise, avec mon expérience internationale je n'aurais pas de problèmes à trouver quelque chose d'autre. Si l'Europe n'existait pas, je n'aurais pas ces possibilités!

Un retraité (80 ans)

Autrefois l'histoire européenne, c'était l'histoire des conflits permanents entre la France et l'Allemagne ou l'Angleterre. Je parle en connaissance de cause° parce que j'ai fait la guerre de 40* et que j'ai passé quatre ans en Allemagne dans un camp de prisonniers. Maintenant, avec la nouvelle Europe, la guerre est devenue impossible. Je suis pour l'intégration politique de l'Europe parce que cela signifie paix° et prospérité pour mes petits-enfants . . . et leurs enfants.

* La guerre de 40, c'est la Deuxième Guerre Mondiale (1940-1944). Voir à la page 252.

dépaysé *lost (in a strange place)*   **cadre** *executive*   **en connaissance de cause** *knowingly*   **paix** *peace*
fond *background*   **suffit = *est suffisant***

Les symboles de l'Europe

Le drapeau européen

Le drapeau européen représente un cercle de 12 étoiles jaunes sur un fond° bleu. Les 12 étoiles ont une valeur symbolique de la perfection.

Le passeport européen

Les citoyens des pays de **l'Union européenne** ont un passeport de format unique, le passeport européen. Cependant, ce passeport n'est pas nécessaire pour aller dans les autres pays de la CE: une simple pièce d'identité suffit.°

deux cent quatre-vingt-treize **293**
Interlude culturel

■ **Note culturelle**

Erasme (1466–1536) était un humaniste hollandais. Pendant la Renaissance (voir page 140), les humanistes étaient des esprits universels qui s'intéressaient à tous les aspects de la connaissance humaine, et plus particulièrement à l'histoire et à la littérature grecque et romaine. Aujourd'hui, Erasme reste le symbole de l'universalité de la connaissance humaine.

■ **Realia Note**

Le passeport européen
Although each country issues its own passport, all the information inside the passport is given in each of the languages of the "CE" members.

■ **Teaching Suggestion**

Have students look at the websites for the consulates of several francophone countries. They should note what services and cultural activities these offices offer to their citizens who are living in the United States and to the general public.

Expansion

Internet Connection – Interlude 7
Visit **http://my.hrw.com** for more information and useful links about the various French-speaking African countries.

Comparisons
Standard 4.2 Students demonstrate understanding of the nature of culture through comparisons of francophone cultures with their own.

■ **Pour en savoir plus**

Pour davantage de renseignements sur la Résistance, voir pages 254–259.

■ **Note culturelle**

Emmaüs est un village au nord de Jérusalem. Dans la tradition chrétienne, c'est là ou Jésus s'est manifesté à ses disciples incrédules la nuit de sa résurrection.

SUPPLEMENTARY VOCABULARY

le squatter *squatter*
squatter *to squat (in a building)*
le chômage *unemployment*
la délinquance *delinquency*
le SDF (Sans Domicile Fixe)
  homeless person
la solidarité *solidarity*
un(e) sans-abri *homeless person*

Nous, c'est les autres!

La France d'aujourd'hui est un pays riche et prospère. Ses habitants ont l'un des niveaux de vie les plus élevés du monde. Pourtant, comme toute société moderne, la société française a ses problèmes et ses victimes.° Il y a les chômeurs,° les sans-abri,° les gens qui ont faim. Que fait-on pour ces déshérités de la société? Certains Français ont répondu à cette question par leurs actions.

L'abbé Pierre et les «Chiffonniers d'Emmaüs»

L'abbé Pierre et deux de ses protégés

L'abbé* **Pierre** a 90 ans ou un peu plus. C'est un homme simple qui, depuis 40 ans, porte le même béret et la même pèlerine° noire. C'est aussi l'un des hommes les plus admirés de France. Issu d'une famille riche, l'abbé Pierre a décidé de mettre sa religion en pratique et de devenir l'apôtre° des pauvres.

En réalité, l'abbé Pierre s'appelle Henri Grouès. C'est pendant la Guerre de 1940, quand il travaillait dans la Résistance, qu'il a pris le nom d'Abbé Pierre. Cette guerre, qui a duré° quatre ans, a causé la destruction d'un très grand nombre de maisons et d'immeubles dans toute la France. À la fin de la guerre, il y avait des milliers de «sans-abri». L'abbé Pierre est devenu leur porte-parole° lorsqu'il a été élu° député° à l'Assemblé Nationale** en 1945.

Mais pour l'abbé Pierre, l'activité politique n'était pas suffisante. Devant l'inaction du gouvernement, il a décidé de passer à l'action tout court.° C'est ainsi qu'il a créé les «Chiffonniers° d'Emmaüs», une organisation qui donnait du travail, un logement, et surtout une raison de vivre° à ceux que personne ne voulait employer: les alcooliques, les anciens repris de justice,° et tous les déshérités de la terre. Pour rappeler° aux Français l'existence des sans-abri, l'abbé Pierre a décidé de «squatériser», d'une manière illégale mais non injuste, les immeubles vides° ou abandonnés. Plus récemment, en 1991, il a créé des «boutiques-solidarité» pour aider les gens qui n'ont pas les moyens° de vivre comme tout le monde.

La misère n'a évidemment pas de frontière° et l'action de l'abbé Pierre est devenue internationale. Il y a aujourd'hui plus de 250 centres Emmaüs en France et 600 dans le monde. L'abbé Pierre est décédé en 2007 après une longue vie au service des déshérités.

---

* **L'abbé:** un titre religieux donné à certains prêtres catholiques.
** **L'Assemblée Nationale:** Avec le Sénat, chambre parlementaire qui vote les lois *(laws)*. C'est l'équivalent du «House of Representatives» du congrès américain.

---

victimes *casualties* **chômeurs** *unemployed* **sans-abri** *homeless* **pèlerine** *cape* **apôtre** *apostle, defender* **duré** *lasted* **porte-parole** *spokesperson*
élu *elected* **député** *congressman* **tout court =** *directement* **chiffonniers** *ragpickers* **raison de vivre** *aim in life* **anciens repris de justice** *former prison inmates* **rappeler** *remind* **vides** *empty* **moyens** *means* **frontière** *border*

Notes culturelles

- L'abbé Pierre est né en 1912. Il entre au monastère à l'âge de 19 ans, après avoir distribué sa part d'héritage et fait voeu de pauvreté. À 34 ans, il est élu député de Meurthe-et-Moselle et devient ainsi le porte-parole des pauvres.
- Le film français intitulé *Hiver 54* relate le combat de l'abbé Pierre pour soulager la misère des pauvres gens et pour fonder les Chiffonniers d'Emmaüs.
- L'abbé Pierre s'est retiré dans un monastère italien à Paglia, près de Padoue, en 1996.
- Ses funérailles ont eu lieu à Notre Dame en présence du président Jacques Chirac.

Coluche et les «Restos du Coeur»

À son époque, **Coluche**, de son vrai nom Michel Colucci, était le comédien le plus célèbre de France. Son visage bonhomme,° ses manières rustres,° sa salopette° étaient universellement connus. Mais pour Coluche, faire des films, se produire° à la télévision et gagner de l'argent, ne suffisait pas. Coluche était un homme généreux, courageux et juste qui ne pouvait pas tolérer la misère ou les inégalités sociales. Alors, un jour il est passé à l'action et il a créé les «Restaurants du coeur». Cette organisation prépare des repas chauds pour les sans-abri, pour les personnes sans ressources, et généralement pour tous ceux qui ont faim et qui n'ont pas d'argent.

En 1986, Coluche s'est tué dans un accident de moto, mais son oeuvre° continue. Aujourd'hui, les 2500 «Restos° du coeur», animés par des milliers de bénévoles,° servent 100 millions de repas gratuits par an.

Coluche, le comédien au grand coeur

Jeunes Français, bénévoles qui servent des repas gratuits au «Restos du Coeur»

bonhomme *good-natured*   **rustres** *boorish, lacking good manners*   **salopette** *overalls*   **se produire** = se montrer   **oeuvre** *charitable works*
restos = restaurants   **bénévoles** = volontaires

RESOURCES

TECHNOLOGY
Teacher One Stop
💻 **Projectable Transparencies**

4, *Le monde francophone:*
L'Afrique, l'Europe, l'Asie

Transparency Copymasters,
pp. A10–A11

■ Notes historiques

LES INVASIONS
- The Roman occupation is described in *Interlude 1*, p. 98.
- Among the invading German tribes were the **Franks**, who gave their name to the country.
- The Scandinavians or Vikings came from Norway, Sweden, and Denmark. They were also known as Norsemen or Normans **(les hommes du Nord)**. See p. 104.

SUPPLEMENTARY VOCABULARY

la carte de séjour *visa, green card*
la naturalisation *naturalization*
l'intégration *assimilation*
le travailleur clandestin *illegal worker*
le réfugié (politique) *(political) refugee*
le demandeur d'asile *asylum seeker*
l'autorisation de travail *work permit*

La France, une mosaïque

Les Français d'aujourd'hui ne s'appellent pas seulement Dupont, Moreau, Petit ou Normand. Ils s'appellent aussi Belkacem, Lopez, Nguyen et Meyer. Ils sont blancs, noirs, bruns et jaunes. Ils vont à l'église, à la mosquée, au temple et à la synagogue* . . . Loin d'être un pays homogène, la France est en réalité une mosaïque marquée par l'intégration, la fusion et la cohabitation de cultures différentes..

Historiquement, la France a d'abord été une terre d'invasion. Au cours° des dix premiers siècles,° elle a été occupée par les Romains, les Germains, les Scandinaves . . . Au 19e siècle, elle est devenue une terre d'asile° pour les milliers de réfugiés politiques venus d'Allemagne, de Pologne, de Hongrie et de Russie.

Au 20e siècle, La France est devenue une terre d'immigration pour des millions de travailleurs étrangers. Le développement économique et industriel a en effet créé un énorme besoin de main d'oeuvre.° Pour répondre à ce besoin, le gouvernement français a invité des étrangers à venir travailler en France. Dans les années 20, ces travailleurs venaient principalement d'Italie et de Pologne. Dans les années 50, ils venaient surtout du Portugal et d'Espagne.

Depuis les années 60, la majorité des travailleurs étrangers qui viennent en France ne sont pas européens. Ce sont principalement des Maghrébins (Algériens, Marocains et Tunisiens) venus des pays d'Afrique du Nord. D'autres, moins nombreux, viennent d'Afrique occidentale° (Mali, Sénégal, Cameroun . . .) et d'Asie (Viêt-nam, Laos, Cambodge).

Après les États-Unis, la France est le pays du monde qui a le plus grand nombre d'immigrants. Les 4,5 millions d'étrangers qui habitent en France représentent 8% de la population du pays. Ces étrangers, d'origine européenne, africaine ou asiatique, donnent à la France d'aujourd'hui un visage véritablement multi-culturel et multi-ethnique.

---

* En France, les **Catholiques** vont **à l'église**, les **Musulmans** *(Moslems)* vont **à la mosquée**, les **Protestants** vont **au temple**, les **Juifs** vont **à la synagogue**.

---

au cours de = pendant   **un siècle** = 100 ans   **terre d'asile** *land of asylum*   **main d'oeuvre** *labor, manpower*   **occidentale** *Western*

Teaching Strategy: Projects

Immigration policy is often a complicated, emotionally charged topic for discussion. It is important that students learn to accept and respect divergent opinions during class debate. Be sure to review rules of appropriate behavior before group work or class discussion. Divide the class into groups and assign a short research project. The project should focus on recent newspaper and magazine articles on immigration in both France and the U.S. Ask students to comment on similarities and differences and write a short description of the articles they read.

Le Maghreb et les Maghrébins

Maghreb est un mot arabe qui signifie *le pays où le soleil se couche.*° Autrefois, le Maghreb représentait l'extrémité occidentale du monde musulman. Le Maghreb désigne les trois pays d'Afrique du Nord: l'**Algérie**, le **Maroc** et la **Tunisie**. Les Maghrébins sont les habitants de ces pays.

La majorité des Maghrébins sont arabes et musulmans. Leur religion est l'**Islam**. Un grand nombre de Maghrébins (environ deux millions) ont émigré en France où ils représentent le groupe le plus important d'étrangers.

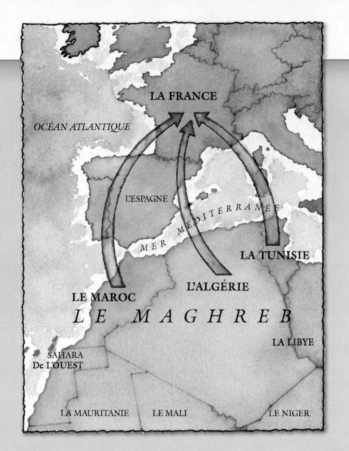

OCÉAN ATLANTIQUE

LA FRANCE

L'ESPAGNE

MER MÉDITERRANÉE

LA TUNISIE

L'ALGÉRIE

LE MAROC

L E   M A G H R E B

LA LIBYE

SAHARA
De L'OUEST

LA MAURITANIE   LE MALI   LE NIGER

LES ÉTRANGERS EN FRANCE

Algériens	700 000	Espagnols	250 000
Marocains	650 000	Tunisiens	240 000
Portugais	580 000	Turcs	240 000
Italiens	320 000	Vietnamiens, Laotiens et Cambodgiens	170 000

se couche *sets*

The Arabs of North Africa are the descendants of the conquerors who came from the Arabian peninsula in the 8th century. However, not all those who live in the Maghreb are Arabs. There are also the Berbers whose ancestors were living in the Maghreb centuries before the Arab invasion. Now both Arabs and Berbers are Muslim.

■ **Note linguistique**

In French-speaking African countries you might hear the following idioms:

gréver (Sénégal) = faire grève
avoir les dents dehors (Congo) = rire
un payé-cousu (Cameroun) = un vêtement acheté en prêt-à-porter
faire l'avion par terre (Côte-d'Ivoire) = se dépêcher, marcher vite

Note linguistique

Le mot **beur** est un néologisme dérivé du **verlan** qui est un argot codé dans lequel on inverse les syllabes des mots.

Par exemple:

l'envers → **verlan**

bizarre → **zarbi**

pourri → **ripou**

Le mot **beur** vient d'une double transformation du mot arabe en **verlan**:

arabe → **rabeu**

rebeu → **beur**

La beurette (féminin de beur) est une jeune fille d'origine maghrébine, née en France.

Additional Information

L'aïd célèbre la fin du Ramadan.

Note culturelle

Mahomet, le fondateur de l'Islam, considérait les patriarches et les prophètes de la Bible commes ses précurseurs.

■ Djamila ou le dilemme de l'intégration

Djamila, 17 ans, est une jeune «beur». Cela signifie qu'elle est fille d'immigrés maghrébins. Ses parents sont venus d'Algérie il y a vingt ans, et elle, elle est née à Marseille. Elle a la nationalité française, parle français, va dans un lycée français où presque tous ses copains sont d'origine française. Après le bac, elle compte aller à l'université et un jour devenir vétérinaire. Est-ce qu'elle se sent vraiment française? Ou bien, est-elle restée algérienne?

Djamila explique son dilemme.

«Fondamentalement, je suis française, mais je suis différente parce que ma famille est différente. Mes parents sont arabes et musulmans pratiquants.° Cela ne signifie pas seulement qu'ils célèbrent l'aïd* et qu'ils ne mangent pas de porc et ne boivent pas d'alcool. Cela signifie aussi qu'ils ont une conception différente de la vie. Mon père, par exemple, ne veut pas que je sorte seule avec un garçon, alors que mes copines françaises n'ont pas besoin de demander la permission. C'est parfois une situation difficile, mais j'obéis parce que j'ai beaucoup de respect et d'admiration pour mon père. C'est un homme honnête qui a travaillé très dur pour donner un minimum de confort à sa famille.

* **L'aïd:** Cette fête musulmane, aussi appelée «fête du mouton», rappelle le sacrifice d'Abraham et d'Isaac.

■ L'influence maghrébine en France

La présence de plus de deux millions de Maghrébins en France a modifié et enrichi la culture française dans beaucoup de domaines. Par exemple:

■ Religion

Aujourd'hui, l'**Islam** est la deuxième religion pratiquée en France, après la religion catholique et avant les religions protestantes et juives. Il y a 6000 mosquées en France et 5 millions de Musulmans.

■ Cuisine

Le **couscous**, plat traditionnel d'Afrique du Nord, est devenu un plat très populaire en France. C'est un plat de semoule° cuit à la vapeur° et servi avec des légumes, de la viande et une sauce très pimentée.° Pour manger un bon couscous, on peut aller dans les restaurants marocains, algériens ou tunisiens. Si on veut manger un couscous chez soi, il suffit d'acheter une boîte de couscous au supermarché.

D'autres spécialités maghrébines sont les gâteaux au miel,° les gâteaux aux amandes° appelés «cornes° de gazelle» et le thé à la menthe.°

■ Vocabulaire

La langue française d'aujourd'hui contient un certain nombre de mots d'origine arabe, comme:

un toubib	*un médecin*
un bled	*un petit village, généralement isolé et sans intérêt*
un méchouï	*une grande fête où on mange généralement du mouton rôti*
avoir la baraka	*avoir de la chance*
c'est kif-kif	*c'est la même chose*

pratiquants = qui observent les préceptes de leur religion **semoule** *semolina* **cuit à la vapeur** *steamed* **pimentée** *hot, spicy* **miel** *honey* **amandes** *almonds* **cornes** *horns* **menthe** *mint*

«Mes parents ont la nostalgie de leur pays. Parfois, ils parlent de rentrer en Algérie et ils voudraient que je vienne avec eux. Je suis allée plusieurs fois en Algérie où nous avons de la famille, mais là-bas, je ne me sens pas chez moi. Chez moi, c'est en France. C'est là où j'habite et c'est là où je vais faire ma vie. Parce que je suis intégrée, je sais que je n'aurai pas de difficulté à trouver un bon emploi. Pourtant, il y a des problèmes. Par exemple, quand je sors avec mes copines beurs et que nous parlons arabe entre nous, j'ai parfois l'impression qu'on nous regarde de travers.° À ce moment-là, je me sens alors algérienne, et fière° d'être différente.»

La grande mosquée de Paris

Quelques prénoms arabes

FILLES

Aïcha	Malika	Soraya
Djamila	Nacera	Yasmina
Farida	Ourida	Zeïna
Leïla	Sakinna	Zohra

GARÇONS

Ahmed	Latif	Omar
Ali	Malek	Rachid
Farid	Malik	Saïd
Hacine	Mohamed	Toufik
Ismaïl	Mouloud	Youssef
Kateb	Mustapha	

Les cinq principes de la religion musulmane

La religion musulmane est l'une des religions les plus importantes du monde. Elle est pratiquée par plus d'un milliard° de personnes, principalement au Moyen Orient, au Pakistan, en Indonésie, en Afrique du Nord et en Afrique occidentale.

La religion musulmane a cinq principes fondamentaux. Ces principes sont assez simples.

- Il y a un seul Dieu,° **Allah**.
- Chaque jour, le Musulman doit faire ses prières° cinq fois, tourné dans la direction de la **Mecque,**° ville natale du prophète Mahomet, et ville sainte° de l'islam.
- Le Musulman doit être charitable. Chaque année, il doit donner un pourcentage de sa fortune aux pauvres.

- Chaque année, le Musulman doit faire le jeûne° du **Ramadan**. Pendant les 30 jours du Ramadan, il doit s'abstenir totalement de manger et de boire du matin jusqu'au soir.
- Durant sa vie, le Musulman doit aller une fois en pèlerinage° à la Mecque. Ce pèlerinage s'appelle le **hadj**.

Horaire des prières

Al-Fajr	4 h 27
Ach-Chrouq	5 h 58
Ad-Dohr	12 h 36
Al-Asr	16 h 10
Al-Maghrib	19 h 08
Al-Ichaa	20 h 37

---

de travers = *d'une manière étrange* **fière** *proud* **un milliard** *one billion* **Dieu** *God* **prières** *prayers*
Mecque *Mecca (today in Saudi Arabia)* **sainte** *holy* **jeûne** *fast* **pèlerinage** *pilgrimage*

■ Realia Note

Whereas standard Muslim practice requires five daily prayers, there are often optional prayers. The fundamental prayers, as they appear in this newspaper announcement, are the following:

Al-Fajr: morning (sunrise)
Ad-Dohr: noon
Al-Asr: mid-afternoon
Al-Maghrib: evening
Al-Ichaa: night

On this particular day, **Ach-Chrouq** was listed an additional optional prayer.

Notes culturelles

- Islam is important in many areas of the French-speaking world: Algeria, Morocco, Tunisia, and several countries of West Africa (see p. 375). It is presented here for general information about the culture of these regions.
- Le prophète **Mahomet** (570–632) a fondé la religion musulmane en 622, l'an zéro du calendrier musulman.

- Le livre sacré des Musulmans s'appelle **le Coran** et est écrit en arabe. Il contient la parole d'Allah telle qu'elle a été transmise à Mahomet par l'archange Gabriel.
- Dans le calendrier musulman, le mois de **Ramadan** est le mois où le Coran a été révélé à Mahomet.

■ Additional Information

- **S.O.S Racisme** was founded in 1984 by Harlem Jean-Philippe Désir.
- **S.O.S Racisme**
  28, rue des Petites Ecuries
  75010 Paris
  Monthly publication: *La lettre de S.O.S. Racisme*
- **MRAP (Mouvement contre le Racisme et pour l'Amitié entre les Peuples**
  89, rue Oberkampf
  75001 Paris
  Monthly publication: *Différences*
- *We are the World* was written in 1985 by Michael Jackson and Lionel Richie, and sung by a group of popular artists.

■ SOS Racisme

Les travailleurs immigrés qui viennent en France apportent avec eux une culture spécifique. Ils ont leurs coutumes, leurs traditions, leur religion, leur langue, leur musique, leur cuisine, leur façon de s'habiller . . . Ces immigrés sont généralement heureux d'habiter en France, même si les conditions de travail et de logement sont souvent difficiles.

De leur côté,° la majorité des Français, les jeunes en particulier, acceptent assez bien les immigrés même si leur culture est différente de la culture traditionnelle française. D'autres, au contraire, ont beaucoup de difficultés à accepter la réalité multi-culturelle de la France d'aujourd'hui. Ils ne comprennent pas que cette réalité est irréversible. Certains pensent que les immigrés sont responsables des problèmes comme le chômage,° la délinquance, ou la drogue.° Des extrémistes voudraient même renvoyer° les immigrés dans leur pays d'origine. En France, comme dans d'autres pays européens, le racisme et la discrimination contre les immigrés sont devenus des problèmes importants à résoudre.°

Comment combattre le racisme? Un jour, il y a dix ans, des copains d'origine diverse discutaient justement° de leurs différences. «Nous sommes blancs, noirs, marron, bronzés!° Nous sommes copains depuis des années et nous le resterons, parce que nous disons oui à la solidarité et non au racisme.» Ce jour-là, un grand mouvement, **SOS Racisme**, était né.

De père martiniquais et de mère alsacienne, **Harlem Désir**, le fondateur et premier président de **SOS Racisme**, est bien le symbole même de la France multi-ethnique. «Chez nous, dit-il, on respecte l'individu et on écoute les autres.»

Les activités de **SOS Racisme** sont très nombreuses: aider les immigrés, trouver des avocats pour les victimes de la discrimination, combattre le racisme sous toutes ses formes, et, plus généralement, changer les attitudes et faire accepter le droit° à la différence. Pour mobiliser l'opinion, **SOS Racisme** organise des campagnes, des marches, et surtout de grands concerts publics où les jeunes viennent manifester leur solidarité au mouvement.

L'emblème° de **SOS Racisme** est une main ouverte, bleue, rouge ou orange, avec un slogan «Touche pas à mon pote!»° Ce slogan signifie «Nous sommes différents, mais nous sommes frères et soeurs. Si tu attaques l'un de nous, nous sommes là pour le défendre et le protéger.» Cette petite main symbolique a eu un succès extraordinaire, non seulement en France, mais aussi en Suisse et en Belgique. Des dizaines de milliers de jeunes, surtout des lycéens, portent cet emblème sur leurs vêtements. C'est une façon de dire à tout le monde: «Je suis pour la justice, pour l'intégration et contre le racisme et la discrimination.»

Une manifestation, SOS Racisme

---

de leur côté *as far as they are concerned*   **chômage** *unemployment*   **drogue** *drug addition*   **renvoyer** *to send back*   **résoudre** *to solve*
justement *as a matter of fact*   **bronzés** *light brown*   **droit** *right*   **emblème** = *logo*   **pote = copain** *(slang)*

Teaching Strategy

Divide the class into pairs. Each pair will role-play an interview between a journalist and **Harlem Désir** twice, allowing each person to play both roles. Students should use their imaginations, asking questions about **S.O.S. Racisme** and its creation, etc.

DOCUMENTS *Éthiopie*

Éthiopie

La chanson *Éthiopie** est chantée sur la musique universellement connue de *We are the world*. Cette chanson exprime la solidarité du peuple français avec les peuples les moins favorisés de la terre° et en particulier avec le peuple éthiopien, victime de la famine et de la guerre civile. Les chanteurs français les plus célèbres l'ont chantée dans de grands concerts publics organisés pour aider les enfants d'Éthiopie.

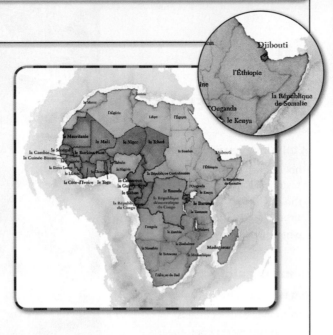

Ils n'ont jamais vu la pluie
Ils ne savent même plus sourire°
Il n'y a même plus de larmes°
Dans leurs yeux si grands

Les enfants d'Éthiopie
Embarqués sur un navire°
Qui n'a plus ni voiles° ni rames°
Attendent le vent.

> Loin du coeur et loin des yeux
> De nos villes, de nos banlieues
> L'Éthiopie meurt peu à peu
> Peu à peu

> Rien° qu'une chanson pour eux
> Pour ne plus fermer les yeux
> C'est beaucoup et c'est bien peu
> C'est bien peu.

Mais à chaque enfant qui tombe
Qui meurt loin des yeux de l'occident°
Notre ciel devient plus sombre°
Et notre avenir moins grand

Sur cette terre de sécheresse°
Ne fleurissent° que les tombes°
Malgré° toutes nos richesses
Leur soleil nous fait de l'ombre.°
> *(refrain)*
> Donnons-leur des lendemains°
> En échange de rien
> Donnons-leur la vie
> Seulement la vie

Chez nous, la forêt succombe°
Là-bas, le désert avance°
Plus vite que la colombe°
Dans un ciel d'indifférence

Les enfants du tiers-monde°
N'ont que l'ombre d'une chance
Chaque jour, chaque seconde
Faisons taire° le silence.

* L'Ethiopie est un pays d'Afrique, voisin de la Somalie.

terre *earth* **sourire** *to smile* **larmes** *tears* **navire** = *bateau* **voiles** *sails* **rames** *oars* **rien que** = *seulement* **l'occident** *Western world* **sombre** = *noir*
sécheresse *drought* **fleurissent** *blossom* **tombes** *tombstones* **malgré** *in spite of* **nous fait de l'ombre** *casts a shadow on us* **lendemains** *tomorrows*
succombe = *meurt* **avance** = *progresse* **colombe** *dove* **tiers-monde** *Third World* **faisons taire** = *mettons fin à*

Teaching Strategy

Divide the class into groups. Ask each group to brainstorm ideas for a logo and motto (in French) to promote peace and tolerance. Each group should choose one of the suggested ideas and complete its logo and motto for display.

MAIN THEME
Cities and City Life

COMMUNICATION
- Making a date
- Discussing city life
- Describing your neighborhood
- Explaining where one lives

CULTURES
- Learning about French neighborhoods
- Learning about street artists in France
- Comparing French paintings

CONNECTIONS
- Judging the validity of a self-quiz
- Supporting an opinion with ideas from a story
- Connecting to Language Arts: Brainstorming activities for posters to promote tourism
- Connecting to Math: Graphing the results of a survey
- Connecting to Science/Health: Investigating science or technology museums and exhibits
- Connecting to Social Studies: Interviewing people about community activities
- Connecting to Art/Music: Finding out about local museums and concerts
- Connecting to Technology: Finding out about technology used in community activities
- Connecting to Language Arts: Writing a poem about one's city or town

COMPARISONS
- Using cognates to guess the main idea
- Comparing the imperfect and pluperfect in French and English
- Comparing the conditional and past conditional in French and English
- Comparing French and U.S. cities.

COMMUNITIES
- Preparing tourism posters
- Examining city vs. country life
- Exploring career choices

Unité 8

En ville

THÈME ET OBJECTIFS

Culture

In this unit, you will discover . . .

- how French cities developed historically and what they look like
- the advantages and disadvantages of urban life
- what types of street artists you might see in Paris or other large cities

Communication

You will learn how . . .

- to arrange to meet friends
- to explain where people live
- to describe your neighborhood

Langue

You will learn how . . .

- to make wishes or suggestions
- to formulate polite requests
- to narrate past actions in sequence
- to indicate what you would do in certain circumstances

DIGITAL FRENCH my.hrw.com
ONLINE STUDENT EDITION with...

performance)**space**

News + **Networking**

@**HOMETUTOR**

- Audio Resources
- Video Resources
- Interactive Flashcards
- WebQuest

PRACTICE FRENCH WITH HOLT MCDOUGAL APPS!

DIGITAL FRENCH

TEACHER TOOLS
- Teacher One Stop
- Interactive Whiteboard Lessons
- Generate Success Rubric Generator and Interactive Graphic Organizers
- Examview Test Generator

ALSO AVAILABLE...
- Online Workbook
- French InterActive Reader
- @HomeTutor
- DVD Program
- Power Presentations
- Interactive Flashcards

FRENCH ON THE GO!
- Performance Space
- Holt McDougal French Apps
- Discovering French Today eTextbook

◆ LES VILLES FRANÇAISES ◆

L es Français sont des citadins°. Aujourd'hui, 90% de la population habite en zone urbaine et presque° la moitié° dans des villes de plus de 100.000 habitants. L'urbanisme est peut-être un phénomène relativement récent, mais les grandes villes françaises sont très anciennes. Marseille et Nice ont été fondées au sixième siècle avant Jésus-Christ par des marins° grecs. Paris, Lyon, Bordeaux, Toulouse, Strasbourg, Rouen et Tours étaient déjà des centres urbains à l'époque romaine, il y a 2000 ans.

À l'origine, les villes ont été créées autour d'un point stratégique important: un port naturel, le croisement° de deux routes, le passage d'une rivière . . .

◆ Au Moyen Age, on a construit° un château et des remparts pour protéger ces villes. ——————

◆ Quand les villes ont grandi° à partir° du XVIIᵉ siècle, les remparts ont été détruits°. Les villes se sont alors développées autour d'un nouveau centre, ou le long° de larges avenues, suivant° un plan d'urbanisme bien établi.

◆ Avec la révolution industrielle au XIXᵉ siècle, de vastes banlieues industrielles se sont développées concentriquement autour des villes. ——————

◆ Au XXᵉ siècle et particulièrement après 1960, les possibilités de travail ont attiré° des millions d'habitants de la campagne vers les grandes villes. Cet exode rural a nécessité la construction d'énormes quartiers résidentiels dans la banlieue de ces villes. ——————

L'histoire des villes françaises explique leur géographie. (Suite à la page 310-311)

1300 200.000 HAB

1650 600.000 HAB

1850 1.000.000 HAB

1960 2.800.000 HAB

et vous?

Faites un bref historique de la ville où vous habitez ou d'une grande ville des États-Unis. Vous pouvez mentionner . . .
• quand cette ville a été fondée: par qui? et pourquoi?
• comment elle s'est développée
• combien d'habitants elle a aujourd'hui et quelles sont ses activités principales

NOM FRANÇAIS	NOM LATIN
Paris	LUTETIA
Lyon	LUGDUNUM
Marseille	MASSILIA
Bordeaux	BURDIGALA
Toulouse	TOLOSA
Nice	NICAEA
Strasbourg	ARGENTORATUM
Rouen	ROTOMAGUS
Tours	CAESARODUNUM

citadins *city people* **presque** *almost* **moitié** *half* **marins** *sailors*
croisement *crossing* ***construire** *to build* **grandi** *grew in size*
à partir *beginning in* ***détruire** *to destroy* **le long de** *along*
suivant *according to* **attiré** *attracted*

INFO MAGAZINE

ASSESSMENT IN UNIT RESOURCE BOOK

Print Resources
• **Workbook TE/PE**
• *Activités pour tous* **TE/PE**
• *Lectures pour tous*
• **Unit Resource Book**
  Audioscripts
  Video Activities
  Videoscripts

Achievement Tests
• **Quizzes, Unit 8**
• **Unit Test 8**
• **Reading and Culture Tests**
• **Assessment Answer Key**

Proficiency Tests
• **Listening Comprehension**
• **Speaking Performance**
• **Writing Performance**
• **Portfolio Assessment**

INFO MAGAZINE

Theme: French cities

Reading Strategy: Reading for information, scanning

RESOURCES

TECHNOLOGY
Teacher One Stop
🖥 **Projectable Transparencies**
  1, *La France*
  1(o), *La France*
  6, *Paris*
  Transparency Copymasters, pp. A5–A6, A13–A14

■ **Interdisciplinary Connections**

Faites une liste de dix grandes villes américaines et indiquez quand et par qui elles ont été fondées.

21ˢᵗ CENTURY SKILLS

• **Communication:** SE: pp. 303, 304, 306, 307, 309, 311, 312, 313, 315, 317, 321, 323, 332, 333; TE: pp. 304–307, 309, 310, 311, 312, 313, 318, 319, 321, 323, 324, 333, 339, 343
• **Critical Thinking and Problem Solving:** TE: pp. 305, 310, 311, 328, 330, 333, 339, 340
• **Creativity and Innovation:** SE: pp. 307, 332, 333; TE: pp. 304, 305, 306, 307, 308, 309, 310, 312, 313, 318, 319, 321, 324, 339
• **Information Literacy:** TE: pp. 302, 310, 325
• **Technology Literacy:** TE: pp. 305, 310, 325, 333, 342, 343
• **Flexibility and Adaptability:** TE: pp. 305, 310, 312, 325
• **Initiative and Self-Direction:** TE: pp. 310, 312, 325
• **Social and Cross-Cultural Skills:** TE: pp. 310, 340
• **Productivity and Accountability:** TE: pp. 306, 308, 310, 319, 321
• **Leadership and Responsibility:** TE: pp. 325

Unité 8 303

VILLE OU CAMPAGNE?

■ **Notes culturelles**

The following U.S. cities have French origins:

- **Detroit,** Michigan, was founded by French explorer **Sieur Antoine de la Mothe Cadillac** in 1701.
- **Chicago,** Illinois, was a fur-trading post founded by **Jean-Baptiste Point du Sable** after the site was visited by French explorer **Robert Cavelier, Sieur de la Salle,** in 1682.
- **Fort Wayne,** Indiana, was a French fort in 1680.
- **Memphis,** Tennessee, was a French fort by 1797.
- **Minneapolis,** Minnesota, started when the site was discovered by the French missionary **Louis Hennepin** in 1680. Hennepin also "discovered" Niagara Falls.
- **Mobile,** Alabama, was settled by the brothers **Pierre** and **Jean-Baptiste Lemoyne** in 1702. It was the capital of French Louisiana between 1710 and 1719.
- **New Orleans,** Louisiana, was founded by **Jean-Baptiste Lemoyne, Sieur de Bienville** in 1718.
- **Saint Louis,** Missouri, was a French fur-trading post in 1764. It became American when bought as part of the Louisiana Purchase in 1803.

Êtes-vous un citadin ou un villageois?
Êtes-vous plutôt fait(e) pour la vie en ville ou pour
la vie à la campagne?
Pour déterminer cela, évaluez les avantages et les inconvénients
des villes. Donnez une note positive de **0 (pas important)** à
+5 (très important) à chacun des avantages.
Donnez une note négative de **0 (pas important)** à **-5 (très important)**
à chacun des inconvénients. °

⊕ AVANTAGES

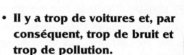

- **Il y a beaucoup d'endroits où on peut aller.**
  On peut aller au ciné, dans les magasins, aux restaurants . . .

- **Il y a beaucoup de choses intéressantes à faire.**
  On peut voir des expositions, assister à des événements culturels . . .

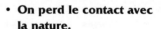

- **On peut faire la connaissance de beaucoup de gens d'origines° différentes.**
  Dans les villes, il y a une grande diversité ethnique, culturelle et sociale.

- **Les villes sont généralement animées.**
  On ne s'ennuie° jamais parce qu'il y a toujours de la vie et du mouvement.

INCONVÉNIENTS ⊖

- **Il y a trop de voitures et, par conséquent, trop de bruit et trop de pollution.**
  On ne peut pas se promener tranquillement.°

- **On perd le contact avec la nature.**
  Il n'y a pas assez d'arbres, pas assez de plantes, pas assez de fleurs.

- **Pour beaucoup de gens, la vie est difficile.**
  Pour cela, les gens des villes sont souvent stressés et irritables.

- **Il y a beaucoup d'inégalités sociales.**
  Il y a trop de gens pauvres et sans-abri.°

inconvénients *drawbacks* **origines** *backgrounds* **s'ennuie** *gets bored* **tranquillement** *safely* ° **sans-abri** *homeless people*

Teaching Strategy

Divide the class into pairs. Have each pair construct an interview based on the information/survey from pp. 303–305. The interviewer should ask questions of the interviewee who will give answers based on the information presented, or on personal opinion.

INTERPRÉTATION

Faites le total des points positifs et négatifs.
Quel total obtenez-vous?

de 15 à 20 points

Vous êtes certainement un(e) citadin(e), mais vous ignorez les charmes de la campagne. Un jour, vous devriez y faire un tour.

de 5 à 14 points

Vous êtes une personne optimiste et vous aimez la proximité des gens. Vous appréciez les avantages de la vie en ville. Pour cela, vous en minimisez les inconvénients.

de 4 à -4 points

Vous êtes une personne réaliste. Vous êtes conscient(e) des problèmes des grandes villes, mais vous les tolérez.

de -5 à -14 points

Vous n'aimez pas vivre là où il y a trop de gens. Vous préférez le calme et la tranquillité.

de -15 à -20 points

La ville n'est évidemment pas faite pour vous. Mais ne soyez pas trop idéaliste! La campagne aussi a ses problèmes.

INTERVIEW DANS LA RUE

Nous sommes place de Jaude à Clermont-Ferrand, un samedi après-midi.

Une journaliste de «La Montagne», le journal local, interviewe les gens qui passent. Elle parle maintenant à un homme d'une cinquantaine d'années qui porte un sac à provisions.°

— Bonjour, Monsieur. Vous êtes d'ici?
— Non, je suis de la campagne.
— Qu'est-ce qui vous attire° à Clermont? Le cinéma? les restaurants? les cafés?
— Non, je n'y vais jamais.
— Pouvez-vous me dire alors pourquoi vous venez ici?
— Ben, vous voyez, je viens pour faire mes courses.
— Il n'y a pas de supermarché chez vous?
— Si, mais en ville il y a un plus grand choix.
— Vous venez souvent à Clermont-Ferrand?
— Oui, toutes les semaines.
— Vous aimez cette ville?
— Pas tellement.°
— Pourquoi donc?
— Ben, il y a trop de circulation,° trop de bruit… Et puis, les gens sont pressés° et malpolis.°
— Alors, pourquoi est-ce que vous ne restez pas chez vous?
— Parce que chez moi, c'est trop calme. Alors, je viens en ville pour trouver un peu d'animation.

sac à provisions *shopping bag* **attire** *attracts* **pas tellement** *not that much* **circulation** *traffic* **pressés** *in a hurry* **malpolis** = impolis

■ **Photo Notes**
• La **FNAC** is a chain of stores that sell media-related goods: books, cameras, CDs, computers, videos…
• **C&A** is a chain of department stores.

■ **Note culturelle**
Clermont-Ferrand is located in the region of Auvergne. Its inhabitants are called **les Clermontois.** The city was founded by the Romans. In 1095 Pope Urban II preached the first crusade in Clermont-Ferrand.

■ **Irregular Verb**
(See Appendix C)
obtenir is conjugated like **tenir**

Teaching Strategy

Assign these activities to pairs of students:
• **Ma ville**
Établissez une liste par ordre d'importance des avantages et des inconvénients d'habiter votre ville. Comparez votre liste avec celle de votre partenaire.
• **Une brochure touristique**
Avec votre partenaire, préparez une brochure où vous expliquez aux touristes français les avantages de visiter votre ville. Soyez spécifiques. Par exemple, décrivez en détail les endroits intéressants, les choses à faire …
• **Expansion questions**
Êtes-vous d'accord avec le résultat du test? Pourquoi? Si vous n'êtes pas d'accord, quel devrait être votre résultat d'après vous?

Unité 8 305

■ **Teaching Note**
To review reflexive verbs, see **Unité 1**, p. 44.

■ **Note linguistique**
In France, you might also hear: **d'acc.!** (instead of **d'accord**) and **O.K.**

■ **Teaching Strategy**
Have students write a group story with each person contributing two sentences. The premise of the story should be that students met their friend/ friends somewhere. Encourage students to be original and creative, and to use as much vocabulary from pp. 306–307 as possible. At least one of each student's sentences should include a vocabulary word. As the story is created, a secretary will copy it onto the board. Switch secretaries after several sentences.

306 Unité 8

Un rendez-vous en ville

> Qu'est-ce que tu fais samedi?
>
> Est-ce que tu veux voir une exposition avec moi?
>
> Je suis libre.
>
> À deux heures et demie.
>
> Bonne idée! À quelle heure est-ce qu'on va se retrouver?

COMMENT SE DONNER RENDEZ-VOUS

— Qu'est-ce que tu fais samedi?
  Je suis libre.

— Est-ce que tu veux | aller au ciné
  voir une exposition
  prendre un pot
  faire un tour en ville | avec moi?

| **prendre un pot** *to have something to drink in a café* |

— Où est-ce qu'on va **se donner rendez-vous?**
  Chez moi.   **Devant** *(in front of)* le ciné.
  Au café «Le Bistro».   **À côté de** *(next to)* la poste.
                             En face de *(across from)* la librairie.

— À quelle heure est-ce qu'on va | **se retrouver?**
                                   se rencontrer?
  À deux heures et demie.

— Alors, | d'accord! | **À samedi**, deux heures et demie devant le ciné.
          | **entendu** *(agreed).* | *(See you on Saturday . . .)*

① *Créa-dialogue: Une invitation*

Il y a un(e) nouvel(le) élève français(e) dans votre classe. Invitez le/la. Composez le dialogue avec votre partenaire qui va jouer le rôle de l'élève.

— Ask your friend what he/she is doing on a date of your choice..	⇄	(He/she is free.)
— Propose something interesting to do.	⇄	(He/she accepts.)
— Ask where you can meet.	⇄	(He/she selects a place close to the activity you proposed.)
— Ask at what time you are going to meet.	⇄	(He/she chooses a time.)
— Say that you will see him/her at the time and place you have agreed on.	→	

Teaching Suggestion: DVD Program

In the Unit 8 *Vidéo-drame: Un rendez-vous en ville,* students will have a chance to observe Mélanie and Nicolas make arrangements to meet with Guillaume, Mélanie's boyfriend. Make sure students pay close attention to the reflexive verbs like **se retrouver** and **se donner rendez-vous**.

Differentiation

Sequential Pair strong and at-risk students. Have them carry out the dialogs on page 307. Ask them to write down the dialogs created. Then ask them to review their dialog out loud with their partner before performing it for the class.

@HOMETUTOR
my.hrw.com

LES RENCONTRES ET LES RENDEZ-VOUS

On peut	**rencontrer** (meet by chance, run into) **faire la connaissance de** (meet for the first time)	**quelqu'un**.

On peut	**sortir avec** **avoir un rendez-vous avec** **donner rendez-vous à** (make a date)	**quelqu'un.**

On peut	**se donner rendez-vous** (agree to meet) **se rencontrer** (meet each other) **se retrouver** (meet each other)	**quelque part** (somewhere).

SUPPLEMENTARY VOCABULARY

aller boire un verre *to go have a drink*
faire les magasins *to go shopping*
faire du lèche-vitrine *to go window shopping*
(se) présenter à *to introduce (oneself) to*
croiser quelqu'un *to pass by someone*
tomber sur quelqu'un *to come across/meet someone*

■ Photo note
The restaurant pictured is called **La Bergerie**, which means *sheepfold*. The two young girls are standing in front of **un kiosque à journaux** (*newsstand*).

■ Looking Ahead
The reciprocal use of reflexive verbs is reviewed and practiced in Unit 9.

Conversations libres

Avec votre partenaire, choisissez l'une des situations suivantes. Composez ensemble un dialogue correspondant à cette situation et jouez ce dialogue en classe.

Digital **performance space**

1 Une jeune fille amoureuse

Jérôme veut téléphoner à sa camarade de classe Véronique. C'est Sylvie, la soeur de Véronique, qui répond. Sylvie, qui est secrètement amoureuse de (*in love with*) Jérôme, essaie d'obtenir un rendez-vous avec lui.
Rôles: Jérôme / Sylvie

3 Rendez-vous

Philippe téléphone à Juliette pour voir une exposition. Juliette a déjà vu cette exposition et propose autre chose.
Rôles: Philippe / Juliette

2 Au Jardin du Luxembourg

Une étudiante américaine est au Jardin du Luxembourg (un parc public à Paris). Un étudiant français engage la conversation. Il veut inviter la jeune Américaine à un concert de rock à la Villette. D'abord la jeune fille refuse poliment. L'étudiant français insiste. Elle finit par accepter l'invitation.
Rôles: l'étudiant français / l'étudiante américaine

4 Une amie de passage (*A visiting friend*)

Marc téléphone souvent à sa cousine. Aujourd'hui, elle n'est pas chez elle et c'est une amie de passage qui répond. Marc s'excuse, puis il continue la conversation. Dans cette conversation il essaie de savoir ce que cette jeune fille aime faire. Finalement, il propose un rendez-vous. La jeune fille accepte, puis refuse.
Rôles: Marc / la jeune fille

Teaching Strategy
Divide the class into pairs and give them the following scenario:
Un rendez-vous
Votre camarade français(e) et vous, vous avez décidé de sortir ensemble ce week-end.

Décidez …
• d'une activité à faire
• d'un endroit pour le rendez-vous
• d'une heure
Composez et jouez le dialogue correspondant avec votre partenaire qui va jouer le rôle de votre camarade français(e).

Langue et Communication

RESOURCES

PRINT
Workbook, pp. 77–79, 152
Unit 8 Resource Book, Partie 1
Audioscripts

AUDIO
Audio Program
CD 8, Tracks 5–6

TECHNOLOGY
@HomeTutor

■ Notes linguistiques

• **Attention:** **si** becomes **s'** before **il** or **ils** only. **S'il venait. S'ils savaient. Si elle venait. Si elles savaient.**

■ Réponses: Activité 1

1. —...si on allait dans une pizzeria?
   —Hm, je n'aime pas le pizza. Si on allait plutôt dans un restaurant chinois?
   —Bonne idée! Allons-y!
2. —... si on faisait un tour dans le centre?
   —Hm, je suis trop fatigué(e). Si on allait plutôt au ciné?
   —Bonne idée. Allons au ciné.
3. —... si on allait voir une exposition?
   —Hm, il fait très beau aujourd'hui. Si on se promenait plutôt dans le parc?
   —Bonne idée. Allons au parc.
4. —... si on allait dans les magasins?
   —Hm, je n'ai pas d'argent. Si on jouait plutôt aux jeux vidéo chez moi?
   —Écoute, je n'ai pas envie de jouer aux jeux vidéo. Si je te prêtais dix euros?
   —D'accord. Allons dans les magasins.

A La construction *si* + imparfait

Note the use of the IMPERFECT in the following sentences:

Ah, si j'**étais** riche...	*Oh, if only I **were** rich...*
Ah, si mon frère me **prêtait** sa voiture...	*Oh, if only my brother **would lend me** his car...*
Dis, Alain, **si on allait** en ville?	*Hey, Alain, **what about going** downtown?*
Dis, Sophie, **si tu m'aidais?**	*Hey, Sophie, **what about helping me?***

Révision p. R5
Formation de l'imparfait

To express a WISH or to make a SUGGESTION, the French often use the construction:

> **si** + IMPERFECT

B Le plus-que-parfait

As in English, the PLUPERFECT **(le plus-que-parfait)** is used to describe what people HAD DONE or WHAT HAD HAPPENED before another past action or event.

Cet été, j'ai visité Québec.	*This summer I visited Quebec City.*
L'année d'avant, **j'avais visité** Montréal.	*The year before, **I had visited** Montreal.*
Quand nous sommes arrivés à la gare, le train **était parti.**	*When we arrived at the station, the train **had left.***

The PLUPERFECT is formed as follows:

> IMPERFECT of **avoir** or **être** + PAST PARTICIPLE

INFINITIVE	voyager	aller	s'amuser
PLUPERFECT	j' **avais voyagé**	j' **étais allé(e)**	je **m'étais amusé(e)**
	tu **avais voyagé**	tu **étais allé(e)**	tu **t'étais amusé(e)**
	il/elle **avait voyagé**	il/elle **était allé(e)**	il/elle **s'était amusé(e)**
	nous **avions voyagé**	nous **étions allé(e)s**	nous **nous étions amusé(e)s**
	vous **aviez voyagé**	vous **étiez allé(e)(s)**	vous **vous étiez amusé(e)(s)**
	ils/elles **avaient voyagé**	ils/elles **étaient allé(e)s**	ils/elles **s'étaient amusé(e)s**
NEGATIVE	je **n'avais pas voyagé**	je **n'étais pas allé(e)**	je **ne m'étais pas amusé(e)**
INTERROGATIVE	est-ce que tu **avais voyagé?** **avais-tu voyagé?**	tu **étais allé(e)?** **étais-tu allé(e)?**	tu **t'étais amusé(e)?** **t'étais-tu amusé(e)?**

→ In the pluperfect, the agreement rules for the past participle are the same as in the passé composé.

J'ai vu Pauline ce matin.   Je l'avais vue hier aussi.

J'ai développé les photos que j'avais prises cet été.

Teaching Strategy: Warm-Up

Have students imagine that they are Cinderella **(Cendrillon)**, Pinochio, or Dumbo, and express a wish using the imperfect. Next, have them make a suggestion to one of their friends, to their parents or to the principal of the school using the imperfect.

Differentiation

Cumulative Review the construction of the **imparfait**, writing out a verb on the board. Then, give a verb stem and ask students to generate the endings. For each verb, ask students to generate a **si**-clause sentence.

1 En ville 💬

Vous rencontrez votre partenaire en ville. Suggérez-lui de faire quelque chose avec vous (colonne A).
Votre partenaire va refuser et expliquer pourquoi. Il/elle va aussi proposer autre chose (colonne B).
Acceptez ou refusez. Continuez le dialogue jusqu'à ce que vous trouviez une chose d'intérêt commun.

Dis, Corinne, si on prenait un pot?

Hm, je n'ai pas soif. Si on allait plutôt au ciné?

Bonne idée! Allons au ciné.

A : VOUS	B : VOTRE PARTENAIRE
• aller dans une pizzeria	• aller dans un restaurant chinois
• prendre un pot	• aller au ciné
• faire un tour dans le centre	• se promener dans le parc
• voir une exposition	• jouer aux jeux vidéo
• aller dans les magasins	• téléphoner à des copains
• ??	• ??

(Écoutez, j'ai vu tous les films de la semaine. Et si on . . .)

2 Et avant?

Lisez ce que ces personnes ont fait et dites ce qu'elles avaient fait avant.

▶ Le week-end dernier, Philippe est sorti avec Alice. (le week-end d'avant / avec Karine)
Le week-end d'avant, il était sorti avec Karine.

1. Dimanche, nous sommes allés au ciné. (samedi soir / à un concert)
2. Hier, j'ai pris un pot au Balto. (avant-hier / au Saint Victor)
3. Cet après-midi, tu t'es promené en ville. (ce matin / dans le parc)
4. Hier, tu as donné rendez-vous à Catherine dans un café. (jeudi / devant le musée)
5. Ce week-end, les touristes ont visité le château d'Amboise. (le week-end dernier / le château de Chenonceaux)

3 Trop tard!

On fait parfois les choses trop tard. Décrivez ce qui est arrivé aux personnes suivantes.

▶ Jean-Claude arrive à l'aéroport.
L'avion est parti.
Quand Jean-Claude est arrivé à l'aéroport, l'avion était parti.

1. Nous arrivons au théâtre.
La pièce *(play)* a commencé.
2. Olivier téléphone à Catherine.
Elle est sortie avec Jean-Paul.
3. La serveuse apporte l'addition.
Les clients sont partis.
4. Monsieur Renaud entre dans la cuisine.
Le chien a mangé le bifteck.
5. Vous arrivez à la pâtisserie.
Le pâtissier a vendu le dernier gâteau.
6. Le lièvre *(hare)* arrive.
La tortue *(tortoise)* a gagné la course.

4 Pourquoi?

Expliquez pourquoi les choses suivantes sont arrivées. Attention: le verbe peut être affirmatif ou négatif.

▶ Les touristes n'ont pas trouvé de chambre d'hôtel. (réserver?)
Ils n'avaient pas réservé.

1. Monsieur Dupont a raté son avion. (se dépêcher?)
2. Tu n'as pas vu l'éclipse de lune *(moon)*. (se coucher trop tôt?)
3. Vous n'êtes pas allés au concert. (acheter les billets?)
4. Thomas n'a pas vu le film à la télé. (rentrer trop tard chez lui?)
5. Nous avons eu une indigestion. (manger trop?)
6. Les élèves ont eu une mauvaise note à l'examen. (étudier?)

■ **Réponses: Activité 2**
1. Samedi soir, nous étions allés à un concert.
2. Avant-hier, j'avais pris un pot au Saint Victor.
3. Ce matin, tu t'étais promené dans le parc.
4. Jeudi, tu avais donné rendez-vous à Catherine devant le musée.
5. Le week-end dernier, les touristes avaient visité le château de Chenonceaux.
6. L'été d'avant, nous étions allés au Mexique.

■ **Réponses: Activité 3**
1. Quand nous sommes arrivés au théâtre, la pièce avait commencé.
2. Quand Olivier a téléphoné à Catherine, elle était sortie avec Jean-Paul.
3. Quand la serveuse a apporté l'addition, les clients étaient partis.
4. Quand Monsieur Renaud est entré dans la cuisine, le chien avait mangé le bifteck.
5. Quand vous êtes arrivés à la pâtisserie, le pâtissier avait vendu le dernier gâteau.

■ **Réponses: Activité 4**
1. Il ne s'était pas dépêché.
2. Tu t'étais couché(e) trop tôt.
3. Vous n'aviez pas acheté les billets.
4. Il était rentré trop tard chez lui.
5. Nous avions trop mangé.
6. Ils n'avaient pas étudié.
Variation:
Demandez pourquoi les choses suivantes sont arrivées. Attention: le verbe peut être affirmatif ou négatif.
Exemple:
Les touristes n'ont pas trouvé de chambre d'hôtel. (réserver?)
N'avaient-ils pas réservé?/ Est-ce qu'ils n'avaient pas réservé?

Teaching Strategy

Divide the class into three groups. Have the first group come up with three or four sentences that explain what students did during summer vacation last year as compared with the year before. Have the second group come up with three or four sentences, imagining that they are Garfield the cat.

What did Garfield notice had happened when he got back from his two-day trip?

Have the third group come up with sentences that give excuses for why people are not getting their holiday presents this year. Each group should be using the pluperfect in all of their sentences.

INFO MAGAZINE

Theme: French cities

Reading Strategy:
Scanning, reading for information

RESOURCES

TECHNOLOGY
Teacher One Stop
🖥 **Projectable Transparencies**
  1, *La France*
  1(o), *La France*
  6, *Paris*
  48, *Où habiter?*
  48(o), *Où habiter?*
  Transparency Copymasters,
  pp. A5–A6, A13–A14,
  A102–A103

■ **Anecdote**
La plus vieille maison de Paris est
située au **51, rue de Montmorency.**
Elle a été construite par **Nicolas
Flamel,** en 1407.

■ **Irregular Verbs**
(see Appendix C)
se distraire:
  je me distrais
  tu te distrais
  il/elle se distrait,
  nous nous distrayons
  vous vous distrayez
  ils/elles se distraient
s'asseoir

INFOMAGAZINE

La géographie des villes françaises

L'histoire des villes françaises, décrite brièvement à la page 303, explique leur aspect et leur structure si différents des villes américaines. Une ville française typique comprend° les quartiers suivants.

LA VILLE MÊME

La «vieille ville»

C'est le quartier historique, aujourd'hui très touristique, où l'on trouve les vestiges du passé: la cathédrale, des rues étroites,° des maisons anciennes très pittoresques, parfois un château, des vestiges de remparts et même des ruines romaines. Les maisons anciennes ont souvent été restaurées. Ce sont des résidences très recherchées° par les habitants des villes qui y trouvent à la fois° le confort du présent et le charme du passé.

Le «centre-ville»

C'est l'endroit le plus dynamique, le plus animé et, pour beaucoup de gens, le plus intéressant de la ville. Situé généralement autour d'une place monumentale, on y trouve les bâtiments administratifs (la mairie, le palais de justice, la poste. . .), les grands magasins, les boutiques de luxe, les cinémas, le théâtre municipal, les cafés et les meilleurs restaurants de la ville. Il y a parfois un jardin public avec des fontaines, des parterres de fleurs° et des bancs.° Le week-end les gens viennent au centre-ville pour faire leur shopping et pour se distraire.° Quand il fait beau, ils s'asseyent° à la terrasse des cafés pour voir le spectacle de la rue et aussi pour être vus.

Les quartiers résidentiels

Ils sont situés autour du centre-ville et le long d'avenues transversales. C'est là que les gens habitent. Les immeubles ont un maximum de six étages. Leur rez-de-chaussée est généralement occupé par des boutiques. Le reste est divisé en appartements.

comprend *includes* **étroites** *narrow* **recherchées** *sought after* **à la fois** *at the same time*
parterres de fleurs *flower beds* **bancs** *benches* **se distraire** *to have fun*
*s'asseoir *to sit down*

Interdisciplinary/Community Connections
This article may be used as the basis for a
class project comparing the geography of
French and U.S. cities and towns. You may
wish to work with the history and social
studies teachers, or your local historical
society or library, to help students to produce a
report complete with maps, photos, and
illustrations.

LA BANLIEUE

Les banlieues qui s'étendent° autour des villes sont modernes, mais la vie y est généralement monotone, banale, même ennuyeuse°. Il y a différentes sortes de banlieues. Dans les banlieues «chic», les gens habitent dans des maisons individuelles entourées° de jardins. Dans les banlieues ouvrières°, les gens habitent dans des «grands ensembles°». Ce sont des immeubles de 10, 20 ou 30 étages, à l'architecture simple mais souvent sans grand intérêt. Dans les banlieues les plus défavorisées, les gens habitent dans des logements précaires sans confort et sans hygiène. Pour aider les habitants des banlieues pauvres, le gouvernement français a financé la construction d'HLM (habitation à loyer modéré°) où les gens pourraient avoir l'occasion de louer ou acheter leur appartement à des conditions avantageuses.

Les «villes nouvelles»

Toutes les grandes villes du monde ont un problème commun: la qualité de la vie y est menacée par une expansion trop rapide et souvent anarchique. Pour limiter l'expansion de Paris et de sa banlieue, le gouvernement français a décidé de créer cinq villes entièrement nouvelles dans la région parisienne: Cergy-Pontoise, Saint-Quentin-en-Yvelines, Évry, Melun-Sénart, Marne-la-Vallée. Ces «villes nouvelles» sont de dimension moyenne°. Elles ont de 80 000 à 250 000 habitants. Tout a été planifié° pour assurer à ceux-ci un bon équilibre entre le travail et les loisirs. Ces villes offrent° à leur population non seulement des logements et des emplois, mais aussi des centres commerciaux, des équipements culturels et sportifs, des parcs de loisirs. Et, pour maintenir le contact avec la nature, des espaces verts et des plans d'eau° y ont été aménagés.°

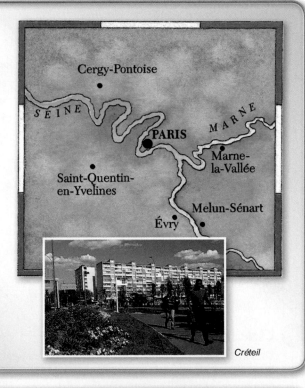

Créteil

et vous?

Imaginez que vous allez passer une année dans une grande ville française. Où préféreriez-vous habiter? dans la vieille ville? au centre-ville? dans un quartier résidentiel? dans la banlieue? dans une «ville nouvelle»? Expliquez pourquoi.

---

s'étendent *extend* **ennuyeuse** *boring* **entourées** *surrounded* **ouvrières** *working class* **grands ensembles** *housing projects*
loyer modéré *low rent* **moyenne** *average* **planifié** *planned* ***offrir** *to offer* **plans d'eau=** *lacs artificiels* **aménagés =** *développés*

Notes Culturelles

- **Euro Disney** opened in April 1992 in Marne-la-Vallée. The theme park is about 20 miles from Paris.
- Although they existed before World War II, more **H.L.M.** started being built in 1947 to deal with the housing crisis brought on by war damages.

- Four other "villes nouvelles" are being developed in France near the following cities:
  Lyon: L'Isle d'Abeau
  Marseille: Rives de l'Étang de Berre
  Lille: Villeneuve-d'Ascq
  Rouen: Le Vaudreuil

■ Notes linguistiques

- The expression **le bidonville** originated in North Africa. A compound of **le bidon** *(can)* and **la ville,** it designates rudimentary shelters made of scraps in the poorest areas.
- The abbreviation **H.L.M.** can be either masculine or feminine: **le H.L.M,** or **la H.L.M.**

■ Teaching Strategy

Assign the following:
- **Photos.** Choisissez une des photos du texte et décrivez ce que vous voyez.
- **Débat.** Votre partenaire et vous, vous allez passer l'été dans une ville française. Vous cherchez un appartement. Votre partenaire voudrait habiter dans un quartier résidentiel moderne. Vous, au contraire, vous préférez habiter dans la vieille ville. Débattez les avantages et les inconvénients de chaque situation.

■ Irregular Verb

(see Appendix C)
offrir *(see* **ouvrir)**

PRINT
Workbook, pp. 153–156
Activités pour tous

Unit 8 Resource Book, Partie 2
  Activités pour tous TE
  Audioscripts
  Lesson Plans
  Block Scheduling Lesson Plans
  Absent Student Copymasters
  Workbook TE

AUDIO
 Audio Program
  CD 9, Tracks 1–5

TECHNOLOGY
@HomeTutor
◣ Interactive Whiteboard Lessons
Teacher One Stop
  Block Scheduling Copymasters
🖥 **Projectable Transparencies**
  49, *Plan de Lyon*
  Transparency Copymasters,
  pp. A104–A106
▶ DVD Program, Unit 8

■ **Teaching Strategy**
Have the students, with a partner, prepare a survey and an interview for the school paper which discusses where the students live with respect to the school and in what type of houses and neighborhoods they live. Dialog should be at least 5–6 lines per person.

■ **Teaching Note**
HLM housing projects were subsidized by French government funds to provide moderately priced housing for low-income families.

Comment expliquer
où on habite

J'habite 18, place Voltaire.

Où habites-tu?

— Où habites-tu?
  J'habite | 10, rue de la République.   dans la 35ᵉ rue.
  | 25, avenue Victor Hugo.   dans la 6ᵉ avenue.
  | 120, boulevard Raspail.
  | 18, place Voltaire.

— Où est-ce exactement?
  C'est | dans **le centre-ville.**
  | dans **la banlieue** *(suburbs).*
  | dans **le quartier** *(district, area, neighborhood)* Saint-Pierre.

> **Révision** p. R10
> Les nombres

— Dans quel genre de résidence habites-tu?
  J'habite dans | **une maison individuelle.**   **un immeuble** *(apartment building)*
  | **un appartement.**   **un HLM*** *(low-income housing project)*
  | **une tour** *(high rise).*

— C'est près d'ici?
  Oui, c'est | **tout près** *(nearby).*   Non, c'est | **loin.**
  | **à 100 mètres.** | **à 3 kilomètres.**
  | **à dix minutes à pied.** | **à 20 minutes en bus.**

— Comment est-ce qu'on peut aller là-bas?
  On peut y aller | à pied.   On peut prendre | un bus.
  | à vélo. | un taxi.
  | | le métro.

* **HLM** = Habitation à Loyer Modéré *(low-rent housing)*

---

1 **Une invitation à dîner**

Vous avez invité votre camarade français(e) à dîner chez vous. Votre camarade accepte, mais il/elle a besoin de renseignements pour aller chez vous. Il/elle veut savoir . . .

- votre adresse
- dans quelle partie de la ville vous habitez
- si c'est loin de l'école
- comment aller chez vous

Vous lui expliquez. Composez le dialogue correspondant avec votre partenaire et jouez-le en classe.

Teaching Suggestion: DVD Program

In this section of the Unit 8 video, *Vidéo-drame: Un rendez-vous en ville,* the theme of giving directions to one's house is covered. As you play the video the first time, have students write down some of the directions being given. Next, review the directions by playing the video one more time.

After watching the video, have each student explain how to get to their house from the school using some of the phrases from the video.

Dans mon quartier, il y a . . .

des boutiques	un centre sportif	un parc
des commerces *(small businesses)*	un centre de loisirs *(recreation center)*	un jardin public
un grand centre commercial *(mall)*	une Maison des Jeunes *(Youth center)*	une mairie *(city hall)*
une station-service	une bibliothèque	une poste *(post office)*
	un musée	un poste de police
		une gendarmerie } *(police station)*
		une caserne de pompiers

FLASH d'information

La police nationale et la gendarmerie sont deux corps de police distincts. Certaines de leurs fonctions sont semblables, mais d'autres sont différentes. L'un des rôles de la gendarmerie est d'assurer la police° des routes. C'est à eux qu'on a affaire° quand on ne respecte pas le code de la route.°

la police *law enforcement*
avoir affaire à *to have to deal with*   **code de la route** *traffic regulations*

2 ## Créa-dialogue: En ville 💬🗨

Votre partenaire, qui est français(e), visite votre ville. Il/elle veut faire l'une des choses suivantes. Dites-lui à quel endroit aller et si c'est loin d'ici.

▶ *Je voudrais envoyer des lettres.*
Est-ce que c'est loin d'ici?
Comment est-ce que je peux aller là-bas?
Va à la poste.
Non, c'est à 500 mètres.
Vas-y à pied.
(Prends le bus.)

- faire réparer ma voiture
- faire une promenade à pied
- jouer au volley
- rencontrer de jeunes Américains
- emprunter un livre
- faire des achats
- déclarer la perte *(loss)* de mon passeport
- interviewer un membre du conseil municipal *(city council)*
- envoyer des lettres
- voir une exposition de photos

SUPPLEMENTARY VOCABULARY

une maison jumelée *two-family house*
un grand ensemble *residential area consisting of large blocks of apartments*
un gratte-ciel *skyscraper*
un studio *studio*
un pavillon *single house*
un pied-à-terre *pied-à-terre (secondary or temporary lodging)*
un meublé *furnished apartment*

200 feet	60 mètres
500 feet	150 mètres
half a mile	800 mètres
a mile	1 kilomètre et demi

Notes culturelles

- **Victor Hugo (1802–1885)** was a very influential writer of his time. He was the author of masterpieces such as *Les Misérables and Notre-Dame de Paris.* (For more information, see p. 224.)
- **François Raspail (1794–1878)** was a chemist and a political activist who went to jail and was exiled for his democratic ideals.

He was elected **député** *(representative)* in 1876.
- **Voltaire (François-Marie Arouet, 1694–1778)** was a writer famous for his sharp wit and ruthless fights against injustice. He was jailed in the Bastille and was exiled for questioning the monarchy. His works include *Candide, Zadig,* and many poems.

@HOMETUTOR
my.hrw.com

Langue et Communication

■ **Teaching Strategy: Variation**

• Activity 1 can be done in pairs with partners comparing their choices.

• It can also be done as a class survey: first the students each write out their answers, and then the results are tabulated.

A Révision: le conditionnel

The CONDITIONAL is used to express what WOULD HAPPEN, what people WOULD DO in certain circumstances.

Review the formation of the conditional:

Révision p. R19

Formation du conditionnel

> FUTURE STEM + IMPERFECT ENDINGS

INFINITIVE		parler	ENDINGS
FUTURE	je	**parler**ai	
	je	**parler**ais	-ais
	tu	**parler**ais	-ais
CONDITIONAL	il/elle/on	**parler**ait	-ait
	nous	**parler**ions	-ions
	vous	**parler**iez	-iez
	ils/elles	**parler**aient	-aient

Verbs with irregular stems:

payer	je **paier**ais	devoir	je **devr**ais
acheter	j'**achèter**ais	pouvoir	je **pourr**ais
		vouloir	je **voudr**ais
appeler	j'**appeller**ais		
être	je **ser**ais		
avoir	j'**aur**ais	envoyer	j'**enverr**ais
aller	j'**ir**ais	recevoir	je **recevr**ais
faire	je **fer**ais	savoir	je **saur**ais
venir	je **viendr**ais	voir	je **verr**ais

① Au choix

Supposez que vous ayez le choix entre les possibilités suivantes. Que choisiriez-vous? (Si vous voulez, expliquez votre choix.)

▶ habiter en ville ou à la campagne?
J'habiterais à la campagne (parce que j'aime la nature).

1. habiter dans le centre-ville ou en banlieue?
2. travailler dans un restaurant ou dans un supermarché?
3. assister à un concert ou à un match de foot?
4. passer les vacances à la mer ou à la campagne?
5. aller au ciné ou au restaurant?
6. voir une comédie ou un film d'aventures?
7. avoir une moto ou une voiture de sport?
8. faire du ski nautique ou du parapente?
9. être acteur (actrice) de cinéma ou athlète professionnel(le)?

Differentiation

Structured Review the formation of the conditional. Then have students copy one regular verb in the conditional for each of the 3 verb groups: **-er, -ir, -re.** Have them write the endings in red. Then have students practice verbs orally and underline all forms pronounced identically in black.

■ **Expansion: Activity 2**

Have students continue the conversation by explaining their positions.

— **Pourquoi?**
— **Parce que je veux aider les gens qui n'ont pas beaucoup d'argent.**

2 Les élections municipales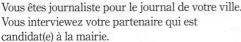

Vous êtes journaliste pour le journal de votre ville. Vous interviewez votre partenaire qui est candidat(e) à la mairie.

▶ construire des HLM?
— **Est-ce que vous construiriez des HLM?**
— **Oui, je construirais des HLM.**
   (Non, je ne construirais pas de HLM.)

- développer les transports publics
- fermer le jardin public la nuit
- contrôler la pollution
- taxer les commerces
- créer un centre de loisirs pour les personnes âgées
- construire une nouvelle caserne de pompiers
- fermer la bibliothèque le dimanche
- interdire la circulation dans le centre-ville

3 La meilleure solution

Imaginez que vous êtes dans les situations suivantes. Qu'est-ce que vous feriez? Comparez votre solution avec celle de votre partenaire.

SITUATION A

Vous habitez la banlieue. Vous êtes allé(e) au cinéma dans le centre-ville. Vous voulez rentrer chez vous, mais vous n'avez pas assez d'argent pour prendre le bus et vos parents ne sont pas à la maison.
Que feriez-vous?

- rentrer à pied?
- demander de l'argent à un passant *(passerby)*?
- faire de l'auto-stop *(hitchhiking)*?
- ??

SITUATION B

Pour son anniversaire, vous avez invité votre meilleur(e) ami(e) à dîner chez vous. Au moment de préparer le repas, vous vous apercevez *(realize)* que la cuisinière *(stove)* ne marche pas. Que feriez-vous?

- téléphoner à votre ami(e) et annuler le repas?
- acheter une pizza?
- inviter votre ami(e) au restaurant?
- ??

SITUATION C

Votre frère a une copine. Un jour vous découvrez que cette copine sort avec un autre garçon. Que feriez-vous?

- dire la vérité à votre frère?
- parler à la copine de votre frère?
- envoyer une lettre d'insultes à l'autre garçon?
- ??

SITUATION D

Vous êtes dans un ascenseur quand une panne d'électricité *(power failure)* paralyse tout l'immeuble. Que feriez-vous?

- attendre calmement l'arrivée des pompiers?
- forcer la porte?
- monter sur le toit de l'ascenseur?
- ??

4 Les vacances idéales

Avec votre partenaire, discutez des vacances idéales. Posez-vous les questions suivantes (en français, bien sûr!)

- *where would you go?*
- *how would you travel?*
- *how long would you stay?*
- *in what type of hotel would you stay?*
- *at what time would you get up?*

- *what would you do in the morning?*
- *what would you do in the afternoon?*
- *what would you do to meet people?*
- *what would you do to stay in shape* **(en forme)?**
- *what would you do in the evenings?*

Puis, mettez-vous d'accord et écrivez un petit paragraphe où vous décrivez ce que vous feriez.

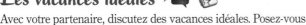

Pour nos vacances idéales, nous irions...

315

■ **Teaching Strategy: Activity 4**

You may wish to practice the questions before students do the activity in pairs.
   Où irais-tu?
   Comment voyagerais-tu?
   etc.

■ **Proverbe**

Avec un si, on mettrait Paris en bouteille. *(In theory, anything is possible.)*

■ **Note culturelle**

Le Parc de la Villette, in Paris, is a popular attraction. In **la Cité des sciences et de l'industrie** you will find an IMAX theater and a science museum, while in **la Cité de la musique,** you will find a concert hall and a music school.

B | Le conditionnel dans les phrases avec *si*

Note the use of the conditional in the following sentences.

Si j'avais une voiture, j'**irais** à la campagne.	*If I had a car (but I don't), I **would go** to the country.*
Si nous habitions à Paris, nous **voyagerions** en métro.	*If we were living in Paris (but we aren't), we **would travel** by subway.*

The CONDITIONAL is used to express what WOULD HAPPEN, <u>if</u> certain conditions contrary to reality <u>were met</u>.
In such sentences, the construction is usually:

si-clause: IMPERFECT	result clause: CONDITIONAL
Si je **gagnais** à la loterie,	j'**achèterais** une moto.

→ In French, the CONDITIONAL is <u>never</u> used in the **si**-clause.

5 **Si j'habitais . . .**

Pour chaque endroit, décrivez 2 ou 3 choses que vous feriez si vous habitiez là.

▶ à Paris

Si j'habitais à Paris, je parlerais français tout le temps.

Je voyagerais en métro.

Je visiterais de temps en temps le musée d'Orsay.

J'irais parfois écouter des concerts à la Villette . . . .

1. à San Francisco
2. en Floride
3. à la Martinique
4. dans le centre-ville
5. dans un petit village à la campagne
6. dans la banlieue d'une grande ville

6 **Rêves** *(Dreams)*

Rêver ne coûte rien. Expliquez les rêves des personnes suivantes en utilisant les éléments des colonnes A et B. Soyez logique!

	A	B
nous	• invisible	• savoir tout
vous	• multi-millionnaire	• protéger les innocents
Sandrine	• extra-lucide	• voyager dans l'espace
Philippe	• Superman/Wonder Woman	• habiter dans un château
mes copains	• Robin des Bois *(Robin Hood)*	• avoir une Rolls-Royce
		• aider les pauvres
		• voler comme des oiseaux
		• passer à travers les murs
		• connaître le passé, le présent et l'avenir

▶ **Si Philippe était Robin des Bois, il aiderait les pauvres.**

Teaching Strategy

Have each student tell you one thing that he or she would like to have, to happen to him or her, to do, etc. — one wish. Jot these on the board. Then ask students to give two sentences about what they would do if their wish came true. Have them write one of their sentences on the board next to their wish. Go over all sentences orally to insure grammatical correctness.

7 Problèmes et solutions

Votre partenaire va choisir l'un des problèmes suivants.
Dites-lui ce que vous feriez à sa place. Donnez-lui
2 ou 3 suggestions (affirmatives ou négatives).

▶ Je grossis.

**Si je grossissais, je mangerais moins.
J'irais au centre sportif et je ferais
de la gymnastique tous les jours.
Je ne prendrais pas le bus pour
aller à l'école. J'irais à pied.**

- Je n'ai pas d'appétit.
- Je dors trop.
- Je ne me sens pas très bien.
- Je perds mon temps.
- Je ne réussis pas à mes examens.
- J'ai besoin d'argent.
- Je suis déprimé(e) *(depressed)*.
- J'ai un problème avec mon copain
  (ma copine).
- J'ai des difficultés avec mes parents.
- Mon frère (ma soeur) m'embête
  tout le temps.

8 Que feriez-vous?

Choisissez l'une des situations suivantes et composez un petit paragraphe où vous décrivez
ce que vous feriez (ou ce que vous ne feriez pas) si vous étiez dans cette situation.
Utilisez le conditionnel . . . et votre imagination!

1. Pour impressionner Stéphanie, sa nouvelle
copine, Raphaël l'a invitée dans un grand
restaurant. Au moment de payer, Raphaël
s'aperçoit *(realizes)* qu'il a perdu son
portefeuille.
Si j'étais Raphaël, . . .

2. Depuis plusieurs semaines, Caroline
reçoit des lettres d'un admirateur inconnu.
Elle veut savoir qui est ce mystérieux
correspondant.
Si j'étais Caroline, . . .

3. Jérôme a emprunté la voiture de Cécile.
Au moment de rendre la voiture à son amie,
il remarque une éraflure *(dent, scratch)*
fraîche. Il n'est pas sûr que cette éraflure
était là quand il a emprunté la voiture.
Si j'étais Jérôme, . . .

4. Jean-Claude a passé la soirée dans une petite
salle de la bibliothèque municipale. Il est
maintenant onze heures. Au moment
de sortir, Jean-Claude s'aperçoit qu'il est seul
et que toutes les portes sont fermées à clé.
Si j'étais Jean-Claude, . . .

5. Madame Lescot a invité ses amis à dîner. Au
moment de préparer le repas, elle s'aperçoit
que sa cuisinière *(stove)* ne marche pas.
Si j'étais Madame Lescot, . . .

6. Monsieur Rimbaud voyage souvent en avion.
Un jour, il prend par erreur une valise qui
n'est pas à lui. Chez lui, il ouvre la valise et
découvre un million de dollars . . . et
l'adresse d'une bande de terroristes.
Si j'étais Monsieur Rimbaud, . . .

9 Qu'est-ce que vous feriez à leur place?

Avec votre partenaire, choisissez une des situations suivantes et dites ce que vous feriez
dans ces situations.

A  **B**  **C**

■ **Teaching Strategy:
Expansion**

Comparez votre paragraphe avec
celui de votre partenaire.

SUPPLEMENTARY VOCABULARY

la barque *small boat*
couler *to sink, drown*
la soucoupe volante *flying saucer*
le martien *martian*
atterrir *to land*
la panne (de voiture) *(car)
  breakdown*
tomber en panne *to break down*

■ **Expansion**

Also: il faut → **il faudrait**
il vaut mieux →
il vaudrait mieux

■ **Teaching Strategy**

You may wish to tell your students
that polite requests with **pouvoir** are
particularly useful when traveling in
French-speaking areas. For example:
Pourriez-vous me dire où
se trouve la banque la plus
proche?, etc.
The conditional in English is similarly
used to express politeness.

■ **Note linguistique**

In indirect speech, a statement
is made using a DECLARATIVE VERB,
such as:
**dire, déclarer, annoncer,
écrire, prédire, promettre,** etc.

C Le conditionnel: autres usages

POLITE REQUESTS

The conditional of verbs such as **vouloir, pouvoir, devoir** is used instead of the present
to express a WISH or REQUEST in a MORE POLITE manner. Compare:

Je veux regarder tes photos.	*I **want** to look at your pictures.*
Je voudrais regarder tes photos.	*I **would like** to look at your pictures.*
Peux-tu me prêter ton vélo?	*Can you loan me your bike?*
Pourrais-tu me prêter ton vélo?	*Could you loan me your bike?*
Vous devez être à l'heure.	*You **must** be on time.*
Vous devriez être à l'heure.	*You **should** be on time.*

INDIRECT SPEECH

The conditional is used to report what people mentioned IN THE PAST about a FUTURE EVENT.
It describes what they said they WOULD DO or what WOULD HAPPEN later.

Maintenant, Éric **dit** qu'il **ira** au ciné.	*Now Eric **says** that he **will go** to the movies.*
Hier, il **a dit** qu'il **irait** au concert.	*Yesterday he **said** that he **would go** to the concert.*

After a declarative verb (such as **dire** or **écrire**), future events are expressed
according to the following tense sequence:

DECLARATIVE VERB	FUTURE EVENT
present	future
past (imperfect, passé composé, pluperfect)	conditional

Qu'est-ce que la météo a annoncé hier?

Elle a annoncé qu'il ferait beau ce weekend!

HOTEL DE LA PLAGE**

Teaching Strategy

Divide the class into pairs and give them the
following situation:

Isabelle et Florent sont sortis ensemble
pendant quatre ans. Ils se sont fait beaucoup de
promesses. Maintenant, Isabelle veut son
indépendance alors elle quitte Florent. Florent
rappelle à Isabelle toutes ses/leurs promesses.

Qu'est-ce que Florent lui dit? (Tu m'as dit
que...)

Each pair of students should come up with an
original dialog to present to the class.

10 Soyons polis!

Montrez que vous êtes poli(e). Pour cela, reformulez les phrases suivantes en utilisant le conditionnel.

▶ Est-ce que tu veux un dessert?
Est-ce que tu voudrais un dessert?

1. Je veux te parler.
2. Nous voulons sortir avec vous.
3. Peux-tu m'inviter à ta boum?
4. Pouvons-nous amener nos amis?

5. Pouvez-vous être à l'heure?
6. Tu dois m'aider.
7. Vous devez être plus généreux.
8. Vous ne devez pas mentir *(tell lies)*.

11 Messages téléphoniques

Votre partenaire a écouté votre répondeur *(answering machine)* et il/elle a noté les messages suivants. Demandez-lui qui a téléphoné et ce que chaque personne a dit.

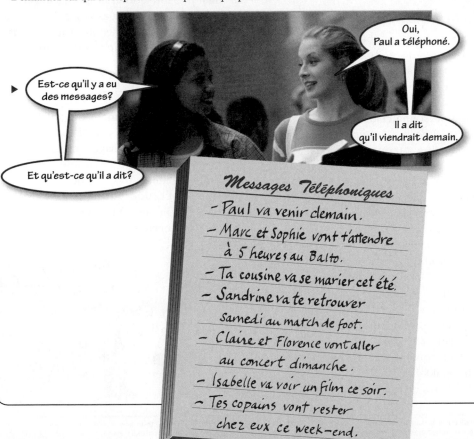

> Est-ce qu'il y a eu des messages?

> Oui, Paul a téléphoné.

> Et qu'est-ce qu'il a dit?

> Il a dit qu'il viendrait demain.

Messages Téléphoniques

- Paul va venir demain.
- Marc et Sophie vont t'attendre à 5 heures au Balto.
- Ta cousine va se marier cet été.
- Sandrine va te retrouver samedi au match de foot.
- Claire et Florence vont aller au concert dimanche.
- Isabelle va voir un film ce soir.
- Tes copains vont rester chez eux ce week-end.

SUPPLEMENTARY VOCABULARY

le publiphone *phone booth (where you can pay with a card)*
la cabine téléphonique *phone booth*
la télécarte *prepaid phone card*
composer (un numéro) *to dial (a number)*
décrocher (le combiné) *to pick up (the receiver)*
le numéro vert *toll-free number*

■ **Notes culturelles**

• Almost all phone booths in France require the use of a phone card instead of change. The **télécarte** is a smart card with a prepaid amount recorded on its electronic chip. These cards are avidly sought after by collectors who seek rare designs and limited editions.

• Like Americans, French people may choose to have an unlisted number (**être sur la liste rouge**).

Teaching Strategy

Have the students write a story (including dialog) in which they employ all the different uses of the conditional (pp. 314-319). Ideas:
• winning the lottery / promised to share with someone
• turning 16 / parents promised a car at 16
• eating grapefruit for 3 weeks / friend said he/she lost 20 lbs. doing same

Encourage students to be creative and to use as much vocabulary and as many verbs in the conditional as possible.

INFO MAGAZINE

Theme: Street entertainers in France

Reading Strategy: Reading for pleasure

■ Note culturelle

Marcel Marceau (1923–2007) reinvented the art of mime with his character, a gentle clown called Bip. Marceau opened an international mime school in Paris and travelled around the world as Bip, his silent alter-ego.

■ Additional Information

In Paris, you will always see various artists performing in front of the **Pompidou Center.** In Montreal (Quebec) the **Place Jacques Cartier** in the old town is a favorite stage for performance artists.

■ Irregular Verbs

(see Appendix C)
vivre
se distraire *(see p. 310)*
plaire
suivre
s'apercevoir *(see **recevoir**)*
rire

Le spectacle EST DANS LA RUE

Pour les Français, la rue n'est pas seulement un endroit où l'on passe pour aller au travail, à l'école, ou dans des magasins. C'est aussi un endroit où l'on vit.° On y rencontre ses amis. On s'y repose (à la terrasse des cafés). On y dîne (à la terrasse des restaurants). Et surtout, on s'y distrait.°

La rue est en effet un théâtre permanent qui offre toutes sortes de spectacles aux «badauds».° Certains spectacles sont spontanés et gratuits: un accident, une querelle entre deux automobilistes, une manifestation,° le passage d'une personne célèbre,° le tournage° d'un film, etc. Les autres spectacles sont organisés par des «artistes» et laissés° à l'appréciation personnelle des passants. Si vous jugez° que le spectacle est bon, vous laisserez° quelques pièces de monnaie° dans le chapeau que vous tendra° l'artiste. Sinon, vous quitterez les lieux avant la fin° du spectacle.

Autrefois, les «artistes des rues» étaient des jongleurs,° des chanteurs, des montreurs° d'animaux (ours,° singes,° chiens savants,° etc. . .). Les artistes d'aujourd'hui ne sont pas tellement° différents des artistes d'autrefois et leur principe est le même: l'artiste s'installe dans un endroit fréquenté; les «badauds» arrivent; l'artiste commence son spectacle; à la fin du spectacle, il fait la quête°. Il y a plusieurs catégories d'artistes de rue:

❖ LES MUSICIENS

Ce sont les plus nombreux.° Suivant° la clientèle ou le quartier, ils jouent du jazz, du rock, de la musique folklorique, de la musique indienne, des rythmes africains, ou même de la musique classique. L'important° est que la musique soit bonne et que le musicien soit sympathique ou ait l'air exotique. Parce que leur musique plaît,° les jeunes musiciens américains qui jouent en France ont généralement beaucoup de succès!

❖ LES MIMES

Ils opèrent° généralement devant la terrasse d'un café. Leur costume est classique: pantalon noir, gilet° rayé,° chapeau noir. La technique du mime consiste à suivre° un passant et à imiter tous ses gestes avec la plus grande exactitude possible. Le passant ne s'aperçoit° de rien, mais les spectateurs qui sont à la terrasse du café rient° . . . et contribuent!

***vivre** to live ***se distraire** to have fun **badauds** onlookers **manifestation** demonstration **célèbre** famous **tournage** making **laissés** left
jugez = pensez **laisserez** = mettrez **monnaie coins** **tendra** = présentera **fin** end **jongleurs** jugglers **montreurs** exhibitor **ours** bears
singes monkeys **savants** trained **tellement** that (much) **fait la quête** passes the hat **nombreux** numerous **suivant** according to
L'important = la chose importante ***plaire** to please **opèrent** = travaillent **gilet** vest **rayé** striped ***suivre** to follow ***s'apercevoir** to notice
***rire** to laugh

Teaching Strategy

This *Info Magazine* article provides additional cultural information on life in French cities. It is designed to provide easy reading practice. Since these readings are optional, you may allow students to choose whether or not to concentrate heavily on this material. If you wish to use the quizzes as a self-check for comprehension, students may find it useful.

❖ LES AUTOMATES

Ils sont déguisés en personnages d'autrefois. Leur visage couvert de poudre° ne manifeste° aucune expression. Leurs gestes sont complètement mécaniques. Ils tournent la tête à droite, à gauche, ils lèvent° le bras comme des marionnettes. On ne sait vraiment pas s'ils sont réels . . . jusqu'au° moment où ils descendent de leur piédestal et passent le chapeau.

et vous?

DÉFINITIONS
Définissez les mots suivants.

- un badaud
- une manifestation
- un animal savant
- un jongleur
- un mime
- un automate
- une marionnette
- faire la quête

EXPRESSION ÉCRITE
Vous êtes en vacances à Paris. Écrivez une lettre à un(e) ami(e) où vous décrivez un spectacle de rue auquel vous avez assisté. Mentionnez, par exemple:
- le genre de spectacle
- ce que «l'artiste» a fait (donnez des détails)
- comment vous avez trouvé le spectacle
- si vous avez donné de l'argent (pourquoi ou pourquoi pas)

L'automate
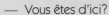

C'est un «automate». Nous l'avons rencontré un jour d'été à Strasbourg. Il était sept heures du soir. Il avait le visage encore° tout blanc, et il portait un chapeau de paille,° à la mode de 1900. Le spectacle était terminé et il allait partir sur sa grosse moto. Nous lui avons parlé.

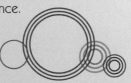

— Vous êtes d'ici?

— Non, je suis de la banlieue. Je viens ici parce que ça marche bien.

— Ça a marché aujourd'hui?

— Pas trop mal. J'ai fait 150 euros!

— Quels sont vos meilleurs clients?

— En général, tout le monde donne quelque chose, mais j'aime beaucoup les Allemands. Ils comprennent l'effort et la qualité du travail.

— Est-ce que votre métier° est dur?°

— Très dur! Il faut se concentrer. . . C'est difficile quand il y a tant° de gens qui passent, le bruit, le vent. . . Et puis il y a la préparation, le maquillage.° Ça prend du temps! Enfin, l'essentiel, c'est que les gens s'amusent. Quand ils s'amusent, comme aujourd'hui, je sais que j'ai bien fait mon travail.

— Merci, et bonne chance.

poudre *powder* **manifeste** = montre **lèvent** *raise* **jusqu'au** *until* **encore** *still* **paille** *straw* **métier** = profession
dur = difficile **tant** *so many* **maquillage** *make-up*

SUPPLEMENTARY VOCABULARY

le caricaturiste *caricaturist*
le portraitiste *portrait artist*
la diseuse de bonne aventure *fortune teller*
le magicien *magician*
l'avaleur *(m.)* **de sabres** *sword swallower*
le cracheur de feu *fire eater*

■ Teaching Strategy: Expansion
Give students the following scenarios:

- **Un spectacle**
  Imaginez que vous allez participer à un «cabaret» organisé par le club français. Choisissez un spectacle (musique, mime, automate, jongleur …) et décrivez ce que vous allez faire.

- **Spectacle à Paris**
  Vous voyagez en France avec votre partenaire. Pour gagner un peu d'argent, vous décidez d'organiser un «spectacle de la rue». Choisissez ce spectacle et décrivez ce que vous allez faire.

Differentiation
Synthetic/Analytic Have students say and write the vocabulary words in the **Et vous?** on flashcards. Have students work in pairs to drill the vocabulary words using the flashcards. Have them write out the main points of the passage and share them with the class.

PRINT

Workbook, p. 84
Activités pour tous

Unit 8 Resource Book, Partie 3

Activités pour tous TE
Audioscripts
Lesson Plans
Block Scheduling Lesson Plans
Absent Student Copymasters
Workbook TE

TECHNOLOGY

@HomeTutor

Teacher One Stop

Block Scheduling Copymasters
Teacher to Teacher Copymasters,
Trouver celui qui ..., pp. 97–98;
Et maintenant ..., pp. 99–100;
Jumeaux/Jumelles, pp. 101–104

■ Note linguistique

• The past conditional is sometimes called the CONDITIONAL PERFECT.

• Stress that the past conditional <u>only</u> occurs in the result clause. It is <u>never</u> used in the **si**-clause, as it is in English.

> Si **j'avais su**, ...
> If **I would have known**
> (If **I had known**), ...
> je ne t'**aurais** pas **écouté**.
> **I would** not **have listened** to you.

• The underlying condition may be expressed by a phrase other than a **si**-clause. For example:

> **À ta place**, je serais parti.
> **In your place, I would have left.**
> **Avec plus d'argent**,
> j'aurais ...
> **With more money, I would have ...**
> acheté une voiture plus grande.
> *bought a bigger car.*

322 Unité 8

A Le conditionnel passé

The PAST CONDITIONAL is used to express what WOULD HAVE HAPPENED under certain circumstances. Note the forms of the verbs in heavy print:

À ta place,   *In your place (If I had been you),*
  je **n'aurais pas pris** ma voiture.   *I **would not have taken** my car.*
Je **serais allé(e)** en ville en bus.   *I **would have gone** downtown by bus.*

FORMS

The PAST CONDITIONAL is formed as follows:

> CONDITIONAL of **avoir** or **être** + PAST PARTICIPLE

> In the past conditional, the agreement rules for the past participle are the same as in the passé composé.
>
> Tu n'as pas invité **ta copine**. À ta place, je l'aurais invité**e**.

INFINITIVE		voyager		aller		s'amuser
	j'	aurais voyagé	je	serais allé(e)	je	me serais amusé(e)
	tu	aurais voyagé	tu	serais allé(e)	tu	te serais amusé(e)
PAST CONDITIONAL	il/elle/on	aurait voyagé	il/elle/on	serait allé(e)	il/elle/on	se serait amusé(e)
	nous	aurions voyagé	nous	serions allé(e)s	nous	nous serions amusé(e)s
	vous	auriez voyagé	vous	seriez allé(e)(s)	vous	vous seriez amusé(e)(s)
	ils/elles	auraient voyagé	ils/elles	seraient allé(e)s	ils/elles	se seraient amusé(e)s
NEGATIVE	je	n'aurais pas voyagé	je	ne serais pas allé(e)	je	ne me serais pas amusé(e)
INTERROGATIVE	est-ce que tu	aurais voyagé?	tu	serais allé(e)?	tu	te serais amusé(e)?
		aurais-tu voyagé?		serais-tu allé(e)?		te serais-tu amusé(e)?

USES

The following sentences express what WOULD HAVE HAPPENED **if** certain past conditions HAD BEEN MET.
Note the use of tenses in the sentences below.

Si j'**avais étudié**,   *If I **had studied**,*
  j'**aurais réussi** à l'examen.   *I **would have passed** the exam.*

Si vous **étiez allés** à la boum,   *If you **had gone** to the party,*
  vous **vous seriez amusés**.   *you **would have had fun**.*

Hypothetical sentences that refer to the past are usually formed according to the pattern:

si-clause	MAIN or RESULT clause
pluperfect	past conditional

si j'avais su, j'aurais pris le métro

Teaching Strategy:

Divide the class into pairs. Have them imagine that they have a very obnoxious friend who enjoys letting them know she/he's always right by saying "I told you so...!" Ask the students to write five sentences, from the point of view of the obnoxious friend, pointing out what you did wrong using the past conditional.

Differentiation

Cumulative Review the conditional form of the verbs **avoir** and **être**. Write some verbs on the board and have students tell if they are conjugated with **avoir** or with **être**. Then, write two columns on the board: 1= Conditional of **avoir** or **être**; 2= Past participle. For each verb, have students generate the forms.

■ **Note linguistique**
Remind students:
The past participle of **devoir** takes a circumflex accent only in the singular masculine form: **dû, due, dus, dues.**

ALLONS PLUS LOIN
Note the English equivalents of the past conditional of **vouloir, pouvoir** and **devoir.**

J'**aurais voulu voir** ce film.   *I **wish I had seen** that movie.*
                                          *(I **would have liked to see** that movie.)*

Tu **aurais pu me téléphoner**.   *You **could have called me**.*

Vous **auriez dû attendre**.   *You **should have waited**.*

❶ L'incendie

Sébastien habite au deuxième étage d'un immeuble. Hier, il y a eu un commencement *(beginning)* d'incendie *(fire)* dans cet immeuble. Voici ce qu'il a fait. Dites si oui ou non vous auriez fait les mêmes choses.

▶ Sébastien est resté calme.
   Moi aussi, je serais resté(e) calme.
   (Moi, je ne serais pas resté(e) calme.)

1. Il a téléphoné aux pompiers.
2. Il a téléphoné à sa copine.
3. Il a fermé la porte de l'appartement à clé.
4. Il a pris sa tablette.
5. Il a laissé son argent dans un tiroir *(drawer)*.
6. Il est allé dans la salle de bains.
7. Il a mis une serviette mouillée *(wet)* sous la porte.
8. Il a ouvert la fenêtre.
9. Il a attendu dix minutes.
10. Il s'est impatienté.
11. Il a sauté *(jumped)* par la fenêtre.
12. Il s'est cassé la jambe.

❷ Vive la différence! 💬

Votre partenaire est allé(e) en ville. Il/elle explique ce qu'il/elle a fait. Dites lui que vous auriez fait quelque chose de différent. (Utilisez le même verbe, mais avec une expression de votre choix.)

▶ aller au musée
   — **Je suis allé(e) au musée.**
   — **Eh bien moi, à ta place, je ne serais pas allé(e) au musée.**
      Je serais allé(e) au ciné (au café, dans les magasins, . . .).

1. voir une exposition
2. déjeuner au café
3. manger un sandwich
4. se promener dans le parc
5. passer à la Maison des Jeunes
6. aller au centre commercial
7. acheter des jeux vidéo
8. rentrer à pied

❸ Tant pis pour toi! 💬

Votre partenaire vous décrit certains problèmes qu'il/elle a eus. Dites-lui que c'est de sa faute et expliquez pourquoi.

▶ rater l'examen / étudier

1. se perdre en ville / prendre ton plan *(map)*?
2. attendre une heure au restaurant / réserver une table?
3. arriver en retard au rendez-vous / regarder ta montre?
4. attraper un coup de soleil / mettre de la crème solaire?

J'ai raté l'examen.

Est-ce que tu avais étudié?

Non, je n'avais pas étudié.

Tant pis pour toi!
Si tu avais étudié, tu n'aurais pas raté l'examen.

Teaching Strategy: Expansion

Give students the following situations:
Avec votre partenaire, choisissez l'une des situations suivantes. Discutez de ce que vous auriez fait et de ce que vous n'auriez pas fait dans cette situation. Si vous voulez, écrivez une composition où vous décrirez les résultats de votre discussion.
1. S'il avait fait très beau (ou très mauvais) le week-end dernier …
2. S'il y avait eu une panne d'électricité *(power failure)* hier soir …
3. Si vous étiez allé(e) en France l'été dernier …
4. Si vous aviez eu plus de temps le mois dernier …
5. Si vous étiez né(e) dans une famille très riche …

@HOMETUTOR
my.hrw.com

4 Dommage!

Les personnes suivantes n'ont pas fait certaines choses. Décrivez ce qui serait arrivé si elles avaient fait ces choses. Attention: le verbe entre parenthèses peut être affirmatif ou négatif.

▶ Jérôme n'a pas fait attention. (tomber dans les escaliers?)
Si Jérôme avait fait attention, il ne serait pas tombé dans les escaliers.

1. Nous ne nous sommes pas dépêchés. (rater le train?)
2. Patrick n'a pas lu les annonces. (trouver un job cet été?)
3. Mes copains n'ont pas acheté de billets. (aller au concert?)
4. Je n'ai pas utilisé ma calculatrice. (se tromper dans le problème?)
5. Les joueurs ne se sont pas entraînés. (gagner le match?)
6. Vous n'avez pas attendu. (voir l'éclipse?)
7. Tu n'as pas mis ton manteau. (attraper une pneumonie?)
8. Les élèves ne se sont pas reposés. (dormir pendant la classe?)
9. Le Petit Chaperon Rouge *(Little Red Riding Hood)* n'a pas écouté sa mère. (rencontrer le loup *[wolf]*?)

B Résumé: l'usage des temps avec *si*

Review the sequence of tenses with **si**.

To describe...	si–clause	main or result clause	
• a possibility (concerning a future event)	PRESENT	FUTURE IMPERATIVE	**Si** je **vais** en ville, j'**achèterai** le journal. **Si** tu **vas** au supermarché, **achète** du pain.
• a hypothetical situation (usually contrary to reality)	IMPERFECT	CONDITIONAL	**Si** j'**avais** un billet, j'**irais** au concert.
• a hypothetical situation in the past	PLUPERFECT	PAST CONDITIONAL	**Si** j'**avais étudié**, je **n'aurais pas raté** l'examen.

5 Vive la différence!

Vous et votre partenaire, vous n'êtes pas d'accord. Votre partenaire vous dit ce qu'il/elle fera. Dites-lui ce que vous feriez si vous étiez dans les mêmes circonstances. (Choisissez une option différente.)

▶ avoir faim / manger quoi?
— Si j'ai faim, je mangerai un sandwich.
— Eh bien, moi, si j'avais faim, je mangerais une pizza.

1. avoir soif / boire quoi?
2. avoir de l'argent / acheter quoi?
3. sortir samedi / aller où ?
4. aller au cinéma / voir quoi?
5. aller à Paris / visiter quoi?
6. aller en Europe / voyager comment?

■ Notes linguistiques

In French, as in English, the sequence of tenses may be modified to reflect the sequence of facts or situations described.

si-clause	→	result clause
IMPERFECT	→	PAST CONDITIONAL

Si tu **étais** généreux, tu m'**aurais prêté** ta voiture.

PLUPERFECT	→	PRESENT CONDITIONAL

Si tu **avais dormi** la nuit dernière, tu **ne serais pas** fatigué maintenant.

■ Teaching Strategy: Review

On a piece of posterboard, draw a 5 x 5 grid with a different verb in each box. Make a spinner with five different tenses (imperfect, pluperfect, conditional, past conditional, future). Put the posterboard in the front of the class, divide the class into pairs, and begin spinning the spinner. The first tense (determined by the spinner) goes with the verb in the top left-hand corner. Give the pairs ten seconds to write the proper conjugation in a 5 x 5 grid that they have drawn on a piece of paper. Continue spinning until the grid has been completed. Do not repeat or slow down. Go over conjugations.

Differentiation

Metacognitive, Gifted & Talented Write the summarizing chart from page 324 on the board, with blanks in each box. Have students generate vocabulary to fill each box and explain their answer (as needed). Then, have them write a poem or song titled "Si," using the vocabulary from the box or additional vocabulary. Have students present their poem or song to the class.

6 Et si cela arrivait . . . ?

Avec votre partenaire, choisissez une des situations suivantes et discutez de ce que vous feriez et de ce que vous ne feriez pas si vous étiez dans cette situation. Puis, écrivez un paragraphe d'au moins 5 lignes où vous décrirez les résultats de votre discussion.

1. Vous êtes témoins d'un cambriolage.
2. Vous êtes prisonniers/prisonnières de dangereux bandits.
3. Vous êtes perdu(e)s dans la jungle tropicale.
4. Vous êtes invité(e)s à la Maison Blanche.
5. Vous assistez au mariage d'un copain français.
6. Un réalisateur *(movie producer)* vous offre un rôle dans son prochain film.
7. Vous découvrez un trésor *(treasure)* dans une maison abandonnée.

7 Achats

Complétez les phrases suivantes avec la forme du verbe **acheter** qui convient.

1. Si je vais à la poste, j'___ des timbres.
2. Si nous ___ des billets, nous aurions pu aller au concert samedi soir.
3. S'il avait de l'argent, mon oncle ___ un appartement dans le centre-ville.
4. Qu'est-ce que tu ___ si tu gagnes de l'argent l'été prochain?
5. Si j'étais passé à la boulangerie, j'___ des croissants.
6. Si tu ___ des CD dans ce magasin, tu paieras moins cher.
7. Est-ce que tu ___ cette veste si elle était en solde?
8. Si Paul ___ une moto, il vendrait son vélo.

8 Un discours électoral

À chaque élection, Monsieur Duroc est candidat à la mairie de Clocheville. Cette année, il se présente à nouveau. Vous êtes son/sa secrétaire. Complétez son discours *(speech)* avec la forme correcte du verbe entre parenthèses.

Messieurs et Mesdames,

J'ai le plaisir d'annoncer pour la sixième fois ma candidature à la mairie de Clocheville. Si vous (voter) pour moi aux dernières élections, vous (voir) les nombreuses améliorations que j'(apporter) à notre bonne ville. Je/j' (construire) une nouvelle gendarmerie, une nouvelle poste et, bien sûr, une nouvelle mairie. J'(éliminer) la pollution et la criminalité. Aujourd'hui, votre ville (être) belle, propre et sans danger.

Malheureusement, aux dernières élections, vous avez voté pour mon adversaire qui est un incapable. Si je/j' (être) à sa place, je/j' (avoir) honte de me présenter à nouveau. Heureusement, vous êtes intelligents. Quand vous (voter) pour moi dimanche prochain, vous (voter) pour quelqu'un de responsable et d'honnête. Si je/j' (être) élu, vous (pouvoir) être fiers à nouveau de votre ville!

Merci!

Notes culturelles

- In France, a mayor is elected by the city council, called **le conseil municipal.** The council itself is elected by the citizens of the city. The mayor and the council are elected for six years. To run for mayor, you must be at least 18.

- In France, elections are always held on Sundays. If none of the candidates for a particular position receives an absolute majority (more than 50% of the vote), a run-off election is held.

Unité 8

Interdisciplinary/ Community Connections

Make posters (in French!) of enjoyable activities for your chamber of commerce or tourism office.

Language Arts
Brainstorm activities available in your area, using the Internet, the library, local sports clubs, and other sources. Be sure to include seasonal activities as well as permanent ones.

Math
Graph the results of the social studies surveys: How many people enjoy town bicycle trails? How many visit a ski hill nearby?

Science/Health
Investigate science or technology museums and exhibits to include.

Social Studies
Interview friends and neighbors about what they do for fun in the area. If possible, ask about activities involving French, such as museum exhibits of French artwork, concerts of music by French composers, or French restaurants.

Art/Music
Find out about museums, art galleries, professional and amateur concerts. Use photos, drawings, or other media in the design of your posters.

Technology
Use the computer to compile information into a report. OR Find out how technology is involved in any of the activities.

Community
Complete and donate your posters for others to enjoy.

■ **Pronunciation**
jungle /ʒɑ̃gl/ or /ʒɔ̃gl/

RESOURCES

PRINT 📖
Activités pour tous

TECHNOLOGY
Teacher One Stop
🖥 **Projectable Transparencies**
    L8, *Les pêches*
    Transparency Copymasters,
    pp. A133–A134
French InterActive Reader

■ **Additional Information**
At the same time he was an author,
André Theuriet also had a career as
a civil servant in the Department of
Finance. Some of his other works
include:
    Le Bleu et le noir,
    Amour d'automne,
    La Fortune d'Angèle,
    Reine des bois.

■ **Note linguistique**
le standing = la position sociale

LECTURE

d'après André Theriet

Les pêches

AVANT DE LIRE

Le contexte historique

Pour bien comprendre une histoire, il faut la placer
dans son contexte historique. L'histoire suivante se passe
à la «Belle Époque», il y a environ° cent ans. La vie était
alors assez différente d'aujourd'hui et deux aspects sont
particulièrement importants pour l'histoire que vous
allez lire.
  • À cette époque, les gens riches organisaient
de temps en temps de grandes réceptions° chez eux.
Ces fêtes, généralement très formelles, étaient des
événements importants de la vie mondaine.° Il était donc
essentiel pour son standing social d'y être invité.
  • Un autre aspect important pour l'histoire concerne l'alimentation
d'alors. Comme les transports étaient très limités (l'automobile et
l'avion n'existaient pas encore!), la distribution des produits frais,°
et particulièrement des fruits, était très localisée et très saisonnière.
Si on voulait manger des fruits frais, il fallait attendre l'été, ou bien,
si on avait beaucoup d'argent, il fallait faire venir° spécialement ces
produits de Provence, d'Italie ou d'Espagne.

environ = approximativement **réception** = soirée de gala **mondaine** = sociale **frais** *fresh*
faire venir *to have shipped*

André Theuriet (1833-1907)
Comme beaucoup d'écrivains
français, André Theuriet s'est
exprimé dans des genres
littéraires différents: le roman, le
conte, la poésie, le théâtre. Dans
ses contes, Theuriet décrit la
société de son époque. Pour
son oeuvre, il a été élu membre
de l'Académie Française.

Teaching Notes
• This story fits the cultural and linguistic
  themes of both Units 8 and 10. Depending on
  your scheduling, you can either present this
  story now or postpone it until Unit 10.
• For a definition of **la Belle Époque,** refer
  your students to *Interlude 6,* p. 252.

• You may wish to use **Projectable
  Transparency L8** to help students get a
  visual overview of the story before beginning
  to read. Use the *Anticipons un peu* questions
  to help students read with a critical focus.

Anticipons un peu!

Imaginez que vous êtes invité(e) à un très grand mariage. Votre meilleur(e) ami(e), qui est malade, ne peut pas vous accompagner. Vous lui avez promis de lui rapporter un morceau° du gâteau nuptial.

Le gâteau a été servi, mais comme vous êtes un peu timide, vous n'avez pas osé° en demander un second morceau à l'hôtesse. Vous n'avez cependant pas oublié votre promesse.

Vous allez au buffet et, quand personne ne regarde, vous prenez un morceau de gâteau pour votre ami(e). Comment feriez-vous pour le ramener° sans être vu(e)?

• Je le mettrais dans ma poche de pantalon ou de jupe.
• Je le cacherais sous ma veste.
• Je le mettrais dans mon sac.
• Je l'envelopperais dans une serviette.°

morceau *piece* **osé** *dared* **ramener** *to bring back* **serviette** *napkin*

LES PÊCHES

1

C'est au cours d'un dîner organisé par les anciens élèves du lycée de province où j'avais fait mes études que j'ai revu mon copain d'enfance Vital Herbelot. C'est lui qui est venu me saluer° après le café. À vrai dire, je ne l'avais pas reconnu. Vêtu d'un costume de velours côtelé° et d'une chemise à carreaux,° les cheveux en brosse et le visage bronzé, il respirait° la santé et la bonne humeur. Certes, ce n'était pas le grand garçon élégant, distingué, mais un peu timide, que j'avais connu vingt-cinq ans avant. Élève très doué, il était promis à l'avenir le plus brillant. Après le bac, il avait tout de suite trouvé un poste dans la plus grande banque de la ville.

Un peu surpris de le revoir, je lui ai demandé:

— Alors, tu es° toujours dans la banque?

— Oh non, il y a bien longtemps que je l'ai quittée. . . J'habite à la campagne maintenant…

Je suis cultivateur!

— Cultivateur, toi?! Mais je croyais que tu t'intéressais à la finance.

— C'est vrai… Et si j'avais continué, j'aurais certainement fait une «brillante carrière», comme on dit . . .Aujourd'hui je serais peut-être le président d'une grande banque nationale ou internationale… Qui sait? Mais tu vois, il m'est arrivé quelque chose°, il y a vingt ans de cela.

— Quoi? Qu'est-ce qui t'est arrivé?

— Oh, une histoire de pêches . . . mais une histoire qui a changé mon existence. Pour le meilleur!

— Tu as dit «une histoire de pêches»?

— Oui, une absurde histoire de pêches.

Voulant satisfaire ma curiosité évidente, Vital Herbelot a commencé à me raconter son histoire.

Mots utiles

un ancien élève	*alumnus*
un cultivateur	*farmer*
une pêche	*peach*
doué	*gifted*
vêtu de	*dressed in*
au cours de	*during, in the course of*
à vrai dire	*to tell the truth*

saluer = dire bonjour **velours côtelé** *corduroy* **à carreaux** *plaid* **respirait** = était l'expression de
tu es = tu travailles **il m'est arrivé quelque chose** *something happened to me*

■ **Pour en savoir plus**
For more information on the history of the **bac,** and the **bac** of today, refer your students to *Info Magazine 1* of Unit 10, pp. 383–385.

Teaching Strategy

You may wish to point out the following homonyms in French:

pêcher *to fish*
pécher *to sin*

la pêche *peach*
la pêche *fishing*

le pêcher *peach tree*
le péché *sin*

le pêcheur *fisherman*
le pécheur *sinner*

(la pêcheuse–*fisherwoman***)**
(la pécheresse–*sinner***)**

Tu sais que j'étais fils et petit-fils d'employés relativement modestes.° C'est ma mère qui a insisté pour que je fasse des études et que j'obtienne mon bac. Tu te souviens, sans doute, que j'aimais les étud et que j'ai obtenu mon bac avec mention.° Aussi, je n'ai pas eu de
35 difficulté à trouver du travail.

Après le bac, j'ai été immédiatement embauché dans une grande banque d'affaires.° Tous mes camarades de classe convoitaient° le poste que je venais d'obtenir. Rappelle-toi comme vous étiez tous un peu jaloux de moi! Comme j'étais très travailleur et très disciplin
40 et que je réussissais bien dans les affaires que je traitais, j'ai vite obtenu plusieurs promotions, et avec celles-ci des augmentations de salaire importantes.

Au bout de trois ans, j'étais devenu l'un des adjoints° principaux
45 du patron de la banque. Je t'assure que je gagnais bien ma vie, mais en contrepartie,° je devais sacrifier tout mon temps aux affaires de la banque. C'est à ce moment-là que je me suis marié avec une jeune fille qui avait toutes les qualités et qui, de plus, était très jolie.

Mots utiles

embaucher	*to hire*
obtenir *	*to get, obtain*
au bout de	*after, at the end of*

Avez-vous compris?

1. À quelle occasion est-ce que le narrateur rencontre Vital Herbelot?
2. Pourquoi est-ce qu'il ne le reconnaît pas?
3. Quelle est la profession de Vital Herbelot maintenant?
4. Quelle était sa profession autrefois?

Irregular Verbs

(see Appendix C)
- **devoir**
- **nuire** is conjugated like **cuire: je nuis, il nuit, nous nuisons, ils nuisent.**
- **obtenir** (see **tenir**)

Avez-vous compris?

(Sample answers)
1. Il le rencontre au cours d'un dîner d'anciens élèves de son lycée.
2. Il ne le reconnaît pas parce qu'avant il était élégant et timide, et maintenant il est moins élégant, bronzé, de bonne humeur.
3. Il est cultivateur.
4. Autrefois, il travaillait dans une banque. Il était adjoint du patron.

Anticipons un peu!

Vital Herbelot avait une situation brillante. Maintenant, il est cultivateur.
À votre avis, qu'est-ce qui s'est passé?
- Il a eu un grave accident.
- Il a commis une faute *(mistake)* professionnelle.
- Sa femme est tombée malade.
- Quelque chose d'autre s'est passé. Imaginez quoi!

2

Mon patron était un homme très riche et très mondain.° De
50 temps en temps il organisait de grandes réceptions où il invitait tous les notables° de la ville et quelques-uns de ses employés supérieurs. Il y avait généralement un repas suivi d'un bal.

Peu de temps après mon mariage, j'ai reçu ma première invitation à l'une de ces réceptions. Malheureusement, quelques jours avant
55 l'événement, ma femme est tombée malade. Je pensais envoyer mes excuses, mais ma femme a insisté pour que j'aille à cette réception.
— Ton patron est un homme généreux, mais très autoritaire. S'il ne t voyait pas à la première réception à laquelle il t'invite, il serait certainement très vexé, et cela nuirait° à ta carrière.

modestes = *assez pauvres* **avec mention** *with honors*
une banque d'affaires *investment bank* **convoitaient** = *désiraient secrètement*
adjoints = *assistants* **en contrepartie** *in exchange* **mondain** *of fashionable society*
notables = *personnes importantes* **employés supérieurs** *top executives* **nuirait à** = *ruinerait*

Teaching Strategy

- Ask students if they have noticed any differences in the presentation of the story on this page versus page 327. (If they do not notice the change in typeface, indicating a change in narrator, point it out to them.) Why is this device used? Is it successful?

- Ask students the following questions: **À votre avis, pourquoi est-il important pour Vital Herbelot d'aller à cette réception? Quelles pourraient être les conséquences de son absence à cette soirée? Pre–AP skill:** Make inferences.

Bien sûr, j'aurais préféré rester avec ma femme, mais, convaincu par ses arguments, j'ai finalement accepté l'invitation.

Ce soir-là, je me suis donc habillé pour l'occasion. Alors qu'elle m'aidait à ajuster ma cravate, ma femme m'a dit:
—Je regrette vraiment de ne pas pouvoir t'accompagner.
Il y aura un très beau buffet . . . et j'ai entendu dire que la femme de ton patron a fait venir° spécialement des primeurs* du Midi. Il paraît même qu'il y aura des pêches… Tu sais comme je les aime. Et pourtant, c'est absolument impossible d'en trouver dans les magasins en cette saison… Oh, ces pêches! Est-ce que tu pourrais m'en rapporter une . . . Une seule . . . S'il te plaît!

Surpris de cette requête inattendue, j'ai essayé d'expliquer à ma femme que c'était difficile. Comment un monsieur en habit noir° pourrait-il prendre une pêche et la mettre dans sa poche sans être vu?

Mais ma femme a insisté: «Rien de plus facile, au contraire . . . Tu profiteras d'un moment où tout le monde sera en train de danser. Tu t'approcheras du buffet et tu prendras une pêche comme si c'était pour toi et tu la dissimuleras° adroitement.° Personne ne te verra… Oh, je sais bien, c'est un caprice,° mais ça me ferait tellement plaisir! Allez, promets-moi . . .»

Comment refuser quelque chose à la femme qu'on aime? J'ai fini par promettre, puis j'ai pris mon manteau et mon chapeau. Au moment où j'allais partir, ma femme m'a regardé de ses grands yeux bleus et m'a dit: «N'oublie pas!»

Mots utiles

un bal	*dance*
un caprice	*whim*
une pêche	*peach*
une requête	*request*
s'approcher de	*to approach*
convaincre *	*to convince*
entendre dire	*to hear (it said)*
faire plaisir à	*to please*
profiter de	*to take advantage of*
inattendu	*unexpected*
alors que	*while*

Avez-vous compris?

1. Pourquoi Madame Herbelot ne va-t-elle pas à la réception?
2. Pourquoi conseille-t-elle à son mari d'y aller?
3. Qu'est-ce qu'elle lui demande de faire?
4. Pourquoi est-ce que son mari hésite?

3

Ce soir-là, toute la société° de la ville était réunie° chez mon patron. Il y avait le maire, le président du tribunal, le général commandant la garnison et ses officiers supérieurs, et toutes les grandes familles de la ville.

Mon patron avait bien fait les choses. Le dîner était exquis. Après le dîner, les invités passèrent au grand salon et le bal commença. Vers

---

* Les primeurs du Midi. À cause de son climat, le Midi (dans le sud de la France) produit des primeurs, c'est-à-dire, des fruits et légumes consommables avant la saison normale.

a fait venir = a commandé   **habit noir** *formal evening dress*   **dissimuleras** = cacheras
adroitement *skillfully*   **caprice** *whim*   **la société** = la haute société   **était réunie** = se trouvait

■ Irregular Verb
(see Appendix C)
convaincre   (see **vaincre**)

■ Avez-vous compris?
(Sample answers)
1. Elle ne va pas à la réception parce qu'elle est tombée malade.
2. Elle lui conseille d'y aller parce que c'est utile pour sa carrière.
3. Elle lui demande de lui rapporter une pêche.
4. Il hésite parce que ce n'est pas facile de le faire discrètement.

■ Teaching Note
In episodes 3 and 4, the narrator shifts to the **passé simple** as he begins to narrate the action. If necessary, you may want to review this tense in Appendix C, pp. R32–R33.

Anticipons un peu!

À votre avis, comment est-ce que Vital Herbelot va satisfaire la requête de sa femme?
- Il va demander à l'hôtesse de la réception la permission de prendre une pêche.
- Il va prendre une pêche sans demander la permission.
- Il va acheter des pêches chez un marchand.
- Il va rentrer chez lui sans pêche.
- Il va faire autre chose. Imaginez quoi!

LECTURE

Note linguistique

Le buffet is the table where cold food, pastries, and refreshments are served during a party.

Irregular Verbs

(see Appendix C)
se produire (see **conduire**)

Avez-vous compris?

(Sample answers)

1. Les pêches sont servies après minuit par le maître d'hôtel, aux personnes indiquées par le patron. Elles sont coupées en deux.
2. Il prend les pêches quand les domestiques sont partis.
3. Il met les pêches dans son chapeau.

---

minuit, il y eut un temps de repos pendant lequel un buffet fut servi dans une petite pièce à côté du salon. Au milieu de la table trônaient les fameuses pêches venues° spécialement du Midi. Disposées° en pyramide sur un plateau de faïence,° elles provoquaient l'admiration
95 générale. Oui vraiment, elles étaient superbes! Je pensais alors à la promesse que j'avais faite à ma femme et me demandais comment j'allais la réaliser. Ce n'était pas facile!

Les domestiques préposés° au service montaient une garde vigilante° autour de ces magnifiques et coûteux fruits. De temps en
100 temps, sur un signe de mon patron, le maître d'hôtel prenait délicatement une pêche, la découpait avec un couteau d'argent, et en présentait les deux moitiés à un invité de marque.° Il en restait encore une demi-douzaine quand l'orchestre se remit° à jouer. Les invités se précipitèrent au salon et on recommença à danser.

105 C'est alors que j'exécutai mon projet. Je pris mon chapeau et mon manteau, comme si j'allais partir. Puis, sous un prétexte quelconque,° je passai dans la petite salle où était dressé° le buffet. Heureusement les domestiques étaient partis. Je me trouvais donc seul. M'assurant que personne ne me regardait, je ne pris non pas une
110 mais deux de ces magnifiques pêches et je les mis discrètement dans mon chapeau. Pressant celui-ci très fort° contre ma poitrine, j'allai saluer° mon hôte et mon hôtesse. Je les remerciai de leur aimable invitation, puis je me dirigeai, digne et fier de moi, vers la sortie.

115 Mon projet avait parfaitement réussi. Que ma femme serait heureuse quand elle verrait le produit de mon larcin inoffensif! C'est alors que se produisit l'incident . . .

---

trônaient = occupaient la place d'honneur   **venues** *brought*   **disposées** = arrangées
faïence *glazed pottery*   **préposés** *assigned*   **montaient une garde vigilante** *kept watchful guard*
de marque = important   **se remit à** = recommença à   **un prétexte quelconque** *some pretext or oth-*
dressé = placé   **fort** *tightly*   **saluer** = dire au revoir à

Mots utiles

un larcin	*small theft*
la moitié	*half*
la poitrine	*chest*
s'assurer	*to make sure*
découper	*to cut (into pieces)*
se demander	*to wonder*
se diriger vers	*to move toward*
se précipiter	*to dash*
se produire	*to happen*
digne	*dignified*
inoffensif	*harmless*
comme si	*as if*
reste . . .	*there is/ are . . . left*

Avez-vous compris?

1. À quel moment de la réception sont servies les pêches? Par qui? À qui? Comment?
2. Comment Vital Herbelot réussit-il à prendre deux pêches?
3. Qu'est-ce qu'il fait pour passer inaperçu *(unnoticed)*?

Anticipons un peu!

À votre avis, qu'est-ce qui va se passer ensuite?

- Vital Herbelot va apporter les pêches à sa femme qui sera très contente.
- Il sera dénoncé par un domestique qui l'a vu et il sera arrêté par la police.
- Après être sorti, il fera tomber *(will drop)* les pêches dans la rue et il ne pourra pas les rapporter à sa femme.
- Quelque chose d'autre arrivera. Imaginez quoi.

---

330 trois cent trente
Unité 8

Teaching Strategy

- Ask students to name a food that would be comparably extravagant today to the peaches in the story. (Exemples: le caviar, le homard, les truffes, le foie gras...)

- Ask students:
  À votre avis, Vital Herbelot a-t-il commis une faute grave? Expliquez votre opinion.

~ 4 ~

Avant de sortir, il fallait que je traverse le salon où les jeunes gens et les jeunes filles continuaient à valser.° On organisait justement une nouvelle figure: une danseuse est placée au centre des danseurs qui exécutent une ronde° autour d'elle. Elle doit tenir un chapeau à la main et en coiffer° le jeune homme avec qui elle veut danser. C'était justement la fille de mon patron qui devait se placer au centre du groupe. Me voyant avec mon chapeau pressé contre la poitrine, elle s'écria:

— Monsieur Herbelot! Monsieur Herbelot! Nous avons besoin de votre chapeau! S'il vous plaît, prêtez-le-nous pour quelques minutes seulement.

Et sans attendre ma réponse, elle me prit le chapeau des mains d'un mouvement brusque. Les pêches tombèrent et roulèrent sur le sol devant les invités ébahis.°

La musique s'arrêta. Tout le monde riait maintenant, sauf mon patron qui avait l'air absolument furieux. Même les domestiques semblaient se moquer de moi… Alors la fille du patron me donna mon chapeau en me disant d'une voix ironique:

— Eh bien, monsieur Herbelot, ramassez donc vos pêches!

J'aurais voulu être cent pieds sous terre.° Rouge de confusion, je pris mon chapeau, balbutiai° quelques mots d'excuses, et partis comme un fou. Je rentrai chez moi et, la mort dans le coeur, je racontai le désastre à ma femme.

Le lendemain, l'histoire courait° la ville. Quand je suis entré à mon bureau ce matin-là, mes collègues savaient ce qui s'était passé. Les plus malicieux° murmuraient° à mon passage: «Hé, Monsieur Herbelot, ramassez donc vos pêches.» Dans la rue, j'entendais les enfants des écoles dire en me montrant du doigt: «Regardez! C'est le monsieur aux pêches!»

Huit jours après, j'ai quitté la banque et la ville. Ma femme et moi, nous nous sommes installés à la campagne, chez un vieil oncle qui avait une grande ferme. Je ne connaissais rien aux travaux des champs,° mais avec l'aide de mon oncle, j'ai vite appris. Quand celui-ci est mort, j'ai hérité de la ferme. C'est comme ça que je suis devenu cultivateur!

Tiens, si tu es libre dimanche prochain, viens donc me rendre visite. Nous déjeunerons ensemble.

valser = danser la valse *(waltz)*   **exécutent une ronde** = dansent dans un cercle   **coiffer** = mettre sur la tête   **ébahis** *open-mouthed*   **sous terre** *underground*   **balbutiai** *mumbled*   **courait** = circulait dans **malicieux** *inclined to tease*   **murmuraient** *would say in a low voice* **travaux des champs** *farm work*

Mots utiles

hériter de	to inherit
s'installer	to settle
montrer du doigt	to point at
se moquer de	to laugh at, to make fun of
ramasser	to pick up
traverser	to go across, to cross
justement	precisely at that moment

Avez-vous compris?

1. De quelle façon le larcin de Vital Herbelot a-t-il été découvert?
2. Quelle a été la réaction des autres invités?
3. Quelle a été la réaction de ses collègues le lendemain?
4. Qu'est-ce qu'il a décidé de faire à la suite de l'incident?

Et vous?

Qu'est-ce que vous auriez fait si vous aviez été à la place de Vital Herbelot? Expliquez pourquoi.

• J'aurais présenté mes excuses à mon patron et j'aurais gardé mon poste.
• J'aurais fait un procès *(filed a suit)* à mes collègues de bureau pour harcèlement professionnel.
• J'aurais quitté la ville et j'aurais cherché un travail similaire dans une autre ville.
• J'aurais fait comme Vital Herbelot.
• J'aurais fait quelque chose d'autre. Expliquez quoi.

■ **Irregular Verb**

(see Appendix C)
courir

■ **Teaching Note**
Have students note that this is the end of the Herbelot narration.

■ *Avez-vous compris?*
(Sample answers)
1. Son larcin a été découvert parce qu'une jeune fille lui a demandé son chapeau pour une danse.
2. Les autres invités ont beaucoup ri.
3. Le lendemain, ses collègues ont dit: «Ramassez vos pêches!»
4. Il a décidé de quitter la banque et la ville, et d'aller chez un oncle qui avait une ferme.

■ Teaching Note

Ask students if they noted that the conclusion is presented by the initial narrator.

■ Irregular Verbs

(see Appendix C)
cueillir
sourire   *(see **rire**)*

■ Note linguistique

The expression **un bureaucrate** is pejorative. It generally refers to a petty civil servant who thinks he is very powerful.

Italicized teaching column on left:

■ Teaching Note

Ask students if they noted that the conclusion is presented by the initial narrator.

■ Irregular Verbs

(see Appendix C)
cueillir
sourire   *(see **rire**)*

■ Note linguistique

The expression **un bureaucrate** is pejorative. It generally refers to a petty civil servant who thinks he is very powerful.

■ *Avez-vous compris?*

(Sample answers)
1. À la ferme, l'atmosphère est sympathique.
2. Il est très heureux de son sort.

Mots utiles

un verger	*orchard*
un pêcher	*peach tree*
cueillir *	*to pick*
sourire *	*to smile*
d'ailleurs	*besides*
en souvenir de	*in memory*

chargé de *laden with*   **travaux des champs** *farm work*

5

155 Intrigué par l'histoire de mon ancien camarade de lycée, j'ai accepté son invitation. Le dimanche suivant, je suis donc allé chez lui. Là, j'ai fait la connaissance de sa femme, toujours jolie à quarante-cinq ans, et de leurs magnifiques enfants. Nous avons fait un excellent déjeuner, accompagné d'un agréable vin blanc que mon ami faisait lui-même.

160 Après le déjeuner, il m'a proposé de faire un tour de la ferme. Il était particulièrement fier de son verger. Alors que j'admirais particulièrement un pêcher chargé de fruits splendides, il m'a dit:

— Celui-là, je l'ai planté en souvenir de l'histoire que je t'ai 165 racontée! J'ai eu de la chance. Sans cette histoire absurde, je serais resté un bureaucrate toute ma vie. D'accord, j'aurais peut-être plus d'argent, mais je ne serais pas plus heureux. D'ailleurs, comment être plus heureux? J'ai tout pour moi.

170 Puis, il a cueilli deux énormes pêches et il me les donna en souriant:

— Tu verras! Ce sera les meilleures pêches que tu aies jamais mangées!

Avez-vous compris?

1. Quelle est l'atmosphère générale à la ferme de Vital Herbelot?
2. Qu'est-ce que Vital Herbelot pense de son sort *(fate)*?

À votre avis

Est-ce que Vital Herbelot a pris la meilleure décision possible? Expliquez pourquoi.

APRÈS LA LECTURE

𝓔xpression orale

La morale de l'histoire
L'histoire des pêches peut avoir plusieurs morales. Choisissez l'une des morales suivantes (ou bien, créez votre propre morale) et expliquez pourquoi elle correspond le mieux à l'histoire.

• L'argent ne fait pas le bonheur.

• Les petits incidents peuvent avoir des conséquences importantes.
• Il vaut mieux être pauvre que ridicule.
• Le crime ne paie pas.
• Il ne faut jamais écouter les mauvais conseils.
• Le ridicule tue.
• Les gens trop ambitieux sont toujours punis.

Notes linguistiques

• When **ce + être** is followed by a plural noun, **être** generally agrees with the noun. The singular form is, however, commonly used in the spoken language. Here:
Ce sera les meilleures pêches... (spoken)
Ce seront les meilleures pêches... (written)
• When **ce + être** is followed by the pronoun **moi, toi, nous,** or **vous,** then **être** is in the 3rd person singular: **C'est moi. / C'est nous qui avons mangé la tarte.**
• When **ce + être** is followed by the pronoun **eux** or **elles,** then **être** is in the 3rd person plural: **Ce sont eux. Ce sont elles.** The singular is commonly used, especially in the negative form: **Ce n'est pas eux. C'est elles.**

Débat

Avec votre partenaire, débattez les avantages et les inconvénients de la vie en ville et à la campagne, en fonction de l'histoire que vous avez lue. Chacun va choisir une opinion différente.

Situations

Avec votre partenaire, choisissez l'une des situations suivantes. Composez le dialogue correspondant et jouez-le en classe.

1	**Détails**

Quand elle voit rentrer son mari le soir de la réception, Madame Herbelot comprend que quelque chose d'extraordinaire s'est passé. Elle veut avoir des détails.

Rôles: Monsieur et Madame Herbelot

2	**À la fête**

Une personne qui a assisté à la fête raconte l'histoire des pêches à un(e) voisin(e). Ce(tte) voisin(e) pose beaucoup de questions. La personne qui a été à la fête a tendance à exagérer un peu pour faire plus d'effet.

Rôles: la personne qui a été à la réception et son(sa) voisin(e)

3	**Une décision**

Le jour après l'incident, Vital Herbelot explique à sa femme ce qui s'est passé au bureau et dans la rue. Ils discutent de ce qu'ils doivent faire pour éviter *(to avoid)* ces problèmes. Ils prennent une décision.

Rôles: Monsieur et Madame Herbelot

4	**Vingt ans après**

Vingt ans après l'incident, l'un des enfants de Vital Herbelot apprend que son père a été cadre *(executive)* dans une banque. Il veut connaître le passé de son père.

Rôles: Monsieur Herbelot et son fils (sa fille)

5	**Ville ou campagne ?**

Après la promenade dans la ferme, le camarade de lycée de Vital Herbelot explique à son ami que la vie en ville a beaucoup d'avantages aussi. Vital Herbelot n'est pas d'accord.

Rôles: Vital Herbelot et son camarade de lycée

Expression écrite

«La Belle époque»

Relisez le texte et faites une liste des détails qui indiquent que cette histoire se passe il y a cent ans.

Lettre à un(e) ami(e)

Imaginez que vous êtes dans la situation de Vital Herbelot. Après avoir terminé vos études, vous avez trouvé un bon poste dans une banque (ou une autre sorte de travail). Vous avez reçu plusieurs promotions et vous gagnez très bien votre vie. Un jour, cependant, vous réalisez que cette existence ne correspond pas à ce que vous voulez vraiment faire.

Écrivez une lettre à un(e) ami(e). Dans cette lettre, informez-le(la) de votre décision de quitter votre travail, expliquez pourquoi et dites ce que vous allez faire.

Sujets de composition

1. Une situation embarrassante.
Décrivez une situation embarrassante, réelle ou imaginaire, dans laquelle une personne que vous connaissez s'est trouvée.

2. Un incident
Décrivez une situation, réelle ou imaginaire, dans laquelle un petit incident a eu des conséquences très importantes pour vous ou pour une personne que vous connaissez.

Student Portfolios

Using the activities in the *Après la lecture* section, have students choose one or two activities for their portfolios. If a group of students decide to work together to produce a debate, see if other students will volunteer to video the event and make copies for the participants' portfolios.

■ **Note linguistique**

Note the following familiar expressions:
- **avoir la pêche** *to be in great form/spirits*
- **se fendre la pêche** *to laugh*

■ **Teaching Note**

You may wish to use the short Lecture quiz as a comprehension check before students begin the activities in the *Après la lecture* section.

■ **Expression écrite**

For writing rubrics, consult the **Generate Success** Rubric Generator on the **Teacher One Stop.** You can also create your own custom rubrics with this tool.

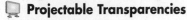
TECHNOLOGY

Teacher One Stop

Pre-AP Digital Resources

📺 **Projectable Transparencies**

H5, *La France et le Nouveau Monde*

3, *Le monde francophone: L'Amérique*

Transparency Copymasters, pp. A145–A146, A6–A7

■ **Notes linguistiques**

• **Martinique** vient du nom Martin, car l'île fut découverte le onze novembre, date qui correspond à la Saint Martin dans le calendrier catholique.

• **Guadeloupe** vient de Notre-Dame de Guadalupe d'Estremadure. Christophe Colomb choisit ce nom pour remercier Notre-Dame qu'il avait priée lors d'une tempête. Avant cela, les habitants appelaient leur île **Calouacaera**.

■ **Pour en savoir plus**

For more information on the events leading up to 1763, see *Interlude 10*, p. 412.

Un peu d'histoire

Les dates	Les événements
1492-1502	■ Christophe Colomb fait plusieurs voyages en Amérique. Au cours de° ces voyages, il «découvre» plusieurs îles qui seront plus tard occupées par les Français: Hispaniola (1492), la Guadeloupe (1493), la Martinique (1502). À l'époque de Christophe Colomb, ces îles étaient habitées depuis des siècles par différents groupes d'«Indiens» — nom donné par Christophe Colomb aux populations caraïbes. Ces Indiens sont rapidement décimés° par les maladies et les mauvais traitements des Européens.
1635	■ Les premiers colons° français arrivent à la Martinique et à la Guadeloupe. Peu après, ils font venir° de force des Africains pour travailler comme esclaves° dans leurs plantations.
vers 1640	■ L'île de la Tortue,° au nord-ouest d'Hispaniola, sert de base à des pirates de toutes nationalités. Des colons français s'installent à Saint-Domingue, la partie ouest d'Hispaniola.
1697	■ Saint-Domingue (Haïti) devient officiellement une colonie française.
1763	■ La France perd ses colonies continentales d'Amérique (le Canada, la Louisiane), mais elle garde ses îles des Antilles.
1791	■ Les Africains de Saint-Domingue se révoltent contre les Français. Toussaint Louverture devient l'un des chefs de cette révolte.
1794	■ La Révolution française déclare l'abolition de l'esclavage dans toutes ses colonies.
1802	■ L'esclavage est rétabli par Napoléon, ce qui provoque une nouvelle insurrection en Haïti. Napoléon envoie ses troupes pour mater° cette insurrection.
1804	■ Après la victoire des Africains révoltés sur les troupes françaises, Saint-Domingue devient un pays indépendant et prend le nom d'Haïti. Les Français quittent Haïti, mais le français reste la langue officielle du pays.
1848	■ L'esclavage est définitivement aboli dans les colonies françaises. Les habitants de la Martinique et de la Guadeloupe deviennent des citoyens° français à part entière.°
1902	■ L'éruption de la montagne Pelée à la Martinique fait plus de 30 000 morts.
1946	■ La Martinique et la Guadeloupe deviennent des départements d'outre-mer.°
1990	■ Jean-Bertrand Aristide est élu démocratiquement Président de la République haïtienne. Quelques mois après, un coup d'État militaire l'oblige à s'exiler.
2010	■ Un sévère tremblement de terre° dévaste Haïti.

au cours de = pendant   **décimés** *killed*   **colons** *settlers*   **ils font venir** = ils amènent   **esclaves** *slaves*   **tortue** *turtle*   **mater** *to put down*
citoyens *citizens*   **à part entière** = 100%   **outre-mer** *overseas*   **tremblement de terre** *earthquake*

Note culturelles

• **Les Antilles** est le nom généralement donné aux îles de la mer Caraïbe. (Les Caraïbes étaient les Indiens qui habitaient ces îles avant l'arrivée de Christophe Colomb.) Les Antilles francophones comprennent les départements français de la Martinique et de la Guadeloupe, et la république d'Haïti.

• La fameuse **Île de la Tortue**, repaire de pirates, était française de 1665 à 1804. Depuis 1804, cette île, connue sous le nom espagnol de Tortuga, fait partie d'Haïti.

La malédiction caraïbe

Nous sommes à la Martinique en 1900. À cette époque, Saint-Pierre est la capitale de l'île. Avec ses distilleries, ses docks, ses magasins, ses banques, c'est un centre économique et commercial très actif. Dans le port, on peut voir des bateaux français, mais aussi des bateaux anglais, des bateaux américains, des bateaux italiens, des bateaux japonais, des bateaux chiliens ... Sur ces bateaux, les marins chargent° le sucre, le rhum et les produits tropicaux de l'île.

Saint-Pierre est aussi une ville artistique et culturelle. Le dimanche, les gens vont au concert ou au théâtre. Il y a, en effet, un théâtre, le seul théâtre de toutes les Antilles. Saint-Pierre mérite bien son nom de «Paris des Antilles».

En réalité, Saint-Pierre est une ville en danger. La ville est située au pied d'un volcan, la montagne Pelée. Le 8 mai 1902, à sept heures cinquante du matin, la montagne Pelée explose! À huit heures, la ville est totalement dévastée. La cathédrale, le théâtre, le jardin botanique, les monuments, les maisons sont maintenant un immense désert de ruines. En moins de cinq minutes, toute la population de Saint-Pierre a péri.° Il y a 30 000 victimes ... et un survivant. Ce survivant est un prisonnier. Ironiquement, les murs de la prison l'ont protégé contre la violence de l'explosion.

L'explosion de la montagne Pelée est une des grandes catastrophes dans l'histoire de l'humanité. Cette catastrophe a été annoncée dans une vieille légende caraïbe. Les Indiens caraïbes sont les premiers habitants de la Martinique. Quand les Français arrivent en 1635, ils veulent faire des Caraïbes leurs esclaves. Les Caraïbes résistent, mais ils sont finalement battus.° Courageusement, ils préfèrent la mort à l'esclavage.

Avant de mourir, le dernier chef caraïbe donne sa malédiction° aux Français:

> «Aujourd'hui, vous êtes les plus forts,
> mais demain
> la montagne de feu va nous venger.»°

La «montagne de feu», c'est bien sûr la montagne Pelée. Le 8 mai 1902, la malédiction caraïbe s'est réalisée!

chargent *load*   **péri** *perished, died*   **battus** *beaten*   **malédiction** *curse*   **venger** *to avenge*

■ Note historique

Fort-de-France est devenue la capitale (ou **chef-lieu**) de la Martinique après la destruction de Saint-Pierre.

■ Anecdote

The survivor of the eruption of **Mt. Pelée**, a man called **Cyparis**, later joined the Barnum and Bailey circus.

■ Additional Information

Guadeloupe is another volcanic island. The volcano **la Soufrière** is the highest point of the island at 1467 meters (4812 feet). It erupted in 1956 and 1976 and is still active today.

Expansion

Internet Connection – Interlude 8
Visit **http://my.hrw.com** for more information and useful links about the French West Indies.

Communities
Standard 5.2 Students show evidence of becoming lifelong learners by using French for personal enjoyment and enrichment.

■ Pour en savoir plus

For historical background on the French Revolution, see *Interlude 5*, pp. 216–225.

■ Note culturelle

More than 50,000 African slaves were sent to Martinique in 1636 to work in the plantations. They came mostly from Angola, Guinea, and Senegal.

■ Additional Information

• Unable to give an heir to Napoleon, **Joséphine** was repudiated in 1809. The civil marriage was annulled on the grounds that one of the witnesses was under age (he was nineteen at the time). Joséphine had two children from her previous marriage with **de Beauharnais.** After the annulment, she kept her imperial title and retired in her castle of **Malmaison** where she died in 1814.

• **La Guyane** (French Guiana) is located in South America and borders the Atlantic Ocean between Suriname and Brazil. Until 1953, it served as a French penal colony. In 1968, the **Centre spatial guyanais** was built at **Kourou.** Today the spaceport is maintained by the European Space Agency and is used to launch the Ariane 5 as well as the Soyuz and Vega rockets.

Deux Martiniquais célèbres

■ L'impératrice Joséphine (1763-1814)

Joséphine Tascher de la Pagerie est née à la Martinique dans la plantation de ses parents. Un jour, quand elle était petite, sa gouvernante° noire lui dit: «Un jour, tu gouverneras la France.» Joséphine évidemment ne croit pas cette prédiction extraordinaire. Elle grandit° et devient une jeune fille très belle et très élégante. À seize ans, elle épouse un jeune officier noble, Alexandre de Beauharnais, mais celui-ci est guillotiné pendant la Révolution. Joséphine elle-même est emprisonnée et échappe de peu° à la mort.

Peu de temps après, Joséphine rencontre Napoléon qui tombe éperdument° amoureux d'elle. Ils se marient en 1796. Quand Napoléon devient empereur en 1804, Joséphine devient impératrice,° réalisant ainsi la prédiction de sa gouvernante. Joséphine et Napoléon n'ont pas d'enfant. Napoléon veut avoir un fils pour assurer la succession de son trône. Il divorce et se remarie avec une princesse autrichienne.° Cependant, Napoléon reste très ami avec Joséphine qui, pour les Français, continue d'être la véritable° impératrice.

L'impératrice Joséphine

Aimé Césaire, poète et homme politique

■ Aimé Césaire (1913- 2008): Poète et homme politique

Originaire de la Martinique, **Aimé Césaire** va à Paris pour faire ses études universitaires. Là, il rencontre d'autres étudiants noirs avec qui il fonde un journal intitulé *L'Étudiant noir.* C'est dans ce journal qu'il définit la notion de **négritude.** Pour exprimer la valeur de la personnalité noire, Césaire choisit la poésie. En 1939, il écrit un livre de poèmes intitulé *Cahier d'un retour au pays natal.* Césaire est aussi un homme d'action et, pour lui, l'action, c'est la politique. Il rentre à la Martinique où il fonde un parti, *le Parti Progressiste Martiniquais.* Il devient maire° de Fort-de-France. Élu° député° de la Martinique, il défend les intérêts des habitants de son île.

■ Qu'est-ce que la négritude?

La négritude est un mouvement littéraire, philosophique et politique, né à Paris dans les années 1930. Les fondateurs de ce mouvement étaient des étudiants noirs, venus de différentes colonies françaises: Aimé Césaire (Martinique), Léon Damas (Guyane française), Léopold Senghor (Sénégal).

En quête de° leur identité, ces écrivains redécouvrent leurs racines° africaines qu'ils veulent valoriser.° La négritude est la reconnaissance d'une identité noire spécifique. Les Noirs ont leur personnalité, leur culture, leur système de valeurs, leur façon de percevoir et de comprendre l'univers. Ils doivent préserver et être fiers de cette identité spécifique liée° à l'Afrique, terre° de leurs ancêtres communs.

> *«La négritude est la conscience d'être noir, simple reconnaissance d'un fait, qui implique acceptation, prise en charge de son destin de noir, de son histoire et de sa culture.»*
>
> — *Aimé Césaire*

---

gouvernante *governess*   **grandit** = devient grande   **échappe de peu** *narrowly escapes*   **éperdument** = passionnément
impératrice = la femme de l'empereur   **autrichienne** *Austrian*   **véritable** = réelle   **maire** *mayor*   **élu** *elected*   **député** *congressman*
en quête de *in search of*   **racines** *roots*   **valoriser** *to emphasize the value of*   **liée** *linked*   **terre** *land*

DOCUMENTS — Pour saluer le Tiers-Monde

POUR SALUER LE TIERS-MONDE

Dans ce poème, écrit en 1960, Aimé Césaire, de son île de la Martinique, salue les pays d'Afrique qui viennent de gagner leur indépendance. Ce poème est dédié à son ami, Léopold Senghor, président du Sénégal.

La Guinée

Madagascar

Le Cameroun

Ah!
mon demi-sommeil d'île si trouble
sur la mer!

Et voici de tous les points du péril
l'histoire qui me fait le signe° que j'attendais.

Je vois pousser° des nations.
Vertes et rouges*, je vous salue,
bannières, gorges° du vent ancien,
Mali, Guinée, Ghana
et je vous vois, hommes,
point maladroits° sous ce soleil nouveau!

Écoutez:
        de mon île lointaine°
        de mon île veilleuse°
je vous dis Hoo!
        Et vos voix me répondent
        et ce qu'elles disent signifie:
«Il y fait clair.» Et c'est vrai:
même à travers orage et nuit
pour nous, il y fait clair.

Vois:
        l'Afrique n'est plus
        au diamant du malheur
            un noir cœur qui se strie;°

notre Afrique est une main hors du ceste,°
c'est une main droite, la paume° devant
et les doigts bien serrés;°

c'est une main tuméfiée°,
une blessée-main-ouverte,
tendue°,
        brunes, jaunes, blanches,
à toutes mains, à toutes les mains blessées
du monde.

* Les drapeaux des pays africains de Mali, de Guinée et de Ghana ont les couleurs vertes, rouges et jaunes

---

le signe = le signe de la liberté **pousser** *grow* **gorges** *pride* **points maladroits** *not at all clumsy* **lointaine** = qui est loin (de l'Afrique)
veilleuse = *lente* **se strie** *is lacerated [by the diamond of misfortune]* **ceste** *boxing glove* **paume** *palm* **bien serrés** *close together*
tuméfiée *swollen* **tendu** *stretched out*

■ **Additional Information**
F.A.O. = *Food and Agriculture Organization* (**Organisation pour l'Alimentation et l'Agriculture**) This U.N. agency offers technical assistance to developing countries in order to increase and promote their agricultural revenues and productions.

Teaching Note

Brief interpretation of *Pour saluer le Tiers-Monde:*

verses 1, 2 From his island that is still half asleep, Césaire recognizes the sign of freedom rising from areas where it was in peril.

verse 3 He sees the banners of the new African nations, and he sees the citizens of these countries under a new sun.

verse 4 From his far-away island, he calls out to the people of Africa who respond that light is dawning in their land.

verse 5 Africa is no longer a bleeding heart.

verse 6 It is a strong hand, recovering from its wounds, reaching out to all the hands of the world.

Unité 8   337

RESOURCES

TECHNOLOGY
DVD Program, Unit 8
Vignette culturelle

■ **Note linguistique**

Haïti is the name that had been given to the island by its pre-Columbian inhabitants, the Arawaks. The word means "mountainous island."

■ **Additional Information**

• **Toussaint Louverture** was jailed in the fort of Joux, France, where he died just before Haiti gained its independence.

• There were many plantations in **Saint-Domingue,** most growing sugar cane, coffee, and indigo.

• U.S. forces occupied **Haiti** between 1915 and 1934 to restore order after political unrest.

Haïti

Un champion de la liberté: Toussaint Louverture (1743–1803)

Haïti est une nation indépendante depuis près de 200 ans.
Le héros de l'indépendance haïtienne s'appelle Toussaint Louverture.
Voici l'histoire de ce grand champion de la liberté.

Cette histoire commence à la fin du 18e siècle. La partie occidentale° d'Haïti s'appelait alors Saint-Domingue. C'était une colonie française où il y avait 20 000 Français et 500 000 Africains qui travaillaient très dur comme esclaves dans les plantations des Français.

En 1789, ces esclaves ont eu un grand espoir. °Une révolution libérale venait d'éclater en France. Est-ce que cette révolution allait émanciper les Noirs? En principe, oui. Les révolutionnaires français ont décidé d'abolir l'esclavage dans les colonies. Malheureusement, Saint-Domingue était loin de Paris et les Français de l'île ont refusé de libérer leurs esclaves. Pour les Africains, il y avait une seule° solution: la révolte. En 1791, les Africains de Saint-Domingue sont entrés en rébellion contre leurs maîtres.

Trois ans plus tard, en 1794, les Anglais, qui étaient en guerre contre la France, ont voulu occuper Saint-Domingue. Pour les Français, la situation était extrêmement grave. Le gouverneur de Saint-Domingue a décidé alors de rencontrer le chef des esclaves révoltés. Ce chef était Toussaint Louverture. Il avait 4 000 hommes sous ses ordres. Il a proposé au gouverneur un marché:° «Garantissez la liberté des Noirs et mes troupes vont combattre avec vous contre les Anglais.» Le gouverneur n'avait pas le choix. Il a accepté.

Quelques semaines après, Toussaint Louverture, l'ancien esclave, a été nommé commandant. C'était un brillant stratège. Ses troupes ont chassé les Anglais de Saint-Domingue. En juillet 1795, Toussaint Louverture a été nommé général de brigade et vice-gouverneur de Saint-Domingue. En réalité, c'était maintenant lui le chef de l'île.

Avec l'émancipation des esclaves, Toussaint Louverture avait réalisé sa première ambition. Cependant, il avait une autre ambition: obtenir l'indépendance de Saint-Domingue. Oui, mais comment? Il fallait d'abord organiser le pays. Toussaint Louverture a créé une administration moderne. Il a ouvert des écoles. Il a développé le commerce. S'il a réussi dans ses projets, c'est parce que c'était un homme juste. Il ne faisait pas de distinction entre les anciens maîtres blancs et les anciens

Toussaint Louverture, un champion de la liberté.

esclaves noirs. Ainsi, il a pu mobiliser tous les talents. Les résultats de cette politique ont été immédiats. En 1800, Saint-Domingue était un pays riche et prospère. Économiquement, c'était un pays indépendant.

Administrativement, cependant, Saint-Domingue était toujours une colonie française. La France, à ce moment-là, était gouvernée par Napoléon Bonaparte. Napoléon était un général brillant mais très autoritaire. Il n'aimait pas l'indépendance de Toussaint Louverture. Pire,° il a décidé de rétablir l'esclavage à Saint-Domingue. Pour cela, il a préparé une formidable expédition. Le premier février 1802, 22 000 soldats français sont arrivés dans l'île. C'était la guerre! La guerre d'indépendance a mal commencé pour les Noirs. Leur chef, Toussaint Louverture a été capturé par traîtrise.° Déporté en France, il est mort après dix mois de captivité.

La mort de Toussaint Louverture a encouragé la résistance des Noirs. Ceux-ci ont finalement battu l'armée française. Le premier janvier 1804, Saint-Domingue est devenue une nation indépendante et a pris le nom d'Haïti.

---

occidentale *western* **espoir** *hope* **une seule** *only one* **un marché** *a deal* **pire** *worse* **traîtrise** *treachery*

Note culturelles

Jean-Jacques Dessalines was born in Guinea, Africa, circa 1758. This former slave and lieutenant of Toussaint Louverture took over the fight, leading the country to declare its independence on January 1st, 1804. He then proceeded to make himself emperor, under the name of **Jacques 1er**.

A tyrannical ruler, he was assassinated in 1806. Haiti became a republic in 1844 after years of internal fighting and political division.

Student Portfolios

Students may enjoy writing and illustrating their own short poems. Begin by asking students to think of adjectives to describe their own city or town, then work toward using the most visual and vivid images in the final product.

DOCUMENTS   Pour Haïti

Pour Haïti

René Depestre est né en Haïti en 1926. À l'âge de vingt ans, il a été exilé de son pays à cause de ses activités politiques. Il habite actuellement° à Paris. Depestre est un poète engagé° qui dénonce l'oppression et l'injustice. Dans ce poème, il évoque sa terre° natale qu'il a quittée il y a longtemps, mais à laquelle il pense sans cesse.°

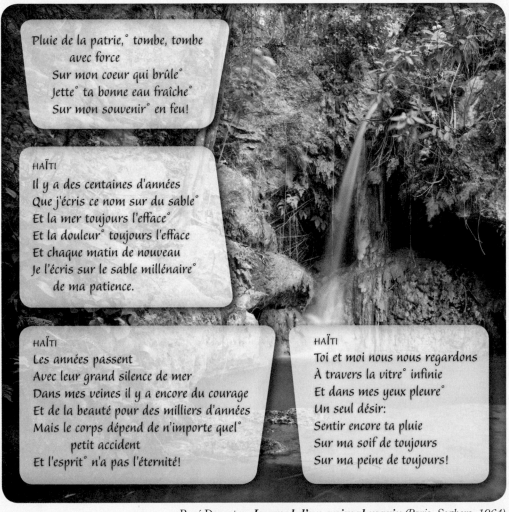

Pluie de la patrie,° tombe, tombe
           avec force
Sur mon cœur qui brûle°
Jette° ta bonne eau fraîche°
Sur mon souvenir° en feu!

HAÏTI

Il y a des centaines d'années
Que j'écris ce nom sur du sable°
Et la mer toujours l'efface°
Et la douleur° toujours l'efface
Et chaque matin de nouveau
Je l'écris sur le sable millénaire°
           de ma patience.

HAÏTI

Les années passent
Avec leur grand silence de mer
Dans mes veines il y a encore du courage
Et de la beauté pour des milliers d'années
Mais le corps dépend de n'importe quel°
           petit accident
Et l'esprit° n'a pas l'éternité!

HAÏTI

Toi et moi nous nous regardons
À travers la vitre° infinie
Et dans mes yeux pleure°
Un seul désir:
Sentir encore ta pluie
Sur ma soif de toujours
Sur ma peine de toujours!

René Depestre, ***Journal d'un animal marin*** (Paris, Seghers, 1964)

actuellement = à présent   **engagé** *politically active*   **terre** *land*   **sans cesse** *unceasingly*   **patrie** *native land* (= Haïti)   **brûle** *is burning*   **jette** *throw*
fraîche *cool*   **souvenir** *memory*   **sable** *sand*   **efface** *erases*   **douleur** *pain, suffering*   **millénaire** = qui a mille ans   **n'importe quel** *any*   **esprit** *soul, spirit*
vitre *glass*   **pleure** *is crying*

Teaching Note

Have students compare the second verse of this poem with *Liberté* by Paul Éluard, page 257.

Teaching Suggestion: DVD Program

To hear the poem read aloud, and to familiarize students with Haïti, play the Unit 8 *Vignette culturelle* entitled *Pour Haïti*.

■ **Teaching Note**

You might want to have students compare the style of these Haitian paintings with the «naïf» style of Rousseau, p. 64.

En Haïti, l'art, c'est la vie

Tous les Haïtiens, ou presque, ont une âme° d'artiste. En Haïti, l'art est partout:° sur les murs, sur les devantures des magasins,° sur les volets° des maisons, dans les églises, sur les autobus, sur les camions° ou sur les voitures. Et maintenant, il se trouve aussi dans les collections privées et dans les musées.

L'art haïtien est avant tout un art populaire: il est issu du peuple et il est fait pour le peuple. À la différence des artistes européens ou américains, les artistes haïtiens n'ont généralement pas reçu de formation technique dans des écoles d'art spécialisées. Ils ont appris eux-mêmes à peindre.° Leur style, souvent appelé «style naïf», est caractérisé par un dessin° relativement simple, l'absence de perspective et l'usage d'une palette aux couleurs chaudes et vibrantes.

Les sources de l'art haïtien sont intérieures et personnelles: c'est l'environnement immédiat de l'artiste, la nature, la culture, la religion et les croyances° d'un peuple aux profondes racines° africaines. Les sujets représentés expriment la vie et l'âme de ce peuple. Ce sont souvent des scènes de la vie quotidienne, la ville avec ses gens aux vêtements multicolores ou la campagne haïtienne avec sa végétation luxuriante, parfois des cérémonies ou des sujets religieux, ou des scènes historiques.

C'est un Américain, DeWitt Peters, qui a fait découvrir au monde les merveilles de l'art haïtien. Peters était venu en Haïti au début° des années 1940 pour enseigner° l'anglais. Lui-même peintre, il a tout de suite été séduit° par l'art simple et coloré des peintres haïtiens. Avec l'aide des gouvernements haïtien et américain, il a ouvert un Centre d'Art où étaient exposées les oeuvres° des meilleurs peintres haïtiens. L'existence de ce centre a encouragé de nombreuses vocations d'artistes. Autrefois méconnu,° l'art haïtien est aujourd'hui apprécié par un nombre croissant° d'amateurs° un peu partout dans le monde.

■ L'art sur roues: le tap-tap

Le tap-tap est un bus privé qui assure le transport public en Haïti. Il a un itinéraire fixe et fait des arrêts° fréquents. Quand un passager veut descendre, il tape plusieurs fois sur la partie métallique du bus. C'est l'origine du nom tap-tap.

Les tap-taps sont peints° en couleurs chaudes et brillantes. Leurs décorations multicolores représentent souvent des scènes de la Bible, des monuments ou des portraits de stars de la télévision et de joueurs de foot célèbres. Moyen de transport essentiel, le tap-tap est aussi une forme d'expression artistique et de promotion culturelle.

âme soul   **partout** *everywhere*   **devantures des magasins** *storefronts*   **volets** *shutters*   **camions** *trucks*   **peindre** *to paint*   **dessin** *design*
croyances *beliefs*   **racines** *roots*   **début** *beginning*   **enseigner** *to teach*   **tout de suite** = immédiatement   **séduit** *attracted, seduced*   **oeuvres** *works*
méconnu = peu connu   **croissant** *increasing*   **amateurs** *art-lovers*   **arrêts** *stops*   **peints** *painted*

Note culturelles

• **Général Dessalines**
Jean-Jacques Dessalines, le général victorieux de la bataille de Vertières, se proclame empereur d'Haïti et prend le nom de Jacques Iᵉʳ.

À la bataille de Vertières, l'armée française était commandée par le général Rochambeau, fils de Rochambeau, héros de l'indépendance américaine. (Voir page 413.)

Quelques artistes haïtiens

Sénèque Obin, «*La création du drapeau haïtien*»

Sénèque Obin est un spécialiste des scènes historiques de l'indépendance haïtienne. Sur ce tableau°, le général Jean-Jacques Dessalines crée le premier drapeau haïtien le 18 mai 1803. Chaque année, l'anniversaire de cet événement est célébré avec grande fanfare non seulement en Haïti mais dans les communautés haïtiennes aux États-Unis. La Fête du Drapeau est un symbole de liberté, de dignité humaine et d'unité nationale pour tous les Haïtiens.

Philomé Obin, «*Mariage à la campagne*»

Philomé Obin, frère de Sénèque, aime illustrer des scènes simples de la vie haïtienne qu'il peint avec des couleurs claires et lumineuses. Ici, des jeunes mariés, accompagnés de leurs parents en habits° de dimanche, traversent une rivière pour se rendre à l'église où sera célébré le mariage.

Hector Hyppolite, «*Agoué et son consort*»

Hector Hyppolite, l'un des premiers peintres exposés au Centre d'Art, était aussi un *houngan*, c'est-à-dire un prêtre vaudou. Dans ce tableau, Hyppolite a peint Agoué, loa de la mer, symbolisée ici par une ancre marine, et son consort.

Castera Bazile, «*Carnaval*»

Castera Bazile a découvert sa vocation artistique en admirant les tableaux exposés au Centre d'Art où il travaillait comme employé de maison. Dans ce tableau il représente une scène typique de Carnaval, l'équivalent de Mardi Gras. Durant cette fête joyeuse, les Haïtiens chantent et dansent dans les rues, déguisés en costumes multicolores.

tableau *painting* **champ** *field* **habits** *clothes*

Note historique

Dessalines created the Haitian flag by taking the French **tricolore** of his oppressors and cutting out the central white band. The red and blue sections were then sewn together by his wife's niece, Catherine Flon, who is the middle figure in Obin's painting.

Teaching Strategy

Ask the students to look at the paintings for three minutes, jotting down their impressions. Then ask students:
Qu'est-ce que ces tableaux évoquent pour vous? Dites lequel vous préférez et pourquoi.

Note culturelles

• **Hector Hyppolite**
The painter Hector Hyppolite (who died in 1948) was one of the first Haitian painters to be discovered not only by DeWitt Peters but also by the French surrealists. On a visit to Haiti, the French writer André Breton was absolutely fascinated by Hyppolite and bought several of his paintings.

Now Hyppolite's works are in collections all over the world.
• **Le houngan**
À la fois prêtre, prophète, pharmacien, médecin et conseiller de sa communauté, **le houngan** joue encore un rôle important dans la société haïtienne d'aujourd'hui.

DOCUMENTS *Rue Cases-nègres*

Rue Cases-nègres est un film entièrement martiniquais. Réalisé par **Euzhan Palcy**, une cinéaste martiniquaise, d'après l'oeuvre° de l'écrivain martiniquais **Joseph Zobel**, il est joué par des acteurs martiniquais, sur une musique de biguine martiniquaise.

L'action du film se passe en 1930 dans une Martinique bien différente de la Martinique d'aujourd'hui. Les différentes scènes sont reliées° entre elles par la présence d'un jeune garçon d'une douzaine d'années, **José Hassam**, un orphelin° élevé° par sa grand-mère, **M'man-Tine** (Grand-maman Amantine). Tous deux habitent rue Cases-Nègres, une rue pauvre d'un petit village de Martinique.

Les conditions de vie sont difficiles. Tout le monde doit travailler très dur° dans les champs de canne à sucre pour ne gagner presque rien. Pour échapper° à cette misère, il n'y a qu'une solution: l'instruction.°

Le jeune José a plusieurs mentors. D'abord, M'man-Tine, la vieille grand-mère pieuse,° qui va tout faire pour que son petit-fils aille à l'école. Il y a aussi le vieux **Médouze**, en quelque sorte le père spirituel de José. Médouze a passé toute sa vie au travail et maintenant son corps est usé° et brisé°. Il rêve° de l'Afrique lointaine, pays des ancêtres où il voudrait un jour retourner. Il raconte à José l'histoire du peuple: le départ forcé d'Afrique, l'esclavage dans les plantations des «Békés»*, l'émancipation qui en réalité n'a pas changé grand-chose, et le travail, le travail, toujours le travail . . . Émerveillé° et attentif, le jeune José écoute le vieillard° évoquer les éléments de la sagesse° africaine: respect de la nature, respect de la vie . . .

Il y a aussi les professeurs de José. Ils ont remarqué l'intelligence du jeune garçon et en sont d'abord surpris. L'un d'eux accuse même José d'avoir triché° à une composition. José est reçu au certificat d'études** et reçoit une bourse° partielle pour aller étudier à Fort-de-France. Malheureusement, la bourse n'est pas suffisante. M'man-Tine est une femme fière et déterminée. Elle a décidé que son petit-fils continuerait ses études, quoi qu'il lui en coûte° à elle. Malgré° son âge, la vieille femme va s'établir° à Fort-de-France où elle travaille comme lingère° pour gagner l'argent des études. L'administration comprend finalement la situation et accorde° une bourse complète à José. M'man-Tine peut retourner à son village où elle meurt heureuse d'avoir accompli son rêve.

*Pour son film **Rue Cases-Nègres**, la réalisatrice° Euzhan Palcy a reçu le César (Oscar français) du meilleur premier film.*

Cette histoire simple sert de trame° générale au film où se succèdent° une série de petites scènes souvent réalistes, parfois comiques (les rapports entre José et sa tante Madame Léonce), parfois pénibles° (les rapports entre son copain Léopold et le père de celui-ci). Par son décor, le monde qu'Euzhan Palcy nous présente dans son film peut paraître archaïque et lointain.° Les gens qui vivent dans ce monde sont pauvres et simples, mais ils sont honnêtes, droits,° généreux, fiers et avant tout ils sont humains!

* «Békés» est un mot créole qui désigne les descendants des anciens colons blancs venus de France
    pour établir des plantations dans les Antilles.

** Le certificat d'études = un diplôme de fin des études primaires.

---

l'oeuvre = le livre   **reliées** *linked*   **orphelin** = enfant qui a perdu son père et sa mère   **élevé** *raised*   **dur** *hard*   **échapper à** *to escape from*
l'instruction *education*   **pieuse** *pious*   **usé** *worn out*   **brisé** *broken*   **rêve** *dreams*   **émerveillé** *amazed*   **vieillard** = vieil homme   **sagesse** *wisdom*
triché *cheated*   **bourse** *scholarship*   **quoi qu'il lui en coûte** *whatever it may cost her*   **malgré** *in spite of*   **s'établir** *to settle*   **accorde** = donne
lingère *laundry woman*   **trame** *plot*   **se succèdent** *follow one another*   **pénibles** *painful*   **lointain** *distant*   **droits** *straightforward*   **réalistatrice** *director*

Notes culturelles

• **Euzhan Palcy** made her first feature film, *Rue Cases-nègres*, at the age of 27. The film, which was produced on a budget of less than one million dollars, was acclaimed as a masterpiece on its release in 1982. In addition to the César award for the Best First Film, it also was honored with a Silver Lion at the Venice Film Festival. All the actors in the film, except two, were non-professional.

In her 1992 film, *Siméon*, Palcy depicts a group of Zouk musicians from Martinique who go to Paris to get a record contract. More recently, Palcy has written and directed a documentary, *Parcours de Dissidents*, as well as an action adventure film set in the 17th century called *Les Mariées de l'îles Bourbon*.

• **Joseph Zobel**, author of the autobiographical novel La rue *Cases-nègres*, makes a brief cameo appearance in the film (as the priest). Born and raised in Martinique in circumstances similar to those of José, Zobel continued his schooling and went to Sénégal to become a teacher.

342 Unité 8

Teaching Notes

The film **Rue Cases-nègres** (*Sugarcane Alley*) has been rated PG. You will definitely want to preview the movie, however, before deciding whether or not it is appropriate for your classes.

• In the scene at Léopold's house, Léopold's mother plays a record that she has just received from France: we hear Joséphine Baker singing her signature piece: «J'ai deux amours, mon pays et Paris» (cf. *Interlude 4*, p. 178).

Quelques scènes du film

Sur cette photo, on peut voir les personnages principaux du film. Au premier plan, le jeune José Hassam en costume et chapeau blancs. Derrière lui, sa grand-mère M'Man Tine. Derrière M'man Tine, on peut remarquer Euzhan Palcy, la réalisatrice du film.

Dans les champs de canne à sucre, les habitants du village travaillent très dur sous l'oeil vigilant d'un contremaître (foreman) à cheval.

Tous les jours, José va à l'école avec les enfants du village.

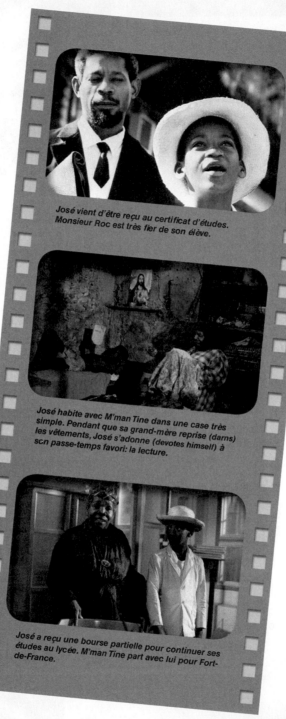

José vient d'être reçu au certificat d'études. Monsieur Roc est très fier de son élève.

José habite avec M'man Tine dans une case très simple. Pendant que sa grand-mère reprise (darns) les vêtements, José s'adonne (devotes himself) à son passe-temps favori: la lecture.

José a reçu une bourse partielle pour continuer ses études au lycée. M'man Tine part avec lui pour Fort-de-France.

trois cent quarante-trois **343**
Interlude culturel

Notes culturelles

In 1882, **Jules Ferry** promulgated a new law, which made schooling mandatory and free for all children between the ages of 7 and 13.

Le certificat d'études used to be awarded to students who finished elementary school and were not going to pursue any higher education. It became obsolete when school became mandatory until the age of 16, since from then on, all children would go on at least to junior high school. The certificate was abrogated in 1989.

Teaching Suggestion
Bring in the film for *La Rue Cases-nègres* to do the following activities:
- Create a cloze activity from the dialogue of a particular scene, leaving certain words, phrases, and sentences blank. Have students watch the scene once, then give them the activity. Show the scene several times while the students listen carefully for the missing pieces.
- Divide the class into pairs, and have each pair give a summary of one scene.

Unité 9

MAIN THEME
Personal Relationships, Friendships, Family Life

COMMUNICATION
- Discussing relationships
- Congratulating, comforting, expressing sympathy
- Describing friendship
- Describing life phases
- Expressing feelings towards other people

CULTURES
- Comparing French and American families
- Learning about the *Restos du coeur*
- Learning about African legends

CONNECTIONS
- Using titles to make predictions
- Connecting to Language Arts: Brainstorming a list of questions
- Connecting to Math: Calculating percentages
- Connecting to Science/Health: Investigating compatibility myths
- Connecting to Social Studies: Researching interesting information to talk about
- Connecting to Art/Music: Writing about art and music preferences
- Connecting to Technology: Using a computer to communicate with pen pals

COMPARISONS
- Comparing how reciprocal actions are expressed in French and English
- Comparing the use of relative pronouns, subject pronouns, and direct object pronouns in French and English
- Comparing ways French and American people volunteer to help others
- Comparing French and American weddings

COMMUNITIES
- Writing to pen pals
- Predicting one's future and setting goals

Unité 9

Les relations personnelles

THÈME ET OBJECTIFS

Culture

In this unit, you will discover . . .

- what friendship and family life mean to the French
- what young people in France do to help the disadvantaged
- what is involved in planning a wedding in France

Communication

You will learn how . . .

- to talk about friends and acquaintances
- to explain how people get along with one another
- how to congratulate people on their success or comfort them when they are feeling down
- to describe the various phases of the life cycle

Langue

You will learn how . . .

- to talk about how people interact with each other
- to describe people and things in a clear and complete manner

DIGITAL FRENCH my.hrw.com
ONLINE STUDENT EDITION with...

performance space

News ✚ Networking

@HOMETUTOR

- Audio Resources
- Video Resources
- Interactive Flashcards
- WebQuest

PRACTICE FRENCH WITH HOLT MCDOUGAL APPS!

 DIGITAL FRENCH

TEACHER TOOLS
- Teacher One Stop
- Interactive Whiteboard Lessons
- Generate Success Rubric Generator and Interactive Graphic Organizers
- Examview Test Generator

ALSO AVAILABLE...
- Online Workbook
- French InterActive Reader
- @HomeTutor
- DVD Program
- Power Presentations
- Interactive Flashcards

FRENCH ON THE GO!
- Performance Space
- Holt McDougal French Apps
- Discovering French Today eTextbook

Les amis et la famille

Pour les Français, les rapports humains ont énormément d'importance. L'amitié, par exemple, est considérée comme la valeur la plus importante de l'existence. Elle passe avant le travail, l'argent et même l'amour. Un ami, évidemment, n'est pas n'importe qui.° Ce n'est pas une personne qu'on rencontre un jour et qu'on oublie le lendemain. C'est généralement quelqu'un qu'on connaît depuis très longtemps, souvent depuis l'enfance et avec qui on a beaucoup d'expériences communes.° C'est la personne spéciale à qui on dit tout, avec qui on partage° ses joies et ses peines° et sur qui on peut compter dans les moments les plus difficiles de l'existence. Les vrais amis sont peu nombreux, mais ces amis-là, c'est pour la vie.

Un autre aspect de la vie en France est la solidité des relations familiales. Autrefois, le milieu familial était très vaste et la vie familiale très active. La famille comprenait° non seulement enfants, parents, grands-parents, cousins, tantes et oncles, mais aussi toutes les autres personnes qui avaient une ascendance° commune ou qui étaient alliées par le mariage. On se réunissait assez régulièrement le dimanche, autour d'un grand repas familial, ou plus occasionnellement pour les fêtes de famille: anniversaires, mariages, cérémonies religieuses, etc.

Aujourd'hui, la famille proche se limite au couple, à leurs enfants et aux parents qu'on voit régulièrement. Cette famille est généralement très unie. Parents et enfants s'entendent° bien, même au moment difficile de l'adolescence. D'après une enquête, 77% des adolescents français considèrent que leurs relations avec leurs parents sont excellentes ou très bonnes. De même, 88% des jeunes de 18 à 24 ans déclarent s'entendre bien avec leurs parents.

Si la vie de famille est moins active qu'autrefois, «l'esprit de famille» est resté intact. La solidarité familiale joue beaucoup dans les différentes phases de l'existence. Les parents font énormément d'efforts et de sacrifices pour assurer une bonne éducation à leurs enfants. Après leurs études, ils continuent à les aider moralement et matériellement. À leur tour, les enfants s'occupent de leurs parents au moment de leur vieillesse.

Pour les Français, la famille, c'est sacré!

n'importe qui *just anyone* **communes** *shared, in common* **partage** *shares* **peines** *sorrows* **comprenait** *included* **ascendance** *ancestry* **s'entendent** *get along*

ASSESSMENT IN UNIT RESOURCE BOOK

Print Resources
- **Workbook TE/PE**
- *Activités pour tous* TE/PE
- *Lectures pour tous*
- **Unit Resource Book**
  Audioscripts
  Video Activities
  Videoscripts

Achievement Tests
- **Quizzes, Unit 9**
- **Unit Test 9**
- **Reading and Culture Tests**
- **Assessment Answer Key**

Proficiency Tests
- **Listening Comprehension**
- **Speaking Performance**
- **Writing Performance**
- **Portfolio Assessment**

INFO MAGAZINE

Theme: Friends and family

Reading Strategy: Skimming, scanning

■ Teaching Strategy
After reading the article, ask students to compare and contrast family life in France and the U.S.

SUPPLEMENTARY VOCABULARY

la famille éclatée *extended family*
le beau-père *stepfather/father-in-law*
la belle-mère *stepmother/mother-in-law*
les beaux grands-parents *step-grandparents*
le demi-frère *stepbrother*
la demi-soeur *stepsister*
le demi-oncle *step-uncle*
la demi-tante *step-aunt*
le fils adoptif *adopted son*
la fille adoptive *adopted daughter*
les parents adoptifs *adoptive parents*

21ST CENTURY SKILLS

- **Communication:** SE: pp. 347, 348, 351, 353, 359, 361, 366, 367, 368, 369, 371; TE: pp. 345, 346, 349, 351, 354, 362, 365, 367, 371, 378, 381
- **Collaboration:** TE: p. 365
- **Critical Thinking and Problem Solving:** SE: pp. 347, 359, 366, 371; TE: pp. 345, 348, 358, 365, 366, 368, 378, 381
- **Creativity and Innovation:** SE: p. 371; TE: pp. 349, 353, 360, 362, 365, 367, 371, 381
- **Information Literacy:** TE: p. 365
- **Technology Literacy:** TE: pp. 365, 381
- **Flexibility and Adaptability:** TE: pp. 351, 365, 381
- **Initiative and Self-Direction:** TE: pp. 346, 365, 367, 381
- **Social and Cross-Cultural Skills:** SE: p. 359; TE: pp. 345, 348, 351, 365, 381
- **Productivity and Accountability:** TE: pp. 349, 351, 353, 357, 360, 367
- **Leadership and Responsibility:** SE: p. 347; TE: pp. 346, 365

Unité 9 345

Les qualités d'un(e) ami(e)

Nous choisissons nos amis parce qu'ils ont beaucoup de qualités. Évidemment, certaines qualités sont plus importantes que d'autres. Parmi les qualités suivantes, choisissez les cinq qui comptent le plus pour vous et classez-les par ordre d'importance.

- l'intelligence
- l'humour
- le courage

- la patience
- la loyauté
- l'apparence physique
- la bonne humeur

- la franchise
- la sincérité
- l'honnêteté
- ??

- la générosité
- la sensibilité
- la discrétion

et vous?

Comparez votre liste de qualités avec celles de vos camarades de classe. Vous pouvez aussi établir une liste des préférences de toute la classe.

NOUS ET LES AUTRES

L'abbé Pierre

La vie moderne a beaucoup d'avantages. La majorité des gens habitent dans des maisons confortables et modernes, gagnent bien leur vie, et ont des loisirs intéressants. Mais en France, comme ailleurs, il y a aussi beaucoup de gens qui ne profitent pas de ces avantages. Il y a des jeunes qui n'ont pas de travail, des familles qui n'ont pas d'argent et parfois pas d'abri,° des personnes âgées qui sont malades et qui n'ont pas de famille pour s'occuper d'elles. Ces personnes aussi font partie de la société, mais la société a tendance à les oublier.

abri *shelter*

Teaching Strategy

Ask students to bring in pictures of family members or friends. Ask them to talk about three of these people in front of the class, including information about where they live, when the student sees them and what they generally do/talk about together. You may also suggest making a collage with multiple photos, realia, notes, and information and using this as a gift for an important family occasion.

Heureusement, tout le monde n'est pas égoïste.
Voici le cas de trois jeunes Français qui ont décidé
de «faire quelque chose» pour les autres.

Patrick Esquivel

(15 ans, lycéen)

Dans l'immeuble où j'habite, il y a une vieille dame qui a perdu
son mari l'année dernière et qui maintenant vit° toute seule dans
son appartement au cinquième étage sans ascenseur. Je fais les
courses pour elle une ou deux fois par semaine. Ça l'aide un peu,
mais le plus important, c'est quand je passe une heure ou deux à
bavarder° avec elle. Je lui parle de ce que je fais au lycée et elle
me raconte sa vie. J'apprends des choses fascinantes, et elle ne
se sent plus seule.°

Claire Delamotte

(19 ans, étudiante)

Je travaille deux jours par mois aux «Restos° du coeur». C'est
une organisation bénévole° qui prépare des repas chauds pour les
sans-abri°, les personnes sans ressources et, plus généralement,
pour tous ceux qui ont faim. Mon travail varie. Parfois je
travaille à la collecte de la nourriture. D'autres fois, je travaille à
la cuisine ou bien je sers les repas.

Dans une société qui glorifie l'argent et la réussite, il est
important de préserver les vraies valeurs qui n'ont rien à voir°
avec celles que nous proposent les médias. Quand je travaille
aux «Restos», je suis en contact avec la réalité de la misère
humaine et je peux faire quelque chose d'utile. Le problème,
c'est que nous avons de plus en plus de clients!

Steevy Gustave

(23 ans, musicien professionnel)

Je suis d'origine martiniquaise, mais maintenant j'habite dans la
région parisienne. Dans ma banlieue, il y a beaucoup de
problèmes de délinquance juvénile et de drogue. Heureusement,
il y a une «Maison des Jeunes» qui attire° pas mal° de monde. J'y
travaille souvent comme animateur. Mon but°, c'est de récupérer
les jeunes drogués en les intéressant à la musique. Ce n'est pas
toujours facile, mais avec de la persévérance et beaucoup
d'encouragement, on y arrive.°

- Selon vous, lequel de ces jeunes Français fait la chose la plus utile? Expliquez pourquoi.
- Avez-vous déjà travaillé comme «volontaire»? Décrivez votre expérience.

vit / vivre *to live*   **bavarder** *to chat*   **seule** *lonely, alone*   **Restos** = *restaurants*   **bénévole** *charitable*   **sans-abri** *homeless*
rien à voir = rien à faire   **attire** *attracts*   **pas mal** = beaucoup   **but** = objectif   **on y arrive** *one can do it*

SUPPLEMENTARY VOCABULARY

le bénévolat *volunteer work*
le bénévole *volunteer*
l'entraide *(f.) mutual assistance*
la charité *charity*
la solidarité *solidarity*
le soutien *support*
l'isolement *(m.) isolation*
l'humanisme *(m.) humanism*

■ Pour en savoir plus

LES RESTOS DU COEUR
For more information on this
organization, see *Interlude 7*, p.295.

■ Note culturelle

**Les Maisons des Jeunes et de la
Culture (M.J.C.)** were created in
1944. They are financed by the cities
with the help of the **Ministère de la
Jeunesse et des Sports** and offer a
wide variety of activities to young
people. At the M.J.C. French young
people may learn a craft, watch
movies, play sports, or even display
their own artwork.

■ Irregular Verb

(see Appendix C)
vivre

Teaching Strategy

After the students have read the profiles of the
young French people on p. 347, have them write
a similar profile of themselves or a friend,
imagining that it is going to be included in an
English textbook to demonstrate American
culture and patterns of community service.

Encourage the students to write longer
sentences as opposed to simple subject-verb
sentences.

Le Français pratique

■ **Proverbe**
Les petits cadeaux entretiennent l'amitié.

■ **Teaching Strategy: Warm-Up**
Have students brainstorm for two minutes, listing all the words meaning "friend" in English, recording all suggestions on the board or on a transparency. Next, list the new vocabulary above and ask students to see if the categories of friendship listed are similar in French and English. Then move into Act. 1, dividing the class into groups for discussion.

Les amis, les copains et les relations personnelles

— Tiens, voilà Catherine.
— Qui est-ce?
— C'est une copine.
— Tu la connais depuis longtemps?
— Oui, depuis deux ans.
— Est-ce que tu peux me la présenter?
— Oui, volontiers!

LES PERSONNES QU'ON CONNAÎT

un ami **une amie**	est quelqu'un	qu'on connaît depuis longtemps pour qui on a beaucoup d'affection en qui on a **une confiance** *(trust)* absolue
un copain **une copine**	est quelqu'un	qu'on connaît bien qu'on voit souvent avec qui on fait beaucoup de choses
un camarade **une camarade**	est quelqu'un	avec qui on va en classe
une connaissance	est quelqu'un	qu'on connaît assez bien qu'on voit de temps en temps

1 Un(e) ami(e) n'est pas n'importe qui *(A friend is not just anybody)*

Quelle est votre définition d'<u>un ami</u>?
  • Considérez la liste suivante et faites une liste des cinq caractéristiques
    les plus importantes. Vous pouvez aussi mentionner d'autres caractéristiques.
  • Comparez votre liste avec celle de votre partenaire.
Faites la même chose pour la définition d'<u>une amie.</u>

Un ami Une amie	est quelqu'un ...	
■ qui est toujours d'accord avec moi ■ qui me comprend ■ à qui je peux parler de tout ■ qui me dit toujours la vérité ■ qui m'aide quand j'ai un problème ■ en qui j'ai complète confiance ■ pour qui j'ai beaucoup d'admiration ■ qui ne me critique jamais		■ qui me donne des conseils ■ qui me prête de l'argent quand j'en ai besoin ■ qui est toujours loyal(e) ■ que je respecte ■ qui me respecte ■ qui me pardonne *(forgives)* toujours ■ ??

Teaching Suggestion: DVD Program

In the Unit 9 *Vidéo-drame: Dispute et réconciliation*, students will learn about relationships. This section focuses on feelings and relations between people. Before watching the video, you may point out to students the different levels of friendship that exist in France.

Next, play the video once without interruption. Then, ask students to explain why Mélanie is upset and what phrases Nicolas uses to console her.

SUPPLEMENTARY VOCABULARY

un(e) camarade de
  chambre *roommate*
un pote *(fam.)* pal
un petit ami *boyfriend*
une petite amie *girlfriend*
un inconnu *stranger*
un voisin *neighbor*
On a confiance en quelqu'un/
  quelque chose *to have
  confidence/faith in*
On fait confiance à quelqu'un/
  quelque chose *to trust*
du mépris *scorn*
de la pitié
de la rancune *resentment*
de la haine *hatred*
détester *to dislike*
haïr *to hate*
faire connaissance avec
  quelqu'un *to become acquainted
  with someone*
faire la connaissance de
  quelqu'un *to meet someone*
perdre/reprendre connaissance *to
  lose/regain consciousness*
prendre connaissance de quelque
  chose *to study, examine something*

■ **If students ask...**

un coup de foudre *lightning bolt
  (love at first sight)*

LES SENTIMENTS

On éprouve . . .   ou au contraire . . .

| | | éprouver *to feel* |

de l'amitié *(friendship)*   de l'envie
de l'affection   de la jalousie *(jealousy)*
de la sympathie *(instinctive liking)* de l'antipathie
de l'admiration   de l'animosité
du respect   de l'aversion

L'amitié et l'amour

On | **aime bien** quelqu'un.
   | **a de l'amitié pour** quelqu'un.

On | **tombe amoureux/amoureuse de**
   | quelqu'un.
   | **aime** quelqu'un.
   | **a le coup de foudre pour** quelqu'un.

aimer bien *to like*
aimer *to love*

tomber amoureux de *to fall
  in love with*

**avoir le coup de foudre
  pour** *to fall in love with
  at first sight*

2 Mes sentiments

Choisissez deux des personnes suivantes et décrivez quel(s) sentiment(s) vous éprouvez
pour chaque personne. Comparez vos sentiments avec ceux de votre partenaire.

Frankenstein   Monsieur Richard   Juliette   Jérôme

Patricia   Claire   Le comte Dracula   Pierre

Teaching Strategy

Divide the class into groups and have them
create numbered cartoons illustrating the
emotions listed in the vocabulary box. (Be sure
that the cartoons do <u>not</u> have the emotion
written on the illustration.) Have the groups
exchange cartoons and write a sentence for
each one that identifies the emotion shown.
Have the groups peer-correct their lists.

LES RELATIONS PERSONNELLES

— Qu'est-ce que tu fais samedi?
— Je sors avec une copine.
— Tu t'entends bien avec elle?
— Oui, en général je m'entends bien avec elle.
  Parfois on se dispute, mais après on se réconcilie.

Qu'est-ce que tu fais samedi?

Je sors avec une copine.

Les rapports / Les relations

On peut . . .

avoir | de **bons rapports** avec | quelqu'un.
| de **bonnes relations** avec |

s'entendre bien avec *(to get along with)*
être d'accord avec *(to agree with)*

se réconcilier avec *(to make up with)*

avoir confiance en *(to trust)*

avoir | de **mauvais rapports** avec | quelqu'un.
| de **mauvaises relations** avec |

s'entendre mal avec
ne pas s'entendre avec

se disputer *(to have an argument)*
avoir une dispute avec
se quereller *(to have a fight)*
se fâcher avec *(to be upset at)*
rompre avec *(to break up with)*

COMMENT FÉLICITER QUELQU'UN

Bravo!
Quelle bonne nouvelle!

Félicitations! *(Congratulations!)*
Je te félicite.

Je suis content(e) | pour toi.
Je me réjouis

féliciter *to congratulate*
se réjouir *to be happy*

COMMENT PLAINDRE ET CONSOLER QUELQU'UN

plaindre* *to feel sorry for*

Mon pauvre! Ma pauvre!
Quel dommage!
Quelle malchance *(bad luck)*!
Tu n'as pas de chance.

Je te plains.
Je suis désolé(e) pour toi.
Ne t'en fais pas! *(Don't worry! Don't feel bad!)*
Ça s'arrangera! *(Things will be okay!*
  Everything will work out all right!)

■ Irregular Verb

(see Appendix C)
Rompre is conjugated like **rendre** except for the 3rd person singular: **il rompt.**

■ Notes linguistiques

To review the forms of **plaindre**, have students refer to page 271.
• **plaindre** *to pity*
  se plaindre *to complain*
• Note the following expressions:
  s'entendre comme les deux doigts de la main to get along very well
  s'entendre comme chien et chat to not get along

■ Vocabulary Expansion

Also: **Tout s'arrange.**

Teaching Strategy: Warm-Up

Using twenty of the vocabulary words from pp. 348–350, have students write twenty sentences about various books, T.V. shows, movies and/or plays they have read or seen. Have them discuss the relationships between the characters using the vocabulary given; avoid obscure characters.

Differentiation

Alphabetic/Phonetic Read the expressions for complimenting, complaining and consoling to show voice inflection (for example, rising at the end of **Quelle bonne nouvelle!** and falling at the end of **Je suis désolé pour toi.**) Have students repeat after you.

SUPPLEMENTARY VOCABULARY

complimenter *to compliment*
s'accorder bien *to get along well*
se fréquenter *to go out with, to see*

3 **Mon copain et moi** 💬

Décrivez vos relations avec votre copain (copine).
Comparez vos réponses avec celles de votre partenaire.

1. J'ai une confiance – – – en lui/elle.
   - complète
   - presque totale
   - assez limitée
   - ??

2. En général, je m'entends – – –
   avec lui/elle.
   - parfaitement
   - très bien
   - relativement bien
   - ??

3. Quand nous nous querellons, c'est
   d'habitude *(usually)* moi qui . . .
   - ai raison
   - gagne
   - cède *(gives in)* le premier/la
     première
   - ??

4. Quand nous avons une dispute
   sérieuse, nous nous réconcilions . . .
   - immédiatement
   - au bout *(after)* d'une heure
   - au bout d'une semaine
   - ??

5. Quand nous nous disputons,
   c'est à cause de . . .
   - ses copains
   - sa famille
   - mes copains
   - ??

6. En ce moment, nos rapports sont . . .
   - excellents
   - relativement bons
   - tendus *(tense)*
   - ??

4 **Mes rapports personnels**

Choisissez l'une des personnes suivantes et décrivez vos rapports avec cette personne.

mon meilleur ami	mon petit/grand frère	mes voisins
ma meilleure amie	ma petite/grande soeur	mon prof de maths
un(e) autre ami(e)	mes cousins	mon prof d'anglais
	un(e) autre membre de ma famille	un autre adulte

▶ **En général je m'entends bien avec ma cousine, mais je ne suis pas tout le temps
d'accord avec elle. De temps en temps je me dispute avec elle. . . .**

5 **Ça va?** 💬

Choisissez d'être l'une des personnes
suivantes. Votre partenaire va vous demander
si ça va et pourquoi. Décrivez un événement
heureux ou malheureux. Il/elle va vous féliciter
ou exprimer sa sympathie.

▶ — Ça va?
— Non, ça ne va pas.
— Qu'est-ce qui t'est arrivé?
— Je viens de me fâcher avec ma copine.
— Ne t'en fais pas. Ça s'arrangera.

■ **Teaching Strategy: Expansion**

Give students the following assignment:
Choisissez deux personnes:
- l'une avec qui vous vous entendez bien
- l'autre avec qui vous vous entendez mal

Décrivez vos rapports avec ces deux personnes.

■ **Teaching Suggestion**

Arrange to have a native French speaker from your community visit your class to talk about his or her native country. You may want to have students prepare questions ahead of time.

Teaching Strategy

Have the students fold a piece of paper into three columns. In Column 1, have them write fifteen difficult vocabulary words (with their books open). Then, have them exchange these papers with the person next to them who must write the English translation or draw a picture representing the French word in Column 2.

Once the second column is completed, the paper should go back to its original owner with the first column folded under so it can't be seen. The original student must then use the English/pictures from Column 2 to write the correct French word in Column 3.

PRINT
Workbook, p. 87

TECHNOLOGY
@HomeTutor

■ **Notes linguistiques**

• In the **passé composé**, the past participle agrees with the reflexive object <u>only</u> if the reflexive pronoun is a <u>direct</u> object. Compare:

Marc a vu **Valérie**.
Valérie a vu **Marc**.
Ils se sont **vus**.
(direct object: AGREEMENT)

Anne a téléphoné **à Pierre**.
Pierre a téléphoné **à Anne**.
Ils se sont **téléphoné**.
(indirect object: no AGREEMENT)

Examples of verbs where the reflexive pronoun is an <u>indirect</u> object:

se parler, se téléphoner, s'écrire

• In French, reflexive verbs may be followed by an expression to reinforce the idea of reciprocity, such as: **l'un(e) l'autre; les un(e)s les autres; entre eux; mutuellement.**

Elles se querellent les unes les autres.
Ils se battent entre eux.

A **Les verbes réfléchis: sens réciproque**

Reflexive verbs may be used to express a RECIPROCAL ACTION. In this case, the reflexive pronouns often correspond to the English expression *each other*. In the examples below, note the form of the verbs in heavy print.

Alain connaît Sophie. Sophie connaît Alain.	Ils **se connaissent**.	They **know each other**.
J'écris à ma copine. Ma copine m'écrit.	Nous **nous écrivons**.	We **write each other**.
Tu téléphones à Claire. Claire te téléphone.	Vous **vous téléphonez**.	You **phone each other**.

Since a reciprocal action involves two or more people, the subject of a reciprocal verb is always plural: **nous, vous, ils, elles.**

→   The subject may also be **on** used in the plural sense of **nous**.

On se verra demain.   *We will see each other* tomorrow.

1 **Entre amis!**

Les personnes suivantes sont des amis. Décrivez leurs relations.

▶ Jérôme et moi / se voir souvent
Nous nous voyons souvent.

1. Marc et Pauline / se téléphoner tous les jours
2. toi et tes amis / s'écrire pendant les vacances
3. Philippe et Cécile / se donner souvent rendez-vous
4. moi et mes copains / se retrouver après les classes
5. toi et François / se rendre visite tous les week-ends
6. toi et tes voisins / s'entendre bien
7. moi et mes cousins / se disputer rarement
8. Caroline et Charlotte / se réconcilier après chaque dispute

Teaching Strategy: Warm-Up

Before class, write out reciprocal verbs for each pair of students. Divide the class into pairs and give each pair one of the verbs. Ask them to act out the verb so that the class can guess their verb. Once the verb has been correctly guessed, that pair should make a complete and detailed sentence using their verb. This activity should be done very quickly.

■ **Proverbe**

Les jours se suivent mais ne se ressemblent pas.
(The days follow each other but are not alike.)

2 Relations personnelles

Informez-vous sur les personnes suivantes et décrivez leurs relations en utilisant les verbes entre parenthèses dans des phrases affirmatives ou négatives.

▶ Jérôme et Alice sont fiancés. (s'aimer?)
Ils s'aiment.

1. Marc et François sont de bons copains.
(s'aider? se disputer? se fâcher souvent?)
2. Mes voisins et moi, nous avons de bons rapports.
(s'entendre? s'inviter? se téléphoner?)
3. Jean-Paul et toi, vous êtes amis mais vous n'habitez pas dans la même ville.
(se voir souvent? se téléphoner? s'écrire?)
4. Claire et sa cousine ne sont jamais d'accord.
(se disputer? s'entendre bien? se réconcilier facilement?)
5. Delphine et moi, nous sommes fâchés.
(se parler? s'entendre mal? se quereller?)

3 Courrier du coeur

Complétez les lettres à Zoé avec les formes appropriées des verbes suggérés.

(1) s'entendre *(présent)*   (3) ne plus se parler *(présent)*   (5) ne pas se revoir *(passé composé)*

(2) se fâcher *(passé composé)*   (4) se disputer *(imparfait)*

Chère Zoé,
Je sors avec une fille depuis trois mois. En général, nous —— (1) très bien, mais la semaine dernière, il y a eu un drame.
Nous —— (2) parce que je suis arrivé à un rendez-vous avec vingt minutes de retard. Depuis, nous —— (3). Je ne veux pas rompre, mais j'ai peur de faire le premier pas!
Désolé

Cher désolé,
C'est toi qui étais en retard. Alors, si tu veux te réconcilier avec ta copine, c'est à toi de faire le premier pas.
Zoé

Chère Zoé,
L'été dernier, j'ai fait la connaissance d'un garçon avec qui je suis sortie pendant quelques temps. Un jour, j'ai rompu avec lui parce que nous —— (4) tout le temps. Depuis, nous —— (5).
Samedi dernier, j'ai appris, par hasard, qu'il sortait avec ma cousine. Maintenant, je ne peux plus dormir. Je pense sans cesse à lui et je crois que je l'aime toujours!
Nostalgique

Chère Nostalgique,
Tu n'es pas amoureuse, seulement jalouse! Oublie ton copain et cherche quelqu'un de plus compatible avec toi.
Zoé

4 À votre tour

Digital
performance space

Maintenant écrivez une lettre à Zoé. Dans cette lettre, vous décrivez un problème que vous avez avec un(e) ami(e) imaginaire. Votre partenaire jouera le rôle de Zoé et vous donnera un conseil.

Teaching Strategy

Have students cut out two comic strips from newspapers, magazines, etc. Have them write French captions to replace the English ones, explaining the relationships between the people speaking. In each caption there should be at least one vocabulary word and/or reciprocal verb. This activity may be done in class or assigned as homework.

@HOMETUTOR
my.hrw.com

■ **Teaching Strategy**
As a teaching help, you may want to present the following diagram:
ANTECEDENT + **qui** + VERB
ANTECEDENT + **que** + SUBJECT + VERB

■ **Notes linguistiques**
• Remind students that **que** becomes **qu'** before a vowel sound:
Jean-Paul téléphone à la fille **qu'**il a rencontrée ce matin.
• This is another case of the agreement of the past participle with a preceding direct object.

■ **Teaching Strategy**
Ask students to bring in photos or pictures from magazines. Have them describe each person in their pictures by using a relative pronoun (either *qui* or *que*). Similarly, cut out pictures of famous people and places before class. Show these to the students and ask them to describe these people/places using both relative pronouns in one sentence.
Picture of Disney World: **C'est un parc qui est très amusant et que j'adore.**
Have each student write one sentence on the board.

B **Révision: Les pronoms relatifs *qui* et *que***

When we want to describe people or things, we often use adjectives. We can also use CLAUSES which refer back or relate to the people and things being described (the ANTECEDENTS). Such clauses are called RELATIVE CLAUSES and are introduced by RELATIVE PRONOUNS. Note how the French relative pronouns **qui** and **que** are used to convert two clauses into a single sentence.

J'ai un ami. **Il** habite à Paris.

→ J'ai un ami **qui** habite à Paris.   *I have a friend **who** lives in Paris.*

J'ai un ami. Je **l'**invite souvent.

→ J'ai un ami **que** j'invite souvent.   *I have a friend **whom (that)** I often invite.*

J'ai lu le livre. **Il** était sur la table.

→ J'ai lu le livre **qui** était sur la table.   *I read the book **that** was on the table.*

J'ai lu le livre. Tu **l'**as apporté.

→ J'ai lu le livre **que** tu as apporté.   *I read the book **that** you brought.*

Both **qui** and **que** may refer to people, things, or ideas.
The choice between **qui** and **que** is determined by their function in the sentence.
• **Qui** *(who, that, which)* is the SUBJECT of the verb of the relative clause.
• **Que** *(whom, that, which)* is the DIRECT OBJECT of the verb of the relative clause.

◆ The verb that follows **qui** always agrees with the ANTECEDENT of **qui**.

Est-ce que c'est **vous qui avez pris** ces photos?

◆ Although the object pronoun *whom, that, which* may be omitted in English, **que** is always expressed in French.

◆ When the verb that follows **que** is in the passé composé, its past participle agrees with the ANTECEDENT of **que**.

J'ai aimé **le film que** j'ai **vu** hier.   J'ai téléphoné **aux filles que** j'ai **vues** au cinéma.

5 **Mes amis** ——————————————————

Ces personnes sont vos amis. Présentez-les à vos copains, d'après le modèle.

▶ Juliette (Elle habite à Québec.)
  Je vous présente Juliette. C'est une fille qui habite à Québec.

1. Thomas (Je le connais depuis cinq ans.)
2. Nathalie (Elle habite près de chez moi.)
3. Sandrine (Elle va à mon école.)
4. Philippe (Je le vois tous les week-ends.)
5. Claire (Elle est dans ma classe de maths.)
6. Antoine (Il est venu chez moi le week-end dernier.)
7. Bruno (Je l'ai rencontré pendant les vacances.)
8. Delphine (Je l'ai invitée à la boum.)

Differentiation
Synthetic/Analytic Teach the chart seen under Teaching Strategy above (**Antecedent + qui + verb** and **Antecedent + que + subject + verb**). Have students generate elements to fit under each column, and then combine them to form sentences. Write their sentences on the board.

6 Pauvre Corinne!

Corinne n'a pas de chance. Expliquez pourquoi en complétant les phrases suivantes avec **qui** ou **que (qu')**.

1. Elle a voulu aller dans un magasin _____ était fermé aujourd'hui.
2. Elle a pris un bus _____ est tombé en panne *(broke down)*.
3. Elle a acheté une montre _____ ne marche pas.
4. Elle n'a pas compris les exercices _____ le professeur a donnés.
5. Elle a vu un film _____ elle a trouvé stupide.
6. Elle a invité à dîner une copine _____ n'est pas venue.
7. Elle a perdu le numéro de téléphone d'un garçon _____ elle a rencontré à une boum.
8. Elle a perdu le bracelet _____ son père lui a donné pour son anniversaire.

7 Compliments . . . et insultes

Votre ami(e) français(e) — votre partenaire — veut avoir votre opinion sur certaines choses qu'il/elle a faites. Faites-lui un compliment . . . ou une insulte.

▶ la veste / acheter
très belle . . . ou moche?

— **Qu'est-ce que tu penses de la veste que j'ai achetée?**
— **Elle est très belle!**
 (Elle est moche!)

1. les copines / inviter
sympathiques . . . ou snobs?
2. l'ami / rencontrer
intelligent . . . ou stupide?
3. le repas / préparer
délicieux . . . ou infect *(disgusting)*?

4. les photos / prendre
jolies . . . ou ratées?
5. le poème / écrire
sublime . . . ou ridicule?
6. l'histoire / raconter
amusante . . . ou idiote?

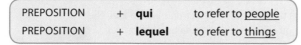

C La construction préposition + pronom relatif

In the examples below, the relative clause is introduced by a preposition (**avec**).
Note the forms of the relative pronouns as they refer to people or things.

Philippe a une copine. Il va souvent au cinéma **avec cette copine.**

→ Philippe a une copine **avec qui** il va souvent au cinéma.
  *Philippe has a friend **with whom** he often goes to the movies.*

Tu as des idées. Je ne suis pas d'accord **avec ces idées.**

→ Tu as des idées **avec lesquelles** je ne suis pas d'accord.
  *You have ideas **with which** I do not agree.*

When relative pronouns are used with prepositions (**avec, pour, sur,** etc.), the constructions are:

PREPOSITION	+ **qui**	to refer to <u>people</u>
PREPOSITION	+ **lequel**	to refer to <u>things</u>

◆ **Lequel** agrees with the noun it represents. It has the same forms as the corresponding interrogative pronoun:

lequel   laquelle   lesquels   lesquelles

◆ In French, the preposition (**avec, pour,** etc.) always comes <u>before</u> the relative pronoun.
(In English, the preposition may come at the end of the sentence.) Compare:
Tu as des idées **avec lesquelles** je ne suis pas d'accord.
  *You have ideas **with which** I do not agree. (You have ideas **that** I do not agree **with**.)*

■ Activité

Qui ou que sont-ils? Complétez les phrases avec **qui** ou **que** selon le cas.

1. **La statue de la liberté.** C'est la statue ___ est dans le port de New York. C'est le cadeau ___ la France a fait aux États-Unis. [*qui, que*]
2. **Le basket de rue.** C'est un sport ___ est à la mode et ___ les jeunes aiment beaucoup. [*qui, que*]
3. **L'internet.** C'est un réseau *(network)* ___ permet d'explorer le monde à partir de chez soi et ___ relie toute la planète. [*qui, qui*]
4. **MTV.** C'est la chaîne ___ je préfère et ___ passe les meilleurs clips. [*que, qui*]
5. **La pollution de l'air.** C'est un problème ___ les écologistes considèrent comme très important et ___ il faut résoudre *(to solve)* rapidement. [*que, qu'*]

■ Notes linguistiques

• Although **qui** is preferred with people, **lequel** may also be used: Qui est la copine **avec qui/avec laquelle** tu es sortie?
• **Lequel** must always be used after the prepositions **entre** *(between)* and **parmi** *(among)*, even when the antecedent is a person.

Teaching Strategy

Using the same pictures from the activity listed in the Teaching Strategy on p. 354, ask the students to define the people/places by giving complete sentences which include a preposition before the relative pronoun **qui** or

lequel/laquelle....
Picture of New York: **C'est une ville <u>dans laquelle</u> je me perds toujours.**

RESOURCES

PRINT
Workbook, pp. 90, 162
Unit 9 Resource Book, Partie 1
Audioscripts

AUDIO
Audio Program
CD 10, Tracks 6–8

TECHNOLOGY
@HomeTutor

■ **Note linguistique**

Lequel is used with **de** only when **de** is part of a prepositional phrase (**près de, loin de, à cause de, ...**). In all other cases, **dont** is used.

C'est l'hôtel près **duquel** j'habite.
C'est l'hôtel **dont** je t'ai parlé.

■ **Teaching Strategy**

You may wish to extend Act. 8 by using the following additional cues:

un aspirateur: nettoyer le salon
un couteau: couper du pain
une brosse à cheveux: se brosser les cheveux
le shampooing: se laver les cheveux
une machine à laver: laver les vêtements
un porte-manteau: ranger sa veste
une éponge: nettoyer la salle de bains

ALLONS PLUS LOIN

The relative pronoun **lequel**, like the interrogative **lequel?**, contracts with **à** and **de**.

Tu as assisté **à ce concert?**   Oui, c'est le concert **auquel** j'ai assisté.

Tu habites **près de ce parc?**   Oui, c'est le parc **près duquel** j'habite.

---

8 *Qu'est-ce qu'on fait avec?*

Définissez les choses suivantes en expliquant ce qu'on fait avec.

un ordinateur	• un objet	tondre la pelouse
un sécateur	• une chose	se brosser les dents
une raquette	• un appareil	repasser les chemises
une tondeuse	• une machine	surfer sur l'Internet
un fer	• un produit	couper des fleurs
le dentifrice	• un instrument	jouer au tennis

▶ **Une tondeuse est une machine avec laquelle on tond la pelouse.**

---

9 *Relations personnelles*

Décrivez vos relations avec trois personnes de votre choix en utilisant les suggestions suivantes.

quelqu'un	aller souvent chez . . .
un(e) ami(e)	téléphoner souvent à . . .
une personne	avoir beaucoup d'admiration pour . . .
un(e) adulte	pouvoir compter sur . . .
une personne de ma famille	éprouver du respect pour . . .
un professeur	éprouver de l'amitié pour . . .
des gens	avoir confiance en . . .
	s'entendre bien avec . . .
	s'entendre mal avec . . .
?? **??**	**??**

▶ **Mon oncle George est une personne de ma famille sur qui je peux compter.**

---

10 *Le job d'Alice*

Alice a trouvé un job dans une entreprise d'électronique. Un jour elle montre à un ami l'endroit où elle travaille. Complétez ses phrases.

▶ Voici la compagnie pour **laquelle je travaille.**

1. Voici le laboratoire dans _____.
2. Voici les collègues avec _____.
3. Voici le projet sur _____.
4. Voici l'ordinateur avec _____.
5. Voici les nouvelles machines avec _____.
6. Voici l'ingénieur pour _____.

D Le pronom relatif *dont*

Note how in the examples below, the relative pronoun **dont** replaces a noun introduced by **de**.

Je ne connais pas la fille. Tu parles **de cette fille**.
→ Je ne connais pas la fille **dont** tu parles.
*I don't know the girl **(whom, that)** you are talking **about**.*

The relative pronoun **dont** replaces

de + NOUN or NOUN PHRASE

Dont is, therefore, often used with verbs and verbal expressions that are followed by **de**:

avoir besoin de	parler de
se souvenir de	faire la connaissance de
avoir envie de	discuter de
s'occuper de	être amoureux de

◆ **Dont** may refer to PEOPLE or THINGS.
◆ **Note** the word order with **dont**:

(antecedent) + **dont** + subject + verb ...

Je connais le restaurant. Tu parles **de ce restaurant.**
→ Je connais le restaurant **dont** tu parles.
*I know the restaurant **(that)** you are talking **about**.*

Marc a trouvé le livre. Il avait besoin **de ce livre**.
→ Marc a trouvé le livre **dont** il avait besoin.
*Marc found the book **(that)** he needed.*

> ### ALLONS PLUS LOIN
> **Dont** is also used to replace **de** + noun in sentences where **de** indicates possession or relationship. In this type of construction, **dont** is the equivalent of *whose*.
>
> Voici l'ami.
> La soeur **de cet ami** habite à Paris.
>
> Voici l'ami **dont** la soeur habite à Paris.
> *This is the friend **whose** sister lives in Paris.*
>
> Voici l'ami.
> Je t'ai donné l'adresse **de cet ami**.
>
> Voici l'ami **dont** je t'ai donné l'adresse.
> *This is the friend **whose** address I gave you.*

11 Tant mieux!

Décrivez ce que les personnes suivantes ont fait.

▶ Christophe / trouver les livres (Il avait besoin de ces livres.)
   Christophe a trouvé les livres dont il avait besoin.

1. Pauline / acheter les chaussures (Elle avait envie de ces chaussures.)
2. Marc / trouver le magazine (Il avait besoin de ce magazine.)
3. Madame Lavoie / acheter la voiture (Elle avait envie de cette voiture.)
4. Thomas / voir le film (Sa copine lui a parlé de ce film.)
5. Véronique / visiter l'exposition (On a parlé de cette exposition dans le journal.)
6. Bruno / sortir avec la fille (Il a fait la connaissance de cette fille chez Sophie.)
7. Christine / avoir des nouvelles des enfants (Elle s'était occupée de ces enfants pendant les vacances.)
8. Caroline / se marier avec le garçon (Elle était amoureuse de ce garçon.)

12 Et vous?

Mentionnez un exemple d'une chose ou d'une personne correspondant aux définitions suivantes. Comparez vos réponses avec celles de votre partenaire.

▶ un objet dont vous avez besoin tous les jours **Mon stylo (mon peigne, ma brosse à dents, . . .) est un objet dont j'ai besoin tous les jours.**

1. un objet dont vous n'avez pas besoin en ce moment
2. une chose dont vous avez envie
3. un sujet dont vous parlez avec vos amis
4. un sujet dont vous discutez avec vos parents.
5. un événement important dont vous vous souvenez bien
6. une personne dont vous avez fait la connaissance récemment

Teaching Strategy
Before class, write out various relative pronouns and prepositions with relative pronouns on index cards. Hand one to each student and ask them to write a complete sentence describing themselves using the word(s) from their card. They should write these on the board so that the class can go over them together. Next, give each student a famous person or place (from the pictures used in the Teaching Strategies on pp. 354–355) and have them write a complete sentence about this person/place using the word(s) from their card.

Teaching Strategy: Warm-Up

As a preliminary activity, you may want to practice the use of **dont** with the expression **avoir besoin**. Ask students if they need the following things:

▶ **l'argent**
   — As-tu besoin d'argent?

— Oui, c'est une chose **dont** j'ai toujours besoin. (Non, c'est une chose **dont** je n'ai pas souvent besoin.)
• ton livre de français
• la voiture de tes parents
• l'amitié de tes copains
• la compréhension de tes professeurs

Unité 9 357

INFO MAGAZINE

Theme: Marriage

SUPPLEMENTARY VOCABULARY

la liste de mariage *bridal registry*
la demoiselle d'honneur *bridesmaid*
le garçon d'honneur *best man*
le bouquet de la mariée *bridal bouquet*
le contrat de mariage *prenuptial agreement*
la lune de miel *honeymoon*

■ Note culturelle

Le mariage civil est le seul mariage reconnu légalement. En général, mais pas toujours, le mariage civil et le mariage religieux ont lieu le même jour.

■ Irregular Verbs

(see Appendix C)
promettre   (*see* **mettre**)
offrir   (*see* **ouvrir**)
inscrire   (*see* **écrire**)

Le mariage
EN FRANCE

Un jour, un jeune homme et une jeune fille qui s'aiment, décident de se marier. Ils annoncent la bonne nouvelle° à leurs familles respectives et à leurs amis proches.° Pour célébrer cet événement, il y a parfois une cérémonie assez simple, les fiançailles,° où le jeune homme et la jeune fille promettent° de se marier. Comme symbole de cette promesse, le fiancé offre° une bague — la bague de fiançailles — à sa fiancée.

Le mariage a lieu six mois ou un an plus tard. C'est un événement qui demande beaucoup de préparation. Il faut fixer la date du mariage, organiser la cérémonie, établir la liste des invités, envoyer les invitations, etc.

Pour se marier, les deux futurs époux doivent chacun être âgés de 18 ans minimum. En réalité, les Français attendent beaucoup plus longtemps avant de se marier. En moyenne,° les hommes se marient à 32 ans et les femmes à 30 ans. Avant le mariage, les fiancés doivent accomplir un certain nombre de formalités administratives: examen médical, publication des bans° de mariage, etc… S'ils le désirent, ils peuvent aussi établir officiellement un «contrat de mariage» qui détermine la disposition de leurs biens.° Quand ces formalités sont faites, ils peuvent se marier. En général, les gens choisissent de se marier le week-end et en été. (80% des mariages français sont célébrés le samedi. 60% ont lieu de juin à septembre.)

La majorité des Français ont deux mariages: un mariage civil et un mariage religieux. Le mariage civil est obligatoire. Il a lieu à la mairie de la ville où l'on habite. C'est d'habitude une cérémonie assez simple à laquelle assistent seulement le jeune couple, leurs familles proches, leurs témoins° et quelques amis intimes. Pour cette occasion, le maire° porte une écharpe° tricolore,° signe de sa fonction officielle. Il marie les époux,° les félicite° et leur délivre° un document officiel, le «livret° de famille» où seront inscrits° les événements importants de leur vie commune (naissance des enfants, décès°…). Le jeune homme et la jeune fille sont maintenant légalement mariés.

Cinquante-deux pour cent des Français décident d'avoir aussi un mariage religieux. Le mariage religieux a toujours lieu *après* le mariage civil. Il est célébré à l'église (pour les catholiques), au temple (pour les protestants) ou à la synagogue (pour les juifs).

---

nouvelle *news* **proches** *close* **fiançailles** *engagement* **promettent / promettre** *to promise* **offre / offrir** *to give* **moyenne** *on the average* **bans** = *annonce officielle* **biens** *assets* **témoins** *witnesses* **maire** *mayor* **écharpe** *sash* **tricolore** = *bleu-blanc-rouge* **époux** *spouses* **félicite** *congratulate* **délivre** = *donne* **livret** *booklet* **inscrits / inscrire** *to inscribe* **décès** *death*

Teaching Strategy

You may wish to limit class discussion or group work if you decide that this article poses sensitivity issues in the class. If so, you may choose to have students read the article on their own and write a short reaction to it.

You might also adapt the **sondage** on p. 359 to a U.S. context and ask students how they think the percentages would differ if the questions were asked in their own community.

C'est généralement une grande cérémonie à laquelle assistent toute la famille et un grand nombre d'invités: amis, voisins, relations, etc. Traditionnellement la mariée porte une longue robe blanche. À la main elle tient° un bouquet de fleurs d'oranger. Sur la tête, elle porte une couronne.° Un voile de dentelle° lui couvre° le visage. Accompagnée de son père, elle avance vers l'autel° où l'attend son fiancé. Pendant la cérémonie, le jeune homme et la jeune fille échangent leurs alliances° en présence de leurs témoins. Après la cérémonie, les jeunes mariés sortent de l'église accompagnés des garçons d'honneur° et des demoiselles d'honneur.° On prend beaucoup de photos. Puis tout le monde va au repas de noces.°

Comme les Français aiment se marier à la campagne, le repas de noces a souvent lieu dans une petite auberge ou dans la maison de campagne des parents de la mariée. C'est un repas très joyeux. On fait des discours.° On porte des toasts au bonheur des jeunes mariés. On raconte des histoires. On chante des chansons. Et surtout, on mange bien. Au dessert, il y a une «pièce montée», c'est-à-dire un gâteau à l'architecture compliquée, que découpent° les mariés. Après le repas, on danse. Les jeunes mariés restent quelque temps avec les invités, puis ils partent en voyage de noces dans leur voiture décorée de rubans° blancs.

COMMENT SE SONT-ILS RENCONTRÉS?

Autrefois les gens qui se mariaient avaient beaucoup de choses en commun. Ils étaient issus du même milieu social et avaient la même religion. Généralement, ils habitaient dans la même ville ou le même village et souvent ils se connaissaient depuis leur enfance.

Aujourd'hui, le mariage unit de plus en plus de gens qui se sont rencontrés par hasard.° Voici comment les futurs couples se forment:

Sur 100 jeunes mariés, se sont rencontrés …

- au bal...18%
- dans un lieu public........................14%
- au travail.....................................13%
- chez des particuliers°.....................10%
- pendant leurs études.......................9%
- dans un club ou une association..........8%
- au cours° d'une fête chez des amis 7%
- à l'occasion d'une sortie ou au spectacle (cinéma, concert, théâtre,. . .).............5%
- pendant les vacances........................5%
- dans une discothèque........................4%
- par relations de voisinage..................3%
- dans une fête publique.......................3%
- par annonces°, agence matrimoniale, Internet..1%

Additional Information
- By law, a French worker may take a four-day paid vacation when he/she gets married.
- Legally, each spouse keeps his/her own name. The wife may take her husband's last name, or husband and wife may adapt both their names by joining them with a hyphen.

et vous?

DÉFINITIONS
Définissez les mots et les expressions suivants.

- les fiançailles
- les bans
- un contrat de mariage
- une alliance
- un mariage civil

- le livret de famille
- le mariage religieux
- la famille proche
- les témoins
- une écharpe tricolore

- les garçons d'honneur
- les demoiselles d'honneur
- le repas de noces
- une «pièce montée»
- un voyage de noces

DISCUSSION
Avec votre partenaire, faites une liste des similarités et des différences entre un mariage français et un mariage américain.

EXPRESSION ORALE
Imaginez que vous allez vous marier. Préférez-vous avoir un mariage simple ou un mariage formel? Expliquez pourquoi.

EXPRESSION ÉCRITE
Décrivez un mariage (réel ou imaginaire) auquel vous avez assisté.
(Qui étaient les mariés? Où a eu lieu la cérémonie? Combien y avait-il d'invités? Comment était habillés le marié et la mariée? les demoiselles et les garçons d'honneur? Comment s'est déroulé la cérémonie? . . .)

---

tient / tenir *to hold* **couronne** *crown, tiara* **voile de dentelle** *lace veil* **couvre / couvrir** *to cover* **autel** *altar*
alliances *wedding rings* **garçons d'honneur** *ushers* **demoiselles d'honneur** *bridesmaids* **noces** = *mariage* **discours** *speeches*
découpent = coupent **rubans** *ribbons* **par hasard** *by chance* **chez des particuliers** *at the home of friends or acquaintances*
au cours de = pendant **annonces** *personal ads*

Irregular Verbs
(see Appendix C)
tenir
couvrir *(see **ouvrir**)*

Notes Culturelles
- In French, the best man and the maid of honor are called **les témoins,** since they sign the official documents at the city hall.
- Generally, engaged couples leave a list of desired gifts in a store of their choice for guests to consult before choosing a present.

- Before the wedding reception, the families may host **un vin d'honneur** to toast the bride and groom with friends and relatives. Wine and snacks are served.

RESOURCES

PRINT
Workbook, pp. 163–164
Activités pour tous
Unit 9 Resource Book, Partie 2
   Activités pour tous TE
   Audioscripts
   Lesson Plans
   Block Scheduling Lesson Plans
   Absent Student Copymasters
   Workbook TE

AUDIO

 Audio Program
   CD 10, Tracks 9–12

TECHNOLOGY

@HomeTutor
 Interactive Whiteboard Lessons
Teacher One Stop
   Block Scheduling Copymasters
   Teacher to Teacher Copymasters,
   Les relations, pp. 105–107;
   Et maintenant ..., pp. 110–111;
   Jumeaux/Jumelles, pp. 112–115
 Projectable Transparencies
   51, *Les phases de la vie*
   Transparency Copymasters,
   pp. A110–A111

SUPPLEMENTARY VOCABULARY

demander en mariage *to propose (marriage)*
fonder un foyer *to set up a household/to get married*
venir au monde *to be born [to come into the world]*
prendre de l'âge *to age*
décéder *to die*
perdre son travail *to lose one's job*
démissionner *to quit (one's job)*
être renvoyé(e) *to be fired*
être mis(e) à la porte *to be fired*
être mis(e) au chômage *to be laid off*

■ Irregular Verbs

To review the conjugations of **naître, vivre,** and mourir, see Appendix C.

360 Unité 9

Les phases de la vie

♻ **RAPPEL**
naître: il/elle est né(e)
mourir: il/elle est mort(e)

L'ENFANCE — on **naît** | **naître*** *to be born*
on **grandit** | **grandir** *to grow up*

LA JEUNESSE
L'ADOLESCENCE
  (la vie scolaire) — on **développe** sa personnalité | **développer** *to develop*
on **fait des études** | élémentaires / secondaires / universitaires

  (la vie sociale) — on **fait connaissance** |
on **rencontre** | d'autres personnes
on **se fait** des amis | **se faire des amis** *to make friends*

L'ÂGE ADULTE
  (la vie familiale) — on **rencontre** quelqu'un de spécial
on **tombe amoureux** de cette personne | **tomber amoureux de** *to fall in love with*
on décide de | **vivre** ensemble | **vivre** *to live*
   se fiancer | **se fiancer** *to get engaged*
   se marier | **se marier** *to get married*
   ou de rester **célibataire** *(single)*

on **élève** une famille | **élever** *to raise*

parfois on | **se sépare** | **se séparer** *to separate*
   divorce | **divorcer** *to get divorced*
   et on **se remarie** | **se remarier** *to remarry*

  (la vie familiale) — on **choisit** un métier ou une profession
on **trouve** un job
on **travaille** dur
on **gagne** sa vie | **gagner sa vie** *to earn a living*
on **obtient** une promotion | **obtenir*** *to get*

LA VIEILLESSE — on **prend** sa retraite | **prendre sa retraite** *to retire*
on **s'occupe** de façons diverses | **s'occuper** *to keep busy*
on **vieillit** | **vieillir** *to grow old*
   parfois on **tombe malade** | **tomber malade** *to get sick*
on **meurt** | **mourir *** *to die*

Teaching Strategy

Have the students predict their futures and write a one-page description of their lives. Obviously, they should only mention main events but give as much humorous or specific information as possible. Their predictions should include as much vocabulary from p. 360 as possible.

Differentiation

Multisensory To drill vocabulary, have students repeat it 3 times, and then write out boldfaced expressions on cards. Pair strong and at-risk students and have them carry out the dialogs on page 361.

@ **HOMETUTOR**
my.hrw.com

1 Mon avenir 💬

Faites une liste de 5 choses que vous voulez accomplir dans votre vie. Classez-les par ordre d'importance. Comparez votre liste avec celle de votre partenaire.

Cinq choses que je voudrais faire dans ma vie

1.
2.
3.
4.
5.

2 Débat 💬

Vous avez décidé de vous marier. Votre partenaire a décidé de rester célibataire (ou vice versa). Chacun va expliquer les raisons et les avantages (et désavantages) de sa décision.

3 Une vie

Catherine parle de son grand-père. Complétez cette description avec le passé composé des verbes de la liste. Soyez logique!

élever	naître
faire la connaissance	prendre sa retraite
faire ses études	tomber amoureux
ne pas gagner	tomber malade
grandir	travailler dur
se marier	trouver un job
mourir	ne pas vieillir

Mon grand-père ___ dans un petit village de la province de Québec où il ___ et où il ___ secondaires. À l'âge de 17 ans, il a immigré aux États-Unis et il ___ dans une usine de textile.

Un jour, il ___ d'une jeune fille, ma grand-mère dont il ___. Ils ___ peu de temps après et ensemble ils ___ une famille de six enfants.

Durant sa vie, mon grand-père ___, mais il ___ beaucoup d'argent. Il ___ après 50 ans de travail dans la même usine. Malheureusement, mon grand-père et ma grand-mère ___ ensemble. Ma grand-mère, en effet, ___ et elle ___ en 1975. Mon grand-père ___ dix ans après, à l'âge de 85 ans.

4 À votre tour ✍

Composez la biographie d'une personne de votre famille (votre grand-père ou votre grand-mère) ou d'une personne âgée imaginaire.

Note linguistique

Le troisième âge est une expression qui désigne les personnes qui sont à la retraite et qui ont quitté la vie active. Les clubs du troisième âge organisent des voyages et diverses activités pour les retraités.

■ Proverbe

Si jeunesse savait, si vieillesse pouvait. *Youth is wasted on the young.*

■ Réponses: Activité 3

est né/a grandi/a fait ses études/a trouvé un job/a fait la connaissance/ est tombé amoureux/se sont mariés/ ont élevé/a travaillé dur/n'a pas gagné/a pris sa retraite/n'ont pas vieilli/est tombée malade/est morte/ est mort

Note: The verb **mourir** is used twice.

Teaching Strategy

Extend Act. 1 by giving students the following assignment:
Votre passé. Faites une liste de cinq choses que vous avez accomplies dans votre vie. Utilisez des mots et expressions du vocabulaire de la page 360.

Sample answers:
Je suis née dans le Missouri.
J'ai fait des études élémentaires à l'école x.
J'ai fait connaissance de mon amie Gail à Boston.
J'ai travaillé dans un supermarché l'été dernier.
Je suis tombée amoureuse de x au mois d'avril.

Langue et Communication

■ **Note linguistique**

As in English, **où** *(where)* is generally used instead of **dans lequel.**
… le bureau **où** je
travaille …

■ **Teaching Note**

In Activity 1, item 5, it is also possible to use **où** rather than **dans laquelle.**

A Résumé: les pronoms relatifs

Review the use of the relative pronouns in the chart below.

The relative pronoun functions as . . .	The relative pronoun refers to: PEOPLE	THINGS
SUBJECT	**QUI** l'ami **qui** est arrivé	**QUI** la lettre **qui** est arrivée
DIRECT OBJECT	**QUE** la fille **que** tu connais	**QUE** le café **que** tu connais
OBJECT OF A PREPOSITION (other than **de**)	**QUI** la personne **avec qui** je travaille	**LEQUEL** la machine **avec laquelle** je travaille
OBJECT OF THE PREPOSITION de	**DONT** le garçon **dont** je te parle	**DONT** le livre **dont** je te parle

1 Photos de vacances

Catherine montre ses photos de vacances à son frère Marc. Jouez les deux rôles en faisant les substitutions suggérées. (Utilisez les pronoms qui conviennent.)

▶ Mélanie / Nous avons rencontré cette fille à la plage.

Tu te souviens de Mélanie?

Non, pas vraiment.

Mais si! C'est la fille que nous avons rencontrée à la plage!

Ah, oui. Je me souviens maintenant.

1. Jean-Paul / Tu jouais au tennis avec ce garçon.
2. Pierre et Jérôme / Ces garçons nous ont invités à une boum.
3. Alice / J'ai dîné chez cette fille un jour.
4. Véronique / Tu as fait la connaissance de cette fille dans un café.
5. La Tulipe noire / Nous passions nos soirées dans cette discothèque.

2 Quel pronom?

Complétez les phrases avec le pronom qui convient.

1. Je n'ai pas trouvé le livre . . .
___ j'avais besoin.
___ était sur la table.
dans ___ il y a des photos de Paris.
___ j'ai acheté ce matin.

2. Ma cousine va se marier avec un jeune homme . . .
avec ___ elle est fiancée depuis un an.
___ elle connaît depuis deux ans.
___ elle a fait la connaissance à la Martinique.
___ travaille pour une agence de voyage.

3. Nous allons dîner dans le restaurant . . .
___ mon frère m'a recommandé.
___ sert des spécialités régionales.
___ tout le monde parle.
devant ___ nous sommes passés ce matin.

4. Je suis sorti avec les amis . . .
___ je t'ai parlé.
___ m'ont téléphoné ce matin.
avec ___ je suis allé en vacances.
___ j'ai vus le week-end dernier.

Teaching Strategy

Divide the class into pairs and have each pair write a dialog between two friends about the relationship of one of the friends with another person/people. Encourage the students to use their imaginations, a wide vocabulary, **ce que**, **ce qui** (p. 364), and at least four other relative pronouns. These dialogs are a synopsis of the chapter's information and should be done carefully: begun in class, worked on at home, turned in, practiced and performed in class. They may be included in student portfolios.

③ La légende de Tristan et Yseult

Complétez le texte suivant avec les formes appropriées des pronoms qui conviennent.

Tristan et Yseult est une très vieille légende (1) date du Moyen Âge et (2) on retrouve dans les littératures anglaise, française et allemande de l'époque.

Cette légende relate la tragique histoire de deux jeunes gens, unis par un amour (3) ils ne peuvent pas contrôler. Dans cette légende, le roi Marc va épouser une jeune fille (4) il ne connaît pas mais (5) ses conseillers lui ont parlé. Il envoie Tristan, son neveu en (6) il a toute confiance, chercher cette jeune fille (7) s'appelle Yseult et (8) habite en Irlande. Tristan trouve Yseult et la ramène en Cornouailles°, le pays du roi Marc. Sur le bateau (9) les transporte, Tristan et Yseult boivent par mégarde° une potion (10) un magicien avait préparée pour assurer l'amour éternel entre Marc et Yseult. Sous l'influence de la potion (11) ils ont bue, Tristan et Yseult tombent éperdument° amoureux l'un de l'autre.

À leur retour, le roi Marc, (12) a découvert la vérité, chasse le pauvre Tristan. Des années passent. Tristan a épousé une autre jeune fille (13) il a fait la connaissance dans son exil. En réalité, il ne cesse de penser à la belle Yseult (14) il est resté amoureux. Un jour, il participe à une bataille au cours de (15) il est très grièvement° blessé! Yseult à (16) on a annoncé la nouvelle veut revoir l'homme (17) elle aime toujours. Malheureusement, quand elle arrive chez Tristan, celui-ci est déjà mort. À son tour, Yseult meurt de désespoir. Les deux amants (18) la vie a séparés sont finalement unis par la mort.

Cornouailles *Cornwall (in southwestern England)* **par mégarde** = par accident **éperdument** *madly*
grièvement = très sérieusement

④ Descriptions

Choisissez l'une des situations suivantes et décrivez la chose ou la personne dont il est question. Pour cela, utilisez la construction relative dans au moins trois phrases différentes.

▶ Vous avez perdu votre cahier d'exercices. Décrivez ce cahier.
 C'est un cahier qui est assez grand.
 C'est le cahier que j'avais avec moi ce matin.
 C'est le cahier dans lequel j'ai pris beaucoup de notes.
 C'est un cahier dont j'ai absolument besoin.

1. Vous avez perdu la montre que votre oncle vous a donnée pour votre anniversaire.
 Décrivez cette montre.
2. Vous avez dîné dans un restaurant qu'un ami vous a recommandé. Décrivez ce restaurant.
3. Vous avez trouvé un job pour l'été. Décrivez ce job.
4. Vous avez inventé une machine. Décrivez cette machine.
5. Vos parents ont acheté une nouvelle voiture. Décrivez cette voiture.
6. Vous avez fait la connaissance d'un(e) étudiant(e) francophone très sympathique
 à la dernière réunion du club français. Décrivez cet(te) étudiant(e).
7. L'été dernier, vous avez rencontré une personne très intéressante. Décrivez cette personne.

Notes culturelles

- The legend of **Tristan et Yseult** probably originated in Cornwall. Several versions were written by the end of the 12th century. The poets **Thomas d'Angleterre** and **Béroul** are two of its most notable authors. The story of Tristan and Yseult was later incorporated in the Arthurian legends.

- In 1900, French author **Joseph Bédier (1864–1938)** compiled several versions of the story into a new and more complete one.
- *Tristan und Isolde* is an opera by **Richard Wagner**, based on the medieval legend.

RESOURCES

PRINT
Workbook, pp. 92–94, 164
Unit 9 Resource Book, Partie 2
  Audioscripts

AUDIO
  Audio Program
  CD 10, Tracks 13–14

TECHNOLOGY
@HomeTutor
Teacher One Stop
  Teacher to Teacher Copymasters,
  Et maintenant ..., pp. 110–111

■ Notes linguistiques

- **Ce** is considered in this case a neutral pronoun that refers to things.
- **Ce que** and **ce qui** are used to form indirect interrogative sentences, e.g.:
    Demande-lui ce qu'il aimerait manger. (qu'est-ce qu'il aimerait manger)
    Demande-lui ce qui est intéressant à voir. (qu'est-ce qui est intéressant à voir)
- **Ce qui** is followed by a singular verb. It is modified by a masculine singular adjective.

B   *Ce qui, ce que* et *ce dont*

Note the use of **ce qui, ce que** and **ce dont** in the following sentences.

Je voudrais savoir **ce qui** t'intéresse.	*I would like to know **what** interests you.*
Dis-moi **ce qui** est arrivé.	*Tell me **what** happened.*
Je ne sais pas **ce que** tu fais.	*I don't know **what** you are doing.*
Montre-moi **ce que** tu as acheté.	*Show me **what** you bought.*
Dis-moi **ce dont** tu as envie.	*Tell me **what** you want.*
Je ne comprends pas **ce dont** tu parles.	*I don't understand **what** you are talking about.*

Ce qui, ce que, and **ce dont** correspond to *what*.

- **Ce qui** is equivalent to **la chose/les choses qui . . . .**
    It functions as the SUBJECT of the verb that follows.

- **Ce que** is equivalent to **la chose/les choses que . . . .**
    It functions as the DIRECT OBJECT of the verb that follows.

- **Ce dont** is equivalent to **la chose/les choses dont . . . .**
    It replaces a phrase with **de**.

Je voudrais savoir ce qui t'intéresse.

Montre-moi ce que tu as acheté.

5 Précisions 🗨

Votre partenaire vous explique certaines choses sans préciser. Demandez-lui de préciser
en utilisant les expressions entre parenthèses avec **ce qui, ce que** ou **ce dont.**

▶ Quelque chose m'amuse. (Dis-moi . . .)
  Dis-moi ce qui t'amuse.

▶ J'ai besoin de quelque chose. (Je voudrais savoir . . .)
  Je voudrais savoir ce dont tu as besoin.

1. Quelque chose m'intéresse. (Explique-moi . . .)
2. Je fais quelque chose. (Je voudrais savoir . . .)
3. J'ai envie de quelque chose. (Dis-moi . . .)
4. Quelque chose m'est arrivé. (Raconte-moi . . .)
5. J'ai acheté quelque chose. (Montre-moi . . .)
6. Mon copain m'a parlé de quelque chose. (Dis-moi . . .)

6 Qu'est-ce qu'ils font?

Complétez les phrases avec **ce qui, ce que (ce qu')** ou **ce dont.**

1. Je suis au supermarché. J'achète . . .
   ___ est sur ma liste
   ___ j'ai besoin
   ___ j'ai oublié hier

2. Marc veut faire un cadeau d'anniversaire à
   Sylvie. Il lui demande . . .
   ___ l'intéresse
   ___ elle a envie
   ___ elle aimerait avoir

3. Christine et Françoise font du shopping. Elles
   regardent . . .
   ___ est en solde
   ___ elles ont envie
   ___ elles voudraient acheter si
       elles avaient de l'argent

4. Le professeur aide les élèves. Il explique . . .
   ___ il a parlé la semaine dernière
   ___ est difficile
   ___ ils ne comprennent pas

5. Monsieur Dumont nettoie son appartement.
   Il range . . .
   ___ est en désordre
   ___ il veut garder
   ___ il n'a pas besoin

6. Madame Moreau a été témoin d'un accident.
   Elle explique à la police . . .
   ___ elle a vu
   ___ elle se souvient
   ___ est arrivé

Compile a pen pal bank to share
with other French classes in your
area or state.

Language Arts
Brainstorm and decide on a list of
questions about background and
interests.

Math
For an overview of your class,
calculate percentages of people
interested in various activities and
display in chart form.

Science/Health
Is there a science to predicting what
types of people get along or will be
attracted to each other? Investigate
various myths and methods.

Social Studies
Explore something interesting about
your heritage, town, or activities you
are interested in; this may provide a
good conversation starter!

Art/Music
Write a paragraph or two—in
French—about the kinds of art and
music you like, and where you go to
enjoy them.

Technology
Communicate with another school
and send pen pal letters
electronically. Or Investigate the use
of technology in dating services. How
do they match people up?

Community
Send letters or e-mail to pen pals
from another French class. Include
information about your school and
community in initial communications.

Reading fiction

RESOURCES

PRINT
Activités pour tous

TECHNOLOGY
Teacher One Stop
🖥 **Projectable Transparencies**
   L9, *Le bracelet*
   Transparency Copymasters,
   p. A135
French InterActive Reader

■ **Pour en savoir plus**
For more information on the
Académie française, refer your
students to p. 56.

LECTURE

Michelle Maurois

Le bracelet

AVANT DE LIRE

Lisez le titre de cette histoire et puis regardez l'illustration.
Décrivez avec le maximum de détails:

- la jeune fille
- la marchande d'antiquités
- le magasin
- le bracelet qui est à la vitrine

Michelle Maurois
(1914 – 1994) vient d'une
famille d'écrivains et
d'intellectuels. Son père,
André Maurois, était
membre de l'Académie
française. Connue pour ses
contes, Michelle Maurois a
aussi écrit des essais et des
romans.

Anticipons un peu!

Répondez aux questions suivantes, en expliquant votre opinion.
- Quel genre d'histoire est-ce? une histoire drôle? une histoire
  policière? une histoire sentimentale?
Maintenant lisez l'histoire pour voir si vous avez raison.
- Quel est le sujet de cette histoire?
- Est-ce que la marchande vendra le bracelet à la jeune fille?
  Pourquoi ou pourquoi pas?
Maintenant lisez l'histoire pour voir si vous avez raison.

Le bracelet

Teaching Strategy

Using **Projectable Transparency L9** and the
Avant de lire activities, help students to use
critical thinking skills to predict the genre of
the story and possible plot points. Before
reading, ask students to look at all the
illustrations to see if they contain "hints" about
the characters and plot. Ask students to
imagine why the girl is looking at the bracelet
in the shop window. List possible reasons on the
board, then have students read the first
segment of the story and answer the
comprehension questions.

I

—Bonjour Madame, dit Denise, entrant dans le magasin de bric-à-brac.°

—Mademoiselle ... Je ne suis pas encore Madame.

—Excusez-moi, dit la jeune fille déconcertée. Bonjour Mademoiselle.

—Entrez ma belle, dit la marchande sans lâcher° son tricot.

Denise se dirige vers la très vieille femme, vêtue d'une longue robe rouge, assise sur une chaise basse. Son visage est usé,° ses cheveux d'un blanc de neige, mais son regard° reste jeune et souriant.°

—S'il vous plaît, Mademoiselle, quel est le prix du bracelet qui se trouve au milieu de la vitrine?

—Il n'est pas à vendre, dit la vieille, souriant toujours.

—Comment cela?

—Tout est à vendre, sauf le bracelet.

—Mais ... vous l'exposez.

—Oui, mais pas pour qu'on l'achète.

—Ah! dit Denise étonnée.° C'est dommage. Il me plaît. J'aime beaucoup les bijoux anciens.

La marchande se lève. Elle est toute voûtée° et avance à petits pas.° La jeune fille regarde autour d'elle avec curiosité; ces vieux objets excitent son imagination, rappellent des époques disparues, des familles éteintes.° Ici sont mêlés° tasses chinoises, assiettes romantiques,° boîtes marquées du «N» napoléonien,* vases de Venise° plus ou moins cassés, verres de Bohême.°

La marchande prend dans la vitrine le bracelet et revient vers la jeune fille. Ce bracelet est en or, recouvert° de pierres de toutes les couleurs. Chaque pierre a la forme d'un cœur.

—Il est fermé par un saphir de la couleur de mes yeux, dit la vieille femme. Il est joli, n'est-ce pas, mon bracelet?

—Très joli, dit Denise en le prenant dans ses mains.

Quand elle le voit de près, la jeune fille est encore plus tentée. Le travail° est fin, délicat. C'est un charmant bijou qui vient d'être nettoyé et qui brille de mille feux. On le remarque d'autant plus que tout ce que contient le magasin° est recouvert de poussière.

Mots utiles

un bracelet	bracelet
des bijoux	(pieces of) jewelry
la marchande d'antiquités	antique dealer
une pierre	stone, gem
la poussière	dust
le tricot	knitting
une vitrine	store window
briller	to shine
se diriger vers	to go toward
exposer	to exhibit
plaire *	to please
tenter	to tempt
d'autant plus que	all the more that
autour de	around
sauf	except

* **Boîtes marquées du «N» napoléonien.** As presents to his courtiers, Napoleon used to give small boxes decorated with the imperial «N».

bric-à-brac = antiquités bon marché   **lâcher** = laisser   **usé** = vieux   **son regard** = les yeux   **souriant** smiling   **étonnée** astonished
voûtée bent over   **pas** steps   **éteintes** = qui n'existent plus   **mêlés** mixed together   **romantiques** = décorées de sujets romantiques
vases de Venise Venitian glass vases   **verres de Bohême** [red] Bohemian glasses   **recouvert de** covered with   **travail** workmanship
ce que contient le magasin = ce qu'il y a dans le magasin

Avez-vous compris?

1. Pourquoi est-ce que Denise entre dans le magasin?
2. À votre avis, quel âge a la marchande (approximativement)? Expliquez pourquoi vous pensez cela.
3. À votre avis, est-ce qu'elle est mariée? Expliquez comment vous savez cela.
4. En quoi le bracelet est-il différent des autres objets? Décrivez ce bracelet.

Anticipons un peu!

À votre avis, pourquoi est-ce que la marchande ne veut pas vendre le bracelet? Expliquez pourquoi vous pensez cela.

- Le bracelet n'est pas à elle.
- C'est un souvenir personnel.
- Elle l'a promis à une personne de sa famille.
- Il coûte trop cher.
- Une autre raison. Imaginez laquelle.

Differentiation

Metacognitive, Gifted & Talented As a pre-reading activity, have students go through the reading and identify cognates. Then, have them write out any unknown vocabulary, and look up the words, writing definitions in their notebooks. Then have students choose at least 10 of the new words they looked up and create a crossword puzzle with the words.

Have students exchange crossword puzzles with another student and complete each others' puzzle. Pair strong and at-risk students to carry out the activity at the bottom of page 367.

SUPPLEMENTARY VOCABULARY

Les bijoux
la bague *ring*
la gourmette *chain bracelet*
les clips *(m.)* **d'oreilles** *clip earrings*
les boucles *(f.)* **d'oreilles** *earrings*
le collier *necklace*
le pendentif *pendant*
le tour de cou *choker*
le sautoir *chain (long necklace)*

■ **Irregular Verbs**

(see Appendix C)
remettre   *(see* mettre*)*
suivre
surprendre   *(see* prendre*)*
tenir

■ ***Avez-vous compris?***

(Sample answers)

1. Frédéric Cottet était le fiancé de la marchande quand elle était jeune.
2. Elle ne veut pas vendre le bracelet parce que c'est un cadeau de Frédéric.
3. Elle continue à l'exposer dans la vitrine parce qu'elle pense que Frédéric reviendra et reconnaîtra le bracelet dans la vitrine.
4. Elle pense que la marchande est folle mais intéressante.

II

Denise adore les bijoux, elle en possède plusieurs, mais elle n'a pas de bracelet. Elle vient de recevoir son salaire du mois et elle a envie de faire une folie.°
—Mais pourquoi, demande-t-elle, pourquoi ne voulez-vous pas me le céder?°
—Parce qu'il est à moi et parce que j'y tiens plus qu'à tout au monde.
—Mais tout, ici, n'est-il pas à vous?
—Non. Les autres objets, je les ai achetés, tandis que ce bracelet m'a été donné.
—Alors, pourquoi l'exposer?
—C'est un cadeau de mon fiancé.
Denise regarde la marchande et se tait. Le mot «fiancé» dans la bouche de la vieille femme est surprenant.
—Frédéric avait vingt ans ... Frédéric Cottet, c'est le nom de mon fiancé. Un jour il m'a apporté ce bracelet pour me tenir compagnie pendant son absence. Il partait pour un très long voyage ... Il n'est pas revenu.
—Excusez-moi, j'ai été indiscrète. Comme c'est triste!
—Oh non! Je l'attends.
—Vous ... vous l'attendez ...? dit la jeune fille.
—Tous les jours, à toutes les heures. Et comme il ne sait sans doute pas où me trouver, je laisse le bracelet au milieu de la vitrine pour qu'il le reconnaisse: voilà pourquoi il n'est pas à vendre.

—Je comprends, dit Denise lentement.
—Je vais d'ailleurs vite le remettre. Si Frédéric passait juste maintenant ...
«La vieille femme est sûrement folle, se dit Denise en la suivant des yeux, mais touchante, mystérieuse. Peut-être ne finit-on jamais de rêver?»
La marchande prend un verre sur lequel on peut lire en lettres dorées,° un peu effacées,° «souvenir» et le tend° à la jeune fille.
—Je vous le donne parce que vous êtes si jolie.
—Oh! C'est trop gentil,° mais je ne peux pas l'accepter...
—Cela me fait plaisir. Et revenez me voir.
Denise part, le verre serré° dans sa main, le cœur un peu lourd. Cette nuit-là, dans son lit, elle ne réussit pas à s'endormir. Son esprit° ne peut pas se détacher° de la vieille marchande, attendant toute sa vie sans se décourager.

une folie = quelque chose d'extravagant   **me le céder** = *to let me have it*   **doré** = d'or   **effacer** *to erase*
tend = donne   **gentil** = généreux   **serré** *held tightly*   **esprit** *mind*   **se détacher** = oublier

Mots utiles

faire plaisir à	*to please*
posséder	*to own, possess*
remettre *	*to put back*
rêver	*to dream*
suivre *	*to follow*
surprendre *	*to surprise*
tenir * **à**	*to hold dear, to cherish*
tenir * **compagnie**	*to keep company*
fou (folle)	*crazy*

Avez-vous compris?

1. Qui est Frédéric Cottet?
2. Pourquoi est-ce que la marchande ne veut pas vendre le bracelet?
3. Pourquoi est-ce qu'elle continue à l'exposer dans la vitrine?
4. Qu'est-ce que Denise pense de la marchande?

À votre avis

Exprimez votre opinion sur les sujets suivants et expliquez pourquoi vous avez cette opinion.

- Est-ce que la vieille femme est bizarre, complètement folle ou simplement sentimentale?
- Est-ce que Frédéric Cottet est une personne réelle ou bien est-ce qu'il existe seulement dans l'imagination de la vieille femme?
- Est-ce que Frédéric Cottet va revenir un jour? Si oui, dans quelles circonstances?

Teaching Strategy

After students have read the first two segments of the story, divide the class into groups to discuss the *À votre avis* questions. If there are differences of opinion, have students tally the responses. Have each group present their answer to <u>one</u> of the questions to the whole class. Compare with other groups' answers.

You may also wish to add an additional question for all groups:
À votre avis, pourquoi la vieille dame n'est-elle pas partie avec son fiancé? (Utilisez votre imagination pour trouver une explication!) Discuss the answers in class.

III

Quelques mois plus tard, l'été est venu. Denise en sortant du bureau, rentre un soir par la rue où se trouve le magasin de bric-à-brac. Brillant de tous ses feux, le bracelet est toujours là. La vieille femme est assise sur le trottoir devant la porte, travaillant au même tricot. Elle reconnaît la jeune fille et lui fait un grand sourire.

—Venez vous asseoir avec moi, ma belle, prenez une chaise à l'intérieur.°

La jeune fille s'installe contre le mur de la maison à côté de la marchande.

—Vous avez eu beaucoup de clients aujourd'hui? demande Denise.

—Oh non! Je n'ai eu personne. J'ai été plus tranquille pour penser. Moi, je ne suis jamais seule ... Frédéric est près de moi ... Et vous? Avez-vous un fiancé?

—Non, dit la jeune fille en rougissant.

—Pourquoi?

—Je connais peu de jeunes gens ...

—Quand Frédéric viendra, je lui demanderai de vous présenter un de ses amis.

Denise frissonne; elle est saisie par une sorte d'anxiété.°

—Je dois rentrer, dit-elle. Ma mère m'attend. Il va être l'heure du dîner.

—Je laisse ouvert° le plus longtemps possible. Frédéric termine peut-être tard son travail. Mais je vais fermer dans quelques minutes.

La marchande se dirige vers la vitrine, sort le bracelet que Denise regarde une fois de plus avec admiration et l'attache à son bras.

—Je le mets tous les soirs pour dormir, dit-elle.

—Je reviendrai vous voir, dit la jeune fille.

—Adieu, ma belle. À bientôt.

Mais quelques jours plus tard, Denise tombe malade et reste couchée° près d'un mois. Elle est obligée d'aller se reposer à la montagne. Les soucis causés par sa maladie lui ont fait un peu oublier la vieille dame et son éternellement jeune fiancé.

à l'intérieur = à l'intérieur du magasin **anxiété** = peur **je laisse ouvert** = je garde le magasin ouvert **couchée** = au lit

Mots utiles

un souci	concern, worry
un sourire	smile
un trottoir	sidewalk
frissonner	to shiver, shudder
saisir	to seize, take

Avez-vous compris?

1. Selon vous, est-ce que les choses ont changé quand Denise revient plus tard?
2. Qu'est-ce que la marchande propose à Denise quand elle apprend que celle-ci n'est pas mariée?
3. Quelle est la réaction de Denise?
4. Pourquoi est-ce que Denise ne revient pas voir la marchande?

Anticipons un peu!

Selon vous, comment va se terminer l'histoire? Expliquez votre réponse.

- Frédéric Cottet reviendra et il se mariera avec la marchande.
- La marchande apprendra la mort de Frédéric Cottet et finalement vendra le bracelet à Denise.
- Un jour Denise fera la connaissance du petit-fils de Frédéric Cottet et se mariera avec lui.
- Quelque chose d'autre arrivera. Imaginez quoi.

■ Avez-vous compris?

(Sample answers)

1. Non, les choses n'ont pas changé. C'est l'été, et la vieille femme est assise devant la porte, mais elle attend toujours Frédéric.
2. Elle lui propose que Frédéric lui présente un de ses amis.
3. Elle trouve que c'est trop bizarre. Elle a peur. Elle part.
4. Elle ne revient pas parce qu'elle tombe malade et va se reposer à la montagne. Elle oublie un peu la vieille femme.

IV

À son retour, Denise passe par hasard, un jour, devant le magasin qui lui plaisait tant. De très loin, elle voit
105 que le bracelet n'est plus dans la vitrine. Elle s'aperçoit aussi que quelque chose a changé. Il y a plus d'ordre, tout paraît plus propre qu'autrefois. Surprise, elle ouvre
110 la porte du magasin et voit une femme brune de cinquante ans environ, installée derrière un bureau.

—La vieille dame n'est plus là? demande la jeune fille.
115 —Non ... elle est morte depuis un mois ...

—Oh! Cela me fait de la peine,° dit Denise. Elle était si charmante.

—Elle est morte brusquement. On
120 l'a trouvée un matin ici, par terre. Vous savez, elle était un peu bizarre ...

—Oui, dit Denise, un peu bizarre ...

—Je ne sais pas ce que je vais faire du magasin ...

—Oh! J'espère que vous le garderez, il a tant de charme.
125 —Est-ce que vous désirez quelque chose?

—Il y avait dans la vitrine, dit la jeune fille, un bracelet avec des pierres de couleur en forme de cœurs: il me plaisait beaucoup.

—En effet, il était très joli. Ma tante l'avait déjà quand j'étais toute petite° ... Je l'ai vendu quelques jours après sa mort. Un
130 matin, un vieux monsieur, tout voûté, est resté longtemps dans la rue à regarder la vitrine. Puis il est entré. Il était complètement sourd° et nous avons eu beaucoup de mal° à nous comprendre. Je crois qu'il trouvait le bracelet trop cher mais il en avait très envie et, à la fin il l'a acheté.
135 —Vous ne savez pas comment il s'appelait?

—Je ne me souviens pas, mais il m'a payée par chèque. Cela vous intéresse de savoir son nom?

—Oui. J'attendais d'avoir assez d'argent pour acheter ce bracelet. Je vais essayer de joindre le vieux monsieur et lui
140 demander de me le céder.°

La femme brune ouvre un secrétaire,° cherche dans des papiers.

—Ah voilà le nom: Frédéric Cottet.

me fait de la peine = me rend triste   toute petite = très jeune
sourd *deaf*   beaucoup de mal = beaucoup de difficultés
me le céder = me le vendre
un secrétaire = un petit bureau

Mots utiles

s'apercevoir *	notice
joindre *	to contact (someone)
paraître *	to look, appear, seem
environ	about, approximately
par hasard	by chance
par terre	on the ground
tant de	so much

Avez-vous compris?

1. Qu'est-ce qui a changé quand Denise retourne au magasin?
2. Qui est la nouvelle marchande par rapport à l'ancienne?
3. Qui a finalement acheté le bracelet?

■ Irregular Verbs

(see Appendix C)

s'apercevoir	(*see* **recevoir**)
joindre	(*see* **peindre**)
paraître	(*see* **connaître**)

■ Avez-vous compris?

(Sample answers)
1. La vieille marchande est morte. Il y a une nouvelle marchande.
2. La nouvelle marchande est la nièce de l'ancienne.
3. Frédéric Cottet a acheté le bracelet.

Teaching Strategy

Using the illustrations and characters from the story, have students list two adjectives to describe as many elements as possible:
- la vieille dame (*patiente, fidèle...*)
- Denise (*curieuse, sympathique...*)
- l'histoire (*romantique, triste...*)

Then have students write a paragraph about the story using the adjectives they compiled.

Pre-AP skill: Brainstorm, organize ideas, make outlines.

APRÈS LA LECTURE

Expression orale

Débat: L'amour éternel

Selon vous, est-ce que l'amour éternel, tel qu'il est décrit dans l'histoire, est possible? Prenez une position pour ou contre et débattez le sujet avec votre partenaire. Si possible, donnez des exemples.

Situations

Avec votre partenaire, choisissez l'une des situations suivantes. Composez le dialogue correspondant et jouez-le en classe.

1	Coup de téléphone

Après chaque visite au magasin, Denise téléphone à un(e) ami(e) pour raconter ce qui s'est passé. L'ami(e) demande des détails.
Rôles: Denise, l'ami(e)

2	Conversation

Denise a réussi à retrouver Frédéric Cottet. Celui-ci lui pose des questions sur sa fiancée d'autrefois.
Rôles: Denise, Frédéric Cottet

Expression écrite

Frédéric Cottet

Écrivez l'histoire de Frédéric Cottet en inventant des détails. Par exemple:

- Où, quand et comment Frédéric a-t-il rencontré la dame de la boutique?
- À quelle occasion est-ce qu'il lui a offert le bracelet?
- Pourquoi est-il parti à l'âge de vingt ans?
- Où est-il allé et qu'est-ce qu'il a fait là-bas?
- Pourquoi a-t-il mis si longtemps à revenir?
- Pourquoi est-ce qu'il est finalement revenu?
- Quelles étaient ses pensées en revoyant le bracelet dans la vitrine? etc.

Une lettre

La vieille dame, avant de mourir, décide d'écrire une lettre à Frédéric Cottet. Dans cette lettre, elle explique ce qu'elle a fait pendant son absence, pourquoi elle l'a attendu si fidèlement *(faithfully)* et comment elle espérait le revoir.

Une autre conclusion

Imaginez une autre conclusion moins triste et plus romantique à l'histoire que vous avez lue. Pour cela, réécrivez complètement le quatrième épisode.

■ **Expression écrite**

For writing rubrics, consult the **Generate Success** Rubric Generator on the **Teacher One Stop.** You can also create your own custom rubrics with this tool.

Student Portfolios

After students have completed the post-reading activities from the *Après la lecture* section, give them the following written activity and dialog scenario to be included in their portfolios:

- **Une lettre**
  Denise est malade. Elle est à la montagne et elle s'ennuie. Elle décide d'écrire à la vieille dame une lettre dans laquelle elle explique où elle est et ce qu'elle fait. Elle exprime aussi sa sympathie envers la vieille dame et écrit qu'elle espère la revoir bientôt.
- **Dialogue**
  Denise explique à la nouvelle vendeuse qui est Frédéric Cottet. La vendeuse est curieuse et pose des questions.
  Rôles: Denise, la vendeuse

Unité 9
Interlude culturel

RESOURCES

TECHNOLOGY

Teacher One Stop

Pre-AP Digital Resources

💻 **Projectable Transparencies**

4, *Le monde francophone: L'Afrique, l'Europe, l'Asie*

H6, *L'Afrique dans la communauté francophone*

Transparency Copymasters, pp. A10–A11, A147–A148

■ Note historique

On a découvert les peintures préhistoriques de Tassili dans le sud de l'Algérie en 1956. Ces peintures témoignent de l'évolution de ce peuple africain: c'était d'abord des chasseurs (de 6000 à 4000 av. J.-Chr.), puis des bergers (de 4000 à 1000 av. J.-Chr.).

■ Additional Information

• Until 1957, **Ghana** was known as the Gold Coast (**La Côte de l'Or**).

Un peu d'histoire

Les dates

- 6000 av. J.-C.
- Tassili
- 0
- 670 *arrivée des Arabes*
- 700 *Empire du Ghana (700-1200)*

Empires africains

- 1200 *Empire du Mali (1200-1500)*
- 1300 *Empire de Songhaï (1350-1600)*
  Royaume de Bénin (1350-1900)
- 1500
- 1600

Colonisation

- 1860
- 1900
- 1960 *Indépendance*

Indépendance

- 2000

rupestres *on rock walls*   **chargées de** *loaded with*   **pépite** *nugget*

Les événements

La préhistoire en Afrique occidentale

Pendant six mille ans avant Jésus-Christ, le Sahara était une savane habitée par un peuple qui a laissé de remarquables peintures rupestres° dans la région de Tassili.

7e - 8e siècles: Conquête de l'Afrique du Nord par les Arabes

En 670, les Arabes arrivent en Afrique du Nord où ils imposent la religion musulmane. Ils établissent progressivement des relations commerciales avec les populations d'Afrique occidentale. Au contact des Arabes, beaucoup d'Africains adoptent la religion musulmane.

10e - 16e siècles: Période de prospérité et de grande civilisation

De puissants et vastes empires se succèdent en Afrique occidentale: empire du **Ghāna**, empire du **Mali**, empire de **Songhaï**. La prospérité de ces empires est basée sur le commerce avec l'Afrique du Nord. Les caravanes chargées de° sel traversent le Sahara. Elles arrivent à Tombouctou, capitale de l'empire du Mali, et repartent avec de l'or et des pierres précieuses. Une civilisation brillante se développe dans toute la région.

Cette illustration, tirée d'un atlas du 14ᵉ siècle, montre un marchand arabe rendant visite au Roi du Mali. Celui-ci tient dans sa main une pépite° d'or.

Note culturelles

• The **Sahara** is the largest desert in the world. It reaches across Africa from the Atlantic Ocean to the Red Sea and beyond as the Arabian desert.

• The discovery of cave paintings representing plants and animals proved that there used to be water in the Sahara in prehistoric times.

• The **Songhaï** empire conquered the empire of Mali in the 15th century. Its dominance lasted until 1591, when it fell to Moroccan soldiers.

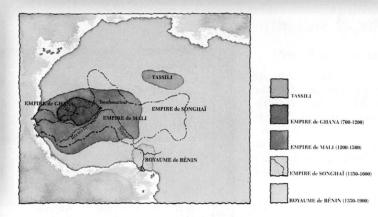

14e - 19e siècles: Le royaume de Bénin

Indépendamment des empires d'Afrique occidentale, le royaume du Bénin se développe dans la région tropicale près du Golfe de Guinée. Le génie de cette civilisation est préservé dans de splendides sculptures de bronze.

17e et 19e siècles: Arrivée des Européens — esclavage et colonisation

À partir du 17ᵉ siècle, l'arrivée des Européens provoque le déclin progressif de cette grande civilisation africaine. Les Européens viennent en Afrique chercher des esclaves pour travailler dans leurs plantations des Antilles, de Louisiane, du Brésil . . . Des centaines de milliers d'Africains sont arrachés° de leur terre° ancestrale et déportés en Amérique dans des conditions épouvantables°. Cet odieux trafic d'êtres° humains dure jusqu'au début du 19ᵉ siècle.

Dans la seconde moitié du 19ᵉ siècle, les Européens, qui ont déjà établi des comptoirs° sur le littoral°, décident de coloniser l'intérieur du continent. C'est ainsi que l'Afrique occidentale et équatoriale est découpée° en colonies anglaises, françaises et belges. Les Européens imposent des structures administratives et économiques qui ne correspondent pas à la culture africaine traditionnelle.

20e siècle: De l'exploitation à l'indépendance

Les pays européens exploitent leurs colonies africaines. Un grand nombre de soldats africains sont recrutés par l'armée française et combattent courageusement en Europe pendant les deux guerres mondiales (1914-1918 et 1939-1945).

Après la deuxième guerre mondiale, les leaders politiques africains réclament l'indépendance des colonies avec de plus en plus d'insistance. À partir de 1960, ces colonies deviennent des pays indépendants, membres des Nations Unies.

*Cette plaque de bronze représente l'**oba** ou roi du Bénin avec sa famille. Ses serviteurs le protègent du soleil.*

■ Notes historiques

- C'est à la suite de la Conférence de Berlin (1884) que les puissances européennes décidèrent de se partager l'Afrique.

France	Afrique de l'ouest
Belgique	région du Congo
Angleterre	Nigeria, Afrique de l'est et du sud
Allemagne	Afrique du sud-ouest et du sud-est
Portugal	Angola, Mozambique

- Depuis l'indépendance, certains pays ont décidé de changer leur nom.

COLONIE		RÉPUBLIQUE
Dahomey	→	Bénin
Haute Volta	→	Burkina Faso
Soudan français	→	Mali

---

arrachés *torn away* **terre** *land* **épouvantables** *ghastly* **êtres** *beings* **comptoirs** *trading posts* **littoral** *coast* **découpée** *cut up*

Expansion

Internet Connection – Interlude 9
Visit **http://my.hrw.com** for more information and useful links about French -speaking Africa.

Cultures

Standard 2.1 Students demonstrate an understanding of the relationship between the practices and perspectives of the cultures of the francophone world.

Notes culturelles

- L'enseignement du français varie de pays en pays. En Côte d'Ivoire, par exemple, il commence dès l'école maternelle.
- En mai 1997, le président Laurent Kabila a changé le nom du Zaïre en République démocratique du Congo (le Congo démocratique).

Note linguistique

Ces expressions franco-africaines sont typiques des pays mentionnés:

l'essencerie = la station-service [Sénégal]

un gros mot = un mot savant [Bénin]

NOTE: In France, un gros mot = swearword

froidir = se calmer [Côte-d'Ivoire]

À NOTER:

Pour plus d'expressions, se référer à la page 297 de ce livre.

Anecdote

In **Congo** (formerly **Zaire**), the expression **avoir l'Apollo** means to suffer from conjunctivitis. This originated in 1969, when an epidemic of conjunctivitis in Africa immediately followed the explosion of an Apollo rocket. People then attributed their red eyes to the fall of the debris.

L'Afrique francophone et sa culture

■ Qu'est-ce que c'est que l'Afrique francophone?

C'est un groupe d'une douzaine de pays d'Afrique occidentale et équatoriale où le français est la langue officielle. Parmi ces pays, les plus importants sont **le Sénégal, la Côte-d'Ivoire, le Mali, la République démocratique du Congo, le Bénin, le Cameroun . . .** Autrefois ces pays étaient des colonies françaises ou belges. Indépendants depuis 1960, ils ont décidé de garder le français comme langue administrative et commerciale. En général, les jeunes apprennent le français à l'école secondaire et parfois dès° l'école primaire.

■ Quelles langues parle-t-on en Afrique?

Il y a un très grand nombre de langues africaines. Au Sénégal, par exemple, on parle **wolof**. En Côte-d'Ivoire, on parle **baoulé** et **dioula**. Au Mali, il y a dix langues régionales. Ces langues reflètent la grande diversité ethnique des peuples d'Afrique. En Côte-d'Ivoire, par exemple, on compte au moins soixante groupes ethniques différents.

Les noms baoulés

Dans les familles baoulés, les noms traditionnels donnés aux enfants correspondent aux jours de la semaine où ils sont nés.

	GARÇONS	FILLES
lundi	**Kouassi**	**Akissi**
mardi	**Kouadio**	**Adjoua**
mercredi	**Konan**	**Amelan**
jeudi	**Koffi**	**Affoué**
vendredi	**Yao**	**Aya**
samedi	**Kouakou**	**Ahou**
dimanche	**Kouamé**	**Amoin**

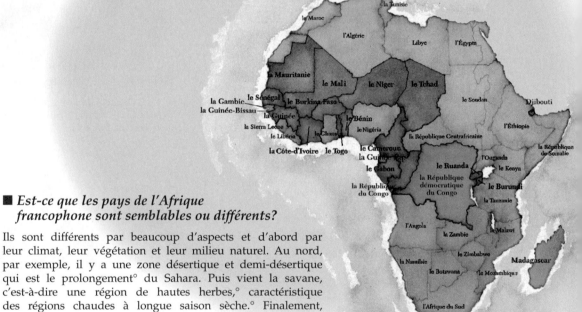

■ Est-ce que les pays de l'Afrique francophone sont semblables ou différents?

Ils sont différents par beaucoup d'aspects et d'abord par leur climat, leur végétation et leur milieu naturel. Au nord, par exemple, il y a une zone désertique et demi-désertique qui est le prolongement° du Sahara. Puis vient la savane, c'est-à-dire une région de hautes herbes,° caractéristique des régions chaudes à longue saison sèche.° Finalement, plus au sud et le long du littoral,° là où le climat est chaud et humide, on trouve la forêt équatoriale avec ses dizaines d'espèces d'arbres différents.

---

dès *as of* **prolongement** = *extension* **herbes** *grass* **sèche** *dry* **littoral** *coast*

■ *Quelles sont les religions de l'Afrique francophone?*

Cela dépend des pays. La religion musulmane est très importante dans les régions de l'ouest et du nord où il y a eu beaucoup de contacts avec les Arabes. C'est le cas, par exemple, au Mali, au Sénégal, et au Niger, où la grande majorité des gens sont musulmans. Au sud et au centre, au contraire, ce sont les religions animistes qui prédominent, par exemple, en Côte d'Ivoire, au Bénin, et au Burkina-Faso. Dans tous ces pays, il y a aussi des minorités catholiques. N'oublions pas, par exemple, que la plus grande basilique catholique du monde, la Basilique de Notre Dame de la Paix, se trouve à Yamoussoukro, en Côte d'Ivoire, et qu'elle a été inaugurée en 1989 par le pape Jean-Paul II.

Mosquée de Djemé, Mali

La Basilique de Notre Dame de la Paix à Yamoussoukro

Une mosquée au Niger

■ *Qu'est-ce que l'animisme?*

C'est la religion traditionnelle de l'Afrique noire. L'animisme attribue une âme° aux plantes, aux animaux, aux phénomènes naturels, et plus généralement à toutes les forces de la nature. Les animistes pratiquent ainsi le culte des ancêtres avec qui on peut communiquer et qui peuvent avoir une influence positive ou négative sur les événements de la vie quotidienne.° L'animisme explique l'importance de la nature, des animaux et des génies dans la littérature africaine.

âme *soul* **quotidienne** *daily*

■ Note historique

Le christianisme a été introduit en Afrique occidentale dans la deuxième moitié du 19ᵉ siècle. Les populations chrétiennes se trouvent principalement le long du littoral, là où arrivaient les missionnaires européens.

■ Additional Information

- The basilica of **Notre Dame de la Paix** has 36 stained-glass windows. Designed by an architect from the Ivory Coast, they were hand-blown in France.
- It took only three years to build the basilica, which cost about $300 million.

■ Note linguistique

Le mot **animisme** vient du latin, **anima** *(soul)*.

■ *Quel est le rôle de la famille dans la société africaine?*

Pour les Africains, la famille représente une structure très importante. Tous les membres de la famille s'aident et doivent s'entraider.° La famille africaine est très vaste. Elle comprend° non seulement les grands-parents, les parents et les enfants, mais aussi tous les oncles, tantes, cousins et cousines unis par les liens de sang° et de mariage.

Dans les villages où la polygamie existe, la famille est encore plus grande puisqu'elle comprend aussi les demi-frères et les demi-soeurs. Le père est le chef de famille. Il est respecté et son autorité n'est pas contestée. S'il a plusieurs femmes, chacune a sa propre case ou maison où elle élève° ses enfants.

À côté de la famille visible, il y a aussi la famille invisible, celle des ancêtres qui restent très présents dans la mémoire des Africains. On peut communiquer avec l'esprit de ses ancêtres et, inversement, ils peuvent communiquer avec nous et influencer les événements de notre vie quotidienne.

En Mauritanie, la décoration des maisons est traditionnellement réservée aux femmes. À cause des conditions climatiques, ces maisons doivent souvent être repeintes. Ici, les femmes utilisent des éléments géométriques pour décorer leurs maisons.

s'entraider *help each other*   **comprend** *includes*   **liens de sang** *blood ties*   **élève** *raises*

■ Additional Information
• **Mauritania** is a desert country, about twice the size of France.

■ Photo Note
The type of house shown is typical of the city of Oualâta, Mauritania. Women use dyes to decorate both the inside and outside of their homes with intricate geometric designs.

■ Note culturelle
In most African cities, Western fashion coexists with more traditional wear. Women traditionally wear **un boubou,** a long embroidered dress, or a loose top over a wrapped skirt **(le pagne).** Men wear **un grand boubou,** a loose embroidered robe worn over pants.

376 Unité 9

Notes culturelles

• La polygamie tend à disparaître, surtout dans les villes. Elle subsiste cependant dans certains villages où la population est musulmane.
• Dans certaines sociétés africaines, chez les Baoulés de la Côte d'Ivoire, par exemple, c'était la mère qui traditionnellement était le chef de la famille.

Aujourd'hui, ce matriarcat a disparu, mais la mère est toujours très écoutée et très respectée.

■ *Quelles sont les caractéristiques de la littérature africaine traditionnelle?*

La littérature africaine traditionnelle est très différente de la littérature européenne. C'est avant tout une littérature orale. Son but° principal est d'expliquer et de transmettre de génération en génération les coutumes, les traditions et les valeurs du groupe. Ses thèmes sont variés: la création du monde, l'origine de l'humanité, l'histoire des ancêtres et de la tribu, les relations entre les gens. Ses formes d'expression sont la poésie, la fable, la légende, et surtout le conte.° Il y a toutes sortes de contes: contes moraux, contes humoristiques, contes d'aventures, contes d'amour, contes du merveilleux . . . Dans ces contes, les personnages sont souvent des animaux qui représentent en réalité les humains avec leurs qualités et leurs défauts.

Les conteurs° africains s'appellent des «griots». Dans les villages de l'Afrique traditionnelle, le griot joue un rôle très important. C'est lui qui transmet l'histoire et les traditions de chaque famille du village.

Aujourd'hui, il y a aussi une littérature écrite très abondante. Cette littérature reprend les thèmes de la littérature orale (contes, fables) ou traite les thèmes plus personnels (poésie, romans, récits autobiographiques). L'un des représentants les plus connus de la littérature africaine moderne est l'écrivain sénégalais Léopold Sédar Senghor. Ce poète s'exprime en français sur des thèmes africains ou des thèmes universels, comme la liberté. Considéré comme l'un des plus grands écrivains d'expression française, il a été élu en 1980 membre de l'Académie française.

Léopold Sédar Senghor: Poète et homme d'action

Homme de lettres et brillant intellectuel, Léopold Senghor (1906 - 2001) a aussi joué un rôle politique très important dans l'histoire de l'Afrique francophone. Après la deuxième guerre mondiale, il a milité pour l'indépendance de son pays, le Sénégal. Quand le Sénégal est devenu une république indépendante en 1958, il en est devenu le premier président (1958-1980).

■ Note culturelle
Quand Senghor était étudiant à Paris dans les années 1920, lui et son ami Aimé Césaire ont fondé le journal *L'Étudiant noir* dans lequel ils ont défini le concept de «négritude» (voir à la page 336).

■ Additional Information
• Born in **Joal**, a town near **Dakar** (Senegal), **Léopold Sédar Senghor** became the mayor of **Thiès** (France) before being elected to the French parliament in 1946.

■ Pour en savoir plus
For more information on the **Académie française,** see p. 56.

DOCUMENTS — Une fable africaine

La gélinotte et la tortue

Un jour, une gélinotte° rencontra une tortue qui avançait lentement à travers la plaine. «Pourquoi est-ce que tu ne vas pas plus vite?» demanda-t-elle à la tortue. «Parce que je suis une tortue» répondit la tortue. «Eh bien, moi, je te suis supérieure non seulement parce que je vais plus vite que toi, mais aussi parce que je peux voler.»°

À ce moment des chasseurs passèrent par là. Ils mirent le feu aux herbes de la plaine pour déloger des gazelles qui s'y étaient cachées.° Le cercle de feu se rapprocha des deux animaux exposés à un péril certain. La tortue se cacha dans le trou° laissé par le pied d'un éléphant, et elle survécut. La gélinotte voulait s'envoler, mais elle fut étouffée° par la fumée° et mourut.

N'est pas supérieur celui qui se vante

but = *objectif* **conte** *short story* **conteurs** *storytellers* **gélinotte** *grouse* **voler** *to fly*
cachées *hidden* **trou** *hole* **étouffée** *suffocated* **fumée** *smoke* **se vante** *boasts*

■ **Note culturelle**
Le nom **baobab** signifie «arbre de mille ans». Ses fruits, de la taille d'une orange, ont le goût un peu amer. Pour Diop, cet arbre majestueux, dont le tronc peut atteindre 23 mètres de circonférence, symbolise le dynamisme et l'avenir de l'Afrique.

DOCUMENTS **Afrique**

Afrique

Afrique mon Afrique
Afrique des fiers guerriers° dans les savanes ancestrales
Afrique que chante ma grand-Mère
Au bord° de son fleuve° lointain°
Je ne t'ai jamais connue

Mais mon regard est plein de ton sang
Ton beau sang noir à travers les champs répandu°
Le sang de ta sueur°
La sueur de ton travail
Le travail de l'esclavage
L'esclavage de tes enfants

Afrique dis-moi Afrique
Est-ce donc toi ce dos qui se courbe°
Et se couche° sous le poids° de l'humilité
Ce dos tremblant à zébrures° rouges
Qui dit oui au fouet° sur les routes de midi

Alors gravement une voix me répondit
Fils impétueux cet arbre robuste et jeune
Cet arbre là-bas
Splendidement seul au milieu de fleurs blanches et fanées°
C'est l'Afrique ton Afrique qui repousse°
Qui repousse patiemment obstinément
Et dont les fruits ont peu à peu
L'amère° saveur° de la liberté.

David Diop (1927-1960)

Né en France d'un père sénégalais et d'une mère camerounaise*, David Diop est l'un des écrivains les plus militants de la littérature africaine. Dans ce poème, publié en 1956, il dénonce le colonialisme et entrevoit° l'indépendance de l'Afrique. Diop est mort dans un accident d'avion alors° qu'il venait s'établir° définitivement au Sénégal, devenu° depuis peu° un état indépendant.

* **Le Cameroun** = un pays de l'Afrique francophone

Baobab dans la savane africaine

---

guerriers *warriors* **au bord** *on the shore* **fleuve** = *rivière* **lointain** = *distant* **répandu** *spilled* **sueur** *sweat* **se courbe** *is bent over*
se couche *is doubled over* **poids** *weight* **zébrures** *stripes (caused by lashing)* **fouet** *whip* **fanées** *withered* **repoussse** *grows back*
amère *bitter* **saveur** *taste* **entrevoit** = *anticipe* **alors que** *when* **s'établir** *to settle* **devenu** = *qui était devenu* **depuis peu** = *récemment*

Teaching Strategy

You may wish to help students with a brief analysis of *Afrique* if they are having difficulty:

Verse 1 The poet evokes the Africa of noble warriors which he has never known.

Verse 2 What he sees is the blood and sweat of slavery.

Verse 3 He wonders if the Africa that he sees bent over and humiliated is the real Africa.

Verse 4 A voice answers him that the tree he sees growing tall and strong is the symbol of the rebirth of a free Africa.

L'art africain
et
son influence sur l'art européen

Parmi les arts africains traditionnels, la forme la plus développée est la sculpture. Les principaux objets sculptés sont des statues et des masques. Pour les Africains, ces objets ne sont pas considérés comme des objets artistiques, mais comme des objets religieux. Dans les cérémonies rituelles, par exemple, les masques sont portés par des danseurs pour honorer l'esprit des ancêtres et demander leur protection.

La majorité des masques africains sont en bois. Ils représentent généralement des figures humaines sous des formes stylisées. On peut noter l'importance des formes géométriques: lignes droites° ou courbes, cercles, ovales, triangles, etc. Cette stylisation transforme le corps et le visage humains et permet l'expression d'émotions très intenses.

Au début du 20e siècle, les Européens ont pris connaissance° de l'art africain grâce à plusieurs expositions coloniales où figuraient masques et statues de l'Afrique noire. L'originalité de cet art a d'abord choqué le public peu habitué° à la représentation non-conventionnelle de l'être humain. Les grands artistes de l'époque, au contraire, ont été très impressionnés par la simplification stylistique de l'art africain. Matisse, Modigliani et surtout Picasso ont incorporé cette simplification dans leurs propres oeuvres.° En particulier, l'usage des formes géométriques, directement inspiré par la sculpture africaine, est à la base du cubisme qui allait révolutionner l'art européen du 20ᵉ siècle.

■ Note culturelle

Le cubisme est un mouvement artistique qui est né à Paris vers 1906. Les fondateurs de ce mouvement sont Georges Braque (1881–1963) et Pablo Picasso (1882–1973). Les artistes cubistes représentent leurs sujets sous des perspectives différentes et les décomposent en formes géométriques fondamentales: cubes, sphères, ovales, un peu à la manière des sculpteurs africains. Dans son tableau révolutionnaire, *Les Demoiselles d'Avignon* (1907), Picasso a peint certains de ses personnages en leur donnant des visages ressemblant d'assez près à des masques

■ Additional Information

- French painter **Maurice de Vlaminck (1876-1958)** was a leader of the fauvism school.
- In Côte-d'Ivoire, **le festival des masques** is celebrated in November. It is famous for its mask-wearing performers who dance on stilts.
- In Mali, masks are an essential symbol for the **Dogon** people who use them for funerals and many festivals, including the **Signi,** a ceremony held only once every sixty years.

À remarquer l'influence des masques africains sur le célèbre tableau de Picasso, *Les Demoiselles d'Avignon.*

Ce masque africain a appartenu au peintre Vlaminck qui l'a montré à ses amis artistes. On peut noter les ressemblances entre ce masque et la sculpture de Modigliani.

Modigliani, *Tête de femme*

Picasso, *Étude pour les Demoiselles d'Avignon*

---

droites *straight*   **ont pris connaissance** *became aware*   **habitué** *accustomed*   **oeuvres** *works*

Teaching Suggestion: DVD Program

The Unit 9 *Vignette culturelle: L'art africain* presents more information about African art. Students will see how **tam-tams,** sand paintings, and **batik** cloths are made.

DOCUMENTS   La légende baoulé

Bernard Dadié

Bernard Dadié, né en 1916, est originaire de la Côte d'Ivoire. C'est l'un des écrivains les plus féconds° de la littérature africaine d'expression française. Il a écrit des contes, des poèmes, des romans et des pièces de théâtre. Militant nationaliste, Dadié a été arrêté en 1949 et a passé seize mois en prison pour ses activités politiques. Après l'indépendance de la Côte d'Ivoire, il a été nommé Ministre de la Culture de son pays.

La légende baoulé est extraite du livre **Légendes africaines**. Dans ce récit, Dadié explique comment son peuple, les Baoulés, ont reçu leur nom grâce au sacrifice de leur reine, la reine Pokou.

Il y a longtemps, très longtemps, vivait au bord d'une lagune calme, une tribu paisible° de nos frères. Ses jeunes hommes étaient nombreux, nobles et courageux, ses femmes étaient belles et joyeuses. Et leur reine, la reine Pokou, était la plus belle parmi les plus belles.

Depuis longtemps, très longtemps, la paix était sur eux et les esclaves mêmes, fils des captifs des temps révolus,° étaient heureux auprès de leurs heureux maîtres.

Un jour, les ennemis vinrent nombreux comme des magnans.° Il fallut quitter les paillotes,° les plantations, la lagune poissonneuse,° laisser les filets,° tout abandonner pour fuir.°

Ils partirent dans la forêt. Ils laissèrent aux épines° leurs pagnes,* puis leur chair.° Il fallait fuir toujours, sans repos, sans trêve,° talonné° par l'ennemi féroce.

Et leur reine, la reine Pokou, marchait la dernière, portant au dos son enfant.

* **Pagne:** a rectangular strip of cloth made of vegetal fibers which is worn as a loincloth or wrapped around the hips to form a short skirt.

---

féconds *prolific* **paisible** *peaceful* **révolus** *long past* **magnans** *red ants* **paillotes** *straw huts* **poissonneuse** = *avec beaucoup de poissons* **filets** *nets* **fuir** *to flee* **épines** *thorns* **chair** *flesh* **sans trêve** *unceasingly* **talonné** *followed close on their heels*

Note culturelle

Les Baoulés Aujourd'hui les Baoulés représentent l'un des groupes ethniques les plus importants de la Côte d'Ivoire. Autrefois, ce peuple habitait dans la région du Ghana actuel. À une époque lointaine et pour des raisons mystérieuses, les Baoulés ont été chassés de leur territoire et ont dû s'enfuir en Côte d'Ivoire. La légende baoulé décrit l'exil de ce peuple et explique l'origine de son nom.

La reine Pokou Le rôle joué par la reine Pokou dans la légende souligne l'importance de la femme, et particulièrement de la mère dans la société baoulé traditionnelle.

À leur passage l'hyène ricanait,° l'éléphant et le sanglier° fuyaient, le chimpanzé grognait° et le lion étonné° s'écartait du chemin.°

Enfin, les broussailles° apparurent, puis la savane et les rôniers° et, encore une fois, la horde entonna° son chant d'exil:

> *Mi houn Ano, Mi houn Ano, blâ ô*
> *Ebolo nigué, mo ba gnan min —*
>
> > *Mon mari Ano, mon mari Ano, viens,*
> > *Les génies de la brousse° m'emportent.*

Harassés, exténués,° amaigris,° ils arrivèrent sur le soir au bord d'un grand fleuve dont la course° se brisait° sur d'énormes rochers.

Et le fleuve mugissait,° les flots° montaient jusqu'aux cimes° des arbres et retombaient et les fugitifs étaient glacés d'effroi.°

Consternés,° ils se regardaient. Était-ce là l'Eau qui les faisait vivre naguère,° l'Eau, leur grande amie? Il avait fallu qu'un mauvais génie l'excitât contre eux.

Et les conquérants devenaient plus proches.°

Et, pour la première fois, le sorcier° parla: «L'eau est devenue mauvaise, dit-il, et elle ne s'apaisera° que quand nous lui aurons donné ce que nous avons de plus cher.»° Et le chant d'espoir° retentit:°

> *Ebe nin flê nin bâ*
> *Ebe nin flâ nin nan*
> *Ebe nin flê nin dja*
> *Yapen'sè ni djà wali*
>
> > *Quelqu'un appelle son fils*
> > *Quelqu'un appelle sa mère*
> > *Quelqu'un appelle son père*
> > *Les belles filles se marieront.*

Et chacun donna ses bracelets d'or et d'ivoire, et tout ce qu'il avait pu sauver.

Mais le sorcier les repoussa du pied° et montra le jeune prince, le bébé de six mois: «Voilà, dit-il, ce que nous avons de plus précieux.»

Et la mère, effrayée,° serra° son enfant sur son coeur. Mais la mère était aussi la reine et, droite° au bord de l'abîme, elle leva l'enfant souriant° au-dessus de sa tête et le lança dans l'eau mugissante.

Alors des hippopotames, d'énormes hippopotames émergèrent et, se plaçant les uns à la suite° des autres, formèrent un pont° et sur ce pont miraculeux le peuple en fuite° passa en chantant:

> *Ebe nin flê nin bâ*
> *Ebe nin flâ nin nan*
> *Ebe nin flê nin dja*
> *Yapen'sè ni djà wali*
>
> > *Quelqu'un appelle son fils*
> > *Quelqu'un appelle sa mère*
> > *Quelqu'un appelle son père*
> > *Les belles filles se marieront.*

Et la reine Pokou passa la dernière et trouva sur la rive° son peuple prosterné.°

Mais la reine était aussi la mère et elle put dire seulement «baouli», ce qui veut dire: l'enfant est mort.

Et c'était la reine Pokou et le peuple garda le nom de Baoulé.

---

ricanait *was laughing* **sanglier** *wild boar* **grognait** *grunted* **étonné** *astonished* **s'écartait** *moved aside* **broussailles** *brush* **rôniers** *palm trees* **entonna** = *commença à chanter* **la brousse** *the bush* **exténués** = *très fatigués* **amaigris** *very thin* **la course** = *l'eau* **se brisait** *was breaking* **mugissait** *was roaring* **flots** *waves* **cimes** = *sommets* **glacés d'effroi** *frozen with fright* **consternés** *in alarm* **naguère** = *dans le passé* **plus proches** *closer* **sorcier** *witch doctor* **s'apaisera** = *deviendra calme* **cher** = *précieux* **espoir** *hope* **retentit** *resounded* **repoussa du pied** *kicked away* **effrayée** *scared* **serra** *clutched* **droite** *standing tall* **souriant** *smiling* **à la suite de** *right behind* **pont** *bridge* **en fuite** *fleeing* **rive** *shore* **prosterné** *prostrate, face to the ground*

■ Teaching Strategy

Ask students:

- Relevez tout ce qui, d'après vous, révèle que l'histoire se passe en Afrique. En quoi ces détails sont-ils significatifs?
- À votre avis, y avait-il une autre solution possible pour traverser le fleuve? Laquelle?
- Connaissez-vous une autre légende? Laquelle? Pouvez-vous la résumer brièvement?

■ Irregular Verb

(See Appendix C)
fuir

■ Note linguistique

Bâ = l'enfant; **ou li** = est mort

Teaching Strategy

Have students create and illustrate a legend, assigning each member of the group a task. This not only gives students practice in expanding their own abilities, but also helps them to appreciate the difficulties others may have in dealing with certain tasks or subject matters. The legends may be displayed in the classroom.

Unité 9 381

MAIN THEME

University studies and careers

COMMUNICATION
- Looking for a job
- Planning for a career
- Deciding on a college major

CULTURES
- Learning about Cajun music

CONNECTIONS
- Writing a curriculum vitae
- Writing questions about the history of the French in America
- Connecting to Language Arts: Writing letters for information about bilingual jobs
- Connecting to Math: Creating a chart of companies that use French in some way
- Connecting to Science: Investigating how scientists who speak different languages communicate
- Connecting to Social Studies: Researching local companies with French branches and French companies with American branches
- Connecting to Art/Music: Writing about a francophone star who is successful in the U.S.
- Connecting to Technology: Finding out how technology is used to communicate or send information overseas

COMPARISONS
- Comparing the use of the infinitive and past infinitive in French and English
- Comparing the use of the present participle in French and English

COMMUNITIES
- Learning about jobs that involve foreign languages
- Creating a French/American timeline
- Exploring career choices
- Role-playing job interviews

■ Note culturelle

The **Bac** series **L**, **ES**, and **S** were implemented in 1995 to allow more flexibility, replacing the old bac A (now **L**), bac B (now **ES**), and bacs C, D, E, and S (now **S**). In each **série** and **spécialité**, students are offered optional courses (**les options**) such as ancient Greek, Latin, science, and art history.

Vers la vie active

THÈME ET OBJECTIFS

Culture

In this unit, you will discover . . .

- what the **bac** is all about and why it is so important for French young people
- which are the most popular professions in France
- how to prepare for an interview with a wedding in France

Communication

You will learn how . . .

- to talk about what you plan to study in the future
- to indicate what type of job or profession you would like to have
- to describe your personal qualifications
- to prepare a a résumé in French

Langue

You will learn how . . .

- to describe simultaneous actions
- to indicate why you do certain things
- to explain under which conditions or constraints you do certain things
- to express how your actions may depend on what others do
- to describe how your actions have an effect on other people

---

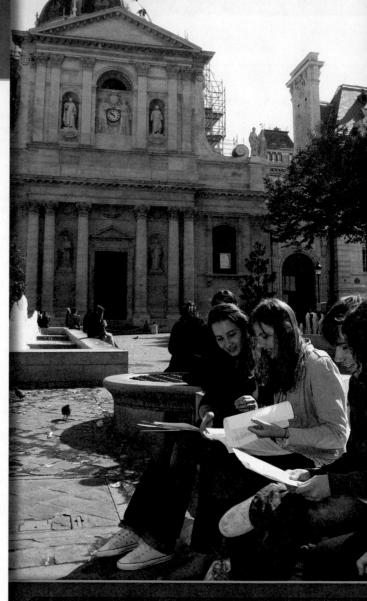

DIGITAL FRENCH my.hrw.com
ONLINE STUDENT EDITION with...

 performance space

 News 💬 Networking

@HOMETUTOR

- Audio Resources
- Video Resources
- Interactive Flashcards
- WebQuest

PRACTICE FRENCH WITH HOLT MCDOUGAL APPS!

DIGITAL FRENCH

TEACHER TOOLS
- **Teacher One Stop**
- **Interactive Whiteboard Lessons**
- **Generate Success Rubric Generator and Interactive Graphic Organizers**
- **Examview Test Generator**

ALSO AVAILABLE...
- **Online Workbook**
- **French InterActive Reader**
- **@HomeTutor**
- **DVD Program**
- **Power Presentations**
- **Interactive Flashcards**

FRENCH ON THE GO!
- **Performance Space**
- **Holt McDougal French Apps**
- **Discovering French Today eTextbook**

CE FAMEUX BAC!

INFO MAGAZINE

Theme: Education in France

Reading Strategy:
Reading for information, skimming, scanning

Corinne, 17 ans, et Guillaume, 18 ans, sont en «terminale», c'est-à-dire, en dernière année de leurs études secondaires. Dans quelques semaines, ils vont passer le bac. Corinne est une excellente élève et pourtant elle a le trac.° «J'ai beaucoup étudié, mais on ne sait jamais. Qu'est-ce que je vais faire si je ne suis pas reçue?° Je n'ai vraiment pas envie de redoubler.»° Guillaume, lui, redouble. Il est plus philosophe et plus décontracté° que Corinne. «Si je n'ai pas mon bac cette fois, je vais m'engager dans l'armée. Après, on verra!»

Chaque année, en juin, 645.000 jeunes Français passent le bac. C'est un examen très important qui marque la fin des études secondaires et qui détermine, en grande partie, l'avenir des lycéens. S'ils sont reçus, ils peuvent aller à l'université et continuer leurs études. S'ils ratent le bac, ils peuvent redoubler et se représenter° l'année suivante, ou bien ils peuvent faire des études techniques, ou entrer dans la vie professionnelle. Heureusement, 80% des candidats sont reçus et pour la majorité, ils continuent leurs études.

Il y a plusieurs types (ou "séries") de bac. Ils sont désignés par des lettres. Dans chaque série, l'élève doit choisir une spécialité. Ces spécialités sont importantes parce qu'elles déterminent le genre d'études universitaires qu'on peut faire et, par conséquent, sa profession future. Par exemple, si on veut être médecin ou pharmacien, il est conseillé° de faire un bac S, spécialité sciences de la vie et de la terre. Si on pense faire des études de droit° et devenir avocat, il est préférable de faire un bac ES, spécialité sciences économiques et sociales. Voici les trois séries principales et leurs spécialités:

Série littéraire, bac L:
- langues vivantes
- philosophie
- art
- mathématiques

Série économique et sociale, bac ES:
- sciences économiques et sociales
- mathématiques
- langues vivantes

Série scientifique, bac S:
- mathématiques
- physique chimie
- sciences de la vie et de la terre
- technologie industrielle

---

a le trac *is scared, nervous* **si je ne suis pas reçue** = si je ne réussis pas **redoubler** *to repeat a grade* **décontracté** *relaxed* **se représenter** *retake (the exam)* **conseillé** = recommandé **droit** *law*

ASSESSMENT IN UNIT RESOURCE BOOK

Print Resources
- Workbook TE/PE
- *Activités pour tous* TE/PE
- *Lectures pour tous*
- Unit Resource Book
- Audioscripts
- Video Activities
- Videoscripts

Achievement Tests
- Quizzes, Unit 10
- Unit Test 10
- Reading and Culture Tests
- Assessment Answer Key

Proficiency Tests
- Listening Comprehension
- Speaking Performance
- Writing Performance
- Portfolio Assessment

■ **Teaching Strategy**
These readings can be done:
- in class or as homework
- to begin or wrap up a unit

■ **Note culturelle**
After passing the **baccalauréat**, most French young people continue their studies. Many go to university where they can study humanities, social sciences, law, science, medicine and pharmacy. Most French universities are government controlled and tuition is minimal. Other students go to professional schools (e.g., business schools, engineering schools) which are private and charge tuition.
- Les classes d'un lycée français sont: **la seconde** (11th grade)**, la première** (12th) et **la terminale**

21ST CENTURY SKILLS
- **Communication:** SE: pp. 384, 385, 386, 387, 391, 393, 395, 397, 405, 407, 408, 409; TE: pp. 386, 387, 392, 395, 398, 402, 405, 407, 408, 417
- **Critical Thinking and Problem Solving:** SE: pp. 384, 385, 402; TE: pp. 383, 403, 408
- **Creativity and Innovation:** TE: pp. 386, 392, 398, 403, 409
- **Information Literacy:** TE: pp. 392, 401, 417
- **Technology Literacy:** TE: pp. 386, 392, 395, 401, 417
- **Flexibility and Adaptability:** SE: p. 393; TE: pp. 386, 392, 401
- **Initiative and Self-Direction:** TE: pp. 386, 392, 395, 401, 417
- **Social and Cross-Cultural Skills:** SE: p. 384; TE: pp. 386, 401, 417, 418, 419
- **Productivity and Accountability:** TE: pp. 387, 389, 390, 398, 402
- **Leadership and Responsibility:** TE: pp. 386, 392, 401, 417

Unité 10 383

Notes culturelles

- Because of the ongoing unemployment crisis in France, many teens choose to remain in school in order to get a college degree. Thirty-one percent of French teens expect to face unemployment.
- The **baccalauréat** tests the students on all subjects, including physical education.

SUPPLEMENTARY VOCABULARY

le programme *curriculum*
la moyenne *average (grade)*
l'orientation *(f.) career choice*
la classe préparatoire *class to prepare students for the entrance exam of "une grande école"*
le manuel scolaire *textbook*

Quelques expressions familières employées par les lycéens français:
 bachoter *to cram (for an exam)*
 sécher *not to know the answer (lit.: to dry up)*
 bûcher *to cram (work hard)*
 la bourse *scholarship*
 le restaurant universitaire (le resto U) *college cafeteria*
 la cité universitaire *dorm*
 l'association des anciens élèves *alumni association*
 les débouchés *(m.) prospects, openings (career)*

■ Irregular Verb

(see Appendix C)
obtenir *(see* **tenir***)*

Les études universitaires durent au moins deux ans. Aussi, certains jeunes qui ont le bac préfèrent étudier en I.U.T. (Institut Supérieur de Technologie) où ils peuvent obtenir un diplôme universitaire de technologie après deux années d'études. Les "grandes écoles" sont une autre option. Ce sont des écoles spécialisées dans certains domaines: commerce, administration publique, professions d'ingénieur, etc. Pour entrer° dans ces écoles prestigieuses, il faut passer un concours° extrêmement difficile, auquel la plupart des candidats échouent.° Cependant, si on est reçu, et si on obtient° le diplôme d'une de ces écoles, on a toutes les chances de faire une brillante carrière dans le commerce, la finance, l'industrie et même la politique.

Comme on peut le voir, les diplômes ont beaucoup d'importance en France. Un diplôme représente une carte d'entrée dans la vie professionnelle. Voilà pourquoi les parents insistent pour que leurs enfants étudient. Les enfants sont généralement d'accord pour faire l'effort nécessaire. En France, les études, c'est sérieux!

Petite histoire du bac

◆ Au Moyen-Âge, un bachelier* était un jeune gentilhomme qui voulait être chevalier.° Vers 1500, c'était un étudiant qui avait écrit une thèse° de philosophie.

◆ Le bac moderne date de Napoléon qui l'a institué° en 1808. La première année, il y avait 32 candidats. En 1900, il y en avait 4 000. Aujourd'hui, il y en a 645 000.

◆ Le bac a d'abord été un examen exclusivement masculin. La première «candidate» se présenta en 1861. (C'était une institutrice° de 37 ans!) Aujourd'hui, 57% des candidats sont en réalité . . . des candidates.

◆ À l'origine, l'examinateur interrogeait° le candidat sur une liste de questions préparées à l'avance et tirées au sort.° En un an, le candidat devait apprendre la réponse à 500 questions différentes. Ce système donna lieu° à la pratique de «bachotage», selon laquelle l'élève apprend par coeur un grand nombre d'informations sans en connaître nécessairement le sens.°

◆ Le bac se démocratise.° En 1900, seulement un jeune Français sur cent passait le bac. Aujourd'hui, cette proportion est de 80%.

* De nos jours, un «bachelier» est une personne qui a son baccalauréat.

---

et vous?

DÉFINITIONS
Définissez les mots ou expressions suivants:
- le «bac»
- la «terminale»
- redoubler
- être reçu à un examen
- l'université
- être prioritaire
- une «grande école»
- un concours

ET VOUS?
Quel genre d'étudiant(e) êtes-vous? Êtes-vous plutôt comme Corinne ou comme Guillaume? Expliquez.

EXPRESSION ORALE
- Avec votre partenaire, discutez les avantages et les inconvénients d'aller à l'université.
- Expliquez à un(e) ami(e) français(e) (votre partenaire) le système d'enseignement aux États-Unis (par exemple, quels sujets on peut choisir à l'école secondaire, comment on obtient son diplôme, ce qu'on doit faire pour aller à l'université, etc.)

EXPRESSION ÉCRITE
Écrivez une lettre à un copain français où vous dites ce que vous allez faire si vous avez votre diplôme d'études secondaires et si vous ne l'avez pas.

---

entrer = être accepté   **concours** *competitive exam*   **échouent** = ne réussissent pas   **obtient / obtenir** *to obtain, get*   **chevalier** *knight*
thèse = essai   **institué** = créé   **institutrice** = professeur d'école primaire   **interrogeait** = posait des questions   **tirées au sort** *chosen at random*
donna lieu *gave rise*   **sens** *meaning*   **se démocratise** = devient démocratique

---

Notes culturelles

Les études universitaires en France sont divisées en trois cycles. Chaque cycle est sanctionné par un diplôme:
- 1er cycle: **le DEUG** (Diplôme d'Études Universitaires Générales; en 2 ans)
- 2e cycle: **la licence** (BA) et ensuite **la maîtrise**

- 3e cycle: **le DESS** (Diplôme d'Études Supérieures Spécialisées), **le DEA** (Diplôme d'Études Approfondies) et **le doctorat**.
- Les **IUT** furent créés en 1966. Ils font partie de l'université et offrent une formation de technicien supérieur en deux ans (avec 35 heures de cours par semaine).

Il a raté le bac

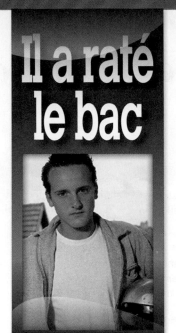

Mathieu gagne très bien sa vie. Il a une voiture de sport, voyage en première classe et, surtout, il fait ce qu'il aime. Pourtant, il a raté le fameux bac. Il raconte:

❝ Je ne suis pas fait° pour les études. Au lycée, ça n'allait vraiment pas. J'étais nul° en maths et en sciences, médiocre° dans les autres disciplines. La seule activité que j'aimais, c'était le sport. Là, j'étais vraiment «top», mais évidemment, ça ne suffisait° pas. J'ai raté mon bac une première fois, j'ai redoublé et je l'ai raté à nouveau. Alors, j'ai abandonné mes études. J'ai cherché un job. Tous les jours, je lisais les petites annonces dans les journaux et je téléphonais, mais sans bac je n'avais aucune chance. Alors, j'ai décidé de m'engager° dans l'armée.° J'ai opté pour un engagement° de trois ans. Pendant ce temps, j'ai continué à faire du sport et, surtout, j'ai fait un stage° de parachutisme.

Malheureusement, après mon service, ma situation n'avait pas changé! J'avais pensé être professeur d'éducation physique, mais sans diplôme, ce n'était pas possible. Alors, j'ai fait des petits boulots.° J'ai été chauffeur de taxi. J'ai travaillé dans un fast-food. J'ai été garde du corps° d'un banquier. Tout cela n'était pas ma vocation, et je cherchais désespérément à faire autre chose.

Un jour, finalement, la chance° m'a souri.° On tournait° un film dans le quartier où j'habitais. Je suis allé là pour regarder. Il y avait une scène où l'acteur principal devait sauter° du troisième étage d'une maison en flamme. Ce jour-là, le cascadeur° qui devait le remplacer n'est pas venu. Le metteur en scène° avait l'air désespéré. Alors, j'ai offert mes services. Ça a si bien marché° qu'on m'a embauché° pour le reste du film.

Depuis, je suis cascadeur professionnel. J'ai déjà une vingtaine de films à mon actif.° Évidemment, je ne suis pas la grande vedette,° mais je suis bien payé. Je voyage dans tous les pays du monde. Je connais des tas° d'acteurs et d'actrices et de temps en temps on me demande mon autographe. . . Et surtout, j'ai trouvé ma voie!° ❞

Les jeunes Français et l'armée

Le service militaire a été longtemps une tradition nationale en France. Symbole de démocratie et d'égalité, il était obligatoire° pour les garçons et volontaire° pour les filles. À 18 ans, les jeunes gens faisaient un service militaire de dix mois. Ce service militaire, aussi appelé «service national,» a été supprimé° en 2002.

Le système traditionnel a été remplacé par un système plus simple. À l'age de 16 ans, tous les jeunes Français, garçons et filles, doivent être recensés° à la mairie.° Avant l'âge de 18 ans, ils doivent suivre «une Journée° défense et citoyenneté° (JDC)» pour laquelle ils reçoivent un certificat de préparation.

Les volontaires° peuvent faire une courte «préparation militaire» ou s'engager° dans l'armée, la police ou chez les pompiers° pour une période plus longue.

et vous?

- Selon vous, quelle est la «morale» de l'histoire de Mathieu?
- Aimeriez-vous être cascadeur / cascadeuse? Expliquez pourquoi ou pourquoi pas.

EXPRESSION ORALE

- Vous êtes journaliste. Interviewez Mathieu (joué par votre partenaire).
- Connaissez-vous des personnes qui n'étaient pas faites pour les études mais qui ont trouvé un job intéressant? Donnez un ou plusieurs exemples.

---

ne suis pas fait *cut out* **nul** = *zéro* **médiocre** *below average* **suffisait** = *c'était suffisant* **m'engager** *enlist* **L'armée** *the army* **engagement** *service*
stage *training session* **petits boulots** = *jobs* **garde de corps** *bodyguard* **chance** *luck* **souri / sourire** *to smile* **tournait** = *filmait* **sauter** *to jump*
cascadeur *stuntman* **metteur en scène** *director* **si bien marché** *went so well* **embauché** *hired* **à mon actif** *behind me* **vedette** = *star* **tas** = *beaucoup*
voie *way* **obligatoire** *compulsory* **volontaire** *optional* **supprimé** *abolished* **recensé** *registered* **mairie** *town hall* **journée** *day* **citoyenneté** *citizenship*
volontaires *volunteers* **s'engager** *enlist* **pompiers** *firefighters*

■ **Notes linguistiques**
- Remind your students that **passer un examen** = *to take a test*. (**être reçu/réussir à un examen** = *to pass a test*
- **les langues étrangères** = les langues vivantes (≠ les langues mortes)
- **les lettres classiques** = le français, la philosophie, le latin et le grec

■ **Additional Information**
- In May 1996, President Chirac called for reform of the military service in France, changing it from a mandatory recruitment to a voluntary system.
- Some French draftees used to do their military service in the United States as technical advisers in French consulates, or as teachers in Canada.

■ **Irregular Verb**
(see Appendix C)
sourire (*see* **rire**)

- Quelques grandes écoles françaises: **HEC** (Haute École de Commerce); **Polytechnique** (Hautes Etudes Scientifiques), **l'ENA** (École Nationale d'Administration qui forme les hauts fonctionnaires de l'état).

■ **Notes linguistiques**
Remind students of the omission of the definite article with professions:
> **Ma mère est professeur.**
Also:
> **faire** + PARTITIVE + NOUN
> Je vais faire du droit/du journalisme/ de la comptabilité.
> NOTE: With certain subject matters or professional schools:
> > **faire** + NOUN
> > Je vais faire médecine/pharmacie/ Sciences-Po/Polytechnique.

■ **Proverbe**
Il n'est point de sot métier.
(All jobs are good.)

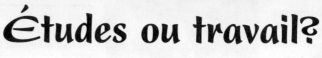

Études ou travail?

Qu'est-ce que tu vas faire après le lycée?

Je vais continuer mes études.

— Qu'est-ce que tu vas faire après le lycée?
Je vais | continuer mes études | chercher | **du travail**
        | aller à l'université | | **un emploi** *job*

gagner ma vie

| **gagner sa vie** *to earn a living* |

— Qu'est-ce que tu vas étudier?
Je vais | **étudier** les sciences
        | **faire des études de** biologie
        | **me spécialiser en** chimie

| **se spécialiser en** *to major in* |

— Qu'est-ce que tu veux faire plus tard?
Je voudrais être médecin.

LES ÉTUDES

Les études scientifiques et techniques
> la **chimie**
> la **physique**
> les **maths**
> l'**informatique**
> les **études d'ingénieur**

Les études médicales
> la **biologie**
> la **médecine**
> les **pharmacie**
> les **études vétérinaires**

Les sciences humaines
> l'**histoire**
> la **psychologie**
> les **sciences économiques**
> les **sciences politiques**

Les études commerciales
> la **commerce** *business*
> la **gestion** *management*
> le **marketing**
> la **publicité** *advertising*
> la **comptabilité** *accounting*

Les études juridiques
> la **droit** *law*

Les études littéraires et artistiques
> la **philosophie**
> la **littérature**
> les **langues étrangères**
> le **journalisme**
> la **musique**
> le **dessin** *art, design*

1 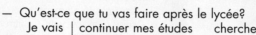 **À l'université**

Imaginez que vous avez décidé d'aller à l'université. Choisissez ...
> • une spécialité principale *(major)*
> • deux spécialités secondaires *(minors)*
Comparez votre choix de spécialité principale avec le reste de la classe.
Quelle est la spécialité favorite?

Teaching Suggestion: DVD Program

The *Vidéo-drame: Guillaume trouve un job* in Unit 10 focuses on a summer job search. After viewing the video, ask students comprehension questions. (eg.: **Qu'est-ce que Mélanie fait quand Guillaume arrive?; Quel est le domaine de Mélanie?**)

Teaching Suggestion

Ask a former French student who has studied in France or another francophone country to visit your class to talk about his/her experiences. Students can ask the student how he/she prepared to live abroad, what he/she studied, what student life is like in another country, etc. Afterward, have your class prepare a brochure promoting studying abroad.

QUELQUES PROFESSIONS

La médecine
- un **médecin**
- un(e) **chirurgien(ne)** *surgeon*
- un(e) **dentiste**
- un(e) **pharmacien(ne)**
- un(e) **vétérinaire**
- un(e) **infirmier (-ère)**

Le commerce, les affaires *business*
- un(e) **vendeur (-euse)** *salesperson*
- un(e) **représentant(e)** *de commerce*
- un(e) **spécialiste** *de marketing*
- un(e) **homme (femme) d'affaires**

Le finance
- un(e) **banquier (-ière)**
- un(e) **agent de change** *stockbroker*

Le droit *law*
- un(e) **avocat(e)** *lawyer*
- un(e) **juge**

La fonction publique *civil service*
- un(e) **fonctionnaire** *civil servant*
- un(e) **diplomate**
- un(e) **assistant(e) social(e)** *social worker*

La technique et les sciences
- un(e) **scientifique**
- un **ingénieur**
- un(e) **chercheur (-euse)** *researcher*
- un(e) **technicien(ne)**
- un(e) **informaticien(ne)**
- un(e) **spécialiste de logiciel** *software*
- un(e) **spécialiste de données** *data*

L'administration
- un(e) **cadre** *executive*
- un(e) **patron(ne)** *boss*
- un(e) **chef** *(head)* **de personnel**
- un(e) **directeur (-trice)** *manager*

Les emplois de bureau *office*
- un(e) **employé(e)** *clerk*
- un(e) **secrétaire**
- un(e) **comptable** *accountant*

La services
- un **agent immobilier** *real estate agent*
- un **agent d'assurances** *insurance agent*

FLASH d'information

Les professions préférées des Français

Ce qui compte le plus dans le choix d'une profession, ce n'est pas nécessairement la possibilité de gagner beaucoup d'argent, c'est avant tout de faire quelque chose d'intéressant. Voici la liste des dix professions préférées des Francais, par ordre d'intérêt.

1. Chercheur scientifique	16%	6. Acteur	10%
2. Pilote	14%	7. Chef de publicité	7%
3. Médecin	14%	8. Professeur d'université	5%
4. Journaliste	14%	9. Avocat	5%
5. Chef d'entreprise	11%	10. Banquier	4%

---

2 Choix professionnels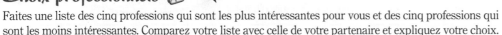

Faites une liste des cinq professions qui sont les plus intéressantes pour vous et des cinq professions qui sont les moins intéressantes. Comparez votre liste avec celle de votre partenaire et expliquez votre choix.

---

3 Après le lycée

Vous avez décidé de continuer vos études, mais votre partenaire a décidé de chercher du travail (ou vice versa). Expliquez votre décision respective en donnant des arguments. Considérez, par exemple, les aspects suivants . . .
- gagner sa vie
- être indépendant(e)
- se perfectionner en . . . *(to increase one's skills in)*
- avoir plus d'options plus tard

■ Teaching Strategy: Warm-Up

Have each student choose a job and describe <u>where</u> it is done (**au bureau, à l'école**, etc.). From that information, the class will try to identify the job itself. If the class is unable to guess from the place of work or the name of the company, students should then give a sentence explaining the job, what is worn to work, or some other hint that will help the class identify the job. Continue until someone guesses it correctly. Keep a list and compare with the survey from p. 387.

SUPPLEMENTARY VOCABULARY

les métiers d'avenir
l'analyste-programmeur *systems analyst*
le concepteur de circuit intégré *integrated circuit designer*
le spécialiste de maintenance informatique *computer maintenance expert*
le cogniticien *engineer specialized in artificial intelligence*
le logisticien *logistics specialist (within a business)*
le juriste d'entreprise *corporate lawyer*
l'analyste de crédit *credit analyst*
ALSO:
un(e) architecte
un(e) décorateur (-trice)
un(e) commerçant(e) *shopkeeper*
un boulanger *baker*
un pâtissier *pastry cook*
un chef, un cuisinier *cook*
un maçon *mason*
un menuisier *cabinet maker*
un plombier *plumber*
un mécanicien
un réparateur *repairman*
un ouvrier qualifié
un ouvrier spécialisé
un contremaître *foreman*
un ouvrier agricole *farm worker*

Teaching Strategy

Have students make up vocabulary flashcards. Next, have them form two circles—one inside the other—with an equal number of students in each circle so that every student has a partner in the other circle. Students from the inside circle test their partners by showing them their flashcards. After testing each card, students should confirm or correct by giving a complete sentence: **Je fais des études de...** or **J'étudie...** or **Je me spécialise en....** After two minutes, call «**Changez de partenaires!**» and the outside circle will rotate.

Langue et Communication

■ **Expansion**
The infinitive is also used after:
au lieu de *instead of*
Étudier **au lieu de** t'amuser.
à condition de *on condition that*
Je gagnerai ma vie **à condition de** trouver un job.
afin de *in order to*
Pauline travaille **afin de** s'acheter une voiture.

■ **Note culturelle**
Molière popularized this saying of Socrates in *L'Avare*:
«Suivant le dire d'un ancien,
il faut manger pour vivre,
et non pas vivre pour manger.»

A La construction préposition + infinitif

Note the use of the infinitive in the following sentences.

Je voudrais aller à l'université
pour me spécialiser en informatique.

Tu ne réussiras pas à ton examen
sans étudier.

Donne-moi ton adresse
avant de partir en vacances.

I would like to go to college
(in order) to major *in computer science.*

You will not pass your exam
without studying.

Give me your address
before leaving *on vacation.*

In French, the INFINITIVE is used after prepositions such as
pour *(in order to)*
avant de *(before)*
sans *(without)*

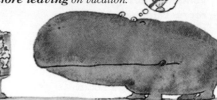

Il faut manger pour vivre, et non pas vivre pour manger.

1 À l'université

Chacun a ses raisons pour aller à l'université. Expliquez les raisons des étudiants suivants.

▶ Christine étudie la physique.
Christine va à l'université pour étudier la physique.

1. Nous étudions la biologie.
2. Vous apprenez la comptabilité.
3. Je fais des études de droit.
4. Jean-Paul se spécialise en chimie.
5. Tu continues tes études de musique.
6. Hélène et Alice retrouvent leurs copains de lycée.
7. Marc est avec sa copine.
8. Philippe et Antoine jouent dans l'équipe de football.

2 Ne t'en fais pas! *(Don't worry!)*

Dites à votre partenaire ce qu'il/elle doit faire. Il/elle va suivre vos conseils.

▶ sortir / prendre la clé

1. aller chez tes copains / téléphoner
2. organiser une boum / demander la permission à tes parents
3. répondre à cette question / réfléchir *(think)*
4. quitter le restaurant / payer l'addition
5. prendre la voiture / faire le plein d'essence
6. partir en vacances / réserver une chambre d'hôtel

▶ *Ne sors pas sans prendre la clé!*

Ne t'en fais pas! Je prendrai la clé avant de sortir.

3 Conseils

Votre partenaire va choisir un objectif de la liste ou un objectif de son choix.
Expliquez-lui ce qu'il faut faire pour atteindre *(to reach)* cet objectif.

OBJECTIFS		
• être interprète	• gagner de l'argent	• devenir professeur
• être avocat	• aller à l'université	• devenir vétérinaire
• être ingénieur	• être millionnaire	• ??

▶ **Pour être ingénieur, il faut faire des études d'ingénieur (être bon en maths, aller dans une université spécialisée, . . .)**

Teaching Strategy

Have every student write a sentence using each of the prepositions from p. 388. These sentences should be about themselves or about friends or family. Have students choose one of their sentences to put on the board. Have three columns on the board: one for **sans**, one for **avant de**, and one for **pour**. Students should write their sentences in the proper column.
Pre-AP skill: Demonstrate knowledge and use of devices that link meaning (transitions).

B L'infinitif passé

The verbs in heavy print are in the PAST INFINITIVE. Note the forms of the past infinitive in the following sentences.

Je suis content d'**avoir trouvé** un emploi.   *I am happy to **have found** a job.*

Nous ne regrettons pas d'**être allés** à l'université.   *We do not regret **to have gone** (having gone) to college.*

Alice a étudié après **s'être reposée.**   *Alice studied after **having** rested.*

FORMS

The PAST INFINITIVE is formed as follows:

> **avoir** or **être** + PAST PARTICIPLE

→ When the past infinitive is a reflexive verb, the reflexive pronoun represents the same person as the subject of the sentence.

> **Je** ne me souviens pas de **m'**être promené dans ce parc.

USES

The PAST INFINITIVE is used instead of the present infinitive to describe an action that takes place <u>before</u> the action of the main verb. It is <u>always</u> used after **après**.

Qu'est-ce que tu vas faire   *What are you going to do*
après avoir fini tes études?   ***after having finished (after finishing)*** *your studies?*

4 Leurs sentiments

Expliquez les sentiments des personnes suivantes en fonction de ce qu'elles ont fait.

> ▶ Patrick / être content / trouver un bon job
> **Patrick est content d'avoir trouvé un bon job.**

1. Alice / être heureuse / aller au Canada l'été dernier
2. Thomas / être enchanté / faire la connaissance de ta cousine
3. nous / avoir peur / rater l'examen
4. Bruno / être furieux / se tromper dans le problème de maths
5. vous / s'excuser / arriver en retard au rendez-vous
6. Madame Simon / être fière / créer sa propre *(own)* entreprise.

5 Hier 💬

Demandez à votre partenaire à quelle heure il/elle a fait les choses suivantes hier et ce qu'il/elle a fait après.

> ▶ te coucher

1. te lever
2. prendre le petit déjeuner
3. arriver à l'école
4. déjeuner
5. rentrer chez toi
6. dîner
7. finir tes devoirs

À quelle heure est-ce que tu t'es couché?

Et qu'est-ce que tu as fait après t'être couché?

À dix heures et demie.

J'ai lu un livre.

(Je me suis endormi. J'ai regardé la télé . . .)

Notes linguistiques

■ FORMS

The rules of agreement of the past participle apply to the past infinitive. Note the following examples of agreement of the past infinitive:

(with subject)
> **Alice** s'excuse d'être **arrivée** en retard.

(with preceding direct object)
> Je ne me souviens pas de **les** avoir **rencontrés.**

(with reflexive pronoun when it is a direct object)
> **Nous** regrettons de **nous** être **disputés.**

■ USES

In the negative, **pas** may come before the auxiliary or between the auxiliary and the past participle.

> Je regrette de ne **pas** avoir appris l'espagnol.

> Je regrette de n'avoir **pas** appris l'espagnol.

ALSO:

The past infinitive in French may correspond in English to a past infinitive *(to have done)* or a verb form ending in *-ing (having done).*

Differentiation

Multisensory Have students draw or cut out pictures from magazines that show the various professions, labeling the pictures. Have them work in pairs to drill each other on the vocabulary, and then carry out Act. 3 on page 388.

Differentiation

Metacognitive Ask students to explain to you the agreement rules of the past participle. Then, write some subjects and verbs on the board and have them tell you whether each verb takes **être** or **avoir,** and then create a sentence with the past participle.

■ **Teaching Strategy: Additional Practice**

You may ask for students to provide the present participles of other irregular verbs:

boire	**buvant**
conduire	**conduisant**
connaître	**connaissant**
croire	**croyant**
devoir	**devant**
dire	**disant**
écrire	**écrivant**
peindre	**peignant**
pouvoir	**pouvant**
recevoir	**recevant**
rire	**riant**
venir	**venant**
vouloir	**voulant**

■ **Notes linguistiques**

• La forme **en + participe présent** forme ce que l'on appelle **le gérondif**. En général, le gérondif se rapporte au sujet de la phrase et décrit les circonstances de l'action.

• Expansion:
   forger *to forge*
   le forgeron *blacksmith*
   la forge *forge*
   le fer forgé *wrought iron*

■ **Teaching Note: Activity 6**

• Quelques titres d'Hemingway en français: *Le Soleil se lève aussi; Pour qui sonne le glas; L'Adieu aux armes; Le Vieil homme et la mer.*

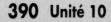
390 Unité 10

C **Le participe présent**

FORMS

Note the forms of the PRESENT PARTICIPLE in the following sentences.

Parlant français et anglais,
   je voudrais travailler pour une firme internationale.

Speaking French and English,
   I would like to work for an international company.

J'ai rencontré mes copains
   en **allant** au cinéma.

*I met my friends
   while **going** to the movies.*

The PRESENT PARTICIPLE always ends in **-ant**. It is formed as follows:

STEM	+	ENDING
nous-form of the present	+	**-ant**

parler:	nous **parl**ons	→ **parlant**	aller:	nous **all**ons	→ **allant**
finir:	nous **finiss**ons	→ **finissant**	faire:	nous **fais**ons	→ **faisant**
attendre:	nous **attend**ons	→ **attendant**	sortir:	nous **sort**ons	→ **sortant**
acheter:	nous **achet**ons	→ **achetant**	voir:	nous **voy**ons	→ **voyant**
commencer:	nous **commenç**ons	→ **commençant**	lire:	nous **lis**ons	→ **lisant**
manger:	nous **mange**ons	→ **mangeant**	prendre:	nous **pren**ons	→ **prenant**

→ There are three irregular present participles:
   être → **étant**   avoir → **ayant**   savior → **sachant**

→ With reflexive verbs, the reflexive pronoun represents the same person as the subject.
   En **me** promenant, **j'**ai rencontré mon professeur d'histoire.

USES

The construction **en** + PRESENT PARTICIPLE is used to express:

• SIMULTANEOUS ACTION (*while, on, upon* doing something)
   Éric écoute la radio
   en lavant sa voiture.

   *Éric is listening to the radio
   while **washing** his car.*

• CAUSE AND EFFECT (*by* doing something)
   Il gagne de l'argent
   en lavant des voitures.

   *He earns money
   by **washing** cars.*

C'est en forgeant qu'on devient forgeron.

6 **Études de langues**

Pour chaque personne, choisissez une langue et dites comment elle apprend cette langue.

moi	l'espagnol
vous	le français
mon copain	l'anglais
Alice et Catherine	

• écouter Radio-France
• étudier à l'Alliance Française
• regarder des westerns à la télé
• écouter des chansons mexicaines
• passer les vacances en Argentine
• surfer sur l'Internet
• sortir avec des amis québécois
• lire des romans d'Hemingway

▶ **Mon copain apprend l'espagnol en écoutant des chansons mexicaines (en passant les vacances en Argentine).**

Teaching Strategy

Give students sentences using **pendant que...** to transform by eliminating **pendant que...** and using the present participle. **Je regarde la télévision pendant que je parle avec ma soeur. = Je regarde la télé en parlant avec ma soeur.**

Next, give students two sentences which explain how one arrives at a goal. Have them rewrite the sentences to explain the process in one logical sentence using the present participle: **Je suis devenu(e) prof de français. J'ai étudié beaucoup. C'est en étudiant beaucoup que je suis devenu(e) prof de français.**

7 C'est simple!

Cet été Céline a travaillé pour gagner de l'argent. Marc lui pose des questions sur son job. Céline lui répond. Avec votre partenaire, jouez les deux rôles.

▶ gagner de l'argent cet été / travailler dans un restaurant

1. trouver ce job / lire les annonces
2. contacter le restaurant / téléphoner à la propriétaire *(owner)*
3. réussir à l'entrevue / avoir une bonne attitude
4. apprendre ton travail / regarder les autres employés
5. recevoir tes pourboires *(tips)* / être attentive et polie avec les clients

Comment as-tu gagné de l'argent cet été?

C'est simple! J'ai gagné de l'argent en travaillant dans un restaurant.

8 Zut alors!

Les personnes suivantes ont eu des problèmes. Expliquez quand ou comment c'est arrivé.

▶ Monsieur Lasalle s'est coupé. (Il se rasait.)
Monsieur Lasalle s'est coupé en se rasant.

1. Stéphanie s'est blessée. (Elle faisait de l'alpinisme.)
2. Je suis tombé. (Je descendais les escaliers.)
3. Tu t'es cassé une dent. (Tu mangeais du homard [*lobster*].)
4. Vincent a perdu son portefeuille. (Il allait au cinéma.)
5. Nous nous sommes perdus. (Nous nous promenions à la montagne.)
6. Vous avez eu un accident. (Vous faisiez du parapente.)

9 Comment?

Dites comment les personnes suivantes font certaines choses.

▶ Philippe célèbre son anniversaire. Il organise une boum.
Philippe célèbre son anniversaire en organisant une boum.

1. Catherine reste en forme. Elle nage tous les jours.
2. Isabelle se repose. Elle écoute de la musique classique.
3. Jérôme amuse ses amis. Il imite Jim Carrey.
4. Alice gagne de l'argent. Elle fait du baby-sitting.
5. Thomas aide ses parents. Il passe l'aspirateur.
6. Stéphanie s'informe. Elle lit des magazines.
7. Carole reste en contact avec ses amis. Elle leur écrit pour leur anniversaire.
8. Marc soigne sa grippe. Il boit du thé chaud.
9. Édouard contribue à la protection de l'environnement. Il ramasse *(picks up)* les vieux papiers.
10. Hélène fait des bonnes actions *(deeds)*. Elle aide une famille d'immigrés.

10 et vous?

Avec votre partenaire, dites comment vous faites les mêmes choses que celles de l'activité 9.

▶ **Moi, je célèbre mon anniversaire en faisant du bowling avec mes copains.**

■ **Teaching Strategy: Variation**

The students playing the role of Céline may use object pronouns in their answers:

J'en ai gagné en travaillant dans un restaurant.
1. Je l'ai trouvé …
2. Je l'ai contacté …
3. J'y ai réussi …
4. Je l'ai appris …
5. Je les ai reçus …

INFO MAGAZINE

Theme: Job interviews

COMMENT SE PRÉSENTER À UNE ENTREVUE

Vous avez surfé sur l'Internet pour trouver un job. Vous avez trouvé une petite annonce qui vous a intéressé(e). Vous avez téléphoné. On vous a demandé d'envoyer votre curriculum vitae. Quelques jours plus tard, on vous a convoqué(e)° pour une entrevue. Finalement le grand jour est arrivé. Ne le ratez pas! Voici quelques conseils.

■ Teaching Strategy

With your partner, role-play two interviews:
- one goes very well, the candidate answers all questions and is clearly qualified and enthusiastic.
- one goes badly when the candidate makes many mistakes, saying the wrong things, asking the wrong questions.

Rôles: le/la candidat(e), l'interviewer

■ Teaching suggestion

Tell students to research and make a list of which French and francophone companies have branches in the United States. Have them look at the companies' job postings to see what types of jobs are available to those who speak French. Make a help wanted bulletin board to put in the corridor or guidance office so that all students can see the advantages of learning French.

■ Irregular Verb

(see Appendix C)
interrompre (*see* **rompre**)

Pour l'entrevue

◆ **Habillez-vous correctement.**

La présentation a beaucoup d'importance. Soignez-la!° Pour les garçons, mettez un costume et une cravate. Pour les filles, mettez une robe classique. Si vous avez le temps, passez chez le coiffeur quelques jours avant l'entrevue. Laissez vos lunettes de soleil chez vous, même s'il fait beau. Évitez les couleurs criardes° et les parfums excessifs. Et pas de coiffure extravagante.

◆ **Arrivez à l'heure ou même un peu avant.**

Soyez poli avec la réceptionniste. Attendez patiemment votre tour, même si la personne avec qui vous avez rendez-vous est en retard.

◆ **Ne soyez pas intimidé.**

Même si vous avez le trac° intérieurement°, ayez l'air décontracté. (Ce n'est pas le dernier jour de votre vie, mais peut-être le premier jour de votre vie professionnelle.) Ne mâchez° pas de chewing-gum pour masquer votre nervosité.

Pendant l'entrevue

◆ **Répondez clairement et distinctement aux questions de l'interviewer.**

Mettez en valeur° vos talents et vos qualifications, mais sans les exagérer. Surtout, ne vous inventez pas un curriculum vitae extraordinaire. (À votre âge, il est normal que votre expérience professionnelle soit limitée.)

◆ **Soyez attentif et respectueux.**

Ayez l'air intéressé par ce qu'on vous dit. N'interrompez pas l'interviewer quand il vous parle. Posez des questions, mais seulement au bon° moment. À l'occasion, prenez des notes. (Pour cela, n'oubliez pas d'apporter un carnet et un stylo à l'entrevue. Cela fera bonne impression.) Ne regardez jamais votre montre pendant l'entrevue.

◆ **Ne soyez pas trop personnel.**

Parlez de votre vie personnelle seulement si cela a un rapport° avec vos qualifications pour le job. Ne soyez pas familier avec votre interviewer. (Par exemple, n'essayez pas de savoir qui sont les personnes sur les photos qui peuvent être sur son bureau!)

---

convoqué(e) *called* **Soignez-la!** *pay careful attention to it* **criardes** *loud* **trac** *are scared, nervous* **intérieurement** *inside* **mâchez** *chew*
mettez en valeur *emphasize* **interrompez / interrompre** *to interrupt* **bon** *right* **rapport** *connection*

INFOMAGAZINE

◆ **Ne parlez jamais de salaire.**
Si vous êtes accepté pour le job, il sera temps d'en discuter à ce moment-là.

Après l'entrevue

◆ **Soyez persévérant sans être trop insistant.**

Si possible, écrivez une lettre assez courte dans laquelle vous remerciez l'interviewer de l'entretien qu'il vous a donné. Cela l'aidera à se souvenir de vous. Ne téléphonez pas tous les jours à la compagnie pour connaître les résultats de l'entrevue. En fait, attendez au moins 15 jours avant de vous informer sur votre sort.°

◆ **Restez optimiste.**

Même en cas de réponse négative, vous avez acquis° l'expérience de l'entrevue. Cela vous sera utile pour la prochaine fois.

et vous?

Avec votre partenaire, déterminez quels sont les trois (3) conseils les plus utiles et dites pourquoi.

EXPRESSION ÉCRITE
Décrivez une entrevue personnelle que vous avez eue. Mentionnez, par exemple:
- comment vous étiez habillé(e)
- quand vous êtes arrivé(e) à l'entrevue
- comment vous vous sentiez
- qui était l'interviewer
- quelles questions il/elle vous a posées
- comment vous avez répondu
- quels problèmes vous avez eus pendant l'entrevue
- qu'est-ce que vous avez fait après l'entrevue
- quel a été le résultat de cette entrevue

CURRICULUM VITAE

et vous?

Vous voulez travailler pour une compagnie française. Préparez votre propre curriculum vitae sur le modèle indiqué.

CURRICULUM VITAE

Karine PERRAUDIN
125, rue de l'Ermitage
37100 Tours
tél. 02-47-31-22-51
19 ans

ÉTUDES	1 année de préparation, École Supérieure de Commerce Bac S, mention assez bien
LANGUES	Anglais (courant°) Allemand Notions d'espagnol
EXPÉRIENCE	été 2012 — Stage d'un mois à CANAL-PLUS (service marketing)
	été 2011 — Réceptionniste dans un hôtel 3 étoiles
	été 2010 — Animatrice dans une colonie de vacances pour enfants handicapés
POSTE SOUHAITÉ	Stage de 4 à 6 semaines, si possible rémunéré, dans un service de publicité ou de marketing. Préférence pour compagnie internationale.
SPORTS ET LOISIRS	Tennis, Natation, Escalade, Musique (violon), Photo
RÉFÉRENCES	Sur demande.°

sort *fate*
acquis / acquérir* *to acquire*
courant *fluent*
sur demande *on request*

Notes culturelles

- **Le C.V.** est l'abréviation usuelle de **curriculum vitae. Curriculum vitae** est une expression invariable d'origine latine signifiant littéralement "la course de la vie."

- Il est d'usage en France d'inclure son âge et son état civil (**marié[e], célibataire, divorcé[e] ou veuf/ veuve**) sur son C.V. De plus, beaucoup de compagnies exigent une lettre d'accompagnement écrite à la main de manière à pouvoir en faire **l'analyse graphologique** avant de décider d'interviewer le candidat ou non.

Irregular Verb
(see Appendix C)
acquérir

INFOMAGAZINE

393

Teaching Strategy

Divide the two pages of reading into three parts: **Pour l'entrevue/Pendant l'entrevue/ Après l'entrevue.** Divide the class into groups and give each group one of the sections. Have them read each section carefully, prepare an explanation/presentation about it and write three questions about the information to give to the class as a mini-quiz.

■ **Note culturelle**

The minimum wage was created in France in 1950. In April 2011, the minimum hourly wage was 9€ (about $12.80). The minimum wage is regularly increased.

■ **Note linguistique**

Les technologies, telles que les ordinateurs personnels, le courrier électronique et l'Internet, permettent à un certain nombre de personnes de travailler chez elles. C'est ce que l'on appelle en France **"le télétravail"** (travail à distance).

La vie professionnelle

Où voudrais-tu travailler?

Je voudrais travailler pour une banque.

— Où voudrais-tu travailler?
  Je voudrais travailler **dans/pour une banque.**

un bureau	**une compagnie internationale**
une usine *factory*	**un cabinet** *(office)* **d'avocat**
une agence de voyages	**un laboratoire de recherches**

— **Dans quelle branche d'activité** voudrais-tu | travailler?
| **faire carrière?**

  J'aimerais travailler dans **la finance**.

le commerce *trade*	**l'informatique**
l'industrie	**la recherche** *(research)* **scientifique**
la communication	**la fonction publique** *civil service*
la publicité *advertising*	**les relations publiques**
les assurances *insurance*	**l'immobilier** *real estate*
les affaires *business*	**l'électronique**

— **Pour quel genre d'entreprise** voudrais-tu travailler?

  Je voudrais travailler **pour une** | **petite** | **entreprise.**
  | **grande** |

une compagnie	**moyenne** *average size*
une firme	**multinationale**
une société	

  Je voudrais | travailler **à mon propre compte** *(for myself).*
  | **créer ma propre** *(own)* **entreprise.**

— Qu'est-ce que tu **recherches** |
  Qu'est-ce qui t'intéresse | dans ce travail?
  Qu'est-ce qui compte le plus |

  rechercher *to look for, search*

  Je recherche **un bon salaire.**

une bonne ambiance *atmosphere*
de bonnes conditions de travail
la possibilité de promotion
des responsabilités importantes
des avantages sociaux *fringe benefits*

Teaching Suggestion: DVD Program

In the Unit 10 *Vidéo-drame: Guillaume trouve un job*, students will learn new vocabulary dealing with employment. As you play the video, ask students to write down some of the new vocabulary they hear. Then, encourage them to discuss what kind of job they would like to have, what qualifications they would need, etc.

1 Choix professionnel 🗨

Votre partenaire et vous, vous allez choisir une profession qui vous intéresse.
(Chacun va choisir une profession différente.) Comparez les avantages
de chaque profession sur la base des éléments suivants.

	faible	moyen(ne)	assez bon(ne)	bon(ne)	excellent(e)
• salaire/rémunération					
• intérêt du travail					
• prestige					
• ambiance de travail					
• possibilité de promotion					
• possibilité de voyager					
• possibilité de rencontrer des gens intéressants					
• ??					

2 La meilleure solution 🗨

Préféreriez-vous travailler pour une compagnie ou créer votre propre entreprise?
Chaque solution a ses avantages, mais aussi ses désavantages. Avec votre partenaire, évaluez
ces avantages et ces désavantages.

- Quelle est la meilleure solution pour vous?
- Quelle est la meilleure solution pour votre partenaire?

AVANTAGES		
peu important	important	très important

DÉSAVANTAGES		

Créer sa propre entreprise	Travailler pour une compagnie
• Satisfaction personnelle	• Horaire régulier
• Indépendance	• Salaire régulier
• Heures flexibles	• Avantages sociaux
• Possibilité de devenir riche	• Responsabilités limitées
• ??	• ??
• Possibilité d'échec (failure)	• Salaire limité
• Risques financiers	• Hiérarchie pesante (heavy)
• Travail très dur	• Travail monotone
• Trop de responsabilités	• Pas assez de responsabilités
• ??	• ??

SUPPLEMENTARY VOCABULARY

la **flexibilité** *flexibility*
les **heures supplémentaires** *overtime*
le **pointage** *clocking in/out*
le **stress**
la **vocation** *vocation*
le **rendement** *output, efficiency*
le **déplacement** *business travel*
un **organisme**
une **organisation**
une **affaire** *business*
la **sécurité de l'emploi** *job security*

■ **Expansion: Activity 2**
Other categories students may want
to consider:
   la **sécurité de l'emploi**
   les **vacances**
   les **congés** *paid vacation*

■ **Note linguistique**
Note that the verb "to commute" has
no direct translation in French.
to commute = **faire la navette (pour
   se rendre au travail tous les jours)**
commuter = **personne qui fait la
   navette (pour se rendre au travail
   tous les jours)**
Attention: the French verb **commuter**
means *to switch over; to commute (as
in a penalty)*

Teaching Strategy

As a week-long project, have each of the students begin by preparing their **curriculum vitae**. Be sure they are very careful to be clear, concise and grammatically correct. Each group should prepare two interviews giving each student a chance to be interviewer/interviewee. The next day have students dress appropriately for the presentation of the interviews to the class.

Le Français pratique
À la recherche d'un emploi

RESOURCES

PRINT
Workbook, pp. 168–171

Unit 10 Resource Book, Partie 2
Audioscripts

AUDIO
Audio Program
CD 12 Tracks 1–5

TECHNOLOGY
@HomeTutor
Interactive Whiteboard Lessons
Teacher One Stop
Teacher to Teacher Copymasters, *Un emploi*, pp. 119–121; *Jumeaux/Jumelles*, pp. 126–129

■ **Note linguistique**
Entrevue/interview/entretien: These three expressions are synonymous.

SUPPLEMENTARY VOCABULARY

mettre une annonce
lire les offres d'emploi

j'ai travaillé dans ...
   un restaurant
   un fast-food

À la recherche d'un emploi

Qu'est-ce que tu vas faire pour trouver du travail?

Je vais lire les annonces.

POUR TROUVER DU TRAVAIL
— Qu'est-ce que tu vas faire pour trouver du travail?
Je vais | **lire les annonces** *classified ads.*
répondre à l'annonce.
téléphoner au chef du personnel.
prendre rendez-vous *to make an appointment.*
envoyer mon curriculum vitae *resume.*
solliciter *to ask for* | **une entrevue** *interview.*
une interview.
un entretien.
aller à l'entretien.

PENDANT L'INTERVIEW
— Quel emploi cherchez-vous?
Je cherche **un emploi temporaire.**

un job d'été	**un emploi à mi-temps** *half time*
un stage *internship*	**un emploi à temps partiel** *part time*
	un emploi à plein temps *full time*

— Avez-vous déjà travaillé?
Oui, j'ai travaillé dans | un hôpital.
une boutique.
un supermarché.
Non, je n'ai **pas d'expérience professionnelle.**

— Qu'est-ce que vous savez faire?
Je sais **parler anglais.**

parler français, espagnol, chinois . . .	**conduire** *to drive*
conduire une voiture	**se servir de** *to use*
utiliser | **un ordinateur**	**classer** *to file*
me servir d'	
classer des documents	

— Quelles sont vos qualifications personnelles?
J'ai **l'esprit d'initiative.**

de l'ambition
le sens des contacts humains
le goût *(liking)* **des responsabilités**
une bonne formation *(education)* **générale**
des connaissances *(knowledge)* **techniques**

Notes culturelles
• One way to find work in France is to use the services of **Pôle Emploi.** This agency helps French citizens find jobs and provides training workshops as well as career counseling.

• In France, you must be at least 16 to be legally allowed to work full time. (See *Info Magazine* article, «Le travail, ça paie!», pp. 82–83, plus accompanying teacher notes, for further information.)

— Quels documents avez-vous apportés?

J'ai **mon curriculum vitae**.

> **des lettres de recommandation**
> **mes références**
> **mes diplômes**

— Merci! **Vous faites l'affaire!** *(You are qualified.)*

Nous allons vous | **offrir** un emploi.
| **embaucher.**

Je suis désolé(e), mais **vous ne faites pas l'affaire**.

> Quels documents avez-vous apportés?
>
> J'ai mon curriculum vitae.

offrir *to offer*
embaucher *to hire*

Conversations libres

Avec votre partenaire, choisissez l'un des sujets suivants. Composez et jouez le dialogue correspondant à ce sujet. Votre partenaire va jouer l'autre personne.

Digital performance space

1   Jobs d'été

Votre camarade et vous, vous habitez en France. Discutez de ce que vous allez faire pour trouver un job cet été.
Rôles: deux étudiants français.

2   Agence de voyages

Une agence de voyages française cherche un(e) assistant(e). Vous avez obtenu une entrevue avec le chef du personnel. C'est le jour de l'entrevue.
Rôles: un(e) candidat(e) /le chef du personnel

3   Télémarketing

Dans le journal, vous avez lu une annonce dans laquelle une firme française de produits cosmétiques cherche des étudiants américains pour vendre ses produits par téléphone. Téléphonez à cette firme pour expliquer vos qualifications.
Rôles: un(e) étudiant(e) américain(e)/ le représentant de la firme

4   Compagnie internationale

Vous venez d'obtenir votre diplôme universitaire avec une spécialité en littérature française. Vous répondez à l'annonce d'une compagnie internationale qui recrute des étudiants pour son département de marketing. Vous n'avez pas fait d'études de marketing. Expliquez à l'interviewer pourquoi vous voulez le job et pourquoi vous êtes tout de même *(nevertheless)* qualifié(e).
Rôles: un(e) candidat(e)/l'interviewer

5   Office de Tourisme

Vous habitez en France. L'Office de Tourisme de votre ville recrute des étudiants parlant anglais pour développer le tourisme dans la région. Vous avez une entrevue avec la directrice de l'Office du Tourisme.
Rôles: un(e) candidat(e)/la directrice

SUPPLEMENTARY VOCABULARY

renvoyer *to fire, let go*
mettre à la porte *to fire*
licencier *to dismiss/lay off*
le demandeur d'emploi *job seeker*
l'intérimaire *(f. & m.) temp (worker)*
les compétences *(f.) qualifications*
le dynamisme *dynamism*
le traitement de texte *word processing*
taper *to type*

■ Note culturelle

• Une façon moderne de trouver un job d'été est de consulter les offres d'emploi sur **l'Internet**, à la page "jobs on line." Si on n'a pas accès à l'Internet chez soi, on peut aller dans **un cyber-café**.

• Pour répondre à une offre d'emploi, il faut accompagner son CV d'une **lettre de motivation**.

• French teens like to find summer jobs. They may find work in such areas as:
  – **la restauration rapide**
  – **les parcs à thème**
  – **les hypermarchés**
  – **les instituts de sondage**

■ **Notes linguistiques**

- The subjunctive is also used after:
  afin que *in order that*
  bien que *although*
  quoi que *although*
  pourvu que *provided that*

- The pleonastic (or redundant) **ne** is optional after **avant que** and **sans que**. It is more frequently used with **à moins que**.
  Je finirai mon travail **avant que** vous **ne** veniez.
  Nous sortirons **à moins qu'**il **ne** fasse mauvais.

- The infinitive is used under the same conditions after:
  à moins de
  à condition de
  afin de

■ **Teaching Strategy**

Before class write the following conjunctions on separate pieces of paper: **pour que ... pour ... à condition que ... à condition de ... à moins que ... sans que ... sans ... avant que ... avant ... jusqu'à ce que** so that each pair of students has two conjunctions. Put the papers into a hat and have each pair pick two conjunctions and write creative sentences using these words. Then write each of the conjunctions on the board and have the students write their sentences under the appropriate conjunction. The whole class could then vote on the most creative/amusing sentence.

A La construction conjonction + subjonctif

Note the use of the subjunctive in the following sentences.

Je te prête le journal **pour que tu lises** les petites annonces.	*I am lending you the paper **so that you read** the ads.*
Téléphone au chef du personnel **avant qu'il parte** en vacances.	*Call the head of personnel **before he leaves** on vacation.*
Nous vous engagerons **à condition que vous ayez** de bonnes recommandations.	*We will hire you **provided that you have** good recommendations.*

The SUBJUNCTIVE is used after certain conjunctions which express:

- **PURPOSE or INTENT**

pour que	*so that*	Le professeur explique **pour que** vous **compreniez**.

- **CONDITION or RESTRICTION**

à condition que	*provided, on condition that*	Nous ferons une promenade à vélo **à condition qu'**il **fasse** beau.
à moins que	*unless*	J'irai à la plage **à moins qu'**il **fasse** mauvais.
sans que	*without*	Philippe est parti **sans que** tu lui **dises** au revoir.

- **TIME LIMITATION**

avant que	*before*	Je vous téléphonerai **avant que** vous **partiez**.
jusqu'à ce que	*until*	Nous attendrons **jusqu'à ce que** vous **veniez**.

→ The INFINITIVE is used after **avant de, pour,** and **sans** when the subject of the main clause and the dependent clause are the same.

Victor est venu ...	Victor est venu ...
pour parler de ses projets.	**pour que vous parliez** de vos projets.
avant d'aller en France.	**avant que vous alliez** en vacances.
sans avoir rendez-vous.	**sans que vous ayez** rendez-vous.

→ Remember that the INDICATIVE is used after conjunctions, such as **parce que, pendant que, depuis que, lorsque**.

Je cherche du travail **parce que j'ai** besoin d'argent.

Differentiation

Cumulative, Gifted & Talented Review the formation of the subjunctive, writing a verb on the board. Write three columns on the board for Subjunctive, Infinitive and Indicative and write the expressions listed in the book under the appropriate column. Then have students create a skit about a young person who wishes to borrow money for college from a rich, but eccentric, aunt or uncle. The aunt or uncle agrees, but with some unusual conditions or restrictions.

1 Prêts

Vous êtes une personne généreuse qui prête ce qu'elle a. Choisissez une chose
et dites à qui vous allez la prêter et pourquoi.

▶ **Je vais prêter dix dollars à mon cousin Christophe (à ma soeur
   Michelle) pour qu'il/elle aille au cinéma.**

QUOI?	POURQUOI?
mon vélo	s'acheter un livre
mon gant de baseball	faire un tour à la campagne
mon lecteur MP3	aller au ciné
mon appareil-photo	prendre des photos
dix dollars	organiser une boum
vingt dollars	écouter de la musique
??	??

2 Il y a toujours une raison

Expliquez pourquoi les personnes suivantes font certaines choses pour d'autres personnes.

▶ Madame Bertrand / donner de l'argent à sa nièce / s'acheter une tablette
   Madame Bertrand donne de l'argent à sa nièce pour qu'elle s'achète une tablette.

1. Thomas / prêter son vélo à son copain / faire une promenade à la campagne
2. Monsieur Thibault / payer les études à sa fille / être avocate
3. Madame Rémi / envoyer un chèque à son fils / payer sa scolarité *(tuition)*
4. le professeur / écrire des lettres de recommandation aux élèves / trouver du travail
5. Marc / inviter sa copine à dîner / faire la connaissance de ses parents
6. Madame Lombard / envoyer ses enfants en Angleterre / apprendre l'anglais

3 Dépêchez-vous!

Dites à votre partenaire de se dépêcher de faire certaines choses.

> Va à la bibliothèque avant qu'elle ferme.

▶ aller à la bibliothèque (elle va fermer)

1. téléphoner à ta copine (elle va sortir)
2. ranger ta chambre (tes copains vont venir)
3. finir tes devoirs (on va aller au ciné)
4. promener le chien (il va faire noir)
5. acheter cette montre (les prix vont augmenter)
6. chercher un job (les vacances vont commencer)
7. demander des lettres de recommandation (tes profs
   vont partir en vacances)
8. répondre à cette annonce (la compagnie va
   embaucher quelqu'un d'autre)

4 Conditions

François demande à sa mère s'il peut faire certaines choses. Sa mère accepte mais à certaines conditions. Avec votre partenaire, jouez les deux rôles.

▶ aller à la boum / rentrer avant minuit

FRANÇOIS: **Dis, est-ce que je peux aller à la soirée?**

SA MÈRE: **Je veux bien, mais à condition que tu rentres avant minuit.**

FRANÇOIS: **Bon, d'accord! Je rentrerai avant minuit.**

1. regarder mon nouveau DVD / finir tes devoirs avant
2. écouter de la musique / ne pas faire de bruit
3. inviter un copain à dîner / mettre la table
4. organiser un pique-nique / faire les courses
5. prendre la voiture / être prudent
6. voyager cet été / réussir à tes examens

5 Négociation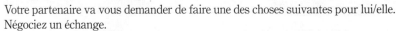

Votre partenaire va vous demander de faire une des choses suivantes pour lui/elle. Négociez un échange.

- prêter ton VTT
- prêter ton portable
- prêter dix dollars
- inviter au café

- inviter à ta boum
- présenter à tes copains
- aider avec le devoir
- aider à ranger ma chambre

▶ — **Dis, est-ce que tu peux me prêter ton VTT?**
 — **D'accord, mais à condition que tu me prêtes ton appareil-photo (que tu m'aides avec le problème de maths, . . .)**

6 Une promenade à vélo

Vous êtes en Touraine avec votre partenaire. Vous organisez une promenade à vélo. Expliquez vos projets à votre partenaire.

▶ Nous ferons une promenade samedi.
  (à condition que / il fait beau)
  Nous ferons une promenade samedi à condition qu'il fasse beau.

le château d'Amboise

1. Le matin, nous visiterons le château d'Amboise.
  (à moins que / il est fermé)
2. Je te prêterai mon appareil-photo.
  (pour que / tu prends des photos)
3. Après, nous ferons un pique-nique.
  (à moins que / nous trouvons une petite auberge sympathique)
4. Nous irons dans cette auberge.
  (à condition que / elle a des spécialités régionales)
5. Ensuite nous continuerons notre promenade.
  (jusqu'à ce que / nous sommes fatigués)
6. Nous rentrerons.
  (avant que / il fait nuit)

7 Double effet

En général, nos actions nous concernent nous-mêmes. Elles peuvent aussi concerner d'autres personnes. Exprimez cela d'après le modèle.

▶ J'achète le journal pour lire les petites annonces. (tu)
J'achète le journal pour que tu lises les petites annonces.

1. Madame Gustave passe un an au Brésil pour apprendre le portugais. (ses enfants)
2. Monsieur Guyon commande un taxi pour être à l'heure au rendez-vous. (son patron)
3. Nous allons dans ce magasin pour regarder les ordinateurs. (vous)
4. Je rendrai visite à mes cousins avant de partir en vacances. (ils)
5. Nous te téléphonerons avant d'aller en France. (tu)
6. Monsieur Durand ne partira pas sans avoir son passeport. (sa femme)
7. Nous ne quitterons pas Paris sans voir Notre Dame. (nos enfants)
8. Monsieur Thomas achète un nouveau logiciel *(software)* pour faire sa comptabilité *(accounting)*. (sa secrétaire)
9. Je téléphone à la directrice pour avoir une entrevue. (tu)
10. Madame Rimbaud relit la lettre avant de signer. (son patron)
11. Le chef du personnel n'engagera pas ces candidats sans parler au président de la compagnie. (ils)

8 C'est vous le président!

C'est vous le président de votre propre entreprise. Tous les mois, vous réunissez votre personnel. Faites votre présentation en complétant les phrases suivantes.

1. Je vous ai demandé de venir pour que . . .
   (vous / discuter des progrès de l'entreprise)
2. Nos ventes *(sale)* ont progressé depuis que . . .
   (je / vous avoir parlé le mois dernier)
3. En particulier, nos exportations vers le Japon ont augmenté depuis que . . .
   (le franc / avoir été dévalué)

4. J'ai contacté notre agence de Tokyo pour que . . .
   (elle / faire de la publicité à la télévision)
5. Nous devons développer de nouveaux produits sans que . . .
   (nos concurrents / le savoir)
6. Pour financer ces produits, je vais emprunter de l'argent à la Banque Nationale de Paris pendant que . . . (les taux [*rates*] d'intérêt / être favorables)
7. Nous allons réussir à moins que . . .
   (la situation économique / devenir mauvaise)

8. J'augmenterai vos salaires à condition que . . .
   (vous / continuer dans vos efforts)
9. Pour ma part, je vais continuer à travailler jusqu'à ce que . . .
   (cette compagnie / être la première compagnie dans sa spécialité)
10. C'est possible parce que . . .
    (nos produits / être les meilleurs produits du monde)

Expansion linguistique

- In France, the CEO of a company is referred to as **le PDG (Président-Directeur-Général)**. An executive is **un cadre**.

- Quelques logiciels populaires en France:
  le traitement de texte *word processing*
  le tableur *spreadsheet*
  la gestion/la comptabilité *accounting*

Unité 10

Interdisciplinary/ Community Connections

Hold a career day featuring professions involving foreign languages. This could be done in conjunction with other foreign-language classes.

Language Arts
Write for information about jobs in local companies that require both French and English.

Math
Find out how many companies in your state use French in some way. Display your information in a chart.

Science
Contact a major university or international company and inquire about language barriers. How do scientists from different countries communicate?

Social Studies
Research a list of local companies with French branches, and French companies with American branches.

Art/Music
Write a biographical profile of a francophone star who is also successful in the U.S.

Technology
Find out how technology is used to communicate or send information overseas. Or find out about technology that translates words from one language into another.

Community
Invite professionals from different fields involving foreign languages to speak at a school assembly or community gathering.

■ **Note culturelle**
Yves Thériault wrote about the natural beauty of Quebec in *Le Dompteur d'ours*. He became interested in the **inuit** (Eskimos) in his book *Agaguk*, and Native Americans in *Askini*.

LECTURE

Yves Thériault

Le portrait

AVANT DE LIRE

Le but d'un conte est de distraire.° Pour cela, un conte doit contenir un élément qui attirera et maintiendra l'attention du lecteur: humour, intrigue, développement psychologique, etc.

Dans le conte que vous allez lire, Hélène, une jeune fille canadienne, découvre un portrait dans le grenier de la ferme où elle habite avec sa famille. Elle apprend que c'est le portrait d'un oncle mort il y a longtemps et dont personne ne veut parler.

D'après cette courte introduction, quel est, selon vous, l'élément que l'auteur utilisera pour retenir l'attention des lecteurs?

- l'humour?
- le mystère?
- l'intrigue?
- le récit d'aventures?
- le développement psychologique?
- autre élément?

distraire *to entertain*

Yves Thériault (1915-1983) est un auteur québécois. Avant de se consacrer à la littérature, il a fait un peu tous les métiers: conducteur de camion, marchand de fromages, présentateur à la radio, traducteur. . . Écrivain très prolifique, il a écrit des essais, des contes sur des thèmes canadiens, aussi bien qu'une série de romans policiers.

LE PORTRAIT

Teaching Strategy

Have students read the material in the *Avant de lire* section and work in groups to discuss the questions. Ask students to summarize the responses from their group and tabulate the results for the whole class. Using **Projectable Transparency L10,** ask students to look at the visuals to determine whether there are any clues to the author's technique.

Differentiation

Synthetic/Analytic Pre-reading: Have students say and write the vocabulary words in the *Mots utiles*. Have students work in pairs to underline the vocabulary words in the passage. Have them write out the main points of the passage and share them with the class.

1

J'ai trouvé le portrait dans le grenier, un matin de juin. J'y étais allée chercher des pots° pour les confitures de fraises, puisque nous étions au temps de l'année pour ces choses.

Le portrait était derrière un bahut.° J'ai vu la dorure° du cadre. J'ai tiré à moi, 5 et voilà que c'était le portrait.

Celui d'un homme jeune, aux cheveux bruns, à la bouche agréable, et des yeux qui me regardaient. De grands yeux noirs, vivants . . .

J'ai descendu le portrait dans la cuisine.

— Voilà, mère, c'était au grenier.

10 Elle regarda le portrait d'un air surpris.

— Nous avions donc ça ici, ma fille? Tiens, tiens . . .

J'ai demandé:

— Qui est l'homme? Parce que c'est un bel homme. Il est vêtu° à la mode ancienne, mais c'est un magnifique gaillard . . .°

15 — Ton oncle, dit-elle, le frère de ton père. Le portrait a été peint alors qu'il était jeune.

— Quel oncle?

Je ne connaissais qu'une vague tante, pâle, anémique, qui vivait à la ville et venait chez nous une fois l'an. C'était, à ma connaissance, la seule parente de mon 20 père.

Je l'ai dit à ma mère.

— Je ne me connais pas d'oncle . . .

— C'était le plus jeune frère de ton père. Ils étaient quatre. Trois garçons, 25 une fille. Il ne reste que ton père et ta tante Valérienne.

— Les autres sont morts?

Elle fit° oui de la tête.

— Même celui-là? dis-je, même ce bel oncle-là?

— Oui.

■ Note linguistique
In the Middle Ages, **un bahut** was a wooden chest used when traveling. Nowadays, it means a cupboard and is familiar teenage slang for **le lycée (aller au bahut = aller au lycée).**

■ Additional Information
Strawberries are in season in June and July.

■ Irregular Verb
(See Appendix C)
mourir

Mots utiles

le cadre	*frame*
la colère	*anger*
le grenier	*attic*
chercher à	= *essayer de*
descendre	*to bring down*
pendre	*to hang*
secouer	*to shake*
tirer	*to pull, draw*
ça n'a pas d'importance	*that doesn't matter*
il ne reste que…	*there is/are only . . . left*
mieux vaut	= *il vaut mieux*

pot *jar* **bahut** *cupboard* **dorure** *gilt* **vêtu** *dressed* **gaillard** *guy* **fit** = *dit*

Teaching Strategy

Ask students to look at the illustrations in the first section of the story <u>without</u> reading the text. Then ask them to write a short caption for each picture that describes what seems to be happening. They may also provide speech bubbles for dialog if they prefer, or even create their own versions of the pictures and write captions. Then have students read the story and determine whether their predictions based on visual cues were accurate.

■ **Note linguistique**

Cru est un adjectif dérivé du latin "crudus" (**saignant:** *bleeding*). **Cru** désigne quelque chose de direct, que rien n'atténue au passage: **la lumière crue, une couleur crue.**

— Ce n'est pas juste de mourir quand on est si jeune et si beau . . . Non, ce n'est pas juste . . . Eh bien, oui, j'avais un bel oncle. Dommage qu'il soit mort . . . 30

Ma mère me regardait curieusement.

—Hélène, tu dis de drôles de choses . . .

Mais je n'écoutais pas ma mère. Je regardais le portrait. Maintenant, à la lumière plus crue° de la cuisine, le portrait me paraissait encore plus beau, 35 encore mieux fait . . . Et j'aimais bien les couleurs.

— Je le pends dans ma chambre, dis-je . . .

— Comme tu voudras, dit ma mère, aujourd'hui, ça n'a plus d'importance. La remarque n'était pas bien claire, et j'ai voulu savoir.

— Vous ne trouvez pas que c'est d'en dire beaucoup, et bien peu, mère? 40

— Peut-être. De celui-là, mieux vaut en dire le moins possible . . .

— Comment se nommait-il?°

— Tout simplement Jean . . .

— Et qu'est-ce qu'il faisait, demandai-je, qu'est-ce qu'il faisait dans la vie? Mais ma mère secoua la tête. 45

— Pends, dit-elle, ce portrait où tu voudras . . . Ça n'a plus d'importance, mais si tu veux un bon conseil, ne dis rien, ne cherche à rien savoir. Et surtout, ne parle de rien à ton père.

Au fond,° ça n'avait pas d'importance. J'aimais le coup de pinceau° de l'artiste. J'aimais sa façon de tracer, de poser° la couleur, j'aimais les teintes° 50 chaudes . . .

crue *direct*   **se nommait-il** = s'appelait-il   **au fond** *deep down*   **coup de pinceau** *brush stroke* **poser** = mettre   **teintes** = couleurs

55   Je trouvais l'oncle bien beau, et bien jeune. Mais ça n'était pas si important que je doive encourir° d'inutiles colères. Et quelque chose me disait, quelque chose dans le ton de la voix de ma mère, dans la détermination de son visage, que mon père n'aimerait pas du tout que j'aborde° le sujet de son frère Jean.

encourir *to incur*   **aborde** = *approche*

Avez-vous compris?

1. Comment Hélène a-t-elle découvert le portrait?
2. Qu'est-ce que sa mère lui explique? Qu'est-ce qu'elle ne lui explique pas?
3. Qu'est-ce qu'Hélène pense de son oncle?
4. Qu'est-ce qu'elle veut faire du portrait?

Anticipons un peu!

Hélène a décidé de mettre le portrait dans sa chambre. D'après vous, qu'est-ce qui va se passer dans l'épisode suivant?

- Le portrait va disparaître.
- Le portrait va vouloir communiquer quelque chose à Hélène.
- Hélène va tomber malade et mourir mystérieusement.
- L'oncle Jean va réapparaître dans la maison familiale bien vivant *(alive)*.
- Autre possibilité?

Expliquez votre choix.

■ **Irregular Verb**

(See Appendix C)
encourir is conjugated like **courir**

■ **Teaching Strategy**

Tell students:
Regardez l'illustration qui représente le tableau de l'oncle. Quelle impression vous donne la personne représentée? Pouvez-vous donner deux adjectifs pour décrire cette personne?

■ *Avez-vous compris?*

(Sample answers)
1. Elle a découvert le portrait au grenier, où elle cherchait des pots pour les confitures de fraises.
2. Sa mère lui explique que l'homme du portrait était le frère de son père, et qu'il est mort. Elle ne lui explique pas pourquoi on ne parle jamais de lui.
3. Elle pense qu'il est très beau.
4. Elle veut pendre le portrait dans sa chambre.

Notes linguistiques

- **Souffler la lampe:** on souffle sur la flamme d'une lampe à pétrole pour l'éteindre.
- The expression **la bougeotte** comes from the verb **bouger** (to move). **Avoir la bougeotte** is a familiar expression meaning to have itchy feet.

2

J'ai pendu le portrait au mur de ma chambre.

Je l'ai regardé chaque matin en m'éveillant, et chaque soir avant de souffler la lampe.

Et puis, au bout de deux semaines, une nuit, j'ai senti que quelqu'un me touchait l'épaule. 60

Je me suis éveillée en sursaut,° j'ai allumé ma lampe de chevet.° J'avais des sueurs froides le long du corps . . . Mais il n'y avait personne dans ma chambre.

Machinalement,° j'ai regardé le portrait, et en le voyant j'ai crié, je crois, pas fort,° mais assez tout de même, et je me suis enfoui° la tête sous l'oreiller.° 65

Dans le portrait, l'oncle Jean, très habilement° rendu,° regardait droit devant lui... Mais lorsque je me suis éveillée, j'ai vu qu'à cette heure-là de la nuit, il regardait ailleurs. En fait il regardait vers la fenêtre. Il regardait dehors . . .

Le matin, je n'ai rien dit. Je n'ai rien dit non plus les jours suivants, même si, chaque nuit, quelqu'un . . . ou quelque chose m'éveillait en me touchant 70 l'épaule. Et même si chaque nuit, l'oncle Jean regardait par la fenêtre . . .

Naturellement, je me demandais bien ce que ça voulait dire. Plusieurs fois je me suis pincée, très fort,° pour être bien sûre que je ne dormais pas.

Chose certaine, j'étais bien éveillée.

Et quelque chose se passait . . . Mais quoi? 75

Au sixième matin . . . vous voyez comme je suis patiente . . . j'ai voulu tout savoir de maman.

— L'oncle Jean, qui est-il? Qu'est-ce qu'il faisait? Pourquoi ne faut-il pas en parler devant papa, de cet oncle?

— Tu as toujours le portrait dans ta chambre? dit ma mère. 80

— Oui.

Elle continua ses occupations pendant quelques minutes, puis elle vint s'asseoir devant moi, à la table.

— Ma fille, me dit-elle, il y a des choses qui sont difficiles à dire. Moi, ton oncle Jean, je l'aimais bien, je le trouvais charmant. Et ça mettait ton père dans 85 tous les états° quand j'osais dire de telles choses.

Je lui ai demandé:

— Mais pourquoi, mère?

— Parce que ton oncle Jean, c'était une sorte de mouton noir dans la famille . . . il a eu des aventures, je t'épargne° les détails. 90 Surtout, il avait la bougeotte.° Il s'est enfui jeune de la maison, on ne l'a revu que plus tard . . .. Puis il est reparti. Un jour, ton père a reçu une lettre. Ton oncle Jean s'était fait tuer,° stupidement, dans un accident aux États-Unis. On a fait transporter son corps ici, pour être enterré dans le lot° familial au cimetière. Il n'aurait pas dû . . . mais . . . 95

en sursaut with a start   **de chevet** bedside   **machinalement** unconsciously   **pas fort** not very loud
enfoui buried   **oreiller** pillow   **habilement** skillfully   **rendu** = peint   **pincée très fort** pinched hard
dans tous les états = en colère   **épargne** spare   **bougeotte** travelling urge
s'était fait tuer was killed   **lot** plot

Mots utiles

l'épaule	shoulder
la sueur	sweat
un testament	will
allumer	to light
crier	to scream
se demander	to wonder
s'enfuir *	to run away
éveiller	to wake up
oser	to dare
souffler	to blow out
vouloir dire	to mean
ailleurs	elsewhere
au bout de	= après
tel (telle)	such

— Pourquoi? ai-je demandé, pourquoi n'aurait-il pas dû?

— Parce que, dans un testament découvert par la suite dans les effets de Jean, celui-ci exigeait d'être enterré n'importe où, mais pas dans le lot° familial . . .

100   Il disait dans cet écrit qu'il n'avait aucunement° le désir de reposer aux côtés de la paisible° et sédentaire famille. Il avait un autre mot pour eux . . . pas très gentil.

    Moi je croyais comprendre, maintenant.

— Est-ce que papa l'a fait transporter ailleurs?

— Euh . . . non . . . question° des dépenses que ça signifiait° . . . Jean n'a rien laissé, il est mort pauvre.

lot *plot*   **aucunement** = *pas du tout*   **paisible** *quiet*   **question des** = *à cause des*   **signifiait** = *représentait*

Note linguistique

les effets *(m.)* = *personal belongings*

Avez-vous compris?

(Sample answers)

1. Elle s'est éveillée en sursaut parce qu'elle a senti que quelqu'un lui touchait l'épaule.
2. L'oncle regardait par la fenêtre.
3. Elle pensait qu'il était charmant.
4. Leurs rapports étaient mauvais.
5. Il est mort dans un accident aux États-Unis.
6. Il voulait être enterré n'importe où, mais pas dans le lot familial. On n'a pas respecté son testament.

Avez-vous compris?

1. Pourquoi est-ce qu'Hélène s'est éveillée en sursaut?
2. En quoi le portrait de son oncle était-il différent à ce moment-là?
3. Que pensait la mère d'Hélène de l'oncle Jean?
4. Quelles étaient les rapports entre le père d'Hélène et son frère Jean?
5. Comment est mort l'oncle Jean?
6. Qu'est-ce que son testament stipulait? Est-ce qu'il a été respecté?

Anticipons un peu!

D'après vous, qu'est-ce que l'oncle Jean voulait communiquer à Hélène?

- Qu'elle ouvre la fenêtre.
- Qu'elle sorte *(take out)* le portrait de la maison.
- Qu'elle prie *(pray)* pour lui.
- Qu'elle quitte elle-même la maison familiale et parte à l'aventure.

Expliquez votre choix.

Teaching Strategy

Divide the class into groups after reading the second section of the story and answering the *Avez-vous compris?* comprehension questions. Ask the group to answer the following questions; if there are differences of opinion, both/all answers should be recorded. Have each group present its answers to the class.

- À votre avis, qui ou quoi touche l'épaule d'Hélène la nuit? Est-ce un fantôme? De qui? Est-ce un insecte? Sa mère? Ou est-ce un rêve *(dream)*? Expliquez votre opinion.
- À votre avis, qu'est-ce que Jean est parti faire aux États-Unis?

Notes linguistiques

Attention à ne pas confondre:
- **soit:** 3e personne singulier du subjonctif du verbe **être**
- **soit...soit:** conjonction *(either...or)*
  Soit Marie, soit Lucie, mais pas Henri.
- **soit:** subjonctif du verbe **être** utilisé pour introduire une supposition *(given [that] a...)*
  Soit un carré dont la surface est de...
- **soit:** adverbe d'affirmation *(so be it)*
  Soit! Allons à Genève demain.

Additional Information

Sigmund Freud (1856-1939) est le père de la psychanalyse. Il a écrit, entre autre, *L'Interprétation des rêves* en 1900.

Avez-vous compris?

(Sample answers)
1. Elle porte le portrait dehors, parce qu'elle pense que l'oncle Jean veut être dehors.
2. Il semble sourire, parce qu'Hélène a compris ce qu'il voulait.
3. Cette nuit-là il l'embrasse, pour la remercier.
4. Le portrait disparaît.
5. Elle n'a pas d'explication. C'est peut-être un rêve, ou peut-être des faits, elle ne sait pas.

3

Ce soir-là, j'ai mieux dormi. J'ai été éveillée vers quatre heures, et toute la scène d'habitude s'est répétée. 105

— Soit,° ai-je déclaré au portrait de l'oncle Jean . . . Demain, je vais faire quelque chose.

Et le lendemain matin, j'ai pris le portrait, et je l'ai porté dehors, derrière la remise.° Je l'ai appuyé là, face au soleil levant.° 110

Plusieurs fois dans la journée, je suis allée voir. L'oncle Jean regardait en face, mais j'ai cru voir comme une lueur° amusée dans ses yeux. Je me suis dit que je n'avais pas remarqué ce sourire auparavant.°

Au crépuscule,° le portrait était encore là . . .

Durant la nuit, je fus éveillée de nouveau. Seulement, au lieu d'une main 115 discrète sur mon épaule, ce fut un très gentil baiser sur la joue qui m'éveilla.

Et je vous jure que pendant les quatre ou cinq secondes entre le sommeil profond et l'éveil complet, j'ai bien senti des lèvres tièdes° sur ma joue.

Je me suis rendormie paisiblement. J'avais comme une sensation de bien-être. 120

Au matin, le portrait n'était plus à sa place.

J'ai demandé à papa s'il l'avait pris, et il m'a dit que non. Maman n'y avait pas touché. Mes petits frères non plus.

Le portrait avait disparu. Et moi j'étais convaincue que sa disparition° coïncidait avec le baiser de reconnaissance si 125 bien donné au cours de la nuit.

Vous voulez une explication? Je n'en ai pas. La chose est arrivée. Elle s'est passée comme ça peut être une suite° de rêves. Freud aurait une explication, 130 je suppose . . . N'empêche° que les faits sont là. Un portrait est disparu, et l'oncle Jean regardait. Pour un homme qui avait toujours eu la bougeotte, c'était tout de même assez significatif . . .

soit *all right, so be it*   **remise** *shed*   **levant** *rising*   **lueur** *gleam*   **auparavant** *= avant*
crépuscule *dusk*   **tièdes** *warm*   **disparition** *disappearance*
suite *series, sequence*   **n'empêche que** *nevertheless*

Mots utiles

un baiser	*kiss*
le bien-être	*well-being*
l'éveil	*wakefulness*
la reconnaissance	*= la gratitude*
un rêve	*dream*
le sommeil	*sleep*
appuyer	*to lean*
jurer	*to swear*
se rendormir *	*to go back to sleep*

Avez-vous compris?

1. Qu'est-ce qu'Hélène fait avec le portrait? Pourquoi?
2. Quelle semble être la réaction du portrait? Pourquoi?
3. Qu'est-ce qui se passe cette nuit-là? Pourquoi?
4. Que devient le portrait?
5. Quelle est l'explication d'Hélène?

Et vous?

D'après vous, qu'est-ce qui est arrivé au portrait?

Teaching Strategy

Ask students to think about what they have learned about the character of the uncle while reading the story and develop a list of adjectives to describe him. Then ask students to look at the list and compare themselves to the character. Are there any adjectives that are the same? Have students note similar adjectives and add a second column of adjectives describing themselves.

SUPPLEMENTARY VOCABULARY

le mystère *mystery*
l'énigme *(f.) enigma*
le fantôme *ghost*
l'apparition *(f.) apparition*
l'esprit *(m.) spirit*
hanter *to haunt*
l'au-delà *(m.) afterlife*

APRÈS LA LECTURE

Expression orale

Situations

Avec votre partenaire, choisissez l'une des situations suivantes. Composez le dialogue correspondant et jouez-le en classe.

1 L'histoire du portrait

Hélène raconte l'histoire du portrait à un(e) copain (copine). Incrédule, celui-ci (celle-ci) veut connaître les détails.
Rôles: Hélène, le copain (la copine)

2 La rupture

Quelques années après, Hélène demande à son père les raisons de la rupture avec son jeune frère Jean. Le père hésite et finalement répond à Hélène qui veut des détails. (Imaginez les raisons de cette rupture.)
Rôles: Hélène, le père

■ Teaching Note

You may wish to use the short *Lecture* quizzes to check comprehension, or use them as a basis for discussion.

Expression écrite

Le journal d'Hélène

Vous êtes Hélène. Dans votre journal, décrivez les événements suivants.
- la découverte du portrait
- ce qui s'est passé la première nuit
- ce qui s'est passé la dernière nuit

La biographie de l'oncle Jean

Un jour Hélène a trouvé dans le grenier le journal de l'oncle Jean dans lequel il décrit sa vie. Avec votre partenaire, imaginez la biographie de l'oncle Jean. Décrivez, par exemple . . .
- où il a passé sa jeunesse
- quelles étaient ses relations avec sa famille (Pourquoi s'est-il disputé avec sa famille?)
- quels problèmes il a eus
- pourquoi il s'est enfui une première fois
- où il est allé et qu'est-ce qu'il a fait
- pourquoi il est revenu
- pourquoi il est reparti une seconde fois
- où il est allé cette fois-là et qu'est-ce qu'il a fait
- comment il est mort

■ Expression écrite

For writing rubrics, consult the **Generate Success** Rubric Generator on the **Teacher One Stop**. You can also create your own custom rubrics with this tool.

Student Portfolios

A variety of portfolio items may be developed from either the *Situations* or the *Expression écrite* activities. More advanced students may write their own stories and illustrate them if desired. Since this is the final *Lecture* in DISCOVERING FRENCH TODAY!–*ROUGE* you may wish to assign a more challenging project (such as writing an original story) to show students and parents how much progress has been made during the year.

Interlude culturel

■ **Photo Note**
Bourbon is the family name of many French kings, including Louis XIII, Louis XIV, Louis XV and Louis XVI.

■ **Notes culturelles**
• **Mont-Royal,** an extinct volcano, was a site where Iroquois Indians lived as early as 1000 B.C.
• **Jacques Cartier** was the first European to explore in the valley of the Saint Lawrence River.
• In 1775, the American revolutionaries took over the city of Montreal but failed to take Quebec in 1776. Benjamin Franklin had hoped to make Montreal the fourteenth colony. Montrealers refused because they could not have retained their French roots and language.

L'histoire franco-américaine en dix questions

Depuis cinq siècles, l'histoire de la France et celle de l'Amérique du Nord sont étroitement liées.° Voici quelques pages d'histoire franco-américaine.

1. *Combien est-ce qu'il y a d'Américains d'origine française?*

Aux États-Unis, il y a plus de trois millions et demi de personnes qui se considèrent d'origine française. En outre,° il y a aussi dix millions de personnes qui ont au moins un ancêtre d'origine française. Ces personnes habitent principalement dans les états de la Nouvelle Angleterre et en Louisiane.

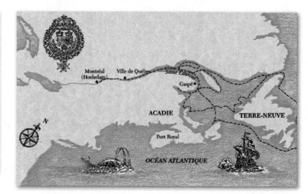
La Nouvelle-Orléans

Festival en Louisiane

2. *Quand est-ce que les premiers Français sont venus sur le continent américain?*

L'arrivée de Jacques Cartier à Gaspé (1534).

Jacques Cartier, un explorateur français, est arrivé au Canada en 1534. Sa mission était de trouver des mines d'or et de diamants pour le roi de France. Au lieu de découvrir des richesses fabuleuses, il a découvert un immense pays inconnu des Européens: le Canada. Il a débarqué° à Gaspé le 24 juillet 1534. Là, il a planté une croix° dans le sol,° et il a pris possession de la région au nom du roi de France. Au cours d'une seconde expédition l'année suivante, il a découvert l'estuaire d'un grand fleuve° qu'il a appelé le Saint-Laurent (parce que c'était le 10 août, fête de Saint Laurent). Puis il a remonté° ce fleuve jusqu'à un petit village indien appelé Hochelaga, site de la future ville de Montréal.

Les premiers colons français sont arrivés au Canada seulement 70 ans plus tard. Ils se sont d'abord installés° en Acadie (aujourd'hui la Nouvelle Écosse°) où ils ont fondé Port Royal (aujourd'hui Annapolis Royal) en 1605. En 1608, **Samuel de Champlain** a fondé la ville de **Québec**.

liées *interwoven* **en outre** *in addition* **a débarqué** *landed* **croix** *cross* **sol** *ground* **fleuve** = *rivière* **a remonté** *sailed up*
se sont installés *settled* **Nouvelle Écosse** *Nova Scotia*

3. *Quand a été fondé Montréal?*

En 1642, une petite expédition de 50 Français sous le commandement de Paul Chomedey de **Maisonneuve** est arrivée sur le site du village indien d'**Hochelaga**. Le but° de cette expédition était de créer une communauté religieuse pour soigner les malades et convertir les Iroquois. C'est ainsi qu'est née la ville de **Montréal**, appelée alors Ville Marie de Montréal. Parmi les membres de l'expédition, il y avait une jeune femme, **Jeanne Mance**, co-fondatrice de Montréal avec Maisonneuve. En 1644, elle a fondé l'Hôtel-Dieu*, un hôpital qui existe toujours aujourd'hui.

Peu à peu, Montréal a grandi.° C'est devenu un important centre du commerce de la fourrure° et le point de départ d'importantes expéditions vers la région des Grands Lacs et le Mississippi. Avec une population de 3 300 000 habitants, en majorité francophones, Montréal est aujourd'hui la seconde ville d'expression française du monde.

Jeanne Mance et Paul Chomedey de Maisonneuve, fondateurs de Montréal

Les «Filles du Roy»

Après la fondation de Québec (1608) et de Montréal (1642), des familles françaises se sont installées au Canada, mais ces familles n'étaient pas nombreuses: quelques dizaines seulement. Le roi Louis XIV, qui voulait établir une grande colonie, a encouragé le départ de centaines de colons. C'étaient des «habitants» qui travaillaient la terre,° des «coureurs des bois»° qui faisaient le commerce de la fourrure° avec les Indiens, et des soldats qui défendaient la colonie contre les attaques des Anglais et de leurs alliés iroquois.

Évidemment, pour assurer la survie° et le développement de cette petite colonie, il fallait que ces hommes se marient et aient des enfants. Oui, mais où trouver des épouses? L'administration royale a eu l'idée de recruter des jeunes filles françaises, volontaires pour partir dans un pays totalement inconnu et y fonder une famille. Pour les encourager, le roi leur donnait une dot° et leur assurait une éducation.

Les «filles du Roy» arrivent au Canada (1665-1675)

C'est ainsi qu'entre 1665 et 1675, plus de mille jeunes Françaises, les «Filles du Roy», ont quitté leur pays pour la grande aventure. Arrivées au Canada, elles étaient accueillies° dans des centres d'apprentissage° fondés par une autre Française, **Marguerite Bourgeoys**. Là, elles apprenaient ce qui était nécessaire pour survivre dans un pays rude° et parfois hostile. Puis, elles se mariaient...

Un très grand nombre de familles québécoises d'aujourd'hui descendent directement de ces courageuses pionnières, arrivées au Canada il y a plus de 300 ans.

* Hôtel-Dieu: nom donné autrefois à l'hôpital public de la ville.

but = *objectif* **a grandi** = *s'est développé* **fourrure** *fur* **terre** *earth* **coureurs des bois** *fur trappers* **survie** *survival* **dot** *dowry* **accueillies** *welcomed* **centres d'apprentissage** = *écoles* **rude** *rough*

Expansion

Internet Connection – Interlude 10
Visit **http://my.hrw.com** for more information and useful links about French culture in North America.

Communication

Standard 1.2 Students understand and interpret spoken and written French on a variety of topics.

4. Qu'est-ce qu'on appelle les «guerres françaises et indiennes» (1689-1763)?

Les Français ont créé une vaste colonie qu'ils ont appelée **la Nouvelle France**. Ce n'était pas les seuls occupants de cette partie de l'Amérique du Nord. Il y avait aussi les Anglais qui s'étaient établis en Nouvelle Angleterre. La rivalité entre ces deux groupes était intense. Chacun avait des alliés indiens. Les alliés des Français étaient les Hurons et les Algonquins. Les alliés des Anglais étaient les Iroquois. De temps en temps, chaque groupe faisait des raids sur le territoire de l'autre.

Finalement en 1756, une guerre générale a éclaté° entre la France et l'Angleterre. Au début, les Français ont été victorieux. Mais l'armée anglaise était bien supérieure en nombre et les forts français sont tombés les uns après les autres. Les Anglais ont pris Québec en 1759 et Montréal

Les «guerres françaises et indiennes»

en 1760. Au traité de Paris de 1763, la France a dû abandonner toutes ses colonies d'Amérique du Nord. Le Canada et toute la rive est du Mississippi sont passés sous contrôle anglais.

5. Quand la Louisiane était-elle française?

LaSalle prend possession de la Louisiane au nom de la France

Vers le milieu du 17ᵉ siècle, des expéditions françaises, parties de Montréal, avaient exploré la région des Grands Lacs. En 1673, le père **Marquette** avait découvert le Mississippi, mais personne ne savait jusqu'où allait ce long fleuve. **Cavelier de La Salle** décida d'entreprendre° cette exploration. En 1681, il organisa une petite expédition et il partit à l'aventure. Après un voyage très difficile, il arriva à l'estuaire du Mississippi le 9 avril 1682.

Au passage, La Salle prit possession des territoires qu'il traversait° au nom de la France. Il nomma cette région **Louisiane** en l'honneur du roi Louis XIV. Plus tard, d'autres Français

arrivèrent dans la région. Ils fondèrent **la Nouvelle Orléans** en 1718 et construisirent des forts le long du Mississippi. À cette époque, la Louisiane était un immense territoire puisqu'elle représentait toute la vallée du Mississippi et ses affluents.°

À la suite° de traités, la France dut abandonner la Louisiane. La rive° ouest du Mississippi devint espagnole en 1762 et la rive est devint anglaise en 1763.

En 1800, la France acquit° par traité la partie espagnole. En 1803, Napoléon, qui avait besoin d'argent pour financer ses guerres, la revendit aux États-Unis pour la somme de 15 millions de dollars.

a éclaté *broke out* **entreprendre** *undertake* **traversait** *crossed* **affluents** *tributaries* **à la suite** *as a result* **rive** *shore, bank* **acquit** *acquired*

Notes culturelles

• In 1774, **l'Acte de Québec** allowed French Canadians to retain their religion, institutions and language. French-speaking Catholics were then called **les canayens**.

• **Peter Minuit (1580–1638)** was sent to America by the Dutch West India Company. He bought the island of Manhattan with trinkets worth about $24.

• **Paul Revere (1735–1818)** was a silversmith from Massachusetts who became a messenger for the colonists in 1774. On the night of April 18, 1775, he rode to warn Adams and Hancock that a British army was marching on Concord and Lexington. This heroic ride was immortalized in a poem by Longfellow.

6. Qui sont les Huguenots français?

«Huguenot» était le nom que les Français donnaient aux Protestants au 16e siècle. À cette époque, il y avait des guerres de religion entre Protestants et Catholiques. Les Protestants, très inférieurs en nombre, ont été persécutés et chassés° de France. Beaucoup sont allés en Hollande et en Allemagne. Certains ont immigré en Amérique. Des Huguenots français venus de La Rochelle, France, ont fondé la ville de New Rochelle, New York, en 1688.

Parmi les Américains d'origine huguenote: Peter Minuit qui a acheté Manhattan pour 24 dollars, Paul Revere, patriote et héros de la Révolution américaine, John Jay, premier juge de la Cour Suprême, Louis Tiffany, joaillier de réputation internationale.

Peter Minuit, arrivant à la Nouvelle Amsterdam, aujourd'hui New York.

Paul Revere, patriote américain d'origine française

7. Comment les Français ont-ils aidé les Américains pendant la guerre d'Indépendance?

Quand ils ont déclaré leur indépendance en 1776, les Américains avaient besoin d'aide. Pour obtenir cette aide, ils ont envoyé Benjamin Franklin comme ambassadeur en France. Franklin, qui était très admiré et très respecté des Français, a pleinement réussi dans cette mission. Conseillé par sa femme Marie-Antoinette, le roi de France, Louis XVI, a reconnu° la jeune république des États-Unis en 1778. Mieux, il a décidé d'envoyer sa flotte° et ses meilleures troupes au secours° des «insurgés» américains.

La bataille de Yorktown

La bataille décisive de la guerre d'Indépendance a eu lieu à Yorktown en octobre 1781. D'un côté° il y avait une armée anglaise commandée par Cornwallis. De l'autre côté, il y avait une armée américaine commandée par Washington et une armée française commandée par **Rochambeau.** Pendant que la bataille faisait rage,° la flotte française empêchait° les renforts° anglais d'arriver. Encerclées, les troupes anglaises ont capitulé. Cette victoire franco-américaine a mis fin aux hostilités. Deux ans plus tard, l'Angleterre reconnaissait l'indépendance des États-Unis.

---

chassés *expelled* **reconnu** *recognized* **flotte** *fleet* **au secours** = *pour aider* **côté** *side* **faisait rage** *was raging* **empêchait** *prevented* **renforts** *reinforcements*

- **John Jay (1745–1829)** helped draft the constitution of New York State. He was governor of New York for two terms.
- **Charles Louis Tiffany (1812–1902)** started to manufacture his own jewelry in 1848. He opened a branch of his store in Paris in 1850.
- **Charles Cornwallis (1738–1805)** led the British army in the Yorktown battle. He later became governor of India and Viceroy of Ireland.
- **Jean Baptiste Donatien de Vimeur, Comte de Rochambeau (1725–1807)** landed in Newport R.I. in 1780 with 6,000 French soldiers. Imprisoned in France after the French Revolution, his rank was later restored to him by Napoleon.

■ Notes historiques

- La Fayette landed at North Island, near Charleston, South Carolina. From there he went overland to Philadelphia where he received his commission from the Continental Congress on July 31, 1777.
- It was La Fayette who gave the order to destroy the fortress of **La Bastille** in July 1789 after it was attacked by the people of Paris.
- In 1802, La Fayette helped in finalizing the **Louisiana Purchase.** (He had acquired land in Louisiana.)
  La Fayette refused the post of governor of Louisiana offered to him by the U.S. Congress.
- In 1824, La Fayette returned to the United States where he was greeted as a hero and given land and a pension by the U.S. government.
- **Adrienne de Noailles de La Fayette** was the daughter of the **Duc d'Ayen.** She married La Fayette in 1774.

8. *Qui était La Fayette?*

Une université, de nombreuses écoles, plusieurs villes portent le nom de ce héros de la guerre d'Indépendance américaine. Qui était exactement **La Fayette?**

La Fayette (1757-1834) était un aristocrate français qui appartenait° à l'une des familles les plus illustres du pays. En 1777, il avait seulement vingt ans et il était immensément riche. Un jour, il a entendu parler° de la Révolution américaine. Il a pris contact avec Benjamin Franklin qui était alors l'ambassadeur des États-Unis en France. Après cette entrevue, il a décidé de rejoindre les «insurgés» américains comme volontaire. Malheureusement, le roi de France était tout à fait opposé à cette idée et lui a interdit de partir. Que faire? La Fayette était un jeune homme déterminé avec beaucoup d'imagination … et beaucoup d'argent. Il a quitté la France en secret. Il est allé en Espagne où il a acheté un bateau qu'il a appelé *La Victoire* et il est parti pour les États-Unis.

Après avoir débarqué° en Caroline du Sud, La Fayette est allé à Philadelphie pour offrir ses services au Congrès américain. Le Congrès, impressionné par ses qualités et son enthousiasme, l'a nommé général auprès° de George Washington. Les deux hommes sont immédiatement devenus de grands amis.* En Octobre 1777, La Fayette a pris part à sa première bataille et il a été blessé à la jambe. Peu de temps après, le Congrès, reconnaissant son courage et ses talents militaires, lui a donné le commandement de la division de Virginie.

En 1779, La Fayette est retourné brièvement en France. Sa mission était de plaider la cause américaine et d'obtenir l'aide de la France. Il est allé voir le roi qui cette fois-ci l'a écouté. Quelques temps après, l'armée française est arrivée aux États-Unis. De retour aux États-Unis, La Fayette a rejoint son poste de commandement. À la bataille décisive de Yorktown, en 1781, il était à la tête d'une division américaine dans l'armée de Washington.

Après la guerre d'Indépendance, La Fayette est rentré en France où il a continué à combattre pour la justice et pour les idées nouvelles de liberté et d'égalité. Quand la Révolution française a éclaté en 1789, c'était l'homme le plus populaire de France. C'est lui qui a proposé la déclaration européenne des *Droits de l'homme et du citoyen* et qui a fait accepter le drapeau tricolore comme drapeau national. La Fayette était aussi un membre très actif du Club des Amis des Noirs, un club politique qui voulait l'abolition de l'esclavage° dans les colonies françaises. À cause du rôle important qu'il a joué aux États-Unis d'abord et en France ensuite, on appelle souvent La Fayette «le héros des deux mondes».

La Fayette, héros de la guerre d'Indépendance américaine.

* Plus tard, La Fayette a nommé son fils George Washington La Fayette.

appartenait *belonged to*   **a entendu parler de** *heard about*   **débarqué** *landed*   **auprès de** *on the staff of*   **esclavage** *slavery*

DOCUMENTS | lettre

Une lettre du Marquis de La Fayette à Madame de La Fayette

La Fayette est arrivé aux États-Unis le 13 juin 1777. Quelques jours plus tard, il était à Charleston où il a écrit la lettre suivante à sa jeune femme. Dans cette lettre, il décrit ses premières impressions sur le pays et ses habitants.

Adrienne de Noailles de La Fayette

1777, à Charlestown

... Je vais à présent vous parler du pays, mon cher cœur, et de ses habitants. Ils sont aussi aimables que mon enthousiasme avait pu se le figurer.° La simplicité des manières, le désir d'obliger,° l'amour de la patrie° et de la liberté, une douce° égalité, règnent ici parmi tout le monde. L'homme le plus riche et le plus pauvre sont de niveau,° et quoiqu'il y ait° des fortunes immenses dans ce pays, je défie° de trouver la moindre° différence entre leurs manières respectives les uns pour les autres.

J'ai commencé par la vie de campagne, chez le major Huger; à présent, me voici à la ville. Tout y ressemble assez à la façon anglaise, excepté qu'il y a plus de simplicité chez eux qu'en Angleterre. La ville de Charlestown est une des plus jolies, des mieux bâties° et des plus agréablement peuplées que j'aie jamais vues. Les femmes américaines sont fort jolies, fort simples et d'une propreté° charmante...

Ce qui m'enchante ici, c'est que tous les citoyens sont frères. Il n'y a en Amérique ni pauvres, ni même ce qu'on appelle paysans.° Tous les citoyens ont un bien honnête,° et tous, les mêmes droits° que le plus puissant° propriétaire du pays.

Les auberges sont bien plus différentes d'Europe; le maître et la maîtresse se mettent à table avec vous, font les honneurs d'un bon repas, et en partant vous payez sans marchander.° Quand on ne veut pas aller dans une auberge, on trouve des maisons de campagne où il suffit d'être bon Américain pour être reçu avec les attentions qu'on aurait en Europe pour un ami.

... Il est fort avant° dans la nuit, il fait une chaleur affreuse, et suis dévoré de moucherons° qui vous couvrent de grosses ampoules,° mais les meilleurs pays ont, comme vous voyez, leurs inconvénients.

Adieu mon cœur, adieu.

Lafayette

figurer = imaginer **obliger** = rendre service **patrie** *fatherland* **douce** *gentle* **de niveau** *at the same level* **quoiqu'il y ait** *although they are* **défie** *challenge* **la moindre** = la plus petite **bâties** *built* **propreté** *cleanliness, hygiene* **paysans** *peasants* **un bien honnête** *a property of their own* **droits** *rights* **puissant** *powerful* **marchander** *to bicker over the price* **fort avant** = très tard **moucherons** *gnats* **ampoules** *swellings*

Notes culturelles

- The sentence **«La Fayette, nous voici!»**, while commonly ascribed to General Pershing, was said by Colonel Charles Stanton during an address honoring La Fayette on July 4, 1917 at the French hero's grave in the Picpus cemetery in Paris.
- World War I ended with the armistice signed on November 11, 1918. It was signed in **Rethondes** (France), in the dining-car of a train.
- In 1943, the first French airforce squadron armed by the U.S. took the name of **Escadrille La Fayette.**

9. *Qui a dit «La Fayette, nous voilà!» et à quelle occasion?*

On attribue cette phrase au général américain John Pershing à son arrivée en France en 1917. En rendant hommage à La Fayette, héros français de la guerre d'Indépendance, il voulait réaffirmer l'amitié et la solidarité qui unissaient le peuple français et le peuple américain. Le général Pershing était le commandant du corps expéditionnaire américain en France pendant la Première Guerre Mondiale (1914-1918).

En réalité, les premiers Américains qui sont venus aider la France pendant cette guerre étaient des volontaires incorporés dans l'armée française. Parmi ceux-ci, il y avait les pilotes de la fameuse «Escadrille Lafayette». Il y avait aussi les ambulanciers de l'«American Field Service Ambulance Corps». C'était des lycéens de 17 ans, des étudiants de Yale et de Harvard, ou de simples citoyens venus par idéalisme.

Les États-Unis sont officiellement entrés en guerre aux côtés° de la France et de l'Angleterre en avril 1917. Cette année-là, des centaines de milliers de soldats américains sont venus combattre sur le sol° français. Parmi ces soldats, il y avait un jeune capitaine d'artillerie venu du Missouri, Harry Truman, futur président des États-Unis. C'est grâce à l'intervention des troupes américaines que les Alliés ont finalement pu gagner la guerre en 1918.

Pilotes de l'Escadrille Lafayette. (Remarquez que ces pilotes américains portent des uniformes français.)

10. *Où se trouve Omaha Beach?*

Omaha Beach se trouve en Normandie. C'est sur cette plage et d'autres plages normandes que le plus grand débarquement° de l'histoire a eu lieu le 6 juin 1944. Ce jour-là, 100 000 soldats américains, anglais, canadiens, français, polonais° ont débarqué sur le sol de France occupé par l'Allemagne nazie. Peu après, les armées alliées commandées par le général Eisenhower ont libéré le reste de la France. Près de Omaha Beach il y a un grand cimetière où se trouvent les tombes de 9 385 soldats américains, héros de la libération de la France.

Le 6 juin 1944 les troupes alliées débarquent sur la plage d'Omaha Beach en Normandie

Un GI réconforte un enfant français

aux côtés de *on the side of* **sol** *soil* **débarquement** *landing* **polonais** *Polish*

Teaching Strategy

Divide the class into groups. Ask each group to prepare two <u>new</u> questions and answers on separate pieces of paper based on the material in the answers provided to the **dix questions** posed in this *Interlude*. (Remind students that their questions must be very different from the existing ones!) Collect all questions, shuffle them, and pass them out to the groups. Each group must answer the questions they receive and check against the "Answer Key" provided by the original groups.

Villes américaines — noms français

Un certain nombre de villes américaines portent des noms français. Ces noms rappellent quelques épisodes de la longue histoire franco-américaine.

■ **Duluth** (Minnesota)
Cette ville porte le nom d'un Français, Daniel **du Luth** (1636-1710), explorateur du Lac Supérieur et ami des Indiens de la région.

■ **Fond du Lac** (Wisconsin)
Cette ville est appelée ainsi à cause de sa position à l'extrémité sud du lac Winnebago. Au 18ᵉ siècle, c'était un centre où les Français faisaient le commerce de la fourrure avec les Indiens.

■ **Détroit** (Michigan)
Cette ville a été fondée en 1701 par un explorateur français, Antoine de la **Mothe Cadillac**, futur gouverneur de la Louisiane. À l'origine, la ville s'appelait Fort Pontchartrain du Détroit, en l'honneur du ministre français de la Marine.

■ **Marietta** (Ohio)
En 1788, d'anciens° soldats de la guerre d'Indépendance ont fondé une petite colonie qu'ils ont appelée Marietta, en l'honneur de la reine de France, **Marie-Antoinette**. Dix ans plus tôt, Marie-Antoinette avait convaincu° son mari d'envoyer ses troupes à l'aide des patriotes américains.

■ **Laramie** (Wyoming)
Cette ville porte le nom de Jacques **La Ramie**, un trappeur canadien qui est arrivé dans la région vers 1820. Il a construit une cabane pour stocker ses fourrures. Plus tard, Fort Laramie, bâti sur ce site, a joué un rôle important dans la conquête de l'ouest.

■ **Fremont** (Californie)
Cette ville porte le nom de John Charles **Fremont** (1813-1890), un explorateur américain d'origine française. Fremont a été le premier sénateur de Californie. Il a aussi été gouverneur de l'Arizona et candidat à la présidence des États-Unis.

■ **Louisville** (Kentucky)
Cette ville a été nommée ainsi en 1780 pour remercier le roi de France, Louis XVI, de l'aide française pendant la Révolution américaine.

■ **Bâton Rouge** (Louisiane)
En 1699, une expédition française découvre le site de la ville actuelle.° Les Indiens de la région appellent ce site «Istrouma» expression qui signifie «bâton° rouge». Les Français donnent ce nom au fort qu'ils construisent là quelques années plus tard.

■ **Saint Louis** (Missouri)
René Chouteau, un jeune homme de la Nouvelle Orléans, avait seulement 15 ans quand il a fondé Saint Louis en 1764. Il a nommé la ville en l'honneur de deux rois de France: **Louis XV** et son patron, **Saint Louis**.

■ **Mobile** (Alabama)
Vers 1700, des explorateurs français sont arrivés dans la région. Ils ont construit un fort qu'ils ont appelé Fort Louis de la Mobile: Fort Louis, en l'honneur du roi de France, Louis XIV; de la Mobile, du nom de Mauvile, une tribu indienne de la région.

■ **Vincennes** (Indiana)
Cette ville porte le nom de son fondateur, l'explorateur canadien Jean-Baptiste **Vincennes** (1668-1719). Elle est restée pendant longtemps une ville française. Pendant la guerre d'Indépendance, ses habitants ont aidé les Américains contre les Anglais.

actuelle *present* **bâton** *stick, pole* **anciens** *former* **convaincu** *convinced*

■ Notes historiques
- **Saint Louis, le roi Louis IX** (1226–1270), was known for his integrity and strong faith. He participated in the Crusades and was responsible for the construction of the Sainte-Chapelle, in Paris.
- In 1763, the Treaty of Paris gave all the French territories *east* of the Mississippi to England. This is why Chouteau chose the *west* bank as a site for St. Louis.

Teaching Strategy: Interdisciplinary/Community Connections

Combine classes with an American history teacher to work on a group project. Prepare an illustrated timeline on long sheets of paper, showing events in American history provided by the history students and additional French-related events provided by the French students. Display the final timeline in a hallway for all students to see.

■ **Note culturelle**
On appelle **le Grand Dérangement** l'exode des Acadiens qui refusèrent de prêter serment à la couronne d'Angleterre. À cette époque, des Acadiens choisirent de retourner en France. Après avoir été libres et propriétaires de leurs terres, beaucoup ne purent se réadapter à la société française. En conséquence, Louis XV mis un bateau à leur disposition pour leur permettre de retourner en Amérique, dans la colonie établie sur les bords du Mississippi.

■ **Pour en savoir plus**
The Cajun culture is known in the rest of the United States for its food and its music. See *Interlude 4*, p. 182, where **la musique cajun** and **zydéco** are presented.

■ **Note culturelle**
While the term **Cajun** is widely used throughout the United States, the French-speaking community in Louisiana more commonly uses the term **cadien**.

Les héritiers de la Louisiane française

Des gens d'origine française, venus surtout du Canada, ont été les premiers blancs à occuper la partie centrale de ce qui allait devenir les États-Unis. C'était pour la plupart des soldats, des missionnaires, des trappeurs. Ils construisirent des comptoirs° et des forts dans la vallée du Mississippi. Après la fondation de la Nouvelle Orléans en 1718, une colonie française s'établit en Louisiane. Au cours des années qui suivirent, cette colonie s'enrichit d'éléments nouveaux: d'abord Acadiens venus du Canada, puis Créoles venus des Antilles françaises. Les descendants de ces deux groupes représentent aujourd'hui la quasi-totalité de la population de la Louisiane d'origine française.

La Mothe-Cadillac, explorateur français

Des musiciens cajuns

■ Les Acadiens ou «Cajuns»

Les Acadiens doivent leur nom à leur région d'origine, l'Acadie, ce territoire du Nord-Est canadien représenté aujourd'hui par les provinces du Nouveau Brunswick et de la Nouvelle Écosse.° C'est dans cette région que s'établirent des colons français dès° 1640. Devenus sujets britanniques à la suite° d'un traité° (1713) qui donnait l'Acadie à l'Angleterre, les Acadiens refusèrent de prêter serment° à leur nouveau gouvernement. Pour cet acte de rébellion, toute la population française fut expulsée d'Acadie par l'armée anglaise. Un grand nombre d'Acadiens retournèrent en France. D'autres s'éparpillèrent° dans les territoires français d'Amérique. Un premier contingent de 231 réfugiés arriva en Louisiane en 1765, suivi d'autres groupes de plusieurs milliers de personnes. Leurs descendants et leurs alliés par mariage (Espagnols, Allemands, Indiens) constituent la population «cajun» actuelle. Aujourd'hui cette population habite principalement dans la région des bayous. Les centres cajuns se reconnaissent facilement à leurs noms français: Lafayette, Abbeville, Saint Martinville, Ville Platte, Thibodaux.

■ Les Créoles

Il existe plusieurs définitions du terme *créole*. La définition généralement acceptée s'applique aux descendants des habitants de Saint Domingue (aujourd'hui Haïti), blancs et noirs, venus en Louisiane pendant la Révolution française (1789-1799) et, plus tard, après l'indépendance d'Haïti (1804). Ces créoles s'établirent à la Nouvelle Orléans et dans les plantations à proximité du Mississippi et des bayous. Beaucoup de créoles de la Nouvelle Orléans habitaient le quartier du Vieux Carré° qu'ils quittèrent vers 1910.

comptoirs *trading posts* **Nouvelle Écosse** *Nova Scotia* **dès** *beginning in* **à la suite de** *as the result of* **traité** *treaty*
prêter serment *to pledge allegiance* **s'éparpillèrent** *were scattered* **Carré** *Square*

Teaching Suggestion: DVD Program
Use the Unit 10 *Vignette culturelle: Les Cajuns* to learn more about Cajun culture. Students will be introduced to Zachary Richard, a Cajun singer, and have a chance to hear his music. After viewing the video, ask students about what they think makes Cajun music so different and original.

DOCUMENTS Réveille

Réveille

Réveille,° réveille! . . .
C'est les goddams* qui viennent
brûler° la récolte.°
Réveille, réveille, hommes acadiens
pour sauver le village.

Mon grand-grand-grand-grand-père
est venu de la Bretagne;
le sang de ma famille est mouillé° l'Acadie
et là les maudits* viennent
nous chasser comme des bêtes,
détruire les saintes familles**
nous jeter° tous au vent.
        Réveille, réveille! . . .

J'ai entendu parler
de monter avec Beausoleil***
pour prendre le fusil,°
battre les sacrés° maudits.
J'ai entendu parler°
d'aller en la Louisiane
pour trouver de la bonne paix
là-bas dans la Louisiane.
        Réveille, réveille! . . .

J'ai vu mon pauvre père
qui était fait prisonnier
pendant que ma mère,
ma belle mère braillait.°
J'ai vu ma belle maison
qui était mise aux flammes.
Et moi j'suis resté orphelin.°
Orphelin de l'Acadie.
        Réveille, réveille! . . .

Réveille, réveille! . . .
C'est les goddams* qui viennent
voler° les enfants.
Réveille, réveille, hommes acadiens
pour sauver l'héritage.

Zachary Richard

Zachary Richard est un poète et chanteur cajun. Dans cette chanson célèbre, il évoque un événement historique important: l'attaque des Acadiens par les Anglais et leur expulsion. La sonnerie de clairon° «Réveille, réveille» alerte la population que les soldats anglais arrivent.

* **les goddams; les maudits** (*cursed ones*): Terme qui désigne les soldats anglais.
** **Les saintes familles:** Les familles acadiennes françaises étaient catholiques. Massacrées par les soldats protestants anglais, elles sont devenues martyres.
*** **Beausoleil:** Capitaine, héros de la Résistance acadienne contre les Anglais.

---

sonnerie de clairon *bugle call* **réveille** *wake up* **brûler** *to burn* **récolte** *crops* **mouillé** *soaked (in)* **jeter** *to throw*
fusil *rifle* **sacrés** *«cursed»* **entendu parler** *heard about* **braillait** *was crying and screaming* **orphelin** *orphan* **voler** *to steal*

quatre cent dix-neuf **419**
Interlude culturel

■ **Notes culturelles**

Quelques créoles célèbres

D'ORIGINE EUROPÉENNE

- **John James Audubon** (1780–1851), né à Haïti, peintre de la célèbre série *Les Oiseaux d'Amérique*.
- **P.G.T. Beauregard** (1818–1893), important général sudiste pendant la Guerre de Sécession.

D'ORIGINE AFRICAINE

- **Homer Plessy** (1862–1925) était issu d'une des nombreuses familles francophones d'origine africaine de la Nouvelle Orléans. En 1890, il fut arrêté pour être monté dans un wagon réservé aux Blancs. Son cas fut plaidé devant la Cour Suprême des États-Unis. La décision célèbre «Plessy contre Ferguson» (1896) est à l'origine de la doctrine raciste de «séparés mais égaux».
- **Sidney Béchet** (1897–1959), était l'un des plus grands musiciens de jazz, style Nouvelle Orléans.

■ **Note linguistiques**

- Le mot créole désigne également la langue parlée aux Antilles, en Louisiane et dans les îles Maurice et de la Réunion.

Standard French equivalents:

- «mon grand-grand-grand-grand-père» = mon arrière-arrière-arrière-grand-père
- «j'ai vu mon pauvre père qui était fait prisonnier» = j'ai vu que mon pauvre père était fait prisonnier

Teaching Strategy

There are many recordings of Cajun music available. You or your students may wish to play these for the class. Zachary Richard's own recordings of "Réveille" are powerful and moving; they may help students to appreciate the written form of the poem more easily.

Le drapeau acadien

Les différents éléments du drapeau des Acadiens de Louisiane rappellent l'histoire du peuple cajun.

Les fleurs de lys sur fond bleu étaient l'emblème des rois de France. Elles représentent l'héritage français des cajuns et leur langue.

La tour jaune sur fond rouge était l'emblème des rois d'Espagne. Quand les premiers Acadiens sont arrivés en Louisiane, celle-ci était devenue espagnole. Cette partie du drapeau rappelle l'hospitalité du gouverneur espagnol.

Le blanc était la couleur de l'ancienne Acadie. Le triangle de cette couleur rappelle l'origine canadienne des Cajuns. L'étoile jaune est un double symbole. Elle représente la dévotion des Acadiens à la Vierge Marie, leur sainte patronne. Elle symbolise aussi le patriotisme des premiers Acadiens et leur participation comme volontaires à la Guerre d'indépendance (1775-1783). À peine arrivés en Louisiane, ils se sont ralliés à la cause américaine. Organisés en milices, ils ont combattu victorieusement contre les Anglais.

Notes culturelles

- Après être restée longtemps française, la Louisiane (côté ouest du Mississippi) est devenue espagnole par le Traité de Fontainebleu de 1762.

- Les milices acadiennes furent créées par le gouverneur espagnol de la Louisiane, Bernardo de Galvez, après qui la ville de Galveston, Texas, est nommée.

Tête à tête Pair Activities

CONTENTS

UNITÉ 1	La rentrée	PA2
UNITÉ 2	Travaux domestiques	PA3
UNITÉ 3	Cambriolage	PA4
UNITÉ 4	Les courses	PA5
UNITÉ 5	À l'agence de voyage	PA6
UNITÉ 6	Vacances	PA7
UNITÉ 7	Chez le médecin	PA8
UNITÉ 8	Rendez-vous parisien	PA9
UNITÉ 9	Marie Curie	PA10
UNITÉ 10	Choix professionnels	PA11

Teaching Note

All of the Tête à tête activities are done in pairs as **Élève A** and **Élève B**. Quickly divide the class into **Élève A** and **Élève B** by going around the classroom and counting off: A...B...A...B. Then, have the "A" students pair up with the nearest "B" students. Instruct students to turn their books upside down in order to begin the activity.

La rentrée — Élève A

Partie 1

Il y a deux nouveaux professeurs à l'école: Mademoiselle Bertin et Monsieur Moreau.

▶ Faites une description détaillée de chaque personne:

- le visage
- les cheveux
- les yeux
- le nez
- la bouche
- le(s) signe(s) particulier(s)

Votre partenaire va dessiner un portrait de ces deux personnes sur la base de vos informations.

 Mlle Bertin

 M. Moreau

Partie 2

Maintenant c'est à votre tour de dessiner. Prenez une feuille de papier. Écoutez bien la description physique de deux autres professeurs, Madame Dubois et de Monsieur Mercier. Dessinez leurs portraits sur la base des informations données par votre partenaire.

Mme Dubois ¿

M. Mercier ¿

La rentrée — Élève B

Partie 1

Il y a deux nouveaux professeurs à l'école: Madame Dubois et Monsieur Mercier. Prenez une feuille de papier. Écoutez bien la description physique de ces personnes faite par votre partenaire. Dessinez leurs portraits sur la base des informations qu'il/elle vous donne.

Partie 2

Maintenant c'est à votre tour de faire la description de deux autres professeurs: Madame Dubois et Monsieur Mercier.

▶ Faites une description détaillée de chaque personne:

- le visage
- les cheveux
- les yeux
- le nez
- la bouche
- le(s) signe(s) particulier(s)

Votre partenaire va dessiner un portrait de ces deux personnes sur la base de vos informations.

? Mlle Bertin

? M. Moreau

 Mme Dubois

 M. Mercier

---

■ Teaching tip

Have students review PHYSICAL DESCRIPTION VOCABULARY by referring them to pp. 36–37 in the textbook. Alternately, you can use **Projectable Transparencies** 12, 14, and 14(o) to review this vocabulary.

■ Answers

Élève A:

Mlle Bertin:
Mlle Bertin a le visage ovale. Elle est blonde et elle a les cheveux frisés et assez longs. Elle a les yeux bleus. Elle porte du rouge à lèvres. Elle a des boucles d'oreilles et un collier.

M. Moreau:
M. Moreau a le visage rectangulaire. Il est brun avec les cheveux courts et un peu frisés. Il porte des lunettes, et il a les yeux noirs. Il a aussi une moustache

Élève B:

Mme Dubois:
Mme Dubois a le visage ovale. Elle a les cheveux châtain clair. Elle a les cheveux courts et lisses. Elle a les yeux marron. Elle porte du rouge à lèvres. Elle a des boucles d'oreilles. Elle a un grain de beauté.

M. Mercier:
M. Mercier a le visage triangulaire. Il est blond avec les cheveux courts et en brosse. Il a les yeux noirs, et il a une cicatrice.

Tête à tête PA3

Travaux domestiques

Élève A

Vous travaillez à la maison et dans le jardin.

▶ Choisissez six petits travaux domestiques et demandez à votre partenaire de vous aider avec chaque tâche *(task)*.

Il/elle accepte et vous demande où trouver l'objet nécessaire à chaque tâche. Répondez-lui.

Élève A: Est-ce que tu peux essuyer la table?

Élève B: D'accord! (Volontiers!) Où est l'éponge?

Élève A: Je crois que l'éponge est dans la cuisine (sous l'évier, ...)

- ☐ essuyer la table
- ☐ couper le pain
- ☐ éplucher les pommes
- ☐ repasser la nappe *(tablecloth)*
- ☐ passer l'aspirateur dans le salon
- ☐ laver la voiture
- ☐ tailler les arbustes
- ☐ arroser les plantes
- ☐ tondre la pelouse
- ☐ balayer le garage
- ☐ nettoyer la salle à manger

TÊTE À TÊTE

Travaux domestiques

Élève B

Votre partenaire vous demande de l'aider dans certains petits travaux domestiques.

▶ Acceptez et demandez-lui où est l'objet nécessaire pour accomplir chaque tâche *(task)*

Il/elle vous va vous dire où trouver l'objet.

Élève A: Est-ce que tu peux essuyer la table?

Élève B: D'accord! (Volontiers!) Où est l'éponge?

Élève A: Je crois que l'éponge est dans la cuisine (sous l'évier, ...)

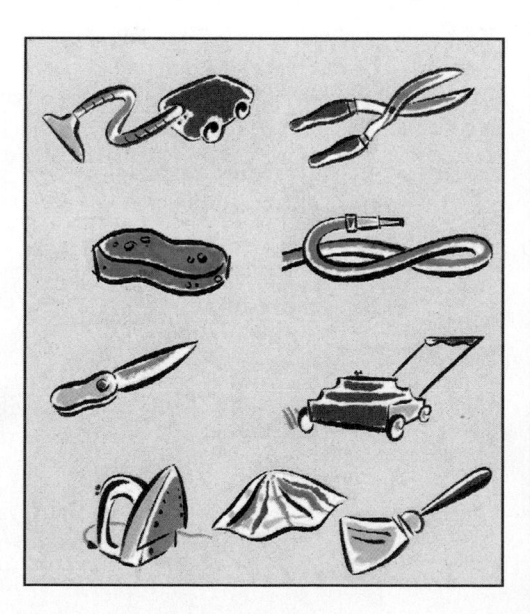

■ Teaching tip

Have students review HOUSEWORK VOCABULARY by referring them to pp. 74–75, and 77 in the textbook. Alternately, you can use

Projectable Transparencies 19 and 19(o) to review this vocabulary.

■ Sample answers

A: Est-ce que tu peux …?
B: D'accord! (Volontiers!) Où est …?
A: Je crois … est …

- essuyer la table/l'éponge
- couper le pain/le couteau
- éplucher les pommes/le couteau
- repasser la nappe/le fer à repasser
- passer l'aspirateur dans le salon/ l'aspirateur
- laver la voiture/le tuyau d'arrosage (l'éponge)
- tailler les arbustes/le sécateur
- arroser les plantes/le tuyau d'arrosage
- tondre la pelouse/la tondeuse
- balayer le garage/le balai
- nettoyer la salle à manger/ le chiffon

■ Teaching tip

Have students review the IMPERFECT by referring them to p. 116 in the textbook.

■ Sample answers

A: Il était trois heures.

B: C'est faux! Il était presque quatre heures et demie.

B: Il y avait une vieille femme qui regardait par la fenêtre.

A: C'est faux! Il y avait un homme qui regardait par la fenêtre.

A: Il pleuvait.

B: C'est vrai.

B: La cambrioleuse sautait de la fenêtre avec l'argent.

A: C'est faux! La cambrioleuse était assise sur la moto. Elle attendait le cambrioleur qui avait l'argent.

A: La cambrioleuse avait les cheveux blonds.

B: C'est faux! La cambrioleuse était rousse.

B: Le cambrioleur portait une casque.

A: C'est faux! Le cambrioleur portait une casquette.

Cambriolage — **Élève B**

Vous avez été témoin d'un cambriolage *(burglary)* avec votre partenaire, mais vos souvenirs *(memories)* de l'accident sont différents. Chacun à son tour va décrire six (6) détails de l'événement d'après l'illustration qu'il a. Si vous n'êtes pas d'accord avec votre partenaire, rectifiez sa description.

Élève A: Il y avait deux voitures dans la rue.

Élève B: C'est vrai.

Élève B: La première voiture était jaune.

Élève A: C'est faux! Elle était bleue.

— **Cambriolage** — **Élève A** —

Vous avez été témoin d'un cambriolage *(burglary)* avec votre partenaire, mais vos souvenirs *(memories)* de l'accident sont différents. Chacun à son tour va décrire six (6) détails de l'événement d'après l'illustration qu'il a. Si vous n'êtes pas d'accord avec votre partenaire, rectifiez sa description.

Élève A: Il y avait deux voitures dans la rue.

Élève B: C'est vrai.

Élève B: La première voiture était jaune.

Élève A: C'est faux! Elle était bleue.

Élève B — Les courses

Cet après-midi, vous allez faire les courses dans les magasins sur votre liste des courses.

Partie 1

Dites à votre partenaire dans quels magasins vous allez aller. Pour chaque magasin, demandez-lui si vous pouvez acheter quelque chose pour lui/elle. Écoutez bien sa réponse. Puis, inscrivez sa requête dans une liste des courses comme celle à droite. (Utilisez une autre feuille de papier.)

Élève B: Je vais passer à la pharmacie.
Qu'est-ce que je peux acheter pour toi?

Élève A: Achète-moi deux boîtes de coton-tiges, s'il te plaît.

Partie 2

Maintenant vérifiez votre liste.

Élève B: À la pharmacie je vais acheter deux boîtes de coton-tiges.

Élève A: Oui, c'est ça. (Non, je voulais…)

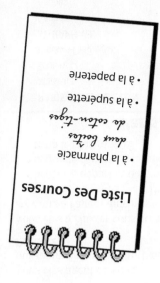

Liste Des Courses

• à la pharmacie
  ~~deux boîtes de coton-tiges~~
• à la supérette
• à la papeterie

Élève A — Les courses

Vous avez besoin des produits suivants. Pour chaque produit, déterminez une certaine quantité (par exemple, deux boîtes de coton-tiges). Indiquez ces quantités sur une autre feuille de papier.

Partie 1

Votre partenaire va faire les courses cet après-midi et vous dit dans quels magasins il/elle va passer. Demandez-lui d'acheter les produits qui figurent sur votre liste.

Élève B: Je vais passer à la pharmacie. Qu'est-ce que je peux acheter pour toi?

Élève A: Achète-moi deux boîtes de coton-tiges, s'il te plaît.

Partie 2

Maintenant votre partenaire va vérifier sa liste.

Élève B: À la pharmacie je vais acheter deux boîtes de coton-tiges

Élève A: Oui, c'est ça. (Non, je voulais…)

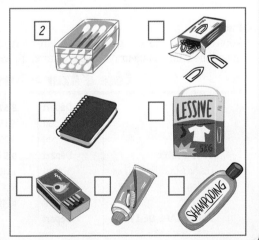

TÊTE À TÊTE

■ Teaching tip

Have students review SHOPPING VOCABULARY by referring them to pp. 152–153 in the textbook. Alternately, you can use **Projectable Transparencies** 28–31 to review this vocabulary.

■ Sample answers
Partie 1

B: Je vais passer … Qu'est-ce que je peux acheter pour toi?

A: Achète-moi …, s'il te plaît.

• à la pharmacie/une bouteille de shampooing (une boîte de coton-tiges), (une tube de dentifrice)
• à la supérette/un paquet de lessive (une boîte d'allumettes)
• à la papeterie/un carnet (une boîte de trombones)

Partie 2

B: À la pharmacie (supérette/papeterie)

A: Oui, c'est ça. (Non, je voulais …)

UNITÉ 5 Pair Activity

Élève B — À l'agence de voyage

Partie 1

Vous êtes agent de voyage. Voici l'horaire du train TGV Paris - Côte d'Azur. Répondez aux questions d'un voyageur (votre partenaire) qui veut aller de Paris à Nice.

Paris / Ile de France > Côte d'Azur

PARIS-GARE-DE-LYON	Départ	11.12	13.49	22.30
Marseille	Arrivée			
Toulon	Arrivée	5.00		
Les Arcs-Draguignan	Arrivée		19.21	
ST-RAPHAEL	Arrivée	16.47	19.39	5.48
Cannes	Arrivée	17.13	20.04	6.14
Antibes	Arrivée	17.26	20.17	6.25
NICE	Arrivée	17.43	20.33	6.44

Partie 2

Vous êtes à Nice et vous voulez aller à Paris en train TGV. Demandez les renseignements suivants à l'agent de voyage (votre partenaire).

- nombre de trains pour Paris?
- heure de départ et d'arrivée du premier train?
- heure de départ du dernier train?
- train le plus rapide?

À l'agence de voyage — Élève A

Partie 1

Vous êtes à Paris et vous voulez aller à Nice en train TGV. Demandez les renseignements suivants à l'agent de voyage (votre partenaire).

- nombre de trains pour Nice?
- heure de départ et d'arrivée du premier train?
- heure de départ du dernier train?
- train le plus rapide?

Partie 2

Vous êtes agent de voyage. Voici l'horaire du train TGV Côte d'Azur - Paris. Répondez aux questions d'un voyageur (votre partenaire) qui veut aller de Nice à Paris.

Côte d'Azur > Paris / Ile de France

NICE	Départ	8.57	9.45	12.16	21.58
Antibes	Départ	9.13	10.01	12.36	22.12
Cannes	Départ	9.25	10.14	12.49	22.24
ST-RAPHAEL	Départ	9.51	10.39	13.14	22.50
Les Arcs-Draguignan	Départ	10.10		13.32	
Toulon	Départ	10.47			23.46
Marseille	Départ	10.40			
PARIS-GARE-DE-LYON	Départ		16.25	19.22	6.46

■ Teaching tip

Have students review TRAVEL VOCABULARY by referring them to pp. 196–198 in the textbook. Alternately, you can use **Projectable Transparancies** 36 and 37 to review this vocabulary.

■ Answers

Partie 1

A: Combien de trains y a-t-il pour Nice?
B: Il y a trois trains pour Nice.

A: À quelle heure est le départ et l'arrivée du premier train?
B: L'heure de départ du premier train est 11h12. L'heure de l'arrivée du premier train est 17h43.

A: À quelle heure est le départ du dernier train?
B: L'heure de départ du dernier train est 22h30.

A: Quel est le train le plus rapide?
B: Le train qui part à 11h12 est le plus rapide.

Partie 2

B: Combien de trains y a-t-il pour Paris?
A: Il y a trois trains pour Paris.

B: À quelle heure est le départ et l'arrivée du premier train?
A: L'heure de départ du premier train est 9h45. L'heure de l'arrivée du premier train est 16h25.

B: À quelle heure est le départ du dernier train?
A: L'heure de départ du dernier train est 21h58.

B: Quel est le train le plus rapide?
A: Le train qui part à 9h45 est le plus rapide.

Vacances — Élève B

Partie 2

Vous voulez passer une semaine dans un petit hôtel: "L'auberge du moulin". Avant de faire votre réservation, vous téléphonez au (à la) réceptionniste — votre partenaire — pour obtenir les renseignements (*information*) suivants.

- **Nombre de chambres?**
- **Prix des chambres?**
- **Prix du petit déjeuner?**
- **Téléphone et télévision?**
- **Piscine et salle d'exercice?**
- **Ascenseur et air conditionné?**

Partie 1

Vous êtes le/la réceptionniste à l'hôtel "Relais Soleil". Répondez à votre client(e) — votre partenaire — qui voudrait quelques renseignements.

Relais Soleil

32 chambres: de 110 € à 180 €
5 suites: de 200 € à 250 €
petit déjeuner complet: 9 €
menus: 28 € et 42 €

Élève A: Quel est le prix des chambres?
Élève B: Les prix vont de 110 € à 180 €
par jour.

Vacances — Élève A

Partie 1

Vous voulez passer une semaine à l'hôtel de luxe "Relais Soleil". Avant de faire votre réservation, vous téléphonez au (à la) réceptionniste — votre partenaire — pour obtenir les renseignements (*information*) suivants.

- **Prix des chambres?**
- **Prix du petit déjeuner?**
- **Prix des repas?**
- **Service en chambre?**
- **Éléments de confort?**
- **Possibilités de faire du sport?**

Élève A: Quel est le prix des chambres?
Élève B: Les prix vont de 110 € à 180 €
par jour.

Partie 2

Vous êtes le/la réceptionniste à "L'auberge du Moulin." Répondez à votre client(e) — votre partenaire — qui voudrait quelques renseignements.

AUBERGE DU MOULIN

12 chambres: de 50 à 100 €
petit déjeuner: 6,50 €
menus: 20 et 30€

■ **Teaching tip**
Have students review HOTEL VOCABULARY by referring them to pp. 230–231 in the textbook. Alternately, you can use **Projectable Transparencies** 39–42 to review this vocabulary.

■ **Answers**
Partie 1
A: Quel est le prix du petit déjeuner?
B: Le prix du petit déjeuner complet est 9 €.
A: Quel est le prix des repas?
B: Les menus vont de 28 à 42 €.
A: Est-ce qu'il y a le service en chambre?
B: Oui, il y a le service en chambre.
A: Quels sont les éléments de confort?
B: Il y a la climatisation, l'air conditionné, la télévision, le service en chambre, un ascenseur, une piscine et une salle d'exercices.
A: Est-ce qu'on peut faire du sport?
B: Oui, on peut jouer au tennis, nager (faire de la natation) et faire du vélo dans la salle d'exercice.

Partie 2
B: Combien de chambres est-ce qu'il y a?
A: Il y a 12 chambres.
B: Quel est le prix des chambres?
A: Les prix vont de 50 à 100 €.
B: Quel est le prix du petit déjeuner?
A: Le prix du petit déjeuner est 6,50 €.
B: Est-ce qu'il y a le téléphone et la télévision?
A: Oui, il y a le téléphone et la télévision.
B: Est-ce qu'il y a une piscine et une salle d'exercice?
A: Il y a une piscine, mais il n'y a pas de salle d'exercice.
B: Est-ce qu'il y a un ascenseur et l'air conditionné (la climatisation)?
A: Il y a l'air conditionné (la climatisation), mais il n'y a pas d'ascenseur.

UNITÉ 7 Pair Activity

■ Teaching tip

Have students review MEDICAL VOCABULARY by referring them to pp. 264–266 in the textbook. Alternately, you can use **Projectable Transparencies** 43 and 45–46 to review this vocabulary.

■ Sample answers

B: Comment allez-vous?
A: Je ne me sens pas bien.
B: Où avez-vous mal?
A: J'ai mal au dos.
B: Qu'est-ce qui s'est passé?
A: Je faisais du snowboard, quand tout à coup j'ai glissé sur la glace et je suis tombé(e).
B: Je vais vous faire une radio. En plus, prenez de l'aspirine toutes les 4 heures. Vous devez aussi vous reposer et surtout ne faites pas de snowboard!

Chez le médecin ————————— Élève B

Vous êtes médecin (ou dentiste)

Vous examinez un(e) patient(e) — votre partenaire.

Faites un diagnostic en complétant la conversation suivante. Puis, proposez un traitement, en vous inspirant des suggestions à droite.

- Ask how your patient feels.
- Ask where it hurts.
- Ask what happened to him/her.
- Tell him/her what you are going to do.

- prendre la température
- faire une radio
- faire une piqûre
- donner des médicaments
- donner un antibiotique
- faire un pansement
- faire un plâtre

****

- faire un plombage
- enlever une dent

Chez le médecin ————————————— Élève A

Vous allez chez le médecin (ou le dentiste). Choisissez l'un des problèmes suggérés par les illustrations. Écoutez le médecin — votre partenaire — et répondez à ses questions.

- Tell the doctor how you feel.
  Je me sens ...
  (Je ne me sens pas ...)

- Tell the doctor where it hurts.
  J'ai mal ...

- Tell the doctor what happened.
  (Use your imagination.)
  Je suis tombé(e) d'un arbre et je me suis fracturé ...

Rendez-vous parisien — Élève A

Votre partenaire visite Paris. Il/elle loge à l'hôtel d'Angleterre situé rue Jacob — "X" sur le plan *(street map)* à droite.

- Choisissez un des cafés marqués 1, 2 ou 3.
- Donnez-lui rendez-vous dans ce café et expliquez-lui en détail comment y aller à pied.

Voici le début du dialogue:

Élève A: Est-ce que tu veux prendre un pot avec moi dans mon café préféré?

Élève B: Oui, bien sûr, comment est-ce que je vais là-bas?

Élève A: Tu sors de l'hôtel et tu tournes à droite dans la rue Jacob.

Élève B: D'accord, je tourne à droite dans la rue Jacob. Et après?

Élève A: ...

À la fin, votre partenaire va confirmer votre rendez-vous.

Tête à tête PA9

Rendez-vous parisien — Élève B

Vous êtes à Paris à l'hôtel d'Angleterre situé rue Jacob — "X" sur le plan *(street map)* à droite. Votre partenaire vous donne rendez-vous dans un café.

- Demandez-lui comment y aller.
- Suivez ses instructions sur le plan.

Voici le début du dialogue:

Élève A: Est-ce que tu veux prendre un pot avec moi dans mon café préféré?

Élève B: Oui, bien sûr, comment est-ce que je vais là-bas?

Élève A: Tu sors de l'hôtel et tu tournes à droite dans la rue Jacob.

Élève B: D'accord, je tourne à droite dans la rue Jacob. Et après?

Élève A: ...

Avez-vous trouvé le café de votre partenaire? Confirmez votre rendez-vous avec lui.

Élève B: Est-ce que c'est le café qui se trouve en face de (à côté de, sur) ...?

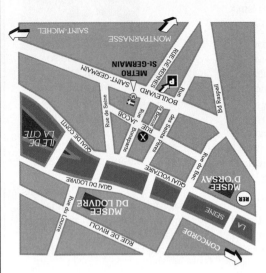

■ Teaching tip
Have students review MEETING DOWNTOWN VOCABULARY by referring them to pp. 306–307 in the textbook. Alternately, you can use **Projectable Transparency** 47 to review this vocabulary. You may also wish to show **Projectable Transparency** 49 so students can see another city map before doing this activity.

■ Sample answers

A: Est-ce que tu veux prendre un pot avec moi dans mon café préféré?

B: Oui, bien sûr, comment est-ce que je vais là-bas?

A: Tu sors de l'hôtel et tu tournes à gauche dans la rue Jacob.

B: D'accord, je tourne à gauche dans la rue Jacob. Et après?

A: Tu tournes à gauche encore dans la rue de Seine.

B: D'accord. Et après ça?

A: Tu continues dans la rue de Seine et puis tu tournes à droite dans le quai de Conti.

B: Très bien—c'est tout?

A: Non! Il faut continuer un tout petit peu dans le quai de Conti et puis tu vas tourner à gauche dans la première rue à gauche.

B: D'accord. Est-ce que c'est le café qui est situé sur l'Île de la Cité?

A: Oui, c'est ça!

Teaching Note

In preparation for this activity, model the pronunciation of the names of the places and streets on the map. Also, review vocabulary such as:

traverser (la rue, la Seine)
continuer tout droit
prendre le pont

After the conversation, have students change roles for a second conversation.

Élève B

Partie 2

Voici la continuation de la biographie de Marie Curie. Lisez le texte deux fois: d'abord en silence, ensuite à haute voix pour votre partenaire.

> Dans leur laboratoire, Pierre et Marie Curie ont travaillé sur les phénomènes de la radioactivité. Dans leurs recherches, ils ont découvert deux éléments nouveaux: le polonium et le radium. Pour ces travaux, ils ont reçu le Prix Nobel de Physique en 1903.
>
> Malheureusement Pierre Curie est mort dans un accident. Marie a continué ses travaux. En 1911, elle a reçu le Prix Nobel de Chimie. Les recherches de Marie Curie sur les rayons-X ont permis les progrès de la médecine moderne. Marie Curie est morte en 1934.

Puis, répondez à ses questions.

Élève B: Quand est née Marie Curie?
Élève A: Elle est née en 1867.

Partie 1

Votre partenaire va vous lire la biographie de Marie Curie, génie scientifique du 20ᵉ siècle. Écoutez bien et prenez des notes sur les sujets suivants:

- date de naissance
- nationalité d'origine
- date de son arrivée à Paris
- nom du mari
- nom de leur fille

Si c'est nécessaire, posez des questions à votre partenaire. Puis écrivez un paragraphe basé sur vos notes.

Marie Curie — Élève A

Partie 1

Voici une courte biographie de Marie Curie, génie scientifique du 20ᵉ siècle. Lisez le texte deux fois: d'abord en silence, ensuite à haute voix pour votre partenaire.

> Marie Curie était d'origine polonaise. Elle est née à Varsovie en 1867. Au lycée, c'était une élève brillante. À l'âge de 16 ans, elle a obtenu son diplôme. Puis elle a travaillé dans un laboratoire de physique expérimentale.
>
> Après quelques années, elle a décidé de continuer ses études scientifiques en France. En 1891, elle a quitté la Pologne, son pays natal. Elle est arrivée à Paris et elle s'est inscrite à l'université.
>
> Là, elle a rencontré un jeune professeur de physique et de chimie. Il s'appelait Pierre Curie. Ils se sont mariés en 1895 et ils ont eu une petite fille, nommée Irène.

Puis, répondez à ses questions.

Élève B: Quand est née Marie Curie?
Élève A: Elle est née en 1867.

Partie 2

Maintenant votre partenaire va continuer la biographie. Écoutez bien et prenez des notes sur les sujets suivants:

- découvertes scientifiques
- première distinction
- événement tragique
- deuxième distinction
- date de la mort

Si c'est nécessaire, posez des questions à votre partenaire. Puis écrivez un paragraphe basé sur vos notes.

Teaching tip

Have students review PHASES OF LIFE VOCABULARY by referring them to p. 360 in the textbook. Alternately, you can use **Projectable Transparency** 51 to review this vocabulary.

Answers

Partie 1

B: Quelle est la nationalité d'origine de Marie Curie?

A: Marie Curie était d'origine polonaise.

B: Quand est-ce qu'elle est arrivée à Paris?

A: Elle est arrivée à Paris en 1891.

B: Comment s'appelait son mari?

A: Son mari s'appelait Pierre Curie.

B: Comment s'appelait leur fille?

A: Leur fille s'appelait Irène.

Partie 2

A: Quelles étaient les découvertes scientifiques de Marie Curie?

B: Pierre et Marie ont travaillé sur les phénomènes de la radioactivité. Ils ont découvert le polonium et le radium—deux éléments nouveaux.

A: Quelle a été sa première distinction?

B: Pierre et Marie ont reçu le Prix Nobel de Physique en 1903.

A: Quel événement tragique a eu lieu dans la vie de Marie Curie?

B: Son mari, Pierre, est mort dans un accident.

A: Quelle a été sa deuxième distinction?

B: Marie a reçu le Prix Nobel de Chimie en 1911.

A: Quand est-ce que Marie Curie est morte?

B: Marie Curie est morte en 1934.

Élève B

Choix professionnels

Vous êtes conseiller(conseillère) professionnel(le).

- Votre client — votre partenaire — va vous indiquer quatre de ses préférences personnelles.
- Pour chaque option, suggérez deux (2) professions qui correspondent à cette préférence.

Élève A: Moi, je préfère [travailler seul(e)].

Élève B: Alors, vous pouvez être [écrivain ou chercheur (chercheuse).]

Élève A: Mais j'aime aussi ...

Élève B: Dans ce cas, vous pouvez devenir ...

- acteur (actrice)
- assistant(e) social(e)
- banquier (banquière)
- chercheur (chercheuse)
- chimiste
- cinéaste
- dessinateur (dessinatrice)
- diplomate
- écrivain
- fonctionnaire
- homme (femme) d'affaires
- infirmier (infirmière)
- journaliste
- médecin
- photographe
- professeur
- représentant(e) de commerce
- secrétaire
- steward (hôtesse de l'air)
- vendeur (vendeuse)

Choix professionnels ──────────────── Élève A

Vous voulez avoir une profession qui corresponde à vos préférences personnelles.

- Choisissez une option dans quatre (4) des catégories suivantes.
- Indiquez votre première préférence à votre conseiller(conseillère) professionnel(le) — votre partenaire — et demandez-lui quelle profession vous convient.
- Il/elle vous donnera deux possibilités.
- Continuez, en lui indiquant les trois autres préférences.

D'après vous, quelle est la meilleure suggestion?

1 ☐ **voyager**		ou	☐	**rester à la maison**
2 ☐ **gagner beaucoup d'argent**		ou	☐	**avoir une vie de famille**
3 ☐ **avoir beaucoup de responsabilités**		ou	☐	**être indépendant(e)**
4 ☐ **avoir une profession artistique**		ou	☐	**avoir une profession scientifique**
5 ☐ **travailler beaucoup**		ou	☐	**avoir des vacances**
6 ☐ **travailler seul(e)**		ou	☐	**travailler avec d'autres**

Élève A: Moi, je préfère [travailler seul(e)].

Élève B: Alors, vous pouvez être [écrivain ou chercheur (chercheuse).]

Élève A: Mais j'aime aussi ...

Élève B: Dans ce cas, vous pouvez devenir ...

■ **Teaching tip**

Have students review PROFESSIONAL VOCABULARY by referring them to pp. 386–387 in the textbook. Alternately, you can use **Projectable Transparencies** 52–53 to review this vocabulary.

■ **Sample answers**

A: Moi, je préfère avoir une profession artistique.

B: Alors, vous pouvez être photographe ou dessinatrice (dessinateur).

A: Mais j'aime aussi gagner beaucoup d'argent.

B: Dans ce cas, vous pouvez devenir femme (homme) d'affaires ou médecin.

Reference Section

CONTENTS

APPENDIX A Reprise   R2–5

    1. Verbes   R2
      A. Le présent   R2
        Les verbes réguliers   R2
        Le verbe **sortir**   R2
        Les verbes **vouloir, pouvoir,** et **devoir**   R2
        Les verbes **prendre** et **mettre**   R2
        Les verbes **être, avoir, aller, faire** et **venir** R3
      B. Le passé composé   R4
        Le passé composé avec **avoir**   R4
        Le passé composé avec **être**   R4
      C. L'imparfait   R5
      D. Passé composé ou imparfait?   R5

    2. Langue et communication   R6–R8
      A. Les articles   R6
      B. Les adjectifs irréguliers   R7
      C. Les noms irréguliers   R7
      D. Les pronoms compléments d'objet   R8
      E. Connaître ou savoir?   R8

    3. Vocabulaire   R10–R15
      A. Les nombres et les dates   R10
        Les nombres cardinaux   R10
        Les nombres ordinaux   R10
      B. La nourriture et les boissons   R11
      C. Les parties du corps   R12
      D. Les vêtements et les accessoires   R13
      E. Les pays   R14
        Les continents et les pays du monde   R14
        Les articles et les prépositions avec les noms des pays R15

APPENDIX B Sound-Spelling Correspondence   R16

APPENDIX C Verbs   R18
    1. Regular verbs   R18
    2. Verbs with spelling changes   R20
    3. Auxiliary forms   R22
    4. Irregular verbs   R22
    5. Passé simple   R32

APPENDIX D Maps   R34
    1. La France   R34
    2. Paris   R35
    3. Le monde francophone   R36

Vocabulaire   R38
    1. Français/Anglais   R38
    2. Anglais/Français   R59

Index   R70

Credits   R74

R1

APPENDIX A: REPRISE

1 Verbes

A. *Le présént* ·

Révision Appendix C, pp. R20–21
present tense of stem-changing verbs

Verbes réguliers

	parler	**-er**	finir	**-ir**	vendre	**-re**
STEM	**parl-**		**fini-**		**vend-**	
je	**parle**	-e	**finis**	-is	**vends**	-s
tu	**parles**	-es	**finis**	-is	**vends**	-s
il/elle/on	**parle**	-e	**finit**	-it	**vend**	—
nous	**parlons**	-ons	**finissons**	-issons	**vendons**	-ons
vous	**parlez**	-ez	**finissez**	-issez	**vendez**	-ez
ils/elles	**parlent**	-ent	**finissent**	-issent	**vendent**	-ent

NEGATIVE	INTERROGATIVE	
je **ne parle pas**	**est-ce qu'**il/elle **parle?**	**parle-t**-il/elle?
je **ne finis pas**	**est-ce qu'**il/elle **finit?**	**finit**-il/elle?
je **ne vends pas**	**est-ce qu'**il/elle **vend?**	**vend**-il/elle?

Le verbe **sortir** *(to go out)*

STEM	**sor-**		**sort-**	
	je	**sors**	nous	**sortons**
	tu	**sors**	vous	**sortez**
	il/elle/on	**sort**	ils/elles	**sortent**

┌─ Verbes comme **sortir** ─────────┐
partir	*to leave*	**je pars**	**nous partons**
dormir	*to sleep*	**je dors**	**nous dormons**
servir	*to serve*	**je sers**	**nous servons**

Les verbes **vouloir** *(want, wish),* **pouvoir** *(can, be able)* **et devoir** *(must, have to)*

	vouloir	**pouvoir**	**devoir**
je	**veux**	**peux**	**dois**
tu	**veux**	**peux**	**dois**
il/elle/on	**veut**	**peut**	**doit**
nous	**voulons**	**pouvons**	**devons**
vous	**voulez**	**pouvez**	**devez**
ils/elles	**veulent**	**peuvent**	**doivent**

Ils doivent travailler.

Les verbes **prendre** *(to take)* **et mettre** *(to put, place)*

	prendre	**mettre**
je	**prends**	**mets**
tu	**prends**	**mets**
il/elle/on	**prend**	**met**
nous	**prenons**	**mettons**
vous	**prenez**	**mettez**
ils/elles	**prennent**	**mettent**

┌─ Verbes comme **prendre** ─────────┐
apprendre	*to learn*
comprendre	*to understand*

┌─ Verbes comme **mettre** ─────────┐
promettre	*to promise*
permettre	*to permit, allow*

Les verbes être, avoir, aller, faire, venir

PRESENT	être *(to be)*	avoir *(to have)*	aller *(to go)*	faire *(to do, make)*	venir *(to come)*
je (j')	suis	ai	vais	fais	viens
tu	es	as	vas	fais	viens
il/elle/on	est	a	va	fait	vient
nous	sommes	avons	allons	faisons	venons
vous	êtes	avez	allez	faites	venez
ils/elles	sont	ont	vont	font	viennent

Quelques expressions avec avoir

avoir chaud/froid	*to be warm, hot/cold*
avoir faim/soif	*to be hungry/thirsty*
avoir raison/tort	*to be right/wrong*
avoir sommeil	*to be sleepy*
avoir peur (de)	*to be afraid (of)*
avoir de la chance	*to be lucky*
avoir . . . ans	*to be . . . years old*
avoir mal	*to hurt*
avoir besoin de	*to need*
avoir envie de	*to feel like, to wish*

Quelques expressions avec faire

faire { **du (de l')** / **de la (de l')** / **des** } + *sport* / *subject (of study)* / *activity*

faire du ski   **faire de la natation**
faire de l'algèbre   **faire des maths**
faire du camping   **faire du théâtre**

faire attention (à)	*to pay attention (to), to be careful (with), to watch out (for)*
faire les courses	*to go shopping (for food)*
faire des achats	*to go shopping (for items other than food)*
faire la cuisine	*to cook*
faire la vaisselle	*to do the dishes*
faire ses devoirs	*to do one's homework*
faire ses valises	*to pack (one's suitcases)*
faire une promenade (à pied)	*to go for a walk*
faire une promenade (en auto, à vélo)	*to go for a ride (by car, by bicycle)*
faire un tour	*to take a walk, ride*
faire une randonnée	*to take a hike, a long drive*
faire un voyage	*to go on a trip, to take a trip*
faire un séjour	*to spend time (in a place away from home)*

Appendix A R3

B. *Le passé composé* ·······································

Le passé composé avec avoir

PAST PARTICIPLE	parler → parlé	finir → fini	vendre → vendu
PASSÉ COMPOSÉ	j'**ai parlé** tu **as parlé** il/elle/on **a parlé** nous **avons parlé** vous **avez parlé** ils/elles **ont parlé**	j'**ai fini** tu **as fini** il/elle/on **a fini** nous **avons fini** vous **avez fini** ils/elles **ont fini**	j'**ai vendu** tu **as vendu** il/elle/on **a vendu** nous **avons vendu** vous **avez vendu** ils/elles **ont vendu**
NEGATIVE	je **n'ai pas parlé**		
INTERROGATIVE	**est-ce que** tu **as parlé**? **as**-tu **parlé**? **a-t**-il/elle **parlé**?		

Le passé composé avec être

PASSÉ COMPOSÉ	je **suis allé** tu **es allé** il/on **est allé** nous **sommes allés** vous **êtes allé(s)** ils **sont allés**	je **suis allée** tu **es allée** elle **est allée** nous **sommes allées** vous **êtes allée(s)** elles **sont allées**
NEGATIVE	je **ne suis pas allé(e)**	
INTERROGATIVE	**est-ce que** tu **es allé(e)**? **es**-tu **allé(e)**? **est**-il/elle **allé(e)**?	

PARTICIPES PASSÉS DES VERBES IRRÉGULIERS

-é	être	j'ai **été**
-ait	faire	j'ai **fait**
-ert	ouvrir découvrir	j'ai **ouvert** j'ai **découvert**
-i	suivre dormir sentir	j'ai **suivi** j'ai **dormi** j'ai **senti**
-is	mettre prendre apprendre	j'ai **mis** j'ai **pris** j'ai **appris**
-it	dire écrire	j'ai **dit** j'ai **écrit**
-uit	conduire détruire	j'ai **conduit** j'ai **détruit**
-u	avoir boire savoir voir pouvoir devoir vouloir recevoir lire courir connaître vivre il y a il faut	j'ai **eu** j'ai **bu** j'ai **su** j'ai **vu** j'ai **pu** j'ai **dû** j'ai **voulu** j'ai **reçu** j'ai **lu** j'ai **couru** j'ai **connu** j'ai **vécu** il y a **eu** il a **fallu**

VERBES CONJUGUÉS AVEC ÊTRE

aller *(to go)*	je suis allé(e)	**passer** *(to pass)*	je suis passé(e)
venir *(to come)*	je suis venu(e)	**rester** *(to stay)*	je suis resté(e)
		rentrer *(to go back)*	je suis rentré(e)
arriver *(to arrive, come)*	je suis arrivé(e)	**retourner** *(to return)*	je suis retourné(e)
partir *(to leave)*	je suis parti(e)	**revenir** *(to come back)*	je suis revenu(e)
entrer *(to enter, come in)*	je suis entré(e)	**devenir** *(to become)*	je suis devenu(e)
sortir *(to go out)*	je suis sorti(e)		
		naître *(to be born)*	je suis né(e)
monter *(to go up)*	je suis monté(e)	**mourir** *(to die)*	je suis mort(e)
descendre *(to go down)*	je suis descendu(e)		
tomber *(to fall)*	je suis tombé(e)		

C. *L'imparfait*

The imperfect tense is formed as follows:

> **nous**-form of the present minus **-ons** + endings

	parler	finir	vendre	faire	endings
(PRESENT) nous	parl**ons**	finiss**ons**	vend**ons**	fais**ons**	
IMPERFECT STEM	parl-	finiss-	vend-	fais-	endings
je	parlais	finissais	vendais	faisais	-ais
tu	parlais	finissais	vendais	faisais	-ais
il/elle/on	parlait	finissait	vendait	faisait	-ait
nous	parlions	finissions	vendions	faisions	-ions
vous	parliez	finissiez	vendiez	faisiez	-iez
ils/elles	parlaient	finissaient	vendaient	faisaient	-aient
NEGATIVE	je **ne parlais pas**				
INTERROGATIVE	est-ce que tu **parlais**? **parlais**-tu?				

APPENDIX A

IMPERFECT STEMS

manger commencer	je mangeais je commençais
être avoir aller venir	j'étais j'avais j'allais je venais
sortir dormir mettre	je sortais je dormais je mettais
suivre	je suivais
devoir pouvoir vouloir	je devais je pouvais je voulais
savoir connaître prendre	je savais je connaissais je prenais
dire lire écrire	je disais je lisais j'écrivais
conduire	je conduisais
boire croire voir	je buvais je croyais je voyais

HIER APRÈS-MIDI, NOUS SOMMES ALLÉS EN VILLE. NOUS AVONS VU UN ACCIDENT.

PENDANT LES VACANCES, J'ALLAIS SOUVENT À LA PLAGE. IL Y AVAIT TOUJOURS BEAUCOUP DE MONDE.

D. *Passé composé ou imparfait?*

Use:	to describe:	
the PASSÉ COMPOSÉ	• what you did • what happened	Hier après-midi, nous **sommes allés** en ville. Nous **avons vu** un accident.
the IMPERFECT	• what you used to do • what used to be	Pendant les vacances, j'**allais** souvent à la plage. Il y **avait** toujours beaucoup de monde.
	• what you were doing • what was going on	Hier à neuf heures, je **regardais** la télé. Il y **avait** une comédie.
	• the circumstances of an event (time, weather)	Quelle heure **était**-il? Quel temps **faisait**-il?

2 Langue et Communication

A. Les articles

In French, nouns are frequently introduced by ARTICLES. The choice of article depends on the context in which the noun is used.

These articles . . .		introduce . . .	
DEFINITE:	**le (l')** **la (l')**	a noun used in a GENERAL or COLLECTIVE sense	J'aime **le** fromage. **La** patience est une qualité.
	les	a SPECIFIC thing (or things)	Voici **le** fromage. *(the one I bought)* **La** patience du professeur est remarquable.
INDEFINITE:	**un** **une**	one (or several) WHOLE items	J'ai acheté **un** fromage. *(a whole cheese)*
	des	one of a kind	Ce boulanger *(baker)* fait **un** pain excellent. Vous avez **une** patience extraordinaire.
PARTITIVE:	**du (de l')** **de la (de l')** **des**	SOME, ANY, A PORTION an UNSPECIFIED AMOUNT of something	Nous mangeons **du** fromage. *(just a piece)* Vous avez **de la** patience. Veux-tu **des** spaghetti?

REMARKS:

→ In <u>negative</u> sentences, **un, une, du, de la, des → de (d').**

    Marc mange **du** fromage.   Alice ne mange pas **de** fromage.
    Philippe a **un** couteau.   Mélanie n'a pas **de** couteau.

→ The DEFINITE article is generally used after the following verbs:

    aimer   J'aime **le** gâteau.
    préférer   Marc préfère **la** glace.

Philippe préfère le gâteau.

→ The PARTITIVE article is often, but <u>not always</u>, used after the following:

    voici   **boire**   **acheter**
    voilà   **manger**   **avoir**
    il y a   **prendre**   **vouloir**

It is the context that determines which article is used. Compare:

    Je mange **la** pizza.   *(= the pizza that I bought)*
    Je mange **une** pizza.   *(= a whole pizza)*
    Je mange **de la** pizza.   *(= a piece of pizza)*

Les boissons sont sur la table.

→ The PARTITIVE article is <u>not</u> used to introduce a subject. Compare:
    Le lait est dans le réfrigérateur.   Il y a **du lait** dans le réfrigérateur.

→ The PARTITIVE article can be used with <u>abstract</u> as well as <u>concrete</u> nouns.
    Vous avez **de l'argent.**   Moi, j'ai **du talent.**

B. *Les adjectifs irréguliers* ···································

Irregular feminine forms

MASCULINE	FEMININE		
-eux	-euse	curieux	curieuse
-f	-ve	actif	active
-en	-enne	canadien	canadienne
-on	-onne	mignon	mignonne
-el	-elle	ponctuel	ponctuelle
-er	-ère	régulier	régulière
-et	-ète	discret	discrète

Ils sont actifs!

Irregular masculine plural forms

SINGULAR	PLURAL		
-eux	-eux	curieux	curieux
-al	-aux	loyal	loyaux

Les adjectifs: beau, nouveau, vieux

SINGULAR			PLURAL	
MASCULINE		**FEMININE**	**MASCULINE**	**FEMININE**
beau	(bel)	belle	beaux	belles
nouveau	(nouvel)	nouvelle	nouveaux	nouvelles
vieux	(vieil)	vieille	vieux	vieilles

Est-ce que ces belles maisons à Annecy sont nouvelles?

REMARKS:

→ In French, adjectives usually come <u>after</u> the noun.

　　J'aime la musique **classique.**　　Anne porte une jupe **rouge** et **noire.**

→ The following adjectives usually come <u>before</u> the noun:

> | grand ≠ petit | jeune ≠ vieux | joli = beau |
> |---|---|---|
> | bon ≠ mauvais | nouveau ≠ ancien | |

　　Nous avons une **grande** maison dans un **vieux** quartier de Tours.

Ce monsieur est-il jeune ou vieux?

Note: Often **des → de** before a plural adjective.
　　Il porte **des** sandales. Il porte **de vieilles** sandales.

C. *Les noms irréguliers* ···································

SINGULAR	PLURAL		
-al	-aux	un animal	des animaux
-eau	-eaux	un chapeau	des chapeaux
-eu	-eux	un cheveu	des cheveux

→ A few nouns in **-al** form their plural by adding **-s:**
　　un festival　　　　　　　**des festivals**

Malice est un animal domestique.

D. *Les pronoms compléments d'objet direct et indirect* ······························

FORMS AND USES

SUBJECT	DIRECT and INDIRECT
je (j')	me (m')
tu	te (t')
nous	nous
vous	vous

SUBJECT	DIRECT	INDIRECT
il	le (l')	lui
elle	la (l')	
ils	les	leur
elles		

A DIRECT OBJECT answers the questions:
qui? *(whom?)* or **quoi?** *(what?)*

qui?	Je vois **Pauline**.	Je **la** vois.
quoi?	Je vois **la voiture**.	Je **la** vois.

VERB + DIRECT OBJECT
(quelqu'un)

aider	inviter
aimer	regarder
chercher	rencontrer
connaître	retrouver
écouter	voir

An INDIRECT OBJECT answers the question:
à qui? *(to whom?)*

à qui?	Je parle **à Pauline.**	Je **lui** parle.

VERB + INDIRECT OBJECT
(à quelqu'un)

dire à
écrire à
parler à
téléphoner à
rendre visite à
rendre service à

donner à *(to give)*
emprunter à *(to borrow)*
montrer à *(to show)*
prêter à *(to lend)*
rendre à *(to return, to give back)*

E. *Connaître ou savoir?* ···

Connaître and **savoir** both mean *to know,* but they are used differently.

Connaître . . .   is used with NOUNS (or pronouns) designating:

je	**connais**
tu	**connais**
il/elle/on	**connaît**
nous	**connaissons**
vous	**connaissez**
ils/elles	**connaissent**

- PEOPLE   **Je connais** Jean-Philippe.
- PLACES   **Je connais** bien Paris.
  Je connais un bon restaurant italien.
- INFORMATION   Je **ne connais pas** ton adresse.

POSITION

Object pronouns come **before** the verb EXCEPT in affirmative commands.

	AFFIRMATIVE	NEGATIVE
Present	Je **t'**invite. Je **le** connais. Je **lui** téléphone.	Je ne **t'**invite pas. Je ne **le** connais pas. Je ne **lui** téléphone pas.
Passé composé	Je **t'**ai vu. Je **l'**ai invité. Je **leur** ai parlé.	Je ne **t'**ai pas vu. Je ne **l'**ai pas invité. Je ne **leur** ai pas parlé.
Imperative (commands)	Écris-**moi**. Invite-**les**. Rends-**leur** visite.	Ne **m'**écris pas. Ne **les** invite pas. Ne **leur** rends pas visite.
Infinitive construction	Je vais **t'**inviter. Je vais **les** voir. Je vais **leur** écrire.	Je ne vais pas **t'**inviter. Je ne vais pas **les** voir. Je ne vais pas **leur** écrire.

Savoir . . . is used (with):

je	**sais**
tu	**sais**
il/elle/on	**sait**
nous	**savons**
vous	**savez**
ils/elles	**savent**

- ALONE
- a CLAUSE introduced by . . .
  - **que** *(that)*
  - **si** *(if, whether)*
  - an INTERROGATIVE expression

- an INFINITIVE
- a NOUN designating something LEARNED

Tu sais? Non, je ne **sais** pas.

Je sais que tu as une nouvelle moto.
Est-ce que tu **sais** si Éric va venir?
Je ne **sais** pas où tu habites.
Sais-tu qui a téléphoné?
Je ne **sais** pas quand je vais aller à Nice.
Savez-vous utiliser un ordinateur?
Les élèves ne **savent** pas la leçon.

3 Vocabulaire

A. Les nombres et les dates

LES NOMBRES CARDINAUX

To count, we use CARDINAL numbers: 1, 2, 3 . . .

———————————————————— **0 à 99** ————————————————————

0	zéro	10	dix	20	vingt	60	soixante
1	un	11	onze	21	vingt et un	61	soixante et un
2	deux	12	douze	22	vingt-deux	70	soixante-dix
3	trois	13	treize	23	vingt-trois	71	soixante et onze
4	quatre	14	quatorze	30	trente	72	soixante-douze
5	cinq	15	quinze	31	trente et un	80	quatre-vingts
6	six	16	seize	40	quarante	81	quatre-vingt-un
7	sept	17	dix-sept	48	quarante-huit	90	quatre-vingt-dix
8	huit	18	dix-huit	49	quarante-neuf	91	quatre-vingt-onze
9	neuf	19	dix-neuf	50	cinquante	99	quatre-vingt-dix-neuf

———————————————————— **100 à 1 000 000** ————————————————————

100	cent	400	quatre cents	1 000	mille
101	cent un	520	cinq cent vingt	1 210	mille deux cent dix
110	cent dix	675	six cent soixante-quinze	2 000	deux mille
200	deux cents	880	huit cent quatre-vingts	15 000	quinze mille
215	deux cent quinze	900	neuf cents	100 000	cent mille
371	trois cent soixante et onze			1 000 000	un million

LES NOMBRES ORDINAUX

To rank or put in sequence, we use ORDINAL numbers: 1st, 2nd, 3rd . . .

> ordinal number = cardinal number + **ième**
> (minus -**e**, if any)

deux	→ **deuxième**	EXCEPTIONS:		
douze	→ **douzième**	un	→	**premier (première)**
vingt et un	→ **vingt et unième**	cinq	→	**cinquième**
cent huit	→ **cent huitième**	neuf	→	**neuvième**

LA DATE

When giving the date in French, use cardinal numbers:

> **le douze octobre**
> **le vingt juillet**

However, use the ordinal number (**premier**) for the first of the month:

> **le premier mai**

B. *La nourriture et les boissons*

Boulangerie Pâtisserie

- **le pain** *bread*
- **un croissant**
- **un gâteau** *cake*
- **une tarte** *pie*

Boucherie

- **la viande** *meat*
- **le rosbif**
- **le jambon** *ham*
- **le porc**
- **le veau** *veal*

Alimentation générale

- **le ketchup**
- **la mayonnaise**
- **le sel** *salt*
- **le poivre** *pepper*
- **le sucre** *sugar*
- **la confiture** *jam*
- **le riz** *rice*
- **les spaghetti**
- **les céréales**

Produits laitiers
(Dairy products)

- **le lait** *milk*
- **le beurre** *butter*
- **la margarine**
- **le fromage** *cheese*
- **la glace** *ice cream*
- **le yaourt** *yogurt*
- **un oeuf** *egg*

Poissonnerie
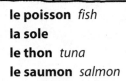

- **le poisson** *fish*
- **la sole**
- **le thon** *tuna*
- **le saumon** *salmon*

Fruits

- **une orange**
- **une banane**
- **un melon**
- **une pomme** *apple*
- **une poire** *pear*
- **une pamplemousse** *grapefruit*
- **une fraise** *strawberry*
- **une cerise** *cherry*
- **du raisin** *grapes*

Légumes

- **le céleri**
- **une salade** *lettuce*
- **une carotte**
- **une tomate**
- **une pomme de terre** *potato*
- **des petits pois** *peas*

Boissons

- **le thé**
- **le café**
- **l'eau** *water*
- **l'eau minérale**
- **le jus de fruits**
- **le jus de pomme**
- **le jus de raisin**

C. *Les parties du corps*

le corps *(body)*

la tête

le nez

la bouche

l'épaule *(f.)*

le doigt

le bras

le ventre
l'estomac *(m.)*

le genou

la jambe

la figure

les cheveux

l'oeil (les yeux)

l'oreille

le cou

le dos

le coeur

la main

le pied

Note the expression **avoir mal à:**

J'ai mal à la tête.	*I have a headache. (My head hurts.)*
J'ai mal au dos.	*I have a backache. (My back hurts.)*
J'ai mal aux dents.	*I have a toothache.*
J'ai mal au coeur.	*I have an upset stomach.*

D. Les vêtements et les accessoires

un sweat
des sandales
un tee-shirt
un short
un maillot de bain
un blazer
un polo
des chaussettes
des tennis
une veste
un pull
une casquette
un survêtement
un chapeau
un blouson
une cravate
un pantalon
un jean
une cravate
un bracelet
des boucles d'oreilles
un chemisier
une bague
des baskets
des lunettes de soleil
un tailleur (woman's suit)
un collier
une ceinture
un impermeable
un costume (man's suit)
une jupe
une robe
un manteau
un parapluie
des collants
un foulard
des bottes
des chaussures
un sac

E. *Les pays* ·······························

LES CONTINENTS ET LES PAYS DU MONDE

L' Amérique du Nord et l'Amérique du Sud
1. le Canada
2. les États-Unis
3. le Mexique
4. le Guatemala
5. le Venezuela
6. le Pérou
7. le Brésil
8. l'Argentine
9. le Chili

L' Afrique
10. le Maroc
11. l'Algérie
12. la Tunisie
13. l'Égypte
14. le Sénégal
15. la Côte d'Ivoire
16. la République démocratique du Congo
17. Madagascar

L' Europe
18. la France
19. l'Espagne
20. le Portugal
21. l'Angleterre
22. l'Irlande
23. l'Écosse
24. la Belgique
25. le Luxembourg
26. la Suisse
27. les Pays-Bas
28. l'Allemagne
29. l'Italie
30. la Grèce
31. le Danemark
32. la Norvège
33. la Suède
34. la Pologne
35. la Russie

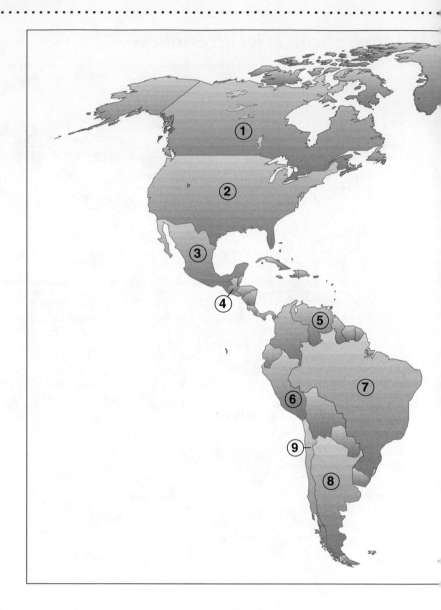

Le Moyen-Orient
36. Israël
37. le Liban
38. l'Arabie Saoudite

L' Asie et l'Océanie
39. la Chine
40. le Japon
41. la Corée
42. le Viêt-nam
43. le Cambodge
44. l'Inde
45. les Philippines
46. l'Australie
47. la Nouvelle Zélande

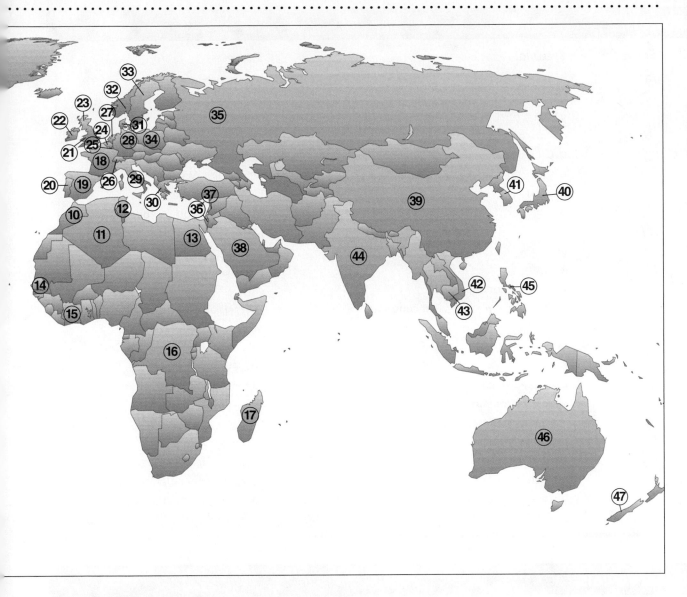

Les articles et les prépositions avec les noms de pays

	masculine country beginning with a consonant	feminine country or masculine country beginning with a vowel	plural country
Je visite . . .	**le** Canada	**la** France **l'**Iran	**les** États-Unis
Je vais . . . J'habite . . .	**au** Canada	**en** France **en** Iran	**aux** États-Unis
Je viens . . .	**du** Canada	**de** France **d'**Iran	**des** États-Unis

APPENDIX B   SOUND-SPELLING CORRESPONDENCE

Vowels

Sound	Spelling	Examples
/a/	a, à, â	Madame, là-bas, théâtre
/i/	i, î	visite, Nice, dîne
	y (initial, final, or between consonants)	Yves, Guy, style
/u/	ou, où, oû	Toulouse, où, août
/y/	u, û	tu, Luc, sûr
/o/	o (final or before silent consonant)	piano, idiot, Margot
	au, eau	jaune, Claude, beau
	ô	hôtel, drôle, Côte-d'Ivoire
/ɔ/	o	Monique, Noël, jolie
	au	Paul, restaurant, Laure
/e/	é	Dédé, Québec, télé
	e (before silent final z, t, r)	chez, et, Roger
	ai (final or before final silent consonant)	j'ai, mai, japonais
/ɛ/	è	Michèle, Ève, père
	ei	seize, neige, Tour Eiffel
	ê	tête, être, Việt-nam
	e (before two consonants)	elle, Pierre, Annette
	e (before pronounced final consonant)	Michel, avec, cher
	ai (before pronounced final consonant)	française, aime, Maine
/ə/	e (final or before single consonant)	je, Denise, venir
/ø/	eu, oeu	deux, Mathieu, euro, oeufs
	eu (before final se)	nerveuse, généreuse, sérieuse
/œ/	eu, oeu (before final pronounced consonant except /z/)	heure, neuf, Lesieur, soeur, coeur, oeuf

Nasal Vowels

Sound	Spelling	Examples
/ɑ̃/	an, am	France, quand, lampe
	en, em	Henri, pendant, décembre
/ɔ̃/	on, om	non, Simon, bombe
/ɛ̃/	in, im	Martin, invite, impossible
	yn, ym	syndicat, sympathique, Olympique
	ain, aim	Alain, américain, faim
	(o) + in	loin, moins, point
	(i) + en	bien, Julien, viens
	un, um	un, Lebrun, parfum
/œ̃/	un, um	un, Lebrun, parfum

Semi-vowels

Sound	Spelling	Examples
/j/	i, y (before vowel sound)	bien, piano, Lyon
	-il, -ill (after vowel sound)	oeil, travaille, Marseille
/ɥ/	u (before vowel sound)	lui, Suisse, juillet
/w/	ou (before vowel sound)	oui, Louis, jouer
/wa/	oi, oî, oy (before vowel)	voici, Benoît, voyage

Consonants

Sound	Spelling	Examples
/b/	b	Barbara, banane, Belgique
/k/	c (before a, o, u, or consonant)	Coca-Cola, cuisine, classe
	ch(r)	Christine, Christian, Christophe
	qu, q (final)	Québec, qu'est-ce que, cinq
	k	kilo, Kiki, ketchup
/ʃ/	ch	Charles, blanche, chez
/d/	d	Didier, dans, médecin
/f/	f	Félix, franc, neuf
	ph	Philippe, téléphone, photo
/g/	g (before a, o, u, or consonant)	Gabriel, gorge, légumes, gris
	gu (before e, i, y)	vague, Guillaume, Guy
/ɲ/	gn	mignon, champagne, Allemagne
/ʒ/	j	je, Jérôme, jaune
	g (before e, i, y)	rouge, Gigi, gymnastique
	ge (before a, o, u)	orangeade, Georges, nageur
/l/	l	Lise, elle, cheval
/m/	m	Maman, moi, tomate
/n/	n	banane, Nancy, nous
/p/	p	peu, Papa, Pierre
/r/	r	arrive, rentre, Paris
/s/	c (before e, i, y)	ce, Cécile, Nancy
	ç (before a, o, u)	ça, garçon, déçu
	s (initial or before consonant)	sac, Sophie, reste
	ss (between vowels)	boisson, dessert, Suisse
	t (before i + vowel)	attention, Nations Unies, natation
	x	dix, six, soixante
/t/	t	trop, télé, Tours
	th	Thérèse, thé, Marthe
/v/	v	Viviane, vous, nouveau
/gz/	x	examen, exemple, exact
/ks/	x	Max, Mexique, excellent
/z/	s (between vowels)	désert, télévision, Louise
	z	Suzanne, zut, zéro

Sound-Spelling Correspondences R17

APPENDIX C VERBES

1 Regular Verbs

INFINITIF	parler (to talk, speak)	finir (to finish)	vendre (to sell)	se laver (to wash oneself)
PRESENT	je **parle** tu **parles** il **parle** nous **parlons** vous **parlez** ils **parlent**	je **finis** tu **finis** il **finit** nous **finissons** vous **finissez** ils **finissent**	je **vends** tu **vends** il **vend** nous **vendons** vous **vendez** ils **vendent**	je **me lave** tu **te laves** il **se lave** nous **nous lavons** vous **vous lavez** ils **se lavent**
IMPÉRATIF	**parle!** **parlons!** **parlez!**	**finis!** **finissons!** **finissez!**	**vends!** **vendons!** **vendez!**	**lave-toi!** **lavons-nous!** **lavez-vous!**
PASSÉ COMPOSÉ	j'**ai parlé** tu **as parlé** il **a parlé** nous **avons parlé** vous **avez parlé** ils **ont parlé**	j'**ai fini** tu **as fini** il **a fini** nous **avons fini** vous **avez fini** ils **ont fini**	j'**ai vendu** tu **as vendu** il **a vendu** nous **avons vendu** vous **avez vendu** ils **ont vendu**	je **me suis lavé(e)** tu **t'es lavé(e)** il/elle **s'est lavé(e)** nous **nous sommes lavé(e)s** vous **vous êtes lavé(e)(s)** ils/elles **se sont lavé(e)s**
IMPARFAIT	je **parlais** tu **parlais** il **parlait** nous **parlions** vous **parliez** ils **parlaient**	je **finissais** tu **finissais** il **finissait** nous **finissions** vous **finissiez** ils **finissaient**	je **vendais** tu **vendais** il **vendait** nous **vendions** vous **vendiez** ils **vendaient**	je **me lavais** tu **te lavais** il **se lavait** nous **nous lavions** vous **vous laviez** ils **se lavaient**
PLUS-QUE-PARFAIT	j'**avais parlé** tu **avais parlé** il **avait parlé** nous **avions parlé** vous **aviez parlé** ils **avaient parlé**	j'**avais fini** tu **avais fini** il **avait fini** nous **avions fini** vous **aviez fini** ils **avaient fini**	j'**avais vendu** tu **avais vendu** il **avait vendu** nous **avions vendu** vous **aviez vendu** ils **avaient vendu**	je **m'étais lavé(e)** tu **t'étais lavé(e)** il/elle **s'était lavé(e)** nous **nous étions lavé(e)s** vous **vous étiez lavé(e)(s)** ils/elles **s'étaient lavé(e)s**
PASSÉ SIMPLE	je **parlai** tu **parlas** il **parla** nous **parlâmes** vous **parlâtes** ils **parlèrent**	je **finis** tu **finis** il **finit** nous **finîmes** vous **finîtes** ils **finirent**	je **vendis** tu **vendis** il **vendit** nous **vendîmes** vous **vendîtes** ils **vendirent**	je **me lavai** tu **te lavas** il **se lava** nous **nous lavâmes** vous **vous lavâtes** ils **se lavèrent**

INFINITIF	**parler** *(to talk, speak)*	**finir** *(to finish)*	**vendre** *(to sell)*	**se laver** *(to wash oneself)*
FUTUR	je **parlerai**	je **finirai**	je **vendrai**	je **me laverai**
	tu **parleras**	tu **finiras**	tu **vendras**	tu **te laveras**
	il **parlera**	il **finira**	il **vendra**	il **se lavera**
	nous **parlerons**	nous **finirons**	nous **vendrons**	nous **nous laverons**
	vous **parlerez**	vous **finirez**	vous **vendrez**	vous **vous laverez**
	ils **parleront**	ils **finiront**	ils **vendront**	ils **se laveront**
CONDITIONNEL	je **parlerais**	je **finirais**	**je vendrais**	je **me laverais**
	tu **parlerais**	tu **finirais**	**tu vendrais**	tu **te laverais**
	il **parlerait**	il **finirait**	**il vendrait**	il **se laverait**
	nous **parlerions**	nous **finirions**	**nous vendrions**	nous **nous laverions**
	vous **parleriez**	vous **finiriez**	**vous vendriez**	vous **vous laveriez**
	ils **parleraient**	ils **finiraient**	**ils vendraient**	ils **se laveraient**
CONDITIONNEL PASSÉ	j'**aurais parlé**	j'**aurais fini**	j'**aurais vendu**	je **me serais lavé(e)**
	tu **aurais parlé**	tu **aurais fini**	tu **aurais vendu**	tu **te serais lavé(e)**
	il **aurait parlé**	il **aurait fini**	il **aurait vendu**	il/elle **se serait lavé(e)**
	nous **aurions parlé**	nous **aurions fini**	nous **aurions vendu**	nous **nous serions lavé(e)(s)**
	vous **auriez parlé**	vous **auriez fini**	vous **auriez vendu**	vous **vous seriez lavé(e)(s)**
	ils **auraient parlé**	ils **auraient fini**	ils **auraient vendu**	ils/elles **se seraient lavé(e)s**
SUBJONCTIF	que **je parle**	que je **finisse**	que je **vende**	que je **me lave**
	que **tu parles**	que tu **finisses**	que tu **vendes**	que tu **te laves**
	qu'**il parle**	qu'il **finisse**	qu'il **vende**	qu'il **se lave**
	que nous **parlions**	que nous **finissions**	que nous **vendions**	que nous **nous lavions**
	que **vous parliez**	que vous **finissiez**	que vous **vendiez**	que vous **vous laviez**
	qu'**ils parlent**	qu'ils **finissent**	qu'ils **vendent**	qu'ils **se lavent**
PASSÉ DU SUBJONCTIF	que j'**aie parlé**	que j'**aie fini**	que j'**aie vendu**	que je **me sois lavé(e)**
	que tu **aies parlé**	que tu **aies fini**	que tu **aies vendu**	que tu **te sois lavé(e)**
	qu'il **ait parlé**	qu'il **ait fini**	qu'il **ait vendu**	qu'il/elle **se soit lavé(e)**
	que nous **ayons parlé**	que nous **ayons fini**	que nous **ayons vendu**	que nous **nous soyons lavé(e)s**
	que vous **ayez parlé**	que nous **ayez fini**	que vous **ayez vendu**	que vous **vous soyez lavé(e)(s)**
	qu'ils **aient parlé**	qu'ils **aient fini**	qu'ils **aient vendu**	qu'ils/elles **se soient lavé(e)s**
PARTICIPE PRESENT	**parlant**	**finissant**	**vendant**	**se lavant**
INFINITIF PASSÉ	**avoir parlé**	**avoir fini**	**avoir vendu**	**s'être lavé(e)**

APPENDIX C VERBES

2 Verbs with spelling changes

Some **-er** verbs have spelling changes in certain tenses. These changes are highlighted in the chart below. All other forms of these verbs are similar to those of regular **-er** verbs.

The verbs listed below follow the pattern of the indicated model verbs. Note that reflexive verbs are conjugated with **être** in the compound tenses. (All others are conjugated with **avoir.**)

verbs like **acheter** *(to buy)*	verbs like **appeler** *(to call)*	verbs like **préférer** *(to prefer)*
amener *(to take, bring along)*	**s'appeler** *(to be named, to be called)*	**accélérer** *(to accelerate)*
élever *(to educate, to raise)*	**empaqueter** *(to bag)*	**célébrer** *(to celebrate)*
enlever *(to take off)*	**épousseter** *(to dust)*	**espérer** *(to hope)*
lever *(to lift, raise)*	**étinceler** *(to twinkle)*	**s'inquiéter** *(to worry)*
se lever *(to get up)*	**jeter** *(to throw)*	**posséder** *(to possess, to own)*
mener *(to take, to lead)*	**rappeler** *(to call back)*	**protéger** *(to protect)*
promener *(to walk [a dog])*	**se rappeler** *(to remember)*	**répéter** *(to repeat)*
se promener *(to take a walk, take a ride)*	**rejeter** *(to reject)*	**sécher** *(to dry)*
		se sécher *(to dry oneself)*
		suggérer *(to suggest)*

INFINITIF	PRÉSENT		IMPÉRATIF	PASSÉ COMPOSÉ	IMPARFAIT
acheter **e → è**	j'**achète** tu **achètes** il **achète**	nous **achetons** vous **achetez** ils **achètent**	**achète!** achetons! achetez!	j'ai acheté	j'achetais nous **achetions**
appeler **l → ll** *(double consonant)*	j'**appelle** tu **appelles** il **appelle**	nous **appelons** vous **appelez** ils **appellent**	**appelle!** appelons! appelez!	j'ai appelé	j'appelais nous **appelions**
préférer **é → è**	je **préfère** tu **préfères** il **préfère**	nous **préférons** vous **préférez** ils **préfèrent**	**préfère!** préférons! préférez!	j'ai préféré	je préférais nous **préférions**
payer **y → i**	je **paie** tu **paies** il **paie**	nous **payons** vous **payez** ils **paient**	**paie!** payons! payez!	j'ai payé	je payais nous **payons**
commencer **c → ç** *(before a,o)*	je **commence** tu **commences** il **commence**	nous **commençons** vous **commencez** ils **commencent**	commence! **commençons!** commencez!	j'ai commencé	je **commençais** nous **commencions**
manger **g → ge** *(before a,o)*	je **mange** tu **manges** il **mange**	nous **mangeons** vous **mangez** ils **mangent**	mange! **mangeons!** mangez!	j'ai mangé	je **mangeais** nous **mangions**

verbs like **payer** (to pay, pay for)

balayer (to sweep)
employer (to use, to employ)
s'ennuyer (to be bored)
essayer (to try)
essuyer (to wipe, to dry)
nettoyer (to clean)

verbs like **commencer** (to begin, start)

annoncer (to announce, proclaim)
divorcer (to divorce)
se fiancer (to get engaged)
menacer (to threaten)

verbs like **manger** (to eat)

arranger (to arrange, to fix)
changer (to change)
charger (to charge)
s'en charger (to take charge)
corriger (to correct)
dégager (to shorten)
déranger (to disturb)
diriger (to direct, to run)
exiger (to demand)
égorger (to slit the throat)
embaucher (to hire)
interroger (to interrogate)
juger (to judge)

mélanger (to mix)
nager (to swim)
négliger (to neglect)
obliger (to oblige)
partager (to share)
plonger (to dive)
protéger (to protect)
ranger (to pick up, to put away)
venger (to avenge)
voyager (to travel)

PASSÉ SIMPLE	FUTUR	CONDITIONNEL	SUBJONCTIF	PARTICIPE PRÉSENT
j'achetai il **acheta** ils **achetèrent**	j'**achèterai**	j'**achèterais**	que j'**achète** que nous **achetions**	**achetant**
j'appelai il **appela** ils **appelèrent**	j'**appellerai**	j'**appellerais**	que j'**appelle** que nous **appelions**	**appelant**
je **préférai** il **préféra** ils **préférèrent**	je **préférerai**	je **préférerais**	que je **préfère** que nous **préférions**	**préférant**
je **payai** il **paya** ils **payèrent**	je **paierai**	je **paierais**	que je **paie** que nous **payions**	**payant**
je **commençai** il **commença** ils **commencèrent**	je **commencerai**	je **commencerais**	que je **commence** que nous **commencions**	**commençant**
je **mangeai** il **mangea** ils **mangèrent**	je **mangerai**	je **mangerais**	que je **mange** que nous **mangions**	**mangeant**

3 Auxiliary Forms

INFINITIF	PRÉSENT		IMPARFAIT		FUTUR	
avoir	j'ai tu as il a	nous avons vous avez ils ont	j'avais tu avais il avait	nous avions vous aviez ils avaient	j'aurai tu auras il aura	nous aurons vous aurez ils auront
être	je suis tu es il est	nous sommes vous êtes ils sont	j'étais tu étais il était	nous étions vous étiez ils étaient	je serai tu seras il sera	nous serons vous serez ils seront

4 Irregular Verbs

For the conjugation of the irregular verbs listed below, follow the pattern of the indicated verbs. Verbs conjugated with **être** as an auxiliary verb in the compound tenses are noted with an asterisk (*). All others are conjugated with **avoir.**

accueillir	*(see cueillir)*	craindre	*(see peindre)*	s'endormir	*(see dormir)*
admettre	*(see mettre)*	cuire	*(see conduire)*	s'enfuir	*(see fuir)*
apercevoir	*(see recevoir)*	débattre	*(see battre)*	entreprendre	*(see prendre)*
apparaître	*(see connaître)*	décevoir	*(see recevoir)*	entretenir	*(see tenir)*
appartenir	*(see tenir)*	découvrir	*(see ouvrir)*	éteindre	*(see peindre)*
apprendre	*(see prendre)*	décrire	*(see écrire)*	s'étendre	*(see rendre)*
atteindre	*(see peindre)*	se déplacer	*(see placer)*	inscrire	*(see écrire)*
attendre	*(see rendre)*	déplaire	*(see plaire)*	interdire	*(see dire)*
combattre	*(see battre)*	détruire	*(see conduire)*	interrompre	*(see rompre)*
comprendre	*(see prendre)*	descendre	*(see rendre)*	intervenir	*(see venir)*
confier	*(see planifier)*	*devenir	*(see venir)*	introduire	*(see conduire)*
conquérir	*(see acquérir)*	disparaître	*(see connaître)*	joindre	*(see peindre)*
construire	*(see conduire)*	effacer	*(see placer)*	lancer	*(see placer)*
contenir	*(see tenir)*	élire	*(see lire)*	maintenir	*(see tenir)*
convaincre	*(see vaincre)*	entendre	*(see rendre)*	se marier	*(see planifier)*
couvrir	*(see ouvrir)*	s'entendre	*(see rendre)*	se méfier	*(see planifier)*

INFINITIF	PRÉSENT		IMPÉRATIF	PASSÉ COMPOSÉ	IMPARFAIT
acquérir *(to acquire, get)*	j'acquiers tu acquiers il acquiert	nous acquérons vous acquérez ils acquièrent	acquiers acquérons acquérez	j'ai acquis	j'acquérais
aller *(to go)*	je vais tu vas il va	nous allons vous allez ils vont	va allons allez	je suis allé(e)	j'allais

CONDITIONNEL		SUBJONCTIF	
j'aurais	nous aurions	que j'aie	que nous ayons
tu aurais	vous auriez	que tu aies	que vous ayez
il aurait	ils auraient	qu'il ait	qu'ils aient
je serais	nous serions	que je sois	que nous soyons
tu serais	vous seriez	que tu sois	que vous soyez
il serait	ils seraient	qu'il soit	que ils soient

mentir	*(see sortir)*	promettre	*(see mettre)*	*revenir	*(see venir)*
obtenir	*(see tenir)*	reconnaître	*(see connaître)*	sentir	*(see sortir)*
offrir	*(see ouvrir)*	réconcilier	*(see planifier)*	servir	*(see sortir)*
opérer	*(see céder)*	reconstruire	*(see conduire)*	souffrir	*(see ouvrir)*
paraître	*(see connaître)*	récupérer	*(see céder)*	sourire	*(see rire)*
parcourir	*(see courir)*	redécouvrir	*(see ouvrir)*	soutenir	*(see tenir)*
*partir	*(see sortir)*	réduire	*(see conduire)*	se souvenir	*(see venir)*
parvenir	*(see venir)*	remarier	*(see planifier)*	subvenir	*(see venir)*
pendre	*(see rendre)*	remercier	*(see planifier)*	succéder	*(see céder)*
se perdre	*(see rendre)*	remettre	*(see mettre)*	surprendre	*(see prendre)*
permettre	*(see mettre)*	se rendre à	*(see rendre)*	survenir	*(see venir)*
peser	*(see acheter)*	renoncer	*(see placer)*	survivre	*(see vivre)*
plaindre	*(see peindre)*	renvoyer	*(see envoyer)*	tondre	*(see rendre)*
poursuivre	*(see suivre)*	répandre	*(see rendre)*	se tordre	*(see rendre)*
prédire	*(see dire)*	répondre	*(see rendre)*	traduire	*(see conduire)*
prévoir	*(see voir)*	ressentir	*(see sortir)*		
produire	*(see conduire)*	retenir	*(see tenir)*		

PASSÉ SIMPLE	FUTUR	CONDITIONNEL	SUBJONCTIF	PARTICIPE PRÉSENT
j'acquis	j'acquerrai	j'acquerrais	que j'acquière que nous acquérions	acquérant
j'allai	j'irai	j'irais	que j'aille que nous allions	allant

APPENDIX C

INFINITIF	PRÉSENT		IMPÉRATIF	PASSÉ COMPOSÉ	IMPARFAIT
appuyer (to push)	j'**appuie** tu **appuies** il **appuie**	nous **appuyons** vous **appuyez** ils **appuient**	**appuie!** **appuyons!** **appuyez!**	j'ai **appuyé**	j'**appuyais**
s'asseoir (to sit down)	je m'**assieds** tu t'**assieds** il s'**assied**	nous **nous asseyons** vous **vous asseyez** ils s'**asseyent**	**assieds-toi!** **asseyons-nous!** **asseyez-vous!**	je me suis **assis(e)**	je m'**asseyais**
avoir (to have)	j'**ai** tu **as** il **a**	nous **avons** vous **avez** ils **ont**	**aie!** **ayons!** **ayez!**	j'ai **eu**	j'**avais**
il y a (there is, are)	**il y a**		– –	**il y a eu**	**il y avait**
battre (to beat)	je **bats** tu **bats** il **bat**	nous **battons** vous **battez** ils **battent**	**bats!** **battons!** **battez!**	j'ai **battu**	je **battais**
boire (to drink)	je **bois** tu **bois** il **boit**	nous **buvons** vous **buvez** ils **boivent**	**bois!** **buvons!** **buvez!**	j'ai **bu**	je **buvais**
céder (to cede)	je **cède** tu **cèdes** il **cède**	nous **cédons** vous **cédez** ils **cèdent**	**cède!** **cédons!** **cédez!**	j'ai **cédé**	je **cédais**
conduire (to drive)	je **conduis** tu **conduis** il **conduit**	nous **conduisons** vous **conduisez** ils **conduisent**	**conduis!** **conduisons!** **conduisez!**	j'ai **conduit**	je **conduisais**
connaître (to know)	je **connais** tu **connais** il **connaît**	nous **connaissons** vous **connaissez** ils **connaissent**	**connais!** **connaissons!** **connaissez!**	j'ai **connu**	je **connaissais**
courir (to run)	je **cours** tu **cours** il **court**	nous **courons** vous **courez** ils **courent**	**cours!** **courons!** **courez!**	j'ai **couru**	je **courais**
croire (to believe, think)	je **crois** tu **crois** il **croit**	nous **croyons** vous **croyez** ils **croient**	**crois!** **croyons!** **croyez!**	j'ai **cru**	je **croyais**
cueillir (to gather, pick)	je **cueille** tu **cueilles** il **cueille**	nous **cueillons** vous **cueillez** ils **cueillent**	**cueille!** **cueillons!** **cueillez!**	j'ai **cueilli**	je **cueillais**
devoir (must, to have to, owe)	je **dois** tu **dois** il **doit**	nous **devons** vous **devez** ils **doivent**	**dois!** **devons!** **devez!**	j'ai **dû**	je **devais**

PASSÉ SIMPLE	FUTUR	CONDITIONNEL	SUBJONCTIF		PARTICIPE PRÉSENT
j'**appuyai**	j'**appuierai**	j'**appuierais**	que j'**appuie** que nous **appuyions**		**appuyant**
je m'**assis**	je m'**assiérai**	je m'**assiérais**	que je m'**asseye** que nous **nous asseyions**		s'**asseyant**
j'**eus**	j'**aurai**	j'**aurais**	que j'**aie** que tu **aies** qu'il **ait**	que nous **ayons** que vous **ayez** qu'ils **aient**	**ayant**
il y **eut**	il y **aura**	il y **aurait**	qu'**il y ait**		--
je **battis**	je **battrai**	je **battrais**	que je **batte** que nous **battions**		**battant**
je **bus**	je **boirai**	je **boirais**	que je **boive** que nous **buvions**		**buvant**
je **cédai**	je **céderai**	je **céderais**	que je **cède** que nous **cédions**		**cédant**
je **conduisis**	je **conduirai**	je **conduirais**	que je **conduise** que nous **conduisions**		**conduisant**
je **connus**	je **connaîtrai**	je **connaîtrais**	que je **connaisse** que nous **connaissions**		**connaissant**
je **courus**	je **courrai**	je **courrais**	que je **coure** que nous **courions**		**courant**
je **crus**	je **croirai**	je **croirais**	que je **croie** que nous **croyions**		**croyant**
je **cueillis**	je **cueillerai**	je **cueillerais**	que je **cueille** que nous **cueillions**		**cueillant**
je **dus**	je **devrai**	je **devrais**	que je **doive** que nous **devions**		**devant**

INFINITIF	PRÉSENT		IMPÉRATIF	PASSÉ COMPOSÉ	IMPARFAIT
dire *(to say, tell)*	je **dis** tu **dis** il **dit**	nous **disons** vous **dites** ils **disent**	**dis!** **disons!** **dites!**	j'**ai dit**	je **disais**
dormir *(to sleep)*	je **dors** tu **dors** il **dort**	nous **dormons** vous **dormez** ils **dorment**	**dors!** **dormons!** **dormez!**	j'**ai dormi**	je **dormais**
écrire *(to write)*	j'**écris** tu **écris** il **écrit**	nous **écrivons** vous **écrivez** ils **écrivent**	**écris!** **écrivons!** **écrivez!**	j'**ai écrit**	j'**écrivais**
envoyer *(to send)*	j'**envoie** tu **envoies** il **envoie**	nous **envoyons** vous **envoyez** ils **envoient**	**envoie!** **envoyons!** **envoyez!**	j'**ai envoyé**	j'**envoyais**
être *(to be)*	je **suis** tu **es** il **est**	nous **sommes** vous **êtes** ils **sont**	**sois!** **soyons!** **soyez!**	j'**ai été**	j'**étais**
faire *(to make, do)*	je **fais** tu **fais** il **fait**	nous **faisons** vous **faites** ils **font**	**fais!** **faisons!** **faites!**	j'**ai fait**	je **faisais**
falloir *(to be necessary)*	il **faut**	– –	– –	il **a fallu**	il **fallait**
fuir *(to flee)*	je **fuis** tu **fuis** il **fuit**	nous **fuyons** vous **fuyez** ils **fuient**	**fuis!** **fuyons!** **fuyez!**	j'**ai fui**	je **fuyais**
lire *(to read)*	je **lis** tu **lis** il **lit**	nous **lisons** vous **lisez** ils **lisent**	**lis!** **lisons!** **lisez!**	j'**ai lu**	je **lisais**
mettre *(to put, place)*	je **mets** tu **mets** il **met**	nous **mettons** vous **mettez** ils **mettent**	**mets!** **mettons!** **mettez!**	j'**ai mis**	je **mettais**
mourir *(to die)*	je **meurs** tu **meurs** il **meurt**	nous **mourons** vous **mourez** ils **meurent**	**meurs!** **mourons!** **mourez!**	je **suis mort(e)**	je **mourais**

PASSÉ SIMPLE	FUTUR	CONDITIONNEL	SUBJONCTIF		PARTICIPE PRÉSENT
je **dis**	je **dirai**	je **dirais**	que je **dise** que nous **disions**		**disant**
je **dormis**	je **dormirai**	je **dormirais**	que je **dorme** que nous **dormions**		**dormant**
j'**écrivis**	j'**écrirai**	j'**écrirais**	que j'**écrive** que nous **écrivions**		**écrivant**
j'**envoyai**	j'**enverrai**	j'**enverrais**	que j'**envoie** que nous **envoyions**		**envoyant**
je **fus**	je **serai**	je **serais**	que je **sois** que tu **sois** qu'il **soit**	que nous **soyons** que vous **soyez** qu'ils **soient**	**étant**
je **fis**	je **ferai**	je **ferais**	que je **fasse** que nous **fassions**		**faisant**
il **fallut**	il **faudra**	il **faudrait**	qu'il **faille**		– –
je **fuis**	je **fuirai**	je **fuirais**	que je **fuie** que nous **fuyions**		**fuyant**
je **lus**	je **lirai**	je **lirais**	que je **lise** que nous **lisions**		**lisant**
je **mis**	je **mettrai**	je **mettrais**	que je **mette** que nous **mettions**		**mettant**
je **mourus**	je **mourrai**	je **mourrais**	que je **meure** que nous **mourions**		**mourant**

INFINITIF	PRÉSENT		IMPERATIF	PASSÉ COMPOSÉ	IMPARFAIT
naître *(to be born)*	je **nais** tu **nais** il **naît**	nous **naissons** vous **naissez** ils **naissent**	**nais!** **naissons!** **naissez!**	je **suis né(e)**	je **naissais**
ouvrir *(to open)*	j'**ouvre** tu **ouvres** il **ouvre**	nous **ouvrons** vous **ouvrez** ils **ouvrent**	**ouvre!** **ouvrons!** **ouvrez!**	j'**ai ouvert**	j'**ouvrais**
peindre *(to paint)*	je **peins** tu **peins** il **peint**	nous **peignons** vous **peignez** ils **peignent**	**peins!** **peignons!** **peignez!**	j'**ai peint**	je **peignais**
placer *(to place)*	je **place** tu **places** il **place**	nous **plaçons** vous **placez** ils **placent**	**place!** **plaçons!** **placez!**	j'**ai placé**	je **plaçais**
plaire *(to please)*	je **plais** tu **plais** il **plaît**	nous **plaisons** vous **plaisez** ils **plaisent**	**plais!** **plaisons!** **plaisez!**	j'**ai plu**	je **plaisais**
planifier *(to plan)*	je **planifie** tu **planifies** il **planifie**	nous **planifions** vous **planifiez** ils **planifient**	**planifie!** **planifions!** **planifiez!**	j'**ai planifié**	je **planifiais**
pleuvoir *(to rain)*	il **pleut**	– –	– –	il **a plu**	il **pleuvait**
pouvoir *(to be able,* *can)*	je **peux** tu **peux** il **peut**	nous **pouvons** vous **pouvez** ils **peuvent**	– –	j'**ai pu**	je **pouvais**
prendre *(to take, have)*	je **prends** tu **prends** il **prend**	nous **prenons** vous **prenez** ils **prennent**	**prends!** **prenons!** **prenez!**	j'**ai pris**	je **prenais**
recevoir *(to receive,* *get, obtain)*	je **reçois** tu **reçois** il **reçoit**	nous **recevons** vous **recevez** ils **reçoivent**	**reçois!** **recevons!** **recevez!**	j'**ai reçu**	je **recevais**
rendre *(to render)*	je **rends** tu **rends** il **rend**	nous **rendons** vous **rendez** ils **rendent**	**rends!** **rendons!** **rendez!**	j'**ai rendu**	je **rendais**
résoudre *(to resolve)*	je **résous** tu **résous** il **résout**	nous **résolvons** vous **résolvez** ils **résolvent**	**résous!** **résolvons!** **résolvez!**	j'**ai résolu**	je **résolvais**
rire *(to laugh)*	je **ris** tu **ris** il **rit**	nous **rions** vous **riez** ils **rient**	**ris!** **rions!** **riez!**	j'**ai ri**	je **riais**

PASSÉ SIMPLE	FUTUR	CONDITIONNEL	SUBJONCTIF	PARTICIPE PRÉSENT
je **naquis**	je **naîtrai**	je **naîtrais**	que je **naisse** que nous **naissions**	**naissant**
j'**ouvris**	j'**ouvrirai**	j'**ouvrirais**	que j'**ouvre** que nous **ouvrions**	**ouvrant**
je **peignis**	je **peindrai**	je **peindrais**	que je **peigne** que nous **peignions**	**peignant**
je **plaçai**	je **placerai**	je **placerais**	que je **place** que nous **placions**	**plaçant**
je **plus**	je **plairai**	je **plairais**	que je **plaise** que nous **plaisions**	**plaisant**
je **planifiai**	je **planifierai**	je **planifierais**	que je **planifie** que nous **planifiions**	**planifiant**
il **plut**	il **pleuvra**	il **pleuvrait**	qu'il **pleuve**	**pleuvant**
je **pus**	je **pourrai**	je **pourrais**	que je **puisse** que nous **puissions**	**pouvant**
je **pris**	je **prendrai**	je **prendrais**	que je **prenne** que nous **prenions**	**prenant**
je **reçus**	je **recevrai**	je **recevrais**	que je **reçoive** que nous **recevions**	**recevant**
je **rendis**	je **rendrai**	je **rendrais**	que je **rende** que nous **rendions**	**rendant**
je **résolus**	je **résoudrai**	je **résoudrais**	que je **résolve** que nous **résolvions**	**résolvant**
je **ris**	je **rirai**	je **rirais**	que je **rie** que nous **riions**	**riant**

INFINITIF	PRÉSENT		IMPÉRATIF	PASSÉ COMPOSÉ	IMPARFAIT
rompre *(to break)*	je **romps** tu **romps** il **rompt**	nous **rompons** vous **rompez** ils **rompent**	**romps!** **rompons!** **rompez!**	j'ai **rompu**	je **rompais**
savoir *(to know)*	je **sais** tu **sais** il **sait**	nous **savons** vous **savez** ils **savent**	**sache!** **sachons!** **sachez!**	j'ai **su**	je **savais**
sortir *(to go out)*	je **sors** tu **sors** il **sort**	nous **sortons** vous **sortez** ils **sortent**	**sors!** **sortons!** **sortez!**	je **suis sorti(e)**	je **sortais**
suivre *(to follow)*	je **suis** tu **suis** il **suit**	nous **suivons** vous **suivez** ils **suivent**	**suis!** **suivons!** **suivez!**	j'ai **suivi**	je **suivais**
se taire *(to be quiet)*	je **me tais** tu **te tais** il **se tait**	nous **nous taisons** vous **vous taisez** ils **se taisent**	**tais-toi!** **taisons-nous!** **taisez-vous!**	je **me suis tu(e)**	je **me taisais**
tenir *(to hold)*	je **tiens** tu **tiens** il **tient**	nous **tenons** vous **tenez** ils **tiennent**	**tiens!** **tenons!** **tenez!**	j'ai **tenu**	je **tenais**
vaincre *(to win, conquer)*	je **vaincs** tu **vaincs** il **vainc**	nous **vainquons** vous **vainquez** ils **vainquent**	**vaincs!** **vainquons!** **vainquez!**	j'ai **vaincu**	je **vainquais**
valoir *(to be worth, deserve, merit)*	je **vaux** tu **vaux** il **vaut**	nous **valons** vous **valez** ils **valent**	**vaux!** **valons!** **valez!**	j'ai **valu**	je **valais**
venir *(to come)*	je **viens** tu **viens** il **vient**	nous **venons** vous **venez** ils **viennent**	**viens!** **venons!** **venez!**	je **suis venu(e)**	je **venais**
vivre *(to live)*	je **vis** tu **vis** il **vit**	nous **vivons** vous **vivez** ils **vivent**	**vis!** **vivons!** **vivez!**	j'ai **vécu**	je **vivais**
voir *(to see)*	je **vois** tu **vois** il **voit**	nous **voyons** vous **voyez** ils **voient**	**vois!** **voyons!** **voyez!**	j'ai **vu**	je **voyais**
vouloir *(to want, wish)*	je **veux** tu **veux** il **veut**	nous **voulons** vous **voulez** ils **veulent**	**veuille!** **veuillons!** **veuillez!**	j'ai **voulu**	je **voulais**

PASSÉ SIMPLE	FUTUR	CONDITIONNEL	SUBJONCTIF	PARTICIPE PRÉSENT
je **rompis**	je **romprai**	je **romprais**	que je **rompe** que nous **rompions**	**rompant**
je **sus**	je **saurai**	je **saurais**	que je **sache** que nous **sachions**	**sachant**
je **sortis**	je **sortirai**	je **sortirais**	que je **sorte** que nous **sortions**	**sortant**
je **suivis**	je **suivrai**	je **suivrais**	que je **suive** que nous **suivions**	**suivant**
je **me tus**	je **me tairai**	je **me tairais**	que je **me taise** que nous **nous taisions**	**se taisant**
je **tins**	je **tiendrai**	je **tiendrais**	que je **tienne** que nous **tenions**	**tenant**
je **vainquis**	je **vaincrai**	je **vaincrais**	que je **vainque** que nous **vainquions**	**vainquant**
je **valus**	je **vaudrai**	je **vaudrais**	que je **vaille** que nous **valions**	**valant**
je **vins**	je **viendrai**	je **viendrais**	que je **vienne** que nous **venions**	**venant**
je **vécus**	je **vivrai**	je **vivrais**	que je **vive** que nous **vivions**	**vivant**
je **vis**	je **verrai**	je **verrais**	que je **voie** que nous **voyions**	**voyant**
je **voulus**	je **voudrai**	je **voudrais**	que je **veuille** que nous **voulions**	**voulant**

5 Passé Simple

The PASSÉ SIMPLE is a past tense which is used mainly in literary French. You may encounter the passé simple in newspaper and magazine articles, in short stories and novels. The passé simple is generally not used in conversational French, nor is it used in informal notes and letters.

FORMS

The PASSÉ SIMPLE is a simple tense.

> PASSÉ SIMPLE = INFINITIVE STEM + PASSÉ SIMPLE ENDINGS

For REGULAR VERBS, this tense is formed as follows:

INFINITIVE	parler	
STEM	parl-	**ENDINGS**
je	**parlai**	-ai
tu	**parlas**	-as
il/elle/on	**parla**	-a
nous	**parlâmes**	-âmes
vous	**parlâtes**	-âtes
ils/elles	**parlèrent**	-èrent

INFINITIVE	finir	
STEM	fin-	**ENDINGS**
je	**finis**	-is
tu	**finis**	-is
il/elle/on	**finit**	-it
nous	**finîmes**	-îmes
vous	**finîtes**	-îtes
ils/elles	**finirent**	-irent

INFINITIVE	vendre	
STEM	vend-	**ENDINGS**
je	**vendis**	-is
tu	**vendis**	-is
il/elle/on	**vendit**	-it
nous	**vendîmes**	-îmes
vous	**vendîtes**	-îtes
ils/elles	**vendirent**	-irent

PASSÉ SIMPLE OF SELECTED IRREGULAR VERBS
(FOR RECOGNITION)

il alla	aller
il but	boire
il conduisit	conduire
il connut	connaître
il craignit	craindre
il crut	croire
il dit	dire
il dormit	dormir
il dut	devoir
il eut	avoir
il écrivit	écrire
il fallut	il faut
il fit	faire
il fut	être
il lut	lire
il mit	mettre
il mourut	mourir
il naquit	naître
il ouvrit	ouvrir
il plut	plaire
il plut	il pleut
il prit	prendre
il put	pouvoir
il reçut	recevoir
il rit	rire
il sortit	sortir
il suivit	suivre
il tint	tenir
il vécut	vivre
il vit	voir
il voulut	vouloir
il sut	savoir

Many IRREGULAR VERBS have irregular stems in the passé simple.
These are always given in the **je**-form in dictionaries and verb charts.

Irregular verbs fall into three groups, according to their endings:

	je-form in **-us** connaître		**je**-form in **-is** prendre		**je**-form in **-ins** venir	
je	**connus**	**-us**	**pris**	**-is**	**vins**	**-ins**
tu	**connus**	**-us**	**pris**	**-is**	**vins**	**-ins**
il/elle/on	**connut**	**-ut**	**prit**	**-it**	**vint**	**-int**
nous	**connûmes**	**-ûmes**	**prîmes**	**-îmes**	**vînmes**	**-înmes**
vous	**connûtes**	**-ûtes**	**prîtes**	**-îtes**	**vîntes**	**-întes**
ils/elles	**connurent**	**-urent**	**prirent**	**-irent**	**vinrent**	**-inrent**

→ Note that **aller** follows the pattern of **-er** verbs: **j'allai, il alla, ils allèrent.**

USES

The passé simple corresponds to the simple past in English.

Champlain **fonda** Québec en 1608.   *Champlain **founded** Quebec in 1608.*

Contrast the use of the past tenses in French:

To express	in LITERARY French:	in CONVERSATIONAL French:
• an on-going event or action *(what was happening)*	IMPERFECT **Il neigeait.** *(It was snowing.)*	IMPERFECT **Il neigeait.** *(It was snowing.)*
• a habitual past action *(what used to happen)*	IMPERFECT **En hiver, nous faisions du ski.** *(In winter, we used to go skiing.)*	IMPERFECT **En hiver, nous faisions du ski.** *(In winter, we used to go skiing.)*
• a specific event completed at a given moment in the past *(what happened)*	PASSÉ SIMPLE **Paul tomba et se cassa le bras.** *(Paul fell and broke his arm.)*	PASSÉ COMPOSÉ **Paul est tombé et il s'est cassé le bras.** *(Paul fell and broke his arm.)*
• an action that took place in the past at an indefinite time and has consequences in the present *(what was happening)*	PASSÉ COMPOSÉ **Personne ne l'a vu depuis l'accident.** *(Nobody has seen him since the accident)*	PASSÉ COMPOSÉ **Personne ne l'a vu depuis l'accident.** *(Nobody has seen him since the accident)*

APPENDIX D   MAPS

La France

L'ANGLETERRE

LA MANCHE

LA BELGIQUE

L'ALLEMAGNE

LE LUXEMBOURG

Lille•
NORD[2]

HAUTE-
NORMANDIE

PICARDIE

Le Havre•
•Rouen

Caen•

BASSE-
NORMANDIE

Versailles• ⊛Paris
RÉGION
PARISIENNE[1]

Nancy•

LORRAINE

CHAMPAGNE-
ARDENNE

Seine

LES VOSGES

•Strasbourg

Colmar•

ALSACE

Rhin

BRETAGNE

Rennes•

PAYS DE
LA LOIRE

CENTRE

Loire

•Tours

Dijon•

FRANCHE-
COMTÉ

•Nantes

BOURGOGNE

LA SUISSE

OCÉAN
ATLANTIQUE

POITOU-
CHARENTES

AUVERGNE

Vichy•

Saône

Annecy•

LIMOUSIN

Clermont-
Ferrand•

•Lyon

RHÔNE-ALPES

LES ALPES

L'ITALIE

Grenoble•

LE MASSIF

•Bordeaux

Garonne

Rhône

CENTRAL

AQUITAINE

Albi•

•Avignon

Nîmes•

PROVENCE-
CÔTE D'AZUR[3]

•Nice

MONACO

MIDI-PYRÉNÉES

Montpellier•

Cannes•

Toulouse•

LANGUEDOC
ROUSSILLON

Marseille•

Saint-
Tropez

Toulon•

LES PYRÉNÉES

L'ESPAGNE

MER MÉDITERRANÉE

LA CORSE

[1]Also known as Île-de-France
[2]Also known as Nord-Pas-de-Calais
[3]Also known as Provence-Alpes-Côte d'Azur *(Bottin 1989)*

Paris

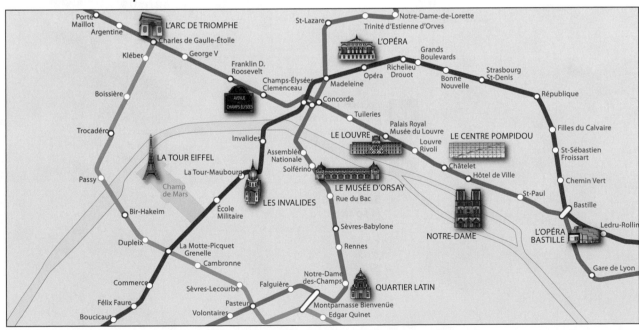

Paris Métro Map

Le Monde francophone

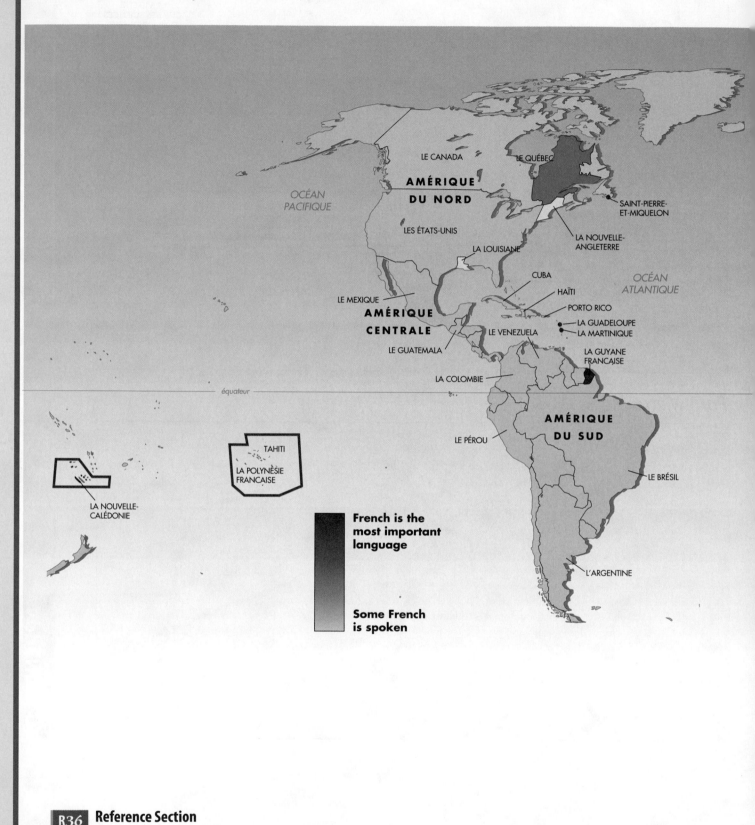

French is the most important language

Some French is spoken

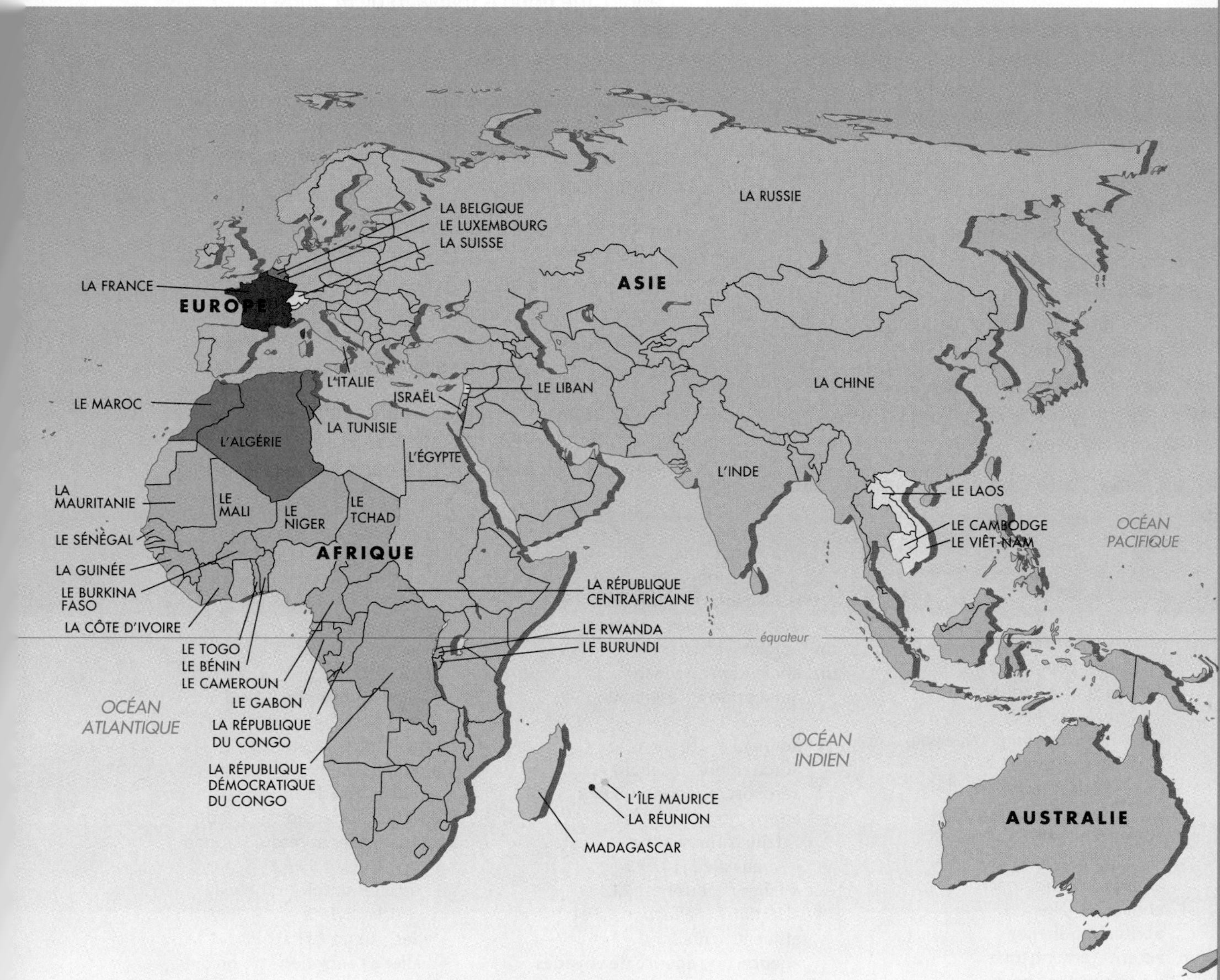

LA RUSSIE

ASIE

LA BELGIQUE
LE LUXEMBOURG
LA SUISSE

LA FRANCE

EUROPE

L'ITALIE

LE MAROC

ISRAËL

LE LIBAN

LA CHINE

L'ALGÉRIE

LA TUNISIE

L'ÉGYPTE

LA
MAURITANIE

LE
MALI

LE
NIGER

LE
TCHAD

L'INDE

LE LAOS

LE SÉNÉGAL

AFRIQUE

LE CAMBODGE
LE VIÊT-NAM

OCÉAN
PACIFIQUE

LA GUINÉE

LE BURKINA
FASO

LA CÔTE D'IVOIRE

LA RÉPUBLIQUE
CENTRAFRICAINE

LE TOGO
LE BÉNIN
LE CAMEROUN

LE RWANDA
LE BURUNDI

équateur

LE GABON

LA RÉPUBLIQUE
DU CONGO

OCÉAN
ATLANTIQUE

OCÉAN
INDIEN

LA RÉPUBLIQUE
DÉMOCRATIQUE
DU CONGO

AUSTRALIE

L'ÎLE MAURICE
LA RÉUNION

MADAGASCAR

VOCABULARY   FRANÇAIS-ANGLAIS

The French-English vocabulary contains active and passive words from the text, as well as the important words of the illustrations used within the units.

The numbers and letters following an entry indicate the first lesson in which the words or phrase is activated. The following abbreviations have been used:

R   Reprise
L   Lecture
IM Info Magazine
IC Interlude Culturel
FP Français Pratique
TA Teacher's Annotation
LC Langue et Communication
A   Appendix

The number after the section abreviation indicates the unit *Partie* in which the vocabulary word is introduced.

An asterisk (*) after the unit reference indicates that the word or phrase is presented in the *Mots utiles* section of the reading.

Nouns: If the article of a noun does not indicate gender, the noun is followed by *m. (masculine)* or *f. (feminine)*. If the plural is irregular, it is given in parentheses.

Adjectives: Adjectives are listed in the masculine form. If the feminine form is irregular, it is given in parentheses. Irregular plural forms are also given in parentheses.

Verbs: Verbs are listed in the infinitive form. An asterisk (*) in front of an active verb means that it is irregular. (For forms, see the verb charts in the Appendix.) Irregular past participle *(p.p.)*, present participle *(pres. part.)*, future *(fut.)*, and subjunctive *(subj.)* forms are listed separately.

Words beginning with an **h** are preceded by a bullet (•) if the **h** is aspirate; that is, if the word is treated as if it begins with a consonant sound.

A

à to, at
   à + *length of time* (length of time) from . . . **8.FP2**
   à + *distance* (distance) from . . . **8.FP2**
   à + *date, time until,* see you at (date, time) **8.FP1**
   à + *mode of transport* by (mode of transport) . . .
abord: d'abord first, at first **3.FP2**
aborder to approach
l' **abri** *m.* shelter
abriter to shelter
un **accent** accent, tone
accès: un accès pour personnes handicapées handicap access **6.FP1**
un **accident** accident **3.FP2**
un **accord** chord
   d'accord OK **2.FP2**
accorder to grant
*accueillir** to provide shelter; to welcome
acheter to buy **5.FP2**
s' **acheter** to buy (oneself) **1.FP3**
l' **acier** *m.* steel **2.FP3**
*acquérir** to acquire
actif: à mon actif to my credit

actuel (actuelle) current, present
actuellement currently
adieu *(pl. adieux)* farewell
un **adjoint** assistant
un **adolescent** teenager
l' **admiration** *f.* admiration **9.FP1**
s' **adresser à** to speak to
adroitement skillfully
l' **aéroport** *m.* airport **5.FP2**
une **affaire** business, affair
   faire l'affaire to be qualified **10.FP3**
les **affaires** *f.* business **2.L***
l' **affection** *f.* affection **9.FP1**
affluent tributary
agence: une agence de voyages travel agency **5.FP2**
agent: un agent d'assurances insurance agent **10.FP1**
   un agent de change stockbroker **10.FP1**
   un agent de police policeman
   un agent immobilier real estate agent **10.FP1**
*agir** to act
*s' agir: il s'agit de** it is about
aider (à) to help **2.FP2**
aïe! ouch! **7.FP1**
ailleurs elsewhere **7.IM**
   d'ailleurs besides **8.L***

aimer to like **2.LC2;** to love **9.FP1**
   aimer bien to like **9.FP1**
l' **aîné** eldest **R.L***
ainsi que as well as
l' **air** *m.* aria
   l'air conditionné air conditioning **6.FP1**
aise: à l'aise comfortable
ajouté added
ajouter to add
alléché attracted, tempted
aller: un aller et retour round-trip ticket **5.FP2**
   un aller simple one-way ticket **5.FP2**
*aller** to go **6.FP1**
   aller à l'entretien to go on an interview **10.FP2**
   aller à la pêche to go fishing **3.FP1**
   aller voir to go look **1.L***
*s' en aller** to go away **1.LC4**
une **allergie** allergy **7.FP1**
une **alliance** wedding ring
allumer to light **10.L***
   allumer un feu to light a fire **2.L***
une **allumette** match **4.FP1**
une **allure** allure, impression
alors que whereas
les **Alpes** *f.* the Alps **1.LC1**
l' **alpinisme** *m.* mountain climbing

faire de l'alpinisme   to go mountain climbing 3.FP1
altier (altière)   proud
l' aluminium m.   aluminum 2.FP3
amaigri   very thin
une amande   almond
un amateur   amateur
une ambiance   atmosphere 10.FP2
l' ambition f.   ambition 10.FP3
l' âme f.   soul
à l'âme tendre   with a soft heart
aménagé   equipped, developed
amer (amère)   bitter
un ami (une amie)   friend 9.FP1
l' amitié f.   friendship 9.FP1
l' amour m.   love
amoureux (amoureuse) de   in love with
l' ampleur f.   extent 4.L*
un ampli   amplifier 4.FP3
l' ampoule f.   swelling
s' amuser   to have fun 1.FP3
ancien (ancienne)   old, former 2.FP3
un ancien élève   alumnus 8.L*
l' angine f.   strep throat 7.FP1
un animal (pl. animaux)   animal 2.FP1
une animateur (une animatrice)   counselor
l' animosité f.   animosity 9.FP1
une annonce   notice, ad 2.IM
annulé   canceled 5.FP2
annuler   to cancel 5.FP2
une antenne   antenna 4.FP3
un antibiotique   antibiotic 7.FP1
l' antipathie f.   antipathy 9.FP1
l' anxiété f.   anxiety
s' apaiser   to calm down
l' appareil-photo m.   camera 4.FP3
apercevoir   to notice 6.L
*s' apercevoir   to notice
un apôtre   apostle, defender
l' apparence f.   appearance 2.FP3
un appartement   apartment 8.FP2
appartenir à   to belong to 2.L
appeler   to call 6.FP2
s' appeler   to be called, named 1.LC4
un apport   contribution
apporter   to bring 6.L*
s' approcher (de)   to approach, come closer 1.LC4
appuyer   to lean 10.L* to push
après   after, afterwards 3.FP2
l' après-rasage m.   aftershave 1.FP2
l' aquarium m.   aquarium 2.FP1
un arbuste   shrub 2.FP1

l' arc-en-ciel m.   rainbow
arche: l'Arche f. de Saint Louis   the Arch of St. Louis 2.FP3
l' argent m.   silver R.L*
l' armée f.   the army
une armoire   wardrobe, closet 1.L*
arraché   torn away
arracher   to pull out
arranger   to fix 4.L*
ça s'arrangera   things will be okay 9.FP1
arrêter   to arrest 5.L*
s' arrêter   to stop (oneself) 1.FP3
l' arrière-garde f.   rear guard
arriver   to happen 3.FP2
arriver à   to manage to 4.L*
il arrive   it happens
il est arrivé quelque chose   something happened
on y arrive   one can do it
arroser   to water (plants, flowers)
l' arrosoir m.   watering can
un article   item 4.FP1
l' ascendance f.   ancestry
un ascenseur   elevator 6.FP1
l' aspirateur m.   vacuum
l' aspirine f.   aspirine 4.FP1
*s' asseoir   to sit down 1.LC4
assez   enough 3.LC1
l' assistance f.   audience
un(e) assistant(e) sociale   social worker 10.FP1
assister à   to be present at; to see 3.FP2
l' assurance f.   insurance
s' assurer   to make sure 8.L*
l' asthme m.   asthma 7.FP1
astucieux (astucieuse)   smart
un atelier   studio
un atelier d'artisan   craftsman workshop
athlétique   athletic 1.FP1
attacher   to attach 5.FP2
*atteindre   to reach
*attendre   to wait 5.FP2
*s' attendre à   to expect
attendant: en attendant   in the meantime
attendrissant   touching
*atterrir   to land 5.FP2
attirant   attractive, alluring
attiré   attracted
attirer   to attract
attraper   to catch, get 3.FP1
attraper un coup de soleil   to get a sunburn 3.FP1
une auberge   inn 6.FP1
une auberge de jeunesse   youth hostel 6.FP1

aucun   no
aucunement   not at all
augmenter   to increase
l' aumône f.   charity
auparavant   before
auprès de   with; next to
aussitôt que   as soon as 5.LC2
autant   as much
d'autant plus que   all the more that 9.L*
un autel   altar
l' autoroute f.   turnpike
autour de   around 9.L*
autre: un autre   another; another one 4.LC1
autre chose?   is there something else? 4.FP1
autre chose à faire   something else to do 2.FP2
d'autres   other(s), some other(s); other ones 4.LC1
les autres   the others
autrefois   in the past
l' Autriche f.   Austria
autrichien (autrichienne)   Austrian
avaler   to swallow 7.FP1
une avance   advance, progress
en avance   early 5.FP2
dix minutes d'avance   ten minutes early 5.FP2
avant: avant de   before 10.LC1
avant tout   above all
l' avant-bras m.   forearm
avant-hier   the day before yesterday 3.FP2
avantage: un avantage social   fringe benefit 10.FP2
l' avenir m.   future
l' aversion f.   aversion 9.FP1
averti   notified
aveu (pl. aveux)   admission
aveugle   blind
avis: à votre avis   in your opinion RA
un avocat (une avocate)   lawyer 10.FP1
*avoir   to have
avoir affaire à   to have to deal with 8.FP2
avoir beau essayer   to try in vain 4.L*
avoir confiance   to trust 9.FP2
avoir de la chance   to have good luck 9.FP1
avoir de la peine   to be sad, in pain 3.L*
avoir l'air décontracté   to look relaxed
avoir le coup de foudre

pour to fall in love with at first sight 9.FP1

avoir le mal de mer to be seasick 3.FP1

avoir le trac to be scared, nervous

avoir lieu to take place 2.L*

avoir mal to hurt, have pain 7.FP1

avoir mal à l'estomac to have an upset stomach 1.L*

avoir mal à la gorge to have a sore throat 7.FP1

avoir mal à la tête to have a headache 1.L*

avoir mal au coeur to feel nauseous 7.FP1

avoir mal au ventre to have a stomach ache 7.FP1

avoir peur to be scared 7.LC1

avouer to admit, avow 2.L*

B

un **badaud** onlooker

les **bagages** *m.* baggage, luggage 5.FP1

un **bagage à main** carry-on luggage 5.FP1

une **bague** ring R.L*

un **bahut** cupboard

se **baigner** to go swimming 3.FP1

un **bain** bath 1.FP3

un **baiser** kiss 7.L*

baisser to turn down, lower 6.FP2

se **baisser** to stoop, bend down 7.L*

un **bal** dance 8.L*

un **balai** broom 2.FP1

une **balance** scale

balayer to sweep 2.FP1

balbutier to mumble

un **balcon** balcony 6.FP1

une **balle** bullet

un **ballon** balloon 2.FP3

un **banc** bench

une **bande** gang 5.L*

en bande in a group

la **banlieue** suburbs

la **banque** bank 10.FP2

une banque d'affaires investment bank

un **banquier (une banquière)** bank teller 10.FP1

des **bans** official announcements

une **barbe** beard 1.FP1

barbu bearded 1.FP1

bas (basse) low 2.FP3

à bas down with

bâtiment: le bâtiment des Nations Unies United Nations building 2.FP3

*bâtir** to build

un **bâton** stick, pole

la **batterie** drums

*battre** to beat 7.L*

*se **battre** to fight

battu beaten

bavarder to chat

beaucoup a lot; very 3.LC1

beaucoup de mal a lot of difficulty, pain

bénéfique beneficial

bénévole voluntary

une **béquille** crutch 7.FP2

berger: un berger allemand shepherd dog

une **bestiole** small animal

une **bête** animal 3.L*

une **bêtise** silliness, stupidity 3.L*

une **bibliothèque** library, bookcase 8.FP2

bien well, good 1.FP4

bien portant in good health 7.FP1

bien serré close together 6.FP1

bien situé well located 6.FP1

bien sûr of course 2.FP2

un **bien** possession; asset

un bien honnête a property of one's own

les **biens** *m.* wealth 2.L*

les **biens immobiliers** *m.* real estate

un **bien-aimé** beloved

le **bien-être** well-being 10.L*

un **bienfait** benefit, blessing

bientôt soon

un **bijou** *(pl. bijoux)* jewel, jewelry 9.L*

un **billet** letter; ticket 5.FP2

la **biologie** biology 10.FP1

le **blé** wheat

blessé injured, wounded

blesser to hurt

se **blesser** to get hurt, injure oneself 3.FP1

bleu blue 1.FP1

un **bloc** pad (of paper) 4.FP1

blond blond 1.FP1

un **bocal** glass jar 3.L*

le **bois** wood 2.FP3

en bois wooden

un **bois** woods

une **boîte** club, nightspot; box 4.FP1

une boîte de couleurs paintbox

le **bonheur** happiness

bon (bonne) right; good

il est bon que it is good that 2.LC2

bonhomme good-natured

un **bonhomme** fellow, man

la **bonté** goodness

le **bord** brim; edge 3.IM

au bord de on the edge of

un **bossu** hunchback

la **bouche** mouth 1.FP1

bouclé curly, wavy

la **boue** mud

la **bouffe** food, grub

la **bougeotte** travelling urge

bouger to move (around)

sans bouger without moving

boule: la boule à zéro bald head 4.L*

bouleversé overwhelmed 7.L*

un **boulot** job

bourdonner to buzz

bourguignon (bourguignonne) people native to Burgundy

une **bourse** scholarship

bout: au bout de after, at the end of 8.L*

une **bouteille** bottle 2.FP3

une **boutique** shop 4.FP1

un **bouton** button (on camera) 4.FP3

des boutons a rash 7.FP1

un **bracelet** bracelet 9.L*

brailler to cry and scream

branche: une branche d'activité branch office 10.FP2

brancher to plug in

le **bras** arm 7.FP2

Bravo! Bravo! 9.FP1

bref brief

les **bretelles** *f.* suspenders

le **bric-à-brac** odds-and-ends

le **bricolage** fixing and building things

un **brigand** bandit

brillant shiny 2.FP3

briller to shine 3.FP3

la **brique** brick 2.FP3

brisé broken

briser to break

se **briser** to break

la **bronchite** bronchitis 7.FP1

bronzé light brown, tan

bronzer to tan oneself 3.FP1

brosse: une brosse à cheveux hairbrush 1.FP2

une **brosse à dents** toothbrush 1.FP2

se **brosser** to brush (one's hair, one's teeth) 1.FP2

se brosser les dents to brush one's teeth 1.FP2

le **brouillard** fog 3.FP3

la **brousse** bush, undergrowth

la **broussaille** brushwood

un **bruit** noise

brûlé burned

brûler to burn

se **brûler** to burn oneself 7.FP2

la **brume** fog 3.FP3

brun brown 1.FP1

bruyant noisy 6.FP1

un **buffet** sideboard 1.L*, food wagon

un **bureau** (pl. bureaux) office

un bureau de tabac tobacco shop

le **but** objective

dans ce but to this end

un **butin** booty

butte: en butte à faced with

C

ça: ça a eu lieu this happened, took place 3.FP2

ça fait combien? how much does that come to? 4.FP1

ça ira things will go well

ça n'a pas d'importance that doesn't matter 10.L*

ça s'est passé . . . this happened . . . 3.FP2

ça vous fait mal? does it hurt you? 7.FP2

une **cabine** booth

cabinet: un cabinet d'avocat lawyer's office 10.FP2

un cabinet de médecin doctor's office

caché hidden

cacher to hide 5.L*

se **cacher** to hide (oneself)

un **cachet** tablet (medicine) 7.FP1

un **cadeau** (pl. cadeaux) gift 6.L*

un **cadre** frame 10.L*

un(e) **cadre** executive

la **cage** cage 2.FP1

la **caisse** check-out counter

calme calm 1.FP4

un(e) **camarade** acquaintance, classmate 9.FP1

un **cambriolage** burglary 3.FP2

un **camion** truck

la **campagne** country (side)

le **Canada** Canada 1.LC1

un **canapé** small sofa 1.L*

les **Canaries** f. Canary Islands 5.FP1

cantonné quartered, stationed

une **carotte** carrot 2.FP1

le **caoutchouc** rubber 2.FP3

la **capacité** capacity, volume 2.FP3

un **caprice** whim 8.L*

un **car** bus

une **carie** cavity 7.FP2

un **carnet** notebook 4.FP1

carré square 1.FP1

carreaux: à carreaux plaid

un **carrosse** horse-drawn carriage

carte: une carte d'embarquement boarding pass 5.FP2

une carte d'identité identification card 5.FP1

une carte de crédit credit card 6.FP1

une carte de mémoire memory card 4.FP1

une carte postale postcard 4.FP1

un **carton** cardboard 2.FP3

cas: un cas d'urgence emergency

un **cascadeur (une cascadeuse)** stuntman

caserne: une caserne de pompiers fire station 8.FP2

une **casquette** cap (hat)

cassé broken 4.FP3

casser to break 3.FP1

se **casser** to break (body part) 3.FP1

se casser la jambe to break one's leg 3.FP1

une **casserole** pot, pan 1.L*

cause: à cause de because of 7.L*

une **caution** deposit

un **cavalier (une cavalière)** horseman (horsewoman)

ce: ce n'est pas croyable! that's not for real! 3.FP2

ce sera prêt this will be ready 4.FP3

c'est arrivé it happened 3.FP2

c'est incroyable! that's unbelievable! 3.FP2

c'est tout? that's all? 4.FP1

c'est votre tour it's your turn 4.FP1

c'est vous le patron (patronne)! you're the boss! 2.LC2

céder to give up

ceinture: une ceinture de sécurité seat belt 5.FP2

célèbre famous

célibataire single

celui (celle) this one 6.LC2

celui-ci (celle-ci) this one 2.L*

celui-là (celle-là) that one

celui (celle) de that of, the one belonging to 6.LC2

celui (celle) qui the one who(m), the one that 6.LC2

la **cendre** ash(es)

centre: un centre d'apprentissage training school

un centre de loisirs recreation center 8.FP2

un centre sportif gym, sports center 8.FP2

le **centre-ville** town center, downtown 8.FP2

certain(e)s some; certain ones 4.LC1

la **chair** flesh

la **chaleur** warmth

chambre: une chambre à air inner tube

une chambre d'hôte guest room

champêtre rural

un **champ** field 6.L*

sur le champ immediately

la **chance** luck

une **chandelle** candle 6.L*

changer: changer d'avis to change one's mind 7.L*

un **chantier** worksite

une **charge** burden 2.L*; rank

chargé loaded; responsible

chargé de laden with; loaded with

charger to load

se **charger** to take care of

un **chariot** shopping cart

chassé expelled

la **chasse** hunting

le **chat** cat 2.FP1

châtain chestnut (hair) 1.FP1

châtain clair gold (hair) 1.FP1

châtain foncé brown (hair) 1.FP1

chaud hot/warm 2.FP3

le **chauffage** heating

une **chaussure** shoe

chauve bald 1.FP1

chef: un chef de personnel head of personnel 10.FP1

un **chef-d'oeuvre** masterpiece

chemin: un chemin de fer railroad

la **cheminée** fireplace

une **chemise** shirt 2.FP1

un **chenil** kennel

chèque: un chèque de voyage
  traveler's check **6.FP1**
    par chèque (paid) by check
      6.FP1
  cher (chère) precious, dear
  chercher to claim (luggage)
    5.FP2
    chercher à to try to **10.L***
un **chercheur (une chercheuse)**
    researcher **10.FP1**
  chéri darling
un **chevalier** knight
  chevet: au chevet bedside
les **cheveux** *m.* hair **1.FP1**
    les cheveux en brosse
      crew-cut **1.FP1**
la **cheville** ankle **7.FP2**
  chez: chez des particuliers at
    private homes
    chez soi at home
le **chien** dog **2.FP1**
un **chiffon** cloth rag **2.FP1**
  chiffonné wrinkled
un **chiffonnier (une chiffonnière)**
    ragpicker
la **chimie** chemistry **10.FP1**
un **chirurgien (une chirurgienne)**
    surgeon **7.FP1**
  *choisir to choose **9.FP2**
le **chômage** unemployment
un **chômeur (une chômeuse)**
    unemployed person
  chouette super **3.L***
la **chrétienté** Christendom
une **cicatrice** scar **1.FP1**
le **ciel** *(pl. cieux)* sky
une **cime** peak
un **cintre** hanger **6.FP2**
  circulaire circular **2.FP3**
la **circulation** traffic **6.L***
les **ciseaux** *m.* scissors **1.FP2**
un **citadin** city dweller
un **citoyen (une citoyenne)** citizen
  clair light; sunny **6.FP1**
  classe: la classe affaires
    business class **5.FP2**
    la classe économie tourist
      class **5.FP2**
    la deuxième classe second
      class **5.FP2**
    la première classe first class
      5.FP2
  classer to file **10.FP3**
la **clé** key
la **climatisation** air conditioning
    6.FP1
le **climatiseur** air conditioner
le **clou** nail (metal) **2.FP3**
  coalisé allied
une **cocarde** cockade

code: le code de la route
  traffic regulations **8.FP2**
un **coffre** safe **R.L***
  coiffer to cover (head)
le **coiffeur** hairdresser **4.FP2**
une **coiffure** hairstyle
un **coin** corner
  au coin on the corner
  du coin from the
    neighborhood, area
la **colère** anger **7.LC1**
  en colère angry **1.FP4**
un **colis** package **4.FP1**
la **colle** glue **4.FP1**
  coller to stick, to glue
une **colombe** dove
un **colon** settler
  combien: combien de
    temps? how long? **6.FP1**
  combien en voulez-vous?
    how many would you like?
    4.FP1
  combien est-ce que je vous
    dois? how much do I owe
    you? **4.FP1**
  comble: à son comble at its
    height
une **commande** order
  comme since
    comme convenu as agreed
    comme d'habitude as usual
    comme si as if **8.L***
le **commerce** business, trade
    10.FP1
un **commerce** (small) business,
    shop **8.FP2**
  commun in common, shared
la **communication**
    communication **10.FP2**
une **compagnie** company **10.FP2**
    une compagnie internationale
      international company
      10.FP2
  complet (complète) complete, full
    (sold out) **5.FP2**
un(e) **complice** accomplice **5.L***
  composer to dial
  composter to punch (ticket)
    5.FP2
le **composteur** ticket-punching
    machine **5.FP2**
  *comprendre to include
  y compris including
un **comprimé** pill (medicine) **7.FP1**
la **comptabilité** accounting **10.FP1**
un(e) **comptable** accountant **10.FP1**
  compte: à son propre
    compte on his own account
    10.FP2
  compter to count on, to plan; to

count **6.FP1**
le **comptoir** trading post; counter
    5.FP2
la **comtesse** countess **7.L***
un **concours** competitive exam
la **condition** condition **2.FP3**
    à condition que provided, on
      condition that **10.LC2**
    de bonnes conditions de
      travail good working
      conditions **10.FP2**
  *conduire to lead **3.L***; to drive
une **confiance** trust **9.FP1**
  confiant trusting
  confier entrust
  confirmer to confirm **5.FP2**
la **confiture** jam
  confortable comfortable **6.FP1**
  confus upset
une **connaissance** acquaintance
    9.FP1
    en connaissance de cause
      knowingly
    faire la connaissance to meet
      (for the first time)
    les connaissances
      techniques technical
      knowledge **10.FP3**
  connu known
un **conseil** advice
  conseillé recommended
la **consigne** baggage-check **5.FP2**
une **consigne** rule
la **consistance** consistency **2.FP3**
  consterné dismaying
  *construire to build
un **conte** short story
  *contenir to contain
  content happy **1.FP4**
un **conteur (conteuse)** storyteller
  continuer to continue
un **contrebandier (une**
    contrebandière) smuggler
  contrepartie: en contrepartie in
    exchange
  contrôle: un contrôle de
    sécurité security check
    5.FP2
    un contrôle de passeports
      passport check **5.FP1**
  *convaincre to convince
  convaincu convinced
  convaincant convincing
  convoiter to desire secretly
  convoquer to call in (for an
    interview)
un **copain (une copine)**
    boy/girlfriend **9.FP1**
la **coqueluche** whooping cough
    7.FP1

un **cor** horn
une **corbeille** wastepaper basket, trash **2.FP1**
un **corbeau** *(pl. corbeaux)* crow
le **cordonnier** shoe repairer **4.FP3**
une **corne** horn
Cornouailles Cornwall (in southwestern England)
le **corps** body
une **correspondance** connection (plane) **5.FP2**
la **Corse** Corsica
cortège: un cortège funèbre funeral procession
costaud solid, well-built **1.FP1**
côté: la Côte d'Azur French Riviera (blue coast)
un **côté** side **4.L***
à côté (de) besides, next to
d'à côté next door
de l'autre côté de on the other side of
de leur côté as far as they are concerned
sur les côtés on the sides **4.FP2**
un **coton-tige** cotton swab **4.FP1**
le **cou** neck **1.FP1**
couché in bed
se **coucher** to go to sleep **1.FP3**; to set (sun); to be doubled over
couler to flow
un **couloir** aisle **5.FP2; corridor**
coup: un coup de main a helping hand, help
un coup de pinceaux brush stroke
un coup de téléphone phone call
une **coupe** (hair) cut
une coupe de cheveux haircut **4.FP2**
une **coupe-brushing** haircut and a blow-dry **4.FP2**
couper to cut **2.FP1**
se **couper** to cut (oneself) **1.FP2**
se couper à la main to cut one's hand **7.FP2**
se couper les cheveux to cut one's hair **4.FP2**
coupez-les-moi courts cut my hair short **4.FP2**
une **cour** courtyard; court
courant fluent
courbé rounded, arched **2.FP3**
se **courber** to bend over
coureur: un coureur (une coureuse) des bois fur trapper
*courir to run **1.L***

une **couronne** crown
le **courrier** mail **4.FP1**
cours: au cours (de) during, in the course of
au cours de l'engagement during battle
la **course** water
court short
un **couteau** *(pl. couteaux)* knife **2.FP1**
couvert overcast **3.FP3**
une **couverture** blanket **2.L***
*couvrir to cover
*craindre to fear, be afraid of **7.LC1**
la **crainte** fear **7.LC1**
le **crâne** skull **4.L***
un **crayon** pencil **4.FP1**
créer: créer sa propre entreprise start one's own business **10.FP2**
crème: la crème à raser shaving cream **1.FP2**
le **crépuscule** dusk
cri: un cri de ralliement rallying cry
criard loud (color)
crier to yell, shout **1.L***
une **crise** fit
*croire to believe **7.LC1**
un **croisement** crossing
se **croiser** to cross, meet
croissant increasing
une **croix** cross
la **croyance** belief
*cueillir to pick (flowers)
cuisiner to cook
cuit: cuit à la vapeur steamed
le **cuivre** copper **2.FP3**
un **cultivateur (une cultivatrice)** farmer **8.L***
un **curriculum vitae** résumé **10.FP3**
cutané of the skin

dans: dans les approximately
dans touts ses états very upset
dame: une dame de compagnie lady-in-waiting
un **débarquement** landing
débarquer to disembark, land **5.FP2**
débarrasser to clear **2.FP1**
débarrasser la table to clear the table **2.FP1**
se **débarrasser** to get rid of **3.L***
se **débloquer** to unlock
débordant overflowing

debout standing
le **début** beginning
un **débutant** beginner
un **décès** death
des **déchets** *m.* trash
décimé killed
décoller to take off (plane) **5.FP2**
un **découpage** division
découpé cut out
découper to cut (into pieces) **8.L***
*découvrir to discover
décrocher to pick up (phone)
déçu disappointed, deceived **1.FP4**
un **défaut** fault, failing
défendu forbidden **3.L***
défier to challenge
dégager to shorten (hair) **4.FP2**
des **dégâts** damage
dehors outside **3.FP2**
en dehors outside
déjà already, yet; ever **3.LC1**
délivrer to give, deliver
demander to ask, necessitate
demande: sur demande on request
se **demander** to wonder **8.L***
démarche: les démarches *f.* amoureuses steps in courtship
démissionner to resign
se **démocratiser** to become democratic
demoiselle: une demoiselle d'honneur bridesmaid
démontable that can be dismantled
démonter to take apart
une **dent** tooth **7.FP2**
une dent de sagesse wisdom tooth **7.FP2**
le **dentifrice** toothpaste **1.FP2**
un **dentiste** dentist **7.FP1**
le **déodorant** deodorant **1.FP2**
dépaysé lost (in a strange place)
se **dépêcher** to hurry (oneself) **1.FP3**
dépens: aux dépens at the expense (of)
se **déplacer** to move (around)
déplorer to deplore **7.LC1**
déprimé depressed **7.FP1**
depuis peu recently
un **député** congressman
déranger to bother
la **dérision** mockery
dernier (dernière) last **3.FP2**
se **dérouler** to take place

derrière   in back **4.FP2**

le   **dérrière**   behind, rear end

dès   as of; beginning in

   dès lors   from then on

   dès que   as soon as **5.LC2**

un   **désastre**   catastrophe **4.L***

   *descendre   to get off (train)
   5.FP2; to bring down 6.FP2

   descendre: avoir +

   descendu   to have taken
   or carried something down
   3.LC1

   descendre: être +

   descendu   to have gone
   down **3.LC1**

se   **déshabiller**   to get undressed
   1.FP3

   désirer   to wish **2.LC2**

   désolé   sorry, sad **2.FP2**

le   **désordre: en désordre**   in
   disorder **2.FP1**

   désormais   henceforth

le   **dessin**   design, art

   dessus: par-dessus   on
   sur le dessus   on top **4.FP2**

se   **détacher**   to separate, break
   away

   **détective: un détective
   privé**   private eye **5.L***

une   **détente**   relaxation

   *détruire   to destroy

   devant   in front (of) **8.FP1**

   sur le devant   in front **4.FP2**

une   **devanture (de magasin)**
   storefront

   développer   to develop (photos,
   personnality) **4.FP3**

   *devenir   to become

   deviner   to guess **3.FP2**

une   **devise**   motto

   *devoir   must; to owe **4.FP1**

   dévoué   devoted **7.L***

un   **dieu (une déesse; pl. dieux)**
   god, deity **2.IC**
   Dieu *m.*   God **2.IC**
   Mon Dieu!   My goodness
   3.FP2

   digne   dignified **8.L***

la   **dimension**   dimension, size
   2.FP3

la   **diminution**   decrease

   dîner   to dine, have dinner **3.LC1**

un(e)   **diplomate**   diplomat **10.FP1**

un   **diplôme**   diploma **10.FP3**

   *dire: à vrai dire   to tell the truth

   direct   direct (flight) **5.FP2**

un   **directeur (une directrice)**
   director **10.FP1**

se   **diriger vers**   to move toward **8.L***

un   **discours**   speech

*disparaître   to disappear, go
   away **5.L***

la   **disparition**   disappearance

   disposé   arranged

   disposer   to have (at one's
   disposal)

une   **dispute**   an argument **9.FP1**

se   **disputer**   to have an argument
   9.FP1

   dissimuler   to hide

   *distraire   to amuse

*se   **distraire**   to have fun

   divorcer   to get a divorce **9.FP2**

un   **docteur**   doctor **1.LC1**

   **dommage: il est dommage
   que**   it is too bad that **2.LC2**

   donner: donner à manger à
   to feed **2.FP1**

   donner lieu   to give rise

   donner rendez-vous à   to
   make an appointment/date
   with **8.FP1**

   donner un coup de main   to
   give a hand **2.FP2**

   donnez-m'en dix   give me ten
   (of them) **4.FP1**

se   **donner rendez-vous**   to agree to
   meet **8.FP1**

   dont   whose

   doré   gilded, golden

la   **dorure**   gilt

une   **dot**   dowry

la   **douane**   customs **5.FP1**

un   **douanier (une douanière)**
   customs officer

   doucement   gently

la   **douceur**   kindness

une   **douche**   shower **1.FP3**

   doué   gifted **8.L***

une   **douleur**   pain, suffering **7.FP2**

   douloureux (douloureuse) painful
   7.L*

se   **douter bien**   to be sure

   doux (douce)   soft, gentle

un   **drap**   sheet (bedding) **6.FP2**

   dressé   placed, prepared

une   **drogue**   drug

   droit   straight, upright **2.FP3;
   straightforward**

le   **droit**   law; right

   drôlement   truly **4.L***

   dur   hard **2.FP3; difficult**

la   **durée**   duration, period

   durer   to last **2.L***

E

eau: l'eau *f.* de toilette
   perfume **1.FP2**

ébahi   open-mouthed

s'   **écarter**   to move aside

   échapper à   to escape from

   échapper de peu   to escape
   narrowly

une   **écharpe**   sash

un   **échec**   failure

une   **échelle**   ladder

   des échelles   in steps (hair),
   uneven **4.L***

   échouer   to fail

un   **éclair**   (flash of) lightning **3.FP3**

   éclatant   very loud

   éclater   to break out

une   **écorce**   bark (tree)

   écossais   Scottish

l'   **écran** *m.*   screen

un   **écrivain**   writer

   écroulé   collapsed

l'   **eczéma** *m.*   rash (skin) **7.FP1**

   effacer   to erase

   effrayé   scared

   également   equally, also

   égorger   to slit the throat of

l'   **égout** *m.*   sewer

un   **élastique**   rubber band **4.FP1**

l'   **électronique** *f.*   electronics
   10.FP2

   élémentaire   elementary

   élevé   raised, high **2.FP3**

   mal élevé   impolite, poorly
   raised

   élever   to raise (children) **2.L***

s'   **élever**   to stand up

   élu   elected

l'   **emballage** *m.*   packaging

   embarquer   to board (plane)
   5.FP2

l'   **embarras** *m.*   difficulty

   embaucher   to hire

   emblème *m.*   emblem, logo

s'   **embêter**   to get bored **1.LC4**

l'   **embouteillage** *m.*   traffic jam

   embrasser   to kiss **1.L***

une   **embuscade**   ambush **2.IC**

   émerveillé   amazed

   emmener (person)   to bring **3.L***

   empaqueter   to bag (groceries)

   empêcher de   to prevent, keep
   from (doing) **1.L***

   n'empêche que
   nevertheless

s'   **empêcher (de)**   to stop, prevent
   oneself from **4.L***

l'   **emplacement** *m.*   site, location

un   **emploi**   employment, job **10.FP1**

   un emploi à mi-temps
   half-time job **10.FP3**

   un emploi à plein temps
   full-time job **10.FP3**

un **emploi à temps partiel**
part-time job **10.FP3**
un **emploi temporaire**
temporary job **10.FP3**
un **employé (une employée)**
employee, clerk **10.FP1**
emporter to take along; to
carry off
ému moved, touched
encore still
encore lui! him again!
*****encourir** to incur
*****s' **endormir** to fall asleep
endroit: cet endroit précis
this very spot
énervé nervous; upset, bothered
1.FP4
s' **énerver** to get upset **1.LC4**
l' **enfance** f. childhood
enfiler to put on (clothes)
enfin at last **3.FP2**
*****enfouir** to bury
*****s' **enfuir** to run away, flee
engagé politically active
un **engagé** volunteer
l' **engagement** m. military service
s' **engager** to enlist
enlever to take off, remove
4.FP3
s' **ennuyer** to be bored
ennuyeux (ennuyeuse) boring
énorme enormous **2.FP3**
*****s' **enquérir de** to inquire
une **enquête** survey
enregistrer to check (luggage)
5.FP2
enseigner to teach
ensuite next **3.FP2**
*****entendre: entendre dire** to
hear (it said) **8.L***
entendre parler de to hear
about
*****s' **entendre** to get along with
entendu agreed **8.FP1**
enterré buried
l' **enterrement** m. funeral
enterrer to bury
entonner to begin to sing
entouré surrounded
s' **entraider** to help each other out
entre among
entre-temps meanwhile
*****entreprendre** to undertake
une **entreprise** company **10.FP2**
entrer to be accepted (school)
*****entretenir** to take care of
entretenu maintained
un **entretien** m. interview
10.FP3
*****entrevoir** to anticipate

une **entrevue** interview **10.FP3**
un **envahisseur** invader
une **enveloppe** envelope **4.FP1**
envelopper to wrap **7.L***
l' **envers** m. reverse
l' **envie** f. envy, desire
environ about, approximately
l' **environnement** m.
environment **3.FP1**
un **envoyé** messenger
envoyer to send
épais (épaisse) thick **2.FP3**
épargne spare
s' **éparpiller** to scatter
l' **épaule** f. shoulder
une **épée** sword
éperdument madly
une **épine** thorn
une **épingle** pin **4.FP1**
une **épingle de sûreté**
safety pin **4.FP1**
éplucher to peel **2.FP1**
une **éponge** sponge **2.FP1**
épouser to marry **2.L***
épouvantable ghastly
les **époux** m. spouses, husband
and wife
épris enamored
éprouver to feel, experience
l' **escalade** f. rock climbing
faire de l'escalade to go rock
climbing
une **escale** stopover, connection
5.FP2
l' **esclavage** m. slavery
une **esclave** slave
espèces: en espèces in cash
6.FP1
un **espion (une espionne)** spy **5.L***
l' **espoir** m. hope
l' **esprit** m. soul, spirit; mind
un esprit d'initiative
enterprising mind **10.FP3**
essayer to try
l' **essence** f. gasoline **6.L***
essentiel: il est essentiel que
it is essential that
2.LC2
essoufflé out of breath
essuyer to wipe **2.FP1**
s' **essuyer** to wipe (oneself) dry
1.FP2
s'essuyer les mains to dry
one's hands **1.FP2**
et and **5.LC1**
s' **établir** to settle, establish
l' **étagère** f. shelf
un **étang** pond
une **étape** step, stage
l' **état** m. condition **2.FP3**

les **États-Unis** m. United States
1.LC1
*****éteindre** to turn off
*****s' **éteindre** to go out, be
extinguished
éteint out, off, extinct
un **étendard** military banner
*****étendre** to extend
*****s' **étendre** to extend
éternuer to sneeze **7.FP1**
l' **étoffe** f. fabric **2.FP3**
une **étoile** star
étonnant amazing **6.LC1**
étonné astonished **7.LC1**
l' **étonnement** m. amazement
7.LC1
étouffé suffocated
étranger: à l'étranger abroad **5.FP1**
*****être** to be
être accueilli to be welcomed,
invited
être d'accord to agree **9.FP2**
être enrhumé to have a cold
7.FP1
être reçu to be accepted
(school)
être témoin de to witness
3.FP2
être tranquille to be alone,
undisturbed **1.L***
un **être** human being
étroit narrow, tight **2.FP3**
une **étude** course of study **10.FP1**
faire des études (de) to study
9.FP3
les études d'ingénieur
engineering studies **10.FP1**
les études vétérinaires
veterinary studies **10.FP1**
étudier to study **10.FP1**
s' **évader** to escape
l' **éveil** m. wakefulness **10.L***
éveiller to wake up **10.L***
un **événement** event **3.FP2**
un **évêque** bishop
l' **évier** m. kitchen sink
avoir plein l'évier to have a
sink full (of pots)
éviter to avoid **3.FP1**
examiner to examine **7.FP1**
s' **excuser** to excuse oneself
apologize **1.FP3**
exécuter: executer une ronde to
dance in a circle
un **exemplaire** copy (books,
magazines)
exiger to insist **2.L***
expérience: l'expérience f.
professionnelle
professional experience
10.FP3

expliquer   to explain **2.L***
exposer   to exhibit **9.L***
exprimé   expressed
exquis   exquisite **7.L***
exténué   exhausted

fabriquer   to do, make **3.L***
face: en face de   opposite **6.L***,
   across from **8.FP1**
fâché   upset **3.L***
se fâcher   to be upset **9.FP1**
la façon   manner
faible   weak **1.FP1**
la faïence   glazed pottery
la faim   hunger
*faire   to make, do
   faire appel   to call; to ask
   faire bouillir   to boil **4.LC3**
   faire carrière   to have a career
      10.FP2
   faire connaître   to make
      known
   faire couper les cheveux
      to get a haircut
   faire cuire   to cook **4.LC3**
   faire de la planche à voile
      to go windsurfing **3.FP1**
   faire de la plongée
      sous-marine   to go scuba
      diving **3.FP1**
   faire du camping   to go
      camping **3.FP1**
   faire (du) mal à   to hurt **3.L***
   faire frire   to fry **4.LC3**
   faire l'innocent   to act
      innocent
   faire la cour   to court
      (somebody)
   faire la vaisselle   to wash the
      dishes **2.FP1**
   faire le ménage   to do
      housework **2.FP1**
   faire partie   to be a part of
   faire rage   to rage
   faire réchauffer   to reheat
   faire taire   to silence, stifle
   faire un pique-nique   to have
      a picnic **3.FP1**
   faire un plâtre   to make a cast
      (broken bone) **7.FP2**
   faire une analyse de sang
      to take a blood sample **7.FP1**
   faire une promenade en
      bateau   to take a boat trip
      3.FP1
*se faire: se faire des amis   to make
      friends **9.FP2**
   se faire mal   to get hurt **3.FP1**

se faire nommer   to name
      oneself
se faire tuer   to have oneself
      killed
*s'en faire   to worry **4.L***
un fait   fact **3.FP2**
   un fait divers   a minor news
      event **3.FP2**
*falloir   to be necessary
   il me faut   I need **4.FP1**
fané   withered
fard: le fard à paupières
      eyeshadow **1.FP2**
fatigué   tired **1.FP4**
la faune   wildlife
une fauve   wild beast
   fécond   prolific
Félicitations!   Congratulations!
      9.FP1
féliciter   to congratulate **9.FP1**
femme: la femme de
      chambre   chambermaid
le fer (metal)   iron **2.FP3**
   un fer à repasser   iron (for
      clothes) **2.FP1**
une ferme   farm **6.L***
   ferroviaire   railroad
un feu (pl. feux)   fire
une feuille   form (paper); leaf (tree)
le feuillage   leaves
les fiançailles *f.*   engagement
se fiancer   to get engaged **9.FP2**
la ficelle   string **4.FP1**
   fichu   ruined
   fidèle   loyal, faithful
   fier (fière)   proud **3.L***
la fierté   pride
la fièvre   fever **7.FP1**
la figure   face **1.FP1**
   figurer   to appear, figure; to
      imagine
un filet   net
le filtre   filter **4.FP3**
   fin   refined
la fin   end
   à la fin   towards the end
   finalement   finally **3.FP2**
la finance   finance **10.FP2**
*finir   to finish **3.LC1**
une firme   firm (company) **10.FP2**
se fixer   to settle
le flash   camera flash **4.FP3**
une fleur   flower **2.FP1**
*fleurir   to bloom
un fleuve   river
   flexible   flexible **2.FP3**
la flore   plant life
un flot   stream, cascade; wave
une flotte   fleet
le foie   liver

fois: une fois   once **7.FP1**
   à la fois   at the same time
   deux fois par jour   twice a day
      7.FP1
une folie   madness, lunacy
fonction: la fonction
      publique   civil service
      10.FP2
fonctionner   to function **4.FP3**
un(e) fonctionnaire   civil servant
      10.FP1
le fond   background; depth
   au fond   in the back; deep
      down
   fonder   to found
*fondre: fondre en larmes   to
      break into tears
la force   strength
la forêt   forest **3.FP1**
la formation   training
la forme   form **2.FP3**
   en forme   in shape **1.FP4**
   formidable   great, terrific
   fort   loud **6.L***; strong **1.FP1**;
      tightly
   fort avant   very late
   fou (folle)   crazy **3.L***
un fou (une folle)   madman/
      madwoman **7.L***
un fouet   whip
   fougueux (fougueuse)   brave
   fouiller   to search
la foule   crowd
se fouler   to sprain **7.FP2**
le four   oven **1.L***
la fourrure   fur
se fracturer   to fracture **7.FP2**
   fragile   weak **2.FP3**
la fraîcheur   coolness
   frais (fraîche)   fresh, cool
   frais et dispos   fresh and
      rested
le français   French (language)
      1.LC1
   à la française   in the French
      manner
*franchir   to cross, to bridge
   frapper   to knock (on door)
      1.L*; to strike
les freins *m.*   brakes **4.FP3**
   fréquenter   to visit
les fringues *f.*   clothing
   frisé   curly, frizzy **1.FP1**
   frissonner   to shiver, shudder
      9.L*
   froid   cold **2.FP3**
   froidure   cold weather
le front   forehead **1.FP1**
la frontière   border
*fuir   to flee

en fuite in flight, fleeing
*s' **enfuir** to flee
la **fumée** smoke
furieux (furieuse) furious **1.FP4**
un **fusil** gun, rifle
fusillé shot and killed

gagner: gagner sa vie to earn one's living **R.L***
un **gaillard** guy
un **gamin** kid
gant: un gant de toilette wash cloth **1.FP2**
un **garçon** bellboy **6.FP2**
  un garçon d'honneur usher (wedding)
garde: un garde du corps bodyguard
garder to keep
la **gare** train station **5.FP2**
gâter to spoil **7.L***
le **gazon** grass
gelé frozen **3.FP3**
une **gélinotte** grouse
gênant bothersome **3.L***
une **gendarmerie** police station **8.FP2**
un **genou (pl. genoux)** knee, lap **7.L***
un **genre** kind
gens: les gens m. **de service** servants
gentil (gentille) nice **2.FP2**
le/la **gérant(e)** manager **6.FP2**
la **gestion** management **10.FP1**
un **gilet** vest
gitan gypsy
un **gîte** simple lodging
glacé: glacé d'effroi frozen with fear
la **glace** ice **3.FP3**; mirror **1.FP2**
glisser to slip **3.FP1**
le **goût** taste
  le goût des responsabilités the inclination for responsibility **10.FP3**
une **goutte** drop **7.FP1**
une **gouvernante** governess
grâce à thanks to
grain: un grain de beauté beauty mark **1.FP1**
grand big **1.FP1**
  un grand centre commercial mall **8.FP2**
  un grand ensemble housing project
  une grande surface shopping center
*__grandir__ to grow (in size) **3.L***;

to grow up **9.FP3**
gratuit free
gratuitement free of charge
la **Grèce** Greece **5.FP1**
grêle frail
le **grenier** attic
une **grenouille** frog **3.L***
grièvement seriously
la **grippe** the flu **7.FP1**
gris grey **1.FP1**
grogner to grunt
gronder to scold
gros (grosse) fat, heavyset; big
la **guerre** war
guerrier (guerrière) warlike
un **guerrier (une guerrière)** warrior
le **guichet** ticket window **5.FP2**

H

habilement skillfully
s' **habiller** to get dressed **1.FP3**
habit: habit m. **noir** formal evening dress
habitué à accustomed to
haie: une haie d'arbustes hedge **6.L***
hardiment boldly
hasard: par hasard by chance
haut high **2.FP3**
le·**haut-parleur** loudspeaker **4.FP3**
héberger to shelter
l' **herbe** f. grass **2.FP1**
hériter (de) to inherit **8.L***
un **héritier (une héritière)** heir/heiress **R.L***
heure: à l'heure on time **5.FP2**
heureux (heureuse) happy **1.FP4**
hier yesterday **3.FP2**
  hier soir last night **3.FP2**
l' **histoire** f. history **10.FP1**
un **HLM (Habitation à Loyer Modéré)** low-income housing **8.IM**
homme: un homme (une femme) d'affaires business man, woman **10.FP1**
  mi-homme half man
honteux (honteuse) ashamed
l' **hôpital** m. hospital **7.FP2**
un **horaire** schedule **5.FP2**
un **hôtel** hotel **6.FP1**
  un hôtel bon marché inexpensive hotel **6.FP1**
  un hôtel de luxe luxury hotel **6.FP1**
hôtesse: l'hôtesse f. **de l'air** stewardess **5.FP2**
l' **humeur** f. mood **4.L***

de bonne humeur in a good mood **1.FP4**
de mauvaise humeur in a bad mood **1.FP4**
humide humid, wet **2.FP3**

I

ici: d'ici une semaine one week from now **4.FP3**
il y a ago **3.FP2**
  il n'y a pas de quoi you're welcome **2.FP2**
  il n'y aura pas there won't be
s' **illuminer** to brighten
un **immeuble** apartment building
l' **immobilier** m. real estate **10.FP2**
s' **impatienter** to get impatient **1.LC4**
une **impératrice** emperor's wife
important important **10.FP2**
l' **important** m. the important thing **8.IM**
  il est important que it is important that **2.LC2**
  n'importe quel any
  n'importe qui (just) anyone
  n'importe quoi anything **7.L***
imprescriptible that which cannot be legally taken away
imprimé printed
imprimer to print
improviste: à l'improviste unannounced
imprudent careless, imprudent
inattendu unexpected **8.L***
incendié burned to the ground
un **incendie** fire
s' **incliner** to bow
un **inconnu** stranger **7.L***
un **inconvénient** inconvenience, drawback
l' **indigestion** f. indigestion **7.FP1**
indispensable: il est indispensable que it is indispensable that **2.LC2**
indisponible unavailable
l' **industrie** f. industry **10.FP2**
inexpérimenté inexperienced
infirme crippled
un **infirmier (une infirmière)** nurse **7.FP1**
un **informaticien (une informaticienne)** computer specialist **10.FP1**
un **ingénieur** engineer **10.FP1**
injuste unfair **R.L***
inoffensif (inoffensive) harmless **8.L***
l' **inondation** f. flood

*inquiet (inquiète)   worried
s' **inquiéter**   to worry
*inscrire   to enroll; to register to inscribe
insensible   insensitive
insister: insister pour que   to insist that **2.LC2**
l' **insolation** *f.*   sunstroke
insouciant   carefree
inspecteur: un inspecteur de police   police detective **5.L***
s' **installer**   to settle **8.L***
instituer   to create, institute
institutrice   (primary school) teacher
l' **instruction** *f.*   education
insu: à l'insu de   without the knowledge of
*interdire   to prohibit
interdit   forbidden
s' **intéresser**   to be interested
intérieur: à l'interieur   inside
intérieurement   internally, inside
interrogé   interviewed, asked
interroger   to interrogate
*interrompre   to interrupt
*intervenir   to intervene
une **interview**   interview **10.FP3**
*introduire   to introduce; to lead
un **invité**   guest

J

la **jalousie**   jealousy **9.FP1**
jardin: un jardin public   public garden **8.FP2**
le **jardinage**   gardening
jeter   to throw **3.FP1**
se **jeter**   to throw oneself
jeûne   fast
job: un job d'été   summer job **10.FP3**
la **joie**   joy **7.LC1**
*joindre   to contact (someone) **9.L***
un **jongleur (une jongleuse)**   juggler
la **joue**   cheek
jour: dans deux jours   in two days' time **4.FP3**
un jour de congé   day off **4.L***
il fait grand jour   the sun is up and shining
le **journalisme**   journalism **10.FP1**
la **journée**   day
un(e) **juge**   judge **10.FP1**
juger   to judge, think
un **Juif (une Juive)**   Jew
jurer   to swear

jusqu'à   up to, until
jusqu'à quand   until when **6.FP1**
jusqu'alors   until then
jusqu'au bout   to the end **7.L***
jusqu'ici   until now **4.L***
juste   fair **R.L***
il est juste que   it is fair that **2.LC2**
justement   precisely at that moment **8.L***; as a matter of fact

L

laboratoire: un laboratoire de recherche   research laboratory **10.FP2**
lâcher   to loosen, let go
laid   ugly
la **laine**   wool
laisser   to leave **R.L***
laisser ouvert   to leave open
laisser tomber   to drop
laissez-les-moi longs   leave my hair long (haircut) **4.FP3**
lancer   to launch **4.L***; to send out
lancer un défi   to challenge
la **langue**   tongue
une langue étrangère   foreign language **10. FP1**
la langue maternelle   native language
un **lapin**   rabbit **2.FP1**
un **larcin**   small theft
le **lard**   salt pork
large   wide **2.FP3**
une **larme**   tear **7.L***
le **lavabo**   bathroom sink **2.FP1**
laver   to wash **2.FP1**
laver le linge   to do laundry **2.FP1**
se **laver**   to wash (oneself) **1.FP3**
se laver la figure   to wash one's face **1.FP2**
léger (légère)   light **2.FP3**
les **légumes** *m.*   vegetables **2.FP1**
le **lendemain**   the day after **6.L***
la **lenteur**   slowness
la **lentille**   (camera) lens **4.FP3**
les lentilles *f.* **de contact**   contact lenses **1.FP1**
lequel (laquelle)   which
lesquels (lesquelles)   which
la **lessive**   detergent **4.FP1**
une **lettre**   letter **4.FP1**

une lettre de recommandation   letter of recommendation **10.FP3**
levant   rising
lever   to raise
se **lever**   to get up
libre   free **2.FP2**
le **libre-échange**   free trade
librement   freely
lié   interwoven, linked
lien: les liens *m.* **de sang**   blood ties
lier: lier conversation   to talk, initiate conversation
un **lieu (pl. lieux)**   location
au lieu de   instead of
le **linge**   laundry
une **lingère**   laundry woman
la **lingerie**   laundry room **2.FP1**
*lire   to read
lisse   straight (hair) **1.FP1**; smooth **2.FP3**
lit: à un lit   with one bed **6.FP1**
faire le lit   to make the bed **2.FP1**
un **litre**   liter **1.LC1**
la **littérature**   literature **10.FP1**
le **littoral (pl. littoraux)**   coast
livraison: la livraison des bagages   baggage claim **5.FP2**
une **livre**   pound
se **livrer**   to give oneself up
un **livret**   booklet
une **locataire**   tenant
loger   to live, lodge **2.L***
la **loi**   law
loin   far, far away **8.FP2**
au loin   in the distance **6.L***
lointain   distant
long (longue)   long **1.FP1**
à la longue   in the long run
le long de   along
lorsque   when **3.LC2**
un **lot**   plot
louer   to rent
une **loupe**   magnifying glass **5.L***
lourd   heavy
loyer: un loyer modéré   low rent
une **lueur**   gleam
la **lumière**   light
lundi   Monday **3.FP2**
la **lune**   moon
une **lutte**   fight, struggle
en lutte   struggling
la lutte pour la vie   the struggle for survival

M

mâcher   to chew
machinalement   unconsciously
un magazine   magazine 2.FP1
un magnan   red ant
maigre   skinny 1.FP1
main: sous la main   at hand, available
la main-d'oeuvre   labor, manpower
maintes   many, several
le maire   mayor
la mairie   city hall 8.FP2
le maïs   corn
maison: une Maison des Jeunes   youth center 8.FP2
une maison individuelle   single-family house 8.FP2
mal   bad 1.FP4, harm
mal au foie   abdominal pain
mal aux dents   toothache 7.FP4
malade   sick 1.FP4
une maladie   sickness, disease 7.FP1
une maladie d'enfance   childhood illness 7.FP1
maladroit   clumsy
une malédiction   curse
maléfique   detrimental
un malfaiteur (une malfaitrice)   criminal
malgré   in spite of
malheureux (malheureuse)   unhappy 1.FP4
malicieux (malicieuse)   inclined to tease, malicious
une mallette   briefcase 5.L*
malpoli   impolite
une manche   sleeve
une manifestation   demonstration
manifester   to show, manifest
manquer   to lack
les maquis   guerilla troops
le maquillage   makeup
se maquiller   to put on makeup
se maquiller les yeux   to apply eye makeup 1.FP2
un marchand   merchant 2.L*
le/la marchand(e) d'antiquités   antique dealer 9.L*
marchander   to bargain over the price
marche: la marche à pied   walking
un marché   deal
marcher   to work, function 4.FP2
faire marcher   to operate (equipment) 4.LC3
marcher bien   to go well
marcher sur   to step on 1.LC3

les marches f.   steps, stairs
marécageux (marécageuse)   swampy
se marier   to get married 9.FP2
marin   marine
un marin   sailor
le marketing   marketing 10.FP1
une marque   designer, brand name
de marque   important
marrant   funny
marron   brown 1.FP1
le mascara   mascara 1.FP2
massif (massive)   massive 2.FP3
massif m. de fleurs   flower bed
mater   to put down
le matériel (pl. matériaux)   material, equipment
les maths f.   mathematics 1.LC1
la matière   material 2.FP3
la matière synthétique   synthetic material 2.FP3
maudit   darned
mauvais   bad
le matin   morning 7.FP1
la matinée   morning
la méchanceté   malice
méchant   mean, nasty 2.L*
une mèche   streak, highlight (hair)
méconnu   unrecognized
la Mecque   Mecca
un médecin   doctor 7.FP1
la médecine   medicine (the practice of) 10.FP1
le médicament   medicine, drugs
médiocre   average, mediocre
se méfier   to be distrustful
mégarde: par mégarde   by accident
mélanger   to mix
mélanger les colorants   to mix dyes
mêlé   mixed together
même   even
Mémé   grandma
mener   to take, lead
la menthe   mint
*mentir: sans mentir   to tell the truth, honestly
mention: avec mention   with honors
le menton   chin 1.FP1
menu   small
merci   thank you 2.FP2
merci beaucoup   thank you very much 2.FP2
merci mille fois   thanks a million 2.FP2
la messe   (Catholic) Mass
Messire   My Lord
mesurer   to measure 1.FP1

le métal (pl. métaux)   metal 2.FP3
la météo   weather forecast 3.FP3
un métier   trade
mètre: à 100 mètres   100 meters away 8.FP2
metteur: le metteur en scène   director
*mettre   to put, place, turn on 6.FP2
mettre des sutures   to put stitches (in a wound) 7.FP2
mettre la table   to set the table 2.FP1
mettre le couvert   to set the table (silverware) 2.FP1
mettre le feu   to set a fire 3.FP1
mettre en garde   to warn
mettre en question   to call
meuble: des meubles m. rustiques   rustic furniture 6.L*
le Mexique   Mexico 5.FP1
le micro   microphone 4.FP3
le miel   honey
millénaire   1000 years old
un milliard   one billion
millier: des milliers   thousands
mince   thin 1.FP1
miné   weakened
minuscule   minuscule 2.FP3
un miroir   mirror 1.FP2
mise: une mise en plis   a set (hair) 4.FP2
le Mississippi   Mississippi 1.LC1
une mode   way
modeste   modest
modique   low, modest
la moindre   the least, the smallest
un moine   monk
moins   less 6.FP1
à moins que   unless 10.LC2
un mois   month 3.FP2
la moitié   half 2.L*
moment: au moment où   just as 3.LC2
mondain   social, of fashionable society
la monnaie   change
les monnaies f.   coins
la mononucléose   mononucleosis 7.FP1
monter   to get on (train) 5.FP2; to bring up, carry up 6.FP2
monter une garde vigilante   to keep watchful guard
monter: avoir + monté   to have taken or carried something up 3.LC1

VOCABULARY FRANÇAIS-ANGLAIS *continued*

monter: être + monté(e) to have gone up **3.LC1**
montrer: montrer du doigt to point at **8.L***
un **montreur (une montreuse)** exhibitor
se **moquer de** to make fun of
un **morceau (pl. morceaux)** piece
morfondu upset
la **mort** death
un **mot** word **6.L***
mou (molle) soft **2.FP3**
un **moucheron** gnat
un **mouchoir** handkerchief **1.L***
  un **mouchoir en papier** paper tissue **4.FP1**
mouillé wet **2.FP3**
un **moulin** coffee grinder
*mourir to die **9.FP2**
  mourir de faim to die of hunger
la **moustache** moustache **1.FP1**
le **moyen** means
moyen (moyenne) average; average size **10.FP2**
  en moyenne on the average
le **Moyen Âge** Middle Ages
  au Moyen Âge in the Middle Ages
muet (muette) silent **7.L***
*mugir to roar
multinational multinational **10.FP2**
un **mur** wall
murmurer to murmur, say in a low voice
un **musée** museum **8.FP2**
la **musique** music **10.FP1**
musulman Moslem

N

nager to swim **3.FP1**
naguère in the past
*naître to be born **9.FP2**
la **nature** nature **3.FP1**
naturel: il est naturel que it is natural that **2.LC2**
la **nausée** nausea **7.FP1**
une **navette** shuttle train
un **navire** boat, ship
ne . . . aucun no, not any **5.LC1**
ne . . . jamais never **3.LC1**
ne . . . ni . . . ni neither . . . nor **5.LC1**
ne . . . nulle part nowhere **5.LC1**
ne . . . pas encore not yet **3.LC1**

ne . . . personne no one, nobody **RC**
ne. . . plus no longer, not anymore **1.L***
ne. . . point not (at all)
ne . . . que only
ne . . . rien nothing **RC**
la **neige** snow **3.FP3**
nerveux (nerveuse) nervous **7.FP1**
le **nettoyage** cleaning **2.FP1**
nettoyer to clean **2.FP1**
neuf (neuve) brand new **2.FP3**
un **neveu (pl. neveux)** nephew **R.L***
le **nez** nose **1.FP1**
ni . . . ni neither . . . nor
un **nid** nest
niveau: de niveaux at the same level
  le niveau de vie standard of living
la **noblesse** nobility
les **noces** f. marriage
nocif (nocive) harmful
noir black **1.FP1**
  il fait noir it's dark **3.FP3**
  il fait nuit noire it's pitch black
nombreux (nombreuses) numerous
se **nommer** to be called, named
normal: il est normal que it is normal that **2.LC2**
la **Norvège** Norway
notable important, notable
la **note** bill **6.FP2**
*nourrir to feed
nouveau: de nouveau again **1.L***
les **nouvelles** news
la **Nouvelle Écosse** Nova Scotia
se **noyer** to drown **3.FP1**
nu naked, nude
un **nuage** cloud **3.FP3**
*nuire à to ruin, damage
nul (nulle) zero. nothing

O

l' **objectif** m. lens (focus) **4.FP3**
obligatoire compulsory
obliger to oblige, do a favor
l' **obscurité** f. darkness **4.L***
obsédé obsessed
observer to observe **3.FP1**
*obtenir to get, obtain
occasion: d'occasion second-hand, used **2.FP3**
l' **occident** m. Western world
occidental (occidentaux) western

occupé busy **2.FP2**
s' **occuper de** to be busy, take care of **1.LC4**
un **oculiste** ophthalmologist **7.FP1**
un **oeil (pl. yeux)** eye **1.FP1**
l' **oeuvre** f. work (of art)
*offrir to offer, give
un **oiseau (pl. oiseaux)** bird **2.FP1**
l' **ombre** f. shadow
  faire de l'ombre to cast a shadow
ondulé wavy **2.FP3**
ongle nail **1.FP2**
opérer to work, operate
opprimé oppressed
l' **or** m. gold **R.L***
un **orage** storm **3.FP3**
un **orchestre** band
un **ordinateur** computer **10.FP3**
une **ordonnance** prescription **7.FP1**
les **ordures** f. garbage **2.FP1**
une **oreille** ear **1.FP1**
un **oreiller** pillow **6.FP2**
les **oreillons** m. mumps **7.FP1**
l' **orgueil** m. pride **7.LC1**
l' **origine** f. background
orner to decorate, embellish
un **orphelin** orphan
oser to dare
ou or **5.LC1**
l' **ouate** f. cotton **4.FP1**
les **oubliés** m. forgotten people
un **ouragan** hurricane **3.FP3**
un **ours** bear
un **outil** tool
outre: en outre in addition
  outre-mer overseas
un **ouvrier (une ouvrière)** worker **R.L***
  les ouvriers working class
*ouvrir to open
ovale oval **1.FP1**

P

un **paillasson** doormat **1.L***
la **paille** straw
une **paillote** straw hut
le **pain** bread **2.FP1**
paisible peaceful, quiet
la **paix** peace
un **palais** palace
un **pansement adhésif** bandage **4.FP1**
  faire un pansement to dress a wound **7.FP2**
une **pantoufle** slipper
la **papeterie** stationery store **4.FP1**
le **papier** paper **2.FP3**
  le papier à lettres

stationery paper **4.FP1**

le papier hygiénique   toilet paper **4.FP1**

un **paquet**   package **4.FP1**

un **parachute**   parachute **2.FP3**

paraître**   to appear **7.L

il paraît que   it seems that

le **parapente**   parasailing

un **parc**   park **8.FP2**

***parcourir**   to travel through

parfait   perfect **3.L***

le **parfum**   perfume **1.FP2**

parier   to bet **7.L***

parler: parler anglais   to speak English **10.FP3**

parmi   among

part: à part entière   one hundred percent

le **partage**   division

partager   to share

parterre: les parterres de fleurs   flower beds

un **parti**   political party

***partir**   to leave **5.LC2**

à partir de   from

partir à (en, pour)   to leave for (destination) **5.LC2**

partir de   to leave from (place) **5.LC2**

partout   everywhere **3.L***

un **pas**   step

pas mal   a lot; not bad

pas possible!   impossible! **3.FP2**

un **passant**   passerby

un **passeport**   passport **5.FP1**

passer   to pass

passer (un vêtement)   to put on

passer l'aspirateur   to vacuum **2.FP1**

passer la nuit   to spend the night **6.FP1**

passer par   to go through **5.FP2**

passer: avoir + passé   to have spent (time) **3.LC1**

passer: être + passé   to have passed by **3.LC1**

se **passer**   to happen **3.FP2**

un **passionné**   real devotee

une **pastille**   tablet (medicine)

pâté: le pâté de cochon   type of meatloaf

la **patrie**   native land

un **patron (une patronne)**   boss **10.FP1**

la **paume**   palm

pauvre: Mon (Ma) pauvre! . . .   My poor . . . ! **10.FP1**

un **pays**   country **5.FP1**

un **paysage**   landscape

un **paysan (une paysanne)**   peasant, farmer

un **péage**   toll (highway)

la **peau (pl. peaux)**   skin

dans sa peau   in one's skin

une **pêche**   peach **8.L***

pêcher   to fish **3.L***

un **pêcher**   peach tree **8.L***

un **pêcheur (une pêcheuse)**   fisherman

le **peigne**   comb **1.FP2**

se **peigner**   to comb one's hair **1.FP2**

***peindre**   to paint

peiné   hurt

la **peine**   effort, trouble; sorrow

à peine   hardly **2.IC**

faire de la peine   to make sad, upset

la **peinture**   painting

un **pèlerinage**   pilgrimage

une **pèlerine**   cape

une **pellicule**   film

une **pelote**   ball (of string) **4.FP1**

la **pelouse**   lawn **2.FP1**

pendant   during **3.LC2**

pendant que   while **3.LC2**

pendre**   to hang (up) **10.L

pénible   painful

pension: la pension complète   full room and board **6.FP1**

la demi-pension   room with breakfast and dinner **6.FP1**

un **pensionnaire**   boarding student

une **pépite**   nugget

***perdre: perdre l'équilibre**   to lose one's balance **3.FP1**

*se **perdre**   to get lost **3.FP1**

perfectionner   to improve

périr   perish, die

une **permanente**   hair perm **4.FP2**

***permettre**   to allow

permis: un permis de conduire   driver's license **5.FP1**

perplexe   perplexed **1.FP4**

la **perruche**   parakeet **2.FP1**

peser   to weigh **1.FP1**

petit   small, short **1.FP1**

peuplé   populated

la **peur**   fright

faire peur à   to scare **3.FP1**

un **phare**   lighthouse

la **pharmacie**   pharmacy **4.FP1;** pharmaceutics (practice of) **10.FP1**

un **pharmacien (une pharmacienne)**   pharmacist **10.FP1**

le **phénix**   phoenix

la **philosophie**   philosophy **10.FP1**

une **photocopie**   photocopy **4.FP1**

le **photographe**   photographer **4.FP1**

la **physique**   physics **10.FP1**

pièce: une pièce d'argent   coin

une pièce d'eau   pool

une pièce d'identité   identity card **5.FP1**

une pièce d'or   gold coin **7.L***

pied: à pied   on foot **8.FP2**

pieds nus   bare feet

une **pierre**   stone **2.FP3**

pieuse (pieux)   pious

une **pile**   battery **4.FP1**

un **pillard**   looter

un **pilote**   pilot **5.FP2**

une **pilule**   pill

pimenté   hot, spicy

le **pinceau (pl. pinceaux)**   brush

pincé   pinched

piquer   to sting **3.FP1**

être piqué par les moustiques   to be bitten by mosquitos **3.FP1**

piqûre: une piqûre de novocaïne   shot of novocaine **7.FP2**

faire une piqûre   to give a shot, injection **7.FP1**

pire   worse **7.L***

une **piscine**   swimming pool **6.FP1**

pitoyable   pitiful **4.L***

une **place**   seat **5.FP2**

de la place   room **5.FP2**

la place d'Armes   parade ground

***plaindre**   to feel sorry for **7.LC1**

*se **plaindre de**   to complain about **7.LC1**

***plaire**   to please

plan: un plan d'eau   artificial lake

plaisanter: tu plaisantes!   you're kidding! **3.FP2**

plaisir: avec plaisir!   with pleasure! **2.FP2**

faire plaisir à   to please **8.L***

planifier   to plan

une **plante**   plant **2.FP1**

plaque: une plaque d'immatriculation   license plate **5.L***

le **plastique**   plastic **2.FP3**

en plastique   plastic **2.FP3**

plat   flat **2.FP3**

plein   full

en plein air   outdoors

plein de   a lot of

pleurer   to cry **1.L***

plier   to fold (up) **3.L***

le **plomb**   lead **2.FP3**

un **plombage**   tooth filling **7.FP2**
plonger   to plunge
la **pluie**   rain **3.FP3**
une **plume**   (quill) pen
la **plupart**   most of them, the majority **4.LC1**
 la plupart de   most of **4.LC1**
plus   more **6.FP1**
 en plus   in addition
 de plus en plus   more and more
 plus d'allure
plusieurs   several **4.LC1**
un **pneu (pl. pneux)**   tire
une **pneumonie**   pneumonia **7.FP1**
une **poche**   pocket **1.L***
le **poids**   weight **1.FP1**
un **poignet**   wrist **7.L***
un **poing**   fist
 point: sur le point de   on the verge
 pointu   pointed **2.FP3**
 poissonneux (poissonneuse)   full of fish
la **poitrine**   chest **8.L***
poli   polished **2.FP3**
la **police**   law enforcement **8.FP2**
la **Pologne**   Poland
polluer   to pollute **3.FP1**
la **pollution**   pollution **8.FP3**
polonais   Polish
une **pommade**   ointment
un **pompier**   firefighter
un **pont**   bridge
la **porte**   door; boarding gate **5.FP2**
un **portemanteau (pl. portemanteaux)**   hanger **6.FP2**
un **porte-parole**   spokesperson
 porter: porter des lunettes   to wear eyeglasses **1.FP1**
 se porter bien   to be in good health **7.FP1**
un **portier (une portière)**   doorman
une **portière**   train door **7.L***
le **Portugal**   Portugal **5.FP1**
poser   to put, to place
posséder to own, possess **9.L***
possibilité: la possibilité de promotion   opportunity for promotion **10.FP2**
la **poste**   post office **4.FP1**
 la poste restante   general delivery **4.FP1**
 poste: le poste de police   police station **8.FP2**
un **pot**   jar
un **pote**   buddy

une **poubelle**   garbage can **1.L***
un **pouce**   inch
la **poudre**   powder
la **poudrerie**   powdery snow
les **poumons** *m.*   lungs
pour   in order to **10.LC1**
 pour que   so that **10.LC2**
un **pourboire**   restaurant tip
pourtant   however
pousser   to grow
 pousser des cris   to scream **3.L***
 pousser un gros soupir   to let out a large sigh
la **poussière**   dust
***pouvoir**   to be able to
le **pouvoir**   power
un **pratiquant**   practitioner (religion)
se **précipiter**   to dash
préconiser   to advocate
***prédire**   to predict **3.FP3**
préférer   to prefer **2.LC2**
***prendre**   to take
 on ne l'y prendrait plus   he wouldn't be taken in again
 prendre connaissance   to become aware
 prendre la température   to take one's temperature **7.FP1**
 prendre la tension   to take one's blood pressure **7.FP1**
 prendre le deuil   to be in mourning
 prendre rendez-vous   to make an appointment, date **7.FP1**
 prendre sa retraite   to retire **9.FP2**
 prendre un bain de soleil   to sunbathe **3.FP1**
 prendre un pot   to go for a drink **8.FP1**
 pris   seized
préoccupé   worried **1.FP4**
se **préparer**   to get ready **1.FP3**
préposé   assigned
près: de près   closely, from close up **4.L***
présenter   to present, show **5.FP2**
se **présenter**   to show up
presque   almost
pressé   in a hurry
se **presser**   to hurry
prêter: prêter serment   to pledge allegiance
prétexte: un prétexte quelconque   some pretext or other

un **prêtre**   priest
la **preuve**   proof
prévenir**   to warn **3.L
***prévoir**   to plan ahead for
prier   to pray
 je t'en prie   you're welcome **2.FP2**
une **prière**   prayer
une **princesse**   princess **1.LC1**
la **prise**   taking; electrical plug **4.FP3**
le **prix**   prize
prochain   next **5.FP2**
proche   close
***produire**   to produce
***se produire**   to happen
profiter de   to take advantage of **1.L***
la **proie**   prey
le **prolongement**   extension
promener   to walk **2.FP1**
***se promener**   to take a walk **1.FP3**
***promettre**   to promise
propre   own; clean
la **propreté**   cleanliness, hygiene
un **propriétaire**   owner **R.L***
prosterné   prostrate, face to the ground
***protéger**   to protect **3.FP1**
provoqué   caused, provoked
la **psychologie**   psychology **10.FP1**
la **publicité**   advertising **10.FP1**
une **puce**   microchip
puis   then **3.FP2**
puisque   since **3.L***
puissant   powerful
un **pupitre**   school desk
pur   fresh

Q

le **quai**   platform **5.FP2**
quand   when **5.LC2**
 quand même   anyhow **3.L***
la **quantité**   quantity **4.FP1**
qu'est-ce que. . . : qu'est-ce qu'il y a?   what's wrong? **1.FP4**
 qu'est-ce qu'il y a eu?   What happened? **3.FP2**
 qu'est-ce que tu as?   what's the matter? **1.FP4**
qu'est-ce qui. . . : qu'est-ce qui a eu lieu?   what happened? **3.FP2**
 qu'est-ce qui est arrivé?   what happened? **3.FP2**

qu'est-ce qui ne marche pas? what doesn't work? **4.FP3**

qu'est-ce qui ne va pas? what's wrong? **7.FP1**

qu'est-ce qui s'est passé? what happened? **3.FP2**

quant à as for

le **quartier** neighborhood, district **8.FP2**

que whom, that, which **9.LC1**

quel (quelle) what, which **4.FP1**

quel dommage! too bad! **9.FP1**

quel est le problème? what is the problem? **4.FP3**

quel genre? what kind, type? **6.FP1**

quelle bonne nouvelle! what good news! **9.FP1**

quelle malchance! what bad luck! **9.FP1**

quelle que soit whatever

quelle sorte de what type of **5.FP2**

quelques some, a few **4.LC1**

quelqu'un someone, somebody **RC**

quelque chose something **RC**

quelque chose à déclarer something to declare **5.FP1**

quelque chose d'autre something else **4.FP1**

quelque part somewhere **5.LC1**

quelques-un(e)s some, a few **4.LC1**

se **quereller** to quarrel, have a fight **9.FP1**

question: question de because of

quête: en quête de in search of

faire la quête to pass the hat

queue: une queue de cheval ponytail **1.FP1**

qui who, that, which **9.LC1**

un **quiproquo** misunderstanding

quitter to leave (place/person) **5.LC2**

quoi: quoi de neuf? what's new? **3.FP2**

quoi que ce soit whatever it is

quoi qu'il arrive whatever happens

quoi qu'il lui en coûte whatever it may cost her

quoi qu'il y ait although there is (are)

quotidien (quotidienne) daily, common

R

la **racine** root

raconter to tell (what happened) **3.FP3**

une **radio** x-ray

faire une radio to x-ray **7.FP1**

une **rafale** gust of wind

raide straight

raison: la raison de vivre aim in life

*se **ralentir** to slow down **7.L***

un **ramage** song

ramasser to pick up **7.L***

une **rame** oar

ramener to bring back **3.L***

une **randonnée** long hike

une randonnée pédestre hiking

un **rang** row

rangé clean, put-away **2.FP1**

ranger to put away **2.FP1**

rappeler to remind

se **rappeler** to remember, to recall **1.LC4**

un **rapport** connection, relation **9.FP1**

bons rapports good relations **9.FP1**

mauvais rapports bad relations **9.FP1**

rapporter to equal, match, relate **3.IM**

se **raser** to shave **1.FP2**

le **rasoir** shaver **1.FP2**

rater to flunk; to miss (bus) **5.FP2**

rattrapé caught

se **rattraper** to catch up with

ravi delighted **7.LC1**

rayé striped

un **rayon** department (in store) **4.FP1**

*réagir** to react

un **réalisateur (réalisatrice)** movie director

recensé registered

le **récepteur** receiver

la **réception** reception desk **6.FP1**; gala, party

le/la **réceptionniste** receptionist, secretary **6.FP2**

*recevoir** to get, receive

recherche: la recherche scientifique scientific research **10.FP2**

recherché sought after

rechercher to research; to look for, search for **10.FP2**

récif: le récif de corail coral reef

un **récit** story

une **récolte** crop

faire la récolte to harvest

récompenser to reward **4.L***

*se **réconcilier** to make up **9.FP1**

la **reconnaissance** gratitude

reconnu recognized

*reconstruire** to rebuild

recouvert: recouvert de covered with

récréatif (récréative) recreational

rectangulaire rectangular **1.FP1**

recueilli adopted, taken in

reculé remote

récupérer to get back, recuperate **5.L***

*redécouvrir** to rediscover

redonner to give back

redoubler to repeat a grade

une **référence** reference **10.FP3**

réfléchir to think things over; to reflect on **7.L***

un **réfrigérateur** refrigerator **2.FP3**

un **regain** renewal

un **regard** glance, look

réglé: réglé par structured according to

le **règlement** rule

le **regret** regret **7.LC1**

regretter to regret **2.FP2**

la **reine** queen **1.LC1**

les **reins** *m.* kidneys

*se **réjouir** to be happy **9.FP1**

relâché released

les **relations** *m.* relations **9.FP1**

les relations publiques public relations **10.FP2**

relié linked

se **remarier** to remarry **9.FP2**

remarquer to notice **2.L***

remercier to thank **2.FP2**

remettre to put back **9.L***

se **remettre** to get back (into shape), restart

une **remise** shed

remonter to put back together; to go back (in time); go up

rempli filled

remplir to fill **2.FP1**

un **renard** fox

rencontrer to meet by chance, run into (person) **8.FP1**

se **rencontrer** to meet each other **8.FP1**

un **rendez-vous** appointment, date **7.FP1**

*se **rendormir** to go back to sleep **10.L***

*rendre grâce** to give thanks

rendre service to do a favor **2.FP2**

*se **rendre** to go, to render oneself
se rendre compte to realize 2.L*

un **renfort** reinforcement
renoncer to give up
un **renseignement** information
renvoyé fired
renvoyer to send away, send back
*se **répandre** to spread
répandu spilled
réparer to fix, repair 4.FP3
repasser to iron 2.FP1
*répondre** to respond 10.FP3
se **reposer** to rest 1.FP3
repousser to grow back
repousser du pied to kick away
un(e) **représentant(e)** representative 10.FP1
la **représentation** performance
se **représenter** to retake (the exam)
repris: un repris de justice prison inmate
une **requête** request 8.L*
une **réservation** reservation 5.FP2
réserver to reserve 6.FP1
une **résidence** apartment complex
*résoudre** to solve, resolve
le **respect** respect 9.FP1
respecter to respect 3.FP1
respirer to breathe
une **responsabilité** responsibility 10.FP2
*ressentir** to feel (pain or emotion) 1.FP4
le **ressort** spring (in watch) 4.FP3
rester: il ne reste que ... there is/are only ... left 10.L*
il reste ... there is/are ... left 8.L*
il vous reste ... you have ... left
rester au lit to stay in bed 7.FP1
un **resto** restaurant
retard: en retard late 5.FP2
une heure de retard one hour late 5.FP2
retentissant big, huge
*retentir** to resound
retirer to withdraw (money)
se **retourner** to turn around 7.L*
se **retrouver** to meet each other 8.FP1
réuni reunited
*se **réunir** to unite, get together
un **rêve** dream

un **réveil** alarm clock
réveiller to wake (something, someone) 6.FP2
se **réveiller** to wake (oneself) up 1.FP3
*revenir** to come back 1.L*
rêver to dream
*revoir** to see again
révolu long past
un **rhume** a cold 7.FP1
un rhume des foins hayfever 7.FP1
ricaner to laugh
rien: de rien you're welcome 2.FP2
rien à déclarer nothing to declare 5.FP1
rien à voir (avec) nothing to do (with)
rien que only
rigolo amusing 3.L*
le **rimmel** mascara 1.FP2
*rire** to laugh
une **rive** bank, shore
robe: une robe de chambre bathrobe
le **robinet** faucet
rocambolesque incredible, fantastic
le **roi** king
le Roi du Ciel King of Heaven
romantique romantic
*rompre** to break 7.L*
rompre (avec) to break up (with) 9.FP1
rond round 1.FP1
la **roue** wheel 4.FP3
rouge red 1.LC1
le rouge à lèvres lipstick 1.FP2
la **rougeole** measles 7.FP1
*rougir** to blush 4.L*
un **rouleau (pl. rouleaux)** roll (of paper towels) 4.FP1
rouler to roll; to travel, drive
roux (rousse) red-headed 1.FP1
un **royaume** kingdom
un **ruban** ribbon
la **rubéole** German measles 7.FP1
une **rubrique** column
rude rough
rugueux (rugueuse) rough, uneven 2.FP3
rupestre on rock walls
rustre boorish, lacking good manners
la **Russie** Russia 5.FP1

S

le **sable** sand
un **sac** bag 5.FP1
un sac à dos backpack
un sac à provisions shopping bag
sacré "cursed"
la **sagesse** wisdom
saigner to bleed 7.FP1
saigner du nez to get a nosebleed 7.FP1
sain healthy, sain
saint holy
saisi seized, taken
*saisir** to seize, take 9.L*
*se **saisir** to seize, take
un **salaire** salary 10.FP2
sale dirty 2.FP1
une **saleté** something gross, dirty
une **salle** hall
la salle d'armes fencing hall
la salle d'attente waiting room 5.FP2
la salle d'exercices exercise gym 6.FP1
la salle de bains bathroom 6.FP1
un **salon** show
une **salopette** overalls
saluer to salute, greet, take one's leave of
samedi on Saturday 1.LC1
le samedi on Saturdays 1.LC1
le **sang** blood
sanglant blood-stained
un **sanglier** wild boar
sans (que) without 10.LC1
sans bouger without moving
sans cesse unceasingly
sans trêve unceasingly
les **sans-abri** *m.* homeless people
la **santé** health
en bonne santé in good health 7.FP1
le **saucisson** sausage
sauf except
sauter to jump 1.L*
sauvage wild
sauver to save 5.L*
se **sauver** to escape
savant trained
un **savant** scientist
la **saveur** taste
le **savon** soap 1.FP2
un **scénario** script
scène: sur scène on the stage
une **scie** saw 2.FP3
science: les sciences *f.*

économiques economics **10.FP1**

les sciences *f.* politiques
  political science **10.FP1**

un(e) scientifique scientist **10.FP1**

le scotch scotch tape **4.FP1**

un seau (pl. seaux) bucket

sec (sèche) dry **2.FP3**

un sécateur shrub clippers **2.FP1**

se *sécher to dry (oneself) **1.FP2**

se sécher les cheveux to dry
  one's hair **1.FP2**

une sécheresse drought

le séchoir (hair) dryer **1.FP2**

secouer to shake **10.L***

*secourir to help

secours: crier au secours to call
  for help

un secrétaire writing desk

un(e) secrétaire secretary **10.FP1**

section: la section fumeur
  smoking section **5.FP2**

la section non-fumeur
  non-smoking section **5.FP2**

séduisant attractive **7.L***

séduit attracted, seduced

le seigneur lord

un séjour stay

faire un séjour to go on
  holiday, spend some time
  5.FP1

séjourner to stay, lodge **6.FP1**

semaine week **3.FP2**

sembler to seem, to appear
  1.FP4

la semoule semolina

le sens sense, direction, meaning

le sens des contacts
  humains ability to network
  10.FP3

la sensation feeling

un sentier trail

*sentir to smell **1.FP4**

*se sentir to feel

comment te sens-tu? how do
  you feel? **1.FP4**

se sentir chez soi to feel at
  home

ne pas se sentir de joie to be
  beside oneself with joy

se séparer to separate (husband &
  wife) **9.FP2**

un serpent serpent **3.FP1**

serré held tightly, close together

serrer to clutch

serrer la main de to shake
  hands with

service: le service dans les
  chambres room service
  6.FP1

la serviette towel **1.FP2**; napkin

*servir to serve **6.FP2**

*se servir de to use **10.FP3**

seul alone, lonely

le seul the only

un seul only one

le shampooing shampoo **1.FP2**

un shampooing a shampoo
  (hair salon) **4.FP2**

si if **5.LC2**

un siècle century

un siège a seat **5.FP2**

siffler to whistle **3.L***

sifflet: un sifflet à roulette
  whistle **3.L***

un signe sign

la signification meaning

signifier to represent, signify

sillonner to travel across

un singe monkey

singulier (singulière) strange

situé: bien situé well located
  6.FP1

mieux situé better located
  6.FP1

une société society, company **10.FP2**

soigner to treat (medical) **7.FP1**

soignez-le (la)! pay careful
  attention to it!

se soigner to take care of one's
  health

le soir evening **7.FP1**

soit all right, so be it

le sol floor **2.FP1**

des soldes sale

le soleil sun

le soleil levant rising sun

solliciter to solicit, ask for **10.FP3**

solide solid **2.FP3**

sombre black, somber

le sommeil sleep

un son beat

sonner to ring; to blow

sonnerie: la sonnerie de
  clairon bugle call

le Sopalin paper towels (brand
  name) **4.FP1**

la sorcellerie witchcraft

un sorcier (une sorcière) witch
  doctor

le sort fate

la sortie exit **5.FP2**

*sortir to take (something) out; to go
  out **2.FP1**

sortir la poubelle to take out
  the trash **2.FP1**

sortir: avoir + sorti to have
  taken something out
  3.LC1

sortir: être + sorti to have
  gone out **3.LC1**

un sot (une sotte) stupid person

souche: de souche native born

un souci concern, worry

souffler to blow out **10.L***; to
  blow **3.FP3**; to prompt

*souffrir to suffer

souhaiter to wish **2.LC2**

soupir: un soupir de
  soulagement sigh of relief

la source spring

sourd deaf

souriant smiling

*sourire to smile

un sourire smile

une souris mouse

*soustraire à to protect from

*soutenir to support

un souvenir memory

en souvenir de in memory of
  8.L*

souvent often **3.LC1**

*se souvenir (de) to remember

spacieux (spacieuse) roomy
  6.FP1

se spécialiser en to specialize,
  major in **10.FP1**

un spécialiste specialist **7.FP1**

un(e) spécialiste de données
  data processor **10.FP1**

un(e) spécialiste de
  logiciel software specialist
  10.FP1

un(e) spécialiste de
  marketing marketing
  specialist **10.FP1**

spirituel (spirituelle) witty

un square public garden

un stage training session,
  internship

faire un stage to do an
  internship

un standard operator **6.FP2**

station: une station thermale
  hot springs resort

une station-service gas station **8.FP2**

statue: la Statue de la
  Liberté Statue of Liberty
  2.FP3

une stèle stele (stone marker with an
  inscription) **6.L***

le steward steward **5.FP2**

une strophe verse

stylo: un stylo à bille ball point
  pen **4.FP1**

subit sudden

*subvenir to meet

subvenir aux besoins to meet
  the needs

une subvention subsidiary

se succéder to follow one another

succomber to die, succumb

la sueur sweat

*suffire   to be sufficient
  il suffit . . .   it is
    sufficient . . .
  il suffit d'y penser   you just
    have to think about it
la suite   series, sequence
  à la suite de   right behind; as a
    result of
suivant   according to; next
  5.FP2
*suivre   to take (a class); to follow
une supérette   convenience store
  4.FP1
supporter   to bear, stand **2.L***
supprimé   abolished
sûr   safe, sure
  bien sûr   of course **2.FP2**
surprenant   surprising
*surprendre   to surprise **9.L***
surpris   surprised **7.LC1**
sursaut: en sursaut   with a start
la survie   survival
susceptible   touchy
sympa   nice, kind **2.FP2**
la sympathie   instinctive liking
  9.FP1
**syndicat: le Syndicat
  d'Initiative**   Chamber of
  Commerce **6.LC1**

T

la table   table **2.FP1**
un tableau (pl. tableaux)   painting
  le tableau d'affichage
    billboard **5.FP2**
une tablette   bar
un tabouret   stool **4.L***
une tache   spot, stain
  les taches *f.* de rousseur
    freckles **1.FP1**
la taille   height, size (person) **1.FP1**
  de taille moyenne   average
    size **1.FP1**
  tailler   to prune, trim **2.FP1**
*se taire   to be quiet, shut up **1.LC4**
un talon   heel (of shoe) **4.FP3**
  talonné   followed close on one's
    heels
le tambour   drum
la Tamise   Thames (River)
une tanière   lair
  tant: tant de   so many; so much
  tant que   as long as
  tant pis!   too bad! **2.LC2**
un tapis   rug **1.L***
la tapisserie   tapestry
  tard   late **3.LC1**
  tas: des tas   tons, a lot
un technicien (une

technicienne)   technician
  10.FP1
le teint   complexion
la teinte   color
le teinturerie   the cleaners **4.FP3**
le téléobjectif   telephoto lens
  4.FP3
le téléphone   telephone **6.FP1**
téléphoner   to telephone, call
  10.FP3
la télévision   television **6.FP1**
tel (telle)   such
  tel qu'on le connaît   as we
    know him
tellement   so much **4.L***
  pas tellement   not that much
téméraire   bold
un témoin   witness
la température   temperature **2.FP3**
la tempête   storm **3.FP3**
  une tempête de neige
    snowstorm **3.FP3**
le temps   time **2.FP2**
  le beau temps   nice weather
    3.FP3
  le mauvais temps   bad
    weather **3.FP3**
  de temps en temps   from time
    to time **4.L***
*tendre   to hand, give **7.L***
tendu   tense, uptight **1.FP4**;
  stretched out
*tenir   to hold **3.L***, to have;
  present
  tenir à   to hold dear, cherish
    9.L*
  tenir compagnie   to keep
    company **9.L***
  tenir un langage   parler
  qu'a cela ne tienne   that won't
    matter
**tentative: une tentative
  d'évasion**   escape attempt
tenter   to tempt **9.L***
terne   dull **2.FP3**
la terre   land, earth, soil
  la terre d'asile   land of asylum
  la terre ferme   solid ground
  par terre   on the ground
  sous terre   underground
  la Terre Sainte   Holy Land
Terre-Neuve   Newfoundland
un testament   will
un têtard   tadpole **3.L***
tête: tête à tête   face to face
  en tête   leading
une thèse   thesis, essay
tiède   warm **2.FP3**
un tiers   one-third
le tiers-monde   third world

une tignasse   unruly mop (of hair)
  4.L*
un timbre   stamp
  tiré   fired
  tirer   to take out; to derive
  tirer au sort   to choose at
    random
  tiré de   based on
le tissu   fabric
la toile   canvas
le toit   roof
une tombe   tombstone
tomber   to fall **3.FP1**
  **tomber amoureux (amoureuse)
  de**   to fall in love with
  tomber dans l'eau   to fall in
    the water **3.FP1**
  tomber malade   to get sick
    9.FP2
une tondeuse   lawn-mower **2.FP1**;
  clippers **4.L***
*tondre   to mow, cut very short
  2.FP1; to clip very short **4.L***
le tonnerre   thunder **3.FP3**
tonte: la tonte des moutons
  sheep-shearing
tort: à tort   wrongly
une tortue   turtle
  tôt   early **3.LC1**
  toujours   still
un tour   turn; trick
  faire des tours   to do tricks
    3.L*
  faire le tour   to go around
  faire un tour   to walk **3.FP1**
une tour   tower, high-rise **8.FP2**
  la Tour Eiffel   Eiffel Tower
    2.FP3
le tournage   making (of a film)
une tournée   tour
  tourner   to film
se tourner   to turn around
  tousser   to cough **7.FP1**
  tout   any
  tout à fait   completely
  tout à l'heure   in a little while
    4.FP3
  tout court   directly
  tout d'un coup   all of a sudden
  tout de même   nevertheless
  tout de suite   immediately
  tout le temps   all the time,
    always
  tous les . . .   every
  toutes les 4 heures   every four
    hours **7.FP1**
  tout petit   very young
  tout près   nearby **8.FP2**
une toux   cough
*trahir   to betray

une **trahison** betrayal
un **train** train 5.FP2
un **trait** feature
un **traité** treaty
traîtrise treachery
une **trame** plot
tranquillement safely
traqué tracked, hunted down
le **travail (pl. travaux)** work 2.FP1
les travaux domestiques housework 2.FP1
les travaux des champs farm work
travailler to work 9.FP2
travers: à travers across, through 1.L*
de travers in a strange way
traverser to cross
tremblement: un tremblement de terre earthquake
trempé soaking wet
triangulaire triangular 2.FP3
tricher to cheat
tricolore blue, white, red
le **tricot** knitting 9.L*
triste sad 1.FP4
la **tristesse** sadness 7.LC1
un **trombone** paper clip 4.FP1
se **tromper** to make a mistake 1.LC4
trôner to occupy a place of honor
trop too 3.LC1
un **trottoir** sidewalk 9.L*
un **trou** hole
trousse: la trousse de toilette toiletry kit 1.FP2
trouver to find 9.FP2
se **trouver** to be (located); to find oneself
un **tube** tube 4.FP1
tuer to kill
tuméfié swollen
tuyau: le tuyau d'arrosage garden hose 2.FP1
un **type** guy, person

usagé worn 2.FP3
usé worn out, old 4.FP3
une **usine** factory 10.FP2
utile: il est utile que it is useful that 2.LC2
utiliser to use 10.FP3

la **vaisselle** dishes 2.FP1
la **valeur** value

une **valise** suitcase 5.FP1
*valoir** to be worth 3.IC
il vaut mieux que it is better that 2.LC2
valoriser to emphasize the value of
valser to waltz
vaniteux (vaniteuse) boastful
se **vanter** to boast
la **varicelle** chicken pox 7.FP1
vase: un vase de Venise Venetian glass vase
un **vassal (pl. vassaux)** subject
une **vedette** star
la **végétation** vegetation 3.FP1
veille previous day
veilleuse low (light)
un **vélodrome** bicycle racetrack
velours: le velours côtelé corduroy
un **vendeur (une vendeuse)** salesperson 10.FP1
venger to avenge
*venir** to come
faire venir to bring
un **verger** orchard 8.L*
le **verglas** sheet ice 3.FP3
véritable true
vernis: le vernis à ongles nail polish 1.FP2
un **verre** glass 2.FP1
les verres de Bohême Bohemian glasses
les verres de contact contact lenses 1.FP1
vers towards; at, about 1.FP3,
verser to pour 3.L*
vert green 1.FP1
le **vertige** dizzy spell, vertigo 7.FP1
les **vêtements** m. clothes 2.FP1
un(e) **vétérinaire** veterinary doctor 10.FP1
vêtu dressed
une **victime** victim, casualty
vide empty 2.FP3
vider to empty 2.FP1
la **vie** life R.V
la vie courante daily life
un **vieillard** elderly man
*vieillir** to grow old 9.FP2
le **vieillissement** aging
vieux (vieille) old 2.FP3
vif (vive) bright
vif d'esprit alert
la **ville** the city
vingt: vingt et un coups de canon 21-gun salute
la **Virginie** Virginia 1.LC1
le **visage** face 1.FP1
une **vitamine** vitamin 4.FP1
la **vitesse** speed

en vitesse quickly
une **vitre** window pane 2.FP1
la **vitrine** store window 9.L*
vivant living
*vivre** to live
une **voie** way
voilà there you go 4.FP1
voile: un voile de dentelle lace veil
une **voile** sail
*voir** to see
faire voir to show 4.LC3
la **voiture** car 2.FP1
voix; à mi-voix in a low voice
un **vol** flight 5.FP2; theft
volé stolen
voler to steal 5.L* to fly 9.C
les **volets** shutters 8.IC
un **voleur (une voleuse)** thief 5.L
la **volonté** will 7.LC2
volontiers! sure! with pleasure! I'd love to! 2.FP2
volumineux (volumineuse) voluminous, large in volume 2.FP3
vomir to throw up 7. FP1
*vouloir** to want, to wish 2.LC2
vouloir bien to want (used to accept an offer), to accept, agree 4.FP1
vouloir dire to mean 10.L*
*voyager** to travel 5.FP1
un **voyage** voyage, trip
vrai true
à vrai dire to tell the truth 8.L*
Vraiment? Really? Truly? 3.FP3
une **vue: une belle vue** a nice view 6.FP2

un **wagon** car (train) 5.FP2
un **wagon-lit** sleeping car (train) 5.IM
un **wagon-restaurant** dining car (train) 5.IM

y: j'y vais there: I'm going (there) 4.LC1
les **yeux** m. (**un oeil**) eyes 1.FP1

Z

les **zébrures** f. stripes, welts 9.IC

VOCABULARY ANGLAIS-FRANÇAIS

The English—French vocabulary contains active and passive words from the text, as well as words introduced in the *Mots utiles* sections of the Lectures.

The numbers and letters following an entry indicate the first unit section in which the words or phrase are activated. The following abbreviations have been used:

R Reprise
L Lecture
IM Info magazine
IC Interlude Culturel
FP Français pratique
TA Teacher's Annotation
LC Langue et communication
A Appendix

The number after the section abbreviation indicates the unit *Partie* in which the vocabulary word is introduced.

An Asterisk (*) after the unit reference indicates that the word or phrase is presented in the *Mots Utiles* section of the reading.

Nouns: If the article of a noun does not indicate gender, the noun is followed by *m. (masculine)* or *f. (feminine)*. If the plural is irregular, it is given in parentheses.

Verbs: Verbs are listed in the infinitive form. An asterisk (*) in front of an active verb means that it is irregular. (For forms, see the verb charts in the Appendix.)

Words beginning with an **h** are preceded by a bullet (•) if the **h** is aspirate; that is, if the word is treated as if it begins with a consonant sound.

A

ability: ability to network le sens des contacts humains **10.FP3**
abroad à l'étranger **5.FP1**
accident un accident **3.FP2**
accomplice un(e) complice **5.L***
accountant un(e) comptable **10.FP1**
accounting la comptabilité **10.FP1**
acquaintance une connaissance, un(e) camarade **9.FP1**
across à travers **1.L***
   across from en face de **8.FP1**
adhesive: adhesive bandage un pansement **4.FP1**
admiration l'admiration *f.* **9.FP1**
to **admit** avouer **2.L***
advertising la publicité **10.FP1**
affection l'affection *f.* **9.FP1**
after au bout de **8.L***; après **3.FP2**
afterwards après **3.FP2**
aftershave l'après-rasage *m.* **1.FP2**
again de nouveau **1.L***
ago il y a **3.FP2**
to **agree** *être d'accord **9.FP2**
   to agree to meet se donner rendez-vous **8.FP1**
agreed entendu **8.FP1**
air conditioning l'air *m.* conditionné **6.FP1**, la climatisation **6.FP1**
airport l'aéroport *m.* **5.FP2**
aisle un couloir **5.FP2**
all: all the more that d'autant plus que **9.L***
allergy une allergie **7.FP1**
Alps les Alpes *f.* **1.LC1**
already déjà **3.LC1**
aluminum l'aluminium *m.* **2.FP3**
alumnus un ancien élève **8.L***
amazement l'étonnement *m.* **7.LC1**
amazing étonnant **6.LC1**
ambition l'ambition *f.* **10.FP3**
amplifier un ampli **4.FP3**
amusing rigolo **3.L***
and et **5.LC1**
anger la colère **7.LC1**
angry en colère **1.FP4**
animal une bête **3.L***, un animal (pl. animaux) **2.FP1**
animosity l'animosité *f.* **9.FP1**
ankle la cheville **7.FP2**
another, another one un autre **4.LC1**
antenna une antenne **4.FP3**
antibiotic un antibiotique **7.FP1**
antipathy l'antipathie *f.* **9.FP1**
antique: antique dealer le/la marchand(e) d'antiquités **9.L***
anyhow quand même **3.L***
anything n'importe quoi **7.L***
apartment un appartement **8.FP2**
to **appear** *paraître **7.L***
appearance l'apparence *f.* **2.FP3**
to **apply: to apply eye make up** se maquiller les yeux **1.FP2**
appointment un rendez-vous **7.FP1**
to **approach** s'approcher (de) **1.LC4**
aquarium l'aquarium *m.* **2.FP1**
arch: Arch of St. Louis l'Arche *f.* de Saint Louis **2.FP3**
argument une dispute **9.FP1**
arm le bras **7.FP2**
around autour de **9.L***
to **arrest** arrêter **5.L***
as: as if comme si **8.L***
   as soon as aussitôt que, dès que **5.LC2**
aspirin l'aspirine *f.* **4.FP1**
asthma l'asthme *m.* **7.FP1**
astonished étonné **7.LC1**
at: at about vers **1.FP3**
   at last enfin **3.FP2**
   at the end of au bout de **8.L***
athletic athlétique **1.FP1**
atmosphere une ambiance **10.FP2**
to **attach** attacher **5.FP2**
attractive séduisant **7.L***
average: average size de taille moyenne **1.FP1**, moyen (moyenne) **10.FP2**
aversion l'aversion *f.* **9.FP1**
to **avoid** éviter **3.FP1**
to **avow** avouer **2.L***

B

bad   mal 1.FP4
bag   un sac 5.FP1
baggage   les bagages *m.* 5.FP1
  baggage claim   la livraison des
    bagages 5.FP2
  baggage-check   la consigne
    5.FP2
balcony   un balcon 6.FP1
bald   chauve 1.FP1
  bald head   la boule à zéro 4.L*
ball (of string)   une pelote (de
    ficelle) 4.FP1
  ball point pen   un stylo à bille
    4.FP1
balloon   un ballon 2.FP3
bank   la banque 10.FP2
banker   un banquier (une
    banquière) 10.FP1
bath   un bain 1.FP3
bathroom   la salle de bains 6.FP1
  bathroom sink   le lavabo
    2.FP1
battery   une pile 4.FP1
to be alone, undisturbed   *être
    tranquille 1.L*
  to be bitten by mosquitos
    *être piqué par des
    moustiques 3.FP1
  to be born   *naître 9.FP2
  to be busy   s'occuper de 1.LC4
  to be called, named   s'appeler
    1.LC4
  to be happy   *se réjouir 9.FP1
  to be in good health   se porter
    bien 7.FP1
  to be present at   assister à
    3.FP2
  to be qualified   *faire l'affaire
    10.FP3
  to be quiet   *se taire 1.LC4
  to be sad, in pain   *avoir de la
    peine 3.L*
  to be scared   *avoir peur 7.LC1
  to be seasick   *avoir le mal de
    mer 3.FP1
  to be upset   se fâcher 9.FP1
to bear   supporter 2.L*
  beard   une barbe 1.FP1
  bearded   barbu 1.FP1
to beat   *battre 7.L*
  beauty: beauty mark   un grain
    de beauté 1.FP1
  because of   à cause de 7.L*
  before   avant de 10.LC1
to begin to   *se mettre à 3.L*

to believe   *croire 7.LC1
  bellboy   le groom 6.FP2
to belong to   *appartenir à 2.L*
  besides   d'ailleurs 8.L*
to bet   parier 7.L*
  big   grand 1.FP1
  bill   la note 6.FP2
  billboard   le tableau d'affichage
    5.FP2
  biology   la biologie 10.FP1
  bird   un oiseau (pl. oiseaux)
    2.FP1
  black   noir 1.FP1
    black and white film   une
      pellicule en noir et blanc
      4.FP1
  blanket   une couverture 2.L*
to bleed   saigner 7.FP1
  blond   blond 1.FP1
to blow   souffler 3.FP3; (out)
    souffler 10.L*
  blue   bleu 1.FP1
to blush   *rougir 4.L*
to board (plane)   embarquer 5.FP2
  boarding: boarding pass   une
    carte d'embarquement 5.FP2
to boil   *faire bouillir 4.LC3
  bookcase   une bibliothèque
    8.FP2
  boss   un patron (une patronne)
    10.FP1
  bothered   énervé 1.FP4
  bothersome   gênant 3.L*
  bottle   une bouteille 2.FP3
  box   une boîte 4.FP1
  boyfriend, (girlfriend)   un copain
    (une copine) 9.FP1
  bracelet   un bracelet 9.L*
  brakes   les freins *m.* 4.FP3
  branch: branch office   une
    branche d'activité 10.FP2
  brand: brand new   neuf (neuve)
    2.FP3
  Bravo!   Bravo! 9.FP1
  bread   le pain 2.FP1
to break   casser 3.FP1, *rompre
    7.L*; (body part) se casser
    3.FP1
    to break a leg   se casser la
      jambe 3.FP1
    to break up (with)   *rompre
      (avec) 9.FP1
  brick   une brique 2.FP3
  briefcase   une mallette 5.L*
to bring (object)   apporter 6.L*;
    (person) emmener 3.L*
    to bring back   ramener 3.L*

to bring down   *descendre
    6.FP2
  to bring up, carry up   monter
    6.FP2
broken   cassé 4.FP3
bronchitis   la bronchite 7.FP1
broom   un balai 2.FP1
brown   brun 1.FP1, châtain
    foncé (hair) 1.FP1, marron
    1.FP1
to brush (one's hair, one's teeth)
    se brosser (les cheveux, les
    dents) 1.FP2
  to brush one's teeth   se
    brosser les dents 1.FP2
burden   une charge 2.L*
burglary   un cambriolage 3.FP2
to burn oneself   se brûler 7.FP2
business   les affaires *f.* 2.L*
  business (small)   un
    commerce 8.FP2
  business   le commerce 10.FP1
  business class   classe affaires
    5.FP2
  businessman, woman   un
    homme (une femme)
    d'affaires 10.FP1
  busy   occupé 2.FP2
button (on camera)   le bouton
    4.FP3
to buy   acheter 5.FP2
  to buy (oneself)   s'acheter
    1.FP3

C

cage   la cage 2.FP1
to call   appeler 6.FP2
  calm   calme 1.FP4
  camera   l'appareil-photo *m.*
    4.FP3
    camera flash   le flash 4.FP3
  Canada   le Canada 1.LC1
  canary: Canary Islands   les îles
    Canaries *f.* 5.FP1
to cancel   annuler 5.FP2
  canceled   annulé 5.FP2
  candle   une chandelle 6.L*
  capacity   la capacité 2.FP3
  car   une voiture 2.FP1; (train) un
    wagon 5.FP2
  cardboard   un carton 2.FP3
  carrot   une carotte 2.FP1
  carry-on: carry-on luggage   un
    bagage à main 5.FP1
  cat   le chat 2.FP1
  catastrophe   un désastre 4.L*
to catch   attraper 3.FP1

cavity une carie **7.FP2**
certain: certain ones certain(e)s **4.LC1**
chamber: Chamber of Commerce le Syndicat d'Initiative **6.LC1**
to change: to change one's mind changer d'avis **7.L***
check: (paid) by check par chèque **6.FP1**
to check (luggage) enregistrer **5.FP2**
chemistry la chimie **10.FP1**
chest la poitrine **8.L***
chestnut (hair) châtain **1.FP1**
chicken: chicken pox la varicelle **7.FP1**
childhood: childhood illness une maladie d'enfance **7.FP1**
chin le menton **1.FP1**
to choose *choisir **9.FP2**
circular circulaire **2.FP3**
city: city hall la mairie **8.FP2**
civil: civil servant un(e) fonctionnaire **10.FP1**
civil service la fonction publique **10.FP2**
to claim (luggage) chercher **5.FP2**
classmate un(e) camarade **9.FP1**
clean, put-away rangé **2.FP1**
to clean nettoyer **2.FP1**
cleaners le teinturier **4.FP3**
to clear débarrasser **2.FP1**
to clear the table débarrasser la table **2.FP1**
to clip: to clip very short *tondre **4.L***
clippers une tondeuse **4.L***
closely, from close up de près **4.L***
cloth: cloth rag un chiffon **2.FP1**
clothes les vêtements *m.* **2.FP1**
cloud un nuage **3.FP3**
cold froid **2.FP3**; un rhume **7.FP1**
color: color film une pellicule-couleurs **4.FP1**
comb le peigne **1.FP2**
to comb: to comb one's hair se peigner **1.FP2**
to come: to come back *revenir **1.L***
to come closer s'approcher (de) **1.LC4**
comfortable confortable **6.FP1**

communication la communication **10.FP2**
company une entreprise, une compagnie **10.FP2**
to complain about *se plaindre de **7.LC1**
complete, full (sold out) complet (complète) **5.FP2**
computer un ordinateur **10.FP3**
computer specialist un informaticien (une informaticienne) **10.FP1**
condition l'état *m.* **2.FP3**; la condition **2.FP3**
to confirm confirmer **5.FP2**
to congratulate féliciter **9.FP1**
Congratulations! Félicitations! **9.FP1**
connection, relation un rapport **9.FP1**; (plane) une correspondance **5.FP2**
consistency la consistance **2.FP3**
contact: contact lenses les lentilles *f.* de contact, les verres *m.* de contact **1.FP1**
to contact (someone) *joindre **9.L***
convenience: convenience store une supérette **4.FP1**
to cook *faire cuire **4.LC3**
copper le cuivre **2.FP3**
cotton l'ouate *f.* **4.FP1**
cotton swab un coton-tige **4.FP1**
to cough tousser **7.FP1**
to count compter **6.FP1**
counter le comptoir **5.FP2**
countess la comtesse **7.L***
country un pays **5.FP1**
course: course of study des études **10.FP1**
crazy fou (folle) **3.L***
credit: credit card une carte de crédit **6.FP1**
crew: crew-cut les cheveux en brosse **1.FP1**
crutch une béquille **7.FP2**
to cry pleurer **1.L***
curly, frizzy frisé **1.FP1**
customs la douane **5.FP1**
to cut couper **2.FP1**; (into pieces) découper **8.L***; (oneself) se couper **1.FP2**
cut my hair short coupez-les-moi courts **4.FP2**
to cut one's hair se couper les cheveux **4.FP2**

to cut one's hand se couper à la main **7.FP2**
to cut very short *tondre **2.FP1**

dance un bal **8.L***
darkness l'obscurité *f.* **4.L***
data processing l'informatique *f.* **10.FP1**
data processor un(e) spécialiste de données **10.FP1**
day after le lendemain **6.L***
day before yesterday avant-hier **3.FP2**
day off un jour de congé **4.L***
date un rendez-vous **7.FP1**
delighted ravi **7.LC1**
dentist un dentiste **7.FP1**
deodorant le déodorant **1.FP2**
department (in store) un rayon **4.FP1**
to deplore déplorer **7.LC1**
depressed déprimé **7.FP1**
detergent la lessive **4.FP1**
to develop (photos, personality) développer **4.FP3**
devoted dévoué **7.L***
to die mourir **9.FP2**
dignified digne **8.L***
dimension, size la dimension **2.FP3**
to dine, have dinner dîner **3.LC1**
diploma un diplôme **10.FP3**
diplomat un(e) diplomate **10.FP1**
direct (flight) direct **5.FP2**
director un directeur (une directrice) **10.FP1**
dirty sale **2.FP1**
to disappear, go away *disparaître **5.L***
disappointed, deceived déçu **1.FP4**
to disembark, land débarquer **5.FP2**
dishes la vaisselle **2.FP1**
distance: distance from . . . à + distance **8.FP2**
dizzy spell, vertigo le vertige **7.FP1**
to do, make fabriquer **3.L***
to do a favor rendre service **2.FP2**
to do housework faire le ménage **2.FP1**
to do laundry laver le linge

2.FP1
to do tricks *faire des tours 3.L*
does it hurt you? ça vous fait mal? 7.FP2
doctor un médecin 7.FP1, **un docteur 1.LC1**
doctor's office un cabinet de médecin 7.FP1
dog le chien 2.FP1
door, boarding gate la porte 5.FP2
doormat un paillasson 1.L*
to **dress a wound** faire un pansement 7.FP2
driver's license un permis de conduire 5.FP1
drop une goutte 7.FP1
to **drown** se noyer 3.FP1
dry sec (sèche) 2.FP3
dryer (hair) le séchoir 1.FP2
to **dry (oneself)** se sécher 1.FP2
to dry one's hair se sécher les cheveux 1.FP2
to dry one's hands s'essuyer les mains 1.FP2
dull terne 2.FP3
during pendant 3.LC2

ear une oreille 1.FP1
early tôt 3.LC1, **en avance 5.FP2**
to **earn: to earn one's living** gagner sa vie R.L*
economics les sciences f. économiques 10.FP1
Eiffel Tower la Tour Eiffel 2.FP3
electrical plug la prise 4.FP3
electronics l'électronique f. 10.FP2
eldest l'aîné R.L*
elevator un ascenseur 6.FP1
employee, clerk un employé (une employée) 10.FP1
employment, job un emploi 10.FP1
empty vide 2.FP3
to **empty** vider 2.FP1
engineer un ingénieur 10.FP1
engineering studies les études f. d'ingénieur 10.FP1
enormous énorme 2.FP3
enough assez 3.LC1
envelope une enveloppe 4.FP1
evening le soir 7.FP1
event un événement 3.FP2
ever déjà 3.LC1

every: every four hours toutes les **4 heures 7.FP1**
everywhere partout 3.L*
to **examine** examiner 7.FP1
to **excuse oneself, apologize** s'excuser 1.FP3
exercise gym la salle d'exercices 6.FP1
to **exhibit** exposer 9.L*
exit la sortie 5.FP2
to **explain** expliquer 2.L*
exquisite exquis 7.L*
extent l'ampleur f. 4.L*
eye un oeil (pl. yeux) 1.FP1
eyeliner l'eye-liner m. 1.FP2
eyeshadow le fard à paupières 1.FP2

fabric l'étoffe f. 2.FP3
face la figure 1.FP1, **le visage 1.FP1**
fact un fait 3.FP2
factory une usine 10.FP2
fair juste R.L*
to **fall** tomber 3.FP1
to fall in love with at first sight avoir le coup de foudre pour 9.FP1
to fall in the water tomber dans l'eau 3.FP1
far, far away loin 8.FP2
farm une ferme 6.L*
farmer un cultivateur (une cultivatrice) 8.L*
fear la crainte 7.LC1
to **fear, be afraid of** craindre 7.LC1
to **feed** donner à manger à 2.FP1
to **feel (pain or emotion)** *ressentir 1.FP4
to feel nauseous avoir mal au coeur 7.FP1
to feel sorry for *plaindre 7.LC1
fever la fièvre 7.FP1
field un champ 6.L*
to **file** classer 10.FP3
to **fill** remplir 2.FP1
film une pellicule
filter le filtre 4.FP3
finally finalement 3.FP2
finance la finance 10.FP2
to **find** trouver 9.FP2
to **finish** finir 3.LC1
fire station une caserne de pompiers 8.FP2

firm (company) une firme 10.FP2
first, at first d'abord 3.FP2
first class la première classe 5.FP2
to **fish** pêcher 3.L*
to **fix, repair** réparer 4.FP3
to **fix** arranger 4.L*
flat plat 2.FP3
flexible flexible 2.FP3
floor le sol 2.FP1
flower une fleur 2.FP1
flu la grippe 7.FP1
fog la brume 3.FP3
to **fold (up)** plier 3.L*
forbidden défendu 3.L*
forehead le front 1.FP1
foreign languages les langues étrangères 10.FP1
forest la forêt 3.FP1
form la forme 2.FP3
to **fracture** se fracturer 7.FP2
frame le cadre 10.L*
freckles les taches f. de rousseur 1.FP1
free libre 2.FP2
French (language) le français 1.LC1
friend un ami (une amie) 9.FP1
friendship l'amitié f. 9.FP1
fringe benefit un avantage social 10.FP2
frog une grenouille 3.L*
from time to time de temps en temps 4.L*
frozen gelé 3.FP3
to **fry** faire frire 4.LC3
full room & board la pension complète 6.FP1
full-time employment un emploi à plein temps 10.FP3
to **function, work** fonctionner 4.FP3; **marcher 4.FP3**
furious furieux (furieuse) 1.FP4

gang une bande 5.L*
garbage les ordures f. 2.FP1
garbage can la poubelle 1.L*
garden hose le tuyau d'arrosage 2.FP1
gas station une station-service 8.FP2
gasoline l'essence f. 6.L*
general delivery la poste restante 4.FP1

German measles la rubéole 7.FP1

to **get a nosebleed** saigner du nez 7.FP1

to **get a sunburn** attraper un coup de soleil 3.FP1

to **get angry** se mettre en colère 1.LC4

to **get back, recuperate** récupérer 5.L*

to **get bored** s'embêter 1.LC4

to **get dressed** s'habiller 1.FP3

to **get engaged** se fiancer 9.FP2

to **get hurt, injure oneself** se faire mal 3.FP1; se blesser 3.FP1

to **get impatient** s'impatienter 1.LC4

to **get lost** se perdre 3.FP1

to **get married** se marier 9.FP2

to **get off (train)** *descendre 5.FP2

to **get on (train)** monter 5.FP2

to **get ready** se préparer 1.FP3

to **get rid of** se débarrasser 3.L*

to **get sick** tomber malade 9.FP2

to **get undressed** se déshabiller 1.FP3

to **get upset** s'énerver 1.LC4

to **get** attraper 3.FP1

give me ten (of them) donnez-m'en dix 4.FP1

to **give a hand** donner un coup de main 2.FP2

to **give a shot, injection** faire une piqûre 7.FP1

gift un cadeau (pl. cadeaux) 6.L*

gifted doué 8.L*

girlfriend une copine 9.FP1

glass un verre 2.FP1

glass jar un bocal 3.L*

glue la colle 4.FP1

to **go** aller 6.FP1

to **go away** s'en aller 1.LC4

to **go back to sleep** *se rendormir 10.L*

to **go camping** faire du camping 3.FP1

to **go fishing** aller à la pêche 3.FP1

to **go for a drink** prendre un pot 8.FP1

to **go look** aller voir 1.L*

to **go mountain climbing** faire de l'alpinisme 3.FP1

to **go on a trip** *faire un voyage 5.FP1

to **go on an interview** aller à un entretien 10.FP3

to **go on holiday, spend some time** faire un séjour 5.FP1

to **go out** *sortir 2.FP1

to **go scuba diving** faire de la plongée sous-marine 3.FP1

to **go swimming** se baigner 3.FP1

to **go through** passer par 5.FP2

to **go to bed** se coucher 1.FP3

to **go windsurfing** faire de la planche à voile 3.FP1

God Dieu *m.* 2.IC

gold l'or *m.* R.L*

gold coin une pièce d'or 7.L*

gold (hair) châtain clair 1.FP1

good working conditions de bonnes conditions de travail 10.FP2

grass l'herbe *f.* 2.FP1

Greece la Grèce 5.FP1

green vert 1.FP1

grey gris 1.FP1

to **grow (in size)** 3.L*

to **grow old** *vieillir 9.FP2

to **grow up** grandir 9.FP3

to **guess** deviner 3.FP2

gym, sports center un centre sportif 8.FP2

H

hair les cheveux *m.* 1.FP1

hair perm une permanente 4.FP2

hairbrush une brosse à cheveux 1.FP2

haircut une coupe de cheveux 4.FP2

haircut and a blow-dry une coupe-brushing 4.FP2

hairdresser le coiffeur 4.FP2

half la moitié 2.L*

half-time employment un emploi à mi-temps 10.FP3

to **hand, give** *tendre 7.L*

handicap access un accès pour personnes handicapées 6.FP1

handkerchief un mouchoir 1.L*

to **hang (up)** *pendre 10.L*

hanger un portemanteau (pl. portemanteaux) 6.FP2; un cintre 6.FP2

to **happen** se passer 3.FP2; arriver 3.FP2

happy heureux (heureuse) 1.FP4; content 1.FP4

hard dur 2.FP3

harmless inoffensif (inoffensive) 8.L*

to **have pain, to hurt** avoir mal 7.FP1

to **have a career** faire carrière 10.FP2

to **have a cold** être enrhumé 7.FP1

to **have a headache** avoir mal à la tête 1.L*

to **have a picnic** faire un pique-nique 3.FP1

to **have a soar throat** avoir mal à la gorge 7.FP1

to **have a stomach ache** avoir mal au ventre 7.FP1

to **have an argument** se disputer 9.FP1

to **have an upset stomach** avoir mal à l'estomac 1.L*

to **have good luck** avoir de la chance 9.FP1

to **have fun** s'amuser 1.FP3

to **have to deal with** avoir affaire à 8.FP2

hayfever un rhume des foins 7.FP1

head of personnel un chef de personnel 10.FP1

in good health en bonne santé 7.FP1

to **hear (it said)** entendre dire 8.L*

hedge une haie d'arbustes 6.L*

heel (of shoe) un talon 4.FP3

height, size (person) la taille 1.FP1

heir (heiress) un héritier (une héritière) R.L*

to **help** aider à 2.FP2

to **hide** cacher 5.L*

high haut 2.FP3

history l'histoire *f.* 10.FP1

to **hold** *tenir 3.L*

to **hold dear, cherish** *tenir à 9.L*

hospital l'hôpital *m.* 7.FP2

hot/warm chaud 2.FP3

hotel un hôtel 6.FP1

housework les travaux *m.* domestiques 2.FP1

how much does that come to? ça fait combien? **4.FP1**

how do you feel? comment te sens-tu? **1.FP4**

how long? combien de temps? **6.FP1**

how many would you like? combien en voulez-vous? **4.FP1**

how much do I owe you? combien est-ce que je vous dois? **4.FP1**

humid, wet humide **2.FP3**

hurricane un ouragan **3.FP3**

to hurry (oneself) se dépêcher **1.FP3**

to hurt faire du mal **3.L***

to hurt one's head se blesser à la tête **7.FP2**

I need il me faut **4.FP1**

ice la glace **3.FP3**

identification card une carte d'identité **5.FP1**

if si **5.LC2**

important important **10.FP2**

impossible! pas possible! **3.FP2**

in disorder en désordre **2.FP1**

in a bad mood de mauvaise humeur **1.FP4**

in a good mood de bonne humeur **1.FP4**

in a little while tout à l'heure **4.FP3**

in back derrière **4.FP2**

in cash en espèces **6.FP1**

in front sur le devant **4.FP2**, (of) devant **8.FP1**

in good health bien portant **7.FP1**

in memory of en souvenir de **8.L***

in order to pour **10.LC1**

in shape en forme **1.FP4**

in steps (hair), uneven des échelles **4.L***

in the distance au loin **6.L***

in two days' time dans deux jours **4.FP3**

in your opinion à votre avis **R.A.**

inclination for responsibility le goût des responsabilités **10.FP3**

indigestion l'indigestion *f.* **7.FP1**

industry l'industrie *f.* **10.FP2**

inexpensive hotel un hôtel bon marché **6.FP1**

to inherit hériter (de) **8.L***

initiative un esprit d'initiative **10.FP3**

inn une auberge **6.FP1**

to insist exiger **2.L***

to insist that insister pour que **2.LC2**

instinctive liking la sympathie **9.FP1**

insurance agent un agent d'assurances **10.FP1**

international company une compagnie internationale **10.FP2**

interview un entretien **10.FP3**, une entrevue **10.FP3**

to iron repasser **2.FP1**

iron (for clothes) un fer à repasser **2.FP1**; (metal) le fer **2.FP3**

is there something else? autre chose? **4.FP1**

it is better that . . . il vaut mieux que . . . **2.LC2**

it is essential that il est essentiel que **2.LC2**

it is fair that il est juste que **2.LC2**

it is good that il est bon que **2.LC2**

it happened c'est arrivé **3.FP2**

it is important that il est important que **2.LC2**

it is indispensable that il est indispensable que **2.LC2**

it is natural that il est naturel que **2.LC2**

it is normal that il est normal que **2.LC2**

it is too bad that il est dommage que **2.LC2**

it is useful that . . . utile: il est utile que . . . **2.LC2**

it's dark il fait noir **3.FP3**

it's your turn c'est votre tour **4.FP1**

item un article **4.FP1**

jealousy la jalousie **9.FP1**

jewel, jewelry un bijou (pl. bijoux) **9.L***

journalism le journalisme **10.FP1**

joy la joie **7.LC1**

judge un(e) juge **10.FP1**

to jump sauter **1.L***

just as au moment où **3.LC2**

to keep company *tenir compagnie **9.L***

kiss un baiser **7.L***

to kiss embrasser **1.L***

knee, lap un genou (pl. genoux) **7.L***

knife un couteau (pl. couteaux) **2.FP1**

knitting le tricot **9.L***

to knock (on door) frapper **1.L***

to land atterrir **5.FP2**

to last durer **2.L***

last dernier (dernière) **3.FP2**

last night hier soir **3.FP2**

late tard **3.LC1**; en retard **5.FP2**

one hour late une heure de retard **5.FP2**

to launch lancer **4.L***

laundry room la lingerie **2.FP1**

law enforcement la police **8.FP2**

lawn la pelouse **2.FP1**

lawn-mower la tondeuse **2.FP1**

lawyer un avocat (une avocate) **10.FP1**

lawyer's office un cabinet d'avocat **10.FP2**

lead le plomb **2.FP3**

to lead *conduire **3.L***

to lean appuyer **10.L***

to leave laisser **R.L***; partir **5.LC2**

to leave my hair long (haircut) laissez-les-moi longs **4.FP2**

to leave (place/person) quitter **5.LC2**

to leave from (place) partir de **5.LC2**

to leave for (destination) partir à (en, pour) **5.LC2**

length: length of time from . . . à + length of time **8.FP2**

lens (camera) la lentille **4.FP3**

lens (focus) l'objectif *m.* **4.FP3**

less moins **6.FP1**

letter une lettre **4.FP1**

letter of recommendation une lettre de recommandation **10.FP3**

library une bibliothèque 8.FP2

license plate une plaque d'immatriculation 5.L*

light léger (légère) 2.FP3

to light allumer 10.L*
  to light a fire allumer un feu 2.L*

lightening (flash of) un éclair 3.FP3

to like aimer 2.LC2
  to like aimer bien 9.FP1

lipstick le rouge à lèvres 1.FP2

liter le litre 1.LC1

literature la littérature 10.FP1

to live, lodge loger 2.L*

long long (longue) 1.FP1

to look for, search for rechercher 10.FP2

to lose one's balance perdre l'équilibre 3.FP1

loud fort 6.L*

loudspeaker le•haut-parleur 4.FP3

to love aimer 9.FP1

low bas (basse) 2.FP3
  low-income housing un HLM (Habitation à Loyer Modéré) 8.FP2

luggage les bagages *m.* 5.FP1

luxury hotel un hôtel de luxe 6.FP1

madman/woman un fou (une folle) 7.L*

magazine un magazine 2.FP1

magnifying glass une loupe 5.L*

mail le courrier 4.FP3

to make a cast (broken bone) faire un plâtre 7.FP2
  to make a mistake se tromper 1.LC4
  to make an appointment/date with donner rendez-vous à 8.FP1
  to make an appointment, date prendre rendez-vous 7.FP1
  to make friends se faire des amis 9.FP2
  to make sure s'assurer 8.L*
  to make the bed faire le lit 2.FP1
  to make up se réconcilier 9.FP1

mall un grand centre commercial 8.FP2

to manage to arriver à 4.L*

management la gestion 10.FP1

manager le/la gérant(e) 6.FP2

marketing le marketing 10.FP1
  marketing specialist un(e) spécialiste de marketing 10.FP1

to marry épouser 2.L*

mascara le mascara 1.FP2, le rimmel 1.FP2

massive massif (massive) 2.FP3

match une allumette 4.FP1

material le matériel 2.FP3

mathematics les maths *f.* 1.LC1

mean, nasty méchant 2.L*

to mean *vouloir dire 10.L*

measles la rougeole 7.FP1

to measure mesurer 1.FP1

medicine (the practice of) la médecine 10.FP1

to meet each other se rencontrer 8.FP1
  to meet by chance, run into (person) rencontrer 8.FP1

memory card une carte de mémoire 4.FP1

merchant un marchand 2.L*

metal le métal (pl. métaux) 2.FP3

Mexico le Mexique 5.FP1

microphone le micro 4.FP3

minuscule minuscule 2.FP3

minor news event un fait divers 3.FP2

mirror un miroir 1.FP2; la glace 1.FP2

to miss (bus) rater 5.FP2

Mississippi le Mississippi 1.LC1

Monday lundi 3.FP2

mononucleosis la mononucléose 7.FP1

month un mois 3.FP2

mood l'humeur *f.* 1.FP4

more plus 6.FP1

morning le matin 7.FP1

most of la plupart de 4.LC1
  most of them, the majority la plupart 4.LC1

moustache la moustache 1.FP1

mouth la bouche 1.FP1

to move toward se diriger vers 8.L*

to mow *tondre 2.FP1

multinational multinational 10.FP2

mumps les oreillons *m.pl.* 7.FP1

museum un musée 8.FP2

music la musique 10.FP1

must devoir 4.FP1

My Goodness! Mon Dieu! 3.FP2

My poor . . . Mon (Ma) pauvre . . . 9.FP1

nail (metal) le clou 2.FP3

nail un ongle 1.FP2
  nail polish le vernis à ongles 1.FP2

narrow, tight étroit 2.FP3

nature la nature 3.FP1

nausea la nausée 7.FP1

nearby tout près 8.FP2

neck le cou 1.FP1

neighborhood, district le quartier 8.FP2

neither . . . nor ni . . . ni 5.LC1

nephew un neveu (pl. neveux) R.L*

nervous nerveux (nerveuse) 7.FP1

never ne . . . jamais 3.LC1

next suivant 5.FP2; ensuite 3.FP2

next prochain 5.FP2

nice, kind sympathique 2.FP2

no longer, not anymore ne . . . plus 1.L*
  no one, nobody ne . . . personne RC
  no, not any ne . . . aucun 5.LC1

noisy bruyant 6.FP1

non-smoking section la section non-fumeur 5.FP2

nose le nez 1.FP1

not yet ne . . . pas encore 3.LC1

notebook un carnet 4.FP1

nothing ne . . . rien RC
  nothing to declare rien à déclarer 5.FP1

to notice remarquer 2.L*; apercevoir 6.L*

nowhere ne . . . nulle part 5.LC1

nurse un infirmier (une infirmière) 7.FP1

to observe observer 3.FP1

of course bien sûr 2.FP2

often souvent 3.LC1

O.K. d'accord 2.FP2

old vieux (vieille) 2.FP3

former ancien (ancienne) 2.FP3
on foot à pied 8.FP2
  on his own account à son propre compte 10.FP2
  on time à l'heure 5.FP2
  on Saturday samedi 1.LC1
  on Saturdays le samedi 1.LC1
  on the sides sur les côtés 4.FP2
  on top sur le dessus 4.FP2
once une fois 7.FP1
one hundred meters away à 100 mètres 8.FP2
  one week from now d'ici une semaine 4.FP3
  one-way ticket un aller simple 5.FP2
  the one who(m), the one that celui (celle) qui 6.LC2
to **operate (equipment)** faire marcher 4.LC3
operator un standard 6.FP2
opportunity for promotion la possibilité de promotion 10.FP2
opposite en face de 6.L*
ophthamologist un oculiste 7.FP1
or ou 5.LC1
orchard un verger 8.L*
  other ones d'autres 4.LC1
ouch! aïe! 7.FP1
outside dehors 3.FP2
oval oval 1.FP1
oven un four 1.L*
overcast couvert 3.FP3
overwhelmed bouleversé 7.L*
to **owe** devoir 4.FP1
to **own, possess** posséder 9.L*
owner un propriétaire R.L*

P

package un paquet 4.FP1; un colis 4.FP1
pad: pad (of paper) un bloc 4.FP1
pain, suffering une douleur 7.FP2
painful douloureux (douloureuse) 7.L*
paper le papier 2.FP3
  paper clip un trombone 4.FP1
  paper tissue un mouchoir en papier 4.FP1
  paper towels (brand name) le Sopalin 4.FP1

parachute un parachute 2.FP3
parakeet la perruche 2.FP1
park un parc 8.FP2
to **pass by** passer 3.LC1
passport un passeport 5.FP1
  passport check un contrôle des passeports 5.FP1
peach une pêche 8.L*
  peach tree un pêcher 8.L*
to **peel** éplucher 2.FP1
pencil un crayon 4.FP1
perfect parfait 3.L*
perfume l'eau *f.* de toilette 1.FP2; le parfum 1.FP2
perplexed perplexe 1.FP4
pharmaceutics (practice of) la pharmacie 10.FP1
pharmacy la pharmacie 4.FP1
pharmacist un pharmacien (une pharmacienne) 10.FP1
philosophy la philosophie 10.FP1
photocopy une photocopie 4.FP1
photographer le photographe 4.FP1
physics la physique 10.FP1
to **pick up** ramasser 7.L*
pillow un oreiller 6.FP2
pill (medicine) un comprimé 7.FP1
pilot le pilote 5.FP2
pin une épingle 4.FP1
pitiful pitoyable 4.L*
plant une plante 2.FP1
plastic en plastique (adj.) 2.FP3; le plastique (n.) 2.FP3
platform le quai 5.FP2
to **please** faire plaisir à 8.L*
pneumonia une pneumonie 7.FP1
pocket une poche 1.L*
to **point: point at** montrer du doigt 8.L*
pointed pointu 2.FP3
police: police detective un inspecteur de police 5.L*
  police station le poste de police 8.FP2; une gendarmerie 8.FP2
polished poli 2.FP3
  political science les sciences *f.* politiques 10.FP1
to **pollute** polluer 3.FP1
ponytail une queue de cheval 1.FP1
Portugal le Portugal 5.FP1

postcard une carte postale 4.FP1
post office la poste 4.FP1
pot, pan une casserole 1.L*
to **pour** verser 3.L*
precisely at that moment justement 8.L*
to **predict** prédire 3.FP3
to **prefer** préférer 2.LC2
prescription une ordonnance 7.FP1
to **present, show** présenter 5.FP2
to **prevent, keep from doing** empêcher de 1.L*
pride l'orgueil *m.* 7.LC1
princess une princesse 1.LC1
private eye un détective privé 5.L*
professional experience l'expérience *f.* professionnelle 10.FP3
proud fier (fière) 3.L*
provided, on condition that à condition que 10.LC2
to **prune, trim** tailler 2.FP1
psychology la psychologie 10.FP1
public: public garden un jardin public 8.FP2
  public relations les relations *f.* publiques 10.FP2
to **punch (ticket)** composter 5.FP2
to **put, place, turn on** mettre 6.FP2
  to put away ranger 2.FP1
  to put back *remettre 9.L*
  to put stitches (in a wound) mettre des sutures 7.FP2

quantity une quantité 4.FP1
to **quarrel, have a fight** se quereller 9.FP1
queen la reine 1.LC1

R

rabbit un lapin 2.FP1
raconter to tell (what happened) 3.FP2
rain la pluie 3.FP3
to **raise (children)** élever 2.L*
raised, high élevé 2.FP3
rash (skin) l'eczéma *m.* 7.FP1; des boutons 7.FP1

real estate l'immobilier *m.* 10.FP2
  real estate agent un agent immobilier 10.FP1
Really? Vraiment? 3.FP2
to **realize** se rendre compte 2.L*
reception desk la réception 6.FP1
receptionist, secretary le/la réceptionniste 6.FP2
recreation center un centre de loisirs 8.FP2
rectangular rectangulaire 1.FP1
red rouge 1.LC1
  redhead roux (rousse) 1.FP1
reference une référence 10.FP3
to **reflect on** réfléchir 7.L*
refrigerator le réfrigérateur 2.FP3
regret le regret 7.LC1
to **regret** regretter 2.FP2
relations les relations *f.* 9.FP1
  good relations bons rapports 9.FP1
  bad relations mauvaises relations 9.FP1
to **remarry** se remarier 9.FP2
to **remember, recall** se rappeler 1.LC4
representative un(e) représentant(e) 10.FP1
request une requête 8.L*
research laboratory un laboratoire de recherche 10.FP2
researcher un chercheur (une chercheuse) 10.FP1
to **reserve** réserver 6.FP1
reservation une réservation 5.FP2
respect le respect 9.FP1
to **respect** respecter 3.FP1
to **respond** répondre 10.FP3
responsibility une responsabilité 10.FP2
to **rest** se reposer 1.FP3
résumé un curriculum vitae 10.FP3
to **retire** prendre sa retraite 9.FP2
to **reward** récompenser 4.L*
ring une bague R.L*
roll (of paper towels) un rouleau (pl. rouleaux) 4.FP1
room de la place 5.FP2
  room service le service dans les chambres 6.FP1

room with breakfast, dinner la demi-pension 6.FP1
roomy spacieux (spacieuse) 6.FP1
rough, uneven rugueux (rugueuse) 2.FP3
round rond 1.FP1
  round-trip ticket un aller et retour 5.FP2
rounded, arched courbé 2.FP3
rubber le caoutchouc 2.FP3
  rubber band un élastique 4.FP1
rug un tapis 1.L*
to **run** *courir 1.L*
Russia la Russie 5.FP1
rustic furniture des meubles *m.* rustiques 6.L*

S

sad triste 1.FP4
sadness la tristesse 7.LC1
safe un coffre R.L*
safety pin une épingle de sûreté 4.FP1
salary un salaire 10.FP2
sales person un vendeur (une vendeuse) 10.FP1
to **save** sauver 5.L*
saw une scie 2.FP3
scar une cicatrice 1.FP1
to **scare** faire peur 3.FP1
schedule un horaire 5.FP2
scientist un(e) scientifique 10.FP1
scientific research la recherche scientifique 10.FP2
scissors les ciseaux *m.* 1.FP2
scotch tape le scotch 4.FP1
to **scream** pousser des cris 3.L*
seat un siège 5.FP2; une place 5.FP2
  seat belt une ceinture de sécurité 5.FP2
second class la deuxième classe 5.FP2
second-hand, used d'occasion 2.FP3
secretary un(e) secrétaire 10.FP1
security check un contrôle de sécurité 5.FP2
see you (date, time) à + date, time 8.FP1
to **see** assister à 3.FP2
to **seem, appear** sembler 1.FP4

to **seize, take** saisir 9.L*
to **separate: to separate (husband & wife)** se séparer 9.FP2
serpent un serpent 3.FP1
to **serve** *servir 6.FP2
set (hair) une mise en plis 4.FP2
to **set a fire** mettre le feu 3.FP1
  to set the table (silverware) mettre le couvert 2.FP1
  to set the table mettre la table 2.FP1
to **settle** s'installer 8.L*
several certain(e)s, plusieurs 4.LC1
to **shake** secouer 10.L*
shampoo le shampooing 1.FP2
  a shampoo (hair salon) un shampooing 4.FP2
to **shave** se raser 1.FP2
shaver le rasoir 1.FP2
shaving cream la crème à raser 1.FP2
sheet: sheet (bedding) un drap 6.FP2
sheet ice le verglas 3.FP3
to **shine** briller 3.FP3
shiny brillant 2.FP3
shirt une chemise 2.FP1
to **shiver, shudder** frissonner 9.L*
shoe repairer le cordonier 4.FP3
shop une boutique 4.FP1; un commerce 8.FP2
to **shorten (hair)** dégager 4.FP2
shot of novocaine une piqûre de novocaïne 7.FP2
to **show** *faire voir 4.LC3
shower une douche 1.FP3
shrub un arbuste 2.FP1
  shrub clippers un sécateur 2.FP1
to **shut up** *se taire 1.LC4
sick malade 1.FP4
sickness, disease une maladie 7.FP1
side un côté 4.L*
sideboard un buffet 1.L*
sidewalk le trottoir 9.L*
silent muet (muette) 7.L*
silver l'argent *m.* R.L*
since puisque 3.L*
  single-family house une maison individuelle 8.FP2
to **sit down** *s'asseoir 1.LC4
  to sit down to eat se mettre à table 1.FP3
skinny maigre 1.FP1
skull le crâne 4.L*

to slip glisser 3.FP1
to slow down *ralentir 7.L*
small, short petit 1.FP1
small sofa un canapé 1.L*
to smell *sentir 1.FP4
smoking section la section fumeur 5.FP2
smooth lisse 2.FP3
to sneeze éternuer 7.FP1
snow la neige 3.FP3
snowstorm une tempête de neige 3.FP3
so much tellement 4.L*
so that pour que 10.LC2
soap le savon 1.FP2
social worker un(e) assistant(e) social(e) 10.FP1
soft mou (molle) 2.FP3
software specialist un(e) spécialiste de logiciel 10.FP1
something else to do autre chose à faire 2.FP2
to solicit, ask for solliciter 10.FP3
solid solide 2.FP3
some, a few quelques 4.LC1; quelques-un(e)s 4.LC1; certain(e)s 4.LC1
someone, somebody quelqu'un RC
something quelque chose RC
something else quelque chose d'autre 4.FP1
something to declare quelque chose à déclarer 5.FP1
somewhere quelque part 5.LC1
very sorry, sad désolé 2.FP2
to speak English parler anglais 10.FP3
to specialize, major in se spécialiser en 10.FP1
specialist un spécialiste 7.FP1
to spend (time) passer 3.LC1
to spend the night passer la nuit 6.FP1
to spoil gâter 7.L*
sponge une éponge 2.FP1
to sprain se fouler 7.FP2
spring (in watch) le ressort 4.FP3
spy un espion (une espionne) 5.L*
square carré 1.FP1
to stand supporter 2.L*
to start *se mettre à 3.L*
to start one's own business créer sa propre entreprise 10.FP2

stationery store la papeterie 4.FP1
stationery paper le papier à lettres 4.FP1
Statue of Liberty la Statue de la Liberté 2.FP3
to stay, lodge séjourner 6.FP1
to stay in bed rester au lit 7.FP1
to steal voler 5.L*
steel l'acier m. 2.FP3
stele (stone marker with an inscription) une stèle 6.L*
to step on marcher sur 1.LC3
steward le steward 5.FP2
stewardess l'hôtesse f. de l'air 5.FP2
to sting piquer 3.FP1
stockbroker un agent de change 10.FP1
stone une pierre 2.FP3
stool un tabouret 4.L*
to stoop, bend down se baisser 7.L*
to stop, prevent oneself from s'arrêter 1.FP3; s'empêcher (de) 4.L*
stopover, connection une escale 5.FP2
store window une vitrine 9.L*
storm la tempête 3.FP3; un orage 3.FP3
straight lisse 1.FP1
straight, upright droit 2.FP3
stranger un inconnu 7.L*
strep throat l'angine f. 7.FP1
string la ficelle 4.FP1
strong fort 1.FP1
to study étudier 10.FP1, faire des études (de) 9.FP3
suitcase une valise 5.FP1
summer job un job d'été 10.FP3
sunny clair 6.FP1
to sunbathe prendre un bain de soleil 3.FP1
super chouette 3.L*
surgeon un chirurgien (une chirurgienne) 7.FP1
to surprise *surprendre 9.L*
surprised surpris 7.LC1
to swallow avaler 7.FP1
to sweep balayer 2.FP1
to swim nager 3.FP1
swimming pool une piscine 6.FP1
synthetic material la matière synthétique 2.FP3

T

table la table 2.FP1
tablet (medicine) un cachet 7.FP1
tadpole un têtard 3.L*
to take *prendre 5.FP2
to take a blood sample faire une analyse de sang 7.FP1
to take a boat trip faire une promenade en bateau 3.FP1
to take a walk se promener 1.FP3
to take advantage of profiter de 1.L*
to take care of s'occuper de 1.LC4
to take off (plane) décoller 5.FP2
to take off, remove enlever 4.FP3
to take one's blood pressure prendre la tension 7.FP1
to have taken or carried something up monter: avoir + monté 3.LC1
to take out the trash sortir la poubelle 2.FP1
to take place avoir lieu 2.L*
to tan oneself bronzer 3.FP1
tear une larme 7.L*
technical knowledge les connaissances f. techniques 10.FP3
technician un technicien (une technicienne) 10.FP1
telephone le téléphone 6.FP1
to telephone, call téléphoner 10.FP3
telephoto lens le téléobjectif 4.FP3
television la télévision 6.FP1
temperature la température 2.FP3
temporary employment un emploi temporaire 10.FP3
to tempt tenter 9.L*
ten minutes early dix minutes d'avance 5.FP2
tense, uptight tendu 1.FP4
to thank remercier 2.FP2
thank you merci 2.FP2
thank you very much merci beaucoup 2.FP2
thanks a million merci mille fois 2.FP2
that que 9.LC1

that doesn't matter ça n'a pas d'importance **10.L***

that of, the one belonging to celui (celle) de **6.LC2**

that's all? c'est tout? **4.FP1**

that's not for real! ce n'est pas croyable! **3.FP2**

that's unbelieveable! c'est incroyable! **3.FP2**

then puis **3.FP2**

there is/are . . . left il reste . . . **8.L***

there is/are only . . . left il ne reste que . . . **10.L***

thick épais (épaisse) **2.FP3**

thief un voleur (une voleuse) **5.L***

thin mince **1.FP1**

things will be okay ça s'arrangera **9.FP1**

this happened, took place ça a eu lieu **3.FP2;** ça s'est passé . . . **3.FP2**

this one celui-ci (celle-ci) **2.L***

this one, the one celui (celle) **6.LC2**

this will be ready ce sera prêt **4.FP3**

through à travers **1.L***

to **throw** *jeter **3.FP1**

to **throw up** *vomir **7.FP1**

thunder le tonnerre **3.FP3**

ticket un billet **5.FP2**

ticket window le guichet **5.FP2**

ticket-punching machine le composteur **5.FP2**

time le temps **2.FP2**

tire la roue **4.FP3**

tired fatigué **1.FP4**

to **the end** jusqu'au bout **7.L***

toilet paper le papier hygiénique **4.FP1**

toiletry bag la trousse de toilette **1.FP2**

too trop **3.LC1**

too bad! tant pis! **2.LC2; quel dommage! 9.FP1**

tooth une dent **7.FP2**

tooth filling un plombage **7.FP2**

toothache mal aux dents **7.FP4**

toothbrush une brosse à dents **1.FP2**

toothpaste le dentifrice **1.FP2**

tourist class la classe économie **5.FP2**

towel la serviette **1.FP2**

tower, high-rise une tour **8.FP2**

town centre, downtown le centre-ville **8.FP2**

trade le commerce **10.FP1**

traffic la circulation **6.L***

traffic regulations le code de la route **8.FP2**

train un train **5.FP2**

train door une portière **7.L***

train station la gare **5.FP2**

travel agency une agence de voyages **5.FP2**

to **travel** voyager **5.FP1**

traveler's check un chèque de voyage **6.FP1**

to **treat (medical)** soigner **7.FP1**

triangular triangulaire **2.FP3**

truly drôlement **4.L***

trust une confiance **9.FP1**

to **trust** avoir confiance **9.FP1**

to **try in vain** avoir beau essayer **4.L***

to try to chercher à **10.L***

tube un tube **4.FP1**

to **turn: to turn around** se tourner **4.L***

to turn down, lower baisser **6.FP2**

twice a day deux fois par jour **7.FP1**

unexpected inattendu **8.L***

unfair injuste **R.L***

unhappy malheureux (malheureuse) **1.FP4**

United Nations building le bâtiment des Nations Unies **2.FP3**

United States les États-Unis *m.* **1.LC1**

unless à moins que **10.LC2**

unruly mop (of hair) la tignasse **4.L***

until now jusqu'ici **4.L***

until when jusqu'à quand **6.FP1**

upset fâché **3.L*; énervé 1.FP4**

to **use** utiliser **10.FP3; *se servir de 10.FP3**

to **vacuum** passer l'aspirateur **2.FP1**

vegetable un légume **2.FP3**

vegetation la végétation **3.FP1**

very much beaucoup **3.LC1**

veterinary: veterinary doctor un(e) vétérinaire **10.FP1**

veterinary studies les études *f.* vétérinaires **10.FP1**

view une vue **6.FP1**

Virginia la Virginie **1.LC1**

vitamin une vitamine **4.FP1**

volume la capacité **2.FP3**

voluminous volumineux (volumineuse) **2.FP3**

to **wait** attendre **5.FP2**

waiting room la salle d'attente **5.FP2**

to **wake up (something, someone)** réveiller **6.FP2**

to **wake (oneself) up** se réveiller **1.FP3; s'éveiller 10.L***

wakefulness l'éveil *m.* **10.L***

to **walk** faire un tour **3.FP1; promener 2.FP1**

to **want** *vouloir **2.LC2**

wardrobe, closet une armoire **1.L***

warm tiède **2.FP3**

to **warn** *prévenir **3.L***

to **wash** laver **2.FP1**

to wash (oneself) se laver **1.FP3**

to wash one's face se laver la figure **1.FP2**

to wash the dishes faire la vaisselle **2.FP1**

wash cloth un gant de toilette **1.FP2**

wastepaper basket, trash la corbeille **2.FP1**

wavy ondulé **2.FP3**

weak faible **1.FP1; fragile 2.FP3**

wealth les biens *m.* **2.L***

to **wear glasses** porter des lunettes **1.FP1**

bad weather le mauvais temps **3.FP3**

nice weather le beau temps **3.FP3**

weather forecast   la météo 3.FP3

week   une semaine 3.FP2

to **weigh**   peser 1.FP1

weight   le poids 1.FP1

well, good   bien 1.FP4

  well-being   le bien-être 10.L*

  well-built, solid   costaud 1.FP1

  well located   bien situé 6.FP1

wet   mouillé 2.FP3

what   quel (quelle) 4.FP1

  what bad luck!   quelle malchance! 9.FP1

  what doesn't work?   qu'est-ce qui ne marche pas? 4.FP2

  what good news!   quelle bonne nouvelle! 9.FP2

  what happened?   qu'est-ce qu'il y a eu? 3.FP2; **qu'est-ce qui a eu lieu?** 3.FP2; qu'est-ce qui est arrivé? 3.FP2; qu'est-ce qui s'est passé? 3.FP2

  what is the problem?   quel est le problème? 4.FP3

  what kind, type?   quel genre? 7.FP1

  what type of   quelle sorte de 5.FP2

  what's new?   quoi de neuf? 3.FP2

  what's the matter?   qu'est-ce que tu as? 1.FP4

  what's wrong?   qu'est-ce qu'il y a? 1.FP4; **qu'est-ce qui ne va pas?** 7.FP1

when   lorsque 3.LC2; **quand** 5.LC2

which   quel (quelle) 4.FP1; **que** 9.LC1

while   pendant que 3.LC2

whim   un caprice 8.L*

whistle   un sifflet à roulette 3.L*

to **whistle**   siffler 3.L*

who, that, which   qui 9.LC1

whom   que 9.LC1

whooping cough   la coqueluche 7.FP1

wide   large 2.FP3

wind   le vent 3.FP3

window pane   une vitre 2.FP1

to **wipe**   essuyer 2.FP1

  to wipe (oneself) dry   s'essuyer 1.FP2

wisdom tooth   une dent de sagesse 7.FP2

to **wish**   souhaiter 2.LC2; **désirer** 2.LC2

with one bed   à un lit 6.FP1

  with pleasure   avec plaisir 2.FP2

without   sans (que) 10.LC1

to **witness**   être témoin 3.FP2

to **wonder**   se demander 8.L*

wood   le bois 2.FP3

word   un mot 6.L*

work   le travail (pl. travaux) 2.FP1

to **work**   travailler 9.FP2

worker   un ouvrier (une ouvrière) R.L*

worn   usagé 2.FP3

  worn out, old   usé 4.FP3

to **worry**   s'en faire 4.L*

worried   préoccupé 1.FP4

worse   pire 7.L*

to **wrap**   envelopper 7.L*

wrist   le poignet 7.L*

to **x-ray**   faire une radio 7.FP1

to **yell, shout**   crier 1.L*

yesterday   hier 3.FP2

you're kidding!   tu plaisantes! 3.FP2

  you're the boss!   c'est vous le patron (patronne)! 2.LC2

  you're welcome   de rien 2.FP2; **je t'en prie** 2.FP2; **il n'y a pas de quoi** 2.FP2

yet   déjà 3.LC1

youth center   une Maison des Jeunes 8.FP2

  youth hostel   une auberge de la jeunesse 6.FP1

INDEX

à + **lequel** 242 + possessive pronoun 244 verbs used with 156

accidents 278 while on vacation 112

adjectives 5 **beau, nouveau, vieux** R7 formation of comparison with 234 irregular R7 possessive adjective in superlative construction 236

adverbs 114 formation of comparison with 234 superlative construction 236 with passé composé 114

agreement direct object with past participle 162 past participle with pluperfect 308 past participle of **être** with subject 15 past participle of reflexive verb with subject 50

airplane travel by 196, 197

aller conditional 207 passé composé 114 imperative 54 passé simple 133 past conditional 322 past subjunctive 280 pluperfect 308 present R3 subjunctive 86 to express future 5

appearance objects 90

articles see definite article, indefinite article, partitive article

avoir conditional R23 expressions with R3 future R22 imperfect R22 passé composé formed with R4, 114

passé simple 133 present R3, R22 subjunctive 86, R23 verbs conjugated with R22–R23

bac, talking about 383–385

bicycle, parts of 167

body, parts of 36, R12 with definite article 38, 39

cameras 166-167

ce + relative pronoun 364

clothing and accessories, talking about R13

commands see imperative

comparative constructions adjectives and adverbs 234 **bon/meilleur/ mieux** 234 nouns 234

conditional formation 207, 314 in phrases with **si** 207, 316 indirect speech 318 past conditional forms and uses 322 to express politeness and requests 318

congratulations, to extend 350

conjunctions construction with subjunctive 398 expressing time 204

connaître vs. **savoir** 23, R8

consolation, to give 350

contractions **à, de** + possessive pronouns 244 **à + le, de + le** 38 **à + lequel** 242, 356 before vowel sound 22, 25 **de + lequel** 242 direct objects (**le→l'**) 25

countries names of R14 articles and prepositions with R15

countryside, vacationing at 109, 111, 112

craindre, and verbs like 271

croire 271

customs (airport) 191

daily routine, describing 48

dates 39, R10

de **de + lequel** 242 in negative sentences 8 verbs used with 156

definite article 8, R6 after reflexive verbs 44 denoting quantity 39 denoting preferences 8 uses of 38, 39 with days of week 39 with geographical names 39 with parts of body 38, 39, 44

demonstrative pronoun **celui** 242 **celui-ci, celui-là** 242 **celui de** 242 **celui qui/celui que** 243

depuis 6

descendre 114

devoir + infinitive 80, 323 present R2

dimensions, describing 90

dîner imperfect 116

dire subjunctive 78

direct object pronouns 22, 25, R8, 162 agreement with past participle 162 in commands 162, 164 position 164, R9 with indirect object pronouns 164

dont   **ce dont** 364   object of preposition 362 relative pronoun 357 uses of 362   verbs used with 357

ecology   109–112, 121

emotions, talking about 52, 272

en (*preposition*)   + present participle 390   with names of countries R15

en (*pronoun*)   + nouns 9, 156   position 156 replacing **du, de la, de l'** 156   replacing expressions of quantity 156 with numbers 156 with **y** 164

être   agreement of past participle and subject 15 conditional R23   **être en train de** 5   imperfect 116   passé composé 12, 114   passé composé of reflexive verbs formed with 114, R4   passé simple 133   present R3 subjunctive 86, R23 verbs conjugated with R4, R22–R23

events, talking about   124, 128, 131

facial features   36–37

faire   + infinitive 168 expressions with R3, 168 imperfect 116   passé simple 133   present R3 **se faire** + infinitive 168 subjunctive 86

favors, asking for, accepting, refusing 84

finir   conditional 207 future 201   passé simple

133   subjunctive 78

food and drink, talking about R11

form, describing 90

friendship and love, expressing 349

future   expressed with aller 5   formation 201 in indirect speech after declarative verb 318 irregular forms 201 with **quand**-clause 204 with **si**-clause 204

garden, activities in 75

geographical names R14–R15   prepositions with 190, R15   with definite articles 39, R15

hair salon 160–161

health   at the dentist 279 talking about 261–266

height, talking about 36

hotel   230–231, 240

household chores, talking about 74–75

household objects 77

il faut   + infinitive 80 + subjunctive 78   **il ne faut pas** 80

il y a 13   **il y a** + *time* 13

imperative   of reflexive verbs 54   with indirect objects 22   with direct object and indirect object pronouns 164   with object pronouns 162 with reflexive pronouns 44   word order with **y** and **en** 156

imperfect   17   describe

circumstances formation 116, R5   imperfect and passé composé in same sentence 131   imperfect stems 116, R5   uses 116 vs. passé composé 118, 128, R5   with **si**-clause 308

indefinite article   8, R6

indirect object pronouns   25, R8   in commands 22, 162 position 164, R9   with direct object pronouns 164   with imperative 162, 164

infinitive   constructions 44 with reflexive verbs 44 following preposition 388 past infinitive 389   vs. subjunctive 272, 398

interdictions 80

interviewing, for a job 392–393, 396

invitations, accepting, extending, refusing 306

-ir verbs   present participle forms and uses 390

irregular verbs   R2, R3 spelling changes chart R20–21   verb chart R22–31

kitchen, activities in 74

laundry, doing 74

lequel   242   **à + lequel** 242, 356   **de + lequel** 242, 356   with preposition 362

limiting expression **ne . . . que** 192

materials 91

meeting people 306–307

INDEX *continued*

mettre R2

monter 114

mood   indicative mood 270
    subjunctive mood 270
    vs. tense 270

mountains, vacationing in 112

negation   **ne . . . jamais**
    114   **ne . . . pas en- core** 114
    ne . . . personne 23, **192**
    ne . . . aucun(e),
    ne . . . ni . . . ni,
    ne . . . nulle part 192   **ne . . . rien**
    23, 192   position 192

neighborhoods 312–313

nouns   formation of
    comparison with 234
    irregular plurals R7

numbers   cardinal R10
    ordinal R10

object pronouns   *see* direct
    object pronouns, indirect
    object pronouns

objects, physical attributes 90

ocean, vacationing at 112

opinions   use of infinitive in
    expressing 87   use of
    subjunctive in
    expressing 87

parler   conditional 207, 314
    future 201   passé simple
    133   past subjunctive 280
    subjunctive 78

partir 203

partitive article 8   forms R6

passé composé   12, R4
    formed with **avoir** 114,
    R4   formed with **être**
    114   of reflexive verbs
    50, 114, R4   vs.
    imperfect 118, 128, R5

passé simple   133   regular
    and irregular uses and
    formation 133, R32–R33

passer 114

past   expressed with **venir**
    de 5

past participles, irregular R4

pendant que   131

people, talking about friends
    and family 345, 348–350

personal care, talking about
    42

pets, taking care of 75

phases, of life 360

physical description and
    condition, describing
    36–37, 52

pluperfect formation   308
    with **si**-clauses 322

possessive pronouns   244

post office 152

pouvoir   R2   past
    conditional 323

prendre R2

prepositions   followed by
    infinitive 388   followed
    by relative pronouns 355
    with **lequel** 362
    replaced by **y** 156

present participle   **en** + 390
    forms and uses 390

present tense   formation of
    regular verbs, chart R2

professions, talking about
    386–387, 394, 396–397

pronouns   **à** + possessive,
    de + possessive 244
    ce + relative pronoun 364

complementary 22, R8–R9
    demonstrative 242
    direct object 162
    function 362   indirect
    object 162   interrogative
    242   positions of direct
    and indirect pronouns
    162, 164, R9   possessive
    244   reflexive 44
    relative 354, 362, 364
    stress pronouns + **même**
    45   with direct and
    indirect objects R9

pronunciation, review of
    R16–R17

quand-clause   with future
    204   with imperfect
    131

quantity   indefinite articles
    in expressing adjectives
    of quantity 158   defined
    quantities 8   replaced
    by **en** 156   with use of
    definite article 39

que   **ce que** 364   direct
    object 354   introducing
    subjunctive clause 78
    relative pronoun 354

quelqu'un, quelque chose
    23

qui   **ce qui** 364   object of
    preposition 362   relative
    pronoun 354   subject
    354

quitter 203

reflexive   construction 44
    idiomatic usage 54
    imperative 44, 54   in
    infinitive constructions 44
    list of reflexive verbs 54
    passé composé 50, R5
    reciprocal action 54, 352
    to describe daily activities
    44, 48   uses 278

regret, expressing 84

regular verbs   R2   chart
R18–R19

relative pronouns   *see* **qui,**
que, and **dont**

répondre   passé simple 133

s'amuser   passé composé
114   past conditional 322
past subjunctive 280
pluperfect 308

savoir vs. **connaîre** 23, R8

se laver   passé composé 50
present 44

se souvenir 54

seasons, talking about 126

sentir 52

shoe repair 166

shopping and errands   152
aisles, sections of store 153
asking for help 152
services 166

si-clause   revision of tenses
used in **si**-clause 324
to express wish 308
with conditional 207, 316
with future 204   with
imperfect 308   with
pluperfect 322

sortir 114, R2

sound-spelling correspondence
chart   R16–R17

stationery store 152, 153

stereo, parts 167

stress pronouns   after
comparative phrases 234
pronouns + **même** 45

studies 386

subjunctive   after emotions

and sentiments 272
after expressions of will
and desire 88   after **il**
faut que 78, 80   after
impersonal expressions
87   concept 270   with
expressions of doubt
274–275   with expressions
of opinion 87   expressions of
mood 270   irregular formation
86
past subjunctive 280
regular formation 78, 81
stems 78   used to
express necessity and
obligation 78   vs.
indicative 270   vs.
infinitive 272   with
conjunction construction 398

superlative construction
236   introduced by
possessive adjective 236
position of adjective 236
with adjectives 236
with adverbs 236
with nouns 236

surprise, expressions of 125

television, parts 167

temperature, describing 90

tense   vs. mood 270

texture, describing 90

thanking 84

time   expressions of 131,
204   **il y a** + *time* 13
depuis 6

toiletry items 42

train, travel by 196–198

vacation   hotel 230–231, 240
talking about 112
traveling 190–191, 196–198

vendre   conditional 207
future 201   subjunctive 78

venir   future 5   present R3
subjunctive 81

volume, describing 90

vouloir   conditional 314
je veux bien 88   past
conditional 323   present
R2   use of subjunctive
with **vouloir que** 88
vouloir + infinitive 88

voyager   passé composé 114
past conditional 322
pluperfect 308

weather, talking about the
seasons and weather
126

weight, talking about 36, 90

wishes, expressing 88, 308,
318

y   to replace **à** + noun 156
position 156   to replace
à + place 9   phrases
introduced by preposition
156   with **en** 164

TEXT CREDITS

"Afrique" from **Coups de Pilon** by David Diop. Text copyright © 1964 by Éditions Seghers. Reprinted by permission of Éditions Présence Africaine.

"Deuxième conte pour enfants de moins de trios ans" from *Présent passé, Passé present* by Eugène Ionesco. Text copyright © Mercure de France. Reprinted by permission of Mercure de France.

Lyrics to "Éthiope." Text copyright © 1985 EMI records. Reprinted by permission of EMI Pathé.

"King" from *Les Aventures de Petit Nicolas* by Sempé and Goscinny. Text and illustrations copyright © 1966 by Macmillan/George Publishing. Reprinted by permission of Editions Denoel.

"La Fourmi" from *Chantefables at chantefleurs* by Robert Desnos. Text copyright © 1944 by Librairie Gründ. Reprinted by permission of Éditions Gründ.

"La légende baoulé" from *Légendes Africaines* by Bernard Dadié. Text copyright © 1966, 1973 by Éditions Seghers. Reprinted by permission of Presence Africaine.

"Le portrait" from *L'île Introuvable* by Yves Thériault. Text copyright © 1968 by Les Éditions du Jour and Yves Thériault. Reprinted by permission of Éditions Gallimard.

"Liberte" from *Oeuvres complètes* by Paul Éluard. Text copyright © 1968 by Éditions Gallimard: Biblothèque de Pléiade. Reprinted by permission of Les Editions de Minuit.

"Pour faire le portrait d'un oiseau" from *Paroles* by Jacques Prévert. Text copyright © 1947 by Les Éditions du Point du Jour. Reprinted by permission of Éditions Gallimard and the Estate of Jacques Prévert.

"Pour saluer le tiers-monde" from *Ferrements* by Aimé Cesaire. Text copyright © 1960 by Éditions Le Seuil. Reprinted by permission of Éditions Le Seuil.

"Soyez Polis" from *Histoires* by Jacques Prévert. Text copyright © 1963 by Éditions Gallimard. Reprinted by permission of Éditions Gallimard and the Estate of Jacques Prévert.

Acknowledgements

The editorial staff would like to extend special thanks to the following people for their help and support in the production of **Discovering French–*Rouge***:

- William Price, Day Junior High School
- Arthur Greenspan, Colby College
- Seldan Rodman
- The staffs of the French Library and the French Consulate in Boston.

PHOTO CREDITS

Front Cover
Front Cover ©Shaen Adey/Gallo Images/Getty Images

Back Cover
Level 1a: ©David Noble/Travel Pictures
Level 1b: ©Patrice Coppee/Workbook Stock/Getty Images
Level 1: ©Travelpix Ltd/Stone/Getty Images
Level 2: ©David Sanger/The Image Bank/Getty Images
Level 3: ©Shaen Adey/Gallo Images/Getty Images

Interior: All photos by HMH except the following:
v (b) ©INTERFOTO/Alamy; vi (b) ©Superstock; vii (b) ©Réunion des Musées Nationaux/Art Resource; viii (b) ©Paris Pierce/Alamy; ix (b) ©Leemage/Getty Images; x (b) ©ARS/Réunion des Musées Nationaux/Art Resource/ © 2012 Artists Rights Society (ARS), New York/ADAGP, Paris; xi (b) ©Gamma-Rapho/Georges Merillon/Getty Images; xii (b) ©culture-images/Lebrecht Photo Library; xiii (b) ©Werner Forman/Art Resource, NY; xiv (b) ©Hemis/Alamy; xv ©Rebecca and Jean-Paul Valette; 2 (br) ©DEA/C. SAPPA/De Agostini/Getty Images; 11 (bl) ©John Zada/Alamy; 11 (bcl) ©Tommy Trenchard/Alamy; 11 (bcr) ©Patrick Orton/Aurora Photos/Alamy; 11 (tcr) ©Comstock/Getty Images; 11 (br) ©Glow Asia/Alamy; 11 ©itanistock/Alamy; 14 (cl) ©TMAX/Fotolia; 33 (tr) ©Paris Market/Alamy; 33 ©Rebecca DeVaney/Alamy; 34 ©Franck Camhi/Alamy; 34 ©Petro Feketa/Alamy; 34 ©Photodisc/Getty Images; 35 (tl) ©Eyewire/Getty Images; 35 (tr) ©John Kellerman/Alamy; 35 (tcl) ©Masterpics/Alamy; 35 (tcr) ©The Art Gallery Collection/Alamy; 35 (bcl) ©Marka/Alamy; 35 (bcr) ©Superstock/© 2012 Estate of Pablo Picasso/Artists Rights Society (ARS), New York; 35 (bl) ©Geoff Dann/Dorling Kindersley/Getty Images; 35 (br) ©Jupiterimages/Getty Images; 36 (tr) ©Digital Vision/Getty Images; 51 (r) ©Eric Ryan/Getty Images; 56 (tl) ©Louis Monier/Gamma-Rapho/Getty Images; 60 (t) ©Imagno/Hulton Archive/Getty Images; 61 (tl) ©Peter Willi/Superstock/Getty Images; 61 (tr) ©Burstein Collection/Corbis; 61 (cl) ©World History Archive/Alamy; 61 (br) ©The Protected Art Archive/Alamy; 62 (tr) ©The Art Gallery Collection/Alamy; 62 (cr) ©INTERFOTO/Alamy; 62 (cl) ©Peter Barritt/Alamy; 63 (tr) ©The Protected Art Archive/Alamy; 63 (cl) ©David Askham/Alamy; 63 (cr) ©INTERFOTO/Alamy; 63 (bl) ©Robert Harding Picture Library Ltd/Alamy; 64 (tl) ©INTERFOTO/Alamy; 64 (cr) ©Peter Horree/Alamy; 65 (cr) ©Masterlines/Alamy; 65 (tl) ©INTERFOTO/Alamy; 65 (b) ©Réunion des Musées Nationaux/Art Resource/ © 2012 Artists Rights Society (ARS), New York/ADAGP, Paris; 66 (c) ©Duane Michals/Pace MacGill Gallery; 66 (tr) ©Bridgeman Art Library/Superstock/ © 2012 C. Herscovici, London/Artists Rights Society (ARS), New York; 66 (br) ©Superstock/ © 2012 C. Herscovici, London/Artists Rights Society (ARS), New York; 67 (b) ©Martinie/Roger-Viollet/Getty Images; 68 (tr) ©Gamma-Keystone/Getty Images; 69 (tr) ©Xavier Rossi/Gamma-Rapho/Getty Images/ © 2012 Artists Rights Society (ARS), New York/ADAGP, Paris.; 69 (bl) ©akg-images/Archives CDA/St-Genès/ © 2012 Artists Rights Society (ARS), New York/ADAGP, Paris; 69 (tl) ©Iconotec/Alamy/ © 2012 Niki Charitable Art Foundation. All

rights reserved/ARS, NY/ADAGP, Paris; 69 (br) ©Ted Russell/Alamy/ © 2012 Artists Rights Society (ARS), New York/ADAGP, Paris; 77 (b) ©Patrick Escudero/Hemis/Alamy; 99 (tr) ©akg-images/VISIOARS; 99 (br) ©Superstock; 99 (cl) ©Mary Evans Picture Library; 100 (tl) ©Jerome Chatin/Gamma-Rapho/Getty Images; 100 (cr) ©akg-images/ullstein bild; 100 (bl) ©Paleolithic/The Bridgeman Art Library/Getty Images; 101 (t) ©akg-images; 101 (b) ©Sisse Brimberg/National Geographic/Getty Images; 103 (br) ©Mary Evans Picture Library/Alamy; 104 (b) ©INTERFOTO/Alamy; 106 (t) ©Tim Graham/Alamy; 109 (bl) ©Jacques Pierre/Alamy; 109 (tr) ©Imagebroker/Alamy; 110 (tc) ©Rene Mattes/Hemis/Alamy; 110 ©Rene Mattes/Hemis/Alamy; 111 (bl) ©Richard Semik/Alamy; 112 (bcl) ©Jacques Pierre/Alamy; 112 (bl) ©Imagebroker/Alamy; 120 (tr) ©Kathy Willens/AP Images; 120 (bl) ©AFP/Getty Images; 120 (cr) ©Albane Navizet/Kipa/Corbis; 122 (t) ©Ian Dagnall/Alamy; 122 (cl) ©Comstock/Jupiterimages/Getty Images; 123 (b) ©Digital Vision/Getty Images; 123 (t) ©Rubberball/Getty Images; 127 (bl) ©Paul Bradbury/OJO Images Ltd/Alamy; 133 (br) ©Bettmann/Corbis; 140 (cr) ©Datacraft Co Ltd/Getty Images; 141 (tl) ©The Art Gallery Collection/Alamy; 141 (tr) ©Eyewire/Getty Images; 141 (br) ©Réunion des Musées Nationaux/Art Resource; 142 (bl) ©Orion Classics/Photofest; 143 (all) ©Orion Classics/Photofest; 144 (all) ©Orion Classics/Photofest; 145 (all) ©Orion Classics/Photofest; 147 (tl) © Pippa West/Alamy; 147 (tcl) ©Pixtal/Superstock; 147 (bcl) ©Guy Heitmann/Design Pics Inc./Alamy; 147 (bl) ©Jeremy Cozannet/Alamy; 147 (tr) ©Jason's Travel Photography/Getty Images; 147 (tcr) ©Jean-Luc Cochonneau/Alamy; 147 (bcr) ©Harald A. Jahn/Corbis; 147 (br) ©Jozef Sedmak/Alamy; 151 (b) ©incamerastock/Alamy; 159 (tr) ©Sean O'Neill/Alamy; 161 (t) ©Franck Camhi/Alamy; 163 (tr) ©Allan Baxter/The Image Bank/Getty Images; 176 (br) ©Paris Pierce/Alamy; 176 (bl) ©Fine Art Images/Leemage/Superstock/ © 2012 Estate of Pablo Picasso/Artists Rights Society (ARS), New York; 177 (l) ©Gamma-Keystone/Getty Images; 177 (cl) ©Gamma-Keystone/Getty Images; 177 (cr) ©Georges Pierre/Sygma/Corbis; 177 (r) ©Pierre Verdy/AFP/Getty Images; 177 (bl) ©Michael Ochs Archives/Getty Images; 178 (tl) ©Michel Ginfray/Gamma-Rapho/Getty Images; 178 (br) ©akg-images/ullstein bild; 179 ©Tony Barson/WireImage/Getty Images; 179 ©Dominique Charriau/WireImage/Getty Images; 179 ©Johanna Geron/AFP/Getty Images; 179 ©Andia/Alamy; 179 ©Frank Hoensch/Getty Images; 180 (bl) ©AFP/Getty Images; 180 (c) ©Kambou Sia/AFP/Getty Images; 181 (tr) ©Carlo Allegri/Getty Images; 181 (cl) ©Pascal Pavani/AFP/Getty Images; 181 (bl) ©Joe Scarnici/WireImage/Getty Images; 182 (tr) ©Kevin Winter/Getty Images; 182 (cl) ©David Redfern/Redferns/Getty Images; 182 (br) ©David Redfern/Redferns/Getty Images; 183 (tr) ©Jacques Morell/Kipa/Corbis; 184 (cr) ©Snark/Art Resource; 184 (b) ©Hendrik Siemiradzki/The Bridgeman Art Library/Getty Images; 185 (c) ©Mary Evans Picture Library/Alamy; 185 (tl) ©Beatriz Schiller/Time Life Pictures/Getty Images; 185 (bl) ©Photo Inc/Photo Researchers, Inc./Getty Images; (c) ©mpworks architecture/Alamy; 189 (t) ©Michael Matisse/Getty Images; 189 ©Comstock Images/Getty Images; 189 ©Age Fotostock America, Inc.; 190 (b) ©Comstock Images/Getty

Images; 190 (b) ©Irène Alastruey/Author's Image Ltd/Alamy; 191 (c) ©Photononstop/Superstock; 194 (t) ©Sami Sarkis/Alamy; 195 (t) ©Denis Charlet/Getty Images; 195 (tr) ©Lightworks Media/Alamy; 197 (b) ©Ocean/Corbis; 217 (t) ©Leemage/Getty Images; 217 (cl) ©Jacques Louis David/Bridgeman Art Library/Getty Images; 217 (bl) ©FPG International/Getty Images; 218 (t) ©Hulton Archive/Getty Images; 219 (tl) ©The Art Gallery Collection/Alamy; 219 (tr) ©Bertrand Langlois/Getty Images; 219 (cr) ©Chris Pancewicz/Alamy; 219 (bl) ©The Art Gallery Collection/Alamy; 219 (br) ©Jupiterimages/Getty Images; 219 (bcr) ©Anna Yu/Alamy; 219 (bcr) ©Stamp Collection/Alamy; 219 (bcr) ©Artville/Getty Images; 221 (tr) ©Comstock Images/Getty Images; 221 (t) ©akg-images/Pietro Baguzzi; 221 (cl) © Carpe Diem - France/Alamy; 221 (c) ©David C. Tomlinson/Getty Images; 221 (br) ©World History Archive/Alamy; 223 (c) ©Prisma Archivo/Alamy; 223 (br) ©INTERFOTO/Alamy; 224 (b) ©Pixtal/Age Fotostock America, Inc.; 224 (t) ©Lebrecht Music and Arts Photo Library/Alamy; 225 (b) ©Jupiterimages/Getty Images; 227 (c) ©Superstock/Alamy; 227 (cr) ©Coutant Marie-Astrid/Corbis; 231 ©Emmanuel Lattes/Alamy; 231 ©Rob Melnychuk/Getty Images; 231 ©UpperCut Images/Alamy; 231 ©Miscellaneoustock/Alamy; 241 ©Emmanuel Lattes/Alamy; 241 ©Rob Melnychuk/Getty Images; 241 ©UpperCut Images/Alamy; 241 ©Miscellaneoustock/Alamy; 245 (tr) ©Franck Guiziou/Hemis/Alamy; 252 (t) ©The Art Gallery Collection/Alamy; 252 (b) Getty Images; 252 (c) ©Roger Viollet/Getty Images; 253 (tr) ©Photo Researchers/Science Source/Getty Images; 253 (c) ©Hulton Archive/Getty Images; 253 (br) ©Micheline Pelletier/Sygma/Corbis; 254 (b) ©akg-images/ullstein bild; 254 (tr) ©AFP/Getty Images; 254 (b) ©Stockbyte/Getty Images; 255 (tr) ©DeA Picture Library/Art Resource, NY; 255 ©Photos 12/Alamy; 255 ©Universal Images Group/Getty Images; 255 (cr) ©Roger Viollet/Getty Images; 255 (bl) ©Roger Viollet/Getty Images; 256 (t) ©Portrait presumed to be of Paul Eluard (1895-1952) 1947 (card) by Leger, Fernand (1881-1955), Musee d'Art et d'Histoire, Saint-Denis, France/Archives Charmet/The Bridgeman Art Library/ © 2012 Artists Rights Society (ARS), New York/ADAGP, Paris; 256 ©Roger Viollet/Getty Images; 256 (b) ©Jeanne Louise Bulliard/Sygma/Corbis; 257 (t) © Réunion des Musées Nationaux/Art Resource/ © 2012 Artists Rights Society (ARS), New York/ADAGP, Paris; 258 (tr) ©Ron Galella/WireImage/Getty Images; 258 ©Photos 12/Alamy; 258 (c) ©Orion Classics/Photofest; 258 ©Orion Classics/Photofest; 259 (br) ©Orion Classics/Photofest; 259 ©Orion Classics/courtesy Everett Collection; (c) ©Jose Luis Pelaez, Inc/Blend Images/Getty Images; 261 ©David Hanover/Getty Images; 261 (b) ©B2M Productions/Getty Images; 262 (t) ©Directphoto.org/Alamy; 265 (b) ©ron levine/Riser/Getty Images; 268 ©Lionel Bonaventure/AFP/Getty Images; 276 ©ALFRED/SIPA/AP Images; 276 ©Kate Geraghty/Sydney Morning Herald/Getty Images; 277 (c) ©2011 MSF All rights reserved.; 282 (cr) ©Hulton Archive/Getty Images; 293 (tr) ©Comstock Images/Getty Images; 293 (br) ©Photononstop/Superstock; 294 (tr) ©Corbis; 294 (bc) ©Micheline Pelletier/Sygma/Corbis; 295 (tr) ©Alexis Duclos/Gamma-Rapho/Getty Images; 296 (c) ©Directphoto.org/Alamy; 299 (c) ©Louise Heusinkveld/Alamy; 300 (b) ©Gamma-Rapho/Georges Merillon/Getty Images; 300 (bl) ©Jack Guez/AFP/Getty Images; 303 (tr) ©Hulton Archive/Getty Images; 311 (tl) ©Yves Talensac/Photononstop/Getty Images; 311 (tr) ©Getty Images; 313 (cl) ©Stephane Gautier/sagaphoto.com/Alamy; 313 (cr) ©Jack Sullivan/

Alamy; 314 (cr) ©STOCKFOLIO/Alamy; 319 (bl) ©Comstock Images/Getty Images; 321 (tr) ©Chuck Pefley/Alamy; 336 (tr) ©Hulton Archive/Getty Images; 336 (cl) ©Vincent Kessler/X00403/Reuters/Corbis; 337 ©DBI Studio/Alamy; 337 ©DBI Studio/Alamy; 337 ©DBI Studio/Alamy; 338 (tr) ©Corbis; 339 (c) ©Robin Moore/National Geographic Society/Corbis; 340 (b) ©Tony Wheeler/Lonely Planet Images/Getty Images; 341 (tr) ©culture-images/Lebrecht Photo Library; 341 Courtesy of the John J. Burns Library, Boston College, Arthur Morrissey, MD, Haitian Painting Collection. Photograph by Gary Gilbert. ; 341 (bl) Peasant Wedding, Obin, Philome (1891-1986)/Private Collection /The Bridgeman Art Library International; 341 (br) Carnival, 1951 (oil on masonite), Bazile, Castera (1923-1965)/Private Collection/Galerie Bonheur, St. Louis, Missouri, USA/The Bridgeman Art Library International; 342 (tr) ©Guillaume Collet/Gamma-Rapho/Getty Images; 343 ©Photos 12/Alamy; 343 ©Photofest; 343 ©Photos 12/Alamy; 343 ©Photos 12/Alamy; 343 ©Photos 12/Alamy; 346 ©Micheline Pelletier/Sygma/Corbis; 360 (tr) ©Directphoto Collection/Alamy; 361 (br) ©Big Cheese Photo/Getty Images; 363 (cr) ©Gianni Dagli Orti/Corbis; 372 (tr) ©Holton Collection/Superstock/Getty Images; 372 (b) ©Fotosearch/Getty Images; 373 (tr) ©Werner Forman/Art Resource, NY; 373 ©Ivan Vdovin/Alamy; 373 ©Ivan Vdovin/Alamy; 373 ©DBI Studio/Alamy; 375 (t) ©Olivier Martel/Corbis; 375 (bl) ©Tommy Trenchard/Alamy; 375 (cr) ©imagegallery/Alamy; 376 (tl) ©Tina Manley/Alamy; 376 (b) ©Margaret Courtney-Clarke/Corbis; 377 (tr) ©Peter Jordan/Alamy; 378 (br) ©Harry Hook/The Image Bank/Getty Images; 379 (bl) ©CNAC/MNAM/Dist. Réunion des Musées Nationaux/Art Resource, NY; 379 (bcl) ©Burstein Collection/Corbis; 379 (bcr) ©Judith Collins/Alamy; 379 (br) ©Réunion des Musées Nationaux/Art Resource/© 2012 Estate of Pablo Picasso/Artists Rights Society (ARS), New York, NY/2012 Estate of Pablo Picasso/Artists Rights Society (ARS), New York; (c) ©David R. Frazier Photolibrary, Inc./Alamy; 383 (b) ©Marco Simola/Photographers Direct; 385 (bc) ©Miguel Medina/AFP/Getty Images; 387 (t) ©Moodboard/Alamy; 392 (t) ©Asia Images Group/Getty Images; 393 (bl) ©Tom Grill/Corbis; 400 (b) ©Jeremy Cozannet/Alamy; 410 (bl) ©Mary Evans Picture Library/Alamy; 410 ©Andy Levin/Alamy; 410 ©Bill Heinsohn/Alamy; 410 ©Thomas Shjarback/Alamy; 411 (br) L'arrivée des Filles du Roi, avant 1927; Source: Bibliothèque et Archives Canada/C-020126; 412 (tr) ©Bettmann/Corbis; 412 (cl) ©PoodlesRock/Corbis; 413 (tr) ©Stock Montage/Getty Images; 413 (c) ©Bettmann/Corbis; 413 (b) ©The Art Gallery Collection/Alamy; 414 (br) ©Hemis/Alamy; 415 (tr) ©Lebrecht Music and Arts Photo Library/Alamy; 416 (t) ©Bettmann/Corbis; 416 (bl) Hulton-Deutsch Collection/CORBIS; 416 (br) ©Bert Brandt/Bettmann/Corbis; 418 (cl) ©North Wind Picture Archives/Alamy; 418 (cr) ©Michael Ventura/Alamy; 419 (tr) ©Tim Mosenfelder/Getty Images; 420 (cr) ©Danita Delimont/Gallo Images/Getty Images; 420 (cl) ©canadabrian/Alamy; PA10 (t) ©Science Source/Photo Researchers/Getty Images; PA10 (b) ©Science Source/Photo Researchers/Getty Images *in His Garden at Argenteuil, l873.* Wadsworth Atheneum, Hartford. Bequest of Anne Parrish Titzell.; bl: Farrell Grehan/.